T0414403

"In *Ruined Sinners to Reclaim*, twenty-six gifted pastors and theologians have joined forces to bequeath the church a rich, fruitful, and comprehensive survey of the doctrine of total depravity from the perspectives of historical theology, biblical exegesis, systematic theology, and polemics. With sensitivity to the contours of our increasingly secular world, the authors demonstrate how our understanding of total depravity should impact our evangelism, counseling, and preaching in modern contexts. Above all, the authors lead us to the spotless Lamb of God who takes away the sins of the world. This magisterial work is one of the most definitive treatments of total depravity available in the Reformed tradition."

Joel R. Beeke, Chancellor and Professor of Homiletics and Systematic Theology, Puritan Reformed Theological Seminary; Pastor, Heritage Reformed Congregation, Grand Rapids, Michigan

"As I read through the rich and deep chapters of *Ruined Sinners to Reclaim*, I not only found myself instructed; I also found myself moved again and again by the goodness and grace of God in Christ toward ruined sinners such as I. This book helps us to look squarely at our pervasive depravity and inability to save ourselves from sin's ruinous grip while also helping us to gaze in wonder and worship at God's pervasive purity and his power to save."

Nancy Guthrie, author; Bible teacher

"Reading a book on total depravity might betray a morbid preoccupation with the subject—or worse, confirmation of its existence in the reader! Yet this outstanding collection of essays is a treasure trove for scholars and students alike. Canvassing the historical, biblical, theological, and pastoral dimensions of this much-neglected and much-misunderstood doctrine of Holy Scripture, the Gibson brothers have provided a perspicacious window into the importance of understanding the depth of our ruin, in order to appreciate the glory of our being reclaimed by Christ. From the opening comprehensive introduction by the editors to the closing pastoral chapters, this book is a richly woven tapestry of insights into the extent of our fallenness and the wonder of God's redeeming grace."

Glenn N. Davies, former Archbishop of Sydney

"It was Seneca who said that if we desire to judge all things justly, we must first persuade ourselves that none of us is without sin. This excellent book—*Ruined Sinners to Reclaim*—does a superb job of persuading us about the complex nature of sin and the comprehensive salvation we find in Christ, and thus enables us to make thoughtful theological judgments for Christian ministry today. All sections, and many of the essays within, will supply good guidance for weary pilgrims through the Slough of Despond and onward toward the Celestial City."

Mark Earngey, Head of Church History and Lecturer in Doctrine, Moore Theological College; author, *Bishop John Ponet (1516–1556): Scholar, Bishop, Insurgent*; coeditor, *Reformation Worship*

"As with the first volume in the Doctrines of Grace series, *Ruined Sinners to Reclaim* provides depth, breadth, and clarity to its chosen topic. Since, as Calvin rightly put it, nearly all the wisdom we possess consists in the knowledge of God and of ourselves, this volume on sin, its nature, and its effects provides rich and practical wisdom so that we might better know ourselves, and thus know God better, as it plumbs the depths of Scripture and the Reformed theology that naturally wells up from Scripture. There is no other volume available that so adeptly gives us a microscope into the human heart."

K. Scott Oliphint, Professor of Apologetics and Systematic Theology, Westminster Theological Seminary

RUINED SINNERS TO RECLAIM

Titles in The Doctrines of Grace Series

Published:

From Heaven He Came and Sought Her

Ruined Sinners to Reclaim

Future titles:

Chosen Not for Good in Me

Then Shone Your Glorious Gospel Ray

Safe in the Arms of Sovereign Love

THE DOCTRINES OF GRACE

RUINED
SINNERS
TO RECLAIM

SIN AND DEPRAVITY
in HISTORICAL, BIBLICAL,
THEOLOGICAL, *and*
PASTORAL PERSPECTIVE

Edited by DAVID GIBSON & JONATHAN GIBSON

Foreword by MICHAEL HORTON

∷ CROSSWAY®

WHEATON, ILLINOIS

Ruined Sinners to Reclaim: Sin and Depravity in Historical, Biblical, Theological, and Pastoral Perspective

© 2024 by David Gibson and Jonathan Gibson

Published by Crossway
        1300 Crescent Street
        Wheaton, Illinois 60187

Cover design: Dual Identity

Cover image: Thomas Cole, *Expulsion from the Garden of Eden*, 1828 (Wikimedia Commons)

First printing 2024

Printed in China

Unless otherwise indicated, Scripture quotations are from the ESV® Bible (The Holy Bible, English Standard Version®), © 2001 by Crossway, a publishing ministry of Good News Publishers. Used by permission. All rights reserved. The ESV text may not be quoted in any publication made available to the public by a Creative Commons license. The ESV may not be translated into any other language.

For other Scripture versions cited, see pages 919–20.

The abbreviation ET denotes English translations.

Translations of Scripture by the authors of this book are identified as such.

All emphases in Scripture quotations added by the authors.

Hardcover ISBN: 978-1-4335-5705-7
ePub ISBN: 978-1-4335-5708-8
PDF ISBN: 978-1-4335-5706-4

Library of Congress Cataloging-in-Publication Data

Names: Gibson, David, 1975- editor. | Gibson, Jonathan, 1977- editor.
Title: Ruined sinners to reclaim : sin and depravity in historical, biblical, theological, and pastoral perspective / David Gibson & Jonathan Gibson.
Description: Wheaton, Illinois : Crossway, 2024. | Series: The grace project | Includes bibliographical references and index.
Identifiers: LCCN 2023014712 (print) | LCCN 2023014713 (ebook) | ISBN 9781433557057 (hardcover) | ISBN 9781433557064 (nook edition) | ISBN 9781433557088 (epub)
Subjects: LCSH: Sin--Christianity. | Sin--Biblical teaching.
Classification: LCC BT715 .R86 2024 (print) | LCC BT715 (ebook) | DDC 241/.3--dc23/ eng/20231108
LC record available at https://lccn.loc.gov/2023014712
LC ebook record available at https://lccn.loc.gov/2023014713

Crossway is a publishing ministry of Good News Publishers.

RRD   33 32 31 30 29 28 27 26 25 24
15 14 13 12 11 10 9 8 7 6 5 4 3 2 1

"Man of Sorrows," what a name
for the Son of God, who came
ruined sinners to reclaim:
Hallelujah, what a Savior!

Philip P. Bliss (1838–1876)

Contents

II. Sin and Depravity in the Bible

III. Sin and Depravity in Theological Perspective

IV. Sin and Depravity in Pastoral Practice

Tables and Diagrams

Foreword

Is it not a little overkill? All this talk of human depravity? After all, we know now that brains are wired in certain ways, genetics playing their part, along with the chemical soup. Plus, there is nurture, which warps us in all sorts of ways: "the woman you gave me" (or mother, father, etc.). Ultimately, is God not on the hook for all this?

Special revelation—that is, Scripture—represents God's own account of what he created us to be, how we have all fallen short of his glory, yet are reconciled to him by his own act in history. Nevertheless, general revelation also tells the same truth if we interpret it properly—with scriptural spectacles. The problem is that we do not want the bad news to be as bad as it is, which keeps us from hearing the good news in all its astounding beauty. In our secular culture, "sin" has been "cancelled." The new *Oxford Junior Dictionary* has deleted sin and other terms related to Christianity and added words like blog, broadband, and celebrity. Already in 1973, Karl Menninger's *Whatever Became of Sin?* astounded the public, as a psychologist not especially known for his Christian beliefs announced that the avoidance of sin had only exacerbated people's anxieties. While psychotherapy may alleviate some of the symptoms, Menninger argued, it does not have the methods or sources to provide a deeper account of human guilt. Everyone experiences shame, he noted, and this is the focus of therapy—but it is just a symptom. The root problem is guilt, which used to be dealt with by religious explanations. People could say, "Oh, well, at least that tells me why I *feel* ashamed." However grim, there was a deeper diagnosis of the condition. That has been forgotten, Menninger observed, leaving people with no sense of solidarity as those who are all "in it together," sharing a common experience of falling short of the purpose for which they exist.

Liberals and fundamentalists have contributed to this crisis in different ways. Both tend to identify sin with particular acts, whether social or individual, often emphasizing external factors. While the lists differ signifi-cantly, sin is often seen as the result of one's environment. Both sides tend to deflect sin onto outsiders. Too rarely is sin considered something that pervades every individual from conception because of Adam's fall.

The biblical doctrine of sin is far more complex. We are warped through-out not just because of deliberate decisions we have made but because of a common human condition. We are sinners and therefore responsible for our own agency. But we are also sinned against, which means we are also victims of other people's attitudes and actions. And we live in a fallen world that is broken not only ethically but also in our decaying bodies, dementia, and other brain illnesses, such as depression, schizophrenia, bipolar disorder, personality disorder, and so forth. To pin sin on any one of these pegs alone is to forget that God created us good and whole creatures in the beginning.

"Total depravity" is one of the most misunderstood doctrines of the Christian faith. Originating as a term no earlier than the twentieth century, it is not a particularly good one. Nor is it peculiar to Calvinism. The classi-cal Augustinian anthropology holds that the whole person, body and soul, is created in God's image and is therefore good—*and*, at the same time, is wholly depraved. As John Calvin taught against the negative ("Manichean") view of bodily nature as inherently depraved, "It is not nature but the cor-ruption of nature" that Scripture teaches. "Depravity" means a decline from an ideal good. The meal I put in the refrigerator may be wonderful, but if I leave the door open while I am gone on a trip and return to find it moldy, it is *depraved*. Depravity presupposes goodness. Or, to change the metaphor, a drop of poison corrupts the entire glass of water. This does not mean that there is no water left, but that the poison has infiltrated every part of it, such that the water is no longer health-giving.

Based on a host of passages unfurled in this volume, it was the common view from the ancient church to Aquinas and the Protestant Reformers that the whole person is good by created nature *and* also wholly defiled by sin: corrupt not in its intensity (as if there is no good left) but in its extensity. There is no part of us that has not been polluted by the guilt and corruption of sin, no island of neutrality—mind, will, or emotions—to make a safe land-ing for grace. Instead, God's grace must come to sinners, raising them from death to life. In salvation, God implants no new "spare part," as if we lost something natural, but saves everything that belonged to us by creation. In fact, he takes it beyond its original righteousness into glorification, immortality, and the impossibility of ever turning away from the Goodness in whom we exist. God's grace liberates the will, mind, and emotions to rest in him.

If we evaluate the alternatives, this biblical diagnosis is severe but also reasonable. Secularists do not have to talk about an ethical "fall" of the human race because they do not think that human beings are uniquely created in God's image and likeness. For us, though, humanity did not trip once upon a time but plunged from the highest position in creation next to the angels. This is one of the problems with the "TULIP" acronym: It starts with the fall rather than with creation.

Thus, total depravity does not mean that we are as bad as we can possibly be, but that the beautiful ways in which we are like God have become weapons to be used against him. We use our reasoning to invent ingenious subterfuges for avoiding the truth; our powerful emotions and imagination to love and invent idols; our excellent skill of deliberation to choose that which harms us; and our elegant bodies to rush toward destruction.

Yet still God gives grace. He never gives up on us. Even the last breath that curses the Creator is a gift of God's common grace. Believers and unbelievers alike enjoy sunsets, romance, families, and the liberal arts and sciences. Surpassing this goodness by far is the saving grace that God gives through the gospel. "God so loved the world that he gave his only begotten Son . . ." (John 3:16). God did not "so love" something that was ugly, contemptible, and disgusting. He loved what he had made. Like an artist whose great masterpiece has been disfigured by rogues, God would not quit until he restored the image to even beyond its original glory.

Yet God's work of reconciliation and restoration makes no sense unless we have a robust understanding of the crisis. As in the Christmas carol "Joy to the World," written by the Calvinist hymn-writer Isaac Watts, God's grace in Christ restores everything "far as the curse is found." The redemption is far greater even than the corruption. Justification is greater than forgiveness of guilt; it is being counted righteous before God. Regeneration and sanctification are not merely a return to Eden, but they lead us finally to glorification, which no human but Jesus has experienced.

From this vista—creation to redemption—we are able to interpret the sinfulness of the human race, the fallen world, and our own appetites in proper perspective. I appreciate how the authors in this book engage the historic Christian tradition but with biblical corrections recognized by the Protestant Reformers. Some readers may encounter for the first time discussions of topics such as *concupiscence* that seem arcane and yet which are essential to contemporary debates over whether not only decisions but also desires should be considered sinful. Once we are safe in Christ's arms, we can confess not only our individual sins but our twisted desires—however influenced by nature and nurture—as truly sinful enemies from which Christ has redeemed us.

The essays contained in this volume will help us navigate the shoals of a negative view of human nature, on the one side; and a recognition that we have all "fallen short of the glory of God" (Rom. 3:23), on the other. For those who worry about where they come from, their fallen condition, particular sins they have committed, and how Christ covers them, this volume will be a rich treasure.

Michael Horton
J. Gresham Machen Professor of Systematic Theology and Apologetics,
Westminster Seminary, California

Preface

In 2013, when *From Heaven He Came and Sought Her* was published, we had no intention of following such a mammoth undertaking with any further editorial projects. The doctrine of definite atonement had always stood out to us as, arguably, the most controversial of "the five points of Calvinism," and therefore the one most in need of defense and contemporary explanation and application. In the years that followed, however, it became clear that the other doctrines of grace were equally as deserving of careful examination and restatement. This volume, now the second in the series, is the next of four more volumes in what we are calling "The Doctrines of Grace" series, in which we hope, God willing, to treat the theology of the Canons of the Synod of Dort (1618–19) in all their historical, biblical, theological, and pastoral richness for our present day.

The focus of these volumes on the theology that was formulated within Reformed orthodoxy in the seventeenth century is not an attempt to make more of it than we should. Indeed, Richard Muller's oft-quoted observation about the Reformation provides some wider context to this project.

> The Reformation, in spite of its substantial contribution to the history of doctrine and the shock it delivered to theology and the church in the sixteenth century, was not an attack upon the whole of medieval theology or upon Christian tradition. The Reformation assaulted a limited spectrum of doctrinal and practical abuses with the intention of reaffirming the values of the historical church catholic. Thus, the mainstream Reformers reconstructed the doctrines of justification and the sacraments and then modified their ideas of the *ordo salutis* and of the church accordingly; but they did not alter the doctrine of God, creation, providence, and Christ, and they maintained the Augustinian tradition concerning predestination, human nature and sin. The reform of individual doctrines, like justification and the sacraments, occurred within the bounds of a traditional, orthodox, and catholic system which, on the grand scale, remained unaltered.[1]

---

[1] Richard A. Muller, *Post-Reformation Reformed Dogmatics*, 4 vols., 2nd ed. (Grand Rapids, MI: Baker Academic, 2003), 1:97.

It is certainly possible to argue, when it comes to human nature and sin, that Muller's "maintenance mode" setting for the Reformation requires important qualification. On the one hand, the Augustinian tradition was not simply monolithic at this point, and, on the other hand, the Reformers were soon engaged in conflict with Rome over the doctrine of concupiscence (the faculty of carnal desire) and the remittance of original sin in baptism. The various ways in which the Reformation sought to maintain the Augustinian tradition on sin came, in time, to be contested with Rome as the heirs of the Reformation settled on following Augustine's understanding of sin and grace in his later period. Nevertheless, the conception of the Reformation as a "limited assault" is a helpful one. Not only does it help to locate its theological upheavals within a broader view of the whole of the Christian tradition, but it also helps to moderate the kind of claims some Protestant theologians (in particular) might be tempted to make about the biblical and doctrinal rediscoveries that came to light in the work of the magisterial Reformers. The Reformation was a distinct and definitive doctrinal revolt, but it did not spring up *de novo* nor did it provide a high point of orthodoxy from which there was never any need of further development or refinement.

The Canons of Dort—and the system of Reformed orthodoxy that they represent and that they further repristinated—should, we suggest, be understood in the same way. The disputes debated at the Synod, which were answered with the "Heads of Doctrine" agreed upon by the assembly of Reformed ministers and professors, can in its own way be seen as a "limited assault" (or, better, a "counterassault") on a nexus of theological questions that were receiving aberrant answers at a certain point in history within a definite context. In publishing afresh today on the context, content, and biblical-theological-pastoral implications of that theology, we are claiming that it is beautiful theology with abiding value and confessional significance for the church; what we are *not* claiming is that the Canons of Dort *de novo* provide a climax of orthodoxy that represents the defining moment of the Christian tradition. Rather, the "Heads of Doctrine" formulated by the Synod represent a historically located instance of theological foment revolving around a certain set of matters related to soteriology.

This is the spirit in which we present the essays in this and all the other volumes. In undertaking the task of "The Doctrines of Grace" series, we are seeking to locate the Synod of Dort in its proper place within church history, such that it is worth stating again that the project is not a presentation of "the five points of Calvinism" or a defense of the "TULIP" acronym, which is so often presented as a summary of the Canons and of Reformed theology. As we stated previously, "It is not that there is no value to such language. But there can be a tendency to use such terminology as the soteriological map *itself*, without realizing that such terms simply feature as historical landmarks *on* the map."[2]

With this overall framework in place, then, it is the effort of this volume to trace the historical debates about sin's debilitating effects, sketch the biblical awfulness of sin's many forms, engage the theological complexities of sin's nature and transmission, and meditate on the pastoral realities of sin's presence in our lives and in the world. We seek to show not only that the doctrine of the total depravity of human creatures is biblical, but that it too, like all the other doctrines of grace confessed at Dort, "comes to us with a textured history, theological integrity, and pastoral riches."[3]

Soli Deo gloria.

---

[2] David Gibson and Jonathan Gibson, "Sacred Theology and the Reading of the Divine Word: Mapping the Doctrine of Definite Atonement," in *From Heaven He Came and Sought Her: Definite Atonement in Historical, Biblical, Theological, and Pastoral Perspective*, ed. David Gibson and Jonathan Gibson (Wheaton, IL: Crossway, 2013), 43 (emphasis original); cf. also Richard A. Muller, "How Many Points?," *CTJ* 28 (1993): 425–33.
[3] Gibson and Gibson, "Sacred Theology and the Reading of the Divine Word," 17.

Acknowledgments

This book, more than seven years in the making, has truly been a team effort, and we wish to express our gratitude to all those who have helped to bring it to fruition.

In 2016 Justin Taylor at Crossway was kind enough to entertain a proposal of four more books on the doctrines of grace to follow *From Heaven He Came and Sought Her*. He and Todd Augustine have extended grace upon grace as we extended the deadline year upon year. We are also indebted to Jill Carter for her handling of the contractual side of things. It has been a delight, as always, to work with the team at Crossway, and we wish especially to thank Bill Deckard for his expertise in editing this book. We are grateful that he came out of retirement for such an undertaking. It is far the better for his keen editorial eye.

We are grateful to those who provided feedback at various stages of the "Doctrines of Grace" series, from the proposal stage to the finished product; in particular, our thanks to Lee Gatiss, Scott Oliphint, Gray Sutanto, and Garry Williams. We express our deep gratitude to Jiang Ningning, our editorial assistant, who has served in preparing the manuscripts to be compatible with Crossway style. She edited each chapter with care and excellence, saving us a huge amount of work. Thanks also to Jeremy Menicucci for his assistance with the Abbreviations and Select Bibliography.

This book would not have been possible at all were it not for the generous support of a patron couple who covered the cost of a writing sabbatical in Cambridge during which time the vision and proposal were birthed. Their support then, and since, have played a significant role in the publication of this book coming to completion. As devoted Christians who understand the seriousness of sin but also the grace of God in the gospel for unworthy sinners, they have exhibited a heart of sacrificial love in partnering with us.

Their humility is testament to the great Reformation principle that God alone deserves the glory. *Ignoti aliis, sed Deo cogniti.*

Our wives, Angela and Jackie, have endured many years of our talking about a book about sin, and wondering if it would ever see the light of day. Yet they have supported us in various ways, not least allowing us time to work for undistracted periods on the book. We are deeply grateful for their support, patience, and grace, as well as their humor that helps to keep everything in perspective.

Our labors in this volume are dedicated to our fellow ministers and elders in the International Presbyterian Church, our band of brothers, whom we count it a great honor and joy to serve alongside. As under-shepherds of God's flock, they know all too well the mess and misery that our innate corruption makes of all our lives; yet, in season and out of season, they faithfully lead their congregations to the Chief Shepherd, who is able to deal with the penalty, power, and presence of sin in his tender grace. May God keep us all clear in our understanding of sin and depravity so that we might remain faithful in the proclamation of our great and glorious Savior.

Abbreviations

AB	Anchor Bible
AUSS	*Andrews University Seminary Studies*
BDAG	Walter Bauer, Frederick W. Danker, William Arndt, and F. Wilbur Gingrich. *A Greek-English Lexicon of the New Testament and Other Early Christian Literature* (Chicago: University of Chicago Press, 2000).
BECNT	Baker Exegetical Commentary on the New Testament
BibInt	*Biblical Interpretation*
BSac	*Bibliotheca Sacra*
BZAW	*Beihefte zur Zeitschrift für die alttestamentliche Wissenschaft*
BZNW	*Beihefte zur Zeitschrift für die neutestamentliche Wissenschaft und die Kunde der älteren Kirche*
CD	Canons of Dort
CE	*The Correspondence of Erasmus*
CR	Corpus Reformatorum, 101 vols. (Halle, Germany: Schwetschke, 1834–60).
CTJ	*Calvin Theological Journal*
CWE	*The Collected Works of Erasmus: Literary and Educational Writings, 1 and 2* (Toronto: University of Toronto Press, 1978).
DCH	David J. A. Clines, ed., *The Dictionary of Classical Hebrew*, 8 vols. (Sheffield, UK: Sheffield Academic, 1993–2011).
ExpTim	*Expository Times*
HALOT	Ludwig Koehler, Walter Baumgartner, and Johann Jakob Stamm, *The Hebrew and Aramaic Lexicon of the Old Testament*, trans. and ed. M. E. J. Richardson, 5 vols. (Leiden, Netherlands: Brill, 1994–2000).
HC	Heidelberg Catechism
HTR	*Harvard Theological Review*
ICC	International Critical Commentary
IJST	*International Journal of Systematic Theology*
JBL	*Journal of Biblical Literature*
JETS	*Journal of the Evangelical Theological Society*

JRT	*Journal of Reformed Theology*
JSOT	*Journal for the Study of the Old Testament*
JSOTSup	Journal for the Study of the Old Testament Supplement Series
JSS	*Journal of Semitic Studies*
LHBOTS	The Library of Hebrew Bible/Old Testament Studies
LW	*Luther's Works*, ed. J. J. Pelikan, H. C. Oswald, and H. T. Lehmann, 55 vols. (St. Louis: Concordia, 1955–86).
NAC	New American Commentary
NICNT	New International Commentary on the New Testament
NICOT	New International Commentary on the Old Testament
NIDNTTE	*New International Dictionary of the New Testament Theology and Exegesis*, ed. Colin Brown, 4 vols. (Grand Rapids, MI: Zondervan, 1986).
NIGTC	The New International Greek Testament Commentary
NIVAC	New International Version Application Commentary
NovT	*Novum Testamentum*
NPNF[1]	*Nicene and Post-Nicene Fathers*, Series 1, ed. Alexander Roberts, James Donaldson, Philip Schaff, and Henry Wace, 14 vols. (repr., Peabody, MA: Hendrickson, 1994).
NSBT	New Studies in Biblical Theology
NTS	*New Testament Studies*
OE	*Opus epistelorum des Erasmi Roterodami*, ed. P. S. Allen, H. M. Allen, H. W. Garrod, and B. Flower, 11 vols. (Oxford: Oxford University Press, 1536).
PG	Patrologia graeca, ed. J.-P. Migne et al. (Paris: Centre for Patristic Publications, 1857–86).
PL	Patrologia latina, ed. J.-P. Migne et al. (Paris: Centre for Patristic Publications, 1878–1890).
PNTC	Pillar New Testament Commentary
PRSt	*Perspectives in Religious Studies*
SJT	*Scottish Journal of Theology*
TDOT	*Theological Dictionary of the Old Testament*, ed. G. Johannes Botterweck and Helmer Ringgren, trans. John T. Willis et al., 15 vols. (Grand Rapids, MI: Eerdmans, 1974–2006).
TJ	*Trinity Journal*
TT	*Theology Today*
VT	*Vetus Testamentum*
VTSup	Supplements to Vetus Testamentum
WA	Martin Luther, *D. Martin Luther's Werke: Kritische Gesamtausgabe (Weimarer Ausgabe)* (Germany: H. Böhlaus Nachfolger, 1963).

WABr	Martin Luther, *D. Martin Luthers Werke: Abteilung. Briefwechsel*, 18 vols. (Germany: Hermann Böhlau, 1966).
WBC	Word Biblical Commentary
WCF	Westminster Confession of Faith
WLC	Westminster Larger Catechism
WSC	Westminster Shorter Catechism
WTJ	*Westminster Theological Journal*
WUNT	Wissenschaftliche Untersuchungen zum Neuen Testament
ZAW	*Zeitschrift für die alttestamentliche Wissenschaft*
ZECNT	Zondervan Exegetical Commentary on the New Testament

Contributors

James N. Anderson is Carl W. McMurray Professor of Theology and Philosophy at Reformed Theological Seminary, Charlotte, and an ordained minister in the Associate Reformed Presbyterian Church. His doctoral thesis in philosophical theology at the University of Edinburgh was published as *Paradox in Christian Theology: Its Presence, Character, and Epistemic Status* (Paternoster/Wipf & Stock, 2007). He is also the author of *What's Your Worldview?* (Crossway, 2014); *Why Should I Believe Christianity?* (Christian Focus, 2016); and *David Hume* (P&R, 2019).

Raymond A. Blacketer is a Reformation historian and is ordained in the Christian Reformed Church in North America. He is currently working on a new translation of John Calvin's *Institutes of the Christian Religion*, edited by A. N. S. Lane, to be published by Crossway. He is the author of numerous articles on Reformation history and of the monograph *The School of God: Pedagogy and Rhetoric in Calvin's Interpretation of Deuteronomy* (Springer, 2006).

Stephen M. Coleman is an ordained teaching elder in the Presbyterian Church in America and serves as Associate Professor of Old Testament and Biblical Languages, and Dean of Biblical and Theological Studies at Westminster Theological Seminary, Philadelphia, where he holds the Stephen Tong chair of Reformed Theology. He is the author of *The Biblical Hebrew Transitivity Alternation in Cognitive Linguistic Perspective* (Harassowitz, 2018); *Haggai, Zechariah, and Malachi: A 12-Week Study* (Crossway, 2018); and has coedited, with Todd Rester, *Faith in the Time of Plague* (WSP, 2021).

Brandon D. Crowe is an ordained teaching elder in the Presbyterian Church in America and serves as Professor of New Testament at Westminster Theological Seminary, Philadelphia. He is the author of *The Message of the*

General Epistles in the History of Redemption: Wisdom from James, Peter, John, and Jude (P&R, 2015); *The Hope of Israel: The Resurrection of Christ in the Acts of the Apostles* (Baker Academic, 2020); *The Path of Faith: A Biblical Theology of Covenant and Law* (IVP Academic, 2021); *The Lord Jesus Christ: The Biblical Doctrine of the Person and Work of Christ* (Lexham, 2023).

Lee Gatiss is Director of Church Society and a lecturer in church history at Union School of Theology. He is the author of a number of books, including *Fight Valiantly: Contending for the Faith against False Teaching in the Church* (Church Society, 2022); *For Us and for Our Salvation: "Limited Atonement" in the Bible, Doctrine, History, and Ministry* (Latimer Trust, 2012); and *Cornerstones of Salvation: Foundations and Debates in the Reformed Tradition* (Evangelical Press, 2017), and has edited volumes, including *The Sermons of George Whitefield*, 2 vols. (Crossway, 2012); *The NIV Proclamation Bible* (Hodder & Stoughton/Zondervan, 2013); and (with Brad Green) *1–2 Thessalonians, 1–2 Timothy, Titus, Philemon*, Reformation Commentary on Scripture (IVP Academic, 2019). He is series editor, with Shawn D. Wright, of *The Complete Works of John Owen*, 40 vols. (Crossway, 2022–); and *The Hodder Bible Commentary*, 50 vols. (Hodder & Stoughton, 2024).

David Gibson is Minister of Trinity Church, Aberdeen, Scotland. He studied theology at Nottingham University and King's College London, and completed a doctorate in historical and systematic theology at the University of Aberdeen. He is the author of *Reading the Decree: Exegesis, Election, and Christology in Calvin and Barth* (London/New York: T&T Clark, 2009); "Barth on Divine Election," in *The Wiley Companion to Karl Barth*, edited by George Hunsinger and Keith L. Johnson (Wiley Blackwell, 2020); and coeditor, with Jonathan Gibson, of *From Heaven He Came and Sought Her: Definite Atonement in Historical, Biblical, Theological, and Pastoral Perspective* (Crossway, 2013).

Jonathan Gibson is an ordained teaching elder in the International Presbyterian Church (UK), and presently serves as Associate Professor of Old Testament at Westminster Theological Seminary, Philadelphia. He is the author of *Covenant Continuity and Fidelity: A Study of Inner-Biblical Allusion and Exegesis in Malachi* (Bloomsbury T&T Clark, 2016); *Lamentations*, in the

ESV Expository Commentary series (Crossway, 2022); coeditor with Mark Earngey of *Reformation Worship: Liturgies from the Past for the Present* (New Growth, 2018); and, with David Gibson, of *From Heaven He Came and Sought Her: Definite Atonement in Historical, Biblical, Theological, and Pastoral Perspective* (Crossway, 2013).

Bradley G. Green (PhD, Baylor University) is Professor of Theological Studies at Union University (Jackson, Tennessee), and Professor of Philosophy and Theology at The Southern Baptist Theological Seminary. He has written essays and reviews for *International Journal of Systematic Theology*, *First Things*, *Chronicles*, and *Touchstone*. He is the author of *The Gospel and the Mind: Recovering and Shaping the Intellectual Life* (Crossway, 2010); *Colin Gunton and the Failure of Augustine: The Theology of Colin Gunton in Light of Augustine* (Wipf & Stock, 2011); *Covenant and Commandment: Works, Obedience, and Faithfulness in the Christian Life* (InterVarsity Press, 2014); *Augustine: His Life and Impact*, in Christian Focus's Church Fathers series (Christian Focus, 2020); and coeditor, with Lee Gatiss, of *Reformation Commentary on Scripture*, vol. 12, *1–2 Thessalonians, 1–2 Timothy, Titus, Philemon* (IVP Academic, 2019). He and his wife, Dianne, were co-founders of Augustine School, a Christian liberal arts school in Jackson, Tennessee.

Francis X. Gumerlock (PhD, Saint Louis University) teaches Latin in Colorado. He was Professor of Historical Theology at Providence Theological Seminary in Colorado Springs and visiting professor of Latin at Colorado College. He writes on the theology of grace in early and medieval Christianity, including *Fulgentius of Ruspe on the Saving Will of God* (Edwin Mellen, 2009); and *Gottschalk and a Medieval Predestination Controversy* (Marquette University Press, 2010).

Michael A. G. Haykin serves as Chair and Professor of Church History at The Southern Baptist Theological Seminary and is Director of the Andrew Fuller Center for Baptist Studies, which operates under the auspices of Southern Seminary. He has an MRel from Wycliffe College, the University of Toronto (1977), and a ThD in church history from the University of Toronto and Wycliffe College (1982). He is the author of a number of books on Christianity in late antiquity and British and Irish Dissent in the eighteenth century.

Mark Jones (PhD, Leiden University) is Senior Pastor at Faith Vancouver Presbyterian Church (PCA). He has authored and edited a number of books, including *Knowing Christ, God Is, Knowing Sin, Antinomianism*, and *A Puritan Theology*. Recently, he edited Stephen Charnock's work, *The Existence and Attributes of God* (Crossway, 2022). He is currently in the process of establishing Trinity Reformed College, a new seminary in Cape Town, South Africa.

Heath Lambert is Senior Pastor of First Baptist Church in Jacksonville, Florida, where he has served since 2016. He also serves as Associate Professor at The Southern Baptist Theological Seminary and formerly served as Executive Director of the Association of Certified Biblical Counselors. He is the author of several books, including *Finally Free*, *A Theology of Biblical Counseling*, and *The Great Love of God*.

Andrew M. Leslie is Head of Theology, Philosophy, and Ethics at Moore Theological College in Sydney. He is the author of a monograph on John Owen's doctrine of Scripture (*The Light of Grace: John Owen on the Authority of Scripture and Christian Faith* [V&R Academic, 2015]), and a volume editor in a forthcoming new edition of John Owen's works (Crossway). In addition to having an interest in Owen and Protestant orthodoxy more generally, he is committed to promoting the expression and defense of Reformed theological convictions in service of the contemporary church.

Ryan M. McGraw is Morton H. Smith Professor of Systematic Theology at Greenville Presbyterian Theological Seminary and a minister in the Orthodox Presbyterian Church. He has pastored and served on session in several churches, and authored twenty-eight books, including editing and contributing to *Charles Hodge: American Reformed Orthodox Theologian* (Vandenhoeck & Ruprecht, 2023). His academic publishing topics include John Owen, Reformed Scholasticism, Peter van Mastricht, Jonathan Edwards, Charles Hodge, and Trinitarian theology.

R. Albert Mohler Jr. is President of The Southern Baptist Theological Seminary. He has written widely on contemporary issues and has been recognized by such influential publications as *Time* and *Christianity Today* as a leader among American evangelicals. In addition to his presidential duties at Southern, he is a professor of Christian theology and hosts two radio programs:

"The Briefing," a daily analysis of news and events from a Christian world-view; and "Thinking in Public," a series of conversations with the day's leading thinkers. He also serves as editor for *WORLD Opinions*. Mohler has authored numerous books, his most recent being, *Tell Me the Stories of Jesus: The Explosive Power of Jesus' Parables*. He served as general editor of the *Grace and Truth Study Bible* (Zondervan). He also writes a popular blog and a regular commentary on moral, cultural, and theological issues.

Douglas Sean O'Donnell is an ordained teaching elder in the Presbyterian Church in America and serves as the Senior Vice President of Bible Editorial at Crossway. He earned an MA from Wheaton College, an MA from Trinity Evangelical Divinity School, and a PhD from the University of Aberdeen. He has pastored several churches, served as a professor, and authored or edited more than twenty books, including commentaries, Bible studies, academic articles, children's books, and a Sunday school curriculum. He coauthored, with Leland Ryken, *The Beauty and Power of Biblical Exposition*, and was contributing editor for *The Pastor's Book*, by R. Kent Hughes.

Nathan D. Shannon (PhD, VU Amsterdam) is Associate Director of Global Curriculum and Assessment as well as Adjunct Professor of Apologetics and Systematic Theology at Westminster Theological Seminary, Philadelphia. Previously he taught systematic theology at Torch Trinity Graduate University in Seoul. He is the author of *Shalom and the Ethics of Belief: Nicholas Wolterstorff's Theory of Situated Rationality* (Pickwick, 2015); and *Absolute Person and Moral Experience: A Study in Neo-Calvinism* (Bloomsbury T&T Clark, 2022), as well as editor of the Great Thinkers series (P&R). He is an ordained teaching elder in the Presbyterian Church in America.

Murray J. Smith serves as Lecturer in Biblical Theology and Exegesis at Christ College, Sydney, and is an ordained elder in the Presbyterian Church of Australia. He holds an MA from the University of Sydney, an MDiv from the Australian College of Theology, and an MA and PhD from Macquarie University. He is the author of *Jesus: All about Life* (Bible Society of Australia, 2009, 2023), and editor of *Effective Eldership* (Eider, 2022) and *Presbyters in the Early Church* (Mohr Siebeck, forthcoming). His published essays include contributions to the *Journal of Biblical Literature* and several edited collections. He also serves as an editor for two forthcoming series that integrate biblical and confessional theology: *We Believe—Studies in Reformed Biblical Doctrine* (Lexham); and the *Reformed Exegetical and Theological Commentary on Scripture* (Crossway).

Daniel Strange is the Director of Crosslands Forum, a center for cultural engagement and missional innovation. Formerly he was College Director and Tutor in Culture, Religion, and Public Theology at Oak Hill College, London. He has a PhD from Bristol University. He is a contributing editor for *Themelios*, and Vice President of The Southgate Fellowship. He is the author of a number of books, including, *Their Rock Is Not Like Our Rock: A Theology of Religions* (Zondervan, 2015); *Plugged In* (The Good Book Company, 2019); and *Making Faith Magnetic* (The Good Book Company, 2021).

Nathaniel Gray Sutanto (PhD, University of Edinburgh) is Assistant Professor of Systematic Theology at Reformed Theological Seminary, Washington, DC. He is the author of *God and Knowledge: Herman Bavinck's Theological Epistemology* (Bloomsbury T&T Clark, 2020); coauthor of *Neo-Calvinism: A Theological Introduction* (Lexham, 2023); cotranslator of Herman Bavinck's *Christian Worldview* and *Christianity and Science* (Crossway, 2019, 2023); and coeditor of the forthcoming *T&T Clark Handbook of Neo-Calvinism*. He is an ordained minister in the International Presbyterian Church.

Mark D. Thompson is Principal of Moore Theological College in Sydney. His doctoral research at Oxford University was published as *A Sure Ground on Which to Stand: The Relation of Authority and Interpretive Method in Luther's Approach to Scripture* (Paternoster, 2004). He is an ordained presbyter in the Anglican Diocese of Sydney, a canon of St. Andrews Cathedral in Sydney, and Chair of the Sydney Diocesan Doctrine Commission. He teaches systematic theology at Moore College, with particular interest in the doctrines of Scripture, Christology, the atonement, and justification by faith alone. He is the author of *A Clear and Present Word* (IVP Academic, 2006) and *The Doctrine of Scripture: An Introduction* (Crossway, 2022). He is currently working on Christology.

Steven Wedgeworth is Rector of Christ Church Anglican in South Bend, Indiana. He holds an MDiv from Reformed Theological Seminary and is an ordained minister in the Anglican Diocese of the Living Word. He is a regular writer for Desiring God, *WORLD Opinions*, and *Ad Fontes: A Journal of Protestant Letters*. He was a founding board member of The Davenant Institute and has contributed to several of their books, including *Protestant Social Teaching: An Introduction*, and *The Lord Is One: Reclaiming Divine Simplicity*.

David F. Wells is Distinguished Senior Research Professor at Gordon-Conwell Theological Seminary. He is the author of several books engaging the modern world with evangelical theology, most notably, *No Place for Truth* (Eerdmans, 1994) and *God in the Wastelands* (Eerdmans, 1995). He has taught at Trinity Evangelical Divinity School and has served as the Academic Dean at Gordon-Conwell Theological Seminary's Charlotte, North Carolina, campus.

Garry J. Williams serves as Pastor of Ebenezer Chapel in Luton, England, and as Director of the Pastors' Academy at London Seminary. His publications include *Silent Witnesses: Lessons on Theology, Life, and the Church from Christians of the Past* (Banner of Truth) and *His Love Endures Forever: Reflections on the Immeasurable Love of God* (Inter-Varsity Press/Crossway).

William M. Wood (PhD, Westminster Theological Seminary) is a minister in the Orthodox Presbyterian Church and serves as Associate Professor of Old Testament at Reformed Theological Seminary, Atlanta, and is a teacher at Christ Orthodox Presbyterian Church, Marietta, Georgia. His doctoral work was on Zephaniah, entitled, "I Will Remove Your Proudly Exultant Ones: A Study in Inner-Biblical Interpretation in the Book of Zephaniah." He has a number of forthcoming articles, chapters, and a book titled *Worship according to the Pattern: Redemptive History and the Regulative Principle of Worship* (Reformed Forum Press).

INTRODUCTION

1

"Salvation Belongs to the Lord"

MAPPING THE DOCTRINE OF THE TOTAL
DEPRAVITY OF HUMAN CREATURES

David Gibson and Jonathan Gibson

Self-deception about our sin is a narcotic, a tranquilizing and disorienting suppression of our spiritual central nervous system. What's devastating about it is that when we lack an ear for the wrong notes in our lives, we cannot play right ones or even recognize them in the performance of others. Eventually we make ourselves religiously so unmusical that we miss both the exposition and the recapitulation of the main themes God plays in human life. The music of creation and the still greater music of grace whistle right through our skulls, causing no catch of breath and leaving no residue. Moral beauty begins to bore us. The idea that the human race needs a Savior sounds quaint.[1]

The doctrine of total depravity states that, with the exception of the Lord Jesus Christ, all of humanity, from the very moment of conception, share a corrupt human nature which renders us liable to God's wrath, incapable of any saving good, inclined toward evil, and which leaves us both dead in sin and enslaved to sin. Left to ourselves, we neither want to nor can return to the God who made us, and, without the regenerating grace of the Holy Spirit, we cannot know him as our heavenly Father. Our mind has lost the pure knowledge of God so that we are blind, self-centered, and self-impressed. Our will has squandered its holiness and surrendered its freedom; we are wicked in our rebellion against a good God and his ways, and, more than this, we are enslaved

---

[1] Cornelius Plantinga Jr., *Not the Way It's Supposed to Be: A Breviary of Sin* (Grand Rapids, MI: Eerdmans, 1995), xiii.

to our rebellion. Our affections are impure and find delight in what is evil. We do not rejoice constantly in God. It is not that we are as bad as we possibly could be; rather, total depravity simply describes the fact that there is not one single aspect of our constitution that is unaffected by sin's derangements.[2]

In much the same way as we argued previously with the doctrine of definite atonement,[3] total depravity says something essential about the corruption of humanity, but it does not say everything there is to say. Strictly speaking, this doctrine refers to the utter pervasiveness of sin's spread just as it has also become linked in particular historical contexts to the understanding of human inability to respond to God's grace apart from his personal intervention. All these ideas have been contested and are complex in themselves, but undergirding these ideas is the fall of humanity and the doctrine of original sin, which together form the bleak backdrop to all that Christian theology has fought for, argued about, and humbly confessed in its doctrine of creation and of humankind. Total depravity does not exhaust the Christian doctrine of sin; indeed, it is so tightly related to several other facets of sin that this volume widens its scope to consider them as well.

The complexities of our subject have generated objections in every age. The moral philosopher Alfred Edward Taylor called the doctrine of original sin "the most vulnerable part of the whole Christian account."[4] The tradition itself recognizes the challenge of a coherent account. Herman Bavinck wrote in his *Reformed Dogmatics* that the event of the fall of the first humans "is of such great weight that the whole of Christian doctrine stands or falls with it."[5] Similarly, for Bavinck, the doctrine of original sin is not only "one of the weightiest but also one of the most difficult subjects in the field of dogmatics."[6] It is one of the weightiest subjects, because, along with the doctrine of God, it is one of the great presuppositions of the Christian gospel:

---

[2] The definition in this paragraph is our own, but it is a composite drawn almost entirely from Articles One and Three of the Third and Fourth Heads of Doctrine in the Canons of Dort, and also from John Calvin's treatment of original sin. See the new translation of the Canons of Dort in W. Robert Godfrey, *Saving the Reformation: The Pastoral Theology of the Canons of Dort* (Sanford, FL: Reformation Trust, 2019), 127–30; John Calvin, *Institutes of the Christian Religion*, ed. John T. McNeill, trans. Ford Lewis Battles, 2 vols. (Philadelphia: Westminster, 1960); 2.1.8 (1:250–52).

[3] David Gibson and Jonathan Gibson, "Sacred Theology and the Reading of the Divine Word: Mapping the Doctrine of Definite Atonement," in *From Heaven He Came and Sought Her: Definite Atonement in Historical, Biblical, Theological, and Pastoral Perspective*, ed. David Gibson and Jonathan Gibson (Wheaton, IL: Crossway, 2013), 33–53.

[4] A. E. Taylor, *The Faith of a Moralist* (London: Macmillan, 1930), 165. Quoted from Hans Madueme, "'The Most Vulnerable Part of the Whole Christian Account': Original Sin and Modern Science," in *Adam, the Fall, and Original Sin: Theological, Biblical, and Scientific Perspectives*, ed. Hans Madueme and Michael Reeves (Grand Rapids, MI: Baker, 2014), 225.

[5] Herman Bavinck, *Reformed Dogmatics*, ed. John Bolt, trans. John Vriend, 4 vols. (Grand Rapids, MI: Baker Academic, 2003–8), 3:38.

[6] Bavinck, *Reformed Dogmatics*, 3:100.

"Christ Jesus came into the world to save *sinners*" (1 Tim. 1:15).[7] It is one of the most difficult subjects, because it is so multifaceted. Blaise Pascal said, "It is astonishing however that the mystery furthest from our understanding is the transmission of sin, the one thing without which we can have no understanding of ourselves!"[8]

The doctrine of original sin presupposes and entails other doctrines, such as the nature of man as body and soul and his state of original righteousness before the fall. A right handling of the doctrine of original sin situates it within the framework of a covenant of works with Adam and in relation to God's law in Eden, before delineating various aspects of the doctrine: the origin of sin (God, man, or the devil?) and the kingdom of evil; the spread of sin (preexistent, realistic, mediate imputation, or immediate imputation?); the nature of sin (a substance, privation of good, negation or nothingness, moral evil or lawlessness?); the scope of sin (body, soul, emotions, mind, and will?); and the effect of sin on the freedom of the will (necessary, contingent, certain?). From this foundation and foreground, we arrive at one specific, significant, and historically influential rendering of sin's nature and effects, namely, the total depravity of human creatures. But it is the full picture of sin and its derelictions that we are concerned with in this volume.

Stand-alone books on sin are invariably self-conscious and, of course, the unease is understandable. Why might a book of Christian theology be so preoccupied with the *bad* news? The posture adopted in this volume, however, is neither defensive nor embarrassed about the need to stare long and hard at the problem of sin and depravity in the human race. Indeed, some methodological throat-clearing at the start of such a collection of essays is an opportunity for us to reflect a little more on what we have already alluded to: the doctrine of sin requires us to grapple with the tightly interwoven fabric of the whole of Christian theology and to recognize that we will not travel far or well along the road of abundant delight in the gospel without a profound understanding of the plight from which we have been saved. Classic texts such as *Dynamics of Spiritual Life* have shown us that, in fact, a depth perception of sin goes hand in hand in Scripture and throughout church history with the lifegiving, restorative,

---

[7] J. Gresham Machen, *Christianity and Liberalism* (Grand Rapids, MI: Eerdmans, 2009), 47: "The two great presuppositions of the gospel are a doctrine of God and a doctrine of man"; John Murray, "Inability," in *Collected Writings of John Murray*, vol. 2, *Systematic Theology* (Edinburgh: Banner of Truth, 1977), 83, 88: "Original sin deals with our depravity. Inability deals with the fact that our depravity is humanly irremediable. . . . The only gospel there is is the gospel which rests upon the assumption of total inability."

[8] Blaise Pascal, *Pensées*, trans. Honor Levi (Oxford: Oxford University Press, 2008), section 164 (p. 42).

reviving work of the Holy Spirit, both individually and corporately.[9] There is significant precedent for our longing and prayer that the present book might serve as a tool in the hands of God to awaken us afresh to the nefarious nadirs of who we are in our rebellion, precisely so that the stunning splendor of who God is in stooping to save us can be confessed anew. As D. A. Carson puts it,

> There can be no agreement as to what salvation *is* unless there is agreement as to that from which salvation rescues us. The problem and the solution hang together: the one explicates the other. It is impossible to gain a deep grasp of what the cross achieves without plunging into a deep grasp of what sin is; conversely, to augment one's understanding of the cross is to augment one's understanding of sin.[10]

The weightiness and difficulty of the doctrine of sin, and its interconnectedness to a whole range of other topics in Christian theology, make the case, we believe, for the same argument advanced in *From Heaven He Came and Sought Her*, namely, that church history, the Bible, theology, and pastoral practice need to coalesce to provide a framework within which the doctrine of total depravity is best articulated today.[11] This volume is a patient attempt to listen to the past and the faithful cloud of witnesses who have thought long and hard about sin; it seeks to submit itself and the tradition to Scripture as our supreme authority; and it wishes to pursue the systematic and dogmatic integration of church history, exegesis, and theological reflection into a coherent whole that is turned toward God in doxology and toward the church in loving, gracious, truthful, and Christ-exalting pastoral practice. The attempt here, as in the first volume, is an exercise in biblical, theological, and confessional faithfulness, which is never less than the ordering of all that the Bible has to say on sin, while also being much more. Part of the rationale for this methodology is that, without it, mistaken or less than helpful paths present themselves all too easily to the Christian disciple thinking about sin.

Consider, for example, the argument that "the normal Christian life is the victorious Christian life," advanced in John Stevens's book, *The Fight of Your Life: Facing and Resisting Temptation*.[12] Written at a popular level for

---

[9] Richard F. Lovelace, *Dynamics of Spiritual Life: An Evangelical Theology of Renewal* (Downers Grove, IL: IVP Academic, 1979).

[10] D. A. Carson, "Sin's Contemporary Significance," in *Fallen: A Theology of Sin*, ed. Christopher W. Morgan and Robert A. Peterson, Theology in Community (Wheaton, IL: Crossway, 2013), 22 (emphasis added).

[11] Gibson and Gibson, "Sacred Theology and the Reading of the Divine Word," 37–41.

[12] John Stevens, *The Fight of Your Life: Facing and Resisting Temptation* (Fearn, Ross-shire, UK: Christian Focus, 2019).

an evangelical audience, this work is driven by the admirable pastoral aim of helping believers in their battle against sin, seeking to free them from false burdens of guilt and failure. In particular, the desire to provide nourishment for Christian living is evident in the book's sensitive handling of sexual temptation, both heterosexual and homosexual. It seeks to tackle an "unintended consequence" of the teaching that "we are sinners not just because of the sins we commit, but because of our desires and thoughts." For Stevens, this theology has had the harmful effect of making "the struggle against sin primarily a battle not to experience certain thoughts and desires."[13] He presses a distinction between temptation and sin: "All Christians experience temptation, but temptation is not itself sin. The proper response to temptation is resistance rather than repentance. Experiencing temptation does not make us guilty before God and in need of his cleansing mercy and forgiveness."[14] It is perhaps fair to say that such a distinction has become commonplace in evangelical theology[15] (although not as commonplace as Stevens might wish, given his own perception of the guilt and shame attached to the teaching he wishes to counter).

It will fall to some of the other essays in this book to explore some of the more substantial responses that should be made to this kind of hamartiology and understanding of fallen human nature; our concern here is simply to register some *methodological* observations that show why the enterprise of this volume is needed.

Stevens is explicit that he sees his book as a challenge both to the "Keswick" teaching of the Wesleyan model of holiness, on the one hand; and the teaching of men like J. C. Ryle and J. I. Packer, who exemplify "the more traditional puritan approach," on the other. Both positions Stevens regards as representing the "extremes" of biblical teaching on the normal Christian life.[16] Such a viewpoint might be entirely defensible, of course, but what is striking about Stevens's book is his choice to situate his own argument historically while not offering any engagement with the competing historical positions he is seeking to balance and critique. The impression, unwittingly or not, is that simple biblical exegesis is an adequate antidote to either extreme. By not laying out the biblical exegesis of the positions he is challenging, Stevens presents his own interpretations as

---

[13] Stevens, *Fight of Your Life*, 11.
[14] Stevens, *Fight of Your Life*, 20.
[15] See Sam Allberry, *Is God Anti-Gay? And Other Questions about Jesus, the Bible, and Same-Sex Sexuality* (Epsom, Surrey, UK: Good Book Company, 2023), 59–61, as one such example.
[16] Stevens, *Fight of Your Life*, 10, 13.

self-evidently true when, in fact, there are significant and weighty challenges to his thesis lying dormant in the great tradition that precedes his book.

At the foundation of Stevens's argument is a reading of James 1:13–15, a text which he believes "draws a definitive contrast between temptation and sin." He holds that "These verses make clear that there is a step between temptation and sin, which is captured by the metaphor of giving birth. The desire which is evil has the potential to become sin, but this is not inevitable."[17] However, what seems self-evident to Stevens is not the case for other readers of the same text. Here, for example, is John Calvin on James 1:13–15:

> It seems, however, improper, and not according to the usage of Scripture, to restrict the word *sin* to outward works, as though indeed lust itself were not a sin, and as though corrupt desires, remaining closed up within and suppressed, were not so many sins . . . For he [James] proceeds gradually, and shows that the consummation of sin is eternal death, and that these depraved desires or affections have their root in lust.[18]

Stevens appears to have a category of evil human desires that are not yet sinful in themselves, whereas, for Calvin, to conceptualize corrupt desires as not intrinsically sinful seems improper, and not according to the usage of Scripture.

So how is a reader of the Bible to choose between different possible interpretations like these?

The contention of this volume is that the further back in church history a doctrine of sin is willing to reach, and the deeper down into theological precision it is willing to mine, then the further forward it will extend in longevity and usefulness for the Christian church. That is to say, to be truly contemporary, a doctrine of sin is required to retrieve the immense riches from the concepts, categories, and distinctions present in the tradition which can both enrich our exegesis and rescue us from error. For instance, without engaging with it at all, and seemingly unaware of it, Stevens's treatment of temptation wades into the deep waters of the doctrine of concupiscence (literally, the faculty of desire and, in church history, the anatomy of sinful desire), and thereby, in an evangelical Protestant book, actually presents a Roman Catholic position on unbidden and unwanted desires as the straightforward reading of the Bible.[19] Further, the wider

---

[17] Stevens, *Fight of Your Life*, 26.

[18] John Calvin, *Commentaries on the Epistle of James*, Calvin's Commentaries, vol. 22, trans. John Owen (Grand Rapids, MI: Baker, 1979), 290.

[19] For more on this, see the essay by Steven Wedgeworth in this volume (ch. 21).

biblical theology used by Stevens to buttress his position—the temptations of Eve and of Christ—takes no account of the considerable theological significance of their *unfallen* human natures at the very points where Stevens wishes to press their analogical usefulness to the temptations of the Christian believer.[20]

But why does all this matter? Recall that Stevens's aim in his book is explicitly pastoral. He particularly wants to help Christians who experience same-sex temptation to understand that while lusting after a person of the same sex would be sinful, "there [are] no grounds to conclude that a person is sinning merely because they experience unwanted and unencouraged attraction towards people of the same sex."[21] The vital significance of such questions is not hard for us to understand in our current milieu and, again, it is possible to argue that Stevens is articulating a view of "same-sex attraction" which has become increasingly popular within evangelical theology. The terms "same-sex attraction" or "same-sex sexual attraction" are now commonly used in contemporary discussion by many evangelicals. Some "same-sex attracted" Christians have chosen to distance themselves from the language of "homosexual" or "gay," replacing it with "same-sex (sexual) attraction" or "same-sex sexuality" on the basis that the former terms often convey identity and lifestyle while the latter terms convey only the desire or experience of same-sex attraction.[22]

However, by treating unwanted and unbidden desires in this way, Stevens ignores the ways in which the theology of the Reformation and the Reformed tradition countered it. Compare, for example, Stevens's pastoral approach with Girolamo Zanchi's view of repentance, which is representative of the Reformed tradition:

> . . . repentance is a changing of the mind and heart, stirred up in us through the Holy Ghost, by the word both of the law and the gospel, wherein we grieve from our heart, we detest, we lament, we loath and bewail, and confess before God all our sins, *and even the corruption of our nature* as things

[20] For a further extensive critique of Stevens, see the excellent book by Matthew P. W. Roberts, *Pride: Identity and the Worship of Self* (Fearn, Ross-shire, UK: Christian Focus, 2023), 70–79. For more on the Roman Catholic position on concupiscence and for an alternative rich reading of James 1:12–18, see the sermon by Kevin DeYoung, "When Desire Destroys," February 28, 2021, https://christcovenant.org/sermons/when-desire-destroys/.
[21] Stevens, *Fight of Your Life*, 31.
[22] For example, Allberry, *Is God Anti-Gay?*, 16–17, 120; Ed Shaw, *The Plausibility Problem* (Nottingham, UK: Inter-Varsity Press, 2015), 35–43. Semantically, however, the distinction fails at a lexical level: "same-sex (sexual) attraction" or "same-sex sexuality" is the same as "homosexual attraction/sexuality," the word "homosexual" being comprised of "homo" (same) and "sexual" (sex). Also, practically, the distinction is not able to be consistently applied in the church. There are celibate Christians who are happy to use the attribute "gay" to describe themselves, as noted, for example, in Greg O. Johnson, *Still Time to Care: What We Can Learn from the Church's Failed Attempt to Cure Homosexuality* (Grand Rapids, MI: Zondervan, 2021); and Gregory Coles, *Single, Gay Christian: A Personal Journey of Faith and Sexual Identity* (Downers Grove, IL: InterVarsity Press, 2017).

utterly repugnant (as the law teaches) to the will of God and to the cleansing, whereof the death of God's own Son (as the gospel preaches) was needful.[23]

Because Stevens eliminates the need for repentance in the case of concupiscence, ironically, he provides less gospel hope and comfort, not more, to those struggling with same-sex desires. For he ends up implying that there are parts of our fallen human natures that God's grace does not need to redeem. Of course, Stevens might reject this conclusion, expressed in this way, yet he is explicit that "as human beings we all experience an emotional attraction to rebellion and disobedience which is not itself sin."[24] But to distinguish, and then to separate, "emotional attraction" (what others might call "propensity" or "inclination") *toward* sin from sin *itself* is wrongly to separate what is rightly distinguished. Being attracted to sin and sinning are distinct but inseparable parts of the sin-guilt complex. Genesis 6:5 is clear that our sinful nature corrupts all the way down to thoughts and inclinations of the heart, which are described as only evil continually.[25] However, Stevens maintains that some unbidden and unencouraged desires do not have an innate corruption that renders us culpable before God. This is, ultimately, to misconstrue original sin and total depravity. This is evident when Stevens says that his book "will assert the twin truths that our temptations are sinful, which gives added motivation for resisting them, but that we are not personally guilty of sin unless we choose to act on them. The sinful desires we experience do not automatically make us guilty sinners."[26] But to tie sin (and therefore also guilt) only to the *consent* of the will and not also to the *corruption* of the will, as Stevens does here, is a departure from Protestant orthodoxy. Doing so allows the terminology of "same-sex (sexual) attraction" to become a morally neutral identity marker for the Christian, one in which a propensity or attraction toward sin is no longer classified as sin.

The Reformed tradition, however, has always held that the corruption of nature, which is ours on account of original sin, *is itself sin* as well as the actual transgressions we commit that flow from it: "This corruption of nature, during

---

[23] Girolamo Zanchi, *De religione christiana fides—Confession of the Christian Religion*, eds. Luca Baschera and Christian Moser, Studies in the History of Christian Traditions (Leiden, Netherlands: Brill, 2007), XVIII.v (Lat. = p. 330; ET = p. 331). We have modernized the wording for our purposes (emphasis added). Thanks to Matthew Mason for pointing us to this quote.

[24] Stevens, *Fight of Your Life*, 33.

[25] WSC Q&A 14 is instructive here: "What is sin? Sin is *any want of conformity unto*, or transgression of, the law of God" (emphasis added). To be attracted to sin is to lack conformity to the law of God, and thus is sin. Also, as Gen. 6:5 indicates, to distinguish between propensity and desire is to make a distinction without a difference.

[26] Stevens, *Fight of Your Life*, 21.

this life, doth remain in those that are regenerated; and although it be, through Christ, pardoned and mortified; yet both itself and all the motions thereof, are truly and properly sin" (Westminster Confession of Faith 6.5). The Thirty-Nine Articles of the Church of England similarly say that, through original sin, the desire of the flesh remains in the believer as an "infection of nature," with the result that "the Apostle doth confess, that concupiscence and lust hath of itself the nature of sin" (Article IX). It is for these reasons that some have seen in the theology of the Canons of Dort the very saving of the Reformation precisely because its theology of grace was now in the crosshairs of an optimistic anthropology which had not sufficiently accounted for human nature.[27] Unless original sin and the depravity that extends to our concupiscence are fully in view, then it is possible for grace to "no longer be grace" (Rom. 11:6).[28]

This contemporary issue shows that our choice of language and terms needs historical awareness, biblical precision, and theological consistency. Our argument is that, as with definite atonement, so the doctrine of sin and depravity in human creatures is neither merely biblical, nor merely a systematic construct with no grounding in the Bible. Rather, total depravity receives its fullest and best expressions as a *biblico-systematic* doctrine that is born from careful exegesis of all the texts where sin is displayed in all its terrible forms, and from synthesis with all other doctrines that are intimately related to it, such as the doctrines of God, creation, anthropology, Christology, and covenant, and that such synthesis is all the richer when it follows contemplation of the tradition that has thought itself clear ahead of us on so many vital matters of definition and distinction. We are seeking in this volume, once again, to provide both a web for holding the doctrine together with all its canonical threads and doctrinal implications so that individual parts can be considered in the light of the whole, and also to provide a map to and through the doctrine of human corruption. Where should we look in Scripture for our doctrine of sin? Who in the tradition should we speak to about what we have found, and what might they say to us in response that could guide our next

---

[27] Note the title of W. Robert Godfrey's study, *Saving the Reformation: The Pastoral Theology of the Canons of Dort* (see note 2, above).

[28] For a full and helpful treatment of these issues in the context of pastoral care for those with same-sex attraction, see "The Ad Interim Committee Report on Human Sexuality" prepared for the forty-eighth General Assembly of the Presbyterian Church in America (https://pcaga.org/wp-content/uploads/2020/05/AIC-Report-to-48th-GA-5-28 -20-1.pdf [accessed March 10, 2023]). The report rejects the Roman Catholic understanding of concupiscence but also conveys how, properly understood, the doctrine of concupiscence helps those with "same-sex attraction" to know they are not the most heinous of sinners. Even further nuance and clarity in engagement with the AIC Report is available in a helpful article by Stephen Spinnenweber, "Homosexuality, Concupiscence, and the PCA," https:// heidelblog.net/2022/08/homosexuality-concupiscence-and-the-pca/ (accessed March 10, 2023).

steps? What clues about sin's origin, nature, and terrible meaning have they left for us as we try to join the dots for the mission of the church in our time and place?

Once again, the overall effect of the volume is meant to be cumulative. Taken together, each essay within each section, and then each section within the book, offers a webbed framework of theological thinking that maps the study of human corruption in the Bible.

Total Depravity in Church History

The series of essays that begins this volume performs a particular service in the early stages of forming the web and shaping the map. Their role is to expose us to the language, concepts, distinctions, and terminology of sin that have been birthed by the Scriptures throughout church history, and to show us clearly the road that others have walked ahead of us. For instance, as Petrus van Mastricht reminds us, "The term *original sin* . . . is not present in the Scriptures but derives from ecclesiastical use."[29] This should no more worry us than the absence of the word "Trinity" from the Scriptures. Instead, viewing church history as "the history of the exegesis of the Word of God,"[30] these essays take us beyond the facile "Calvinist vs. Arminian" conception of the history of soteriology and instead lead us through the Patristic, Medieval, Reformation, and post-Reformation periods to see how sin has been understood and misunderstood in the theological landscape that we have inherited. Church history affords many examples of varied interpretations of the biblical data: from Pelagians and semi-Pelagians, Arminians and rationalists, Romanists and evolutionists, there has been no era in the history of the Christian church in which the doctrine of sin has not been debated.

One such debate over the doctrine of sin came to a head in the seventeenth century when the Remonstrants, following Jacob Arminius's teaching, argued that man's will was free and was not completely enslaved to sin. The response from the Reformed churches of Europe was a robust defense of the doctrine of man's nature. The Reformed delegates at the Synod of Dort understood the theological connectedness involved in the issue of man's fallen nature and his inability to respond to the gospel. The "Heads of Doctrine"

---

[29] Petrus van Mastricht, *Theoretical-Practical Theology: The Works of God and the Fall of Man*, vol. 3, ed. Joel R. Beeke, trans. Todd M. Rester (Grand Rapids, MI: Reformation Heritage, 2021), 450.
[30] Karl Barth, *Church Dogmatics*, ed. G. W. Bromiley and Thomas F. Torrance, 4 vols. (Edinburgh: T&T Clark, 1956–75), I/2.681.

and "Rejection of Errors" produced by the Synod refer to the state of man in original righteousness, the image of God, the systemic effects of the fall on the whole man (including emotional and noetic effects), common grace, the propagation of sin from Adam to his race, the inability of man's will, and the inadequacy of the light of nature and the law to save.

Modern advocates of Reformed theology and the "Five Points" have at times been guilty of neglecting the historical context out of which the Canons of Dort were articulated, while at the same time failing to grasp the interdependence of theological issues involved in the doctrines. Presenting the doctrines of grace as historically dislocated and theologically disconnected robs them of their beauty and power. In particular, it is worth noting how "total depravity" is not a phrase that summarizes just one paragraph of response to the Remonstrants in the Canons; rather, it summarizes seventeen articles in the Third and Fourth Heads of Doctrine in the Canons of Dort and also the "Rejection of Errors" that accompany the articles, because the issues at stake in the Synod were more far-reaching than solely the teaching of the Remonstrants of 1610. As many have previously argued, and as Lee Gatiss shows in this volume, article three of the Remonstrants on sin is not problematic for Reformed theology when taken on its own and considered at face value, but rather takes on a defective hue when considered in connection with its development in their fourth point on the nature of conversion. In other words, total depravity as a summary statement does the work the Reformed want it to do only when as full a picture as possible is developed.

Total Depravity in the Bible

The doctrines of total depravity and of the total inability of human creatures to save ourselves can seem impossibly stark when stated in abstract theological and philosophical terms. But on turning to Scripture itself we are quickly overwhelmed by the sheer scale of the textual data and its rich variety in depicting what ails us. There are matters of careful definition to be settled, for sure; and there are matters of enormous theological significance that require precision, yes; but the scriptural vocabulary and grammar of sin creates a cascading cacophony of darkness that leaves us in little doubt about the pervasive, inveterate depravity of the human heart: "The sin of Judah is written with a pen of iron; with a point of diamond it is engraved on the tablet of their heart, and on the horns of their altars" (Jer. 17:1).

The biblical essays in this volume trace the linguistic data of sin to show its multifaceted nature and power. Sin is named by specific words but also by an attending army of ideas and themes that paint the full picture of its horrors. In the OT three main words for sin appear most frequently: "sin," with the meaning of missing a mark, failing to hit a target; "transgression," with the sense of crossing a boundary line set by the divine lawgiver; and "iniquity," which speaks to the moral pollution of our evil. All three terms occur together in Psalm 51:1–2, "Have mercy on me, O God, according to your steadfast love; according to your abundant mercy blot out my transgressions. Wash me thoroughly from my iniquity, and cleanse me from my sin!" From a trinity of words, a picture begins to emerge: "Overlapping in meaning and comprehensive in scope, the three terms function together to teach us that when a person sins, he wilfully fails to attain his created purpose and defiantly rebels against the Lord's authority, and consequently incurs guilt and liability to punishment."[31] The circle widens further in Scripture through both Old and New Testaments. We meet specific words for wickedness, evil, rebellion, infidelity, stubbornness, ignorance, wandering or straying, uncleanness and defilement, unrighteousness and lawlessness, disobedience, and trespass—these terms and more are considered in detail in this volume's essays tracing sin in the Bible.

However, in many ways, the key contention of this volume's biblical essays is that words about sin combine to tell a *story* of sin and rebellion, and that it is the unfolding narrative of humanity's fall from original righteousness in Eden into ruinous rebellion, which paints full the picture of human depravity and corruption in Scripture's pages. We are not to understand sin merely from etiology but from covenant theology, as William Wood's two essays show. A true understanding of sin arises from the context of the covenant of works, from the law of God revealed in the garden, and from the doctrine of a holy God, so that it is offending against him, before either injuring or offending my neighbor, which gives to sin its grotesque nature. Sin in the Prophets is a breach of covenant, but it is also conveyed in language of disloyalty and adultery when one of the fundamental metaphors for God's relationship with his people is taken into consideration: the husband-wife relation of conjugal union. In this way the meaning of sin is played out in

---

[31] Joel R. Beeke and Paul M. Smalley, *Man and Christ*, vol. 2 of *Reformed Systematic Theology* (Wheaton, IL: Crossway, 2020), 328. Beeke and Smalley further elaborate that the "core of sin is rebellion against God rooted in unbelief toward his revelation" (347); they argue that this takes the form of doubting, distorting, denying, and defying God's word (347–50).

story form, in the account of our disordered loves, so that sin does not have merely legal definition; it also has relational forms. The cumulative effects of sin's follies are for human creatures to experience shame and disgrace, to be rendered guilty before God and liable to punishment from his righteous and holy hand. Sin's distortion of all that is good sees us grappling with consciences that accuse and condemn us; we live often with horror and fear, and our direction of travel is to flee the presence of God rather than seek to move toward him as a child to a benevolent father. "Sin wraps itself in a cloak, spreads abroad dense fog, waits for darkest night, and moves stealthily."[32] Sin's repercussions are our estrangement from God and his abandonment of us to the idolatry we have chosen to pursue.

When these narrative elements of depravity are each studied on their own and then patiently integrated with each other, after listening to the tradition of church history that has reflected on them in depth ahead of us, then, as before with the doctrine of definite atonement, the language of total depravity and, concomitantly, of total inability, emerges as illuminating heuristic terminology to describe "a pattern of judgment present in the texts."[33] This moves us beyond a biblicist reading of biblical texts and toward a biblico-systematic reading, where the words about sin illumine and in turn are illumined by the story of sin, so that by the end of a complete reading of the whole Bible the pervasiveness of sin in the human person is beyond doubt. For instance, we note how the verb "to hear" plays a prominent role in references to sin, so that refusing to hear the divine word makes the God of the covenant out to be evil and his spoken word out to be untrustworthy. The resultant spiritual hardness permeates the human person. "Though the sinner retains his essential faculties as a human being, he loses his spiritual eyes and ears, so to speak, and his inner man becomes dead in disbelief and disobedience . . . , [t]he result is slavery."[34]

This is one example of how the doctrine of sin's pervasiveness is not reliant on the "sin" word-group alone. It is patterns such as these in the texts that leads contemporary Reformed theologians to follow Augustine in defining sin's center and roots as a preference for sensuality over rationality, pride instead of humility, selfishness in place of love, idolatry above true worship, unbelief eclipsing faith, and rebellion instead of wholehearted and delighted

[32] Beeke and Smalley, *Man and Christ*, 325.
[33] The phrase is David S. Yeago's, in his seminal article, "The New Testament and the Nicene Dogma: A Contribution to the Recovery of Theological Exegesis," *Pro Ecclesia* 3.2 (1994): 152–64 (153).
[34] Beeke and Smalley, *Man and Christ*, 333.

obedience.[35] This panoply of replacements of several divine goods with substitute human evils leads to a truly awful reality: sin is vandalism of shalom; it is spiritual filth and corruption; it leads us to be perverted, polluted, and disintegrated; it is parasitic on the good; it masquerades in deceit as something it is not; it is folly; and it is, ultimately, addictive.[36] Little wonder that Augustine argued that "sin becomes the punishment of sin."[37]

Total Depravity in Theological Perspective

Given the awfulness of our subject, the self-consciousness many feel in attending so closely and fully to sin leads some to methodological overstatement in defense of the cause. "There is no subject of greater importance to Christian theology than its understanding of the concept of sin and its effects."[38] No doubt such a statement is intended in the same vein as D. A. Carson's admonition that we will not grasp the glories of our salvation if we have not plumbed the depths of our plight. Yet the truth is that, to make sin the most important subject in Christian theology is precisely to dislocate sin from a truly *theological* perspective.

"Sin is lawlessness" (1 John 3:4)—what can this mean unless there is a law; but what law and whose law? Reformed orthodoxy in its embrace of sin's definition as lawlessness "also identified sin's first motion as unbelief towards God's word (Gen. 3:1–5)."[39] John Webster points us in this direction: "Sin is trespass against creatureliness, but beneath that lies an even deeper wickedness, contempt for the creator in all its forms. . . . Sin humiliates the creature, robbing the creature of the dignity which it can have only as it fulfils its destiny for fellowship with God."[40] This means, of course, that "Salvation occurs as part of the divine self-exposition; its final end is the reiteration of God's majesty and the glorification of God by all creatures. Soteriology therefore has its place within the theology of the *mysterium trinitatis*, that is, God's inherent and communicated richness of life as Father, Son and Holy Spirit."[41] As Richard Lints says,

[35] Beeke and Smalley, *Man and Christ*, 334–343.
[36] This presentation is our summary of the format of Cornelius Plantinga Jr.'s argument in *Not the Way It's Supposed to Be*.
[37] Cited in Plantinga, *Not the Way It's Supposed to Be*, 33.
[38] Gerald Bray, "Sin in Historical Theology," in Morgan and Peterson, *Fallen: A Theology of Sin*, 163.
[39] Beeke and Smalley, *Man and Christ*, 342.
[40] John B. Webster, " 'It Was the Will of the Lord to Bruise Him': Soteriology and the Doctrine of God," in *God of Salvation: Soteriology in Theological Perspective*, ed. Ivor J. Davidson and Murray A. Rae (Farnham, Surrey, UK: Ashgate, 2011), 15–34 (19).
[41] Webster, "It Was the Will of the Lord to Bruise Him," 20.

To put it simply, the eternal God is the starting point for salvation. It is God who saves; it is creatures who are saved. Locating the nature and character of salvation in God in the first place protects salvation from becoming a human project in which God may (or may not) participate.[42]

In the same vein, Thomas McCall eloquently depicts the bleakness of sin against the backdrop of God's pure holiness and perfect goodness:

Sin is whatever is opposed to God's will as that will reflects God's holy character and as that will is expressed by God's commands. Sin is fundamentally opposed to nature and reason, and it is ultimately opposed to God. The results of sin are truly catastrophic. Sin wreaks havoc on our relationships with God, one another, and the rest of creation. It is universal in human history and manifests itself in various cultural expressions. Sin is rebellion against our Lord and treason against our Creator—and it is our fault. It wrecks human lives and leaves us vulnerable; apart from the grace that we so readily reject, it utterly destroys us.[43]

In this volume, the theological essays seek to explore the profound depths of the simple claim that it is a holy God who saves and it is depraved creatures who are saved. How can this best be articulated in a world of competing philosophies of sin (or alternatives to sin), and in a world where such terrible suffering and evil exists that the claim that God is present to save begins to look patently absurd at best or callously cruel at worst? How is Adam's sin propagated to his offspring? How are we to make sense of individual responsibility and corporate solidarity and federal headship in the complex of issues involved in the proliferation of Adam's sin to his offspring? Imputation of guilt, transmission of sin, and the distinction between original sin and actual sins, are each areas of significant importance and difficulty.

Amid these challenges, however (and they are all addressed in thoughtful and insightful ways in the essays that follow), it is vital not to lose sight of the fact that a theological account of sin and depravity is fundamentally hopeful and positive, not miserable or defeatist. The ugliness and awfulness of sin is no match for the goodness and beauty of God. Divine providence is neither compromised in part nor undone in full by human intransigence. The picture of God that you will find in these pages gives no space to any form

---

[42] Richard Lints, "Soteriology," in *Mapping Modern Theology: A Thematic and Historical Introduction*, ed. Kelly M. Kapic and Bruce L. McCormack (Grand Rapids, MI: Baker Academic, 2012), 259–92 (284).
[43] Thomas McCall, *Against God and Nature: The Doctrine of Sin* (Wheaton, IL: Crossway, 2019), 379.

of mechanistic deism, with the presence of evil best accounted for by God's "mere permission." Instead, we present an understanding of God's nature and attributes which secures divinely ordered justice in the world and sin as a tool in God's hand in the perfect and upright execution of his decree. As Herman Bavinck argues, Scripture shows us repeatedly that God uses sin as punishment for the wicked, as a means of saving his people as well as disciplining and testing them, and as something to glorify his own divine name:

> Precisely because God is the absolutely Holy and Almighty One, he can use sin as a means in his hand. Creatures cannot do that; with the least contact, they themselves become polluted and impure. But God is so infinitely far removed from wickedness that he can make sin, as an unresisting instrument, subservient to his glorification.[44]

Indeed, we want to argue that it is precisely this vista of God's glory and the eternal fame of his name that makes the study of sin in Scripture so profoundly important and moving. It is the doctrine of sin that helps us to see the divine majesty for what it is. In confessing that "Salvation belongs to the LORD" (Jonah 2:9), we confess that we are so lost and so unable to save ourselves, but that he is so gracious and so powerful to save. The gospel is the story of human depravity and inability conquered by divine purity and ability, human death overcome by divine life, human corruption countered by divine plenitude. And in it all, sin is not a challenge to divine glory but rather the very means God uses to display his attributes in a way that humbles us and exalts himself. Bavinck's treatment of this reaches beautiful, even poetic, heights in a depiction of God's power and wisdom:

> [God] would not have tolerated [sin] had he not been able to govern it in an absolute holy and sovereign manner. He would not have put up with it if he were not God, the Holy and Omnipotent One. But being God, he did not fear its existence and power. He willed it so that in it and against it he might bring to light his divine attributes. If he had not allowed it to exist, there would always have been a rationale for the idea that he was not in all his attributes superior to a power whose possibility was inherent in creation itself. For all rational creatures as creatures, as finite, limited, changeable beings, have the possibility of apostatizing. But God, because he is God, never feared the way of freedom, the reality of sin, the eruption of wickedness, or the power of Satan. So, both in its origin and its development, God

always exercises his rule over sin. He does not force it, nor does he block it with violence but rather allows it to reach its full dynamic potential. He remains king yet still gives it free rein in his kingdom. He allows it to have everything—his world, his creatures, even his Anointed—for evils cannot exist without goods. He allows it to use all that is his; he gives it opportunity to show what it can do in order, in the end, as King of kings, to leave the theater of battle. For sin is of such a nature that it destroys itself by the very freedom granted it; it dies of its own diseases; it dooms itself to death. At the apex of its power, it is, by the cross alone, publicly shown up in its powerlessness (Col. 2:15).[45]

Total Depravity in Pastoral Perspective

In the essays that close out this book you will meet the application of this strong view of God's sovereignty and providence in the joyful confession that God has used sin to doom itself to death in the cross of the Lord Jesus Christ. For our ruinous corruption and depravity is so profound that the human being who knows himself or herself truly cries out with the apostle Paul, "Wretched man that I am! Who will deliver me from this body of death? Thanks be to God through Jesus Christ our Lord!" (Rom. 7:24). Depravity in pastoral perspective holds that sin is doomed but the sinner need not be. The good news of divine rescue for lost humanity comes to us in all our brokenness and the manifold imperfections of our lives and the perverted loves of our hearts, and it comes to us as a promise and hope of a world made new where "nothing unclean will ever enter it" (Rev. 21:27).

The pastoral essays in the final section seek to provide a consistent application of the volume's framework for theological thinking. The malady of sin in human creatures is not considered first and foremost through the lens of things we *do* that are wrong and that harm and destroy. Rather, the imputation of Adam's sin means that human beings sin by trans-liturgical identity choices that mar who we *are* as creatures, and that then, from our pseudo-identities, our actual sins flow. All of life flows from worship, and the greatest of our evils is not what we *do* but whom we *love* and *serve* instead of God. As Beeke and Smalley eloquently express, we reject our filial relationship with our heavenly Father "so that natural self-love descends into the pit of self-deification." This self-worship distorts the very essence of what it means to be human:

---

[45] Bavinck, *Reformed Dogmatics*, 3:64–65.

The image of God and the covenant with Adam engage man as God's covenant servant according to the threefold office of prophet, priest and king. Sin twists man into a false prophet who refuses to receive God's Word by faith and speaks lies; an unholy priest who pollutes God's worship and seeks after created idols; and a rebellious king who transgresses God's laws and incurs liability to his sovereign retribution.[46]

Our pseudo-prophet-priest-king identities, now lived out in our self-centered narratives with which we create the meaning of our lives, mean that, as David Wells and Al Mohler each argue in different ways, sin is no longer defined by God but by the self; the self is so dominant it has come to eclipse human nature; and psychological shame has come to replace objective guilt.

Yet, wonderfully, the combined effect of all the essays in this book is to point in one direction for the cure of souls: the gospel for sinners is not a command to stop sinning, or an exhortation to sin less, or a warning to flee from sin, as essential and morally upright as all these imperatives are. The greatest movement in pastoral practice is the application of Christology to the maladies of the human person. "But as sin is opposed to God, so also is God opposed to sin. And this fact—grounded as it is in the utter goodness of God—is our hope."[47] The gospel is that God has sent us the true and the last Adam, in whom there was no sin or deceit in any form; the only Man who ever lived who did not deserve to die, and who offered up to God his sinless body as a sacrifice for sin. "For our sake he made him to be sin who knew no sin, so that in him we might become the righteousness of God" (2 Cor. 5:21). The sinless and perfect obedience of the Lord Jesus—the God-*man*—is the hope of a dying world and the comfort of a broken sinner. This volume restates the central confession of Reformed soteriology and the catholic Christian faith, that *God saves sinners* and that *Christ redeemed us by his blood* as "the witness both of the Bible and of the believing heart."[48] *Soli Deo gloria.*

---

[46] Beeke and Smalley, *Man and Christ*, 342.
[47] McCall, *Against God and Nature*, 381.
[48] J. I. Packer, "Introductory Essay," in John Owen, *The Death of Death in the Death of Christ* (London: Banner of Truth, 1959), 10.

I

SIN AND DEPRAVITY
IN CHURCH HISTORY

2

"Rivers of Dragons and Mouths of Lions and Dark Forces"

SIN IN THE PATRISTIC TRADITION[1]

Michael A. G. Haykin

In his annotated translation of the celebrated treatise of Jean Claude (1619–87) on the composition of a sermon, the Particular Baptist Robert Robinson (1735–90) observed with regard to the ancient church that the "primitive fathers held different opinions about grace and free will, and most of them speak obscurely and contradictorily about human depravity and divine assistance." Robinson had just detailed what he considered to be the clear position of Augustine (354–430), namely, that "conversion flows from the influence of the Holy Spirit, and not from the unassisted efforts of the human mind."[2] His generalization about the obscurity of the patristic doctrine of sin cannot, therefore, be meant to include Augustine. While Robinson is correct about the overall shape of Augustine's doctrine of sin and salvation, his comments are not at all a helpful guide to patristic anthropology. In general, up until the anthropological controversies raised by Pelagius (c. 354–c. 427) in the West and the Messalians in the East, Christian authors

---

[1] Unless otherwise indicated, all of the translations from Greek and Latin are those of the author. Material from the section on Macarius has appeared in Michael A. G. Haykin, *The Empire of the Holy Spirit*, 3rd ed. (Peterborough, ON: H&E, 2020). Used by permission. I am indebted to my former student Jon Cleland of Cambridge, Ontario, for help in certain aspects of the preparation of this essay.
[2] Jean Claude, *An Essay on the Composition of a Sermon*, trans. and annotated by Robert Robinson, 2nd ed., 2 vols. (London: W. Lepard, 1782), 1:108–9.

had tended to stress human freedom and responsibility in response to the *mentalité* of Roman Hellenism and the distortions of Gnosticism. During the first century or so of the Roman Imperium, what had been the classical view of human responsibility became increasingly muted as fate or fortune were regarded as the true determinants of humanity's future. Critical in heightening this sense of inevitability and human powerlessness in the face of it were two strange bedfellows, popular Stoicism and astrology. Then, within the church, Christian apologists had to do battle with various Gnostics who highlighted human inability in the face of sin and the inevitability of salvation for those who were among the elect.[3] In the face of what must have appeared as identical twin dangers, authors such as the late-second-century writer of the *Letter to Diognetus* stressed that God willed "to save us by persuasion, and not by compulsion, for there is no compulsion found with God."[4] The North African theologian Tertullian (fl. 190–220), in his polemic against the arch-heretic Marcion, similarly maintained that "man was created by God as a free man, with power to choose, and power to act, for himself."[5] And Irenaeus (c. 130–c. 200) was certain that "disobedience to God and the rejection of the good is within man's power . . . since man possesses free choice."[6]

"Lawless and Godless": Second-Century Christian Perspectives on Sin

Nevertheless, despite the necessity of this apologetic emphasis on human freedom, the dire predicament of humanity could not be forgotten. Irenaeus knew that Adam's disobedience in the garden had had radical consequences for the entire human race: "through the disobedience of the one man, who was first formed from the untilled earth, the many were made sinners and

---

[3] Jaroslav Pelikan, *The Emergence of the Catholic Tradition (100–600)*, The Christian Tradition, vol. 1 (Chicago; London: University of Chicago Press, 1971), 280–84; see also Julius Gross, *Gechichte des Erbsündendogmas: Ein Beitrag zur Gechichte des Problems vom Ursprung des Übels*, 4 vols. (Munich: E. Reinhardt, 1960), 1:69–255.

[4] *Letter to Diognetus* 7.4, trans. Maxwell Staniforth, *Early Christian Writings* (Harmondsworth, Middlesex, UK: Penguin, 1968), 146. For the late-second-century dating of this letter, see Robert M. Grant, *Greek Apologists of the Second Century* (Philadelphia: Westminster, 1988), 178–79; and Theofried Baumeister, "Zur Datierung der Schrift an Diognet," *Vigiliae Christianae* 42 (1988): 105–11. W. S. Walford, *Epistle to Diognetus* (London: James Nisbet & Co., 1908), 7–9; and L. W. Barnard, "The Enigma of the Epistle to Diognetus," in his *Studies in the Apostolic Fathers and Their Background* (New York: Schocken, 1966), 172–73, would date it no later than 140.

[5] Tertullian, *Against Marcion* 2.5, in *Tertullian: Adversus Marcionem*, trans. Ernest Evans (Oxford: Oxford University Press, 1972), 99.

[6] Irenaeus, *Against Heresies* 4.37.4, in Irenaeus, *Libros quinque adversus haereses*, ed. W. Wigan Harvey, 2 vols. (Cambridge: Cambridge University Press, 1857), 2:288–89. The numbering of the chapters and sections in Harvey's edition do not align with the standard numeration.

lost life."[7] And thinking of the "mystical solidarity" between Adam and humanity, Irenaeus wrote that "at the beginning disobedient man was stricken (*percussus est*) in Adam."[8] Fifteen or so years later, Tertullian reasoned regarding baptism,

> We have one baptism, and one only, on the evidence both of our Lord's gospel and of the apostle's letter, [where he says] that there is one God and one baptism, and one Church [which is] in heaven. . . . So then, we enter into the bath once only, once only are our sins washed away, because these ought not to be committed a second time. . . . Happy is that water which cleanses once for all, which is not a toy for sinners to amuse themselves with, and is not tainted with repeated applications of filth, so as to defile once more those whom it cleanses.[9]

Here Tertullian argued for the unique nature of the sacrament on the basis of the number "one" in Ephesians 4:4–6 and the evidence of probably John 13:10, where Jesus had said that the person who had bathed once does not need to wash again. Tertullian held to an understanding of sin in which Adam's willful disobedience had led to his posterity's loss of their likeness to God and the deprivation of the Holy Spirit, irrationality, corruption, and physical death.[10] Post-baptismal volitional sins were thus a problem for him. Their remedy, Tertullian went on to argue, was martyrdom: "We have indeed a second washing, it too a single one, that of blood."[11] And yet tellingly, at the very close of this treatise, Tertullian, himself a baptized believer, requested prayer for himself: "remember Tertullian, a sinner [*Tertulliani peccatoris memineritis*]."[12] This extremely personal aside reveals an ongoing awareness of the power of sin even in the lives of believers.[13]

Another powerful depiction of the power of sin and the impotency of sinners occurs in *The Letter to Diognetus*. This anonymous letter has been well described by Avery Dulles as "the pearl of early Christian apologetics."[14] *In*

---

[7] Irenaeus, *Against Heresies* 3.18.7, trans. J. N. D. Kelly, in J. N. D. Kelly, *Early Christian Doctrines*, 4th ed. (London: Adam & Charles Black, 1968), 171, altered.

[8] Irenaeus, *Against Heresies* 5.34.2, in Irenaeus, *Libros quinque adversus haereses*, ed. Harvey, 2:420. The phrase "mystical solidarity" is from Kelly, *Early Christian Doctrines*, 172.

[9] Tertullian, *On Baptism* 15, in *Tertullian's Homily on Baptism*, trans. Ernest Evans (London: Society Promoting Christian Knowledge, 1964), 33, 35.

[10] Christopher Bounds, "Tertullian's Doctrine of Christian Perfection and Its Theological Context," *Wesleyan Theological Journal* 51.2 (Fall 2016): 130.

[11] Tertullian, *On Baptism* 16, 35.

[12] Tertullian, *On Baptism* 20, 42, and 43.

[13] For other texts in which Tertullian discusses the nature of sin, see esp. *On the Soul* 39–41; and *On Repentance* 2 and 6.

[14] Avery Dulles, *A History of Apologetics* (New York: Corpus Instrumentorum; Philadelphia: Westminster, 1971), 28. For studies of the *Letter to Diognetus*, see esp. Henry G. Meecham, *The Epistle to Diognetus: The Greek Text*

nuce, this letter, which sought to persuade a pagan named Diognetus of the truth of the Christian religion, was the joyous expression of a man who stood utterly amazed at the gracious liberation of impotent sinners by God's love through the death of his Son for those very men and women. The letter sought to answer a series of specific questions from Diognetus, one of which had its basis in Graeco-Roman reverence for antiquity.[15] For Roman Hellenism, what was true had to be ancient; if it was recent, it was suspect.[16] Thus, if Christianity was true, why had Graeco-Roman culture not known of it in the past? This question is answered in what is the theological core of the *Letter to Diognetus*, namely, chapters 7–9.[17]

The author first affirmed unequivocally that Christian truth was ultimately not a matter of human reason or religious speculation. Rather, it was rooted in God's revelation of himself.[18] Unlike some of his Christian contemporaries, notably Justin Martyr (c. 100–c. 165), who regarded Greek philosophical thought as playing an important, albeit subordinate, role in preparing Graeco-Roman civilization for the gospel, the writer of this letter flatly asserted the opposite. In the words of H. G. Meecham, "All such strivings after God are discredited."[19] Christianity was ultimately founded on God's revelation of himself, and that in a person, his Son. This discussion of the way in which God has revealed himself opened the way for the author to provide an answer to the query about the antiquity of Christianity. The standard approach among second-century Christian apologists like Justin Martyr or Theophilus of Antioch (fl. 180s) was to refer to the history of salvation in the OT that finds its fulfillment in Christian faith, or to engage in a typological exegesis of the OT, which was then seen to foreshadow the coming of Christianity. In the light of these approaches, Christianity had a much better

---

with *Introduction, Translation, and Notes* (Manchester, UK: Manchester University Press, 1949); Barnard, "Enigma of the Epistle to Diognetus," 165–73; Joseph T. Lienhard, "The Christology of *the Epistle to Diognetus*," *Vigiliae Christianae* 24 (1970): 280–89; A. L. Townsley, "Notes for an Interpretation of the Epistle to Diognetus," *Rivista di studi classici* 24 (1976): 5–20; Charles E. Hill, *From the Lost Teaching of Polycarp: Identifying Irenaeus' Apostolic Presbyter and the Author of Ad Diognetum*, Wissenschaftliche Untersuchungen zum Neuen Testament, vol. 186 (Tübingen: Mohr Siebeck, 2006); Paul Foster, "The *Epistle to Diognetus*," *ExpTim* 118 (2007): 162–68; Horacio E. Lona, "Diognetus," in *The Apostolic Fathers: An Introduction*, ed. William Pratscher (Waco, TX: Baylor University Press, 2010), 197–213.

[15] *Letter to Diognetus* 1.

[16] Stephen Benko, *Pagan Rome and the Early Christians* (Bloomington: Indiana University Press, 1984), 21–22; Wolfram Kinzig, "The Idea of Progress in the Early Church until the Age of Constantine," in *Studia Patristica*, ed. Elizabeth A. Livingstone (Louvain: Peeters, 1993), 24:123–25.

[17] Markus Bockmuehl, *Revelation and Mystery in Ancient Judaism and Pauline Christianity* (Grand Rapids, MI: Eerdmans, 1997), 219.

[18] *Letter to Diognetus* 7.1–2 and 8.6; cf. also *Letter to Diognetus* 5.3.

[19] H. G. Meecham, "The Theology of the Epistle to Diognetus," *ExpTim* 54 (1942–1943): 98. For Justin's views about pre-Christian Graeco-Roman philosophical thought, see, e.g., *1 Apology* 44.8–10; 46.3; and *2 Apology* 13.

claim to antiquity than either Greek or Roman thought, neither of which was over a millennium old.

The *Letter to Diognetus*, however, took neither of these approaches. This was probably due to the fact that, earlier in the letter, in sections dealing with Judaism, the impression was given that Judaism was of little value as a forerunner of Christianity.[20] Thus, the author was forced to argue that God's design of sending his Son to redeem humanity was divulged at first to none but the Son. He waited until men and women had shown by their "unbridled passions . . . pleasures and lusts" that they were both "unworthy of life" and "incapable of entering into the kingdom of God by their own power." Then, at the opportune time, God sent forth his Son.[21] As this argument stands, without any hint of the OT period of preparation and the history prior to the incarnation, it was an inadequate response to the query about Christianity's antiquity. A pagan respondent could easily ask for proof of these claims and, in the terms in which they had been given, none would be forthcoming. Moreover, although it was very evident that the author is not a Gnostic, this dismissal of history was characteristic of the various Gnostic systems on the second-century religious landscape.

Yet, in the wake of this weak argument for the antiquity of Christianity, a powerful Pauline apologetic for Christianity was given. The author argued that God revealed his plan of salvation to none but his "beloved Son" until human beings realized their utter and complete inability to gain the kingdom of God by their own strength. It was then, and only then, that God

> did not hate or reject us or bear us ill-will. Rather, he was long-suffering, bore with us, and in mercy he took our sins upon himself [αὐτὸς τὰς ἡμετέρας ἁμαρτίας ἀνεδέξατο]. He himself gave his own Son as a ransom for us—the Holy One for the godless, the Innocent One for the wicked, the Righteous One for the unrighteous, the Incorruptible for the corruptible, the Immortal for the mortal. For what else was able to cover our sins except his righteousness? In whom could we, who were lawless and godless, have been justified, but in the Son of God alone? O the sweet exchange! O the inscrutable work of God! O blessings beyond all expectation!—that the wickedness of many should be hidden in the one Righteous Man, and the righteousness of the One should justify the many wicked![22]

---

[20] See *Letter to Diognetus* 3–4.
[21] *Letter to Diognetus* 8.9–9.2. The Greek text can be found in *The Apostolic Fathers*, ed. and trans. Michael W. Holmes (Grand Rapids, MI: Baker Academic, 2007), 708 and 710.
[22] *Letter to Diognetus* 9.2–5. The Greek text can be found in Holmes, ed., *Apostolic Fathers*, 710.

In the Greek papyri, the verb ἀναδέχομαι is often used with a legal meaning, namely "to become surety for," and G. W. H. Lampe has listed its usage
with this meaning in patristic literature dealing with the atonement.[23] Meecham thus rightly observes that here it "means that God in his concern for
man acted as though man's sin was his own and hence planned to do away
with it by giving his own Son as ransom."[24] Five dialectical expressions then
delineated this act of substitution, one of which—"the Righteous One for
the unrighteous"—almost exactly reproduced a phrase from 1 Peter 3:18.
What was highlighted in this dialectic were the twin soteriological themes of
the Son's utter sinlessness and humanity's radical depravity.[25] The author's
doxological expressions of amazement at the kindness of God bespeak the
humility appropriate to thought about Christ's death for sinners unable to
free themselves: "O the sweet exchange! O the inscrutable work of God! O
blessings beyond all expectation!"

André Benoit has argued that the concept of original sin is essentially absent from the Greek patristic tradition of the second century.[26] To be sure, this
mini-apology to Diognetus did not discuss how it was that men and women
came to be in the predicament of spiritual bondage to sin. Yet, Benoit did not
take stock of another text from this era, namely, the sermon *On the Pascha*
by Melito of Sardis (d. c. 190). Contemporaries regarded Melito as having
lived a life remarkable for its spirituality, though knowledge of his career is
scanty. Of his sixteen or so writings whose titles are known, only the sermon
On the Pascha is extant in full. Of the rest only fragments exist.[27] *On the
Pascha* began with an explanation of the origins of the OT Passover and how
it was a type of the redemption wrought by Christ. But why did Christ have
to suffer? Melito's answer was a delineation of Adam's death-dealing "inheritance" (κληρονομία) to his progeny: lust, decay, dishonor, bondage, and

---

[23] Meecham, *Epistle to Diognetus*, 101.

[24] Meecham, *Epistle to Diognetus*, 129. For drawing my attention to this comment by Meecham, I am indebted to
Matthew R. Crawford, " 'O, the Sweet Exchange': Soteriology in *The Epistle to Diognetus*" (advanced MDiv thesis,
The Southern Baptist Theological Seminary, 2008), 70.

[25] This dialectic recalls such Pauline texts as Rom. 5:6–10.

[26] André Benoit, *Le baptême chrétien au second siècle: La théologie des Pères* (Paris: Presses universitaires de
France, 1953), 223.

[27] On these writings, see Stuart G. Hall, trans., *Melito of Sardis: On Pascha and Fragments* (Oxford: Clarendon,
1979), 63–79. See also Melito of Sardis, *On Pascha with the Fragments of Melito and Other Material Related to
the Quartodecimans*, trans., introduced, and annotated Alistair Stewart-Sykes, Popular Patristics Series (Crestwood,
NY: St. Vladimir's Seminary Press, 2001). For a helpful bibliography of studies on Melito, see esp. Stuart G.
Hall, "Meliton von Sardes," *Theologische Realenzyklopädie* (Berlin, NY: Walter de Gruyter, 1992), 22:424–28.
This bibliography built upon those of Rudolf M. Mainka, "Melito von Sardes: Eine bibliographischen Übersicht,"
Claretianum 5 (1965): 225–55; and Hubertus Drobner, "15 Jahre Forschung zu Melito von Sardes (1965–1980):
Eine kritische Bibliographie," *Vigiliae Christianae* 36 (1982): 313–33.

finally destruction.[28] Personifying sin as a tyrant (τῆς τυραννικῆς ἁμαρτίας), Melito listed in graphic detail the multitude of ways in which men and women do the bidding of this seemingly unstoppable ruler, including all types of sexual sin and perversions, along with murder and infanticide.[29] No human being was free from sin's footstep or presence (εἰς πᾶσαν δὲ ψυχὴν ἐτίθει ἡ ἁμαρτία ἴχνος): "all flesh has fallen under sin and every body under death."[30] As Pier Franco Beatrice has noted, Melito was drawing this delineation from Romans 5:12: sin has permeated the entirety of creation by means of Adam's disobedience and brought in its train the overwhelming devastation of death.[31]

Since Melito made no mention of the way in which Adam's disobedience has let loose this devastating flood of sin, namely, through hereditary transmission by sexual conception, and given that the term κληρονομία is too general to convey this idea, Beatrice further concludes that Melito also had no concept of original sin.[32] But such a conclusion seems unwarranted. The genre of this text needs to be taken into account—it is a homily and not a theological treatise per se. Moreover, Melito was clear on the solidarity of humanity with fallen Adam as well as the irresistible power of sin present in human life. And an anti-Gnostic orientation would discourage him from making any sort of statement that might potentially undermine human responsibility for sin.[33]

Before we leave the second century, it is noteworthy that the NT pattern of listing various types of vice and sinners[34] is continued in a number of second-century Christian texts.[35] Collectively, these vices are designated as either the "way of death [τοῦ θανάτου ὁδός]" or the "way of blackness [τοῦ μέλανος ὁδός]."[36] In the following century, a list of sinful occupations was

---

[28] Melito of Sardis, *On Pascha*, 46, 49.

[29] Melito of Sardis, *On Pascha*, 30–53.

[30] Melito of Sardis, *On Pascha*, 55.

[31] Pier Franco Beatrice, *The Transmission of Sin: Augustine and the Pre-Augustinian Sources*, trans. Adam Kamesar (Oxford: Oxford University Press, 2013), 172–73.

[32] Beatrice, *Transmission of Sin*, 171–74; see also the discussion of Fernando Mendoza, "El pecado original en la Homilía sobre la Pascua de Melitón de Sardes," *Scripta Theologica* 2 (1970): 287–302.

[33] A. Trapè and L. Longobardo, "Sin. II. Original Sin," in *Encyclopedia of Ancient Christianity*, ed. Angelo di Berardino et al., 3 vols. (Downers Grove, IL: IVP Academic, 2014), 3:596. For Melito's anti-Gnosticism, see Hall, "Introduction," *Melito of Sardis*, xli.

[34] See, e.g., Rom. 1:28–31; 1 Cor. 5:10–11; 6:9–10; Col. 3:5–9; 1 Tim. 1:9–10; 2 Tim. 3:2–4; Rev. 21:8; 22:15. See the discussion by J. D. Charles, "Vice and Virtue Lists," in *Dictionary of New Testament Background: A Compendium of Contemporary Biblical Scholarship*, ed. Stanley E. Porter and Craig A. Evans (Downers Grove, IL: InterVarsity Press, 2000), s.v.

[35] *Didache* 3.1–6; 5.1; *1 Clement* 30.1; *2 Clement* 6.4; *Letter of Barnabas* 20.1; Theophilus of Antioch, *To Autolycus* 2.34. See the study of the vice lists in the *Didache* by Shawn J. Wilhite, *The Didache: A Commentary*, Apostolic Fathers Commentary Series (Eugene, OR: Cascade, 2019), 128–133, 150–55. I am indebted to Wilhite for help with these references and for drawing my attention to his work on them.

[36] *Didache* 5.1; *Letter of Barnabas* 20.1. The latter is an important passage, as it is one of the earliest texts in the Christian tradition to identify the color μέλαν with sin. Cf. Theophilus of Antioch, *To Autolycus* 2.36, where

drawn up to supplement these lists of sins and sinners, as in *The Apostolic Tradition* (c. early third century),[37] which forbade Christians from being involved in such obviously sinful occupations as being a pimp or a prostitute, a sculptor of idols, a gladiator or anyone involved in the promotion of the gladiatorial games, "an enchanter, an astrologer, a diviner, a soothsayer . . . an amulet-maker," or a magician.[38] Other occupations—less immediately obvious as being sinful—that nonetheless brought a person potentially into contact with sin included being an actor (due to the nature of the plays in which he had to act), a school teacher (because of what he must teach by way of pagan Graeco-Roman literature), a soldier (in light of the idolatrous nature of military oaths of allegiance), or "a military commander or civic magistrate that wears the purple" (presumably because of the political decisions he must render).[39]

"The Contagion of Ancient Death": Cyprian and Sin

Amid the chaos that plagued the Roman *Imperium* during the third century—the rapid and violent turnover of emperors, the constant warfare against the Sassanians in the east and the Germanic tribes to the north, the collapse of key aspects of the monetary system, the political eclipse of the Senate, and the significant decline in fresh architectural projects[40]— a North African *rhetor* from the curial class, Caecilius Cyprianus qui et Thascius (c. 200–258),[41] better known as simply Cyprian of Carthage, suggested a radical solution to the anxieties and fears of the day: conversion to the one true God who had revealed himself in Jesus Christ. This was the "one sure means to peace and to calm," Cyprian affirmed in a tract written

---

Theophilus quotes a fragment from the *Sibylline Oracles*, Book 3—from a Hellenistic Jewish provenance—that speaks of humanity wandering in the "dark and black night [σκοτίῃ . . . νυκτὶ μελαίνῃ]."

[37] For a synopsis of the date and authorship of *The Apostolic Tradition*, see A. Stewart-Sykes, "Apostolic Tradition," in *Encyclopedia of Ancient Christianity*, 1:199–200.

[38] Hippolytus, *The Apostolic Tradition* 16.10, 20, 11, 15, 21–22, in *The Apostolic Tradition of Hippolytus*, trans. Burton Scott Easton (Cambridge: Cambridge University Press, 1934; repr. Hamden, CT: Archon, 1962), 42–43.

[39] Hippolytus, *Apostolic Tradition* 16.12–13, 17–19 (p. 42).

[40] For a succinct summary of these military, political, and social ills, see Averil Cameron, *The Later Roman Empire AD 284–430* (Cambridge, MA: Harvard University Press, 1993), 1–12.

[41] For Cyprian's social status, see Michael M. Sage, *Cyprian*, Patristic Monograph Series 1 (Philadelphia: Philadelphia Patristic Foundation, 1975), 98–100 and 105–10. As Maurice Wiles has noted, Cyprian "was a man of wealth with a considerable personal fortune" (Wiles, "The Theological Legacy of St. Cyprian," in his *Working Papers in Doctrine* [London: SCM, 1976], 68).

On his name, see W. D. Niven, "Leaders of the Ancient Church. V. Cyprian of Carthage," *ExpTim* 44 (1932–1933): 363; Sage, *Cyprian*, 98–100. For recent studies on the life and impact of Cyprian, see Henk Bakker, Paul van Geest, and Hans van Loon, eds., *Cyprian of Carthage: Studies in His Life, Language, and Thought* (Leuven, Paris, Walpole, MA: Peeters, 2010); Brian J. Arnold, *Cyprian of Carthage: His Life and Impact* (Fearn, Ross-shire, UK: Christian Focus, 2017).

for a Christian friend named Donatus,[42] the only "genuine and steadfast place of security" amid "the storms of this restless age."[43] This tract, *To Donatus*, was the earliest of the authentic writings of the North African theologian and appears to have been written in the autumn of 246, not long after Cyprian's conversion and baptism.[44] Both Michael Sage, in his detailed theological biography of Cyprian, and Allen Brent, a translator of this work, have argued that it was intended to be an evangelistic tract that would lead Cyprian's pagan contemporaries in Roman North Africa to see the folly and vanity of their entire culture, and so turn to Christ.[45] In point of fact, both the military and political turmoil and the massive moral declension, which Cyprian scathingly details in *To Donatus* 6–13, may well have played a role in Cyprian's own conversion.[46]

What is so striking about Cyprian's salvific solution to the problems of his day was his insistence that salvation was ultimately not attainable by human energy—it was a free gift of God by means of the Holy Spirit. Prior to launching into his overview of the breakdown of Roman society and moral order, Cyprian argued this point through an account of his own encounter with the message of Christianity. When Cyprian first heard the gospel, he was a man in the meridian of life, a patron with numerous clients and laden with the public honors that his social status brought. He was used to extravagance in food and dress, and, in a word, was so immersed in the privileges and pleasures of the Roman world that, although he disliked the man he had become and the way in which he lived, he could not envision how his lifestyle could ever be changed.[47] And for a period of time after hearing the Christian message, Cyprian despaired of ever changing his life. He thus plunged back into his personal maelstrom of sin.[48] But during this time he was befriended by one of the elders in the Carthaginian church,

---

[42] For the difficulty in identifying this individual, see Cyprian, *A Donat et La Vertue de Patience*, trans. Jean Molager, Sources chrétiennes, 291 (Paris: Les Éditions du Cerf, 1982), 9 n. 2.

[43] Cyprian, *To Donatus* 14, trans. Allen Brent, in Cyprian, *On the Church: Select Treatises*, Popular Patristics Series 32 (Crestwood, NY: St. Vladimir's Seminary Press, 2006), 64. Subsequent quotations from *To Donatus* will be taken from either this translation—cited simply as "Brent" with the page number—or from that of Cyprian, *Treatises*, trans. Roy J. Deferrari (New York: Fathers of the Church, Inc., 1958), 7–21. The Latin, when referenced, is from *A Donat*, trans. Molager, 74–116.

[44] Sage, *Cyprian*, 110, 118, 380, 383; *A Donat*, trans. Molager, 12. On the time of year, see Cyprian, *To Donatus* 1. Cyprian alludes to the relatively brief time he had been a Christian in *To Donatus* 2.

[45] Sage, *Cyprian*, 128; Brent, *On the Church: Select Treatises*, 47.

[46] Sage, *Cyprian*, 126–27.

[47] For these details, see *To Donatus* 3, which I am taking to be a somewhat autobiographical reflection. Support for this interpretation can be found in the first sentence of *To Donatus* 4, where Cyprian notes that what he describes in the previous sentences "often applied to me" (*To Donatus* 4 [Brent, 52]). See also Sage, *Cyprian*, 111.

[48] Cyprian, *To Donatus*, 4.

Caecilianus, who persuaded him to study the Scriptures,[49] and in due course, Cyprian became a Christian.

As Michael Sage has noted, Cyprian's account of his conversion high-lights the fact that "the major propulsion" toward the Christian "way of life came from God."[50] In Cyprian's own words, "everything we are able to do is of God. From him we live, by him we are empowered."[51] In particular, Cyprian emphasized the role played by the Holy Spirit:

> When I drank in the Spirit from heaven a second birth made me into a new man. Immediately in a marvellous manner what was doubtful was con-firmed, what was closed opened, what was shadowy shone with light, what before seemed difficult I was granted the means to do, [and] it was possible to practice what I had thought impossible.[52]

Maurice Wiles has argued that this conversion account does not bespeak "a deep transformation of personal life or moral ideals." It is that of a man who wishes to make a clean break with his past, but who did not have the capacity to "make that break effective at the deeper levels of his thinking." The result is that Cyprian cannot really be reckoned as a "profound Christian theologian."[53] While Wiles definitely has a point regarding the depth of Cyprian as a Chris-tian thinker, a close reading of the text cited above, alongside Cyprian's earlier statements about his pagan past, actually conveys quite a different impression about his conversion. The change wrought by the Spirit in Cyprian's life gave him a deep sense of the truth of the Christian faith. It illuminated key aspects of that faith that had hitherto been totally unclear. And, most significantly, it gave him a real measure of moral victory over his sins. Before, it seemed as if his sins and bent to sinning were insuperable. God's power, as experienced through the Holy Spirit, proved otherwise. As Rowan A. Greer has rightly pointed out, Cyprian's experience of deliverance, which gave him the "power to live in hope and freedom" and enabled him to have a life of true virtue, was actually an experience "central to early Christianity."[54]

Jaroslav Pelikan has argued that it was Cyprian who clearly pioneered the formulation of the doctrine of original sin, and that he did so as a way

---

[49] Pontius the Deacon, *The Life of Cyprian* 4, 2.
[50] Sage, *Cyprian*, 129.
[51] Cyprian, *To Donatus* 4 (Brent, 53). See also Cyprian, *To Donatus* 14.
[52] Cyprian, *To Donatus* 4 (Brent, 52, altered).
[53] Wiles, "Theological Legacy of St. Cyprian," 69–70.
[54] Rowan A. Greer, *Broken Lights and Mended Lives: Theology and Common Life in the Early Church* (University Park, PA: Pennsylvania State University Press, 1986), 22–23.

of undergirding his thinking about the necessity of infant baptism.[55] The key text to which Pelikan points for this formulation is Cyprian's *Letter 64*, which was written by Cyprian on behalf of a synod of sixty-six African bishops, probably in the spring of 252, to a certain Fidus, who occupied an episcopal see to the west of Carthage in the western regions of the province of Proconsularis.[56] Fidus had written to Cyprian about a couple of concerns, one of which involved the baptism of infants. He objected to the baptism of infants immediately following their birth and indicated that he preferred to wait until the eighth day after birth to conduct their baptisms. He defended this practice on the basis of the fact that it corresponded to the OT practice of circumcision on the eighth day and that having to kiss the foot of a newly born infant—seemingly a part of the baptismal ceremony in the North African churches[57]—was simply repugnant.[58]

Cyprian responded to Fidus's two reasons for baptizing on the eighth day by stressing that the OT rite of circumcision on the eighth day prefigured Christ's resurrection and the gift of the Spirit, both of which had taken place on the day after the Sabbath, that is, the eighth day, and as such, the OT eighth day had its fulfillment day.[59] And rather than shrinking in repugnance from a new-born babe, Fidus must "think of the very hands of God from which that infant has so freshly come; in a sense, therefore, in a human being recently formed and newly born we are kissing . . . [the] hands of God" that created the child.[60] "The divine Scriptures in which we put our trust" indicate that the Spirit is given equally to all—both adults and infants—and who then can refuse, or delay, baptism that, by implication, gives the heavenly grace of the Spirit.[61] As Cyprian urged Fidus to remember,

> Even in the case of those who have sinned most grievously, offending many times in their past lives against God, they are granted remission of their sins, subsequently, on becoming believers. No one is denied access to baptism

---

[55] Jaroslav Pelikan, *Development of Christian Doctrine: Some Historical Prolegomena* (New Haven, CT: Yale University Press, 1969), 73–94; cf. the discussion of Beatrice, *Transmission of Sin*, 152–57, who questions whether or not Cyprian was the pioneer that Pelikan claims him to be (esp. 154 n. 43).

[56] For the date of the letter and the location of the see of Fidus, see G. W. Clarke, trans. and annotated, *The Letters of St. Cyprian of Carthage*, 4 vols., Ancient Christian Writers 46 (New York; Mahwah, NJ: Newman, 1986), 3:302–303, 305–306; see also G. W. Clarke, "Cyprian's Epistle 64 and the Kissing of Feet in Baptism," *HTR* 66 (1973): 147–48.

[57] See the discussion by Clarke, "Cyprian's Epistle 64 and the Kissing of Feet in Baptism," 147–52; and Clarke, *Letters of St. Cyprian of Carthage*, 3:310–11.

[58] Cyprian, *Epistle* 64.2–4.

[59] Cyprian, *Epistle* 64.4.3.

[60] Cyprian, *Epistle* 64.4.1–2, trans. Clarke, *Letters of St. Cyprian of Carthage*, 3:111.

[61] Cyprian, *Epistle* 64.3; 64.5.1, trans. Clarke, *Letters of St. Cyprian of Carthage*, 3:110.

and grace. How much less reason is there then for denying it to an infant who, being newly born, can have committed no sins. The only thing that he has done is that, being born after the flesh as a descendant of Adam, he has contracted from that first birth the contagion of ancient death [*contagium mortis antiquae*]. And he is admitted to receive remission of his sins all the more readily in that what are being remitted to him are not his own sins but another's.[62]

Cyprian's argument here is *a maiori ad minus*: if baptism was a crucial part of the way in which forgiveness was extended for actual sins, how much more would it convey grace to those whose only sin was that of another, namely, Adam.[63] The *contagium mortis antiquae* has been transmitted to the infant by virtue of its physical descent from Adam. And from the context, which mentions the "remission of his sins," the nature of the *mortis* is best construed as spiritual death.[64] Of the importance of this text, Pelikan notes, "Cyprian would thus appear to have been the first teacher of the Church to connect an explicit argument for the baptism of infants with an explicit statement of the doctrine that, through their physical birth, children inherited the sins of Adam and the death that was the wages of sin."[65]

"Rivers of Dragons and Mouths of Lions and Dark Forces": Macarius on Sin[66]

The fourth century is usually remembered for its debates about the deity of Christ and the Holy Spirit, but at the close of the century, after the theological settlement at Constantinople (381), there was quite evidently a growing interest in theological anthropology. This can be seen, for example, in the profound reflections of Gregory of Nyssa (c. 335–c. 395) on human spirituality and the somewhat different reasonings of Pelagius about innocence and sin. Now, the Eastern fathers like Nyssen have often been interpreted in such a way as to align them with Pelagius and his thought. As J. N. D. Kelly has pointed out, however, this is to do a serious injustice to their thinking.

---

[62] Cyprian, *Epistle* 64.5.2, trans. Clarke, *Letters of St. Cyprian of Carthage*, 3:112, altered.

[63] Pelikan, *Development of Christian Doctrine*, 82–85; Everett Ferguson, "Book Review: *Development of Christian Doctrine: Some Historical Prolegomena*. By Jaroslav Pelikan," *Church History* 39 (1970): 132.

[64] Beatrice, *Transmission of Sin*, 154.

[65] Pelikan, *Development of Christian Doctrine*, 87. On the role of Tertullian in the background of this development, see also 88–91.

[66] The quote in the subtitle is from Macarius, *Homily* 16.13 (in George A. Maloney, trans., *Pseudo-Macarius: The Fifty Spiritual Homilies and the Great Letter*, The Classics of Western Spirituality [New York; Mahwah, NJ: Paulist, 1992]). For this expression, see also Macarius, *Homily* 15.50; 43.3.

Nyssen, for instance, spoke of sin as being "innate [συναποτικτομένη] to human nature" and as proof of the assertion he adduced Psalm 51:5b.[67] Again, this Cappadocian theologian stressed that "sin takes its rise in us as we are born; it grows with us and keeps us company till life's end."[68] Just as plainly, Didymus the Blind (313–398) reasoned that Christ was free from sin by virtue of the fact that he was conceived and born of a virgin. But this is not so with the rest of humanity. Given that all other human beings are conceived in sexual union, Didymus reckoned that Adam's ancient sin had became theirs "by transmission [κατὰ διαδοχὴν]" at conception.[69]

Yet there were Eastern theologians like Theodore of Mopsuestia (c. 350–429) whose thought seems to place them comfortably within the Pelagian camp. Theodore took a purely volitional approach to sin and, as such, argued that "death is punishment for personal sins, not punishment for Adam's sins."[70] It is no surprise that Theodore wrote a treatise with the provocative title *Against Those Who Say Men Sin out of Nature and Not with Will*. It may well be the case that Theodore had the Messalians in his sights when he wrote this work.[71] Be this as it may, an author who is sometimes associated with this group of ascetics, namely, Macarius, does form quite a contrast to Theodore.

Macarius appears to have been especially active between the 380s and the first decade of the fifth century.[72] He had strong ties to Syrian Christianity, although his mother tongue was most likely Greek. He would thus have been very comfortable with the theological ambience of Greek Christian life and piety.[73] His ministry seems to have been situated on the frontier of the Roman Empire in upper Syria and in southern Asia Minor, where he was the spiritual mentor of a number of monastic communities.[74]

---

[67] Gregory of Nyssa, *Homily on Psalm 6* (PG 44 609D).
[68] Gregory of Nyssa, *Homily 6 on the Beatitudes* (PG 44.1273A–B), trans. Kelly, *Early Christian Doctrines*, 351.
[69] Didymus the Blind, *Against the Manichaeans* 8 (PG 39.1096B); Beatrice, *Transmission of Sin*, 175.
[70] Arthur Vööbus, "Regarding the Theological Anthropology of Theodore of Mopsuestia," *Church History* 33 (1964): 118; cf., however, Kelly's reading of Theodore, in *Early Christian Doctrines*, 373–74.
[71] Beatrice, *Transmission of Sin*, 205–6.
[72] For major studies of Macarius's life and theology, see Hermann Dörries, *Die Theologie des Makarios-Symeon* (Göttingen, Germany: Vandenhoeck & Ruprecht, 1978); Columba Stewart, *"Working the Earth of the Heart": The Messalian Controversy in History, Texts, and Language to AD 431* (Oxford: Clarendon, 1991); Marcus Plested, *The Macarian Legacy: The Place of Macarius-Symeon in the Eastern Christian Tradition* (Oxford: Oxford University Press, 2004). See also the helpful studies by Maloney, "Introduction," in *Pseudo-Macarius: The Fifty Spiritual Homilies and the Great Letter*, 1–33; and Alexander Golitzin, "A Testimony to Christianity as Transfiguration: The Macarian Homilies and Orthodox Spirituality," in S. T. Kimbrough Jr., *Orthodox and Wesleyan Spirituality* (Crestwood, NY: St. Vladimir's Seminary Press, 2002), 129–56.
[73] Plested, *Macarian Legacy*, 14–15.
[74] Plested, *Macarian Legacy*, 15–16.

Four collections of Macarius's homilies are extant.[75] These homilies have been historically linked to Messalianism, an ascetic movement that was condemned at various councils, including the ecumenical Council of Ephesus in 431 as well as the earlier Synod of Side in Pamphylia (c. 395). According to those who condemned them, the Messalians argued that there was an indwelling demonic power in each human soul, and that only intense and ceaseless prayer could break the power that the demonic power held over the soul. Consequently, they were said to refuse to work so that they could devote their entire time to prayer. They were also said to affirm physical experiences of the Spirit, and to make light of the sacraments of the church as well as the ministry of those in official positions of power.[76] Although there are a number of clear points of contact between the Messalians and Macarius, the burden of current scholarly opinion is that Macarius cannot be regarded as a Messalian.[77]

The awful devastation caused by the fall of Adam and the experiential reality of the tyranny of sin that ensued for his progeny as a result of his disobedience regularly impressed themselves upon the mind of Macarius.[78] Prior to the fall, Adam was clothed with the glory of the Holy Spirit,[79] and thus knew the Spirit's personal instruction as well as that of the word of

---

[75] For discussion of the four collections, see Stuart K. Burns, "Pseudo-Macarius and the Messalians: The Use of Time for the Common Good," in *The Use and Abuse of Time in Christian History*, ed. R. N. Swanson (Woodbridge, Suffolk, UK: Boydell Press for The Ecclesiastical History Society, 2002), 3 n. 7; Plested, *Macarian Legacy*, 9–12.

I have used Maloney's translation of what is termed Collection II in what follows, since it is most readily available. The other major English translation of Collection II is A. J. Mason, *Fifty Spiritual Homilies of St. Macarius the Egyptian* (London: Society for Promoting Christian Knowledge, 1921). When reference is made to the Greek in the text, then the relevant column and section in J.-P. Migne, ed., *Patrologiae cursus completes . . . series Graeca* (Paris: Centre for Patristic Publications, 1860), 34:449–822, henceforth abbreviated as PG 34, is given in brackets after the citation of the primary source.

I have also made very occasional use of the seven untranslated homilies edited by G. L. Marriott: *Macarii Anecdota: Seven Unpublished Homilies of Macarius*, Harvard Theological Studies, vol. 5 (Cambridge, MA: Harvard University Press, 1918). Following the numbering of Plested (*Macarian Legacy*, 10 and n. 5), these are Homilies 51–57. Where they are used, I have designated the reference by the name of Marriott with the appropriate page number in brackets.

[76] Stewart, *"Working the Earth of the Heart,"* 52–69; Maloney, "Introduction," 8–9; David Roach, "Macarius the Augustinian: Grace and Salvation in the Spiritual Homilies of Macarius-Symeon," *Eusebeia* 8 (Fall 2007): 77–78. In the words of Robert Murray, the Messalians "laid too much stress on experience of the Spirit for the liking of ecclesiastics in the institutional Church" (*Symbols of Church and Kingdom: A Study in Early Syriac Tradition* [Cambridge: Cambridge University Press, 1975], 35).

On the question of the relationship of Macarius to the Messalians, see John Meyendorff, "Messalianism or Anti-Messalianism? A Fresh Look at the 'Macarian' Problem," in *Kyriakon: Festschrift Johannes Quasten*, ed. Patrick Granfield and Josef A. Jungmann, 2 vols. (Münster: Verlag Aschendorff, 1970), 2:585–590; Reinhart Staats, "Messalianism and AntiMessalianism in Gregory of Nyssa's De Virignitate," *The Patristic and Byzantine Review* 2 (1983): 27–44; Stuart K. Burns, "Charisma and Spirituality in the Early Church: A Study of Messalianism and Pseudo-Macarius" (PhD thesis, University of Leeds, 1990); and Alexander Golitzin, "Temple and Throne of the Divine Glory: 'Pseudo-Macarius' and Purity of Heart, Together with Some Remarks on the Limitations and Usefulness of Scholarship," in *Purity of Heart in Early Ascetic and Monastic Literature: Essays in Honor of Juana Raasch, O.S.B.*, ed. Harriet A. Luckman and Linda Kulzer (Collegeville, MN: Liturgical Press, 1999), 107–17.

[77] See, e.g., Stewart, *"Working the Earth of the Heart"*; and Burns, "Pseudo-Macarius and the Messalians," 1–12.

[78] See Plested, *Macarian Legacy*, 35–36; and Roach, "Macarius the Augustinian," 78–79, for an overview of Macarius's thinking about the impact of the fall.

[79] Macarius, *Homily* 5.11, 12; 12.6–8; 20.1.

God—the "Word was everything to him."[80] He lived in total purity, was pleasing to God in all areas of his life, and had sovereign control over his thoughts and actions.[81] When he disobeyed God's word of his own free will, though, his disobedience became the doorway through which all kinds of evil were sowed in the world, as well as being the vehicle for the entrance of "tumult, confusion, and battle" into the inner being of men and women.[82] After the fall, Adam and his descendants lost both God and their God-given beauty. God, ever "the Lover of mankind," wept over his fallen creation,[83] for they were now marred by corruption, spiritual ugliness, and "a great stench" that emanated from their souls.[84] Fallen men and women were now, in one of Macarius's most trenchant descriptions, like "houses of prostitution and ill-fame in which all sorts of immoral debaucheries go on."[85] Dominating their lives was a love of this age and its passions and concerns.[86] Instead of their Maker being their Lord, Satan himself became their prince and ruler, and filled their hearts with spiritual darkness.[87] Ever true to his nature as a wicked tyrant, Satan did not spare any area of human existence from his deadly touch and control. The "evil prince corrupted" the human frame "completely, not sparing any of its members from its slavery, not its thoughts, neither the mind nor the body."[88] When men and women act under the impulse of these evils, they think that they are doing so on the basis of their "own determination [ἰδίας φρονήσεως]." But the reality is they are controlled by the power of sin.[89] From Macarius's vantage-point, every fallen human being is so under sin's dominion that he or she can "no longer see freely but sees evilly, hears evilly, and has swift feet to perpetrate evil acts."[90]

Although this extremely realistic view of the fall and its impact would appear to commit Macarius to a strongly determinist perspective with regard to the human condition, Macarius vehemently maintained that men and women ultimately commit evil of their own free will. As he asserted on one occasion, "Our nature . . . is capable of both good and evil, either of divine grace or of

---

[80] Macarius, *Homily* 12.6–8 (Maloney, *Fifty Spiritual Homilies*, 99–100).
[81] Macarius, *Homily* 12.7–8; 15.25.
[82] Macarius, *Homily* 15.49; see also Macarius, *Homily* 1.7.
[83] Macarius, *Homily* 4.16; 30.7; 46.3.
[84] Macarius, *Homily* 30.7–8; see also Macarius, *Homily* 24.4.
[85] Macarius, *Homily* 12.2.
[86] Macarius, *Homily* 21.2; 24.2.
[87] Macarius, *Homily* 5.2; 21.2.
[88] Macarius, *Homily* 2.1 (Maloney, *Fifty Spiritual Homilies*, 44); see also Macarius, *Homily* 16.6.
[89] Macarius, *Homily* 15.49.
[90] Macarius, *Homily* 2.2 (Maloney, *Fifty Spiritual Homilies*, 45).

the opposing power, but never through compulsion [ἀναγκαστική]."[91] However, this ability to choose appears to extend solely to individual sinful acts.[92] What human beings cannot do is remove the deeply rooted interiority of sin itself. Its dominion within the human heart is far too strong to be defeated by human energy alone.[93] It is "impossible," Macarius stated on one occasion, "to separate the soul from sin unless God should calm and turn back this evil wind, inhabiting both the soul and body."[94] Again, as he put it elsewhere, "without the Lord Jesus and the working of divine power," that is, the Holy Spirit, "no one can . . . be a Christian."[95]

This situation can be changed for the better, in Macarius's thinking, only through a person persistently crying out to God for help to transform him or her from "bitterness to sweetness."[96] So it is that Macarius can argue that "even the man confirmed in evil, or the one completely immersed in sin and making himself a vessel of the devil . . . still has freedom [ἐλευθερίαν] to become a chosen vessel."[97] Given Macarius's views about the devastation that has resulted from the fall, some of which has been detailed above, this statement must be taken to mean that Macarius believes human beings have enough freedom to cry out to God for salvation.[98] Without God's aid through the gift of the Spirit, no one will ever "return to their senses from their intoxication with the material realm [τῆς μέθης τῆς ὕλης]."[99] Without the life-giving power of the Spirit, one is dead "as far as the kingdom goes, being unable to do any of the things of God," for "the Spirit is the life of the soul."[100] And so great is the plague of sin in the human heart, healing is found only through the medicine of the Holy Spirit.[101]

Macarius also likens the conversion of a person to the taming of a horse. Prior to being tamed, an unconverted person is like a "wild and indomitable" horse. But once "he hears the Word of God and believes, he is bridled by the

---

[91] Macarius, *Homily* 15.25 (PG 34.592D).
[92] Mariette Canévet, "Macaire," in A. Rayez, A. Derville, and A. Solignac, *Dictionnaire de spiritualité* (Paris: Beauchesne, 1980), 10:31–32; Golitzin, "Testimony to Christianity as Transfiguration," 132.
[93] Macarius, *Homily* 3.4; 27.22; Stewart, *"Working the Earth of the Heart,"* 74; Golitzin, "Temple and Throne of the Divine Glory," 124–25.
[94] Macarius, *Homily* 2.3 (Maloney, *Fifty Spiritual Homilies*, 45); see also *Homily* 3.4.
[95] Macarius, *Homily* 17.10 (Maloney, *Fifty Spiritual Homilies*, 139).
[96] Macarius, *Homily* 2.3; 4.4, 8; 18.2; 20.1; 31.1; 44.9; 47.7, 10; see also Golitzin, "Testimony to Christianity as Transfiguration," 132.
[97] Macarius, *Homily* 15.40 (PG 34.604A); Maloney, *Fifty Spiritual Homilies*, 123, altered.
[98] Macarius, *Homily* 46.3.
[99] Macarius, *Homily* 24.5 (PG 34.665B–C).
[100] Macarius, *Homily* 30.3, 6 (Maloney, *Fifty Spiritual Homilies*, 191, 192).
[101] Macarius, *Homily* 20.7 (PG 34.653A).

Spirit. He puts away his wild habits and carnal thoughts, being now guided by Christ, his rider."[102] The apostle Paul was, for Macarius, a prime example of such conversion. He had been living under the "tyrannical spirit of sin," and as a persecutor of the church he can be rightly described as being "steeped in evil and turned back to a wild state." But Christ arrested his progress in sin, and "flooding him with ineffable light," liberated him from sin's domination. Here, Macarius stated, we see Christ's "goodness . . . and his power to change."[103] From another angle, the Spirit comes into the entirety of a person's being to put it in order and beautify it just as "a house that has its master at home shows forth an abundance of orderliness, and beauty and harmony."[104]

This gift of the Spirit in conversion, though, is only the beginning of what formed a major aspect of Macarius's theological reflections, namely, the remarkable nature of life in the Spirit. Sometimes the believer's life is flooded with the joy of the Spirit and he is like "a spouse who enjoys conjugal union with her bridegroom."[105] On other occasions, he finds himself overwhelmed by grief as he prays in accordance with the "love of the Spirit towards mankind."[106] Other times there is "a burning of the Spirit" which enflames the heart with regard to the things of God.[107] Then, just as "deep, conjugal love" between man and a woman lead them to marry and leave father and mother and all other earthly loves, so "true fellowship with the Holy Spirit, the heavenly and loving Spirit" ultimately brings freedom from the loves of this age.[108]

It bears noting that the gift of the Spirit is dependent on the cross-work of Christ. Likening the cross to the work of a gardener, Macarius argued that through the cross Christ, "the heavenly and true gardener" removed from the barren soul "the thorns and thistles of evil spirits" as well as uprooting and burning with fire "the weeds of sin." With the removal of these, he can now plant in the soul "the most beautiful paradise of the Spirit."[109] The gift of the Spirit is a fruit of the death of Christ.

The gift of the indwelling Spirit, though, does not mean that the one whom he indwells is now exempt from spiritual warfare, for, "where the Holy

---

[102] Macarius, *Homily* 23.2 (Maloney, *Fifty Spiritual Homilies*, 156).
[103] Macarius, *Homily* 44.8 (Maloney, *Fifty Spiritual Homilies*, 225–26).
[104] Macarius, *Homily* 11.3; 33.3 (Maloney, *Fifty Spiritual Homilies*, 202); see also *Homily* 5.9; 27.19.
[105] Macarius, *Homily* 18.7.
[106] Macarius, *Homily* 18.8 (Maloney, *Fifty Spiritual Homilies*, 144).
[107] Macarius, *Homily* 25.9 (Maloney, *Fifty Spiritual Homilies*, 163).
[108] Macarius, *Homily* 4.15 (Maloney, *Fifty Spiritual Homilies*, 56–57, altered).
[109] Macarius, *Homily* 28.4 (Maloney, *Fifty Spiritual Homilies*, 185, altered).

Spirit is, there follows . . . persecution and struggle."[110] As Marcus Plested has noted, Macarius argued for "a profoundly militant Christianity."[111] There is persecution of the church by the powers of this age.[112] The faithful believer is "nailed to the cross of Christ" and knows what it is to experience "the stigmata and wounds of the Lord."[113] And there is struggle within the heart of the Christian, such that even the most mature Christian can fall back into a life of sin.[114] In part, Macarius argued, this is because of the malice of Satan, who is "without mercy and hates humans," and thus never hesitates to attack Christians.[115] In part, though, it is because Christians, even "those who are intoxicated with God" and "bound [δεδεμένοι] by the Holy Spirit," are not under constraint to do that which pleases God, for they still have their free will [τὸ αὐτεξούσιον].[116] Thus Macarius read Ephesians 4:30 to mean that it was up to the Christian's "will and freedom of choice to honor the Holy Spirit and not to grieve him" through sin.[117]

Macarius personally knew people who seemed to be making great progress in the Christian life and then, through yielding to sin, lost everything. One man, who was a Roman aristocrat, seeking to follow Christ, sold his possessions and freed all of his slaves. He soon gained a reputation for being a holy man. But pride entered in and eventually he "fell completely into debaucheries and a thousand evils."[118] Yet another suffered as a confessor in what was probably a period of persecution in the Sassanian Empire during the long rule of Shapur II (309–379). He was horribly tortured. While in prison, a Christian woman sought to minister to him, but, tempted by sexual lust, they "fell into fornication."[119] The Christian experience of life in the Spirit in this world was thus one of great struggle against evil powers, whom, in a memorable turn of phrase, Macarius likened to "rivers of dragons and mouths of lions and dark forces."[120]

[110] Macarius, *Homily* 15.12 (Maloney, *Fifty Spiritual Homilies*, 112).

[111] Plested, *Macarian Legacy*, 37. For discussion of this theme, see Plested, *Macarian Legacy*, 36–38; Christine Mengus, "Le 'cœur' dans les 'Cinquante Homélies spirituelles' du Pseudo-Macaire (II)," *Collectanea Cisterciensia* 59 (1997): 36–38; Golitzin, "Temple and Throne of the Divine Glory," 125.

[112] Macarius, *Homily* 15.12; see also *Homily* 9.2–7.

[113] Macarius, *Homily* 10.1 (PG 34.541A); 53.17 (Marriott, 36); see also Macarius, *Homily* 12.5.

[114] Macarius, *Homily* 8.5; 15.4, 14, 16, 36; 26.17.

[115] Macarius, *Homily* 15.18 (Maloney, *Fifty Spiritual Homilies*, 114).

[116] Macarius, *Homily* 15.40 (PG 34.604B). The phrase "bound by the Spirit" is taken from Paul's statement in Acts 20:22. See also *Homily* 15.36; 27.10–11.

[117] Macarius, *Homily* 27.9 (Maloney, *Fifty Spiritual Homilies*, 178).

[118] Macarius, *Homily* 27.14 (Maloney, *Fifty Spiritual Homilies*, 180).

[119] Macarius, *Homily* 27.15 (Maloney, *Fifty Spiritual Homilies*, 180).

[120] Macarius, *Homily* 16.13 (Maloney, *Fifty Spiritual Homilies*, 134).

Ultimately, though, it is not the human will that is the determinant factor in perseverance. It is "the power of the divine Spirit" that is the critical necessity for a person to attain to eternal life. True to the pneumatological focus in much of his thought, Macarius thus concluded, "if [a person] thinks he can effect a perfect work by himself without the help of the Spirit, he is totally in error. Such an attitude is unbecoming one who strives for heavenly places, for the kingdom."[121]

A Concluding Word

One standard narrative regarding the development of the doctrine of sin in the ancient church is that the Latin tradition, from its inchoate origins in the thought of Cyprian to its mature expression in the corpus of Augustine, is the acme of patristic hamartiology. But Macarius's deeply realistic approach to the human condition reveals him also to be a thinker worthy of attention in our day that is marked by both a passionate interest in what it means to be truly human as well as a failure to take seriously the dire reality of sin in framing such an anthropology. Macarius's vision of the Christian life took seriously the fact that, prior to conversion, the human heart was dominated by evil, due to Adam's disobedience, and was under the tyranny of sin. Conversion brought liberty from this dreadful state of affairs but also plunged the believer into a warfare with indwelling sin and external spiritual enemies. Ultimately it was the Spirit and his grace that spelled victory in this war with sin.[122]

Later theological reflection on the inescapable bondage of sinners under the thralldom of sin, and thus the necessity of an insuperable work of the Spirit to free those held in this prison house—both so central to the Augustinian and Reformed understanding of the human condition—were not therefore without precedent in the early patristic era. Of course, the theological precision of how mankind ended up in this predicament, especially with respect to the imputation of Adam's sin, is not present before Augustine. However, it would be wrong to say that Augustine's theologico-anthropological concerns, which he was forced to develop in the light of Pelagius's erroneous conceptions, arrived unheralded.

---

121 Macarius, *Homily* 24.3, 5 (Maloney, *Fifty Spiritual Homilies*, 158).
122 Plested, *Macarian Legacy*, 78–79.

"Give What You Command, and Then Command Whatever You Will"

AUGUSTINE, PELAGIUS, AND THE QUESTION OF ORIGINAL SIN

Bradley G. Green

> It is no wonder that [Augustine's] version of the Fall-doctrine has stamped itself so deeply upon the imagination of his descendants that it is still very generally believed to be the only Fall-doctrine.[1]

Introduction

Original sin, in particular the relationship between Adam and the rest of humanity, is perhaps one of the most vexing doctrines in the history of Christian thought. Henri Blocher captures it well when he refers to the doctrine as a "riddle."[2] Often the best way to come to terms with a difficult theological issue is to come at it through a close study of a key historical controversy that surrounds the doctrine. With the doctrine of original sin, this would entail a study of the pitched theological struggle between Augustine and Pelagius (and the Pelagians). This was a literary battle, as Augustine never met Pelagius, although they both were in Rome at the same time.

---

[1] Norman Powell Williams, *The Ideas of the Fall and of Original Sin*, The Bampton Lectures, 1924 (New York: Longmans, Green, 1927), 322.
[2] Henri Blocher, *Original Sin: Illuminating the Riddle*, NSBT 5 (Grand Rapids, MI: Eerdmans, 1997).

In this chapter I will aim to get at the heart of the theological issue which separated Augustine and Pelagius (and the Pelagians), especially on the question of original sin. Attempting to understand Augustine—in particular, to grasp how, in some ways, his thought developed over time; and how in other ways, it remained constant over time—requires a deep immersion in several of his writings, including more than a couple dozen works spanning from near the beginning of his ministry up until the time of his death. In this chapter we will look at a number of Augustine's works,[3] as well as the key works of Pelagius and the Pelagians.[4] I will proceed along the following lines: First, I will offer some preliminary thoughts to orient our study and draw attention to the text in *Confessions* that appears to have triggered Pelagius's concerns. Second, I will explore the thought of Pelagius in relation to Adam, sin, and Adam's relationship to the rest of humanity. Third, I will proceed to explore the heart of Augustine's concerns with, and responses to, Pelagius and the Pelagians. Fourth, I will offer some theological reflections on the significance of Pelagianism and why it is necessary to deal forthrightly with these lines of thought today.

Pelagius and the Pelagians

Pelagius was a British man who desired to see moral reform in the church of his day. He was an active layman, and perhaps a monk.[5] He would eventually travel to Rome, and it is almost assuredly because of the protracted literary debate with Augustine (by Pelagius and those Pelagians who followed him) that he is today a "household name" in church history. He lived from (approximately) 360–420, close to Augustine's own life span (354–430).

Much of our knowledge of Pelagius's thought comes by way of his main adversary—Augustine, which means one must work extra hard to be fair to Pelagius. Nonetheless, there are some extant writings from Pelagius, including a commentary on Romans and an intriguing letter to one

---

[3] Unless otherwise noted I will be utilizing the New City Press translation of Augustine's works. When I have chosen to offer my own translation of Augustine, I will make this clear. Additionally, I will be using English titles for Augustine's works, and will generally use the titles found in the opening pages of Allan Fitzgerald, ed., *Augustine through the Ages: An Encyclopedia* (Grand Rapids, MI: Eerdmans, 1999), xxxv–il.

[4] I had originally planned to include the semi-Pelagians in this chapter. After reading the semi-Pelagians, and Augustine's responses, it became clear that the semi-Pelagians would be better treated in my other chapters on Augustine in forthcoming volumes in this series.

[5] It is common to describe Pelagius as a British monk. This is debated. B. R. Rees suggests that he might be called an "honorary monk," "in view of his undoubted adoption of an ascetic way of life." See B. R. Rees, *Pelagius: Life and Letters*, 2 vols. (Suffolk, UK: Boydell, 1991), 1:xiv.

Demetrius.[6] With the Pelagians who followed Pelagius, we have at least some of their own writings. Of particular interest is Augustine's second large anti-Julian writing, *Unfinished Work in Answer to Julian*, in which he quotes a lengthy work by Julian and offers his own response. One may assume that Augustine is quoting Julian accurately, since *not* to do so would have been easily called out by any number of persons, including Julian himself.[7]

Origins of the Pelagian Controversy

Pelagius's opposition to Augustine's teaching was triggered by a snippet he heard from the African doctor's book of personal confessions. In his *Confessions* Augustine had written,

> On your exceedingly great mercy rests all my hope. Give what you command, and then command whatever you will. You order us to practice continence. . . . O Love, ever burning, never extinguished, O Charity, my God, set me on fire! You command continence: give what you command, and then command whatever you will.[8]

It was Augustine's maxim, "Give what you command, and then command whatever you will," that gravely concerned Pelagius. For him, Augustine seemed to be saying that the ability to obey God must somehow come from God. That is, what animated (and agitated) Pelagius, was that Augustine appeared to be saying that if a sinner were to be able to obey God's commands, God himself must be somehow intricately related to human obedience. This is, of course, exactly what Augustine would proceed to argue throughout a lifetime of writing. Indeed, in his anti-Pelagian writings (including his writings against the so-called "semi-Pelagians") Augustine speaks clearly, and at length, about the priority of God's grace, the efficacy of God's grace, and the life-transforming nature of God's grace. Given Pelagius's commitment to the freedom of the will, in which a person

---

[6] The Romans commentary, however, as it has come down to us today, appears to have been significantly edited.

[7] There are a number of studies on Pelagius and the Pelagian controversy. Two twentieth-century studies would be Robert F. Evans, *Pelagius: Inquiries and Reappraisals* (Eugene, OR: Wipf & Stock, 2010 [1968]); B. R. Rees, *Pelagius: A Reluctant Heretic* (Suffolk, UK: Boydell, 1988). Most recently, Stuart Squires has written *The Pelagian Controversy: An Introduction to the Enemies of Grace and the Conspiracy of Lost Souls* (Eugene, OR: Pickwick, 2019). One could also consult the essays by R. A. Markus and L. Wickham in *The Making of Orthodoxy: Essays in Honour of Henry Chadwick*, ed. Rowan Williams (Cambridge: Cambridge University Press, 1989); Peter Brown, *Religion and Society in the Age of St. Augustine* (Eugene, OR: Wipf & Stock, 2007); Gerald Bonner, *Church and Faith in the Patristic Tradition: Augustine, Pelagianism, and Early Christian Northumbria*, Variorum Collected Studies (Abingdon-on-Thames, UK: Routledge, 1998).

[8] Augustine, *Confessions* X.29.40, emphasis added.

could choose or not choose how to act, Augustine's position was unacceptable. Behind Pelagius's opposition lay commendable motives. As B. R. Rees comments,

> He was at heart a moral reformer who, as he became familiar with Christian society in Rome at the turn of the fourth century, became also more and more critical of its moral standards and responded to the general laxity and extravagance he saw around him by preaching the need for simple and virtuous living based on man's freedom to choose for himself what he would, and would not, do.[9]

For Pelagius, to wrest the responsibility from man and place it in God's hands would lead only to more licentious living. That is, Pelagius thought Augustine's notion that God must "grant" the ability to obey the Lord in effect was a denial of the importance of human agency in human obedience. Throughout his literary corpus Augustine circles back to this issue repeatedly (especially in his anti-Pelagian writings). In particular, Augustine often turns to key texts like Philippians 2:12–13 and Ezekiel 36:26–27 to show that God "granting" the ability to obey the Lord does not diminish human agency in obedience, but rather *grounds* human obedience.

Pelagius (and fellow Pelagians) would criticize Augustine's position in print, leading to an astonishing literary output on Augustine's part. Interestingly, given the nature of literary exchange at the time, literary combatants would often "write past" one another, as their writings traveled from one interlocutor to the other. Augustine's writing and thinking were honed as he responded to Pelagius and the Pelagian position, although it is probably correct to say that the essential seeds of his own position were present in 396 (the date of his writing *To Simplicianus*).

The Thought of Pelagius

We turn now to the writings of Pelagius himself, starting with his commentary on Romans, to understand the main contours of his thought on original sin.

PELAGIUS'S ROMANS COMMENTARY

On the crucial text of Romans 5:12, Pelagius argues that when Paul wrote, "Therefore, just as sin came into the world through one man, and death

---

[9] Rees, *Pelagius: Life and Letters*, 1:3.

through sin," he meant that sin entered the world "by example or by pattern."[10] That is, Adam was an "example" or a "pattern," but this does *not* mean that we are *truly* and *really* bound up with Adam's transgression. Pelagius makes this clear when he comments on the latter part of the verse: "and so death spread to all men because all sinned." Pelagius writes, "As long as they sin the same way, they likewise die." Strikingly, Pelagius even says, "For death did not pass on to Abraham and Isaac."[11]

Pelagius makes an interesting move at Romans 5:15: "But the free gift is not like the trespass. For if many died through one man's trespass, much more have the grace of God and the free gift by the grace of that one man Jesus Christ abounded for many." Pelagius interprets the verse to mean, "Righteousness had more power in bringing to life than sin in putting to death, because Adam killed only himself and his own descendants, but Christ freed both those who at that time were in the body and the following generations."[12] In other words, rather than speak in asymmetrical terms in order to highlight and magnify the superabundant and glorious and majestic nature of God's grace, Pelagius does the opposite. He highlights the asymmetrical nature of the passage by downplaying the destructive and universal nature of Adam's trespass. That is to say, Pelagius (rightly) picks up on Paul's emphasis on the *asymmetrical* relationship of (1) *Christ's act of obedience*—and accompanying life/righteousness to (2) *Adam's act of disobedience*—and its consequence of death, corruption, and condemnation. But Pelagius uses the asymmetry to draw attention to the "lesser" nature of Adam's transgression: Adam "killed only himself and his own [immediate] descendants," but not the rest of the human race. Adam "became only the model for transgression" for the human race.[13] Hence, Pelagius argues, "Just as *by example of* Adam's disobedience many sinned, so also many are justified by Christ's obedience."[14]

Pelagius's commentary on Romans reveals a clear articulation of the tenets of classical Pelagianism, especially that of Pelagius's denial that Adam's

---

[10] Pelagius, *Pelagius' Commentary on St. Paul's Epistle to the Romans*, ed. Theodore De Bruyn, Henry Chadwick, and Rowan Williams, Oxford Early Christian Studies (Oxford: Clarendon, 1993), 92.

[11] Pelagius, *Romans* 92. It is worth noting that Pelagius says *death* did not pass on. The (Eastern) Orthodox (at least in general) deny that *guilt* passes on from Adam to his posterity, but they do argue that *death* passes on to Adam's posterity. Pelagius here clearly denies that *death* itself passes on from Adam to his posterity.

[12] The line "himself and his own descendants" is intriguing. We see from Pelagius's comments on Rom. 5:12 that, for him, death did *not* pass on to Abraham and Isaac. It is therefore hard to know exactly what Pelagius meant by "and his descendants." Perhaps he meant his *immediate* descendants, but not farther down the line, with Abraham and Isaac?

[13] Pelagius, *Romans* 95.

[14] Pelagius, *Romans* 95.

progeny is in any meaningful way bound up with Adam's transgression. In short, for Pelagius, Adam's sin serves simply as an example for those persons who follow Adam.

PELAGIUS'S "LETTER TO DEMETRIUS"

In his "Letter to Demetrius" (413), Pelagius writes to a certain Demetrius, who—on the verge of getting married—is considering pledging herself to virginity. Her mother, understandably concerned, had written to Pelagius for advice. In his communication to Demetrius, Pelagius says a number of interesting things, and consistently speaks of the goodness of man, his freedom, and his ability to choose, etc.[15] From the letter it is clear that Pelagius rejects original sin. Sin, for him, is simply "habit" that has been ingrained due to repetition:

> Nor is there any reason why it is made difficult for us to do good other than that long habit of doing wrong which has infected us from childhood and corrupted us little by little over many years and ever after holds us in bondage and slavery to itself, so that it seems somehow to have acquired the force of nature. We now find ourselves being resisted and opposed by all that long period in which we were carelessly instructed, that is, educated in evil, in which we even strove to be evil, since, to add to the other incentives to evil, innocence itself was held to be folly. That old habit now attacks our new-found freedom of will, and, as we languish in ignorance through our sloth and idleness, unaccustomed to doing good after having for so long learned to do only evil, we wonder why sanctity is also conferred on us as if from an outside source.[16]

It is important to note that when Pelagius writes here of the importance of "habit," he is actually using the language of Augustine, even if his overall understanding of man and the human dilemma due to sin is different from Augustine's. Augustine speaks of the importance of habit, and how we continue to tie ourselves into knots as we repeatedly engage in sin. But there is a clear difference. Augustine affirms, in his own words, both original sin and actual sin. For Augustine, as we engage in actual sin through habit, we—in a sense—reinforce and compound the problem of original sin with which we entered the world. By contrast, for Pelagius, there is no link between original sin and actual sin, for original sin—in the sense of someone being corrupted

---

[15] Pelagius, *Letter to Demetrius* 2.2.
[16] Pelagius, *Letter to Demetrius* 8.3.

by or guilty of Adam's sin—does not exist. According to Pelagius, Adam had original sin; we have only actual sin.

PELAGIUS'S *ON THE CHRISTIAN LIFE*[17]

In this work, there is a striking section on Adam (13.2). Intriguingly, Pelagius says of Adam's sin, "I find that there was no disbelief in him but only disobedience, which was the reason why he was condemned and why all are condemned for following his example."[18] Pelagius's point is a straightforward one: Adam was condemned for his disobedience; all those after Adam are condemned for following his example.[19] That is, those who follow Adam *do* in fact engage in disobedience, but the problem for those who are subsequent to Adam does not really lie in *Adam's* transgression; the problem lies in their following Adam's *example*. In other words, for Pelagius, the condemnation for sin is not for being guilty *in* Adam but for imitation *of* Adam. According to B. R. Rees, there is "no more explicit refutation in Pelagius of Augustine's doctrine on the fall and original sin than this: Adam was condemned for disobedience and so are we ever after for our imitation of his example."[20]

PELAGIUS'S *LITTLE BOOK OF FAITH*

Around 417, Pelagius wrote a letter to Pope Innocent I, and included a statement of faith with it, which he called *Little Book of Faith*. On the whole, the statement is orthodox: Pelagius affirms the Trinity, condemns Arius and Apollinaris, and adheres to the full humanity and deity of Christ. However, he is critical of Augustine at points, the first of which occurs in section 21. Pelagius pushes back against the notion in Augustine's *Confessions* that God is required to enable man toward obedience; he engages again the maxim that triggered the controversy in the first place: "Give what you command, and then command whatever you will."[21] In response, Pelagius writes,

---

[17] With this piece, there is an assumption that it is from the pen of Pelagius, since key wording from this writing is quoted at the Synod of Diospolis (415). For further, see the introduction by Rees in *Pelagius: Life and Letters*, 2:105–6.
[18] Pelagius, *On the Christian Life* 13.2. The disjunction between *disbelief* and *disobedience* is intriguing. Might not it be better to see *every* act of disobedience as *at least in some mysterious sense* rooted in a kind of "disbelief"—not believing that the path of obedience is the better path, the path that brings the most joy and happiness to someone? When we sin (when we *disobey*), is that not in some sense inextricably tied to a (mysterious) kind of *disbelief*, for when we sin are we not in a sense acting like unbelievers at that point?
[19] See footnote 22 in Rees, *Pelagius: Life and Letters*, 2:121.
[20] Rees, *Pelagius: Life and Letters*, 2:121 n. 2.
[21] Augustine, *Confessions* X.29.40. As previously noted, the larger context in Augustine is, "You command continence: give what you command, and then command whatever you will."

> We do also abhor the blasphemy of those who say that any impossible thing
> is commanded to man by God; or that the commandments of God cannot be
> performed by any one man, but that by all men taken together they may.[22]

In section 25, Pelagius has Augustine in view again when he writes,

> Free will we do so own, as to say that we always stand in need of God's
> help; and that as well they are in an error who say with Manichaeus that a
> man cannot avoid sin, as they who affirm with Jovinian that a man cannot
> sin; for both of these take away the freedom of the will. But we say that a
> man always is in a state that he may sin, or may not sin, so as to own our-
> selves always to be of a free will.[23]

The term "free will" is of course contested in Christian history. Some, like
Augustine himself, can use the term, but define it in his own way—such that
indeed man has "free will," but that man (especially in his unregenerate state) is
"free" to obey a will which is inextricably bound up with sinful desires. Pelagius
can sound almost "Augustinian" when he says that "we always stand in need of
God's help." But this statement must be interpreted in light of the context. Especially important is the end of this quotation, where Pelagius affirms, it seems,
what is generally called a "libertarian" view of free will: "a man always is in a
state that he may sin, or may not sin, so as to own ourselves always to be of a
free will." In short, "free will" *really* seems to mean for Pelagius that our act of
the will (again, especially in an unregenerate state) is in no meaningful way connected to, hampered by, or bound up with a deep and intractable sin problem.

On the Deeds of Pelagius

Having surveyed a number of works from Pelagius, we turn now to the results of the Council of Carthage (411/412). The council offered a helpful
seven-point summary of the views of one of the key Pelagians—Caelestius,
a fourth-century, contemporary follower of Pelagius and one of the key proponents of his views. A certain Paulinus saw seven key errors in Caelestius,
which were debated at the Council of Carthage. Augustine lists them in his
On the Deeds of Pelagius:[24]

---

[22] Pelagius, *Confession of Faith* 21, https://earlychurchtexts.com/public/pelagius_letter_and_confession_to_innocent.htm.

[23] Pelagius, *Confession of Faith* 25; https://earlychurchtexts.com/public/pelagius_letter_and_confession_to_innocent.htm.

[24] Augustine, *On the Deeds of Pelagius* 11.23; see also Augustine, *On the Grace of Christ, and Original Sin* 1.3 and 4. Augustine was not at this council, and so is relying on testimony.

1. "Adam was created mortal so that he would die whether he sinned or did not sin."
2. "The sin of Adam harmed him alone and not the human race."
3. "The law leads to the kingdom just as the gospel does."
4. "Before the coming of Christ there were human beings without sin."
5. "Newly born infants are in the same state in which Adam was before his transgression."
6. "The whole human race does not die through the death or transgression of Adam."
7. ". . . nor does the whole human race rise through the resurrection of Christ."

These seven axioms or principles reveal the inner logic and nature of Pelagianism.

Summary

It is perhaps worth summarizing some of the key tenets of Pelagius and the Pelagians before moving to Augustine's response.

First, Pelagius is quite clear that persons subsequent to Adam (i.e., Adam's descendants) follow Adam by *imitation* rather than by *propagation*. This is central to understanding Pelagius: there is no real connection to Adam, in the sense that Adam's act of disobedience fundamentally shapes or marks those who follow him.

Second, Pelagius tends to emphasize that there is a fundamental *continuity* between pre-fall man (Adam before the fall) and post-fall man (all of Adam's descendants). To grasp this is to begin truly to understand Pelagius's theology and mindset. Pelagius can look at pre-fall man and post-fall man and see a real and fundamental continuity. There is no fundamental rupture as one moves from the pre-fall era of history to the post-fall era of history.

Third, Pelagius has a lower view of what man was before the fall. This is tied to the previous point. Pelagius sees all man's current failures and sins as not *fundamentally* a rupture in man. That is, since there is not a pre-fall realm from which Adam tragically fell—and with Adam, his progeny—there is in a sense a "lower" view of man *in his very nature*. Not to get too far ahead of things, but one might say that with Augustine there is a *grandeur* and a *magnificence* of man that is simply absent in Pelagius. When man—in the present—sins, it is as if Pelagius believes, "Well, this is simply what man does. Sometimes he obeys, sometimes he disobeys."

Fourth, Pelagius, in his attempt to *secure* man's freedom or liberty, perhaps constructs his anthropology so as actually to render incomprehensible a meaningful understanding of human freedom and nature. On this point, B. B. Warfield makes a penetrating observation, suggesting that one of Pelagius's chief errors was his emphasis on

(1) *each individual act* of man over against, or at the expense of,

(2) man's *character*.

As Warfield writes, "[Pelagius] looked upon freedom in its *form* only, and not in its *matter*."[25] Likewise, with Pelagius, "the will was isolated from its acts, and the acts from each other, and all organic connection or continuity of life was not only overlooked but denied."[26]

Fifth, Pelagius's way of reading the old covenant and new covenant (only briefly touched on here) reveals a fundamental hermeneutical weakness. It appears that there was virtually no sense of a historical-redemptive reading of Scripture in Pelagius. The great biblical tensions of the already–not yet, and of the law's holiness, righteousness, and goodness, combined with its pedagogical role which culminates in Christ, the end of the law, are strangely missing in Pelagius. The idea that the old covenant was good, but had a fading glory, while the new covenant is truly *better*, with an unfading glory, seems to have no purchase in Pelagius's theologizing.

Augustine's Response to Pelagius and Pelagianism

Augustine summarizes and critiques the thought of Pelagius in many places. We begin with his *To Simplicianus*, since this work is a turning point in his thought in the controversy with Pelagius.

TO SIMPLICIANUS

Written around 396 to 398, this was Augustine's first work as a bishop. Some consider it the "early" Augustine, but there appears to be a significant shift in this work to what becomes his fully developed thought in the

---

[25] Benjamin Breckenridge Warfield, "The Pelagian Controversy," in *Studies in Tertullian and Augustine* (New York: Oxford University Press, 1930), 296.

[26] Warfield, "Pelagian Controversy," 296.

last three decades or so of his life. There are some positions in his early work which Augustine later disavows. First, Augustine at this point affirms something like semi-Pelagianism (or, if one likes, semi-Augustinianism): Man has within himself the ability to turn to God for salvation, and then God's grace enters the scene.[27] Second, Augustine thinks that the classic struggle described in Romans 7 must be a struggle experienced by the non-Christian. Later, Augustine will come to see this as a Pelagian interpretation, for how could a *non-Christian* have such an extreme moral battle or struggle?[28]

In section I.2.20, Augustine speaks of *tradux peccati* (the passing on of sin) and *originalis reatus* (original liability). Commenting on Sirach 33:11, he says that God made a "single mass" of those who had been separated from paradise: "Then a single mass was made of all of them, which came from the transmission of sin and the punishment of mortality, although, thanks to God's forming and creating them, they are good." It is striking how highly Augustine speaks of fallen mankind:

> For in all people there is a beauty and cohesion of body with such harmony among its members that the Apostle used this to illustrate how charity should be maintained; in all people there is also a vital spirit that gives life to their earthly members; and the whole nature of the human person is regulated in marvelous fashion by the mastery of the soul and the servitude of the body.

However, Augustine then turns explicitly to sin: "But the fleshly desire that results from the punishment for sin has, because of the original guilt [or "liability"[29]], cast abiding confusion into everything, and now it presides over the whole human race as one complete lump."[30] While Augustine does not give a final interpretation of how sin is passed on, it is part of the matrix of this chapter to show that he clearly affirms that sin is passed on from Adam to all of his descendants. Augustine also affirms "original guilt" or "original liability"—*originalis reatus*: Adam was responsible for original liability or guilt, and Adam's act "cast an abiding confusion onto everything." When

---

[27] Augustine, *To Simplicianus* I.1.14.

[28] The debate over how much Augustine's thought on these issues changed over time is an intriguing issue. Of course, it is possible that Augustine may himself overplay the difference between the "earlier" and the "later" Augustine. For example, see Carol Harrison, *Rethinking Augustine's Early Theology: An Argument for Continuity* (Oxford: Oxford University Press, 2006).

[29] The Latin here is "originali reatu," which could also be translated "original liability."

[30] Augustine, *To Simplicianus* I.2.20.

Augustine then says that "it presides over the whole human race," the ante-cedent of "it" clearly seems to be this "original liability" or "original guilt," which now pervades the entire human race. It seems clear that Pelagius never grasped a biblical anthropology: the whole human race is truly "in" Adam, and Adam truly represents all of his descendants. Because Pelagius did not seem to grasp such an anthropology, he did not seem to grasp the all-pervasive and radically universal nature of sin—a sin bound up with the first man, and which has been passed on (however mysteriously) to the entire human race.

In short, *To Simplicianus* is a transitional work. The seeds sown in this early work of Augustine flower and blossom throughout the rest of his corpus.

CONFESSIONS

Augustine's *Confessions* was written between 397 and 400. While there are many places in which Augustine reflects on the reality, allure, and experi-ence of sin, we draw attention to Book V, where he explicitly speaks of original sin:

> For me too a scourge was waiting there, in the guise of a bodily illness that brought me to death's door loaded with all the sins I had committed against you, against myself and against other people, evil deeds many and grievous over and above the original sin that binds all of us who die in Adam.[31]

Here Augustine affirms actual sin that we commit "over and above" the origi-nal sin we have in Adam.

THE PUNISHMENT AND FORGIVENESS OF SINS AND THE BAPTISM OF LITTLE ONES

Augustine wrote this volume in 412. It consists of an Introduction plus three "books" (essentially modern-day chapters). The work was a response to a certain Marcellinus, who had written to Augustine with questions about Pe-lagianism. One of the ways in which Augustine attempts to critique Pelagius and the Pelagians is by a discussion of infant baptism, and the Pelagian posi-tion on original sin in relationship to infant baptism. Augustine returns to this

---

[31] Augustine, *Confessions* V.9.16.

theme of infant baptism at a number of points in his writings. There are three key lines of (Pelagian) argument to which Augustine responds.[32]

First Line of (Pelagian) Argument: Adam's Death Was by Necessity of Nature

The Pelagians essentially argued that death is a natural reality, and that Adam would have died whether he sinned or not.[33] In contrast, for Augustine, death enters the world through the sin of Adam, and is not ultimately a "natural" reality. Augustine argues that if Adam had not sinned but had continued to obey the Lord, then he would have been eventually translated into an elevated existence, where temptation to sin would no longer exist and where death would not exist. Augustine does clarify that Adam could have been *mortal* by nature, but that does not mean that *death* is by nature. As he writes, "the body could be mortal without being destined to die, before being changed into that state of incorruption which is promised to the saints at the resurrection."[34]

Second Line of (Pelagian) Argument: There Are in This Life Those Who Have No Sin

In Book II Augustine addresses the second of the three Pelagian arguments. He states the key question as follows: "Is there anyone now living, or has anyone ever lived, or will anyone ever live in this world without any sin whatever?"[35] In response, Augustine points to the Lord's Prayer and the line "lead us not into temptation," which, he argues, would make little sense if combating sin was not a significantly challenging and difficult issue.[36]

Third Line of (Pelagian) Argument: Another Way to Deny the Transmission of Sin

In Book III of *The Punishment and Forgiveness of Sins and the Baptism of Little Ones* Augustine summarizes and responds to a third significant argument of Pelagius, summarized in his Romans commentary.[37] "They say 'If the sin of Adam did harm even to *those who are not sinners*, then the righteousness of Christ also benefits *those who are not believers*, because he says that human

---

[32] These three are found at the beginning of Book III of *The Punishment and Forgiveness of Sins and the Baptism of Little Ones*, the first and second in 1.1 and the third in 2.2.

[33] See also Augustine, *On the Deeds of Pelagius* 11.23, and *On the Grace of Christ, and Original Sin*, II.11.12. In these places Augustine summarizes the thought of Caelestius, a Pelagian.

[34] Augustine, *Punishment and Forgiveness of Sins and the Baptism of Little Ones* I.5.5.

[35] Augustine, *Punishment and Forgiveness of Sins and the Baptism of Little Ones* II.1.1.

[36] That is, Augustine seems to think that, for Pelagius to argue that it is certainly the case that there could be someone having no sin, simply overlooks the seriousness of sin.

[37] When Pelagius speaks of "they" in the following quote, he is putting this "Pelagian" argument on the "lips" of others.

beings are saved through the one man in a similar way and in fact to a greater extent than they perished through the other.' "[38] The Pelagian argument—against original sin being in any way passed on to Adam's descendants—appears to be as follows: Since we know that *Christ's act of obedience* does not (at least ultimately) benefit all persons (i.e., those who are not believers), we have to say that *Adam's sin* does not affect all persons.[39] In response, Augustine turns to both Scripture and two key early Christian leaders—Cyprian and Jerome—to try and show that Scripture and the historical Christian church have consistently taught the truth of original sin. There is, of course, Romans 5: sin entered the world through one man. But interestingly, Augustine is quite happy to say that even if one might contest the exact meaning of Romans 5, Scripture as a whole consistently teaches the universal sinfulness of man.[40]

AUGUSTINE ON *NATURE AND GRACE*

Augustine's *Nature and Grace* (415) was written to answer certain questions posed by some persons perplexed by the thought of Pelagius. In it, Augustine seems to respond to Pelagius's work *Nature*, which had been given to him by two former followers of Pelagius, men by the names of Timasius and James.[41] It appears that, upon reading Pelagius's *Nature*, Augustine shifts his stance significantly regarding Pelagius: from (1) criticizing a mistaken brother in the Lord, to (2) criticizing someone who was opposing the very gospel of Christ.[42] Looking back at this work, Augustine wrote in his *Retractations*,

> There also came into my hands at that time a book of Pelagius in which he defended human nature, with as much argumentation as he could, in opposition to the grace of God by which the sinner is justified and by which we are Christians. I, therefore, called the book by which I answered him, *Nature and Grace*. In it I did not defend grace in opposition to nature, but the grace by which nature is set free and ruled.[43]

---

[38] Pelagius, quoted in Augustine, *Punishment and Forgiveness of Sins and the Baptism of Little Ones* III.2.2; emphasis added. Augustine can speak of those who are sinful *originaliter*, and those who are sinful *actualiter*. Those who are sinful *originaliter* (all persons excepting Christ) *will indeed and in fact* sin *actualiter*. Augustine has categories that Pelagius does not have, which is the heart of the issue.

[39] Interestingly, the argument comes from Pelagius's commentary on Romans (5:15), as noted earlier, but Pelagius does not state it as his own. He attributes it to "those who oppose the transmission of sin" (Pelagius, *Pelagius' Commentary on St. Paul's Epistle to the Romans*, 94).

[40] Augustine, *Punishment and Forgiveness of Sins and the Baptism of Little Ones* III.4.8.

[41] The introductory material in the New City Press edition of *Nature and Grace* is very helpful.

[42] Augustine, *Retractations* II.68.42.

[43] Augustine, *Retractations* II.68.42 (on *Nature and Grace*). I use here the common English translation "Retractations" for the Latin "Retractationes." The Latin title "Retractationes" can be something of a "false friend" when translated. In English, it does not really mean "retractions." It probably means something like "revisions" or "recon-

It would be hard to find a better summary of at least a strand of Augustine's understanding of grace, than this last line: "In it I did not defend grace in opposition to nature, but the grace by which nature is set free and ruled." Pelagius had written an intriguing (if nefariously clever) work entitled *Nature*, in which he wrote along the following lines: (1) God by grace creates nature; (2) hence, nature is inherently "graced"; (3) thus, when one—*out of one's own "nature"*—comes to saving faith, or obeys the Lord, one does so by "grace." Augustine notes more than once that it took a while for him to grasp exactly what Pelagius was doing. But Augustine eventually came to see that what Pelagius was doing, in terms of grace, was thoroughly different from what he read in Scripture. One of the literary results of coming to terms with Pelagius's thought was *Nature and Grace*. This final line by Augustine encapsulates a precious Augustinian insight: while grace need not be viewed in "opposition" to nature, yet it *is* the case that grace is needed to "set free" nature and to "rule" nature.

As noted above, a key question in the debate is whether there are any who have never sinned.[44] Augustine summarizes Pelagius (not mentioned by name) as follows: the Pelagian notion is that human nature is "capable by itself of fulfilling the law and attaining perfect righteousness."[45] But, if this is *really* possible, Augustine replies, Christ died in vain.[46] He goes on to argue, "But if Christ has not died in vain, then the whole of human nature can be justified and redeemed from the perfectly just anger of God, that is, from punishment, in no other way than by faith and the mystery of Christ's blood."[47]

Pelagius's argument was based on the following:

1. It is God by his grace who has created all things, including human nature.
2. Man, *by nature*, can obey the Lord and fulfill God's commands.
3. Since man's *nature* is provided by God's *grace*, man can come to saving faith, or obey God with the "help" of God's grace.

Augustine finds (at least) two things questionable in Pelagius's argument:

(1) First, Pelagius ignores the distinction between *pre-fall man* and *post-fall man* (and a big part of Augustine's subsequent response is to highlight that

---

siderations"—and some English translations use one of those latter terms. I use the older translation "retractations" simply because of its historic, common usage.

[44] This question is raised at the very beginning of *Nature and Grace* (1.1) and is treated repeatedly throughout the volume.

[45] Augustine, *Nature and Grace* II.2.

[46] Augustine, *Nature and Grace* II.2.

[47] Augustine, *Nature and Grace* II.2.

after the fall we all start with wounded natures in need of healing). That is, for Pelagius, *post-fall man* has all the powers and abilities that *pre-fall man* had. Indeed, the fall did not bring about any change in man's fundamental situation.[48]

(2) Second, Pelagius seems to argue that man at present needs no *additional* help or grace from God if he is going to obey God, which sounds essentially like saying that man *really* does not need help or grace if he is going to obey God.

Augustine's response is to say that,

(1) There is a significant difference between pre-fall and post-fall man in regard to his "nature." Pre-fall man is innocent; post-fall man is corrupt and guilty.

(2) Even apart from this pre-fall/post-fall distinction, it is inadequate to say that since our created nature comes from God, somehow this "counts" as God "helping" us to live a sinless life:[49] "He has attributed the ability not to sin to God's grace, precisely because God is the author of the nature in which he claims that the ability not to sin is inseparably implanted."[50]

Augustine's assessment is that Pelagius needs to admit that we need a savior. That is, we need a savior from outside of us to rescue us. We need something more than simply the "grace" given in nature to deliver us from the problem of sin.

THE CITY OF GOD

In his classic work *The City of God* (426) Augustine treats the question of sin, and especially original sin, in some detail. All the key elements of Augustine's mature thought appear in two key books (books 13 and 14) of *The City of God*.[51]

Augustine affirms that all of humanity was "in" Adam:

But as man the parent is, such is man the offspring. In the first man, therefore, there existed the whole human nature, which was to be transmitted by the woman to posterity, when that conjugal union received the divine sentence of its own condemnation; and what man was made, not when

---

[48] The importance of the distinction between *pre-fall* man and *post-fall* man is hard to overestimate. For Augustine, something radical happened with Adam's transgression, and Adam's act *truly* or *really* affected both Adam and his progeny. For Pelagius, since Adam's transgression has no real effect on Adam's progeny, there is *no real distinction* between pre-fall man and post-fall man. This distinction is largely in terms of moral or ethical state and ability, rather than in terms of metaphysics or ontology. That is, both pre-fall man and post-fall man are human, and both bear the image of God (i.e., at the metaphysical or ontological level). However, there is a chasm between pre-fall man and post-fall man in terms of moral or ethical state and ability.

[49] Augustine begins his line of argument in *Nature and Grace*, starting in XLIV.53.

[50] Augustine, *Nature and Grace* LI.59.

[51] The *City of God* selections in this section are from the Marcus Dods translation of 1950 (Modern Library Classics [New York: Random House]).

created, but when he sinned and was punished, this he propagated, so far as the origin of sin and death are concerned.[52]

A few lines later, Augustine continues to describe the way in which Adam's posterity came into the world corrupted and changed by Adam's transgression:

> [T]he first man did not fall by his lawless presumption and just sentence; but human nature was in his person vitiated and altered to such an extent, that he suffered in his members the warring of disobedient lust, and became subject to the necessity of dying. And what he himself had become by sin and punishment, such he generated those whom he begot; that is to say, subject to sin and death.[53]

At points, Augustine says not only that all persons were *in* Adam in some sense, but that all persons *are* Adam: "For we were all in that one man, since we all *were* that one man who fell into sin through the woman who was made from him prior to sin."[54] Indeed, all persons after Adam come into the world with a vitiated nature: "And, once this nature was vitiated on account of sin, and bound by the chain of death, and justly condemned, man could not be born of man in any other condition."[55]

It should be noted that for Augustine, Adam and Eve, in a sense, sinned *before* they sinned. That is, there was a kind of "secret" turning of the will in on itself before the actual eating of the fruit of the tree of the knowledge of good and evil. As Augustine writes, "Thus, the evil act—that is, the transgression of eating the forbidden food—was committed by people who were already evil, and it would not have been committed if they had not already been evil."[56] He goes on: "The first evil, then, is this: when man is pleased with himself, as if he were himself light, he turns away from the light which, if it pleased him, would have made him light himself."[57]

For Augustine, human nature itself was changed due to Adam's sin: "human nature was changed for the worse and was also transmitted to their posterity under the bondage of sin and the necessity of death."[58] He expands:

---

52 Augustine, *City of God* XIII.3.
53 Augustine, *City of God* XIII.3.
54 Augustine, *City of God* XIII.14, emphasis added.
55 Augustine, *City of God* XIII.14.
56 Augustine, *City of God* XIII.13.
57 Augustine, *City of God* XIII.13.
58 Augustine, *City of God* XIV.1.

> For God, the author of natures, not vices, created man upright; but man, being of his own will corrupted, and justly condemned, begot corrupted and condemned children. For we all were *in* that one man, since *we all were that one man* who fell into sin by the woman who was made from him before the sin.[59]

Thus, after Adam's sin, Augustine describes Adam's progeny as "the whole mass . . . condemned, so to speak, in its vitiated root."[60]

We now turn to some of Augustine's final works, his responses to the Pelagian Julian of Eclanum.

Augustine and Julian of Eclanum

When we speak of Augustine and the Pelagian controversy, we are dealing with Pelagius and several people besides him who articulated a similar understanding of key issues related to man, sin, and grace. The "last of the Pelagians"—as far as Augustine was concerned—was Julian of Eclanum, whom Serge Lancel calls a "hotheaded youngster."[61] Augustine would be still dealing with Julian up to virtually his dying day. In fact, upon his death, Augustine would leave unfinished his lengthier response to Julian.[62]

We will look at the following works of Augustine in which he is responding to Julian: *Marriage and Desire*; *Answer to the Two Letters of the Pelagians*; *Against Julian*; and *Unfinished Work in Answer to Julian*.

MARRIAGE AND DESIRE

In his work *Marriage and Desire* Augustine is responding to Julian of Eclanum's criticism of him. Julian had accused Augustine of condemning marriage. Augustine responded to this criticism with Book I of *Marriage and Desire* (written in the winter of 418–419). Julian in turn responded to Augustine, leading Augustine to pen Book II of *Marriage and Desire*[63] (written either in 420 or 421).

---

[59] Augustine, *City of God* XIII.14, emphasis added.
[60] Augustine, *City of God* XIV.26. The Latin is "*universa massa tamquam in vitiata radice damnata est.*"
[61] Serge Lancel, *Saint Augustine*, trans. Antonia Nevill (Norwich: Hymns Ancient & Modern, 2002), 418. The literary dispute between Augustine and Julian was, to put it mildly, acerbic.
[62] Augustine's *Against Julian* (AD 421) is close to 300 pages, and Augustine's *Unfinished Work in Answer to Julian* is almost 700 pages long (both in the New City Press editions).
[63] A helpful summary of this history can be found in the "Introduction" to the New City Press edition of *Marriage and Desire*. See Augustine, *Answer to the Pelagians II*, in *The Works of Saint Augustine: A Translation for the 21st Century*, vol. I/24 (Hyde Park, NY: New City Press, 1998). Roland J. Teske wrote the "Introduction" and translated the works in this volume.

Book I

In the opening lines of *Marriage and Desire* Augustine gets right to the point about what is really at stake in the debate over original sin:

> The new heretics, my dear son, Valerius, maintain that the medicine of Christ which heals sins is not necessary for little ones born in the flesh, and they keep shouting in a most hateful manner that we condemn marriage and the divine work by which God creates human beings from men and women.[64]

Why did these "new heretics" (Julian and those in agreement with him) view Augustine (and his position) as condemning marriage? Because since Augustine views the infant as already sinful and in need of grace, he in fact is condemning marriage (since the sexual union through which children come into being is simply part and parcel of the marriage relationship). Augustine clarifies the issue: "The aim, then of this book is to distinguish, insofar as the Lord grants us his help, [1] the goodness of marriage from [2] the evil of carnal desire on account of which a human being who is born through it contracts original sin."[65] Augustine appears to argue that sexual intercourse *in and of itself* is in no way bad or evil, for man and woman were created to procreate. After the entry of sin into the world, however, the sexual act seems inextricably bound up with "the evil of carnal desire."[66] And on account of this evil of carnal desire, "a human being is born," and through such carnal desire the person "contracts original sin."[67]

Later in *Marriage and Desire*, Augustine turns more directly to the state of the newborn child, or children. Augustine turns again and again to variations of a certain phrase: "The child that is born from this concupiscence of the flesh is, of course, born for the world, not for God, but is born for God when it is reborn from water and the Spirit."[68] Indeed, even if the parents have been baptized, their offspring are still born with original sin: "That what has been forgiven in the parent is contracted by the child is a strange fact, but it is, nonetheless, a fact."[69]

[64] Augustine, *Marriage and Desire* I.1.1.
[65] Augustine, *Marriage and Desire* I.1.1. My enumeration. We will try and come to terms with what Augustine is or is not saying about sexual desire.
[66] Augustine, *Marriage and Desire* I.1.1.
[67] Augustine, *Marriage and Desire* I.1.1.
[68] Augustine, *Marriage and Desire* I.19.21.
[69] Augustine, *Marriage and Desire* I.19.21.

Book II

After Augustine wrote the first book of *Marriage and Desire*, Julian of Eclanum responded with a four-book work entitled *To Turbantius*. Book II of *Marriage and Desire* is Augustine's response to those four books. Augustine apparently had access to excerpts from Julian's *To Turbantius*, collected or collated by an unknown Pelagian.[70]

As in so much of the exchange between Augustine and the various Pelagians over the years, one key stumbling block repeatedly asserts itself: *the failure of the Pelagians to distinguish between (1) pre-fall reality and (2) post-fall reality*. As with Pelagius, Julian denies that with Adam's fall the world shifted on its axis. As Augustine states, "[W]e say, as the Catholics maintain, that the first evil of human beings was incurred by the first couple, and was passed on from them to all human beings."[71]

Augustine criticizes Julian for advocating the notion that persons are related to Adam only if they *imitate* Adam. Augustine, in contrast, emphasizes the agency of Adam in Romans 5:12, "Through one man sin entered this world"; similarly, verse 16, "after the one"—and what can this mean except after one *sin*? Augustine writes, "Let these people explain how condemnation followed after one sin, if it was not that even the one original sin sufficed for condemnation, because it was passed on to all human beings."[72]

AGAINST TWO LETTERS OF THE PELAGIANS

In 421, Augustine wrote *Against Two Letters of the Pelagians*, a response to Julian of Eclanum's two letters to Pope Boniface in Rome. In this work, Augustine returns to Pelagius's view of baptism, putting a challenge to him: if original sin does not exist, then why believe in infant baptism? He quotes Pelagius as saying that baptism of infants was *not* necessary for forgiveness of sins, but it *was* necessary for entrance into the kingdom of heaven. Augustine responds,

> [I]n the Church of the savior little ones believe through others, just as from others they contracted those sins which are forgiven them in baptism. You do not bear in mind that they cannot have eternal life who have not partaken of the body and blood of Christ.[73]

---

[70] See the "Introduction" to Augustine, *Marriage and Desire*, 14.
[71] Augustine, *Marriage and Desire* II.23.38.
[72] Augustine, *Marriage and Desire* II.27.46.
[73] Augustine, *Against Two Letters of the Pelagians* I.22.40.

In other words, just as children believe through their parents when they have them baptized, so children contract sin through others, that is, through their parents. Augustine's line of argumentation here is a not-so-subtle affirmation of original sin.

In the second book of *Against Two Letters of the Pelagians*, Augustine recounts or summarizes a saying by Caelestius: "[T]he sin of Adam harmed Adam alone and not the human race and that newborn infants are in the same state in which Adam was before the sin."[74] In response to this, Augustine gives a strident affirmation of original sin:

> [W]e read the letters of the pontiff I just mentioned in which he writes that unbaptized little ones cannot have eternal life. Who is going to deny that it follows that those who do not have life are dead? What, then, is the source of this terrible punishment in infants, if there is no original sin?[75]

One need not follow Augustine on the necessity and importance of baptism to follow his argument: The reason infant baptism is so important is that there is an original sin that all contract, and this original sin must be dealt with. In Augustine's thinking, baptism is that which cleanses one of original sin.

In this same section Augustine elaborates on the inheritance of our sin from Adam:

> The Catholic faith, of course, does not say that the nature of human beings is evil insofar as human beings were originally made by the creator. Nor is what God now creates in that nature, when he produces human beings from human beings, an evil in it; rather, its evil is what it derives from that defect of the first human being.[76]

Again, for Augustine, in contrast to the Pelagians, there is a fundamental difference between (1) pre-fall man and (2) post-fall man. According to Augustine, man, after the fall, is fundamentally damaged in a way that pre-fall man was not. Indeed, "[A]ll are born subject to sin on account of the defect they inherit and are, therefore, under the power of the devil until they are reborn in Christ."[77] This is not a question about whether pre-fall and post-fall man are both created beings who bear the image of God. Rather, it is a

---

[74] Augustine, *Against Two Letters of the Pelagians* II.4.6.
[75] Augustine, *Against Two Letters of the Pelagians* II.4.8.
[76] Augustine, *Against Two Letters of the Pelagians* II.4.8.
[77] Augustine, *Against Two Letters of the Pelagians* II.5.9.

question of the moral ability or state of the person who comes into the world as corrupt and guilty due to Adam's transgression.

AGAINST JULIAN

In *Against Julian* (421) Augustine engages Julian most directly. The work was comprised of six books and engaged (again) the main fundamental criticism that Julian leveled against Augustine: that since Augustine believed that children come into the world already sinful, he must logically believe that marriage itself (instituted by God) is sinful or bad, since children are the result of the marriage relationship. In this respect, according to Julian, Augustine reveals his Manichean background, since he attributes sin or evil to something God has created.

Against Julian, Book I

In Book I of *Against Julian* Augustine's purpose is, generally, to show that the church fathers have essentially affirmed the doctrine of original sin that he affirms. Augustine summarizes his position and Julian's on original sin in relation to marriage and children: "I [Augustine] say that marriage should be praised in such a way that the fact that all human beings are born subject to the sin of those first human beings in no way involves blame or reproach for marriage."[78] What exactly is it, then, to which Julian objects? Julian's point seems to be that Augustine cannot logically hold together (1) the notion that marriage can be praised as a good thing, alongside (2) the notion that "all human beings are born subject to sin." In contrast, Augustine replies, "you [Julian] claim that marriage is undoubtedly condemned if what is born from it is not free from every debt of original sin."[79] Augustine affirms original sin hundreds of times in this book. Three will suffice. First, Augustine states what Pope Innocent believed along with others: "He [Pope Innocent] holds with them the one, true and Christian position that the poor little ones must be set free by the grace of Christ from the original evil which they contracted from Adam."[80] Likewise, ". . . original sin that entered the world through one man and is passed on to all human beings."[81] Second, Augustine cites fourteen bishops from the Council of Diospolis: "all are

---

[78] Augustine, *Against Julian* I.2.4.
[79] Augustine, *Against Julian* I.2.4.
[80] Augustine, *Against Julian* I.4.13.25.
[81] Augustine, *Against Julian* I.5.16.

born subject to the sin of that first human being."[82] Third, Augustine quotes John Chrysostom, who can affirm with him that there is both original sin inherited from Adam, and personal sin that persons engage in throughout life: "Christ came once; he found our paternal debt that Adam had signed. Adam introduced the beginning of the debt; we have increased the interest by later sins."[83]

Against Julian, Book II

In Book II of *Against Julian,* Augustine's purpose is to critique Julian's own particular arguments. Augustine summarizes Julian's five chief arguments against him. As Julian sees it, Augustine and those like him: (1) believe that "the devil is author of newborn human beings"; (2) "condemn marriage"; (3) "deny that all sins are forgiven in marriage"; (4) "accuse God of the crime of injustice"; and (5) "inculcate a despair of attaining perfection."[84] In his defense, Augustine appeals to numerous persons: Ambrose, Cyprian of Carthage, Gregory of Nazianzus, and Hilary. As Augustine works through these figures, he makes multiple affirmations of original sin. For example, "From this law of the flesh that resists the law of the mind none failed to contract that same law by their first birth, for no woman conceived them except as a result of that law [i.e., the law of flesh]."[85]

One of Julian's most central, and potentially most effective, criticisms is that if someone is *created*, he or she cannot be *sinful*. There is a certain logic here that requires a response. And Augustine engages it:

> When we say that flesh comes from flesh and flesh comes from human beings, do we deny that it also comes from God? Hence, it comes from God because he creates it, and it comes from human beings because they beget it, and it comes from sin because sin corrupts it.[86]

For Augustine, our natures have been damaged by original sin and need to be healed: "Our nature, then, was damaged by the transgression of the first human being; it does not need to be separated from another nature by any divines, but to be healed."[87] In summarizing the argument of Book II Augustine

---

[82] Augustine, *Against Julian* I.5.20.
[83] Augustine, *Against Julian* I.6.26.
[84] Augustine, *Against Julian* II.1.2.
[85] Augustine, *Against Julian* II.4.8.
[86] Augustine, *Against Julian* II.4.8.
[87] Augustine, *Against Julian* II.8.28.

writes, "human beings are born subject to the damaged origin which they inherit from the first human being and that for this reason they face condemnation unless they are reborn in Christ."[88]

Against Julian, Book III

In Book III of *Against Julian*, Augustine engages Book I of Julian's *To Turbantius*. We see Pelagian arguments similar to those noted above. The first key issue relates to the Pelagian (here Julian's) understanding of the baptism of infants. Julian happily admits that infants ought to be baptized, but Augustine presses him: *Why* ought they to be baptized? Are they bound up in Adam's transgression, and therefore need their sin washed away? That would make sense, says Augustine. But why, *on Julian's own grounds*, ought infants to be baptized? Augustine writes,

> You do not deny that they should be baptized, but in your great wisdom you say these astounding things: They are baptized in the sacrament of the savior, but they are not saved; they are redeemed, but they are not set free; they are washed, but they are not cleansed; they undergo exorcism and exsufflation, but they are not rescued from the power of the devil.[89]

Against Julian, Book IV

Augustine continues his response to Julian in Book IV, and we draw attention to one main insight from this book: the question of the "virtuous unbeliever," or what some have called, the "virtuous pagan." Given the nature of his debate with Julian, it is not surprising that the question arises in the context of a discussion about marriage. Augustine poses the issue as follows: "what one should say when some unbelievers are also seen to live chastely with their wives."[90] Should such chaste persons be considered virtuous? We quickly get a sense of Augustine's response, which he develops at some length: "one lives rightly only on the basis of faith in Jesus Christ our Lord, the one mediator between God and human beings . . ."[91] Augustine also goes on to quote himself from *Marriage and Desire*:

---

[88] Augustine, *Against Julian* II.9.31.
[89] Augustine, *Against Julian* III.3.8. "Exsufflation" is not a word often used today. It means essentially a strongly forced expiration of air. Roland Teske, the editor and translator of *Unfinished Work in Answer to Julian*, writes, "The rites of exsufflation and exorcism were parts of the ritual for baptism until recent years. Both rites aimed at the expulsion of the devil from the person about to be baptized" (see the New City Press edition of *Unfinished Work in Answer to Julian*, I.1.50 [153 n. 70]).
[90] Augustine, *Against Julian* IV.3.14.
[91] Augustine, *Against Julian* IV.3.14.

After all, chastity is a virtue, whose contrary vice is unchasteness. Since all the virtues, even those whose actions are carried out by the body, reside in the mind, how can the body truly be called chaste, when the mind itself turns away from its God in fornication?[92]

In short, "true chastity cannot exist in the mind of one without faith."[93] While Augustine will work out this line of reasoning at some length, he will suggest that Julian would have been more consistent to attribute any "virtues" in unbelievers to the gift of God: "How much more acceptable it would be for you to attribute those virtues, which you claim exist in unbelievers, to the gift of God rather than merely to their will."[94] But he quickly turns to his main line of argument: only those with faith can be righteous (referencing, understandably, Rom. 1:17).[95] Hence, "if unbelievers do not have true righteousness, then, even if they have some virtues, they will not have any true virtues, which are its companions and colleagues." Thus, for Augustine: "the continence or the chastity of unbelievers is not true virtue."[96] Augustine affirms Cicero's *definition* of virtue, but he also argues that Cicero did not have the resources or insights to *bring about* such virtue—for ultimately virtue can exist only where there is faith in Christ: "Because of this faith they live prudently, courageously, temperately, and justly, and thus they live correctly and wisely with all the true virtues, because they live with faith." Indeed, "If, then, virtues are of no use to human beings for obtaining the true happiness which true faith in Christ promises will be immortal, they can in no sense be true virtues."[97]

As Augustine works through his argument, he raises the issue of "ends." He writes, "the virtues are to be distinguished from the vices, not by the actions, but by their ends."[98] And the end which should motivate one's actions ought to be God and his service: "When persons do some action in which they seem not to sin, if they do not do the action on account of that for which they ought to do it, they are found to be guilty of sinning."[99] Augustine continues, "True virtues in human beings serve God who gives them to human beings."[100]

---

[92] Augustine, *Against Julian* IV.3.14. He is quoting himself from *Marriage and Desire* I.4.5.

[93] Augustine, *Against Julian* IV.3.14.

[94] Augustine, *Against Julian* IV. 3.16.

[95] Augustine, *Against Julian* IV.3.17.

[96] Augustine, *Against Julian* IV.3.17. In this quotation, Augustine seems to be contrasting "some virtues" with "true virtues," such that the "some virtues" are not, ultimately, "true virtues."

[97] Augustine, *Against Julian* IV.3.17.

[98] Augustine, *Against Julian* IV.3.21.

[99] Augustine, *Against Julian* IV.3.21.

[100] Augustine, *Against Julian* IV.3.21.

In sum, for Augustine, all virtuous behavior comes about by faith in Christ and not by any willpower in the person, since that person, being a descendant of Adam, has inherited his corrupt nature. Augustine closes Book IV with a pointed assertion of original sin:

> But since God is neither unjust nor weak, there remains the view you do not want, but are forced to admit, namely, that the heavy yoke upon the children of Adam from the day they leave the womb of their mother until the day of their burial in the mother of all would not have existed if original sin had not come first and merited it.[101]

Against Julian, Book V

In Book V Augustine insists on linking the transmission of original sin with the reality of concupiscence, or sexual desire. Augustine contends, "With regard to the transmission of original sin to all human beings, since it is passed on by concupiscence of the flesh, it could not be passed on to that flesh [i.e., Jesus's flesh] which the Virgin did not conceive by it."[102] He goes on:

> Adam did not, therefore, infect the flesh which was conceived without this corruption. The flesh of Christ, then, contracted mortality from the mortality of his mother's body, because it encountered in her a mortal body, but it did not contract the infection of original sin, because it did not encounter in her the concupiscence of sexual union.[103]

A little later Augustine writes, "one who is born of morally good intercourse [i.e., intercourse engaged in for the purpose of having children] contracts what is removed by being reborn, because even in morally good intercourse there is present the evil [i.e., concupiscence] of which the goodness of marriage makes good use."[104]

Against Julian, Book VI

The sixth and final book of Augustine's *Against Julian* is a response to the fourth and final book of Julian's *To Turbantius*. One of Julian's chief accusations is that Augustine is, in fact, a Manichee (i.e., Julian claims that with his doctrine of original sin, Augustine affirms that God creates, or brings into

---

[101] Augustine, *Against Julian* IV.16.83.
[102] Augustine, *Against Julian* V.15.54.
[103] Augustine, *Against Julian* V.15.54.
[104] Augustine, *Against Julian* V.16.63.

being, a world that is inherently evil or sinful). But, as Augustine has said many times, man does not have an evil *nature*, per se: "God is good, God is just; there is, of course, no foreign evil nature which, as the Manichees believe, is mixed in with our nature." So where is the problem, exactly? The first problem one has is original sin: "From where do such great evils of human beings come, unless our human origin is corrupted and the human mass condemned?"[105] Augustine returns to a common theme: a person is created, yet sinful: "The whole world, then, is guilty because of Adam, and yet God does not hold back his hand from the work he forms, for he made the seeds, though they have been corrupted by the transgression of their father."[106]

One of Julian's objections is, how can one be held responsible for an act that occurred before one was even alive? In response, Augustine, as he often does, makes a distinction between *original* sin and *personal* sin. He points to 2 Corinthians 5:14: "one has died for all; all have, therefore, died."[107] Augustine admits that *in one sense* the sins of our parents are indeed the sins of others. But in *another sense* the sins of our parents are also our sins: "they [the sins of our parents] are ours because their offspring have been infected."[108]

Augustine offers a helpful summary of this thought, but it includes a note not heard as often in Augustine, of a mother and father passing on *unbelief* to a child:

> And so in a believing woman a child without faith is created, and the parents pass on to it a state of unbelief which they did not have when their child was born, but which they had when they themselves were born. They passed on, then, what was no longer present in them on account of the spiritual seed by which they were reborn, but it was in the carnal seed by which they begot the child.[109]

Augustine also addresses Julian's understanding of Romans 5:12: "Through one man sin entered the world, and through sin death, and in that way it was passed on to all human beings, in whom all have sinned." Whereas Julian seemed to posit that persons (you and I) simply *imitate* Adam (but that

---

[105] Augustine, *Against Julian* VI.1.2.
[106] Augustine, *Against Julian* VI.2.5.
[107] Augustine, *Against Julian* VI.9.24.
[108] Augustine, *Against Julian* VI.10.28.
[109] Augustine, *Against Julian* VI.14.44.

we are in no way tainted or infected by Adam's transgression), Augustine
held that all persons somehow sinned *in* Adam:

> In that way [i.e., in Julian's understanding] all human beings are not un-
> derstood to have sinned at their origin in the one man and in common as
> in a single mass; rather, they sinned because that first man sinned, that is,
> because they imitate him, not because they are his offspring.[110]

This is an important section of *Against Julian*, for in it Augustine explicitly
deals with the key Latin phrase which has been so essential in how later
centuries of Christians have accepted, or rejected, or modified Augustine's
understanding of original sin. It is the controversial prepositional phrase "in
quo" in Romans 5:12: "In quo omnes peccaverunt." Augustine follows the
Latin and takes Paul to be saying, "in whom all sinned." Julian interprets Paul
to be saying something different: "because of which all sinned." One should
give credit where credit is due. Julian's interpretation concurs with the Greek
text (ἐφ' ᾧ πάντες ἥμαρτον), which most agree should be translated "because
of whom all sinned." However, Julian does not appear to be driven by the
Greek, but by a principled opposition to any notion that all persons might
somehow have sinned in Adam.

Augustine's initial response to Julian is intriguing. For Augustine, it is
strange to suggest that when someone sins, they are somehow reflecting upon
Adam's first sin. For example, when someone engages in murder, is it really
because they somehow have Adam as an example to be imitated? Augustine
argues that the Pelagian (Julian's) position is the real logical oddity: Can it be
the case that the person who is sinning today somehow looks back at Adam
as an example to be imitated?

Augustine believes that Paul presents us with two Adams in Romans—
the first and second Adam: "the anger of God came upon the human race
through one man and . . . reconciliation with God comes through one man
for those who are gratuitously set free from the condemnation of the whole
race."[111] Augustine then lines up a number of Scriptures to argue that all
persons are under the wrath of God, and this first comes about "through one
man."[112] Of particular interest, Augustine turns to Romans 5:16: "For after

---

[110] Augustine, *Against Julian* VI.24.75.
[111] Augustine, *Against Julian* VI.24.77.
[112] Augustine, *Against Julian* VI.24.77. Augustine lists Rom. 5:8–9; Eph. 2:3; Jer. 20:14; Job 3:3; 14:15; Sir. 14:18;
40:1; Eccl. 1:2–3; Rom. 8:20; and Pss. 39:6; 90:5.

the one [sin] there came judgment leading to condemnation, but after many sins there came grace leading to justification." Augustine's query: "Why does grace lead to justification after many sins unless besides that one sin at the origin it found many additional sins to destroy?"[113] In other words, there is "one sin" at first, but this one sin is then followed by many sins.

Augustine also ties his argument to infant baptism. He contends that if a child is affected by the sin of the first Adam, then a child can experience the grace of the second Adam. If Julian *truly* wants to sever infants from the sin of the first Adam, he is—in principle—severing infants from the possibility of receiving the grace of the second Adam:

> But if you want them [infants] to be separate from the sin of the first human being, because they have not imitated him by their own will, you will by this same argument also keep them separate from the righteousness of Christ, because they have not imitated him either by their own will.[114]

UNFINISHED WORK IN ANSWER TO JULIAN

Augustine's *Unfinished Work in Answer to Julian* is some 700 pages long. It was written in Augustine's final years before his death and was uncompleted when he died on August 28, 430. Augustine wrote his *Unfinished Work* in response to Julian's *Ad Florum*, which is a response to the second book of Augustine's *Marriage and Desire*.[115] Augustine's *Unfinished Work* appears to quote the first six books of Julian's *Ad Florum* in their entirety: Augustine provides the text of Julian, with interspersed responses after quotations.

Unfinished Work, Book I

A key component of Book I (there are many) is whether infants can rightly be said to possess sin; or, whether one can call infants sinful. Related to this, if infants are *not* sinful, why baptize infants? Augustine also returns to a common theme: to reject the notion that one can be somehow bound up with Adam's sin is (at least theoretically) to reject the notion that one can benefit from Christ's obedience or righteousness.

---

[113] Augustine, *Against Julian* VI.24.79.
[114] Augustine, *Against Julian* VI.24.79.
[115] The "General Introduction" to *Unfinished Work in Answer to Julian* in the New City Press edition is worth reading. A number of persons have lamented the "negative" nature of this work, or Augustine's "cold competence," or his "intransigence," with one person even suggesting that this work is "a work of senility." The first page of the "General Introduction" summarizes some of these more negative readings.

One of Julian's arguments is that there cannot be sin in infants because in order to *sin*, one must have a will, and an infant does not have a will—at least in the sense that one usually means when speaking of a will. In reply, Augustine is happy to say, "all who were going to be born from Adam through concupiscence of the flesh were present in his loins."[116] Augustine also returns to a key point in relation to infant baptism: *Why* should infants be baptized, on Julian's view, if infants have no sin with which to deal? Augustine writes, "you do not want that gift which you put first to pertain to little ones, namely, that it gives pardon to the guilty, for you deny that little ones contract any guilt from Adam."[117] Julian's "answer" is that the grace of baptism, while it *does* provide pardon to the *guilty*, works differently with infants, who are innocent (in his view):

> This grace, which gives pardon to the guilty [e.g., an adult who is baptized], gives to other mortals [e.g., an infant] spiritual enlightenment, adoption as children of God, citizenship in the heavenly Jerusalem, sanctification, transformation into members of Christ, and possession of the kingdom of heaven."[118]

Augustine at times points to the inextricable link between what Adam did in relation to us, and what Christ has done in relation to us. He argues that to deny a real link to Adam entails that one deny (logically, at least) a real link to Christ. Thus, "the sin of Adam harmed those who do not yet have a will able to sin, just as the righteousness of Christ benefits those who do not yet have a will able to believe."[119]

Unfinished Work, Book II

Some of the key components of Book II (again, there are many) is that all persons are truly "in" Adam. Indeed, Adam sins in our place, but, Augustine argues, Adam's sin *is* our sin. Augustine even goes on to say that each person—in a sense—*is* Adam. Augustine returns at numerous points in this book to a common theme: that central to the Bible are two key men—Adam and Christ—and one's primary identity is either in Adam or in Christ.

---

[116] Augustine, *Unfinished Work in Answer to Julian* I.48.
[117] Augustine, *Unfinished Work in Answer to Julian* I.53.
[118] Augustine, *Unfinished Work in Answer to Julian* I.53.
[119] Augustine, *Unfinished Work in Answer to Julian* I.56.

Augustine is clear that all persons are, in some sense, "in" Adam:

> He did, after all, create Adam as such a human being, and we were all in
> that man. But by sinning he destroyed himself and all of us in himself. As a
> result, it is not now in the power of his descendants to be set free from evil
> unless the grace of God gives them the power to become children of God.[120]

In contrast, "the Pelagians refuse to believe that in the one human being the
lump of clay was damaged as a whole and condemned as a whole, and from
that damage and condemnation only grace heals and sets anyone free."[121]

For Augustine, Adam's sin is in one sense the sin of another, and in another sense my sin too:

> The disobedience of the one human being is, of course, not absurdly said
> to be the sin of someone else, because when we were not yet born, we did
> no action of our own, whether good or bad, but we all were in that one who
> committed this sin when he committed it, and that sin was so great and so
> powerful that the whole of human nature was damaged by it.[122]

Augustine, of course, recognizes that the woman sinned first. He understands
Paul to have emphasized the man for perhaps a couple of reasons:

> But because the apostle wanted us to understand generation and not imita-
> tion, he said, "Through one man sin entered the world" (Rom. 5:12). He ei-
> ther included them both under the singular term, for which reason scripture
> said, "They are, therefore, no longer two, but one flesh" (Matt. 19:6), or he
> mentioned the man as the more important one, since generation begins with
> him when the seed is sown so that conception follows.[123]

Augustine offers a helpful summary in which he contrasts the sin of
Adam to the sin of the devil: "The apostle [Paul in Rom. 5], then, quite appropriately spoke of one man by whom there entered the world the sin which
is contracted by generation rather than of the devil by whom there entered
the world that sin which is followed by imitation."[124] Augustine contends
not only that all persons were *in* Adam, but that, in some sense, all persons

---

[120] Augustine, *Unfinished Work in Answer to Julian* II.7.
[121] Augustine, *Unfinished Work in Answer to Julian* II.142.2.
[122] Augustine, *Unfinished Work in Answer to Julian* II.163.1.
[123] Augustine, *Unfinished Work in Answer to Julian* II.194.
[124] Augustine, *Unfinished Work in Answer to Julian* II.199.3. If I am following Augustine here, it can be said that
Adam and Eve *did* "imitate" the devil, who sinned before them. But the sinful link of the rest of humanity to Adam
is by *generation*, not *imitation*.

are Adam. Julian accuses Augustine of being a traducianist, and in response Augustine simply reaffirms his point that all persons *are* Adam: "And I said about all their offspring that, when the sin was committed, they all were that one [man]."[125]

In numerous places, Augustine points out the relationship between Adam and Christ. For example, "The apostle, however, knew what he was saying and set forth Adam as the author of sin and Christ as the author of righteousness, because he knew that the first [Adam] was the origin of our birth and the latter [Christ] the origin of our rebirth."[126] Augustine also writes, "All sinned in him in whom all died. That is Adam. And if the little ones do not die in him, they will certainly not be brought to life in Christ."[127] For Augustine, Adam and Christ rise or fall together: "If Adam did not pass on sin to human beings who are born, Christ does not give righteousness to the little ones who are reborn, because neither as born nor as reborn did the little ones use their own will."[128] He goes on: "And for this reason it is clear that everyone who is born through that series of generations belongs to that first man, just as everyone belongs to the second man who is reborn in him by the gift of grace. As a result, two men, the first and the second, are in a sense the whole human race."[129]

Unfinished Work, Book III

Book III covers several key themes: (1) the question of justice, and the vexing question of how a just God could ever condemn an infant; (2) the relation of nature itself to nature as corrupted by sin; (3) the uniqueness of Adam (in comparison to other parents); (4) the question of free choice.

Augustine spends time responding to Julian's concerns about justice, especially the notion that a just God would never condemn an infant, since an infant has not matured to the level where he or she could exercise a truly free will.[130] Augustine's general response is that *of course* God always acts with justice, including God's actions toward infants. But God is just to condemn Adam's descendants, for they possess Adam's transgression: "not even an infant who has lived one day on earth is free from the filth of sin, and for

---

[125] Augustine, *Unfinished Work in Answer to Julian* II.178.2d; cf. II.178.3 and II.179.
[126] Augustine, *Unfinished Work in Answer to Julian* II.54.
[127] Augustine, *Unfinished Work in Answer to Julian* II.68.
[128] Augustine, *Unfinished Work in Answer to Julian* II.101.1.
[129] Augustine, *Unfinished Work in Answer to Julian* II.163.2.
[130] Augustine, *Unfinished Work in Answer to Julian* III.1 (and following).

that reason we recognize in the evils which the infant suffers not an unjust, but a just God."[131]

In his presentation, Augustine returns to a familiar theme over and over: the difference between (1) *nature* itself and (2) nature *as corrupted by sin*. Augustine writes, "our nature was created good, but corrupted by sin, and from the infants to the elderly it needs Christ as a physician, 'because he has died for all; all have, therefore, died' (2 Cor. 5:14)."[132] For Augustine,

> Human nature that was created good by the good God was injured by the great sin of disobedience so that even their descendants contracted from it the merit and punishment of death, but . . . the good God does not deny to those descendants his good workmanship.[133]

He goes on: "so we do not say that God is the author of evil, and yet we can correctly say that human beings are born evil as a result of the bond of original sin with God alone as their creator, because he alone creates human beings."[134] And again: "But nature has not remained as it was created. Therefore, it is proved to be subject to sin, and it has made the rest of the human race subject to this sin as if it were its heritage. Insofar as it is created by God, this nature is, nonetheless, good."[135] And similarly: "human beings, insofar as they are creatures, are good, but insofar as they are born from a damaged origin, they are not good and, for this reason, need to be reborn."[136]

Augustine is also clear, contra Julian, that a distinction must be made between (1) the unique nature of the parenthood of Adam and (2) other parents: "That one sin, however, by which human nature was changed so that it had to die, even if there were no other sins, is sufficient for condemnation unless the bonds of birth are untied by rebirth."[137]

One thing Augustine repeatedly emphasizes is that Paul spoke of sin entering the world *through one man* (Rom. 5:12) for a reason. According to Augustine, Paul was trying to emphasize that Adam was the first "in the process of generation."[138] Likewise, Paul spoke this way "so that we would understand in those words the beginning of generation which comes from the

---

[131] Augustine, *Unfinished Work in Answer to Julian* III.7.
[132] Augustine, *Unfinished Work in Answer to Julian* III.110.1.
[133] Augustine, *Unfinished Work in Answer to Julian* III.110.3.
[134] Augustine, *Unfinished Work in Answer to Julian* III.109.1.
[135] Augustine, *Unfinished Work in Answer to Julian* III.112.2.
[136] Augustine, *Unfinished Work in Answer to Julian,* III.159.
[137] Augustine, *Unfinished Work in Answer to Julian* III.110.3.
[138] Augustine, *Unfinished Work in Answer to Julian* III.88.3.

man, not an example to imitate which in the human race entered the world through one woman rather than through one man."[139]

As in other works, in his battle with Julian one of the issues to which Augustine repeatedly returns is the radical and fundamental difference between (1) pre-fall man and (2) post-fall man. We see this on the question of "free choice." Augustine writes,

> You, though a human being, do not consider in what condition you are [i.e., now as fallen], and you are as blindly proud in evil days as if these were the good days [i.e., before the fall] when there existed the sort of free choice which you describe; then human beings had not yet become like a vanity so that their days passed like a shadow.[140]

That is to say, things were different before the fall: "This evil [i.e., sin] was not present in Adam when he was created upright, because human nature was not yet corrupted; he had a ruler whom he abandoned by free choice and did not as yet look for a deliverer by whom he might become free from sin."[141]

In holding these views, Augustine does not deny "free choice." For him, man retains "free choice" throughout his existence (including fallen man before conversion), in the sense of having the capacity to choose. For example, commenting on 2 Corinthians 13:7, Augustine writes, "The apostle prayed for this help for the faithful, but he did not remove from human nature free choice."[142] However, in another sense, Augustine does hold that certain conditions must be present if there is to be free choice. That is, to have (true) free choice, Christ must be present with the person. As Augustine asserts, "No one can have the free choice of the will to do the good which one wills or not to do the evil which one hates except by the grace of Christ."[143]

Unfinished Work, Book IV

In Book IV Augustine returns to a common theme, that of created human nature and its fallenness. How can God create persons who are fundamentally *good* yet who also come into the world *sinful*? Augustine wishes to distinguish between God as creator of life (which he is) and as author of sin (which he is not): "there is inborn in human beings a defect from their origin

---

[139] Augustine, *Unfinished Work in Answer to Julian* III.88.4.
[140] Augustine, *Unfinished Work in Answer to Julian* III.37.1.
[141] Augustine, *Unfinished Work in Answer to Julian* III.154.1.
[142] Augustine, *Unfinished Work in Answer to Julian* III.156.
[143] Augustine, *Unfinished Work in Answer to Julian* III.158.

of which God is not the author, though God alone is the creator of human beings."[144] At times, Augustine speaks of fallen mankind as the "mass of perdition" (*massa perditionis*). In commenting on what "nature" means in Ephesians 2:3 ("For we too were once by nature children of anger, just as the rest"), he writes, "But when he [Paul] says, 'Just as the rest,' he shows that all are by nature children of anger unless the grace of God separates some of them from the mass of perdition."[145] In reflecting on what Paul means by "nature" here, Augustine offers a helpful summary of the implications of denying original sin. When Julian denies original sin, Augustine asserts, he is left unable to explain coherently why infants come into the world so often with so many problems: "feeblemindedness," physical deformity, etc. By *denying* original sin, and by insisting on a certain understanding of what it means to say God creates all things, Julian is left (at least logically, according to Augustine) having to say that God *creates* "feeblemindedness," deformity, suffering, etc.

One of Julian's common criticisms of Augustine on original sin is that there must be an act of the *will* if there is to be *sin*. That is, how can a child or infant be seen as sinful if there is not really a will that has acted? Augustine's response is to agree with the basic principle: a will must be present if there is really to be sin present. But Augustine points to the will of *Adam* as central:

> We, however, also say that sin cannot exist without free will, and our teaching, nonetheless, is not destroyed on this account, as you say, when we say that there is original sin. For this kind of sin also came about as a result of free will, not as a result of the personal free will of the one who is born, but as a result of the will of Adam in whom we all originally existed when he damaged our common nature by his evil will.[146]

In other words, the will *is* necessary if there is to be sin.

Unfinished Work, Book V

In Book V Augustine develops a line of argument only somewhat developed in the first four books: the evidence from human experience over time. He

---

[144] Augustine, *Unfinished Work in Answer to Julian* IV.8.2.
[145] Augustine, *Unfinished Work in Answer to Julian* IV.123.2. Augustine speaks of "mass of perdition" or similar language in a number of places: IV.131; VI.1.1 ("this whole mass of rational and mortal animals").
[146] Augustine, *Unfinished Work in Answer to Julian* IV.90.1.

asks, if people are naturally good, why do we see such an overwhelming pattern of human evil and cowardice and laziness, etc.? "Why does this race of mortals fall into the depths of ignorance and softness of cowardice, as if some burden or other were pushing it downhill?"[147]

As he does often, Augustine asserts that Julian's denial of original sin leaves him with no way of explaining why infants suffer various things, including physical deformity. To make things worse, Augustine argues, Julian is then guilty of what he accuses Augustine of, of making God unjust: "you are forced to praise all natural defects to the point that you say that not only physically deformed, sick, and monstrous babies, but even feeble-minded ones would have come into existence in paradise, even if no one had sinned."[148]

Augustine is generally careful not to try and "get behind" the first sin to speculate about *why* Adam originally sinned. Rather, Augustine is generally happy to say that Adam sinned because he wanted to sin. Thus, he says,

> But the angel or the human being from which and in which sins first arose were not compelled to sin by anything; rather, they sinned by free will. And they could have willed not to, because they were not compelled to will to sin, and yet they could not have willed to sin if they had the nature of God and were not made out of nothing.[149]

Unfinished Work, Book VI

In Book VI Augustine continues with a treatment of human nature. Using different imagery, Augustine argues that human nature has been corrupted or tainted or wounded or scarred due to original sin. But for him there has also been a change to our nature. It is not that nature *qua nature* (nature *as nature*) is sinful or evil, but it is the case that there has been a change in, or to, our nature. So, he writes, "This defect by which the flesh has desires opposed to the spirit was turned into our nature by the transgression of the first human being."[150] In other words, due to the first sin, "the nature, not of the one human being, but of the whole human race, was changed.[151]

---

[147] Augustine, *Unfinished Work in Answer to Julian* V.1.2.
[148] Augustine, *Unfinished Work in Answer to Julian* V.22.3.
[149] Augustine, *Unfinished Work in Answer to Julian* V.35.
[150] Augustine, *Unfinished Work in Answer to Julian* VI.8.3.
[151] Augustine, *Unfinished Work in Answer to Julian* VI.7.4.

Summary of Augustine on Original Sin

This survey of Augustine's doctrine of original sin has covered a dozen or so works by the Bishop of Hippo, written over some 35 years from around 396 to his death in 430. Before offering a few theological reflections and conclusions, it may be helpful to briefly summarize what we have learned thus far.

First, Augustine affirms the goodness of creation, including—even after the fall—the goodness of man, rightly considered. That is, man *as creature* (i.e., as one who continues to possess "createdness" even after the fall), can be said—again, in a sense—to be "good." Augustine thinks this way because, especially after his departure from Manichaeism, Augustine has a robust doctrine of the goodness of creation. This is not to deny radical sinfulness. Rather, if man lost all trace of goodness as a creature, he would—on Augustine's view—cease to exist (given Augustine's understanding of evil as a "privatio boni"—a privation of good).

Second, and following from above, there has been a radical and real rupture in the universe—especially in terms of mankind—with Adam's sin. Something has radically shifted or changed with Adam's sin. Man (both Adam and his descendants) is still human, but there is a deep deformity in post-fall Adam and his descendants.

Third, Augustine—contra Pelagius and the Pelagians—sees a strong relationship or continuity between Adam and his descendants or progeny. Augustine may not have worked this out in detail in ways we would prefer, but there is no doubt that Augustine saw all of mankind subsequent to the fall of humanity as wrapped up in, or bound up in, Adam's transgression. Indeed, Adam's sin is transmitted, somehow, to all of his progeny. Later Christian theology, especially among the covenantal emphases of the Reformed tradition, will speak more explicitly about Adam's covenantal or federal headship. Augustine is not as explicit with this kind of terminology, but he certainly lays the groundwork in such a way that later Protestants might be seen as developing strands of thought found in the Bishop of Hippo.

Fourth, Augustine takes seriously that death enters the world through sin, and that therefore death does not preexist the fall. Pelagius indeed has to deny this, and Augustine's awareness of Pelagius's thought at this point heightens Augustine's concerns about the theology of Pelagius and the Pelagians.

Fifth, for Augustine fallen sinners (especially before salvation) act out of who they are, and who they are is radically fallen beings. Augustine speaks of the fallen person, in a sense, as "free," but it is a fallen freedom, a limited freedom, and indeed a "freedom" in need of redemption. The unconverted person is indeed free to do what he wants, but he is not free, really, to choose his wants. Thus, Augustine talks of the unconverted person as "free," but it is a freedom to act in accord with who he is, and the unconverted person is thus also "bound" to act in accord with his will—which is a will bound up with Adam's sin. Augustine employs the language of being sinful *originaliter* and being sinful *actualiter*. All persons after Adam come into the world sinful *originally*, and add to this predicament by their *actual* sin—in the course of their lifespan.

THEOLOGICAL REFLECTIONS

In summarizing the key tenets of Augustine's doctrine of original sin, I present the following theological reflections.

First, Augustine and Pelagius fundamentally disagree on whether there is a true difference between pre-fall man and post-fall man. This almost seems too basic to state, but it is important to note that this fundamental difference runs through much of the Augustine-Pelagius debate. Is creation good? Of course, says Pelagius, and hence man does have the ability to obey God by his nature (a *good* nature given by grace). Of course, says Augustine, creation (and man's *nature*, ultimately) is good, but one must remember that there is a radical and fundamental fracture which runs through the heart of creation because of the fall, and this radical and fundamental fracture runs especially through the heart of man. Man is different after the fall from what he was before the fall. That is, post-fall Adam and his heirs are all guilty, corrupted, and have a proclivity to sin. Pre-fall man possesses *neither* guilt, *nor* corruption, *nor* a proclivity to sin. It is here that we face squarely the importance of a historical Adam and a pre-fall era in which man was originally righteous. If an affirmation of a historical Adam is lost, it seems that the rejection of a pre-fall era is certain to follow, and thus too the original innocence of the first man.

Second, Pelagius has a lower view than Augustine of what man was before the fall. Pelagius sees all man's current failures and sins as not *fundamentally* due to a rupture in man. That is, since there is no pre-fall realm or era from which Adam tragically fell—and with Adam his progeny—there is in a sense a "lower" view of man *in his very nature*. That is, when man, in the present, sins, it is as if Pelagius believes, "Well, this is simply what man does. Sometimes he obeys, sometimes he disobeys." Because Pelagius has a lower view of who or what man is *before* the fall, it makes sense that Pelagius would see man's plight *after* the fall to be less desperate and less significant. Man does not fall from any great height, so to speak. Indeed, since there is no serious link (in terms of sin, etc.) between Adam and the rest of mankind, the Pelagian theological substructure seems to sit nicely with both (1) a lower view of man *before* the fall—persons after Adam are in essentially the same situation as Adam himself; and (2) a higher view of man *after* the fall—man is in a less desperate situation than envisaged in the traditional Augustinian framework.

Third, if one posits that one follows Adam only by *imitation* rather than by *generation* or *propagation*, then one could easily begin to posit that we "follow" Christ only by imitation, and not by a more profound and intimate and significant connection. Augustine repeatedly drew attention to this: to the extent that one denies that someone can be caught in the *transgression* of Adam, one denies, at least in principle, that someone can also *benefit* from the obedience of Christ.

Fourth, Pelagius, in his attempt to *secure* man's "freedom" or "liberty," has perhaps constructed his anthropology so as to render incomprehensible a meaningful understanding of human freedom and nature. B. B. Warfield offers a perceptive insight on Pelagius in this regard. Warfield suggests that one of Pelagius's chief errors is his emphasis on *each individual act* of man over against, or at the expense of, man's *character*. As Warfield writes, "[Pelagius] looked upon freedom in its *form* only, and not in its *matter* . . . the will was isolated from its acts, and the acts from each other, and all organic connection or continuity of life was not only overlooked but denied."[152] If Warfield is correct, in Pelagius's attempt to safeguard or defend the free individual— by emphasizing the free individual *acts* of the person's will, he is actually engaged in a kind of deracination of what it means to be human. That is, in emphasizing the freedom of each individual act of the will, Pelagius does not give attention to how our various acts as persons can shape us over time, whether in a more- or a less-moral direction. As Warfield notes, "After each act of the will, man stood exactly where he did before: indeed, this conception scarcely allows for the existence of a 'man'—only a willing machine is left,

---

[152] Warfield, "Pelagian Controversy," 296.

at each click of the action of which the spring regains its original position, and is equally ready as before to reperform its function."[153] In short, while trying to secure the freedom of man, Pelagius may have been helping, conceptually, at least, to destroy the freedom of man.[154]

Warfield notes that lurking in the background of Pelagius's error is a failure to grasp the fundamental unity of the human race in Adam. He writes, "the type of [Pelagian] thought which thus dissolved the organism of the man into a congeries of disconnected voluntary acts, failed to comprehend the solidarity of the race."[155] Thus, while traditional Christianity has affirmed that man is a fundamental unity—we are all *in Adam*—Pelagius severed the link between mankind and Adam. Warfield notes, "The same alembic [here, "chemical"] that dissolved the individual into a succession of voluntary acts, could not fail to separate the race into a heap of unconnected units."[156] Warfield continues: "If sin, as Julian declared, is nothing but will, and the will itself remained intact after each act, how could the individual act of an individual will condition the acts of men as yet unborn?"[157] Or, we might ask, If the act of one's own will—that is, a particular act of the will—does not affect *oneself*, ultimately, how could one man's (Adam's) act affect the *rest* of the human race? Thus, a certain kind of *philosophical* commitment by Pelagius to the notion of the radical disjunction of a person's individual acts makes it conceptually impossible for Pelagius to consider that an actual *person* (and his acts) could be somehow meaningfully tied to the rest of the race.[158]

Fifth, a comment on Romans 5:12 is necessary. It is important to recognize that rarely is a theological construct so built on one or two words, such that a difference of interpretation on that word or words will render the whole theological construct suspect. As we have noted, Augustine was at least happy to surrender this passage, and to argue for his position on the basis of other Scriptures and biblical and theological reasoning. As John Rist

---

[153] Warfield, "Pelagian Controversy," 296.

[154] We will not pursue it here, but it is worth noting that the French existentialists, like Camus and Sartre, liked to argue that we are always shaped and determined by each of our decisions throughout life. That is, we find ourselves today as that person who is shaped by all of life's decisions over time. Our actions and decisions throughout life really do matter, and ultimately shape who we are. We are not just—contra Pelagius—willing or acting "machines." We are truly persons.

[155] Warfield, "Pelagian Controversy," 296.

[156] Warfield, "Pelagian Controversy," 296–97.

[157] Warfield, "Pelagian Controversy," 297.

[158] This is a brilliant line of argument, and I suspect Warfield is correct. It is possible that Warfield did not give quite enough attention to Pelagius's notion of habit, and how one's habits will or will not shape one's response to temptation over time. My thanks to Mark Ellis for raising this point in a question-and-answer session several years ago when I gave a version of this chapter at the 2018 national meeting of the Evangelical Theological Society.

has asserted, "if Augustine were deprived of the use of it [Romans 5:12], his theology would not be affected."[159] Especially as one reads through *Against Julian* and *An Unfinished Work*, it becomes clear that Augustine's position on original sin is not tied only or simply to a certain way of reading Romans 5:12, and it certainly does not necessarily hinge on the Latin *in quo* or the Greek ἐφ᾽ ᾧ. Rather, Augustine's position is a biblical-theological construct built on a more general reading of Scripture.

Sixth, Pelagius's way of reading the old covenant and new covenant (only briefly touched on here) reveals a fundamental hermeneutical weakness. There is virtually no sense of a redemptive-historical reading of Scripture in Pelagius, as far as I can tell. The great biblical tensions of the already–not yet, of the law's goodness and righteousness, combined with its pedagogical role which culminates in Christ, the end of the law, is strangely missing in Pelagius. The idea that the old covenant was good, but had a fading glory, while the new covenant is truly *better*, with an unfading glory, gets no purchase in Pelagius's theologizing. In Pelagius, the Bible is essentially a very flat book. Pelagius has no problem saying that surely at least some OT saints would have lived perfectly holy and righteous lives. Whereas the Christian church has wrestled with the realities of old and new covenant, the ways in which we have moved from shadow to reality, from type to antitype, these fundamental biblical categories and hermeneutical queries are strangely lacking in Pelagius's theologizing. Did his hermeneutic lead him astray? Or did fundamental theological commitments keep him from attending to Scripture as he ought?

Conclusion

The debate between Augustine and Pelagius (and the Pelagians) on the question of original sin is one of the most important and intriguing in all of church history. To be an "Augustinian" on this issue is—almost—shorthand simply for being a traditional Christian. Reflection and study of this debate is also a reminder of how much hinges on key theological decisions. With this central debate, we see the importance of grasping the distinction between a pre-fall era and a post-fall era. When this distinction is lost it is impossible to affirm

---

[159] John Rist, *Augustine Deformed: Love, Sin, and Freedom in the Western Moral Tradition* (Cambridge: Cambridge University Press, 2016), 20.

and propagate the remainder of the traditional Christian theological structure: death coming into the world through sin; the last Adam (Christ)—of whom the first Adam was a type —overcoming death in his own death, burial, and resurrection; the fundamental distinction between a pre-fall world (including mankind) and a post-fall world; the fundamental unity of the race as contained in, and derived from, the first couple; and the necessity of radical grace if sinners are going to be rescued and brought to saving faith. I suspect that the extent to which the Christian church remains faithful over time will depend in large part on how faithfully the church understands and perpetuates key truths found in the works of Augustine, Bishop of Hippo.

Ruined Sinners in a Pseudo-Augustinian Treatise on Predestination

Francis X. Gumerlock

Introduction

From the controversies about grace, free will, and predestination in the fifth and sixth centuries, at least six treatises devoted to the topic of predestination have survived. Of these, all written in Latin, the authors of three are known with certainty: Augustine, Arnobius the Younger, and Fulgentius of Ruspe. These three texts have been published in English translation.[1] The authors of the three other texts on predestination are uncertain, and none has been published in English.[2] One of them, which circulated in the name of Augustine throughout the Middle Ages, entitled *On Predestination*, is the subject of the

---

[1] Augustine's *On the Predestination of the Saints* is in Roland J. Teske, trans., *Answer to the Pelagians IV: To the Monks of Hadrumetum and Provence*, in *The Works of Saint Augustine: A Translation for the 21st Century*, vol. I/26, ed. John E. Rotelle (Hyde Park, NY: New City Press, 1999), 147–87. Books 2 and 3 of Arnobius's *Praedestinatus* are translated in Guido Stucco, *Not without Us: A Brief History of the Forgotten Catholic Doctrine of Predestination during the Semipelagian Controversy* (Tucson, AZ: Fenestra, 2006), 193–263. Fulgentius's *On the Truth of Predestination and Grace* is in Rob Roy McGregor and Donald Fairbairn, trans., *Fulgentius and the Scythian Monks: Correspondence on Christology and Grace*, in *The Fathers of the Church: A New Translation*, vol. 126 (Washington, DC: Catholic University of America Press, 2013), 121–231.

[2] The first of the two anonymous texts, which are not the subject of this essay, is *On Predestination and Grace (De praedestinatione et gratia)*, in J.-P. Migne, *Patrologiae cursus completes, series Latina* (Paris: Petit-Montrouge, 1844–1864 [hereafter PL]), 45:1665–1678 and 65:843–54. Written before the Council of Orange in 529, this text seems to have been composed in response to Faustus of Riez's *On the Grace of God and Free Will*, written in 474. The second anonymous text is *On the Predestination of God: A Little Book of an Unknown Author (De praedestinatione Dei, libellus ignoti auctoris)*, in PL 45:1677–80. It is possible that this text may not be from the fifth and sixth century controversy, but from the seventh, eighth, or ninth century.

present essay. In particular, the essay examines its teaching on the inability of humans, who are ruined by sin, to choose Christ apart from a special work of divine grace.

After discussing the title, date, provenance, probable authorship, purpose, and content of the text of *On Predestination*, this essay focuses on its teaching on the effects of sin on the human will. The essay then draws a few conclusions, summarizes the findings, and adds two appendices, one of which is a translation of a significant portion of the text.

On Predestination

TITLE, DATE, AND AUTHORSHIP

The short treatise *On Predestination* is actually part of a larger work, the pseudo-Augustinian *Hypomnesticon contra Pelagianos et Caelestianos* (*Response against the Pelagians and Celestians*).[3] *On Predestination* makes up Book VI of the work, or more precisely *Response Six: On Predestination* (*Responsio VI: De praedestinatione*). In the preface to the *Hypomnesticon* the author reveals his intention to write responses to five Pelagian errors, which he does.[4] Later, however, the same author feels it necessary to add a sixth response in answer to accusations against predestination.[5] This response, *On Predestination*, covering more than fifty medieval manuscripts, circulated as a text by itself apart from the other five books of the *Hypomnesticon*.[6]

Written between the years 430 and 435, the *Hypomnesticon* in the early Middle Ages was often attributed to Augustine (d. 430).[7] However, in the ninth century Prudentius of Troyes and Florus of Lyons challenged that attribution, noting that it was not contained in the list of writings that Augustine published at the end of his life in his *Retractationes*, nor was it mentioned in the list of Augustine's writings by Possidius (d. after 437). However, after the ninth century it continued to be ascribed to Augustine; and in the sixteenth

---

[3] The word *hypomnesticon* (or *hypognosticon*, as it appears in some manuscripts) means a memorandum, a written remark, a note, or a response. A Latin edition of the entire *Hypomnesticon* is in *The Pseudo-Augustinian Hypomnesticon against the Pelagians and Celestians*, ed. with introduction by John Edward Chisholm, 2 vols. (Fribourg, Switzerland: University Press [vol 1: introduction, 1967; vol. 2: text edited from the manuscripts, 1980]). *Responsio VI: De praedestinatione* is in vol. 2, pp. 191–208.

[4] Chisholm, *Hypomnesticon*, 2:102–3.

[5] Chisholm, *Hypomnesticon*, 2:191: *Addere etiam hoc quam maxime huic operi oportet . . .* "Also, as much as possible, it is necessary to add this [response] to this work . . ." (my translation).

[6] The medieval manuscripts, in which Response VI circulated alone, are listed and described in Chisholm, *Hypomnesticon*, 2:42–62.

[7] Chisholm, *Hypomnesticon*, 1:40. Alexander Y. Hwang, *Intrepid Lover of Perfect Grace: The Life and Thought of Prosper of Aquitaine* (Washington, DC: Catholic University of America Press, 2009), 25, 180, dates it more precisely to between 433 and 435.

century the Lutheran author of the 1530 Confession of Augsburg, in a discussion on free will, quoted from it as a work of Augustine. According to John Chisholm, by the end of the seventeenth century Augustine's authorship of it "was decisively disproved, and almost universally abandoned." However, between the seventeenth and twentieth centuries searches for its true author, among whom Marius Mercator and Sixtus of Rome had been suggested, were unsuccessful.[8]

In 1967, Chisholm presented a lengthy case of more than fifty pages claiming that the author of *On Predestination* was the defender of Augustine, Prosper of Aquitaine. In the late 420s and early 430s Prosper was living in Provence in southern Gaul, where monastic luminaries like John Cassian and Vincent of Lerins were opposing Augustine's view of predestination. Chisholm noted the similarity between the *Hypomnesticon* and Prosper's works with respect to titles, doctrine, quotations of Scripture, style, and vocabulary.[9] While I am convinced by Chisholm's arguments and accept Prosper as the author of the *Hypomnesticon*, as does Guido Stucco, in 1983 Jean de Savignac rejected Chisholm's attribution of the *Hypomnesticon* to Prosper and concluded that its author was probably someone from Africa.[10] Alexander Hwang, who wrote on Prosper's life and thought in 2009, also did not think that Prosper was the author of the *Hypomnesticon*. Listing it under "Works Falsely Attributed to Prosper," he did concede that it was written "probably by a member of Prosper's Augustinian faction in Marseilles."[11]

Chisholm's critical edition of the Latin text of the *Hypomnesticon* was published in 1980. Up to the present time, no English translation of the *Hypomnesticon* has been published. A five-page English summary of its sixth response, *On Predestination*, is in Stucco's *Not without Us*.[12] Zachary Maxcey, formerly a graduate student at Providence Theological Seminary, translated the entire sixth response *On Predestination* in a 2011 paper for one of his courses. For this essay, Maxcey has graciously permitted me to use his translation, a portion of which is provided in appendix 2 at the end of this chapter.[13]

---

[8] The contents of this paragraph are from Chisholm, *Hypomnesticon*, 1:41–73. Quotation from p. 61.

[9] Chisholm, *Hypomnesticon*, 1:77–129. See also John Edward Chisholm, "The Authorship of the Pseudo-Augustinian *Hypomnesticon* against the Pelagians and Celestians," *Studia Patristica* 11 (1972): 307–10.

[10] Stucco, *Not without Us*, 60–61; Jean de Savignac, "Une attribution nouvelle et une edition critique de l'*Hypomnesticon*," *Scriptorium* 37 (1983): 134–40.

[11] Hwang, *Intrepid Lover of Perfect Grace*, 22–25, 180.

[12] Stucco, *Not without Us*, 63–67.

[13] Zachary S. Maxcey, "An English Translation of Prosper of Aquitaine's Hypomnesticon: A Paper Presented in Partial Fulfillment of the Requirements for the Course 'Predestination from Augustine to the Reformation: Readings, Research, and Translations'" (Colorado Springs: Providence Theological Seminary, May 2011), unpublished.

Purpose and Overall Content

The purpose for writing *On Predestination*, which is subdivided into eight chapters, was to respond to false accusations about what the author and those who thought similarly to him were believing and preaching about predestination. This reason for his writing is set forth in its first chapter. They are accused of saying that God predestines certain people to eternal life in such a way that even if they do not want to pray or fast or be vigilant, they have nothing to worry about because they are not able to perish. They are also accused of saying that God predestined certain people to hell, and that even if those predestined to hell wanted to believe and obey God's will, eternal life cannot be granted to them. Finally, they are accused of teaching that God is an "acceptor" of persons, meaning that God shows partiality, a concept that directly contradicts passages of Scripture such as Acts 10:34, Romans 2:11, and Colossians 3:25.

In the second chapter, the author explains that God does in fact both predestine and foreknow. While he foreknows and predestines good things, however, in the case of moral evils he only foreknows them but does not predestine them.[14] God is not an acceptor of persons, but from the mass of the condemned human race he predestined some to eternal life and deservedly punishes the rest. The third and fourth chapters repeat that God is not an acceptor of persons. However, if the accuser wants to know why God punishes some with justice and frees others with mercy, it is a mystery, according to the apostle Paul (Rom. 9:20–21). Humans cannot know God's unsearchable ways nor comprehend his inscrutable decisions (Rom. 11:34–35). Turning the tables on his accusers, the author writes that they, even more so than the fearless apostle Paul, claim to be able to comprehend the judgments of God, for example, when they say that the reason God forbade Paul and Barnabas to preach in Asia (Acts 16:6–7) was that God foreknew that the Asian people were not going to believe.

Chapters 5 and 6 of *On Predestination* focus on those who will perish out of the mass of condemned humanity. God foreknew them in their impious works, but did not impel them to commit evil deeds. However, their punishment was predestined. Judas Iscariot is a prime example of this. His evil deed of betrayal of Jesus was foreknown, but God did not cause it. Otherwise, it would have been a work of God and not of Judas, who would then be without

---

[14] Cf. Augustine, *On the Predestination of the Saints* 10, 19, in Teske, trans., *Answer to the Pelagians IV*, 165.

fault and whose condemnation would be unjust. Rather, by a just judgment God handed Judas over to a reprobate mind (Rom. 1:18) and permitted his evil deed. Judas's punishment, however, was predestined. To support his teaching that merited punishment for the wicked has been predestined, the author quotes Acts 1:25, 2 Peter 2:3, Jude 4, and Matthew 25:41. For those predestined to life, salvation is entirely a gift and not dependent on one's merits. This is supported with an extended quotation and commentary on passages from the first and second chapters of Ephesians.

The seventh chapter of *On Predestination* counters the accusation that the author and those in agreement with him preach that, even if some want to believe, God refuses to bestow salvation to them. He also addresses other accusations, not mentioned in the first chapter, that his teaching of predestination excludes free will and that he does not think it is necessary for people to be devout in good works. He answers the latter with passages from the Gospels that tell people to watch and pray and do what the Savior commands. The predestined do these things because God has enabled them. Concerning those without the grace of predestination, God is not responsible for their evil behavior, for God does not will iniquity nor command anyone to act wickedly (Ps. 5:5; Sir. 15:20). Predestination is not done out of any malice in God nor out of an accepting of persons by him, but rather the cause is secret.

In the last chapter the author asks his interlocutors to stop making false accusations, and challenges them, saying that if they want to be argumentative, they should argue with the Lord Jesus himself, who said things like, "No one is able to come to me unless the Father, who sent me, will have drawn him" (John 6:44). The author addresses one last accusation: that he believes that what the apostle said, that God "wants all people to be saved" (1 Tim. 2:4), is false. In response, he shows from the Gospels that God does blind and harden the hearts of some (Mark 4:11–12; John 12:39–40), and states that not everyone will be saved. The author also teaches that God's will is not impeded by man's will. He then interprets the Pauline passage to mean that all who are saved, are saved by God's will, which corresponds with one of the interpretations of Augustine.[15] He concludes the treatise by declaring that it is blasphemy to deny predestination, an undeserved grace that imparts desperation to none and encourages all to engage in good works.

---

[15] Augustine, *Enchiridion on Faith, Hope, and Love* 103; Henry Paolucci, ed., *St. Augustine. The Enchiridion on Faith, Hope, and Love* (Chicago: Regnery Gateway, 1961), 119–20.

RUINED SINNERS IN THIS TEXT

Besides the topic of predestination, the treatise *On Predestination* discusses the fall and its consequences for all humans. Those consequences include mortality, condemnation, and an inability of the human will to choose righteousness. Chapter 2 teaches that "in the transgression of Adam and Eve" the human race was made "mortal and worthy of condemnation."[16] According to the sixth chapter, the sin of Adam "passes down to those who are born."[17] Accordingly, death and condemnation come to all humans through the sin of our first parents. This makes predestination and election necessary for people to be saved. From this mass of people, who are justly under a sentence of condemnation, God mercifully predestines some to eternal life, but justly punishes the rest.

In the case of the elect, according to the fourth, fifth, and sixth chapters, the merit of a right choice plays no role. In the sixth and eighth chapters this is shown in the election of infants who have not yet grown to use their faculty of choice. Through an inscrutable decision, God gives baptismal grace to one infant, while allowing another infant to die before being born of water and Spirit (John 3:5), which the author understands as taking place in infant baptism. Those latter infants are guilty of "the sin of Adam only" but "are liable to punishment," which is in accordance with divine justice.[18] In the case of those chosen for salvation who are old enough to use their faculty of choice, the human will does not go before God, but rather God himself "precedes the will of man with his mercy. For it says, 'My God will precede me with his mercy' (Ps. 59:10)."[19] This is because humans, according to chapters 6 and 7, "are able to do absolutely nothing without him," a clear statement of their inability.[20] Only "through him," that is, through Christ, are they able to do what he commands.

Chapter 5 teaches that, in the case of those who are perishing (excluding unbaptized infants), they perish because of their own vices and works of impiety. In the case of Judas, these included the sins of greed, betrayal, and using his office of apostleship wickedly. God did not cause these evil deeds of Judas, but foreknew them and permitted them. Two additional teachings

---

[16] Pseudo-Augustine, *On Predestination* 2; Maxcey, "An English Translation," 2.
[17] Pseudo-Augustine, *On Predestination* 5; Maxcey, "An English Translation," 11.
[18] Pseudo-Augustine, *On Predestination* 6; Maxcey, "An English Translation," 11; cf. Augustine, *On the Predestination of the Saints* 12, 24, in Teske, trans., *Answer to the Pelagians IV*, 168–69.
[19] Pseudo-Augustine, *On Predestination* 4; Maxcey, "An English Translation," 5.
[20] Pseudo-Augustine, *On Predestination* 6; Maxcey, "An English Translation," 13.

about ruined sinners are gleaned from the fifth chapter. The first concerns God handing one over to a reprobate mind (Rom. 1:18), which the author says that God did in the case of Judas by a "just judgment."[21] In other words, handing one over to a reprobate mind is not an act in which God *makes* a person a sinner. Rather, it is a just punishment for one who has previously sinned and is deserving of punishment. This distinction is important so that God is not thought to be the author of sin. The fifth chapter also reveals that there are degrees of culpability that depend upon the severity of the sin. The author ended the chapter, which focused largely on the deeds of Judas, acknowledging that the fault or blame of one may be dissimilar from that of another. In other words, some sins, because of their severity, carry more culpability than others.

In the sixth and seventh chapters the author says that if anyone is able to do anything good, he should give thanks to God who enabled him, citing twice the words of the Savior: "Without me you are able to do nothing" (John 15:5). When one is enabled to do good works, he should not boast as if these had derived from his own will, because they came from the work of God. To support this, the author quotes Romans 9:16, which says, "It is not of those who will nor of those who run, but of God who has mercy"; and John 3:27, "A man is not able from himself to do anything unless it will have been given to him from above." Divine grace changes a person's will and makes an unwilling person willing. According to the eighth chapter, even for the initial act of believing, God opens the heart of some people "for the purpose of believing, and illumines their eyes for the purpose of seeing and knowing the mystery of the kingdom of heaven, that is, that they may be able to be saved."[22]

Conclusion

The Authorship of This Text

The treatise *On Predestination* was attributed to Augustine throughout the Middle Ages, but by the seventeenth century scholars almost unanimously recognized that it was not his. In the twentieth century, Chisholm argued that Prosper of Aquitaine was its author, but reception of that attribution has been mixed. I lean toward affirming Prosper of Aquitaine as its author. The correspondence between it and Prosper's other writings with regard to vocabulary, style, and

---

[21] Pseudo-Augustine, *On Predestination* 5; Maxcey, "An English Translation," 10.
[22] Pseudo-Augustine, *On Predestination* 8; Maxcey, "An English Translation," 17.

use of certain Scripture passages, is clear. Furthermore, the contents of *On Predestination* fit the historical circumstances surrounding Prosper in 432–435. At that time some monks in southern Gaul, especially Vincent of Lerins, were severely criticizing Augustine's doctrine of predestination. According to Prosper's *Answers to the Objections of the Gauls* and *Answers to the Vincentian Articles*, they were saying that he was teaching that "By God's predestination men are compelled to sin," "God will not have all to be saved," and "God is the author of our sins," all of which are answered in *On Predestination.*[23]

Hwang's conjecture, that a person in Prosper's faction in Marseilles wrote the *Hypomnesticon* (of which *On Predestination* was its sixth response) has merit in that it links the text with Prosper. But its weakness is that there is little evidence that a "faction" of Prosper in Marseilles ever existed. Prosper was not a bishop with priests under his care, nor an abbot with monks he instructed, nor a schoolmaster with students, but simply an educated layperson who tended to work somewhat independently. His only known associate in Marseilles to join in his defense of Augustine was another layperson, named Hilary. This Hilary, like Prosper, wrote a letter to Augustine about 427, to which Augustine replied with *On the Predestination of the Saints* and *On the Gift of Perseverance*, addressed to both Prosper and Hilary. After this, almost nothing is known of Hilary.[24]

Another circumstance for Prosper writing *On Predestination* is also possible. About that same time, an abbot named Arnobius the Younger, presiding over a monastery outside Rome, was also opposing Prosper's teaching.[25] Arnobius wrote *Praedestinatus*, which portrayed predestination in the most horrific ways and labeled it as a heresy. It is very possible that *On Predestination* was not written in response to the Gauls, but in dialogue with Arnobius. Arnobius's accusations against predestinarians in Book 2 of his *Praedestinatus* correspond with those stated in the first chapter of *On Predestination*, namely, that they teach that prayer, fasting, and being solicitous about virtue is useless because different ends for people were predestined and are irreversible.[26]

---

[23] Prosper of Aquitaine, *Answers to the Objections of the Gauls*, Articles 1 and 8; *Answers to the Vincentian Articles*, Articles 2 and 5; De Letter, *Prosper of Aquitaine: Defense of St. Augustine*, 140, 146, 165, 167.

[24] Hilary's letter to Augustine is *Letter 226* among the works of Augustine, and is translated in Teske, trans., *Answer to the Pelagians IV*, 60–68.

[25] On the conflict between Prosper and Arnobius, see Francis X. Gumerlock, "Arnobius the Younger against the 'Predestined One': Was Prosper of Aquitaine the Predestinarian Opponent of Arnobius the Younger?" *Augustinian Studies* 44.2 (2013): 249–63.

[26] In Book 2 of *Praedestinatus* Arnobius claims to be quoting from a little book written by predestinarians, which says that sins are committed because of God's predestination; but the little book is believed to be a fabrication of Arnobius himself.

See appendix 1 at the end of this chapter for a comparison of the two texts. Additionally, the case of Judas Iscariot does not seem to have been important to the Gallic opponents of Prosper, but it was an issue for Arnobius. His *Praedestinatus* criticized predestinarians for allegedly believing that Judas was predestined to death. If *On Predestination* was written in dialogue with Arnobius, this explains the long discussion in its fifth chapter about God not predestining and impelling Judas's evil deeds and about Judas being responsible for his own sins, which were foreknown but not predestined.

If Prosper did write *On Predestination*, this has bearing on the question of why he was relatively silent about predestination in his later writings on grace. These later writings include *Official Pronouncements of the Apostolic See on Divine Grace and Free Will* and his *Call of All Nations*.[27] Elsewhere I have shown that Prosper's relative silence on predestination in these writings is because he wrote them after his relocation to Rome about 435. After that time, it seems Prosper focused on the theology of grace that the Roman bishops had endorsed. In their various pronouncements, the Roman bishops had not taken a stand on Augustine's teaching of predestination, but they clearly taught that in salvation grace precedes and enables the human will to choose well, and that became the focus of Prosper's writings.[28] I still hold to this argument. However, there may be another very simple reason Prosper did not write on the topic of predestination after 435. There was no need to, since if Prosper was the author of *On Predestination*, he would have already written on predestination. Therefore, if someone after 435 had asked Prosper about predestination, he did not need to write another treatise for them. He could simply direct the person to his earlier work *On Predestination*, the sixth response he added to his *Hypomnesticon*.

TEACHING ABOUT RUINED SINNERS

According to the author of *On Predestination*, all of humanity fell in the transgression of Adam and Eve and received mortality and the sentence of condemnation. Out of this mass of people, God mercifully predestined some for eternal life and justly punishes the rest. The ground of their perdition is

---

[27] *Official Pronouncements* is in Prudentius De Letter, trans., *Prosper of Aquitaine: Defense of St. Augustine*, Ancient Christian Writers 32 (New York: Newman, 1963), 178–85; De Letter, *St. Prosper of Aquitaine: The Call of All Nations*, Ancient Christian Writers 14 (New York: Newman, 1952).
[28] Francis X. Gumerlock, "The 'Romanization' of Prosper of Aquitaine's Doctrine of Grace" (MA thesis, St. Louis University, 2001), unpublished.

their own impiety, except in unbaptized infants, in whom the inherited sin of Adam is the ground of their just judgment. God foreknows the evil of those perishing but did not predestine it.

Concerning the elect, the Lord opens their hearts to believe. When a person chooses well or does good works, it is because God enables the previously unwilling person to choose rightly. Therefore, that person should not boast as if the good work came from his own will.

The author of *On Predestination* devoted many of his words to defending himself from false accusations, especially with respect to those who eventually perish. God, he says, foreknows but does not predestine the *sins* of the reprobate, but their *punishment* was predestined. This distinction between foreknowledge and predestination, mentioned in a cursory way by Augustine, is amplified in *On Predestination*.[29] It was its author's way of demonstrating that God predestines without being the author of sin.

In summary, *On Predestination* sets forth a view of election in which it is not based on the foreseen faith or foreseen choice of the elect person. Its cause is in a secret decree unknown to humans. The grace of predestination is necessary because all humans transgressed in Adam and are ruined sinners unable to believe in God or choose God without it. In other words, the text affirms the imputation of Adam's sin and the total infirmity of a sinner to turn to God without his effectual call and the regenerating work of the Holy Spirit. Through that special grace, God opens the hearts of some, illumines their minds, and makes them willing to believe. Thus, there is no cause for boasting by a Christian, only thanks for being set free from just condemnation and for obtaining divine mercy.

Appendix 1:

THE CORRESPONDENCE BETWEEN THE ACCUSATIONS STATED IN *ON PREDESTINATION* AND THOSE STATED IN ARNOBIUS'S *PRAEDESTINATUS*

When the author of *On Predestination* stated his reason for writing, he mentioned that it was to respond to accusations that were being thrown at him. This appendix will compare the accusations stated in the first chapter of *On Predestination* with those leveled by Arnobius the Younger in Book 2 of his

---

[29] Augustine, *On the Predestination of the Saints* 10, 19, in Teske, trans., *Answer to the Pelagians IV*, 165–66.

Praedestinatus by providing an excerpt from each. I have placed some of the words of correspondence in bold. According to the author of *On Predestination*,

> Also it is especially necessary to add this [response] to this work, so that both your false accusation, which you are accustomed to throw at us, may be defeated, indeed refuted, through the illumination of the grace of the Savior, and the integrity of our faith may be proven. Indeed, [you accuse] us of saying that we believe and preach openly in predestination, in agreement with the law of God and the prophets and with the gospel of Christ and his Apostles, in that God predestines certain people to life in the kingdom of heaven in such a manner, that [even] if they refuse to **pray** or **fast** or to be **vigilant in every divine work,** that they are in **no way able to perish nor should they be at all solicitous** for themselves, **because God willed** that they [be saved, and] by choosing them once for all he predestined them to life. But he predestined certain others to the punishment of hell in this manner, that even if they want to believe [and] subject themselves to **fasting, prayers, and all the divine will,** that God is not pleased by these things [and] eternal life absolutely cannot be given to them; thus, by election they **have been predestined to perish.**[30]

In Book 2 of the *Praedestinatus*, Arnobius says that the predestinarians say the following:

> Therefore, why do you, who remain in sin, become frightened? If God deigns, you will be holy. Or why is it that you, who live in holiness, remain **solicitous,** as if your solicitude will save you? If God does not will [otherwise], **both** [the one who remains in sin and the one who lives in holiness] **will never perish.** Both, be secure in God! You, who are holy so that you do not perish, who both offer up **prayers** day and night, who engage in **fasting,** who diligently persevere in the **divine** readings, who are free from exhortations, and who every day **pursue all kinds of holy exercises,** will you be saved by this devotion of yours? Will you be holier than Judas, who received the power of curing the sick, of putting demons to flight, of raising the dead, [and] of walking upon snakes and scorpions,[31] who was a colleague of the Apostles [and] a disciple of Christ, and who, nevertheless, because he **was predestined to death,** incurred eternal death? O man, **cease to be solicitous** about yourself; cease, I say, **to be solicitous** about your virtue, and only **trust securely in the will of God.**[32]

---

[30] See Chisholm, *Hypomnesticon*, 2:191, my translation.
[31] Luke 10:19.
[32] See Franco Gori, ed., *Arnobi Iunioris Praedestinatus qui dicitur*, Corpus Christianorum Series Latina 25B (Turnhout, Belgium: Brepols, 2000), 59–60, my translation.

Arnobius wrote that the predestinarians believe that one who engages in "prayer," "fasting," and "all kinds of holy exercises" should not think that he will be saved because of such devotion. Similarly, the author of *On Predestination* wrote that he was being accused of teaching that even if a person did not want "to pray," or "fast," or to be vigilant "in every good work," he should not worry about it because God's predestination cannot be reversed.

Arnobius spoke of one who "was predestined to death," and the author of *On Predestination* spoke of those "predestined to perish." Arnobius spoke of those who "will never perish," and the author of *On Predestination* spoke of those who are "in no way able to perish." Finally, both texts say that a person does not have to be "solicitous" because salvation or damnation depends upon God's "will."

These verbal correspondences between Arnobius's *Praedestinatus* and *On Predestination* may be indicative that the authors of both texts were writing in dialogue with each other. In an article published in 2013, I demonstrated that Arnobius's chief predestinarian opponent was Prosper of Aquitaine. I did this with examples of correspondence between the writings of Arnobius and those known to be from Prosper's pen.[33] The comparison above, of a paragraph from the first chapter of *On Predestination* and a paragraph from Book 2 of Arnobius's *Praedestinatus*, might be further evidence to support the hypothesis of Chisholm that Prosper of Aquitaine was the author of the *Hypomnesticon*, which contains *On Predestination* as its sixth response.

Appendix 2: Translation of Chapters 3–7 of *On Predestination*[34]

CHAPTER THREE

If you demand to know this from me, if he is not an acceptor of persons[35] why God has done these two things differently, that generally he either should punish with justice, or free with mercy, then dispute with Paul. Yes indeed, if you dare, argue with Paul, who has said, with Christ speaking

---

[33] Gumerlock, "Arnobius the Younger against the 'Predestined One,'" (see note 25, above).
[34] This translation of *On Predestination* 3–7 is from Maxcey, "An English Translation," 3–15, with slight modifications by me. Used by permission.
[35] Acts 10:34; Rom. 2:11; Col. 3:25.

through him:[36] "O man, who are you who answers back to God? Surely the thing formed does not say to him who formed him, 'Why have you made me in this way?' Does not the potter have the power to make from the same lump of clay one indeed as a vessel for honor but another as a vessel for dishonor?" (Rom. 9:20–21). Moreover, I am saying this which I have said, that whatever God does mercifully, he does justly and in holiness, since he alone knows by foreknowing, what man does not know by being ignorant. "For who has known the mind of the Lord, who should instruct him? Or who has been his counselor? Or who has first given to him, and it will be repaid to him?" (Rom. 11:34–35). "Or who says to him, 'What have you done?' " (Wis. 12:12). God cannot be said to be only just, or only merciful, but both just and merciful. Thus, we speak; thus, we believe. Therefore, when we with David, while fearing his mercy and judgment, sing,[37] we do not question as those seeking what his will is in judgment and mercy. But if these responses are still not yet sufficient for your animosity, by which having been caught up in a chariot of controversy, you will be brought out through fields of questioning, listen as we bring forth other things with sole consideration of the faith concerning the depth of the riches of the wisdom and knowledge of God, while trembling at his incomprehensible judgments and his unsearchable ways;[38] because if we would have wished to investigate the secret of God, what is known of his justice alone, we are not able to comprehend it, and so it is fulfilled in us what has been written: "Searching they have failed the search." How? Since "man comes near," it is said, "to a deep heart, and God shall be exalted" (Ps. 64:6). But perhaps although you are reprehensible, if you say that you are comprehensible of the judgments of God, certainly you are more pleasing to God than the Apostle Paul, who has preached through the Holy Spirit that his judgments are incomprehensible.[39] Therefore, explain that judgment, as it has been spoken by Paul and Barnabas preaching the word of God in Lystra:[40] "In past generations, he allowed all nations to walk in their own ways" (Acts 14:16), that they might perish in the idolatry of images; and only one nation, that is Jacob, the Lord has chosen for himself and Israel as his possession,[41] to whom alone certainly he gave the law for examining oneself, while, as I have said, the rest of the generations have been set aside. Or why again did the loss of the Jews happen, so that the reconciliation of the world, that is, of all nations, might occur, just as the Apostle has declared: "For if their rejection is the reconciliation of the world, what will their acceptance be except life from the dead?" (Rom. 11:15), as if it

---

[36] Second Corinthians 13:3.
[37] Psalm 100:1.
[38] Romans 11:33.
[39] Romans 11:33.
[40] Acts 14:6.
[41] Deuteronomy 7:6; 26:18.

was impossible for the omnipotent God to give the law to the whole world at one time, to confer the salvation of the grace of Christ, or, rather as I will say, to do it from the beginning, from the fall of Adam? What happens in the difference of the times exists by his decision. Also teach why Paul and Barnabas, having been sent by the Holy Spirit to carry the name of the Lord for the cause of salvation among the nations, when they, while preaching, were crossing Phrygia and the region of Galatia, "were forbidden by the Holy Spirit to speak the word in Asia; and when they had come to Mysia, wanting to go into Bithynia, the Spirit of Jesus," it says, "did not permit them" (Acts 16:6–7).

Chapter Four

You will say: "God knew that they were not going to believe, and for that reason he did not permit them to go for the purpose of speaking the word." Fool, God is he who justifies the wicked.[42] He is not preceded by the human will, but he himself precedes the will of man with his mercy. For it says: "My God will precede me with his mercy" (Ps. 59:10). Listen also to another prophet who says: "Change me, Lord, and I shall be changed; heal me, Lord, and I shall be healed" (Jer. 17:14). Accordingly, the Apostle also says: "Having been justified freely through his grace, through the redemption, which is in Christ Jesus" (Rom. 3:24). Hear [the word] "freely" and be silent concerning merits. Is not that prohibition of the Holy Spirit shown in another [passage], as the word of the Lord Jesus says in the Gospel: "The wind blows where it pleases" (John 3:8). Consider this and explain this other thing, why he said "where it pleases" and not "everywhere." Also tell us why when Paul and Barnabas with forewarnings were preaching salvation to the Gentiles and Jews in Pisidian Antioch,[43] that no one believed, unless thereupon the Lord predestined them that they might believe. For, thus also the sacred page bears witness about them. It says: "And they believed, as many had been foreordained," that is, predestined, "to eternal life" (Acts 13:48). Behold, in everything which we have brought forth from divine authority, you have mercy and judgment; and it is certain that God is not an acceptor of persons,[44] nor does he respect any person. Descend therefore, if you are able, into the depths of the mercy of God; ascend, if you are capable, into the loftiness of the righteousness of his judgments; stretch out into the length and breadth of his unsearchable ways;[45] and if you will have clearly penetrated, explain such dreaded and

---

[42] Romans 4:5.
[43] Acts 13:14.
[44] Acts 10:34; Rom. 2:11; Col. 3:25.
[45] Romans 11:33.

incomprehensible secrets[46] as these to us, about which Paul, himself fearless, becomes frightened.

If, moreover, as I have said above, you will fall, having been thrown from the chariot of worthless questionings into a flood of vain controversy; and just as a ship deserted by its captain, you will have rolled along through diverse and unknown shores. You will not be able to sail when you speed up, nor return and dock in the port of the Catholic faith, where no tempest of unfruitful curiosity is able to disturb or drown you. For however great a thing you attempt to know, you are not able to understand the judgments of God, nor will you [ever] be able, because just as no man knows the things which are of a man, except the spirit which is in him; so also, the things which are of God, "no one knows except the Spirit of God" (1 Cor. 2:11). Therefore, if we will have been able to grasp anything, we ought to know that it was not by our skill, but it was revealed by the gift of the Holy Spirit. Moreover, if it is not given us to know what is above us, it should not be sought by our insignificance. For it was said beforehand by the holy Scriptures: "You shall not seek the things higher than you, and you shall not search the things more powerful than you in vanity; also, do not [seek] to understand the deep thing, but fear" (Sir. 3:21). The depths of God[47] shall be utterly feared[48] and venerated, since we solemnly confess that we are not able to search them out. It says: "All things you have established in measure and number and weight, Lord" (Wis. 11:22). Consequently, who is sufficient to understand this measure, this number, and this weight of God, that he may be able to describe all his decisions in these three pronouncements? In measure, I think of what consists of quality, in number quantity, in weight an equalized ratio. But these three (that is, quality and quantity and an equalized ratio) are constant in the judgment and mercy of God, because in these two holy boundaries they have been set, by which he establishes, governs, and is going to judge throughout this world. In these things, God, the just Judge, is not able to be comprehended; he is not able to be blamed. Therefore, all the things which we have said above, or shall say, lie hidden to us now in the enclosure of these three, which at that time will be unsealed only by the keys of the judgment and mercy of God, so that they may be known, when at the Lord's advent the secret things of darkness will be illuminated, and the plans of the hearts will be revealed,[49] so that praise or punishment may be given to each one from God.[50] Therefore, it is necessary that we return to those things which we have begun to debate above.

---

[46] Romans 11:33.
[47] First Corinthians 1:20.
[48] Romans 11:20.
[49] Romans 2:16; Heb. 4:12.
[50] First Corinthians 4:5.

CHAPTER FIVE

On the other hand, we have said concerning the damnable mass of the human race, that God has foreknown them whom by his mercy, not by their merits, and by the election of grace, he predestined to life; but that he only foreknew that the rest, who by the judgment of his justice are made to have no part in this grace, would perish through their own vices, not that he predestined them to perish. But, as I have said, those whom he foreknew in works of impiety and death, he did not predestine, nor did he impel [them to do so]; in those who provoke God to wrath, they are neither willing to accept for themselves the faith or the preaching of salvation, nor are they able, or they wickedly make use of his favors, and on account of this they are handed over to a reprobate mind by God the Judge,[51] so that they may not do the things which are proper; with these, we confess that punishment has been predestined. Insofar as we may be able to demonstrate, I think that Judas alone is sufficient for an example. Namely, although God had foreknown that he would be the worst in the vices of his own will, that is—that he would wickedly make use of his election of discipleship which was conferred by Christ righteously, and that he, burning with greed, would betray the Lord to the Jews for a price; he predestined punishment for him from merit, as the Holy Spirit says through David, "O God, pass not over my praise in silence, because the mouth of the sinner and the crafty one has been opened against me" (Ps. 109:1–2). This is [the mouth] of Judas or the Jews with regard to Christ. [Of the mouth] of Judas, when he says: "What are you willing to give to me, and I will hand him over to you?" (Matt. 26:15). And after the promise of money, giving them a sign of betrayal, he says: "The one I will kiss is the man; seize him" (Matt. 26:48). Therefore, it says "it has been opened against me." Indeed, when he gave them the sign, they seized him whom he disclosed by his crafty mouth. Also, [of the mouth of] the Jews, when wishing to destroy him by treachery, as the Gospel explains, they shouted saying: "Crucify, crucify!" (John 19:6). And after a little while, it follows: "Appoint a sinner over him," that is, over Judas, "and may the devil stand by his right hand. When he is judged, may he emerge as one condemned, and may his prayer be made in sin. May his days be made few; and may another receive his office" (Ps. 109:6–8). And after other things which [are written] about him there follows: "Because he did not remember to do mercy," it says, "and he persecuted the poor and destitute man, and he handed over to death the one pricked in the heart" (Ps. 109:16), and the remaining [things which] follow, what had been predicted with regard to his punishment. For instance, as the book of the Acts of the Apostles relates, it has been predicted about him and what had been

---

[51] Romans 1:28.

fulfilled in him, the holy Apostle Peter demonstrates, when he announces that it is necessary that, for the purpose of testifying of the resurrection of Jesus, one be elected to his place from those, who had been assembled with the Apostles, saying:

> Men, brethren, it is necessary that the Scripture be fulfilled, which the Holy Spirit spoke beforehand through the mouth of David concerning Judas, who was the leader of those who arrested Jesus, who had been numbered among us, and was allotted a portion in this ministry. And, indeed, this man took possession of a field from the reward of iniquity, and having been hung, he burst in the middle, and all his entrails were poured out. Moreover, it became well known to all the inhabitants of Jerusalem, so that in their language that field was named Akel Dama, that is, the field of blood. For it was written in the book of Psalms: "May his dwelling be deserted, and may there not be one who dwells in it, and may another receive his office." (Acts 1:16–20)

And after a few things these things that follow:

> They set up two, it says, Joseph, who is called Barsabbas, who was surnamed Justus, and Matthias. And while praying, they said: "You, Lord, who know the hearts of all, reveal which one from these two you have chosen to receive a place in this ministry and apostleship, from which Judas fell, that he might go away unto his own place," and the rest. (Acts 1:23–25)

When, therefore, mention of his evil works is made by the Holy Spirit in the Psalms, that which was going to happen against the Son of God was foreknown, not caused, before it occurred. For, if it has been caused, he would be inculpable, and it would be attributed to a work of God, not of Judas; also, the condemnation manifested upon him would be unjust. But God forbid that this be from the consummately good Judge, from God the author of all good, but the One who condemns all evil, since, as I said before, he foreknew the evil deeds of Judas but did not cause them. And yet with regard to the things he foreknew, handing him over to a reprobate mind[52] by just judgment, he permitted that he would fulfill them. And therefore, he permitted it, since he predicted it through the Holy Spirit before he would perish. Since just as it was necessary that Christ suffer through Judas, having been foretold by the Holy Spirit through the prophets, so it was necessary that Judas perish, having been foretold by the same Holy Spirit. For, it was said concerning him: "No one has perished, except the son of perdition" (John 17:12). For we clearly recognize that for him punishment

[52] Romans 1:18.

was predestined for his own evils—which with regard to those things, as I have often said, he[53] was only foreknown, not predestined—in that passage where it is spoken concerning him by the Apostle Peter "that he might go away unto his own place" (Acts 1:25), that is, his office was honorably transferred unto another. And we explain the other things, such as when it is read that he was condemned before he was born, according to that which we have said before in the discussion. Therefore, this is the cause of all those who shall perish, although blame may be different from blame.

CHAPTER SIX

Moreover, we have said what is true, although it is being abundantly debated, that is, that the punishment for those who shall perish has been predestined. Listen to the Apostle Peter, when he says that there will be false prophets and false teachers and apostates in the church,[54] just as they were among the ancient people: "For whom," he says, "judgment from long ago does not cease even now, and their destruction does not sleep" (2 Pet. 2:3). Likewise, the Apostle Jude says: "Certain men have entered, who were written of beforehand long ago for this judgment, ungodly men, turning the grace of our Lord into wantonness, and denying the only Lord and the Lord Jesus Christ" (Jude 4). And the Lord in the Gospel says to sinners: "Go into eternal fire, which my Father prepared for the devil and his angels" (Matt. 25:41), but to the predestined: "Come, blessed of my Father, take possession of the kingdom prepared," that is, predestined, "for you from the beginning of the world" (Matt. 25:34). Therefore, the rule of this discussion should be held firmly, which has been illuminated by divine testimonies: sinners before they were in the world have only been foreknown in their own evils, not predestined; but the punishment for them has been predestined according to what has been foreknown; likewise, children not having been born again from water and the Holy Spirit[55] are liable for predestined punishment, who have been foreknown not on the basis of their own wills, of which there are no good or evil actions, except in the sin of Adam only, which passes down to those who are born, and remaining in this, they leave the time of this present life. Indeed, what he may do concerning these, to whom mercy does not rescue, is a judgment of justice. He, who by pure faith trusts in the Lord who says that one who "does not eat my flesh and does not drink my blood" will not have life in himself (John 6:53), understands this and withdraws from controversy.

[53] Judas Iscariot.
[54] Second Peter 2:1.
[55] John 3:5.

But it must be said without wavering that those who live according to the purpose of God have been foreknown and predestined by the election of his gratuitous grace, and the kingdom of heaven has been predestined for them. Indeed, the Apostle Paul demonstrates this, when he testifies that they were predestined and elected before the world was established. Writing to the Ephesians he says: "Just as he chose us in him," that is, in Christ, "before the foundation of the world, that we might be holy and blameless in his sight in love, who predestined us to the adoption of sons through Jesus Christ to himself" (Eph. 1:4–5). Let the human tongue be silent, nor let it be lifted up concerning merits by any means with regard to predestination. Let it pay attention to the saying, "before the foundation of the world." This is a gift of the divine will, not the merit of human frailty. Finally, pay attention to that which follows:

> In whom, it says, we have redemption through his blood, the remission of sin, according to the riches of his grace, which he has abundantly supplied to us in all wisdom and prudence; to make known to us the mystery of his will, according to his good pleasure which he purposed in him, in the dispensation of the fullness of times to renew in Christ all things, which are in the heavens and which are on earth—in Him. In whom also we have been predestined according to his purpose, who works all things according to the counsel of his own will, that we, who have first hoped in Christ, may be to the praise of his glory. (Eph. 1:7–12)

Listen! He says, "according to the riches of his grace, which he has abundantly supplied to us," that is, by which he precedes us. Why? "To make known to us the mystery of his will." Listen! "Who works all things according to the counsel of his own will." Can it be that it depends on the merits of me, or you, or another? God forbid! But "his [will]," by which also with regard to these whom he predestines, he prepares works of good will, that in these they might walk, according to that which he again says in the same epistle:

> For, by grace you have been saved through faith. And this is not your own doing; it is the gift of God, not a result of works, so that no one may boast. For we are his workmanship, created in Christ Jesus for good works, which God prepared beforehand, that we should walk in them. (Eph. 2:8–10)

Listen! "For good works, which God prepared beforehand." And if you see that you are able to do anything good, give thanks to the one who prepares beforehand what you are able to do, not from your own will, since you are able to do absolutely nothing without him who said: "Apart from me you can do nothing" (John 15:5).

CHAPTER SEVEN

And so do not believe those saying anything of this kind: that we exclude the free choice of will, since it is still certain that those things which we speak hang upon divine authority; or, as you falsely throw at us, that we do not think that it is necessary to be devoted in the purpose of God by doing good works. But rather, we exhort those who understand that they obtain the mercy of God by the gift of grace, that it is necessary to press on in prayers, in supplications, in fasting, in vigils, and every work of the divine will. For it is said to the predestined Apostles, although nevertheless what is said to them by Christ, who was predestined according to the flesh from the seed of David, but predestined according to the power of God the Father with the Father and Holy Spirit,[56] is general: "Watch and pray that you may not enter into temptation" (Matt. 26:41). Likewise: "Watch, praying at all times, that you may be considered worthy to escape all these things, which are about to happen, and to stand before the Son of Man" (Luke 21:36). Also: "Strive to enter through the narrow gate" (Luke 13:24). Likewise: "You are my friends if you do what I command you" (John 15:14), and many other things, which are too lengthy to explain. But, as I have mentioned above, he said to them: "Without me, you are able to do nothing" (John 15:5). Through him they are able to do that which they are commanded. In this manner the Apostle says that the elect of God[57] are in Christ, in whom also they have been predestined "according to the purpose of him who works all things" (Eph. 1:11). Understand the saying, "who works all things," and believe that the works[58] of those who walk according to the purpose of God[59] is the work of God.

Therefore, those who are without the grace of predestination, that is, strangers from the purpose of God,[60] and continue in evil works, if they also will have departed from this life in such a manner, we do not say, as you think, that they have been ordained thus by God, the Creator of men, that they should perish, as if he created for them the behaviors of an evil life, or as if he will cast down those who were invited to every work of death. God forbid that this be from the divine purpose! For God does not will iniquity,[61] "neither has he commanded anyone to act wickedly, nor has he given to

---

[56] Romans 1:3–4. Cf. Augustine, *On the Predestination of the Saints* 15, 30, in Teske, trans., *Answer to the Pelagians IV*, 174.
[57] Romans 8:33.
[58] Ephesians 2:10.
[59] Ephesians 1:4–5.
[60] Ephesians 2:12.
[61] Psalm 5:4–5.

anyone a relaxation for sinning" (Sir. 15:20). "For he made all things that they might be and the nations of the earth curable" (Wis. 1:14). "But by envy of the devil, death entered into the world. Therefore, those who are of his faction follow him" (Wis. 2:24). Nor do we say, as you contrive: "And if they wish to believe, or to be occupied with the good works of God, God refuses to bestow this to them, since to choose in this manner is the gift of God." If therefore what they will is from God, God wills that what he gave becomes finished. If however it is not from God, but it is from the boasting of one's own will, by which they think that they earn God by merits, what they will, they are obviously not able to grasp, since "it is not of those who will," the Apostle says, "nor of those who run, but of God who has mercy" (Rom. 9:16); and since "a man is not able from himself to do anything, unless it will have been given to him from above" (John 3:27). God, the highest good, does not do this with malice, but with justice; he does this not by an accepting of persons,[62] but by a decreeing of secret causes. We know that often some strive to receive eternal life; and some do not. Also, some are unwilling to follow, but when divine grace comes in them so that they may be willing, they change their will; others do not. We also know that some, advanced [in the faith] from the labor of many years, having fallen into ruin at the end of their life, perished. But others from their young age have endured in every crime and damnable offense continuously to a very old age, and unexpectedly inspired by heavenly salvation, have been carried off to the rest of the kingdom of heaven. We also know that children, in whom there is no use of free will that we may judge concerning their good or bad merits, have been carried by the hands of their parents to the grace of holy baptism. In one of them through the hand of the priest the mystery of the faith is fulfilled, at other times another dies in the hands of the parents, denied the grace of the Savior.

"Who is wise and will understand these things?" (Hos. 14:9). Or who will be suitable to render a reason for these things? We say with David, "The Lord is righteous in all his ways and holy in all his works" (Ps. 145:17); and "How magnificent are your works, Lord! Your thoughts have been framed exceedingly deep" (Ps. 92:5). We say also with Paul, "O the depth of the riches of the wisdom and knowledge of God! How incomprehensible are his judgments, and unsearchable his ways!" (Rom. 11:33).

---

[62] Acts 10:34; Rom. 2:11; Col. 3:25.

5

The Bondage of the Will

LUTHER VERSUS ERASMUS

Mark D. Thompson

Erasmus—An Odd but Obvious Opponent

Desiderius Erasmus was the obvious choice to take on Martin Luther as the Reformation began to gather speed in the 1520s. After all, he was the "Prince of Humanists," with an unrivalled reputation as a scholar. He was universally recognized as one of the leading intellectuals of the northern Renaissance.[1] Among his friends and correspondents he could list Thomas More, Henry VIII, John Fisher, John Cole, Jacques Lefèvre d'Etaples, Guillaume Budè, Ulrich Zasius, Johann Reuchlin, and successive popes. He was also a convinced Catholic. "For my own part," he wrote in April 1522, "neither death nor life shall tear me from the society of the Catholic church."[2] And in the same month, "I would sooner meet death ten times over than start or encourage a perilous schism [periculosi dissidii]."[3]

Yet, at the same time, he was an odd choice. In the early decades of the sixteenth century, doubts had arisen about Erasmus. His critique of corruption within the church had raised questions about his loyalty, which were themselves the context for Erasmus's emphatic insistence that he was a faithful son of the church. Furthermore, Erasmus resisted being drawn into the

[1] Harold J. Grimm, *The Reformation Era: 1500–1650*, 2nd ed. (New York: Macmillan, 1973), 65.
[2] Desiderius Erasmus, *Epistola* 1273 (to Pedro Ruiz de la Mota, Bishop of Palencia, April 21, 1522), in *CE* 9:60.30–31 = *OE* 5:44.26–27.
[3] Erasmus, *Epistola* 1274 (to Luis Núñez Coronel, April 21, 1522), in *CE* 9:64.63–64 = *OE* 5:47.57.

Reformation debates, at least on the public stage, for the best part of a decade, despite extraordinary pressure to do so. As early as September 9, 1520, he wrote to Gerard Geldenhouwer, "There is actually a bishopric waiting for me, if I will attack Luther in print."[4] Immediately following the publication of Luther's excommunication, in January 1521, the pope himself (Leo X) wrote to Erasmus, "Never was the time more opportune or the cause more just for setting your erudition and your powers of mind against the impious, nor is anyone better suited than yourself—such is our high opinion of your learning—for this praiseworthy task."[5] Almost two years later, a new pope, Adrian VI, a Dutchman who had been at the University of Leuven at the same time as Erasmus, repeated the appeal:

> The affection however which we feel for you and the concern we have for your reputation and true glory prompt us to urge you to employ in an attack on these new heresies the literary skill with which a generous providence has endowed you so effectually; for there are many reasons why you ought properly to believe that the task has been reserved by God especially for you.[6]

Erasmus preferred consensus, compromise, and cooperation to controversy and conflict. While he certainly was capable of sharp criticism and satire, an irenic tone was his preferred register. So despite the pressure, and the infuriating suggestions that his silence signified his agreement with Luther and the Reformation program in general, Erasmus held back from public comment, while privately voicing his displeasure with Luther's tone and the upheaval he had caused.[7] Even as late as 1523 he would still insist, "I have constantly declared, in countless letters, booklets, and personal statements, that I do not want to be involved with either party."[8] Erasmus the peacemaker, the man perennially sitting on the fence: was he really the one to take on Luther in this crisis?

It is not difficult to see why the pressure continued to be applied. Not only his towering reputation as a scholar, but also the credibility he had established

---

[4] Erasmus, *Epistola* 1141 (to Gerard Geldenhouwer, September 9, 1520), in *CE* 8:45.36–37 = *OE* 4:340.30–31.
[5] Leo X to Erasmus, *Epistola* 1180 (January 15, 1521), in *CE* 8:145.19–22 = *OE* 4:435.17–436.21. *Decet Romanum Pontificem*, the papal decree by which Luther was formally excommunicated, was promulgated on January 3.
[6] Adrian VI to Erasmus, *Epistola* 1324 (December 1, 1522), in *CE* 9:205.24–29 = *OE* 5:145.22–26.
[7] Erasmus, *Epistola* 947 (to Philippus Melanchthon, April 22, 1519), in *CE* 6:309.41–3 = *OE* 3:540.34–35; *Epistola* 993 (to Leonardus Priccardus, July, 1, 1519), in *CE* 7:3.52–55 = *OE* 4:2.44–47; *Epistola* 1041 (to the Reader, October–November 1519), in *CE* 7:129.38–130.46 = *OE* 4:121.32–39; *Epistola* 1113 (to Philippus Melanchthon, before June 21, 1520), in *CE* 7:313.24–27 = *OE* 4:287.22–24; *The Sponge of Erasmus against the Aspersions of Hutten* (*Spongia Erasmi adversus Aspergines Hutteni*) (September 1523), in *CWE* 78:90.
[8] *Sponge of Erasmus*, 78:88.

among those who were disenchanted with the church, suggested him as the ideal voice to be raised against Luther. Prior to 1517, Erasmus himself had been seen as "a leader of the reform movement within the church."[9] He had long presented a bold and clear challenge to corruption among the clergy and the encrusted formalism in church practice, which he believed stifled genuine Christian faith and virtue.[10] In 1503 he had written in his *Enchiridion Militis Christiani*,

> Do not think something is right because the ruling class or the majority do it. The only right conduct is that which conforms to the rule of Christ [*regulam Christi*]. . . . Our example is Christ, in whom alone are all the patterns of the holy life. You may imitate him without exception [*hunc sine exceptione licebit imitari*].[11]

Significantly, Erasmus's reform program of imitative virtue required a neutrality of the soul which allowed for either a positive or a negative response to exhortation and command. "The spirit makes us religious [*pios*]," he wrote, while "the flesh [makes us] irreligious [*impios*]" and "the soul constitutes us as human beings . . . neither one nor the other [*neutros*]."[12] Precisely because this is so, the Christian life requires discipline, since "those who exercise themselves diligently will be inspired by the Spirit, the fosterer of pious impulses."[13] Here was his *philosophia Christi*, a simple religion of ethical duty modeled on and made possible by Christ. In a famous letter to Jan Šlechta, written on November 1, 1519, he wrote,

> The whole of Christian philosophy [*philosophiae Christianae summa*] lies in this, our understanding that all our hope is placed in God, who freely gives us all things through Jesus his son, that we were redeemed by his death and engrafted through baptism with his body, that we might be dead to the desires of this world and live by his teaching and example, not merely harbouring no evil but deserving well of all men; so that, if adversity befall, we may bear it bravely in hope of the future reward which beyond question awaits all good men [*omnes pios*] at Christ's coming, and that we may ever advance from one virtue to another, yet in such a way

---

[9] Charles Trinkaus, "Introduction," in *CWE* 76:xxi.

[10] On the corruption of the priests, see Desiderius Erasmus, *Praise of Folly* (*Moriae encomium*) (1511), in *CWE* 27:83–153.

[11] Erasmus, "The Handbook of the Christian Soldier" (*Enchiridion Militis Christiani*), 40A, in *CWE* 66:86. *Enchiridion Militis Christiani saluberrimis preceptis refertum* (repr. Lyons, France: Ioannis Maire, 1641), 162.

[12] Erasmus, "Handbook," in *CWE* 66:52; *Enchiridion*, 92.

[13] Erasmus, "Handbook," in *CWE* 66:54; *Enchiridion*, 96.

that we claim nothing for ourselves, but ascribe any good we do to God [*ut nihil tamen nobis arrogemus, sed quicquid est boni Deo transscribamus*].[14]

Erasmus believed in grace, even in the necessity of grace, but he was also thoroughly committed, long before his dispute with Luther, to ethical endeavour and the freedom of the will which it presupposed. It was Christ's teaching and example that was Erasmus's central reference point, rather than the cross, the resurrection, and the gift of the Spirit.

It is often overlooked that Erasmus was not simply a humanist scholar but had some claim to being a theologian in the broadest sense. He attended lectures in theology in the University of Paris, during which he grew tired of scholastic theology;[15] he then planned to move to Bologna to study for a doctorate there,[16] but was eventually awarded the Doctor of Divinity degree *per saltem* (examined by the theology faculty but not fulfilling the other customary requirements) by the University of Turin on September 4, 1506.[17] His correspondence with John Colet included an invitation to lecture on the OT in Oxford in 1499 and an extended discussion of the nature of Christ as evident from his struggle in the garden of Gethsemane, later in that same year.[18] From 1511 to 1515 he was the Lady Margaret Professor of Divinity in the University of Cambridge. He acted like a theologian, drawing up a curriculum for theological students, commenting on theological questions and publishing devotional material.[19] A special focus during his time in Cambridge was his revised Latin translation of the NT, the *Novum Instrumentum omne*, in which he called into question the Vulgate translation at a number of critical points.[20] Erasmus would describe that particular work to his friend Jakob Wimpfeling as "the New Testament translated by me, with the Greek text facing, and notes on it by me."[21] It was these notes (*Annotationes*) that would provoke Luther to

---

[14] Erasmus, *Epistolae* 1039 (November 1, 1519), in *CE* 7:126.245–127.254 = *OE* 4:118.228–37.
[15] Erasmus, *Epistolae* 64 (to Thomas Grey, August 1497), in *CE* 1:138.94–101 = *OE* 1:192.86–193.92.
[16] Erasmus, *Epistolae* 75 (to Arnoldus Bostius, April 1498), in *CE* 2:123.15–7 = *OE* 1:202.13–15.
[17] Erasmus, *Epistolae* 200 (to Servatius Rogerus, November 4, 1506), in *CE* 1:151.9–10 = *OE* 1:432.8–9. Earlier, Erasmus had made clear his disdain for and yet the necessity of gaining a doctorate (*Epistolae* 145 [to Anna von Borssele, January 27, 1501], in *CE* 2:16.120–37 = *OE* 1:344.105–345.120; Erika Rummel, "The Theology of Erasmus," in *The Cambridge Companion to Reformation Theology*, ed. D. Bagchi and D. C. Steinmetz [Cambridge: Cambridge University Press, 2004], 29).
[18] Erasmus, *Epistolae* 108, 109, 111 (to John Colet, October 1499), in *CE* 1:205.85–95, 207.42–210.151, 214.58–219.252 = *OE* 1:248.76–84; 250.37–253.139; 255.49–259.210.
[19] Rummel, "Theology of Erasmus," 28. See also Rummel, *Erasmus' Annotations on the New Testament: From Philologist to Theologian* (Toronto: University of Toronto Press, 1986).
[20] On Erasmus's correction of the Vulgate, see *Nouum Instrumentum Omne* (Basel: Froben, 1516). See also C. A. L. Jarrott, "Erasmus' Biblical Humanism," *Studies in the Renaissance* 17 (1980): 125–56.
[21] Erasmus, *Epistola* 305 (to Jakob Wimpfeling, September 21, 1514), in *CE* 3:32.228–9 = *OE* 2:23.222–24.

write critically about Erasmus to their mutual friend Spalatin in October 1516, suggesting he pass on the substance of the critique to "that most learned man":

> What disturbs me most about Erasmus, that most learned man, my Spalatin, is the following: in explaining the Apostle [Paul], he understands the righteousness which originates in "works" or in "the Law" or "our own righteousness" (the Apostle calls it that) as referring to those ceremonial and figurative observances [of the Old Testament]. Moreover, he does not clearly state that in Romans, chapter 5, the Apostle is speaking of original sin, although he admits that there is such a thing.[22]

Erasmus's explanation left room for human moral effort and an understanding of original sin as an impediment rather than a mortal wound that introduced an incapacitating bias to the will. Just a few months later, still without any direct contact with Erasmus, Luther wrote to Johann Lang in similar terms:

> I am reading our Erasmus but daily I dislike him more and more . . . he does not advance the cause of Christ and the grace of God sufficiently. . . . Human things weigh more with him than the divine . . . the discernment of one who attributes weight to man's will is different from that of him who knows of nothing else but grace.[23]

Erasmus might well have been a theologian, though some raised doubts about that even in his own time.[24] However, even if that description can be claimed for him, he was, as we shall see, a theologian heading in entirely the opposite direction to that of Luther. An unbridgeable theological divide had opened up between the two men. As Ernst-Wilhelm Kohls suggested, even at this early stage Luther "attacks the foundation of Erasmian theology, the summit of which is the comprehension of free will. The real public quarrel between Erasmus and Luther and the confrontation between the two systems was no more than a question of time."[25]

---

[22] Martin Luther, "An Spalatin" (October 19, 1516), in *WABr* 1:70.4–8 = *LW* 48:24. Erasmus, commenting on Rom. 5:12, had said, "There is, then, nothing in the words here that cannot be accommodated to sin of imitation" (Erasmus, *Annotations on Romans* [*Annotationes in epistolam ad Romanos*], 586B, in *CWE* 66:141).

[23] Luther, "An Joh. Lang in Erfurt" (March 1, 1517), in *WABr* 1:90.15, 18, 19–20, 25–26 = *LW* 48:40.

[24] Erasmus himself reported what was said about him by Vincentius Theoderici, a theologian working in Louvain: ". . . and Erasmus knows no theology. What an imposter Erasmus is! He writes paraphrases on the Epistles and annotations on the New Testament. He publishes replies to sundry theologians; but he does not know a word of theology." This led to Erasmus's admission, "I . . . think little of myself in theology" (Erasmus, *Epistolae* 1196 [to Vincentius Theoderici, March 1521], in *CE* 8:81.184–87, 187–88 = *OE* 4:467.169–72, 173).

[25] Ernst-Wilhelm Kohls, "*La position théologique d'Érasme et la Tradition dans le 'De libero arbitrio'*," in *Colloquium Erasmianum* (Mons, Belgium: Centre Universitaire de l'Etat, 1968), 73.

Erasmus and Luther Prior to 1524

Very early in his teaching and writing career, Luther had become convinced of the incapacitated nature of human willing on this side of the fall. In early 1516, lecturing on Romans 8:28, Luther told his students, "The free will without grace has absolutely no power to achieve righteousness, but of necessity it is sin. Therefore blessed Augustine is correct in his book *Against Julian* when he calls it 'a bound will rather than a free will' [*servum potius quam liberum arbitrium*]."[26] Later that year, in the disputation celebrating the promotion of Bernhard Bernardi, Luther argued, "Man, apart from the grace of God, is not able [*nequaquam potest*] to serve him or his commandments, nor to prepare for grace either congruently [*de congruo*] or condignly [*de condigno*], but remains by true necessity under sin."[27] With those words, Luther was clearly challenging the scholastic doctrines of human nature and salvation. That challenge would reach far beyond the little university in Wittenberg when, a year later, Luther published his explosive *Disputatio contra scholasticam theologiam*:

> 4. It is therefore true that man, being a bad tree, can only will and do evil [*non potest nisi malum velle et facere*].
> 5. It is false to state that man's inclination is free to choose between either of two opposites. Indeed, the inclination is not free, but captive [*nec liber sed captivus est*]. This is said in opposition to common opinion.
> 6. It is false to state that the will can by nature conform to correct precept. This is said in opposition to Scotus and Gabriel.
> 7. As a matter of fact, without the grace of God the will produces [*necessario elicit*] an act that is perverse and evil.
> 10. One must concede that the will is not free [*voluntas non est libera*] to strive toward whatever is declared good. This in opposition to Scotus and Gabriel.[28]

These controversial theses were soon overshadowed by Luther's *Disputatio pro declaratione virtutis indulgentiarum* of October 31, 1517, the critical

---

[26] Luther, *WA* 56:385.15–18 = *LW* 25:375. It is this and earlier statements in this series of lectures (e.g., on Rom. 8:3 [*WA* 56:355.3–11 = *LW* 25:344]; and famously on Rom. 4:7 [*WA* 56:272.16–20 = *LW* 25:260]) that led Alister McGrath to date Luther's "crucial step" in the development of his understanding of justification to his Romans lectures of 1515 and to argue that, in contrast to Augustine, "Luther's doctrine of justification is based upon the concept of *servum arbitrium* [an enslaved will]" (Alister E. McGrath, *Iustitia Dei: A History of the Christian Doctrine of Justification*, 3rd ed. [Cambridge: Cambridge University Press, 2005], 220, 232).

[27] Luther, *Questio de viribus et voluntate hominis sine gratia disputata* (September 25, 1516), in *WA* 1:147.10–13. For the significance of this disputation, and its impact on Karlstadt in particular, see Martin Brecht, *Martin Luther: His Road to Reformation 1483–1521*, trans. James L. Schaaf (1981; English translation, Philadelphia: Fortress, 1985), 166–70.

[28] Luther, *Disputation against Scholastic Theology (Disputatio contra scholasticam theologiam)* (September 1517), in *WA* 1:224.13–19, 23–4 = *LW* 31:9, 10.

catalyst for the Reformation. However, they do reveal that Luther was clear from a very early stage on the anthropological implications of his discoveries about the biblical doctrine of justification. This is confirmed by the theses Luther prepared for his defense before the Augustinian friars in Heidelberg in April 1518. Among these, and providing the immediate context for his famous contrast between a theology of glory and a theology of the cross, Luther wrote,

13. Free will, after the fall, exists in name only, and as long as it does what it is able to do [*facit quod in se est*], it commits a mortal sin.
14. Free will, after the fall, has power to do good only in a passive capacity [*subiectiva*], but it can always do evil in an active capacity [*activa*].
18. It is certain that man must utterly despair of his own ability before he is prepared to receive the grace of Christ.[29]

In his explanation of these theses, Luther quoted Augustine: "Free will without grace has the power to do nothing but sin"; and "You call the will free, but in fact it is an enslaved will."[30] Luther himself pushed even harder. Even the justified person cannot claim a totally free will or the capacity to do unalloyed good works. "There is no such thing as a total will [*Tota . . . voluntas*] in this life," Luther wrote in his extended comment on his sixth thesis. "Therefore, we constantly sin while doing good [*semper peccamus, dum benefacimus*], sometimes less and sometimes more. . . . Whoever does less than he ought, sins. But every righteous person in doing good does less than he ought."[31] This is one of the theses that would be picked up by the papal bull threatening his excommunication, *Exsurge Domine*, in its list of Luther's damnable errors: "31. The righteous person sins in every good work [*In omni opera bono iustus peccat*]."[32]

A third and critically important part of the evidence for Luther's settled position is provided by his final published defense of his theology prior to his excommunication, the *Assertio omnium articulorum M. Lutheri per Bullam Leonis X novissimam damnatorum*. In Article 36, where Luther was defending, or rather amending, the thirteenth thesis from the Heidelberg Disputation, he wrote,

I was wrong in saying that free will before grace is a reality only in name. I should have said simply: "free will is in reality a fiction, or a name without

---

[29] Luther, *Heidelberg Disputation (Disputatio Heidelbergae habita)* (1518), in *WA* 1:354.5–8, 15–16 = *LW* 31:40.
[30] Augustine, *Spirit and Letter* iii.5 (PL 44:203); *Against Julian* II.viii.23 (PL 44:689).
[31] Luther, *Heidelberg Disputation*, in *WA* 1:367.25–27, 368.10–11 = *LW* 31:61.
[32] "*LXXXI. Errores 41 Martini Lutheri damnati a Leone V per Bullam, Exsurge Domine*" *16 Maji 1520*, in H. Denzinger, *Enchiridion Symbolorum et Definitionum que de Rebus Fide et Morum a Conciliis Oecoumenicis et Summus Pontificibus Emanarunt* (Wirceburgi: Stahl, 1854), 220.

reality" [*liberum arbitrium est figmentum in rebus seu titulus sine re*]. For no one has it in his own power to think a good or bad thought, but everything (as Wycliffe's article condemned at Constance rightly teaches) happens by absolute necessity [*omnia . . . de necessitate absoluta eveniunt*].[33]

Luther's willingness to cite a condemned heretic (Wycliffe) with approval and to speak of "absolute necessity" drew the line between himself and Erasmus even more starkly.

Meanwhile, as we have seen, pressure mounted on Erasmus to come out publicly against Luther and his theology. In February 1522 he wrote to Pirckheimer,

> I . . . am a heretic to both sides. Among our own people, a few who have other reasons to dislike me are actually trying to persuade the emperor that I am a leader of the rebels, for no better reasons than my failure to publish against Luther. Luther's party in their public utterance tear me to pieces as a Pelagian, because they think I give more weight than they do to free will.[34]

Two months later, Erasmus told a friend that, while he had "already made a fair start with a short treatise on how to end this business of Luther," he had been stymied by ill health and by the approaches from "many people who were greatly attracted by Luther."[35] This proposed three-way dialogue (between Luther, given the name Thrasymachus, an opponent, named Eubulus, and an arbiter, named Pilalethes) never actually appeared in print.[36]

Two pieces of writing tipped the balance and finally brought Erasmus out into the open. On June 20, 1523, Luther wrote to Johannes Oecolampadius at the University of Basel with one of his most scathing assessments of Erasmus:

> Do not be disturbed by his displeasure. What Erasmus thinks, or pretends to think, in his judgment of spiritual matters is abundantly shown in his booklets from the first to the last. Although I myself feel his stings all over, yet since he pretends not to be my open foe I, too, pretend not to understand his cunning; however, I understand him better than he thinks. He has accomplished

---

[33] Martin Luther, *Assertion of the All the Articles of Martin Luther Recently Condemned by the Bull of Leo X (Assertio omnium articulorum M. Lutheri per Bullam Leonis X novissimam damnatorum)* (December 1520), in *WA* 7:146.4–8. Luther proceeds to cite either the poet Marcus Manilius or Vergil (scholarly opinion is divided on this) and then a variation on Matt. 10:29, replacing "sparrow" with a "leaf of a tree." See H. J. McSorley, *Luther: Right or Wrong? An Ecumenical-Theological Study of Luther's Major Work, The Bondage of the Will* (New York: Newman, 1969), 255 n. 192.

[34] Erasmus, *Epistola* 1259 (to Willibald Pirckheimer, February 12, 1522), in *CE* 9:23.10–15 = *OE* 5:16.9–13.

[35] Erasmus, *Epistola* 1275 (to Jean Glapion, April 21, 1522), in *CE* 9:65.23–6 = *OE* 5:16.9–13.

[36] Erasmus, *Epistola* 1341A (to Jean Glapion, April 21, 1522), in *CE* 9:65.1338–53 = *Catalogus omnium Erasmi Roterodami lucubrationum* (Basel: Froben, 1523), c.

what he was called to do: he has introduced among us the languages and has called us away from the sacrilegious studies. Perhaps he himself will die with Moses in the plains of Moab, for he does not advance to the better studies (those which pertain to piety). I greatly wish he would restrain himself from dealing with Holy Scripture and writing his *Paraphrases*, for he is not up to this task; he takes the time of readers in vain and he hinders them in studying Scripture. He has done enough in showing us the evil. He is (in my opinion) unable to show us the good and to lead us into the promised land.[37]

It was not long until Erasmus learned the contents of this letter. He was deeply offended. In a letter to Zwingli in August he would mention the allusion to Moses and write, "I only wish he himself were the Joshua who is to bring us all into the promised land."[38] He was more candid when writing to his Catholic friend Johannes Fabri. Recalling the same comment about Moses and the wilderness he remarked, "This sort of thing means war."[39]

In the midst of this, Ulrich von Hutten published his *Expostulatio* in July 1523.[40] In it he explained Erasmus's public silence about Luther and his theology in terms of Erasmus's preoccupation with his own reputation (*inexplebilis famae*) and his personal cowardice.[41] There had been mounting tension between the two men since they had met while Erasmus was in Louvain in May 1520.[42] Erasmus's response to the *Expostulatio* was published within two months and entitled *Spongia Erasmi adversus aspergines Hutteni*. In it, Erasmus challenged the portrait of him that Hutten presented and then wrote of "the things that offend me in Luther's writings—his unrestrained abuse and his seeming arrogance." If only from the outset "Luther had explained his teachings in a candid and gentle way, refraining from the kind of language that is patently offensive, we would not have this tumult." He continued, "His prose is tight and sparing of words when he makes an argument, but in taunts and insults he knows no bounds, often indulging in mockery and sarcasm where there is no call for it."[43]

Erasmus wrote this in September 1523. In the same month he wrote to King Henry VIII of England, "I have something on the stocks against the

---

[37] Luther, "An Joh. Ökolampad in Basel" (June 20, 1523), in *WABr* 3:96.13–25 = *LW* 49:44.
[38] Erasmus, *Epistola* 1384 (to Huldrych Zwingli, August 31, 1523), in *CE* 10:83.62–63 = *OE* 5:329.57–58.
[39] Erasmus, *Epistola* 1397 (to Johannes Fabri, November 21, 1523), in *CE* 10:110.12 = *OE* 5:349.11.
[40] Ulrich von Hutten, *Ulrichi ab Hutten cum Erasmo Roterodamo, Presbytero, Theologo Expostulatio* (Strasburg: John Schott, 1523), in *Ulrichi de Hutten Equitis Germani Opera quae extant omnia* (Berlin: Reimer, 1824), 343–94. The English translation of the title is, *Expostulation with Erasmus of Rotterdam, Priest and Theologian*.
[41] Von Hutten, *Ulrichi ab Hutten cum Erasmo*, 348.
[42] J. D. Tracy, "Introductory Note to 'The Sponge of Erasmus against the Aspersions of Hutten,'" in *CWE* 78:19–29.
[43] Erasmus, *Sponge of Erasmus*, in *CWE* 78:111, 112, 113.

new doctrines, but I dare not publish it unless I have left Germany first, for fear I prove a casualty before I enter the arena."[44] He would send an unfinished draft of the work, "a book on the freedom of the will directed against Luther," to Henry in March 1524.[45] Luther must have gotten wind of it somehow. He wrote directly to Erasmus in April, ". . . do not give comfort to my enemies and join their ranks against us. Above all, do not publish booklets against me, as I shall publish nothing against you."[46] In retrospect, Erasmus's reply was ominous: "If you are ready to give an account to every man of the faith that is in you, why should it upset you if someone wants to argue with you in the hope of deepening his understanding? Perhaps Erasmus's opposition will do more for the gospel than all the support you receive from dullards . . ."[47]

Erasmus's Defense of a Free or Unbound Will

On September 6, 1524 Erasmus wrote to Henry VIII again: "The die is cast. The little book on free will has seen the light of day."[48] In light of the background we have traced, the choice of subject was neither accidental nor arbitrary. The nature of the human condition, and in particular the nature of human willing this side of the fall, was a primary presupposition both of Erasmus's *philosophia Christi* and of Luther's doctrine of justification only by faith.[49] Both had mentioned how critical this was in correspondence with friends, and both were appalled at the stance taken by the other on this issue. In defense of his *Annotationes* on Romans, Erasmus wrote,

> . . . when I wrote this, I had no idea that there had been anyone who entirely abolished all the force of free will. . . . I would rather teach the doctrines that encourage us to try for the best in every way we can, while yet at the same time claiming no credit for ourselves.[50]

---

[44] Erasmus, *Epistola* 1385 (to Henry VIII, September 4, 1523), in *CE* 10:85.15–7 = *OE* 5:330.11–13.

[45] Erasmus, *Epistola* 1430 (to Henry VIII, March 1524), in *CE* 10:201.15–6 = *OE* 5:417.12–13. He had previously sent a copy to Ludwig Baer at the University of Basel in February (*Epistola* 1419 [to Ludwig Baer, February 1524], in *CE* 10.180.1–2 = *OE* 5.400.1–2).

[46] Luther, "An Erasmus in Basel" (April 18, 1524), in *WABr* 3:268.61–62 = *LW* 49:80.

[47] Erasmus, *Epistola* 1445 (to Martin Luther, May 8, 1524), in *CE* 10:255.27–31 = *OE* 5:452.24–27.

[48] Erasmus, *Epistola* 1493 (to Henry VIII, September 6, 1524), in *CE* 10:373.6–7 = *OE* 5:541.4.

[49] Contra E. G. Schwiebert, *Luther and His Times: The Reformation from a New Perspective* (St. Louis: Concordia, 1950), 691: "Perhaps the chief difference in the disputants was that to Erasmus the entire subject was essentially a rhetorical exercise in curious and superfluous speculation; to Luther it was the very essence of the Christian faith." See Robert Kolb, *Bound Choice, Election, and Wittenberg Theological Method: From Martin Luther to the Formula of Concord* (Grand Rapids, MI: Eerdmans, 2005), 13–14.

[50] Erasmus, *Epistola* 1342 (to Marcus Laurinus, February 1, 1523), in *CE* 9:400.1066–7, 1074–6 = *OE* 5:226. 967–69, 975–77.

Luther, for his part, would applaud Erasmus for choosing this topic for their confrontation:

> I praise and commend you highly for this also, that unlike all the rest you alone have attacked the real issue [*rem ipsam*], the essence of the matter in dispute [*summam caussae*]. . . . You and you alone have seen the question on which everything hinges [*cardinem rerum*], and have aimed at the vital spot [*iugulum petisti*].[51]

Erasmus couched his treatise *De Libero Arbitrio DIATRIBE sive Collatio* as a response to Luther's *Assertio*. He began by expressing his distaste for assertions and would later quote Article 36 (see above) in full.[52] He was troubled by Luther's strong language and his denial of any reality to "free will," but especially by his use of the expression "all things happen by absolute necessity [*omnia de necessitate absoluta eveniunt*]," which raised for Erasmus the spectre of "necessitarianism or theological determinism."[53] As far as he was concerned, the use of this expression, alongside the unqualified rejection of free will, put Luther at an extreme end of the spectrum of opinion on this issue. Erasmus himself preferred to leave room for free will, which he defined as "a power of the human will by which man may be able to direct himself towards, or turn away from, what leads to eternal salvation [*uim humanae uoluntatis qua se possit homo applicare ad ea, quae perducunt ad aeternam salutem, aut ab ysdem auertere*]."[54]

The form of Erasmus's treatise was to be a *collatio*, a bringing together of authorities on either side of the question, most especially the biblical texts that could and had been cited for and against the proposition of free will. It presents, therefore, in large measure as a piece of inductive biblical scholarship.[55] Erasmus acknowledged that "there are many passages in Holy

---

[51] Luther, *The Bondage of the Will* (1525), in *WA* 18:786.26–7, 30 = *LW* 33:294.
[52] "And I take so little pleasure in assertions (*et adeo non delector assertionibus*) that I would gladly seek refuge in Scepticism whenever this is allowed by the inviolable authority of Holy Scripture and the church's decrees" (Erasmus, "A Discussion of Free Will," in *CWE* 76:7 = *De Libero Arbitrio DIATRIBE, sive Collatio* [Basel: Froben, 1524], 2). The quotation of Luther's article is found at *CWE* 76:45 = *De Libero Arbitrio*, 41.
[53] McSorley, *Luther: Right or Wrong?*, 254.
[54] Erasmus, *Free Will*, in *CWE* 76:21 = *De Libero Arbitrio*, 16.
[55] In this, Erasmus's approach is somewhat different from his friend John Fisher's *Assertio Lutheranae Confutatio*, with which, it appears, Erasmus was deeply familiar. After an introduction in which he put forward ten *veritae*, functioning as general methodological axioms, Fisher worked his way through each of the articles in Luther's *Assertio* and responded to each of them in turn (R. D. D. Ioannis Fischerii, *Roffensis in Anglia Episcopi Opera* [Würzburg: Fleishmann, 1597], cols. 274–745). The treatment of Luther's Article 36 is found in cols. 660–716, where many of the same biblical and patristic texts as Erasmus would later use are cited (Richard Rex, *The Theology of John Fisher* [Cambridge: Cambridge University Press, 1991], 117–28; Thomas P. Scheck, "Bishop John Fisher's Response to Martin Luther," *Franciscan Studies* 71 [2013]; 463–509).

Scripture [*in sacris literis plurima esse loca*] which clearly seem to support the freedom of the human will; and on the other hand, some [*nonnulla*] which seem to deny it completely." This requires explanation, since "it is certain that Scripture cannot contradict itself [*scripturam secum pugnare non posse*], since it all proceeds from the same Spirit."[56]

Part of the explanation, Erasmus insisted, arises from the nature of Scripture itself: "For in Holy Scripture there are some secret places [*adyta*] into which God did not intend us [*deus noluit nos*] to penetrate very far, and if we attempt to do so, the farther in we go the less and less clearly we see [*magis ac magis caligamus*]. . . . It is more reverent to adore the unknown (*incognita*) than analyse the incomprehensible [*imperuestigabilia*]."[57] There are some things of which "God intended us to remain entirely ignorant [*deus omnino uoluit nobis esse ignota*]," other things that he "intended us to examine so that we might venerate him in mystical silence [*in mystic silentio veneremur*]," and still other things that "he intended to be absolutely clear [*notissima*] to us: such are the precepts for a good life." It is this last category which should be the focus of our attention and energy; "other things are more properly committed to God."[58] Erasmus suggested that Scripture is ambiguous, or at best unclear, on the relation of God's sovereign purpose and the exercise of human will. However, this lack of clarity is divinely intended, which is why the topic should not be pursued and we should be satisfied with the consensus of the fathers as expressed in the teaching of the church. These comments by Erasmus would provoke from Luther the strongest affirmations of *claritas scripturae*.

However, part of the explanation for the disagreements between pastors and theologians on this issue arose from the differing concerns of those who expounded certain biblical texts. Erasmus recognized that each interpreted what they read "in the light of their individual aims":

> Some reflected on the great extent of human religious apathy and on the great evil of despairing of salvation; in the attempt to remedy these ills, they fell unawares into another evil and exaggerated the role of free will [*ac plus satis tribuerunt libero hominis arbitrio*]. Others, however, considered how destructive it is of true godliness for man to rely on his own strength and merits, and how intolerable is the arrogance of certain parties who display their own good deeds . . . (and) in their valiant efforts to avoid this evil, they

---

[56] Erasmus, *Free Will*, in *CWE* 76:21 = *De Libero Arbitrio*, 16.
[57] Erasmus, *Free Will*, in *CWE* 76:8, 10 = *De Libero Arbitrio*, 4, 6.
[58] Erasmus, *Free Will*, in *CWE* 76:10 = *De Libero Arbitrio*, 6.

have either taken half of free will away [*dimidiarunt liberum arbitrium*], to the extent that it plays no part at all in a good work, or they have destroyed it altogether [*totum iugularunt*] by propounding the absolute necessity of all events.[59]

Erasmus's "little book" has a simple structure (made transparent by the headings inserted in modern translations). After a preface and introduction, in which he explained his approach to the question and drew attention to the fact that there are scholars and sinners on both sides—and then asked, "What am I to do if many people assert different opinions, every one of them swearing he has the Spirit?"—he turned his attention to the biblical texts.[60] He first examined passages from the OT which he believed support the freedom of the human will. He broke off quickly, though, to track a spectrum of scholarly thought on the issue with Pelagius and Scotus at one end, Karlstadt and Luther (together with Wycliffe) at the other, and Augustine in between.[61] He then returned to the OT, listing texts where there is an exhortation to do or choose good, to repent or depart from evil, and texts where the commands of God are pressed upon his people.[62] "What is the purpose of such a vast number of commandments," Erasmus asked, "if not a single person has it at all in his power to do what is commanded?"[63]

Erasmus next treated the NT texts he believed supported his position.[64] Would not "Christ's excellent commandments" be emptied of their meaning "if nothing is attributed to human will?" he asked.[65] Does not Jesus's own language of "good and bad deeds" and even "reward" call into question Luther's language of absolute necessity?[66] What point would there be in Jesus's reproaches to the scribes, Pharisees, and others, if they did not have the capacity to perform what Jesus finds lacking in them?[67] Erasmus asked similar questions of key Pauline exhortations. "How can the accusation of contempt for God's commandment (Rom. 2:4) be made if the will is not free? How can God invite us to repentance if he is the cause of impenitence?

[59] Erasmus, *Free Will*, in *CWE* 76:74 = *De Libero Arbitrio*, 73.
[60] Erasmus, *Free Will*, in *CWE* 76:18, 19 = *De Libero Arbitrio*, 13, 15.
[61] Erasmus, *Free Will*, in *CWE* 76:27–33 = *De Libero Arbitrio*, 21–27.
[62] Genesis 2:17; 4:6–7; Deut. 30:15, 19; Ps. 33:15; Isa. 1:19–20; 21:12; 45:20, 22; Jer. 15:19; Ezek. 18:21–22, 31–32; Zech. 1:3.
[63] Erasmus, *Free Will*, in *CWE* 76:37 = *De Libero Arbitrio*, 31.
[64] Matthew 5:12; 7:20; 19:17, 21; 20:1–16; 23:37; 25:35–36; Luke 9:23; John 1:12; Rom. 2:4; 7:18; 13:12; 1 Cor. 14:32; 15:10; Col. 3:9; 1 Tim. 4:4, 7–8; 6:12; 2 Tim. 2:5, 21; James 1:13–15; 2 Pet. 1:5, 10; 1 John 3:3.
[65] Erasmus, *Free Will*, in *CWE* 76:40 = *De Libero Arbitrio*, 34.
[66] Erasmus, *Free Will*, in *CWE* 76:40 = *De Libero Arbitrio*, 34.
[67] Erasmus, *Free Will*, in *CWE* 76:41 = *De Libero Arbitrio*, 35.

How can the accused be justly condemned when the judge compels him to crime?"[68] "And how can Paul's comparisons with the runners in the stadium, the trophy, and the victor's crown be valid if we can ascribe nothing to our own efforts?"[69] Erasmus quoted Paul in 2 Timothy 2:21, Romans 13:12, and Colossians 3:9, and asked, "How can (a person) cleanse himself if he does nothing at all?" "How can we be ordered to 'throw off' or 'strip off' if we cannot do anything?"[70]

Throughout this section, Erasmus adopts a strategy of considering what was necessary for each text to mean what it appears to mean on a first and straightforward reading. "I find difficulty in reconciling the terms 'fight,' 'crown,' 'just judge,' 'award,' and 'fighting,'" he wrote, "with the absolute necessity of all events and a will that does nothing but is merely passive."[71] It is at the end of this section that Erasmus quoted Article 36 from Luther's *Assertio*.

Erasmus then turned his attention to texts from Scripture which seemed to oppose the freedom of the human will. His engagement with these texts was a little more extensive and he focused on fewer of them, primarily Romans 9 and the OT texts to which it appeals and which form its conceptual background. The hardness of Pharaoh's heart (Ex. 9:12, 16; 33:19) was explained as an act of Pharaoh's free will: "He was created with a will that he could turn in either direction, and by his own choice he directed it to evil, for he preferred to follow his own will rather than to obey God's commandments."[72] God's hardening of Pharaoh's heart was, according to Erasmus, his judgment on Pharaoh's prior decision: God gave him over to his own depravity.[73] In the case of Jacob and Esau (Gen. 25:23; Mal. 1:2), Erasmus insisted this was not a question of eternal salvation but of a temporal condition. "God can will a man to be a slave," he wrote, "without excluding him from eternal salvation." Such texts are used by the prophets and Paul, he argued, "to refute the arrogance of the Jews," not as a "proof of necessity."[74]

Erasmus concluded that the passages Luther and others cite in support of their argument for an enslaved human will this side of the fall can be reconciled with the texts he had already cited "if we join the efforts of our will to the

---

[68] Erasmus, *Free Will*, in *CWE* 76:42 = *De Libero Arbitrio*, 36.
[69] Erasmus, *Free Will*, in *CWE* 76:42 = *De Libero Arbitrio*, 37.
[70] Erasmus, *Free Will*, in *CWE* 76:44 = *De Libero Arbitrio*, 39.
[71] Erasmus, *Free Will*, in *CWE* 76:43 = *De Libero Arbitrio*, 38.
[72] Erasmus, *Free Will*, in *CWE* 76:47–48 = *De Libero Arbitrio*, 44.
[73] Erasmus, *Free Will*, in *CWE* 76:52 = *De Libero Arbitrio*, 48.
[74] Erasmus, *Free Will*, in *CWE* 76:53 = *De Libero Arbitrio*, 49.

assistance of God's grace."[75] The language of cooperation became increasingly important in the last third of Erasmus's treatise. After quoting Paul's words in 1 Corinthians 15:10, he wrote, "it is the impression of insolence which this correction seeks to rule out, not the possibility of cooperation."[76] Quoting Philippians 2:13, and Ambrose as an interpreter, he wrote, "it means that man's good will works together with the action of grace."[77] Erasmus may have thought he had avoided the Pelagian error, but his conclusions were decidedly synergistic and would easily attract the charge of semi-Pelagianism. This is clear in the illustration he famously used at this point:

> A child who cannot yet walk has fallen, however hard he tried: his father sets him back on his feet and shows him an apple some distance away. The boy very much wants to run towards it, but because his limbs are so helpless, he would soon have fallen again if the father did not put out his hand to support him and did not guide his steps. So, with his father guiding him, he reaches the apple, which his father gladly gives him as a reward for having run. The child could not have stood up unless his father had supported him; he would not have seen the apple unless his father had shown it to him; he would not have been able to walk unless his father had constantly aided his tottering steps; he could not have reached the apple unless his father had placed it in his hands. What claim can the child make for himself in this? And still he had done something, yet he has no reason to glory in his own powers, for he is completely in his father's debt.[78]

Erasmus was aware that it was not simply a matter of who could marshall the most texts on their side of the argument. In the final section of "the little book," he put forward his own "moderate opinion" (*sententiae moderationem*), based on both the textual work he had done and the consensus of the church in interpreting those texts. Three themes were woven together in this final argument: (1) Acknowledging free will preserves the integrity of judgment. "Why are we made to appear before the judgment-seat if we have done nothing through our own will, but everything has been done in us by absolute necessity?"[79] (2) More importantly, an affirmation of free will guards against any suggestion that God himself is arbitrary and unjust in the way he deals with his human creatures. Those who deny free will might think they are

---

[75] Erasmus, *Free Will*, in *CWE* 76:58 = *De Libero Arbitrio*, 55.
[76] Erasmus, *Free Will*, in *CWE* 76:70 = *De Libero Arbitrio*, 68.
[77] Erasmus, *Free Will*, in *CWE* 76:68 = *De Libero Arbitrio*, 67.
[78] Erasmus, *Free Will*, in *CWE* 76:80–81 = *De Libero Arbitrio*, 81–82.
[79] Erasmus, *Free Will*, in *CWE* 76:76 = *De Libero Arbitrio*, 75.

elevating the grace and mercy of God, but they do this in one place only to diminish it in another, for God becomes the judge who condemns a person for not doing what they were unable to do or for doing what he determined they would do.[80] "They exaggerate God's mercy in good men in such a way as to make him almost cruel towards others."[81] In Erasmus's view, the denial of free will ends up being an assault upon God's character. (3) Third, the affirmation of free will preserves the incentive to moral endeavour, making sense of the biblical exhortations to justice, mercy, and love. Those who deny it, by "vastly exaggerating original sin, by which they claim even the highest powers of human nature have been corrupted," leave no room for a capacity to do what we are commanded to do, resulting in either indolence or despair.[82] Erasmus summed up his argument with characteristic clarity:

> Why, you may ask, attribute anything at all to free will? To allow the ungodly, who have deliberately fallen short of the grace of God, to be deservedly condemned; to clear God of the false accusation of cruelty and injustice; to free us from despair, protect us from complacency, and spur us on to moral endeavour. For these reasons nearly everyone admits the existence of free will; but lest we claim anything for ourselves, they assert that it can achieve nothing without the perpetual grace of God.[83]

Erasmus believed he had managed successfully to navigate between "the Scylla of arrogance" and "the Charybdis of despair or indolence," and that by the juxtaposition of texts properly interpreted so had the Scriptures.[84] Pelagius attributed too much to free will, Duns Scotus not so much but an ample amount, Augustine very little, yet Luther (according to Erasmus) made away with it all together.[85] The irenic Erasmus offered a middle way: a place for the freedom of the will but always with a clear confession that God's grace is necessary if we are to accomplish anything that might be considered "good." Yes, he had conceded very early in this treatise that the human will has been impacted by the fall, but not so as to make choice impossible:

> For although the freedom of the will has been wounded [*uulnus accepit*] by sin, it is not dead [*non . . . extincta est*]; and although it has been lamed, so

---

[80] Erasmus, *Free Will*, in *CWE* 76:82–84 = *De Libero Arbitrio*, 83–87.
[81] Erasmus, *Free Will*, in *CWE* 76:76 = *De Libero Arbitrio*, 76.
[82] Erasmus, *Free Will*, in *CWE* 76:84 = *De Libero Arbitrio*, 86.
[83] Erasmus, *Free Will*, in *CWE* 76:87 = *De Libero Arbitrio*, 89.
[84] Erasmus, *Free Will*, in *CWE* 76:87 = *De Libero Arbitrio*, 89–90.
[85] Erasmus, *Free Will*, in *CWE* 76:87, 30, 78–9 = *De Libero Arbitrio*, 89, 23, 78–79.

that we are more inclined [*propensiores simus*] to evil than to good before we receive grace, it has not been destroyed [*excisa non est*]; it is just that the enormity of our misdeeds and our habit of sinning [*assuetudo peccandi*], which has become second nature, sometimes so cloud our powers of judgment and so smother [*obruit*] the freedom of our will that the one seems to be snuffed out and the other dead.[86]

Luther's Response on the Bondage of the Human Will

Luther took some time to reply to Erasmus. There were other things to occupy him in the first half of 1525: the peasants' revolt and its aftermath, and his marriage to Katharina von Bora in June. Luther's supporters grew impatient. In later life, Luther mused on the catalyst for responding to Erasmus at last: "Erasmus believed no one could respond to [his] diatribe. I wanted to be silent but Joachim [Camerarius] persuaded my Kathe to press me. She begged me to write."[87] By September 1525 he was at work. He paused briefly to write to Spalatin near the end of the month: "I am now fully engaged in refuting Erasmus and free will . . . truly nothing he says is right [*vere nihil dixit recte*]."[88] When his reply, *De servo arbitrio*, was finally published on December 31, Luther suggested he had completed it "as best I could in a short time and in a hurry [*in brevi et festinantia*]," and in the book itself he insisted, "It was . . . neither pressure of work, nor the difficulty of the task, nor your great eloquence, nor any fear of you, but sheer disgust, anger and contempt, or—to put it plainly— my considered judgment on your *Diatribe* that damped my eagerness to answer you."[89] Luther clearly was not impressed by Erasmus's "little book."

Luther took head-on the larger methodological questions Erasmus had raised. First, in contrast to Erasmus's "distaste for assertions," Luther insisted that assertions are a necessary element of Christian faith. "A man must delight in assertions or he will be no Christian," Luther wrote. "Nothing is better known or more common among Christians than assertion. Take away assertions and you take away Christianity."[90] Christian confession necessarily involves assertion of the truth that has been made known to us in Scripture. Luther appealed to Romans 10:10, Matthew 10:32, and 1 Peter 3:15 in support of this.

---

[86] Erasmus, *Free Will*, in *CWE* 76:26–7 = *De Libero Arbitrio*, 23.
[87] Martin Luther, Table Talk #5069 (June 1540), *WATr* 4:641.10–13.
[88] Luther, "Luther an Spalatin" (September 28, 1525), in *WABr* 3:583.14–16.
[89] Luther, "Luther an Michael Stifel in Tolleth" (December 31, 1525) (*WABr* 3:653.1–2 = *LW* 49:140); *Bondage of the Will* (*WA* 18:601.29–32 = *LW* 33:17).
[90] Luther, *Bondage of the Will* (*WA* 18:603.11–12, 28–29 = *LW* 33:20, 21).

Second, in answer to Erasmus's suggestion that there are truths in Scripture too profound for us to understand or even seek to understand, a divinely intended obscurity in parts of the Bible, Luther drew a distinction between the person of God and what God has made known to us in Scripture. "God and the Scripture of God are two things. . . . That in God there are many things hidden, of which we are ignorant, no one doubts. . . . But that in Scripture there are some things abstruse, and everything is not plain—this is an idea put about by the ungodly Sophists." Turning to Paul's words in Romans 11:33, "Unsearchable are his judgments," Luther pointed out, "Paul does not say that the judgments *of Scripture* are unsearchable, but the judgments *of God*."[91]

This led Luther to insist in the strongest terms on the clarity of Scripture, a subject he had addressed in passing in the *Assertio*.[92] Against Erasmus he wrote, "The subject matter of the Scriptures, therefore, is all quite accessible, even though some texts are still obscure owing to our ignorance of the terms . . . (and) to the blindness or indolence of those who will not take the trouble to look at the very clearest truth."[93] Now that "the seals have been broken, the stone rolled away from the door of the sepulcher," we know the heart of the Scriptures: "Take Christ out of the Scriptures, and what will you find left in them?"[94] Sure, "the Spirit is required for the understanding of Scripture, both as a whole and in any part of it," yet God did not mean us to stumble around in darkness but to make a confident stand in the light.[95]

Luther answered Erasmus's two objections. First, anticipating the protest "I do not say that the Scriptures are obscure in all parts . . . but only in this and similar parts," Luther insisted the word of God is "a lamp shining in a dark place" (2 Pet. 1:19) and "if part of this lamp does not shine, it will be a part of the dark place rather than of the lamp itself." "In opposition to you," he wrote, "I say with respect to the whole Scripture, I will not have any part of it called obscure."[96] Second, to the objection with which Erasmus had concluded his *Diatribe*—why, if this is so clear, have thirteen hundred years of learned and godly scholars disagreed?—Luther replied, "It is . . .

[91] Luther, *Bondage of the Will* (*WA* 18:606.11, 12–13, 16–17; 607.19–20 = *LW* 33:25, 27 [emphasis added]).
[92] "Or tell me, if you can, who finally decides when two statements of the fathers contradict themselves? Scripture ought to provide this judgment, which cannot be delivered unless we give to Scripture the chief place in everything, that which was acknowledged by the fathers: that is, that it is in and of itself the most certain [*certissima*], the most accessible [*facillima*], the most clear of all [*apertissima*], interpreting itself [*sui ipsius interpres*], approving, judging and illuminating all things" (Luther, *Assertion*, *WA* 7:97.19–24).
[93] Luther, *Bondage of the Will* (*WA* 18:606.30–31; 607.10–11 = *LW* 33:26, 27).
[94] Luther, *Bondage of the Will* (*WA* 18:606.25–26, 29 = *LW* 33:26).
[95] Luther, *Bondage of the Will* (*WA* 18:609.11–12 = *LW* 33:28).
[96] Luther, *Bondage of the Will* (*WA* 18:656.12–13, 17–18, 15–16 = *LW* 33:94, 95, 94).

not astonishing that in divine things men of outstanding talent through so many centuries have been blind. In human things it would be astonishing. In divine things the wonder is rather if there are one or two who are not blind, but it is no wonder if all without exception are blind." It is not so much "the weakness of the human mind" but "the malice of Satan" that is at work defying the truth.[97] Furthermore, the true church has always been in the minority; witness the seven thousand in Elijah's day (1 Kings 19:18), the remnant in Israel (Isa. 10:22), Nicodemus and Joseph of Arimathea in the wake of the crucifixion (Matt. 26:31, 56; John 19:38–39), and the small band of faithful bishops in the time of the Arians.[98]

Erasmus had suggested that this was not really an important doctrine and certainly not one that should be "prostituted to the ears of all and sundry [*prostituere promiscuis auribus*]."[99] Luther responded,

> . . . it is not irreverent, inquisitive, or superfluous, but essentially salutary and necessary [*imprimis salutare et necessarium*] for a Christian, to find out whether the will does anything or nothing in matters pertaining to eternal salvation. . . . For if I am ignorant of what, how far, and how much I can and may do in relation to God, it will be equally uncertain and unknown to me, what, how far, and how much God can and may do in me, although it is God who works everything in everyone. . . . It therefore behooves us to be very certain about the distinction between God's power and our own, God's work and our own, if we want to live a godly life [*pie vivere*].[100]

In other words, Erasmus's approach would harm the very thing he wanted to uphold most, namely, Christian piety.

Luther carefully dissected Erasmus's definition of free will. If, as Luther had demonstrated, only God is truly free in terms of being totally sovereign and without contingency of any sort (i.e., bound only by his own character and will), and human beings "cannot subsist for a moment by their own strength," then free will might be predicated of God but not of his human creatures. "You might perhaps rightly attribute some measure of choice to man, but to attribute free choice to him in relation to divine things is too much."[101] In fact, Luther showed that Erasmus's definition contradicted what Erasmus himself

[97] Luther, *Bondage of the Will* (*WA* 18:659.3–6, 27–31 = *LW* 33:98, 99–100).
[98] Luther, *Bondage of the Will* (*WA* 18:650.6–35 = *LW* 33:85–86).
[99] Erasmus, *Free Will*, in *CWE* 76:11, 14 = *De Libero Arbitrio*, 9, 11.
[100] Luther, *Bondage of the Will* (*WA* 18:614.1–3, 9–12, 15–6 = *LW* 33:35).
[101] Luther, *Bondage of the Will* (*WA* 18.662.6–7 = *LW* 33:103).

had written elsewhere in the *Diatribe*. In one breath, Erasmus spoke of the necessity of grace, while in the next (in his definition) he insisted that the human will is itself "capable of applying itself to the things which belong to eternal salvation."[102] Luther suggested that Erasmus had even moved further from the teaching of Scripture than Pelagius and the medieval theologians, since he had argued that "free choice not only moves itself by its own power, but also applies itself to things which are eternal, that is, incomprehensible to itself."[103] Given what we have seen, it would appear that Luther exaggerated Erasmus's position. Erasmus did not completely exclude grace or the action of the Holy Spirit as Luther suggested, but rather had stressed a cooperation of grace and the human will.[104] Nevertheless, Luther saw this as mere sophistry, since the very idea of cooperation itself must mean that not everything in our salvation is ascribed to God.[105] Just as Augustine (or more properly, Prosper of Aquitaine) had seen the synergistic soteriology of John Cassian as a revival of the Pelagian heresy, so Luther saw the synergism of medieval theology, and of Erasmus too, as ultimately a denial of grace.[106] "This is just the song Pelagius sang," he wrote.[107]

The *Bondage of the Will* followed the basic structure of Erasmus's *Diatribe*. Luther addressed the texts which Erasmus had cited in support of the freedom of the human will, beginning, as Erasmus had, with Sir. 15:14–17 (and not without a brief comment about its canonicity). Luther described Erasmus's use of biblical texts as "thoughtlessness [*incogitantia*]."[108] Along with those before him who had appealed to this apocryphal text, Erasmus had not paid careful enough attention to what is actually being said (while rushing to the interpretation he believed was necessary for the text to say what he believed it was saying). He had not attended to the fact "that this and similar passages—'If thou wilt, if thou shalt hear, if thou shalt do'— show not what men *can* do but what they *ought to* do."[109] Luther distinguished between the imperatives of Scripture and the indicatives, the commands and

---

[102] Luther, *Bondage of the Will* (*WA* 18:664.27, 32–35 = *LW* 33:107–8).
[103] Luther, *Bondage of the Will* (*WA* 18:664.27–29 = *LW* 33:107).
[104] Luther, *Bondage of the Will* (*WA* 18:665.15–16 = *LW* 33:109).
[105] Luther, *Bondage of the Will* (*WA* 18:614.22–24 = *LW* 33:35).
[106] Augustine, *De praedestinatione sanctorum* 2 (428), in *NPNF*¹ 5:498 = *PL* 44.961; Prosper of Aquitaine, *De gratia Dei et libero arbitrio liber contra collatorem* 3.1, 5.3, 11.2, 16.1 (AD 432), in *The Fathers of the Church: A New Translation*, vol. 7 (Washington, DC : Catholic University of America Press, 1947–2013), 350, 357, 376, 397 = *PL* 51:221–22, 227, 243, 259.
[107] Luther, *Bondage of the Will* (*WA* 18:683.4–5 = *LW* 33:136).
[108] Luther, *Bondage of the Will* (*WA* 18:676.15 = *LW* 33:125).
[109] Luther, *Bondage of the Will* (*WA* 18:664.1–3 = *LW* 33:124–45 [emphasis added]).

the promises, and made the grammatical point that in Hebrew the future indicative ("you will, you will not") is often used for the imperative, for example in the Decalogue. Luther's argument was that Erasmus had gathered texts which in the end do not make his case. He had not considered an alternative that Luther found compelling: "Human reason [*ratio carnalis*]," Luther argued, "thinks man is mocked by an impossible precept, whereas we say that he is warned and aroused by it to see his own impotence."[110] Instead of asking, "What must be true for this command or precept to be possible?" Erasmus should have been asking, "Why would God give this command, knowing that those to whom he gave it would prove incapable of obeying it in their own strength?"

The answer, Luther insisted, lay in the distinction between law and gospel. Our inability to fulfil the law drives us to Christ and his gospel. Taking up Zechariah 1:3, one of the verses cited by Erasmus—"Return to me, says the LORD of hosts, and I will return to you"—Luther pointed out that "the word 'return' has two uses in the Scriptures, one legal, the other evangelical. . . . Zechariah, therefore, has given us the briefest possible epitome of both kinds of preaching, both of law and of grace; for it is nothing but law, law at its peak, when he says, 'Return to me,' and it is grace when he says, 'I will return to you.' "[111] This movement from law to grace was something Luther saw throughout Scripture, indeed as a key to the right interpretation of Scripture.[112] What he saw Erasmus doing was obscuring the word of grace, the glorious and comforting word of the gospel. With reference to Ezekiel 18:32, Luther argued that the meaning of the words had been obscured by Erasmus's emphasis on what we must do. It is as if God said, "I desire not the sin of man," rather than what he did say, "I desire not the death of a sinner."[113] That "evangelical word" is "the sweetest comfort in every way to miserable sinners,"[114] Luther concluded his response to Erasmus's appeal to the OT with the scathing judgment, "Nothing is farther from being proved by all that long, repetitive, and emphatic disputation than what had to be proved."[115]

---

[110] Luther, *Bondage of the Will* (*WA* 18:676.38 = *LW* 33:126). "For (Diatribe) can quote nothing but imperative or subjunctive or optative expressions, which signify, not what we do or can do . . . but what we ought to do and what is demanded of us, in order that we may be made aware of our impotence and brought to the knowledge of sin" (*WA* 18:688.13–17 = *LW* 33:144).
[111] Luther, *Bondage of the Will* (*WA* 18:682.10–11, 18–20 = *LW* 33:135).
[112] Luther had elsewhere made this point in a sermon from 1521 (*WA* 7:502.34–35), and would at more length later in his commentary on Galatians of 1535 (*WA* 40/1:469.32–470.14 = *LW* 26:302).
[113] Luther, *Bondage of the Will* (*WA* 18:683.28–37 = *LW* 33:137).
[114] Luther, *Bondage of the Will* (*WA* 18:683.11 = *LW* 33:136).
[115] Luther, *Bondage of the Will* (*WA* 18:688.21–22 = *LW* 33:144).

Luther saw just as many problems with Erasmus's appeal to NT texts. He isolated two key questions from Erasmus's list of citations, one to do with the precepts of the NT and the other regarding the concepts of merit and reward. In answer to the first, Luther did not doubt for a moment that the NT contained exhortations, commands, and precepts. However, how these are used, and when, is important. He argued,

> in the New Testament the gospel is preached, which is nothing else but a message in which the Spirit and grace are offered with a view to the remission of sins, which has been obtained for us by Christ crucified; and all this freely, and by the sole mercy of God the Father. . . . Then follow exhortations, in order to stir up those who are already justified and have obtained mercy, so that they may be active in the fruits of the freely given righteousness and of the Spirit . . .[116]

The exhortations, commands, and precepts concern our response to grace, which is itself made possible only by grace. What then of the language of reward in the NT? Luther distinguished between seeing reward in terms of worthiness, which would result in no reward, since "the good will, the merit and the reward all come from grace alone" (i.e., the reward is not something achieved but given); and in terms of consequence, which simply means that one state of affairs is the consequence of another. However, in neither case is the language of reward a statement about human ability to attain the reward, aided or unaided. So, in the end,

> it is God alone who by his Spirit works in us both merit and reward, though he discloses and proclaims them both to the whole world by his external Word, in order that his power and glory and our impotence and ignominy may be proclaimed even among the ungodly and unbelieving and ignorant.[117]

Luther, clearly tiring of Erasmus's presentation, concluded his account of Erasmus's appeal to the NT by protesting,

> it would be much too tiresome to repeat every single imperative verb that *Diatribe* enumerates from the New Testament, always tacking on her own inferences and speciously arguing that the things said are ineffectual, point-less, ridiculous empty nothings if the will is not free. For we have long

---

[116] Luther, *Bondage of the Will* (*WA* 18:692.20–23, 693.1–3 = *LW* 33:150).
[117] Luther, *Bondage of the Will* (*WA* 18:696.6–10 = *LW* 33:155).

since pointed out with quite nauseating frequency how nothing is achieved by such arguments.[118]

Next, Luther challenged Erasmus's treatment of those texts which seem at face value to speak against free will. Here, too, he took issue with Erasmus's general approach to the texts he had cited: "For just as previously, when she [*Diatribe*] was pleading for free choice, she eluded all the imperative and subjunctive expressions of the law by tacking on inferences and similes, so now, when she is going to plead against us, she twists all the words of divine promise and affirmation in any way she pleases, by discovering a trope in them."[119] Erasmus's handling of the biblical texts was determined by a prior commitment to the necessity of free will. Luther warned of the consequence: "all heresies and errors in connection with the Scriptures have arisen, not from the simplicity of the words, as is almost universally stated, but from neglect of the simplicity of the words, and from tropes and inferences hatched out of men's own heads."[120] Again and again Luther would insist, "the words must be taken as they stand"; "nor are the similes that are adduced at all relevant"; "it is not enough to say that there may be a trope here, but the question is whether there ought to be and must be a trope here"; and "it is the foolishness of the flesh that compels you to speak like this, for it treats the words of God as a game, not believing them to be meant seriously."[121]

Luther recognized that Erasmus had concentrated his effort on two OT texts in particular, Exodus 9:12 and Malachi 1:2, both of which were taken up by Paul in his argument in Romans 9:11–21. The Exodus text speaks of God hardening Pharaoh's heart, which Erasmus explained, following Origen, as a "figure of speech by which the person who has provided the opportunity for something is said to have done it."[122] Luther saw this as just another evasion of the words as they stand. "It is not for us to decide to make and remake the words of God just as we please," he wrote.[123] "To put it in a word, this license of interpretation comes to this, that by a new and unprecedented use of grammar everything is jumbled up, so that when God says 'I will harden

[118] Luther, *Bondage of the Will* (*WA* 18:696.12–16 = *LW* 33:156).
[119] Luther, *Bondage of the Will* (*WA* 18:700.13–17 = *LW* 33:162).
[120] Luther, *Bondage of the Will* (*WA* 18:701.11–13 = *LW* 33:163).
[121] Luther, *Bondage of the Will* (*WA* 18:703.9, 705.37, 702.7–8, 704.38–40 = *LW* 33:166, 170, 164, 169).
[122] Erasmus, *Free Will*, in *CWE* 76:47 = *De Libero Arbitrio*, 44. Erasmus cites Origen, *On First Principles*, 3.1.10–11.
[123] Luther, *Bondage of the Will* (*WA* 18:703.1–3 = *LW* 33:166).

Pharaoh's heart,' you change the person and take it to mean 'Pharaoh hardens himself through my forbearance.' "[124] Luther thought this ludicrous:

> Truly this is by far your best effort: God is said to harden when he indulges sinners with his forbearance, but to have mercy when he visits and afflicts them, inviting them to repentance by severity. What, I ask you, did God leave undone in the way of afflicting and punishing Pharaoh and calling him to repentance? Are there not ten plagues recorded?[125]

Erasmus had considered it absurd that a good God should harden a man's heart so that he might display his power. Luther countered with a question: "But what article of faith does this absurdity sin against?" Is this more absurd than a crucified Christ, who is foolishness to the Gentiles and a stumbling block to Jews (1 Cor. 1:23)? God remains sovereign and directs all things according to his will, but Luther argued that this becomes a problem only "if you wish to maintain at the same time both God's foreknowledge and man's freedom."[126] At this point Luther directly addressed Erasmus's concern about the language of absolute necessity. He distinguished between necessity and coercion, taking up the example of Judas Iscariot:

> If God foreknew that Judas would be a traitor, Judas necessarily became a traitor, and it was not in the power of Judas or any creature to do differently or to change his will, though he did what he did willingly and not under compulsion, but that act of will was a work of God, which he set in motion by his omnipotence, like everything else. . . . if God is not deceived in what he foreknows, then the thing foreknown must of necessity take place.[127]

Just as in the case of Judas, the hardening of Pharaoh's heart was necessary in the purpose of God for the salvation of his people and the glory of his name. Yet Pharaoh was not compelled against his will to harden his heart. That is the true nature of the interplay between God hardening Pharaoh's heart and Pharaoh hardening his own heart. Necessity and compulsion are not the same thing, though they were repeatedly confused in Erasmus's treatment of the subject.

---

[124] Luther, *Bondage of the Will* (*WA* 18:703.29–32 = *LW* 33:167).
[125] Luther, *Bondage of the Will* (*WA* 18:704.28–31 = *LW* 33:168).
[126] Luther, *Bondage of the Will* (*WA* 18:707.21, 717.25–27 = *LW* 33:173, 188).
[127] Luther, *Bondage of the Will* (*WA* 18:715.18–716.1, 716.5 = *LW* 33:185).

The text from Malachi treats God's choice of Jacob over Esau: "I have loved Jacob but Esau I have hated." Erasmus had suggested this concerned "temporal affliction," not "eternal salvation."[128] Luther saw in this another evasion of what the text actually says. Erasmus's explanation would result in the conclusion that Paul had misunderstood Malachi 1 (and Gen. 25) when he cited this passage in Romans 9.[129] Luther outlined the three moves ("a three-fold piece of ingenuity") Erasmus had made: transforming the question posed by the text in its context (both in Malachi and in Romans) from why God loves and hates to how God loves and hates; narrowing the focus from eternal damnation to temporal misfortune; and introducing a distinction within each group in order to say that God "neither loves all Gentiles nor hates all Jews."[130] In contrast, Luther argued that, in the context of Romans 9, Paul was teaching that faith and salvation do not come about by our own work, "but solely by the love and hate of God; though when it has come about, he exhorts them to persevere lest they be cut off."[131]

Erasmus had insisted repeatedly that only an affirmation of free will could secure the justice of God and resolve the difficulty arising from the suggestion that God condemns those who could not do otherwise. Luther saw this as yet another example of human reason demanding God be answerable to it and on its own terms. His answer was to let God be God and to recognize that now we see only "through a glass darkly." What seems unjust by our standards will be revealed to be entirely just, when we see things as God sees them and in view of the end, where all things are brought into the light. As Luther put it,

> Let us take it that there are three lights—the light of nature, the light of grace, and the light of glory. . . . By the light of nature it is an insoluble problem how it can be just that a good man should suffer and a bad man prosper; but this problem is solved by the light of grace. By the light of grace it is an insoluble problem how God can damn one who is unable by any power of his own to do anything but sin and be guilty. . . . But the light of glory tells us differently, and it will show us hereafter that the God whose judgment here is one of incomprehensible righteousness is a God of most perfect and manifest righteousness.[132]

---

[128] Erasmus, *Free Will*, in *CWE* 76:53 = *De Libero Arbitrio*, 49.
[129] Luther, *Bondage of the Will* (*WA* 18:722.33–723.2 = *LW* 33:196).
[130] Luther, *Bondage of the Will* (*WA* 18:724.27–726.37 = *LW* 33:199–202).
[131] Luther, *Bondage of the Will* (*WA* 18:726.35–37 = *LW* 33:202).
[132] Luther, *Bondage of the Will* (*WA* 18:785.26–7, 28–31, 35–37 = *LW* 33:292; cf. *WA* 18:730.28–731.13 = *LW* 33:208).

As he drew his treatise to a close, Luther reasserted the claims of his *Assertio*. The universal sinfulness of human creatures is evident from Genesis 6:3, 5 and 8:21, despite Erasmus's attempt to evade the meaning of those texts by redefining the word "flesh." He demonstrated that human inability to accomplish salvation and to secure righteousness in God's sight, both in the Old Testament ("the way of man is not in himself, . . . it is not in man who walks to direct his steps"; Jer. 10:23) and in the New ("apart from me you can do nothing"; John 15:5). He pointed out that in the latter case, Erasmus's "long out-of-date and moth-eaten gloss" had twisted "nothing" into "not very much," "only a little," or "nothing perfectly."[133]

Erasmus's own proposal had been a cooperative work, in which God's grace is recognized as necessary but, alongside it, and making its own contribution to the outcome, is human moral effort. Luther saw that proposal as creating more problems than it solved in the reading of biblical texts and as representing, in effect, a revival of the Pelagian heresy. "Scripture every–where preaches Christ by contrast and antithesis, as I have said, putting everything that is without the Spirit of Christ in subjection to Satan, ungod-liness, error, darkness, sin, death, and the wrath of God . . . all the texts that speak of Christ must consequently stand opposed to free choice; and they are innumerable, indeed they are the entire Scripture."[134]

"The Question on Which Everything Hinges"

Luther was entirely unconvinced by Erasmus's erudite *Diatribe*. He saw it, not as a careful piece of scholarly biblical study, but as an evasion of the teaching of Scripture that would ultimately undermine grace, for all Erasmus's protests to the contrary. Yet in attacking Luther at this point, Erasmus had done him a service, for even "so distinguished and powerful a mind" could not successfully defend free will. Erasmus had said "nothing on this important subject that [had] not been said before," and his deliberately careful and moderate treatment of the subject had actually made things "worse than before."[135] This long-anticipated clash of the intellectual titans had proved decidedly one-sided in the end.

Erasmus sought to respond to Luther's work. He published a detailed refutation of Luther in two parts, the *Hyperaspistes Diatribae Adversus*

---

[133] Luther, *Bondage of the Will* (*WA* 18:748.27–30 = *LW* 33:234).
[134] Luther, *Bondage of the Will* (*WA* 18:782.21–25 = *LW* 33:287).
[135] Luther, *Bondage of the Will* (*WA* 18:600.19–20, 600.21–601.1, 602.22–26 = *LW* 33:16, 18).

Servum Arbitrium Martini Lutheri, but the battle was over and the "warrior" was left stranded.[136] Erasmus's learned appeal to the history of interpretation and the authority of the church convinced very few. Though he himself was convinced that he had "demolished whatever argument he [Luther] can introduce," he privately conceded, "if I follow Paul and Augustine, very little is left to free will. . . . Augustine, in fact, . . . makes such a case for the power of grace that I do not see what is left to free will."[137] So before long Erasmus's *Diatribe* and the *Hyperaspistes* faded from view, while Luther's *De servo arbitrio* remained one of his most important pieces of writing. Luther would later tell his friends he was reluctant to see published a collection of his writings, for "I acknowledge none of them to be really a book of mine, except perhaps the one on the enslaved will and the *Catechism*."[138]

The fire of Luther's reply, which stood out in contrast with the irenic tone which Erasmus had affected (though itself not without the occasional barb), stemmed from the critical importance he placed on a sober recognition of the reality and depth of the guilt, corruption, and enslavement brought about by human sin—the sin of the first man and woman and the sin of every human being since, save one. Without such an acknowledgment of our helplessness, our incapacity to contribute even the smallest amount to our salvation, we will not despair of helping ourselves and will not flee to Christ, as Luther had made clear as early as the Heidelberg Disputation of 1518. The human inclination is to seek a place for our own contribution (even if, with Erasmus, it is one that cooperates rather than acts on its own), and even if we embrace grace, we position our moral effort alongside it. We are reluctant to face the truth about ourselves and admit that we are entirely dependent on God and his mercy. Luther saw that as a danger of phenomenal proportions. Whatever Erasmus's good intentions, he had compromised grace and the gospel of Christ and so dishonored God our Savior:

> For we cannot have it both ways; the grace of God cannot be both so cheap
> as to be obtainable anywhere and everywhere by any man's puny endeavour,

---

[136] Erasmus, *A Warrior Shielding a Discussion of Free Will against the Enslaved Will by Martin Luther* (Part 1, February 1526; Part 2, September 1527), in *CWE* 76:91–297; 77:333–749.

[137] Erasmus, *Epistola* 1804 (to Thomas More, March 30, 1527), in *CE* 13:13.53–5, 15.88–16.92 = *OE* 7:7.50–1, 8.81–82, 84–85.

[138] Luther, "An Wolfgang Capito" (July 9, 1537), in *WABr* 8:99.7–8 = *LW* 50:172–73.

and at the same time so dear as to be given us only in and through the grace of one Man and so great a Man.[139]

To sum up: If we believe that Christ has redeemed men by his blood, we are bound to confess that the whole man was lost; otherwise, we should make Christ either superfluous or the Redeemer of only the lowest part of man, which would be blasphemy and sacrilege.[140]

---

[139] Luther, *Bondage of the Will* (*WA* 18:777.30–33 = *LW* 33:279).
[140] Luther, *Bondage of the Will* (*WA* 18:786.17–20 = *LW* 33:293).

"Whatever Remains Is a Horrible Deformity"

SIN IN EARLY TO POST-REFORMATION THEOLOGY

Raymond A. Blacketer

Introduction: The Depths of Depravity

> We say that these deficiencies, and this *total depravity*, are sin, not only a punishment for sin, and something indifferent, as many of the Sentences Commentators say, that these evils are only a punishment, and something indifferent, but not sin. And they water down the original evil, and then they pretend that persons can satisfy the law of God and become righteous through their own fulfilling of the law.

This is how one Reformer described the Protestant understanding of how the primal sin of Adam affects the entire human race, Christ himself being the only exception. But despite his posthumous association with the term *total depravity*, it was not John Calvin (1509–64) who wrote these words. The author is Philip Melanchthon (1497–1560) in his 1551 Saxon Confession, a full 68 years before the promulgation of the Canons of Dort.[1] The Canons

---

[1] "Hos defectus et hanc totam depravationem dicimus esse peccatum . . ." (Philip Melanchthon, *Confessio doctrinae Saxonicarum ecclesiarum*, in vol. 28 of *Philippi Melanthonis Opera quae supersunt omnia*, ed. C. G. Bretschneider and H. E. Bindseil, vols. 1–28 of Corpus Reformatorum [hereafter CR] [Halle, Germany: Schwetschke, 1834–60], 28:379). Calvin certainly agreed with the concept, however; see below, n. 63.

actually do not use the term *total depravity*, which became famous in the early twentieth century due to the otherwise unfortunate TULIP acronym, but the delegates at Dort certainly agreed with the concept.[2] Not that human beings are as bad as one could possibly imagine; rather, the corruption in human beings is total in two senses. First, there is no faculty or component of the human being that is not affected by the corruption of inherited sin: neither body nor soul; neither intellect nor will; thus, this depravity is pervasive. Second, this depravity is also spiritually debilitating. This corruption in human nature renders sinners entirely unable to merit eternal life, to choose to exercise saving faith, or even to desire God's salvation in Jesus Christ.

On this there was general agreement among first-generation Protestants, even if Melanchthon himself eventually attributed more cooperation to the human will in conversion than would Martin Luther (1483–1546) or representatives of Reformed Protestantism. But it is a common mistake to make the blanket statement that the Reformers rejected Roman Catholic teaching on sin. On the contrary, they affirmed the traditional definition of original sin as it had come to embrace both the loss of original righteousness that God had instilled in the first human couple in their state of integrity and the resultant corruption of human nature, identified as concupiscence.[3]

There were rather specific developments in the doctrine of sin that the Reformers found unbiblical and objectionable. The Reformers called into question the entire penitential system of confession and reconciliation, which gave priests the power of spiritual life and death over Christ's people. They sought to rid God's people of the burden of this system, including temporal satisfactions assigned to penitents by the clergy and the granting or even purchasing of indulgences to reduce purgatorial punishment, as well as the doctrines that underpinned these practices, such as the existence of purgatory

---

[2] The teaching of a pervasive and debilitating depravity was already present in the Heidelberg Catechism, Q&A 8, and occurs especially in the Canons of Dort, 3/4, art. 3, and Rejection of Errors 4. See *Our Faith: Ecumenical Creeds, Reformed Confessions, and Other Resources* (Grand Rapids, MI: Faith Alive, 2013), 72, 130, 135.

[3] For surveys of the doctrine of sin, see Robert W. Landis, *The Doctrine of Original Sin as Received and Taught by the Churches of the Reformation, Stated and Defended, and the Error of Dr. Hodge in Claiming That This Doctrine Recognizes the Gratuitous Imputation of Sin, Pointed Out and Refuted* (Richmond, VA: Whittet & Shepperson, 1884); R. S. Moxon, *The Doctrine of Sin: A Critical and Historical Investigation into the Views of the Concept of Sin Held in Early Christian, Mediaeval, and Modern Times* (London: George Allen & Unwin, 1922); Julius Gross, *Geschichte des Erbsündendogmas: Ein Beitrag zur Geschichte des Problems vom Ursprung des Übels*, 4 vols. (Munich: E. Reinhardt, 1960–1972); Tatha Wiley, *Original Sin: Origins, Developments, Contemporary Meanings* (New York: Paulist, 2002), 56–100; and Keith L. Johnson and David Lauber, eds., *T&T Clark Companion to the Doctrine of Sin* (London: Bloomsbury T&T Clark, 2016 [hereafter *TTCC*]). Note the rather biased approaches of Moxon, who seeks to demote Augustine's views and promote Pelagius as a defender of human virtue and free will; and of Gross, who thinks the doctrine of original sin should be repudiated.

itself, the gradation of sins as venial or mortal, an emphasis on human merit and moral striving, and the inclusion of good works not only as a result but as a cause of salvation. And in the words of the Saxon Confession cited above, Melanchthon argued against the view that the hereditary depravity in human beings is not a sin, but only a punishment for Adam's sin. But then Melanchthon pivots to the preeminent objection of Lutherans and Reformed alike: the increasingly prominent trend among some theologians to minimize the effects of original sin on human moral capacities, and to offer a rather positive estimation of human moral and spiritual ability apart from grace or with merely supplemental assistance from grace.

Nonetheless, Protestant thinkers drew heavily not only from the early church but also from traditional scholastic theology in their own doctrinal formulations on the doctrine of sin. Many Reformed authors found considerable value, for example, in the mature work of Thomas Aquinas (1225–74),[4] although Calvin was not among them, and betrays little knowledge of the Angelic Doctor. Thomas's doctrine of sin is robust, and his *Summa Theologiae* "is quite Augustinian in its assumption that salvation occurs by grace alone."[5] This fact stands in stark contrast to older, confessionally driven assertions that Thomas's teaching is at the root of the Reformers' objections.[6] We may not assume that the entire medieval tradition of theology promoted an anemic view of sin that basically left human beings with unimpeded free choice. It is misleading to ask, as one otherwise fine study does, "Is original sin merely the absence of righteousness or the active presence of sin?" followed by an assertion that the apostle Paul does not characterize original sin or its effects "merely as a privation of righteousness as medieval theologians believed."[7] To characterize this doctrine as a "mere" loss of original righteousness adopts a polemical stance based on early Reformed criticism

---

[4] David S. Sytsma, for example, demonstrates how Peter Martyr Vermigli drew directly on Thomas in his doctrine of predestination, particularly, the Angelic Doctor's argumentation that rejects a predestination based on foreseen merit (Sytsma, "Vermigli Replicating Aquinas: An Overlooked Continuity in the Doctrine of Predestination," *Reformation and Renaissance Review* 20.2 [2018]: 155–67).

[5] Richard A. Muller, "Scholasticism, Reformation, Orthodoxy, and the Persistence of Christian Aristotelianism," *TJ* (NS) 19 (1998): 84.

[6] For critiques of modern Protestant misinterpretations of Thomas, see Arvin Vos, *Aquinas, Calvin, and Contemporary Protestant Thought: A Critique of Protestant Views on the Thought of Thomas Aquinas* (Washington, DC: Christian College Consortium, 1985); Richard A. Muller, "Reading Aquinas from a Reformed Perspective: A Review Essay," *CTJ* 53.2 (2018): 255–88. A recent collection of studies documents the reception of Thomas by Protestant theologians: Manfred Svensson and David VanDrunen, eds., *Aquinas among the Protestants* (Hoboken, NJ: Wiley-Blackwell, 2018).

[7] J. V. Fesko, *Death in Adam, Life in Christ: The Doctrine of Imputation* (Geanies House, UK: Christian Focus, 2016), 226.

of certain late medieval and early modern theologians as well as humanists like Erasmus (1466–1536) and the doctors of the Sorbonne, who left
human nature basically intact after the fall. To call sin an "active presence"
also requires further clarification. The Reformers concur with Augustine
(354–430) and against the Manicheans that sin is *not* a substance and is in
fact a privation of justice or righteousness that leads to corruption and evil
habits; this condition can then be characterized as active or positive in a
moral sense.[8]

To continue with the example of Thomas, original sin is formally the
loss of original righteousness; materially, it is the infection and corruption
of human nature which is called concupiscence.[9] By making this distinction,
Thomas combined the two major views of original sin. While Peter Lombard
(c. 1096–1160) had followed Augustine in identifying the essence of original
sin as concupiscence, Anselm of Canterbury (1033/1034–1109) had identified it as a lack of original justice or righteousness.[10] Anselm's conception,
however, is also Augustinian in that it builds on the Bishop of Hippo's idea
that evil is not a substance, but rather a *privatio boni*, a privation of something good; "injustice, like blindness, is simply non-being."[11] Not only that,
but Augustine had also essentially taught the doctrine of the loss of original
righteousness, which in turn results in the disordering of loves that is carnal concupiscence.[12] Peter Martyr Vermigli (1499–1562), in fact, says that
Anselm's view "does not really differ from that of Augustine," but he also
observes that one can misinterpret it as a mere privation that does not result
in corruption.[13] For Anselm himself, this deprivation was not the loss of some
optional equipment; it meant that the "whole being" of Adam and Eve "was
weakened and corrupted." He says that original sin is "so grave that no one
can show it to be more so."[14] Without original righteousness, like a body

---

[8] See Francis Turretin, *Institutes of Elenctic Theology*, ed. James T. Dennison Jr., trans. George Musgrave Giger, 3 vols. (Phillipsburg, NJ: P&R, 1992–97), 9.11.14–16 (1:638).
[9] For a summary of Aquinas's doctrine of original sin, see Frederick Christian Bauerschmidt, "Aquinas," in *TTCC*, 199–216.
[10] Peter Lombard, *Sententiarum libri quatuor*, 2.30.4, in J.-P. Migne, ed., *Patrologiae cursus completus, series La-tina* (Paris: Vives, 1844–1865 [hereafter PL]), 192:721; Lombard, *The Sentences*, trans. Giulio Silano, 4 vols. (To-ronto: Pontifical Institute of Mediaeval Studies, 2007–10), 2:147 (2.30.5). See also Bauerschmidt, "Aquinas," 203; Heiko A. Oberman, *The Harvest of Medieval Theology: Gabriel Biel and Late Medieval Nominalism* (Cambridge, MA: Harvard University Press, 1963), 122–25; Anselm of Canterbury, *De Conceptu Virginali* 2 (PL 158:434–35; *Complete Philosophical and Theological Treatises of Anselm of Canterbury*, trans. Jasper Hopkins and Herbert Richardson [Minneapolis: Banning, 2000], 430–31).
[11] Anselm, *De Conceptu Virginali* 5 (PL 158:438–39; *Treatises*, 436–37).
[12] Augustine, *De civitate Dei* 13.13; Jesse Couenhoven, "Augustine," *TTCC*, 181–98 (188).
[13] Peter Martyr Vermigli, *On Original Sin*, trans. and ed. Kirk Summers (Leesburg, VA: Davenant, 2019), 35.
[14] Anselm, *De Conceptu Virginali* 2 (PL 158:434, 435; *Treatises*, 430, 431).

lacking an immune system or an automobile that lacks brakes, human nature is profoundly broken and headed for disaster.[15]

By the sixteenth century, however, there were, in fact, even Thomists who were teaching a minimalist view of sin's effects on humanity and were twisting Thomas's rather Augustinian and predestinarian teachings in a synergistic direction. This was the result of debates concerning the legacy of the theologians John Duns Scotus (c. 1266–1308)[16] and William of Ockham (c. 1287–1347) and many who were influenced by their teachings.[17] In short, a number of theologians had begun to teach that human nature was left relatively unscathed after Adam's fall. Sin stripped the human race of its supernatural gifts, such as original righteousness, but the human mind and will were basically left intact, in a state of pure nature (*in puris naturalibus*). Henri de Lubac has argued that later Thomists, particularly Thomas Cardinal Cajetan, OP (1469–1534), misread Aquinas in a way that left humanity with its natural faculties unharmed after the loss of grace. This resulted in a two-storied universe in which nature is independent and has its own ends, and supernatural grace merely adds to nature.[18]

Thus, sinners were still capable of preparing themselves to receive God's grace in a number of ways, primarily by exerting themselves morally. Human beings are still capable of renouncing sin and loving God above all, and thereby meriting God's grace. This unaided effort, then, begins a process that may (or may not) result in the sinner's salvation. Sinners must "do what is in them" (*facere quod in se est*); they must exert themselves to the best of their ability. Although this effort is not inherently worthy, God graciously accepts it as a half-merit, a congruent merit (*meritum de congruo*), which God has determined to accept as if it were inherently worthy, a condign merit (*meritum de condigno*). And in response, God rewards the sinner's best efforts with initial or first grace. Having received this first grace, the sinner must cooperate

[13] See Oberman, *Harvest of Medieval Theology*, 125.

[16] On Scotus and Ockham, see Heiko A. Oberman, *Forerunners of the Reformation: The Shape of Late Medieval Thought* (Philadelphia: Fortress, 1981 [1966]), 130–31. See also Oberman, "*Facientibus quod in se est Deus non denegat Gratiam:* Robert Holcot, O.P. and the Beginnings of Luther's Theology," *HTR* 55.4 (1962): 317–42; and Oberman, *Harvest of Medieval Theology*.

[17] The term "nominalism" and the distinction between the *via antiqua* and *via moderna* that was later used to describe realists and anti-realists, respectively, is common but problematic. See Robert Pasnau, *Metaphysical Themes 1274–1671* (Oxford: Oxford University Press, 2011), 83–88.

[18] See Henri de Lubac, *Augustinianism and Modern Theology*, trans. Lancelot Sheppard (New York: Crossroad, 2000), 105–46; Paul Helm, "Nature and Grace," in *Aquinas among the Protestants*, ed. M. Svensson and D. VanDrunen (Hoboken, NJ: Wiley-Blackwell, 2018), 238. See also Vos, *Aquinas, Calvin, and Contemporary Protestant Thought*, 152–57; Daniel A. Rober, *Recognizing the Gift: Toward a Renewed Theology of Nature and Grace* (Minneapolis: Fortress, 2016); and Fergus Kerr, *After Aquinas: Versions of Thomism* (Oxford: Blackwell, 2002), 134–38.

with grace in order to merit salvation. Heiko Oberman has concluded that the thought of these theologians, such as Robert Holcot (c. 1290–1349) and Gabriel Biel (c. 1420–95), could only be characterized as Pelagian.[19] Martin Luther would pronounce the same verdict on this theology of human effort and merit,[20] as would theologians of the Reformed tradition.

Where Biel and others had common ground with Pelagius (fl. 390–418), the British heretic, was in their conclusion that the "difference between the elect and the reprobate amounts to the difference between those who fulfill the requirements of God's law and those who do not fulfill the requirements."[21] Human beings could still make the first move toward God, and in fact must do so in order to have any chance of salvation. That unimpaired freedom of the will, and the crucial need for an initial human effort, and one of maximal moral exertion, were factors that raised the specter of Pelagius. It should also be noted that there were other thinkers of the fourteenth century who opposed this trajectory and emphasized divine predestination and prevenient grace, including Thomas Bradwardine (c. 1295–1349) and the Augustinian Friar Gregory of Rimini (d. 1358).

Early Reformation Views of Sin

Martin Luther objected to the prevailing doctrinal tendency to minimize the effects of sin, and therefore the crucial nature of grace. Luther, moreover, was wary of those who made original righteousness little more than an optional accessory. Scotus and Ockham had interpreted the loss of original righteousness in a way that minimized the effects of original sin on human moral powers.[22] Thus, Luther condemns those "who have impiously asserted that natural powers remain undiminished after sin in men as well as in demons."[23] Elsewhere, he exclaims, "the scholastic statement that 'the natural powers are unimpaired' is a horrible blasphemy."[24] "The scholastics argue," Luther asserts in his Genesis commentary, "that original righteousness was not a

---

[19] Oberman, "*Facientibus*," 328; *Harvest of Medieval Theology*, 177, 196.
[20] See his *Lectures on Romans,* scholia on Romans 14:13 (*LW* 25:496 = *WA* 56:503); cf. the study by Leif Grane, *Contra Gabrielem: Luthers Auseinandersetzung mit Gabriel Biel in der Disputatio Contra Scholasticam Theologiam 1517* (Copenhagen: Gyldendal, 1962).
[21] Thomas H. McCall, *Against God and Nature: The Doctrine of Sin*, Foundations of Evangelical Theology (Wheaton, IL: Crossway, 2019), 296. McCall summarizes the work of Oberman.
[22] Jairzinho Lopes Pereira, *Augustine of Hippo and Martin Luther on Original Sin and Justification of the Sinner* (Göttingen, Germany: Vandenhoeck & Ruprecht, 2013), 331. On Scotus's exceptionally weak view of sin, see Richard Cross, *Duns Scotus* (New York: Oxford University Press, 1999), 95–100.
[23] Luther, *The Disputation concerning Justification* (*LW* 34:154–55, and n. 6).
[24] Luther, *Lectures on Psalms 2, 45, and 51* (1532), on Psalm 51 (*LW* 12:307–8 = *WA* 40.2:322).

part of man's nature but, like some adornment, was added to man as a gift, as when someone places a wreath on a pretty girl." When the loss of original righteousness is defined in this way, leaving the natural endowments of human beings intact, Luther says, "this idea must be shunned like poison, for it minimizes original sin." Instead, Luther teaches that Adam's "righteousness was not a gift which came from without, separate from man's nature, but that it was truly part of his nature, so that it was Adam's nature to love God, to believe God, to know God, etc."[25]

Luther concluded that the scholastic theologians of his day had come to see sin and righteousness merely in terms of human moral effort because they failed to see that Aristotle's ethical theories, which were fine in themselves, had nothing to do with the theology of sin and grace.[26] For Luther, it was not a matter of doing more or fewer good works, but of becoming a new person by grace.[27] Sin is not merely something a person *does*; sin is what a person *is*. For Luther, "it is great wisdom to know that we are nothing but sin [*nos nihil esse quam peccatum*], so that we do not think of sin as lightly as do the pope's theologians, who define sin as 'anything said, done, or thought against the Law of God.'"[28] Sin is not peripheral or external for Luther, but radical; concupiscence is a corruption at the root (*radix*) of human nature.[29] He specifically makes reference to the nominalist doctrine of *facere quod in se est* in his *Heidelberg Disputation*, thesis 13: "Free will, after the fall, exists in name only, and as long as it does what it is able to do, it commits a mortal sin."[30] Luther reinterprets the traditional distinction between venial and mortal sins in light of his doctrine of justification by grace through faith; the distinction is not to be found in the sin, but in the sinner. All sins are mortal to unbelievers; all sins are venial for believers, for they are not imputed to them because of Christ.[31]

The humanist scholar Erasmus, himself no friend of academic theology, nonetheless also held that sin's effects on human nature were far less severe,

---

[25] Luther, *Lectures on Genesis*, on Genesis 3:7 (*LW* 1:164–65 = *WA* 42:123–24).
[26] See Muller, "Persistence of Christian Aristotelianism," 87–88; Brian A. Gerrish, *Grace and Reason: A Study in the Theology of Luther* (Oxford: Oxford University Press, 1962), 34 and n. 5; Grane, *Contra Gabrielem*, 312–15.
[27] See Luther, *The Freedom of a Christian* (*LW* 31:361 = *WA* 7:62); Robert Kolb, "Martin Luther," in *TTCC*, 217–33 (224).
[28] Luther, *Lectures on Psalms 2, 45, and 51* (1532), on Psalm 51 (*LW* 12:307 = *WA* 40.2:322).
[29] See Bernhard Lohse, *Martin Luther's Theology: Its Historical and Systematic Development*, trans. and ed. Roy A. Harrisville (Minneapolis: Fortress, 2006), 71.
[30] Luther, *Heidelberg Disputation* 13, in *LW* 31:40 = *WA* 1:354: "Liberum arbitrium post peccatum res est de solo titulo, et dum facit quod in se est, peccat mortaliter."
[31] Luther, *Lectures on Galatians* (1535), in *LW* 27:76 = *WA* 40.2:95–96.

and said of Luther and his followers, "They vastly exaggerate original sin, by which they claim that even the highest powers of human nature have been corrupted, so that of himself man can only be ignorant of God, and hate him, and even when justified by grace through faith can perform no action which is not a sin."[32]

Luther's view of original sin includes the Augustinian concept of concupiscence as well as the Anselmian idea of the loss of original righteousness, along with the doctrine, possibly derived from Ockham, that God forensically imputes Adam's sin to all his posterity. Luther, however, reshapes these concepts in his own distinctive way, identifying Adam and Eve's first sin as a failure to believe God's word.[33] Rather than defining a sin solely in terms of a transgression of the law, Luther emphasizes that sin reflects a lack of trust in the Creator, and that all sins arise out of a corrupt human trust in anyone or anything other than the Creator. Sin takes the form of idolatry, and all sins are in a sense a violation of the first commandment,[34] and "where the heart is right with God and this commandment is kept, fulfillment of all the others will follow of its own accord."[35]

Moreover, Luther asserted that the concupiscence which remains in a person is in fact sin, and that original sin is not removed by baptism, but remains with a person throughout life, so that the believer is *simul iustus et peccator* (simultaneously just and a sinner). Believers continue to struggle with sin all their lives, for, as Luther said in the first of his Ninety-Five Theses, the whole life of the believer is to be one of repentance.[36] Luther did, however, teach that a person could lose their salvation by allowing sin to reign in their lives—a significant point on which the Reformed would disagree.[37]

Luther frequently speaks of the condition of sin as being "curved in upon oneself" (*incurvatus in se ipsum*); that is, sinners neglect the love of others because they are captivated by self-love.[38] Though he taught that original sin

---

[32] Desiderius Erasmus, *A Discussion of Free Will (De Libero Arbitrio διατριβή sive collatio)*, in *CWE*, 76:84. See Mark Thompson's chapter 5 in this volume.

[33] Lohse, *Martin Luther's Theology*, 252; Kolb, "Martin Luther," 219.

[34] Kolb, "Martin Luther," 220–21.

[35] See, e.g., Luther's *Large Catechism*, on the first commandment, in Theodore G. Tappert, ed., *The Book of Concord: The Confessions of the Evangelical Lutheran Church* (Philadelphia: Mühlenberg, 1959), 371.

[36] Luther, in *LW* 31:25 = *WA* 1:233; cf. Kolb, "Martin Luther," 230–31.

[37] See Luther, *Lectures on the First Epistle of St. John*, 3:9 (*LW* 30:273 = *WA* 20:706).

[38] See, e.g., Luther's 1513/15 *Lectures on the Psalms*, scholia on Psalm 51:10 (*LW* 10:241; 3:292). See also Kolb, "Martin Luther," 223; Lopes Pereira, *Augustine of Hippo and Martin Luther on Original Sin*, 336–42. Lopes Pereira calls this *incurvatus* motif "Augustinian" but fails to identify any place where Augustine uses the image. The origin could very well be Augustine, *En. Psalm* 50.15 (Psalm 51:12) (*PL* 36:595): *Et quando se homo pronum facit ad terrenas concupiscentias, incurvatur quodammodo; cum autem erigitur in superna, rectum fit cor ejus, ut*

is forgiven in baptism, Luther also affirmed that "tinder of sin" (*fomes pec-cati*), the concupiscence or inclination to sin that remains in a person after baptism, is in fact sin, and not merely a penalty and a weakness or defect. This was one of Luther's teachings that was specifically condemned by the Council of Trent.[39]

Melanchthon and Later Lutheranism

For Luther's close associate Philip Melanchthon, the most important and practical theological *loci* were sin, law, and grace.[40] In the first edition of his *Loci Communes* (1521), Melanchthon takes aim at those theologians who minimize the effects of sin on human capacities. "[W]hen the Sophists say that original sin is the lack of original righteousness, as they express it, they are right. But why do they not add that where there is no original righteous-ness or the Spirit, there in reality is flesh, godlessness, a contempt for spiritual things?"[41] Anselm's definition of original sin is still Melanchthon's starting point in the third, 1543 Latin edition:

> Original sin is the lack of original righteousness which is required to be present in us. But this brief and unclear description requires a longer explanation. For we must inquire what "original righteousness" means. Therefore, we must add this explanation: original righteousness was the acceptance of the human race before God, and, in the very nature of man, light in his mind by which he could firmly assent to the Word of God and turning of his will to God and obedience of his heart in harmony with the judgment of God's law, which had been planted in his mind.[42]

Melanchthon also refers to God's imputation of sin to the human race, but he is concerned that imputation lessens the severity of sin, in contrast to the real corruption of human nature. In the second edition of his *Loci*, he writes,

> The scholastic doctors say many inconsistent things about original sin, but in sum this is their opinion: original sin is guilt, that is, an imputation, by which the progeny of Adam are guilty and condemned on the basis of his

---

bonus illi sit Deus ("And when a person makes oneself bent over toward earthly lusts, one is in a way curved in; but when that person is raised up for things above, their heart is made upright, so that God may be good to them").
[39] Luther, "Defense and Explanation of All the Articles," 2, 3 (*LW* 32:25, 29–31 and n. 21).
[40] Melanchthon, *Theologia Institutio in epistolam Pauli ad Romanos*, ante cap. 1, in CR 21:49.
[41] Melanchthon, *Loci communes rerum theologicarum* (1521), in CR 21:98; trans. in *Melanchthon and Bucer*, ed. Wilhelm Pauck (Louisville: Westminster/John Knox, 1969), 31.
[42] Melanchthon, *Loci theologici* (1543), in CR 21:668–69; *Loci Communes 1543*, trans. J. A. O. Preus (St. Louis: Concordia, 1992), 48.

transgression. Next, they add that sin is a certain kind of weakness. This is a matter worthy of condemnation in itself. But they make punishment for sin an indifferent matter. Moreover, they teach that human nature is able to obey the law of God and to be without sin. . . . We then, on the contrary, hold that original sin is not only imputation or guilt but is also a corruption of human nature, as a result of which we are not able to truly obey the law of God or to be without sin.[43]

The Lutherans later experienced their own controversy over original sin. Following the defeat of the Schmalkaldic League in 1547, Melanchthon formulated a compromise proposal for living as Protestants in the Empire. But the Leipzig interim, as it was called, created a severe rift among Lutheran leaders who squared off into the Philippist and Gnesio-Lutheran parties. The former party, like Melanchthon himself, especially in his later years, entertained a more optimistic view of human nature and human capabilities after the fall into sin. The latter camp (the "True Lutherans") rejected this soteriological synergism and stressed the radical sinfulness of human nature and the sinful person's utter dependence on God's grace. In 1560, the brilliant, productive, and zealous Matthias Flacius Illyricus (1520–75) engaged his Philippist colleague at the University of Jena, Viktorin Strigel (1524–69), in a formal disputation on original sin. During the debate, Flacius went so far as to claim that original sin is not merely accidental to human beings; original sin is, in fact, the substance of human beings. Not only that, in the fall into sin, human beings lost the image of God and took on the image of Satan. While Flacius's statements were considered extreme by both camps, the substance of his statements was similar to other Protestant formulations of the doctrine. He claimed that the formal substance of human beings is sin and the image of Satan, in the same way that theologians said that human beings lost the image of God in a certain sense and lost original righteousness completely. But the material substance, Flacius contended, the human faculties such as reason and volition, were only damaged, and not eradicated. Nonetheless, Flacius's excessive rhetoric branded him for the rest of his days.[44]

---

[43] "Scholastici doctores de peccato originis multa pugnantia dicunt, sed tamen in summa hoc sentiunt, peccatum originis esse reatum, hoc est Imputationem, qua posteri Adae propter ipsius delictum rei ac damnati sint, Deinde addunt esse quandam imbecillitatem esse peccatum, hoc est rem dignam damnatione per sese: sed faciunt poenam peccati et rem mediam. Caeterum docent naturam hominis posse obedire legi dei et sine peccato esse. . . . Nos igitur contra sic sentimus peccatum originis non tantum esse imputationem seu reatum sed etiam naturae hominis corruptionem, qua fit ne possimus vere obedire legi dei et sine peccato esse" (*Loci Communes* [1535], in CR 21:285).
[44] On the controversy, see Robert Kolb, "Dynamics of Party Conflict in the Saxon Late Reformation: Gnesio-Lutherans vs. Philippists," *The Journal of Modern History* 49.3, On Demand Supplement (1977): D1289–D1305;

The Early Reformed Tradition

The Reformed tradition likewise emphasized the profound effects of sin on human moral and spiritual capabilities. Like Luther, Huldrych Zwingli (1484–1531) stressed that sinners cannot contribute anything to their salvation. Zwingli, however, held an unusual perspective on original sin. Like the medieval theologian Peter Abelard (c. 1079–1142), Zwingli claimed that original sin is a tendency to sin, but not sin itself; original sin is a disease, but it is not guilt.[45] The Augsburg Confession (art. 2), echoing Luther's accusation of Zwingli, rejects this teaching as a form of Pelagianism; but in fact, Zwingli has no place in his theology for sinners meriting or contributing to their own salvation.[46] His successor in Zürich, Heinrich Bullinger (1504–75), defended Zwingli's orthodoxy on this point.[47] Zwingli is also known for his rather generous view of predestination; he assumes that virtuous pagans are among the elect, and he is certain that they are holier than the Franciscans and Dominicans.[48]

Like Luther before him, John Calvin put considerable emphasis on the depth of sin in order to highlight salvation as entirely the gracious work of God in Christ.[49] And, like Luther, Calvin's views follow the main lines of traditional Roman Catholic teaching, that sin is both a deprivation of original

---

on Flacius, see Luka Ilić, *Theologian of Sin and Grace: The Process of Radicalization in the Theology of Matthias Flacius Illyricus* (Göttingen, Germany: Vandenhoeck & Ruprecht, 2014).

[45] See Huldrych Zwingli, *De peccato originalio declaratio* etc., in *Huldrici Zwingli Opera*, ed. Melchior Schuler and Johannes Schulthess, 8 vols. in 11 (Zurich, 1828–42), 3:629; Zwingli, *Original Sin*, in *The Latin Works of Huldreich Zwingli*, ed. S. M. Jackson et al., 3 vols. (New York: Putnam; Philadelphia: Heidelberg, 1912–29), 2:5. This is the interpretation of W. P. Stephens, *Zwingli: An Introduction to His Thought* (Oxford: Oxford University Press, 1994), 73–75; Stephens, *The Theology of Huldrych Zwingli* (Oxford: Oxford University Press, 1986), 146–53. Gottfried W. Locher disputes this interpretation; see his "The Change in the Understanding of Zwingli in Recent Research," *Church History* 34.1 (1965): 9–10; cf. the harsh evaluation of Zwingli's doctrine in Gross, *Geschichte des Erbsündendogmas*, 37–58.

[46] See Stephens, *Theology of Huldrych Zwingli*, 153.

[47] See W. P. Stephens, *The Theology of Heinrich Bullinger*, ed. Jim West and Joe Mock (Göttingen, Germany: Vandenhoeck & Ruprecht, 2019), 235–36, 241–42.

[48] Huldrych Zwingli, *De providentia Dei*, in *Opera*, 4:123; trans. in *Latin Works of Huldreich Zwingli*, 2:201. Bullinger held this generous view of election as well; see Stephens, *Theology of Heinrich Bullinger*, 238.

[49] On Calvin's teaching on sin in general, note Lanier Burns, "From Ordered Soul to Corrupted Nature: Calvin's View of Sin," in *John Calvin and Evangelical Theology: Legacy and Prospect*, ed. Sung Wook Chung (Louisville: Westminster/John Knox, 2009), 85–106; and Randall C. Zachman, "John Calvin," in *TTCC*, 235–50, neither of which addresses the core issues. For more focused studies, see John H. Leith, "The Doctrine of the Will in the *Institutes of the Christian Religion*," in *Reformatio Perennis*, ed. Brian A. Gerrish and Robert Benedetto (Pittsburgh: Pickwick, 1981), 49–66; A. N. S. Lane, "Did Calvin Believe in Freewill?" *Vox Evangelica* 12 (1981): 72–90; Barbara Pitkin, "Nothing but Concupiscence: Calvin's Understanding of Sin and the *Via Augustini*," *CTJ* 34.2 (1999): 347–69; Aaron C. Denlinger, "Calvin's Understanding of Adam's Relationship to His Posterity: Recent Assertions of the Reformer's 'Federalism' Evaluated," *CTJ* 44 (2009): 226–50; Nico Vorster, "Calvin's Modification of Augustine's Doctrine of Original Sin," *In die Skriflig* 44, Supplement 3 (2010): 71–89; Luca Baschera, "Total Depravity? The Consequences of Original Sin in John Calvin and Later Reformed Theology," in *Calvinus Clarissimus Theologus: Papers of the Tenth International Congress on Calvin Research*, ed. Herman J. Selderhuis (Göttingen, Germany: Vandenhoeck & Ruprecht, 2012), 37–58.

righteousness and the corruption of human nature, while rejecting entirely any claims that human powers are left largely intact.

John Murray asserts that "Calvin's view of original sin is radically different from that of Rome."[50] This is quite an exaggeration, as one readily observes in Calvin's *Antidote* for the Council of Trent's poisonous condemnation of the Protestants.[51] Commenting on the first decree of the fifth session, Calvin rebukes the delegates for issuing so many statements on the doctrine of original sin in order to give the false impression that the Reformers had substantial differences with traditional Roman Catholic teaching on the subject.[52] The delegates, Calvin says, "borrow the first four headings from the ancient and approved doctrine of the church—matters, namely, about which there was no controversy at all."[53] The first of these statements affirms that Adam's transgression incurred the loss of original righteousness, God's wrath, and the penalty of death, and that Adam was changed for the worse in body and soul, that is, that he suffered corruption. The second statement affirms that the consequences of Adam's sin were not restricted to him alone, but are transmitted to his progeny, including the transmission of sin itself. The third statement denies that the transmission of Adam's sin occurs by imitation, as the Pelagians taught, but asserts that it occurs by propagation; it also denies that this sin can be removed by human nature or by any means other than the merit of Christ, which is applied to both infants and adults in baptism. The fourth statement emphasizes that infants are indeed to be baptized for the remission of sins. Calvin does not disagree.[54]

The fifth of the statements from Trent condemns those who deny that the guilt (*reatus*) of original sin is remitted by the grace of Christ conferred in baptism or who claim that what has the "true and proper nature of sin" is not completely removed, but that it is only "shaved off" (*radi*) or not

---

[50] John Murray, *The Imputation of Adam's Sin* (Grand Rapids, MI: Eerdmans, 1959), 17.

[51] On Calvin's *Antidote*, see Robert P. Swierenga, "Calvin and the Council of Trent: A Reappraisal" (in three parts: *Reformed Journal* 16.3 [1966]: 35–37; 16.4 [1966]: 16–21; 16.5 [1966]: 20–23). Swierenga observes that Calvin agrees with Trent about as often as he disagrees, and he argues that part of Calvin's disagreement with Trent was due to Calvin's "insensitivity to the nuances of Tridentine theology. The Roman Church was not as monolithic as he imagined it to be and the delegates at Trent expressed a wide range of varying opinions" (16.4 [1966]: 21).

[52] *Canons and Decrees of the Council of Trent, with the Antidote* (1547), fifth session, first decree; Latin text in *Ioannis Calvini opera quae supersunt omnia*, ed. J. W. Baum, A. E. Cunitz, and E. Reuss, 59 vols. (Braunschweig, Germany: Schwetschke, 1863–1900 [hereafter *CO*]), 7:423–28; cf. trans. in *Tracts Relating to the Reformation*, trans. Henry Beveridge, 3 vols. (Edinburgh: Calvin Translation Society, 1844–51), 3:85–89; unless otherwise indicated, translations of Calvin are my own. On Trent's theology of original sin, see Hubert Jedin, *A History of the Council of Trent*, trans. E. Graf, 2 vols. (London: Thomas Nelson, 1957–61), 2:136–37.

[53] ". . . prima quatuor capita ex veteri probataque ecclesiae doctrina mutuantur: de quibus scilicet nihil erat controversiae" (*CO* 7:423).

[54] *CO* 7:419–20.

imputed.[55] It is here that Calvin has objections. Calvin denies that original sin is entirely removed by baptism. The guilt (*reatus*; technically, the liability for guilt or punishment[56]) is totally taken away, but sin, though not imputed, still remains, and not merely as an inclination toward sin that one may resist by an exercise of the will. Here Calvin reminds his readers that he teaches a twofold grace (*duplex gratia*) of baptism, or, in other words, the distinction between justification and sanctification, a significant difference between the Reformers and the Church of Rome: "In baptism both remission of sins and regeneration are offered to us. We teach that remission of sins is effected fully, but regeneration is only begun, and people make progress over the course of their whole lives. So then, sin truly remains in us, and it is not immediately extinguished by baptism in a single day. But because the guilt (*reatus*, liability) is removed, there is none with respect to imputation."[57]

Calvin explains that there remains something in believers that is blameworthy (*culpa*), but the liability (*reatus*) is gone, and, for him, this is the proper meaning of Romans 8:28, that there is no condemnation for those who are in Christ. It is not as if believers "were pure and immune from every sin, but they are only freed from the liability"[58] of what is blameworthy in them, the sin that the Reformers insist remains in persons even after baptism, and indeed, throughout their lives.

Calvin's problems with the Roman Catholic teaching of his day, he says in his commentary on Psalm 51, is that "the papists, although they do not deny that human nature is corrupt, nevertheless minimize it such that original sin is almost nothing else than a depraved inclination toward sin."[59] This is the crux of the Reformer's objection. Moreover, he criticizes Rome for locating original sin in the lower, inferior parts of the soul and for saying that it no longer remains after baptism, whereas he affirms that sin infects all the faculties of human nature, and that it is rather obvious that persons continue to be corrupted by sin throughout their lives. Calvin then proceeds to refute

---

[55] *CO* 7:420; *radere*, "to shave off," was a term used by the Pelagians; see Augustine, *Contra Duas Epistolas Pelagianorum* 1.13.26 (PL 44:563). Calvin suspects that the delegates of Trent are attempting a guilt-by-association tactic.
[56] See Richard A. Muller, *Dictionary of Latin and Greek Theological Terms: Drawn Principally from Protestant Scholastic Theology*, 2nd ed. (Grand Rapids, MI: Baker Academic, 2017), 306–7 (s.v. *reatus*).
[57] "nam et peccatorum remissio illic, et regeneratio nobis offertur. Remissionem plenam fieri docemus: regenerationem inchoari duntaxat, suosque tota vita facere progressus. Proinde manet vere peccatum in nobis, neque per baptismum statim uno die exstinguitur: sed quia deletur reatus, imputatione nullum est" (*CO* 7:425).
[58] ". . . quia fideles his verbis non ex/imit a culpa, quasi puri sint, et omni peccato immunes, sed tantum reatu liberat . . ." (*CO* 7:425); cf. Vermigli's similar comments, though he is more conciliatory toward those who say that the concupiscence that remains in a person after baptism is not sin (*On Original Sin*, 62).
[59] "Hodie papistae, tametsi non negant vitiatam esse hominum naturam, sic tamen extenuant ut peccatum originale nihil fere aliud sit, quam prava ad peccatum inclinatio" (*CO* 31:513).

Trent's claim that corruption in the will, the concupiscence that remains in a person, is not properly sin, but only the tinder of sin (*fomes peccati*), given that Paul says in Romans 7 that he continues to struggle with sin, and that he tells believers to put off the old man.[60]

Later, when Calvin examines the very substantial differences with Rome on the doctrine of justification, the matter of human depravity also comes up in connection with what the Reformers considered Rome's excessive emphasis on human good works. Our inherent depravity disfigures any good we do. Thus, it is a "godless delusion" to think that our tainted good works can merit God's grace; rather, God's grace is what renders our good works acceptable.[61]

Calvin's main objection, however, is his conclusion that Trent's decrees minimize sin's continuing consequences for human faculties and thus significantly underestimate sin's effect on the will. Commenting on the sixth session, he complains that, while the delegates concede that original sin diminishes and distorts the will, they do not believe that it extinguishes the will.[62] "Thus, if we believe them, original sin has impaired us such that the defect of our will is not depravity but weakness. For if the will were wholly depraved, its health would not only be distorted and weakened, but lost, until such time that it might be made new."[63] But, Calvin asserts, the latter is precisely what Scripture teaches. What Calvin did not know was that there was a diversity of views among the delegates. He was not privy to the fact that Girolamo Seripando (1493–1563), a newly minted cardinal who, importantly, hailed from the Augustinian order and was a papal legate of the council, argued for positions that were significantly closer to those of the Reformers.[64]

When Bucer, Calvin, Vermigli, and other Reformers criticized the Roman Catholic theologian Albert Pighius's (c. 1490–1542) doctrine of sin, this was a judgment they shared with Trent.[65] Pighius taught that Adam's sin had only

[60] Vermigli, *On Original Sin*, 28–29 (cf. *CO* 7:425–26), makes a similar argument, though he directs it against Pighius's teachings.
[61] *CO* 7:472.
[62] *CO* 7:442–443: ". . . ubi de peccato originali disserunt, liberum arbitrium pronunciant viribus fuisse attenuatum, et inclinatum, non tamen exstinctum." *Inclinatus* here means, "turned away from its original purpose or goal, prejudiced, predisposed." Calvin likely has in mind concupiscence as merely an inclination to sin, but not genuinely sin.
[63] *CO* 7:443: "Ergo, si illis credimus, debilitavit nos peccatum originale, ut voluntatis nostrae vitium non pravitas sit, sed infirmitas. Nam si prava omnino voluntas esset, non inclinatae modo esset sanitatis et attenuatae, sed perditae, donec nova fieret."
[64] See Jedin, *History of the Council of Trent*, 2:146–48, 155–56.
[65] See John Calvin, *The Bondage and Liberation of the Will: A Defense of the Orthodox Doctrine of Human Choice against Pighius*, ed. A. N. S. Lane, trans. G. I. Davies (Grand Rapids, MI: Baker, 1998), xvii; Vermigli, *On Original*

the effects of introducing physical death to the human race and the imputation of Adam's first sin to all human beings. For Pighius, concupiscence was
natural, not the result of the fall, nor did he speak of human nature as corrupted. The Council of Trent censured Pighius's teachings and put one of his
treatises on the Index of Prohibited Books.[66]

For early Reformed thinkers, Adam's sin results in the distortion (and in
some sense the loss) of the image of God in Adam and his posterity. Johannes
Oecolampadius writes, "After he had fallen into sin, however, the image was
obscured, the excellence lost, and thus, too, the capacity for doing good."[67] In
his 1559 *Institutes of the Christian Religion*, Calvin declares that "the image
of God was originally evident in the light of the mind, in the rectitude of the
heart, and in soundness in every part," and further, "the image of God is the
excellence of unfallen human nature, which glimmered in Adam before his
rebellion. . . ."[68] The image of God does not consist in the faculties themselves, but in their integrity.[69] Like Oecolampadius, Calvin does not accept
the traditional interpretation of the words *image* and *likeness* in Genesis 1:26
as the distinction between the image as the substance or essence of the soul
and the likeness as its qualities, or as original righteousness.[70] The content of
the original image of God can be inferred from its restoration in Christ: "we
are restored in such a way that we bear the image of God in true devotion,
righteousness, purity, and understanding."[71]

In the rebellion and fall, the image of God in Adam was lost in some
sense and distorted in another. Calvin's rhetorical vehemence can lead him
to declare that the image of God in human beings is now "obliterated,"[72] but

---

Sin, 11–31 and passim; A. N. S. Lane, "Albert Pighius's Controversial Work on Original Sin," *Reformation and Renaissance Review* 4 (2000): 29–61.

[66] See Jedin, *History of the Council of Trent*, 2:153: "Pighius had taught that original sin was not a sin proper to every child of Adam but that it was due to the imputation of the one original, or first sin of Adam to all his descendants."

[67] Johannes Oecolampadius, *An Exposition of Genesis*, trans. and ed. Mickey L. Mattox (Milwaukee: Marquette University Press, 2013), 99.

[68] ". . . initio in luce mentis, in cordis rectitudine, partiumque omnium sanitate conspicuam fuisse Dei imaginem. . . . Dei imago sit integra naturae humanae praestantia, quae refulsit in Adam ante defectionem . . ." (Calvin, *Institutes*, 1.15.4; in *Joannis Calvini Opera Selecta*, ed. Peter Barth, Wilhelm Niesel, and Dora Scheuner, 5 vols. [vol. 2, 2nd ed.; vols. 3–5, 3rd ed.] [Munich: Christian Kaiser Verlag, 1926–1974 (hereafter *OS*)], 3:179).

[69] Denlinger's assertion that "higher faculties *constitute* the divine image in Adam" (239 and n. 53) is incorrect; his references to Calvin's commentary on Gen. 1:26 and 2:7 both fail to substantiate his claim, and the first, which corresponds closely to *Institutes*, 1.15.4, refutes it. In the second, Calvin explicitly speaks of the *lower* parts of the soul and not the higher faculties. See also Heinrich Heppe, *Reformed Dogmatics: Set Out and Illustrated from the Sources*, rev. and ed. Ernst Bizer, trans. G. T. Thomson (London: George Allen & Unwin, 1950), 232.

[70] On Calvin's doctrine of the image of God, see Jason Van Vliet, *Children of God: The* Imago Dei *in John Calvin and His Context* (Göttingen, Germany: Vandenhoeck & Ruprecht, 2009), and on this distinction, see 53–54, 58, 61; see also Baschera, *Total Depravity?*, 38–39; cf. Oecolampadius, *Exposition of Genesis*, 102–3.

[71] Calvin, *Institutes*, 1.15.4; in *OS* 3:180.

[72] "obliterata fuit caelestis imago" (Calvin, *Institutes*, 2.1.5; in *OS* 3:232–33).

at other times he concedes that "the image of God was not utterly eradicated and annihilated" in Adam; nevertheless it was "so corrupted that whatever remains is a horrible deformity."[73] In Calvin the image of God is closely related, if not identical, to the gifts with which Adam was endowed in his creation.[74] Calvin adopts the traditional distinction between natural and supernatural gifts, and he approves of the statement that he believes is from Augustine (actually from Lombard[75]) that "the natural gifts in human beings have been corrupted by sin, but they have been deprived of the supernatural gifts." The supernatural gifts, Calvin explains, are the light of faith and (original) righteousness, which would have enabled human beings to obtain eternal life. Calvin adds that these include "faith, love for God, charity toward one's neighbors, and the pursuit of holiness and righteousness." The corruption of the natural gifts includes the loss of "soundness of mind and rectitude of heart," the latter including the depravity of the will.[76]

Original sin, as Calvin defines it, is "a hereditary depravity and corruption of our nature, diffused through all parts of the soul, that first makes us liable to the penalty of God's wrath and then produces works in us that the Scripture calls 'the works of the flesh.'"[77] Calvin generally approves of both traditional concepts of original sin, that of the loss of original righteousness and that of corruption in the form of disordered concupiscence, but he also criticizes how the two concepts are used in his day, because theologians minimize the extent and severity of sin.[78] Regarding the loss of original righteousness, Calvin says that those who use this definition, "although they encompass the totality of what is contained in the matter, they still have not expressed its force and energy significantly enough. For our nature is not only destitute and devoid of good but is so abundant and productive of all evils that it cannot remain inactive."[79] If one were to consider the loss of original righteousness as something that still leaves human faculties basically intact,

---

[73] "Quare etsi demus non prorsus exinanitam ac deletam in eo fuisse Dei imaginem, sic tamen corrupta fuit, ut quiequid superest, horrenda sit deformitas" (Calvin, *Institutes*, 1.15.4; in *OS* 3:179).
[74] See Van Vliet, *Children of God*, 32, who cites Calvin's sermon on Gen. 1:26–28; and p. 70, where he cites Calvin's 1536 *Institutes*.
[75] Lombard, *Sentences*, 2.25.8 (PL 192:707); *Sentences*, 2:119.
[76] Calvin, *Institutes*, 2.2.12 (*OS* 3:254); see also 2.2.4, 16.
[77] Calvin, *Institutes*, 2.1.8 (*OS* 3:236–37): "Videtur ergo peccatum originale haereditaria naturae nostrae pravitas et corruptio, in omnes animae partes diffusa: quae primum facit reos irae Dei, tum etiam opera in nobis profert quae Scriptura vocat opera carnis."
[78] See Pitkin, "Nothing but Concupiscence," 359; contrast somewhat Denlinger, "Calvin's Understanding," 240.
[79] ". . . quanquam id totum complectuntur quod in re est, non tamen satis significanter vim atque energiam ipsius expresserunt. Non enim natura nostra boni tantum inops et vacua est: sed malorum omnium adeo fertilis et ferax, ut otiosa esse non possit" (Calvin, *Institutes*, 2.1.8 [*OS* 3:238]).

as some later theologians do, then the definition would be inadequate. Martin Bucer had stated the matter rather clearly:

> The Schoolmen make the loss of original righteousness, the state in which all our parts were rightly ordered within us, the chief aspect of this evil of original sin. But surely it is a necessary consequence of this loss that everything in us is now disordered and distorted, and the habit of corrupt desire has possession of man.[80]

But Calvin also criticizes those (particularly Peter Lombard) who define original sin largely in terms of concupiscence. He says that they also minimize the power of sin by restricting its effect to the will and by locating it primarily in the flesh.[81] Calvin extends sin's effects to the entire human being, body and soul, although Lombard does affirm that the soul is so affected, and Vermigli, more well-versed in the tradition, affirms that the soul "draws the filthiness of sin from the sinful body, to which it is joined."[82] Calvin affirms, "the entire human being is of itself nothing but concupiscence."[83] Like Vermigli,[84] Calvin also strongly emphasizes the noetic effects of sin, sin's corruption of the intellect, an emphasis he thinks is lacking in Lombard.

On the transmission of original sin, early Reformed thinkers generally reflect the realistic tradition, though there are hints of Adam's representative function that later Reformed theologians would develop in detail. Vermigli speaks of sin being passed on through the seminal reason of Adam (λόγοι σπερματικοί, a term that Augustine borrowed from the Stoics), but Vermigli did not exploit this idea in terms of original sin. The notion was adopted by some medieval theologians, such as Bonaventure and Albertus Magnus.[85] It is the idea that God created creatures with potentialities that contain within themselves a sort of blueprint for their development. Adam's seminal reason, damaged by original sin, is passed down to all his progeny.

Just as Luther had described sin as a radical corruption, Calvin affirms that "Adam was not only the progenitor, but also, as it were, the root of human

---

[80] Martin Bucer, *Common Places of Martin Bucer*, ed. and trans. D. F. Wright (Appleford, UK: Sutton Courtenay, 1972), 123.

[81] Calvin, *Institutes*, 2.1.9.

[82] Vermigli, *On Original Sin*, 57.

[83] ". . . totum hominem non aliud ex seipso esse quam concupiscentiam" (Calvin, *Institutes*, 2.1.8 [*OS* 3:238]). Pitkin's article ("Nothing but Concupiscence") is essential reading on this point.

[84] Vermigli, *On Original Sin*, 37–41.

[85] Vermigli, *On Original Sin*, 23; see also Jules M. Brady, "St. Augustine's Theory of Seminal Reasons," *New Scholasticism* 38.2 (1964): 141–58.

nature, and for that reason the human race was also deservedly harmed by his corruption."[86] Calvin goes on to describe the destruction of human nature that occurred in Adam in rather realistic terms, as a contagion: "And this happened not through his offense, the offense of one individual, which had nothing to do with us, but because he had infected his entire seed with that corruption into which he had fallen."[87] But Calvin, unlike Augustine, does not relate the transmission of original sin to the lust of the sexual act. Adam's seed is corrupted somehow, perhaps in a way analogous to Vermigli's seminal reason.

Calvin incorporates Anselm's definition as well. In the fall, Adam and the whole human race lost original righteousness, lost those exceptional gifts, lost the pristine image of God; but this is not a "mere" privation, but results in profound corruption: "Therefore, it is not at all absurd to think that, [Adam] being stripped of those distinctions, human nature is left bare and destitute, that by his pollution with sin, the contagion slithers into our nature. Accordingly, a rotten root produces rotten branches. . . ."[88] Nor is Calvin unique here. Vermigli defines original sin primarily in terms of the loss of original righteousness that results in corruption, affirming that "as soon as God withdrew the gifts bestowed on man, immediately sin and corruption followed of their own accord."[89]

Nevertheless, Calvin argues that the source of corruption is not located in the substance of either the body or the soul, "but in the fact that God ordained that the first human being would simultaneously either keep or lose, both for himself and for his descendants, the gifts conferred on him."[90] One could interpret this statement such that Adam plays a representative role, but even then, it is far from a full-fledged federal image.

Calvin's nuance in his commentary on John 3:6 leans further toward emphasizing God's ordination of the consequences of Adam's fall. God ordained that Adam would keep or lose the supernatural gifts (original righteousness) on behalf of the human race. But here Calvin says corruption "did not proceed from generation, but from the appointment of God. . . . Instead of

---

86 ". . . fuisse Adamum humanae naturae non progenitorem modo, sed quasi radicem, atque ideo in illius corruptione merito vitiatum fuisse hominum genus" (Calvin, *Institutes*, 2.1.6 [*OS* 3:234]).
87 "Neque id suo unius vitio, quod nihil ad nos pertineat: sed quoniam universum suum semen ea in quam lapsus erat vitiositate infecit" (Calvin, *Institutes*, 2.1.6 [*OS* 3:235]).
88 "Nihil ergo absurdi, si spoliato eo, natura nuda inopsque destituitur: si illo per peccatum inquinato, in naturam contagio serpit. Proinde a radice putrefacta rami putridi prodierunt . . ." (Calvin, *Institutes*, 2.1.7 [*OS* 3:236]).
89 Vermigli, *On Original Sin*, 24; cf. his specific comments on Anselm's definition (29–31), and on both concupiscence and lack of original righteousness as the material and formal aspect of original sin, respectively (40–41).
90 "Neque enim in substantia carnis aut animae causam habet contagio: sed quia a Deo ita fuit ordinatum, ut quae primo homini dona contulerat, ille tam sibi quam suis haberet simul ac perderet" (Calvin, *Institutes*, 2.1.7 [*OS* 3:236]).

saying, therefore, that each of us draws vice and corruption from his parents, it would be more correct to say that we are all alike corrupted in Adam alone, because immediately after his revolt God took away from human nature what he had bestowed upon it."[91]

In his commentary on Romans 5:12, Calvin notes that some say we incurred death through no fault of our own, but as if Adam had sinned for us.[92] On the contrary, Calvin affirms that Paul expressly says that we have all sinned, but Calvin specifies that this means that we have all become corrupted and defective. For when Adam sinned, he ruined human nature, and he lost the gifts that God intended to confer on human nature.[93] Augustine, too, had said that it was human nature that sinned in Adam.[94]

Commenting on Psalm 51:5, Calvin interprets David's words, "Surely I was sinful at birth," as a confession that human beings are born completely corrupted by nature.[95] He describes original sin as a hereditary contagion, contrary to Pelagius's assertion that sin is only transmitted by imitation. But on the nature of the transmission itself, Calvin is more reticent; the exact manner of transmission is a "labyrinth" to be avoided—Calvin's standard term for a subject that goes beyond human knowledge.[96] Calvin writes that "God did not adorn Adam with the gifts of his Spirit as any private person whatsoever but assigned to his role (*persona*) that which he willed to be common to the entire human race. Because of that, in him we have all been cut off from that original integrity."[97] Here Calvin does assign a certain, perhaps representative, role to Adam as the first human being, but Calvin does not get into the specifics of Adam's relationship to his posterity or the specifics of transmission.

---

[91] "Nam quod in persona unius Adae totum genus humanum corruptum fuit, non tam ex genitura provenit quam ex Dei ordinatione, qui sicut in uno homine nos omnes ornaverat, ita spoliavit suis donis. Quare non tam unusquisque nostrum a parentibus suis vitium et corruptionem contrahit, quam omnes pariter in uno Adam corrupti sumus, quia statim post eius defectionem Deus, quod naturae humanae dederat, abstulit" (Calvin, *Comm.* John 3:6 [*CO* 47:57]).
[92] "quasi ille nobis peccasset" (*CO* 49:95); cf. the French translation: *comme si nous ne perissions point par nostre propre faute, et seulement pource qu'iceluy a peché en nostre nom* ("as if we did not perish through our own fault, and only because he sinned in our name") (*Commentaire de M. Jean Calvin sur l'Epistre aux Romains* [Geneva: J. Girard, 1550], 185).
[93] Cf. Calvin, *Institutes*, 2.1.7; see Denlinger, "Calvin's Understanding," 241.
[94] See Augustine, *De diversis quaestionibus LXXXIII* 66.3: *"natura nostra peccavit, amissa beatitudine spirituali"* (PL 40:62); cf. also in *The Fathers of the Church: A New Translation*, vol. 70, trans. David L. Mosher (Washington, DC: Catholic University of America Press, 1982), 141: "our nature had sinned and lost the spiritual blessedness." See Paula Fredriksen, "Beyond the Body/Soul Dichotomy: Augustine on Paul against the Manichees and the Pelagians," *Recherches augustiniennes* 23 (1988): 87–114 (91).
[95] "naturaliter se totum corruptum esse" (*CO* 31:513).
[96] John Calvin, *Commentary on the Book of Psalms*, trans. James Anderson, 5 vols. (Edinburgh: Calvin Translation Society, 1845–1849), 2:291. Anderson's translation is wildly inaccurate. Cf. the older translation by Arthur Golding, *The Psalmes of David and Others: With M. John Calvin's Commentaries* (London: Thomas East & Henry Middleton, 1571), fol. 203 r°.
[97] "Quia Deus Adam non ornaverat spiritus sui donis tanquam privatum quemlibet hominem, sed in eius personam contulerat quod volebat commune esse toti humano generi, nos omnes in ipso a prima integritate excidisse" (*CO* 31:514).

One notable aspect of Calvin's doctrine of sin is the stress he places on its noetic effects. Calvin affirms that the seat of sin is the will,[98] but here he involves himself in considerable inconsistency, because Calvin describes human beings in the state of integrity, before the fall into sin, in a manner that places priority on the intellect rather than the will. Apart from this pristine state, however, Calvin underscores the priority of the will over the intellect.[99] Calvin's inconsistency may be explained by the fact that he did not fully understand the issues of philosophical anthropology that were at stake, as well as the fact that he simply had a distaste for traditional metaphysical questions and for medieval theology's concern with such questions.[100] Richard A. Muller speaks of "Calvin's lack of theological training and his continuing wariness of the medieval scholastics" that prevented him from adopting the scholastic distinctions that helped later Reformed thinkers develop much more precise formulations of doctrine.[101]

Post-Reformation Reformed Theology on Sin

After the establishment of Reformed confessional communities and regions, theologians continued to refine and develop Reformed theology in the context of confessional consolidation and codification, as well as continued debates both inside and outside the boundaries of the Reformed faith.[102] This development, of course, included the doctrine of sin.[103] Whereas Calvin's representation of Reformed doctrine was rhetorically powerful, if sometimes imprecise, succeeding generations of Reformed theologians continued to bring increased refinement and a deepening knowledge of the theological tradition and of biblical and cognate languages. Reformed theologians delved further into classic questions; thus, in the theological locus of sin, theologians examined further the matter of how the image of God could be

---

[98] Calvin, *Institutes*, 2.2.27.
[99] See Richard A. Muller, "*Fides* and *Cognitio* in Relation to the Problem of Intellect and Will in the Theology of John Calvin," *CTJ* 25.2 (1990): 207–24; Dewey J. Hoitenga Jr., *John Calvin and the Will: A Critique and Corrective*, foreword by Richard A. Muller (Grand Rapids, MI: Baker, 1997).
[100] Note Calvin's lack of interest in "the minutiae of Aristotle" (Calvin, *Institutes*, 1.15.7).
[101] Richard A. Muller, *Divine Will and Human Choice: Freedom, Contingency, and Necessity in Early Modern Reformed Thought* (Grand Rapids, MI: Baker, 2017), 186.
[102] On the development of theological formulation in this era, see Richard A. Muller, *Post-Reformation Reformed Dogmatics*, 4 vols. (vols. 1–2, 2nd ed.) (Grand Rapids, MI: Baker Academic, 2003), 1:49–52, 60–84; Willem J. van Asselt, "Reformed Orthodoxy: A Short History of Research," in *A Companion to Reformed Orthodoxy*, ed. Herman J. Selderhuis (Leiden, Netherlands: Brill, 2013), 11–26.
[103] On the doctrine of sin in this period, see Heppe, *Reformed Dogmatics*, 320–70; Stephen Hampton, "Sin, Grace, and Free Choice in Post-Reformation Reformed Theology," in *The Oxford Handbook of Early Modern Theology, 1600–1800*, ed. Ulrich L. Lehner, Richard A. Muller, and A. G. Roeber (New York: Oxford University Press, 2014), 228–41.

said to be lost, and in what manner it was retained, albeit damaged, after the fall into sin.[104] Like theologians of the Reformation era, Protestant orthodox theologians continued to characterize original sin as comprising both the loss of original righteousness and the corruption of concupiscence. And, like the early Reformers, they continued to reject views of sin that might leave human beings morally and spiritually intact after the fall of Adam.

In addition, a new emphasis, that of God's covenant, came to the fore. Wolfgang Musculus (1497–1563), who, incidentally, paid virtually no attention to the traditional definitions of original sin, dedicated a separate locus to the covenant and closely tied the concepts of covenant and law. But he did not formulate a covenant of works or consider Adam the federal head of humanity.[105] In his early work, Zacharias Ursinus (1534–83) speaks of a covenant established with human beings at creation, but it was not an enduring theme in his thought.[106]

One of the first theologians who did, in fact, formulate a federal schema in which Adam represents all humanity as its federal head was not even Protestant. The Dominican Ambrosius Catharinus (Ambrogio Catarino, 1483–1553) was an opponent of Lutheranism and a delegate to the Council of Trent.[107] In his 1541 treatise *On the Fall of Mankind and Original Sin*, Catharinus asserts that God "established a covenant with Adam from the beginning so that he himself would possess grace and righteousness and the rest of the gifts, as would his wife and his children, and he would retain them, as long as he abstained from the fruit of one specific tree; but he did not.[108] On the basis of this covenant, Adam would retain or lose original righteousness. As we have seen, it was not unusual to say that all human beings were included in Adam, but Catharinus bases this inclusion on a pre-fall covenant between God and Adam rather than on organic solidarity. Catharinus pairs this initial covenant with a "new covenant" in Christ. Other Roman Catholic theologians maintained a twofold covenant schema, though without the

---

[104] See Heppe, *Reformed Dogmatics*, 232–38.

[105] Wolfgang Musculus, *Loci communes sacrae theologiae*, etc. (Basel: Hervagius, 1567), 305–14. See Jordan J. Ballor, *Covenant, Causality, and Law: A Study in the Theology of Wolfgang Musculus* (Göttingen, Germany: Vandenhoeck & Ruprecht, 2012), 217–23.

[106] Lyle D. Bierma, "Law and Grace in Ursinus' Doctrine of the Natural Covenant: A Reappraisal," in *Protestant Scholasticism: Essays in Reassessment*, ed. Carl R. Trueman and R. Scott Clark (Carlisle, UK: Paternoster, 1999), 96–110.

[107] See Aaron C. Denlinger, *Omnes in Adam ex pacto Dei: Ambrogio Catarino's Doctrine of Covenantal Solidarity and Its Influence on Post-Reformation Reformed Theologians* (Göttingen, Germany: Vandenhoeck & Ruprecht, 2010); Murray, *Imputation of Adam's Sin*, 12; Fesko, *Death in Adam*, 73–74.

[108] Ambrosius Catharinus, *De lapsu* [or *casu*] *hominis et peccato originali*, in *Opuscula* (Lyons, France: M Bonhomme, 1542), 189–190. The table of contents reads "lapsu"; the document itself reads "casu."

covenantal imputation of sin that Catharinus affirmed.[109] The likely background to Catharinus's thought lies with the so-called nominalists, who had employed a covenantal framework in connection with their important distinction between God's absolute and ordained power.[110]

It would be another four decades before Reformed theologians began to develop their own federal schemas, in the final years of the sixteenth century.[111] The first theologian to use the term *foedus operum* (covenant of works) was the English Puritan Dudley Fenner (c. 1558–87), who correlated that prefall covenant with the *foedus gratuitae promissionis* (covenant of gracious promise).[112] Other pioneers of federalism were William Perkins (1558–1602), Robert Rollock (c. 1555–99), and Amandus Polanus von Polansdorf (1561–1610). James Arminius (1560–1609) and his successors in the Remonstrant tradition also employed federal motifs in their theological systems.[113] The height of covenant theology is represented by Johannes Cocceius (1603–69), for whom covenant is an overarching structure to his system and his view of redemptive history.[114]

Within its covenantal schema, Reformed federal theology eventually[115] offered an additional solution to the question of how Adam's individual transgression implicates all of humanity. Perhaps the first to do so was Rollock, in his 1597 *Tractatus de vocatione*.[116] There he writes,

> You will ask where is that effectiveness of this first sin to propagate sin in all and in each individual descendent of Adam? I respond that the effectiveness of this sin comes from a certain word and covenant of God that was stipulated in the initial creation with Adam by these solemn declarations, as it were.[117]

---

[109] Denlinger, *Omnes in Adam*, 11; Fesko, *Death in Adam*, 73–74.

[110] As Denlinger argues, *Omnes in Adam*, 216–31.

[111] See Muller, *Post-Reformation Reformed Dogmatics*, 2:119–23, 206–7; Muller, "Divine Covenants, Absolute and Conditional: John Cameron and the Early Orthodox Development of Reformed Covenant Theology," *Mid-America Journal of Theology* 17 (2006): 11–56; R. Scott Clark, "Christ and Covenant: Federal Theology in Orthodoxy," in *A Companion to Reformed Orthodoxy*, ed. Herman J. Selderhuis (Leiden, Netherlands: Brill, 2013), 403–28.

[112] Dudley Fenner, *Sacra theologia sive veritas qua est secundum pietatem ad unicae et verae methodi leges descripta* (London: T. Dawson, 1585), 4.1, 87–88; see Muller, "Divine Covenants," 21–22.

[113] See Richard A. Muller, "The Federal Motif in Seventeenth-Century Arminian Theology," *Nederlands Archief voor Kerkgeschiedenis* 62.1 (1982): 102–22.

[114] For an introduction to Cocceius's thought, see Willem J. Van Asselt, *The Federal Theology of Johannes Cocceius (1603–1669)*, trans. Raymond A. Blacketer (Leiden, Netherlands: Brill, 2001).

[115] See William Perkins, *A Golden Chain*, in *The Works of William Perkins*, ed. Joel R. Beeke and Derek W. H. Thomas, 10 vols. (Grand Rapids, MI: Reformation Heritage, 2014–20), 6:36.

[116] Robert Rollock, *Tractatus de vocatione efficaci* etc. (Edinburgh: R. Waldegrave, 1597); see Aaron Denlinger's introduction to his translation of Rollock, *Some Questions and Answers about God's Covenant and the Sacrament That Is a Seal of God's Covenant* (Eugene, OR: Pickwick, 2016), 14–15.

[117] Rollock, *Tractatus*, 193–194: "Quaeres unde sit ista efficacia primi illius peccati, ad propagandum peccatum in omnes et singulos Adami posteros? R. efficaciam illius peccati ex verbo et foedere quodam Dei esse quod in prima creatione pepigit cum Adamo, his quasi conceptis verbis."

Nevertheless, Rollock and subsequent federal theologians did not deny the realist or natural connection between Adam and his posterity in the transmission of sin; it was, rather, a matter of both Adam's federal representation, in which God imputes Adam's first sin to all Adam's descendants, and the natural corruption that results from the loss of Adam's original righteousness.[118]

Natural corruption, concupiscence, and the loss of original righteousness continued to figure in Protestant orthodox definitions of sin. Nonetheless, it was common for later Reformed theologians to identify Anselm (and presumably some unnamed Roman Catholic thinkers in their own age) as teaching a "mere privation." Amandus Polanus von Polansdorf, for example, affirms that original sin is "not merely a bare privation or absence of original righteousness that ought to be in human beings, as Anselm has defined it. For our nature is not only empty and destitute of good, but also so prolific and productive of every evil that it cannot be at rest."[119]

Similarly, Francis Turretin (1623–87) claims that the Roman Catholics define sin as a bare privation of original justice, without any positive effect on or corruption of human nature.[120] But even more interesting is that, in his argument to define original sin as both a privation and the corruption of concupiscence, he calls as his star witnesses Thomas Aquinas, followed by Cardinal Cajetan, Peter Lombard, Henry of Ghent (d. 1293), and Gregory of Rimini. Turretin observes that Robert Bellarmine (1542–1621) takes issue with Rimini, but Bellarmine is primarily objecting to the idea of original sin as a created substance.[121] Here again, Turretin's characterization of Roman Catholic teachings on sin seem to be directed at the teachings of some of his Romanist contemporaries.

New controversies provided further impulse to doctrinal refinement. Socinianism, as well as the theology of Jacob Arminius and the Remonstrant party, constituted significant threats to Reformed doctrinal and confessional

---

[118] Denlinger, "Introduction," in Rollock, *Some Questions*, 15–16. See, e.g., Turretin, *Institutes of Elenctic Theology*, 9.9.11 (1:616); Westminster Confession of Faith 6.2–4.

[119] ". . . non est nuda tantum privatio seu carentia iustitiae originalis debita inesse hominibus, ut Anselmus definivit. Non enim natura nostra boni tantum inops et vacua est: sed etiam malorum omnium adeo fertilis et ferax, ut otiosa esse non possit" (*De peccato originis capita aliquot* etc. [Basel: Konrad Waldkirch, 1597], fol. A3 r°).

[120] Turretin, *Institutes of Elenctic Theology*, 9.11.7–23 (1:637–40); cf. 9.1.5–8 (1:592).

[121] Bellarmine here denies that concupiscence is a positive quality in the sense of being a created substance, something that Turretin is also at pains to avoid. Bellarmine accuses the Protestants (specifically Melanchthon) of holding concupiscence to be a created substance (see Bellarmine, *De controversiis Christianae fidei*, the third controversy, *De amissione gratiae et statu peccati*, 5.15, in *Opera Omnia*, 6 vols. in 8 [Naples: J. Giuliano, 1856–1862], 4.1:222–25). De Lubac identifies Bellarmine as the originator of the concept of human beings having both a natural and a supernatural end, the former pertaining to human beings *in puris naturalibus*, but for Bellarmine this is purely a theoretical concept (see de Lubac, *Augustinianism and Modern Theology*, 147–57).

integrity. Once again, the matter at stake was the question of human capacity to contribute to one's salvation. With Arminius and the Remonstrants the issue was not merit and good works, but the free choice and voluntary act of faith. The Remonstrant crisis, like Calvin's conflict with the delegates at Trent, had less to do with the formal elements of the doctrine of sin than with the Remonstrants' insistence that universal grace was available to all persons. In fact, there was nothing overtly objectionable in the third article of the *Remonstrance* (1610), which deals with human depravity. Nevertheless, they held this in common with the late medieval theologians against whom Luther reacted: they claimed that the decisive impetus for salvation lies with human beings.[122]

Theological disputes, however, did not always result in the breaking of fellowship. The French Reformed Academy of Saumur, founded in 1599 and particularly influential between 1635 and 1660, gained a reputation for pushing the boundaries of Reformed doctrine. Scottish theologian John Cameron's (c. 1579–1625) tenure there was followed by Saumur's triumvirate of maverick thinkers.[123] Moïses Amyraut (1596–1664) proposed a theory of hypothetical universalism that created a tremendous stir in the Reformed world; nevertheless, three French synods failed to declare his teachings unorthodox, much to the chagrin of his opponents. Louis Cappel (1585–1658) was a scholar of the Hebrew Scriptures and pioneer of biblical textual criticism who argued that the vowel points of the Masoretic text were a later addition— a theory that to some of his contemporaries seemed to endanger the reliability of Scripture. The third member of this controversial trio was Josué de La Place (1596–1655), whose contribution to Saumur's reputation for testing the limits of Reformed teaching pertained to the doctrine of original sin.

La Place caused a stir by affirming that Adam's sin is passed on to his posterity not by God's immediate imputation of the guilt and punishment for that initial sin to the human race as a whole, but through the corruption of human nature that resulted from the first sin.[124] His views on this matter

---

[122] On Arminius's doctrine of original sin and its development by the Remonstrant party, see Lee Gatiss's contribution to this volume. See also Richard A. Muller, *God, Creation, and Providence in the Thought of Jacob Arminius: Sources and Directions of Scholastic Protestantism in the Era of Early Orthodoxy* (Grand Rapids, MI: Baker, 1991); Keith D. Stanglin and Thomas H. McCall, *Jacob Arminius: Theologian of Grace* (Oxford: Oxford University Press, 2012); and Raymond A. Blacketer, "Arminius's Concept of the Covenant in Its Historical Context," *Nederlands Archief voor Kerkgeschiedenis* 80.2 (2000): 193–220.

[123] On Saumur and its place within the diversity of orthodox Reformed thought, see F. P. van Stam, *The Controversy over the Theology of Saumur, 1635–1650: Disrupting Debates among the Huguenots in Complicated Circumstances* (Amsterdam: APA–Holland University Press, 1988); Muller, *Post-Reformation Reformed Dogmatics*, 1:76–77; 2:123–25.

[124] On La Place and the controversy over his teaching, see Charles Hodge, *Theological Essays: Reprinted from the Princeton Review* (New York: Wiley & Putnam, 1846), 195–96; Hodge, *Systematic Theology*, 3 vols. (New York: Scribner, 1872–73), 2:205–14; Heppe, *Reformed Dogmatics*, 331–34; Murray, *Imputation of Adam's Sin*, 42–46; van

appeared in the published disputations from the Saumur Academy, particularly in his disputation on the state of fallen human beings before or apart from grace.[125] La Place denies that the harm of Adam's sin, the guilt (*culpa*), is passed down merely through imitation, as the Pelagians asserted. He then concludes,

> Therefore, that harm must necessarily be either Adam's actual disobedience itself, which is imputed to us, or a defect arising from that disobedience and inhering in us. The first *cannot be deduced from the sacred writings*, unless it is in this sense, that we are worthy of it on account of the sin inhering in us from the beginning, we who in the same passage (Rom. 5:12) are considered as if we had committed the same disobedience.[126]

Among the numerous reasons La Place marshals for rejecting the imputation of Adam's first sin to the entire human race, he argues (rather soundly) that the phrase ἐφ᾽ ᾧ πάντες ἥμαρτον does not mean "in whom" all sinned but "because of whom" all sinned—a meaning that La Place says is reflected in the Bible translation used in the French Reformed churches. La Place denies that the comparison between Adam and Christ is such that Adam fulfills an office parallel to that of Christ, in which Adam plays the part of our surety and violates the law of God for us or in our place. He notes that Levi may have paid tithes while he was still in Abraham's loins, but this does not mean that either Abraham's sins or his good works were imputed to Levi. Nor does it comport with what Ezekiel says (18:4), that the son shall not bear the sins of the father.[127]

The French Reformed Synod meeting in Charenton (1644–45) responded to complaints about La Place's teaching on this subject. Pierre Bayle relates that Amyraut defended his colleague, even though he did not agree with La Place on this point.[128] Nevertheless, the Synod, without mentioning La Place's name, condemned the doctrine that original sin is wholly defined as

---

Stam, *Controversy*, 178–80, 209–12; Feṣko, *Death in Adam*, 102–108; Anselm Schubert, *Das Ende der Sünde: Anthropologie und Erbsünde zwischen Reformation und Aufklärung*, Forschungen zur Kirchen und Dogmengeschichte (Göttingen, Germany: Vandenhoeck & Ruprecht, 2002), 183–88; Hampton, "Sin, Grace, and Free Choice," 234–35.
[125] Louis Cappel, Moïses Amyraut, and Josué de la Place, *Syntagma thesium theologicarum in Academia Salmuriensi disputatarum*, 2nd ed., 2 vols. (Saumur, France: Jean Lesnier, 1664–65), 1:205–11; cf. the summary in Hampton, "Sin, Grace, and Free Choice," 234.
[126] "Si igitur malum illud necesse est, aut ipsa actualis inobedientia Adami, quae nobis imputetur, aut vitium ex illa natum, nobisque inhaerens. Prius, (nisi hoc sensu, quod ob peccatum nobis ab origine inhaerens digni sumus, qui eodem loco habeamur ac si inobedientiam illam admisissemus,) *Non potest colligi ex Sacris Litteris*" (Cappel, Amyraut, and La Place, *Syntagma*, 1:206, emphasis original).
[127] See Cappel, Amyraut, and La Place, *Syntagma*, 1:206–7.
[128] Pierre Bayle, *The Dictionary Historical and Critical of Mr. Peter Bayle*, 2nd ed., 4 vols. (London: J. J. & P. Knapton, 1734–38), 1:262.

the hereditary corruption of all the descendants of Adam, and that Adam's first transgression is not imputed to Adam's posterity. The Synod prohibited pastors and teachers, on pain of censure, from departing from "the common received opinion of the Protestant churches who (over and besides that corruption) have all acknowledged the imputation of Adam's first sin unto his posterity."[129]

La Place did not back down after the Synod of Charenton's condemnation. Instead, he contended that the Synod's declaration did not apply to his teaching. He denied that he rejected entirely the imputation of Adam's first sin, and, as implausible as that assertion might seem, he justified that denial with a distinction between *immediate* and *mediate imputation*. He published these views a decade after the Synod, in 1655, in a disputation in which he claimed to defend the assembly's declaration. It was there that he distinguished mediate from immediate imputation, which, in Reformed circles at least, was a novelty.[130]

Surprisingly, however, La Place did not invent this distinction. That honor goes to the Gnesio-Lutheran Aegidius Hunnius (1550–1603), who came up with the innovation rather incidentally while trying (and apparently failing) to classify the teaching of the Socinians on original sin.[131] Because Hunnius could not really conceive of the Socinians denying any imputation of Adam's sin to humanity whatsoever, which in fact they did, he presumed that they must have taught a direct or immediate imputation, as opposed to the Lutheran emphasis on the corruption of nature, which he classifies as mediate imputation.[132] This connection deserves further study, as does La Place's theology in general, which remains largely unmined by scholarly research.

At the next and last of the French National Synods, that of Loudun in 1659, some of the French churches urged rather insistently that Charenton's article condemning mediate imputation be moderated, but the Synod, on the contrary, reaffirmed its previous decision and prohibited preaching or publishing anything that would contradict the imputation of sin as described by Charenton.[133] La Place had died by this time, but some theologians in

---

[129] See John Quick, *Synodicon in Gallia reformata, or, The Acts, Decisions, Decrees, and Canons of Those Famous National Councils of the Reformed Churches in France*, 2 vols. (London: T. Parkhurst & J. Robinson, 1692), 2:473–74.

[130] Josué de la Place, *De imputatione primi peccati Adami . . . disputatio* (Saumur, France, 1655).

[131] See Schubert, *Das Ende der Sünde*, 178–82.

[132] See Aegidius Hunnius, *Articulus de peccato* etc., in *Operum Latinorum*, ed. H. Garthius, 5 vols. (Wittenberg: G. Muller, 1607–9), 1:445.

[133] Quick, *Synodicon*, 2:532, and note the statement on p. 500 in the summary, printed in the wrong place: "The Canons about the Imputation of Adam's Sin not to be altered." This seems to contradict the assertion by Brian G. Armstrong that at the Synod "the condemnation of La Place's views of the imputation of Adam's sin was . . .

the Reformed world had reacted strongly against La Place, just as they did against Saumur's other leading lights, Amyraut and Cappel. Reformed leaders in Geneva and the Netherlands were highly suspicious of the Saumur theology and its influence,[134] and Turretin engaged in an extended polemic against La Place's views in his *Institutes of Elenctic Theology.*[135] Interestingly, both La Place and Turretin claimed the support of Calvin for their position.[136] André Rivet (1572–1651) was a fierce opponent of La Place, and he compiled a large catalogue of excerpts from Reformed thinkers intended to demonstrate that La Place's views were foreign and novel, though many of the statements Rivet collected had no real bearing on the issue.[137]

Those in Zürich, Geneva, and the Netherlands who were concerned that the new ideas emanating from Saumur were eroding Reformed orthodoxy were of the opinion that its teachings should be proscribed by means of a confessional statement. The Helvetic Consensus Formula (1675) was designed for just that purpose.[138] Though the leading lights had all died, their ideas continued on in such thinkers as Alexander Morus (1616–70), who had been appointed to succeed Friedrich Spanheim (1600–49) as professor of theology in Geneva. Opposition from the more conservative thinkers such as Turretin forced Morus out of Geneva, but his replacement also espoused the tendencies of Saumur. Johannes Heidegger (1633–98), with Turretin's assistance, composed this confessional codicil to exclude the more controversial teachings of Amyraut, La Place, and Cappel. It rejected hypothetical universalism, affirmed the immediate imputation of Adam's sin, affirmed the integrity of the vowel points in the Hebrew Masoretic text, and enshrined the covenant of works in a confessional document as the Presbyterians had done at Westminster. But it was too late. The document was embraced only within Switzerland and was controversial even there; Geneva itself was the last to adopt it. Its

---

somewhat softened" (*Calvinism and the Amyraut Heresy; Protestant Scholasticism and Humanism in Seventeenth-Century France* [Madison. University of Wisconsin Press, 1969], 118; as well as the claim that at the synod "La Place's views were accepted," made by James T. Dennison Jr., "The Life and Career of Francis Turretin," in Turretin, *Institutes of Elenctic Theology*, 3:645). Again, further study is needed.

[134] See van Stam, *Controversy*; Dennison, "Life and Career of Francis Turretin," 643–45.

[135] Turretin, *Institutes of Elenctic Theology*, 9.9.4–45 (1:614–29).

[136] Amyraut had done the same, perhaps with less justification, for his views on hypothetical universalism.

[137] André Rivet, *Decretum synodi nationalis ecclesiarum in Gallia reformatum. . . . De imputatione primi peccati omnibus Adami posteris* etc. (Geneva: Chouët, 1647); cf. Fesko, *Death in Adam*, 103–4; Murray, *Imputation of Adam's Sin*, 45–46. Hodge translates most of this treatise in *Theological Essays*, 195–217.

[138] On this document, and for what follows, see Martin I. Klauber, "The Helvetic Formula Consensus (1675): An Introduction and Translation," *t11.1* (1990): 103–23; Richard A. Muller, "The Debate over the Vowel Points and the Crisis in Orthodox Hermeneutics," *Journal of Medieval and Renaissance Studies* 10.1 (1980): 53–72; Philip Schaff, *The Creeds of Christendom*, 6th ed., 3 vols. (1931; repr., Grand Rapids, MI: Baker, 1993), 1:477–89.

limited influence lasted only about half a century, until, as Philip Schaff so vividly narrates, it "was allowed to die and be buried without mourners."[139] Nevertheless, the question of the imputation of Adam's sin continued to be a matter of debate, even long after the waning of Reformed orthodoxy. The American revivalist Jonathan Edwards (1703–58) attempted to represent the essence of the old Reformed faith adapted to the new philosophical milieu of the Enlightenment. Whether he was successful in this is a matter of considerable controversy.[140] Edwards's last work appeared after his untimely death following a smallpox inoculation in 1758. In *The Great Christian Doctrine of Original Sin Defended*, Edwards attempted to deflect charges by deists and rationalists, particularly the English dissenter John Taylor (1694–1761), who attacked the traditional doctrine as unreasonable and unjust.[141]

Edwards's doctrinal project has been aptly characterized as "an attempt to re-envision Reformed theology using aspects of early Enlightenment philosophy,"[142] particularly the thought of G. W. Leibniz, John Locke, and David Hume. Edwards's willingness freely to embrace aspects of the rationalist philosophy of his day[143] resulted in a "fully deterministic" approach to God's sovereignty, one that effectively eliminated any meaningful human choice,[144] and to which the Reformed tradition "owes much of its reputation for being a form of determinism or compatibilism."[145] The charge that Edwards

---

[139] Schaff, *Creeds of Christendom*, 1:486.
[140] On Edwards's teachings, particularly on occasionalism and original sin, see Murray, *Imputation of Adam's Sin*, 52–64; Fesko, *Death in Adam*, 115–19; Clyde A. Holbrook, "Editor's Introduction," in Jonathan Edwards, *Original Sin*, ed. Holbrook, vol. 3 of *The Works of Jonathan Edwards*, 26 vols. (New Haven, CT: Yale University Press, 1970), 1–101, esp. 53–60; Holbrook, "Jonathan Edwards Addresses Some 'Modern Critics' of Original Sin," *Journal of Religion* 63.3 (1983): 211–30; C. Samuel Storms, *Tragedy in Eden: Original Sin in the Theology of Jonathan Edwards* (Lanham, MD: University Press of America, 1985); Robert W. Jenson, *America's Theologian: A Recommendation of Jonathan Edwards* (New York: Oxford University Press, 1988), 143–53; Paul Helm, "Jonathan Edwards on Original Sin," in Helm, *Faith and Understanding* (Edinburgh: Edinburgh University Press, 1997), 152–76; Helm, "A Forensic Dilemma: John Locke and Jonathan Edwards on Personal Identity," in *Jonathan Edwards: Philosophical Theologian*, ed. Paul Helm and Oliver D. Crisp (Aldershot, UK: Ashgate, 2003), 45–60; Michael J. McClymond and Gerald R. McDermott, *The Theology of Jonathan Edwards* (New York: Oxford University Press, 2011), 339–56; Oliver D. Crisp and Kyle C. Strobel, *Jonathan Edwards: An Introduction to His Thought* (Grand Rapids, MI: Eerdmans, 2018), esp. 106–20; Oliver D. Crisp, "Jonathan Edwards on the Imputation of Sin," in Crisp, *Retrieving Doctrine: Essays in Reformed Theology* (Downers Grove, IL: IVP Academic, 2010), 47–68; Crisp, "Edwards on Original Sin: Another Look," in Crisp, *Jonathan Edwards among the Theologians* (Grand Rapids, MI: Eerdmans, 2015), 107–23; Michael Allen, "Jonathan Edwards and the Lapsarian Debate," *SJT* 62.3 (2009): 299–315.
[141] John Taylor, *The Scripture-Doctrine of Original Sin Proposed to Free and Candid Examination* (London: J. Wilson, 1740).
[142] Crisp, *Jonathan Edwards among the Theologians*, 4.
[143] See Edwards, *Freedom of the Will*, ed. Paul Ramsey, vol. 1 of *The Works of Jonathan Edwards*, 26 vols. (New Haven, CT: Yale University Press, 1957), 372–75.
[144] Richard A. Muller, "Goading the Determinists: Thomas Goad (1576–1638) on Necessity, Contingency, and God's Eternal Decree," *Mid-America Journal of Theology* 26 (2015): 59–75 (75); and see Muller, "Jonathan Edwards and the Absence of Free Choice: A Parting of Ways in the Reformed Tradition," *Jonathan Edwards Studies* 1.1 (2011): 3–22; Muller, "Jonathan Edwards and Francis Turretin on Necessity, Contingency, and Freedom of Will: In Response to Paul Helm," *Jonathan Edwards Studies* 4.3 (2014): 266–85.
[145] Muller, "Jonathan Edwards and the Absence of Free Choice," 21.

made God the author of sin appeared already in the eighteenth century, most notably from his determined opponent James Dana (1735–1812), whose two volumes refuting Edward's *Freedom of the Will* was "the single longest piece of sustained philosophical invective in eighteenth-century American literature."[146]

Numerous conflicting interpretations of Edwards's thought have arisen from the fact that Edwards discusses traditional doctrines but jettisons the traditional philosophical categories that underlay them, including something as essential to the entire history of Christian thought as secondary causality, while adopting nineteenth-century rationalist metaphysics. Most notable is Edwards's novel and speculative doctrine of continuous creation, or occasionalism. Edwards asserts that God is the sole and immediate cause of all things; there is no secondary causality. Moreover, all things exist for a mere moment of time, and God re-creates the entire creation *ex nihilo* moment-by-moment. These individual moments are not related causally to each other, nor are objects or persons in successive moments identical except by God declaring them to be so.[147] All continuity of identity depends on "an arbitrary constitution of the Creator."[148] This occasionalism enables Edwards to treat all of humanity as a single agent,[149] thus solving, he thinks, the objection that God's imputation of Adam's sin to all humanity is unjust. All human beings are identical with Adam by God's declaration, and thus all human beings consented to and concurred with Adam's sin, and so God imputes this sin to all.[150] The apostasy of Adam does not belong to the whole human race "merely because God imputes it to them; but it is truly and properly theirs, and on that ground, God imputes it to them."[151] In contrast to those who claim that Edwards advocated either the mediate or immediate imputation of Adam's sin, Edwards incorporates elements of both in his thought, aspects of both federal headship and realist solidarity, and yet he goes considerably beyond them by means of his unique—if dubious and problematic—metaphysics.[152]

It is difficult to see how this metaphysic, denying as it does any real causality on the creaturely level, can avoid making God the author of sin, and

---

[146] Allen C. Guelzo, "From Calvinist Metaphysics to Republican Theory: Jonathan Edwards and James Dana on Freedom of the Will," *Journal of the History of Ideas* 56.3 (1995): 399–418 (400).

[147] Crisp, *Retrieving Doctrine*, 66 and n. 44; Fesko, *Death in Adam*, 118; McClymond and McDermott, *Theology of Jonathan Edwards*, 351–52.

[148] Edwards, *Original Sin*, 399.

[149] See Crisp, *Retrieving Doctrine*, 66–68; Jenson, *America's Theologian*, 150.

[150] McClymond and McDermott, *Theology of Jonathan Edwards*, 352.

[151] Edwards, *Original Sin*, 408.

[152] As Crisp argues (*Retrieving Doctrine*, 47–68; cf. Fesko, *Death in Adam*, 115–19).

human choices less than authentic choices, a fact that leads Thomas McCall to go so far as to conclude that for Edwards, as the only causal agent "God is the only sinner," and that these "implications are outrageous. Indeed, they are blasphemous."[153]

In addition to raising this theological concern, Edwards's deterministic view of God's sovereignty, along with the fact that he at best strongly relativizes human choice and agency, has profound implications for Christian experience, despite Edwards's famous emphasis on the religious affections. Ironically, Edwards's system has the potential to result in a view of reality that is not vastly different from the deism he set out to counter, in that it elevates God so far above creaturely existence and agency that there is little room left in Christian experience for genuine lament or robust questioning of God, which are both profoundly biblical themes. Edwards commends desiring God for his own sake in a way that he himself finds intoxicating, but which may leave an ordinary believer feeling more isolated from their Creator and Redeemer.[154]

Edwards's solution vastly complicates a matter that was relatively more straightforward for the Reformers and their successors in the era of Protestant Orthodoxy, though not without its difficulties and unexplained enigmas. Through Adam's transgression, the entire human race is rendered sinful and liable to just condemnation before God, so much so that sinners do not desire, nor are their wills sound enough to choose faith in Christ and repentance. Sinners have lost the gifts of righteousness and integrity, and all their faculties are corrupted and disordered. Thus, only an intervention by the Holy Spirit can bring about conversion. This act depends entirely on the Spirit because sin, as the Reformers and their successors affirmed, renders persons morally and spiritually helpless. Their doctrine of original sin, then, serves to highlight the centrality of divine grace in salvation.

---

[153] Thomas H. McCall, "Divine Providence," in *T&T Clark Companion to the Doctrine of Sin*, ed. Keith L. Johnson and David Lauber (London: Bloomsbury T&T Clark, 2016), 328. Elsewhere McCall observes that "[John] Wesley is arguably in closer continuity with the confessional Reformed tradition than is Edwards. For while Wesley defends the treatment of hamartiology in the Westminster Confession of Faith (1646)—even down to the details of the federalist account of imputation—Edwards is more willing to diverge in creative ways" (McCall, *Against God and Nature*, 24).
[154] The author has observed congregants pastored by advocates of a Christian hedonism who were left cold and uncomfortable by this modern manifestation of Edwardsean theology.

Sin and the Synod of Dort

Lee Gatiss

Missionary Concern in the Canons of Dort

Hadrian Saravia (1532–1613) was an evangelist, and later professor of theology at Leiden in the United Provinces of the Netherlands. He helped to draw up the Belgic Confession, to which members of the Dutch church subscribed.[1] In his book *De Diversis Gradibus Ministrorum Evangelii* (1590) he asserted of Matthew 28:18–20 that,

> The injunction to preach the gospel to all nations of unbelievers had respect not only to the age of the Apostles, but to all ages to come till the end of the world. . . . Christ commanded his Church to provide that the Gospel should be preached to unbelievers, after the departure of the Apostles, according as opportunities of time, place, and persons should admit.[2]

Saravia wondered, however, whether the lack of world mission in his day was due to "a lack of persons fit to be sent" or "a lack of zeal for the extension of Christ's kingdom."[3] Global evangelism had not yet become a major concern of the Protestant powers of Europe, for various reasons.[4]

---

[1] See Frederick Calder, *Memoirs of Simon Episcopius* (London, 1838), 116, on Saravia's letter to Uitenbogaerdt to this effect.

[2] Hadrian Saravia, *A Treatise on the Different Degrees of the Christian Priesthood* (Oxford: John Henry Parker, 1840), 161–62.

[3] Saravia, *Treatise*, 164–65.

[4] I have explored some of the reasons for the slowness of Protestant missionary activity outside of Europe in Lee Gatiss, *Light after Darkness: How the Reformers Regained, Retold, and Relied on the Gospel of Grace* (Fearn, Ross-shire, UK: Christian Focus, 2019), 73–82.

Yet in the twenty-five years leading up to the Synod of Dort, all of that was changing. Dutch merchants began to build an impressive commercial empire in Southern Africa, South America, and especially the East Indies. Having first captured control of the distribution networks for Portuguese pepper and spice imports, Dutch companies were by 1601 sending out larger and larger fleets, and far outstripping the Portuguese and British in the East Indian trade. This culminated at the end of May 1619, just as the Synod of Dort was ending, in the Dutch seizure of Jakarta in Indonesia, and the founding of Batavia—"the foremost European military, naval, and commercial base in Asia."[5] The Dutch Reformed Church had a monopoly as the sole public church in Dutch colonies, but they were soon organizing church services not only in Dutch and Portuguese but also in Malay. As influential pastor Willem Teellinck (1578–1629) put it, "the Lord our great God has not opened up for us these Lands and Coasts only so that we may obtain temporal treasures from them, but also, and much more, so that we would bring our spiritual treasures to them, and *to preach to the Gentiles the unsearchable riches of Christ* (Eph. 3:8)."[6] In the Maluku Islands, the Reformed faith went wherever the Dutch did. As Jonathan Israel states, "Calvinism in Amboina, preached in Malay, put down enduring roots."[7] In Ceylon, many Tamils and Sinhalese were converted to the Reformed faith, as also were many non-Christians living on islands off the coast of China.

This turning outward of the Dutch is reflected in the delegates who assembled for the Synod of Dort in 1618. Antonius Walaeus (1573–1639), a Dutch delegate at the Synod, for example, was even commissioned to establish a missionary training college at Leiden.[8] The theologians and pastors assembled for that international ecumenical gathering were very much aware of issues that are raised when the gospel enters new territory. One of their first discussions was about the baptism of the children of heathens, which they hoped to decide upon quickly because ships were just about to leave for

---

[5] Jonathan Israel, *The Dutch Republic: Its Rise, Greatness, and Fall* (Oxford: Clarendon, 1998), 319–23.
[6] Willem Teellinck, *Ecce Homo, ofte Ooghen-Salve voor die noch sitten in blintheyt des Ghemoets* (Middelburg, Netherlands, 1622), 15, as translated in Chauncey Knegt, "That Christ Be Honored: The Push for Foreign Missions in the Seventeenth-Century Reformed Church in the Netherlands," in *Puritan Reformed Journal* 10.2 (2018): 263–77, 272. On the next page, Teellinck anchored the need for world evangelism in Matt. 28, as Saravia had and as Johannes Hoornbeek would also do later in *De Convincendis et Convertendis Judaeis et Gentilibus Libri VIII* (1655) and *De Conversione Indorum et Gentium Libri Duo* (1669), along with Gisbertus Voetius in his *Politica Ecclesiastica* (1676).
[7] Israel, *Dutch Republic*, 953.
[8] See Michael Laffan, *The Makings of Indonesian Islam: Orientalism and the Narration of a Sufi Past* (Princeton, NJ: Princeton University Press, 2011), 70.

the East Indies on the next fair wind.[9] One of their final acts was to implore the government that,

> Whereas all true Christians, through the Love which they ought to bear for the spread of God's glory among mankind, and for the salvation of their neighbours, are obliged to use every means for this end, and [whereas] the Lords of these lands have opened up the way to various Lands in the Indies and elsewhere, which are destitute of the true and saving knowledge of God, therefore it is the Synod's humble petition, that their Excellencies might be pleased, with Christian seriousness and zeal, to tend to these matters, devise plans, and take in hand every means as shall be serviceable and most apt for achieving the goal of the propagation of the holy Gospel in these Lands.[10]

This missionary concern is especially apparent in the Synod's pronouncements on the "Third and Fourth Heads of Doctrine" concerning the corruption of humans and their conversion to God.[11] It is indeed essential background for understanding Dort. For example, the Synod insisted that all humans are made in the image of God and were originally pure in mind, will, and affections,[12] and yet since the fall are all conceived in sin.[13] Some light of nature remains in them, as can be seen from experience, and yet this does not bring them a saving knowledge of God or enable them to convert to him.[14] As the Canons say, "What neither the light of nature nor the law could do, God accomplished by the power of the Holy Spirit. Through preaching or the ministry of reconciliation—which is the gospel of the Messiah—God is pleased to save humans who believe."[15] But why is this gospel revealed to some (e.g., the Dutch, the British, the Swiss) and not to others (the Hindus, Buddhists, Muslims, and others) whom they had encountered in their colonial adventures? God reveals the mystery of his will "to many without any distinction among the peoples," say the Canons, i.e., there is nothing in the

---

[9] See Donald Sinnema, Christian Moser, and Herman J. Selderhuis, eds., *Acta et Documenta Synodi Nationalis Dordrechtanae (1618 1619)*, vol. 1 *Acta of the Synod of Dort* (Göttingen, Germany: Vandenhoeck & Ruprecht, 2015), 1:30 (November 30, 1618).

[10] See, *Acta et Documenta Synodi Nationalis Dordrechtanae*, 1:181 (May 27, 1619). See Knegt, "That Christ Be Honored," 267, for the translation. See also Justus Heurnius, *De Legatione Evangelica ad Indos Capessenda Admonitio* (Groningen, Netherlands, 1618) for an admonition to undertake gospel mission to the Indies, dedicated to the political and commercial authorities in the year the Synod of Dort began.

[11] It can also be seen in the individual papers on the Third and Fourth Heads of Doctrine submitted by the delegations. E.g., those from Emden were concerned about Indians, Chinese, Turks, Tartars, Brazilians, Peruvians, and others (*Acta*, 2:229).

[12] Canons of Dort, 3/4.1. The text of the Canons here is taken throughout from the new translation in W. Robert Godfrey, *Saving the Reformation: The Pastoral Theology of the Canons of Dort* (Sanford, FL: Reformation Trust, 2019).

[13] Canons of Dort, 3/4.3.

[14] Canons of Dort, 3/4.4.

[15] Canons of Dort, 3/4.6.

gospel about racial superiority or God's preference for any particular people groups. "The cause of this dispensation is not in the value of one nation above others or the better use of the light of nature. It results from the most free good pleasure and gracious love of God."[16]

The frustrations of missionary activity are also acknowledged in the Canons. Many are seriously called through the gospel, but not all will come to Christ and be converted. Why? "The fault for this is not in the gospel," they said clearly, "nor in Christ offered in the gospel, nor in God who calls them through the gospel and who confers gifts on them. Rather, the fault lies in those called."[17] So why is it that others, as the parable of the sower predicts, do actually come to Christ and bear fruit? Is it something within them, that makes this possible? No, said the Canons, "This cannot be ascribed to man as if by his free will he distinguishes himself from others provided with equal or sufficient grace for faith and conversion." It is all down to God. There ought to be no sense of spiritual superiority among Christians encountering non-Christian cultures, as the Dutch (and others) were now doing with increasing frequency. "We ought in no way to be haughty toward those who do not believe as if we made ourselves to differ," said the Synod.[18] The Bible's teaching on the universalism of sin undercuts white supremacy, European exceptionalism, and all spiritual pride. And yet we are still impelled by the gospel to proclaim the truth of Christ to those who do not know him. When William Carey was told in the eighteenth century that if God wanted to convert the heathen he would do it without his help, he famously wrote a book about God's use of means, and then just got on with it.[19] Yet the Canons of Dort said exactly the same in 1619:

> The omnipotent work of God, by which He produces and sustains our natural life, does not exclude but rather requires the use of means. . . . So also this supernatural work of God, which was described before, by which He regenerates us, does not at all exclude or overturn the use of the gospel. The most wise God ordained the gospel as the seed of regeneration and the food of the soul.[20]

Thus, I think it is clear that, lying behind the formulations of the Canons of Dort on human corruption and conversion, is a desire to foster and

---

[16] Canons of Dort, 3/4.7.
[17] Canons of Dort, 3/4.8–9.
[18] Canons of Dort, 3/4.15.
[19] William Carey, *An Enquiry into the Obligations of Christians to Use Means for the Conversion of the Heathens* (1792; repr., London: Carey Kingsgate, 1961), iii.
[20] Canons of Dort, 3/4.17.

encourage gospel missions, and to rightly understand the task theologically. That these clarifying and invigorating statements should be made by a group of gathered theologians at precisely the time when the Protestant and Reformed powers of Europe were beginning to exert themselves on the world's trading stage is an instance of singular providence.[21] Yet it was by no means inevitable that the Reformed churches should take this view of things. The Synod of Dort had gathered, after all, to assess a challenge to the Reformed doctrine of sin and conversion from the Remonstrants and others, including some who taught that eternal life was not necessarily found in Christ alone, and could be obtained apart from a knowledge of him.[22] To understand better what the Canons of Dort were saying, therefore, it is necessary to examine the alternative teaching on the fall and the effects of sin that they were opposing and why it was considered such a threat.

Arminius's Doctrine of Sin

It is usually assumed that the theology of James Arminius (1559–1609) is what prompted the Reformed response at the Synod of Dort. It may, therefore, be a surprise to learn how Augustinian a doctrine of original sin and its effects Arminius himself had. For example, consider this statement in his *Declaration of Sentiments*:

> This is my opinion concerning the Free-will of man: *In his primitive condition* as he came out of the hands of his Creator, man was endowed with such a portion of knowledge, holiness and power, as enabled him to understand, esteem, consider, will, and to perform THE TRUE GOOD, according to the commandment delivered to him. Yet none of these acts could he do, *except through the assistance of Divine Grace.* But in his *lapsed and sinful state*, man is not capable, of and by himself, either to think, to will, or to do that which is really good; but it is necessary for him to be regenerated and renewed in his intellect, affections or will, and in all his powers, by God in Christ through the Holy Spirit, that he may be qualified rightly to understand,

---

[21] Alas, Dutch and British colonists did not all take to heart what the Canons of Dort taught. See Godfrey, *Saving the Reformation*, 112, who says, "At the heart of European failures was their profound sense of their superiority to the peoples they colonized and enslaved. How different that history might have been had those Europeans really grasped the teaching here and understood that they were not more worthy than others in the eyes of God. Then they might have embraced the virtue of humility implied in this teaching. Very regrettably, many Calvinists were no better than most non-Calvinists in really living out this teaching."

[22] Calder, *Memoirs of Simon Episcopius*, 221–22, on the Dutch minister Venator, whose book *Theologia Vera et Mera Infantium et Lactantium in Christo* (1616) was accused of speaking against "the absolute necessity of the reception of Christianity, in order to salvation . . . thereby intimating that Jews, Turks, or Heathens, as well as all sorts of Christians, may be admitted to eternal life, which is contrary to Scripture." Venator was a supporter of Episcopius, and his book was endorsed by Uitenbogaerdt, the leading Remonstrant.

esteem, consider, will, and perform whatever is truly good. When he is made a partaker of this regeneration or renovation, I consider that, since he is delivered from sin, he is capable of thinking, willing and doing that which is good, but yet *not without the continued aids of Divine Grace*.[23]

He uses the same faculty psychology as the Canons of Dort: humans possess intellect, will, and affections.[24] Furthermore, the fall affects our whole being: "in his lapsed and sinful state, man is not capable, of and by himself, either to think, to will, or to do that which is really good; but it is necessary for him to be regenerated and renewed in his intellect, affections or will, and in all his powers," says Arminius here. As William den Boer points out, "In connection with the results of the fall and original sin, Arminius makes it clear that the will is not just injured, but is trapped, ruined and useless. It has lost its freedom, and is powerless without the aid of grace."[25] In a public letter of 1608, Arminius also wrote, "I confess that the mind of a natural and carnal man is obscure and dark, that his affections are corrupt and inordinate, that his will is stubborn and disobedient, and that the man himself is dead in sins."[26] This is why Keith Stanglin and Thomas McCall can assert that,

> Although Arminius never uses the phrase *total depravity*, nevertheless he teaches precisely what later Reformed writers mean when they use this phrase: the damage is "total" in the sense that no aspect of human nature—especially the intellect, will, and affections—remains unaffected and that no one is able to merit salvation.[27]

Arminius taught that the sin of Adam and Eve offended and displeased God. It also led to a twofold infliction of punishment: first, they became liable to two deaths; and second, the Holy Spirit was removed from them. Furthermore,

---

[23] James Arminius, *The Works of James Arminius*, trans. James Nichols and W. R. Bagnall, 3 vols. (London, 1825; repr. Grand Rapids, MI: Baker, 1956), 1:252–53, emphasis original.

[24] Canons of Dort, 3/4.1. Most of the delegations at Dort had identified these powers in the soul, using a variety of Latin terms in their submissions. E.g., in *Acta Synodi Nationalis* (Dort, 1620 [hereafter *Acta*]), 2:178, the Palatinate delegates refer to *mens*, *voluntas*, and *affectus*; in *Acta*, 2:192, the Swiss refer to *intellectus*, *voluntas*, and *affectus*; and in *Acta*, 2:185–86, the Hessians refer to *intellectus*, *voluntate*, and *cor*.

[25] William den Boer, *God's Twofold Love: The Theology of Jacob Arminius*, Reformed Historical Theology 14 (Göttingen, Germany: Vandenhoeck & Ruprecht, 2010), 188.

[26] "Fateor mentem Hominis animalis & carnalis esse obscuratam, affectus pravos & inordinates, voluntatem immorigeram, hominemque in peccatis esse mortuum" (from Arminius's Letter to Hippolytus a Collibus, in Arminius, *Opera Theologica* [Leiden, Netherlands, 1629], 944; cf. den Boer, *God's Twofold Love*, 199).

[27] Keith D. Stanglin and Thomas H. McCall, *Jacob Arminius: Theologian of Grace* (Oxford: Oxford University Press, 2012), 150.

The whole of this sin, however, is not peculiar to our first parents, but is common to the entire race and to all their posterity, who, at the time when this sin was committed, were in their loins, and who have since descended from them by the natural mode of propagation, according to the primitive benediction.[28]

All sinned in Adam, and became children of wrath (liable to both temporal and eternal death), devoid of original righteousness and holiness. Arminius was happy with the language of covenant theology here:

> the condition of the covenant into which God entered with our first parents was this, that, if they continued in the favor and grace of God by an observance of this command and of others, the gifts conferred on them should be transmitted to their posterity, by the same divine grace which they had, themselves, received; but that, if by disobedience they rendered themselves unworthy of those blessings, their posterity, likewise, [*carerent*] should not possess them, and should be [*obnoxii*] liable to the contrary evils.[29]

This is why everyone who is naturally descended from Adam is liable to "death temporal and death eternal" as well as being "devoid of this gift of the Holy Spirit or original righteousness." This, Arminius says, is the punishment known as original sin. In all this, Arminius considered himself part of the church catholic in its stance against Pelagius.[30] Arminius's follower, the classical historian Gerhard Johann Vossius (1577–1649), who grew up in Dort and later taught at Leiden, summarized the doctrine in his well-timed history of the Pelagian controversy:

> The catholic church has always thus judged: That that first sin is imputed to all, that is, by the just judgment of God, as to its effects, it is transmitted to all the sons of Adam: and the Church believed the effects of it to be that it is on that account that we are born destitute of original righteousness, subject to the necessity of death, and liable to eternal separation from God.[31]

---

[28] Arminius, *Works*, 1:485–86.

[29] Arminius, *Works*, 2:78–79.

[30] Stanglin and McCall, *Jacob Arminius*, 159–64, make a good case against seeing Arminius as Pelagian, an identification he himself rejected. Rustin E. Brian, *Jacob Arminius: The Man from Oudewater* (Eugene, OR: Cascade, 2015), 83, also rejects this, although John S. Knox, *Jacobus Arminius Stands His Ground* (Eugene, OR: Wipf & Stock, 2018), 77, concedes that some identified as Arminians later are in fact more properly Pelagian. In *Works*, 1:324, Arminius accuses the Reformed of Pelagianism.

[31] Gerhard Johann Vossius, *Historiæ de Controversiis, Quas Pelagius Eiusque Reliquiæ Moverunt, Libri Septem* (Leiden, Netherlands, 1618), 1.ii p. 1 th. 1, 134. I am indebted to Samuel David Fornecker, "Arminianism and Anti-Remonstrant Polemic in the Later Stuart and Early Hanoverian Church of England" (unpublished PhD diss., University of Cambridge, 2019), 110, for the translation.

Arminius was not so sure, however, whether there was something else besides the absence of original righteousness, which was part of original sin. "We think it much more probable," he said, "that this absence of original righteousness, only, is original sin itself, as being that which alone is sufficient to commit and produce any actual sins whatsoever."[32] Was there also a "certain infused habit" contrary to righteousness in human nature, as Aquinas and others had discussed?[33] Though Arminius may at first have thought that there *is* a positive corruption in us which replaces righteousness,[34] his more mature teaching was that privation alone was sufficient, without this "certain corrupt habit" being added to it as well. Stanglin and McCall are right therefore to conclude that "Arminius, in his doctrine of original sin, stresses deprivation more than depravation."[35] He was not alone in this (medieval scholastics such as John Duns Scotus and William of Ockham had thought the same), but most Reformed theologians would have asserted with Augustine and Lombard that original sin is concupiscence, a disordered desire not focused on God, as well as a privation of some sort. As Article 9 of the Thirty-Nine Articles summarized the Reformed doctrine, original sin is

> the fault and corruption of the Nature of every man, that naturally is engendered of the offspring of Adam; whereby man is very far gone from original righteousness, and is of his own nature inclined to evil, so that the flesh lusteth always contrary to the Spirit; and therefore in every person born into this world, it deserveth [*meretur*] God's wrath and damnation.[36]

---

[32] Arminius, *Works*, 2:79.

[33] Arminius, *Works*, 2:492. Thomas Aquinas, *Summa Theologiae* 1a2ae, 82, discusses the question of whether original sin is a habit (*habitus*), concluding that in the sense of being a disposition of a complex nature, which becomes ill-disposed to righteousness, like a second nature, original sin *is* a habit. It is a disordered disposition which comes from the dissolution of that harmony in which original righteousness is reckoned to consist ("Et hoc modo peccatum originale est habitus. Est enim quaedam inordinata dispositio proveniens ex dissolutione illius harmoniae in qua consistebat ratio originalis iustitiae.") Responding to Anselm, who spoke of original sin as a privation (a taking away), Aquinas said it was not *purely* a privation but *also* a certain corrupt habit ("Unde non est privatio pura, sed est quidam habitus corruptus").

[34] Arminius's *Public Disputation* 32 (sections 5–6) emphasizes both absence of righteousness and presence of positive corruption in us, but there may be some doubts as to the authenticity of this disputation or of Arminius's authorship of it. See Keith D. Stanglin, *The Missing Public Disputations of Jacobus Arminius: Introduction, Texts, and Notes* (Leiden, Netherlands: Brill, 2010), 43–100, 75–81.

[35] Stanglin and McCall, *Jacob Arminius*, 149; cf. Carl Bangs, *Arminius: A Study in the Dutch Reformation* (Nashville: Abingdon, 1971), 339.

[36] Articles 14 and 15 of the Belgic Confession speak similarly: Mankind "by sin separated himself from God, who was his true life, having corrupted his whole nature, whereby he made himself liable to corporal and spiritual death. And being thus become wicked, perverse, and corrupt in all his ways, he hath lost all his excellent gifts which he had received from God, and only retained a few remains thereof. . . . Therefore we reject all that is taught repugnant to this concerning the free will of man, since man is but a slave to sin. . . . We believe that, through the disobedience of Adam, original sin is extended to all mankind; which is a corruption of the whole nature [*totius naturæ*

As well as denying half of this definition, Arminius also said that original sin is punishment (*poena*) but not liability or guilt (*reatus* or *culpa*).[37] This would lead some to conclude that Arminius thought original sin does not merit condemnation as such.[38] Yet the upshot of all this is an emphasis on the grace of God. "Arminius emphasized the total inability of humans to turn to God on their own. The natural person does not will the good, indeed *cannot* will, think, or do the good," say Stanglin and McCall, so that, "Between Arminius and his Reformed contemporaries there is no real difference regarding the event of sin and the need for grace."[39]

Arminius's view seems to be summed up well in the third article of the *Remonstrance* (1610), written just after his death, which states:

> That man has not saving grace [faith, *fidem*] of himself, nor of the energy of his free will [*liberi arbitrii*], inasmuch as he, in the state of apostasy and sin, can of and by himself neither think, will, nor do anything that is truly good (such as saving Faith eminently is); but that it is needful that he be born again of God in Christ, through his Holy Spirit, and renewed in understanding, inclination, or will, and all his powers, in order that he may rightly understand, think, will, and effect what is truly good, according to the Word of Christ, John 15:5: "Without me ye can do nothing."[40]

Article 4 continues:

> That this grace of God is the beginning, continuance, and accomplishment of all good, even to this extent, that the regenerate man himself, without prevenient or assisting, awakening, following and co-operative grace, can neither think, will, nor do good, nor withstand any temptations to evil; so that all good deeds or movements, that can be conceived, must be ascribed to the grace of God in Christ.[41]

---

corruptio], and an hereditary disease, wherewith infants themselves are infected even in their mother's womb, and which produceth in man all sorts of sin, being in him as a root thereof; and therefore is so vile and abominable in the sight of God that it is sufficient to condemn all mankind. Wherefore we reject the error of the Pelagians, who assert that sin proceeds only from imitation" (quoted from Schaff, ed., *The Creeds of Christendom, with a History and Critical Notes: The Evangelical Protestant Creeds, with Translations*, 3 vols. [New York: Harper & Brothers, 1882], 3:399–401).

[37] See, e.g., Arminius, *Works*, 2:79: "Original sin is in itself the punishment inflicted by God," as Mark Ellis summarizes Arminius; and so, "original sin itself does not make one liable to further punishment," as Stanglin and McCall put it (Mark A. Ellis, *Simon Episcopius' Doctrine of Original Sin*, American University Studies 240 [New York: Peter Lang, 2008], 78; Stanglin and McCall, *Jacob Arminius*, 149).

[38] Arminius, *Works*, 2:317–21. See Ellis, *Simon Episcopius*, 77, on how Arminius can sound Reformed on this point but has actually redefined significant terminology, in order to deny the eternal damnation of children as a result of the fall, something which Episcopius would later develop.

[39] Stanglin and McCall, *Jacob Arminius*, 151, 155.

[40] In Schaff, *Creeds of Christendom*, 3:547.

[41] In Schaff, *Creeds of Christendom*, 3:547.

Episcopius and the Remonstrants

It is crucial to note that there are significant differences between Arminius and later Arminianism, even as presented by the Remonstrants at the Synod of Dort. As the Arminian Anglican scholar Jonathan Edwards (c. 1638–1712) said, this doctrine that "all men are *conceiv'd and born in sin*, and that this is the effect of our first Parents' Fall and transgression" was believed and retained by all churches—East and West, Greek and Latin, Roman or Reformed, Lutheran or Calvinist. Indeed, "Arminius and his followers very clearly and fully own'd this Doctrine," he claimed. The problem was that some Remonstrants, such as Episcopius (along with the Socinians), did not affirm this.[42] So who was Episcopius, and what did he and the Remonstrants at Dort say that deviated from the consensus on original sin that Arminius had, it seems, in many respects happily followed?

Simon Bisschop, or "Episcopius" (1583–1643), was a family friend and student of Arminius and later a professor at Leiden. His brother Rembert (1571–1625) was the leading Remonstrant layman in Amsterdam. Episcopius became the most prominent spokesman for the Remonstrants at Dort, and was later Rector of the Remonstrant seminary in Amsterdam after his return from exile following the Synod. Along with Arminius himself and Johannes Arnoldus Corvinus (1582–1650), he is one of the most cited Remonstrants in the papers of the Synod. He was suspected by some of having Jesuit sympathies, and is reported to have confessed that he agreed with the Jesuits on predestination.[43] It was not unusual at the time to make such links.[44] One British delegate to Dort, John Davenant, commented that the

---

[42] Jonathan Edwards, *The Doctrine of Original Sin, As It Was Always Held in the Catholick Church, and Particularly in the Church of England* (Oxford, 1711), 12–13. This is Jonathan Edwards the Principal of Jesus College, Oxford, who was part of an Arminian response to later Remonstrant theology, and not the later Reformed New England divine of the same name. As Fornecker, "Arminianism and Anti-Remonstrant Polemic," 123, says, "For Edwards, the orthodoxy of Jacob Arminius and early followers like Gerhard Vossius was beyond dispute; his quarrel was with the heirs of Episcopius."

[43] Calder, *Memoirs of Simon Episcopius*, 135–36. Gomarus accused Arminius of also agreeing with the Jesuits (Caspar Brandt, *The Life of James Arminius*, trans. John Guthrie [Nashville, 1857], 343–44); Richard A. Muller (*God, Creation, and Providence in the Thought of Jacob Arminius: Sources and Directions of Scholastic Protestantism in the Era of Early Orthodoxy* [Grand Rapids, MI: Baker, 1991], 29), denies that Arminius was a crypto-Catholic or Jesuit sympathizer.

[44] See Jordan Ballor, Matthew Gaetano, and David Sytsma, eds., *Beyond Dordt and De Auxiliis: The Dynamics of Protestant and Catholic Soteriology in the Sixteenth and Seventeenth Centuries* (Leiden, Netherlands: Brill, 2019) for the often surprising parallels between the debates at Dort and those in the Congregatio De Auxiliis between Dominicans and Jesuits. The Jesuit Cardinal Bellarmine, and the Council of Trent, are often cited in error on certain points by the delegates at Dort (e.g., *Acta*, 2:217). Cf. Johann Gerhard, *On Sin and Free Choice*, Theological Commonplaces XII–XIV, trans. Richard J. Dinda, ed. Benjamin T. G. Mayes and Heath R. Curtis (1611; repr., St. Louis: Concordia, 2014), Commonplace XII, ch. 4, § 57, who quotes various "Papists" speaking against the idea of concupiscence having the nature of sin, and of total depravity.

arguments of the Jesuits and Arminians plainly depend on the same foundation.[45] Episcopius was also accused of pandering to Socinianism. Edwards, for example, speaks of *"Episcopius*, who hath transcrib'd a great part of the *Racovian* Divinity into his writings."[46] Episcopius began his leadership of the official opposition at the Synod of Dort by giving a ninety-minute speech, making various accusations and calling for tolerance rather than hairsplitting divisiveness. The president of the Synod, Johannes Bogerman, described this as "a premeditated harangue."[47] It seems relevant to his doctrine of sin to point out that in this speech, Episcopius also declared that "all of us are more or less faulty, and easily subject to mistakes in Divine and Heavenly matters."[48]

Episcopius preferred to stay away from the standard categories of academic debate, and appeals made to logical implications, and tried to avoid the terminology of intellect and will (*intellectus* and *voluntate*) in his discussions of sin.[49] For him, there was no Adamic covenant, and the "eternal death" suffered by Adam as a result of his expulsion from Eden was "purely and simply physical death."[50] As he would later say, "the natural necessity of dying" arose from the sin of Adam, but no-one is condemned to hell for Adam's sin.[51] While Arminius had affirmed that original sin consists in a privation of the Holy Spirit, Episcopius did not hold to this idea.[52] According to the *Confessio Remonstrantium* (1621), which he drafted following the Synod, it is "proper or actual sins" which "obscure our mind concerning spiritual matters," "blind us," and "finally deprave our will more and more by the habit of sinning."

[45] John Davenant, *Dissertationes Duae* (Cambridge, 1650), 174: "Neque opus est ut accurate distinguantur argumenta Jesuitarum & Arminianorum: nam iisdem plane fundamentis nituntur." Joseph Hall alluded to the scholastic battles of the Dominicans and Jesuits in his sermon to the Synod in November 1618 (Anthony Milton, *The British Delegation and the Synod of Dort* [Woodbridge, UK: Boydell, 2005], 130). The connection is also made in the delegation submissions, e.g., *Acta*, 3:269, where the Friesland delegates link Remonstrant doctrine with "Pelagii, Scholasticorum, & Iesuitarum."
[46] Edwards, *Doctrine of Original Sin*, 115. Seeing, or imagining, links between Socinianism and Arminianism was common in the seventeenth century (Lee Gatiss, "Socinianism and John Owen," in *Southern Baptist Journal of Theology* 20.4 [2016]: 43–62).
[47] Geeraert Brandt, *The History of the Reformation and Other Ecclesiastical Transactions in and about the Low-Countries*, 4 vols. (London, 1720), 3:62 (the speech itself is on pp. 52–61).
[48] Brandt, *History of the Reformation*, 3:53.
[49] See Ellis, *Simon Episcopius*, 104, 113, 150. See Calder, *Memoirs of Simon Episcopius*, 249–251 for a sample of his rhetoric against systematic theology with its "dark theological enigmas," its "barbarous and far-fetched phraseology," and its "interminable labyrinths" as opposed to "the simple phraseology of the apostles, which is so easy to be understood by everyone"; cf. Muller, *God, Creation, and Providence*, 27, for similar sentiments from Arminius against "Scholastic Divinity."
[50] Ellis, *Simon Episcopius*, 115, 150.
[51] Simon Episcopius, *Institutiones Theologicae* 4.5.1.4, in *Opera Theologica*, 2 vols. (Amsterdam: Joannes Blaev, 1650), 1:401 (col. 1): "*In Adam omnes moriuntur.* quia mors illa non est pæna peccatorum nostrorum, sed naturalis tantum moriendi necessitas orta quidem ex peccato Adami" (emphasis original).
[52] Ellis, *Simon Episcopius*, 116.

It is not original sin which does this.[53] Mark Ellis may be correct that "Episcopius's colleagues were not supportive of his departure from Arminius in several of the key issues of the Arminian controversy,"[54] but Arminius was dead, and it was Episcopius who was now in the driver's seat, leading the opposition to the majority Reformed consensus. Arminius had said that, because of sin, grace must always precede and sustain faith; but Episcopius thought that sufficient grace had been given to all, even to those who do not use it to believe.[55] This, of course, was an important point of consideration for those involved in missionary endeavors at the time, as it would make a difference to both their practice and their prayers.

Some of the things affirmed or denied in the Canons of Dort may seem unnecessary, if the only background one has is the *Remonstrance* of 1610 and the works of Arminius (who died in 1609). That is because Episcopius was a much more important figure, at the time of the Synod and beyond, for the actual development of Remonstrant theology—and the Reformed response. Episcopius's theology may well affirm the same theological tendencies as Arminius, and may indeed be a development of them, but they were not identical in their teaching on sin and its effects. However, contemporaries may have sensed a certain slippage and slipperiness in Arminius, despite his protestations to the contrary at times, which would become apparent only later, as his heirs worked through his ideas in more detail. As Mark Ellis has concluded, "even in his most questionable departures from Arminius's soteriology, Episcopius was merely working out what was implicit in his precursor's theology."[56] Arminius may in some senses have been Reformed; but Episcopius and the Remonstrants were not Reformed, but Arminian.

The Canons of Dort

It is noticeable, as we turn to the Canons of Dort, that the Synod did not choose to address the issues of human corruption and conversion separately.

---

[53] Mark A. Ellis, trans. and ed., *The Arminian Confession of 1621* (Eugene, OR: Pickwick, 2005), 65 (§ 7.5). See Ellis, *Simon Episcopius*, 122, 157, on Episcopius's confusing use of *mortem aeternam* to mean mere physical death.
[54] Ellis, *Simon Episcopius*, 127.
[55] He says, "itaque gratia sufficiens ad fidem & conversionem non tantum ijs obtingit, qui actu credunt et convertuntur . . . qui actu ipso non credunt, nec reipsa convertuntur" (cf. Ellis, *Arminian Confession*, 109 [§ 17.8]; Ellis, *Simon Episcopius*, 180). This is reminiscent of John Wesley's idea of universal enablement or "prevenient grace," which appears therefore to be more Episcopian than Arminian. See my comments on Wesley's doctrine of original sin in Lee Gatiss, *The True Profession of the Gospel: Augustus Toplady and Reclaiming Our Reformed Foundations* (London: Latimer Trust, 2010), 63, 105–7, particularly the ideas that no one is damned for original sin, and that it no longer functions so as to render us unable to respond to God for salvation.
[56] Ellis, *Simon Episcopius*, 183.

They dealt with "the Third and Fourth Heads of Doctrine" from the *Remonstrance* together, thus rolling together the T and the I of the infamous TULIP acronym.[57] They did this to make one point: the *Remonstrance* may sound orthodox on the third point, but it is seen properly only when this is placed alongside its doctrine of conversion in the fourth point.[58] Peter Lombard has an interesting illustration which helps us see this. He says,

> At night, there is blindness in the eye of a blind person, but it is not readily apparent, and one cannot discern between one who sees and one who is blind until the arrival of the light. In the same way, this vice [original sin, concupiscence] is not apparent in a child, until the arrival of a more advanced age.[59]

We might also say that one's doctrine of sin is not completely apparent until it confronts the light of the gospel, and we see how much spiritual ability it has left us with. Lutheran theologians such as Johann Gerhard (1582–1637) noted this same point and dealt with the issue in a similar way, saying that "the whole question concerns the state of man corrupted through the fall, that is, what he is capable of either before or in conversion with his own natural powers of free choice."[60] Our particular focus in this chapter, however, is what is taught about sin; an exposition of the Synod's teaching on conversion and irresistible grace must wait for another volume.

As usual, the Canons of Dort present their teaching in a way that would be understandable to ordinary churchgoers, rather than in academic jargon. They begin with positive statements before moving to refutations of specific errors, and they move from statements that almost all could affirm, to more contentious points, to try and demonstrate that "Reformed distinctives are the proper development of catholic theology."[61] Each delegation, however,

[57] Dortian Calvinism was in a sense, therefore, only ever really four-point Calvinism! I have dealt with the appropriateness or otherwise of the oft-used mnemonic in Lee Gatiss, "The Synod of Dort and Definite Atonement," in *From Heaven He Came and Sought Her: Definite Atonement in Historical, Biblical, Theological and Pastoral Perspective*, ed. David Gibson and Jonathan Gibson (Wheaton, IL: Crossway, 2013), 148–49; and Lee Gatiss, *For Us and for Our Salvation: Limited Atonement" in the Bible, Doctrine, History, and Ministry* (London: Latimer Trust, 2012), 14–16.
[58] Daniel R. Hyde, *Grace Worth Fighting For: Recapturing the Vision of God's Grace in the Canons of Dort* (Landrum, SC: Davenant Institute, 2019), 227; cf. Christopher J. Gordon, "Dead in Sin: The Utter Depravity of Mankind," in *A Faith Worth Defending: The Synod of Dort's Enduring Heritage*, ed. Jon D. Payne and Sebastian Heck (Grand Rapids, MI: Reformation Heritage Books), 57: "If our starting point is wrong and we attempt to downgrade Scripture's serious diagnosis of human nature, it will have a direct consequence on how we understand the nature of grace in the gospel of Jesus Christ."
[59] Peter Lombard, *Sentences*, 2.30.9.2, in *The Sentences Book 2: On Creation*, trans. Giulio Silano (Toronto: Pontifical Institute of Mediaeval Studies, 2008), 149–50.
[60] Gerhard, *On Sin and Free Choice*, Commonplace XIV, ch. 3, § 32.3.
[61] W. Robert Godfrey, "Popular and Catholic: The *Modus Docendi* of the Canons of Dordt," in *Revisiting the Synod of Dort*, ed. Aza Goudriaan and Fred van Lieburg (Leiden, Netherlands: Brill, 2011), 243–60, 258.

submitted its own judgments on the various points, and these were often couched in the well-worn and precise terminology of university discussions.[62] There is some overlap between the different sections of the Canons, such that each "head of doctrine" is complete of itself, and yet, in order to be so, it must sometimes make statements that impinge on other areas of teaching, because doctrine is a coherent whole. Hence, although sin and corruption are not the explicit subject of discussion until point 3/4, the Canons do actually begin with a statement about sin in their opening section on predestination:

> All people have sinned in Adam and so are subject to the curse and eternal death. God would not have been unfair to anyone if He had left everyone in sin and under the curse, and had willed to damn them all on account of sin. The Apostle teaches this: "The whole world is guilty under the condemnation of God"; "all have sinned and fallen short of the glory of God"; and "the wages of sin is death." (Rom. 3:19, 23; 6:23)[63]

Similarly, the Canons on the fifth head of doctrine (the preservation of the saints) also open by talking about people being liberated "from the dominion and servitude of sin," and of experiencing "daily sins of weakness" even when liberated. Yet the focus of the first half of the Canons on corruption and conversion (3/4) are the key on this doctrine, as well as several of the *"Rejectio Errorum"* sections outlining particular false teachings which the Synod wanted to oppose.

The Canons teach that mankind suffered privation in the fall, which also produced in us "horrible darkness, vanity, and perverseness of judgment" as well as impure affections.[64] They therefore go further than Arminius and speak of depravation as well as deprivation, though without using the exact terminology Aquinas employed about "a certain corrupt habit."[65] They say, "all men are conceived in sin. They are born children of wrath, incapable of any saving good, prone to evil [*propensi ad malum*], dead in sin, and

---

[62] We have access to these papers in, e.g., *Acta*, 2:164–246 (the papers from the foreigners, such as Britain, the Palatinate, Switzerland, Bremen, etc.), and *Acta*, 3:212–307 (the "home team" of the Dutch professors and delegations from Gelderland, North Holland, South Holland, Utrecht, etc.).

[63] Canons of Dort, 1.1.

[64] Canons of Dort, 3/4.1.

[65] The British delegation put it strongly when they said, "after the Fall, there was over and above added, a greedy thirst and desire to sinne . . . such is the nature of the will, that it cannot remaine single or utterly unfurnished, but falling fro[m] one object, to which it did adhere, it pursues another eagerly to embrace it. And therefore being by a voluntary Apostasie habitually turned from God the Creator, it runnes to the creature, with an unbridled appetite, and in a lustful and base manner commits fornication with it" (Milton, *British Delegation*, 252, from *The Collegiat Suffrage of the Divines of Great Britaine* [London, 1629]).

servants of sin."[66] The alternative to this was what the contemporary Huguenot theologian Andreas Rivetus (1572–1651) called "the doctrine of the Pelagians . . . who state that no sin comes with man's birth, but that in man when he is born one finds only what God has created."[67] So if someone has certain inclinations and orientations, the Pelagian instinct is to attribute these to God, who made them like this, rather than to posit a corruption of God's good design through the influence of original sin. The Canons of Dort, however, say that "Corruption produced corruption," which is passed on to all Adam's posterity (except Christ).[68] Original sin is not picked up merely by imitation, as Pelagius was said to have taught. Every part of human nature is adversely affected by the fall. Original sin, as Rivetus would put it, "is nothing else than the perversion and deformity of the whole human nature [*depravation illa et deformities totes humanae naturae*]."[69] Not that we are as bad as we could be, but that every aspect of our nature is dark, perverse, wicked, and impure.

The third Article under this head summarizes the Synod's doctrine of totally pervasive depravity:

> So all men are conceived in sin. They are born children of wrath, incapable of any saving good, prone to evil, dead in sin, and servants of sin. Without the regenerating grace of the Holy Spirit, they neither can nor want to return to God, correct their depraved nature, or dispose themselves to such correction.[70]

We are *born* this way, not made this way only by our own *actual* sins, as the Remonstrant Confession would say. Contrary to those who might give heathen nations a chance at salvation apart from Christ, the Canons make

---

[66] Canons of Dort, 3/4.3.
[67] Antonius Walaeus et al., *Synopsis Purioris Theologiae (Synopsis of a Purer Theology): Latin Text and English Translation* (3 vols.), vol. 1, *Disputations 1–23*, ed. Dolf te Velde, trans. Riemer A. Faber (Leiden, Netherlands: Brill, 2015) (the modern critical edition of *Synopsis Purioris Theologiae* [Leiden, 1625], 358–59) (XV: De Peccato Originali); cf. pp. 376–77, on Pelagius saying "that such concupiscence was implanted by God as something good by nature." Rivetus criticizes (as most Protestant commentators do) the Council of Trent for saying that, although "concupiscence should not be loved but hated as a sin that distracts and diverts us from what we should love most dearly," it is not properly sin until "it bursts forth into actual sin."
[68] Canons of Dort, 3/4.2.
[69] Te Velde (ed.), *Synopsis Purioris Theologiae*, 368–69. Rivetus (370–71) also speaks of concupiscence as a kind of "habit" in man (*concupiscentiam quandam habitualem esse in homine*), saying that original sin is not simply the lack of righteousness but also "an evil tendency" (*pravae inclinationis*), or "an inclination towards every wickedness" (*proclivitatis ad omne malum*) because "actions are not a property of a deficiency, while Scripture does attribute actions to original sin." The point is that Reformed theologians at this point did not have to use the precise Thomistic vocabulary of *habitus* to express this same thought, but could speak of inclination, or proclivity, or propensity (as the Canons do). Rivetus actually quotes Aquinas precisely on pp. 372–73.
[70] Canons of Dort, 3/4.3.

clear that "some light of nature remains in humans," and yet it is "far from bringing a saving knowledge of God or enabling anyone to convert to God." Rather, it only renders them inexcusable, because "they completely pervert it in various ways and suppress it in unrighteousness."[71] There is thus no hope for non-Christian people in European colonies around the world without the light of the gospel and the grace of God.

These people remain *people*, though, to be drawn by persuasion through the gospel; they are not dumb animals or lesser human beings to be merely subjugated:

> Man by the Fall did not cease to be man, endowed with understanding and will. And sin, which pervades the whole human race, did not destroy the nature of the human race, but depraved it and killed it spiritually. So also the divine grace of regeneration does not act in men as if they were tree trunks or logs, or take away the will and its properties, or force it violently and unwillingly.[72]

Dort delegate Antonius Thysius (1565–1640) likewise asserted that "Man does not, however, behave with his free choice like some block of wood; for God works in man as a subject endowed with the faculties of mind and will, and He works through his Word."[73] As Dutch professor Franciscus Gomarus (1563–1641) also said, "no sane person will deny that [man after the fall] remains a human being, though a wounded one" retaining freedom from coercion and necessity.[74] Humanity does not, however, have absolute freedom of will to choose between good and evil, or to choose to believe, as the Remonstrants claimed.[75]

Rejecting Errors

After these positive statements, the Canons reject nine particular errors of those who teach falsely on this head. First, they reject the view of those who say that original sin in itself is not sufficient to condemn us or to deserve

---

[71] Canons of Dort, 3/4.4; cf. Rom. 1:18.
[72] Canons of Dort, 3/4.16.
[73] Te Velde (ed.), *Synopsis Purioris Theologiae*, 420–21 (XVII: De Libero Arbitrio).
[74] The disputation of Gomarus, in *Reformed Thought on Freedom: The Concept of Free Choice in Early Modern Reformed Theology*, ed. Willem J. van Asselt, J. Martin Bac, and Roelf T. te Velde (Grand Rapids, MI: Baker Academic, 2010), 129–32, 141; cf. Thysius, in *Synopsis Purioris Theologiae*, 412–13.
[75] E.g., the Remonstrants' view at the Hague Conference in Henricus Brand, ed., *Collatio Scripto habits Hagae Comitis* (Zierikzee, Netherlands, 1615), 298, 300, 301, which was supported by, for example, Uitenbogaert, Corvinus, Grevinchovius, and Episcopius. Cf. Aza Goudriaan, "The Synod of Dort on Arminian Anthropology," in *Revisiting the Synod of Dort*, ed. Aza Goudriaan and Fred van Lieburg (Leiden, Netherlands: Brill, 2011), 97–99.

temporal or eternal punishments.[76] To this is brought Romans 5:12, 16, and Romans 6:23, to show that death and condemnation are both the result of the fall. This closes off the error which some seemed to detect in Arminius and which Episcopius affirmed (though in an ambiguous way).[77] For Arminius, original sin was itself a punishment but did not merit further punishment; and for Episcopius it led only to the natural necessity of death, not eternal condemnation in hell.[78] Dort, on the contrary, affirmed, as the Irish Articles (1615) did just a few years earlier, that because of original sin, "man is deprived of original righteousness, and by nature is bent unto sin. And therefore, in every person born into the world, it deserveth God's wrath and damnation."[79] The Westminster Confession (1646) would similarly declare that original sin itself "and all the motions thereof are true and properly sin," and that

> Every sin, both original and actual, being a transgression of the righteous law of God, and contrary thereunto, doth, in its own nature, bring guilt upon the sinner, whereby he is bound over to the wrath of God and curse of the law, and so made subject to death, with all miseries spiritual, temporal, and eternal.[80]

Second, the Canons reject the idea that Adam was not created with original righteousness and holiness, on the grounds that Ephesians 4:24 describes the image of God in those terms. The British delegation made the point that, since Ephesians 4:24 says that the image of God restored in believers consists in "righteousness and true holiness," the will of man must have been originally endowed with those excellent graces.[81] As Goudriaan states, "The delegations repeatedly cited the Arminian statement that the human will was not equipped with 'gifts' at the time of its creation, and that these gifts could not be lost because of human sin either."[82] Caspar Barlaeus (1584–1648) had claimed that Adam and Eve had no infused good habits, because God wanted

---

[76] Canons of Dort, 3/4, Rejection 1.

[77] See above on Episcopius's confusing use of the term *mortem aeternam*.

[78] Rivetus, by contrast, says that "By itself original sin earns [*meretur*, cf. article 9 of the Thirty-Nine Articles] not just temporal or bodily death, but also eternal punishment" (te Velde [ed.], *Synopsis Purioris Theologiae*, 380–381; cf. Antonius Walaeus on pp. 394–95).

[79] Schaff, *Creeds of Christendom*, 3:530; cf. Article 9 of the Thirty-Nine Articles.

[80] Schaff, *Creeds of Christendom*, 3:615–16; cf. the Westminster Shorter Catechism Qs 16–19, in James T. Dennison Jr., *Reformed Confessions of the 16th and 17th Centuries in English Translation*, 4 vols. (Grand Rapids, MI: Reformation Heritage, 2014), 4:355. Arminius would be happy with the covenant with Adam in Q. 16, but Episcopius and later Remonstrants would object to the idea that original sin merits "the pains of hell forever." Yet there is some ambiguity here because Qs 18–19 refer to both original *and* actual sins together. The Savoy Declaration, ch. 6 (Dennison, *Reformed Confessions*, 4:465) and the London Baptist Confession (1677) (Dennison, *Reformed Confessions*, 4:540–541) make the same points.

[81] Milton, *British Delegation*, 251; cf. 261.

[82] Goudriaan, "Synod of Dort on Arminian Anthropology," 98, citing a large number of delegation submissions.

their obedience to be completely free.[83] This worried several delegations,[84] and so this denial was included in the final Canons.[85]

Third, the Synod rejected teaching which they claimed was "elevating the powers of the free will," contrary to Jeremiah's statement that "the heart is deceitful above all things" (Jer. 17:9) as well as Ephesians 2:3. The Reformed made clear distinctions allowing for a certain power of the will which humans retain even after the fall, such as freedom from coercion and necessity.[86] Humanity does not, however, have absolute freedom of will to choose between good and evil, or to choose to believe. Rather, since the fall, human will "is not free with regard to the spiritual good, but only and totally inclined to evil," as the North Holland delegation put it.[87] So the Canons reject the error of those who teach that

> The spiritual gifts are not separated from the will of man in spiritual death since the will in itself has never been corrupted. It was only impeded through the darkness of the mind and the disordering of the affections. When these impediments are removed, the will makes natural use of its free faculty, that is, it can either will or choose the good put before it, or it can not will or not choose the good.

This, the Synod said, was "a novelty and an error."[88] It is worth remembering that early modern Reformed argumentation on these points, as on many points, was not of course homogeneous or monolithic. As Richard Muller concludes, the Reformed tradition "was capable of affirming human free choice as defined by intellective deliberation and multiple volitional potencies and as embodying genuine alternativity in a manner that does not comport with the assumptions of modern compatibility theology and philosophy."[89] Yet however they chose to present their own particular approaches to this,

---

[83] Caspar Barlaeus, *Epistola Ecclesiastarum quos in Belgio Remonstrantes vocant, ad exterarum ecclesiarum Reformatos doctores, pastores, theologos* (Leiden, Netherlands, 1617), 56–57.

[84] E.g., Emden (*Acta*, 2:235), Zeeland (*Acta*, 3:251), and the Dutch theologians (*Acta*, 3:213).

[85] Canons of Dort, 3/4, Rejection 2.

[86] Gomarus in *Reformed Thought on Freedom*, 129; cf. Thysius, in *Synopsis Purioris Theologiae*, 412–13. Other delegates at Dort made similar points about the types of freedom which the fallen will does retain, e.g., Nassau-Wetteravia in *Acta*, 2:195–96; Bremen in *Acta*, 2:210; Gelderland in *Acta*, 3:220.

[87] *Acta*, 3:238 (North Holland). See also, e.g., the Friesland delegation (*Acta*, 3:262); the Walloon delegation (*Acta* 3:303); and the Utrecht delegation (*Acta*, 3:257) (Milton, *British Delegation*, 258). Substantially the same doctrine is declared in other Confessions from elsewhere in the seventeenth century, such as the statement from The Colloquy of Thorn (1645), and in the New Confession of Faith (1654) (Dennison, *Reformed Confessions*, 4:211, 430) and other confessional documents noted below.

[88] Canons of Dort, 3/4, Rejection 3.

[89] Muller, *Divine Will and Human Choice: Freedom, Contingency, and Necessity in Early Modern Reformed Thought* (Grand Rapids, MI: Baker Academic, 2017), 311.

the delegates at Dort were united in rejecting these specific errors which they had detected in the Remonstrants.

Fourth, the Synod rejected the teaching that "Unregenerate man is not properly or totally dead in sin or destitute of all powers for spiritual good. Rather, he can hunger and thirst after righteousness and life, and can offer the sacrifice of a contrite and broken spirit, which is acceptable to God." Arminius had written in his *Apology or Defence* that, in some sense, "we speak what is right when we say: 'Serious sorrow on account of sin is so far pleasing to God, that by it, according to the multitude of his mercies, he is moved to bestow grace on a man who is a sinner.' "[90] This, said Arminius, was spoken of a man who is "not yet actually born again." In his *Dissertation on Romans 7*, Arminius had also said,

> To acknowledge themselves to be sinners, to mourn and lament on account of personal transgressions, and to seek deliverance from sin, are good things; *and they belong to some who are unregenerate*. Nay, no man can be made partaker of regeneration, unless he has previously had within him such things as these. From these passages, it is evident that it cannot be said with truth, that nothing of good can be attributed to the unregenerate, what kind of men soever they may be.[91]

The Synod chose to reject this idea, that before regeneration someone can please God with their contrition, on the basis of Ephesians 2:1–5 and of Genesis 6:5 and 8:21, which state that "The imagination of the thoughts of the heart of man is only evil all the time."[92] We will see below how Remonstrant interpreters differed on the interpretation of these verses, but it is clear that the Synod was not simply making up false opinions here and then attributing them to the Remonstrants, as some have accused it of doing.[93] It was open to individuals to repudiate such an opinion, but it was clearly something being affirmed, or seeming to be affirmed, that the Synod thought it important to counter. After all, if, for example, the non-Christian inhabitants of Ceylon could be acceptable to God without having

---

[90] Arminius, *Works*, 1:327.
[91] Arminius, *Works*, 2:281 (emphasis added). This may be contrasted with the statement in *Works*, 1:329, where Arminius asks, "How can a man, without the assistance of Divine Grace, perform any thing which is acceptable to God, and which he will remunerate with the saving reward either of further grace or of life eternal?" Cf. 1:324, 328–29, on his addition of a prevenient grace into the medieval doctrine of *Facientibus quod in se est, Deus non denegat gratiam* ("God will not deny grace to those who do what is in them").
[92] Canons of Dort, 3/4, Rejection 4.
[93] Calder, *Memoirs of Simon Episcopius*, 244.

accepted the good news of Jesus and having been born again, was it urgently necessary to expend time, treasure, and talents on trying to reach them with gospel preaching?

This is also why the Canons also reject the idea, which seemed to be present in Arminius's work, that "corrupt, natural man could so rightly use common grace . . . so that by using this good he could gradually obtain more grace, indeed evangelical and saving grace and salvation."[94] Indeed, Arminius had written against William Perkins's treatise on predestination in just these terms. He said about those to whom Christ has not yet been made known, that

> while they were destitute of the knowledge of Christ, God "left not himself without witness" (Acts 14:17) but even then revealed to them some truth concerning His power and goodness, and the law also, which He kept inscribed on their minds. If they had made a right use of those blessings, even according to their own conscience, *He would have bestowed upon them greater grace*, according to that declaration, "to him that hath shall be given."

Salvation could come from this vocation "*if it is rightly used*," he said.[95] Several delegations at Dort cited these passages by Arminius, along with a work of Corvinus against Tilenus, in which he had defended Arminius.[96] On the contrary, say the Canons, God has sovereignly chosen not to reveal his saving truth to every nation in this way.[97] As Aza Goudriaan has pointed out, "The Synod, in short, criticized the Arminian notion that if a human being makes a good use of his natural capacity, he may thereby be given more grace." It also "rejected the Arminian view that the natural abilities of humans could function as a bridge and starting-point from where grace could be acquired. Thus, in the Synod's judgment, the Arminians did not sufficiently take into account the depravity of the human being."[98] In and by themselves, people cannot correct their depraved nature "or dispose themselves to such correction," as the Canons of Dort 3/4.3 said.

---

[94] Canons of Dort, 3/4, Rejection 5.
[95] Arminius, *Works*, 3:524–25 (emphasis added); cf. also 486.
[96] *Acta*, 2:178 (Palatinate); 2:187, 188, 191 (Hesse); 2:216, 224–25 (Emden); and 3:280 (Groningen); Johannes Arnoldus Corvinus, *Defensio Sententiæ D. Iacobi Arminij* (Leiden, 1613).
[97] The Canons cite Ps. 147:19–20 here: "He has shown His words to Jacob, His statutes and laws to Israel; He has not done this to any other nation; they do not know His Laws." This is cited by, for example, the Utrecht delegation, in *Acta*, 3:253, who also cite Acts 16:6–7 as the final Canons do.
[98] Goudriaan, "Synod of Dort on Arminian Anthropology," 93.

The Exegesis of Key Texts

The Synod of Dort included a number of people who were not simply pastors or systematic theologians but were also keenly interested (and skilled) in Bible translation and proper exegesis. The Synod's authorized translation of the Bible into Dutch and its accompanying annotations gives us an insight into how they understood the texts which were most at issue in these controversies. Comparing this to other commentaries and annotations from both sides of the arguments, and to the use of Scripture in various papers and books, demonstrates how important the interpretation of Scripture was for those fighting these battles.

In their submission on the Third and Fourth Heads of Doctrine, the British delegation explicitly cite and quote from over sixty different Bible texts, ranging from Genesis, Job, 2 Chronicles, Jeremiah, Ezekiel, and Psalms, to all four Gospels, Romans, Ephesians, Hebrews, 1 Peter, 2 Peter, 1 John, and Revelation.[99] The Palatinate delegation cite and interact with around a hundred texts, including Exodus, 1 Kings, Zechariah, 2 Corinthians, 2 Timothy, Titus, and many of the same passages as the British.[100] There are a number of allusions to biblical phraseology in the Canons of Dort on the Third and Fourth Heads of Doctrine,[101] but the texts actually cited in support of various arguments are: Genesis 6:5, Genesis 8:21, Psalm 147:19–20, Isaiah 44:3, Jeremiah 17:9, Jeremiah 31:8, Jeremiah 31:33, Ezekiel 36:26, Matthew 13, Acts 14:16, Acts 16:6–7, Romans 5:5, Romans 5:12, Romans 5:16, Romans 6:23, Romans 9:16, 1 Corinthians 4:7, Ephesians 1:19, Ephesians 2:1, Ephesians 2:3, Ephesians 2:5, Ephesians 4:24, Philippians 2:13, 2 Thessalonians 1:11, and 2 Peter 1:3. All of these, apart from the reference to the parable of the sower, appear in the "Rejection of Errors" section of the Canons, because it was important to show how Scripture was being brought to bear in correcting the Remonstrant errors. All this indicates something of the breadth of scriptural engagement going on at the Synod. However, to feel the depth of exegetical work behind the doctrinal conclusions they reached, we also need to take a look at annotations and commentaries from different sides of the debate. We can get only a snapshot of this here, but it is worth doing so by taking soundings in four key texts, which are often addressed together in

---

[99] *Acta*, 2:162–76.
[100] *Acta*, 2:176–84.
[101] E.g., the Canons of Dort, 3/4.3, speaks about being "born children of wrath," clearly alluding to Eph. 2:3; and the Canons of Dort, 3/4.14, speaks of "God, who works both to will and to do," alluding to Phil. 2:13.

184 SIN AND DEPRAVITY IN CHURCH HISTORY

discussions of this doctrine: Genesis 6:5 and 8:21; Psalm 51:5; Romans 5:12; and Ephesians 2:1–3.[102]

GENESIS 6:5 AND 8:21

Genesis tells us, "The LORD saw that the wickedness of man was great in the earth, and that every intention of the thoughts of his heart was only evil continually" (Gen. 6:5). Similarly, after the flood, the Lord declares, "I will never again curse the ground because of man, for the intention of man's heart is evil from his youth" (Gen. 8:21). These verses are cited together in Rejection 4 of the Canons, to prove that it is incorrect to say, "Unregenerate man is not properly or totally dead in sin or destitute of all powers for spiritual good."[103] They are some of the most cited verses in all the delegation papers.[104]

The *Dutch Annotations* produced by the Synod's committee for Bible translation comment on Genesis 6:5 that "In this verse there is contained a very naked and fundamental description of original Sin, and the fruits thereof."[105] The Genevan delegate to Dort, Giovanni (or John) Diodati (1576–1649) also wrote annotations on the whole of Scripture.[106] He tells us that Genesis 6:5 refers to "internall conceits and secret discourses, which are as it were the modell of all externall humane actions." So in some way, the behavior and secret thoughts of these people are the epitome of all human conduct. The *English Annotations* (sometimes called the Westminster Annotations because several members of the Westminster Assembly were involved in their publication) take a similar approach. They tell us that the Hebrew word יֵצֶר here

---

[102] These are often used in confessions and other theological works of this period as proof texts for a Reformed doctrine of sin. E.g., the Genesis texts appear in the Lutheran "Formula of Concord" (*Concordia: The Lutheran Confessions*, ed. P. T. McCain [St. Louis: Concordia, 2006], 476–77); Romans, Genesis, and Ephesians texts are used in The Confession of the Evangelical Church in Germany (1614) (Dennison, *Reformed Confessions*, 4:59); the Romans and Ephesians texts are in the London Baptist Confession (1644) (Dennison, *Reformed Confessions*, 4:185, 275 [1646]); the Midlands Confession of Particular Baptists (1655) cites Ps. 51:5 and Rom. 5:12–15, and includes the phrase "children of wrath" (Dennison, *Reformed Confession*, 4:433 [cf. the Somerset confession of a year later, at 4:447]); similarly, the Waldensian Confession (1655) (Dennison, *Reformed Confessions*, 4:439, 502–3). The Formula Consensus Helvetica (1675) also cites Rom. 5:12 (Dennison, *Reformed Confessions*, 4:523). All four texts are quoted (along with Job 14:4 and John 3:6, which are also classic texts on this subject) in te Velde (ed.), *Synopsis Purioris Theologiae*, 352–53, 358–59.
[103] Canons of Dort, 3/4, Rejection 4. Arminius cites them together in Arminius, *Works*, 1:527.
[104] They are cited by the delegations from Hesse (*Acta*, 2:186–87), Geneva (*Acta*, 2:202), the universities (*Acta*, 3:214), South Holland (*Acta*, 3:229), North Holland (*Acta*, 3:238), Zeeland (*Acta*, 3:247), Utrecht (*Acta*, 3:258–59), Friesland (*Acta*, 3:263), Overijssel (*Acta*, 3:272, 275), Groningen (*Acta*, 3:282), Drenthe (*Acta*, 3:299), and the Walloon church (*Acta*, 3:306).
[105] Theodore Haak, *The Dutch Annotations upon the Whole Bible . . . Ordered and Appointed by the Synod of Dort* (London, 1657).
[106] John Diodati, *Pious and Learned Annotations upon the Holy Bible: Plainly Expounding the Most Difficult Places Thereof* (London, 1643).

signifieth not onely the imagination, but also the purpose and desire of man: and hereby is meant that internall taint of corrupt nature, which makes a mint of evill imaginations in the head, a sinke of inordinate affections in the heart, useth the memory as a closet or store-house of sinfull fancies and impure impressions.[107]

On the other side of the debate we might put Philip van Limborch (1633–1712). He was a relation and follower of Episcopius, and professor at the Remonstrant Seminary in Amsterdam. In his *Theologia Christiana*, he defends the Episcopian system both theologically and exegetically. He denies the imputation of Adam's sin, that original sin has of itself the nature of sin, and that the understanding, will, and affections (*intellectus, voluntate*, and *affectus*) are so depraved as to be only inclined to evil (as the Contra-Remonstrants alleged). Such a doctrine of corruption is "reconcilable neither with Sacred Scripture, nor with right reason," he asserted.[108] He objected to the Reformed use of Genesis 6:5 and 8:21, because those verses are not about sin universally, the sin of all people. Noah was an exception, for example, as a "righteous and perfect man" (Gen. 6:9), and it was not original sin which caused the flood but *actual* sins.[109] Original sin is always the same, so if that had prompted the flood, why had it not prompted it before?[110]

Cardinal Bellarmine (1542–1621) also denied that these verses were relevant to the discussion of original sin, saying that they described the *actual* sins of those who lived before the flood. They describe an inclination to evil left over from original sin, but which "is not properly sin unless it comes forth in a voluntary action." Johann Gerhard countered this by saying,

> If the imagination of the human heart is only evil at all times, surely corrupt concupiscence cannot be absolved of the accusation that it is sin. . . . Moses intended to show the very source of actual sin, namely, what sort

---

[107] John Downame, *Annotations upon All the Books of the Old and New Testament*, 2 vols. (London: J. Legatt & J. Raworth, 1645) (also known as the *English Annotations*).

[108] Philip van Limborch, *Theologia Christiana*, 4 vols. (Amsterdam, 1686), 2:188 (book 3, ch. 4, sec. 3): "Sed vero ejusmodi corruptio nec cum S. Scripturâ, nec cum rectâ rations conciliari potest."

[109] Limborch, *Theologia Christiana*, 2:191–92: "Non agitur hic de peccato omnibus hominibus communi; Noachus enim ut vir justus & perfectus expresse excipitur. . . . Peccatum originis proprie non est causa diluvii, sed peccata actualia exinde profluentia iram Dei accenderunt."

[110] The same approach to this text is taken by Episcopius. See Ellis, *Simon Episcopius*, 150–51, where Episcopius speaks about discipline, upbringing, and environment as negative influences on children, rather than *peccati virus* or *peccati contagio* infecting everyone from the cradle. Episcopius also denied that the description of the depraved antediluvians could be applied to all people and societies. Cf. Episcopius, *Institutiones Theologicae* 4.5.2, in *Opera Theologica*, 1:406.

of human nature remained after the Spirit of God had been removed. . . . Also, because the same words are repeated to Noah when he left the ark with his family, it is obvious that they cannot be assigned only to those who lived before the flood but are being said in general about the nature of man after the flood as it is in itself, if considered outside of the regeneration and renewal of the Spirit.[111]

In answer to the point about Noah being excepted, Anglican commentator Andrew Willet (1561–1621) also added that "Noah's righteousness was by grace, not by nature."[112]

PSALM 51:5

David confesses, "Behold, I was brought forth in iniquity, and in sin did my mother conceive me" (Ps. 51:5). The *Dutch Annotations* on this verse (Ps. 51:7 in the numbering then in use, following the LXX), say that by this we must "understand the originall sin, inbred corruption, the flesh and the inhabiting sin. See John 3:6. Romans 7:17."[113] Diodati takes a similar approach, making David say, "I do not only confesse my sin in this action, but in generall also by reason of the corruption of nature through originall sinne, which hath passed into me in my begetting: As if he should say, I have not only sinned, but am also wicked of nature, see Job 14:4, John 3:6, Romans 5:12, Ephesians 2:3."[114] The *English Annotations* say that, in verse 5, David "here brings all his actuall transgressions to the fountain of them, originall corruption, Rom. 7:8, etc. By this phrase, *in sin*, expressing that sins possessing the whole man, John 9:34, Acts 8:23, Eph. 2:1 are as waters wherein a man is over-whelmed."[115]

Hugo Grotius (1583–1645) was a leading Remonstrant jurist and biblical commentator. His annotations on Scripture, running into several volumes, were influential throughout the seventeenth century and beyond.[116] Grotius says that Psalm 51:5 is hyperbole, and means "not only now, but also from my childhood I have often sinned."[117] This is demonstrated, he says, by

---

[111] Gerhard, *On Sin and Free Choice*, Commonplace XIII, ch. 11, § 52, with the quote from Bellarmine there.
[112] Andrew Willet, *Hexapla in Genesin, That Is, A Sixfold Commentary upon Genesis*, 2nd ed. (London, 1608), 84, citing also Eph. 2:3 and John 3:6 in his answer to Bellarmine and Pererius.
[113] Haak, *Dutch Annotations*.
[114] Diodati, *Pious Annotations*.
[115] Downame, *Annotations upon All the Books of the Old and New Testament*.
[116] John Owen, *A Review of the Annotations of Hugo Grotius* (Oxford, 1656), complains that they were "in the hands of most students."
[117] *Hugonis Grotii Annotationes in Vetus Testamentum. Tomus I*, ed. G. Vogel (Halae, 1775), 391. "Sensus est: *Non nunc tantum, sed et a pueritia mea, saepius peccaui*. Est enim loquendi genus ὑπερβολικὸν [*superiectiuum*]."

comparing Psalm 51 to the idiom seen in Job 31:18 ("from my mother's womb I guided the widow"), Psalm 22:10 ("On you was I cast from my birth, and from my mother's womb you have been my God"), Psalm 58:3 ("The wicked are estranged from the womb; they go astray from birth, speaking lies"), as well as Psalm 71:5–6 and Isaiah 48:8. However, Psalm 51:5 does not actually use any of the Hebrew words מִבֶּטֶן or מֵרֶחֶם or מִמְּעֵי (from the womb or belly) which are used in these supposed parallels. Even in the Latin Vulgate, the terminology is different (the parallels Grotius adduces use *ab infantia, de utero, de ventre, a vulva*, or *a juventute*), whereas Psalm 51:5 (50:7 in the Vulgate) has "Ecce enim in iniquitatibus *conceptus sum*, et in peccatis *concepit me* mater mea" (with the same Latin verb being used for the two different Hebrew words חוֹלָלְתִּי and יֶחֱמַתְנִי). So Grotius avoids seeing here a confession of original sin, or a biblical testimony to that idea, as he also does with Genesis 8:21 (similarly dismissed as hyperbole, with cross-references again to the same verses in Ps. 58, Ps. 71, Isa. 48, and Job 31).[118] He interprets it simply as the psalmist remembering less serious *actual* sins from his youth as well as his more recent grave crime. The basis on which Grotius does so, however, does not seem to be as sound as he conceives it to be.

Henry Hammond (1605–60) was a prolific and influential commentator, of an Arminian persuasion. All that Hammond will say on Psalm 51:5 is, "Lord, I am a most polluted creature," speaking of "the corruption of my nature," and of "inclinations of my will" toward unlawful objects, but not of how he (i.e., David) became such a polluted or corrupted being.[119] Limborch claims that, even if the psalm is interpreted literally, that does not help the cause of those who claim it is about original sin. It is, after all, about David's mother's sin, not David's own, and certainly not Adam's, and there is nothing here about everybody else. It must therefore simply be hyperbole, David confessing that he is a grievous sinner.[120]

---

[118] Grotius has no comment to make on Gen. 6:5 in his annotations. On Gen. 8:21, however, he says, "Id est, non ob id quod corrupti sunt homines, posthac puniam universos, sed sceleratiores. Bene fert hunk sensum Hebraea constructio" (i.e., the best way to understand the Hebrew here is that, although all men have been corrupted, God won't punish all of them, only the more wicked ones). He adds that *ad adolescentia sua* is "*hyperbole tali qualis est* Psalm 58:3, 71:6, Isaiah 48:8, Job 31:18" (*Hugonis Grotii Annotationes in Vetus Testamentum. Tomus I*, 19).
[119] Henry Hammond, *The Works of the Reverend and Learned Henry Hammond, D. D. The Fourth Volume Containing A Paraphrase and Annotations upon the Psalms*, 2nd ed. (Oxford, 1683), 151.
[120] Limborch, *Theologia Christiana*, 2:192 (§ 16): "Non enim David dicit se in matre sua peccasse; sed matris suæ peccatum commemorat? Non facit ullam mentionem Adami, sed non altius quam ad matrem suam adscendit. Nec etiam omnes homines in iniquitate genitos dicit, sui solius tantum mentionem facit." He compares the alleged hyperbole here with that in Pss. 22, 58, 71, and Job 31, just as Grotius does. Cf. also Episcopius, *Institutiones Theologicae* 4.5.2, in *Opera Theologica*, 1:406, who does the same.

ROMANS 5:12, 16

The Canons of Dort adduce Romans 5:16, "the guilt of one leads to condemnation," as a proof text against those who see no eternal punishment
due as a result of original sin. Arminius himself had said that "On account
of this transgression, man fell under the displeasure and the wrath of God,
rendered himself subject to a double death, and deserving to be deprived of
the primeval righteousness and holiness in which a great part of the image
of God consisted." He cited Romans 5:12, 16, alongside Genesis 3:3–6, 23,
24, as proof of this.[121] The *Dutch Annotations*, authorized by the Synod of
Dort, explain that Romans 5 shows us "that therefore it is not absurd that
we are all justified by one man's obedience, seeing we were all made sinners by one man's disobedience. . . . Eve is also comprehended forasmuch
as these two were one flesh, and one common stock of all mankind." They
add that "all men that dy have not committed any actual sin in themselves,
as appears in infants, many of which dy in their infancy: and therefore, must
have sinned in this one man in whose loyns they were: as Levi is said to have
given Tithes, being in the Loynes of *Abraham*, Hebrews 7:9." We are then
referred to "a large exposition hereof" in Job 14:4, Psalm 51:7 (ET 51:5),
John 3:5–6, and Ephesians 2:3. On Romans 5:16 we are told that "we for
sin are guilty before God's judgement of temporal and eternal death, as appears by what follows," i.e., the guilt of one leads to "condemnation." The
inclusion of eternal death is again made clear in the exposition of verse 21,
because the opposite of "death" there is "*eternal life* through Jesus Christ
our Lord" (cf. Rom. 6:23).

Diodati on Romans 5:12 says of Adam's posterity that "by his sinne
imputed to al his Seed, it was all under God's curse deprived of originall
righteousness, corruption its whole naturall, and subject to death." He speaks
under verse 13 of how

> this original corruption is verified by the effects of all men's actual sinnes,
> in all ages even before the law of Moises which sheweth that there was
> before that another generall law namely that of nature the reliques of which
> doe yet remaine in man (Romans 2:14–15) against which Adam having
> actually sinned, hath enfolded all his posterity in the same fault and hath
> propagated originall sinne in it.[122]

---

[121] Arminius, *Works*, 1:480; cf. 1:485, "liability to two deaths" and how this sin "is common to the entire race and to
all their posterity, who, at the time when this sin was committed, were in their loins" (an image also found in 1:585).
[122] Diodati, *Pious Annotations*.

The *English Annotations* are plagiarized from Diodati here, also saying that mankind is "deprived of originall righteousnesse, corrupted through their whole nature, and subject to death eternall." Note, however, that it is spelled out about death here being eternal death, not simply corporal, so that there is no misunderstanding. They also add that "by sinne, is meant that disease which is ours by inheritance, and men commonly call originall sinne, for so he useth to call that sinne in the singular number; whereas when he speaketh of the fruits thereof, he useth the plurall number, calling them sinnes."[123]

On the other side, Episcopius's exegesis of Romans 5 was, says Mark Ellis, "creative and perhaps unprecedented." Episcopius argued that Romans 5 referred only to sinners who lived between the fall and the Mosaic law, which enabled him to avoid the idea of original sin in the passage, but, as Ellis says, this interpretation "also negated the Reformed doctrine of justification by grace through faith alone."[124] Similarly, the Arminian Anglican Henry Hammond speaks on Romans 5:12, 16, and 6:23 only of death and mortality, and never of eternal death or punishment, even when the contrast in Romans 6:23 with eternal life might suggest it.[125] Likewise, Grotius claims that the word "condemnation" in Romans 5:16 (εἰς κατάκριμα [*ad damnationem*]) really just means "death."[126] Limborch is keen to make the point that Romans 5:12 is about nothing other than the *actual* sin, the personal sin, of Adam, by which death was first introduced. Adam died for his sin, and all those who *imitate* Adam in his transgression have been subjected to the same death.[127]

EPHESIANS 2:1–3

The apostle Paul writes,

> [You] were dead in the trespasses and sins in which you once walked, following the course of this world, following the prince of the power of the air, the spirit that is now at work in the sons of disobedience—among whom

---

[123] Downame, *Annotations upon All the Books of the Old and New Testament*.

[124] Ellis, *Simon Episcopius*, 161; cf. Episcopius, *Institutiones Theologicae* 4.5.2, in *Opera Theologica*, 1:404–5.

[125] Henry Hammond, *A Paraphrase and Annotations upon All the Books of the New Testament* (London, 1659), 461–65.

[126] "Frequens est Hebraeis causam nominare pro effectu, quamvis ex alia causa procedente. Ita, quia damnati mori solent, *damnatio* hic dicitur pro *morte*" (Hugo Grotius, *Hugonis Grotii Annotationes in Novum Testamentum. Volumen VI* [Groningae, 1828], 106).

[127] Limborch, *Theologia Christiana*, 2:191. "Intelligitur mors Adami: dicitur nempe peccandi initium esse factum ab Adamo, eumque propterea mortuum: atque ita ad exemplum Adami reliquos esse mortuos, quia Adamum peccantem imitati sunt."

we all once lived in the passions of our flesh, carrying out the desires of the body and the mind, and were by nature children of wrath, like the rest of mankind. (Eph. 2:1–3)

These verses are cited often in the submissions at Dort,[128] and are both alluded to and quoted in the Canons.[129] Arminius had said that "Whatever punishment was brought down upon our first parents, has likewise pervaded and yet pursues all their posterity. So that all men 'are by nature the children of wrath' (Eph. 2:3), obnoxious to condemnation, and to temporal as well as to eternal death."[130]

More expansively, the *Dutch Annotations* tell us that "you were dead" means we were "not only subject to temporal and eternal death, but also without any life and motion in spiritual things, as this word *to be dead* is also taken elsewhere."[131] They also point out that "carrying out the desires" is plural in the Greek (θελήματα), glossing this as the "lusts and inclinations" of "our corrupt nature." We are by nature, they say, "i.e. from our birth, or even from our mother's womb, as this word *nature* is also taken . . . *children of wrath*, that is, subject to the wrath of God by reason of sin, in which we were born."[132] The *Annotations* also tells us here to "see Job 14:4, Psalm 51:7, John 3:6, and Romans 5:12, 13, 14."

Dortian delegate Diodati says that "the spirit that is now at work in the sons of disobedience" is "the authour of the evill inclination, and motion that is in corrupt men." God is not the author of sin, but Satan is. He adds that "being born in sin and corruption we were by our birth subject to the wrath and curse of God."[133] The *English Annotations* add to this, that

Children of wrath may be understood, either actively, such as deserve wrath, as Judas is said to be the childe of perdition (John 17:12), and the Pharisees Proselytes, the children of hell: (Matt. 23:15) or passively, such as are lyable to the wrath of God, and the sentence of eternall death; men in God's hatred, as well as others, that is, profane people which know not God.[134]

---

[128] They are cited by the delegations from Hesse (*Acta*, 2:189), Emden (*Acta*, 2:216, 241), the universities (*Acta*, 3:214), Gelderland (*Acta*, 3:219–20), South Holland (*Acta*, 3:229), North Holland (*Acta*, 3:238), Zeeland (*Acta*, 3:247–48), Utrecht (*Acta*, 3:259), Overijssel (*Acta*, 3:271, 275), Groningen (*Acta*, 3:282–283), Drenthe (*Acta*, 3:297), and the Walloon church (*Acta*, 3:306).

[129] They are alluded to in Canons of Dort 3/4.3, and quoted in Canons of Dort 3/4, Rejection 3 and Rejection 4.

[130] Arminius, *Works*, 1:486.

[131] Haak, *Dutch Annotations*, citing Rom. 6:13, Eph. 5:14, Col. 2:13, and 1 Tim. 5:6 for this meaning of "dead."

[132] Haak, *Dutch Annotations*, citing Gal. 2:15 (which has the same word, φύσει), "and elsewhere" for this meaning of "by nature" (perhaps they had in mind Gal. 4:8, "those that *by nature* are not gods").

[133] Diodati, *Pious Annotations*.

[134] Downame, *Annotations upon All the Books of the Old and New Testament*.

Hammond, however, does not understand "children of wrath" to mean this. He understands it to refer to how the Gentile church of Rome, from which Paul writes, "went on in those heathen customes, which did universally overspread them, and were born, and lived, and continued in a damning condition."[135] He refers here to a note on 1 Corinthians 11, that we might understand what he means by this. There he tells us that φύσει ("by nature") in Ephesians 2:3 "applied to the national universal custome of idolatry among the Gentiles." He seems therefore to understand this to be talking about a *customary* idolatry that some have fallen into, not a state of fallen nature as such.[136] Hence, in Ephesians 2:4 he interprets "dead in sins" as being in "this heathen state of all kind of impieties, a state so farre from meriting any such dealing, that it deserved nothing but utter desertion."[137] What he means by "desertion" or "damning condition," however, is not quite clear.

Similarly, Grotius sees "dead in sins" to mean something less than *dead* in sins and spiritually lifeless. Rather, he sees it simply as an expression meaning "they are immersed in vice," with "*scarcely* any hope of rising to a better life"—though not, it is implied, without *any* hope.[138] He parallels this with Romans 6:2, "How can we who died to sin still live in it?," to show that the dead nevertheless can in some sense live.[139] On the phrase "we are *by nature* children of wrath" in Ephesians 2:3, Grotius says that φύσει just means "truly" or "genuinely."[140] So Paul is saying we truly deserve to be punished for our sins, but *not* that we are incapacitated by them or that this is a condition we are born into as descendants of Adam. Rather, we merit punishment because of our actual sins, as the Remonstrant Confession teaches and as the Remonstrants such as Episcopius maintained.

Limborch says that the apostle manifestly contradicts the Reformed reading of Ephesians 2:3. The cause of God's wrath in this verse is not natural

---

[135] Hammond, *Paraphrase and Annotations*, 617
[136] Hammond, *Paraphrase and Annotations*, 549.
[137] Hammond, *Paraphrase and Annotations*, 617.
[138] "Alioqui si dativus in proprio suo sensu sumatur, ἀποθνήσκειν τῇ ἁμαρτίᾳ longe aliud indicat ad eo quod hic significatur, ut videre est Rom. 6:2. *Mortui in peccatis* sunt homines immersi vitiis, ita ut vix ulla spes sit eos ad vitam meliorem posse resurgere" (Hugo Grotius, *Hugonis Grotii Annotationes in Novum Testamentum. Volumen VII* [Groningae, 1829], 18).
[139] As Gerhard, *On Sin and Free Choice*, Commonplace XIV, ch. 4, § 40, says on this verse, "just as a dead person can provide no help for his physical resuscitation, so a person spiritually dead in sins can provide no help for his spiritual resuscitation," against Bellarmine, who claimed those who are "dead in sins" here are merely "men living in one kind of life" who can "cooperate toward their own vivification."
[140] "*Ira* in his libris saepe est poena, *filii irae* sunt qui poenam meruere, sicut *filii mortis*, qui mortem, 2 Samuel 12:5, John 17:12, 2 Thessalonians 2:3. φύσει autem significat *non opinione, sed revera*, ut Gal. 4:8, ἀληθῶς, γνησίως" (Grotius, *Annotationes in Novum Testamentum. Volumen VII*, 20).

corruption, but *actual sins*, in which the Ephesians "once walked," as the verse says.[141] Like Grotius, he appeals to Galatians 4:8 to interpret φύσει as "truly" or "genuinely" (just as false gods are not God by nature, i.e., not *truly* God, so we are by nature, that is, we are *genuinely* deserving of God's anger). This makes better sense in the whole context, he claims.[142] Elsewhere he also points out that the main verb is "we were," not "we are" by nature children of wrath, so it cannot be talking about our "natural state." It only refers to those who walk in the lusts of concupiscence and the desires of the flesh. Echoing what Hammond says about "customary idolatry," he concludes that such people "by reason of this *custom* of sinning were truly the children of wrath."[143]

It is noticeable in all this exegetical work that there are patterns of textual relationships and exegetical moves made by our interpreters. For example, Arminian expositors tend to resort to the device of hyperbole, and link various Psalms together, just as they cross-reference to Galatians 4:8 when interpreting Ephesians 2:3 (see Grotius, Episcopius, and Limborch above); whereas Reformed interpreters often appeal to a nexus of texts to build a cumulative picture and explain the larger context into which Ephesians 2:3 fits, or they note the parallels between references to "death" and "eternal life" to interpret death as more than simply physical (see the *Dutch Annotations*, Diodati, and common cross-references and lists of proof texts in the *Acta* and annotations). The Reformed shared their understanding of certain verses with Lutherans such as Johann Gerhard, while the Remonstrants shared theirs with Jesuits such as Cardinal Bellarmine. The interpretation of these verses is always part of a larger picture drawn from Scripture as a whole, which is sensitive to the key terminology as used elsewhere in the Bible. Whether one finds particular exegetical moves convincing or not may perhaps have more to do with one's wider commitments, but it is worth being aware of how exegesis and doctrine interact with one another in these particular debates, as in many others. Exegetical traditions can be established or developed and confirmed

---

[141] Limborch, *Theologia Christiana*, 2:193: "Causa irae hujus non assignatur corruptio aliqua naturalis, sed peccata actualia, in quibus Ephesii ante *ambulaverant* . . ." (cf. the same approach in Episcopius, *Institutiones Theologicae* 4.5.2, in *Opera Theologica*, 1:406).

[142] Limborch, *Theologia Christiana*, 2:193: "Unde evincitur, phrasin *naturâ* hic non significare, à nativitate, sed vere, seu reverâ: perinde ut *Gal.* IV. 8. *Serviebatis iis qui naturâ non sunt Dii:* hoc est, qui reverâ non sunt Dii. Atque ita verba hæc optime conveniunt cum toto contextu." Episcopius, *Institutiones Theologicae* 4.5.2, in *Opera Theologica*, 1:406, also appeals to Gal. 2:15.

[143] Limborch, *Theologia Christiana*, 1:81 (book 2, ch. 10, sec. 15): "Non dicitur, *sumus naturâ* filii irae, sed *eramus.* Et vox *naturâ*, non denotat statum nostrum naturalem; quasi in eo filii iræ esse possemus; sed tantundem sonat, atque reverâ; perinde ut *Gal.* IV. 8. Loquitur Apostolos de peccatoribus, qui in concupiscentiis ac desideriis carnis ambulaverant, & ob istam peccandi consuetudinem reverâ filii iræ fuerant."

as new generations of interpreters address themselves to the text, with their own pressing concerns or new questions in mind, which in turn helps to advance our understanding of the unerring word of God and its application.

Conclusion

The upsurge in East Indian trade launched a period of political, economic, and religious strife in the Netherlands. The Synod of Dort was part of the religious changing of the tides that was ushered in as a result.[144] The Synod contained a number of strong advocates for foreign mission, keen to make the most of the new opportunities. For example, Gisbertus Voetius (1589–1676) was concerned about best practice for the conversion of the heathen and how to foster ministry in the Malay language.[145] Jan Jongeneel even describes Dort as "the first national synod to be self-consciously busy with the issues of missions."[146] This heart for the lost is reflected in the Canons of Dort at several points,[147] and it was certainly a driving factor when it came to the Synod's debates and pronouncements on the third head of doctrine as raised by the *Remonstrance* of 1610. It was crucial to know the spiritual state of those outside of Christ who were being encountered by the Dutch in their overseas endeavors. It was vital to be clear on how, if at all, the dominant Dutch could be distinguished from those they sought to evangelize. There was an urgency to evangelism if original sin condemns everyone to a double death, which might not have been so apparent if Episcopius and the Remonstrants had been declared right. These things needed to be addressed by those seeking to fulfil the Great Commission of Matthew 28, particularly when there were rival interpretations of these critical doctrines at work behind the scenes in Dutch political life as well. The clarifying work of the Synod on the areas of human corruption and conversion, therefore, was hugely important for the future of the nation, the international Reformed movement, and the many places around the world which were now being touched by the hands of Protestant powers.

[144] Bangs, *Arminius*, 176–85.
[145] Knegt, "That Christ Be Honored," 265.
[146] Jan Jongeneel, "The Missiology of Gisbertus Voetius: The First Comprehensive Protestant Theology of Missions," in *CTJ* 26 (1991): 48.
[147] As well as my opening section above, see also Anthony A. Hoekema, "The Missionary Focus of the Canons of Dordt," in *CTJ* 7 (November 1972); and Lyle Bierma, "The Canons of Dordt as a Missional Document," in *Pro Rege* 48.1 (September 2019): 1–6.

8

"By a Divine Constitution"

OLD PRINCETON AND THE
IMPUTATION OF ADAM'S SIN

Ryan M. McGraw

Introduction

The Presbyterian Church U.S.A. founded Princeton Seminary in 1812 in order to produce Reformed and Presbyterian ministers of the gospel in an American context.[1] After Archibald Alexander (1772–1851) served as its first professor, Samuel Miller (1769–1850) joined him in 1813 and Charles Hodge (1779–1878), intermittently due to his international travel, in 1820. Other prominent Princeton theologians during this period included Ashbel Green (1762–1848), Charles Hodge's son A. A. Hodge (1823–86), Caspar Wistar Hodge (1830–91), Benjamin Breckenridge Warfield (1887–1921), and Geerhardus Vos (1862–1949). This school continued as a bastion for training Reformed and Presbyterian ministers and missionaries until its theological reorganization by the General Assembly of the church in 1929.[2] References to Princeton theology before this date typically use the term "Old Princeton."

[1] Useful histories of Princeton Seminary include David B. Calhoun, *Princeton Seminary*, 2 vols. (Edinburgh: Banner of Truth, 1996); James H. Moorhead, *Princeton Seminary in American Religion and Culture* (Grand Rapids, MI: Eerdmans, 2012); Gary Steward, *Princeton Seminary (1812–1929): The Leaders' Lives and Works* (Phillipsburg, NJ: P&R, 2014); William K. Selden, *Princeton Theological Seminary: A Narrative History, 1812–1992* (Princeton, NJ: Princeton University Press, 1992). This last volume goes beyond Old Princeton, up to the 1990s.
[2] See Daryl G. Hart, "The Reorganization of Princeton Theological Seminary and the Exhaustion of American Presbyterianism," *Confessional Presbyterian* 8 (2012): 109–19.

This essay focuses on Old Princeton's teaching on the imputation of Adam's sin to his descendants. Its thesis is that major Old Princeton theologians retained a classic Reformed emphasis on the imputation of Adam's sin to his posterity, while adapting the doctrine to an American context. They did so primarily by appealing to the covenant of works, as carried over from high orthodox Reformed theology.[3] We can understand their teaching by summarizing the development of classic Reformed views on imputation, by surveying Princeton's American context, and by asking on what grounds they taught that God imputed original sin to the human race. In order to narrow our focus, I will examine the writings of Archibald Alexander, Charles Hodge, A. A. Hodge, and B. B. Warfield. Charles Hodge, who wrote more on original sin and the imputation of Adam's sin than any other Princeton theologian, will supply the main narrative, with appropriate references to Alexander, A. A. Hodge, and Warfield. Old Princeton's teaching on the imputation of Adam's sin is important because it provides readers with a broader view of the ways in which contemporary contexts influenced how these theologians received and promoted Reformed doctrine. This can help us draw lessons for doing so in our own day.

Setting the Reformed Orthodox Context

Old Princeton drew from Reformed scholastic conversations with the entire Christian tradition and applied Reformed theology in a complex American context.[4] This makes setting a historical context for Princeton theology much more complicated than studying this earlier period. Princeton adapted Reformed scholastic theology to recent theological, philosophical, and scientific trends. While the Princeton theologians selected below are highly readable, these features of their work can make it harder at times for modern readers to appreciate their connection to the broader Christian tradition.

---

[3] For the periodization of Reformed orthodoxy, see Richard A. Muller, *Post-Reformation Reformed Dogmatics: The Rise and Development of Reformed Orthodoxy, Ca. 1520 to Ca. 1725,* 2nd ed. (Grand Rapids, MI: Baker Academic, 2003), 1:30–32. Generally, the "high orthodox" period began with the Synod of Dort in 1619 and closed around 1700 with the dawn of the Enlightenment.

[4] Treatments of Reformed scholastic theology include Willem J. van Asselt, "Scholasticism Revisited: Methodological Reflections on the Study of Seventeenth-Century Reformed Thought," in *Seeing Things Their Way,* ed. Alister Chapman, John Coffey, and Brad S. Gregory (Notre Dame, IN: University of Notre Dame Press, 2009), 154–74; Willem J. van Asselt et al., *Introduction to Reformed Scholasticism,* trans. Albert Gootjes (Grand Rapids, MI: Reformation Heritage, 2011); *Scholasticism Reformed: Essays in Honour of Willem J. Van Asselt,* ed. Maarten Wisse, Marcel Sarot, and Willemien Otten, vol. 14, *Studies in Theology and Religion* (Leiden, Netherlands: Brill, 2010); Dolf te Velde, "Reformed Theology and Scholasticism," in *Cambridge Companion to Reformed Theology,* ed. Paul T. Nimmo and David A. F. Ferguson (New York: Cambridge University Press, 2016), 215–29; Ryan M. McGraw, *Reformed Scholasticism: Recovering the Tools of Reformed Theology* (Edinburgh: T&T Clark, 2019).

This section wades through some of this material by setting a wider Reformed context. It treats the early seventeenth-century development of the doctrine of original sin with an aim toward the eventual function of the covenant of works in this doctrine. After doing so, I will introduce some of the key issues that affected Princeton's American context. While the story of the doctrine of original sin began in the early church and continued through the medieval period, we must narrow our focus to the areas listed here.[5]

Reformed Orthodox Developments on the Imputation of Adam's Sin

In the early seventeenth century, the idea of the imputation of Adam's sin existed prior to explicit statements of the covenant of works. However, by the end of the century these ideas were bound together. This section provides representative samples of this development from William Bucanus, Franciscus Gomarus, and Herman Ravensperger, concluding with the Westminster Standards and Francis Turretin. This background is relevant to Old Princeton because of the way in which the covenant of works became vital to Reformed arguments for the imputation of Adam's sin.

WILLIAM BUCANUS

William Bucanus (d. 1603) was a Swiss-French theologian who wrote one of the first Reformed systems of doctrine. His system remained influential in Reformed universities for some time, including in America. This makes him an important representative of early Reformed views of the imputation of Adam's sin.

Bucanus began with the doctrine of God,[6] moving immediately to Christology and God's plan of redemption.[7] Locus III focuses on the Holy Spirit, who applies Christ's redemption to his elect.[8] This places both the triune God and the gospel at the forefront of his system. Locus IV introduces Scripture as the means by which God communicates himself today.[9] Creation comes

---

[5] While literature on original sin and the early church is legion, some examples include George A. Riggan, "Original Sin in the Thought of Augustine" (PhD diss., Yale University, 1949); Isabella Image, *The Human Condition in Hilary of Poitiers: The Will and Original Sin between Origen and Augustine* (Oxford: Oxford University Press, 2017); John E. Toews, *The Story of Original Sin* (Cambridge: James Clarke, 2013).
[6] William Bucanus, *Institutiones Theologicae, Seu, Locorum Communium Christanae Religionis* (Geneva, 1648), 1–12.
[7] Bucanus, *Institutiones Theologicae*, 12–26.
[8] Bucanus, *Institutiones Theologicae*, 26–35.
[9] Bucanus, *Institutiones Theologicae*, 35–45.

next.[10] Before turning to mankind, Bucanus treated angels,[11] including special attention to fallen angels.[12] He introduced the topic of sin in relation to angels first, whom original sin does not affect, and whom he regarded as exemplifying the sin against the Holy Spirit.[13]

In Locus VIII (*de Homine*), Bucanus commented briefly on the transmission of original sin. His creationist (as opposed to traducian) account of the origin of the human soul raised the question as to how the guilt of Adam's sin could pass to his posterity.[14] He answered that the transmission of sin was not by reason of the soul or of the body, but by reason of propagation from one, namely Adam, who corrupted the whole genus of mankind.[15] Bucanus stated simply that this happened by the order of God.[16] This is where the covenant of works later came in to explain how this was possible. Bucanus added that Adam was both root and head of all mankind, and that the human soul is corrupted at conception by God's just ordination.[17] He stated as a fact that the guilt of Adam's sin is imputed to his posterity, citing Romans 5:12, with little explanation. He reiterated that the imputation of Adam's disobedience stands by just ordination of God.[18] Adam's sin is imputed in the same way that Christ's obedience is imputed to us in our justification,[19] resulting in a parallel between the imputation of Adam's disobedience and the imputation of Christ's obedience.[20] Finally, there is a similar parallel between regeneration and the habit and *radix* (root) of sin, which comes by propagation.[21] These parallels between Adam and Christ, and man's corrupt disposition and the Spirit's work in regeneration would become prominent in Princeton theology.

---

[10] Bucanus, *Institutiones Theologicae*, 45–60 (Locus V).
[11] Bucanus, *Institutiones Theologicae*, 45–60 (Locus VI).
[12] Bucanus, *Institutiones Theologicae*, 74–84 (Locus VII).
[13] Bucanus, *Institutiones Theologicae*, 76.
[14] Bucanus, *Institutiones Theologicae*, 91–92. "Creationism" here refers to the idea that God creates each human soul directly in the case of every human being at their conception. Traducianism is the opposing theory, that the soul is created through natural generation in the same way as the body is. These terms will be relevant in the discussion of Old Princeton below.
[15] Bucanus, *Institutiones Theologicae*, 92.
[16] Bucanus, *Institutiones Theologicae*, 92.
[17] Bucanus, *Institutiones Theologicae*, 92; citing Calvin, *Institutes*, 1.2.7.
[18] Bucanus, *Institutiones Theologicae*, 93.
[19] Bucanus, *Institutiones Theologicae*, 93.
[20] Heber de Campos expertly shows the development of the Reformed teaching that God imputed Christ's righteous life (active obedience) as well as his suffering and death (passive obedience) to believers in response to Johannes Piscator (1546–1625), who taught the imputation of Christ's work on the cross only. De Campos's treatment of the gradual development of Reformed theology on this point is methodologically similar to my narrative here on the development of the covenant of works in relation to imputation (Heber Carlos de Campos, *Doctrine in Development: Johannes Piscator and Debates over Christ's Active Obedience*, Reformed Historical-Theological Studies [Grand Rapids, MI: Reformation Heritage, 2018]).
[21] Bucanus, *Institutiones Theologicae*, 93.

Before turning to sin proper, Bucanus treated the image of God in man,[22] man's original righteousness,[23] free will prior to the fall,[24] and marriage.[25] Locus XIII treats divorce.[26] Locus XIV then introduces providence.[27] Only in Locus XV did he treat the topic of sin directly.[28] Original sin occupies pages 161–167, while Locus XVI focuses on actual sin distinctly,[29] followed by a treatment of the sin against the Holy Spirit.[30] Subsequent loci then stress the effects of sin.

After noting that Adam's sin affected his posterity, Bucanus asked how original sin was derived.[31] Citing Romans 5:12, he stated that original sin is in all Adam's posterity, including infants, making them odious to God. Since infants cannot commit actual sin, this must refer to original sin. Christ alone is exempted from original sin because the Spirit sanctified him in his mother's womb.[32] Original sin is alien to us rather than being our own proper sin.[33] Adam was not a private person, but he was the head of humanity and he sinned as such. Though Bucanus did not use the term, this entailed imputation. Again, this point about the imputation of Adam's sin is where "covenant of works" language appeared among later authors, in order to explain this relationship between Adam and his posterity.[34] Original sin is propagated through generation. The parallel with Christ communicating his obedience to his members demonstrates as well that Adam's sin was first communicated to his in like manner. Adam is the only man who bears this relation to his descendants.[35] Bucanus noted that original sin is accidental to humanity and it does not change human substance. Here he cited Augustine, who noted explicitly that original sin involved imputed guilt.[36] Original sin also affects the whole human nature, corrupting all of its parts.[37]

---

[22] Bucanus, *Institutiones Theologicae*, 95–99 (Locus IX).
[23] Bucanus, *Institutiones Theologicae*, 99–102 (Locus X).
[24] Bucanus, *Institutiones Theologicae*, 102–8 (Locus XI).
[25] Bucanus, *Institutiones Theologicae*, 102–8 (Locus XII).
[26] Bucanus, *Institutiones Theologicae*, 128–40.
[27] Bucanus, *Institutiones Theologicae*, 140–52.
[28] Bucanus, *Institutiones Theologicae*, 153–67.
[29] Bucanus, *Institutiones Theologicae*, 167–71.
[30] Bucanus, *Institutiones Theologicae*, 171–77 (Locus XVII).
[31] Bucanus, *Institutiones Theologicae*, 161.
[32] Bucanus, *Institutiones Theologicae*, 161. He added that infants are sanctified to God in the church only in accord with 1 Cor. 7:14 (162).
[33] Bucanus, *Institutiones Theologicae*, 162.
[34] As we will see below, Michael McGiffert incorrectly treated the covenant of works as a breach with authors like Bucanus, rather than a seamless development (Michael McGiffert, "Grace and Works: The Rise and Division of Covenant Divinity in Elizabethan Puritanism," *HTR* 75.4 [1982]: 475).
[35] Bucanus, *Institutiones Theologicae*, 162.
[36] Bucanus, *Institutiones Theologicae*, 163.
[37] Bucanus, *Institutiones Theologicae*, 163–64.

According to Bucanus, what, then, is original sin? It is not only privation of good, but the depravation and corruption of human nature.[38] Infants are born with this corruption, though Bucanus noted above that they are also born with Adam's guilt imputed to them.[39] Original sin creates a habit, or disposition, toward sin, which is distinct from actual sin.[40] The wages of original sin include death and every inconvenience throughout life. This doctrine has uses. It should lead us to flee to Christ as our propitiation. We must also confess that Christ alone is our righteousness.[41] Original sin also demonstrates our need for regeneration.[42] The remainder of this section refutes eight errors, which includes the Pelagians, the Manicheans, and those denying the imputation of Adam's sin.[43] Bucanus's treatment clearly includes the fact of the imputation of Adam's sin by a sovereign disposition of God, while leaving the grounds of imputed sin largely unexplained.

FRANCISCUS GOMARUS

Franciscus Gomarus (1563–1641) was a professor at Leiden University. He is best known as one of the primary opponents of Jacob Arminius (1560–1609) and as a member of the Synod of Dort. Though he wrote slightly later than Bucanus, his discussion of original sin is less developed, even though his exposition of sin itself was fairly extensive. He is an important internationally acclaimed representative of the early high orthodox period of the seventeenth century. His treatment of original sin is taken here from his *Locorum Communium Theologicarum Epitome.*[44]

Gomarus began his chapter on sin with a definition of what sin is, accompanied by a brief introduction to original sin. He described sin as the vitiation of the law of God.[45] Properly, sin signifies aberration from what we ought to do.[46] Improperly and metaphorically, sin refers to injustice.[47] He then asserted that original sin is the fountain of all other sin.[48] This is where Gomarus's treatment is less developed than Bucanus's. He took only a passing glance at

[38] Bucanus, *Institutiones Theologicae*, 164.
[39] Bucanus, *Institutiones Theologicae*, 165.
[40] Bucanus, *Institutiones Theologicae*, 165.
[41] Bucanus, *Institutiones Theologicae*, 166, citing Rom. 5:15 ff.
[42] Bucanus, *Institutiones Theologicae*, 166, citing John 3:5.
[43] Bucanus, *Institutiones Theologicae*, 167–68.
[44] Franciscus Gomarus, *Locorum Communium Theologicorum Epitome* (Amstelodami, 1653).
[45] Gomarus, *Locorum Communium Theologicorum Epitome*, 144.
[46] Gomarus, *Locorum Communium Theologicorum Epitome*, 145.
[47] Gomarus, *Locorum Communium Theologicorum Epitome*, 145, citing 1 John 3:4.
[48] Gomarus, *Locorum Communium Theologicorum Epitome*, 146.

Adam's sin being counted to his posterity in order to focus on habitual and actual sin.[49] While Bucanus treated the sin of angels before the sin of mankind, Gomarus lumped them together.[50] In both cases, sin involves transgression of God's law and defect from original righteousness. He then examined the sin of angels.[51] There are some parallels between the sin of men and angels. The angels, by their fall, lost God's grace and favor; fell from heaven into the air; are punished by loss and by sense; they lost holiness of nature and are given to evil; and they will be sent to flames of fire.[52] However, the parallel between angels and men breaks down in that Christ came to save human beings only.[53] The parallel between Adam and Christ with regard to the imputation of sin and righteousness is not explicit.

As we saw with Bucanus, habitual sin, resulting from the depravation of original righteousness, lay at the core of original sin. Gomarus argued that the penalty of death and the privation of original righteousness passed to Adam's descendants by divine institution.[54] Citing Romans 5:12, 14 as evidence, he stated without further explanation that both Adam's sin and his punishment came to his posterity through natural generation. Like Bucanus, he added that this was the only case in which God counted the sins of a father to his posterity.[55] Gomarus virtually reduced original sin to innate habitual sin.[56] As a result, he drew less attention to the parallels between Adam and Christ than Bucanus did. Gomarus's treatment of habitual sin enveloped a creationist account of the origins of the human soul.[57] The bulk of his material is devoted to actual sin, including a detailed exposition of the sin against the Holy Spirit.[58]

HERMAN RAVENSPERGER

Herman Ravensperger (1586–1625) was a German-born professor at the University of Groningen. Unlike Bucanus and Gomarus, he is not well known.[59] Yet he is important in illustrating the Reformed development of the imputation of Adam's sin because he was one of the earliest authors to couch this

[49] Gomarus, *Locorum Communium Theologicorum Epitome*, 147.
[50] Gomarus, *Locorum Communium Theologicorum Epitome*, 148.
[51] Gomarus, *Locorum Communium Theologicorum Epitome*, 149–54.
[52] Gomarus, *Locorum Communium Theologicorum Epitome*, 153.
[53] Gomarus, *Locorum Communium Theologicorum Epitome*, 154.
[54] Gomarus, *Locorum Communium Theologicorum Epitome*, 158 (*ex Dei instituto*).
[55] Gomarus, *Locorum Communium Theologicorum Epitome*, 158.
[56] Gomarus, *Locorum Communium Theologicorum Epitome*, 158–19.
[57] Gomarus, *Locorum Communium Theologicorum Epitome*, 159.
[58] Gomarus, *Locorum Communium Theologicorum Epitome*, 162–69.
[59] I am grateful to Henk van den Belt for alerting my attention to Ravensperger's work.

doctrine explicitly in the context of a covenant of works between God and Adam. His use of the covenant of works, though not his expression of it, would soon become standard fare among Reformed authors.[60]

In his *Catechismus Religione Christianae*, Ravensperger structured the entire system of theology around the covenants of works and of grace.[61] From the time of the ancient church, catechetical instruction followed the pattern of the Apostle's Creed, the Ten Commandments, and the Lord's Prayer. The Creed became a grid through which Reformed authors taught the major doctrines of their theological systems.[62] This order is detectable, for instance, in both Westminster Catechisms, which proceed from "what man is to believe concerning God" to the duty that God requires of man. Ravensperger, however, chose a fivefold division consisting of the Decalogue, the Apostle's Creed, the sacraments, the Lord's Prayer, and ecclesiastical discipline.[63]

The reason why Ravensperger began with the Decalogue was that it enabled him to introduce the covenants of works and of grace. Questions 10–17 explain the nature of covenants in Scripture by way of prologue.[64] A covenant (*foedus*) of God is a pact (*pactum*) between God and man in which God promises life based on a certain condition. Such covenants consist in two parts: reciprocal promises on both sides.[65] Man promises to worship and obey God, while God, in turn, promises to be his God if man fulfills the stipulations of the covenant. This effectively collapsed the promises and stipulations of covenants into one, which later Reformed authors distinguished into parts.[66] God's promise of life included temporal and eternal blessings, which are exhibited to us in Christ.[67] Ravensperger concluded this prologue by stating that the only two covenants between God and man were a covenant of works and a covenant of grace.

---

[60] Reformed covenant theology, including the covenant of works, developed earlier and more clearly in German Reformed theology than in most other parts of the Reformed world. This likely explains Ravensperger's dependence on the covenant idea. For this German context, see Lyle D. Bierma, *The Covenant Theology of Caspar Olevianus* (Grand Rapids, MI: Reformation Heritage, 2005); R. Scott Clark, *Caspar Olevian and the Substance of the Covenant: The Double Benefit of Christ*, Reformed Historical-Theological Studies (Grand Rapids, MI: Reformation Heritage, 2008).

[61] Herman Ravensperger, *Catechismus Religionis Christianae, Juxta Authentica Bibliorum Summari Dispositus* (Herborn, Germany, 1611).

[62] For an example, see Herman Witsius, *Sacred Dissertations: On the Apostles' Creed*, trans. Donald Fraser, 2 vols. (Grand Rapids, MI: Reformation Heritage, 2010).

[63] Ravensperger, *Catechismus Religionis Christianae*, 4.

[64] Ravensperger, *Catechismus Religionis Christianae*, 5.

[65] Ravensperger, *Catechismus Religionis Christianae*, 5 (*Hominis promisso et Dei repromisso*).

[66] For example, see Patrick Gillespie, *The Ark of the Testament Opened, or, the Secret of the Lord's Covenant Unsealed in a Treatise of the Covenant of Grace, Wherein an Essay Is Made for the Promoving [Sic] and Increase of Knowledge in the Misterie of the Gospel-Covenant Which Hath Been Hid from Ages and Generations but Now Is Made Manifest to the Saints . . .* (London, 1681), 49–51.

[67] Ravensperger, *Catechismus Religionis Christianae*, 5.

In Ravensperger's view, the covenant of works was the covenant of God with Adam upon the condition of perfect obedience, standing by the strength of nature, and expressed under the law of Moses.[68] This is why the Mosaic law is called the legal covenant.[69] The moral law is the doctrine of the word of God impressed in our first creation and afterwards given on Mount Sinai under ten precepts. Its annexes include promises of salvation for the perfect observance of the law, as well as comminations (threats) of perdition for breaking the law. The Decalogue epitomized the moral law as well as the covenant of works.[70] Treating the Decalogue inherently as a covenant of works quickly fell out of favor in Reformed theology. John Owen (1616–83) is representative when he argued that the covenant of works was present declaratively at Sinai, though not covenantally.[71] In other words, the law, which was the rule of the covenant of works, was declared at Sinai without making Sinai itself that covenant.[72] Most later Reformed authors believed that the Mosaic covenant belonged to the covenant of grace instead of to the covenant of works.[73]

The point here is not to explore the development of Reformed covenant theology, but to see the connections between Ravensperger's covenant theology and original sin.[74] Following a lengthy exposition of the Ten Commandments,[75] he concluded by summarizing the uses of the law for regenerate and unregenerate people. For the elect unregenerate, the law leads them to salvation in Christ.[76] It also leaves the reprobate inexcusable for their sins. In spite of treating the Decalogue as a covenant of works, Ravensperger maintained a twofold use of the law for the regenerate. The law should humble them for remaining sin, and it is a rule of life with God.[77] It is unclear

---

[68] Ravensperger, *Catechismus Religionis Christianae*, 6 (questions 18–20).
[69] Ravensperger, *Catechismus Religionis Christianae*, 6.
[70] Ravensperger, *Catechismus Religionis Christianae*, 6.
[71] John Owen, *The Works of John Owen, D.D.*, ed. William H. Goold, 24 vols. (Edinburgh: Johnstone & Hunter, 1850–55), 23:77.
[72] For more detail on this point, see Ryan M. McGraw, "The Threats of the Gospel: John Owen on What the Law/Gospel Distinction Is Not," *CTJ* 51 (2016): 79–111.
[73] This is a thorny question historically. For a survey of Reformed views on the Mosaic covenant, see Mark Jones, "The 'Old' Covenant," in *Drawn into Controversie: Reformed Theological Diversity and Debates within Seventeenth-Century British Puritanism*, ed. Michael A. G. Haykin and Mark Jones, Reformed Historical Theology 17 (Göttingen, Germany: Vandenhoeck & Ruprecht, 2011), 183–203. Owen believed that Sinai was neither the covenant of works nor the convent of grace.
[74] For a sound treatment of this development, see Andrew A. Woolsey, *Unity and Continuity in Covenantal Thought: A Study in the Reformed Tradition to the Westminster Assembly*, Reformed Historical-Theological Studies (Grand Rapids, MI: Reformation Heritage, 2012).
[75] Ravensperger, *Catechismus Religionis Christianae*, 6–19.
[76] Ravensperger, *Catechismus Religionis Christianae*, 19.
[77] Ravensperger, *Catechismus Religionis Christianae*, 19.

how this could be, if the law was inherently a covenant of works, though Ravensperger assumed that the law as written on man's heart in creation reflected God's character.[78] Here, he introduced the covenant of grace, writing, "The covenant of grace is the covenant of God, by which he promises Christ to men with all of his benefits, under this condition, if they believe in Christ and worship God through him."[79] This covenant is described most powerfully in the gospel, which Ravensperger taught by way of the Apostle's Creed.

Ravensperger left his doctrine of sin and its connection to the covenant of works largely underdeveloped. He returned to the doctrine of sin under his treatment of the Creed. He argued that the Creed could be divided into the doctrines of God and of the church.[80] The doctrine of God includes God and his works.[81] The creation of man and his fall into sin come under the study of God's works.[82] Before the fall, man was blessed, created in God's image with free will, and disposed to good. After the fall, man is either under the condition of corrupt nature or under grace.[83] Fallen man bears by nature the image of the devil, his will serving evil.[84] There are two parts of misery: sin and its punishment. Similar to Gomarus, Ravensperger defined sin as *aberratio a lege Dei*.[85] Temporal and eternal suffering, and death, are the penalties of sin. We are liberated from the misery of sin by grace through Christ, and the Spirit renews us in the image of God. This led Ravensperger to treat the person and offices of Christ under the heading of redemption.[86]

If Bucanus and Gomarus taught the imputation of Adam's sin without appealing to a covenant of works, then Ravensperger taught a covenant of works without addressing the imputation of Adam's sin. To be fair, Ravensperger's work is only a catechetical summary of theology. Bucanus's clear assessment of the imputation of Adam's sin characterized the later Reformed tradition. Yet so did Gomarus's emphasis on the habits and acts of sin. Ravensperger's treatment of Adam's relation to mankind through the covenant of works was the missing piece that later Reformed theologians used to explain how and why God imputed Adam's sin to the human race. While none

---

[78] By contrast, Westminster Confession of Faith 19.1–2 distinguished the use of the law as a covenant of works and the law's use as a rule of life. The concept of law is distinct from and prior to the covenant of works here.
[79] Ravensperger, *Catechismus Religionis Christianae*, 19 (my translation).
[80] Ravensperger, *Catechismus Religionis Christianae*, 20.
[81] Ravensperger, *Catechismus Religionis Christianae*, 21.
[82] Ravensperger, *Catechismus Religionis Christianae*, 24.
[83] Ravensperger, *Catechismus Religionis Christianae*, 25.
[84] Ravensperger, *Catechismus Religionis Christianae*, 26.
[85] Ravensperger, *Catechismus Religionis Christianae*, 26.
[86] Ravensperger, *Catechismus Religionis Christianae*, 26.

of these three authors combined all the elements of what would soon become the standard Reformed treatment of the doctrine, every strand of the later teaching is present here.

Conclusion: High Orthodoxy on the Imputation of Adam's Sin

Old Princeton was a confessionally Presbyterian institution, seeking to stand solidly in the Reformed tradition as represented in the Westminster Confession of Faith and the Catechisms. The school also used Francis Turretin's *Institutes* as their primary theological text until Hodge published his *Systematic Theology*.[87] Westminster and Turretin, therefore, summarized helpfully the developed seventeenth-century doctrine of the imputation of Adam's sin, which became the backdrop for Princeton's position on the subject.[88]

The Shorter Catechism defined sin as "any want of conformity unto or transgression of the law of God" (WSC 14). Paragraphs 1–2 of chapter 6 of the Confession of Faith state the fact of Adam's fall and its primary effects in terms of loss of righteousness and communion with God, which resulted in death and defilement. Paragraph 3 adds, "They being the root of all mankind, the guilt of this sin was imputed; and the same death in sin, and corrupted nature, conveyed to all their posterity descending from them by ordinary generation." The remaining three paragraphs stress that original sin included the habits of sin and it led to all "actual" sin, making mankind liable to the curses due to sin. Chapter 7, paragraphs 2–3, add the ideas that God promised life to Adam and his posterity in the covenant of works, and that his fall made obtaining life through that covenant impossible, paving the way for the covenant of grace in Christ. Larger Catechism 22 explained, "The covenant being made with Adam as a public person, not for himself only, but for his posterity, all mankind descending from him by ordinary generation, sinned in him, and fell with him in that first transgression." Question 25 then placed "the guilt of Adam's first sin" at the head of the effects of original sin on mankind, with Questions 30–31 explaining that Christ came to bring the elect out of the state of sin and misery, which came through the broken "covenant of works." Redemption comes through Christ's role in the covenant of grace

---

[87] Paul C. Gutjahr, *Charles Hodge: Guardian of American Orthodoxy* (New York: Oxford University Press, 2011), 70, 124. Gutjahr cites Hodge as calling Turretin "the best systematic theological writer with whom we are acquainted" (70).

[88] For a treatment of high orthodox expressions of the covenant of works, see Richard A. Muller, "The Covenant of Works and the Stability of Divine Law in Seventeenth-Century Reformed Orthodoxy: A Study in the Theology of Herman Witsius and Wilhelmus à Brakel," *CTJ* 29.1 (1994): 75–101.

and the work of the Spirit in applying Christ's benefits to believers (WSC 32). This seamlessly integrates the strands of thought outlined in authors like Bucanus, Gomarus, and Ravensperger.

Francis Turretin (1623–87), who taught theology in Geneva, shows how such high orthodox statements of the subject became standard fare in the Reformed tradition by the mid to late seventeenth century.[89] He taught a creationist view of the origin of the human soul.[90] His entire eighth topic treated the covenant of works before exploring sin in the ninth topic. He believed that Adam's relation to his descendants was both natural and "forensic," meaning that Adam could "hold or lose the goods bestowed upon him" for himself and for them.[91] In his view, Pelagians and Anabaptists denied the imputation of Adam's sin to his posterity, and Josue de la Place (1596–1665) in Saumur rejected the imputation of Adam's sin in favor of actual participation in his sin.[92] We will see below that Charles Hodge mirrored Turretin exactly on these points, citing the same opponents. By virtue of being our federal head in the covenant of works, "Adam stood in that sin not as a private person, but as a public and representative person—representing all his posterity in that action and whose demerit equally pertains to all."[93] He added that while original sin could include imputed and inherent sin, he and other Reformed authors focused on inherent or habitual sin, without denying imputed sin.[94] This matches Bucanus, with the addition of a covenant of works integrated into the narrative.

The tight connection that Turretin made between the covenant of works and the imputation of Adam's sin gave Old Princeton a carefully worked out expression of the theology that they found in the Westminster Standards.[95] The covenant of works had become so integral to explaining the imputation of Adam's sin by the late seventeenth century that Dutch Theologian

---

[89] For a solid treatment of Turretin's covenant theology, see J. Mark Beach, *Christ and the Covenant: Francis Turretin's Federal Theology as a Defense of the Doctrine of Grace* (Göttingen, Germany: Vandenhoeck & Ruprecht, 2007).

[90] Francis Turretin, *Institutes of Elenctic Theology*, ed. James T. Dennison Jr., trans. George Musgrave Giger, 3 vols. (Phillipsburg, NJ: P&R, 1992–97), 5.13 (1:477–82). (The first set of numbers in the citation represent topic and question numbers. The second set reflects the volume and page numbers in the English translation. All reference to Turretin below follow this pattern.)

[91] Turretin, *Institutes*, 8.3.11 (1:577).

[92] Turretin, *Institutes*, 9.9.2–4 (1:613–14). We will see below that Turretin's flow of thought reappears in Charles Hodge's treatment of the subject, including the same references to Josué de la Place and his condemnation at the French National Synod in 1644.

[93] Turretin, *Institutes*, 9.9.12 (1:616). Paragraphs 16–18 next develop a lengthy exposition of Rom. 5:12, followed by other passages of Scripture.

[94] Turretin, *Institutes*, 9.10.2 (1:629–30).

[95] Gutjahr's comments on Charles Hodge apply to the entire Princeton tradition: "In fact, it is nearly impossible to overstate the importance of the Westminster Confession on Hodge's thought" (Gutjahr, *Charles Hodge*, 26).

Wilhelmus à Brakel (1635–1711) could write, "Acquaintance with this covenant is of the greatest importance, for whoever errs here or denies the existence of the covenant of works, will not understand the covenant of grace, and will readily err concerning the mediatorship of the Lord Jesus."[96] A few decades after Bucanus, Gomarus, and Ravensperger died, the covenant of works had become vital to the Reformed system of doctrine. This gives us a vantage point from which we can more accurately understand the position of early Princeton on this subject.

The Imputation of Adam's Sin in the American Context

Old Princeton drew from and built upon Reformed orthodox expressions of the imputation of Adam's sin to his posterity through the covenant of works. These theologians regarded themselves as in line with the early church on this subject, with some passing glances at key medieval theologians, as well as with the Reformed tradition. Yet their American context was complicated by the proliferation of scientific, philosophical, and theological developments. These included issues such as evolutionary science, pantheistic philosophies and theologies, Scottish Common Sense Realism, realist and traducian views, and the New England theology that followed Jonathan Edwards.

This section introduces briefly some of these eighteenth- and nineteenth-century developments. For the sake of space, I will draw these concerns primarily from both Hodges and from Warfield, including references to secondary literature along the way for those interested in further study. The narrative here largely follows the topics as they appear in A. A. Hodge's *Outlines of Theology.*

EVOLUTIONARY SCIENCE

Princeton's position on original sin is undoubtedly couched in the context of nineteenth-century theories of evolution.[97] If man evolved from lower life forms, then both the idea that he is uniquely God's image and the notion of

[96] Wilhelmus à Brakel, *The Christian's Reasonable Service*, ed. Joel R. Beeke, trans. Bartel Elshout, 4 vols. (Grand Rapids, MI: Reformation Heritage, 2012), 1:355.
[97] Charles Hodge wrote a book-length response to Darwinism, as did his southern contemporary and fellow Presbyterian Robert Lewis Dabney (1820–1898) (Charles Hodge, *What Is Darwinism?* [New York: Scribner, Armstrong, 1874]; Robert Lewis Dabney, *The Sensualistic Philosophy of the Nineteenth Century* [New York: Anson D. F. Randolph, 1887]). For a detailed analysis of Warfield's voluminous interactions with evolution, see Bradley J. Gundlach, *Process and Providence: The Evolution Question at Princeton, 1845–1929* (Grand Rapids, MI: Eerdmans, 2013), 199–262. Hodge and Warfield were agnostic toward some limited forms of evolution, while Dabney staunchly opposed it.

Adam's federal headship are called into question. A. A. Hodge noted that the question was whether or not God made man by an immediate act of creation.[98] He added that if man had dominion over nature, then he could not be a product of nature. It was essential, in his view, that God did not create any new creatures after creating man, since man was the pinnacle of creation due to his creation in God's image.[99] Charles Hodge noted likewise that evolutionary science called into question the unity of the human race under a single head.[100] This would preclude the idea of Adam being a federal head of humanity in the covenant of works, which would negate the imputation of his sin to his posterity. Such issues continue to confront the church today.[101]

REALISM AND TRADUCIANISM

A. A. Hodge regarded realist views of participation in Adam's sin as a threat to the imputation of Adam's sin as well.[102] The realist position taught that mankind actually participated in Adam's sin, on the view that he acted on behalf of all people by inclusion in a common conception of humanity. The result was that, rather than God imputing Adam's sin to his posterity immediately by virtue of the broken covenant of works, sin was "imputed" mediately because all mankind really participated in Adam's sin.[103] This involved, in Hodge's view, a denial of the covenant of works as well as of imputation, because real participation in Adam's sin took the theological place of imputation.[104]

Traducianism became tied to realism, though not inseparably so. Traducianism was a theory of the origin of the human soul. The idea was that, while God created Adam's soul immediately, all other human souls originate with the body through natural generation. Creationism, the opposing view, taught that God created every human soul directly at conception. Charles Hodge argued that creationism was "almost universally received" in both

---

[98] A. A. Hodge, *Outlines of Theology* (Edinburgh: Banner of Truth, 1999), 296.
[99] A. A. Hodge, *Outlines of Theology*, 297.
[100] Charles Hodge, *Systematic Theology*, 3 vols. (Grand Rapids, MI: Eerdmans, 1999), 2:77.
[101] For recent attempts to reconcile evolutionary ideas with key biblical doctrines, see *Finding Ourselves after Darwin: Conversations on the Image of God, Original Sin, and the Problem of Evil*, ed. Stanley P. Rosenberg et al. (Grand Rapids, MI: Baker Academic, 2018).
[102] A. A. Hodge, *Outlines of Theology*, 193.
[103] A. A. Hodge, *Outlines of Theology*, 193. Readers should not confuse this issue with the debate over realism versus nominalism in the Middle Ages. While overlapping only slightly, this debate asked whether universal ideas were real things (realism) or only convenient names (nominalism) people use to group common phenomena together. For the relevance of this debate in late medieval theology, especially as it related to justification, see Heiko A. Oberman, *The Harvest of Medieval Theology: Gabriel Biel and Late Medieval Nominalism* (Grand Rapids, MI: Baker Academic, 2000).
[104] A. A. Hodge, *Outlines of Theology*, 211.

the East and the West, though Post-Reformation Lutheranism became traducian. Though not all traducians must be realists, all realists must adopt the traducian viewpoint in order to sustain their theory of realistic participation in humanity through Adam.[105] Hodge added that the transmission of original sin is the strongest argument for traducianism because it sought to explain how and why Adam could transmit his sin to his posterity.[106] He objected, however, that traducianism would make Christ's humanity sinful because he too would participate in Adam's sin by virtue of his participation in human nature.[107] In spite of his objections to this view, Hodge concluded that the transmission of life is a mystery "in all its forms" and that a theory on the origin of the soul cannot become the ground of a fundamental doctrine like original sin.[108]

A. A. Hodge targeted New York Presbyterian theologian W. G. T. Shedd (1820–94).[109] According to Hodge, Shedd's traducianism led him to teach that all human beings acted with Adam in his sin in the garden of Eden.[110] He noted that Shedd made sin material, rather than spiritual and personal, by consequence of his scheme.[111] Charles Hodge targeted Shedd as well.[112] The important point is that both Hodges regarded realism, which supposed traducianism, as virtually replacing the role of the covenant of works in the imputation of Adam's sin and as effectively mitigating imputation.[113]

PANTHEISM

Pantheism particularly occupied Charles Hodge's attention as a modern philosophical threat to theology.[114] Pantheism is the idea that God is the world and the world is God, making God the only true actor in the world. This was the view of philosophers such as Baruch Spinoza (1632–77). Hodge also labeled the philosophy of Friedrich Schleiermacher (1768–1834) as "pantheistic," in

---

[105] Charles Hodge, *Systematic Theology*, 2:67.
[106] Charles Hodge, *Systematic Theology*, 2:69.
[107] Charles Hodge, *Systematic Theology*, 2:72.
[108] Charles Hodge, *Systematic Theology*, 2:73.
[109] For a treatment of the interchange between Charles Hodge and Shedd on this point, see Oliver D. Crisp, "Federalism vs. Realism: Charles Hodge, Augustus Strong, and William Shedd on the Imputation of Sin," *IJST* 8.1 (2006): 55–71. In this essay, Crisp defended the realist account.
[110] A. A. Hodge, *Outlines of Theology*, 362.
[111] A. A. Hodge, *Outlines of Theology*, 365.
[112] Charles Hodge, *Systematic Theology*, 2:52.
[113] For a fuller exploration of such issues, see George P. Hutchinson, *The Problem of Original Sin in American Presbyterian Theology* (Phillipsburg, NJ: P&R, 1972). The primary area that Hutchinson omitted was the New England theology (ix), and he wished to expand his treatment of Charles Hodge. This present essay fills in these gaps to some extent.
[114] For examples, see Charles Hodge, *Systematic Theology*, 2:46, 55, 146, 219.

spite of his charitable view of Schleiermacher as a genuine Christian.[115] As we will see below, the issue of pantheism became prominent in the context of Charles Hodge's treatment of Jonathan Edwards and the New England theology. It is sufficient to note that Hodge regarded pantheism as antithetical to the biblical view of the relationship between God and the world. He wrote simply, "The universe is not our God."[116] Because pantheism made God the only real actor in the world, the imputation of Adam's sin to his posterity became a moot point, with or without a covenant of works.

SCOTTISH COMMON SENSE REALISM

Scottish Common Sense Realism was a philosophical method related to epistemology and developed largely by Thomas Reid (1710–96) in Scotland.[117] This philosophy greatly affected Old Princeton, especially Charles Hodge, in the way that he defended the truths of Scripture.[118] While this is a complex topic that deserves further attention, for our purposes it is sufficient to understand that Common Sense Realism taught that human beings have common ideas at the root of all judgments and perceptions.[119] Such intuitive commonsense notions became the foundation of human inquiry and knowledge. This philosophical system opposed David Hume's (1711–76) denial of the clear relationship between effects and their causes.

An example of the application of Common Sense Realism to theological principles is A. A. Hodge's assertions that people intuitively reject metaphysical arguments asserting that there is no physical world, and that we know inescapably that we cannot regenerate ourselves regardless of what philosophers and theologians tell us.[120] Another example is where he argued that, although children have differing dispositions, it is the "universal judgment" of people that those born with bad dispositions are morally responsible for their actions.[121] The number of such appeals to universal and intuitive

[115] Charles Hodge, *Systematic Theology*, 2:138.
[116] Charles Hodge, *Systematic Theology*, 2:146.
[117] For a survey of the rise of Common Sense Realism in Scotland, see Alexander Broadie, *A History of Scottish Philosophy* (Cambridge: Cambridge University Press, 2012), 235–300. Broadie summarizes Common Sense Realism in five points: 1. A set of universally recognized commonsense principles that lie at the base of every belief system. 2. A rejection of "Humean skepticism" as being contrary to these principles. 3. Belief in "a providential God" who created human powers. 4. A Newtonian and Baconian belief that humans are part of the natural world. 5. Stress on "the place of consciousness in our lives and in philosophy" (236–37).
[118] For a theological appraisal of Hodge's approach, see Owen Anderson, *Reason and Faith in the Theology of Charles Hodge: American Common Sense Realism* (New York: Palgrave Macmillan, 2014).
[119] I am grateful to Scott Cook for helping me refine this section.
[120] A. A. Hodge, *Outlines of Theology*, 271.
[121] A. A. Hodge, *Outlines of Theology*, 303.

judgments among Old Princeton theologians is too great to cite adequately. Charles Hodge, in whom the most frequent references appear, appealed repeatedly to the "testimony of consciousness" to argue that people knew better than their claimed denial of Christian doctrines.[122] From a modern vantage point, Common Sense Realism can come across as intellectually bullying opponents into a position rather than arguing for it.

THE NEW ENGLAND THEOLOGY

The so-called New England Theology, which arose in the wake of Jonathan Edwards (1703–58), enveloped realist, traducian, and pantheistic views.[123] For our purposes, Princeton's perception of Edwards is more important here than Edwards's actual teaching on original sin. B. B. Warfield represented the most positive assessment of Edwards among the Princeton theologians. He stated that Edwards argued for the identity of the human race with Adam based on "an arbitrary constitution" by God "binding its successive moments together."[124] Warfield wrote that this idea was "peculiar to himself." However, as demonstrated above, it appears that Gomarus and Bucanus taught something like the first half of this assertion, while not touching the second idea. Warfield added that Edwards argued in one place for the "mediate imputation" of Adam's sin, but he observed that this statement was less clear than the covenantal ideas present in his work on *Original Sin*.[125] Warfield defended Edwards's continuity with the classic Reformed teaching on imputation. He noted that Edwards "strove to show no originality," seeking to defend rather than improve "Calvinism."[126] He added that Edwards's teaching on the will was "precisely the doctrine of the Calvinistic schoolmen," and that, "Edwards's originality thus consisted less in the content of his thought than in his manner of thinking."[127]

According to Warfield, the Edwards party (New England Theology) that followed him was much more interested in practical rather than doctrinal theology[128] This method imitated Edwards's way of thinking while departing

---

[122] A. A. Hodge, *Outlines of Theology*, 2:49, 107, 111, 131, 141, 148, 155, 183, 221–222, 256, 272, 274, 333.
[123] For a treatment arguing that the New England Theology marked a departure from Reformed theology, see Douglas A. Sweeney, *Nathaniel Taylor, New Haven Theology, and the Legacy of Jonathan Edwards* (Oxford: Oxford University Press, 2003).
[124] B. B. Warfield, "Edwards and the New England Theology," in *The Works of Benjamin B. Warfield*, 10 vols. (Grand Rapids, MI: Baker, 2003), 9:530.
[125] Warfield, "Edwards and the New England Theology," 530.
[126] Warfield, "Edwards and the New England Theology," 531.
[127] Warfield, "Edwards and the New England Theology," 531.
[128] Warfield, "Edwards and the New England Theology," 532.

from his Reformed content.[129] Timothy Dwight (1752–1817), whose mother was Jonathan Edwards's daughter, was a key player in the "New Divinity" in his role as president at Yale.[130] Warfield believed that "probably no written system of theology has ever enjoyed wider acceptance than Dwight's 'Sermons.'"[131] The main problem was that New England theologians like Dwight blunted imputation and other effects of original sin. Dwight still maintained that God created Adam in a covenant of works representing his posterity.[132] However, while maintaining the parallels between Adam and Christ generally,[133] Dwight passed over the imputation of sin and argued that all people die because "every child of Adam is a sinner."[134] His treatment of original sin focused on human depravity. Dwight later explicitly repudiated the Reformed view of imputation, stating, "When I assert, that in consequence of the Apostasy of Adam all men have sinned; I do not intend, that the posterity of Adam are guilty of his transgression."[135] He seemed to believe that the corruption of human nature, which resulted from Adam's first sin, made humanity guilty, rather than the imputation of Adam's sin.[136] Warfield tried to distance Edwards from the later New England Theology, which included this diminished emphasis on imputation.[137]

A. A. Hodge shared Warfield's positive assessment of Edwards, citing his views on original sin approvingly at key points.[138] Charles Hodge was less optimistic, stating that "President Edwards" taught mediate imputation while still holding to Adam's federal headship.[139] He regarded these two positions as incompatible because, as we will see below, Charles believed that mediate imputation amounted to denying the imputation of Adam's sin through the covenant of works. Charles Hodge identified Edwards's realism, by which all humanity participated in Adam's sin, as the real culprit.[140] He blamed

[129] Warfield, "Edwards and the New England Theology," 533.
[130] Warfield, "Edwards and the New England Theology," 534.
[131] Warfield, "Edwards and the New England Theology," 535–36.
[132] Timothy Dwight, Theology, Explained and Defended in a Series of Sermons, 5 vols. (New York: Harper & Brothers, 1850), 1:397.
[133] Dwight, Theology, Explained, 1:426.
[134] Dwight, Theology, Explained, 1:436.
[135] Dwight, Theology, Explained, 1:478.
[136] Dwight, Theology, Explained, 1:480. Dwight thus retained the habits of sin in his doctrine of original sin, while excising the imputation of Adam's sin to his posterity.
[137] For a treatment of original sin in New England Theology, see John D. Hannah, "Doctrine of Original Sin in Post-revolutionary America," Bibliotheca Sacra 134:535 (1977): 238–56. Hannah treats Jonathan Edwards Jr., Timothy Dwight, and Nathaniel Taylor. He shows the effects of shifts in politics and religion on the doctrine.
[138] A. A. Hodge, Outlines of Theology, 303, 320, 326, 331.
[139] Charles Hodge, Systematic Theology, 2:207.
[140] Charles Hodge, Systematic Theology, 2:208.

Edwards's brand of realism, in turn, on his view that providence was an act of continual creation rather than of preservation of creation. In Hodge's estimation, this made God the only real actor in the world, and the idea bordered on pantheism as a result.[141] In contrast to A. A. Hodge, who liked such terminology, Charles Hodge rejected Edwards's distinction between man's natural and moral inability, arguing that natural ability implied that fallen man could potentially regenerate himself.[142]

If Warfield and A. A. Hodge exempted Edwards from the doctrinal departures of the New England theology in relation to original sin, then Charles Hodge placed the blame squarely on his shoulders. While evolutionary views and Scottish Common Sense Realism form part of the backdrop of the treatment of Princeton on imputation below, Edwards's realism and Charles Hodge's concern over mediate imputation and pantheism were integral to his defense of the doctrine.[143]

Old Princeton on the Imputation of Adam's Sin Proper

Building on a Reformed orthodox foundation, with challenges of nineteenth-century America in view, we can better appreciate how Old Princeton theologians taught and defended the imputation of Adam's sin to his posterity. After surveying this teaching via Archibald Alexander, I will trace Charles Hodge's more detailed exposition of the doctrine, with comparisons to A. A. Hodge and Warfield along the way.[144]

ARCHIBALD ALEXANDER ON THE IMPUTATION OF ADAM'S SIN

Archibald Alexander is an ideal starting point to gain a simple overview of Princeton's teaching on the imputation of Adam sin.[145] As noted in the introduction, the General Assembly of the Presbyterian Church U.S.A. appointed Alexander to be the first professor at Princeton. Alexander was a pastor and evangelist as well as a professor, and the small body of works that survive

---

[141] Charles Hodge, *Systematic Theology*, 2:219.

[142] Charles Hodge, *Systematic Theology*, 2:265–66.

[143] Gutjahr lists several articles on imputation and original sin by Charles Hodge and Alexander from the 1830s, along with articles by their New England opponents (Gutjahr, *Charles Hodge*, 409–10). For the sake of space, I will omit these articles from the narrative below.

[144] For the lives and thought of A. A. Hodge and Warfield, see Steward, *Princeton Seminary (1812–1929)*, 241–62; Kim Riddlebarger, *The Lion of Princeton: B. B. Warfield as Apologist and Theologian* (Bellingham, WA: Lexham, 2015); Gary L. W. Johnson, *B. B. Warfield: Essays on His Life and Thought* (Phillipsburg, NJ: P&R, 2007).

[145] For Alexander's biography, see James W. Alexander, *The Life of Archibald Alexander* (Philadelphia: Presbyterian Board of Publication, 1870).

from his pen are marked by pastoral simplicity and evangelistic zeal. Most of the material below is summarized from his *Brief Compendium of Bible Truth*. The chapters of Alexander's work of primary relevance treat man's original state, the law of God, and man's fall into sin. He began by noting that God created man in his image, yet mutable, and with the end of enjoying the glory of God.[146] Loving God with the whole heart was easy to him and it was his highest happiness. His probation would have continued "without limit" if God had not introduced a covenant.[147] We will see below that this covenant was the covenant of works. Keeping the covenant by obeying God would end Adam's trial period at some point, confirming him in everlasting life. God made Adam a "federal head" of this covenant. If he obeyed, then all of his posterity would have obeyed in him. If he failed, then his sin "should be so imputed to them, as that they should be brought into existence in the same moral condition in which he should fall, and be subject to the same penalties."[148] It is important to note that the imputation of Adam's sin rested on his character as representative of the whole human race in the garden of Eden. The tree of the knowledge of good and evil was a test of entire obedience to God, while the tree of life was "sacramental."[149] It was a "sign and seal of eternal life" to our first parents. In this original condition, our first parents had "nothing to fear but sin."[150] He concluded simply that, after the fall, the image of God "has been defaced."[151]

The next chapter, which treats the law of God, is an important bridge between Alexander's discussion of the covenant of works and his discussion of the fall. Alexander appealed to the law to describe mankind's proper relation to God by creation and the obedience that Adam owed God, with a promise of eternal life added by virtue of the covenant. He noted that God deserves our supreme love as the fulfillment of his law, but that we would be mere unprofitable servants even if we did all of our duty as his creatures.[152]

---

[146] Archibald Alexander, *A Brief Compendium of Bible Truth* (Grand Rapids, MI: Reformation Heritage, 2005), 80.
[147] Alexander, *Brief Compendium*, 80.
[148] Alexander, *Brief Compendium*, 81.
[149] For some examples of Reformed orthodox views on this point, see Antonius Walaeus et al., *Synopsis Purioris Theologiae (Synopsis of a Purer Theology): Latin Text and English Translation* (3 vols.), vol. 1, ed. Dolf (Roelf T.) te Velde, trans. Riemer A. Faber (Leiden, Netherlands: Brill, 2015), 331; Turretin, *Institutes*, 8.5 (2:580–83); Herman Witsius, *The Economy of the Covenants between God and Man*, ed. Joel R Beeke, trans. William Crookshank, 2 vols. (Grand Rapids, MI: Reformation Heritage, 2010), 1:110–14, § IX–XI; Johannes Cocceius, *The Doctrine of the Covenant and Testament of God*, trans. Casey Carmichael, vol. 3, Classic Reformed Theology (Grand Rapids, MI: Reformation Heritage, 2016), 33. Cocceius and Witsius both denied that the tree of the knowledge of good and evil was a sacrament of the covenant of works because it was a sign, but not a seal of grace.
[150] Alexander, *Brief Compendium*, 82.
[151] Alexander, *Brief Compendium*, 83.
[152] Alexander, *Brief Compendium*, 84.

While moral likeness to God was lost in the fall, "some knowledge of duty, and feeling of moral obligation remained."[153] The Decalogue given under Moses became a "new revelation" of the same moral law, which God wrote on Adam's heart, to clarify our sin and duty.[154] The principles of obedience in this law are simple, but the acts of obedience may be "infinitely diversified."[155] The law "has been justly called a transcript of the moral perfections of God."[156] This is important because it roots all legitimate moral requirements in the character of God. God created human beings to be like him and to imitate him.

The moral law "is also the measure of man's supreme happiness."[157] In light of the preceding chapter, Adam's obedience in the covenant of works would have secured this happiness for his descendants. The law cannot lower its demands due to our sinful inability. Inability is our own fault, while the law remains unchanged. Alexander explained, "No moral change, however, affects the essence of the soul; its faculties remain the same under all moral conditions. Sin destroys no constitutional faculty, and regeneration produces no new faculty. Man, in all stages of his existence, continues to be a free moral agent."[158] Moral precepts are permanent, while what Alexander called "positive" laws can be changed. Positive laws included things like the prohibition against eating of the tree of the knowledge of good and evil, the priesthood and sacrifices of the OT, and the day of the Sabbath. Alexander then listed eight rules for interpreting the Decalogue that parallel Westminster Larger Catechism 99, without citing it.[159] This material was designed to help people understand the obedience that they owe to God as his creatures, and what Adam owed God in covenant. This treatment of the law of God creates a backdrop for what Christ will restore in redemption as well.

Next, Alexander described the nature and results of man's fall into sin. He opened by observing that we do not know how long Adam and Eve stayed in Paradise, but that most authors agree that it was a short time.[160] He focused more on what happened when Adam sinned rather than explaining how it

---

[153] Alexander, *Brief Compendium*, 84.
[154] Alexander, *Brief Compendium*, 85.
[155] Alexander, *Brief Compendium*, 85.
[156] Alexander, *Brief Compendium*, 86.
[157] Alexander, *Brief Compendium*, 87.
[158] Alexander, *Brief Compendium*, 88.
[159] Alexander, *Brief Compendium*, 89–95. Though he quibbles that Rule 7 "is of very little use" because it is "obvious" (94).
[160] Alexander, *Brief Compendium*, 96.

happened, stating, "Here the positive commandment of God was violated, the covenant of life broken, and the curse of death incurred, not only for himself, but for all his posterity."[161] Alexander noted that while the fall of a holy creature into sin is difficult to explain philosophically, "as a practical matter the thing is not difficult."[162] In other words, we know what happened even if we cannot fully explain how. The "immediate consequences" of the fall were guilt, shame, and fear. Adam and Eve were driven from the garden, the ground was cursed, "and the sentence of death was also confirmed."[163] This sentence began that very day when man became mortal. Spiritual death, rather than temporal death, "was the principal thing." Adam was destitute of any principle of holiness and became "capable of unlimited increase in wickedness."[164] This describes man's moral depravity.

Alexander next drew attention to imputation, observing that Adam's posterity "sinned in him and fell with him in his first transgression."[165] Moreover, people come into the world destitute of Adam's original righteousness. Death is universal to the human race as a consequence of Adam's sin. Alexander added that those who "had not sinned after the likeness of Adam's transgression" in Romans 5:14 referred to infants, who were included in the guilt of Adam's first sin.[166] Arguments from the sinfulness and redemption of infants will reappear in both Hodges and Warfield below. Alexander answered a potential moral objection at this point, stating,

> Whether it was just in God to constitute Adam the representative of all his posterity and suspend their salvation on his obedience is not a question for us to discuss. Whatever God does is just, and not only just, but wise; though darkness may rest on this transaction, this is owing to our ignorance and prejudice. We need not fear that the Judge of all the earth will not be able to vindicate His own dispensations to the whole universe.[167]

In any case, Alexander was clear that Adam's sin was imputed to his descendants and that this represented the clear teaching of Scripture. He closed the chapter with a qualifying statement on human depravity: "When it is

---

[161] Alexander, *Brief Compendium*, 97. Readers should be aware that the phrase "covenant of life" comes from WSC 12, and that it is synonymous with the covenant of works.
[162] Alexander, *Brief Compendium*, 97.
[163] Alexander, *Brief Compendium*, 98.
[164] Alexander, *Brief Compendium*, 98.
[165] Alexander, *Brief Compendium*, 99. This language comes from WSC 16, without attribution.
[166] Alexander, *Brief Compendium*, 100.
[167] Alexander, *Brief Compendium*, 100.

asserted that man is totally depraved, the meaning is not that he is as wicked as he is capable of being, or that all men are sinners in an equal degree; but that all men are by nature destitute of any principle of true holiness."[168] This doctrine of sin established man's need of redemption and set the stage for Alexander's treatment of salvation in Christ later in the work. His treatment of sin and original sin is clearly evangelical in its focus, as Charles Hodge's would be later.

Alexander's straightforward presentation of the imputation of Adam's sin is devoid of philosophical questions and contemporary debates. He also left many important questions unanswered. He did not expound relevant texts of Scripture, such as Romans 5:12–21, at length. Nor did he explain the manner of the imputation of Adam's sin, beyond stating that all people fell in Adam when he broke the covenant of works. Alexander's treatment of man as the image of God is largely underdeveloped, and he did not explain the nature of the promised life or threatened death in detail. However, his treatment of sin, including the imputation of Adam's sin, reflects the earlier Reformed tradition and serves as a good summary of the primary points elaborated by other Princeton theologians.

Charles Hodge, A. A. Hodge, and B. B. Warfield on the Imputation of Adam's Sin

Charles Hodge helps give direction and focus to Princeton's teaching on original sin, including the imputation of Adam's sin, in more detail.[169] After a few key statements in a chapter on "the Original State of Man" (ch. 5), most of his foundational material on Adam's imputed sin appears in his chapter on the "covenant of works" (ch. 6). The parallels between Hodge and Turretin regarding the order of topics in treating the covenant of works, sin, and original sin, stand out on the surface. The primary thing that we will see is that the imputation of Adam's sin to his descendants was rooted firmly in the covenant of works. While Hodge's book *The Way of Life* targeted New England views on imputation and original sin as well, the narrative below largely follows his *Systematic Theology*, for the sake of space.[170]

---

168 Alexander, *Brief Compendium*, 101.
169 The first biography of Charles Hodge following A. A. Hodge's biography of his father in 1878 is Gutjahr, *Charles Hodge*. This volume remains an impressive treatment of Hodge's thought, life, and times.
170 Charles Hodge, *The Way of Life* (Philadelphia: American Sunday School Union, 1841).

The Covenant of Works

In chapter 5, Charles Hodge introduces what becomes a repeated refrain in his treatment of the imputation of Adam's sin. In his view, representation in Adam and Christ are the key to understanding our sinful estate. The idea of covenant is tied inextricably to these assertions.[171] This is a tacit argument, in line with à Brakel's statement noted above, that the gospel stands or falls with the parallel between the covenants of works and of grace.

Charles Hodge's treatment on the covenant of works is the linchpin to his explanation of the imputation of Adam's sin, as it was for Alexander and A. A. Hodge. His defense of the imputation of Adam's sin cannot stand without it. In a manner typical throughout his *Systematic Theology*, he opened his chapter by citing the WSC (question 12).[172] Such confessional references both explain the general structure of his material and remind readers that he sought to situate his teaching in the historic Reformed orthodox tradition.

Charles Hodge listed four characteristics of a covenant that he then applied to the covenant of works. The parties of the covenant were God and Adam, the promise of the covenant was life, "the condition was perfect obedience," and the threatened penalty was death.[173] Similarly to Alexander, A. A. Hodge noted that while we owe obedience to God by reason of creation, our enjoyment of him "is a matter of free and sovereign grace."[174] Charles Hodge expanded each element of a covenant to show that, even though the term does not appear in Genesis 2–3, a covenant between God and Adam truly existed. The promise entailed the "happy, holy, and immortal existence of the soul and body."[175] Keeping God's law perfectly and perpetually was the condition of the covenant, exemplified by the prohibition against eating from the tree of the knowledge of good and evil. He added that the idea that God put Adam on probation is probable in light of the situation in the garden.[176] He was a bit more cautious at this point than the Reformed tradition, which largely assumed that the situation in the garden was temporary and that it would lead

---

[171] Charles Hodge, *Systematic Theology*, 2:114.
[172] Charles Hodge, *Systematic Theology*, 2:117.
[173] Charles Hodge, *Systematic Theology*, 2:117.
[174] A. A. Hodge, *The Confession of Faith* (Edinburgh: Banner of Truth, 1998), 120. Curiously, he implied here that God gave a covenant promise to the angels as well, though he did not elaborate the point. In his *Outlines of Theology*, he added, "It was also essentially a gracious covenant, because although every creature is, as such, bound to serve the Creator to the full extent of his powers, the Creator cannot be bound as a mere matter of justice to grant the creature fellowship with himself, or to raise him to an infallible standard of moral power, or to crown him with eternal life and inalienable felicity" (310–311).
[175] Charles Hodge, *Systematic Theology*, 2:118.
[176] Charles Hodge, *Systematic Theology*, 2:120.

to confirmation in everlasting life.[177] The question was whether Adam would enjoy life while remaining on trial before God with the possibility of falling, or whether God would confirm and preserve him in eternal life without the possibility of a fall. Like Alexander, A. A. Hodge had little difficulty with the language of probation.[178] The penalty for breaking the covenant of works was death. Charles Hodge noted, "The death threatened was the opposite of the life promised,"[179] being physical, spiritual, and eternal. He added that our redemption in Christ shows the nature of the penalty most clearly.[180]

Again, in Charles Hodge's view, the Adam-Christ parallel holds throughout. Adam acted as a public person in the covenant of works just as Christ does in the covenant of grace. Underscoring this point, he added, "This great fact is made the ground on which the whole plan of redemption is founded."[181] A. A. Hodge made the Adam-Christ parallel his first argument in favor of a covenant of works, while Charles Hodge introduced it last.[182] Yet the parallel was essential to both men's accounts. Drawing his treatment to a conclusion, Charles Hodge observed, "Men may dispute the ground of the headship of Adam," but they cannot deny its reality.[183] This rings true with early Reformed authors, like Gomarus and Bucanus, who did not appeal to a covenant of works in their treatments of original sin while still teaching imputation. Charles Hodge concluded that while the covenant of works no longer continues, its penalty is still in force and its promise is held forth to believers in Christ. This is similar to the observations of Herman Witsius (1636–1708), who added that Christ obtained the promise of eternal life that Adam lost by breaking the covenant of works.[184]

While Charles Hodge's most significant exegetical defense of the imputation of Adam's sin comes later by way of Romans 5:12–21, its theological underpinnings are here. This fact harmonizes well with the kind of early covenant of works and grace scheme in Ravensperger. Adam's covenantal,

---

[177] Turretin, *Institutes*, 8.6 (1:583–86). While noting that Reformed divines differed over whether Adam would receive a heavenly or an earthly life, Turretin defended the former position, saying that God would have confirmed Adam in life after a trial period.

[178] A. A. Hodge, *Confession of Faith*, 122–26.

[179] Charles Hodge, *Systematic Theology*, 2:120.

[180] Charles Hodge, *Systematic Theology*, 2:120.

[181] Charles Hodge, *Systematic Theology*, 2:120.

[182] Charles Hodge, *Systematic Theology*, 2:311.

[183] Charles Hodge, *Systematic Theology*, 2:122.

[184] Witsius, *Economy of the Covenants between God and Man*, 1:160: "The covenant of grace is not the abolition, but rather the confirmation of the covenant of works, in so far as the Mediator has fulfilled all the conditions of that covenant, so that all believers may be justified and saved, according to the covenant of works, to which satisfaction was made by the Mediator."

or representative, relationship to his posterity was vital to Hodge's argument for imputation. The covenant of works showed how imputation was possible and why it happened.

The Doctrine of Sin

In his chapter on sin proper (ch. 8), Charles Hodge included a lengthy treatment of the imputation of sin.[185] He defined sin as a vitiation of God's law, citing Campegius Vitringa (1669–1722) to this effect.[186] A. A. Hodge followed his father closely at this point, commenting further on Vitringa's definition.[187] Charles Hodge opened his section on the imputation of Adam's sin by asserting, "The whole Christian world" admits that Adam's sin affected his posterity."[188] This appeal to the general testimony of the Christian church resurfaces below. Hodge aimed to show both that Protestant teaching was biblical and that it was not novel. He noted that imputation, corruption, and inability are the three ideas presented in the Westminster Standards regarding sin.[189] He added that Protestants, and most of the Latin church, held to immediate imputation based on a "federal relation" to Adam.[190] While federal language overstates the case a bit in relation to early Reformed covenant theology, it illustrates how the idea of the imputation of Adam's sin became wedded to the covenant idea. The alternative view, known as mediate imputation, respected the transmission of corruption alone rather than the proper imputation of guilt,[191] often reflecting the comments above to this end related to realist and traducian views. Hodge added that some people denied imputation while others appealed to realism to explain it. Still others, such as the Pelagians, denied any such connections to Adam's sin, mediate or immediate.[192]

Charles Hodge next argued that the imputation of Adam's guilt to his posterity brings punishment.[193] In his view, imputed sin was not a legal fiction. We bear real guilt by virtue of Adam's role as our federal head. The ground of the imputation of his sin to us is "both natural and federal."[194]

---

[185] I have omitted chapter 7, which examines the nature and fact of Adam and Eve's fall into sin and the manner of Satan's temptation.
[186] Charles Hodge, *Systematic Theology*, 2:180.
[187] A. A. Hodge, *Outlines of Theology*, 315–16.
[188] Charles Hodge, *Systematic Theology*, 2:192.
[189] Charles Hodge, *Systematic Theology*, 2:192.
[190] Charles Hodge, *Systematic Theology*, 2:192.
[191] Charles Hodge, *Systematic Theology*, 2:193.
[192] Charles Hodge, *Systematic Theology*, 2:193.
[193] Charles Hodge, *Systematic Theology*, 2:194.
[194] Charles Hodge, *Systematic Theology*, 2:196.

It is natural because all who descend from Adam "by ordinary generation" inherit his sin.[195] It is federal because imputation comes to us by virtue of the broken covenant of works, in which Adam represented us. This corresponds to Bucanus's and Gomarus's appeal to imputation by a special disposition of God. It also mirrors Turretin's inclusion of Adam as our natural and federal head. A. A. Hodge similarly stated that mankind sinned in Adam "by a divine constitution."[196] Charles Hodge's appeal to federal terminology sought to clarify how God disposed this arrangement. He repeated here the point that "The whole plan of redemption rests on this same principle."[197] If there is no imputation of Adam's guilt, then there can be no imputation of Christ's righteousness.

Charles Hodge drew an interesting conclusion at this point. He stated that to bear sin "is to bear its penalty" and we are liable to punishment because we bear the guilt of Adam's first sin.[198] It is unclear whether he meant that imputed guilt was equivalent to liability to punishment, or if imputed guilt *resulted in* liability to punishment. Westminster Shorter Catechism 18 included both the guilt of Adam's sin and the resultant punishments as two distinct items. In a short essay answering the question of whether we should repent of original sin, Warfield possibly sheds some light on Hodge's statement. Warfield noted that our answer to this question depends on whether we regard original sin as imputed sin or as the corruption of our natures.[199] Warfield wrote, "By original sin we are to mean not merely adherent but also inherent sin, not merely the sinful act of Adam imputed to us, but also the sinful state of our own souls conveyed to us by the just judgment of God."[200] In his view, we should repent of original sin as inherent sin because we want "not only to do better but to be better."[201]

However, Warfield added curiously, "It is not the personal ill-desert of Adam's sin that is transferred to us by 'imputation,' but only the law-relation to it; not the *reatus culpae* but only the *reatus poenae*."[202] Thus, while we should repent of inherent corruption, we can only have

---

[195] WSC 16.
[196] A. A. Hodge, *Outlines of Theology*, 113. This is where the title of this essay comes from.
[197] Charles Hodge, *Systematic Theology*, 2:199.
[198] Charles Hodge, *Systematic Theology*, 2:201.
[199] B. B. Warfield, "Repentance and Original Sin," in *Selected Shorter Writings of Benjamin B. Warfield* (Phillipsburg, NJ: P&R, 2001), 2:278.
[200] Warfield, "Repentance and Original Sin," 279.
[201] Warfield, "Repentance and Original Sin," 280.
[202] Warfield, "Repentance and Original Sin," 280. In this context, *reatus culpae* means "the cause of guilt," while *reatus poenae* means "the cause of punishment."

"sympathetic identification" with imputed sin, "which very closely sim-
ulates repentance."[203] Sorrow for imputed sin may promote holiness, but
Warfield argued that it cannot involve any real turning from sin to God.[204]
Both Warfield and Charles Hodge drew a parallel between these ideas and
God's work in justifying sinners in Christ.[205] However, this raises numerous
problems in light of historic Reformed views on imputation. Restricting
"imputation" to punishment appears to deny imputation altogether. Just as
Christ's righteousness is imputed to his people in union with him so that
they receive his reward, so Adam's sin is imputed to his people in union
with him so that they receive his punishment. What Warfield wrote, at least,
appears to be a halfway point between Reformed orthodoxy on the one side,
and Timothy Dwight on the other. While affirming imputation, this presentation obscured its meaning.

Charles Hodge's narrative on imputed sin continued with Romans
5:12–21. His primary opponents at this time were New England theologians such as Moses Stuart (1780–1852) and Albert Barnes (1798–1870).
He wrote that this text is "the most formal and explicit" expression of this
truth taught in Scripture.[206] Verse 12 stood out in this regard, in his view,
because it came close to being an explicit statement that God imputed
Adam's sin to his posterity. In his commentary on Romans, Hodge's exposition of this passage occupied thirty-three closely printed pages,[207] followed
by twenty-three pages of doctrinal exposition.[208] In relation to verse 12,
he commented, "The whole race was in him, so that his act was the act of
humanity."[209] Hinting at the New England theology, he classed any view
that made sin purely voluntary as "Pelagian."[210] He added that while Luther
and Calvin virtually reduced this verse to hereditary depravity, Turretin
was better by including imputation.[211] He next rejected realism, treating it
much more briefly than he did in his *Systematic Theology*.[212] In his view,
this verse taught Adam's natural and federal relation to mankind. His sin

---

[203] Warfield, "Repentance and Original Sin," 281.
[204] Warfield, "Repentance and Original Sin," 282.
[205] Warfield, "Repentance and Original Sin," 282; Charles Hodge, *Systematic Theology*, 2:201.
[206] Charles Hodge, *Systematic Theology*, 2:202.
[207] Charles Hodge, *Romans* (Edinburgh: Banner of Truth, 1989), 144–78.
[208] Charles Hodge, *Romans*, 178–91.
[209] Charles Hodge, *Romans*, 145.
[210] Charles Hodge, *Romans*, 149.
[211] Charles Hodge, *Romans*, 150.
[212] Charles Hodge, *Romans*, 151.

became the "judicial ground" on which death passed to all people.[213] He was clear that Adam's sin "was regarded as theirs."[214] His treatment of verse 12 directed his explanation of verses 13–21. His doctrinal appendix began by asserting, "The doctrine of imputation is clearly taught in this passage,"[215] which he defended at length on pages 178–191. He concluded this section by stressing that the imputation of Christ's righteousness and the imputation of Adam's sin stood or fell together.[216] Though his opponents differed to some extent, this material confirms what we see in his *Systematic Theology*.

After passing by the views of the Greek church, which he estimated as among the "lowest" views of sin available in any Christian church, Hodge drew attention to the mediate imputation views represented in the Academy of Saumur in the seventeenth century.[217] This entailed "imputation" by virtue of participation in Adam's sin rather than by covenantal relationship. As a result, Hodge argued that these French theologians reduced imputation to inherent guilt, excluding real imputation. According to Hodge, Josue de la Place coined the term "mediate imputation," while Andreas Rivetus (1572–1651) opposed him.[218] Rivetus was a French theologian who became well known as a professor at the University of Leiden, where he coauthored the *Synopsis Purioris Theologiae* with three other professors in order to combat Remonstrant, or Arminian, theology.[219] As noted above, Charles Hodge's citation of de la Place and the French Synod that condemned his views follow Turretin closely. Hodge reiterated that denying the imputation of Adam's guilt thus threatens, if not denies, the gospel.[220]

"The Strange Doctrine of Jonathan Edwards"

Mediate imputation led Charles Hodge to focus on Jonathan Edwards. He asserted that "President Edwards" taught mediate imputation while still holding to Adam's federal headship.[221] Hodge believed that, though these ideas

---

213 Charles Hodge, *Romans*, 151.
214 Charles Hodge, *Romans*, 152.
215 Charles Hodge, *Romans*, 178.
216 Charles Hodge, *Romans*, 190.
217 Charles Hodge, *Systematic Theology*, 2:205.
218 Charles Hodge, *Systematic Theology*, 2:206.
219 Walaeus et al., *Synopsis Purioris Theologiae* (vol. 1, 2015); Antonius Walaeus et al., *Synopsis Purioris Theologiae (Synopsis of a Purer Theology): Latin Text and English Translation* (3 vols.), vol. 2, *Disputations 24–42*, ed. Henk van den Belt, trans. Riemer A. Faber (Leiden, Netherlands: Brill, 2016).
220 Charles Hodge, *Systematic Theology*, 2:207.
221 Charles Hodge, *Systematic Theology*, 2:207.

were inconsistent, including federal headship redeemed Edwards from the logical consequences of this view. However, rather than pinning Edwards's view on mediate imputation, Hodge blamed his realism.[222] As we have seen above, realism involved the idea that humanity participated ontologically in Adam's sin. This, of necessity, led to a traducian theory on the origin of the human soul. Hodge's concern was that this view threatened the parallel between Adam and Christ via the covenant of works. He noted that William Cunningham (1805–61) stated that the Westminster Confession was more explicit than earlier Reformed creeds on the importance of immediate imputation in order to oppose authors like de la Place.[223]

Charles Hodge then moved to a full refutation of mediate imputation.[224] In line with other Princeton theologians, he believed that all people dying in infancy are saved by the grace of God.[225] He did not argue his case here beyond stating that if infants need salvation from birth, then they are born with guilt. A. A. Hodge observed similarly, "Original sin as well as actual sin is a violation of God's law." Conviction of sin always begins with "what we are" rather than in our actual transgressions.[226] For this reason, "Even infants are redeemed by Christ."[227] Charles Hodge added that mediate imputation denied actual imputation by turning it into a form of realistic participation in sin.[228] Edwards's realism came into Hodge's crosshairs at this juncture.[229] Edwards's view, in Hodge's estimation, was linked to his teaching that providence was an act of continual creation.[230] Hodge referred to this as "the strange doctrine of Jonathan Edwards."[231]

My concern here is to understand Hodge's understanding of Edwards rather than Edwards's own teaching.[232] As noted above, Charles Hodge differed from both A. A. Hodge and Warfield, who read Edwards more favorably. Charles Hodge contended, "In short, [Edwards's] doctrine subverts all

---

[222] Charles Hodge, *Systematic Theology*, 2:208.
[223] Charles Hodge, *Systematic Theology*, 2:209. This point is worth exploring further, but it is beyond the scope of this chapter.
[224] Charles Hodge, *Systematic Theology*, 2:210–14.
[225] Charles Hodge, *Systematic Theology*, 2:211; David K. Clark, "Warfield, Infant Salvation, and the Logic of Calvinism," *JETS* 27.4 (1984): 459–64.
[226] A. A. Hodge, *Confession of Faith*, 116.
[227] A. A. Hodge, *Confession of Faith*, 117.
[228] A. A. Hodge, *Confession of Faith*, 2:216.
[229] Charles Hodge, *Systematic Theology*, 2:216–17.
[230] Charles Hodge, *Systematic Theology*, 2:218.
[231] Charles Hodge, *Systematic Theology*, 2:220.
[232] For a recent treatment on Edwards on original sin, see Oliver D. Crisp, *Jonathan Edwards on the Metaphysics of Sin* (Abingdon-on-Thames, UK: Routledge, 2017).

our ideas."[233] He argued that Edwards generally agreed with the realists while denying "numerical sameness in any case."[234] In other words, the idea of "humanity" as grounded in Adam did not negate, in Edwards's thought, the reality of individually accountable human persons.[235]

Charles Hodge listed seven objections to realism.[236] First, this view is possible, but not probable. Second, it has no support from Scripture. Third, our "consciousness" militates against it. This reflects Hodge's use of Common Sense Realism. Fourth, it contradicts the separate existence of individual souls. While he exempted Edwards from this charge initially, he pinned him with it in the end. Fifth, it violates principles drawn from Trinitarian theology. The idea here is that as God is one essence in three persons, realism would make humanity one essence in many persons. Sixth, this view would deny Christ's sinlessness, since his humanity would be part of an overarching sinful human essence that all humanity participates in. Seventh, there are philosophical objections to realism as well, which I will not explore here. The bottom line was that realism would mean that all sinned in Adam personally rather than by covenantal representation.[237] He added that teaching that we sinned in Adam's act personally is like saying that "a nonentity should act."

Charles Hodge's reasoning here is a bit circular, since it assumes that "humanity" is a nonentity in favor of the idea that each individual has being in his own right. This was precisely the point in dispute. He added that the realist theory would involve imputing all of the acts of Adam's life to us rather than merely his violation of the covenant, because the covenant no longer served as a limiting factor in this regard.[238] Hodge noted that the realistic theory should also attach our sin to Eve more than to Adam, since she sinned first. He appealed again here to Romans 5:12–21 as the decisive scriptural proof against realism, concluding that its great error was that people can be responsible only for their own voluntary and personal actions. Imputed guilt could not be guilt, under this view.[239] John Hannah has observed that this was precisely the ground on which the New England theology rejected

---

[233] Charles Hodge, *Systematic Theology*, 2:220.
[234] Charles Hodge, *Systematic Theology*, 2:221.
[235] For Edwards on mankind's personal participation in Adam's sin, see Michael James McClymond and Gerald R. McDermott, *The Theology of Jonathan Edwards* (New York: Oxford University Press, 2012), 352. On p. 353, they take a passing glance at Charles Hodge's objections to Edwards.
[236] Charles Hodge, *Systematic Theology*, 2:221–22.
[237] Charles Hodge, *Systematic Theology*, 2:224.
[238] Charles Hodge, *Systematic Theology*, 2:225.
[239] Charles Hodge, *Systematic Theology*, 2:225.

the imputation of sin.[240] In light of his firm conviction that Romans 5 taught the imputation of Adam's sin via an implied covenant of works, Hodge concluded, "Realism is a purely philosophical theory."[241]

Original Sin Proper

While Charles Hodge's discussion of imputation appeared in earlier chapters of his *Systematic Theology*, chapter 9 treats original sin directly. Yet again, he opened his chapter with references to the Westminster Standards, focusing on Shorter Catechism 18. Hodge noted that the Westminster Standards' teaching on original can be reduced to the guilt of Adam's first sin, the want of original righteousness, and "the corruption of our whole nature."[242] Because our attention lies on the first of these three elements, I will summarize his teaching as it surrounds the issue of imputation.

After introducing summaries of the doctrine of original sin from various Lutheran and Reformed creeds,[243] Hodge set forth a series of affirmations and denials of what original sin is and is not. Negatively, original sin is not corruption of substance or merely the loss of righteousness or inherent depravity. Positively, original sin includes five things: (1) "This corruption of nature affects the whole soul." (2) It brings with it the loss of original righteousness and inherent depravity. (3) Original sin properly bears the nature of sin, involving both guilt and pollution. (4) "That it retains its character as sin even in the regenerated." (5) "That it renders the soul spiritually dead" and unable to assist in its recovery.[244] He shared the last point in common with Dwight, as seen above, while going beyond him in point three. A. A. Hodge argued for hereditary depravity as the primary idea in original sin, while denying that imputed guilt could bring judgment or condemnation.[245] In line with Warfield, this stressed imputation as punishment rather than culpability.

Charles Hodge focused on destitution of righteousness and corruption of man's whole nature, the effects of the corruption of sin on the whole person,

[240] Hannah, "Doctrine of Original Sin in Postrevolutionary America," 249–50.
[241] Charles Hodge, *Systematic Theology*, 2:226. He summarized here what he believed the proper relation between philosophy and theology should be: (1) It is intimate and necessary. (2) "there is a philosophy which underlies all Scriptural doctrines." (3) Philosophy must accord with the inspired teachings of the Bible. (4) Philosophy helps us understand facts concerning God, man, and nature "in accordance with the divine word" (2:226). He concluded, "The objection to realism is that it inverts this order" (2:227).
[242] Charles Hodge, *Systematic Theology*, 2:227.
[243] Charles Hodge, *Systematic Theology*, 2:228–29.
[244] Charles Hodge, *Systematic Theology*, 2:230.
[245] A. A. Hodge, *Outlines of Theology*, 323–27.

indisposition, inability, and opposition to all spiritual good.[246] Some familiar themes resurface here. For example, Hodge asserted, "If men are not sinners, Christ is not the *Salvator Hominum.*"[247] He added that God is not culpable for this sinful state of mankind.[248] We are not merely prone to sin, but "born in a state of sin," which includes both our guilty status and our dispositions.[249] Both circumcision and baptism show that even infants need to be delivered from this state, which, he again noted, created problems for Pelagians with regard to the meaning of infant baptism.[250]

Romans 5:12–21 resurfaced in this discussion, though with a shift of focus from imputation to death as the penalty for sin.[251] This view, said Hodge, was "the common consent of Christians," adding that Protestants "do not reject the authority of the Church as a teacher. . . . This is a sound principle recognized by all Protestants."[252] Amandus Polanus (1561–1610) represented the classic Reformed view on this point when he argued that God gave the church ministerial authority to interpret Scripture, as opposed to Roman Catholicism, which assigned magisterial authority to her.[253] Charles Hodge added that original sin was seated in the whole person.[254] The resultant spiritual death entailed moral inability.[255]

In spite of this statement, Charles Hodge distanced himself from Edwards's distinction between natural and moral inability on the ground that such terms are ambiguous at best.[256] He argued that natural ability implied that sinners had the ability to change their own hearts. A. A. Hodge did not share his father's reservations at this point.[257] Charles Hodge next proved in detail that inability to do spiritual good was part of original sin.[258] By way of summary and conclusion, with a dash of Common Sense Realism, he wrote,

> There is scarcely a single doctrine of the Scriptures either more clearly taught or more abundantly confirmed by the common consciousness of mankind, whether saints or sinners, than the doctrine that fallen man is

---

[246] Charles Hodge, *Systematic Theology*, 2:231, these points occupying 231–54, 254–57, and 257–77, respectively.
[247] Charles Hodge, *Systematic Theology*, 2:233.
[248] Charles Hodge, *Systematic Theology*, 2:238.
[249] Charles Hodge, *Systematic Theology*, 2:243.
[250] Charles Hodge, *Systematic Theology*, 2:246–47.
[251] Charles Hodge, *Systematic Theology*, 2:248.
[252] Charles Hodge, *Systematic Theology*, 2:249–50.
[253] Amandus Polanus, *Syntagma theologiae christianae ab Amando Polano a Polansdorf: Juxta leges ordinis Methodici conformatum, atque in libros decem digestum jamque demum in unum volumen compactum, novissime emendatum* (Hanoviae [Germany], 1610), 673.
[254] Charles Hodge, *Systematic Theology*, 2:254–57.
[255] Charles Hodge, *Systematic Theology*, 2:257.
[256] Charles Hodge, *Systematic Theology*, 2:265.
[257] A. A. Hodge, *Outlines of Theology*, 327.
[258] Charles Hodge, *Systematic Theology*, 2:267–73.

destitute of all ability to convert himself or to perform any holy act until renewed by the almighty power of the Spirit of God.[259]

The drift of his treatment of original sin was to convict sinners of their sin and to drive them to faith and repentance without delay. The imputation of Adam's sin to his posterity is not stated here, but it is an important backdrop. The primary reason for its importance is that sinners do not merely need new hearts. They need Christ as a new representative, which includes his imputed righteousness in their justification before God, grounded in their "federal union" with him.[260]

Conclusion

The above analysis shows that Old Princeton rooted the imputation of Adam's sin to his posterity in the covenant of works. For Charles Hodge, Jonathan Edwards's realism pervaded his treatment. While this differed to some extent from A. A. Hodge and Warfield's assessments of Edwards, all three theologians, with Alexander, built their views of imputation on the covenant of works. Alexander wrote nothing about Edwards, likely due to the genre of his brief summary of biblical doctrines. Warfield's, and possibly both Hodges', view of imputation as *reatus poenae* to the exclusion of *reatus culpae* is peculiar in the light of earlier Reformed theology and it deserves further exploration. In any case, Adam's breach of the covenant of works brought both the imputation of his sin as well as death and condemnation to the human race.

Closing Evaluation

We can now evaluate Old Princeton on the imputation of Adam's sin and the extent to which their teachings incorporated Reformed orthodoxy and how their American context affected their expression of the doctrine.

First, the imputation of Adam's sin in Reformed theology predated an explicit doctrine of the covenant of works. Bucanus and Gomarus taught the imputation of sin by a sovereign disposition of God without appealing to the covenant as the mechanism through which God did this. In his evaluation of Edwards, Warfield treated this sovereign disposition as the core of

---

[259] Charles Hodge, *Systematic Theology*, 2:274.
[260] Charles Hodge, *Systematic Theology*, 2:551.

the doctrine. While Ravensperger taught a somewhat underdeveloped covenant of works, the Westminster Standards, Turretin, and à Brakel represent the high orthodox integration of the covenant of works into the doctrine of imputation and into the gospel itself. The covenant of works built on and clarified earlier views. Old Princeton's appeal to the covenant of works as the ground of imputation drew from the synthesized expressions found in high Reformed orthodoxy.

Second, many things that Old Princeton theologians attributed to "the testimony of consciousness," via Common Sense Realism, can no longer be taken for granted. For example, Charles Hodge stated that denying that sinful dispositions were properly sin was "opposed to the testimony of consciousness."[261] Yet his arguments apply only under a strong cultural influence of Christianity. It is questionable, for instance, whether such arguments are acceptable in an age when homosexuality is excused precisely on the grounds that it is a disposition. The assumption of modern Western society appears to be that dispositions are not and cannot be wrong. Scripture must correct such views where human consciousness can no longer do so. In this respect, Common Sense Realism effectively leaves many theological arguments underdeveloped in Old Princeton Theology.[262]

Third, the nineteenth-century American context complicated Reformed theology. The changes introduced through the Enlightenment were far-reaching. Realism and traducianism had been around for centuries, but they took on new forms in the New England Theology and in relation to pantheistic philosophy. Evolutionary science threatened the solidarity of the human race, on which the covenant of works hinged. Schleiermacher and the rise of German liberal theology was a new threat to orthodoxy. Transcendentalist philosophy had occupied Charles Hodge's attention also. The American Civil War affected this period as well, dividing the Presbyterian Church U.S.A. along northern and southern lines. New theological institutions arose alongside Princeton during this time as well.[263] I have omitted

---

[261] Charles Hodge, *Systematic Theology*, 2:107.
[262] See J. Ligon Duncan, "Common Sense Realism and American Presbyterianism: An Evaluation of the Impact of Scottish Realism on Princeton and the South" (MA thesis, Covenant Theological Seminary, 1987), 17. He wrote, "Common sense beliefs require no justification since they are foundational." While Duncan defends Old Princeton from the rationalistic tendencies of Common Sense Realism, the fact that key "commonsense beliefs" have shifted in our society shows the problems inherent in the use of this philosophy.
[263] Gutjahr, *Charles Hodge*, 68. "By 1838, there were twelve Presbyterian seminaries, spanning a theological spectrum from conservative Calvinism to Arminian-inflected views of human agency."

such issues to prevent the American context from becoming too unwieldy, but they may shed further light on the topic of this essay.[264]

Old Princeton aimed to take up the mantle of Reformed orthodoxy, applying it to fresh challenges. Moreover, other Princeton theologians, such as Caspar Wistar Hodge Jr. (1870–1937), Geerhardus Vos, and J. Gresham Machen (1881–1937) carried these concerns into the twentieth century. After some professors broke with Princeton and founded Westminster Theological Seminary in 1929 as an alternative institution for training ministers, John Murray (1898–1975) wrote a substantial monograph on the imputation of Adam's sin.[265] Murray also questioned the legitimacy of referring to a covenant of works between God and Adam on some level.[266] This twentieth-century trajectory is worthy of further exploration. In any case, it is clear that Old Princeton aimed to propagate Reformed doctrine on the imputation of Adam's sin via the covenant of works.

---

[264] For an intriguing overview of Hodge's American context and his distinction from other Old Princeton authors as a "public theologian," see John W. Stewart, "Introducing Charles Hodge to Postmoderns," in *Charles Hodge Revisited: A Critical Appraisal of His Life and Work* (Grand Rapids, MI: Eerdmans, 2002), 1–40.

[265] John Murray, *The Imputation of Adam's Sin* (Grand Rapids, MI: Eerdmans, 1959).

[266] John Murray, "The Adamic Administration," in *Collected Writings of John Murray*, 4 vols. (Edinburgh: Banner of Truth, 1977), 2:47–59.

9

"The Chief Evil of Human Life"

SIN IN THE LIFE AND THOUGHT OF THE
ENGLISH PARTICULAR BAPTISTS, 1680s–1830s

Michael A. G. Haykin

Accounts of conversion in the Particular Baptist community during the long eighteenth century are replete with the mention of sin and deliverance from its power and bondage. The pathway that led Londoner Hannah Hurst (1643/53–1720), for instance, to become a Baptist in her late twenties was one of "great fear and anguish," for "my sins," she later recalled, "appeared as a great mountain of lead dragging me down to hell." She was quite conscious that she deserved to go to hell "on the account of original and actual transgression," that is, because of her inheritance of Adam's bent and fallen nature as well as for actual sins she had committed.[1]

The West Yorkshire Particular Baptist pastor William Crabtree (1720–1811) was orphaned as a young child and by his late teens was living in a village that he described as being "next door to hell itself." He became closely acquainted with "a company of rogues" who led him down a path of "drunkenness, profane cursing and swearing." At the time he regarded all of this as evidence of true manliness. But Crabtree went to hear the eccentric Anglican preacher William Grimshaw (1708–1763) of Haworth, and one sentence from Grimshaw's lips

---

[1] *A Brief Narrative of the Dealings of God with Mrs. Hannah Hurst, Taken from Her Own Writings*, in Thomas Harrison, *A Funeral Sermon Occasion'd by the Death of Mrs. Hannah Hurst* (London: J. Clark, E. Matthews, and T. Saunders, 1720), 23–24. I am indebted to Stephen McKay for drawing my attention to this text. The spelling in various eighteenth-century quotations cited in this essay has been modernized.

proved to be the turning point in his life, for it led to a journey that brought him to a living faith in Christ: "One sin would damn a soul as well as a thousand."[2]

Nearly thirty years later, Mary Fox (d. 1823), née Tabor, and her husband William Fox (1736–1826), who was one of the architects of the Sunday school movement and an extremely wealthy merchant, decided to purchase a country home near William's birthplace in Clapton-on-the-Hill in Gloucestershire. William Fox had once been a member of the nearby Baptist church at Bourton-on-the-Water,[3] about one and a half miles distant, and so, in 1781, Mary asked for the privilege of occasional communion at this church. To receive such, Mary was asked to give her testimony of conversion. She told the minister, Benjamin Beddome (1718–95), how, before her conversion, she had been "concerned many years at times under great distresses, her soul overwhelmed within her, both on account of the guilt and power of sin."[4]

A fourth example took place at the beginning of the following decade. In 1792, two English Particular Baptist pastors, John Rippon (1751–1836) and Samuel Pearce (1766–99), sat down in London with an African-American Baptist, David George (1743–1810), as he narrated to them the story of his conversion and his call to ministry. Some, though not all, of his story, would have sounded quite familiar to Rippon and Pearce, especially the way in which George came to see himself as a sinner. When he was told by an acquaintance that if he continued to live as he did, he would "never see the face of God in glory," he experienced such conviction of sin that he was certain that he "must go to hell." As he put it, "I saw myself a mass of sin."[5] He went on relating his story to the two English Baptists: "I could not read, and had no Scriptures. I did not think of Adam and Eve's sin, but *I* was sin. I felt my *own* plague; and . . . that my sins had crucified Christ."[6]

"I Find It Impossible to Deny Universal Depravity"

All of these various experiences substantiated the reality of sin as defined in the leading confessional text of the English Particular Baptists throughout

[2] Cited in Isaac Mann, *Memoirs of the Late Rev. Wm Crabtree* (London: Button & Son, 1815), 16.
[3] "Memoir of William Fox, Esq.," *The Baptist Magazine* 19 (1827): 250, 297.
[4] August 12, 1781, entry in "Bourton-on-the-Water Church Book, 1765–1920" (Angus Library, Regent's Park College, University of Oxford), 41.
[5] It is intriguing to note that this phrase "mass of sin [*massa peccati*]" is ultimately Augustinian. See Augustine, *Miscellany of Questions in Response to Simplicianus* 2.16.
[6] David George, "An Account of the Life of Mr. David George, from Sierra Leone in Africa; Given by Himself in a Conversation with Brother Rippon of London, and Brother Pearce of Birmingham," in *"Face Zion Forward": First Writers of the Black Atlantic, 1785–1798*, ed. Joanna Brooks and John Saillant (Boston, MA: Northeastern University Press, 2002), 180.

this century, namely, *The Second London Confession of Faith* (1677/1688), where it was stated that the disobedience of humanity's "first parents" led to their posterity being "utterly indisposed, disabled, and made opposite to all good, and wholly inclined to all evil."[7] This Confession had been affirmed as the doctrinal standard of the Particular Baptists by this denomination's first national assembly in 1689, though it must be admitted that relatively few Particular Baptist authors or communities referred to it during the eighteenth century.[8] There were no editions of this text for the seventy years between 1720 and 1790,[9] and thus few Baptists would have read its description of sin. And yet, there were confessional documents aplenty in this era that included hamartiological statements dependent on this Confession. A number of these confessions were drawn up by local churches, while a good number were drafted and read at ordinations where prospective pastors were responsible for drafting their own individual statements of faith. Examples of the former include one drawn up by the doyen of Particular Baptists, John Gill (1697–1771), in 1729 for his London church at Horselydown Chapel,[10] and another written over the course of ten months, from August, 1743, to June, 1744, by the Baptist congregation in Barnoldswick, whose minister was the evangelical Calvinist Alvery Jackson (1700–63).[11] Some printed instances of the latter are those of Caleb Evans (1737–91), the Principal of Bristol Baptist Academy; Thomas Davis (1734–96)[12] and Abraham Booth

[7] *A Confession of Faith* 6.2, 4 (London: John Harris, 1688), 24, 25.
[8] Robert W. Oliver, *History of the English Calvinistic Baptists 1771–1892: From John Gill to C. H. Spurgeon* (Edinburgh; Carlisle, PA: The Banner of Truth, 2006), xix.
[9] See *A Confession of Faith*, 5th ed. (London: John Marshall, 1720), and *A Confession of Faith* (London, 1790).
[10] The only copy of this Confession is in the church minute book. No printed copy of this original exists. It was printed again in 1739. Again, there is no extant copy of this second edition. It was printed again in 1764 and 1768, of which editions but three or four copies exist. See Seymour J. Price, "Dr. John Gill's Confession of 1729," *The Baptist Quarterly* 4 (1928–1929): 366–67.
[11] See Evan R. Lewis, *History of the Bethesda Baptist Church, Barnoldswick, Yorks* (Cwmavon, Wales, UK: L. I. Griffiths, 1893), 45–52.
[12] Unlike the other three Particular Baptists mentioned in this sentence, Thomas Davis is almost completely unknown today. On his life, see John Rippon, *A History of the English Baptists* (London: Isaac Taylor Hinton; Holdsworth & Ball, 1830), 4:423–27; Ernest A. Payne, *The Baptists of Berkshire through Three Centuries* (London: Carey Kingsgate, 1951), 90–91. Apart from this Confession, there appears to be nothing extant from Davis's pen. His preaching was vigorous and evangelical, and led to significant growth in the Baptist church at Reading.
   One interesting incident in Davis's ministry occurred when the High Calvinist Baptist William Augustus Clarke (fl. 1770s–1790s), who was accused of being an antinomian, dedicated his autobiographical *A Full and Faithful Narrative of the Dealings of Divine Providence with Mathetes* (London: J. Moore, [1786]) to Davis. Clarke had become a Baptist as a result of conversations with Davis, who had also been instrumental in affirming Clarke's calling as a Baptist preacher in 1774 (*Full and Faithful Narrative*, 100–103, 108–13, 115–16). But Clarke's High Calvinism was patent throughout the autobiography. For example, he stated his "disapprobation of the sentiments of Mr. Andrew Fuller, which by the way is an old error, introduced in a modern dress, which in my view is as detestable as the principles of an Arminian" (*Full and Faithful Narrative*, x; see also pp. 27–28, note*, where Clarke identified the views of John Wesley with those of Fuller). And near the end of his narrative, Clarke set forth his theological convictions, which included the sentiment that "offers of salvation and overtures of mercy are the weak or wicked inventions of unsound teachers," and that "Christ's Gospel is only to be preached to regenerated children." Thus, he

(1734–1806), both London pastors; and that of Andrew Fuller (1754–1815), the most significant theological figure of the Particular Baptist movement in this era.[13]

The Barnoldswick Confession has little to say about sin, which is quite surprising, but Gill's Confession forthrightly declared that Adam "sinning, all his posterity sinned in him & came short of the glory of God," which meant that all of his descendants inherited the guilt of his sin and "a corrupt nature."[14] Booth provided more detail regarding Adam: the first man was "not only the natural but federal head and representative of his unborn posterity."[15] Hence, when he sinned, all of his "unborn posterity . . . sinned in him and fell with him."[16] In Thomas Davis's Confession, it is noteworthy that even before he came to discuss the impact of the sin of Adam, he stressed that "God is not the author of sin, nor is there violence offered to the will of the creature, nor the liberty of second causes taken away."[17] Divine sovereignty over all things, which Davis also affirmed, did not mean that human responsibility was thereby relinquished. Adam, "the natural and publick head, root and representative" of humanity was "left to the freedom of his own will" and "sinned against God."[18]

For Evans, it was important to highlight that both the Scriptures—here he cited a catena of Pauline texts from Romans and 1 Corinthians—and human

---

stated with fierce determination, "The idea therefore that the Gospel is to be preached to all without discrimination, I reprobate, as a fallacious sentiment" (*Full and Faithful Narrative*, 163, 165, 166).

Needless to say, Davis was none too happy to find his name linked to that of a man who was accused of being an antinomian and who was implacably hostile to Fuller's evangelical Calvinism (Clarke later accused Davis of trying to imitate the "Kettering Oracle," by which he meant Fuller, who pastored in Kettering (W. A. Clarke, *A Reply to the Rev. Thomas Davis of Reading, in Berkshire* [London: W. Justins, 1786], 31). Davis appears to have written a response to Clarke's *Full and Faithful Narrative*, in which he described this book as "a compound of nauseous ingredients," an abominable "display of pride, ignorance, censoriousness, and impudence." If Davis had known of Clarke's intention to dedicate it to him, he said he would have endeavoured to suppress its publication. So deep was Davis's revulsion upon reading Clarke's autobiography that he averred he would sooner have had his name affixed to the Qur'an than to the *Full and Faithful Narrative* (for these remarks, see the quotes by Clarke, *Reply to the Rev. Thomas Davis*, 16–17, 28, 36). Davis's response to Clarke's book is not extant.

[13] Caleb Evans, "A Confession of Faith," in *A Charge and Sermon Together with an Introductory Discourse and Confession of Faith Delivered at the Ordination of the Rev. Mr. Caleb Evans* (Bristol: S. Farley, 1767), 12–35; *A Confession of Faith, Delivered at the Ordination of Mr. Thomas Davis, At Reading, September 14th, 1768* (London: Robert M'Gregor, 1776); Abraham Booth, "A Confession of Faith," in *A Charge and Sermon Together with an Introductory Discourse and Confession of Faith Delivered at the Ordination of the Rev. Mr. Abraham Booth* (London: G. Keith; J. Buckland; W. Harris; B. Tomkins; J. Gurney, 1769), 12–26; and Andrew Fuller, "Confession of Faith," in *The Last Remains of the Rev. Andrew Fuller*, ed. J. Belcher (Philadelphia: American Baptist Publication Society, 1856), 209–17. Fuller delivered his confession in the autumn of 1783 at his formal appointment as pastor over the Baptist church in Kettering, Northamptonshire.

[14] Price, "Dr. John Gill's Confession of 1729," 368.

[15] Caleb Evans's words are almost identical: Adam was "not only the natural but federal head and representative of his offspring" ("Confession of Faith," 23).

[16] Booth, "Confession of Faith," 18. Thomas Davis has almost identical words: "all his [i.e., Adam's] posterity sinned in him, and fell with him" (*Confession of Faith, Delivered at the Ordination of Mr. Thomas Davis*, 3).

[17] *Confession of Faith, Delivered at the Ordination of Mr. Thomas Davis*, 2.

[18] *Confession of Faith, Delivered at the Ordination of Mr. Thomas Davis*, 3.

experience underscore the reality of original sin.[19] As Evans observed with regard to the latter realm of proof,

> Indeed when I reflect upon the multiplicity of pains and sorrows and the various kinds of death to which I see innumerable infants daily exposed, notwithstanding they are personally innocent and have not sinned "after the similitude of Adam's transgression" (Romans 5:14), I have no other way of accounting for so plain and flagrant a fact than that which my Bible teaches me, which is that all these calamities flow from Adam's sin "in whom all have sinned" (Romans 5:12) or in the guilt of whose sin all must be involved or they would not share in the punishment. When I observe moreover the early propensities to sin discovered by children as soon as ever they are capable of acting, the general disregard of spiritual and eternal things, the prevalence of vice in the world, and the remains there are of sin in the best of men, I find it impossible to deny universal depravity unless I could suppose poisonous streams to flow from a pure fountain.[20]

Andrew Fuller, on the other hand, cited the "unerring" Bible as well as human reason as evidence for the reality of original sin and then drew implications for three theological perspectives of his day, namely, Arminianism, antinomianism, and Socinianism:

> I own there are some things in these subjects, which appear to me profound and awful. But seeing God hath so plainly revealed them in his Word, especially in the fifth chapter of the epistle to the Romans, I dare not but bow my shallow conceptions to the unerring testimony of God, not doubting but that he will clear his own character sufficiently at the last day. At the same time, I know of no other system that represents these subjects in a more rational light.
>
> I believe, as I before stated, that men are now born and grow up with a vile propensity to moral evil, and that herein lies their inability to keep God's law, and as such, it is a moral and a criminal inability. Were they but of a right disposition of mind, there is nothing now in the law of God but what they could perform; but, being wholly under the dominion of sin, they have no heart remaining for God, but are full of wicked aversion to him. Their very "mind and conscience are defiled" (Titus 1:15). Their ideas of the excellence of good and of the evil of sin are as it were obliterated.
>
> These are subjects which seem to me of very great importance. I conceive that the whole Arminian, Socinian, and Antinomian systems, so far as I understand them, rest upon the supposition of these principles being false. So that, if it should be found, at last, that God is an infinitely excellent being,

---

[19] Evans interwove selections from Rom. 5:12, 18–19; 3:10; and 1 Cor. 15:22 ("Confession of Faith," 23).
[20] Evans, "Confession of Faith," 24. The punctuation of this passage has been modernized.

worthy of being loved with all the love which his law requires; that, as such, his law is entirely fair and equitable and that for God to have required less, would have been denying himself to be what he is; and if it should appear, at last, that man is utterly lost, and lies absolutely at the discretion of God; then, I think it is easy to prove, the whole of these systems must fall to the ground. If men, on account of sin, lie at the discretion of God, the equity, and even necessity, of predestination cannot be denied, and so the Arminian system falls. If the law of God is right and good, and arises from the very nature of God, Antinomianism cannot stand. And if we are such great sinners, we need a great Saviour, infinitely greater than the Socinian Saviour.[21]

If Romans 5 be believed, Fuller averred, then Arminianism with its stress on the freedom of the human will, antinomianism with its lackadaisical attitude to sin, and Socinianism with its optimistic view of human nature, are all fatally undermined.

A "Fretting Leprosy"

Now, Fuller wrote treatises and tracts against all three of these theological perspectives,[22] but during the 1780s and '90s he became increasingly concerned about the presence of antinomianism among his fellow Particular Baptists.[23] In his words, "of late we have been taken as it were by surprise: while our best writers and preachers have been directing their whole force against Socinian, Arian, or Arminian heterodoxy, we are insensibly overrun by a system of false religion which has arisen and grown up among us under the names and forms of orthodoxy." Fuller believed that one of the reasons for this rise of antinomianism was a failure properly to understand the impact of the fall of Adam. The antinomian system of his day, Fuller argued, functioned in such a way as "nearly to remove all accountableness from his [i.e., Adam's] posterity."[24] In the West Country, Caleb Evans gave voice to similar

---

[21] Fuller, "Confession of Faith," 211–12.

[22] See the responses to these perspectives in volume 2 of *The Complete Works of the Rev. Andrew Fuller*, rev. Joseph Belcher, 3rd London ed. (1845; repr., Harrisonburg, VA: Sprinkle Publications, 1988): against the Arminianism of Dan Taylor (1738–1816): *A Defence of a Treatise Entitled The Gospel of Christ Worthy of All Acceptation: Containing a Reply to Mr. Button's Remarks and the Observations of Philanthropos* (pp. 459–511), and *The Reality and Efficacy of Divine Grace, with the Certain Success of Christ's Kingdom, considered in a Series of Letters* (pp. 512–60); against antinomianism: *Antinomianism Contrasted with the Religion Taught and Exemplified in the Holy Scriptures* (pp. 737–62); against the Socinianism of Joseph Priestley (1733–1804): *The Calvinistic and Socinian Systems Examined and Compared, as to their Moral Tendency* (pp. 108–242); and the Socinianism of Joshua Toulmin (1740–1815) and John Kentish (1768–1853): *Socinianism Indefensible on the Ground of Its Moral Tendency* (pp. 243–87).

[23] For some details, see Oliver, *History of the English Calvinistic Baptists 1771–1892*, 112–45.

[24] Fuller, *Antinomianism Contrasted with the Religion Taught and Exemplified in the Holy Scriptures* (*Complete Works of the Rev. Andrew Fuller*, 2:737 and 739).

concerns. In the annual circular letter of the Western Association that he drew up in 1789, he warned the churches of the association about the dangers of both Socinianism, the fastest growing form of heterodoxy at the time, and antinomianism. Of the two, Evans actually feared the latter more:

> We have more reason to guard you against the poisonous influence of a corrupt Antinomian leaven, than the more open attack of Socinianism. Antinomianism comes to you under the guise of an angel of light, and is therefore the more dangerous. It pretends to exalt the free and sovereign grace of God, to reduce the creature to nothing, and make God and Christ all in all. . . . But wherein does salvation consist? Is sanctification no part of it? . . . Few will openly deny the necessity of personal holiness and good works, but there are many who by their doctrine degrade the one and the other, and brand those with legality who express the least concern about them. If God sees fit to make us holy, say some, he will, and if not, we cannot make ourselves holy.[25]

The following year, the Western Association asked Philip Gibbs (1729–1801), the pastor of the Baptist cause in Plymouth, to draw up the annual circular letter. He too warned the churches in the Association to be on their guard against "the baneful and pernicious poison of Antinomianism," which he asserted was an error that was all too prevalent in their day and was, in fact, a "growing evil."[26] Gibbs was careful to emphasize that he was not at all referring to the biblical doctrine of justification by faith alone, which had been wrongly attacked in the eighteenth century by opponents of the Evangelical Revival as antinomianism. Rather, he was speaking of "that horrid doctrine which makes God the author of sin, by charging it on his absolute decrees; and the minister of sin, by denying the sanctification of the Spirit, and substituting the holiness of Christ as imputed for our sanctification; and which further asserts, that God does not punish or chasten his people for sin, though he expressly declares the contrary in his holy Word."[27] As with

---

[25] Caleb Evans, *The Elders, Ministers, and Messengers of the Several Baptist Churches [of the Western Association]* (Bristol?: Western Association, 1789), 6, 7.

[26] Philip Gibbs, *On Truth and Error* in *The Baptist Annual Register, For 1790, 1791, 1792, and Part of 1793*, ed. John Rippon, 4 vols. (London, 1793), 1:56–57. Gibbs had been converted under the preaching of George Whitefield (1714–1770) in 1745. He initially associated himself with the Calvinistic Methodists, but soon became convinced of Baptist principles. In 1748 he began his ministry at the Baptist cause in Plymouth, which prospered under his pastoral care. It is noteworthy that Gibbs had warned of the danger of antinomianism in the Western Association's circular letter of 1776: see *Elders, Ministers, and Messengers of the Several Baptist Churches [of the Western Association]*, 4–5. For these details, see "Recent Deaths," *The Evangelical Magazine* 9 (1801): 35; W. T. Adey, *The History of the Baptist Church, Kingsbridge, Devon* (Kingsbridge, 1899), 11–13; Edwin Welch, *Two Calvinistic Methodist Chapels 1743–1811* (London: London Record Society, 1975), 34–38.

[27] Gibbs, *On Truth and Error*, in *Baptist Annual Register*, 1:56–57.

Caleb Evans's circular letter the previous year, there was a concern here with the denial of the need for a vigorous pursuit of holiness. Gibbs concluded his discussion of this error with an admonition to his readers to "contend earnestly" for the biblical assertion that union with Christ was evidenced "through sanctification and 'holiness, without which no man shall see the Lord' [Heb. 12:14]; for 'anyone who does not have the Spirit of Christ does not belong to him' [Rom. 8:9]."[28] By citing the verse from Romans 8 immediately after that from Hebrews 12, Gibbs was clearly affirming that a sure mark of the indwelling of the Spirit is the pursuit of a holy life and the doing of good works.

John Ryland Jr. (1753–1825), the Principal of Bristol Baptist Academy who became a leading figure in the Western Association in the three decades following Gibbs's circular letter, and was a close friend of Andrew Fuller, was also deeply exercised by the growth of antinomianism. In a preface that Ryland wrote in 1816 for Fuller's posthumously published *Antinomianism Contrasted with the Religion Taught & Exemplified in the Holy Scriptures*, Ryland cited the words of one of their mutual friends, Thomas Steevens (1745–1802) of Colchester, to describe the state of those churches within the Particular Baptist community infected with antinomianism—they were afflicted with a "fretting leprosy" that was teaching professing believers to play fast and loose with their battle with sin.[29] Little wonder that Robert Hall Jr. (1764–1831), in his funeral sermon for Ryland in 1825, noted that an "extreme" against which Ryland had regularly warned believers was "Antinomian licentiousness . . . which he detested as an insult . . . on the majesty and authority of the law."[30] This constant concern with antinomianism was partly the result of the fact that Ryland had been bitterly attacked in the early 1790s by William Huntington (1745–1813) as one who was subverting the gospel of free grace.

William Huntington, London preacher popular with many, and one who enjoyed a curious and heady mix of bombast, Tory politics, and rancorous de-

---

[28] Gibbs, *On Truth and Error*, in *Baptist Annual Register*, 1:57.

[29] John Ryland, "Preface" to Andrew Fuller, *Antinomianism Contrasted with the Religion Taught and Exemplified in the Holy Scriptures*, 2nd ed. (Bristol: J. G. Fuller, 1817), v, xii–xiv. Ryland called his friend "Mr. Stephens of Colchester."

[30] Robert Hall Jr., "A Sermon, Occasioned by the Death of the Rev. John Ryland, D. D." in *The Works of the Rev. Robert Hall, A.M.*, ed. Olinthus Gregory and Joseph Belcher, 4 vols. (New York: Harper & Brothers, 1854), 1:221. The other extreme against which Ryland spoke according to Hall was "Pelagian pride." For a similar warning against "Arminian legality and Antinomian licentiousness," see Charles Whitfield, *The Form and Order of a Church of Christ* (Newcastle upon Tyne, 1775), v.

nunciation of any who dared to criticize him,[31] played a significant role in the propagation of antinomian principles in the late eighteenth century. Though he was not a Baptist, numerous Baptists imbibed his argument that the moral law should not be considered as a pattern for the Christian life, and that any, like Ryland, who did regard it as such were simply nothing more than "Pharisees" and guilty of "undervaluing Christ's imputed righteousness."[32] Huntington was also insistent that the Bible knows only of imputed sanctification and that there is no scriptural basis at all for the doctrine of progressive sanctification. In his words,

> As to sanctification being a progressive work, it is best to consent to the wholesome words of our Lord Jesus Christ, lest we set poor weak believers to inquiring how long this progressive work is to be on the wheels, what part of it is wrought, what measure of it is required, and how much remains to be done: and like Sarah with her bondwoman, they begin to forward the business by the works of the flesh, instead of lying passive to be worked on. "He that believeth shall not make haste" (Isa. 28:16), but he that hasteth with his feet sinneth.[33]

There is no evidence that Huntington himself was guilty of practical antinomianism, but it is quite understandable that opponents like Ryland viewed Huntington's teaching as the foundation of such. As Ryland summed up Huntingtonianism: it is "a false gospel, which . . . [promotes] a redemption, not from sin, but from duty. A perseverance, not in grace, but in security. A mere witness of the Spirit, without the works of the Spirit."[34]

A classic example of the sort of antinomianism that bedeviled some of the Particular Baptist churches concerns a certain James Levit, who had

---

[31] For contrasting perspectives on Huntington, see George M. Ella, *William Huntington: Pastor of Providence* (Darlington, Durham, UK: Evangelical Press, 1994); and Oliver, *History of the English Calvinistic Baptists*, 119–45. See also Casey G. McCall, " 'The Poisonous Influence of a Corrupt Antinomian Leaven': Caleb Evans' Response to the Antinomianism of William Huntington," *The Journal of Andrew Fuller Studies 1* (September 2020): 47–57. Huntington went so far as to imply that any who strenuously opposed him would be struck dead by God. See John Ryland, *Serious Remarks on the Different Representations of Evangelical Doctrine by the Professed Friends of the Gospel* (Bristol: J. Ryland, 1817), 2:39–41. I am grateful to Thomas J. Nettles for making me a photocopy of this important treatise by Ryland.

[32] Robert W. Oliver, "The Emergence of a Strict and Particular Baptist Community among the English Calvinistic Baptists, 1770–1850" (PhD thesis, London Bible College, 1986), 130; John Ryland Jr., *The Practical Influence of Evangelical Religion* (London: B. J. Holdsworth, 1819), 38. Oliver's thesis is essentially the same as his book, *History of the English Calvinistic Baptists*, though not all of the material in the thesis appears in the book and vice versa.

[33] Citing Oliver, *History of the English Calvinistic Baptists*, 127. This text appears in a letter directed against Caleb Evans.

[34] John Ryland, "The Enmity of the Carnal Mind," in *Pastoral Memorials: Selected from the Manuscripts of the Late Revd. John Ryland, D.D.*, 2 vols. (London: B. J. Holdsworth, 1828), 2:12–13. See also his *The Necessity of the Trumpet's Giving a Certain Sound* (Bristol, UK: E. Bryan, 1813), 33; Ryland, "The Believer's Conflict Distinguished from the Struggle of Natural Conscience," in his *Pastoral Memorials*, 2:121: "I am greatly afraid that some modern professors wish to substitute an immediate witness of the Spirit for the extensive and important work of the Spirit. They seem to deny all internal sanctification." (See also Ryland, *Serious Remarks*, 2:53, where he notes that "some, of late, deny all internal sanctification. They are for imputed sanctification.")

become a member of Soham Baptist Church, Cambridgeshire, in May of 1761.[35] In the fall of 1770, Andrew Fuller, who had joined the church that spring as a young convert, discovered that Levit was given to immoderate drinking and getting inebriated "repeatedly." Fuller, and some other members in the church, remonstrated with Levit that this was entirely inappropriate for a Christian believer. Levit replied that "the propensity of his nature was such that he could not avoid it and that if left to himself he should act the same again." By "left to himself," Levit seems to have had in mind the idea that the power to resist sin must come from strength given by God, and since he had not received said strength, he should not be blamed for the sin of drunkenness. Fuller's reproof of Levit could not stay hidden, and soon the entire church was consumed by a conflict over, among other things, the power of the believer's will to do what is good and refrain from evil.

Fuller's own grandmother, Philippa Gunton, one of the founding members of the Soham Church, argued that Levit's conviction about the necessity of divine grace to do anything good was actually biblical, though she suspected that Levit might be using this idea to excuse his sin. She held that believers, though never totally abandoned by God, may be left to their own devices such that they are "unable to persevere in acts of holiness, and to abstain from acts of evil." The pastor, John Eve (d. 1782), originally a sievemaker from Chesterton, near Cambridge, strongly disagreed with Gunton by asserting that the Spirit of God constantly gave believers "a continual power . . . for the performance of all good works and abstaining from all evils." Eventually, when the matter was brought before the entire church and debated publicly on two or three occasions with "somewhat of warmth," Gunton's opinion, with the support of one of the deacons, Thomas Irons, carried the day.

Peace was restored to the church for a brief period, but in the spring of 1771 the controversy broke out afresh. Again, it was "debated warmly," and the church seemed to be headed for complete dissolution. In the autumn of 1771, Eve took the opportunity to quit the Soham pastorate for that of Wisbech, also in Cambridgeshire, and the controversy finally petered out.

---

[35] For what follows in this paragraph and the next two, see "Soham Baptist Church Book 1752–1868" (Cambridgeshire County Archives, Cambridge), pp. 16–22. Notice of Levit's membership can be found in this text on pp. 8 and 11. See also Peter J. Morden, *The Life and Thought of Andrew Fuller (1754–1815)*, Studies in Evangelical History and Thought (Milton Keynes, UK: Paternoster, 2015), 33–35.

Fuller had initially sided with the pastor, but over the course of 1771, he had become convinced that his grandmother's position was the right one. In the long run, the controversy forced him to delve into the Scriptures to find solid answers to the question of the impact of Adam's fall upon the human will and the spheres of human responsibility and divine sovereignty. In doing so, he came to loathe antinomianism as an especial bane of the Particular Baptist denomination; and he would have heartily agreed with his friends Ryland and Steevens that it was indeed a "fretting leprosy." Alan Sell has questioned to what extent these fears of the extent of antinomianism were justifiable. Huntington and Levit reveal in different ways that the deep-seated fears of Ryland, Evans, Gibbs, and Fuller were not entirely without reason. Of course, in the final analysis, Sell is right to cite James Buchanan's observation: "the last day only will declare how much practical Antinomianism has prevailed even in evangelical congregations, which theoretically disowned it."[36]

"Sinful Actings"

As the incident surrounding the repeated drunkenness of James Levit reveals, human depravity and sin within the eighteenth-century Particular Baptist community was not a merely theoretical matter. It brought distress and destruction to these churches. Benjamin Beddome once exhorted his fellow church members in the Midland Association, "Take heed lest your hearts be at any time harden'd thro' the deceitfulness of sin. One corruption favoured and indulged, has sometimes made dreadful havoc even in the gracious soul."[37] And this "dreadful havoc" caused by sin inevitably led to church discipline. Michael R. Watts has noted that the majority of discipline cases within Baptist churches during the eighteenth century had to do with "neglect of worship, drunkenness, and sexual lapses."[38] For example, April 4, 1759, saw the excommunication of George Death and Elizabeth Langly from Colchester Baptist Church for having "joyned themselves with the people called Methodists, thereby wickedly endeavouring to rend and divide our

[36] Citing Alan P. F. Sell, *The Great Debate: Calvinism, Arminianism, and Salvation* (1982; repr., Eugene, OR: Wipf & Stock, 1998), 46–47. Sell sketches the history of antinomianism in the seventeenth century (42–57). But what is needed is a monograph on antinomianism in the period this essay is considering, the long eighteenth century.
[37] Benjamin Beddome, *The Circular Letter from the Elders and Messengers of the Several Baptist Churches [of the Western Association]* (Worcester: R. Lewis, 1765), 3. It is noteworthy that the normal abstract of theological principles that stood at the head of the circular letter was replaced in this case with the statement that the churches of this Association upheld "the doctrines of Free Grace, in opposition to Arminianism and Socinianism: and the necessity of good works in opposition to Libertinism and real Antinomianism" (Beddome, *Circular Letter*, 1).
[38] Michael R. Watts, *The Dissenters*, vol. 1, *From the Reformation to the French Revolution* (Oxford: Clarendon, 1978), 326.

Church."[39] Five years earlier, St. Mary's Baptist Church, Norwich, had ruled that it was "unlawful for any [member] . . . to attend upon the meetings of the Methodists, or to join in any worship which is contrary to the doctrines and ordinances of our Lord Jesus."[40]

Before the passage of Lord Hardwicke's Marriage Act of 1753, which required the presence of an Anglican minister for a valid marriage, Dissenting churches were allowed to perform common-law marriages. Not surprisingly, though, some couples married in Dissenting chapels were not happy with having to settle for a common-law marriage. But this caused problems for the leadership of their churches, who regarded the worship of the Church of England as "spiritual whoredom," to cite the words of Benjamin Winckles (1653–1732), the pastor of Arnesby Baptist Church for the first three decades of the eighteenth century.[41] Thus, when William Matham and Elizabeth Sleater decided that their common-law marriage in the Arnesby meeting-house in 1706 was inadequate and went to the Anglican church for a "proper" wedding, Winckles led the church to disfellowship the couple for the "sin [of] going and joining in with the anti-Christian way of marriage in the carnal Church" of England.[42]

Eighteenth-century Baptists were not at all teetotallers—the minute book of the Luton Baptists, for instance, recorded that the church provided beer for church members who had come from nearby villages and stayed at the church "all Lord's day."[43] But these churches frowned deeply upon drunkenness. Benjamin Dutton (1691–1747) was a clothier who had studied for the ministry of the gospel in various places, among them Glasgow University. For a period of time in the 1720s he was a member of the Arnesby church, but he struggled with alcohol, occasionally "drinking to excess," and, though he was deeply ashamed and sorry for this sin, the church disfellowshipped him.[44] Later, Dutton found deliverance from this crippling addiction, was restored spiritually, and went on to become the pastor of the Baptist work at Great Gransden in Huntingdonshire. In Dutton's own words, he said that he now "stood not in need of wine, or strong drink. The Lord also, of his great

[39] Henry Spyvee, *Colchester Baptist Church—The First 300 Years, 1689–1989* (Colchester: Colchester Baptist Church, 1989), 30.

[40] Charles B. Jewson, "St. Mary's, Norwich," *The Baptist Quarterly* 10 (1940–1941): 283.

[41] Richard Hunt, "Record and Representation: The Minute Book of the Arnesby Particular Baptist Church," *Transactions of the Leicestershire Archaeological and Historical Society* 84 (2010): 158.

[42] Hunt, "Record and Representation," 158.

[43] Watts, *Dissenters*, 327.

[44] Benjamin Dutton, *The Superaboundings of the Exceeding Riches of God's Free-Grace, towards the Chief of the Chief of Sinners* (London: J. Hart, 1743), 80; Hunt, "Record and Representation," 157.

goodness, took away my inclination thereto; so that I had no more inclination to it, or desire after it, than if I had never tasted any in my whole life." In fact, Dutton now had a distinct aversion to drink and even found the smell of it entirely disagreeable.[45]

Another pastor who found restoration after falling deep into sin was David Crosley (1669–1744), a Baptist evangelist from the Pennine hills in Northern England, who pastored a London church between 1705 and 1709. In 1709, he was disfellowshipped for drunkenness, unchaste conduct with women, and lying to the church about these matters when accused. Crosley genuinely repented, and some thirty years later, having lived a life in accord with genuine repentance, he knew some usefulness again in the Lord's work.[46] Around the same time—in April of 1705, to be exact—James Bartlemew and Jane Wells, both of whom came from Coventry, were excommunicated from the Arnesby Church for "their sinful actings with [one] another," but were later readmitted to the church when they married in 1707.[47]

One discipline case that did not end with the restoration of the person disciplined involved a certain William Peace, a member of Olney Baptist Church. According to the church minutes, "A scandalous report having been raised of Wm. Peace, he was suspended" on Thursday, December 23, 1784.[48] Our knowledge of what exactly was entailed by this "scandalous report" is derived from a letter written by the evangelical poet William Cowper (1733–1800), resident in Olney at the time, to his close friend John Newton (1725–1807), who had once been the curate of the town's parish church. Writing on Christmas Eve, 1784, the day following Peace's suspension, Cowper informed his friend that for more than six months a report about Peace had been "current in this place in the way of whisper, but lately with much noise and clamour," namely, that Peace had been involved in pederasty.[49] Apparently, he had either

---

[45] Dutton, *Superaboundings of the Exceeding Riches of God's Free-Grace*, 119. It is noteworthy that Benjamin Winckles wrote a letter of support for Dutton around this time in 1731, in which he expressed his confidence that Dutton had been 'given afresh . . . repentance and remission of sins" (*Superaboundings of the Exceeding Riches of God's Free-Grace*, 102–3).

[46] For his story, see the excellent study by B. A. Ramsbottom, *The Puritan Samson: The Life of David Crosley 1669–1744* (Harpenden, Hertfordshire, UK: Gospel Standard Trust, 1991). Crosley carried on a correspondence with George Whitefield, who noted that their "sentiments as the essential doctrines of the gospel, exactly harmonize[d]," and who wrote a commendatory preface for a sermon Crosley published on Samson. See George Whitefield, "Preface to the Reader," in David Crosley, *Samson a Type of Christ* (1744; repr., Newburyport, MA: William Barrett, 1796), iii.

[47] Hunt, "Record and Representation," 158.

[48] "Olney Church Book III" (Sutcliff Baptist Church, Olney, Buckinghamshire), entry for December 23, 1784.

[49] William Cowper, Letter to John Newton, December 14, 1784, in *The Letters and Prose Writings of William Cowper*, ed. James King and Charles Ryskamp, 5 vols. (Oxford: Clarendon, 1981), 2:314–15. Unless referenced otherwise, what follows is based on this letter by Cowper.

sexually molested two boys or attempted to do so. Cowper identified the boys merely by their surnames: "one called Butcher, and the other Beryl." These two boys may well have been James Butcher and Jonathan Berril, who became members of the Baptist church in 1799 and 1792 respectively.[50]

When Peace was initially confronted with the charge by one of the boys in the presence of his wife, his reply was a "clenched fist and a thrust [of the boy] into the street." The boys refused to let the matter drop and appear to have taken it to John Sutcliff (1752–1814), Peace's pastor. Sutcliff raised the matter with Peace, either on the last Sunday in November or one of the first three Sundays of December. Peace, according to Cowper, "denied it with the most solemn asseverations." Peace was told, however, that the church needed more satisfactory proof of his innocence than simply his word, especially in view of the fact that knowledge of the matter was all over town. Peace refused to try to clear his name. Sutcliff had no choice but to take it to the church at the next monthly business meeting on December 23. It was at this meeting that Peace's privileges as a member were suspended, and three members of the church delegated to visit him. Their first impressions, which one of them communicated to Cowper, were that Peace was indeed guilty, his refusal to attempt to clear his name evincing rather "a hardness of heart, than a consciousness of innocence."

At the next monthly business meeting, held on January 20, 1785, the three members reported that they had met with Peace and his accusers separately. The boys' "testimony appeared credible," but Peace refused to face the boys, though he vehemently denied their charge. After some deliberation, the church was convinced that Peace's whole attitude to the affair bespoke his guilt, and he was "immediately excluded."[51] In disciplining Peace in this manner the Olney Baptists would have been hopeful that exclusion would shock Peace into genuine repentance for his sin and a reformed life. There is no evidence, though, that it did, and behind these textual accounts lies the devastating ugliness of human sin.

One last example of the disruptive nature of sin concerns a member of the Baptist cause at Bourton-on-the-Water, a "Sister Hardiman," who was baptized in 1778 and who lived four miles north of Bourton at Stow-in-the-Wold. Her pastor at the time was Benjamin Beddome, who conducted a service at Stow on a number of Sundays a month, but when the Lord's Table was celebrated at

---

[50] Olney Church Book III, entries for March 10, 1799, and April 29, 1792.
[51] Olney Church Book III, entry for January 20, 1785.

Bourton she would come down from Stow to take it at Bourton. She appears to have been either single or widowed and had come to an age when she needed financial support. She insisted that the Bourton church completely support her financially. When the church refused to comply, she began publicly to criticize Beddome. Part of the reason for the church's reluctance in this regard may have been the fact she held "erroneous opinions bordering on Quakerism, Antinomianism and Mysticism." Things came to a head between 1784 and 1786. On September 17, 1784, she came to Bourton for the Lord's Supper. Afterwards, not being invited to stay over in anyone's house, she told Beddome that she was going to bed down in the meeting house. He tried to persuade her not to, but she insisted and eventually it appears she did stay the night there. That week Beddome and the leadership of the church determined that if she did not behave herself in the future, they would have to exercise discipline by asking her to refrain from taking communion. She must have behaved herself for a while at least, since it was not until March of 1786 that she was finally asked to withdraw from communion. She refused, but came to church and as the bread was being distributed, she brazenly snatched a piece and ate it, but the cup was not given her. Afterwards, before the afternoon worship service, she went into hysterics in the vestry, and had to be carried out bodily![52]

"Millions of Sins of Crimson Red"

A final set of texts that graphically depicted the nature of human sin for this community of Baptists was their hymnals. Probably the best of the earliest of these hymnals was that of the Seventh-day Baptist Joseph Stennett I (1663–1713), which he designed to be used at the celebration of the Lord's Supper.[53] Here sin is associated with a range of negative terms—"stain,"[54] "vileness,"[55] "curse,"[56] "leprous,"[57] "loathsome"/"loath"[58] "foul,"[59] "sores,"[60] "blots"[61] and

---

[52] Bourton-on-the-Water Church Book (F.P.C. F.1[a], Angus Library and Archives, Regent's Park College, University of Oxford), entries for September 17 and 26, 1784, and March 3 and 5, 1786.

[53] Joseph Stennett, *Hymns in Commemoration of the Sufferings of Our Blessed Saviour Jesus Christ, Compos'd for the Celebration of His Holy Supper*, 3rd ed., enlarged ed. (London: John Baker, 1713). On Stennett, see "Stennett, Joseph," in *A Dictionary of Hymnology*, rev. ed., ed. John Julian (London: John Murray, 1907), 1091–92. The capitalization in extracts cited below from these hymns has been modernized.

[54] Stennett, *Hymns in Commemoration*, 7 (Hymn VI, stanza 4); 20 (Hymn XVII, stanza 4); 51 (Hymn XXXVIII, stanza 4).

[55] Stennett, *Hymns in Commemoration*, 11 (Hymn IX, stanza 7).

[56] Stennett, *Hymns in Commemoration*, 12 (Hymn X, stanza 4); 14 (Hymn XII, stanza 4).

[57] Stennett, *Hymns in Commemoration*, 14 (Hymn XII, stanza 4); 42 (Hymn XXXII, stanza 8); 45 (Hymn XXXIV, stanza 9).

[58] Stennett, *Hymns in Commemoration*, 18 (Hymn XV, stanza 5); 36 (Hymn XXVIII, stanza 4).

[59] Stennett, *Hymns in Commemoration*, 20 (Hymn XVII, stanza 4).

[60] Stennett, *Hymns in Commemoration*, 25 (Hymn XX, stanza 7); 44 (Hymn XXXIII, stanza 8): "putrid sores."

[61] Stennett, *Hymns in Commemoration*, 53 (Hymn XXXIX, stanza 7).

"depraved"[62]—though it is two legal terms that are mainly linked to sin: "guilt"/"guilty"[63] and "crimes."[64] It is noteworthy that Stennett never used the chromatic adjective "black" to characterize sin, as has frequently been done in the Western tradition.[65] Rather, he spoke of "millions of sins of crimson red,"[66] a reference to the biblical depiction of sin in Isaiah 1:18. Adamic sin is responsible for death and misery:

> When sin had brought death with a train
> Of miseries on the guilty world . . .[67]

Along the same lines, humanity's sins are described as a "viprous brood of vice/That bring a train of endless woes."[68] But it is only through the prism of Christ's death—referred to as "that crimson fountain," an allusion to Zechariah 13:1—that sins can be seen for what they truly are:

> Ah cruel sins, how odious now,
> And how deform'd are they,
> While in that crimson fountain we
> Their monstrous hue survey.[69]

A couple of Stennett's eucharistic hymns found their way into the first English Baptist congregational hymnbook, *A Collection of Hymns Adapted to Public Worship*. Published in 1769 by Caleb Evans and his close friend John Ash (1724–79), pastor of the Baptist cause in Pershore, Worcestershire, this

---

[62] Stennett, *Hymns in Commemoration*, 64 (Hymn XLVII, stanza 2).
[63] Stennett, *Hymns in Commemoration*, 5 (Hymn IV, stanza 4); 11 (Hymn IX, stanza 6); 14 (Hymn XII, stanza 4); 20 (Hymn XVII, stanza 4); 24–25 (Hymn XX, stanzas 2 and 7); 30 (Hymn XXIV, stanza 3); 32 (Hymn XXV, stanza 2); "Adam's guilty seed"; 36 (Hymn XXVIII, stanza 2); 40 (Hymn XXXI, stanza 2); 51 (Hymn XXXVIII, stanza 4); 54 (Hymn XL, stanza 4); 56 (Hymn XLII, stanza 3); 61 (Hymn XLV, stanza 6); 63 (Hymn XLVI, stanzas 8–9); 64 (Hymn XLIII, stanzas 2–3).
[64] Stennett, *Hymns in Commemoration*, 11 (Hymn IX, stanza 6); 13 (Hymn XI, stanza 2); 16 (Hymn XIII, stanza 6); 17 (Hymn XIV, stanza 4); 20 (Hymn XVII, stanza 3); 30 (Hymn XXIV, stanza 3); 37 (Hymn XXVIII, stanza 7); 53 (Hymn XXXIX, stanza 9); 54 (Hymn XL, stanza 4); 56 (Hymn XLII, stanza 3).
[65] See Michael A. G. Haykin, "'I am Black and Beautiful': Blackness and the Patristic Exegesis of Song of Songs 1:5," in Michael A. G. Haykin and Barry H. Howson, eds., *Reading Scripture, Learning Wisdom: Essays in Honour of David G. Barker* (Peterborough, ON: Joshua Press, 2021), 159–170. See also Michael A. G. Haykin, "Rear View Mirror: Our Sins 'Red' or 'Black,'" *Evangelicals Now* (January 2020): 14.
[66] Stennett, *Hymns in Commemoration*, 26 (Hymn XXI, stanza 2). See also Joseph Stennett, *Hymns Compos'd for the Celebration of the Holy Ordinance of Baptism*, 2nd ed. (London: John Marshall, 1712), 14: "sins of crimson dye" (Hymn X, stanza 4).
[67] Stennett, *Hymns in Commemoration*, 16 (Hymn XIV, stanza 1).
[68] Stennett, *Hymns in Commemoration*, 52 (Hymn XXXIX, stanza 3).
[69] Stennett, *Hymns in Commemoration*, 10 (Hymn IX, stanza 4). Hymn XXXII, stanza 8 describes "Adam's sons" as "deform'd and odious" (Stennett, *Hymns*, 42). See also stanza 4 of Hymn XXXI, where Stennett speaks of "this crimson stream" that provided "a bath" for sinners, "in which they're cleans'd and heal'd" (*Hymns*, 40). See also *Hymns*, 47 (Hymn XXXVI, stanza 1): "crimson flood"; *Hymns*, 63 (Hymn XLVI, stanza 7): "crimson rivers." And in his poem "Love to a Crucified Jesus," Stennett urged readers to "see crimson streams flow from his wounded side" (*The Works of the Late Reverend and Learned Mr. Joseph Stennett*, 5 vols. [London, 1722], 4:274).

hymnal went through eight editions, the last one being published in Norwich by Joseph Kinghorn (1766–1832). It contains hymns by a number of Baptist luminaries, including sixty-two by Anne Steele (1717–78) and thirteen by Benjamin Beddome.[70] One by Anne Steele captured well the totality of sin's devastation of every faculty of the human person:

> How helpless guilty nature lies . . .
> The will perverse, the passions blind,
> In paths of ruin stray;
> Reason, debas'd can never find
> The safe, the narrow way.[71]

A hymn by Isaac Watts (1674–1748), whose style deeply influenced the hymnody of Anne Steele, gave the reason behind such radical depravity:

> We from the stock of Adam came,
> Unholy and unclean;
> All our original is shame,
> And all our nature sin . . .
> Born in a world of guilt, we drew
> Contagion with our breath . . .[72]

In other hymns, sin is graphically depicted under various medical images—it is a "leprosy"[73] and is "like a raging fever,"[74] a "plague,"[75] a "dire contagion" that "spreads its poison to the heart"[76]—or political ones—sin has "tyrant power,"[77] is "reigning" in fallen men and women,[78] who paradoxically

---

[70] See Nancy Jiwon Cho, "Caleb Evans," in *The Canterbury Dictionary of Hymnology*, https://hymnology-hymns am-co-uk.ezproxy.sbts.edu/c/caleb-evans (accessed September 24, 2020).

[71] Caleb Evans, and John Ash, *A Collection of Hymns Adapted to Public Worship*, 6th ed. (Bristol: W. Pine, 1788), 126 (Hymn CLVII, stanzas 1–2). The capitalization in extracts cited below from these hymns has been modernized.

[72] Evans and Ash, *Collection of Hymns*, 70 (Hymn LXXXV, stanzas 1–2). Watts entitled his hymn, one of his paraphrases of Ps. 51, "Original and Actual Sin Confessed and Pardoned" (*The Psalms, Hymns, and Spiritual Songs of the Rev. Isaac Watts, D.D.*, ed. Chris Fenner [Frisco, TX: Doxology and Theology Press; Louisville: The Institute for Biblical Worship of The Southern Baptist Theological Seminary, 2016], 126–27). Evans and Ash replaced Watts's first stanza with his third stanza and altered all of Watts's first-person singular references to the corporate "we," etc. Thus, for instance, Watts had written, "I from the stock of Adam came," which Evans and Ash rendered, "We from the stock of Adam came."

See also similar ideas in Evans and Ash, *Collection of Hymns*, 69 (Hymn LXXXIV, stanzas 1–2), which is also a hymn by Watts ("Original Sin; or, The First and Second Adam" [*Psalms, Hymns, and Spiritual Songs*, 376–77]), and which again Evans and Ash have adapted.

[73] Evans and Ash, *Collection of Hymns*, 93, 94, and 294 (Hymns CXIV, stanza 4; CXV, stanza 4; and CCCXCIV, stanza 2).

[74] Evans and Ash, *Collection of Hymns*, 94 (Hymn CXVI, stanza 2). This is from a hymn by Anne Steele.

[75] Evans and Ash, *Collection of Hymns*, 93 (Hymn CXIV, stanza 4).

[76] Evans and Ash, *Collection of Hymns*, 95 (Hymn CXVI, stanza 2).

[77] Evans and Ash, *Collection of Hymns*, 122 (Hymn CLI, stanza 4).

[78] Evans and Ash, *Collection of Hymns*, 128 (Hymn CLIX, stanza 5).

are its "willing slaves."[79] And in one striking turn of phrase, one hymn speaks of "the wild labyrinth of sin."[80]

These hymnic descriptions of sin would have driven home to the congregations in which they were sung the powerful realities of sin that have been discussed in this essay. It is no wonder then that Evans, one of the editors of this hymnal, once argued that sin has to be "considered as the chief evil of human life," for more than anything else it despoils human beings of "all their excellency and beauty, deforms and debases their very nature and character, and lays the ax to the root of all their happiness."[81]

---

[79] Evans and Ash, *Collection of Hymns*, 125 (Hymn CLVI, stanza 2).
[80] Evans and Ash, *Collection of Hymns*, 96 (Hymn CXVIII, stanza 6).
[81] Caleb Evans, *The Deceitfulness of Sin* (Bristol, UK: W. Pine, 1792), 10.

II

SIN AND DEPRAVITY
IN THE BIBLE

10

From Eden to Exile

THE STORY OF SIN IN GENESIS–2 KINGS

William M. Wood

Introduction

Westminster Larger Catechism (WLC) Q&A 24 answers the question "What is sin?" with "Sin is any want of conformity unto, or transgression of, any law of God given as a rule to the reasonable creature." While this definition is theologically and dogmatically true, articulated in the numerous texts that present such a view (e.g., Lev. 5:17; James 4:17; 1 John 3:4; Gal. 3:10, 12; etc.), it is nonetheless the case that this theological portrait is more often cast in a narrative and historical fashion correspondent to the eschatological telos of God's covenant than in a strictly dogmatic portrait. And yet, the narrative-historical and the dogmatic portrait must not be set in fundamental conflict. As Geerhardus Vos notes, "it should be remembered that on the line of historical progress there is at several points already a beginning of correlation among elements of truth in which the beginnings of the systematizing process may be discerned."[1]

With this in mind, the basic assumption of the following analysis is that there is an inseparable relation between the dogmatic portrait of sin in WLC Q&A 24 and the more narrative portrait of the OT as God works *in history* to redeem fallen man from his sinful state. The dogmatic presentation of what

---

[1] Geerhardus Vos, *Biblical Theology of the Old and New Testaments* (Carlisle, PA: Banner of Truth, 2007), 16. See also Richard B. Gaffin, "Systematic Theology and Biblical Theology," *WTJ* 38.3 (Spring 1976): 281–99.

252 SIN AND DEPRAVITY IN THE BIBLE

sin by definition *is* will have a correspondent portrait to the way sin is *presented* in narrative form in the history under examination. One may therefore analyze sin within the overarching program of God's covenant with man and the historical progression toward its eschatological climax. The foundational contours of this covenant may be summarized by a covenantal kingdom structure where God seeks to confer himself in a bond of communion on a holy people in a holy realm by means of an obedient federal head unto the praise of his glory.[2] The consequences of sin in the OT historical narratives will portray a breach of covenant that has ramifications for all the various aspects of the covenantal kingdom, especially on the loss of the essence of that kingdom in communion with God. Sin is first, foremost, and always something done *against* God as a breach of this covenant relation. As Vos states, "Sin, in the strict sense, is only conceivable as sin against God . . . the feature of a relationship to God is essential for the concept of sin and so has to be made part of the definition."[3] While the following chapter must be necessarily brief, we will examine this consideration of sin as breaking the covenant along particular covenantal kingdom contours as follows: (1) the structure of the covenantal kingdom in the garden (Gen. 1–2); (2) the entrance and advance of sin and misery (Gen. 3–11); (3) restoration promised to sinful patriarchs (Gen. 12–50); (4) restoration begun under Moses and the granting of the law (Exodus–Deuteronomy); (5) securing a holy realm (Joshua); (6) Israel's spiral into sin and misery (Judges); and (7) restoration typologically granted and sinfully lost (Samuel–Kings).

I. The Structure of the Covenantal Kingdom in the Garden (Gen. 1–2)

Adam, created in the image of God, was made in an original state of righteousness from which he may advance to a state of confirmed righteousness by means of perfect, personal, exact, and entire obedience to the stipulations of the covenant of works highlighted in the prohibition concerning the tree of the knowledge of good and evil.[4] By means of *ex pactum merit*, Adam (a holy covenant representative) and all his posterity (a holy people) could

---

[2] This outline is slightly adapted from that presented by Lane G. Tipton in many conversations and lectures.
[3] Geerhardus Vos, *Reformed Dogmatics*, vol. 2, *Anthropology*, trans. and ed. Richard B. Gaffin Jr. (Grand Rapids, MI: Lexham, 2014), 23.
[4] For a good treatment of the covenant of works, also called the "covenant of nature," see Francis Turretin, *Institutes of Elenctic Theology*, ed. James T. Dennison Jr., trans. George Musgrave Giger (Phillipsburg, NJ: P&R, 1992–97), 1:574–78.

advance into an eschatological state of blessedness and reward in a place (a holy realm) of perfect union and communion with God unto the praise of his glory (in worship). Genesis 1–2 reveals these four aspects in the following ways:

1. Adam, the federal head, is commissioned as prophet, priest, and king of the prelapsarian order and charged with obedience to the covenant stipulations pertaining to the probationary tree prior to the creation of any other person (Gen. 2:16–17).[5]
2. Adam's progeny (a holy people) is observable in the commands to "be fruitful and multiply" and "fill the earth" (Gen. 1:26–28) by means of the marriage institution (Gen. 2:18–25).[6]
3. The garden of Eden is the protological "holy realm," a temple-mountain where man dwells in the presence of God. That Adam is called to "work and keep" this realm (his priestly function) *as well as* to "subdue" and "rule" the created order as its vice-regent (Gen. 1:26–28) shows the need for the holy realm to expand further in an ever-increasing manner until all of creation is a holy temple-realm (which is the eschatological kingdom).[7]
4. The creation ordinance of Sabbath keeping (Gen. 2:1–3; Ex. 20:8–11), the covenantal commission in the garden to work in the presence of God, and the promised fellowship meal at the tree of life all express the call for Adam to do this unto the glory of God in heaven (i.e., to worship).[8] Sabbath worship and the sacramental meal are likewise the *goal* of creation, since what is offered to Adam is entrance into God's end-time Sabbath rest in a new-creational kingdom where the fellowship meal is not a promise but a reality.[9]

---

[5] For Adam functioning as a federal head in the threefold office of prophet, priest, and king, see Richard P. Belcher Jr., *Prophet, Priest, and King: The Roles of Christ and Our Roles Today* (Phillipsburg, NJ: P&R, 2016), 5–13. While scholars regularly note the role of Adam as priest and king, the role of Adam as a prophet is largely ignored and sometimes even downplayed; see, e.g., Meredith G. Kline, *Images of the Spirit* (Eugene, OR: Wipf & Stock, 1999), 89–90.

[6] G. K. Beale, *A New Testament Biblical Theology. The Unfolding of the Old Testament in the New* (Grand Rapids, MI: Baker Academic, 2011), 30–33, 46–58; T. Desmond Alexander, *From Paradise to Promise Land: An Introduction to the Pentateuch*, 3rd ed. (Grand Rapids, MI: Baker Academic, 2012), 134–45; Meredith G. Kline, *Kingdom Prologue: Genesis Foundations for a Covenantal Worldview* (Eugene, OR: Wipf & Stock, 2006), 68–82; John Murray, *Principles of Conduct: Aspects of Biblical Ethics* (Grand Rapids, MI: Eerdmans, 1957), 27–30, 45–81.

[7] G. K. Beale, *The Temple and the Church's Mission: A Biblical Theology of the Dwelling Place of God*, NSBT 17, ed. D. A. Carson (Downers Grove, IL: IVP Academic, 2004), 66–80; Margaret Barker, *The Gate of Heaven: The History of Symbolism of the Temple in Jerusalem* (London: SPCK, 1991), 68–103; Gordon J. Wenham, "Sanctuary Symbolism in the Garden of Eden Story," in *"I Studied Inscriptions before the Flood": Ancient Near Eastern, Literary, and Linguistic Approaches to Genesis 1–11*, ed. Richard S. Hess and David Toshio Tsumura (Winona Lake, IN: Eisenbrauns, 1994), 399–404; John H. Walton, *Ancient Near Eastern Thought and the Old Testament: Introducing the Conceptual World View of the Hebrew Bible* (Grand Rapids, MI: Baker Academic, 2018): 113–34.

[8] Murray, *Principles of Conduct*, 30–35; cf. also Jonathan Gibson, "Worship on Earth as It Is in Heaven," in *Reformation Worship: Liturgies from the Past for the Present*, ed. by Jonathan Gibson and Mark Earngey (Greensboro, NC: New Growth, 2018), 4–5.

[9] L. Michael Morales, *Who Shall Ascend the Mountain of the Lord?: A Biblical Theology of the Book of Leviticus*, NSBT 37 (Downers Grove, IL: IVP Academic, 2015), 43–49.

It is within these covenant contours that the *breach* of this order by disobedience and sin in Genesis 3 must be set, for while Adam was created with original righteousness, the order of the covenant was such that he was yet "able to sin." It is likewise here that we see the initial union between the narrative-historical or covenant-historical and the dogmatic presentation of sin. By means of the covenant of works in the relation between God and man along the fourfold contours outlined above, God had *already* revealed to Adam the essential nature of sin as nonconformity to his law by means of the covenant of works, and had placed Adam in position as the federal head and natural father of all humanity.[10]

II. The Entrance and Advance of Sin and Misery (Gen. 3–11)

The narrative of sin begins in earnest in Genesis 3 with the entrance of sin and misery that follows the covenant contours from Genesis 1–2. As Satan approaches in the temptation narrative, he does so in a manner that subverts the created authority structure of the covenantal kingdom with Adam as federal head. Satan did this by encroaching into the garden-temple as a "beast of the field" (Gen. 3:1) that Adam was to have authority over (Gen. 1:28; 2:18–20), as well as first approaching Adam's wife, whom Adam was head over (Gen. 2:23–24; Eph. 5:22–33), thereby subverting Adam's kingly authority. Similarly, by promoting sin in a holy place, Satan confronted Adam's priestly task to "keep" the garden; and by questioning the law of God concerning the probationary tree, he subverted Adam's prophetic task. It is likewise significant that in the entire narrative of Genesis 3:2–7, the covenant name YHWH is absent. In his attack on the covenant head, Satan seeks to subvert and replace the covenant Lord.[11] Because of this, Satan's approach is a direct attack *on Adam* as covenant head of all humanity, because if Adam falls into sin, then all of humanity falls with him (Rom. 5:12–14). In Adam we see not only the origin of sin, but also, in light of his covenant headship and status as natural father of all humanity, the notion of original sin as his corrupt nature is passed down to his posterity. Adam's sin is not

---

[10] For the close association between the covenant of works and law more generally, see Wilhelmus à Brakel, *The Christian's Reasonable Service*, ed. Joel R. Beeke, trans. Bartel Elshout, 4 vols. (Grand Rapids, MI: Reformation Heritage, 2015), 1:356–60.

[11] Notably, the covenant name *is* used in Gen. 3:1, stating that YHWH had created the serpent. This serves to recollect the creational work of YHWH in Gen. 1 while simultaneously keying the reader into the context of the call for Adam to rule over this particular creature. Thus, while Gen. 3:1 recollects the proper covenant authority structure, Gen. 3:2–6 shows its subversion.

merely personal; rather, it is sin by a covenant head that has consequences for all who descend from him.

Upon Adam's breach of the covenant by partaking of the tree (Gen. 3:6; recall WLC Q&A 24), the original righteousness that mankind had in Adam prior to the fall is replaced by man's shameful nakedness in his fallen state (Gen. 3:7). This is a narrative presentation of a new guilt-ridden and corrupt state of human nature.[12] That Adam and Eve are described as "knowing" their shameful state expresses the fallen condition of Adam (and all humanity in him) in a new subjective condition that is characterized by sin.[13] The concept of federal representation includes within it the notion of imputation, where this new corrupt nature and subjective condition of sin are passed on to all those under the headship of the representative. A significant exegetical detail in the text emphasizes this representative headship. When Eve partakes of the tree, nothing happens. It is only after *Adam* partakes that their eyes are opened, and they "know" their shameful nakedness. The narrative progression therefore informs our theological claim: it is with the sin of Adam as man's representative or covenant head that this corrupt, sinful nature is now endemic to humanity.

It is this context of Adam's sinful, shameful nakedness that prompts the approach of God in Genesis 3:8. Again, Adam's covenant headship is highlighted. Unlike the Satanic advance in Genesis 3:2–6, the Lord approaches sinful man within the covenant authority structure by addressing Adam first, then Eve, then the serpent (Gen. 3:8–13 inverts the order of Gen. 3:1–6). Similarly, when the Lord proclaims his curse on Adam, Adam's is the climactic curse (the narrative is inverted once again by the order of serpent-Eve-Adam), with a focus on the stipulation of death as the consequence of sin (Gen. 3:19) and the frustration of the entire created order that was under Adam's rule (Gen. 3:18–19).[14]

Just as Adam's covenant headship is a prime focus of the fall and curse narrative, so also the other aspects of the covenantal kingdom Adam and Eve's progeny and marriage become a key focus in the post-fall curses in

---

[12] It is significant that the Masoretes pointed verse 6 with the *atnach* accent in the middle of the apodosis clause rather than at the end of the protasis, where it is to be expected. By doing so, they place an emphatic portrait of sin in the act of Adam eating from the tree.

[13] John Murray, *Collected Writings of John Murray*, 4 vols. (Carlisle, PA: Banner of Truth, 2009), 2:71–72; see also Kline, *Kingdom Prologue*, 150–53.

[14] For the effect of the fall on creation, see C. John Collins, "The Place of the 'Fall' in the Overall Vision of the Hebrew Bible," *TJ* (2019): 171–80. It is important to note that, while sin impacts all creation, it remains at bottom an ethical issue; see also Herman Bavinck, *Reformed Dogmatics*, ed. John Bolt, trans. John Vriend, 4 vols. (Grand Rapids, MI: Baker Academic, 2003–8), 3:138–40.

Genesis 3:17–19. Even though the marital pair will maintain the original commission to "be fruitful and multiply" within the contours of marriage,[15] the
institutions of progeny and marriage are impacted by the fall in the following
ways: (1) childbirth will be with increased pain (Gen. 3:16a); (2) the marriage
relation is distorted with improper husband-wife relations (Gen. 3:16b); and
especially (3) instead of a single, holy seed progressing from a holy couple,
there will be *two* seeds descending from the woman with two radically different spiritual characters (Gen. 3:15). Adam's federal representation as covenant
head therefore dovetails in the narrative portrait with him as the natural origin
of all mankind. As John Murray states, "on the representative construction natural headship and representative headship are correlative."[16] Similarly Herman
Bavinck, "The way in which this 'originated sin' becomes the experience of all
of us is not through imitation but through generation based on imputation."[17]

In terms of Adam's worship, there are two notable transitions. First, in the
fall Adam and Eve not merely breached covenant with God but they engaged
in a covenant relation with Satan. They worshiped the creature rather than the
Creator as they partook in a rebellious fellowship meal with him rather than a
consummate fellowship meal with God.[18] The fall marks the entrance of false
worship and idolatry into human history as an essential part of the sinful condition. And yet, second, in his work of redemption, the Lord institutes a new
form of worship focused on the offering up of a sacrifice from which he will
renew his people into his image as holy and righteous worshipers. In Genesis
3:21 God de-vests Adam and Eve of their sinfully constructed idolatrous garments intended to cover their exposed shame (Gen. 3:7), creates new clothes by
means of a sacrifice being offered up, and then re-vests them with those clothes
of his own making.[19] After the fall, worship may only be conducted within the
context of redemption, where the Lord spiritually renews a sinner to a proper
covenantal relation with him. It is likewise within this redemptive context that
the proto-evangelion of Genesis 3:15 may be set, as one is prophesied who will
come and conquer sin and Satan by being struck; a new covenant head who will
not only succeed where Adam failed but will bear the curse for Adam's sin.[20]

---

[15] For a collection of passages, see Beale, *New Testament Biblical Theology*, 46–51.
[16] John Murray, *The Imputation of Adam's Sin* (Phillipsburg, NJ: P&R, 1959), 37–38.
[17] Bavinck, *Reformed Dogmatics*, 3:110.
[18] Cf. comments by Gibson, "Worship on Earth as It Is in Heaven," 4–5.
[19] Kline, *Kingdom Prologue*, 130; Beale, *New Testament Biblical Theology*, 41; William Wilder, "Illumination and Investiture: The Royal Significance of the Tree of Wisdom in Genesis 3," *WTJ* 68.1 (Spring 2006): 53, 56–69.
[20] It is notable that within Gen. 3:15 we find already the principles of the active and passive obedience of Christ, where he *not only* perfectly keeps covenant but *also* bears the curse of the fall as a substitutionary sacrifice.

Finally, Adam and Eve's presence in the holy realm of Eden is compromised in the fall as they are cast out of the garden to the east and a guardian cherub bars entry back into the garden (Gen. 3:23–24). Beyond merely presenting a new priestly figure to guard the garden of God, the cherub's flaming sword likewise illustrates that the only way back into the presence of God is by undergoing the judgment of fire and knife. Within this single narrative, all of the consequences of sin are manifest in their terrible multiformity: Adam is the head of a fallen humanity; he and his family (humanity) are cast out to the east and barred entry back into the garden-realm of God; and his children will be marred with a corrupt, sinful nature engaging in false worship. Adam and Eve, with all humanity in them, were exiled out of the place of intimate union and communion with God due to Adam's breach of covenant by sin.

This loss of intimate union and communion with God is a particular focus point where, for the first time in covenant history, man is the enemy of God. As Adam and Eve obeyed the word of the serpent rather than the word of the Lord, they covenanted themselves to and worshiped Satan rather than God and as such became enemies of God. The once-intimate fellowship that Adam and Eve had with God is replaced with hostility as God approaches them in judgment as the divine warrior with a cloud theophany on a protological "day of the Lord."[21]

The rationale for this interpretation is from the translation of the line לְרוּחַ הַיּוֹם in Genesis 3:8 that is most often translated as the "cool of the day" (ESV), likely following a proposed line of interpretation from the LXX that renders the phrase simply, "in the evening" (τὸ δειλινόν). However, some have proposed that this line expresses God's approach in a theophanic storm, like that which is heard upon Mount Sinai in the exodus and which has a corresponding sound (קוֹל; cf. Gen. 3:8; Ex. 19:19; 20:18; Deut. 5:22–27), inciting fear in those who hear it (Gen. 3:10; Ex. 20:18; Deut. 5:5, 22–27).[22] This interpretation provides a drastically different translation, such as "in

---

[21] Kline, *Images of the Spirit*, 98–102; and Meredith G. Kline, "Primal Parousia," *WTJ* 40.2 (Spring 1978): 245–80. For the connection between the day of the Lord and the divine warrior, see Gerhard von Rad, *Old Testament Theology*, 2 vols. (Louisville: Westminster/John Knox, 1965), 2:119–25.

[22] Various arguments are used to make this connection. Kline is by far the most unique in that he further argues that the theophany is a "spirit-theophany," as emphasized by the ל preposition on רוּחַ, rendering the mode of God's approach as "in the capacity of the Spirit" (Kline, *Images of the Spirit*, 106; cf. also Kline, *Kingdom Prologue*, 128–31). Most, however, will stop short of Kline's spirit-theophany connection and merely argue for a storm theophany (see Jeffrey Niehaus, "In the Wind of the Storm: Another Look at Genesis III 8," *VT* 44 [1944]: 263–67; Niehaus, *God at Sinai: Covenant and Theology in the Bible and the Ancient Near East* [Grand Rapids, MI: Zondervan, 1995], 155–59; Douglas K. Stuart, "'The Cool of the Day' [Gen. 3:8] and 'The Way He Should Go' [Prov. 22:6]," *BSac* 171 [July–September 2014]: 259–73).

the wind of the storm"[23] or "as the spirit of the day,"[24] in order to focus on this storm-theophany with God coming in covenant judgment. If this is the case, then the same theophanic image from when Israel enters covenant with God at Sinai appears in Genesis 3:8 in an instance of proclaiming judgment against man for his breach of covenant.

This animosity between God and man is also in Genesis 3:15 as the promise of restoration is made by means of God sowing *enmity* between the woman and the serpent, his seed and her seed. If in the fall Adam and Eve covenanted themselves with Satan, thereby allying themselves against God, then the only hope of redemption is for God to sow enmity in that covenant alignment, break man away from his sinfully chosen anti-lord, and reinstitute a bond of fellowship between him and his elect. In the fall, man chose enmity with God and fellowship with Satan; in redemption, God sows enmity with Satan and promises fellowship with himself, principally focused on redemption accomplished by a new federal head, the seed of the woman, who will defeat the serpent by himself being struck.

With all of this in mind, a few summary points on sin in Genesis 1–3 may be in order. First, the essential nature of sin as a transgression of God's law is part of the covenant of works, where Adam, with mankind in him, is called to obedience to the terms of the covenant. Second, there is an internal, subjective fallen condition in all those who naturally descend from Adam, their federal head, illustrated by Adam and Eve "knowing" their nakedness.[25] Third, animosity is sown between God and man, such that man is no longer in the original intimate fellowship with God, but is an idolater cast out of the Eden-temple by the theophanic divine warrior on a protological "day of the Lord." Fourth, due to Adam's headship of the entire created order, there are cosmic effects of sin where all of creation is frustrated, including mankind's rule of that order (Gen. 3:18–19). Fifth, the origin of sin with Adam has ramifications for original sin in all those who descend from him, which is reinforced by how the narrative of Genesis proceeds. Finally, with the entrance of sin there is the consequence of sin in death, the loss of holy communion with God in a holy realm, the twisting of spiritual persons into idolaters

---

[23] This is Niehaus's take. His full translation is, "Then the man and his wife heard the thunder of Yahweh God as he was going back and forth in the garden *in the wind of the storm* and they hid from Yahweh God among the trees of the garden."
[24] This is the translation proposed and defended by Kline in *Images of the Spirit*, 102–6.
[25] This point is meant to highlight the impact of sin on the heart and mind of man, where man's whole "person" is affected by the fall into sin. This is what Murray calls the "internal revolution" (Murray, *Collected Writings*, 2:71).

(cf. Rom. 1:24–27), and the disintegration of interpersonal relations. It is only upon the entrance of sin that a "return to dust" (see Gen. 3:19) and all of the other miseries of sin become part of man's experience in the created world.[26]

The "story of sin" continues with Cain and Abel in Genesis 4 with a further advance of sin and decline of righteousness, where the two seeds of Genesis 3:15 are observed in the two brothers. Cain, the main focus of Genesis 4, associates himself with sin and Satan (cf. 1 John 3:12–15) by murdering his righteous brother Abel. Here the connection between sin and a corrupt, polluted nature passed on from father to son becomes clear in Cain's consistent pursuit of his own gains against the Lord. It is in the Cain and Abel narrative that we therefore see the first tangible instance of the imputation of Adam's sin and corrupt nature to his posterity, where those who are covenantally aligned to Adam as their corporate head, and who descend from him by natural generation, possess a depraved, sinful nature.[27]

In the punishment of Cain's wicked deeds, two things are noteworthy. First, just as with Adam, his labor is subjected to increased futility when the ground refuses to yield its fruit for him (Gen. 3:17–19; 4:12a); again, the relation between the rulers of creation and the created order is frustrated. And second, just as Adam and Eve are cast east of Eden, so now Cain is cast further east as a "sojourner and wanderer" (נָע וָנָד) on the earth (Gen. 3:24; 4:12b). The advance in sin leads to an advance in the punishment for sin as Cain's labor is subjected to increased futility and he is cast further away from the presence of God. This advance of sin in the life of Cain progresses in a trans-generational fashion in his descendants, who become even more wicked, illustrated by the climactic Lamech (Gen. 4:19–24). As Vos states, there is a "rapid development of sin in the line of Cain."[28]

After a brief genealogy of the righteous line descending from Seth to Noah (Gen. 5), the narrative returns in Genesis 6 to the same theme of advanced corruption and correspondent judgment in the flood narrative. In Genesis 6:1–4 the wickedness of man is principally the intermingling of the righteous and wicked lines to such an extent that the righteous line is dwindled down to a single individual in Noah.[29] This intermingling and advance of

---

[26] For summary points 2–6, I am following Murray, *Collected Writings*, 2:71–72.

[27] For an in-depth discussion on the relation between natural generation and corporate representation, see Murray, *Imputation of Adam's Sin*, 42–70, 90–95.

[28] Vos, *Biblical Theology*, 45.

[29] The interpretation of Gen. 6:1–4 is one of the more hotly debated issues regarding these narratives. Three main theses have been put forward: (1) angelic beings intermarrying with women; (2) the intermarrying of the righteous

the seed of the serpent was such that "The LORD saw that the wickedness of man was great in the earth, and that every intention of the thoughts of [man's] heart was only evil continually" (Gen. 6:5), and that "the earth was corrupt in God's sight, and the earth was filled with violence" (Gen. 6:11, 12). As previously mentioned, the introduction of sin with Adam includes the notion that all who descend from Adam by natural descent are likewise in sin, and no narrative could be clearer on this reality than the universal portrait of sin in Genesis 6:1–8, 11–13.

Geerhardus Vos states concerning these verses, "in the strongest terms the extreme wickedness at the end of the period is described."[30] He then continues to note four important features of sin from Genesis 6:1–13 (esp. vv. 5–7). First, the "intensity and extent" of sin is highlighted in how it is "great in the earth." There was not merely sin, but "great" sin, and it was not isolated but was "in the earth" (i.e., worldwide). Similar statements are made in verses 11 and 13, describing how "the earth was filled with violence" and "the earth was corrupt." Second, the "inwardness" of sin in the line, "every intention of the thoughts of his heart," escalates the subjective condition of sin already noted in Adam and Eve's shameful nakedness. Third, the "absoluteness of the sway of evil" in man's heart, set on "only evil," lacks any notion of what is good in the eyes of God. And finally, sin is "habitual" and "continuous" as these sinful deeds are sought after "all the day" (כָּל־הַיּוֹם).[31] What precipitates the judgment of God in the flood is nothing less than a universal expression of total depravity—the intensity, extent, escalated subjective condition, absolute sway, and continuous nature of sin highlighted here shows an advance of sin that requires a cataclysmic response from the holy God of heaven.

This advance of sin, precipitating God's judgment, is based on what the Lord "sees" (וַיַּרְא יְהוָה). The only other narrative up to this point in Genesis where God's evaluation of an object is declared via the line "and God saw" (וַיַּרְא אֱלֹהִים) is the seven-time repeated refrain in Genesis 1 with the recurrent declaration that creation was made "good" (טוֹב). The closest parallel between

---

and wicked lines; and (3) the "sons of god" as dynastic rulers from the line of Cain. For a good summary of these options, see Willem A. VanGemeren, "The Sons of God in Genesis 6:1–4 (An Example of Evangelical Demythologization?), *WTJ* 43.2 (1981): 320–48. Some among the Reformed tradition have accepted the first interpretation but the majority opt for the second and, primarily, Meredith Kline, for the third, on which, see his "Divine Kingship and Genesis 6:1–4," *WTJ* 24.2 (1962): 187–204. However, a union of views 2 and 3 is possible, such that the narrative presents the *kings* of the godly line (rather than the wicked line) leading the people in wickedness by intermarrying with the wicked line (see Rita F. Cefalu, "Royal Priestly Heirs to the Restoration Promise of Genesis 3:15: A Biblical-Theological Perspective on the Sons of God in Genesis 6," *WTJ* 76.2 [2014]: 351–70).
[30] Vos, *Biblical Theology*, 50–51.
[31] Vos, *Biblical Theology*, 51.

Genesis 1 and 6 is the climactic statement in Genesis 1:31 and the statement of wickedness in Genesis 6:12, where both passages use the identical line "and God saw" (וַיַּרְא אֱלֹהִים), followed by the direct object marker אֶת identifying the object of what God saw, and then an additional line beginning with וְהִנֵּה ("Now, behold"), followed by a divine evaluation. With this allusion, man is no longer deemed "good" (טוֹב) in God's sight (Gen. 1, esp. 1:31) but "corrupt" (שָׁחַת) (Gen. 6:12)[32] since their heart is set on "only evil all the day" (רַק רַע כָּל־הַיּוֹם).

This advanced state of wickedness is the context from which God's deluge judgment is poured forth against all mankind in an episode of cataclysmic de-creation, a type of eschatological judgment (2 Pet. 3:5–7).[33] As the waters of the flood cover the entire face of the earth, the world that God created in Genesis 1 reverts back to its pre-ordered state as "formless and void," with the "waters" as its primary physical descriptor (Gen. 1:2). As T. D. Alexander states, "The flood narrative in 6:9–9:19 exhibits close parallels with Genesis 1. The description of the flood waters gradually covering the entire earth, including the highest mountains, portrays a return to the earth's original state before the separation of the land and sea (cf. 1:9–10)."[34] This de-creative act of judgment was to re-create an earthly realm that "has been cleansed from the pollution caused by unrighteous behavior."[35]

As Noah and his family are brought through the waters of judgment to new life in a re-created world order, the life of man quickly disintegrates into sin and misery once again. Ham exposes the shameful drunkenness and nakedness of his father (Gen. 9:22), whose state is remarkably similar to the shameful nakedness of Adam and Eve after the fall.[36] Again, similar to the fall narrative, the two other sons Shem and Japheth come and cover over their father's naked shame with a garment in a fashion reminiscent of God's own covering of Adam and Eve in Genesis 3:21. Because of this, the line of Ham is cursed (Gen. 9:25) to carry forward the wicked line of the seed of the serpent, while blessing is applied to Shem and Japheth (Gen. 9:26–27). The progress of these lines is the content of the "Table of Nations" in Genesis 10.

---

[32] A similar connection is made by Gordon Wenham in "Original Sin in Genesis 1–11," *Churchman* 104.4 (1990): 13.
[33] The de-creation of the flood narrative becomes a prototypical image of judgment utilized regularly in the OT, particularly among the prophets. See Loya M. Tubbs, *"I Will Utterly Sweep Everything away from the Face of the Earth": Decreation in Israel's Prophetic Literature* (PhD diss., Boston College, 2010).
[34] Alexander, *Paradise to Promise Land*, 165.
[35] Alexander, *Paradise to Promise Land*, 165.
[36] The parallels are the garden/vineyard location, the partaking of fruit leading to nakedness, as well as the subsequent "covering" of shameful nakedness (see Kline, *Kingdom Prologue*, 264).

After the "Table of Nations" concerning Noah's sons in Genesis 10, we find sinful humanity advancing once again in the Babel narrative of Genesis 11, where they begin to construct a city with its tower "in the heavens," attempting in pride to reverse the exilic curse of the fall (Gen. 11:4). However, as sinful man takes it upon himself to construct a would-be heavenly city and reverse the results of sin, the Lord once again emphasizes the results of sin in the confusion of man's language and the expulsion of these peoples across the face of the earth (Gen. 11:9). The combined notes of the "dispersion" of humanity in Genesis 9:19 and 11:1–9 expresses the continuation of the exile of Adam from the presence of God,[37] such that "the picture is that of a diaspora of mankind, a postdiluvian continuation of the exile of Adamic humanity from the focal Presence in the garden of God."[38]

Much more could be stated concerning the entrance and advance of sin in Genesis 3–11; however, enough has been said to illustrate the nature of sin and its entrance into, and advance in, history. Sin entered the world through Adam's breach of God's covenant and then advanced through the line of Cain until it reached cataclysmic proportions in Genesis 6. After the deluge judgment, the world order is re-created, sin advances once again, and is met with the exilic dispersion of the Babelites. And yet, at the same time, God is working to provide redemption for sinners by means of the covenant of grace wherein a new representative head—the seed of the woman—would defeat sin and Satan while redeeming his holy people unto himself, situating them in a holy realm, and restoring them to true, unadulterated worship.

III. Restoration Promised to Sinful Patriarchs

God's work of redemption is the focus of the following chapters of Genesis, with the call of Abram and the promise that he will become the father of a vast nation situated in a holy realm (Gen. 12:1–9). It is notable that these promises given to Abraham follow along the covenant contours outlined above of a holy people in a holy realm by means of an obedient federal head called to worship the Lord alone. Overwhelmingly, the redemptive, promissory covenant that is made with Abraham is discussed within the focus of blessing and restoration. While this is certainly proper, it is vital to note that

---

[37] For a good work discussing the association between the Table of Nations and Babel, see Carol M. Kaminski, *From Noah to Israel: Realization of the Primaeval Blessing after the Flood*, JSOTSup 413 (New York, T&T Clark, 2004), 30–42.

[38] Kline, *Kingdom Prologue*, 272.

this restoration is set along the terms of sin and its consequences met by the redemptive work of God within the contours of his covenantal kingdom. Four main observations draw this out from the Abrahamic narrative.

First, in terms of the postlapsarian result of sin in exilic dispersion out of the presence of God to the east (Gen. 3:24), with Cain moving farther east (Gen. 4:16), and the Babel narrative emphasizing an exilic dispersion of humanity in the east (Gen. 11:1–9; cf. Gen. 9:19), the call of Abram in Genesis 12 from the land of Ur *in the east* signifies a redemptive reversal of the fall. Abram, the representative father of the promised holy people, is called *westward* to a promised Eden-like realm where God will dwell with his people. The tying together of Abram's westward journey with his progeny is made explicit in Genesis 12, as the promise to Abraham that God will "make of you a great nation" (v. 2) is tied to the land: "to your offspring I will give this land" (v. 7). Further, there is a focus on worship in the land. As Abram enters and arrives at Bethel, he immediately constructs an altar and calls "upon the name of the Lord" (v. 8). Abram is promised that he and his descendants will worship God in this holy realm. The exilic alienation from God due to sin is reversed in the redemptive work of God in history: Abram's entrance into the land is a return to a realm where God's blessed presence is found—a new, redemptively acquired and eschatologically advanced Eden where God is faithfully worshiped.[39]

Second, in addition to the east-to-west trajectory of land entry reversing the results of the fall, when the covenant promises in Genesis 12 of progeny and realm are ratified by a covenant ceremony in Genesis 15, the consequences of sin are redemptively met by God. The practice of cutting animals in two, laying them in rows, and passing through the split animals is an ancient Near Eastern covenant ratification ceremony that invoked the curse of death if the covenant were to be broken.[40] As Kline comments,

> Graphically symbolized by the slain and halved animals, soon to be consumed by the birds of prey (Gen. 15:11; cf. Jer. 34:20), was the curse of

---

[39] Morales argues that the trajectory of the Gen. 2–3 narrative is from intimacy with God in Eden to alienation from God out of Eden, and the following narratives express further alienation. As such, when Abram is called in a reverse trajectory, we observe the resolution of alienation from God due to sin in redemptive promises (see Morales, *Who Shall Ascend?*, 56–64). It is likewise important to note that the narrative is not a bare "return to Eden." The goal of the biblical narrative is to advance *beyond* the Edenic realm that was lost to an eschatological realm that remains eternal, and as such the typological significance of this narrative must likewise be linked to this better, heavenly inheritance that can never fade (see Heb. 11:13–16).

[40] For a collection of many of these covenant documents and comments relating to the OT, see Kenton L. Sparks, *Ancient Texts for the Study of the Hebrew Bible: A Guide to Background Literature* (Grand Rapids, MI: Baker Academic, 2005), 435–448. Note esp. his bibliography on 447–48; cf. also Kenneth A. Kitchen, *Ancient Orient and Old Testament* (London: Tyndale, 1996), 90–102.

dereliction and destruction. To pass through the way between the rows of severed carcasses was to walk through the valley of the shadow of death . . . such was the malediction that the LORD conditionally invoked upon himself.[41]

This image of death by cutting is reminiscent of the implement of judgment from Genesis 3:24, where the sword-bearing cherubim guarded the way back into the blessed presence of God (symbolized in the tree of life), such that the only way back into God's presence was to undergo the curse of the sword, to be "cut in two," like these sacrificial animals.[42]

As the covenant ratification ceremony proceeds, Abram is placed in a deep sleep that *prevents him* from passing through the slain animals and thus invoking the curse upon himself on the condition of disobedience (Gen. 15:12). Instead, the Lord, in a theophany of a smoking pot and torch, passes through the animals.[43] The Lord passing through shows that he takes upon himself the curse, that if he is not faithful to his promises then *he* would bear the covenant curse of death-by-knife. This narrative is properly called an oath of self-malediction, where God calls the curses of the covenant upon *himself* if he does not fulfill his word. At this point, the unilateral nature of this covenant must be emphasized. The Lord swears by himself to keep these covenant promises to Abraham in a fashion that recollects the monergistic nature of salvation. While God can never and will never be unfaithful to his promises (it is man who breaches covenant in sin, not God), his promise of salvation rests upon his monergistic work to bear the curse for covenant breakers.

Thus, while the promissory note is clearly present as God proclaims his fidelity to Abram and invokes a self-maledictory oath, the depths of the gospel-promise and God's work to bear the curse of sin are not yet plumbed in this narrative. The Genesis 3:15 promise is that the seed of the woman will conquer sin, death, and Satan by himself being struck. This background provides a lens to the Genesis 15 ratification ceremony where, while God will not (and could not) undergo the curse as a covenant breaker, it is nevertheless by bearing the curse that he will keep this covenant. Kline is again insightful: "so it transpires that though the LORD would not undergo the curse line of

[41] Kline, *Kingdom Prologue*, 296.
[42] It is significant that, as the nation of Israel reenters the land from the east, they encounter a sword-bearing angelic guardian of the land (Josh. 5:13–15).
[43] This imagery is closely associated with the pillars of smoke and fire in the exodus narrative (see, e.g., Ex. 19:18; 24:17–18; Num. 9:15–23; etc.).

the Genesis 15 oath-ritual as a covenant breaker, it was nevertheless only by suffering this curse that he could keep the covenant."[44]

This covenant ratification ceremony is a restoration ceremony, where, in the promise of God, the curse of the fall is to be borne by God himself in the covenant of redemption. At the same time, the animals in Genesis 15 proleptically look forward to the sacrificial animals of the Mosaic covenant. The animals referenced here are in the Mosaic economy proper sacrifices before the Lord. The burnt offerings in Leviticus 1 follow the same order as that listed in Genesis 15:9, of cattle (cf. Lev. 1:3–9), goats/sheep (cf. Lev. 1:10–13), and birds (cf. Lev. 1:14–16).[45] Not only is the progression the same, but also the treatment of the particular sacrifices: cattle and goats are "cut in pieces," while the birds are not (cf. Gen. 15:10; Lev. 1:6, 12, 16). As such, the covenant ratification with the Lord's self-maledictory oath forms the redemptive-historical seed from which the sacrificial system in the cultic life under the Mosaic covenant blossoms forth. Since this sacrificial system is proleptically revealed in the Lord's self-maledictory oath, it will be of no redemptive-historical surprise that God himself, in his Son, must ultimately bear the sacrificial death for sin symbolized in Israel's cult (cf. Gen. 15:10; Lev. 1:6, 12, 16), since the cultic sacrifice always alluded back to the Lord's own self-malediction.

Third, the Abrahamic covenant details the specific promise of God redeeming unto himself a holy seed kept by God's grace, whom he will restore into his presence. While this emphasis has been made previously, it is particularly prominent as the Abrahamic narrative proceeds into the covenant sign in Genesis 17 and the sacrificial offering in Genesis 22. The covenant sign of circumcision (which images the covenant ratification as a knife-sign[46]) focuses on Abram's progeny. As the Lord says to Abram, "walk before me and be blameless, that I may make my covenant between me and you, *and may multiply you greatly*" (Gen. 17·1–2). This promise of a greatly multiplied nation is then reiterated in Abram's name-change to Abraham—from "exalted father" to "father of a multitude."[47] Here the promise of God secures an obedient, holy people in the line of Abraham, whereas the result of the fall

---

[44] Kline, *Kingdom Prologue*, 297.
[45] Gershon Hepner, "The Sacrifices in the Covenant between the Pieces Allude to the Laws of Leviticus and the Covenant of the Flesh," *Biblische Notizen* 112 (2002): 38–73.
[46] Meredith G. Kline, *By Oath Consigned: A Reinterpretation of the Covenant Signs of Circumcision and Baptism* (Grand Rapids, MI: Eerdmans, 1968), 39–49; Kline, *Kingdom Prologue*, 312–18.
[47] See discussion in William J. Dumbrell, *The Search for Order: Biblical Eschatology in Focus* (Eugene, OR: Wipf & Stock, 2001), 35–36.

is that all are alike *in sin* and therefore unholy and disobedient. This promised progeny is secured in Genesis 22 by a substitutionary sacrifice when Abraham ascends Mount Moriah with fire and knife (Gen. 22:6),[48] and the promised seed is placed under the threat of death.[49] That the Lord then provides a substitute in the ram (Gen. 22:13) further reflects on the substitutionary nature of Israel's cultic sacrificial system, where redemption is found by means of the curse of fire and knife being borne by another.[50]

The book of Genesis also reveals the divine work of establishing a promised, redemptive seed with the repeated emphasis on barrenness among the wives of the patriarchs. Sarah (Gen. 11:30), Rebekah (Gen. 25:21), and Rachel (Gen. 29:31) are all barren, such that in each of the three main patriarchal generations there is the danger of the promised line not continuing. Yet, repeatedly God heals the barren womb, such that by grace the promised line continues to advance toward the nation of Israel that will be brought into a land where "none shall miscarry or be barren" (Ex. 23:26). This tie between barrenness and a promised people being brought into a realm of fruitful progeny shows the absolute monergistic work of God in meeting the demands of sin; he alone is the one who can grant life where there was once barrenness and death.

The monergistic work of God is also highlighted in the many instances of failed personal attempts among the patriarchs to gain the promised blessings. While more could be mentioned, two such attempts are worth noting. First, in order to resolve the problem of her barrenness, Sarai offers to Abram her female servant Hagar (Gen. 16:1–2). As Abram "listened to the voice of Sarai" (Gen. 16:2) rather than trusting in the promise of God, he and Hagar begot Ishmael, who was notably *not* the promised son Isaac.[51] Second, a large part of the Jacob narrative describes him as a man who craftily seeks to gain a blessing that was already promised to him (Gen. 25:23). The actions of Jacob in coercing the birthright from his brother (Gen. 25:29–34) and deceiving in order to get a blessing from his father (Gen. 27:1–29) lead to a temporary exile out of the land *on a reverse trajectory of Abram's entrance.* Jacob is tricked by

---

[48] This fire and knife combination recollects both the covenant ratification in Gen. 15 and the fire-and-knife-wielding guardian cherub of Gen. 3:24.

[49] For the close association between the covenant sign of circumcision and Gen. 22 see T. D. Alexander, "Genesis 22 and the Covenant of Circumcision," *JSOT* 25 (1983): 17–22, who even goes so far as to argue that Gen. 22 *is* the ratification of the promises given in Gen. 17.

[50] Moriah is also the location of the Solomonic temple (2 Chron. 3:1).

[51] The act of Abram "listening" to someone other than God in Gen. 16:2 may echo the fall narrative in Gen. 3, where the beginning breach of the covenant started with an identical act. It is likewise worth noting that this act leads to further sin among the family of Abram rather than blessing (Gen. 16:5ff.). Notably, all of Abraham's children *except Isaac* eventually settle back *in the east* from which Abraham had come (Gen. 25:6, 18).

Laban into marrying Leah rather than Rachel (Gen. 29) before finally returning to the land on a trajectory similar to Abraham's (Gen. 32:22–32). On each
occasion that a member of the promised line seeks to gain the blessings by
their own work, the result is catastrophe, and yet along the way God continues
to work in accord with his promises to bring his fallen people a blessing.[52]

Fourth, it is not *merely* that Abraham is promised a seed and a place: the
manner in which the land is going to be granted to his seed is also revealed in
Genesis 15:13–16. As was true for Abraham, his descendants are going to be
sojourners in a foreign land (later revealed to be Egypt) before being restored
to the land that is promised. Here, while Abraham undergoes the westward
trajectory from sojourning to the land, the whole nation that descends from
him likewise progresses from sojourning to the land, not in the form of promise but in the form of *fulfillment* of the promise. A reason is likewise given for
the delay in the fulfillment: "the iniquity of the Amorites is not yet complete"
(Gen. 15:16). As the nation of Israel comes back into the land, the treatment
of "iniquity" comes to the fore (cf. Joshua). However, the book of Genesis
ends with Abraham's seed sojourning in a foreign land as the patriarchal family, in order to avoid a famine, follows Joseph to Egypt (cf. Gen. 12:10–20;
41:56–57), where they will remain and prosper as a people until the time of
the rising up of an oppressive Pharaoh (Ex. 1) and the exodus (Ex. 12).

IV. Restoration Begun under Moses and the Granting of the Law (Exodus–Deuteronomy)

The close association between sin and law is a central focus in the Mosaic
epoch, especially in the redemptive events of the exodus, the Ten Commandments and moral law, the cultic regulations, and the civil structure of Israel.
This focus on the law is set within the covenantal context of the initial fulfillment of Abrahamic blessings as the prophetic proclamations concerning Abraham's descendants are brought to fruition This realization places the giving
of the law within the overarching context of the covenant of grace and God's
work of redemption to gather unto himself a holy people and situate them in
a holy place characterized by worship by means of an obedient federal head.

The exodus-event is the paradigmatic image of redemption and blessing
in the OT. Vos even comments, "the exodus from Egypt *is* the Old Testament

---

[52] For notes on the redemptive work of God amid a fallen people where the curse and sin are still active, see Arie C.
Leder, *Waiting for the Land: The Story Line of the Pentateuch* (Phillipsburg, NJ: P&R, 2010), 82–89.

redemption."[53] Similarly, Bryan Estelle notes, "The exodus motif offers a way of explaining God's grand narrative—or mega-narrative—of redemption for sullied, sinful men, women, and children."[54] It is in this "grand narrative" of the exodus that the initial typological granting of redemptive blessings to the people of Israel is revealed in a few key ways:

1. The promise given to Abraham and the patriarchs of a large nation, derivative of the command given to Adam in the garden and threatened in the fall, is typologically fulfilled in the nation of Israel (Ex. 1:7; cf. Gen. 1:28; 12:2; 15:4–5; 17:2; 22:17; 26:4, 24; 28:14; 35:11; 46:3–4; 47:27; 48:4).

2. Moses is a holy, prophetic representative who leads the people through the wilderness to a place of incipient worship at Mount Sinai, from which he will receive the legislation for proper life and worship in the land. The entire goal of the exodus is for the sake of worship in the presence of God.[55]

3. The exodus trajectory is one of departure from an oppressive land, through the wilderness, and ultimately to the realm promised to Abraham and his seed in a manner similar to that of Abraham himself in Genesis 12:10–20.[56] Further, the exodus event is more than simply God saving the people from oppression; it is a deliverance from a kingdom ruled by sin and Satan and even the people's own sin as the blood of the Passover lamb and Moses intercede on their behalf.[57]

A few narrative features in the Pentateuch help illustrate the redemptive work of God in the exodus. As previously mentioned, Abram's trajectory from east to west represents a reverse of the trajectory of the exile of Adam from the garden. A similar observation may be made of Israel's wilderness wandering as they traverse a realm that has characteristics of the place that Adam was cast out of God's presence into, a realm of thorns and thistles, characterized by death (cf. Gen. 3:17–19).[58] As Israel is on its way toward a

---

[53] Vos, *Biblical Theology*, 109.

[54] Bryan D. Estelle, *Echoes of Exodus: Tracing a Biblical Motif* (Downers Grove, IL: IVP Academic, 2018), 5.

[55] Morales, *Who Shall Ascend?*, 82.

[56] The parallels: famine leads to sojourning in Egypt (Gen. 12:10; 41:1–46:7); there is an initial good treatment from Pharaoh (Gen. 12:16; 47:1–12); the situation in Egypt leads to plagues (note the use of נֶגַע in Gen. 12:17; Ex. 7–12, esp. 11:1); the plagues lead to departure from Egypt (Gen. 12:19–20; Ex. 12:37–42; note the repetition of קַח וָלֵךְ in Gen. 12:19 and וָלְכוּ with קְחוּ in Ex. 12:32); and in both accounts Abraham/Israel gains wealth (Gen. 12:16; Ex. 12:36). See Thomas Römer, "The Exodus in the Book of Genesis," *Svensk Exegetisk Årsbok* 75 (2010): 7–9. For notable differences, see Richard P. Belcher Jr., *Genesis* (Christian Focus, 2012), 116.

[57] Vos, *Biblical Theology*, 110–112. The association between Egypt and Satan is so close that later the prophet Isaiah would liken the exodus, specifically the crossing of the sea, to piercing the dragon (Isa. 51:9–11).

[58] The wilderness is an inverse realm of Eden, characterized as the earth in Gen. 1:2 prior to its forming and filling with life. The terms used to describe the earth pre-formation and pre-filling (תֹהוּ וָבֹהוּ) are likewise used to describe the wilderness: תֹהוּ in Deut. 32:10; Isa. 34:11; and בֹהוּ in Isa. 34:11.

new Eden-like realm, they must traverse *the wilderness* before being brought once more into a place of God's presence. Moreover, it is God's presence in the pillar of fire and cloud with his people *in the wilderness* that leads them on this trajectory. Once again we find emphasized the absolute divine monergistic work of salvation. This monergism is highlighted in how the wilderness is the place of specific divine provision for the people as God fills their need for bread and water (Ex. 15:22–17:7; Num. 11; 20:2–13). Due to the fall, man lost his access to the immediately present sustenance of the garden (Gen. 1:30; 2:9, 16), but in God's redemptive work he sustains his people *through the wilderness* as he works to re-create them as his people and bring them to his holy realm.

In the exodus narrative, the wilderness is not only the place that must be traversed in order once again to enter into the blessed presence of God in a redemptively advanced Edenic realm; it is also the place where sin is dealt with and the covenant is made. It is in the wilderness, specifically at the sea, that the kingdom of Satan is defeated by the work of God as the floodwaters of the Red Sea reenact the deluge judgment of Genesis 6–8 (cf. Ex. 14–15) against Satan's representative in Egypt. It is likewise in the wilderness that the people of Israel themselves are brought into covenant relation with the Lord (Ex. 19–24) and are forgiven their sin in breaching that covenant by the mediatorial work of Moses. Immediately after the ratification of the covenant, the reception of the law, and receiving the pattern for the tabernacle upon Mount Sinai, Moses returns to the camp of Israel to find the people led by Aaron in idolatrous worship of the golden calf (Ex. 32). It is only after Moses's intercession as the holy representative of God's people (Ex. 32:30–35; 33:12–22) that God's blessed presence remains with them, rather than destroying them in the wilderness, and the covenant is renewed

Finally, the wilderness is the place of transfer for the people of Israel, where they are re-created and brought under the reign of God rather than remaining a people in submission to Egyptian rule. Like the waters of the flood in Noah's day, the waters of the Red Sea mark the re-creation of the nation of Israel as the people of God.[59] Israel is renewed through baptismal waters (1 Cor. 10:2) as the presence of the Spirit is a re-creative force hovering over his people in the wilderness, just as he did at creation (cf. Gen. 1:2;

---

[59] Beale, *New Testament Biblical Theology*, 58–63; William J. Dumbrell, *The End of the Beginning: Revelation 21–22 and the Old Testament* (Eugene, OR: Wipf & Stock, 2001), 167–71.

Deut. 32:10–12).[60] In this work of God, the people are transferred from a position under their Egyptian overlords, who are an image of sin and Satan, to one under the rule of God himself.

The conflict between the Lord and Pharaoh (via the Lord's representative Moses), in determining whom Israel will serve, illustrates this transfer. In Exodus there is a repeated call for Pharaoh to release Israel to "serve" the Lord (Ex. 3:12; 4:23; 7:16; 8:1, 20; 9:1, 13; 10:3, 7, 11, 24, 26; 12:31; 14:5, 12). The building projects that begin and end the narrative of the book make a similar point. In Exodus 1–2 the construction of Egyptian store-house cities (Pithom and Raamses; Ex. 1:8–14) under the threat of death by water in the Nile (Ex. 1:15–22) is a main image of Israel's oppression. However, when the people are brought through the waters of the sea and granted life on the other side, they are commissioned by the Lord at the mountain to construct the tabernacle of his presence. In this construction project, they are brought into a new covenant relation with the Lord as their overlord rather than Pharaoh. A people once under the reign of the kingdom of Satan and his unholy representative (Pharaoh) in Egypt as they constructed the city of man are now a holy covenant people under the reign of God as they construct the tabernacle of God (Ex. 35–40).[61]

The construction of the tabernacle and the reception of its "pattern" (Ex. 25:40) on Sinai is a vital part of this narrative portrait in dealing with sin. Israel is brought into the wilderness to a mountain of God as a place of worship and covenant making, recalling the context of Eden as the mountain of God and the place of covenant. This connection is highlighted in the sabbatical 6 + 1 pattern of ascending the mountain that Moses follows as he ascends into the glory-presence of God (Ex. 24:15–18),[62] where he receives the instructions for the tabernacle (Ex. 25–31, esp. 25:40). The tabernacle is likewise constructed following the creational pattern of fiat (Ex. 25–31) and fulfillment (Ex. 35–40)[63] that climaxes once again in the presence of fire and

---

[60] Kline, *Images of the Spirit*, 14–15, 112. In fact, the entire narrative of Exodus is on a trajectory from de-creation to re-creation, where, in the plagues and in the waters of the sea, Egypt is de-created, but in the construction of the tabernacle and the guidance of the Spirit through the waters and the wilderness there is a re-creation motif, as noted by: (1) the aforementioned connections with Gen. 1; (2) the waters and their connection to Gen. 6–8; and (3) the tabernacle construction narrative, patterned after the Genesis creation week (see Morales, *Who Shall Ascend?*, 78ff.).
[61] This connection between "service" and "building" is made by Leder, *Waiting for the Land*, 93–114, who follows Charles Isbell, "Exodus 1–2 in the Context of Exodus 1–14: Story Lines and Key Words," in *Art and Meaning: Rhetoric and Biblical Literature*, ed. David J. A. Clines, David M. Gunn, and Alan J. Hauser, JSOTSup 19 (Sheffield, UK: Sheffield Academic Press, 2009), 37–61. In an earlier publication, Leder likewise connects these two different "building" projects by means of wordplay between "storage cities" (מסכנות) and "tabernacle" (משכן) (see A. C. Leder, "Reading Exodus to Learn and Learning to Read Exodus," *CTJ* 34 [1999]: 21).
[62] Morales, *Who Shall Ascend?*, 88.
[63] Kline, *Images of the Spirit*, 37–42.

glory akin to the top of Sinai (Ex. 40:34–38). The tabernacle, therefore, is a horizontalized mountain of God where the entrance into the holy of holies is a functional ascent to its summit. With this connection, the redemptive renewal into the presence of God is his work to bring the people back into his presence in a new Edenic realm *through the wilderness*, with the mountain and tabernacle as redemptively and covenantally re-acquired places of worship in the presence of God. However, Sinai and the tabernacle remain provisional, as they are *on the way* to Zion in the land, the primary OT expression of the mountain of God and the place of temple worship in the redemptively re-acquired and eschatologically advanced Eden.[64]

This initial fulfillment does not see its final resolution on the typological level until the time of David, and even then, as Estelle properly remarks, "the final goal of the exodus deliverance and salvation itself includes something greater than the Promised Land. It is nothing less than the grandest gift imaginable: heaven itself."[65] These great, epoch-making redemptive blessings in the fulfillment of the Abrahamic promises and meeting the needs of sinful man in reversing the fall are typological. That is, by their very nature they relate to the greater eschatological blessings in the new heavens and new earth (a better realm) under a better representative (Christ; Heb. 3:1–6) in a climactic ecclesial context (the Jew-Gentile church) with eschatologically enhanced worship in the heavenly places (Heb. 8–10; 12:22–24).

It is in close relation to this act of redemption that the law and sin are related in the Mosaic epoch. This connection between the great, programmatic act of redemption, and the giving of the law, is made explicit in the prologue to the Ten Commandments (Ex. 20:1; Deut. 5:1–6) and thereby shows that the only way that obedience to the law occurs is *within* the proper covenant relation with God as his redeemed people (cf. discussion on Gen. 3:21 above).[66] Without the indicative of God's redemptive work, the deliverance from the dominion of sin and misery that is needed in order to carry out God's imperatival commands in the law is lost. Covenant and law therefore go hand in hand: to breach the law is to breach covenant; to obey the law is to be faithful to the covenant. God has both redeemed his people *and* called

---

[64] Estelle, *Echoes of Exodus*, 122.
[65] Estelle, *Echoes of Exodus*, 3.
[66] William J. Dumbrell, *Covenant and Creation: A Theology of Old Testament Covenants* (Eugene, OR: Wipf & Stock, 1984), 91–92.

them to obedience.[67] This association is also clearly present in the blessings and curses of the covenant, where blessing is predicated upon obedience to the covenant stipulations (i.e., law), and cursing upon disobedience.[68] While the law may not establish the covenant relation, it is nonetheless an integral part of covenant life. With this covenantal and redemptive context established, one may then begin to consider the distinct advances in regard to the treatment of sin in the Mosaic law.

An initial observation is that, in the law, there is an increase of revelation as a further expression of what is *righteous* as well as what is *sinful*. This is not to say that sin with its substance as rebellion against God and a failure to conform to his law had not already been revealed; rather, the granting of the Mosaic law and its relation to sin fits within the overarching progressive character of revelation. As redemptive history progresses forward, there is a corresponding increase of revelation, such that God provides greater clarity about the nature of sin and rebellion (along with all other aspects of theology). Because of this, with the granting of the Mosaic law the nature of sin as a breach of law and covenant is sharpened and brought into clearer focus. It is in the law that the standards for sin and righteousness are revealed. In a day where subjective feelings are the prime expression of wrongfulness, the words of Bavinck have never rung more true: "the standard of sin is not the consciousness of guilt but the law of God."[69]

As the law reveals both what is sinful and what is righteous, it likewise reveals the character of God and the character necessary for those who will commune with God. Union and communion with God are a principal function of the law, relating to how God wishes to commune with a holy people. In essence, then, the law reveals the way God's people are to be more like God in their ethical and religious lives, an expression of how they are to reflect, in a more particular fashion, ethical likeness to the Lord of glory.[70] Thus, the law does not merely reveal sin and righteousness; it also reveals the God who declares what is sinful as well as what is righteous, and the manner of life and worship in his presence. As such, the law was a blessing for the people of Israel, not a yoke of oppression, as it revealed the proper confines of a holy life (cf. Deut. 4:7–8).

---

[67] Space does not allow a full exposition of the relation between law and grace. For a good summary, see Murray, *Principles of Conduct*, 181–201.
[68] See Meredith G. Kline, "Law Covenant," *WTJ* 27.1 (1964): 1–20.
[69] Bavinck, *Reformed Dogmatics*, 3:150.
[70] For this function of the law, see esp. Vern S. Poythress, *The Shadow of Christ in the Law of Moses* (Phillipsburg, NJ: P&R, 1995), 78–79. For the necessity of ethical likeness to God in restoration, see Kline, *Images of the Spirit*, 31–34.

"The law is represented in the Old Testament, not as the burden and yoke which it later came to be in the religious experience of the Jews, but as one of the greatest blessings and distinctions that Jehovah had conferred upon his people."[71]

This sharpening in revelation is primarily in the giving of the Ten Commandments that form the central core of the moral law, which are further expanded in the book of Deuteronomy in specific applications to Israel's life in the land.[72] Traditionally, these commandments are divided into two parts (or "tables"): duties to God (commandments 1–4) and duties to fellow man (commandments 5–10). Together, they form a summary of the entire law (Matt. 22:37–40). It is in these commandments that sin is addressed in its terrible multiformity against God and man, and those in covenant with God are called to live righteous lives in obedience to God's moral character revealed in his law. This moral law revealed in the Ten Commandments is lasting and eternal, never abrogated in any epoch of redemptive history.

Following the standard threefold division of the law (WCF 19.2–4), the same cannot be said for the remaining two categories of law in the cultic and the civil regulations for the old covenant people of God.[73] With the revelation of the cultic or ceremonial law, found especially in the book of Leviticus, one learns of the necessary parameters of holiness required for the OT people of God to dwell in his presence in the land, as well as the means by which unholiness and sin are to be dealt with. The sacrificial system established under Moses is the manner in which sin is dealt with, especially the Day of Atonement, where a substitutionary sacrifice would be offered as recompense for a sinner (Lev. 16). As Gordon Wenham comments, "sacrificial blood is necessary to cleanse and sanctify. Sacrifice can undo the effects of sin and human infirmity. Sin and disease lead to profanation of the holy and pollution of the clean. Sacrifice can reverse this process."[74]

It is significant that, in these laws, sin will be dealt with on both the national *and* individual levels. The great festivals and particularly the Day of Atonement illustrate the national level, while the prescriptions for sin offerings illustrate the individual level (Lev. 4:1–6:7). Thus, while there is a national

---

[71] Vos, *Biblical Theology*, 128; cf. also J. Douma, *The Ten Commandments: Manual for the Christian Life*, trans. Nelson D. Kloosterman (Phillipsburg, NJ: P&R, 1996), 4.
[72] For Deuteronomy as an expansion of the Ten Commandments, see John Scott Redd, "Deuteronomy," in *A Biblical-Theological Introduction to the Old Testament: The Gospel Promised*, ed. Miles V. Van Pelt (Wheaton, IL: Crossway, 2016), 133–57.
[73] Calvin, *Institutes*, 2:1502–4.
[74] Gordon J. Wenham, *The Book of Leviticus*, NICOT (Grand Rapids, MI: Eerdmans, 1979), 26.

focus on sin in the theocratic state (see comments on civil law, below), this does not abrogate the responsibility for holiness and a sacrifice for sin on the part of the individual. Cultic regulations express the means by which sin is dealt with among the people of God, both national and individual. It is no surprise, then, that Leviticus is the narrative center of the Pentateuch, revealing the manner in which sinners may be brought into union and communion with God and have their sins forgiven.[75]

While the ceremonial regulations reveal the manner in which sin will be treated in the sacrificial system, they likewise reveal the central regulations of worship for the old covenant people of God. Regulations like those found in the religious festivals (Lev. 23), the maintenance of the tabernacle/temple (Lev. 24:1–16), the place of worship (Lev. 17:1–9; Deut. 12:1–28), and all other occasions when the proper mode of worship is revealed, express that the manner of Israel's worship is tied to how God reveals himself to be worshiped. Israel was not allowed to approach the worship of God in a syncretistic fashion, utilizing the manners of the nations, but rather in accord with the law of God given at Sinai. Thus, just as the tabernacle must be constructed "according to the pattern" received from God, so also the attendant worship is conducted on the same principle.[76]

At the same time, unlike the eternal substance of the moral law, the cultic or ceremonial law is implicitly provisional. This system is sufficient and efficacious to deal with sin in this epoch of redemptive history because of the intimate connection these sacrifices have with the once-for-all sacrifice of Christ (Heb. 9:23–28; WCF 7.5). Due to this typological relation with the coming Messiah, the saints of the old covenant under the ceremonial law found full remission of sins in Christ, who was yet to come. It is because of the final coming of Christ, the antitype to Israel's sacrificial system, that these particular regulations are no longer in effect for the church today. The worship of the church is now modified in light of the new redemptive-historical situation of worship in union with Christ, the once-for-all sacrifice, in the heavenly places rather than at the earthly tabernacle (Heb. 8–10).

Finally, the civil law reveals the way Israel is to live as a theocratic state in the land under the law. Unlike the present epoch of redemptive history,

---

[75] See the structural comments on the Pentateuch by Morales, *Who Shall Ascend?*, 23–34; cf. Leder, *Waiting for the Land*, 33–40.

[76] The same may also be said of the temple and the worship at the temple, which is to be done "according to the pattern" revealed to David (1 Chron. 28:11–21).

the covenant made at Sinai was a national covenant where the nation-state of Israel had a national culpability for sin and national punishment for disobedience or blessing for obedience. While the previous observations concerning the ceremonial law dealing with sin on both the national and individual level must be heeded, Vos is correct to note that "Jehovah dealt primarily with the nation and through the nation with the individual."[77] In this particular epoch of redemptive history, the civil regulations express a union between the religious and the national. The organization of Israel as a theocratic state produces a situation where "the union of the religious lordship and the national kingship of the one Person of Jehovah involved that among Israel civil and religious life were inextricably interwoven."[78] This civil and religious union presents the way sin is treated on the national level in the historical books.

At the same time, one must take care to note that this union is unique to this epoch of history and is where the typological significance of the theocratic state rests: "it can be rightly measured only by remembering that the theocracy typified nothing short of the perfected kingdom of God, the consummate state of Heaven."[79] It is because of the status of the theocratic state of Israel *in the land*, typifying the heavenly kingdom, that the "ideal of absolute conformity to God's law" is presented before the nation-state of Israel.[80] Without this eschatological typology in place, the function of the law in Israel cannot be properly assessed in relation to their national sins, for it presents not merely the *need* for their conformity to God's law, but also the ground upon which they will disqualify themselves from their land blessing in the exile. As Israel progresses into further apostasy throughout its history, they lose the right to dwell in a land to be characterized by holiness and are therefore cast into exilic captivity *as a nation*.

V. Securing a Holy Realm (Joshua)

The narrative of sin in the book of Joshua centers around four primary axes: (1) entrance into the land as gaining a new, redemptively re-acquired and advanced Eden; (2) *herem* warfare as judgment for sin;[81] (3) Israel's sin as a corporate entity; and (4) covenant renewal in the land.

---

[77] Vos, *Biblical Theology*, 128.
[78] Vos, *Biblical Theology*, 125.
[79] Vos, *Biblical Theology*, 126. The three theocratic arrangements in Scripture being: Eden, Israel in the land, and the new creation.
[80] Vos, *Biblical Theology*, 127.
[81] For a treatment of the main uses of *herem* and its warfare context, see Lohfink, "חרם," in *TDOT* 5:180–99.

The opening observation concerning the narrative of sin is in God's work to bring his people into the redemptively promised Edenic realm through Joshua as their wartime mediator. This aspect is especially highlighted in the opening chapters of Joshua (1–5), but is the main theme of the entire book, which may be structured as: entering the land by crossing the Jordan (Josh. 1–5; key word עָבַר); taking the land (Josh. 6–12; key word לָקַח); allotting the land (Josh. 13–21; key word חָלַק); and retaining the land in covenant fidelity (Josh. 22–24; key word עָבַד).[82] In the opening chapter, Joshua is called by God as a holy representative commissioned to complete the task of bringing the people of Israel across the Jordan and into the land (Josh. 1:1–18).[83] Joshua is the executor of Mosaic Torah (Josh. 1:7–8) to lead the people in war to acquire their promised inheritance until rest is gained in the land (Josh. 1:15) sworn to the patriarchs (Josh. 1:6). The previous discussions on covenant, redemptive fulfillment of the Abrahamic promises, and law come to the fore once again in Joshua.

The focus on entering into the Edenic realm is the main theme of Joshua 1–5. In Joshua 3–4 the crossing of the Jordan River reenacts the Red Sea crossing, where the waters "pile up" and the people cross on dry ground, this time led by the ark of God's presence. If the crossing of the Red Sea was an instance of redemptive re-creation, then the same must be said concerning the crossing of the Jordan, with a new generation entering the realm. Thus, more than being a simple miracle to show the power of the God of Israel, the Jordan crossing illustrates that this particular people are redemptively renewed by God and thereby invited to live in his holy realm.

This theme is emphasized again in chapter 5 of Joshua, where the generation that crossed the Jordan is circumcised in the land. After the act of circumcision, the Lord proclaims its import: "today I have rolled away the reproach of Egypt from you" (Josh. 5:9). With the connections made above between the exodus from Egypt and redemption more generally, circumcision becomes a sign of redemption accomplished where, finally, the exodus trajectory from Egypt through the wilderness to the land reaches its terminus. It is likewise after the people have been circumcised that they partake of

---

[82] Daniel Timmer, "Joshua," in *Biblical-Theological Introduction to the Old Testament*, 162.
[83] Some argue that Joshua's call identifies him as a kingly representative of Israel (see Richard D. Nelson, "Joshua in the Book of Joshua," *JBL* 100.4 [1981]: 531–40). However, Joshua's ministry is described as an extension of Moses's (Num. 27:18–20; Deut. 31:1–8; 34:9), which would seem to indicate that his ministry should be viewed as more closely tied to the prophetic office.

the Passover feast and begin their trek through the land (Ex. 12:1–28; Josh. 5:10–12), with the wilderness provision of manna giving way to the produce of the promised realm (Josh. 5:11–12). Having been brought out of bondage and through the wilderness, where God provided for and guided his people, they are now located once again in a land with bountiful harvests that provide for the people of God, a realm like Eden.

The final explicit tie to the redemptively re-acquired and advanced Edenic realm in the early chapters of Joshua is the presence of a sword-bearing angelic figure barring further entry into the land. It is important to note in this connection the direction of entry into the land. The meandering track of the exodus led the people of Israel to enter the land from the eastern side, at the plain of Jericho on a westward trajectory. Like Abraham before them, this east-west trajectory is to image a reversal of the Edenic exile and a restoration to a blessed land. This connection is furthered in the Joshua narrative by the presence of this sword-bearing angel barring advance from the east, just as the guardian cherub was placed at the eastern entrance to the garden in Genesis 3:24.

As previously mentioned, the presence of the cherubim in Genesis 3:24 signifies that the only manner of entry back into the blessed realm of God is through a trial-by-knife ordeal wherein the curse of death is applied. In the narrative structure of Joshua 5, these are the very images utilized in the cultic acts conducted in 5:1–12, where in circumcision the generation underwent a trial-by-knife and then partook of the Passover meal that signified salvation from death, with the lamb standing as a substitute for the death of the people. It is in this context that the commander of the Lord of hosts, rather than executing the death-dealing judgment on Joshua and Israel, calls Joshua to remove his sandals because he is on holy ground (Josh. 5:15), a verbatim repetition of what the Lord himself said to Moses in Exodus 3:5. With the previous connections made with Sinai as a "mountain of God" like Eden, this identification of the land with the same phrase used to designate the top of Sinai identifies the entire realm as like unto Sinai. The promised land is a redemptively granted Edenic realm, a mountain-realm where God dwells in the midst of his people—in short, a holy realm where a holy God dwells with a redeemed, holy people.

While it is certainly the case that the narrative presents the people led by Joshua as entering a holy, Eden-like realm, there is a significant difference in the present quality of Canaan compared to the original Eden: it has been over-run with wickedness. In the fall narrative, the holy realm was infiltrated by

278 SIN AND DEPRAVITY IN THE BIBLE

Satan, now in Joshua the holy realm must be purged of Satan's seed and made holy once again. Only then may rest in the land be acquired. The progression of the narrative illustrates this: the sword-bearing commander of God's armies, which once barred Joshua's entry into the land, now turns his gaze to Jericho and leads the hosts of Israel in war against the land's unholy inhabitants.

It is within these contours that the warfare with the inhabitants of the land must be treated. As previously mentioned in connection with Genesis 15, the delay in granting the land promise was that the "iniquity" of its inhabitants was not yet complete (specifically the Amorites; Gen. 15:16). With the angelic warrior now leading Israel in battle against the inhabitants of the land, the proper theological conclusion is that the inhabitants' iniquity *is* now complete, and the time of divine judgment is at hand. This notion leads to what Kline terms an "intruded eschatology," where the warfare conducted against the Canaanites is a temporary and localized intrusion of eschatological warfare into history.[84] This association fits well with the aforementioned overarching typological function of the land: an image of the perfectly righteous heavenly realm.

It is likewise this typological and intrusionary connection with eschatology that provides the contours for the type of warfare conducted. Often, the command of *herem* warfare, with its absolute destruction of man, woman, child, and even animals, is described as the most difficult ethical issue in the entire Bible.[85] However, if this notion is correct, the warfare conducted by Israel is set under the auspices of God's own eschatological judgment poured out against sinners. The warfare in the book of Joshua is therefore an image of the eschaton, the Lord pouring out his wrath on unrepentant sinners at the end of an age.

The theme of "rest" in the book of Joshua is also understood within the related categories of eschatology and typology. Rest in the land is primarily security from Israel's enemies so that they may properly live in fidelity to God's covenant. The rest is completed under David and his war-efforts in securing the realm (especially Jerusalem).[86] However, this rest is also intimately connected with the typological function of the realm generally, with the new creation and the eternal, Sabbatical rest promised in the garden.[87] Thus, in

---

[84] Meredith G. Kline, "Intrusion and the Decalogue," *WTJ* 16.1 (1953): 1–22.

[85] For a discussion on this, see Stanley N. Gundry, ed., *Show Them No Mercy: Four Views on God and the Canaanite Genocide* (Grand Rapids, MI: Zondervan, 2003).

[86] Timmer, "Joshua," 164–66, following J. Gordon McConville, *God and Earthly Power: An Old Testament Political Theology, Genesis–Kings*, LHBOTS 454 (London: T&T Clark, 2006), 105.

[87] Contra Timmer, "Joshua," 165, who inorganically divides the two, following Jon Laansma, *"I Will Give You Rest": The "Rest" Motif in the New Testament with Special Reference to Mt. 11 and Heb. 3–4*, WUNT 98 (Tübingen: Mohr Siebeck, 1997); also represented in Timmer's earlier work, *Creation, Tabernacle, and Sabbath: The Sabbath*

the postlapsarian setting the work-rest pattern of the covenant of works is replaced with a war-rest pattern. This war-rest pattern is adapted to the typological setting of Israel's entrance into the land to secure the holy realm by waging war on the seed of the serpent, and in which they are to live faithfully within the terms of the covenant (Josh. 24).

In Joshua, sin is treated in a fashion consistent with the national organization of Israel deduced from the Mosaic law and national covenant: on the corporate, national level. The sin of Achan in Joshua 7 shows how the sin of an individual has drastic ramifications for the nation with their defeat at Ai. Due to Achan's violation of the terms of *herem* warfare, by stealing an item that was under the ban, Achan himself is placed under the sanction of *herem* warfare (Josh. 7:25–26). While Achan may be a representative figure of a more general sentiment among the Israelites,[88] a core concept of sin in the passage is that the entire "people of Israel" breached the covenant (Josh. 7:1, 11) in the representative acts of an individual. As such, the initial example of sin in the land is presented within the context of the theocratic state of Israel previously mentioned, where God deals with the people and their relation to the land on the national level.

Finally, the life of the people in the land is once again tied to covenant as the people are called to covenant fidelity in Joshua 22–24. The main sin of the book in chapter 7 is a breach of covenant (Josh. 7:1, 11) that is in need of immediate renewal at Ebal (Josh. 8:30–35),[89] and the covenant is renewed again in chapter 24. The renewals of the covenant at Shechem express the continuation of the covenant arrangement at Sinai for Israel in the land, including the Deuteronomic promise of blessing for obedience and the threat of curse for disobedience. These curses are manifold, but particularly focus on the loss of the land as a consequence of infidelity (Josh. 23:16; Deut. 4:25–26; 28:15–68). As such, Joshua 24 sets the stage for the rest of Israel's life in the land under the rubric of covenant, with the curse of exile as the prime threat for disobedience.[90]

Frame of Exodus 31:12–17; 35:1–3 in Exegetical and Theological Perspective, Forschungen zur Religion und Literatur des Alten und Neuen Testaments 227 (Göttingen, Germany: Vandenhoeck & Ruprecht, 2009).
[88] Joshua Berman, "The Making of the Sin of Achan (Joshua 7)," *BibInt* 22 (2014): 115–31.
[89] It is worth mentioning that there are very few explicit sins mentioned in the book of Joshua. That the prime example of sin has a repeated focus on covenant fidelity marks covenant as the key concept for considering sin in the book.
[90] See Paul R. House, "Examining the Narratives of Old Testament Narrative: An Exploration in Biblical Theology," *WTJ* 67.2 (Fall 2005): 235–37; also Nancy L. de Claissé-Walford, "Covenant in the Book of Joshua," *Review and Expositor* 95 (1988): 227–34.

VI. Israel's Spiral into Sin and Misery (Judges)

With the covenant renewed in the land under Joshua (Josh. 24), the narrative question is whether or not Israel will maintain covenant fidelity after Joshua and therefore remain in the land, or whether the covenant curses will be placed upon them. The book of Judges answers that question with a preliminary assessment of the people of Israel in the land as regular, multigenerational covenant breakers. The repeated failure in *herem* warfare illustrates this as it leads to an advance in idolatry and wickedness, the covenant lawsuit of Judges 2:1–4, the disintegration of intertribal cooperation, and a lack of trans-generational fidelity—all of which are part of the book's downward spiral of sin and misery, leading to a depiction of Israel as sojourners in the land.

Judges is broadly structured with a twofold prologue (Prologue I: 1:1–2:5; Prologue II: 2:6–3:6) and twofold epilogue (Epilogue I: 17:1–18:31; Epilogue II: 19:1–21:25) with a center narrative (3:7–16:31) that forms the main content of the book and moves along a progressive downward spiral of sin among the people of Israel.[91] This downward spiral of sin in the main narrative is introduced in Prologue II with a pattern of sin; punishment in being handed over to oppressors; crying out to the Lord; the Lord moved to pity and raising a deliverer (judge) who grants the people rest from their enemies (until after Gideon); and the death of the judge, upon which the people return to their sin once again in a manner even worse than the previous generation (Judg. 2:11–19).[92] Within the main narrative, this downward trajectory moves from the paradigmatic righteous judge Othniel to the vow-breaking and self-centered judge Samson, with Gideon (Judg. 6–8) as the turning point after which there is no longer rest in the land.[93]

The initial point of failure in Judges upon which this downward spiral begins is the failure properly to carry out the *herem* warfare in Prologue I. This constitutes progressive failure by Israel to complete the conquest of the land begun by Joshua. Two features in the prologue reveal this progressive failure: an overarching summary of Israel's conquest, and five vignettes of that conquest (Judg. 1:1–3, 5–7, 12–15, 23–26; 2:1–5).[94] The overarching summary of the *herem* warfare in the land progresses from an initially

[91] J. P. U. Lilley, "A Literary Appreciation of the Book of Judges," *Tyndale Bulletin* 18 (1967): 94–102.
[92] Susanne Gillmayr-Bucher, "Framework and Discourse in the Book of Judges," *JBL* 128.4 (2009): 687–702.
[93] J. Paul Tanner, "The Gideon Narrative as the Focal Point of Judges," *BSac* 149.594 (April–June 1992): 146–61.
[94] For this organization, see Gregory T. K. Wong, *Compositional Strategy of the Book of Judges: An Inductive Rhetorical Study*, VTSup 111 (Leiden, Netherlands: Brill, 2006), 145–46.

positive portrait with Judah and Simeon in the southern regions, to an increasingly negative portrait as the focus shifts northward, such that by the time the narrator reaches Asher, Naphtali, and Dan, the people of Israel dwell among the inhabitants of the land rather than destroying them.[95] This context of living among the Canaanites presents the danger of the book as a progressive Canaanization of the people of Israel. Due to their failure to drive out the nations, they become *like the nations* that were to be judged in *herem* warfare (Judg. 2:3, 12).[96] The vignettes follow a similar pattern where, while there are some positive elements (e.g., Judg. 1:1–3, 12–15), there is also a focus on compromising the terms of *herem* warfare (Judg. 1:5–7, 23–26).

The fifth vignette in Judges 2:1–5 offers a summary presentation of how sin in the book of Judges is a breach of covenant. This vignette is the first example in Scripture of a covenant lawsuit, where the angel of the Lord confronts Israel for their failure regarding *herem* warfare (Judg. 1:1–31).[97] Upon recounting the fidelity of the Lord in keeping the covenant made with their ancestors and bringing the people into the land (Judg. 2:1), the angel continues to address how the people have broken the covenant by making covenants with the people of the land (2:2a) and by not breaking down their altars (i.e., by compromising religious fidelity; 2:2b). Summarily, the angel indicts them for a lack of obedience, in that they have "not obeyed my voice" (לֹא־שְׁמַעְתֶּם בְּקֹלִי), followed by a climactic rhetorical question marking their breach of covenant: "What is this you have done?" (מַה־זֹּאת עֲשִׂיתֶם). Finally, in Judges 2:3 the sentencing for this breach of covenant is that the people of the land will not be driven out but rather will become a thorn for the Lord's people and their gods will become a snare, the very things that occur in the main narrative cycles of the book. Thus, the entire rationale for the sin-judgment-restoration-rest cycles in the book of Judges is the covenant, where sin and judgment are tied to Israel's breach of covenant, and restoration and rest are tied to the continued longsuffering mercy of the God of the covenant (Judg. 2:18).[98]

While the relation between Israel and the Canaanites is a key feature in the book of Judges, intertribal relations also provide a key portrait of this

---

[95] This northward trajectory of failure in *herem* warfare is likewise observed by Wong, *Compositional Strategy*, 150–56, as well as by Daniel I. Block, *Judges and Ruth*, NAC 6 (Nashville: Broadman & Holman, 1999), 132.

[96] This process is so pronounced that, by the end of the book, Israel is associated not merely with the Canaanites, but the worst form of them in Sodom and Gomorrah, in Judg. 19 (see Block, *Judges and Ruth*, 532–34).

[97] Kline, *Images of the Spirit*, 75–77; cf. also Block, *Judges and Ruth*, 112, who notes the same features but prefers the term "judgment oracle."

[98] This notion of sin as breach of covenant is likewise in the narrative presentation of Samson, the judge at the bottom of this spiral of sin, as a programmatic vow-breaker.

downward spiral of sin. From the outset, the people inquire of the Lord for a proper representative to lead them in the task of completing *herem* warfare after the death of Joshua (Judg. 1:1–2). While this initial act is positive, in the remainder of the book there is a progressive deterioration in the relation between the judge-leaders of Israel and the people, such that by the end of the judges epoch the people are engaged more in intertribal civil war than in war with the inhabitants of the land.[99] Particularly noteworthy for the Judges narrative is the fact that the representative leaders undergo the same pattern of progressive deterioration as the people writ large, emphasizing once again the close association between the people and their corporate heads as part of the main substructure of the covenantal kingdom.[100]

The narrative portrait of Ephraim, the Samson narrative, and the epilogues illustrate this disintegration of intertribal relations. There are three primary narratives with Ephraim in the main body of the book that express a progressive downward trajectory. First, with Ehud the people of Ephraim are called out to join their representative judge in war against the Moabites at the fords of the Jordan (Judg. 3:27–29) in a good example of cooperation between judge and tribe. However, in the same locale there is a struggle between Gideon and Ephraim that shows an increased instability in the judge-people relations, one which is resolved politically (Judg. 7:24–8:3). This progression then reaches its climax in the relation between Ephraim and Jephthah, where, again at the fords of the Jordan, the judge-tribe relation deteriorates to the point of civil war and the near annihilation of the tribe of Ephraim (Judg. 12:1–6).[101] The Samson narrative marks a similar deterioration, where, rather than representatively saving the people from their oppressors, Samson's acts are more along the lines of personal vendettas. Lastly, in Epilogue II civil war breaks out again and leads to the near annihilation of an Israelite tribe (Judg. 19:1–21:25).

Finally, this pattern of progressive deterioration in the downward spiral of sin in the book of Judges shows a failure in trans-generational fidelity. As

---

[99] For a good discussion on intertribal relations in Judges, see Gordon Oeste, "Butchered Brothers and Betrayed Families: Degenerating Kinship Structures in the Book of Judges," *JSOT* 35.3 (2011): 295–316.

[100] For a good analysis of the presentation of the judges as participating in this downward spiral of sin, see Mary L. Conway, *Judging the Judges: A Narrative Appraisal Analysis*, Linguistic Studies in Ancient West Semitic 15 (University Park, PA: Eisenbrauns, 2020).

[101] The interrelation of these narratives is widely recognized; see Elie Assis, *Self-Interest or Communal Interest: An Ideology of Leadership in the Gideon, Abimelech, and Jephthah Narratives (Judges 6–12)*, VTSup 106 (Leiden, Netherlands: Brill, 2005); Lawson Grant Stone, *From Tribal Confederation to Monarchic State: The Editorial Perspective of the Book of Judges* (PhD diss., Yale University, 1988), 366–69; Oeste, "Butchered Brothers," 305; Block, *Judges and Ruth*, 285–86; etc.

the book progresses, the remark in Judges 2:10 of a generation rising up that "did not know the LORD or the work that he had done for Israel" becomes programmatic. With each new generation, faithful teaching of the work and word of God is necessary for continued fidelity (Deut. 6:7); failure in this responsibility leads to the progressive deterioration throughout the book.

Israel's failure to pass their faith on to their children is what leads to the dire straits of Israel in the land in Epilogues I and II of Judges. By the end of the judges epoch, the moral and religious depravity of the people has led to the situation where the people who were to inhabit the land as part of the covenant promises are instead sojourners in the land. The tribe of Dan's northward migration (Judg. 18) and the sojourning of the Levite that leads to civil war (Judg. 19–21) both illustrate this sojourn. In climactic fashion, the events in Epilogue II, with the treatment of the Levite's concubine, depict the people of Benjamin in a worse light than even the paradigmatic wicked cities of Sodom and Gomorrah.[102] Far from being a holy people dwelling in a holy realm, Israel has become worse than the vilest cities of Canaan, living as sojourners rather than inhabitants in the land. Rather than pursuing holiness, "Everyone did what was right in [their] own eyes" (Judg. 21:25).[103]

With the people living as sojourners in the land of promise, and everyone doing "what was right in [their] own eyes," as "there was no king in Israel," the end of Judges leaves the reader wondering what will break this cycle of sin and misery. Is a king the answer to the failure in *herem* warfare, the disintegration of intertribal relations, and the need for maintaining covenant fidelity beyond a single generation?

VII. Restoration Typologically Granted and Sinfully Lost (Samuel–Kings)

While with Joshua one may observe the initial granting of rest in the land, and with Judges the subsequent loss of that rest in the Canaanizing spiral of sin and misery, the portrait of the books of Samuel is one of rest typologically achieved under David as God's righteous representative in the climactic fulfillment of the Abrahamic blessings. The books of Samuel, and into the

---

[102] Block, *Judges and Ruth*, 532–34.
[103] This picture of Israel being "sojourners" in the land, just as they were in the wilderness, is reinforced in the Ruth narrative (which occurred in the period of the judges), in which there is a transition from famine and sojourning to fullness and dwelling in the land, the same progress observed with the transition from wilderness sojourning and the need for food to the abundant produce of the land.

beginning of 1 Kings, reveal the typological realization of the covenantal kingdom under holy representatives (prophets, priests, and kings) who lead a holy people (Israel) in a holy realm characterized by holy worship. This typological fulfillment of rest under a holy representative is the main focus in the narratives of 1–2 Samuel, where there is a transition from an epoch of judge-representatives to kings (1 Sam. 12). The primary narrative tool used to express the progress of the kingdom and kingship in 1–2 Samuel is that of characterization, or, more particularly, character contrasts.[104] The main character contrast in these books is between Saul and David as a jux- taposition of two fundamentally different types of king, where Saul is a king like those of "all the nations" (1 Sam. 8:5) and David is a king after God's own heart (1 Sam. 13:14). With this in mind, the need at the end of Judges and answered in Samuel is not merely for a king, but for the right *kind* of king, one not like those of the nations but like the God of Israel—a holy representative king.[105]

The book of 1 Samuel presents this kingly representative in a remarkable narrative fashion to illustrate the need for holiness. When Saul is first brought to the throne as king of Israel, there is a near immediate exaltation and recog- nition of his reign (1 Sam. 11:12–15). However, from this exalted state, Saul acts as a rash and self-exalting king like the kings of the nations, rather than as a holy king of a holy people (1 Sam. 13:8–14; 14:24–46; 15:1–9). Because of this, his throne will be taken from him (1 Sam. 13:13–14; 15:10–23). With Saul one observes a representative whose sin is principally an act of disobedience in rejecting and disobeying the word of the Lord (1 Sam. 15:23; cf. 1 Sam. 2:22–25), like Adam before him. In contrast, David's kingship be- gins in humility as a shepherd-king, who then regularly pursues fidelity to the Lord (and even to Saul) in an extended state of humiliation (1 Sam. 16–31) before his final exaltation to the throne of Judah (2 Sam. 2:1–7) and all Israel (2 Sam. 5:1–5).

This presents fundamentally different portraits of these two kings. On the one hand, because of his disobedience Saul is brought from an exalted state to his ultimate humiliation in death, whereas David is brought through

---

[104] J. P. Fokkelman, *Narrative Art and Poetry in the Books of Samuel: A Full Interpretation Based on Stylistic and Structural Analysis*, 4 vols. (Assen, Netherlands: Van Gorcum, 1981–1986). See also Bruce K. Waltke and Charles Yu, *An Old Testament Theology: An Exegetical, Canonical, and Thematic Approach* (Grand Rapids, MI: Zondervan, 2007), 624–79.

[105] For the offices of prophet and priest, the character of Samuel is contrasted to that of the sons of Eli in 1 Sam. 2 as the faithful priest, and he is called as a prophet in 1 Sam. 3.

an extended state of humiliation into a state of exaltation as a righteous king. These two kings are thus representative of the fall and of redemption: Saul, an exalted king in the promised realm, is humbled because of disobedience (like Adam), while David, a redemptive leader faithful to the prophetic word, is brought out of the state of humiliation and into exaltation. This pattern of humiliation to exaltation by a holy representative serves as the pattern of redemption and is formative for the life of Christ in his humiliation unto death and subsequent exaltation in the resurrection and ascension (Rom. 1:1–4).

The presentation of David as the holy representative of a redeemed people is highlighted in the covenant that God makes with David in 2 Samuel 7, where the core promises made to Abraham are typologically fulfilled. The following parallels illustrate close association with the Abrahamic covenant: the representative's name will be made great (Gen. 12:2; 2 Sam. 7:9b); both heads are promised a seed/son (Gen. 15:4b; 2 Sam. 7:12), a kingly throne (Gen. 17:6; 2 Sam. 7:13), a continual relationship with the Lord (Gen. 17:7; 2 Sam. 7:14); a holy place (Gen. 12:7; 2 Sam. 7:10); and, finally, there is a promise of an everlasting covenant (Gen. 17:7; 2 Sam. 7:16). In David's kingship, the holy people of Israel are at rest in the holy land (2 Sam. 7:1) and the covenant is renewed once again under the representative head.[106] It is in 2 Samuel 7 that one may observe the initial-level fulfillment of the Abrahamic promises in the theocratic state of Israel in a fashion that maintains a forward-looking gaze and ties together the work of redemption with the Davidic line as the redemptive "house" that God promises to construct (2 Sam. 7:11).

As such, there is a significant advance in how sin will be finally remedied in the Davidic covenant. Within the terms of the covenantal kingdom, the manner in which salvation will be granted is by means of a holy representative. With the Davidic covenant, the added contour is that this representative will descend from the kingly line of David. It is within the terms of this covenant as it looks forward to David's "seed," which is Christ (Rom. 1:1–4), that the plague of sin and misery will be resolved.

This redemptive house-building work of God in 2 Samuel 7 contains a promise that David's son will construct God a house, a temple, as a holy place of worship for the holy people. In this covenant, the trans-generational

---

[106] These associations are a summary presentation slightly adapted from personal correspondence with Jonathan Gibson.

infidelity of the judges epoch finds an initial resolution in the trans-generational nature of the Davidic covenant, with a promised transition from a faithful father (David) to a faithful son (Solomon) to lead God's people in faithful worship. It is with Solomon that we observe not merely a realm where rest is finally gained after extended warfare, as with David, but a realm in a long-term state of peace and rest. As such, while with David the initial fulfillment of the typological blessings promised to Abraham are fulfilled, it is with Solomon as a new Adamic figure that there is a climactic expression of a redemptively re-acquired and advanced Eden.[107]

A number of key observations show Solomon to be a second Adam figure in an Edenic realm.[108] First, Solomon is anointed king at Gihon (1 Kings 1:33, 38, 45), which is a water source on the slope of Mount Zion (Jerusalem) that bears the same name as one of the rivers on Mount Eden (Gen. 2:13).[109] Second, similar to how Adam is to "work" (עָבַד) and "guard" (שָׁמַר) the garden as part of the covenant of works, Solomon is described as a covenant servant (עֶבֶד) at the temple dedication (1 Kings 8:23–24) and is charged to guard (שָׁמַר) the covenant as king of Israel (1 Kings 2:2–3).[110] Third, Solomon's wisdom as king is tied to horticultural and zoological interests (1 Kings 4:26–28, 33), just as with Adam (Gen. 2:15, 19–20). Fourth, the abundance of precious metals in Solomon's kingdom (1 Kings 9:28; 10:10–12, 14–15) recalls the same in the garden (Gen. 2:12). Fifth, Solomon, like Adam, exhibits the offices of prophet, priest, and king.[111] And, finally, Solomon constructs the temple of God's presence that images the Eden-temple.[112]

The presence of the temple in Jerusalem in a redemptively re-acquired and advanced Edenic realm is vital for the manner of life under the covenant of redemption. Adapted to its postlapsarian context, the temple in Jerusalem is not only the place where God dwells amid his people, but also the place where sin is dealt with in the cultic system of Israel as it looks forward to and gains its efficacy from the sacrificial death of Christ (cf. WCF 7.5–6). Within this context, it is also significant that Solomon is granted the prospect of life

---

[107] For Solomon as an Adam-like figure, see John A. Davies, "'Discerning between Good and Evil': Solomon as a New Adam in 1 Kings," *WTJ* 73.1 (Spring 2011): 39–57.

[108] For these I am following Davies, "Discerning between Good and Evil," 41–44.

[109] Contrast this with the place where the usurper Adonijah made himself king, at אֶבֶן הַזֹּחֶלֶת, often translated "the Serpent's Stone" (1 Kings 1:9); it was near En-Rogel, a place closely associated with the tribe of Benjamin (see Donald J. Wiseman, *1 and 2 Kings* TOTC 9 [Downers Grove, IL: InterVarsity Press, 1993], 76).

[110] Beale, *Temple and the Church's Mission*, 66–70.

[111] For argumentation, see Davies, "Discerning between Good and Evil," 44–55.

[112] Beale, *Temple and the Church's Mission*, 66–81.

in the land under the condition of obedience to the covenant (1 Kings 3:14; 6:12; 9:4, 6; 11:10) in a way similar to how Adam was promised life in the garden on the condition of obedience to the covenant of works (Gen. 2:16).[113] With this in mind, Solomon is a representative Adam-like figure in a holy realm at a holy temple charged with obedience in a manner adapted to the postlapsarian context, where the wages of sin are met within the contours of the covenant of redemption.[114]

At the same time that Solomon is a new Adam figure in a realm at peace and in intimate union with God at his temple, the narrative moves to the subsequent "fall" of Solomon. In 1 Kings 10:14–11:8 Solomon violates various aspects of the law of the king from Deuteronomy 17:14–20, which may be summarily portrayed by the statement in 1 Kings 11:6: "Solomon did what was evil in the sight of the LORD and did not wholly follow the LORD." Like Adam, Solomon's life progresses from a state of blessedness to one of judgment as the Lord's anger is kindled against him for a breach of covenant law, such that eventually even this kingdom will be broken in two (1 Kings 11:9–13). This presentation of an initially holy but ultimately sinful representative expresses the need for a completely holy representative, a need for the coming of great David's greater Son, Jesus Christ.

The division of the kingdom due to sin is the focus of the following narrative of Kings, where under Solomon's son Rehoboam the kingdom splits to form the northern and southern kingdoms.[115] While the narrative in the following chapters will oscillate between the northern and southern kingdoms, the primary focus of 1 Kings is on the northern kingdom of Israel and its habitual sin in following their first king, Jeroboam. Rather than faithfully worshiping the Lord, Jeroboam constructed two golden calves (reminiscent of the golden calf of the exodus) and established them at his own high places with his own self-made cultic worship that he "devised from his own heart" (1 Kings 12:25–33, esp. 33). It is this idolatrous act that "became sin to the house of Jeroboam" (1 Kings 13:34) and led to the curse of the covenant in a violent death applied to him and his entire household (1 Kings 14:9–16; cf. Deut. 28:26). It is likewise this sin of Jeroboam and its curse that carries on throughout the various generations and kings of the northern kingdom and on

---

[113] Davies, "Discerning between Good and Evil," 43.
[114] Vos, *Reformed Dogmatics*, 2:130.
[115] It is notable that a "division" of people is a prime result of the fall from Gen. 3 forward, and is keenly represented in the division of the brothers Cain and Abel in Gen. 4 and the split of the kingdom in 1 Kings 12.

account of which God "will give Israel up because of the sins of Jeroboam, which he sinned and made Israel to sin" (1 Kings 14:16). In fact, virtually every king of the northern kingdom, regardless of family line, commits the sins of Jeroboam.[116] This is why it is this very sin that leads to the exile of the northern kingdom to the north and east, to Assyria (2 Kings 17:21–23), which the text describes as being "thrust from the presence of God"—reminiscent of the expulsion of Adam from Eden.

Another key feature of the Kings narrative highlighted in the treatment of the northern kingdom is a consistent failure to listen to the prophetic word (as with Saul). This failure is so pervasive that Bruce Waltke argues that this is the main theme of Kings.[117] A particularly poignant picture of this emerges in the center of the Kings narrative with the Omride dynasty,[118] where the extended narrative on the Elijah-Elisha ministries, and the negative response to them from the northern kingdom, shows failure to listen to the prophetic word as a central feature of sin.[119] It is in this time of failure to listen to the prophetic word that there is a corresponding increase in idolatry (especially Baal worship; 1 Kings 16:32; 18:17–46) as well as moral depravity (e.g., Ahab's murderous seizure of Naboth's vineyard; 1 Kings 21:1–16). In this connection, both tables of the Ten Commandments (in relation to God and man) are violated by the rebellious kings—in violation of the law and the prophetic word.

Due to this fast-paced introduction of and acquiescence to sin, the northern kingdom undergoes increasing political instability that eventually leads to their exile to Assyria in 722 BC (2 Kings 17). Particularly noteworthy is why the exile happened: "because the people of Israel had sinned against the Lord their God" (2 Kings 17:7). In 2 Kings 17, the essence of sin in idolatry (2 Kings 17:8–12) is failing to listen to the prophets who called the people to obedience to the law of God, and thereby breaking the covenant (17:13–18), as paradigmatically seen in the sins of Jeroboam (17:21–23). Due to this continued sin, the northern kingdom is brought to a ruinous exile; only the southern kingdom remains (17:18).[120]

---

[116] First Kings 11:26, 28, 31; 12:26, 31; 13:1, 4, 33; 14:16; 15:29, 34; 16:2, 7, 19, 26, 31; 21:22; 22:52; 2 Kings 3:3; 9:9; 10:29, 31; 13:2, 6, 11; 14:24; 15:9, 18, 24, 28; 17:21–23.

[117] Waltke, *Old Testament Theology*, 702.

[118] For the Omride dynasty and the Elijah-Elisha narrative as the center of 1–2 Kings, see Jerome T. Walsh, *1 Kings*, Berit Olam (Collegeville, MN: Liturgical Press, 1996), 373.

[119] This is comparable to how Adam failed to keep the word he was commissioned to maintain as the prophet in the garden.

[120] It is notable that there is no explicit "return" narrative for the northern kingdom; rather, the northern tribes are subsumed under the restoration of the southern kingdom in the genealogies of returned exiles in 1 Chron. 1–9.

In contrast to the consistent sin and subsequent demise of the northern kingdom, the southern kingdom of Judah has some faithful kings and a more consistent trend of fidelity to the Lord, largely due to the promise given to David and his faithfulness to the Lord. This is initially given as the reason for the kingdom not being immediately ripped away from Solomon (1 Kings 11:12), and yet there is a pattern in the history of Judah similar to what happened with Israel (e.g., with Hezekiah in 2 Kings 20:12–19 and Josiah in 2 Kings 22:19–20). The pattern shows that, while sin remains an issue in the southern kingdom, the repentance of the leader in pursuit of fidelity leads to a far more consistent kingdom under the dynasty of David.[121]

So long as the representative king pursues fidelity to the Lord, the people remain holy with him in the land. However, when the king pursues wickedness, the people quickly follow. If the programmatic sin of the northern kingdom leading to its ultimate demise is that of Jeroboam, a similar thing may be said about the sins of Manasseh, on account of which the exile of Judah is a foregone conclusion (2 Kings 21:10–18). Moreover, as with the sins in the northern kingdom, the sins of Manasseh breach both tables of the covenant in idolatry (2 Kings 21:3–6) and the mistreatment of fellow man (2 Kings 21:16).

This association with the representative in both the northern and southern kingdoms is important for how sin is treated in the books of 1 and 2 Kings. While individual sins are certainly a reality, the focus is on the sins of the representatives (especially the kings); the kings are indicative of the nation, such that as the king goes, so goes the people. This is also part of the regal formulas of each reign that contain evaluation of the kings' fidelity as doing what was "right" or "evil" in the sight of God (for the southern kingdom, also a comparison with David). This was the basis upon which the national judgments were meted out. As mentioned above, sin in the theocratic state is dealt with primarily on the national level, and the representative role of the kings illustrates this point.

The sin treated on the national level, tied to its representative, leads to national and political consequences in the exile of the southern kingdom. While the southern kingdom is the prime expression of the people of God in the land under a Davidic line, it is with the exile of Judah that the exile of

---

[121] The northern kingdom of Israel has 20 kings in 10 dynasties over 209 years, while the southern kingdom of Judah has 19 kings in 1 Davidic dynasty over 345 years.

Adam is recapitulated once again, as the nation that bears the name "son of God" (Ex. 4:22–23) is removed from the mountain of God (Zion) to the east, to Babylon, the same direction to which Adam was exiled from Mount Eden, and from which Abram was called. Due to their violation of the terms of the covenant, the paradisiacal promised realm, granted by redemptive re-creation in the exodus, is lost in the destructive judgment of God. The once-Edenic realm, with its capital city of Jerusalem on Mount Zion, is destroyed, and the people are exiled out of the place of union and communion with God, east of Zion, just as Adam was cast east of Eden.

Conclusion

In this chapter the "story of sin" has been set within the covenant contours of the kingdom of God, in which God seeks to confer himself in a bond of communion with a holy people in a holy realm by means of an obedient federal head, unto the praise of his glory. Each section has sought to trace the development of this covenantal kingdom within the main features of each redemptive-historical epoch, from the entrance of sin and misery, through the advance of sin leading to the flood, all the way to the presence of Israel in the promised Edenic-realm and their subsequent loss of the land due to their sin in the breach of the covenant. Just as with Adam and his exile from the garden, so also with Israel in their exile from the land because of their breach of the covenant; the place of intimate union and communion with God was lost. And yet, the *promise* of God remains, revealed in the Davidic covenant, where the Lord will meet the consequences of sin and death in an entirely holy representative (Jesus Christ, great David's greater Son), who will not only obey the covenant but also bear its curse. It is in union with this representative that the hope of redemption is found for sinners, a hope of re-creation in the image of Christ, where those who call upon his name will be set in his holy realm, bear his holy image, and worship his holy name forevermore. They will be found in a place of climactic union and communion with God that was forfeited by Adam, typified and lost by Israel, and granted in Christ.

At the same time, the "story of sin" reveals a corresponding process of systemization all along the way. Recall the words of Vos, that "it should be remembered that on the line of historical progress there is at several points already a beginning of correlation among elements of truth in which the beginnings of the systematizing process may be discerned."[122] A few points illustrate this "systematizing process" amid the "story of sin." First, all along, the definition of sin as a transgression of God's law and covenant is maintained. There is no epoch of redemptive history that counters this basic definition of sin. Second, postlapsarian history illustrates the impact of sin on the whole human race in vivid fashion in the murderous acts of Cain and the advance of sin leading to the deluge judgment (Gen. 4–9). Prior to the flood, sin's terrible impact dovetails with the doctrine of total depravity, in which sin is manifest in its intensity and extent, its inwardness, its absolute sway over man, and man's habitual pursuit of it "all the day" (Gen. 6:1–13).[123] Third, sin and idolatry go together; to be a sinner is to be idolatrous, and idolatry is sin. It is not merely that man has a corrupt nature, but his corrupt nature is revealed in what he worships. Fourth, simultaneous with the impact of sin on the whole human race leading to the flood narrative, the fundamental reality that man is a slave to sin in need of redemptive re-creation is revealed at every point. It is the Lord's monergistic work of redemption that meets the redemptive needs of fallen man to be restored back into God's holy presence as a holy people by a holy representative in holy worship. This emphasis comes to the fore in the postdiluvian narrative with the call of Abram and the promises of the covenant of redemption that reach their typological fulfillment in the covenant with David. This "story of sin," with its remedy in the covenant of redemption, implicitly, and on its own terms, looks forward to its climax where great David's greater Son will bear the curse of the covenant and live an entirely righteous life, so that all who are united to this king by Spirit-wrought faith are redeemed and restored in his ethical likeness, to the praise of his glory.

[122] Vos, *Biblical Theology*, 16; Gaffin, "Systematic Theology and Biblical Theology," 281–99.
[123] Vos, *Biblical Theology*, 51.

11

The Folly, Mystery, and Absurdity of Sin in the Wisdom Literature

Stephen M. Coleman

For many scholars, wisdom literature presents something of a foreign element within the OT canon.[1] The absence of any explicit reference to Israel's history or covenants has caused such scholars to regard biblical wisdom literature as peripheral, if not antithetical, to the theological mainstream of the OT.[2] John Bright, for example, asserts, "some parts of the Old Testament are far less obviously expressive of Israel's distinctive understanding of reality than others. Indeed, some parts (and one thinks of such a book as Proverbs) seem to be only peripherally related to it, while others (for example, Ecclesiastes) even question its essential features."[3] In fact, this foreign or alien quality has led one scholar, H. D. Preuss, to suggest that the god of wisdom was an altogether different deity, more closely resembling the gods of Israel's pagan neighbors than the God of the Law and Prophets.[4]

---

[1] As early as 1958, Hartmut Gese could assume a consensus on this point when he wrote, "it is recognized that the wisdom literature represents an alien body in the world of the Old Testament" (Hartmut Gese, *Lehre und Wirklichkeit in der alten Weisheit: Studien zu den Spüchen Salomos und zu dem Buche Hiob* [Tübingen: J. C. B. Mohr (Paul Siebeck), 1958], 2).
[2] In the words of James Crenshaw, "This 'alien corpus' is altogether silent with regard to the dominant themes found in the rest of the Bible, for example[,] the promise to the patriarchs, the deliverance from Egypt, the Mosaic covenant, the centrality of Jerusalem and the Davidic dynasty, the prophetic word, and so forth. In place of such emphases, one finds ideas and literary forms that are closer to certain Egyptian and Mesopotamian works" ("Wisdom Literature: Biblical Books," in *Urgent Advice and Probing Questions: Collected Writings on Old Testament Wisdom* [Macon, GA: Mercer, 1995], 1).
[3] John Bright, *The Authority of the Old Testament* (Grand Rapids, MI: Baker, 1975), 136.
[4] Horst Dietrich Preuss, "Das Gottesbild der älteren Weisheit Israels," in *Studies in the Religion of Ancient Israel*, VTSup 23 (Leiden, Netherlands: Brill, 1972), 117–45. Though Preuss is often cited for his extreme views regarding biblical wisdom literature, Leo Perdue helpfully notes that, "later in his career, Preuss did find an important place

In his magisterial *Old Testament Theology* (and later developed in his *Wisdom in Israel*), Gerhard von Rad offered one of the earliest responses to this atomization of OT theology, by casting biblical wisdom literature (along with the Psalms) as "Israel Before Jahweh [Israel's answer]," that is, Israel's grateful and obedient response to God for his great acts of salvation.[5] Von Rad's program, if not his conclusion, was taken up by numerous scholars, notably Walther Zimmerli, H. H. Schmid, Claus Westermann, Roland Murphy, and Leo Perdue.[6] Among conservative scholars, comprehensive and coherent integrations of biblical wisdom literature with Old Testament and Biblical theology have been offered by Derek Kidner, Graeme Goldsworthy, Bruce Waltke, and, most recently, O. Palmer Robertson.[7] The purpose of this chapter is to support and, hopefully, further such efforts at integration by offering a focused consideration of just one aspect of wisdom theology that has been identified as dissonant with (if not contradictory to) the mainstream of biblical theology, namely, the sages' understanding of sin and the human condition.[8]

Walter Brueggemann, for instance, contrasts the theology that has "emerged from the Paul-Augustine-Luther line," and which takes a "dim view of ourselves and our fellows," with that of wisdom, which he says, "makes no sense if it is assumed that man's decision-making machinery is hopelessly warped or crippled."[9] Brueggemann describes wisdom's distinctively anthropocentric outlook as follows:

---

for the ethics of wisdom literature in his OT theology. However, he lessened its value in his remarks that sapiential ethical instructions and admonitions belong neither to the covenant at Sinai nor to the saving acts of Yahweh. For him, this diminished their revelatory and authoritative role" (Leo Perdue, *Wisdom Literature: A Theological History* [Louisville: Westminster/John Knox, 2007], 31).

[5] Gerhard von Rad, *Old Testament Theology*, 2 vols. (New York: Harper & Row, 1962, 1965), esp. 1:355ff.; and Von Rad, *Wisdom in Israel*, trans. James D. Martin (Harrisburg, PA, Trinity Press International, 1972).

[6] Notable works of synthesis include the following: Walther Zimmerli, "The Place and Limit of Wisdom in the Framework of Old Testament Theology," *SJT* 17 (1964): 146–58; H. H. Schmid, *Wesen und Geschichte der Weisheit*, BZAW 101 (Berlin: Töpelmann, 1966); Claus Westermann, "*Weisheit im Sprichwort*," in *Forschung am Alten Testament: Gesammelte Studien* II, Theologische Buecherei 55 (Munich: Kaiser Verlag, 1974): 149–61; Westermann, *Blessing in the Bible and the Life of the Church*, trans. Keith Crim (Philadelphia: Fortress, 1978); Roland Murphy, "The Kerygma of the Book of Proverbs," *Interpretation* 20 (1966): 3–14; Leo G. Perdue, *Wisdom and Creation* (Nashville: Abingdon, 1994).

[7] Derek Kidner, *The Wisdom of Proverbs, Job, and Ecclesiastes: An Introduction to Wisdom Literature* (Downers Grove, IL: InterVarsity Press, 1985); Graeme Goldsworthy, "Gospel and Wisdom," in *The Goldsworthy Trilogy* (Carlisle, UK: Paternoster, 2000); Bruce K. Waltke, "The Book of Proverbs and Old Testament Theology," *BSac* (1979): 302–17; Waltke, *An Old Testament Theology: An Exegetical, Canonical, and Thematic Approach* (Grand Rapids, MI: Zondervan, 2007), 897–969; O. Palmer Robertson, *The Christ of Wisdom: A Redemptive-Historical Exploration of the Wisdom Books of the Old Testament* (Phillipsburg, NJ: P&R, 2017).

[8] The extent to which the designation "sages" was used in ancient Israel to refer to an identifiable and delimited group of scribes, scholars, and/or "wise men" is a vigorously debated issue (see, e.g., Stuart Weeks, *Early Israelite Wisdom* [Oxford: Clarendon, 1994], esp. ch. 5). The term "sage(s)" in this chapter is used simply as a convenient designation to refer to the individuals or groups who composed the corpus traditionally identified as canonical wisdom literature, namely Proverbs, Job, and Ecclesiastes, and who shared a broadly unified approach to theological, anthropological, and ethical reflection.

[9] Walter Brueggemann, *In Man We Trust* (Richmond, VA: John Knox, 1972), 20–21.

There is no authority to which [mankind] can appeal. He is now man come of age in a world from which the gods have fled: it is his world. He is charged with overseeing it, and whatever future he would have he must choose for himself and his community.[10]

Put briefly, therefore, my aim is twofold: (1) to demonstrate the coherence of the theology of sin developed in the wisdom literature with the theology of sin found in the rest of Scripture; and (2) to consider the unique contributions of wisdom literature's treatment of sin to the biblical doctrine.

What were the sages' view(s) of the fundamental human predicament? What did they have to say about the effects of sin in human life and society? And, perhaps most importantly, what did the sages hold forth as the solution to sin and its woeful consequences? It may be stated at the outset that, consonant with the rest of Scripture, sin, for the sages, is *a violation of the will and word of God*. The father's epigram in Proverbs 6:16–19, for example, is framed in terms of things detestable to God:

> There are six things that the LORD hates,
>> seven that are an abomination to him:
> haughty eyes, a lying tongue,
>> and hands that shed innocent blood,
> a heart that devises wicked plans,
>> feet that hasten to run to evil,
> a false witness who breathes lies,
>> and one who sows discord among brothers. (cf. Job 31:1–8; Eccl. 5:6–7)

That the word and will of God includes the specific laws and commandments given to Israel at Sinai is clear from the final words of Qoheleth's epilogist: "The end of the matter; all has been heard. Fear God and keep his commandments, for this is the whole duty of man" (Eccl. 12:13)

Though, for the sages, sin certainly includes any violation of God's will and word as expressed in his commands, their starting point and controlling method for theological, anthropological, and ethical reflection is principally God's will and word as it is revealed in the order of creation. This creational perspective in no way denies, minimizes, or contradicts special revelation; rather, it serves as a necessary complement to God's revelation of himself in history and Scripture. For the sages, sin affects everything. It distorts both the human person as well

---

[10] Brueggemann, *In Man We Trust*, 21.

as human society. It disrupts mankind's relation to the creation as well as the Creator. Yet, a good life (good as defined by God) may still be enjoyed in a sin-cursed world as one seeks to appropriate and to live according to divine wisdom.

Proverbs: The Folly of Sin

Neither the concept of, nor the word(s) for, sin are foreign to biblical pro-verbial literature. Proverbs 5:22 says, "The iniquities [עֲוֹנוֹתָיו] of the wicked ensnare him, and in the cords of his sin [חַטָּאת] he is seized" (my translation). However, far outnumbering the mentions of sinners and their sins are the mentions of fools and their follies. Sin is foolish, and folly is sin. Both are an offense against a holy God, and both receive God's just judgment (Prov. 3:33–35). What, then, is the relation of folly to sin? To answer this question, we must consider the theological outlook and methodology of the Israelite sages who produced the biblical wisdom literature.

CREATION AND THE NATURE OF FOLLY

The theological enterprise of Israel's sages begins with God as Creator.[11] This does not imply that Israelite sages denied, ignored, or minimized God's iden-tity as Redeemer who had entered into covenant with a particular people, Israel, at a particular place and time, Mount Sinai in the days of Moses. After all, God is referred to throughout the book of Proverbs by his cove-nant name, Yahweh (יהוה), the name revealed to Moses on Mount Sinai (Ex. 3:6, 14).[12] It is Israel's God, Yahweh, who is in fact the creator and sustainer of the universe (Prov. 8:22). In both the created order established at the be-ginning, and in his providential upholding, governing, and guiding of his creation, God reveals himself to his creation. The opening verses of Psalm 19, arguably a wisdom psalm itself, capture the theological starting point for Israel's sages: "The heavens declare the glory of God, and the sky above pro-claims his handiwork. Day to day pours out speech, and night to night reveals

---

[11] Walther Zimmerli overstated the case only slightly, when he wrote, famously, "The wisdom of the OT stays quite determinedly within the horizon of creation. Its theology is creation theology" (Zimmerli, "Ort und Grenze der Weisheit im Rahmen der alttestamentlichen Theologie," *Gottes Offenbarung. Gesammelte Aufsätze zum Alten Testament*, Theologische Bucherei 19 [Munich: Kaiser, 1963], 302).

[12] Some have seen the presence of the divine name in Proverbs as evidence of a theological redaction of an other-wise secular collection of sayings (e.g., Norman Whybray, *Wisdom in Proverbs* [London: SCM, 1974]). In his later work, Whybray himself acknowledges this view as untenable (*The Composition of the Book of Proverbs*, JSOTSup 168 [Sheffield, UK: Sheffield Academic Press, 1994], 158–59; cf. Katharine Dell, *The Book of Proverbs in Social and Theological Context* [Cambridge: Cambridge University Press, 2006], 90–124; Knut Heim, *Like Grapes of Gold Set in Silver: Proverbial Clusters in Proverbs 10:1–22:16*, BZAW 273 [Berlin: Walter de Gruyter, 2001]).

knowledge" (Ps. 19:1–2).[13] Though to the human ear the heavens are literally silent, they are nevertheless described anthropomorphically as "speaking," or perhaps more vividly, "declaring" (מְסַפְּרִים) and "proclaiming" (מַגִּיד). The heavens, the sky, the days, the nights work in concert to reveal the glory of God and to instill the knowledge of him in his creation. The implication is clear: the created order itself, in every respect, has a revelatory quality to it. Creation reveals the glory and, as we will see, the wisdom of her Creator.

In his second interlude (Prov. 3:13–20) the sage enumerates and celebrates the manifold blessings that come from laying hold of wisdom. He concludes his soaring commendation of wisdom by directing the reader's/hearer's attention to God's use of wisdom in creation: "The Lord by wisdom [בְּחָכְמָה] founded the earth; by understanding he established the heavens; by his knowledge the deeps broke open, and the clouds drop down the dew" (Prov. 3:19). By identifying wisdom (חָכְמָה) and its near synonyms, understanding (תְּבוּנָה) and knowledge (דַעַת), as the instruments God employed in his acts of creation, the sage is not only ascribing to these virtues the highest praise, but also, effectively setting them before the reader as the most precious commodities that can be obtained in this life, freely available for those who would diligently seek them (cf. 3:13–18).[14]

The theology of creation expressed concisely in Proverbs 3:19 is developed in greater detail in Lady Wisdom's encomium in 8:22–31. So programmatic is the creational theology expressed in these verses, not just for Proverbs but for biblical wisdom literature generally, that Lady Wisdom deserves to be quoted at length:

> The Lord created me as the first of his way,
>   The first of his acts of old.
> Ages ago I was fashioned,
>   At the first, before the beginning of the earth.
> When there were no depths I was brought forth,
>   when there were no springs abounding with water.
> Before the mountains were planted,
>   Before the hills, I was brought forth,
> Before he had made the earth with its fields,
>   Or the first of the dust of the world.

---

[13] For a discussion of Ps. 19 as a wisdom psalm, see Bruce K. Waltke and James M. Houston, *The Psalms as Christian Worship: A Historical Commentary* (Grand Rapids, MI: Eerdmans, 2010), 356.
[14] Though debated, the instrumental use of the preposition בְּ ("by/through"), with בְּחָכְמָה seems to be the most natural reading (Roland Murphy, *Proverbs*, WBC 22 [Nashville: Thomas Nelson, 1998], 22).

When he established the heavens, there was I;
when he engraved a circle on the face of the deep,
when he made firm the skies above,
when he established the foundations of the deep,
when he set the sea its limit,
so that the waters do not transgress his command,
when he marked out the foundations of the earth,
then I was beside him like a master workman,
and I was his delight daily,
rejoicing before him always,
rejoicing in his habitable world
and delighting in the children of man. (my translation)

Much ink has been spilled over the meaning of key words in this passage, specifically קְנָנִי (8:22; from קנה, which can mean "possess," "acquire," or, as translated above, "create") and אָמוֹן (8:30; which may mean "artisan," "constantly," or, with revocalization, "ward/nursling").[15] Even a cursory treatment of the issues presented by these words is beyond the scope of this study. For our purposes, it is sufficient to observe Wisdom's presence with God at the beginning (8:22), and her observation of, if not participation in, his great acts of creation. Her divine origin, her antiquity, and her instrumentality in creation (3:19) afford Wisdom an unimaginably elevated status in the economy of creation and qualifies her as an authoritative source of revelation of God and his purposes. As David VanDrunen observes, "What is so remarkable is that the very wisdom commended to human beings throughout Proverbs resides ultimately and prototypically in God, exhibited in the way the world is structured and ordered. The world from which human beings are to learn wisdom reflects the wisdom of God."[16] All of creation is ordered analogically after the pattern of divine wisdom and serves therefore as revelation of that wisdom.

Entailed in God's revelation of himself in and through the creational order is each person's moral obligation to conform his or her life to the pattern of

---

[15] For a detailed discussion of the philological, exegetical, and theological issues involved with these words, see Waltke, *The Book of Proverbs: Chapters 1–15*, NICOT (Grand Rapids, MI: Eerdmans, 2004), 408–9, 417–22; and Michael V. Fox, *Proverbs 1–9: A New Translation with Introduction and Commentary*, AB 18A (New York: Doubleday, 2000), 279–81, 285–87. Fox makes the important observation that the distinction between *create* and *acquire* is a feature of English and not of Hebrew. Creation is one means of the acquiring (coming into possession) of a reality (cf. Gen. 4:1). The verb קנה, however, does not mean *possess* in the sense of exhibiting a continuous state of possession (Fox, *Proverbs 1–9*, 279).

[16] David VanDrunen, "Wisdom and the Natural Moral Order: The Contribution of Proverbs to a Christian Theology of Natural Law," *Journal of the Society of Christian Ethics* 33 (2013): 153–68, 154.

that order in such a way as to promote their own and their neighbor's welfare. The ability to do this well is called wisdom; and, at its most basic level, the refusal to do so is called folly.[17] Commenting on the connection between the creational order and ethical obligation, James Loader writes, "If the cosmic order was constituted through wisdom and humans are required to find and apply that same wisdom, it means that, for humans, wisdom entails attuning to the creational order of things."[18] For the sages, this divinely established "creational order of things" pertains to every sphere of human life and society. Just as there is a physical order to the universe, so too is there an order that pertains to marriage (Prov. 21:9), family (Prov. 15:20), friendship (Prov. 27:6), neighbors (Prov. 25:17), society (Prov. 14:34), economy (Prov. 22:7), and politics (Prov. 29:4). There is an order to an individual's mental (Prov. 18:11), emotional (Prov. 15:18), and spiritual (Prov. 18:10) constitution. Those who would enjoy the blessings that wisdom promises must first know the God of wisdom (Prov. 1:7), and second must seek to understand how God has ordered his creation in such a way as to promote life and human flourishing.

In contrast, folly is any violation of or veering from this order which God designed to promote life. It is the stubborn refusal to bring one's life into conformity to the pattern of creation. As is customary in proverbial literature, the sages eschew technical definition in favor of portraiture. To take the example of wise/foolish speech, where the wise use their words to promote life and community (Prov. 10:11, 21; 15:2; 18:21), the fool's words sow discord (Prov. 17:9), alienation (Prov. 16:27–28), and death (Prov. 10:14; 15:4). Where the wise person seeks out and heeds counsel from others (Prov. 10:17; 15:22), the fool listens to no one's advice but his own (Prov. 12:15; 18:2). Where the wise person internalizes parental instruction, the fool disregards the most basic means by which wisdom is obtained (Prov. 1:8–9; 10:1). God has ordered creation in such a way that "death and life are in the power of the

---

[17] BH חָכְמָה does not necessarily have moral or virtuous overtones. At a basic level, it refers to skill or ability in everything from craft to statecraft. However, within Israel's wisdom literature, חָכְמָה is used to describe a virtuous quality or ability for which Von Rad's oft quoted description, to be "competent with regard to the realities of life," is still eminently useful (Von Rad, *Wisdom in Israel*, 310).

[18] James A. Loader, *Proverbs 1–9*, Historical Commentary on the Old Testament (Leuven: Peeters, 2014), 175. Similarly, William Brown writes, "The order of creation, as it is featured in 8:22–31, plays a defining role in the development of ethical character. In Proverbs, the language of creation functions to establish wisdom's unequaled position within the conflictual context of the 'strange woman.' The similarities between these two female characters are striking: Both share the same social domains of street and square (7:12); they even share a common core of language. But the strange woman's speech is revealed by wisdom for what it is, crooked and devious. Her house is a façade of Sheol, whereas wisdom's seven-pillar abode is the fountain of life, perhaps suggesting the temple (cf. Ps. 36:7–9) or its literary replacement" (William P. Brown, *Character in Crisis: A Fresh Approach to the Wisdom Literature of the Old Testament* [Grand Rapids, MI: Eerdmans, 1996], 40).

tongue" (Prov. 18:21). Through instruction, observation, and reflection, the wise discern this order and use their words to promote truth and life, thereby imaging their Creator. The fool, by contrast, consciously or unconsciously, refuses to acknowledge this order and as a result uses his words to sow death. Of course, the human capacity for folly extends far beyond the use of words. Folly is as expansive as the order of creation, a sad reality testified to throughout the book of Proverbs.

For the sages, then, the order of creation grounds ethical behavior. William Brown puts it well when he says, "By wisdom Yahweh founded the earth (Prov. 3:19); by wisdom the contours of normative character are decisively shaped."[19] At every conceivable level, God has ordered his creation with intentionality and purpose, and those who bear God's image are obligated to observe, to assess, and to understand that order so that they might conform their lives to its pattern in such a way that they reflect the life and goodness and beauty of their Creator.

THE ORIGIN OF FOLLY

Proverbs does not offer a redemptive-historical explanation for the origin and persistence of sin in the human experience (i.e., the transgression of the first man and woman in the garden, the guilt and corruption for which was passed on to posterity through ordinary generation [WCF 6; WLC Q&A 21–27; WSC Q&A 15–19]). The sages do, however, offer an anthropological explanation. Though God is the Creator of all that exists, though he is the absolute sovereign over even the greatest sovereigns of the world (Prov. 21:1), at no point do the sages locate the origin of or blame for folly in God himself. The origin of folly, rather, lies exclusively within the human heart. Out of the human heart flow both wisdom and folly. But which of the two is more basic to the human person? This question may be answered by considering the means by which one attains wisdom in contrast to folly.

The sages are not unaware that folly may be cultivated through the influence of realities external to an individual. Thus, in the opening lecture the son is warned to avoid the enticements of violent gangs (Prov. 1:8–19), and throughout the book he is warned about the dangers of bad company (Prov. 13:20; 14:7). It would be a mistake, however, to conclude on the basis of such warnings that folly is exclusively or even primarily something learned

<hr>

[19] Brown, *Character in Crisis*, 41.

from one's environment. The real danger for the youth is that the manifold external temptations to sin and folly would be encountered with a heart that has failed to lay hold of wisdom.

Though it would be going too far to read the entirety of the Reformed doctrine of original sin and total depravity into Proverbs 22:15, the raw materials are, nevertheless, present: "Folly is bound up in the heart of a youth, the rod of discipline drives it far from him" (my translation). Folly is consistently cast as something natural and native to every individual from their earliest age. It is universal, innate, and ubiquitous, affecting every faculty of the human person (e.g., heart, Prov. 24:17; mind, Prov. 15:22; will, Prov. 6:25; 22:6; and emotions, Prov. 14:29). One does not have to seek out folly with any intentionality or discipline in order to obtain it. One merely needs to refuse Wisdom's summons, and to persist in the simplicity characteristic of infants and small children.[20] Fools are, almost by definition, those whose only source of wisdom is themselves, and whose understanding comes only by looking inward: "There is a way that seems right to a man, but its end is the way to death" (Prov. 14:12; cf. 26:12; 28:26). This finds its earliest expression in the refusal to heed the most basic means God has appointed to instill wisdom, namely, parental instruction (Prov. 1:8; 10:1; 13:1).

By contrast, wisdom is consistently presented as a reality external to an individual, one that must be pursued, internalized, and, once internalized, guarded and treasured. Consider the force dynamics at work in the metaphors employed by the verbs in Proverbs 2:1–2, 4–6, 9–10:

> My son, if you receive my words
>   and treasure up my commandments with you,
> making your ear attentive to wisdom
>   and inclining your heart to understanding, . . .
> if you seek it like silver,
>   and search for it as for hidden treasures,
> then you will understand the fear of the LORD,
>   and find the knowledge of God.
> For the LORD gives wisdom;
>   from his mouth come knowledge and understanding . . .

---

[20] To be sure, simplicity is not necessarily a morally culpable category. Proverbs was written with the express purpose of "endowing the simple with shrewdness" (Prov. 1:4 [my translation]). Children are by nature simple. The simple, however, become morally culpable as they refuse the divinely appointed means of growing in wisdom. Thus, Lady Wisdom, adopting the posture of a prophet, denounces the simple along with the fool: "How long O simple ones, will you love simplicity [פֶּתִי]? How long will scoffers delight in their scoffing? And fools hate knowledge?" (my translation).

302 SIN AND DEPRAVITY IN THE BIBLE

Then you will understand righteousness and justice,
and equity, every good path;
for wisdom will come into your heart,
and knowledge will be pleasant to your soul.

The verbs "receive" (לקח), "attend to" (קשב), "incline to" (נטה), "seek" (בקש), and "search" (חפש) all construe wisdom as an external reality which must "come in" (בוא) to one's heart (v. 10). Ultimately, wisdom resides in God, and is given by God both to protect and to delight. According to the sages, even that growth in wisdom, insight, and understanding which is attained through one's own experience and intellectual aptitude is acknowledged to be a gift of God (Prov. 2:6).

To be sure, *both* wisdom and folly are, at times, depicted as external realities desirous (anthropomorphically speaking) of the youth's loyalties, the most obvious example being the conclusion of the opening lectures (Prov. 9:1–6, 13–18), in which both Lady Wisdom and Dame Folly issue competing invitations for the passersby to turn aside to their "hospitality." Interestingly, both Lady Wisdom and Dame Folly address the same audience, namely, the simple, with the same invitation: "Whoever is simple, let him turn in here!" (Prov. 9:4, 16). Like her victims, Dame Folly is herself "simple" (פְּתַיּוּת) (9:13b, see ESV mg.), and her invitation is for the simple to join her in an illicit meal that is in reality a banquet in the grave (Prov. 9:18). The simple who enter her home need do nothing more than what is already consistent with their character. However, unlike that of Dame Folly, Lady Wisdom's invitation is for the simple to make a fundamental break with their character, that is, to forsake their simplicity and adopt a fundamentally new way of life characterized by understanding. Lady Wisdom calls out, "Give up simpleness and live, Walk in the way of understanding" (9:6, my translation). The audience envisioned, in other words, is not neutral. Rather, they are the simple, whose gullible character already inclines them toward the door of Dame Folly. Nevertheless, the call of Wisdom persists, as God's bears witness to himself and his truth continually in all that he has made. The entire created order, therefore, serves as God's witness against fools and their folly.

The dynamics of becoming either wise or foolish present a portrait that is consistent with the portrait of sin found in the other portions of the OT. Jeremiah's insight that, "The heart is deceitful above all things, and desperately sick; who can understand it?" (Jer. 17:9) is mirrored by the sages, who ask (rhetorically), "Who can say, 'I have made my heart pure; I am clean from my sin'?" (Prov. 20:9). David's penitential prayer, "Behold, I was brought forth in iniquity, and in sin did my mother conceive me" (Ps. 51:5), finds its sapiential counterpart in Proverbs 23:13: "Do not withhold discipline from a child; if you strike him with a rod, he will not die."[21] Death, as we will see, is the consequence of the folly bound up in the heart of a youth (Prov. 22:15). William Brown summarizes the matter well when he says,

> Wisdom does not come from within; our sages make that quite clear. Nor is she identified with God, the sole object of praise and petition. She is rather created, fashioned, and uttered by God. . . . At base, wisdom is profiled as the voice of God, the language of the Creator that is embodied and disseminated by the community.[22]

Wisdom comes principally from without—first through parental instruction and discipline, and then, as the child grows into adulthood, through the wise counsel of siblings, friends, and counselors, as well as through intentional and careful observation and experience of the way the world works. All of this, to adapt the words of Paul, is from God. By nature, mankind is foolish, but, by God's grace, they may become wise.

CONSEQUENCES OF FOLLY

The correspondence of actions and consequences undergirds the instructions and axioms that comprise the book of Proverbs. This concept, often called the deed-consequence nexus or the doctrine of retribution, is foundational to biblical wisdom, and is exemplified in, for example, Proverbs 13:21, which says, "Misfortune pursues sinners, but the righteous are well rewarded" (Prov. 13:21, JPS). The deed-consequence nexus is not the function of a mechanistic universe abandoned by her Creator, but rather the evidence of God's providential upholding and governing of the creation he brought into being.[23] That the sages did not adopt a simplistic or ironclad view of the deed-consequence network is evident from the clear exceptions implied throughout. For example, Proverbs 21:6 says, "The getting of treasures by a lying tongue is a fleeting

---

[21] Interestingly, the following verse in Ps. 51 reflects the same dynamic just described: "Behold, you delight in truth in the inward being, and you teach me wisdom in the secret heart" (Ps. 51:6). The solution to David's original sin is the truth and wisdom that comes from God.
[22] Brown, *Character in Crisis*, 38.
[23] Lennart Boström, *The God of the Sages*, Coniectanea Biblica: OT Series 29 (Stockholm: Almqvist & Wiksell, 1990), 136.

vapor and a snare of death." Clearly, it is possible that someone might prosper, at least financially, on account of their wickedness. A similar reality is attested in the many "better-than" sayings: "Better is a little with righteousness than great revenues with injustice" (Prov. 16:8); "It is better to be of a lowly spirit with the poor than to divide the spoil with the proud" (Prov. 16:19). Both imply that injustice may, at times, yield profit, a reality that would be at odds with a low-resolution understanding of the deed-consequence nexus. Though exceptions to the doctrine of retribution are not the central focus of Israel's traditional wisdom, such examples demonstrate that the sages were fully aware of the deep and far-reaching consequences of human sin and the brokenness (what Qoheleth will call "absurdity") that affect the created order.

However, exceptions (or apparent exceptions) do not change the basic principle that, to modify Paul's expression, "the wages of folly is death" (cf. Prov. 10:16). Wages are what one is owed. It is what is earned, and therefore, deserved. Wages may be seen as the natural, or at least expected, outcome of a particular course of action. Importantly, however, death, for the sages, does not refer primarily to the mere cessation of biological life, but to all that opposes or inhibits the human flourishing that God designed for them in creation.[24] Death as a principle experienced in life would involve, for example, the want of food, clothing, shelter, health, friends, emotional and mental well-being, intimacy with friends and spouse. Life, by contrast, is the opposite: the experience of joy, abundance, community, family, good health, and a general thriving that is the fruit of a life lived wisely before God.[25] The consequences of sin are not reserved exclusively for a future judgment but are experienced in the here and now as the effects of the divinely appointed created order. For this reason, both life and death are experienced in this lifetime as one reaps the consequences of one's actions either for good or for ill.

---

[24] Jon Levenson's remarks about the psalmists' theology of life and death apply equally well to that of the sages: "Whereas we think of a person who is gravely ill, under lethal assault, or sentenced to capital punishment as still alive, the Israelites were quite capable of seeing such an individual as dead. Or, to be more precise, they could do so in their poetic literature without, it seems to me, implying that in a more prosaic genre (like historiography or religious law) they would make the same categorization. In other words, for us death is radically discontinuous with life, a quantum leap, as it were, lying between the two. For the psalmists, by contrast, the discontinuity lay between the healthy and successful life and one marked by adversity, in physical health or otherwise" (Levenson, *Resurrection and the Restoration of Israel: The Ultimate Victory of the God of Life* [New Haven, CT: Yale University Press, 2006], 38).

[25] "In the wisdom literature, life means significantly more than biological life. . . . A true measure of life is its quality: dignity, prestige, reputation, prosperity, a large family. This ambience constitutes real life for a person; life is a network of proper relationships to God, to other human beings, and to nature" (Roland Murphy, "Death and Afterlife in the Wisdom Literature," in *Judaism in Late Antiquity*, ed. Alan Avery-Peck and Jacob Neusner, vol. 4 [Leiden, Netherlands: Brill, 1999], 101–16, 101–2).

The sages' focus on the here-and-now consequences of actions does not imply a disinterest in, much less a denial of, an afterlife. It is certainly true that a full-blown doctrine of the resurrection as understood by the NT authors is not taught in Proverbs; however, it is nevertheless incorrect to suggest, as many have, that the sages were ignorant of (or uninterested in) the consequences of actions for a life beyond this life.[26] The this-worldly experiences of life and death adumbrate a future, other-worldly experience that the sages envision as the ultimate outcome of lives lived either wisely or foolishly.[27]

The view that the sages were uninterested in an afterlife fails to do justice to the numerous intimations of an afterlife present in the proverbial literature, as well as to the rich symbolic and typological substructure of their literature which points to an eternal significance to one's actions in this life. Intimations of an afterlife may be discerned in the following sayings: "Riches do not profit in the day of wrath [בְּיוֹם עֶבְרָה], but righteousness delivers from death" (Prov. 11:4; cf. 10:2); "When the wicked dies, his hope will perish, and the expectation of wealth perishes too" (Prov. 11:7); and, though it suffers from a significant text-critical issue, the preferable reading of Proverbs 14:32 is suggestive: "The wicked is overthrown through his wickedness, but the righteous finds refuge in his death" (בְּרָעָתוֹ יִדָּחֶה רָשָׁע וְחֹסֶה בְמוֹתוֹ צַדִּיק).[28] Perhaps the most compelling, however, is Proverbs 15:24: "The path of life leads upward for the prudent, that he may turn away from Sheol beneath." Countering the many interpretations that read this verse as having in view a long life in this world, Waltke writes, "Salvation from the grave is more than being spared an untimely death, for otherwise the path of life is swallowed up by death, an unthinkable thought in Proverbs."[29] The metaphor of life-as-path is common in Proverbs and is here employed to distinguish the end-goal of life for the wise from that of the foolish/wicked.

At the symbolic and typological level, mentions of land tenure as the reward for the wise/righteous remind us that, whatever their origin, these sayings have been taken up into a thoroughly Yahwistic theology. Proverbs

---

[26] Murphy, "Death and the Afterlife in Wisdom Literature," 103–5. Though Murphy does admit that Woman Wisdom "seems to be promising more than prosperity in the here and now, a life that transcends the death/sheol that is associated with her opposite number Dame Folly. The surplus is not specified, but there is a hint of something special."

[27] The image of unjust gain (בֶּצַע) "taking away the life of its possessors" suggests that the experience of death is not reserved for the end of life but is the character or quality of life for those who pursue unjust gain (Prov. 1:18–19).

[28] The Hebrew בְמוֹתוֹ, translated "in his death," is rendered by the LXX τῇ ἑαυτοῦ ὁσιότητι, which means, "in his piety/integrity." Thus, the NRSV renders the verse, "The wicked are overthrown by their evildoing, but the righteous find refuge in their integrity."

[29] Waltke, *Book of Proverbs: Chapters 1–15*, 634.

2:21–22, for example, says, "For the upright will inhabit the land, and those with integrity will remain in it, but the wicked will be cut off from the land, and the treacherous will be rooted out of it."[30] In the conceptual world of ancient Israel, the enjoyment of long life in the land as well as the producing of many children (Prov. 17:6; 20:7) was a picture of eternal life with God (Gen. 13:15; Ezek. 37:25; cf. Heb. 11:10). Such images, types, and symbols of eternal life are set in contrast with the ultimate destiny of the wicked and foolish, namely, Sheol and its terrifying inhabitants. The father warns his son of the dangers of consorting with the "forbidden woman," saying, "for her house sinks down to death and her course to the shades; none who go to her come back, nor do they regain the paths of life" (2:18–19, my translation).

Proverbs teaches that a crooked way leads to a crooked end. The painful and sorrowful consequences of folly experienced in life adumbrate the ultimate end of a life lived foolishly, namely judgment and death. Conversely, the blessings of wisdom enjoyed in this life through faith in the one who gives both wisdom and her blessings (Prov. 1:7) provide a foretaste of an eternal life lived in the presence of the God of life. Though cast in terms of this-worldly types and symbols, the sages set forth a future for the wise that is different from that of the fool.

In sum, the portrait of the origin, scope, and effects of sin on the human person in Proverbs is consistent with the portrait found in the non-Wisdom portions of the Scriptures. The corruption of sin and the folly it produces is as extensive internally as it is externally. Internally, sin has corrupted every faculty of the human person: heart, mind, will, emotions; externally, sin has affected every human relationship: familial, social, political, economic, etc. Folly is manifest not just in how one thinks but how one feels. It is manifest not just in one's relationship to parents but also to neighbors and kings. The remedy, however, comes not from within but from without. Though it must be pursued with intentionality, diligence, and discipline, the wisdom that leads to life ultimately comes as a gift of divine grace and is received by faith, or, to use the language of the sages, in "the fear of the LORD" (Prov. 1:7).

Job: Sin and the Mystery of Providence

Central to the Joban drama is the issue of sin, primarily (though not exclusively) Job's sin. The narrator's description of Job as "blameless" (תָּם),

---

[30] Similarly, "Know that wisdom is such to your soul; if you find it, there will be a future, and your hope will not be cut off" (Prov. 24:14; cf. Prov. 10:30).

"upright" (יָשָׁר), "one who fears God" (אֱלֹהִים יְרֵא), and who "turns from evil" (סָר מֵרָע) (Job 1:1)—a judgment twice affirmed by Yahweh himself (1:8; 2:3)—in no way implies sinlessness or moral perfection on the part of the patriarch. Job acknowledges his sinfulness, for example, when he declares, "How many are my iniquities and my sins? Make me know my transgression and my sin. . . . For you write bitter things against me and make me inherit the iniquities of my youth" (Job 13:23, 26).[31]

The central question of the narrative is manifestly not *has* Job sinned in the past, *does* Job sin the present, or *will* Job sin in the future. The central question, rather, is whether Job's unimaginable suffering is the result of a *particular* sin and offense against the Almighty. Job's three friends are certain that it is; Job, though he cannot explain it, certain that it is not. Through the author's masterful use of dramatic irony, the reader, aware of the events narrated in the prologue, knows that Job is correct.

WISDOM MISAPPLIED: THE SIN OF JOB'S THREE FRIENDS

Surprisingly, words for "fool" and "folly," as well as their near synonyms which are commonplace in Proverbs, appear infrequently in the book of Job. "Folly" (נְבָלָה) does, however, appear at a critical point at the conclusion of the narrative, such that it invites the reader to understand all that has come before within the framework of wisdom's teaching on proper speech. In the aftermath of Job's dramatic and transforming encounter with God in the whirlwind (chs. 38–41), Yahweh addresses Eliphaz the Temanite as follows:

> My anger burns against you and against your two friends, for you have not spoken of me what is right, as my servant Job has. Now therefore take seven bulls and seven rams and go to my servant Job and offer up a burnt offering for yourselves. And my servant Job shall pray for you, for I will accept his prayer not to deal with you *according to your folly*. For you have not spoken of me what is right, as my servant Job has. (42:7b–8)

God designates the sin of the three friends as "folly" (נְבָלָה) and twice specifies that their folly consists of their not speaking of God "what is right."

---

[31] Contra D. J. A. Clines, who maintains that Job does "not for a moment admit to any wrongdoing" (*Job 1–20* [Nashville: Thomas Nelson], 318–19). Most commentators understand these verses to imply that Job understands himself to be a sinner both in the past and the present (cf. Job 14:16–17). For example, Samuel Rolles Driver and George Buchanan Gray aver, "Job, though 'perfect,' does not deny that he has sinned" (*Job*, ICC [Edinburgh: T&T Clark, 1921], 125). Similarly, C. L. Seow: "It is not that Job denies having committed any of these (see 7:21; 10:6, 14), but he wants to know the specific charges, not just general possibilities" (Seow, *Job 1–21* [Grand Rapids, MI: Eerdmans, 2013], 649; cf. Francis I. Anderson, *Job* [Downers Grove, IL: InterVarsity Press, 1976], 167–68).

In an ironic twist, the three friends, who were certain of Job's guilt, and who on more than one occasion accused Job of not speaking rightly of God (e.g., Job 8:2–3; 11:2–3), are revealed to be sinners and fools themselves who have not spoken rightly (נְכוֹנָה) of God, and who, as a result, need righteous Job to act as their priest and mediator (Job 42:8).[32]

Yahweh's verdict against the three friends in Job 42:8 clearly identifies their offense as related to their speech. But this raises the question, how have the friends not spoken rightly of God? In answering this question, it is critical to acknowledge the fact that the friends' wisdom, especially their axiomatic sayings, fits comfortably within Israel's wisdom tradition found in the book of Proverbs. The friends clearly understand the deed-consequence nexus and the doctrine of retribution that it entails. Eliphaz, for example, remarks, "Remember: who that was innocent ever perished? Or where were the upright cut off? As I have seen, those who plow iniquity and sow trouble, reap the same" (Job 4:7). Similarly, Bildad reasons, "Can papyrus grow where there is no marsh? Can reeds flourish where there is no water?" (Job 8:11). The reasoning of the three friends is recognizably traditional; it affirms God's sovereignty as the Creator, it affirms an order of creation, and it affirms perhaps above all else the doctrine of retribution. On this last point especially, all three friends have the same theology: a wise and upright life leads to prosperity and blessing, and a wicked and crooked life leads to suffering, disaster, and death. Their theology is in fact well summarized by Proverbs 13:21: "Misfortune pursues sinners, but the righteous are well rewarded" (JPS).

The folly of Job's three friends is not principally in their knowledge of traditional wisdom (or lack thereof), but in their application of traditional wisdom to the situation at hand. This is no small matter. One of the chief characteristics of the wise person in ancient Israel is the ability to speak or apply the right proverb to a situation. This is the reason a proverb in the mouth of a fool is useless if not dangerous, not because the proverb is untrue but because it is misapplied and thus results in harm to themselves and possibly others. So, for example, Proverbs 26:9 says, "Like a thorn that goes up into the hand of a drunkard is a proverb in the mouth of fools." Clearly, for the sages, it was

---

[32] The import of Yahweh's verdict is not the declaration of Job's righteousness, but the integrity of Job's words or speech about Yahweh in distinction from that of the friends. Norman Habel says, "The term rendered 'truth' [$n^e k \hat{o} n \hat{a}$] refers to what is correct and consistent with the facts (Deut. 17:4; 1 Sam. 23:23). Job's answers correspond with reality. They are devoid of dissembling and flattery, a trait against which Job warned the friends (23:7–12)" (Habel, *The Book of Job: A Commentary* [Philadelphia: Westminster, 1985], 583).

not enough to know traditional wisdom; fools may know traditional wisdom. The wise person knows how to *apply* traditional wisdom to the variegated circumstances and issues they encounter. Though they express it in different ways, the wisdom that the three friends offer Job is an unbending doctrine of retribution that interprets Job's great suffering as clear evidence of Job's great sin, for which Job's only recourse is to confess and repent.[33] In their shortsighted and clumsy application of traditional wisdom to Job's desperate circumstances, the three friends thus reveal themselves to be fools in whose mouths a proverb is useless (Prov. 26:7).

In Deuteronomy 29:29, Moses instructs Israel that, "the secret things belong to the Lord our God, but the things that are revealed belong to us and to our children forever, that we may do all the words of this law." Job's three friends believed that, at least as it pertains to Job's plight, they had plumbed the depths of God's mind exhaustively, and had discerned the Almighty's ways in the world with such clarity and precision that they could assume the role of judge and jury, presuming to posture as God's spokesmen and to issue God's verdict.[34] Ironically, in light of the narrative prologue, it is evident to the reader that Job's three friends serve as the mouthpiece of the Satan ("the satan" or "the accuser" being a literal translation of the Hebrew). Like Satan in the garden, the three friends speak, not blatant lies but deceptive words. Their wisdom is recognizably true as expressions of how the world often works, but when it comes to Job's situation their so-called wisdom is ill-informed and inadequate. The truly wise person understands that ultimate, perfect, and complete wisdom resides in God alone, an understanding exemplified in Job himself (Job 28). There is a provisional quality to human wisdom that implicitly acknowledges the limitations of human finitude.

Thus, in Job's friends we see the woeful consequences of "wisdom" in the hands of sinners. The sin-darkened heart and mind can take the truth of God displayed and proclaimed in all creation and distort it so as to exalt self and diminish God. The friends were deceived, thinking that their wisdom gave them exhaustive access to the mind of God and the ways of God in the world. They clearly understood something of the deed-consequence nexus;

---

[33] On the friends' individual perspectives on Job's situation and their characterizations, see Robert Gordis, *The Book of God and Man: A Study of Job* (Chicago: University of Chicago Press, 1965), 77.

[34] "They are self-appointed spokesmen for God and what they say is exposed in all its shallowness by the devastating grandeur expressed in chapters 38–41. They have a mechanical view of creation and providence and fail utterly to glimpse the supernatural dimensions of Job's agony" (Robert Fyall, *Now My Eyes Have Seen You: Images of Creation and Evil in the Book of Job* [NSBT 12; Downers Grove, IL: IVP Academic, 2002], 181).

but they misunderstood the greatness, wisdom, mystery, and indeed freedom of the God who established and upholds the created order of which the deed-consequence nexus is a part.[35] While the sorrows, suffering, and brokenness of this world may at times be explained with reference to folly yielding its natural fruit, Job offers the important reminder that this is by no means the only explanation. Jesus's disciples evidence a similar deficiency of reasoning when they ask, "Rabbi, who sinned, this man or his parents, that he was born blind?" To which Jesus responded, "It was not that this man sinned, or his parents, but that the works of God might be displayed in him" (John 9:2–3).[36] The same may be said of Job. His suffering is not the result of his sin (or his parents' sin), but that the works of God might be displayed in him.

GOD'S RESPONSE TO THE FRIENDS' FOLLY: JOB THE SUFFERING SERVANT

Neither Job nor his friends are ever made aware of the heavenly contest between Yahweh and Satan, nor God's purposes in vindicating himself and his servant before the heavenly court. Job's suffering is, in this regard, never explained. What *is* revealed to Job and the three friends is what God has purposed to do about the sin and suffering in this world. In Job, God sets on display the mediatorial work of his servant who endures suffering which leads to glory. Six times in the book of Job, God refers to Job as "my servant Job" (1:8; 2:3; 42:7, 8 [3x]). This designation places the patriarch in the company of Abraham (Gen. 26:24), Moses (Num. 12:7), and David (2 Sam. 7:5), each of whom served, in their own way, as a type of Christ.

Perhaps the most striking intertextual allusion in the book, however, is to Isaiah's mysterious servant of the Lord. John Hartley identifies numerous parallels between Job and the suffering servant described in Isaiah's Servant Songs.[37] Both are despised:

---

[35] "They rightly assert that God is all powerful, righteous, and wise, but they deny his freedom by not allowing God the freedom to use evil to accomplish his sovereign purposes. Ever since the death of Abel, the innocent have perished (cf. Job 4:7). It is often alleged that the three friends represent the viewpoint of Proverbs. If so, they were poor students of that book" (Waltke, *Old Testament Theology*, 933).

[36] Jesus addressed a similar, and no doubt common, misconception of God's ways in the world when he said, "Do you think that these Galileans were worse sinners than all the other Galileans, because they suffered in this way? No, I tell you; but unless you repent, you will all likewise perish. Or those eighteen on whom the tower in Siloam fell and killed them: do you think that they were worse offenders than all the others who lived in Jerusalem? No, I tell you; but unless you repent, you will all likewise perish" (Luke 13:2–5).

[37] The following examples are taken from John Hartley, *The Book of Job*, NICOT (Grand Rapids, MI: Eerdmans, 1988), 14. Citing Robert Pfeiffer and Samuel Terrien, Hartley believes Job to have been written before Isaiah, "for [Job] only alludes to the vicarious merit of innocent suffering; Isaiah develops this theme more fully. If this position is correct, the message of the book of Job prepared the people to understand and receive Isaiah's bold new message that God was going to redeem his people and the world through the innocent suffering of his obedient Servant" (Hartley, *Book of Job*, 15).

Isaiah 53:3: "as one from whom men hide their faces he was despised and we esteemed him not."

Job 19:18–19: "Even young children despise me; when I rise they talk against me. All my intimate friends abhor me, and those whom I loved have turned against me."[38]

Both are humiliated, mocked, and spat upon:

Isaiah 50:6: "I gave my back to those who strike, and my cheeks to those who pull out the beard; I hid not my face from disgrace and *spitting* [רֹק]."

Job 30:10: "They abhor me; they keep aloof from me; they do not hesitate to *spit* [רֹק] at the sight of me."

Both are deserted by family and closest friends:

Isaiah 53:3: "He was despised and rejected by men, a man of sorrows and acquainted with grief."

Job 19:13–15: "He has put my brothers far from me, and those who knew me are wholly estranged from me. My relatives have failed me, my close friends have forgotten me. The guests in my house and my maidservants count me as a stranger; I have become a foreigner in their eyes."

Both are regarded as one who is smitten by God:

Isaiah 53:4: "Surely he has borne our griefs and carried our sorrows; yet we esteemed him *stricken* [נָגוּעַ], smitten by God, and afflicted."

Job 19:21: "Have mercy on me, have mercy on me, O you my friends, for the hand of God has *struck* [נָגְעָה] me" (my translation).

Though neither has committed violence or spoken deceitful words, both experience unspeakable suffering:

Isaiah 53:9: "And they made his grave with the wicked and with a rich man in his death, *although he had done no violence* [עַל לֹא חָמָס עָשָׂה], and there was no deceit in his mouth."

---

[38] Lexical connections have been noted in text, the non-lexical connections, as here, are conceptual in nature.

Job 16:16–17: "My face is red with weeping, and on my eyelids is deep darkness, *although there is no violence in my hands* [עַל לֹא חָמָס בְּכַפַּי], and my prayer is pure."

Both rest their case in the hands of God:

Isaiah 49:4b: "Yet surely my right is with the LORD, and my recompense with my God."

Job 16:19: "Even now, behold, my witness is in heaven, and he who testifies for me is on high."

Job suffered though he was innocent; he was falsely accused by his friends and neighbors. Yet it was Job's obedience, represented by his integrity and faith, that qualified him as an intercessor who would offer prayers and sacrifices on behalf of sinners. Yahweh accepts Job's mediation, and Job's foolish friends avoid the strokes due for their folly. In Job, therefore, we see not only a model of Christian perseverance in suffering, steadfastness in times of hardship (James 5:11), but also, and perhaps more importantly, we see a type of Christ, the Servant of the Lord who would suffer unjustly, and whose faithfulness to God in and through unspeakable suffering vindicates God, silences the accusations of the devil, qualifies him to be the mediator for sinners, and results in his being glorified.

The great wealth that Job receives at the conclusion of the narrative (Job 42:10–17) is therefore a picture of God who is able to restore to his people all that is lost to them in life.[39] It is a type of resurrection life in which glory and honor and life in abundance is bestowed upon the faithful. Job is God's gracious gift to the foolish friends. The one for whom Job longs in his poignant expressions of faith (e.g., Job 19:25–26) is prefigured in his own life as one who through faithfulness in suffering is exalted and honored. The glory of Job is a picture of the glory of Christ. It is a glory that is bestowed on the Servant of the Lord, who though he is righteous endures unspeakable suffering with steadfastness and is in turn rewarded with riches and glory for his faithfulness.

Though sin is the root cause of all the sorrow and misery God's image-bearers experience in this life, personal and particular sin is not the only

---

[39] Fyall notes that the expression, "the LORD restored the fortunes" is "characteristically used for the nation restored from exile" (e.g., Deut. 30:3; Jer. 29:14; Ps. 126:4) (Fyall, *Now My Eyes Have Seen You*, 182). For restoration from exile as a picture of resurrection glory, see Bryan Estelle, *Echoes of Exodus* (Downers Grove, IL: IVP Academic, 2018), 182–87; cf. Levenson, *Resurrection and the Restoration of Israel*, 156.

explanation for personal and particular suffering. God in his mysterious providence has ordained that his children pass through valleys of deep darkness for reasons they cannot understand. What Job teaches is that God in his infinite wisdom is working through the seemingly senseless tragedies and inexpressible sorrows that his people experience in this life to bring glory to himself and to his Son, the ultimate Suffering Servant. Job never knows why he suffered so terribly, but he is comforted with the knowledge that God does know. He is, in the end, able to take comfort in God's goodness, God's sovereignty, and God's inscrutable wisdom.

Ecclesiastes: Living Well in a Sin-Cursed World

The rabbinic dispute surrounding the canonicity of *Qoheleth* was motivated, in part, by the book's seemingly secular character.[40] On more than one occasion the preacher appears to advocate a sort of epicureanism, as, for example, when he says, "Rejoice, O young man, in your youth, and let your heart cheer you in the days of your youth. Walk in the ways of your heart and the sight of your eyes" (Eccl. 11:9). Furthermore, questions regarding Qoheleth's commitment to personal holiness have been raised based on statements like, "Be not overly righteous, and do not make yourself too wise. Why should you destroy yourself? Be not overly wicked, neither be a fool. Why should you die before your time?" (Eccl. 7:16–17). Perhaps most puzzling from the perspective of traditional wisdom and Israelite faith is Qoheleth's apparent denial of an afterlife evident in such expressions as, "Who knows whether the spirit of man goes upward and the spirit of the beast goes down into the earth?" (Eccl. 3:21).

Nevertheless, the epilogist—Qoheleth's preeminent (not to mention inspired) interpreter—presents the sage in glowing terms: "Besides being wise, the Preacher also taught the people knowledge, weighing and studying and arranging many proverbs with great care. The Preacher sought to find words of delight, and uprightly he wrote words of truth" (Eccl. 12:9–10). Thus, the many challenging teachings of Qoheleth are not regarded by the editor as being at odds with Israelite theology generally nor with traditional wisdom specifically. Qoheleth is best interpreted as offering a realistic view of the

---

[40] Major sources for rabbinic discussion of the issues are: *m. Yad.* 3:5; *b. Meg.* 7a; *b. Shab.* 30b; *Pesiq. Rab. Kah.* 68b; *Lev. Rab.* 28.1. For treatments of the issues, see Roger Beckwith, *The Old Testament Canon of the New Testament Church* (Grand Rapids, MI: Eerdmans, 1985), 278–91; Katharine Dell, *Interpreting Ecclesiastes: Readers Old and New* (Winona Lake, IN: Eisenbrauns, 2013), 21–26.

limits and limitations of human wisdom as it is employed in a world that stands under the curse of sin with all the sorrow and senselessness that this entails.

LIFE UNDER THE SUN

Throughout the book bearing his name, Qoheleth describes the context of his observations with the recurring expression "under the sun" (תַּחַת הַשֶּׁמֶשׁ). Though occurring twenty-eight times in Ecclesiastes, the expression occurs nowhere else in the OT. Insight into its significance, however, may be gleaned from the associated and parallel expressions, "under heaven" (1:13) and "on the earth" (12:7).[41] Qoheleth opens his autobiography with a description of his quest for wisdom, saying, "I applied my heart to seek and to search out by wisdom all that is done *under heaven*. It is an unhappy business that God has given to the children of man to be busy with. I have seen everything that is done *under the sun*, and behold, all is absurd and a striving after wind" (1:13–14, my translation).[42] The report of having observed "everything that is done under the sun" is clearly the accomplishment of Qoheleth's mission "to search out by wisdom all that is done under heaven." Unlike the expression "under the sun," the expression "under heaven" does occur outside of Ecclesiastes, and, as Meredith M. Kline observes, it appears "primarily in biblical passages describing eschatological extermination."[43]

Genesis 6:17 is of particular significance as the expressions "under heaven" and "on the earth" appear together in the context of worldwide judgment by flood, a judgment typical of the eschatological judgment (2 Pet. 3:5–7). God says to Noah, "For behold, I will bring a flood of waters upon the earth [עַל הָאָרֶץ] to destroy all flesh in which is the breath of life under heaven [מִתַּחַת הַשָּׁמָיִם]" (Gen. 6:17). The significance of Qoheleth's expression "under the sun" is well-summarized by Kline:

> The phrase "under the sun" acquires by association the connotations of "under the heavens" and "on the earth." "Under the sun" can be a benefit (4:15; 8:15; 11:7) but it is predominantly correlated with a realm where bad things happen, whether the evil of humans (4:2–3; 8:9; 10:5) or the imposition of God (1:13–15; cf. 7:13; 9:3, 11). Both the oppression of people and the oppressiveness of the common curse sicken Qoheleth (5:12, 15 [5:13,

---

[41] The following discussion is indebted to Meredith M. Kline, "Is Qoheleth Unorthodox?: A Review Article," *Kerux* 13.3 (1998), 16–39.
[42] For a defense of the translation "absurd" for the important *leitwort* הבל, see below.
[43] Kline, "Is Qoheleth Unorthodox?," 23.

16]; 6:2), and cause him to despair in toil (2:20) and to hate life (2:17). Qoheleth is weighed down by the common curse that foreshadows the eschatological curse.[44]

Try as he might, Qoheleth cannot find a single aspect of human existence unaffected by the common curse. The common curse has made the entirety of human experience twisted, senseless, or, to use Qoheleth's favorite word, *hebel*.

It has long been recognized that one's interpretation of Ecclesiastes hinges in large measure on one's understanding of the Hebrew word *hebel* (הֶבֶל), a word which appears throughout the book both alone and in the expression *hᵃbel hᵃbālim* (הֶבֶל הֲבָלִים), often translated (somewhat misleadingly, in this author's opinion) as "vanity of vanities."[45] The significance of *hebel* (הֶבֶל) for Qohelet is signaled in part by its frequency of use and in part by its appearance at strategic locations as a summary assessment of and verdict on his observations of life under the sun. With this expression Qoheleth is clearly describing the character of life lived under the sun as well as the preacher's evaluation of certain experiences. The word means, literally, "vapor," and so it is obvious to most interpreters that we are dealing with a metaphor. But what does the metaphor mean? Space does not permit an evaluation of the seemingly countless translations and their attending interpretations. To mention just a few, suggestions have ranged from vanity, meaningless, ephemeral, elusive, fleeting, incomprehensible, mysterious, nothingness, and deceitful.[46] Michael Fox's proposal that *hebel* carries the sense of "absurdity" has the value of making the most sense of the most passages in which this lexeme is used in this admittedly enigmatic book. In Fox's words,

> The absurd is a disjunction between two phenomena that are thought to be linked by a bond of harmony or causality, or that should be so linked. Such bonds are the *sine qua non* of rationality, and all deduction and explanation presuppose them. Thus the absurd is irrational, an affront to reason—the human faculty that seeks and discovers order in the world about us. The quality of absurdity is not inherent in a phenomenon but is a relational

---

[44] Kline, "Is Qoheleth Unorthodox?," 28.

[45] Douglas Miller, *Symbol and Rhetoric in Ecclesiastes: The Place of Hebel in Qohelet's Work* (Atlanta: SBL, 2002), 2.

[46] For exhaustive studies on the meaning of הֶבֶל in Ecclesiastes, see Klaus Seybold, "הֶבֶל," in *TDOT*, vol. 3, ed. G. J. Botterweck and H. Ringgren (Grand Rapids, MI: Eerdmans, 1978), 313–20; Daniel Frederick, *Coping with Transience* (Sheffield, UK: JSOT Press, 1993); and most recently, Miller, *Symbol and Rhetoric in Ecclesiastes*.

concept, residing in the tension between a certain reality and a framework of expectations.[47]

Consider the usage of the *heḇel* in the following:

> There is a *heḇel* that takes place on earth, that there are righteous people to whom it happens according to the deeds of the wicked, and there are wicked people to whom it happens according to the deeds of the righteous. I said that this also is *heḇel*. (Eccl. 8:14)

Here *heḇel* describes the disconnect between how things are and how things should be. Where there should be a connection between cause and effect, where one would expect there to be harmony and order, Qoheleth finds chance and chaos. Though the verdict *heḇel* does not occur until later, the notion of absurdity is evident in Qoheleth's many observations of a world turned on its head: "Again I saw that under the sun the race is not to the swift, nor the battle to the strong, nor bread to the wise, nor riches to the intelligent, nor favor to those with knowledge" (Eccl. 9:11); and "folly is set in many high places, and the rich sit in a low place. I have seen slaves on horses, and princes walking on the ground like slaves" (Eccl. 10:6); and "I saw under the sun that in the place of justice, even there was wickedness, and in the place of righteousness, even there was wickedness" (Eccl. 3:16). As Qoheleth observes life lived in this sin-cursed world, he concludes that at the center of human experience lies an inescapable and inexplicable absurdity.

The many clear allusions to the creation and fall narratives of Genesis 1–4 suggests that Qoheleth is inviting his hearers/readers to interpret his teaching in light of the history and theology of these accounts.[48] For example, the allusion to Genesis 3:19 in Ecclesiastes 3:20 ("All are from the dust, and to dust all return") establishes the context for the preacher's observations of life as it is lived east of Eden. When Qoheleth says, "Consider the work of God: who can make straight what he has made crooked?" (Eccl. 7:13), he is therefore not referring to God's work in creation deemed "very good"

---

[47] Michael V. Fox, *A Time to Tear Down and a Time to Build Up: A Rereading of Ecclesiastes* (Grand Rapids, MI: Eerdmans, 1999), 31. "Absurd" is preferable to "zero" or "nothing" or "transient" in that the former communicates the sense that what is so evaluated is not as it appears to be or should be. True, vapor is transient and (ultimately) nothing, but Qoheleth's point is that it does not appear to be so.

[48] Charles C. Forman, "Koheleth's Use of Genesis," *JSS* 5 (1960): 256–63; William H. U. Anderson, "The Curse of Work in Qoheleth: An Exposé of Gen. 3:17–10 in Ecclesiastes," *Evangelical Quarterly* 70 (1998): 99–113; Carolyn J. Sharp, "Ironic Representation, Authorial Voice, and Meaning in Qohelet," *BibInt* 12 (2004): 37–68; Radiša Antic, "Cain, Abel, Seth and the Meaning of Human Life as Portrayed in the Books of Genesis and Ecclesiastes," *AUSS* 44 (2006): 203–11.

in Genesis 1:31, but to God's work in subjecting the world (and especially mankind's experience of it) to the absurdity and futility which he promised the first man and first woman when he said,

> Cursed is the ground because of you;
> in pain you shall eat of it all the days of your life;
> thorns and thistles it shall bring forth for you. . . .
> By the sweat of your face
> you shall eat bread,
> till you return to the ground,
> for out of it you were taken;
> for you are dust
> and to dust you shall return, (Gen. 3:17b–19)

The universality of sin expressed in Ecclesiastes 7:20 ("Surely there is not a righteous man on earth who does good and never sins") is a feature not of God's design for creation but of mankind's present condition within it. Sin disrupts not only the human person but the human person's relation to the created order which, after the fall, is characterized by strife or futility.

LIFE AND THE AFTERLIFE ACCORDING TO QOHELETH

For Qoheleth, perhaps the principal way humans experience life under the sun as absurd is in the ineluctable desire for "gain" (יִתְרֹון) combined with the impossibility of ever achieving it. "Gain" is a concept that entails permanence, certainty, control, progress—all of which are an illusion in a life lived under the specter of death. Commenting on the use of "gain" in the preacher's programmatic question, "What does man gain from all the toil at which he toils under the sun?" (Eccl. 1:3), Iain Provan writes, "the idea is that of surplus, and the question is asked from the perspective of someone who thinks of life in a particular way, as if it were raw material to be invested in, manipulated, and shaped, given added value by what is done with it, and marketed as a means of accruing capital."[49] Gain, for Qoheleth, stands for the ways in which mankind seeks mastery over the universe and especially over his or her destiny in it. The chief reason there can be no ultimate gain in this life is that death relativizes the value of every human action. Nothing that mankind can do is of permanent, ultimate, or lasting value.

---

[49] Iain Provan, *Ecclesiastes, Song of Songs*, NIVAC (Grand Rapids, MI: Zondervan, 2001), 54.

In contrast to life-as-gain stands the alternative outlook of life-as-gift. This contrast is seen most clearly in Ecclesiastes 3:9–13. Though the answer to the rhetorical question posed in verse 9, "What gain has the worker from his toil [עָמֵל]?" is clearly, "Nothing!," Qoheleth observes an alternative when he says, "I perceived that there is nothing better for them than to be joyful and to do good as long as they live; also that everyone should eat and drink and take pleasure in all his toil [עֲמָלוֹ]—that is God's gift [מַתַּת אֱלֹהִים] to man" (Eccl. 3:12–13). When viewed as an instrument of absolute gain, toil is a "weariness" and "vexation." When viewed from the perspective of gift, the same reality becomes an inducement to joy. These contrasting perspectives undergird contrasting ethics. When life is viewed as a gift, and the "gains" received therein are also regarded as gifts, then there is genuine joy to be had in food, family, clothing, work, and wife.

Qoheleth's concept of life-as-gain explains the preacher's surprising instruction, "Be not overly righteous, and do not make yourself too wise [וְאַל־תִּתְחַכַּם יוֹתֵר]. Why should you destroy yourself? Be not overly wicked, neither be a fool. Why should you die before your time?" (Eccl. 7:16–17). Though often interpreted as advocating an Aristotelian *via media*, the context suggests the preacher again has in view gifts, in this case righteousness and wisdom, being employed as a means of achieving gain. Immediately prior to this, Qoheleth relates an anecdote that demonstrates the limitations of traditional wisdom: "There is a righteous man who perishes in his righteousness, and there is a wicked man who prolongs his life in his evildoing" (Eccl. 7:15). Righteousness does not exempt one from experiencing the crookedness of life under the sun (Eccl. 7:13). Making oneself "too righteous" or "too wise" is the pursuit of these virtues under the illusion that doing so guarantees a long life.[50] As is true for all attempts at "gain" in life, this too will result in disappointment and destruction of the one who labors under such an illusion. As Provan observes,

> Those who pursue wisdom or righteousness for "profit" in this sense . . . hoping to gain an edge over God and force his hand, are in no different a position to those who pursue foolishness and wickedness. Both are guilty

[50] This interpretation is very similar to that of Norman Whybray, who argues that אַל־תְּהִי צַדִּיק הַרְבֵּה וְאַל־תִּתְחַכַּם יוֹתֵר carries the sense of "do not be self-righteous and do not make pretensions to wisdom" (Whybray, "Qoheleth the Immoralist? [Qoh. 7:16–17]," in *Israelite Wisdom: Theological and Literary Essays in Honor of Samuel Terrien*, ed. J. G. Gammie, W. A. Brueggemann, et al. (Missoula, MT: Scholars Press, 1978], 191–204). Self-righteousness would be another expression of Qoheleth's concept of "gain."

of *hubris*—the arrogant self-deification in which mortal beings so regularly indulge as they seek to fashion reality after their own liking. Both are guilty of sin. It is, indeed, self-delusional to think it possible to escape sin and become the kind of blameless person that verse 16 implies.[51]

In contrast to both the overly righteous and the overly wicked stands the "one who fears God" and who will depart from both extremes (Eccl. 7:18), that is, leave behind both temptations toward "gain."

The second common charge of secularism laid at the foot of the preacher pertains to his alleged skepticism about an afterlife. To be sure, Qoheleth does teach that knowledge about life after death cannot be derived from observation and experience. Mankind dies just like the animals, returning to the dust from which they came. The righteous dies just like the wicked, and the benefit of the wise life is relativized by the inevitable reality of death. Experiences of absolute gain are revealed to be an illusion as names are forgotten and wealth is squandered by foolish children. Nevertheless, Qoheleth's emphasis on the finality of death is somewhat attenuated by his assertions that mankind will be held accountable for his actions in a future judgment. Qoheleth's encouragement to live life to the fullest in the days of your youth, for example, is accompanied by the warning, "But know that for all these things God will bring you into judgment" (Eccl. 11:9).

In contrast to life under the sun, in which gain is relative, stands another realm or order of reality that Qoheleth references with the word "eternity" (עוֹלָם). Qoheleth says, "Also, [God] has put eternity [אֶת־הָעֹלָם] into man's heart, yet so that he cannot find out what God has done from beginning to the end" (Eccl. 3:11). This sense of and longing for eternity, a longing unfulfilled in this life, appears to find satisfaction on the far side of death: "the almond tree blossoms, the grasshopper drags itself along, and desire fails, because man is going to his eternal [עוֹלָמוֹ] home, and the mourners go about the streets" (Eccl. 12:5). Eternity is the realm in which God works apart from the limitations and restrictions of those who live under the sun. Scott Jones writes, "Unlike human works, God's work is not delimited by time. Without temporal bounds, the calculation of values so typical of humans under the sun breaks down, and the possibility of another system of calculation opens up. The dichotomy between these two ways of reckoning is central to the book,

---

[51] Provan, *Ecclesiastes, Song of Songs*, 152.

setting God's works apart from those of humanity."[52] Though ultimate judgment and justice is not to be found under the sun, Qoheleth's sober warnings and exhortations toward piety suggest that what is done under the sun is of consequence in eternity, in which God, not man, will make straight what he has made crooked. Again, Jones writes,

> Yet Qohelet knows of another way of adding things up which is effective in a realm called עוֹלָם. This term simultaneously evokes the limits of time-under-the-sun and points to something beyond those limits. The breakdown of temporal boundaries signals the collapse of human calculations which characterized life under the sun. At the same time, however, it offers new possibilities for assessing value and making sums. Qohelet refuses to set out the details of a new economy, but his claims about divine judgment, the ultimate value of piety, and the reversal of the created order point to another kind of reckoning in which God-fearers will reap absolute benefit and the impious will experience permanent loss.[53]

The above readings of Qoheleth are not meant to blunt the preacher's undeniably sharp goads. The goal, rather, is to demonstrate that the sage's theology (especially as it touches on the doctrine of sin and judgment) does not stand in irreconcilable tension with that of his admiring editor, who closes his work saying, "Fear God and keep his commandments, for this is the whole duty of man. For God will bring every deed into judgment, with every secret thing, whether good or evil" (Eccl. 12:13–14).

Conclusion

Far from peripheral (much less foreign) to the theological mainstream of OT theology, biblical wisdom provides not only a helpful but also a critical perspective on what it means to live by faith in a world groaning under the curse of sin. Regarding the nature, origin, effects, and scope of sin, the sages are of one accord with Moses and the prophets. All mankind is, by nature, prone to folly and thus set on a path characterized by and ending in death. As a concept, sin may be conceived of and construed in a variety of ways. Folly, it has been argued, is a violation of the will and word of God as it has been expressed principally in the pattern of creation. It profiles the destructive consequences that inevitably follow behavior that cuts against the grain of

---

[52] Scott Jones, "The Values and Limits of Qoheleth's Sub-Celestial Economy," *VT* 64 (2014), 21–33, 28.
[53] Jones, "Values and Limits of Qoheleth's Sub-Celestial Economy," 22.

the created order. Just as there is a physical pattern to creation, so too is there a social, relational, marital, familial, economic order as well; and a violation of these latter orders results in harm no less consequential than the former. It is much easier, of course, to discern the harm that results from stepping off a roof than the harm that results from slandering one's neighbor. But the sages remind us that both are antithetical to wisdom and life as God designed it for his image-bearers; and both introduce disorder and death into the human experience. Folly, in this sense, is stupid. It is stupid because it fails to discern the disastrous consequences of foolish behavior, and it fails to consider the ultimate end of folly, namely, eternal death.

God has ordered creation to reveal his wisdom, and by his grace (both common and saving) has enabled mankind to discern wisdom so that they might order their lives accordingly. Wisdom, therefore, is both an obligation and a gift. It is an obligation in the sense that any time or place God's wisdom shines forth in his creation, mankind (ideally in their youth) is obligated to recognize it for what it is and to order their lives to promote their own good and the good of their neighbors, all to the glory of God. Anything less is sin and folly. Yet the sages are clear, that though the attainment of wisdom requires much discipline, hard work, and careful reflection, its ultimate source is the Lord, who is the giver of wisdom, knowledge, and understanding (Prov. 2:6).

However, the mastery of life that Wisdom affords those who lay hold of her is only a relative and limited mastery. Both Job and Ecclesiastes offer an important counterpoint to the traditional wisdom of Proverbs. Even great wisdom does not allow mankind to transgress the boundary separating the Creator from the creature, nor does it give one full access to the ways and purposes of God in the world. To labor under the illusion that it does, is perhaps the height of folly. Though man may gain great understanding in life, man remains man, a creature, limited, dependent, sinful, and, apart from God's grace and the gift of wisdom, death-bound. God's purposes and ways in the world remain elusive even to the most wise, and the truly wise man or woman adopts a posture of humility before the majesty and mystery of divine wisdom.

God's will, word, and ways, expressed in the created order, and discerned through experience and observation, are no less authoritative and binding than his will expressed in his laws and commandments. Those who bear God's image are obligated not simply to choose right over wrong but also to choose the best over the good or permissible. This, in one respect, raises the bar on how we think of the obedience God requires of man, but in another respect, this sets in fuller and more brilliant display the gift of Christ, who, as Paul says, "became to us *wisdom* from God, righteousness and sanctification and redemption, so that, as it is written, 'Let the one who boasts, boast in the Lord'" (1 Cor. 1:30–31).

12

Breaching the Covenant

SIN IN THE PROPHETS

William M. Wood

Introduction

Writing a chapter on sin in the Prophets is a daunting task. Not only is the pro-phetic material of the OT expansive as to its content, but each book contains its own historical context and theological nuances pertaining to the question of sin. As such, any short work on "sin in the Prophets" will, in a sense, be truncated and introductory rather than a thoroughgoing presentation. This, however, is not to say that there are no broad theological considerations that may be brought to the discussion. For the purposes of this chapter, three main sections will discuss some of the central emphases in relation to sin in the Prophets, followed by a final section presenting various sins in terse fashion. These sections are (1) sin as a breach of covenant: the covenant lawsuit; (2) sin as adulterous infidelity: the marriage metaphor; (3) sin and the day of the Lord; and (4) particular sins in the Prophets. In these sections, breach of covenant is the overarching view of sin in the Prophets that merits God coming to administer the curse on the day of the Lord. Sin for the prophets is first and foremost an affront to the Lord in breach of covenant.

I. Sin as a Breach of Covenant: The Covenant Lawsuit

The relation between the prophets and covenant has long been recognized. The pronouncement of curses for breach of the covenant and blessings for obedience to the covenant, along with a hope of restoration after judgment, are central aspects of prophetic theology that provide guiding contours for analyzing the corpus. This perspective on the prophets views them as messengers of the Lord's covenant, and is immediately juxtaposed to the manifold discussions among scholars that the prophets function simply on the level of social commentary or religious innovation and ethics. R. E. Clements, discussing this juxtaposition, argues that the attention given to the broader social function of the prophets led to a situation where

> attention was diverted from their primary role as messengers of Yahweh who were concerned with the covenant relationship between Yahweh and Israel. It is in their concern with this unique position of Israel before Yahweh, and in the threat of the dissolution of the covenant with a hope of its subsequent restoration, that the heart of the prophetic message is to be found.[1]

In other words, the function of the prophets was not in social commentary but rather in bringing God's word to God's people, a word revealed in the covenant. The theme of Israel breaching covenant with the Lord is in fact so prominent that George Mendenhall claims that the prophetic message is "essentially indictment of Israel for breach of covenant."[2] While the category of "messenger of the covenant" is broader than Israel's breach of the covenant in sin, the following analysis focuses on this aspect since the present topic concerns sin in the Prophets.

As messengers of the covenant, it is not surprising that the prophets regularly draw from the covenant idea and specific covenant passages to convey their message. One particular aspect of this among some of the prophets is the so-called covenant lawsuit genre. While the genre is not used by every prophet and may, relatively speaking, be a minor feature of prophetic communication, the administration of this "lawsuit" provides a significant lens with which one may consider the prophetic treatment of sin more generally. Within the lawsuit, the Lord sends his prophets to condemn the people of Israel and Judah for their breach of covenant, which then leads to the application of the covenant curse. To better understand this genre and its function, a few orientating comments are necessary concerning the exact notion of the "covenant lawsuit," followed by an examination of Isaiah 1 as an example.

---

[1] R. E. Clements, *Prophecy and Covenant*, Studies in Biblical Theology 43 (London: SCM, 1965), 25–26.
[2] George E. Mendenhall, *Law and Covenant in Israel and the Ancient Near East* (Pittsburgh: Biblical Colloquium, 1955), 19; cf. also Dilbert Hillers, *Treaty Curses and the Old Testament Prophets* (Rome: Pontifical Biblical Institute, 1964).

The discussion of the prophetic lawsuit as a genre has its origins with the form-critical work of Hermann Gunkel. Gunkel argued for a distinct "lawsuit speech" (*Gerichtsrede*) among the preexilic prophets tied to the Hebrew term רִיב, with the proposal of a רִיב-pattern or רִיב-oracle (*Rechtsverhandlung*).[3] Gunkel's initial analysis focused on a proposed social context (*Sitz im Leben*) for the *Gerichtsrede Gattung* and attendant *Rechtsverhandlung* as a civil judgment rendered at the city gates.[4] Moreover, this lawsuit, according to Gunkel, is conducted with Israel as the defendant, God as the plaintiff, and the "heavens and earth" as judges.

The current discussion concerning the lawsuit parties treats Israel as the defendant and the Lord as both plaintiff and judge, with the "heavens and earth" summoned as witnesses to the proceedings.[5] However, the role of the various parties as well as the proposed *Sitz im Leben* have come under significant scrutiny by later scholars. The proposed *Sitz im Leben* has shifted focus from civil proceedings at the city gate to the ancient Near Eastern legal context of treaties (especially Hittite treaties), building especially off the work of Herbert Huffmon.[6]

Huffmon placed the *Gerichtsrede* into an outline form as follows:

I. A description of the scene of judgment
II. The speech of the plaintiff
    A. Heaven and earth appointed as judges [witnesses]
    B. Summons to the defendant (or judges)
    C. Address in the second person to the defendant

---

[3] See, e.g., Hermann Gunkel and Joachim Begrich, *Einleitung in die Psalmen: Die Gattungen der religiösen Lyrik Israels* (Göttingen, Germany: Vandenhoeck & Ruprecht, 1933), 329, 364–66; cf. also Claus Westermann, *Basic Forms of Prophetic Speech*, trans. Hugh Clayton White (Philadelphia: Westminster, 1967).
[4] For city gates and lawsuits, see Hans Jochen Boecker, *Redeformen des Rechtslebens im Alten Testament* (Neukirchen, Germany: Neukirchener Verlag, 1970), 10; D. A. McKenzie, "Judicial Procedure at the Town Gate," *VT* 14 (1964): 100–104; L. Köhler, "Justice in the Gate," in *Hebrew Man*, trans. Peter R. Ackroyd (London: SCM, 1956), 149–75; J. W. McKay, "Exodus 23:1–3, 6–8: A Decalogue for the Administration of Justice in the City Gate," *VT* 21.3 (1971): 311–25.
[5] B. Gemser, "The Rib- or Controversy-Pattern in Hebrew Mentality," *Wisdom in Israel and the Ancient Near East*, VTSup 3 (Leiden, Netherlands: Brill, 1960), 120–33; Kirsten Nielsen, *Yahweh as Prosecutor and Judge: An Investigation of the Prophetic Lawsuit (Rib-Pattern)*, JSOTSup 9 (Sheffield, UK: JSOT Press, 1978); George E. Wright, "The Lawsuit of God: A Form-Critical Study of Deuteronomy 32," in *Israel's Prophetic Heritage*, ed. B. W. Anderson and W. Harrelson (New York: Harper & Row, 1962), 26–67; J. Limburg, "The Root רִיב and the Prophetic Lawsuit Speeches," *JBL* 88 (1969): 301–4; W. G. Ramsey, "Speech-Forms in Hebrew Law and Prophetic Oracles," *JBL* 96 (1977): 45–58; J. Harvey, *Le Plaidoyer Prophétique Contre Israël après la Rupture de l'Alliance*, Studia 22 (Montréal: Bellarmin, 1967).
[6] Herbert B. Huffmon, "The Covenant Lawsuit in the Prophets," *JBL* 78.4 (1959): 285–95. This is the majority position, and is also extensively argued by Harvey, *Le Plaidoyer Prophétique*, as well as Eberhard von Waldow, *Der traditionsgeschichtliche Hintergrund der prophetischen Gerichtsreden*, BZAW 85 (Berlin: A. Topelman, 1963). A minority position argues for the prophetic lawsuit conducted in a cultic setting during an oral pronouncement of the law (see Ernst Würthewein, "Der Ursprung der prophetischen Gerichtsrede," *Zeitschrift für Theologie und Kirche* 49 [1952]: 1–16; which is refuted by Franz Hesse, "Wurzelt die prophetische Gerichtsrede im israelitischen Kult?" *ZAW* 65 [1953]: 45–53).

1. Accusation in question form to the defendant
2. Refutation of the defendant's possible arguments
3. Specific indictment[7]

While this was the main form, Huffmon also allowed for some possible alternate forms.[8] However, this organization has likewise come under scrutiny as these various parts are not always present and are not always in the same order.[9] The summary statement by Dylan Johnson, that "little consensus was ever reached regarding its [the lawsuit's] constituent elements, the textual material inspiring the ריב format, or the historical setting in which it was performed," must be well heeded.[10] Indeed, even the use of רִיב as a technical term for a lawsuit generally, let alone the prophetic/covenant lawsuit in particular, has been called into question.[11]

With a vast amount of disagreement and discussion as to the nature (or even existence) of the covenant/prophetic lawsuit, one must wonder if there is anything to be gleaned from the discussion. With a few qualifications and the following treatment of Isaiah 1, the answer is in the affirmative.

First, there was far more flexibility in the use of genre categories in the ancient world than one observes in the modern era (or that is often expected by modern scholars). As such, it is unsurprising that strict, formal categories and outlines for the *Gattung* of the covenant lawsuit have resisted classification. An author may use any combination of legal features in any number of ways to present the concept of a covenant disputation with Israel. Concerning legal contracts documented in the ancient Near East, Johnson notes that the methods of study by scribes allowed "students to memorize the necessary structural elements of legal contracts, but this method also granted some degree of flexibility for their deployment in specific cases."[12] While there is no

---

[7] Huffmon, "Covenant Lawsuit," 285.
[8] Huffmon, "Covenant Lawsuit," 286–89.
[9] Huffmon himself recognizes this as he often mentions parts in different orders, as in, e.g., Jer. 2 (discussed on p. 288) and Deut. 32 (288–89). See esp. the reflection on this form in Robert Wilson, "Form-Critical Investigation of the Prophetic Literature: The Present Situation," in *Society of Biblical Literature Papers I* (Chicago: Scholars Press, 1973), 100–21.
[10] Dylan R. Johnson, "The Prophetic Lawsuit of Jeremiah 2–3: Text, Law, and Education in Biblical Prophecy," *Zeitschrift für Altorientalische und Biblotesche Rechtsgeschichte* 23 (2017): 229–40.
[11] Michael de Roche, "Yahweh's *Rîb* against Israel: A Reassessment of the So-Called 'Prophetic Lawsuit' in the Preexilic Prophets," *JBL* 102.4 (1983): 563–74. De Roche notes that there are uses of רִיב that present different ways in which a disputation may be resolved, using a threefold classification for disputations by Simon Roberts, *Order and Dispute: An Introduction to Legal Anthropology* (Harmondsworth, Middlesex, UK: Penguin, 1979), 17–29.
[12] Johnson, "Prophetic Lawsuit of Jeremiah 2–3," 238; following Martha Roth, "Scholastic Tradition and Mesopotamian Law: A Study of FLP 1287, a Prism in the Collection of the Free Library of Philadelphia" (PhD diss., University of Pennsylvania, 1979).

substantial evidence to make the link between ancient Near Eastern scribes and Israelite *prophets* to the extent that Johnson argues, the "degree of flexibility" for the "deployment" of a particular genre in various cases and for an author's own literary purposes is a point worth noting.

Second, earlier studies made too much of the term רִיב. This term is used in a broader sense than a lawsuit in general or the prophetic lawsuit in particular and carries the general notion of "quarrel," "grievance," or "disputation," which may or may not be used in a legal context.[13] As such, Michael de Roche rightly claims that a "lawsuit" is "a modern technical term that has no real Hebrew equivalent,"[14] because "unlike in Roman jurisprudence, there was no specialized legal terminology in New Eastern law."[15] It is the use of the term *in context* that determines its import, and since context is the key feature for the "prophetic lawsuit," the category may be present even without the use of רִיב.[16] Due to this reality, it is perhaps better to categorize the passages commonly described as "prophetic" or "covenant" lawsuits as "covenant disputations" or "covenant grievances" to avoid over-importation from the term "lawsuit."[17] However, in light of the use of the terms "prophetic" or "covenant lawsuit" in academic works, the employment of the term is likely to continue and simply needs to be cast within the particular historical and cultural milieu of ancient Israel rather than our modern expectations.

Third, attempts to isolate a particular *Sitz im Leben* for the proposed covenant lawsuit must be avoided. Barring any discovery of an explicit mention of a social event from which all prophetic lawsuits are understood to arise, the isolation of a singular *Sitz im Leben* that explains the origins of the genre will be speculative. It is better simply to maintain that the prophets are communicating God's divine judgment against Israel for their breach of covenant in a broad sense, one which may have been used in any number of social situations in the religious life of ancient Israel.[18]

---

[13] See "רִיב," in *DCH*, 7:478–81.
[14] De Roche, "Yahweh's *Rîb* against Israel," 564.
[15] Johnson, "Prophetic Lawsuit of Jeremiah 2–3," 232. This, of course, does *not* mean that there is no legal language; rather, that the language that is used in legal disputes also covers more basic (or more broad) semantic domains.
[16] רִיב may also be used in a context that has nothing to do with the covenant lawsuit.
[17] De Roche's main concern in over-importation from the term "lawsuit" seems to be the notion of two parties coming before a third party who is an impartial judge. Since God is both plaintiff and judge, this concept of "lawsuit" is improper (see de Roche, "Yahweh's *Rîb* against Israel," 567–69). He also concludes that the use of רִיב in other places indicates that it is most appropriate to see it as "something that occurs prior to any judicial procedure" (569).
[18] The issue of isolating a particular *Sitz im Leben* that is not explicitly mentioned in the text is fraught with difficulty. It is better to focus on literary and theological contexts rather than social ones.

Finally, while it is the case that strict classifications of genre categories and the use of רִיב as a highly technical term are to be avoided, this does not mean that there are no patterned expectations or legal proceedings. The presence of extensive legal material (including but not limited to רִיב), as well as features such as the summoning of witnesses, marks some unity and formality to the passages typically labeled as "prophetic lawsuit." However, as has been implied, a particular prophet may willingly alter various aspects and use distinct lexemes for their own literary, rhetorical, and theological purposes. Every specific "disputation" must be appreciated on its own terms rather than being forced through strict form-critical grids. This vocabulary and literary patterning, moreover, is closely related to the literary presentation of the book of Deuteronomy, which is the source from which much of the material in these passages is derived, rather than from social settings or broad ancient Near Eastern treaty vocabulary.[19]

Johnson reaches a similar conclusion when he states, "The legal aspect of Jeremiah 2–3 and the other רִיב oracles need not be defined by tenuously reconstructed models of Israelite litigation, but rather by scribal involvement in the administration of law."[20] The present analysis agrees with the first proposition, that רִיב oracles should not be defined by the overly strict genre (*Gattungen*) expectations or the search for social context (*Sitz im Leben*) of former form-critical scholars. However, Johnson's second proposition may be better qualified not by "scribal involvement in the administration of law" but rather by *prophetic* involvement in the proclamation of a covenant disputation against a party (Israel) who has breached the Lord's covenant or law. The covenant lawsuit is the Lord's word through his prophets that his people have breached the covenant and are now in disputation and grievance with YHWH, the God of the covenant, rather than in the blessed state of rest in the land.

With this in mind, a brief examination of Isaiah 1 as a "covenant lawsuit" or "covenant disputation" adds flesh to the previous discussion.[21] Isaiah 1 may

---

[19] As such, the present author prefers terms such as *covenant* lawsuit (or covenant disputation) rather than *prophetic* lawsuit. This use of the term *covenant* highlights the central core of the prophetic witness as messengers of the covenant, as well as the distinct origins of their message derived from the covenant dealings of the Lord with Israel, principally in the book of Deuteronomy.

[20] Johnson, "Prophetic Lawsuit of Jeremiah 2–3," 239.

[21] The importance of Isa. 1 to the whole of Isaiah cannot be understated. It has often been recognized that Isa. 1 forms an introduction to the book as a whole *as well as* an inclusio with Isa. 65–66; for more on this, see the essay by David M. Carr, "Reading Isaiah from Beginning (Isaiah 1) to the End (Isaiah 65–66): Multiple Modern Possibilities," in *New Visions of Isaiah*, ed. Roy F. Melugin and Marvin A. Sweeney (Atlanta: SBL, 2006), 188–218. The notion of Isa. 1 as an introduction to the whole was first popularized by G. Fohrer, "Jesaja 1 als Zusammenfassung der Verkündigung Jesaja," *ZAW* 74 (1962): 251–68.

be broadly organized into two sections, with verses 2–20 functioning as the "covenant lawsuit/disputation" and verses 21–31 as the divine verdict of the preceding disputation.[22] Verses 2–20 are initially separated from 21–31 by means of an inclusio of the phrase "for the LORD has spoken" (כִּי יְהוָה דִּבֵּר) and "for the mouth of the LORD has spoken" (כִּי פִּי יְהוָה דִּבֵּר) in verses 2 and 20, along with the shift in verse 21 by means of the rhetorical question beginning with אֵיכָה. Verses 2–20 are then broken up into three parts, each beginning with a summons, where verses 2 and 10 begin new sections with the command to "hear" (שִׁמְעוּ) and verse 18 begins with the command to "come" (לְכוּ) and to "let us reason" (וְנִוָּכְחָה). The covenant lawsuit/disputation of Isaiah 1:2–20 therefore has three parts to examine: verses 2–9, 10–17, and 18–20.

The first section of the covenant disputation in Isaiah 1:2–9 is itself divided into two parts, with verses 2–3 as an introductory summons and verses 4–9 as an indictment against sinful Israel.[23] The introductory summons in verses 2–3 begins the covenantal context of the "lawsuit" genre by summoning covenant witnesses to the legal proceedings. The Lord calls the "heavens" (שָׁמַיִם) to "hear" (שִׁמְעוּ) and the "earth" (אֶרֶץ) to "listen" (וְהַאֲזִינִי) to the disputation. These "witnesses" are the same as those that were summoned to "testify" (עוֹד) concerning the covenant in Deuteronomy 30:19 (cf. Deut. 4:26; 31:28; 32:1; Ps. 50:4; Mic. 6:1–2), in which Israel will gain life in the land for obedience and experience exile and death for disobedience. The opening summons indicates that the Lord had raised up Israel like a child who then rebelled against its heavenly father (Isa. 1:2), along with a testimony of witnesses to their infidelity.[24]

With this introduction of Israel as a rebellious child, Isaiah 1:4–9 depicts that rebelliousness as *sin*: they are called the "sinful nation" (גּוֹי חֹטֵא), a "people laden with iniquity" (עַם כֶּבֶד עָוֹן), and even the "seed of evildoers" (זֶרַע מְרֵעִים) and "children of corrupt ones" (בָּנִים מַשְׁחִיתִים).[25] As such, they

---

[22] This division is widely recognized; see, e.g., Marvin Sweeney, *Isaiah 1–4 and the Post-Exilic Understanding of the Isaianic Tradition*, BZAW 171 (Berlin: Walter de Gruyter, 1988), 119–23. Sweeney likewise connects the speech of vv. 21–31 with the preceding as a speech of the Lord as judge (122–23), which fits the description here as well. He likewise calls the genre here "prophetic judgment speech" that makes up "YHWH's announcement of judgment" (Sweeney, *Isaiah 1–39 with an Introduction to the Prophetic Literature*, Forms of the Old Testament Literature 16 [Grand Rapids, MI: Eerdmans, 1996], 85).

[23] R. E. Clements separates vv. 2–3 and 4–9 as two separate sections (see R. E. Clements, *Isaiah 1–39*, New Century Bible [Grand Rapids, MI: Eerdmans, 1980], 30–35). However, in light of the observation concerning the calls to "hear" that occur in v. 2 and v. 10, it is better to see vv. 2–3 and 4–9 as subsections of a major section extending from vv. 2–9.

[24] Israel as a stubborn and rebellious child as an image for sinfulness also comes up in Isa. 30:1, 9.

[25] This indictment would have been particularly poignant as Israel was called to be a "holy seed" rather than the seed of corruption.

have "forsaken" (עָזַב) the Lord as their God[26] and have "despised the holy one of Israel" (נִאֲצוּ אֶת־קְדוֹשׁ יִשְׂרָאֵל). The forsaking and despising of the Lord is their rebellious and sinful actions in juxtaposition to the holiness of the God of the covenant.

Holiness is a key motif in the book of Isaiah, where the Lord is identified as the "Holy One of Israel" (קְדוֹשׁ יִשְׂרָאֵל), a phrase that occurs another twenty-six times in the book.[27] This emphasis on God's holiness is also part of Isaiah's prophetic call in Isaiah 6:3, where the seraphim declare the thrice-holy nature of the Lord of Hosts.[28] In light of this, sin is something done *against* the holy God of the covenant, the father who redeemed and raised the nation of Israel as his own. Sin is an afront not simply to the covenant, but more particularly to the *God of the covenant*. To breach the covenant in sin is to forsake the Lord and despise him, for the covenant reveals the holy nature of God himself. As O. Palmer Robertson notes, "the whole message of Isaiah has been affected by this identity of God as the Holy One of Israel."[29] It is the presence of Israel near to the "Holy One of Israel" (קְדוֹשׁ יִשְׂרָאֵל) that precipitates the legal proceedings in Isaiah 1, as the Holy God confronts Israel for their defilement in sin.

There are two primary results of this sinful defilement in Isaiah 1:5–9. First, in verses 5–6 the people are closer to *death* by means of bodily harm. The curses of the covenant in Deuteronomy 30 are summarized by association with death and the blessings with life. Now the sin of the people in Isaiah 1:4 results in bodily ailments and harm (vv. 5–6). Rather than health and life, the people are "sick" (לָחֳלִי); from "toe" to "head" (מִכַּף־רֶגֶל וְעַד־רֹאשׁ) they are "unsound" (אֵין־בּוֹ מְתֹם). Psalm 38:4 (ET 38:3) highlights this connection between sin and the "unsoundness" of flesh: "there is no soundness [מְתֹם] in my flesh, because of your indignation; there is no wellness in my bones,

---

[26] עָזַב is a covenantal term also used in marriage/divorce contexts; see below.
[27] Isaiah 1:4; 5:19, 24; 10:20; 12:6; 17:7; 29:19; 30:11–12 (2x), 15; 31:1; 37:23; 41:14, 16, 20; 43:3, 14; 45:11; 47:4; 48:17; 49:7 (2x); 54:5; 55:5; 60:9, 14 (cf. "Holy One of Jacob," Isa. 29:23). This description of YHWH is used in only two other places among the prophets: Jer. 50:29 and 51:5.
[28] While Isa. 1 may form the introduction to the book as well as an inclusio with its conclusion, the prophetic call of Isa. 6 may be described as the "thematic center" of the book, where all the main themes are tersely represented at Isaiah's call. As such, the focus on holiness in both 1:4 and 6:3 presents a strong case for the central theme of the book being God's holiness and how Israel has sinned against it. For Isa. 6 as the thematic center, see Thomas Wagner, "More Than a Source?: The Impact of Isaiah 6 on the Formation of the Book of Isaiah," in *"I Lifted My Eyes and Saw": Reading Dream and Vision Reports in the Hebrew Bible*, ed. Elizabeth R. Hayes and Lena-Sofia Tiemeyer, LHBOTS 584 (London: T&T Clark, 2016), 183–95; cf. also O. Palmer Robertson, *The Christ of the Prophets* (Phillipsburg, NJ: P&R, 2008), 173–87. Isaiah 1 and 6 are particularly close together; see Willem A. M. Beuken, "The Manifestation of Yahweh and the Commission of Isaiah: Isaiah 6 Read against the Background of Isaiah 1," *CTJ* 39 (2004): 72–87.
[29] Robertson, *Christ of the Prophets*, 177.

because of my sin."[30] As such, the depiction of sin in Isaiah 1:5–6 is that it has led the people closer to death; they are so sick and unsound with sin that no healing balm may aid their distress.

Second, in Isaiah 1:7–9 the result of sin is connected with the desolation of the exile. The defilement of the people meant not only the loss of bodily health, which brought them in their sin nearer to death, but also the defilement of the realm meant to be holy. In sin, Zion, the holy place for the Holy One of Israel, is defiled, with the result that the land itself is made desolate in judgment. Verse 7 is the most explicit on this as the land becomes a desolation (שְׁמָמָה), and the cities a waste (שְׂרֻפוֹת), as God summons foreign powers (v. 7c–d) to lay waste the realm of Israel. This realization dovetails with the presentation of sin in my previous chapter in this volume (ch. 10) on its relation to the covenantal kingdom focused on the people, their representatives, the realm, and their worship. Here, as the people called to holiness have rebelliously become a "sinful nation," the realm that they inhabit has become a desolate place.

Verses 8–9 of Isaiah 1 likewise present this desolation of the land as a result of sin. Verse 8 describes the exile, with the drastically diminished nature of the people and their dwelling places. The discussions concerning these verses largely focus on possible historical circumstances surrounding the imagery of the drastically reduced Zion and Jerusalem, with most scholars arguing for the invasion of Sennacherib in Isaiah 36–37.[31] While this context is possible and fits the theological portrait of these verses, no specific historical situation is mentioned in this passage. As such, isolating the *theological* portrait of the results of sin and the desolation of the realm to the events of 701 BC is unjustified.[32] Rather, the theological portrait of a desolate vineyard[33] shows that the inevitable result of the breach of the covenant by Israel is the application of the curse in the exile.[34]

---

[30] מְחֹם is a fairly rare word, occurring only three times in Scripture (Isa. 1:6; Ps. 38:4, 8), all of which present the results of sin. It is notable that in Ps. 38 there is a connection between the "unsoundness" of flesh due to sin and the wounds that David has, similar to Isa. 1:5–6.
[31] Sweeney, *Isaiah 1–39*, 75–78; Ehud Ben Zvi, "Isaiah 1, 4–9, and the Events of 701 BCE in Judah," *Scandinavian Journal of the Old Testament* 5 (1991): 95–111.
[32] Similar comments are also made by Roy F. Melugin, "Figurative Speech and Reading Isaiah 1 as Scripture," in *New Visions of Isaiah*, 283–84.
[33] Vineyard imagery is fairly common in Isaiah, particularly Isa. 1–39 and the infamous desolate vineyard passage in Isa. 5 (see Andrew T. Abernethy, "The Ruined Vineyard Motif in Isaiah 1–39: Insight from Cognitive Linguistics," *Biblica* 99.3 [2018]: 334–50).
[34] The events in 701 BC themselves reflect this reality as the defeat, subjugation, and exile of Judah is a near certainty until Hezekiah humbles himself before God and the Lord restores the humble king and his kingdom. As such, Sennacherib's invasion is an image of the curse that will be applied later when Babylon will invade. However, the

Except for the Lord's gracious act to save a remnant, the people would end up "like Sodom" (כִּסְדֹם) and "like Gomorrah" (לַעֲמֹרָה) (Isa. 1:9). Becoming like Sodom and Gomorrah is an aspect of the covenant curses from Deuteronomy 29:23 (cf. Zeph. 2:9). In fact, every aspect of judgment in Isaiah 1:4–9 is related to the curses of the covenant. Breaching the covenant (Isa. 1:4; Deut. 28:15–19) by forsaking the Lord (עָזַב) (Isa. 1:4; Deut. 28:20) leads to the curses, including bodily ailments (Isa. 1:5–6; Deut. 28:22, 27, 35, 59), defeat by enemies (Isa. 1:7; Deut. 28:25, 33, 49–57), desolation of the vineyard (Isa. 1:8; Deut. 28:30, 39), and that they will be "like Sodom and Gomorrah" (Isa. 1:9; Deut. 29:23).

In the span of this first section of the covenant lawsuit/disputation, the Lord has summoned his witnesses and indicted Israel for breaching the covenant, and therefore the curses of the covenant—especially death and exile—are presented before them. The following section, Isaiah 1:10–17, continues this disputation by providing a category for its resolution. It is initially worth recognizing that the opening exhortation is to Israel now (not the witnesses), being viewed in association with Sodom and Gomorrah, just as in verse 9. The people have made themselves *ethically* like the paradigmatically wicked cities from Genesis 19. This poses the question as to what remedy may resolve the issue of the defiled Israel in the presence of the "Holy One of Israel," an issue that leads to "utter estrangement" (Isa. 1:4).[35] The following passage (vv. 11–15) shows that religious formalism does nothing to resolve the issue of sin and restore fellowship with God. In so doing, this passage indicts the people of Israel for an additional aspect of sin in their religious practices (vv. 11–15) as well as calling the people to repent (vv. 16–17). Isaiah 1:4–9 presents two aspects of the covenantal kingdom mentioned in my previous chapter in this volume (ch. 10), with sinful people (vv. 4, 5–6) and the land desolate and lost (vv. 7–9). Now, this section focuses on the other aspects of the covenantal kingdom: the representatives of the sinful people are the "rulers of Sodom" (i.e., unholy representatives) in verse 10, and there is a focus on worship in verses 11–15.

Commenting on these matters, J. J. M. Roberts argues that the Lord "rejects the sacrificial ritual as an adequate remedy for the situation. Yahweh,

---

latter is an escalation of the former, as the people and their king do *not* repent and the full force of judgment in the exile is applied. Notably, this may likewise be part of Isa. 1, where the hope of restoration is through repentance. For this theme in Isa. 1, see Mark J. Boda, *A Severe Mercy: Sin and Its Remedy in the Old Testament*, Literature and Theology of the Hebrew Scriptures 1 (Winona Lake, IN: Eisenbrauns, 2009), 191–93.

[35] This notion marks that exile is far more than simply expulsion from the land; it is estrangement from God.

who ordained the cult, is tired of church services."[36] While Roberts is certainly correct that these verses express the Lord's exasperation with Israel's cultic life, it is better to agree with Marvin Sweeney that the Lord is not frustrated with the cultic system per se, as though it were a "blanket condemnation of cultic practice."[37] Rather, he is frustrated with the manner in which it was implemented in Israel. The cultic system in Israel was instituted by God as a means of restoring the fellowship between him and his people which was broken by sin. However, Isaiah 1:11–15 illustrates that even this system could be corrupted by Israel's evil intentions, and there was *always* a requirement of faithful, heartfelt service conjoined to the cultic system.[38] As E. J. Young remarks, "What Isaiah opposes is not sacrifice in itself, but the misuse thereof. . . . [Isaiah] clearly condemns mere formalism in religion."[39]

A few places in this passage illustrate this. Verse 12 describes the coming before God in worship as a "trampling of my courts" (רְמֹס חֲצֵרָי). This trampling of the temple courts brings sin and iniquity into the worship of the Lord and therefore profanes the temple. Verse 13 makes this explicit, where the Lord states that he is not able to endure the union of iniquity (אָוֶן) and solemn assembly (עֲצָרָה). By not repenting of their wicked deeds (Isa. 1:4), the people's approach in the cultic system had become defiled by sin. As such, the system had become a "burden" (טֹרַח) to the Lord and something that "my soul hates" (שָׂנְאָה נַפְשִׁי). This "iniquity" brought into the courts in the final clause of verse 15 is the people's "hands" being "full of blood" (יְדֵיכֶם דָּמִים מָלֵאוּ). Likely, this image is a play on the sacrifices mentioned in verse 11. While those who offer up sacrifices would have had bloody hands, the blood mentioned here is that of bloodshed in murder. Instead of the blood of the sacrifice pleading for the life of the offeror, the blood of the victim stands as the indictment against the false worshipers.[40] Young states, "The people worshiped God with their lips, but their hearts were far from Him. . . . Hence, their worship had become mere idolatry."[41]

[36] J. J. M. Roberts, *First Isaiah*, Hermeneia (Minneapolis: Fortress, 2015), 23.
[37] Sweeney, *Isaiah 1–39*, 80.
[38] Michael Barrett, "The Danger of Heartless Religion: An Exposition of Isaiah 1:2–18," *Puritan Reformed Journal* 6.2 (2014): 5–15.
[39] E. J. Young, *The Book of Isaiah*, 3 vols. (Grand Rapids, MI: Eerdmans, 1965), 1:61.
[40] This is a fairly common interpretation of the "blood" in v. 15 (see Young, *Book of Isaiah*, 1:69–70; Hans Wildberger, *Isaiah 1–12* [Minneapolis: Fortress, 1991], 48). However, this position is not universal. Young points out that Calvin's view is that it is the blood of the sacrifice rather than of murder.
[41] Young, *Book of Isaiah*, 1:66.

Verses 16–17 are distinct from the negative portrait of verses 11–15 by presenting nine imperatives that focus on the people's need to repent from sinful wrongdoing. Only then can they be restored to right fellowship with the Holy One of Israel. The various sins which they commit in breaching the covenant must be "removed" (סוּר) from before the Lord's eyes, and they must learn to "do what is good" (לִמְדוּ הֵיטֵב) and to "seek justice" (דִּרְשׁוּ מִשְׁפָּט). That is, they must learn to be *obedient* to the covenant.

The final section of the "covenant lawsuit/disputation" proper in Isaiah 1:18–20 reflects upon this call to obedience as the Lord calls the people to "reason" (יָכַח) with him. Roberts notes that the verb יָכַח has a "legal background and refers to the arbitration of legal disputes."[42] The covenantal nature of this legal dispute is made clear in verses 19–20, where the two destinies of blessing for obedience (v. 19) and curse for disobedience (v. 20) are outlined as the final part of the disputation (cf. Deut. 30:15–20). In obedience the people will be granted the right to eat of the fruit of the land, but if they disobey, they will be consumed by the sword. And yet, even in the midst of this disputation and the following verdict on their breach of covenant, verse 18 reveals the essentially redemptive nature of this covenant: the Lord's work is to redeem people from sin, to make their scarlet sins white as snow.

With Isaiah 1:18–20, the covenant lawsuit/disputation proper is brought to a close. In 1:21–31, the Lord's verdict is declared: rather than pursuing faithfulness, the people have become harlots; instead of pursuing righteousness, they have become murderers (v. 21). Because of this (לָכֵן) (v. 24a), God declares the judgment against them: he will turn his hand against them in a refining judgment.[43] Israel, who was chosen and raised

---

[42] Roberts, *First Isaiah*, 24; Heinz-Josef Fabry, "יָכַח," in *TDOT* 6:64–71; "יָכַח," in *DCH*, 4:209–10.

[43] For the Lord to "turn his hand" against Israel/Judah is an image of a reversed exodus (cf. also Isa. 5:25). The hand that was once lifted for the redemption of the people is now turned against them in judgment. Numerous works have been written on the Lord's hand or arm being raised against/for a person or group. Many focus on the phrase as an image of judgment, such as Paul Humbert, "Entendre la main' (Note de Lexicographie Hebra-ique)," *VT* 12.4 (1962): 383–95; and Ron Bell, "The Lord's Outstretched Hand: Invective Threat and the Refrain of Isaiah 5:25," *Didaskalia* 12.2 (2001): 81–100. Others argue for some sort of magic ritual, such as M. Striek, *Das Vordeuteronomistische Zephanjabuch* (Frankfurt am Main: Lang, 1999), 92–93; or a liturgical one, as with James L. Crenshaw, "A Liturgy of Wasted Opportunity (Amos 4:6–12; Isaiah 9:7–10:4; 5:25–29)," *Semitics* 1 (1970): 27–37; and William P. Brown, "The So-Called Refrain in Isaiah 5:25–30 and 9:7–10:4," *Catholic Biblical Quarterly* 52 (1990): 432–33. For the development of this as *both* a judgment and a salvific motif, see Matthew R. Akers, "The Soteriological Development of the 'Arm of the Lord' Motif," *JESOT* 3 (2014): 29–48. In this way, the *heilsgeschichte* of the exodus was simultaneously an *unheilsgeschichte* for Egypt, and now that *unheilsgeschichte* is proclaimed against Israel for their breach of covenant. G. K. Beale makes similar observations concerning the hardening of Pharoah's heart in G. K. Beale, "An Exegetical and Theological Consideration of Pharaoh's Heart in Exodus 4–14 and Romans 9," *TJ* 5 (1984): 129–154.

by the Lord as his own child (Isa. 1:2), is now his enemy due to their rebellion (Isa. 1:24–25). It is the sinful deeds of the people that merits the Lord's disciplinary action to "break" (שֶׁבֶר) the "rebels and sinners" (פֹּשְׁעִים וְחַטָּאִים) who have forsaken (עָזַב) him (Isa. 1:28).[44] And yet, just as with the conclusion of the disputation in Isaiah 1:18–20, there is a hope of redemption for those who heed the prophet's warning and "repent" in "righteousness" (וְשָׁבֶיהָ בִּצְדָקָה) (v. 27), such that after restoration, the city described as a harlot (זוֹנָה) (v. 21) will be called the "city of righteousness" (עִיר הַצֶּדֶק) and "city of faith" (קִרְיָה נֶאֱמָנָה) (v. 26).

This brief examination of Isaiah 1 and the covenant lawsuit/disputation generally presents a core aspect of how sin according to the prophets is a breach of covenant. God had entered a covenant relation with Israel in the exodus, promising life and blessing for obedience but death and cursing for disobedience (Deut. 30:15–20). The prophets regularly address Israel as a rebellious people who have breached covenant, who have sinned against the "Holy One of Israel" and therefore the curses of the covenant (Deut. 28:15–69) are proclaimed against them. At the same time, the covenant made with Israel is a *redemptive* covenant. Even while judgment is proclaimed against the nation of Israel for their breach of covenant and they are judged nationally for the same in the exile, the hope of redemption is never abrogated. It is the God of the covenant who has promised to redeem from sin, and this vision is not lost even in the covenant disputation (Isa. 1:18, 26–27).

One final consequence of this *covenantal* treatment of sin in the Prophets must be mentioned before we proceed. Overwhelmingly, sin in our modern conception is something done by an individual and therefore there is individual culpability. While this is certainly true and part of the prophetic revelation and treatment of sin (e.g., Hos. 14:9), the covenantal nature of the relation between Israel *as a nation* and the Lord means that sin is primarily dealt with by the prophets at the *national* rather than individual level. As Geerhardus Vos states, "the sin which the prophets condemn is largely collective national sin."[45] Because of this, the righteous among Israel and Judah suffer along with the wicked, and it is the nature of the *national* covenant enacted in the exodus that explains this reality.

---

[44] These are the same terms used to describe the people as sinful and rebellious in Isa. 1:2, 4.
[45] Geerhardus Vos, *Biblical Theology of the Old and New Testaments* (Carlisle, PA: Banner of Truth, 2007), 264.

II. Sin as Adulterous Infidelity: The Marriage Metaphor

Geerhardus Vos in his *Biblical Theology* adds nuance to the discussion of the covenantal bond mentioned above, noting that it is expressed, especially in Hosea, in marital terms. He argues that according to Hosea the marriage metaphor and the idea of covenant are so similar that they are nearly identical; Vos even calls it a "marriage-*berith*."[46] This union of marriage and covenant is seen especially in Hosea 1–3 and Jeremiah 2:2–3:20, although similar language and motifs may also be found elsewhere (e.g., Mal. 2:10–16).[47] Briefly examining these two prophetic passages (Hos. 1–3 and Jer. 2:2–3:20) on the marriage-*berith* adds to the concept of a covenantal breach, where sin is not merely the breaking of the law or covenant, but *adulterous infidelity* to the God of the covenant, who is the faithful husband of his unfaithful bride. Thus, there is a union between the covenant grievance and the marriage metaphor in Hosea 1–3 and Jeremiah 2:2–3:20. Sin is a violation of the marriage contract, the marriage covenant, between the Lord and Israel.

THE UNION OF THE MARRIAGE AND COVENANT CONCEPTS

Prior to discussing the particulars of Hosea and Jeremiah on the prophetic portrait of sin as adulterous infidelity, a few brief comments on the union of the marriage and covenant concepts will provide important contours for our discussion. This connection is part of the first marriage in Genesis 2:21–25. While space does not allow a full exposition of the context for this marriage, two important points must be made. First, Adam has just finished noting the *incompatibility* of all other creatures upon the earth for this marital bond, which expresses a need of appropriateness for the united parties. The subsequent creation of Eve *from Adam* indicates this appropriateness, such that she is quite literally "bone of my bones and flesh of my flesh" (Gen. 2:23). In this sense, Eve is created in the likeness of Adam. In conjunction with the creation of mankind (male and female) in Genesis 1:26–31, the appropriateness of relation is in how mankind is created in the image of God. Far from being an

---

[46] Vos, *Biblical Theology*, 259–60.

[47] Malachi 2:10–16 is particularly important as well since the marriage relation between man and woman is described with the line "wife of your covenant" (אֵשֶׁת בְּרִיתֶךָ) in v. 14. The passage also unites the notion of the inter-marital relations between a husband and wife and the relation between God and Israel. The faithlessness of Israel in their marriages (Mal. 2:13–16) is their "profaning the covenant of our fathers" (לְחַלֵּל בְּרִית אֲבֹתֵינוּ) by marrying a "daughter of a foreign god" (בַּת־אֵל נֵכָר). For discussion of issues regarding this passage and Israel's marriage to non-Israelite (foreign) women as a breach of the Mosaic covenant, see Jonathan Gibson, *Covenant Continuity and Fidelity: A Study of Inner-Biblical Allusion and Exegesis in Malachi*, LHBOTS 625 (London: T&T Clark, 2016), 116–55.

ancillary addition on the part of the creation narrative, the depiction of Eve's creation in Genesis 2 is reflective of God's creation of humanity generally in Genesis 1:26–31, functioning as an expansion of the original creation account.[48] Thus, the creation of Eve and her appropriateness for marital relation to Adam is expressive of the appropriateness of humanity for relation with God.

Second, the context of Genesis 2 and Adam's marriage is the covenant of works. Upon the creation of Adam earlier in the narrative (v. 7), the Lord entered into a covenant of works with him in verses 15–17. In this covenant Adam, and all humanity with him, by means of *ex pactum* merit in obedience to the probationary command concerning the tree of the knowledge of good and evil, could advance into eschatological blessedness and reward. It is immediately upon the enactment of this covenant in verse 17 that verse 18 presents the situation of Adam's need for a marriage partner, that it is "not good" (לֹא טוֹב) for him to be alone.[49] As God had created for himself a covenant partner in humanity, so now in Genesis 2:18–25 he creates for Adam a covenant partner as well, that is, his "helper" (עֵזֶר), one "like what is before him" (כְּנֶגְדוֹ).[50]

The entire context of Genesis 2:5–25 is therefore the covenant, expressed in the relation between God and Adam and then in how it is reflected in the marriage relation between Adam and his wife. This covenant connection is likewise part of the description of marriage as the man "leaving" (עָזַב) his parents and "cleaving" (דָּבַק) to his wife as "one flesh" (לְבָשָׂר אֶחָד). The language of "leaving" is a breach of a covenant bond. The covenant curse section of Deuteronomy makes this clear, where the breach of covenant leading to the curses is "because you have forsaken me [עֲזַבְתָּנִי]" (Deut. 28:20; cf. also Deut. 29:25).[51] Similarly, the language of "cleaving" is the establishment of a bond, used especially in the call to "cling" or "hold fast" (דָּבַק) to God as part of the covenant enacted in Deuteronomy (Deut. 10:20; 11:22; 13:4; 30:20; cf. also Jer. 13:11). Covenant

---

[48] A common Hebrew narrative tool used here is resumption and expansion. The current analysis fits in this category as the creation of mankind in Gen. 1 is expanded upon in Gen. 2. The creation of Adam and then Eve in the more detailed expression in Gen. 2 is an expansion of their initial creation in Gen. 1:26–31. For this relation between Gen. 1 and 2, see Mark D. Futato, "Because It Had Rained: A Study of Genesis 2:5–7 with Implications for Genesis 2:4–24 and Genesis 1:1–2:3," *WTJ* 6.1 (1998): 1–21.

[49] In light of the repeated refrain of things described as "good" (טוֹב) in Gen. 1, that something is now described as "not good" (לֹא טוֹב) is a significant narrative feature, which will be resolved in the following passage.

[50] The language of כְּנֶגְדוֹ is unique to Gen. 2. However, נֶגֶד is often used to express something that is "corresponding to" or "proper." See "נֶגֶד," in *DCH*, 5:603–4. With this in mind, the notion of something "fit for him" may be better seen as something "according to his correspondence," that is, something that is *like him*. The translation of "like what is before him" is expressive of this, and comes from Kenneth A. Matthews, *Genesis 1–11:26*, NAC 1A (Nashville: Broadman & Holman, 1996), 213.

[51] The opposite is also the case: covenant *faithfulness* is observed in how the Lord states in Deut. 31:6 that he will "not forsake" (עָזַב + לֹא) Israel. Recall that this same term was expressive of the breach of covenant in Isa. 1.

faithfulness is "clinging" to the Lord (2 Kings 18:6). Thus, just as marriage is a "cleaving" between man and woman (Gen. 2:24; cf. also Josh. 23:12; 1 Kings 11:2), so also the bond of the covenant is a "cleaving" between God and Israel.[52] This informs the language of "one flesh," where the דָּבַק-bond between man and woman expresses intimate union and communion, a communion that is made by covenant in marriage just as it is between the Lord and Israel.[53]

This background explains Paul's quotation of Genesis 2:24 in Ephesians 5:22–33, concluding that the marriage bond "refers to Christ and the church" (Eph. 5:32). The covenant of marriage had *always*, from its inception, expressed the relation between God and his people.[54] The covenant between God and his people is the archetype (original) of which human marriage between a man and woman is the ectype (copy). As such, this marital covenant bond forms the background for its explicit use among the prophets, where Israel's breaching of the covenant is expressed as adulterous infidelity. In other words, when Israel sins, she is an *unfaithful bride*.

Hosea 1–3

The most explicit and extensive use of the marriage metaphor for sin and the breach of covenant is Hosea 1–3.[55] Broadly, this section may be organized into three parts, with 1:2–2:1 and 3:1–5 as biographical information concerning Hosea and his role to marry an adulterous wife, and 2:2–23 as the Lord's divorce proceedings in a covenant lawsuit/disputation (cf. Isa. 1).[56] The marriage metaphor with Israel as an adulterous bride is therefore an image of covenant unfaithfulness.

---

[52] The *breach* of covenant is "clinging" to sin (2 Kings 3:3) and the application of the covenant curses is the Lord causing the curse to "cling" to them (Deut. 28:60). The language of "cleaving" is also used to express the relation of faithful servants to their king (see, e.g., 2 Sam. 20:2).

[53] This union between covenant and marriage is frequently recognized, but not always with the same features outlined above (see, e.g., Raymond C. Ortlund Jr., *God's Unfaithful Wife: A Biblical Theology of Spiritual Idolatry*, NSBT 2 [Nottingham, UK: Apollos/Downers Grove, IL: InterVarsity Press, 1996], 22–23; G. P. Hugenberger, *Marriage as a Covenant: A Study of Biblical Law and Ethics Governing Marriage Developed from the Perspective of Malachi* [Eugene, OR: Wipf & Stock, 1994]; Gerlinde Baumann, *Love and Violence: Marriage as Metaphor for the Relationship between YHWH and Israel in the Prophetic Books* [Collegeville, MN: Liturgical Press, 2003]; Călin Sechelea, "The Relationship between God's Covenant with His People and Marriage in the Old Testament," *Studia Theologica* 8.4 [2009]: 250–73).

[54] Some in recent times have grown accustomed to speaking of the marital relation as a reflection of the intra-trinitarian life of the Godhead. Our present analysis shows that the marital relation is *not* a reflection of intra-trinitarian relations—which is wholly unique unto itself—but is a reflection of God's covenant with man.

[55] The literature on Hos. 1–3 is fairly extensive, since early modern Hosea scholarship focused almost exclusively on these chapters. The particular focus of OT scholarship from the late nineteenth to the early twentieth centuries on social and historical context explains this focus, as these chapters reveal extensive details about the prophet's life. For an overview of scholarship on these chapters, see Brad E. Kelle, "Hosea 1–3 in Twentieth-Century Scholarship," *Currents in Biblical Research* 7.2 (2009): 179–216; and Yvonne Sherwood, *The Prostitute and the Prophet: Reading Hosea in the Late Twentieth Century* (London: T&T Clark, 2004).

[56] See Charles H. Silva, "The Literary Structure of Hosea 1–3," *BSac* 164 (2007): 181–97.

This section opens in Hosea 1:2–9 with Hosea being called to marry a "wife of whoredom" (זְנוּנִים אֵשֶׁת) and to have "children of whoredom" (זְנוּנִים וְיַלְדֵי). The reason for this is explicitly stated: because (כִּי) "the land" (i.e., Israel) has "committed great whoredom" (זָנֹה תִזְנֶה) against the Lord. Hosea's taking of the adulterous Gomer as his bride functions as a prophetic sign-act illustrating the actions of Israel in relation to God, showing via Hosea's marriage the infidelity of Israel to their Divine Husband.

This sign-act extends into the naming of the three children of their adultery: Jezreel (יִזְרְעֶאל), No Mercy (רֻחָמָה לֹא), and Not My People (עַמִּי לֹא). Each of these names presents a particular judgment against the adulterous people. Jezreel (Hos. 1:3–5) recollects a geographic location associated with violence and bloodshed.[57] The mention of the house of Jehu here is illuminating in that it was at Jezreel that Jehu slaughtered the entire household of Ahab and brought an end to the wicked Omride dynasty (2 Kings 9–10). The Lord will "punish the house of Jehu for the blood of Jezreel" (Hos. 1:4). There is some debate concerning the meaning of this pronouncement because Jehu was largely faithful (2 Kings 10:30). The most likely scenario is that the house of Jehu undergoes the same fate as that of Ahab and the Omride dynasty. As with the previous ruling family, Jehu's family and dynasty will be enthralled in spiritual adultery that will lead to their ultimate demise.[58] With this naming of Jezreel and its association with bloodshed, it is likewise important to note that the spiritual adultery of Israel is broader than idolatry. Rather, the infidelity of Israel is any breach of covenant; as Ray Ortlund rightly comments, "spiritual adultery entails more than religious offenses."[59]

The names "No Mercy" and "Not My People" aptly express the pouring out of covenant wrath. The root typically translated "mercy" (רחם) is most basically associated with love, with mercy seen as an agent of love—the name may as easily be translated as "not loved." This term is used in covenantal context where the Lord has mercy (love; רְחַם) on those whom he chooses (Ex. 33.19), and the promise of restoration is his "love and compassion" (וְרִחַמְךָ רַחֲמִים) on his people (Deut. 13:17), a love that is tied to the patriarchal promises (2 Kings

---

[57] Jezreel is the place where the Philistines defeated Israel (1 Sam. 29:1), Jezebel's cohort murdered Naboth (1 Kings 21:1), and the Omride dynasty was brought to destruction (2 Kings 9:24–10:11).
[58] See discussion by Duane A. Garrett, *Hosea, Joel*, NAC 19A (Nashville: Broadman & Holman, 1997), 55–57. It is notable that the narrative in 2 Kings 10 lends to this interpretation, where immediately after stating Jehu's faithfulness against the house of Ahab, he commits the "sins of Jeroboam," which form a refrain throughout the history of the northern kingdom from their first king until their final destruction in the exile of 722 BC (1 Kings 14:1–18).
[59] Ortlund, *God's Unfaithful Wife*, 52.

13:23). As such, now that they are "not loved," expressed by the sign-name of לֹא רֻחָמָה, a people who once received mercy and divine love now receive the curse due to infidelity. The same conclusion is reached with the final name, "Not My People" (לֹא עַמִּי), as "the covenant of 'my People, your God' is cancelled."[60] Richard Patterson remarks similarly, "God would no longer call this generation his people. Rather, because they had violated the basis of their covenant relation with the Lord, they would suffer his alienation."[61]

Based on these observations, the union of the covenant idea and the marriage metaphor is clearly established. This is made even more explicit in Hosea 2:2–9, where the *legal* nature of the passage has long been recognized as part of the covenant lawsuit/disputation; it even begins with the oft-discussed term רִיב.[62] The exact context of this particular "disputation" bridges together the legal discussion of breaching covenant with filial and relational perspectives focused on marriage and family. When the Lord joined in covenant with Israel, it was not *merely* a legal union but a relational one where he chose to join himself to Israel as his bride.[63] These two concepts should not be separated: the breach of the relational aspect is *legally* a breach of the marriage-covenant, and the breach of the legal violates the *relational love and union* between God and Israel.[64] As such, while not ignoring the legal aspect, Vos is correct to note that "sin is to Hosea want of conformity to the ideal of marriage-affection and loyalty."[65]

The covenantal nature of this filial breach is signified not merely by opening the dispute with legal language, but also by the use of covenant

---

[60] Ortlund, *God's Unfaithful Wife*, 53.
[61] Richard D. Patterson, *Hosea: An Exegetical Commentary* (Richardson, TX: Biblical Studies Press, 2003), 24; cf. also Marvin A. Sweeney, *The Twelve Prophets*, 2 vols., Berit Olam (Collegeville, MN: Liturgical Press, 2000), 1:21–22.
[62] Recall again the qualifications concerning this term mentioned above. For the legal aspect of Hos. 2, see Stephen C. Russell, "The Syntax of the Legal Metaphor in Hosea 2:4," *JSS* 61.2 (2016): 389–402. It is significant that the term is used *again* in Hos. 4:4, in a passage similar to the covenant lawsuit genre. Thus, while it is true that the use of רִיב in Hos. 2:2 does not immediately reflect the lawsuit genre, the context with Hos. 4 ties the divorce proceedings of Hos. 1–3 closely together with the more legal depiction of the רִיב in Hos. 4:1–3, 4. Again the flexibility of רִיב and the use of particular *Gattungen* must be emphasized. The passage of Hos. 4:1–3 may be more accurately described as an introduction to the following material in 4:4–14, rather than adhering to a strict concept of the covenant lawsuit genre; however, this must *not* diminish both the legal and covenantal nature of this passage, as it clearly indicts Israel for breaching the covenant (see comments by Garrett, *Hosea–Joel*, 109; John L. Mackay, *Hosea* [Fearn, Ross-shire, UK: Mentor, 2012], 126–35). Even Andersen and Freedman, after stating that this passage is "a general preface rather than a fragment of a lawsuit between Yahweh and Israel," continue to say that "the speech is identified as the indictment in a lawsuit (cf. Mic. 6:1–8)" (Francis I. Andersen and David Noel Freedman, *Hosea: A New Translation with Introduction and Commentary*, AB 24 [New Haven, CT: Yale University Press, 1980], 331–32).
[63] Sonship language is also used as part of this metaphor, where Israel is God's son. This was part of Isa. 1:2, where the covenant lawsuit was against the Lord's unfaithful *son*. Note as well that in Exodus Israel is called God's *son* (Ex. 4:23). This is likewise in the context of Hos. 1, where Hosea not merely takes on a wife of whoredom but has *children of whoredom* as well.
[64] This concept is derived from Vos in his discussion on the nature of Hosea's covenant idea; he highlights the *affectionate* aspect of the relation with "divine-marriage-love" granted in a "spiritualized union" (Vos, *Biblical Theology*, 260–61). Vos also continues to speak of the *legal* aspect (262–63).
[65] Vos, *Biblical Theology*, 276.

terminology that reflects the curses from Deuteronomy 28. For one specific example, Ryan Hanley convincingly argues that the "stripping bare"
(אַפְשִׁיטֶנָּה עֲרֻמָּה) of the faithless wife is derived from the curse in Deuteronomy 28:48: they will be brought into a state of "nakedness" (עֵירֹם) due to their
infidelity.[66] The adulterous bride will seek after grain, wine, and oil, but due
to the curse these things will be taken away, such that she will be in a state of
naked desolation (Deut. 28:48, 51).[67] With this overarching introduction to the
disputation in Hosea 2:2–9, the category for the judgment described therein
is one of covenant curse and judgment, where the adulterous bride Israel
receives the curse of shameful nakedness for her infidelity (cf. Gen. 3:7–10).[68]

Finally, in Hosea 3:1–5 the *resolution* of the divorce proceedings and
restoration of the adulterous bride is observed.[69] As in chapter 1, Hosea is
again charged to perform a prophetic sign-act that represents the Lord's love
for Israel. This time, however, it is for Hosea to love (אָהַב) Gomer[70] as the
Lord has loved Israel, *even in light of their spiritual adultery* (Hos. 3:1). This
particular act expresses one necessary element to the resolution of adulterous
infidelity: it rests *not* on the deeds of the adulterous bride but rather on the
loving actions of the husband. Even though there will be a time of punishment (Hos. 3:4), God promises a restoration of the covenantal communion
bond *after* (אַחַר) the days of judgment.

Jeremiah 2

Jeremiah 2 may be treated more briefly than Hosea 1–3, since it presents
much of the same material. Jeremiah may even be dependent on Hosea for
his message as he reapplies the adulterous infidelity Hosea observed in Israel

---

[66] Ryan C. Hanley, "The Background and Purpose of Stripping the Adulteress in Hosea 2," *JETS* 60.1 (2017): 89–103.
[67] Hanley, "Background," 100.
[68] Redemption in the biblical narrative is often depicted with the idiom of *clothing*, which is observed in the earliest depiction of redemption in Gen. 3, where in response to the nakedness of the fall, the Lord provides redemptive garments for Adam and Eve. Now, in judgment, those redemptive garments are taken away and the unfaithful bride is stripped bare. Kline remarks that the "nakedness" of the fall is a sign of the loss of the image of original righteousness in the *imago Dei* (see Meredith G. Kline, *Kingdom Prologue: Genesis Foundations for a Covenantal Worldview* [Eugene, OR: Wipf & Stock, 2006], 130–50; Kline, *Images of the Spirit* [Eugene, OR: Wipf & Stock, 1980], 32). The loss of *redemptive clothing* here expresses the same thing: an image of lost blessing and righteous-ness and the application of the curse. For more on clothing as an image metaphor and its redemptive purposes, see William Wilder, "Illumination and Investiture: The Royal Significance of the Tree of Wisdom in Genesis 3," *WTJ* 68.1 (2006): 51–69, esp. 53. Clothing signifies reward and covenant blessing, while its loss images covenant curs-ing. See similar comments in G. K. Beale, *A New Testament Biblical Theology: The Unfolding of the Old Testament in the New* (Grand Rapids, MI: Baker Academic, 2011), 41.
[69] This restoration has been alluded to all along in Hosea (1:10–11; 2:14–23).
[70] The identity of this "woman" (3:1) is debated. However, that there is no other woman introduced, and that the situation is a resolution to the problems of Hos. 1 would seem to indicate that the woman is Gomer. It must be noted, however, that the Hebrew simply mentions a "woman" (אִשָּׁה) and is ambiguous (see discussion in Garrett, *Hosea–Joel*, 97–100).

to the southern kingdom of Judah.[71] Instead of digging into the particulars of the passage, I will simply present some observations here in relation to the conclusions reached by Dylan Johnson and the relation to the covenant lawsuit/disputation.

Jeremiah 2–3 (esp. 2:4–13) has long been part of the covenant lawsuit/disputation discussion.[72] However, as Johnson claims, the passage has remarkable similarity to divorce proceedings, using vocabulary similar to Hosea 1 and other marriage/divorce passages.[73] Thus, the present analysis stands in agreement with Johnson's conclusion on Jeremiah 3, that "Yahweh's abandonment of Israel was a husband's divorce from his wife."[74] However, it stands in contrast to Johnson's entailed conclusion that "[t]his metaphor may have drawn on the theme of covenant as a marriage contract, but very little within Jeremiah 2–3 points to this theme and far too much emphasis has been placed on all relationships between Israel and Yahweh as defined through the model of covenant."[75] Instead, the marriage contract in the OT has always been based on the model of covenant, where the relation between man and wife as ectype relates to the covenant relation between God and man. Covenant is the more basic category for the relation, after which marriage is derived and imaged. Therefore, as the Lord divorces his bride Israel, it expresses in conclusive terms that the covenant made between the two has been breached by Israel's adulterous infidelity to her husband and covenant King. As mentioned above, the legal and the relational are never opposed to each other in the covenantal bond between the Lord and his people, but rather operate simultaneously and mutually inform each other.

These comments on the nature of marriage and covenant bring to the fore a key concept in the prophetic treatment of sin where sin is adulterous infidelity to the Lord. As part of this relation, the affections of members of the covenant are brought to mind. It is out of love for God that people pursue faithfulness; it is out of hatred toward God and the love of sin that they breach the covenant in unfaithfulness. As such, covenant faithfulness is not simply mechanical obedience to legal terms (although obedience is always

---

[71] Douglas Stephen Abel, "The Marriage Metaphor in Hosea 4 and Jeremiah 2: How Prophetic Speech 'Kills Two Birds with One Stone,' " *Proceedings* 29 (2009): 15–27.

[72] Huffmon, "Covenant Lawsuit," 287–88; cf. also J. A. Thompson, *The Book of Jeremiah*, NICOT (Grand Rapids, MI: Eerdmans, 1980), 159–60.

[73] Johnson, "Prophetic Lawsuit of Jeremiah 2–3," 231–35.

[74] Johnson, "Prophetic Lawsuit," 240.

[75] Johnson, "Prophetic Lawsuit," 240.

required) but is also the love *for* the King of the covenant and affection for the God who saves. Part of covenant faithfulness is the proper relation between covenant partners, and unfaithfulness is adultery. Moreover, it is the love *of* the King that Hosea 3:1–5 sees as the ultimate hope for the restoration of the bond ruptured by the sin of adulterous infidelity.

III. Sin and the Day of the Lord

Another feature that gains prominence in the prophetic treatment of sin is judgment on the day of the Lord.[76] While space does not allow a full exposition of this concept, a few comments are in order. The exact phrase "day of the LORD" (יוֹם יְהוָה) occurs sixteen times in the Prophets,[77] with copious amounts of time and effort spent on its analysis.[78] While there is extensive discussion of this theme, there is no clear consensus as to the exact nature of the day of the Lord. Scholars have made various arguments for the origins of the day of the Lord concept in the OT with cultic ritual,[79] holy war traditions,[80] theophany,[81] and covenant[82] as the main ones. Due to dissatisfaction with

[76] The Prophets contain the most clear expressions concerning the day of the Lord. However, there are other places in the OT where a similar concept is found; as in Gen. 3:8, where YHWH comes in the "Spirit of the Day" to judge Adam for his breach of covenant (see Kline, *Images of the Spirit*, 97–115).

[77] Isaiah 13:6, 9; Ezek. 13:5; Joel 1:15; 2:1, 11, 31; 3:14; Amos 5:18 (2x), 20; Obad. 15; Zeph. 1:7, 14 (2x); Mal. 4:5. This is only the *explicit* use of the phrase; the concept is used numerous other times in a manner that must be deduced from the context.

[78] To list but a few, see, e.g., K. J. Cathcart, "Day of Yahweh," in *The Anchor Bible Dictionary*, ed. David N. Freedman, 6 vols. (York: Doubleday, 1992), 2:84–85; Ladislav Cerny, *The Day of YHWH and Some Relevant Problems* (Prague: Karlovy University, 1948); A. Joseph Everson, "The Day of Yahweh," *JBL* 93 (1974): 329–37; Yair Hoffmann, "The Day of the LORD as a Concept and a Term in the Prophetic Literature," *ZAW* 93.1 (1981): 37–50; Ralph W. Klein, "The Day of the LORD," *Concordia Theological Monthly* 39 (1968): 517–25; Richard L. Mayhue, "The Prophet's Watchword: The Day of the LORD," *Grace Theological Journal* 6.2 (1985): 231–46; Michael S. Moore, "Yahweh's Day," *Restoration Quarterly* 29.4 (1987): 193–208; James D. Nogalski, "The Day(s) of YHWH in the Book of the Twelve," in *Thematic Threads in the Book of the Twelve*, ed. Paul L. Redditt and Aaron Schart (Berlin: Walter de Gruyter, 2003), 192–213; J. M. P. Smith, "The Day of Yahweh," *American Journal of Theology* 4.5 (1901): 505–33; Gerhard von Rad, *Holy War in Ancient Israel*, trans. Marva J. Dawn (Grand Rapids, MI: Eerdmans, 1991); von Rad, "The Origin of the Concept of the Day of Yahweh," *JSS* 4 (1959): 97–108; von Rad, *Old Testament Theology*, vol. 2, trans. D. M. G. Stalker (New York: Harper, 1965), 119–25; von Rad, *The Message of the Prophets* (New York: Harper, 1965), 95–99; Meir Weiss, "The Origin of the Day of the LORD—Reconsidered," *HUCA* 37 (1966): 29–62.

[79] This is Mowinckle's position; see Sigmund Mowinckle, *He That Cometh* (Nashville: Abingdon, 1956); Mowinckle, "Jahves Dag," *Nederlands Theologisch Tijdschrift* 59 (1958): 1–56.

[80] Gerhard von Rad and those who follow him are the main proponents of this view (see von Rad, "Day of Yahweh," 103; von Rad, *Old Testament Theology*, 119–25). Von Rad's thesis has been further developed by Jean-Georges Heintz to tie the motif of the "Day of YHWH" not only with the OT but with a broader ancient Near Eastern context focused on the Akkadian phrase *ūmūšū gerbū*, meaning "his days are near," and tying it together with an ancient Near Eastern battle cry (Jean-Georges Heintz, "Oracles and Prophetiques et 'guerre sainte' selon les archives royales de Mari et l'Ancient Testament," in *Congress Volume: Rome 1968*, VTSup 17 [Leiden, Netherlands: Brill, 1969]: 112–38; Heintz, "Aux origines d'une expression biblique: *ūmūšū gerbū* in A R M 10/6, 8?," *VT* 21.5 [Dec 1971]: 528–40).

[81] Cerny, *Day of YHWH*; Weiss, "Origin of the Day of the LORD"; Jörg Jeremias, *Theophanie* (Neukirchen, Germany: Neukirchener Verlag, 1965).

[82] F. C. Fensham, "A Possible Origin of the Concept of the Day of the LORD," in *Biblical Essays: Die Ou Testamentiese Werkgemeenskap in Suid-Afrika 9th Congress* (Potchefstroom: Rege Pers Beperk, 1966), 90–97. This view is particularly important for Zephaniah in his work to tie together the concept of the day of the Lord with the covenant via sacrifice language in Zeph. 1:7. This view is shared by O. Palmer Robertson, *The Books of Nahum, Habakkuk, and Zephaniah*, NICOT (Grand Rapids, MI: Eerdmans, 1990), 268. Zephaniah's prophecy (esp. ch. 1) is perhaps more

these narrow approaches, others have opted for more mediating positions. Frank Cross, for example, joins together the cultic and holy war traditions, anchoring them in the divine warrior and conquest-exodus motifs, conclud- ing that "the day of Yahweh is the day of victory in holy warfare; it is also the day of Yahweh's festival."[83] H. W. Wolff expounds on Cross by taking his view a step further and arguing for a joined theophanic, cultic, and warfare background.[84] However, Wolff struggles to accept the reality of both blessing and curse occurring together at the same time with יוֹם יְהוָה. He settles the issue with a complex prehistory, where the concept of the day of the Lord among the prophets gradually shifted from one against Israel's enemies to judgment against Israel itself.[85]

It is perhaps better to seek a more basic understanding of the day of the Lord than is typically articulated among scholars. Various passages present, in one way or another, all the facets mentioned above. The Lord's "day" is when he "rouses himself" from his temple (Hab. 2:20; Zeph. 1:7), when he comes as the divine warrior (Isa. 13:6), when he comes to administer covenant curses (Isa. 1–2) or blessings (Zeph. 3:14–20), and the day when he comes in theophanic glory (Zeph. 1:15; Joel 2:1–2). As such, the day of the Lord is best described as the day of the Lord's coming, with all the various other portraits as facets detailing the nature of that coming. Willem VanGemeren is on the right track when he states, "The day of the Lord signifies first and foremost Yahweh's intrusion into human affairs. His coming (theophany) is portrayed in the conceptual imagery of the Warrior, Judge, and the Great King."[86]

Joining this discussion with the prophetic portrait of sin, the day of the Lord is the day when the King of the covenant comes to deal with those who have breached that covenant by sinning. It is this realization that ties together the historical images of the day of the Lord as he comes against Israel and Judah to administer the covenant curse, with the eschatological image of the Lord coming in finality to deal with all sinners. This approach of God in the Prophets coming against Israel or Judah has two main two facets. First, it is a type to the eschatological antitype where the Lord will deal with sin at the end

---

focused on the day of the Lord theme than any other, with various references to the "day" totaling 29 in the space of 53 verses. Greg King is therefore correct to note that "every major section of [Zephaniah] and even every unit should be linked to the day of the Lord" (see Greg King, "The Day of the LORD in Zephaniah," *BSac* 152:605 [1995], 17).
[83] Frank M. Cross, *Canaanite Myth and Hebrew Epic* (Cambridge, MA: Harvard University Press, 1997), 111.
[84] H. W. Wolff, *Joel and Amos*, Hermeneia (Philadelphia: Fortress, 1977), 33–34.
[85] Wolff, *Joel and Amos*, 33–34. This historical progression of the day of the Lord concept is common among scholars.
[86] Willem VanGemeren, *Interpreting the Prophetic Word: An Introduction to the Prophetic Literature of the Old Testament* (Grand Rapids, MI: Zondervan, 2010), 174.

of the ages. As a type, the day of the Lord that Judah and Israel experience in history looks forward to a greater, climactic "day" at the end of days. And second, the day of the Lord is an intrusion of eschatological judgment into history when God comes to pour out his wrath upon sinful Israel/Judah. It is not merely that the eschatological coming of the Lord bears a semblance to those in previous history; rather, the historical comings of the Lord in judgment *bear the substance* of the eschaton. Types are not empty shells until their antitypes come to illustrate their true nature; rather, they contain the substance of their antitypes from their very outset.

Because of this, the prophetic depictions of the day of the Lord pertain *both* to their age *and* to the age to come.[87] At times, the particulars of this relation may be debated or difficult to ascertain, but it is nonetheless the case that the prophets' dealing with sin often relates to both the near history of the people of Israel and the future dealings of God with all sinners in general. Many passages illustrate this relation, but one example draws this out. Zephaniah 1 is focused on the day of the Lord theme that forms the core message of verses 7–18. The message in this chapter, however, merges together the particular, historical judgment to come against Judah for their breach of covenant (vv. 7–16) with the *universal* judgment of God at the end of days (vv. 2–3, 17–18). There is an inclusio of universal judgment between verses 17–18 and verses 2–3, where the judgment on "all the inhabitants of the earth" (כָּל יֹשְׁבֵי הָאָרֶץ) (v. 18) is set within the terms of the cataclysmic events of the flood and de-creational reversal of Genesis 1 (Zeph. 1:2–3; cf. 2 Pet. 3:1–13).[88] Zephaniah then particularizes that judgment upon the nation of Judah in 1:4–6, a judgment which then becomes the focus from verses 7–16. As such, for Zephaniah there is a conceptual union between the day of the Lord poured out against Judah in history and the final day of the Lord at the culmination of history. Separating these two from each other obfuscates the prophetic image of God's judgment against sin on the "day" of his coming.

---

[87] This stands against the portrait of many scholars today that the prophets must have been of *their* time only, and not of the end times. A good example of this is the article by Marvin Sweeney, "Zephaniah: A Prophet of His Time—Not the End Time!" *Biblical Research* 26.6 (2004): 34–40, 43.

[88] For this relation between Zeph. 1:2–3 and Gen. 1 and 6, see Michael de Roche, "Zephaniah I.2–3: The 'Sweeping' of Creation," *VT* 30.1 (1980): 104–109; David A. R. Clark, "Reversing Genesis: A Theological Reading of Creation Undone in Zephaniah," *ExpTim* 123.4 (2012): 166–70; James D. Nogalski, "Zephaniah's Use of Genesis 1–11," *HBAI* 2.2 (2013): 351–72; Nicholas R. Werse, "Realigning the Cosmos: The Intertextual Image of Judgment and Restoration in Zephaniah," *JSOT* 45.1 (2020): 111–27; David Melvin, "Making All Things New (Again): Zephaniah's Eschatological Vision of Return to Primeval Time," in *Chaos and Creation: A Reconsideration of Hermann Gunkel's Chaoskampf Hypothesis*, ed. J. Scurlock and R. H. Beal (Winona Lake, IN: Eisenbrauns, 2013): 269–81. It is also mentioned by numerous commentators, see, e.g., Adele Berlin, *Zephaniah: A New Translation with Introduction and Commentary*, AB 25a (New York: Doubleday, 1994), 13–14.

In sum, the day of the Lord is the time when God comes in his theophanic glory to deal with sin as well as to save those who turn to him in faith and repentance. This day of the Lord theme is a key element of the prophetic message of sin as the prophets proclaim the day of the Lord's judgment against covenant breakers. Moreover, this "day" contains within it an eschatological notion whereby sin will be judged not merely in the historical dealings with Israel and Judah climaxing in the exile, but also with God's eschatological judgment at the end of days, the final day of the Lord. Both the sin of Israel *and* the sin of all mankind will be dealt with on the day of the Lord.

IV. Particular Sins in the Prophets

In order to examine the manifold nature of the Prophetic Books and their treatment(s) of sin, I have organized the preceding material in three broad categories: (1) sin as a breach of the covenant; (2) sin as adulterous infidelity; and (3) sin and the day of the Lord. However, a few brief comments about particular sins that run through prophetic literature are also requisite. While many sins could be listed in the Prophets, the following discussion will examine idolatry, pride, and injustice.

IDOLATRY

One would be hard pressed to find a prophet that did not, in one way or another, address the sin of idolatry among the people of Israel. Idolatry is far more than simply the worship of false gods (although it certainly includes that); it is anything that one *reveres* and rests upon for "ultimate security" that is not the Lord.[89] This concept of idolatry contains both of the main features of breaching the covenant outlined above. Idolatry as worshiping an image or a false God is explicitly included as a breach of the covenant (Ex. 20:3, 4–6). However, in the marriage metaphor, the covenant is likewise breached by misplaced affections. God is jealous for his own worship and glory, and "to worship an image of any part of creation is to take away from the incomparable glory of God."[90]

Among the prophets, Isaiah is particularly focused on idolatry, with an extensive section in Isaiah 41–48 that presents a remarkable idol polemic to

---

[89] This identification of idolatry is made by G. K. Beale, *We Become What We Worship: A Biblical Theology of Idolatry* (Downers Grove, IL: IVP Academic, 2008), 17. In this definition, Beale is building on Luther, as cited in B. S. Rosner, "Idolatry," in *New Dictionary of Biblical Theology*, ed. T. D. Alexander and B. S. Rosner (Downers Grove, IL: IVP Academic, 2000), 571. He is likewise extensively drawing on Christopher Wright, *The Mission of God* (Downers Grove, IL: InterVarsity Press, 2006), 187–88.
[90] Beale, *We Become What We Worship*, 19.

express the ultimate futility of idols and the humiliation of all who trust in them. In these chapters, the Lord is the one who "is," and there is no other like him (Isa. 44:6–8; 45:5, 18; 46:5, 9; 48:12, 17). In contrast to the God who "is," idols are "vain nothings" that are merely the work of human hands, which cannot see, hear, or know (Isa. 44:9–20; cf. Pss. 115:4–7; 135:15–18). In exchanging the worship of the God who *is* for these idols of man's own making, the worshipers become like them: blind, deaf, and unable to know (Isa. 44:9, 18; cf. Isa. 6:9–10). As G. K. Beale states, the judgment upon idolaters is that they become like what they worship: "we resemble what we revere, either for ruin or restoration."[91] This misplaced affection and worship of idols leads to the humiliation of judgment, as all who "trust in carved idols" are "utterly put to shame" (Isa. 42:17).

PRIDE AND THE HUMBLING OF THE PROUD

One of the most common idols among mankind is the idol of *self*. Mankind, in sin, is self-exalting and self-exulting, as people seek to exalt their own name over that of the Lord. This is again a key message of Isaiah, where the refrain of the God who "is" and there is no other (וְאֵין עוֹד אֱנִי יְהוָה), mentioned above, is taken upon the self-exalting lips of Babylon. Babylon, rather than submitting to the God who "is," instead is one who says in his heart, " 'I am, and there is none beside me' " (אֲנִי וְאַפְסִי עוֹד) (Isa. 47:8, 10). Proud Assyria takes up this same line in Zephaniah 2:13–15. Self-exalting pride is an essential attribute of man's idolatry and sin.

Beyond this connection between pride and idolatry in Isaiah 44–48, pride is itself explicitly condemned by the prophets on multiple occasions. In Isaiah 2:12, the day of the Lord is proclaimed "against all the proud and lofty" (עַל כָּל גֵּאֶה וָרָם) and "against all the lifted up" (וְעַל כָּל נִשָּׂא). In other words, sin may itself be categorized broadly as pride.[92] Any rebellion against God is man's self-exaltation in pride, man seeking to place himself in a position in which only God belongs. In fact, the first sin in the garden is pride, as Adam sought the exaltation of divine likeness *without submission* to the divine command.[93] That is, he sought to exalt himself without humbling himself in obedience before the God of heaven, therefore seeking

---

[91] Beale, *We Become What We Worship*, 49.
[92] The prophet Hosea likewise presents this in Hos. 5:5; 7:10, where the sin of Israel is treated under the heading of pride.
[93] This conclusion fits well with the description of Adam and the fall in Ezek. 28, where Adam is cast from Mount Eden (Ezek. 28:16) because "your heart was proud" (גָּבַהּ לִבְּךָ).

to make himself God.[94] As Vos states, "Pride is in its essence a form of self-deification."[95]

The consequence of this self-exalting sin is also dealt with in the Prophets: those who pridefully exalt themselves in sin will be brought low in judgment. Isaiah 2:17 is clear on this when, on the day of the Lord, "the haughtiness [גַּבְהוּת] of man shall be humbled [שָׁחַח], and the lofty pride [רוּם אֲנָשִׁים] of men shall be brought low [שָׁפֵל], and the LORD alone will be exalted in that day."[96] The day of the Lord, briefly described above, presents an inversion of destinies. The pridefully self-exalting who make themselves great on the day of the Lord will be "brought low" in judgment, but the humble and lowly who "seek the LORD" will be exalted (Zeph. 2:1–3; 3:9–20). The statement of Jesus in Matthew 23:12 is a good summary of the prophetic treatment of sin as pride: "those who exalt themselves will be humbled, but those who humble themselves will be exalted" (NIV).[97]

INJUSTICE IN THE THEOCRACY

A final feature of sin in the Prophets is the sin of injustice, or the maltreatment of one's neighbor broadly described as social sin. Injustice in the Prophets is a broad concept that extends from murder (Ezek. 18:10) to a lack of care for orphans and widows (Ezek. 18:12) to financial matters (Ezek. 18:13) and just about everything in between.[98]

However, one must take care in the simple one-to-one application of the prophetic treatment of social sin to modern socioeconomic problems and proposed solutions.[99] Too often, the modern use of the prophetic proclamation against

---

[94] While focusing on the sin of idolatry in the fall, Beale likewise moves in this direction when he states concerning the fall that, "Adam's allegiance shifted from God to himself and probably also to Satan" (133). Adam, like Babylon, sought God-likeness through self-exaltation, to "become like God" in a way "that was not good; indeed it was blasphemous" (134). Beale likewise roots this in the notion of blurring the Creator-creature distinction as man seeks to exalt himself to God-like states, quoting Christopher Wright, that, "Therein lies the root of all other forms of idolatry: we deify our own capacities, and thereby make gods of ourselves and our choices and all their implications" (Wright, *Mission of God*, 164, quoted in Beale, *We Become What We Worship*, 135).
[95] Vos, *Biblical Theology*, 281.
[96] Cf. also Isa. 2:9, 11; 5:15; 10:33; 13:11; 25:11–12; 26:5; 29:4; Ezek. 17:24; 21:26.
[97] This is also the subject of my own doctoral work on Zephaniah, in which I argue that his conception of the day of the Lord via inner-biblical interpretation presents a humbling of the proud but an exaltation of the humble (William M. Wood, "'I Will Remove Your Proudly Exultant Ones:' A Study of Inner-Biblical Interpretation in Zephaniah" [PhD diss., Westminster Theological Seminary, 2021]).
[98] I have chosen to use Ezek. 18 here because it extensively treats social sins and regularly uses the vocabulary of "justice" between people (Ezek. 18:8–9). However, it must be readily observed that the sins mentioned here are broader than what is typically seen as "social sin" today, as they include the sin of false worship in Judah's society (Ezek. 18:6). It must likewise be admitted that the references to various social sins in the Prophets is quite expansive.
[99] The theocratic nature of Israel's society must be recalled in every discussion of social sin and application today. Since we no longer inhabit a theocratic state, there will *always* be a level of disconnect in the application from the prophet in his time to the preacher in ours. Without this appreciation, improper application will run rampant in the church.

social sin is divorced from its inherently *religious and theocentric core*. The justice that the prophets support is one established by God (i.e., a divine justice) and revealed in the covenant order made with his people. Similarly, the *injustice* that the prophets condemn is one that is condemned by the revealed order of God in his covenant. While this should be clear by taking into account the essential task of the prophets as covenant mediators, the treatment of social sin in Ezekiel 18 makes this explicit.[100] Ezekiel 18:5–9 presents the life of the righteous man who is just in his dealings with his fellow man, such that it is said of him that he "turns his hand from iniquity, he deals true justice between man and man" (מֵעָוֶל יָשִׁיב יָדוֹ מִשְׁפַּט אֱמֶת יַעֲשֶׂה בֵּין אִישׁ לְאִישׁ) (v. 8). This dealing of "true justice" among people is stated in terms of *faithfulness to YHWH and his covenant* (v. 9). The just one is one who walks in the Lord's statutes (בְּחֻקּוֹתַי יְהַלֵּךְ), guards the Lord's justice in faithfulness (וּמִשְׁפָּטַי שָׁמַר לַעֲשׂוֹת אֱמֶת), and thereby gains the promised blessing of the covenant as "he will surely live" (הוּא חָיֹה יִחְיֶה). Conversely, the destiny of the unjust murderer and oppressor (vv. 10–12) is that the covenant curse of death is applied in how he will "surely die" (מוֹת יוּמָת) because of his "abominations" (הַתּוֹעֵבוֹת) (v. 13).[101] In light of this, injustice against one's neighbor is part of the overarching category of breaching the covenant. According to the prophets, social sin is *religious* in its core.

Once again Vos is helpful in his treatment of social sin. In discussing the essentially religious core of social sin, he highlights that this sin is first and foremost an afront to God:

> [I]njustice is sin against God, and no consequence, however deplorable from the manward point of view, could equal the terrible significance of the religious fact to the prophetic consciousness. . . . what shocks and excites the prophets' resentment is the bearing of the wicked conduct upon Jehovah and His rights.[102]

Because social sin is first and foremost against God and has an essentially religious core, man is in need of a divine and religious remedy. Again, Ezekiel 18

---

[100] The proximity of features in this passage to the terms of the covenant are so close that Iain Duguid is willing to describe the required features outlined in Ezek. 18 as "a kind of miniature ten commandments" (Iain M. Duguid, *Ezekiel*, NIVAC [Grand Rapids, MI: Zondervan, 1999], 235). Similar connections are likewise made by Joseph Blenkinsopp, *Ezekiel*, Interpretation (Louisville: John Knox, 1990), 81–84.

[101] While the term תּוֹעֵבָה is more broad than simply abominations to God, it is regularly used in the Pentateuch to express things that are breaches of covenant as they are abominable to the Lord. This connection is especially important in light of the "statutes" and "justice" mentioned in Ezek. 18:8–9 that are likewise used as part of obedience to the covenant. All three of these terms are often used together (see, e.g., Lev. 18:26–27). Moreover, every occurrence of "these abominations" found in Ezek. 18:13 is used in context to express a breach of covenant that leads to death, as the one who does them is "cut off" from the people of God (Lev. 18:26, 29; Deut. 12; 2 Kings 21:11; Jer. 7:10; Ezek. 18:13; Ezra 9:14).

[102] Vos, *Biblical Theology*, 275.

is clear on this. Anyone who turns from righteousness and pursues wickedness in social sin merits the curse of death (Ezek. 18:13, 24). The only hope for remedy to social sin is to repent and turn to the Lord. As the prophet proclaims, "repent; namely, repent from all of your transgressions, lest iniquity becomes for you a stumbling block" (שׁוּבוּ וְהָשִׁיבוּ מִכָּל פִּשְׁעֵיכֶם וְלֹא־יִהְיֶה לָכֶם לְמִכְשׁוֹל עָוֹן) (Ezek. 18:30, my translation). This repentance is a divinely enabled turn from the abominations of man, and the Lord's granting of a "new heart and a new spirit" (לֵב חָדָשׁ וְרוּחַ חֲדָשָׁה) (Ezek. 18:31) to those who turn to him in faith.

Herein lies one of the great scandals of modern social preaching: that in examining social sin, they stop at the social offense rather than the more basic offense against God. As a result, in presenting the remedy they fall short of man's true need to repent of sin and turn to the God of heaven. Social activity, regardless of how positive it may be for society, has no power to resolve the root issues of social sin. Social sin, like all sin, is a breach of covenant that requires Spirit-wrought repentance as its remedy. Vos is again helpful in his treatment of modern social preachers and the treatment of social sin:

> All this is of importance, because it marks a great difference between the social image of the prophets, and much that passes as social preaching nowadays. To the prophet it is the *sinfulness* of the wrong social conduct, to the modern social preacher it is too often the injuriousness to the social organism, that stands in the foreground. The prophets view the facts in their relation to God, as measured by the standards of absolute ethics and religion; the modern sociological enthusiast views them mainly, if not exclusively, in their bearing upon the welfare of man. What the prophets feature is *the religious in the social*; what many at the present time proclaim is the social devoid of or indifferent to the religious.[103]

So long as the root offense of social sin is not found in its afront to the holiness and majesty of the God of heaven as a breach of his covenant and meriting his divine wrath, neither the gravity of its sinfulness nor the remedy for sinful man will be grasped.

Conclusion

The definition of sin provided by Westminster Larger Catechism Q&A 24 is that it is "any want of conformity unto, or transgression of, any law of God given as a rule to the reasonable creature." This discussion on sin in the

[103] Vos, *Biblical Theology*, 276, emphasis added.

Prophets sees that terse summary definition of sin as being reflected in the Prophets under the auspices of covenant. For the prophets, the "transgression" of sin is a transgression against the covenant made between the Lord and his people. This was the subject of the first section on the covenant disputation or "lawsuit," where we saw a passage like Isaiah 1 indict Israel for their breach of faith. This covenant disputation was then cast in the light of the marriage metaphor through passages like Hosea 1–3 and Jeremiah 2 which add to the legal emphasis of Isaiah 1 a relational and affectional sense. According to the prophets, sin is not merely a breach of God's law; it is also adulterous infidelity to their covenant King and Husband. Sin includes the affections of the sinner, as love for God is exchanged for a love of sin or something other than God. The third section considered the prophetic treatment of the day of the Lord as the day of his visitation. It is the day when he comes to deal with sin and sinners as well as to redeem the faithful who repent of sin and turn to him—a day that is both historical, typological, and intrusionary, as well as eschatological. Finally, brief notes were made on three prominent categories of sin in the Prophets being idolatry, pride, and injustice—all of which exist under the rubric of a breach of covenant. Sin, according to the prophets, is any want of conformity to or breach of the covenant—which is the established means by which the Lord chose both to reveal his law to man and to relate to his creatures (WCF 7.1).

13

"If You, Then, Who Are Evil"

SIN IN THE SYNOPTIC GOSPELS AND ACTS

Douglas Sean O'Donnell

According to the scriptural testimony of Matthew, Mark, and Luke, it is clear that there is a sin problem that Jesus has come to solve. But how serious is the problem? Are humans "ruined sinners," to use Philip Bliss's less than blissful designation for the Calvinistic doctrine of total depravity? Or, to use the language of the sixteenth-century Dutch Calvinists, has Adam's original sin spread through the whole human race in such a way that the whole human nature, from the moment of conception, is infected with an inherited depravity that produces in humanity every sort of sin, and that this corrupted condition is so vile and enormous in God's sight that it is enough to condemn the human race?[1] In this article I will demonstrate that the Synoptic Gospels and Acts answer that question in the affirmative. While the Evangelists do not cover in equal depth or theological precision the Calvinistic perspective as defined above,[2] I will show how the teachings of both Jesus and the apostles explain and illustrate humanity's nature as "so poisoned" and "so corrupt" that humans are both "inclined toward all evil" and "totally unable to do any good" without help from God.[3]

---

[1] The language above is either directly from, or a slight paraphrase of, the Belgic Confession, Article 15.

[2] To use WSC language (A18), the Synoptics and Acts speak on "all actual transgressions which proceed from it [original sin]," but are silent on "the guilt of Adam's first sin, the want of original righteous, and the corruption of our whole nature." Put differently, the Evangelists give ample evidence of the fruit of inherited depravity, while other NT writers (esp. John and Paul) explain the root (federal representation in Adam) and condition (spiritual deadness, inability).

[3] See the Heidelberg Catechism, Q&A 7 and 8. By "any good" is meant "what indeed is truly good, such as saving faith in the first place" (*The Remonstrance*, article 3).

354 SIN AND DEPRAVITY IN THE BIBLE

The Whole Human Race

Matthew, Mark, and Luke do not directly answer the questions posed above in propositional language or with sermonic prose. Rather, they show in narrative form, and in the discourses and discussions found within, their theological perspectives. For example, in answering the question, "Has Adam's original sin spread through the whole human race?" the Evangelists will not clearly state, as Paul does, "Just as sin came into the world through one man, and death through sin, and so death spread to all men because all sinned" (Rom. 5:12). However, they will show, through their use of language for "sin" and illustrations of its effects, that they hold the same truth, namely, that "all the posterity of Adam, Christ only excepted, have derived corruption from their original parent."[4]

THE CURSE IS FOUND

While Adam is mentioned only twice (and not in reference to his sin),[5] the authors of the Synoptics and Acts describe the world into which sinless Jesus enters as being spiritually dark and blind, under the sway of Satan, demon-infested, filled with disease and death, plagued with poverty, famine, wars, broken relationships, and the upheaval of creation, and thus in need of a savior from sin (Matt. 1:21).[6]

The first fifty-seven verses of the Gospel of Mark paint a vivid picture of fallen humanity, a snapshot of the situation. Satan exists (Mark 1:13), and his influence is experienced everywhere, as Jesus encounters sickness ("various

---

[4] Article 2 of the Third and Fourth Heads of Doctrine, the Canons of Dort.

[5] In Luke's genealogy, Jesus is called "the son of Adam" (Luke 3:38). In Acts 17:26, Paul proclaims that God "made from one man every nation of mankind."

[6] The verb ἁμαρτάνω appears 43x in the NT, but only in three contexts in the Synoptics: Jesus's instruction to Peter on the nature of forgiveness ("If your brother sins against you"; Matt. 18:15); Judas's admission ("I have sinned by betraying innocent blood"; 27:4); and the parable of the prodigal son ("Father, I have sinned"; Luke 15:18). The noun ἁμάρτημα appears four times in the NT, twice in Paul (Rom. 3:25; 1 Cor. 6:18) and twice in Mark 3:28–29, where Jesus speaks of "an eternal sin" (v. 29) that is contrasted with "all sins," the latter of which "will be forgiven" (v. 28). A second noun, ἁμαρτία, which appears 173x in the NT, is found 7x in Matthew, 6x in Mark, 11x in Luke, and 8x in Acts. It is often connected (21x) to the concept of forgiveness (e.g., "God exalted him at his right hand as Leader and Savior, to give repentance to Israel and forgiveness of sins"; Acts 5:31). The adjective ἁμαρτωλός occurs 47x, with over half of its uses in the Synoptics (29x). It is paired eight times with "tax collectors," as in Luke 15:1: "the tax collectors and sinners were all drawing near to hear him." Echoing the LXX, these words in the Synoptics and Acts are used "exclusively in a moral sense," and can be defined as "falling away from a relationship of faithfulness toward God and disobedience to the commandments" ("ἁμαρτάνω," *NIDNTTE*, 258).

Sin (ἁμαρτία), which is also labeled "iniquity" (ἀδικίας) (Acts 8:23) and "trespasses" (παραπτώματα) (Matt. 6:14–15; Mark 11:25), includes breaking God's law (e.g., Stephen's pronouncement of the Jewish religious leaders, "you who received the law . . . did not keep it"; Acts 7:53). However, the concept is broader than the language of what is "unlawful" in relation to the Mosaic law, and perhaps more serious than humans breaking the clear commands of written revelation. The Evangelists employ metaphors like indebtedness, defilement, stumbling, crookedness, and lostness to paint a bleak picture of human depravity.

diseases") and unclean spirits ("many demons"; Mark 1:34) at every turn. The powers of the underworld understand Jesus's identity ("the Holy One of God"; Mark 1:24) but refuse to bow before him. They even fight ("convulsing him and crying out with a loud voice"; Mark 1:26) before giving up their reign over people. Jesus overcomes Satan and his minions (Mark 1:13, 25–27, 34, 39). He heals every illness (Mark 1:31, 32, 34).

The chapter ends with a leper, whom Jesus cleansed and told to obey the law of Moses ("show yourself to the priest and offer" a sacrifice) and his own commandment ("say nothing to anyone"; Mark 1:44), blatantly disobeying both divine laws: "But he [the sense is "immediately"—without stopping to see the priest] went out and began to talk freely about it"; Mark 1:45). Then, in case the point of human depravity is not clear enough, chapter 2 begins with a story that highlights the absolute need of everyone to heed the message of repentance that opened chapter 1 (Mark 1:4, 15). For Jesus to say to a paralyzed man, lying flat on his backside, "Son, your sins are forgiven" (Mark 2:5) implies that either this man's physical condition was caused by some sin, or, like every human created in God's image but deformed by the effects of Adam's original sin, he is a sinner from birth. The latter meaning is more likely, as "Mark intends the forgiveness of sins to be understood in the general context of repentance and faith that Jesus demands in view of the coming kingdom of God."[7] Even if the man never lifted a finger to sin against his fellow man, he is a sinner in God's sight! Thus, in Jesus's mercy, before he remedies this man's physical condition, he points out the spiritual condition of all people.

"You without Sin, Cast the First Stone"

While Jesus's statement, "Let him who is without sin among you be the first to throw a stone at her" (John 8:7), is not found in our earliest and best Greek manuscripts, the assumption of universal guilt before God is evident throughout the Gospels and Acts. Proof of this reality is manifold. Below I provide seven evidences to support this claim.

First, creation is depicted as being in need of restoration. Famines (Acts 11:28), earthquakes (Mark 13:8), and natural disasters (Luke 13:1–5) all indicate "that the whole creation has been groaning together" (Rom. 8:22)

---

[7] Eckhard J. Schnabel, *Mark: An Introduction and Commentary*, Tyndale New Testament Commentaries (Downers Grove, IL: IVP Academic, 2017), 66.

since the fall for "the time for restoring all things" (Acts 3:21). "This cosmic disruption" and the need for "cosmic redemption" is "an index of the seriousness of human sin." As John Frame says, "Sin affects us all. But not only us—also the entire creation. . . . Natural evil is the result of moral evil. Natural disasters are among God's means of punishing sin and reminding us of our need for redemption."[8]

Second, everyone dies. This is a simple but important point. While Jesus and the apostles raise the dead, only Jesus dies and rises and ascends into heaven (i.e., does not die again). For example, the promise for Adam's sin— "you shall surely die" (Gen. 2:17)—is fulfilled in the deaths of Herod, John the Baptist, and the apostle James. Death plays no favorites, as villains and prophets, apostates and apostles, rich and poor, Jew and Gentile, young and old, men and women and children, all fall under its power.

Third, Jesus teaches that all people are "evil." In his teaching on prayer, Jesus uses an analogy between the heavenly Father's generosity and that of an earthly father: "Or which one of you, if his son asks him for bread, will give him a stone? Or if he asks for a fish, will give him a serpent? If you then, *who are evil*, know how to give good gifts to your children, how much more will your Father who is in heaven give good things to those who ask him!" (Matt. 7:9–11). The point of the comparison is not to highlight the sinful nature of humankind but to show the abundant generosity of God. However, Jesus's statement about the earthly fathers who "give good gifts" being "evil" (ὑμεῖς πονηροί), in an ontological sense, is in striking contrast with a view of man's innate goodness. According to Jesus, that we might do "good things" and "give good gifts" does not mean we are "good." Even "good" people are fundamentally "evil."

Fourth, in the parable of the Pharisee and tax collector (Luke 18:9–14), Jesus commends the tax collector's realistic view of himself as "a sinner." The Pharisee, who holds a high view of himself and an optimistic opinion of his own nature, with his wordy prayer in the temple about his overt piety (Luke 18:11–12), is contrasted with the tax collector, who, away from the notice of the crowd ("standing far off"), offers the postures (he "would not even lift up his eyes to heaven, but beat his breast") and prayer of humble confession ("God, be merciful to me, a sinner!"; Luke 18:13). The point of the parable, told to those "who trusted in themselves that they were righteous"

---

[8] John Frame, *Systematic Theology: An Introduction to Christian Belief* (Phillipsburg, NJ: P&R, 2013), 859.

(Luke 18:9), is that the self-acknowledging "sinner" (Luke 18:13) was "justi-fied" (Luke 18:14) by God and the so-called "righteous" (Luke 18:9) Pharisee was not.[9]

Fifth, Jesus teaches that all humans are morally indebted to God. As mentioned above, Jesus compares the forgiveness of the sinful woman ("a woman of the city, who was a sinner"; Luke 7:37) to canceling a large debt (v. 43). Another example can be found in the final two petitions of the Lord's Prayer: "forgive us our sins [we will sin], for we ourselves forgive everyone who is indebted to us [others will sin against us]. And lead us not into temp-tation [everyone will be regularly tempted]" (Luke 11:4; Matt. 6:12–13).[10] A final example is found in Jesus's parable of the unforgiving servant (Matt. 18:23–35), where God's forgiveness of our sin is compared to forgiving a debt of "ten thousand talents" (v. 24). Since "a talent was the highest unit of currency, and ten thousand was then the highest Greek numeral," this debt "was the highest or largest imaginable amount."[11] Robert Gundry labels it "zillions."[12] Therefore, the point of this part of the parable is this: like the servant who could not pay the ten thousand talents of debt (one of the king's "servants . . . could not pay"; Matt. 18:23–25), all humans are "in the deepest possible debt to God,"[13] and, since we cannot possibly cover the astronomi-cal costs, our only hope for forgiveness is that "out of pity" for us God will cancel the balance ("the master . . . forgave him the debt"; Matt. 18:27).[14]

Sixth, it is clear that even God's covenant people are sinners. For ex-ample, in Jesus's answer to the Canaanite woman's plea ("Have mercy . . . my daughter is severely oppressed by a demon"; Matt. 15:22) and the disciples' strong suggestion ("Send her away . . ."; v. 23), he speaks of being "sent . . . to

[9] It is clear from this parable, and especially from Jesus's condemnation of the scribes and the Pharisees in Matt. 23, that Jesus's statement about "the righteous" in Mark 2:17 ("I came not to call the righteous, but sinners") means "those who *considered themselves* righteous."

[10] Matthew adds "and deliver us from evil" or "the evil one" (Matt. 6:13b). Here, every Christian who prays for daily bread also prays for daily deliverance (ῥῦσαι). The Christian is asking God to help him not surrender to the persistent lure of sin and the grasp of Satan.

[11] Douglas Sean O'Donnell, *Matthew*, Preaching the Word (Wheaton, IL: Crossway, 2013), 524.

[12] Robert H. Gundry, *Matthew: A Commentary on His Literary and Theological Art* (Grand Rapids, MI: Eerdmans, 1982), 373.

[13] O'Donnell, *Matthew*, 524. Notice that Jesus's anthropology is connected with his soteriology. "Here Jesus depicts human beings, due to their sin . . . as being zillions of dollars in debt to God," which means that "Jesus thinks deep down (and not so deep down) people are really, really bad. Perhaps more visual than debt, think zillion-mile chasm between God's goodness and our badness. Or think both. With Jesus's calculation, the implications are obvious. He puts to rest any notion of works righteousness. It is a zillion-mile chasm! It's a zillion-dollar debt! Good luck with the climb. Good luck with bank loan. You will not balance that budget or bridge that chasm by yourself. You will only balance it and bridge it by clinging to that old, rugged, and *colossal* cross! A cross deeper and wider and vaster than you can ever fathom. For if one person's debt (one person!) is a zillion dollars, what is the debt for the sins of the whole world for which Christ pays?" (524).

[14] Our indebtedness can be forgiven *only* because Jesus came "to give his life as a *ransom*"—a full payment (Matt. 20:28).

the lost sheep of the house of Israel" (v. 24). The "sent" language emphasizes the Father's role. Jesus is an agent of God, commissioned by God, and sent to "save his people [the Jews] from their sins" (Matt. 1:21). The phrase "the lost sheep of the house of Israel" (Matt. 15:24), which is probably epexegetical ("the lost sheep *which are* the house of Israel"),[15] depicts the whole nation (God's "people Israel"; Matt. 2:6; cf. Ezek. 34:23) as "lost." They are "lost" either in the sense of needing salvation from sin (Matt. 1:21; cf. Isa. 6:5; Luke 15:24, 32; 19:10) or in the sense of needing godly leadership (like "sheep without a shepherd"; Matt. 9:36; cf. Jer. 27:6 LXX). When the twelve are "sent" by Jesus (Matt. 10:5) to "the lost sheep of the house of Israel" (Matt. 10:6), the emphasis appears to be on Israel's need to receive Jesus (Matt. 10:40) and acknowledge him publicly (Matt. 10:32), thereby accepting the proclamation of the kingdom of heaven and experiencing its power (Matt. 7–8).[16] Israel is not alone in its sin. In Jesus's instruction on prayer (Matt. 6:12, 14), relational reconciliation (Matt. 5:23–25), church discipline (Matt. 18:15–20), and the forgiveness of sins (Matt. 18:21–35), he assumes that Christians, even under the new covenant, will regularly and repeatedly sin against other Christians.[17]

Seventh, the solution offered for the sin problem is universal. Put differently, salvation is seen as something everyone needs. Just as in the "days of Noah" (Matt. 24:37) when all humanity was either saved or judged, so when Jesus returns, his adjudication will be universal. Like Jesus, who proclaimed "light" both to the Jews ("our people") and to "the Gentiles" (Acts 26:23), the apostles are also commanded to preach the gospel to "all nations" (Matt. 28:19; cf. Acts 1:8) so that God "may bring salvation to the ends of the earth" (Acts 13:47). Obviously, the whole world, which dwells in darkness (cf. Matt. 4:16; Luke 1:79) needs the "light" of this good news.

THE UNIVERSAL CALL TO REPENTANCE

The effects of sin are so prevalent that John the Baptist, Jesus, and his disciples preached a universal call for repentance in light of universal judgment. There is not a sermon recorded in the Synoptics and Acts that does not

[15] This is similar to Matt. 10:6, where the Jews as a whole ("the house of Israel") are the "lost sheep," as set in contrast to "the Gentiles and . . . the Samaritans" (Matt. 10:5).
[16] Some of the sentences in the above paragraph come from Douglas Sean O'Donnell, "The Canaanite Woman's Great Faith: An Exploration into the Nature of Faith in Matthew" (PhD diss., University of Aberdeen, 2019), 99–100.
[17] Jesus's teaching in Luke 17:3–4 is striking. If another believer sins, rebuke that person; then, if there is repentance, forgive. Even if that person wrongs a fellow believer seven times a day (that is a possibility to Jesus!) and each time turns again and asks forgiveness, that believer must forgive.

assume everyone is a sinner, under the judgment of God, and thus in need of "repentance toward God and of faith in our Lord Jesus Christ" (Acts 20:21). The consistent proclamation is that "all people everywhere" should "repent" (Acts 17:30) and "believe in the gospel" (Mark 1:15).

John the Baptist prepares the way for the coming Christ by "proclaiming a baptism of repentance for the forgiveness of sins" (Mark 1:4; cf. Acts 13:24). His call to repentance—"Repent, for the kingdom of heaven is at hand" (Matt. 3:2)—was indiscriminate. Mark's use of the word "all"—"all the country of Judea and all Jerusalem were going out to him and were being baptized by him in the river Jordan, confessing their sins" (Mark 1:5)— is viewed as the proper response to John's universal summons. To John, there is no need to explain the nature of sin or to offer an apologetic for its existence. Everyone has sins to confess; everyone should confess those sins; everyone can receive baptism as a sign of God's cleansing of sin. Moreover, while John himself is not baptized (or at least it is not recorded), he does admit that, compared with Jesus, he is unworthy: "After me comes he who is mightier than I, the strap of whose sandals I am not worthy [οὐκ εἰμὶ ἱκανός] to stoop down and untie" (Mark 1:7). The phrase οὐκ εἰμὶ ἱκανός certainly designates a distinction of authority (i.e., Jesus is far greater than John), but it also connotes, based on other uses of ἱκανός in the NT, an unworthiness due to personal sinfulness (Matt. 8:8; 1 Cor. 15:9).[18] If this is correct, then Jesus's call to repentance ("repent and believe in the gospel"; Mark 1:15) not only builds on John's message but is a message that John himself should heed.

Like John, Jesus indiscriminately preaches repentance ("Repent, for the kingdom of heaven is at hand"; Matt. 4:17). Jesus also illustrates the nature of true repentance. In the parables of the two sons (Matt. 21:28–32) and the prodigal son (Luke 15:11–32), Jesus makes it clear that repentance involves a change of mind followed by an action that involves turning toward God. In the first parable, the son who said that he would not obey his father "changed his mind and went" (Matt. 21:29); in the second parable, the prodigal "came to his senses" (Luke 15:17 NLT; the English for the Greek idiom εἰς ἑαυτὸν δὲ ἐλθὼν) and then rehearsed to himself the proper steps

---

[18] In Matt. 8:8, the sense of the centurion's οὐκ εἰμὶ ἱκανός "likely goes beyond this man's acknowledgment of racial and religious distinctions. It was not merely ceremonial uncleanness but personal unworthiness that led this centurion to say what he said. In the face of Jesus's majestic authority . . . and in light of his own moral fallenness, he admits, as Peter did before Jesus's powerful presence, that he is 'a sinful man' (Luke 5:8)" (O'Donnell, "Canaanite Woman's Great Faith," 128).

of repentance: walking home, confessing sin, and admitting unworthiness ("I will arise and go to my father, and I will say to him, 'Father, I have sinned against heaven and before you. I am no longer worthy to be called your son' "; Luke 15:18–19a).

In case there is any doubt that Jesus thought all people everywhere must repent, his statement to those who shared with him about a certain sin of their northern covenant comrades ("the Galileans whose blood Pilate had mingled with their sacrifices"; Luke 13:1) should put to rest all opposition to the notion of universal sin:

> And he answered them, "Do you think that these Galileans were worse sinners than all the other Galileans, because they suffered in this way? No, I tell you; but unless you repent, you will all likewise perish. Or those eighteen on whom the tower in Siloam fell and killed them: do you think that they were worse offenders than all the others who lived in Jerusalem? No, I tell you; but unless you repent, you will all likewise perish." (Luke 13:2–4)

Jesus's point here, as Philip Ryken summarizes, is that "we are all sinful enough to deserve the wrath of God." Ryken continues,

> Notice the precise place where Jesus disagreed with his listeners. He did not say they were wrong to hold God responsible for the fall of the tower. Jesus knew that this too was under God's sovereign control. No, the place he disagreed with them was in their assumption that they were morally superior to the people who died at Siloam. On the contrary, the people who died in that tragic accident were no better and no worse than anyone else. The word Jesus used to describe the victims is spiritually significant. The word translated "offenders" is the Greek word for debtors (*ophei-letai*), which is the best word to describe people who owe something to God for their sin. "The fact is," writes Michael Wilcock, "that we are all sinners, all in need of repentance, all deserving of punishment, and all preserved from the wrath of God—at least until judgment day—purely by his mercy."[19]

Jesus's apostles followed this pattern we find in the sayings of Jesus and John. Repeatedly, in their sermons in Acts, the apostles call for repentance.[20]

---

[19] Philip Graham Ryken, *Luke*, 2 vols., Reformed Expository Commentary (Phillipsburg, NJ: P&R, 2009), 2:6. Ryken quotes from Michael Wilcock, *The Message of Luke*, The Bible Speaks Today (Downers Grove, IL: InterVarsity Press, 1979), 138.

[20] Acts 2:38; 3:19, 26; 5:31; 8:22; 17:30; 26:18, 20.

Both Jews (e.g., every single person in Jerusalem for the Passover) and Gentiles (e.g., every single Gentile Paul encounters on his missionary journeys), are called to repent and believe in light of the coming judgment: the message "declared first to those in Damascus, then in Jerusalem and throughout all the region of Judea, and also to the Gentiles, [was] that they should repent and turn to God" (Acts 26:20). They are also promised forgiveness of sins if they trust this gospel about Jesus.[21]

The Whole of Human Nature

As demonstrated above, Matthew, Mark, and Luke present sin as universal. This is why the consistent message throughout the Synoptics and Acts is for "all people everywhere to repent" (Acts 17:30) and "believe in the gospel" (Mark 1:15) in light of God's coming wrath upon all people.

Next, I will demonstrate that "the whole human nature" of the whole human race "is infected with an inherited depravity which produces in humanity every sort of sin." That is, we will see how sin, which is universal, is also so pervasive that the whole person, in the unconverted state, is "wholly defiled in all the parts and faculties of soul and body."[22] Those "parts and faculties" can be described as "the body and its desires," along with "the soul, mind, heart, and will."[23] Since this is a study on the Synoptics, perhaps the language most befitting the aspects of man is the division that Jesus offers in his answer to the teacher of the law: "You shall love the Lord your God with all your heart and with all your soul and with all your strength and with all you mind" (Luke 10:27).

Of course, determining what Jesus meant by these four qualifiers concerning his "call for absolute, singular, and total devotion to YHWH,"[24] is not straightforward. That admission made, it is unlikely that Jesus is formulating a Hellenistic-influenced statement about the partitive psychological makeup of human beings. Rather, he is using common metaphors to personify the whole person, the inner and outer being—the entire feeling, thinking, and doing of אָדָם. He is, without doubt, pointing to Deuteronomy 6:5, speaking

---

[21] Acts 2:38; 3:19; 5:31; 13:38; 26:28.
[22] WCF 6.2.
[23] See Michael S. Horton, *The Christian Faith: A Systematic Theology for Pilgrims on the Way* (Grand Rapids, MI: Zondervan, 2011), 433, on Berkhof. Article 1 of the Third and Fourth Heads of Doctrine, the Canons of Dort lists "blindness of mind . . . vanity, and perverseness of judgment," and that man is "obdurate in heart and will, and impure in his affections."
[24] This is Daniel I. Block's (*For the Glory of God: Recovering a Biblical Theology of Worship* [Grand Rapids, MI: Baker Academic, 2014], 101) summary of Deut. 6:4.

of what humans feel and think (the "heart" and "mind") and what we do with those thoughts and desires.[25]

PERVASIVELY DEPRAVED

There are various texts within the first three Gospels where our Lord highlights man's inner and outer depravity. Perhaps the clearest example is recorded in Mark 7:15–16, 18–23, where he taught:

> "There is nothing outside a person that by going into him can defile him, but the things that come out of a person are what defile him. . . . Do you not see that whatever goes into a person from outside cannot defile him, since it enters not his heart but his stomach, and is expelled?" (Thus he declared all foods clean). . . . "What comes out of a person is what defiles him. For from within, out of the heart of man, come evil thoughts, sexual immorality, theft, murder, adultery, coveting, wickedness, deceit, sensuality, envy, slander, pride, foolishness. All these evil things come from within, and they defile a person."

While there are other theological issues discussed here (the nature of what is clean and unclean in regard to Jewish ritual purity), it is evident that Jesus does not present an optimistic anthropology. He does not merely declare "all foods clean" (Mark 7:19), but he announces that all humans are *not* clean. What is found in a septic tank ("whatever . . . is expelled"; Mark 7:19) is cleaner than what is found in the human heart (cf. Jer. 17:9). Like Paul in Romans 1:29–31, where he describes sin as both interior attitudes (like greed and arrogance) and exterior acts (like murder and disobeying parents), Jesus sees internal sins (evil thoughts, coveting, envy, pride) and external sins (sexual immorality, theft, murder, adultery, wickedness, deceit, sensuality,

---

[25] I take the structure of Luke 10:27 to be chiastic (see below):

heart
    soul
        strength
mind

and that "heart" and "mind" are synonymous parallels (Jesus's "original addition of 'mind' to the list . . . is probably to be related to the fact that διάνοια, 'mind,' is a variant reading for καρδία, 'heart,' in Deuteronomy 6:5 and elsewhere in the LXX" (John Nolland, *Luke*, 3 vols., WBC 35A–C, [Dallas: Word, 1989–1993], 2:583–84), as are "soul" and "strength" (cf. "the strong shall not retain his strength [אמיץ = ψυχήν LXX]," and the fighter shall not save his soul [נַפְשׁוֹ = ψυχήν LXX]," Amos 2:14, NETS [Septuagint]; cf. Sir. 9:2, "Give not the power of thy *soul* to a woman, lest she enter upon thy *strength*, and thou be confounded"). Nolland (584) takes "heart" to denote "a response to God from the inner-most personal center of one's being," and "mind" to include "the thinking and planning process," while "soul" speaks of "the role of the life force that energizes us," and "'strength' introduces the element of energetic physical processes."

slander, foolishness; Mark 7:21–22) as inseparable and at the very core of fallen humanity ("from within, out of the heart of man"; Mark 7:21).

Elsewhere Jesus says, "What comes out of the mouth proceeds from the heart" (Matt. 15:18) and, "On the day of judgment people will give account for every careless word they speak, for by your words you will be justified, and by your words you will be condemned" (Matt. 12:36–37). Words are windows to our hearts. Our lips are unclean because our hearts are unclean. The "evil things" we see on the outside "come from within" (Mark 7:23). From head to toe, body to soul, all aspects of ourselves are pervasively depraved.[26]

EVERY SORT OF SIN

Having demonstrated above that the Synoptics explain and illustrate that "the whole human nature is infected with an inherited depravity," next we turn to how the Evangelists showcase how that fallen core "produces . . . every sort of sin."

As a preliminary summary of the sins recorded in the Synoptics and Acts, my list includes blasphemy (Acts 26:11), hardness of heart (Mark 3:5; synonymous terms would include "stiff-necked" and "uncircumcised in heart"; Acts 7:51), adding to and omitting from God's word (see Matt. 15:1–14), "condemn[ing] the guiltless" (Matt. 12:7), false worship (Luke 20:47), unbelief (Mark 6:6), doubt (Luke 24:38), hatred (Matt. 5:43), theft (Matt. 6:19), idolatry (Acts 19:27–28), coveting wealth (Matt. 6:24), testing God (Mark 8:11–12), an unforgiving spirit (Matt. 18:28–30), ungodly divisions within the church (Acts 15:39), pride (Mark 9:34), worldly ambition (Matt. 20:21), greed (see Mark 11:15–19), flattery (Mark 12:14), murder (Matt. 2:16), envy (Mark 15:10), infanticide (Acts 7:19), rebellion against the government, presumption (Matt. 3:8), judgmentalism (Matt. 7:1), racism (Matt. 15:23), favoritism (including neglecting the poor, Acts 6:1), sexism (Matt. 19:10), discrimination (Luke 18:15), callousness (Matt. 27:4), bribery (Acts 24:26), unjust affliction (Acts 7:34), violence (Matt. 26:27), suicide (Matt. 27:5), false testimony (Mark 14:55–57), lying (Matt. 2:8), tempting others to sin (Luke 17:1), the self-security of religiosity (Luke 19:46), defrauding the weak (Luke 20:47), dissipation and drunkenness (Luke 21:34), resisting the Holy Spirit (Acts 7:51), magic (Acts 8:9), simony (Acts 8:18–19),

---

[26] "The whole man is overwhelmed—as by a deluge—from head to foot, so that no part is immune from sin and all that proceeds from him is to be imputed to sin" (John Calvin, *Institutes of the Christian Religion*, LCC 20, ed. John T. McNeill, trans. Ford Lewis Battles, 2 vols. [Philadelphia: Westminster, 1960], 2:253).

neglecting the needy (Matt. 25:41–46), a host of sexual sins (e.g., Luke 3:19; 15:30; 16:18), and hypocrisy (Mark 7:7) in all its varied forms.

A helpful way to categorize sin, both in these four books and in the whole of the Bible, is to use John Frame's "tri-perspectival definition of sin." Frame states that sin consists of "disobedience, self-glorification, and unbelief/hatred," each represented as a tip of a triangle.[27] Our sin against God is complete!

Regarding *disobedience*, it is not just that God's people in Matthew, Mark, Luke, and Acts are depicted as breaking all ten of the Ten Commandments (see table 13.1), both in the letter and the spirit of those laws, but that Israel fails to keep "the great [twofold] commandment" that summarizes the ethics of the OT ("the Law and the Prophets"—to love God with heart, soul, and mind, and one's neighbor as oneself; see Matt. 22:36–40). Also, Israel's religious leaders, whom Jesus describes as being inwardly "full of greed and self-indulgence" (Matt. 23:25), "break the commandment of God for the sake" of their many man-made traditions (e.g., Matt. 15:3), while they neglect "the weightier matters of the law: justice and mercy and faithfulness" (Matt. 23:23). Of course, the "Gentile sinners" (Gal. 2:15), to borrow a Pauline term, only add to the awful image of iniquity. Sins from idolatry to injustice, drunkenness to deceit, are on full display.

TABLE 13.1: Breaking the Ten Commandments

Ten Commandments in Exodus 20	Samples of Sin in the Synoptics and Acts
1 You shall have no other gods before me. (Ex. 20:3)	By walking away from Jesus's command to follow him by first giving away his possessions, the rich young ruler demonstrates that his love of money takes priority over the kingdom of God (Matt. 19:16–22; cf. 6:24; 13:22).
2 You shall not make for yourself a carved image, or any likeness of anything. (Ex. 20:4)	In Ephesus, "a man named Demetrius, a silversmith, who made silver shrines of Artemis" (Acts 19:24), gathered other idol makers to oppose Paul because he feared that Paul's preaching would hurt their business and that "the temple of the great goddess Artemis [would] be counted as nothing, and that she may even be deposed from her magnificence, she whom all Asia and the world worship" (Acts 19:27).

[27] Frame, *Systematic Theology*, 849.

3	You shall not take the name of the LORD your God in vain. (Ex. 20:7)	The "hypocrites" offer long public prayers to God in the hope of gaining the esteem of man. (see Matt. 6:5)
4	Remember the Sabbath day, to keep it holy. (Ex. 20:8)	In a number of the Sabbath controversies (e.g., Matt. 12:1–14), the religious leaders add to God's word and thus twist the original intention.
5	Honor your father and your mother. (Ex. 20:12)	Jesus sets up what the scribes and Pharisees say ("but you say"; Matt. 15:5) against what God said in the fifth commandment ("for God commanded"; Matt. 15:4), showing how they set aside God's law for the man-made and man-centered tradition of "Corban" (Mark 7:11), the practice of pledging money to the temple to be paid upon one's death (*Mishnah Medarim* 1:2–4; 9:7). This was used as a religious justification for not helping one's parents in their old age.
6	You shall not murder. (Ex. 20:13)	Herod orders the murder of "all the male children in Bethlehem and in all that region who were two years old or under." (Matt. 2:16)
7	You shall not commit adultery. (Ex. 20:14)	Herod committed adultery with his brother's wife, Herodias. (see Luke 3:19)
8	You shall not steal. (Ex. 20:15)	In Zacchaeus's repentance, he admits that he had defrauded people. (see Luke 19:8)
9	You shall not bear false witness against your neighbor. (Ex. 20:16)	False testimony is brought against Jesus at his trial. (Mark 14:55–57)
10	You shall not covet. (Ex. 20:17)	In the parable of the rich fool, Jesus highlights the foolishness of this sin. (see Luke 12:13–21)

Beyond sins that could be classified as sins of disobedience, there are many examples of sins that would fall under *self-glorification*. The most striking example is found in Acts 12:21–23: "On an appointed day Herod put on his royal robes, took his seat upon the throne, and delivered an oration to them. And the people were shouting, 'The voice of a god, and not of a man!' Immediately an angel of the Lord struck him down, because he did not give God the glory, and he was eaten by worms and breathed his last."

While their sin is not as severe, the Jewish religious leaders recurrently succumb to the sin of self-glorification. Thus, Jesus repeatedly scolds them for it (see below) and warns of the coming punishment ("Whoever exalts himself will be humbled"; Matt. 23:12):

They do all their deeds to be seen by others. For they make their phylacteries broad and their fringes long, and they love the place of honor at feasts and the best seats in the synagogues and greetings in the marketplaces and being called rabbi by others. (Matt. 23:5–7)

Beware of the scribes, who like to walk around in long robes and like greetings in the marketplaces and have the best seats in the synagogues and the places of honor at feasts, who devour widows' houses and for a pretense make long prayers. They will receive the greater condemnation. (Mark 12:38–40)

Furthermore, Jesus's own disciples are not immune from this same sin. Shortly after Jesus talks about his coming cross and their need to follow him, deny themselves, and pick up their own cross (Mark 8:34), Mark records that they "argued with one another about who was the greatest" (Mark 9:34). Later, James and John seek to sit on thrones two and three in Jesus's coming kingdom ("Grant us to sit, one at your right hand and one at your left in your glory"; Mark 10:37; cf. Matt. 20:21).

The Synoptics and Acts, as shown above, certainly showcase sin as disobedience and self-glorification. But the sin of *unbelief*—to reject and oppose Jesus and his gospel—is a far more prevalent theme,[28] and it is not viewed merely as a slight offense (e.g., Matt. 10:15). In some way or other, every character group in the Gospels demonstrates opposition to Christ and his kingdom. Jesus provides an overarching judgment against the people he encountered, calling the generation that witnessed his wisdom and works "evil and adulterous" (Matt. 12:39; 16:4).[29]

Offering the most consistent and fiercest opposition to Jesus are the Jewish religious leaders. Their rejection comes in many forms. They are angry with him (Luke 6:11), ridicule him (Luke 16:14), grumble against him (Luke 5:30; cf. John 6:41), and label him an "impostor" (Matt. 27:63) and as "possessed by Beelzebul" (Mark 3:22).[30] Like Satan,[31] they "test" Jesus

---

[28] For texts featuring opposition to God, Jesus, the church, and/or the gospel in Acts, see Acts 4:26; 5:17–18, 33, 40; 7:41, 51, 58; 8:1, 2; 9:1, 23–24, 29; 11:19; 12:15; 13:45, 50; 14:2, 5, 19; 16:19, 22–24; 17:5–6, 8, 13, 32; 18:6, 12, 17; 19:9, 21–41 (esp. v. 29); 20:3, 19, 23; 21:11, 27, 30–36; 22:19, 24; 23:2, 10, 12, 14, 27; 24:27; 25:3; 26:9–11, 21; 28:27.

[29] Cf. "evil" (Matt. 12:45); "twisted" (Matt. 17:17; cf. "crooked," Acts 2:40); "sinful" (Mark 8:38); "faithless" (Mark 9:19).

[30] This final sin Jesus calls the unforgiveable of sin of blasphemy against the Holy Spirit (Mark 3:28–30).

[31] As Yuanhui Ye points out, the conflict between Jesus and the religious leaders in Matt. 16:1–4 mirrors the conflict between God and Satan in Matt. 4:1–7, in that: (1) Matthew uses πειράζω for only two characters—Satan (Matt. 4:1, 3, 7) and the religious leaders (Matt. 19:3–9; 22:15–22, 34–40); (2) the conflict of Matt. 16:1–4 resembles the temptation narrative of Matt. 4:1–11 in that both opponents ask Jesus to perform a miraculous sign; and (3) parallel

(Mark 10:2), seeking to "trap him" (Mark 12:13), "entangle him" (Matt. 22:15), or "catch him in something he said" (Luke 20:20). They seek to kill him (Matt. 12:14), conspire against him (Matt. 27:20), receive false testimony against him at trial (Mark 14:55–57), beat and mock him (Mark 14:65; 15:31), and condemn him to death (Matt. 26:66; Acts 13:27–28). Of course, the Jewish and Gentiles political leaders play their part in the death of the Messiah—Jesus is "delivered into the hands of sinful men and . . . crucified" (Luke 24:7).[32] However, all three Evangelists also speak of the Jewish religious leaders as killing Jesus.[33]

While the Jewish religious leaders are more sinister and harsher in their opposition to Jesus, they are not alone in their rejection of Jesus. In their own ways, the Jewish crowd, the people of Jesus's hometown, Jesus's family, and even the twelve deny him. The crowd, with their cry, "Crucify him" (Mark 15:13), help sentence him to death. His biological family misunderstands, and thus opposes, his mission ("his family . . . went to seize him, for they were saying, 'He is out of his mind,'" Mark 3:21). The people of Nazareth, in "their unbelief" (Mark 6:6), "took offense at him" (Mark 6:3), so much so that "all in the synagogue" were so "filled with wrath" (Luke 4:28) that they sought to "throw him down the cliff" (Luke 4:29).

As every member of the synagogue in Jesus's hometown opposed him, so too did twelve out of the twelve. As Jesus predicted ("You will all fall away"; Mark 14:27), each and every apostle eventually denies him ("And they all left him and fled"; Mark 14:50). Judas and Peter are the most obvious and ominous examples (see Matt. 26:14–16, 47–56). Judas will deny his friend with a kiss (Mark 14:44–45), and Peter's last word in the Gospel of Mark is "I do not know this man" (Mark 14:71). Thus, I agree with Frederick Dale Bruner that "one of the purposes of the Trial Stories in the Passion Narrative is to teach the sinfulness of all strata of the human race."[34] I also agree with what Bruner says elsewhere, which shaped my description as follows:

Whether we call it "total depravity" or "total undependability," what is clearly illustrated in our text (Matt. 26:47–56) is sheep after sheep going astray while the Lamb of God is led away to the slaughter (Isa. 53:6, 7). God is about to

vocabulary is employed (καὶ προσελθὼν ὁ πειράζων) (Matt. 4:3); Καὶ προσελθόντες οἱ Φαρισαῖοι καὶ Σαδδουκαῖοι πειράζοντες) (Matt. 16:1) (Yuanhui Ye, "'By What Authority?': The Literary Function and Impact of Conflict Stories in the Gospel of Matthew" [PhD diss., University of Edinburgh, 2014], 136).
[32] Cf. Matt. 27:26, 27–44; Mark 15:24; Acts 2:23; 4:25–27.
[33] See Matt. 12:39; 20:18; cf. Matt. 26:66; Mark 12:38–39; 14:64; Luke 20:14–15; Acts 2:23; 3:14; 4:10; 5:30; 10:39.
[34] Frederick Dale Bruner, The Churchbook: Matthew 13–28, 2nd and rev. ed. (Grand Rapids, MI: Eerdmans, 2004), 668.

place the "iniquity of us all . . . on him" (Isa. 53:6b). *All* have gone astray . . . *all* our sin on him. . . . From the trial scenes to the crucifixion itself, don't miss that everybody (but Jesus) sins and falls short of the glory of God (Rom. 3:10, 23)—Jews, Gentiles, and even inner-circle disciples. There are the "big and little disciples (Peter and Judas), big and little Israel (Sanhedrin and people), and big and little Rome (Pilate and soldiers)" and at the cross itself again Gentile and Jew (the disciples still hiding) stroll by to shake their heads at Jesus, the colossal failure of a Christ. Ah, but then as it is now "against this awful backdrop of infidelity, Jesus's fidelity looms high and lonely, and that is the point: amid all human failure, there is one who is *totally dependable*."[35]

Vile in God's Sight

Thus far, we have answered two questions. First, "Has Adam's original sin spread through the whole human race?" Second, "Has it spread in such a way that the whole human nature, from the moment of conception, is infected with an inherited depravity which produces in humanity every sort of sin?" We have shown that, while Mark, Matthew, and Luke do not mention Adam in relation to sin, or speak in terms of "original sin" or "inherited corruption,"[36] they do consistently portray every human, with the exception of Jesus, as a sinner who sins. Moreover, while this corpus offers no direct evidence that humanity's sinful nature is birthed at conception, these four books consistently show and teach that every aspect of man—heart and mind; soul and strength—yields every imaginable iniquity. The third question follows: "Is this corrupted condition so vile and enormous in God's sight that it is enough to condemn the human race?" The answer is an absolute and undeniable *yes*. In fact, the three Evangelists offer some of the strongest testimonies in all of Scripture that God takes sin seriously. Their coherent witness comes in two forms: first, the severity of God's condemnation of sinners, namely, the Evangelists' clear espousal of divine judgment, especially of the doctrine of hell; second, in Jesus's hellish forsakenness for sinners.

DIVINE JUDGMENT

John Piper summarizes well the first point, saying, "The reality of hell is God's clear indictment of the infiniteness of our guilt. If our corruption were

---

[35] O'Donnell, *Matthew*, 810. The quoted portions are from Bruner, *Churchbook*, 665–66.
[36] John Calvin, *Institutes*, 2.1.5. Calvin defines the term as "a hereditary depravity and corruption of our nature, diffused into all parts of the soul, which first makes us liable to God's wrath, then also brings forth in us those works which Scripture calls 'works of the flesh' (Gal. 5:19)" (2.1.8).

not deserving of an eternal punishment, God would be unjust to threaten us with a punishment so severe as eternal torment."[37] The word "hell" is used fourteen times in the NT, with only two of those times occurring outside of the Synoptic Gospels.[38] Jesus speaks of hell as divine judgment (see Matt. 5:22; 23:33; Luke 12:5) for those who reject him, his royal reign, and his kingdom ethics. It is a place ("go to hell"; Mark 9:43) wherein a person will experience great pain ("the unquenchable fire," Mark 9:43; "the fire is not quenched," Mark 9:48) and destruction (Matt. 10:28), and thus is to be avoided at all costs (see Matt. 5:29–30; 18:9; cf. Mark 9:43–47).

Whatever we make of Jesus's hyperboles and metaphors as they describe "the 'hell' of eschatological condemnation,"[39] it is clear that the punishments for sin he speaks of are far greater than being sent "into exile" (Acts 7:43), deported "to Babylon" (Matt. 1:12), sentenced to death (see Acts 5:5, 10; 12:23), or experiencing God's judgment against Herod's temple and its authorities (the "days of vengeance"; Luke 21:22).[40] Moreover, it is not simply Jesus's statements on γέεννα that show the severity of sin. It is his consistent mention and vivid imagery of "the coming judgment" (Acts 24:25); that divinely "appointed" day wherein God will "judge . . . the living and the dead" (Acts 10:42; cf. Acts 17:30–31); "the day of judgment" (Matt. 11:24); "the wrath to come" for unbelievers (cf. Matt. 3:7).[41] Jesus teaches that those who reject and oppose the kingdom will be "thrown into hell" (see Matt. 5:29). What a graphic and horrific image! But it is not the only image. In the parable of the talents, God (the "master") commands that the "wicked and slothful [and 'worthless'] servant" be "cast . . . into the outer darkness," a "place" where "there will be weeping and gnashing of teeth" (Matt. 25:26, 30).[42] This is a worse image than what Jesus gives at the end of the parable of the ten minas. There God is depicted as destroying those who oppose him and his Son: "as for these enemies of mine ['citizens (of Israel who) hated him'], who did not want me to reign over them, bring them here and slaughter

---

[37] John Piper, *Five Points: Towards a Deeper Experience of God's Grace*, rev. ed. (Fearn, Ross-shire, UK: Christian Focus, 2013), 22.

[38] Jesus speaks of hell in Matt. 5:22, 29; 10:28; 16:18; 18:9; 23:15, 33; Mark 9:43; Luke 12:5. Even the teachings in James and 2 Peter, by using the metaphors of fire ("set on fire by hell"; James 3:6) and being "cast . . . into . . . darkness" (2 Pet. 2:4), are influenced by the sayings of Jesus.

[39] Joel B. Green, "Heaven and Hell," in *Dictionary of Jesus and the Gospels*, 2nd ed., ed. Joel B. Green, Jeannine K. Brown, and Nicholas Perrin (Downers Grove, IL: IVP Academic, 2020), 375.

[40] Cf. Matt. 21:41; 22:7, 13; 24:2; Luke 19:43–44.

[41] This coming day, as John the Baptist declares, is not only for "all" people, but even for "the Pharisees and Sadducees," whom John calls a "brood of vipers" (Matt. 3:7; cf. Luke 3:7–9). In fact, Jesus also uses the phrase "brood of vipers" (Matt. 23:33) to speak of the religious leaders and their "greater condemnation" (Luke 20:47).

[42] Cf. Matt. 8:12; 13:42, 50; 22:13; 24:51; 25:30; Luke 13:28.

them before me" (Luke 19:27, with 19:14).[43] The image is worse because it is not just that of destruction then annihilation, but of an existence through the ongoing judgment. This is more than Jesus's pronouncement to the foolish virgins in the parable of the ten virgins, where the bridegroom (symbolizing Jesus) says, "I do not know you" and the door is "shut" (Matt. 25:10–12), or his call to "repent" or "perish" (see Luke 13:3, 5). It is like his sentence on Judas: "Woe to that man by whom the Son of Man is betrayed! It would have been better for that man if he had not been born" (Mark 14:21; cf. Matt. 26:24).[44] It is worse because the punishment of that horrendous sin, along with every other great or little sin, is eternal. The "eternal fire" (Matt. 25:41) is an "eternal punishment" (Matt. 25:46) for those "cursed" by God (Matt. 25:41). The fate of the rich man in Jesus's symbolic story of Lazarus and the rich man is a true story for multitudes: the "place of torment" is a real place where real people are "in torment" (Luke 16:23, 28).

Why would compassionate Jesus speak of a permanent separation from him ("Depart from me, all you workers of evil"; Luke 13:27) and that that separation would involve seemingly unendurable and unending pain (an "unquenchable fire"; Luke 3:17)? Why would he speak of, and warn against, people made in God's image being gathered like weeds and burned, caught like fish and discarded, falling from high cliffs to their death, trampled under feet, and cut in pieces?[45] The reason is the sinfulness of human sin in the sight of a "holy, holy, holy" God (Isa. 6:3). The darkness that covered the cross is but a portion of the shades of human darkness that God deals with then, and daily in his judgment of unbelievers.

GOD-FORSAKENNESS

To God, the human condition is so vile and enormous that "he has fixed a day on which he will judge the world" (Acts 17:31). Divine judgment is one way that Matthew, Mark, and Luke testify that God takes sin seriously. A second way is their detail of Jesus's hellish forsakenness for sinners.

---

[43] For other statements on and images of destruction, see Matt. 10:28 ("Rather fear him who can destroy both soul and body in hell"), and Acts 3:23 ("every soul who does not listen . . . shall be destroyed from the people"). Without faith in Jesus (the subject of Matt. 8:5–10), even "the sons of the kingdom [i.e., Jews] will be thrown into the outer darkness," a "place" where they will experience great physical and emotional anguish ("there will be weeping and gnashing of teeth"; Matt. 8:12).
[44] For another comparison related to divine judgment, see Luke 17:2, where Jesus states that "it would be better" for the one who tempts others to sin, especially children, "if a millstone were hung around his neck and he were cast into the sea." That awful punishment would be better than falling into the hands of the living God!
[45] See Luke 3:17; Matt. 7:27; 13:30, 38–42, 47–50; 22:44; 24:51; cf. Luke 12:46–47.

At Gethsemane, at the heart of Jesus's hours-long prayers was the plea, "Father . . . Remove this cup from me" (Mark 14:36). The cup is a metaphor for his awful sufferings (cf. Mark 10:38–39). Jesus knows what lies ahead. He knows he will suffer betrayal, denial, an official sentence of condemnation from his own people, brutal torture from the Romans, and a slow and embarrassing death (see Mark 10:33–34; 14:18, 27, 30). He eyes "the hour" (Mark 14:41) ahead, and he knows that it is paved with unspeakable agony. He knows he has to die and how he will die. This is why he is "greatly distressed and troubled" (Mark 14:33); that at the very core of his being the "sorrow is so deep that it feels as if he is dying"[46] ("My soul is very sorrowful, even to death"; Mark 14:34).

Jesus must drink that cup of pain. But there is more to the "cup" than those horrific sufferings. There is one particular detail of his death that has him sweating ("his sweat became like great drops of blood falling to the ground"; Luke 22:44).[47] After his prayers at Gethsemane, Jesus will be delivered into the hands of "the power of darkness" (Luke 22:53). But it is not until the crucifixion itself, where the darkness of Jesus's enemies, the sky, and his own inner darkness collide. "At the ninth hour," the very light of the world, and the Creator who brought light into the world, "cried with a loud voice, . . . 'My God, my God, why have you forsaken me?'" (Mark 15:34). Jesus selects the dark words of Psalm 22:1 because it fits the dark setting, but also because it fits what is happening to him on the cross.[48] He is forsaken. He has been forsaken by his own people, the Jews. He has been forsaken by his closest friends, the apostles. And now he is forsaken by his own Father.

What then is the nature of this God-forsakenness? Calvin summarizes it in this way in his *Institutes*: Jesus "bore the weight of divine severity, since he was 'stricken and afflicted' [cf. Isa. 53:4] by God's hand and experienced all the signs of a wrathful and avenging God."[49] Earlier in the same passage Calvin states that Christ "suffered the death that God in his wrath had inflicted upon the wicked . . . that invisible and incomprehensible judgment which

---

[46] Mark L. Strauss, *Mark*, ZECNT (Grand Rapids, MI: Zondervan, 2014), 633.

[47] Calvin, *Institutes*, 2.16.12, comments, "What shameful softness would it have been . . . for Christ to be so tortured by the dread of common death as to sweat blood . . . ? Does not that prayer [Matt. 26:39], coming from unbelievable bitterness of heart and repeated three times . . . show that Christ had a harsher and more difficult struggle than with common death?"

[48] "Jesus expresses this horror of great darkness, this God-forsakenness, by quoting the only verse of Scripture which actually described it and which he had perfectly fulfilled" (John Calvin, *A Harmony of the Gospels: Matthew, Mark, and Luke, and the Epistles of James and Jude*, vol. 3, trans. A. W. Morrison [Grand Rapids, MI: Eerdmans, 1975], 81).

[49] Calvin, *Institutes*, 2.16.11.

he underwent in the sight of God in order that we might know not only that Christ's body was given as the price of our redemption, but that he paid a greater and more excellent price in suffering in his soul the terrible torments of a condemned and forsaken man."[50] Thus, Jesus's forsakenness was "an objective reality as well as a subjective experience."[51] The Father forsook the Son in that his wrath was upon him in his *profession* as mediator, but not in his *person* as Son. As Arthur Pink explains, "Never was God more 'well-pleased' with his beloved Son than when he hung on the cross in obedience to him (Phil. 2:10), yet he withdrew from him every effect or manifestation of his love during those three hours of awful darkness, yea, poured out his wrath upon him as our sin-bearer, so that he exclaimed 'Your wrath lies hard upon me, and you have afflicted me with all Your waves' (Ps. 88:7)."[52] The forsakenness is that God left him to die, and in that death he suffered the punishment for sin. Jonty Rhodes uses the analogy of Jesus having a blocked view of the Father's smiling face: "Just as darkness covered the land but the sun didn't cease to shine, so the experience of bearing the covenant curse overwhelmed Jesus in his human nature, clouding his view of his Father's love, steadfast though he remained. . . . Christ felt the anger of God . . . on account of our sin," and "for a short while," the Father "suspended Christ's enjoyment of the grace, happiness, and consolation that he normally enjoyed."[53]

Thus, the "cup" of God's wrath (Mark 14:36; cf. Isa. 53:4–6) that Jesus wanted removed is now—on the cross—felt on his lips and in the pit of his stomach. "The Son of Man" is giving "his life as a ransom for many" (Mark 10:45); he is pouring out his blood for many (Mark 14:24). And the best summary, then, of what Mark shows in story form is what Paul says propositionally in 2 Corinthians 5:18–21: God made sinless Jesus "to be sin" so that all who believe in him might be forgiven of sin. Thus, Jesus is not a martyr facing death. Like Stephen in Acts 7:54–60, "most martyrs face death with courage and confidence, expressing steadfast faith in God and hope for the resurrection."[54] Jesus is a propitiatory sacrifice. He will drink "the cup" of "the wine of [God's] wrath" (see Jer. 25:15–28; cf. Isa. 51:17, 22). That is what is causing him to sweat.

---

[50] Calvin, *Institutes*, 2.16.10.
[51] Jonty Rhodes, *Man of Sorrows, King of Glory: What the Humiliation and Exaltation of Jesus Mean for Us* (Wheaton, IL: Crossway, 2021), 84.
[52] Arthur W. Pink, *The Doctrine of Reconciliation* (1946; repr., Lafayette, IN: Sovereign Grace, 2006), 91.
[53] Rhodes, *Man of Sorrows*, 81, 84.
[54] Strauss, *Mark*, 637.

Totally Unable

In light of the previous section, the words of the classic hymn are only apropos:

Ye who think of sin but lightly
Nor suppose the evil great
Here may view its nature rightly,
here its guilt may estimate.[55]

However, even if our guilt is estimated at its proper value (10,000 denarii of debt!), a final question arises: While the human condition is bad, is it so bad that we cannot come to Christ? Put differently, are we "totally unable" to seek, know, and please God without his help? I will argue that our sinful corruption is so complete that we are not only inclined toward evil, but also so dead and bound in sin that we are morally incapable of overcoming our rebellion against God. Thus, we are absolutely dependent on his grace to breathe spiritual life into us and draw us to himself.[56]

"THE GLIMMERINGS OF NATURAL LIGHT"[57]

The doctrine of total depravity does not mean that unregenerate people act as badly as possible all the time. The fall shattered, but did not destroy, the image of God in all human beings. We still have our faculties. This explains why, throughout the Synoptic Gospels and Acts, we find expressions of sincere curiosity about the Christ (Matt. 2:1–2), devout piety and generosity (Acts 10:2),[58] people caring for a friend (Mark 2:3), financial generosity (Mark 12:42), sacrificial love (Mark 14:3–9), "unusual kindness" (Acts 28:2), and obedience to divine revelation

---

[55] Thomas Kelly, "Stricken, Smitten, and Afflicted" (1804).

[56] See Article 3 of the Third and Fourth Heads of Doctrine, the Canons of Dort.

[57] Article 4 of the Third and Fourth Heads of Doctrine, the Canons of Dort.

[58] Regarding Cornelius, David G. Peterson (*Acts of the Apostles*, PNTC [Grand Rapids, MI: Eerdmans, 2009], 328) suggests that Luke records "the transition of a godly believer (dependent upon OT revelation) into the new age of the Spirit, rather than the conversion of an unbeliever." Similarly, Brandon D. Crowe (*The Hope of Israel: The Resurrection of the Christ in the Acts of the Apostles* [Grand Rapids, MI: Baker Academic, 2020], 135) speaks of Cornelius as a Gentile who is "part of God's righteous remnant," who "occupied a unique place in the outworking of redemption." He was "already . . . a true believer in Israel's God when Peter meets him." If this is true, then what happens to Cornelius could be best labeled an "alteration" rather than a "conversion" (B. R. Gaventa, *From Darkness to Light: Aspects of Conversion in the New Testament*, Overtures to Biblical Theology 20 [Philadelphia: Fortress, 1986], 122). However, even if what happens to Cornelius is viewed as a conversion, as understood in the traditional sense, still, God's acceptance of Cornelius ("acceptable to him"; Acts 10:35) does not equal "justified before God," but rather his prayers and almsgiving are viewed as "commendable" actions in God's sight. For if Cornelius was already justified by this piety, then it would be unnecessary for God to send a vision to him, followed by Peter's sermon and the pouring out of the Spirit. Cornelius and his household were justified before God because they believed in Jesus ("everyone who believes in him receives forgiveness of sins through his name"; Acts 10:43). Peter's clarification of what happened that day makes this clear: they were "saved" through Peter's gospel "message" (Acts 11:14) when the "Holy Spirit fell on them" (Acts 11:15). Their salvation was a "gift" from God (Acts 11:17). It was God who "granted [them] repentance that leads to life" (Acts 11:18).

(Matt. 2:14). It also explains why "every unregenerate man" is not depicted as indulging in "every form of sin" all the time (even Herod cares about John, whom he will behead!).[59] However, just because we are not deprived of a mind that can think, a heart that can feel, and a will that can act, that does not mean that our faculties are spiritually sound enough to seek God so as to find salvation, or to know and love God so as to please him. As Michael Horton explains,

> The "total" in total depravity refers to its extensiveness, not intensiveness: that is, to the all-encompassing scope of our fallenness. It does not mean that we are as bad as we can possibly be, but that we are all guilty and corrupt to such an extent that there is no hope of pulling ourselves together, brushing ourselves off, and striving (with the help of grace) to overcome God's judgment and our own rebellion.[60]

With that explanation made, next I will demonstrate three ways in which this scriptural corpus highlights, in Jesus's own words, that what is "impossible" for man is possible "with God" (Matt. 19:26). That is, while I am aware of John's clarity on the topic (Jesus's statement: "No one can come to me unless the Father who sent me draws him"; John 6:44; cf. 3:27; 6:65; 8:36); and I agree with the hermeneutic *scriptura scripturae interpres* ("Scripture interprets Scripture"), nevertheless, I shall seek to show how the Synoptics and Acts add their own voice. Thus, the basic premise of my argument will be that, in these four books, God's action leads to a human response which in turn points to an underlying inability.

RANSOM THE CAPTIVES

Donald Guthrie summarizes "Jesus's estimate of man's sin in the Synoptic Gospels," stating that sin is universal, internal, enslavement, rebellion, and it

---

[59] Louis Berkhof, *Systematic Theology* (Grand Rapids, MI: Eerdmans, 1996), 246–47. So, while people are occasionally labeled "righteous" (Mark 6:20), "devout" (Luke 2:25), and "worthy" (Matt. 10:13), those labels do not indicate absolute internal and external purity or some intrinsic salvific righteousness before God. "No one is good expect God alone" (Luke 18:19). That Paul can say to the Jewish Council that he has "lived [his] life before God in all good conscience up to this day" (Acts 23:1) does not mean he was not acting like the chief of sinners earlier in Acts (Acts 8:1–3; 9:1–2; cf. 1 Tim. 1:15). He might have had a clear conscience before God, but he was still "a blasphemer, persecutor, and insolent opponent" of Jesus (1 Tim. 1:13). Moses could be viewed as "beautiful in God's sight" (Acts 7:20), but such beauty was not flawless, as evidenced by his murder of an Egyptian. King David could be labeled "a man after [God's] heart, who will do all my will" (Acts 13:22), but David's adultery is a clear indication that not "all" of God's moral will was fulfilled by him. The same can be said of the "good and righteous" Joseph of Arimathea, who was a secret disciple of Jesus because he feared what others might think or do to him (see John 19:38). Similarly, Zechariah, who receives the high praise in Luke 1:6 of being "righteous before God" and "walking blamelessly in all the commandments and statutes of the Lord," is judged moments later for his unbelief (he "did not believe" the angel's "words"; Luke 1:20).
[60] Michael Horton, *For Calvinism* (Grand Rapids, MI: Zondervan Academic, 2011), 41. Or, as he summarizes the final point above elsewhere (*Christian Faith*, 433), "Total depravity . . . means . . . there is no Archimedean point within us that is left unfallen, from which we might begin to bargain or to restore our condition (righteousness before God)."

merits condemnation. Under the heading of "enslavement," he states, "When seen against the background of adverse satanic forces, man in his sinful state is seen to be in the grip of Satan."[61] We are "slaves of sin" (Rom. 6:17, 20; cf. John 8:34). Yet, through Jesus, even those "in the bond of iniquity" (Acts 8:23) can be forgiven and set free (see Acts 13:38–41).

On this theme, Elizabeth Shively argues that the exorcism of the Gerasene demoniac recorded in Mark 5:1–19 depicts Mark's "basic story line in microcosm that develops throughout the Gospel as Jesus inaugurates the kingdom of God: Jesus is the Spirit-filled one who struggles against Satan and his hosts to liberate people in order to form a new community that does God's will."[62] While there is more to Mark than this theme (e.g., the major themes of Christology and discipleship), Shively is correct to see how both the Olivet Discourse (where "Mark envisions Jesus appearing as the Son of Man to triumph over hostile powers, freeing the elect and gathering them into an eschatological community") and the cross demonstrate "Jesus's victory over satanic power."[63] On the cross, Jesus bound Satan ("the strong man") and "plundered his goods" (Mark 3:27). That is, he gave "his life as a ransom for many" (Mark 10:45); he bought with his blood the forgiveness and freedom of God's elect.

SEEKERS ARE SOUGHT

A second way in which the power of God unto salvation is displayed in the Synoptics and Acts is through the work of the Son in calling people to himself. Throughout the Synoptics, Jesus issues universal calls to all people within the sound of his voice. For example, Jesus calls people to "repent and believe" (Mark 1:15), to "enter by the narrow gate" (Matt. 7:13), and to follow him (Mark 8:34). Jesus makes some people who were disinterested, interested in him through his irresistible call. For example, how else can we explain the conversions of Levi and Saul? How does the one man in all of Capernaum who is "sitting" (at his tax booth, no less!) as Jesus arrives in

---

[61] Donald Guthrie, *New Testament Theology* (Downers Grove, IL: InterVarsity Press, 1991), 191–92. I would add concepts of sin that Guthrie sees in the Johannine literature (193–97) to also apply to the Synoptics, such as sin as unbelief, ignorance, and lawlessness.

[62] Elizabeth E. Shively, *Apocalyptic Imagination in the Gospel of Mark: The Literary and Theological Role of Mark 3:22–30*, BZNW 189 (Berlin: Walter de Gruyter, 2012), 2.

[63] Shively, *Apocalyptic Imagination*, 220; cf. E. W. Klink: "The exodus liberation becomes in the NT a type of Christ's liberation of those enslaved to sin and death. Freedom is deepened to include liberation from our sinful imprisonment, and service is restored to its proper ruler, God. In the Synoptics this is displayed throughout the ministry of Jesus, who liberated slaves of sin and those held captive by demons (Mark 5:15) and opposed by disease and handicaps (e.g., Mark 5:29; Luke 13:12)" (E. W. Klink III, "Freedom," in *Dictionary of Jesus and the Gospels*, 295).

town suddenly get up and follow Jesus (Matt. 9:9) and take on his kingdom mission (Matt. 10:5–42; 28:18–20)? How does Saul the persecutor (he "was ravaging the church, and entering house after house, he dragged off men and women and committed them to prison"; Acts 8:3) become Paul the gospel preacher ("And immediately he proclaimed Jesus in the synagogues, saying, 'He is the Son of God' "; Acts 9:20)? Indeed, the conversion of Saul is the clearest examples of monergistic salvation.[64]

Moreover, the response to Jesus's call, "Follow me" (Mark 1:17; cf. Mark 1:20), to Simon, Andrew, James, and John—"And immediately they left their nets and followed" (Mark 1:18; cf. Mark 1:20)—is also remarkable. It is certainly a demonstration of the human will to leave family ("they left their father Zebedee"), household ("with the hired servants"), and occupation/finances ("the boat," Mark 1:20; "their nets," Mark 1:18). But, if any emphasis is to be placed on Mark's usual καὶ εὐθύς associated with the first apostles' actions, it is the immediacy of Christ's sovereign call. In the Johannine tradition, Jesus's teaching in John 6:44 comes to mind: "No one can come to me unless the Father who sent me draws him." In the Synoptics, Jesus's claim in Matthew 11:27 is even more precise to the point: "All things have been handed over to me by my Father, and no one knows the Son except the Father, and no one knows the Father except the Son and anyone to whom the Son chooses to reveal him."[65] That remarkable claim of sovereignty is followed by a call: "Come to me" (Matt. 11:28). Surely, the ordering of ideas is important. God's calling precedes human coming. The pattern of their mission is the pattern of salvation: Jesus "called to him those whom he desired, and they came to him" (Mark 3:13).

Such statements instruct us that even those who seemingly sought after a relationship with Jesus were first sought out by God. Sinners might call out to Jesus for mercy, but it is only because Jesus "came . . . to call . . . sinners" (Luke 5:32). For example, the conversion of Zacchaeus features this

---

[64] Would Thomas Oden's definition of prevenient grace, which follows, fit Saul's story? No! Prevenient grace, says Oden, is "the grace that begins to enable one to choose further to cooperate with saving grace. By offering the will the restored capacity to respond to grace, the person then may freely and increasingly become an active, willing participant in receiving the conditions for justification" (Thomas C. Oden, *John Wesley's Scriptural Christianity* [Grand Rapids, MI: Zondervan, 1994], 243).

[65] According to Jesus, whenever a person comes to know him in a saving manner, it is not based on human ability (e.g., our wisdom or resources), but solely on the work of the Father and the Son (cf. Matt. 16:17; John 1:13; 1 Cor. 4:7). To say that "all things have been handed over" to Jesus is to say that absolutely everything, even a person's salvation, has been "given . . . into his hands" (John 13:3; cf. 3:35). As Irenaeus of Lyons said, "For the Son . . . reveals the Father to all—to whom he wills, when he wills, and as the Father wills" (D. H. Williams, trans. and ed., *Matthew: Interpreted by Early Christian Commentators* [Grand Rapids, MI: Eerdmans, 2018], 235).

rich man's efforts to see Jesus. Because "he was seeking to see Jesus" (Luke 19:3), "he ran on ahead" of the crowd "and climbed up into a sycamore tree" (Luke 19:4). Yet, Jesus's final line in that conversion story helps us interpret the whole text: "For the Son of Man came to seek and to save the lost" (Luke 19:10). All of Zacchaeus's actions relate to Jesus's ultimate action. Jesus stopped under the tree, called the man down, and invited himself over ("I *must* stay at your house"; Luke 19:5), because he was in Jericho for the very purpose of seeking and saving this once notorious sinner. In the conversion of this "chief tax collector" (Luke 19:2) Jesus accomplishes the impossible: he pulls a camel through the eye of the needle (Luke 18:24, 27).

THE ACTS OF GOD IN ACTS

A third way the Evangelists showcase the theme that what is "impossible" for man is possible "with God" (Matt. 19:26) is in the acts of God in the salvation of people as recorded in the Acts of the Apostles. Do we see in Acts "the light of nature" or "the law" leading people to a saving relationship with God, or do we see "the Holy Spirit through the word" leading people to repent and believe?[66] We see the latter, that "faith is . . . the gift of God," that "God bestows the power or ability to believe," that only by the "grace of God" are sinners "enabled to believe."[67] Throughout Acts the work of God comes before the response of man, and, the positive response of men and women to the gospel is repeatedly declared a work of God.

For example, after the apostles were "filled with the Holy Spirit" (Acts 2:4; 13:9) or "clothed with power from on high" (Luke 24:49), they "began to speak" (Acts 2:4; cf. 4:8, 31).[68] Their message was effective only because the Lord was working on their hearers ("they were cut to the heart"; Acts 2:37) and because God determined to "add to their number . . . those who were being saved" (Acts 2:47).[69] People might ask, as they do after Peter's Pentecost sermon, "What shall we do?" (Acts 2:37), and they might act in obedience to the command to "repent and be baptized" (Acts 2:38), but it is

---

[66] Article 6 of the Third and Fourth Heads of Doctrine, the Canons of Dort.

[67] Articles 13 and 14 of the Third and Fourth Heads of Doctrine, the Canons of Dort.

[68] "And the disciples were filled with joy and with the Holy Spirit . . . spoke . . . a great number of both Jews and Greeks believed. . . . So they remained for a long time, speaking boldly for the Lord, who bore witness to the word of his grace" (Acts 13:52; 14:1, 3).

[69] The phrases Luke uses for the saints in Ephesus ("those who through grace had believed"; Acts 18:27) and Corinth ("I have many in this city who are my people"; Acts 18:10) helps us understand the dynamics of "Crispus, the ruler of the synagogue . . . together with his entire household" who "believed in the Lord" (v. 8). They believed due to God's election and saving grace.

clear that their salvation from start to finish is all of God's grace (e.g., "everyone whom the Lord our God calls to himself"; Acts 2:39). The pattern is consistent throughout Acts: the Lord first sends his Spirit ("I will pour out my Spirit"; Acts 2:17; cf. Acts 15:8), then the Spirit falls upon the hearers (Acts 10:44; cf. 11:15), and finally those hearers respond ("everyone who calls upon . . ."; see Acts 2:18, 21). It is God who opens hearts "to pay attention" (Acts 16:14) to "the word of his grace" (Acts 20:32) and grants both "repentance that leads to life" (Acts 11:18) and faith that leads to "eternal life" ("as many as were appointed to eternal life believed"; Acts 13:48; God "opened a door of faith"; Acts 14:27). The only reason "a great number" believe and turn to the Lord (Acts 11:21) is that they had experienced "the grace of God" (Acts 11:23). This is why the apostles boast not in their own power (e.g., "why do you stare at us, as though by our own power or piety we have made him walk?"; Acts 3:12), but in "the things that God has done" (Acts 21:19), in "the gospel of the grace of God" (Acts 20:24).

Conclusion

Matthew, Mark, and Luke do not write from the angle of the inherited guilt of Adam's first sin. They do not focus on the root (federal representation in Adam) and condition (our spiritual deadness and inability). However, as they record the life of Jesus and the acts of the early church, they clearly show the fruits of man's inherited depravity—from the disbelief of the righteous priest Zechariah to Herod's horrific murder of toddlers to the most abhorrent of all evil acts, namely, the crucifixion of God's beloved Son. "All the actual transgressions which proceed from" Adam's transgression are evident.[70] A bad tree produced lots of bad fruit. The first sinner surely brought forth a thousand denarii of debt for each and every human created in God's image but tainted by Adam's fall.

As demonstrated from the three Evangelists' views, I have shown that they see something of how the whole human nature of the whole human race is infected with an inherited depravity which produces every sort of sin, and that human inability is a serious issue that only God can solve. Moreover, and most importantly, perhaps none of the authors of the NT paint a bleaker picture than these three writers of how vile such sins are in God's sight.

[70] WSC A18.

Matthew, Mark, and Luke not only give a clear view of God's coming judgment (the "hell" of eschatological condemnation), but also they all focus on the greatest act of infamy and yet of grace. God's Son is God-forsaken on the cross so that "many" (Matt. 20:28) hell-bound sinners might experience on the final day the pronouncement not only of acceptance ("your sins are forgiven"; Matt. 9:5) but approval ("Well done"; Matt. 25:21). Amazing grace. Inexpressible bliss! Ruined sinners reclaimed.

14

"Everyone Who Practices Sin Is a Slave to Sin"

SIN IN THE JOHANNINE LITERATURE

Murray J. Smith

1. The Surprising Lack of Interest in Johannine Hamartiology

Martin Luther, preaching on John 3:18, declared with characteristic confidence and clarity, "There is no greater sin than unbelief." In fact, he continued, "the sum of it all is that unbelief in the Son is our *only* sin."[1] Following Luther, modern scholarship on the Gospel of John has tended to emphasize "unbelief" as the sum of sin. According to Rudolf Bultmann, "Sin" in the Gospel of John "is not primarily immoral behavior" and "does not consist in any particular action, but is unbelief."[2] This view has been common in modern accounts of John's Gospel.[3] Ernst Haenchen even concluded that "the concept of sin plays no constitutive role in the

---

[1] Luther's *Sermon on Pentecost Monday at Home* (1532), reflecting on John 3:18, in Craig S. Farmer, *John 1–12*, Reformation Commentary on Scripture–New Testament 4 (Downers Grove, IL: IVP Academic, 2014), 106 (emphasis added).
[2] Rudolf Bultmann, *The Gospel of John: A Commentary*, trans. G. R. Beasley-Murray (Philadelphia: Westminster, 1971), 551; cf. Bultmann, *Theology of the New Testament*, trans. K. Grobel, 2 vols. (New York: Scribner, 1955), 2:53–54.
[3] More recently: G. R. Greene, "God's Lamb: Divine Provision for Sin," *PRSt* 37 (2010): 161: "Sin in John is the willful refusal to 'believe' in Jesus"; Gary M. Burge, "The Gospel and Epistles of John," in *T&T Clark Companion to the Doctrine of Sin*, ed. K. L. Johnson and D. Lauber (London: Bloomsbury, 2016), 79–80: "In the Gospel of John, the primary sin we witness is the rejection of God's revelation in Christ. Sin, therefore, is tied to revelation rather than the usual moral categories we find elsewhere in the New Testament . . . disbelief is their fundamental sin. . . . The failure to believe, to embrace Jesus, to acknowledge the revelation of what God is doing in Christ—this is what brings the ultimate crisis to the world in Johannine thought."

Gospel of John."[4] This helps to explain why modern scholarship has given relatively little attention to the question of sin in John. If sin is simply "unbelief," what more is there to say? Further, the tendency to deny that the apostle John was the author of the Gospel, Letters, and Revelation has worked against attempts to construct a *Johannine* hamartiology.[5] While recent scholarship provides some notable exceptions,[6] there seems to have been only one major study of John's doctrine of sin published in the last one hundred years, and even this work is limited to the Gospel.[7]

This relative lack of interest in Johannine hamartiology is surprising for at least two reasons. First, the Gospel, Letters, and Revelation of John explicitly frame their understanding of Christ and salvation in terms of sin: Jesus is "the Lamb of God, who *takes away the sin of the world*" (John 1:29); Christ "appeared in order *to take away sins*, and in him there is no sin" (1 John 3:5); Jesus Christ is the one "who loves us and has *freed us from our sins* by his blood" (Rev. 1:5). Moreover, John's works include statements which—perhaps more than any others among the apostolic writings—might be taken as holistic assessments of the human condition in sin, or even as definitions of sin: "everyone who practices sin is a slave to sin" (John 8:34); "Everyone who makes a practice of sinning also practices lawlessness; sin is lawlessness" (1 John 3:4).[8] My goal in this chapter is to make a small contribution to our understanding of this relatively under-examined aspect of John's works, and to construct a theology of sin in the Johannine literature, with a view to its implications for the Christian doctrine of sin.

---

[4] Ernst Haenchen, *Das Johannesevangelium: ein Kommentar* (Tübingen: Mohr, 1980), 493: ". . . *der Sündenbegriff im Johannesevangelium keine konstitutive Rolle spielt*" (my translation).

[5] For a defense of the apostle John's authorship of the Gospel and Letters, see: Andreas J. Köstenberger, *A Theology of John's Gospel and Letters*. Biblical Theology of the New Testament (Grand Rapids, MI: Zondervan, 2009), 69–76, 82–88. For the apostle John as the author of Revelation, see R. H. Mounce, *The Book of Revelation*, NICNT, rev. ed. (Grand Rapids, MI: Eerdmans, 1998), 8–15; Grant R. Osborne, *Revelation*, BECNT (Grand Rapids, MI: Baker, 2002), 2–6.

[6] Craig R. Koester, *The Word of Life: A Theology of John's Gospel* (Grand Rapids, MI: Eerdmans, 2008), 53–81; Köstenberger, *Theology of John's Gospel and Letters*, 474–79; Jean Zumstein, "Die Sünde im Johannesevangelium," *Zeitschrift für Neues Testament* 12 (2009): 27–35; Greene, "God's Lamb," 147–64; E.-G. Lyu, "Das Verständnis von Sünde im Johannesevangelium," *Korean New Testament Studies* 18.1 (2011): 131–61; Robert W. Yarbrough, "Sin in the Gospels, Acts, and Hebrews to Revelation," in *Fallen: A Theology of Sin*, ed. Christopher W. Morgan and Robert A. Peterson, Theology in Community (Wheaton, IL: Crossway, 2013), 83–106; Paul A. Rainbow, *Johannine Theology: The Gospel, the Epistles, and the Apocalypse* (Downers Grove, IL: IVP Academic, 2014), 115–45; Burge, "Gospel and Epistles," 79–96; Thomas H. McCall, *Against God and Nature: The Doctrine of Sin*, Foundations of Evangelical Theology (Wheaton, IL: Crossway, 2019), 97–101.

[7] Rainer Metzner, *Das Verständnis der Sünde im Johannesevangelium*, WUNT 122 (Tübingen: Mohr Siebeck, 2000); cf. also Timothy Owings, "The Concept of Sin in the Fourth Gospel" (unpublished PhD diss., Southern Baptist Theological Seminary, 1983).

[8] The Westminster Catechisms employ 1 John 3:4 in their definitions of sin (WSC Q14; WLC Q24).

2. The Dark Web of Sin: Tracing the Threads

A number of recent works have begun to recognize that "The Johannine literature presents a rich and multifaceted account of sin."[9] Given the subject matter, however, it is perhaps more appropriate to describe John's doctrine of sin as a dark web with many interwoven threads. Unravelling these threads is the task before us.

The place to start is with John's *language* for "sin." Purely at the linguistic level, "sin" is certainly prominent in John's works.[10] The Gospel employs the ἁμαρτ- root twenty-five times;[11] John's first letter, though only a brief five chapters, has it a further twenty-seven times;[12] and Revelation three times.[13] The Greek ἁμαρτ- word group, like the Hebrew term חטא, which ἁμαρτ- words commonly translate in the LXX, seems to have originally carried the sense of "missing the mark." In both Hebrew and Greek, however, the terms are commonly used in the more general moral sense of "wrongdoing," and in the biblical texts, this "wrongdoing" is especially related to God and his word.[14] But John also has other words for "sin," and these fill out the picture even further. The Gospel employs the adjectives πονηρός ("evil" or "wicked") and φαῦλος ("base" or "wicked") to describe sinful behavior.[15] The Letters also speak of "wicked" (πονηρός) words and works,[16] of "unrighteous" actions (ἀδικία),[17] and—only in one place, but it is a crucial text—of "lawlessness" (ἀνομία [2x]; 1 John 3:4). Moreover, in tracing the threads of the web of sin in John's works, we also need to set the Johannine terminology for sin within the *context* of "the world" (ὁ κόσμος),[18] and "the

---

[9] McCall, *Against God and Nature*, 97; cf. Metzner, *Verständnis der Sünde*, 355: "*Das Spectrum des johanneischen Sündenbegriffs ist ausgesprochen vielfältig*" ("The spectrum of Johannine concept of sin is extremely diverse").

[10] Burge, "Gospel and Epistles," 79, is technically correct that "John refers to *hamartia* (sin) more than any other Gospel." John has the noun "sin" (ἡ ἁμαρτία) 17 times, while Matthew has it 7 times, Mark 6 times, and Luke 11 times. The statement, however, may be misleading. As Burge acknowledges in a footnote (79 n. 1), when all of the cognate words for sin in the ἁμαρτ- word group are taken into account, Luke has the ἁμαρτ- root more than John (33x).

[11] (1) ἡ ἁμαρτία (17x; "sin"): singular: John 1:29; 8:21, 34 (2x), 46; 9:41 (2x); 15:22 (2x), 24; 16:8, 9; 19:11; plural: 8:24 (2x); 9:34; 20:23; (2) ἁμαρτωλός (4x; "sinner"): John 9:16, 24–25, 31; (3) ἁμαρτάνω (4x; "I sin"): John 5:14; 8:11; 9:2–3. Note that this last list includes Jesus's command to the woman caught in adultery to "sin no more" (8:11), which may not be part of the original text of the Gospel.

[12] (1) ἡ ἁμαρτία (17x): singular: 1 John 1:7, 8; 3:4 (2x), 5, 8, 9; 5:16 (2x), 17 (2x); plural: 1 John 1:9 (2x); 2:2, 12; 3:5; 4:10; (2) ἁμαρτάνω (11x): 1 John 1:10; 2:1 (2x); 3:6 (2x), 8, 9 (2x); 5:16 (2x), 18.

[13] ἡ ἁμαρτία: Rev. 1:5; 18:4, 5 (all plural).

[14] For extended discussion of the lexical data, see esp. Moisés Silva, ed. *New International Dictionary of New Testament Theology and Exegesis*, 4 vols. (Grand Rapids, MI: Zondervan, 2014), 1:255–63.

[15] πονηρός: John 3:19; 7:7; φαῦλος: John 3:20; 5:29.

[16] πονηρός: 1 John 3:12 (2x); 2 John 11; 3 John 10.

[17] ἀδικία: 1 John 1:9; 5:17; cf. John 7:18.

[18] ὁ κόσμος in the Gospel of John (77x): 1:9–10 (4x), 29; 3:16–17 (4x), 19; 4:42; 6:14, 33, 51; 7:4, 7; 8:12, 23 (2x), 26; 9:5 (2x), 39; 10:36; 11:9, 27; 12:19, 25, 31 (2x), 46–47 (3x); 13:1 (2x); 14:17, 19, 22, 27, 30–31 (2x); 15:18–19 (6x); 16:8, 11, 20–21 (2x), 28 (2x), 33 (2x); 17:5–6, 9, 11, 13–16 (7x), 18 (2x), 21, 23–25 (3x); 18:20, 36–37

devil" (ὁ διάβολος),[19] as well as relating it to the *consequences* of sin, namely, "death" (ὁ θάνατος, ἀποθνῄσκω),[20] and God's "judgment" (ἡ κρίσις, κρίνω),[21] or "wrath" (ἡ ὀργή).[22] All of this needs to be understood within the frame of John's distinctive dualisms: "light *and darkness*," "love *and hate*," "sight *and blindness*," "faith *and unbelief*."[23]

In order to focus the discussion in the present chapter, and to keep it within reasonable limits, I concentrate in what follows on John's language for sin, within the web of connections just noted. This approach reveals that John's language for sin coalesces around three major threads, namely: (1) sin and revelation; (2) sin, suffering, death, and judgment within God's sovereignty; and, (3) sin and sacrifice.[24] These three threads broadly correspond to John's teaching about: (1) the nature of sin; (2) the effects and consequences of sin; and, (3) the removal of sin. As we trace these threads, first in the Gospel and then in the Letters and Revelation, it will become clear that John especially relates the whole complex web of sin to God's climactic revelation of himself in Christ. John's understanding of sin is Christologically conditioned. My argument throughout, therefore, is that Luther was correct to recognize "unbelief in the Son" as the *center* of John's teaching on sin, but that he overstated the case when he asserted that "unbelief in the Son is

---

(3x); 21:25. In the Letters (24x): 1 John 2:2, 15 (3x), 16 (2x), 17; 3:1, 13, 17; 4:1, 3, 4, 5 (3x), 9, 14, 17; 5:4 (2x), 5, 19; 2 John 7. In Revelation (3x): 11:15; 13:8; 17:8.

[19] ὁ διάβολος in the Gospel (2x): 8:44; 13:2; cf. 6:70. In the Letters (4x): 1 John 3:8 (3x), 10. In Revelation (5x): 2:10; 12:9, 12; 20:2, 10. Also: (1) ὁ Σατανᾶς ("the Satan"): John 13:27; Rev. 2:9, 13 (2x), 24; 3:9; 12:9; 20:2, 7; (2) ὁ ἄρχων τοῦ κόσμου τούτου ("the ruler of this world"): John 12:31; 14:30; 16:11; (3) ὁ πονηρός ("the evil one"): John 17:15; 1 John 2:13, 14; 3:12; 5:18, 19.

[20] ὁ θάνατος in the Gospel (8x): 5:24; 8:51–52 (2x); 11:4, 13; 12:33; 18:32; 21:19. In the Letters (5x): 1 John 3:14; 5:16. In Revelation (19x): 1:18; 2:10, 11, 23; 6:8 (2x); 9:6 (2x); 12:11; 13:3 (2x), 12; 18:8; 20:6, 13, 14 (2x); 21:4, 8. ἀποθνῄσκω in the Gospel (28x): 4:47, 49; 6:49–50 (2x), 58; 8:21, 24 (2x), 52–53 (3x); 11:14, 16, 21, 25–26 (2x), 32, 37, 50–51 (2x); 12:24 (2x), 33; 18:14, 32; 19:7; 21:23 (2x). In Revelation (6x): 3:2; 8:9, 11; 9:6; 14:13; 16:3. Also: ἀπόλλυμι (in the sense of death/loss of life) in the Gospel (8x): John 3:16; 6:39; 10:10, 28; 11:50; 12:25; 17:12; 18:9. In the Letters (1x): 2 John 8. In Revelation (1x): 18:14. ἀπώλεια in the Gospel (1x): 17:12. In Revelation (2x): 17:8, 11.

[21] ἡ κρίσις in the Gospel (11x): 3:19; 5:22, 24, 27, 29, 30; 7:24; 8:16; 12:31; 16:8, 11. In the Letters (1x): 1 John 4:17. In Revelation (4x): 14:7; 16:7; 18:10; 19:2. κρίνω in the Gospel (19x): 3:17, 18 (2x); 5:22, 30; 7:24 (2x), 51; 8:15 (2x), 16, 26, 50; 12:47 (2x), 48 (2x); 16:11; 18:31. In Revelation (9x): 6:10; 11:18; 16:5; 18:8, 20; 19:2, 11; 20:12, 13; cf. κατακρίνω (2x): John 8:10, 11. Also: ἐλέγχω in the Gospel (3x): 3:20; 8:46; 16:8. In Revelation (1x): 3:19.

[22] ἡ ὀργή in the Gospel (1x): 3:36. In Revelation (6x): 6:16, 17; 11:18; 14:10; 16:19; 19:15.

[23] John also refers to "the flesh" (ἡ σάρξ), but does not relate it to sin in any systematic way. The incarnation of "the Word" in "flesh" (1:14; 1 John 4:2; 2 John 7) shows that "flesh" fundamentally refers to embodied humanity as part of God's good creation. Jesus can therefore speak of his "flesh" in salvific terms as "the bread that I will give for the life of the world" (6:51; cf. 6:52–56 [5x]). The "flesh" is weak in relation to the power of God, but not necessarily corrupt or culpable (1:13; 3:6 [2x]; 6:63; 17:2). In Revelation, "flesh" (σάρξ) refers to the weakness of creaturely embodiment, especially when it comes under judgment, but there is, again, no indication that the flesh itself is the problem (Rev. 17:16; 19:18 [5x]; 19:21). There are two exceptions to this pattern of usage, where "flesh" seems to have more negative moral connotations: in John 8:15 Jesus speaks of the Jews judging "according to the flesh" (κατὰ τὴν σάρκα); 1 John 2:16 speaks of "the desires of the flesh" (ἡ ἐπιθυμία τῆς σαρκὸς) as an aspect of human corruption.

[24] These three threads are similar to those traced by Burge, "Gospel and Epistles," 79–96, who treats John's doctrine of sin under the headings "Sin and Revelation," "Sin and Infirmity," and "Sin and Sacrifice." The points at which my analysis differs from that of Burge will become clear.

our *only* sin." John traces a thick web of sin which penetrates deep into the human condition, and reaches far and wide in its implications for the world. As a means of articulating this complex web, I suggest in my conclusion that the Johannine material yields an appropriately sevenfold anatomy of sin.[25] In the Johannine literature, sin is: (1) personal, (2) practical, (3) powerful, (4) perverted, (5) pervasive, (6) persistent, and (7) punishable.[26] This comprehensive assessment of the human condition with regard to sin provides firm support for the classic Reformed understanding of humanity's "total depravity" in sin.[27] Even more importantly, it provides the dark backdrop for John's glorious declaration of the gospel: God in Christ is "the light," who "shines in the darkness" (John 1:5), who makes it possible to "walk in the light" (1 John 1:7), and who will finally "be light" for his people, banishing the darkness of sin forever (Rev. 22:5).

3. Sin in the Gospel of John: The Light Shines in the Darkness

3.1. Sin and Revelation: The Light of the World Exposes the Nature of Sin

3.1.1. Introduction

The Gospel of John, first of all, relates sin to God's climactic revelation of himself in Christ. Jesus's coming from God as "the light of the world" *exposes* the nature of sin. John especially develops this first thread in John 1, 3, and 8–9, where he strongly ties Jesus's identity as "the light of the world" to the language of sin (John 1:5, 9; 3:19–20; 8:12; 9:5; cf. 12:36, 46). He further develops the same thread in John 15–16 in relation to the work of the Spirit. As "the light of the world," Jesus reveals God in a new and climactic way. This also means that he exposes more fully than ever the true nature of the sin of those who reject God and refuse to come to him.

3.1.2. The Light Shines in the Dark World: John 1

The Gospel prologue already introduces sin as the rejection of God as he reveals himself in Christ (John 1:1–18). The subject of the Gospel is "the

---

[25] I allude here to the influential work of R. Alan Culpepper, *Anatomy of the Fourth Gospel: A Study in Literary Design* (Philadelphia: Fortress, 1983), but do not intend any direct reference to his various theses.

[26] My thinking toward this taxonomy was stimulated by a conversation with Chris Seglenieks at the Sydney College of Divinity "Jesus of Nazareth" Conference in September 2017.

[27] For the confessional treatments, see esp. Belgic Confession 14–15; Heidelberg Catechism Q3–14; Canons of Dort 3/4.1–4; WCF 6.1–6; WLC Q21–29; WSC Q13–19.

Word," who was "with God . . . in the beginning," who indeed "was God" from all eternity, and who brought "life" and "light" to humanity (1:1–4). There are strong echoes here of the Genesis creation account (Gen. 1:1–5), but the Gospel immediately shifts to the present tense and introduces the drama that will shape its entire narrative: "the light shines in the darkness [τὸ φῶς ἐν τῇ σκοτίᾳ φαίνει], and the darkness has not overcome it [ἡ σκοτία αὐτὸ οὐ κατέλαβεν]" (John 1:5). It quickly becomes apparent that the "darkness" (ἡ σκοτία) to which John refers is not merely the absence of physical light, but a sinister, evil reality opposed to God and the Word. "The true light," John continues, "which gives light to everyone" came into "the world," but was rejected by the world (1:9–11). In this way, even though the Gospel's prologue does not explicitly mention "sin," it begins to reveal that the fundamental problem with the world is its rejection of God's "light" in Christ.

The prologue also provides an important introduction to the Johannine characterization of "the world" (ὁ κόσμος). In this initial reference, and at the broadest possible level, "the world" refers to created reality (1:10; cf. 12:25; 13:1; 16:21; 17:5, 24; 21:25). Immediately, however, the Gospel introduces a second layer of meaning, which dominates its presentation: "he was in the world, and the world was made through him, *yet the world did not know him* [καὶ ὁ κόσμος αὐτὸν οὐκ ἔγνω]" (1:10). "The world" here, and throughout the Gospel, is humanity in rebellion against God: humanity ignorant of its Creator (1:10; 17:25), hating its Savior (7:7; 15:18), and therefore facing its righteous Judge (3:19; 9:39; 12:31; 16:8, 11). In this context, John's first explicit reference to "sin" (ἡ ἁμαρτία) confirms the negative portrayal of "the world": John the Baptist identifies Jesus as "the Lamb of God who takes away *the sin of the world* [τὴν ἁμαρτίαν τοῦ κόσμου]" (1:29). The reference to "sin" in the singular and "the world" as a collective whole communicates that it is not only the Jews but people everywhere who are involved in the problem of sin.[28] As the Gospel develops, "the world" (ὁ κόσμος) sometimes refers particularly to "the Jews" (1:11; cf. 7:4; 18:20), but elsewhere unambiguously extends to include Samaritans, Greeks, and all people (1:29; 3:16; 4:42; 12:19–20, 46–47). This first explicit reference to "sin," therefore,

---

[28] τοῦ κόσμου could be: (1) a possessive genitive ("sin belonging to the world"), (2) a source genitive ("sin coming from/produced by the world"), or (3) a subjective genitive ("sin committed by the world"). These possibilities do not significantly change the sense of the statement. The singular τὴν ἁμαρτίαν ("the sin") refers to the world's "sin" as "one huge entity" (Murray J. Harris, *John, Exegetical Guide to the Greek New Testament*, ed. A. J. Köstenberger and R. W. Yarbrough [Nashville: Broadman & Holman, 2015], 45).

establishes the first fundamental element in John's anatomy of sin, namely, that sin is a universal problem; it is *pervasive*.[29] At the same time, John the Baptist's declaration of Jesus as "the Lamb of God" provides reason for hope, for the sinful, rebellious "world" remains the object of God's love, expressed in the gift of his Son (cf. 3:16–17; 6:33, 51; 12:47).[30] There is more to say about this below.

3.1.3. *The Light Rejected by the World: John 3*

John 3:16–21 picks up the prologue's introduction of Jesus as "the light," and explicitly relates it to the language of sin. This key passage confirms that the core of sin is the rejection of God as he reveals himself in his Son. This is clear from John's statement that many have "not believed [μὴ πεπίστευκεν] in the name of the only Son of God."[31] The astounding reality is that many of the people of the world reject the God who made them, and refuse to receive "his only begotten Son" (KJV), whom "God sent" out of "love" for "the world" to be "the light" (3:16, 19–21).[32] It was while preaching on this verse that Luther understandably made the comment with which we began— "unbelief in the Son is our only sin." His fundamental insight is that sin has a theological or—better—a Christological center. At its heart, sin is the refusal to humbly trust in God; its climactic expression is the rejection of God's Son, sent in love as "the Savior of the world" (4:42).[33]

The Gospel, however, presses further, to explain *why* people do not believe in the Son, and *how* their sin is expressed. First, people do not believe in the Son because they have "loved the darkness rather than the light [ἠγάπησαν οἱ ἄνθρωποι μᾶλλον τὸ σκότος ἢ τὸ φῶς]" (3:19). In the context

---

[29] Cf. John Calvin, *The Gospel according to St. John 1–10*, trans. T. H. L. Parker, *Calvin's Commentaries* 4 (Grand Rapids, MI: Eerdmans, 1959), 32: "From this we infer that the whole world is bound in the same condemnation; and that since all men without exception are guilty of unrighteousness before God, they have need of reconciliation." Granted, John 1:29 does not teach *explicitly* that all people everywhere, without exception, are guilty of sin, but John's teaching on the pervasive nature of sin is certainly consistent with that truth (cf. Rom. 3:9–20, 23).

[30] Koester, *Word of Life*, 81: "John's ominous portrayal of 'the world' gives depth to his understanding of the love of God and the work of Jesus. The 'world' in John's Gospel is not characterized by soft summer breezes and the graceful light of dawn, by meadows filled with flowers or gentle waves upon the shore. It requires little effort to love a world like that. But in John's Gospel God loves the world that hates him; he gives his Son for the world that rejects him. He offers his love to a world estranged from him in order to overcome its hostility and bring the world back into relationship with its Creator (3:16)."

[31] It is unclear where Jesus's speech ends and the Gospel's commentary begins. For recent discussion, favoring a transition at John 3:16, see Edward W. Klink, *John*, ZECNT (Grand Rapids, MI: Zondervan, 2016), 204–5.

[32] Most modern translations render the Greek adjective μονογενής with "only" (ESV, NRSV) or "one and only" (CSB, NIV) in its five Johannine occurrences (John 1:14, 18; 3:16, 18; 1 John 4:9). For the traditional rendering "only begotten," see Charles Lee Irons, "A Lexical Defence of the Johannine 'Only Begotten'," in *Retrieving Eternal Generation*, ed. F. Sanders and S. R. Swain (Grand Rapids, MI: Zondervan Academic, 2017), 98–116.

[33] For unbelief as the beginning of sin, see Francis Turretin, *Institutes of Elenctic Theology*, 3 vols. (Phillipsburg, NJ: P&R, 1992–97), 1:605–6.

of the most fundamental human duty to "love the LORD your God with all your heart and with all your soul and with all your might" (Deut. 6:5; cf. Matt. 22:37–38; Mark 12:29–30; Luke 10:27–28), the refusal to love God, combined with a disordered love for the "darkness," implies a deep inner corruption, a perversion that is pervasive throughout the whole human person (cf. WCF 6.2, 4).[34] Jesus later explicates this same inner corruption in terms of the lack of "the love of God" and the failure to "seek the glory that comes from God," which culminates in the rejection of Jesus, whom God the Father has sent (John 5:30–47, esp. vv. 42, 44). Second, sin is expressed in actual immoral behavior. People loved the darkness, John explains, "because their works were evil [ἦν γὰρ αὐτῶν πονηρὰ τὰ ἔργα]" (3:19). It is those who "do wicked things" (πᾶς . . . ὁ φαῦλα πράσσων) who "hate the light" and "do not come to the light, lest [their] works should be exposed [ἵνα μὴ ἐλεγχθῇ τὰ ἔργα αὐτοῦ]" (3:20). John's constructions here leave no doubt that he speaks of a pattern of actual immoral behavior—of evil *works*, and wicked *deeds*—just as Jesus later speaks of "those who have done evil [οἱ . . . τὰ φαῦλα πράξαντες]" (5:29).

In this first key passage, then, John begins to weave together several threads of the web of sin. The core of sin is the rejection of God, climactically expressed in the refusal to trust in his Son. But this sin also involves a deep inner corruption, and has an active, ethical dimension. Sin is a deeply *personal* rejection of God in Christ, entails an inner *perversion*, and has eminently *practical* implications in the life of the sinner. It is no wonder that, in John 3, Jesus teaches Nicodemus that the only possible hope for a person "to see" or "to enter the kingdom of God" comes from outside themselves, indeed, "from above" (3:3 ESV mg.), that is, from God's gracious and miraculous initiative in giving "new birth" by his Spirit (3:3–8; cf. 1:13).[35]

---

[34] Cf. John Calvin, *Institutes of the Christian Religion*, ed. John T. McNeill, trans. Ford Lewis Battles, 2 vols. (Philadelphia: Westminster, 1960), 2.1.8 (1:251): ". . . we are so vitiated and perverted in every part of our nature that by this great corruption we stand justly condemned and convicted before God"; Turretin, *Institutes*, 1:637: "Men are not only destitute of righteousness, but also full of unrighteousness; incapable of good, but also inclined to evil; turned away from God, as the immutable and eternal good, but also turned toward the creature and inclined to every vice"; Herman Bavinck, *Reformed Dogmatics*, ed. John Bolt, trans. John Vriend, 4 vols. (Grand Rapids, MI: Baker Academic, 2003–8), 3:119: "As extensive as original sin is in humanity as a whole, so it is also in the individual person. It holds sway over the whole person, over mind and will, heart and conscience, soul and body, over all one's capacities and powers."

[35] The Greek adverb ἄνωθεν can mean either "from above" or "again" (BDAG 92). In John 3:3, this creates an ambiguity, which seems deliberate. Nicodemus thinks that Jesus speaks of a second natural birth (John 3:4), when in reality Jesus affirms that entry into the kingdom of God is possible only through the sovereign work of God's Spirit. Cf. Klink, *John*, 196: "The intentional ambiguity of this adverb is part of the plot."

3.1.4. The Light Exposes Sin: John 8–9

John 8 and 9 further develop the relationship between Jesus, "the light of the world," and the exposure of sin. In these two chapters, where Jesus twice declares himself to be "the light of the world [Ἐγώ εἰμι τὸ φῶς τοῦ κόσμου]" (8:12; cf. 9:5), the language of sin is particularly prominent.[36] The revelation of the light exposes sin in its darkest forms; it shows that the Jews are not only guilty of sin and sins, but also enslaved to sin.

In John 8, Jesus reveals that the Jews are guilty of sin because they fail to recognize and accept that, in Jesus, God himself is present in their midst. The exchange takes place in Jerusalem during the Feast of Tabernacles (7:2, 10), which celebrated God's presence with his people in the wilderness as the light-giving "pillar of fire" (Ex. 13:21).[37] In this context, Jesus's claim to be "the light of the world" recalls God's self-revelation as "light" throughout the OT and evocatively hints at his identity as the one who embodies the divine presence, and so brings "the light of life" (John 8:12).[38] This is confirmed when Jesus declares that he bears the divine name, which the Lord revealed to Moses, and charges that "unless you believe that *I am*, you will die in your sins [ἐὰν γὰρ μὴ πιστεύσητε ὅτι ἐγώ εἰμι, ἀποθανεῖσθε ἐν ταῖς ἁμαρτίαις ὑμῶν]" (John 8:24; cf. Ex. 3:14 LXX: Ἐγώ εἰμι ὁ ὤν).[39] In rejecting Jesus, "the light of the world," the Jews are rejecting nothing less than God's life-giving presence in him.[40] Jesus's statement, of course, does not mean that there was no sin in the world, or among the Jews, before he came: the Gospel prologue presupposes a dark world (1:5); John the Baptist acknowledges sin prior to Jesus's revelation to the world (1:29); Jesus himself characterizes "the devil" as a "murderer *from the beginning* [ἀπ' ἀρχῆς]" (8:44). The sin to

---

[36] Sixteen of the twenty-five occurrences of the ἁμαρτ- root in the Gospel are found in John 8–9: ἡ ἁμαρτία: 8:21, 24, 34, 46; 9:34, 41; ἁμαρτάνω: 8:11; 9:2–3; ἁμαρτωλός: 9:16, 24–25, 31.

[37] In the first century, the Lord's light-giving presence was remembered and celebrated by large lamps set up in the Jerusalem temple, which illuminated the whole city, such that "there was not a courtyard in Jerusalem that was not illuminated by the light" (*m. Sukkah* 5:3).

[38] In the OT, it is preeminently God himself who is "light" (Pss. 27:1; 36:9; 2 Sam. 22:29; Isa. 10:17; cf. Dan. 2:22) and who gives "light" to the world (e.g., Gen. 1:3; Ex. 13:21), even if this "light" is also sometimes mediated by his "law" (Ps. 119:105; Prov. 6:23) or his "servant" (Isa. 42:6; 49:6). The prophets sometimes picture God's eschatological presence with his people in terms of a glorious, bright, "light," which outshines even the sun (Isa. 24:23; 60:19–22; Zech. 14:7; cf. Rev. 21:23–24).

[39] On this theme, see now esp. Joshua J. F. Coutts, *The Divine Name in the Gospel of John: Significance and Impetus*, WUNT 2/447 (Tübingen: Mohr Siebeck, 2016); Charles A. Gieschen, "The Divine Name That the Son Shares with the Father in the Gospel of John," in *Reading the Gospel of John's Christology as Jewish Messianism: Royal, Prophetic, and Divine Messiahs*, ed. B. Reynolds and G. Boccaccini, Ancient Judaism and Early Christianity 106 (Leiden and Boston: Brill, 2018), 387–410; Grant Macaskill, "Name Christology, Divine Aseity, and the I Am Sayings in the Fourth Gospel," *Journal of Theological Interpretation* 12.2 (2018): 217–41.

[40] C. K. Barrett, *The Gospel according to St. John: An Introduction with Commentary and Notes on the Greek Text*, 2nd ed. (Philadelphia: Westminster, 1978), 340.

which Jesus refers is not a radically new kind of sin, provoked only by Jesus's appearance in the flesh, but the climactic, eschatological, and Christologically focused manifestation of unbelief in God, which has characterized the human condition from the fall onward.[41] Those who refuse to accept Jesus as the one who embodies God's life-giving presence will remain in their sin, and die in their sin, because they show by their rejection of him that they do not trust the God of life. Sin, again, is thoroughly *personal*; it is, at its heart, the rejection of God as he reveals himself in Christ.

More than this, Jesus's twice-repeated warning, "you will die in your sin(s)" (8:21, 24) also underscores the Gospel's emphasis on the active and ethical nature of sin. Jesus's switch from the singular "sin" (τῇ ἁμαρτίᾳ; 8:21) to the plural "sins" (ταῖς ἁμαρτίαις [2x]; 8:24) is significant. It suggests a development from Jesus's initial focus on the heart of sin as unbelief, to a more expansive understanding of sin, which includes a plurality of discrete acts. Jesus's coming as "the light of the world" thus not only exposes the essence of sin, but also its extent. As Calvin says on this verse, the "sin" of "unbelief is the fountain and cause of all evils."[42] Sin is not only personal but *practical*; it begins with unbelief, and it manifests in wicked deeds.

Yet further, the dialogue between Jesus and the Jews reveals that they are enslaved to sin. Jesus expands his claim to bring "the light of life" by asserting that he also brings "the truth" which sets people "free" (ἡ ἀλήθεια ἐλευθερώσει ὑμᾶς) (8:12, 32); indeed, Jesus himself is that truth (1:14; 4:23–24; 14:6). In a classic case of Johannine irony, Jesus's interlocutors claim that they "have never been enslaved to anyone [ἐσμεν καὶ οὐδενὶ δεδουλεύκαμεν πώποτε]" (8:33). This claim evinces remarkable self-deception either at the historical level or—more probably and more seriously—at the spiritual level.[43] Certainly, Jesus speaks of that deeper slavery when he declares that "everyone who practices sin is a slave to sin [πᾶς ὁ ποιῶν τὴν ἁμαρτίαν δοῦλός ἐστιν τῆς ἁμαρτίας]" (8:34).[44] Jesus here personifies sin as a tyrannical

---

[41] Bavinck, *Reformed Dogmatics*, 3:141: "sin only comes to its most appalling manifestation vis-à-vis the gospel of the grace of God in Christ."

[42] Calvin, *Gospel according to St. John 1–10*, 215.

[43] The Jews had, of course, been "enslaved" in different ways by the Egyptians, Babylonians, Persians, Greeks, and Romans. There is deep irony in the fact that Jesus's interlocutors make their claim in the midst of the Feast of Tabernacles, which celebrated their release from slavery in Egypt, while also under Roman rule. Most likely, however, "the Jews" perceive that Jesus speaks of a spiritual slavery and assert their spiritual freedom as "offspring of Abraham" (8:33). See: D. A. Carson, *The Gospel according to John*, PNTC (Leicester, UK: Inter-Varsity Press, 1991), 349; Klink, *John*, 415.

[44] The genitive τῆς ἁμαρτίας is omitted in some MSS and versions (D, it^{b. d}, syr^s, cop^{bomss}), but has early and strong support (𝔓^{66, 75}, ℵ, B, C, W), and fits the context, making explicit the nature of the slavery. It is almost certainly original and is best taken as a subjective genitive; sin actively enslaves those who practice it.

Pharaoh-like slave-master.[45] He thus reveals that sin is not only a rejection of God, and a pattern of behavior that corresponds to it, but a power that enslaves; not only a series of discrete acts which people perform, but an authority which acts upon them.[46] This does not mean that sin has some kind of ontological status independent of the heart and the life that rejects God. In a good world created by a good God, "sin"—as Augustine recognized—can be nothing other than the "privation of the good."[47] Thus Jesus's personification of sin is exactly that: a rhetorical device which attributes human characteristics to a nonhuman reality (cf. Gen. 4:7; Rom. 5:12–8:4).[48] Nevertheless, the personification effectively communicates an important truth about sin. It is an "active privation"; not a mere falling away from the good, but "an active and corrupting principle, a dissolving, destructive power."[49] As Frodo observes of the evil orcs in J. R. R. Tolkien's classic *The Lord of the Rings*, "the Shadow that bred them can only mock, it cannot make"; "I do not think it gave life to the orcs," Frodo concludes, "it only ruined them and twisted them."[50] In light of this, we might even say that in John 8:34 Jesus declares a God-given "law of sin": the nature of sin—as God has decreed its existence and now governs its activities—is that those who sin find themselves ever more dominated by sin until it leads them to death.[51] Those who sin are thus both perpetrators and prisoners of sin, both culprits and captives, simultaneously guilty and needy, both deserving punishment and requiring rescue.

---

[45] The echo of the plight of the Hebrews under Pharaoh is created by: (1) Jesus's self-declaration, "before Abraham was, I am" (πρὶν Ἀβραὰμ γενέσθαι ἐγὼ εἰμί: John 8:58); (2) his references to the "offspring" or "children of Abraham" (σπέρμα Ἀβραάμ: 8:37; τέκνα τοῦ Ἀβραάμ: 8:39); and (3) the mention of "slaves" (ὁ δοῦλός: 8:34–35) and the promise of "freedom" (ἐλευθερόω, ἐλεύθερος: 8:36). See Paul M. Hoskins, "Freedom from Slavery to Sin and the Devil: John 8:31–47 and the Passover Theme of the Gospel of John," *TJ* 31 (2010): 47–53.

[46] Although Jesus speaks to "the Jews," the timeless and universal application of his statement is created by the combination of his solemn introduction (Ἀμὴν ἀμὴν λέγω ὑμῖν), his universalizing description of "*everyone* who practices sin" (πᾶς ὁ ποιῶν τὴν ἁμαρτίαν), and the present tense of the verb "to be" (ἐστιν).

[47] Augustine, *Enchiridion* 11; *De civitate Dei* 11.9.

[48] See esp.: J. R. Dodson, *The "Powers" of Personification: Rhetorical Purpose in the Book of Wisdom and the Letter to the Romans*, BZNW 161 (Berlin: Walter de Gruyter, 2008), 27–40: definitional issues; 123–39: personification of sin and death in Romans.

[49] *Reformed Dogmatics*, 3:137; cf. Thomas Aquinas, *Summa Theologiae* (New York: Benziger, 1947–48), § 1–2.q82.a1 (p. 956): "original sin denotes the privation of original justice, and besides this, the inordinate disposition of the parts of the soul. Consequently it is not a pure privation, but a corrupt habit"; Calvin, *Institutes*, 2.1.8: "For our nature is not only destitute and empty of good, but so fertile and fruitful of every evil that it cannot be idle"; Turretin, *Institutes*, 1:592: "this privation is not pure or simple, but corrupting; not idle, but energetic; not of pure negation, but of depraved disposition, by which not only is the due rectitude taken away, but also an undue unrectitude and a depraved quality laid down, infecting all the faculties."

[50] J. R. R. Tolkien, *The Return of the King* (London: Harper Collins, 1997), 893.

[51] Cf. Bavinck, *Reformed Dogmatics*, 3:106–7: "human sins are subject to God's government; the laws and ordinances that apply to the life of sin have been laid down and are being maintained by him. And to that category of laws belongs also this one: 'The curse of an evil deed is above all that it must continually give birth to evil.' The nature of sin is such that it progressively renders sinners more foolish and hard, entangles them ever more firmly in its snares, and propels them ever more rapidly down a slippery slope toward the abyss."

This, in turn, makes it clear that Jesus here again speaks of sin in the fundamental sense of rejecting God; he speaks of those who remain in the "state of sin" (cf. WCF 9.3).[52] "The one who practices sin" (ὁ ποιῶν τὴν ἁμαρτίαν), and who is therefore "a slave to sin," is not the believer who continues to struggle with sin.[53] As Jesus declares immediately, his mission as "the Son" is to set his people "free" from sin, so that they might be "free indeed" (8:36). Rather, as in 1 John 3:4 and 8, "the one who practices sin" is the unbeliever who rejects God and so remains enslaved to sin. In all of this, we see the *powerful* nature of sin in the Gospel of John, as it depicts what the Westminster Confession rightly calls the sinner's "natural bondage under sin" (WCF 9.4).

John 9 underlines the tragic irony of this slavery to sin, and shows that those so enslaved often falsely consider themselves to be free (cf. 8:33). Jesus heals a blind man, and this leads to a division among the Pharisees (9:1–16). The debate that ensues focuses on whether Jesus himself is "a sinner" (ἁμαρτωλός; 9:16, 24, 25, 31). At the climax of the episode, the Pharisees finally reject the blind man's testimony that Jesus is not "a sinner" but "from God" (παρὰ θεοῦ; 9:16, 33). They cast the blind man out, charging that he was "born in utter sin" (Ἐν ἁμαρτίαις σὺ ἐγεννήθης ὅλος; 9:34). But Jesus exposes the bitter irony of the whole situation. The Pharisees, who reject the blind man's testimony while insisting that they "see," have actually made themselves spiritually blind. They refuse to accept the signs of Jesus's authority, and are culpable for their rejection of him. And so Jesus says to them, "If you were blind, you would have no sin [οὐκ ἂν εἴχετε ἁμαρτίαν]; but now that you say, 'We see,' your sin remains [ἡ ἁμαρτία ὑμῶν μένει]" (9:41 ESV mg.). This, again, cannot mean that the Pharisees were innocent of sin in an absolute sense prior to this episode. It means, rather, that their sin has reached a climactic new expression in their rejection of Jesus. Sin so blinds those caught in it that they do not recognize their own predicament. John 9 thus underlines the *powerful* enslaving nature of sin, as well as the way in which this whole dark web is exposed by the presence of Jesus, "the light of the world" (9:5).

---

[52] See Calvin, *Gospel according to St. John 1–10*, 223: "here [John 8:34] Christ maintains, that all who are not delivered by him are in a state of slavery"; cf. Andreas J. Köstenberger, *John*, BECNT (Grand Rapids, MI: Baker Academic, 2004), 263.
[53] The phrase ὁ ποιῶν τὴν ἁμαρτίαν ("the one who practices sin") employs the substantival participle (ὁ ποιῶν) with the arthrous singular noun (τὴν ἁμαρτίαν). In its three occurrences in the Johannine literature (John 8:34; 1 John 3:4, 8), it does not refer to repeated sin in the Christian life. It is semi-technical language for those who remain in the state of sin, and who commit the fundamental sin of rejecting God, together with the habitual sins that flow from it.

3.1.5. The Light Exposes the Work of the Devil: John 8 and 13

The Gospel of John also reveals that sin is closely related to the rule of an evil spiritual power, whom the Gospel variously refers to as "the devil [ὁ διάβολος]" (8:44; 13:2; cf. 6:70), "the Satan [ὁ Σατανᾶς]" (13:27), "the ruler of this world [ὁ ἄρχων τοῦ κόσμου τούτου]" (12:31; 14:30; 16:11), and "the evil one [ὁ πονηρός]" (17:15).

The first reference to "the devil," in John 8, adds new depth to John's depiction of human slavery to sin. In the context of Jesus's sharp interaction with the Jews, he teaches that "from the beginning [ἀπ᾽ ἀρχῆς]," "the devil" has been both "a liar and the father of lies [ψεύστης ἐστὶν καὶ ὁ πατὴρ αὐτοῦ]"—devoid of all truth (ὅτι οὐκ ἔστιν ἀλήθεια ἐν αὐτῷ)—and "a murderer" (ἀνθρωποκτόνος)—opposed to all life (8:44; cf. 1 John 3:8).[54] Humanity's fall into sin, and slavery in sin, was preceded by the fall of the devil, who sinned "from the beginning [ἀπ᾽ ἀρχῆς]" (8:44; 1 John 3:8).[55] Jesus then lays his most shocking charge at the Jews: "You are of your father, the devil [ὑμεῖς ἐκ τοῦ πατρὸς τοῦ διαβόλου ἐστέ], and your will is to do your father's desires" (8:44).[56] In opposing Jesus, who brings them the truth, and in seeking to kill him, who promises life, the Jews reveal that they are children of the devil: they do his "works" (τὰ ἔργα τοῦ πατρὸς ὑμῶν; 8:41) and follow his "desires" (τὰς ἐπιθυμίας τοῦ πατρὸς ὑμῶν; 8:44). This interaction thus confirms the *powerful* nature of "sin" in John's Gospel, but adds another dimension to it. Those who reject God in Christ, and perform the evil works which result from that rejection, are "the children of the devil [τὰ τέκνα τοῦ διαβόλου]" (1 John 3:10), the evil spiritual power who holds them captive to do his will.

John's other reference to "the devil" (ὁ διάβολος; 13:2) and the related reference to "the Satan" (ὁ Σατανᾶς; 13:27) together provide, in the person of Judas, a shocking case study of the way in which this evil power is at work in those who do not believe. Already in John 6:70 Jesus reveals that,

---

[54] There is, therefore, a difference between the devil's original sin, which came entirely from within himself, and the fall of Adam and Eve, in which the devil's temptation exerted an external influence toward sin. See WCF 6.1. Cf. Bavinck, *Reformed Dogmatics*, 3:148: "Satan was not led astray, but he produced sin—the lie—from within himself (John 8:44) and became all at once confirmed in it."

[55] The fall of the devil and wicked angels predates humanity's fall in Adam, but beyond this its precise timing has not been revealed. As Turretin observes, "If the Devil is said to have sinned 'from the beginning' (1 Jn. 3:8), it does not follow that he sinned from the very beginning of creation; for some movement of time does not hinder us from saying it was done from the beginning" (*Institutes*, 1:602).

[56] The genitive τοῦ διαβόλου is best read in apposition to τοῦ πατρός and hence as "your father, the devil." See S. R. Llewelyn, A. Robinson, and B. E. Wassell, "Does John 8:44 Imply That the Devil Has a Father?: Contesting the Pro-Gnostic Reading," *NovT* 60.1 (2018): 14–23. Cf. H. N. Ridderbos, *The Gospel according to John: A Theological Commentary*, trans. John Vriend (Grand Rapids, MI: Eerdmans, 1997), 315–16.

although he chose the twelve disciples, one of them is "a devil" (διάβολός). John immediately clarifies that "He spoke of Judas the son of Simon Iscariot, for he, one of the twelve, was going to betray him" (6:71). It is no surprise, then, when we later read that "the devil [τοῦ διαβόλου] had already put it into the heart of Judas Iscariot, Simon's son, to betray him" (13:2), or that after Jesus identified Judas as the traitor, "the Satan entered into him [εἰσῆλθεν εἰς ἐκεῖνον ὁ Σατανᾶς]" (13:27). These texts make it clear that Judas acted under the direct influence of this malevolent spiritual power. At the same time, they in no way suggest either that the evil one acted outside of God's sovereign control of events, or that Judas was thereby absolved of any guilt. The Gospel, that is, holds together divine sovereignty, satanic influence, and human responsibility. There is more to say about this below. The point for now is to notice again the *powerful* nature of sin in the Gospel of John; by it, the devil was able to control even one of Jesus's twelve disciples.

3.1.6. The Spirit Shines the Light on Christ and Sin: John 14–16

Jesus's farewell discourse (John 14–16) further highlights the way in which Jesus himself, and the Spirit he promises to give, expose the nature of sin. First, Jesus explains that since his words and works reveal God in a new and climactic way, those who reject him are left without excuse (15:18–25). Speaking especially of "the Jews," he affirms, "If I had not come and spoken to them, *they would not have been guilty of sin* [ἁμαρτίαν οὐκ εἴχοσαν], but now they have no excuse for their sin [νῦν δὲ πρόφασιν οὐκ ἔχουσιν περὶ τῆς ἁμαρτίας αὐτῶν]" (15:22). Again, he says, "If I had not done among them the works that no one else did, *they would not be guilty of sin* [ἁμαρτίαν οὐκ εἴχοσαν], but now they have seen and hated both me and my Father" (15:24). Again, this cannot mean that there was no sin of any kind in the world, or among the Jews, before the coming of Christ. Rather, since Jesus reveals God in a new and climactic way (esp. 1:14; 12:45; 14:6–7, 9), the Jews' sin also reaches a new climax in their rejection of him. This rejection of Jesus reveals the heart of sin in the most striking of terms: sin is nothing less than "hating" (μισέω) God and his Son, and this inevitably also leads to "hating" God's people (15:18–19, 23–24; cf. 7:7). Again we see that sin, in this very strong sense, is both utterly *personal* and thoroughly *practical*: it involves hatred toward God and Christ, manifested in hatred and persecution of those whom he has "chosen" for himself.

Second, in this same speech, Jesus explains that after his departure the Holy Spirit will continue his work of revealing God, exposing sin, and convicting the world of its evil. In John's theology, Jesus himself is our "advocate" (παράκλητος) with the Father (cf. 1 John 2:1). In the Farewell Discourse, however, Jesus speaks of the Holy Spirit as *another* advocate" (ἄλλος παράκλητος; John 14:16; cf. 14:26; 15:26; 16:7) who will continue Jesus's work: "when he comes," Jesus says, "he will convict the world (ἐλέγξει τὸν κόσμον) concerning sin and righteousness and judgment" (16:8; cf. 3:20). The key verb ἐλέγχω can mean both "expose" and "convict."[57] In John's Gospel, it carries strong judicial connotations[58] and plays an important role in the "lawsuit motif," according to which "the world" places Jesus on trial, but is itself convicted of sin (3:20; 8:46; 16:8; cf. 7:7).[59] The Spirit's role is thus not merely to "expose" sin, or to "prove [the world] wrong" in an intellectual sense, but to "convict" the world in the judicial sense of demonstrating its guilt before God. The precise role Jesus assigns to the Spirit in John 16:8–11 has been interpreted in various ways, but it is probably best understood as Christologically focused.[60] The three "because [ὅτι]" clauses in John 16:9–11 refer to three moments in the work of Christ: his cross; his exaltation; and his return.[61] The Spirit will convict the world: (1) of its sin in rejecting Jesus, manifested in his crucifixion ("because they do not believe in me"); (2) of Jesus's righteousness, evident in his resurrection and ascension ("because I am going to the Father"); and (3) of the coming judgment on the world at Jesus's return, anticipated already in the judgment of "the evil one"

---

[57] BDAG 315.

[58] ἐλέγχω: (1) 3:20 with 3:17–19: κρίνω, κρίσις, (2) 8:46: ἀλήθεια; (3) 16:8–11: δικαιοσύνη, κρίσις, κρίνω. For John 16:8, see esp. J. Aloisi, "The Paraclete's Ministry of Conviction: Another Look at John 16:8–11," *JETS* 47.1 (2004): 56–60.

[59] See esp. A. E. Harvey, *Jesus on Trial: A Study in the Fourth Gospel* (London: SPCK, 1976); A. T. Lincoln, *Truth on Trial. The Lawsuit Motif in the Fourth Gospel* (Peabody, MA: Hendrickson, 2000).

[60] D. A. Carson, "The Function of the Paraclete in John 16:7–11," *JBL* 98 (1979): 547–66, provides a survey of the interpretive options. Carson's own view is that Jesus speaks of the Spirit convicting the world of its "sin," of its "inadequate" and "empty righteousness," and of its "false judgment" (cf. D. A. Carson, *The Farewell Discourse and Final Prayer of Jesus: An Exposition of John 14–17* [Grand Rapids, MI: Baker, 1980], 138–48; Carson, *Gospel according to John*, 534–39; also Barrett, *Gospel according to St. John*, 487; Klink, *John*, 678–81). The strength of this view is that it maintains the parallelism between the three ὅτι clauses by reading "the world" as the subject of all three nouns—Jesus speaks of the world's sin, the world's empty righteousness, and the world's false judgment. This interpretation struggles, however, to make sense of the reasons Jesus gives in 16:10–11, which refer not to the world's actions as subject, but to Jesus's exaltation (16:10), and to the ruler of the world as the object of judgment (16:11). It also requires taking "righteousness" and "judgment" ironically, and thus supplying the adjectives "inadequate" or "empty" and "false' in translation to bring out the meaning. For a similar critique, see Aloisi, "Paraclete's Ministry of Conviction," 61–65.

[61] For this insight, see esp. Oliver O'Donovan, *Resurrection and Moral Order: An Outline of Evangelical Ethics*, 2nd ed. (Leicester, UK/Grand Rapids, MI: Apollos/Eerdmans, 1994), 105. This reading has the additional advantage of being consistent with Jesus's teaching regarding the work of the Spirit throughout the Farewell Discourse, where the emphasis repeatedly falls on the Spirit's work of shining a bright spotlight on Christ himself (John 14:26; 15:26; 16:13–15).

at the cross ("because the ruler of this world is judged"; 16:11; cf. 12:31–32).[62] In this way, Jesus again teaches that the climactic expression of the world's sin is its rejection of God's self-revelation in him. The good news, however, is that by the work of the Spirit, through the preaching of the apostolic gospel, some will be convicted of sin, and convinced of the truth of Christ, and so—through repentance and faith—will find salvation and life in him.[63]

3.1.7. The Death of Jesus Reveals Degrees of Sin: John 18–19

At the climax of the Gospel, Jesus's trial before Pilate takes us even deeper into John's hamartiology and reveals that there are *degrees* of sin. As Jesus stands before Pilate, he states plainly that "he who delivered me over to you has the greater sin [μείζονα ἁμαρτίαν]" (19:11). The "sin" Jesus refers to here, as always in this Gospel, is closely related to Jesus himself, and especially to the rejection of Jesus by those who should have received him. Jesus in no way absolves Pilate of his part in the saga, but also indicates that his impending death is the result of multiple sins—a complex of sin. Jesus refers to the "greater sin" of "the one who delivered me over" (ὁ παραδούς μέ), but the identity of this "one" is ambiguous, perhaps deliberately so. It could refer: (1) to Caiaphas, the high priest, representing the Jewish Sanhedrin, who in the immediate context "handed Jesus over [παραδίδωμι]" to Pilate (see 18:30, 35 NIV); (2) to Judas, one of Jesus's own disciples who, under the influence of the devil, "handed Jesus over [παραδίδωμι]" to the high priests (see 6:71; 13:21; 18:2); or (3) even to "the devil," since the Gospel repeatedly makes it clear that he was active in Judas's "handing over" of Jesus (6:70–71; 13:2; παραδίδωμι; cf. 13:26–27). Jesus's crucifixion was thus the result of multiple sins. Indeed, in addition to this "greater sin" of handing Jesus over, there is also the "lesser sin" of Pilate, who condemns Jesus despite the fact that, by his own admission, he finds "no cause" in Jesus for crucifixion (18:38; 19:4, 6). Jesus thus distinguishes between the *proactive* sin of the devil, Judas, and Caiaphas, and the *reactive* sin of Pilate; the former took the initiative, and orchestrated, manipulated, and planned for Jesus's demise; the latter responded to that initiative.[64] And so we

---

[62] For similar interpretations, though without recognition of the final judgment anticipated at the cross, see W. H. P. Hatch, "The Meaning of John XVI, 8–11," *HTR* 14 (1921): 103–5; Craig S. Keener, *The Gospel of John: A Commentary*, 2 vols. (Peabody, MA: Hendrickson, 2003), 2:1034; Burge, "Gospel and Epistles," 82–83.

[63] Cf. John Calvin, *The Gospel according to St. John 11–21 and the First Epistle of John*, trans. T. H. L. Parker, *Calvin's Commentaries* 5 (Grand Rapids, MI: Eerdmans, 1961), 116: "the Spirit convicts men in the preaching of the Gospel in two ways" (either for salvation or for condemnation).

[64] Cf. Carson, *Gospel according to John*, 602. "Pilate's guilt is mitigated because he takes a *relatively* passive role. True, Pilate remains responsible for his spineless, politically-motivated judicial decision; but he did not initiate the trial

learn from Jesus here that there are greater and lesser sins.[65] Although all sin equally rejects God, and equally proceeds from the same corrupt heart, and equally deserves God's righteous condemnation, sin manifests itself in different ways, and is expressed to varying degrees, and results in diverse consequences, such that we can rightly speak of lesser and greater sins.[66]

3.1.8. Conclusion

The first major thread in the web of sin—as traced by John—relates sin to God's climactic revelation of himself in Christ. God's "light," especially revealed in Jesus, exposes the darkness of human sin. This sin is, in its essence, utterly *personal*: it rejects, indeed, it hates God, and so refuses to embrace his Son, sent in love as the Savior of the world (1:9–11; 3:18–20; 8:24; 15:23–24; 16:9). This sin is also: *perverted*, arising from a deep inner corruption (3:19–20); *powerful*, such that those who sin become enslaved to it (8:34; 9:41); *practical*, in that it works its way out in a pattern of immoral behavior opposed to God and his word (3:19–20; 5:29; 8:24); and *pervasive*, in that it is a universal problem with the world (1:29). This is, indeed, a dark web. Nevertheless, the Gospel of John also holds out a bright shining hope. Jesus, "the light of the world," who reveals God in a climactic way, and so exposes sin more than ever before, also reveals God's provision for sin; more, he *is* God's provision for sin, the light that shines in the darkness and which has not been overcome (1:5).[67]

3.2. SIN, SUFFERING, DEATH, AND JUDGMENT WITHIN GOD'S SOVEREIGNTY: THE SINLESS ONE SUFFERS THE CONSEQUENCES OF SIN

3.2.1. Introduction

The Gospel of John lays out a second major thread within the web of sin: it relates sin to suffering, death, and judgment, and locates the whole complex

---

or engineer the betrayal that brought Jesus into court. . . . But Pilate would not have had judicial authority over Jesus unless the event of the betrayal itself had been given to him *from above*. . . . *Therefore* the one who handed Jesus over to Pilate, the one who from the human vantage point took the initiative to bring Jesus down, is guilty of the greater sin."

[65] Cf. WLC Q150.

[66] Cf. WLC Q151. For discussion, see Bavinck, *Reformed Dogmatics*, 3:149–52. Bavinck shows that sins differ in at least five ways, according to: (1) the intention of the sinner; (2) the object against which the sin is committed; (3) the subject who commits the sin; (4) the degree to which the sin is embraced; (5) the circumstances under which it is committed; also, "Qualitatively, there is no difference, but this does not rule out a quantitative difference. Though all have turned away from God and are by nature on the road that leads to destruction, not all have progressed equally far down that wrong road and not all are equally far removed from the kingdom of heaven" (175). Cf. Turretin, *Institutes*, 1:597: "If all sins agree in being mortal, it does not follow that they are equal in all things because they can differ from each other as to degree of demerit, so as to deserve a greater or lesser punishment."

[67] Cf. Carson, *Gospel according to John*, 527: "This revelation simultaneously exposes sin and provides its remedy."

of sin, with its effects and consequences, within God's sovereign purposes. This is especially clear in the two paired healing accounts in John 5 and 9, in Jesus's teaching about the judgment (esp. John 5:19–29), and in the account of Jesus's own death (John 18–19). The whole thread, once again, receives its fullest development in relation to Jesus himself: he is the sinless one, who nevertheless suffers the full consequences of God's condemnation of sin.

3.2.2. Sin and Suffering: John 5 and 9

John's Gospel explores the relationship between sin and suffering in the two closely related healing accounts in John 5 and 9. On the surface, Jesus appears to offer two different answers to the question of sin and suffering: his warning to the healed lame man suggests that sin causes personal suffering (5:14); his response to the disciples about the blind man seems to deny the same (9:2–3). The Gospel, however, sets the two accounts in parallel, and so indicates that they are to be read together, as mutually interpretive perspectives on one complex reality.[68]

On the one hand, Jesus's warning in John 5:14 implies that the lame man's suffering is the result of his personal sin.[69] Jesus heals the man (5:1–9),[70] and then commands him to "sin no more [μηκέτι ἁμάρτανε]" (5:14). The construction μηκέτι + present imperative, together with the logic of the following purpose-result clause—"that nothing worse may happen to you [ἵνα μὴ χεῖρόν σοί τι γένηται]"—suggests that the man's past suffering was the result of his past sin.[71] This sense is strengthened if the specific reference

---

[68] The accounts share: (1) a setting in Jerusalem during one of the Jewish feasts (5:1; 7:2, 10, 14, 37; 8:59); (2) a pool of water (5:2, Bethesda; 9:7, 11, Siloam); (3) Jesus healing a man with a long-term ailment (5:5; 9:1); (4) healing on the Sabbath (5:9–10; 9:14); (5) controversy in which "the Jews" or "the Pharisees" persecute Jesus or his followers (5:16, 18; 9:22, 24); (6) the report that Jesus subsequently "finds" (εὑρίσκω) the one he has healed and calls him to personal faith in himself (5:14; 9:35); and (7) revelation of Jesus as "the Son of Man" who bears God's authority to judge and to save (5:17–29; 9:30–33, 35–39).

[69] So, Calvin, *Gospel according to St. John 1–10*, 122: "This admonition also teaches us that all the ills we suffer should be imputed to our sins. The afflictions of men are not accidental but are so many stripes to chastise us." Cf. Carson, *Gospel according to John*, 245–46.

[70] John 5 consistently describes the man using the language of "weakness, illness [ἀσθένεια, ἀσθενέω]." On the basis of John 5:8 he is customarily described as "lame," but the weakness/illness could have been anything that caused him to be chronically bedridden.

[71] The construction μη + present imperative can be used to prohibit an action already in progress, with the sense "stop sinning" (NIV). Against a tendency to overly apply this "rule," the grammars and some commentators are correct to note that this "cessation-of-activity-in-progress" meaning is a function of the context, and is not necessarily indicated by the morpho-syntactical construction on its own (e.g., Carson, *Gospel according to John*, 246 n. 80; Klink, *John*, 274; D. B. Wallace, *Greek Grammar beyond the Basics: An Exegetical Syntax of the New Testament* [Grand Rapids, MI: Zondervan, 1996], 724–25; A. J. Köstenberger, B. L. Merkle, and R. L. Plummer, *Going Deeper with New Testament Greek: An Intermediate Study of the Grammar and Syntax of the New Testament* [Nashville: B&H Academic, 2016], 209). In John 5:14, however, the use of μηκέτι ("no longer") must be given due weight. Together with the present imperative, this adverb creates the strong sense that Jesus is commanding the man to stop the sin which caused his illness in the first place. The construction μηκέτι + present imperative

to his "thirty-eight years" (τριάκοντα [καὶ] ὀκτὼ ἔτη) of suffering is an allusion to Israel's "thirty-eight years" of wandering in the wilderness (5:5; cf. Deut. 2:14 LXX): the experience of this unnamed Israelite seems to mirror the history of the wilderness generation, who suffered God's judgment on their sin. Certainly, the testimony of Scripture, taken as a whole, indicates that all suffering is the result of Adam and Eve's first sin, and our culpability in it (Gen. 2:17; 3:16–19; Rom. 5:12–21; 8:18–25; 1 Cor. 15:22), and that particular personal sins can and do lead to personal suffering, either as the outworking of God's providential ordering of cause and effect, or more directly as the result of God's punishment of the wicked, or God's discipline of his people.[72] In his charge to the healed man, Jesus affirms this general principle, and implies that, at least in his case, his suffering was the result of his personal sin, and that continued sin would result in something "worse [χείρων]" (John 5:14).

Still, Jesus's primary concern in John 5 is with the more fundamental sin of rejecting God, and the future judgment it brings. Jesus does not identify any particular sin from which the man should refrain, and the sin most evident throughout the chapter is the refusal to believe in God, who is powerfully "at work" in Jesus (5:17).[73] The man himself seems to believe that God can heal, but looks for healing in the impersonal superstition of the "magical" waters of the pool (5:7). The Jews also believe that God can heal, but when God, in Jesus, heals in their midst, they see nothing more than a Sabbath "violation" (see 5:10). They "persecute" him (5:16), who has demonstrated among them the healing, health, and wholeness for which the Sabbath was designed (5:6, 9, 11, 14, 15 [ὑγιής]; 5:10 [θεραπεύω]; 5:13 [ἰάομαι]; cf. 7:23 [ὅλον ἄνθρωπον ὑγιῆ ἐποίησα ἐν σαββάτῳ]). In this context, Jesus's command to "sin no more" (5:14) ultimately concerns a kind of sin far more fundamental than any particular immoral action, and his warning of something "worse" (χείρων) ultimately concerns a reality far greater than the recurrence of the man's illness: Jesus is warning the healed man to avoid God's final condemnation (cf. 3:18,

---

certainly carries this sense elsewhere in the NT (John 8:11; Luke 8:49; Eph. 4:28; 1 Tim. 5:23; cf. Ex. 36:6 LXX; 1 Macc. 13:39).
[72] For God's providential ordering of cause and effect, see WCF 5.2. For the distinction between God's punishment of the wicked and fatherly discipline of his children, compare WCF 5.5–6; 6.6; 8.5; 11.3, 5; 12.1; 17.3; 33.2. The key biblical texts are: Job 5:17; Prov. 3:11–12; 1 Cor. 11:32; Heb. 12:5–11; Rev. 3:19; cf. Calvin, *Institutes*, 3.4.31–34; Bavinck, *Reformed Dogmatics*, 4:169.
[73] Cf. S. M. Bryan, "Power in the Pool: The Healing of the Man at Bethesda and Jesus's Violation of the Sabbath (John 5:1–18)," *Tyndale Bulletin* 54 (2003): 16: "The essence of sin" in John 5 and throughout the Gospel "is to see the power of God at work through Jesus and yet refuse to acknowledge that power as evidence of the self-revealing action of God in Jesus."

36; 5:29; 8:21, 24).[74] In John 5:14, then, Jesus affirms that personal sin can and does lead to personal suffering, but especially warns against the fundamental sin of rejecting God, which results in God's final condemnation.

On the other hand, Jesus's response to the disciples about the blind man in John 9:3–4 teaches that personal suffering is certainly not always the direct result of particular personal sin. The disciples' question assumes a tight connection between particular sin and suffering (9:2), and allows for only two possibilities: either the blind man's suffering is the result of his own sin, or it is the result of his parents' sin.[75] Jesus, however, denies the basic assumption in their question. He refuses to link the man's blindness to any particular sin committed by him or his parents. This, again, is consistent with the testimony of Scripture, taken as a whole. While suffering is always the result of Adam's and Eve's sin and God's judgment upon it (Gen. 3:17–19; Rom. 5:12–21; 8:18–25; 1 Cor. 15:22), and suffering is sometimes the result of Satan's work, or the sins of others, it is certainly not always the direct result of any particular sin on the part of the sufferer (e.g., Gen. 50:15–21; Job 1–2; 1 Chron. 21:1–30; Pss. 35:7; 69:4; Luke 13:1–5; 2 Cor. 12:7).[76] The relationship between sin and suffering in God's purposes cannot be reduced to a simple formula of cause and effect. God's good, wise, and sovereign providence is far more complex than that (cf. WCF 5.4–7 and 6.1). Thus, while we cannot speak of "righteous" or "innocent" suffering in any absolute sense—"for there is no one who does not sin" (1 Kings 8:46 // 2 Chron. 6:36; cf. Gen. 6:5; 8:21; Pss. 14:1–3; 53:1–3; Prov. 20:9; Eccl. 7:20; Rom. 3:10–19, 23; Eph. 2:3; 1 John 1:8, 10)—we can speak of innocent suffering in a relative sense.[77] This biblical teaching has immense pastoral and personal significance: personal suffering is often not the direct result of any particular personal sin.[78]

---

[74] Carson, *Gospel according to John*, 246.

[75] The general principle that sin leads to suffering and death is expressed in the Babylonian Talmud: "There is no death without sin and no suffering without iniquity" (b. Shabbat 55a). More particularly, some Jewish texts, on the basis of Exodus 20:5 and Psalm 89:32, suggest that the sin of the parents could be the cause of a child's disability (e.g., Canticles Rabbah I, 6, § 3). Other Jewish texts point to the possibility of the child's own prenatal sin being the cause of suffering (e.g., Genesis Rabbah 63:6, on Gen. 25:22). Note, however, that the Jewish and Graeco-Roman sources from the period, taken as a whole, explain physical deformities in a range of ways. See esp. N. Kelley, "The Theological Significance of Physical Deformity in the Pseudo-Clementine Homilies," *PRSt* 34 (2007): 77–90.

[76] Cf. Bavinck, *Reformed Dogmatics*, 3:170.

[77] Cf. Turretin, *Institutes*, 1:635: "When Christ says that the man born blind had not sinned (Jn. 9:3), he does not absolutely assert that he was free from all sin (whose punishment this calamity of his was), but only comparatively denies that he sinned more than others that he was so afflicted; that his native blindness was the punishment of some special sin." For biblical affirmations of "innocent suffering" in this relative sense, see, e.g., Deut. 19:10; 27:25; Job 9:23; Pss. 10:8; 94:21; 106:38; Prov. 1:11; 6:17; 1 Sam. 19:5; 2 Kings 21:16; 24:4; Isa. 59:7; Jer. 2:34; 7:6; 19:4; 22:3, 17; 26:15; Joel 3:19.

[78] Cf. Carson, *Gospel according to John*, 362: "Although Jesus does not disavow the generalizing connection between sin and suffering, he completely disavows a universalizing of *particular* connections."

In John 9, then, Jesus clearly denies the premise of the disciples' question. There is, however, still some debate as to whether Jesus's affirmation—"that the works of God might be displayed in him [ἵνα φανερωθῇ τὰ ἔργα τοῦ θεοῦ ἐν αὐτῷ]" (9:3)—provides any alternative explanation for the blind man's predicament.[79] It is possible, with some recent interpreters, to read Jesus's response as a comment on the *goal* of his own work, rather than on the *cause* of the man's blindness: "Neither this man nor his parents sinned, but in order that the works of God might be revealed in him we must work the works of the one who sent me while it is day" (9:3–4).[80] On this reading, Jesus speaks only of how his work in healing the blind man will glorify God; the direct cause of the man's blindness remains a mystery.[81] Alternatively, it is possible, with most English translations, and the majority of interpreters, to read Jesus's purpose statement as indicating the *cause* of the man's blindness: "he was born blind *so that* God's works might be revealed in him" (9:3 NRSV).[82] This reading implies that God more directly caused the man's blindness in order to reveal his glory through the man's healing.[83] While some interpreters recoil from this reading because it seems to "blame" God for the man's blindness, and make his suffering instrumental to God's glory,[84] the Gospel is clear, as we will see, that God is sovereign over all things—including even the worst of sins and the deepest of suffering. Indeed, this reading of John 9:3–4 is confirmed by Jesus's later affirmation that Lazarus's illness and death is "for the glory of God [ὑπὲρ τῆς δόξης τοῦ θεοῦ], so that the Son of

---

[79] Grammatically speaking, the final ἵνα + subjunctive clause could indicate either purpose or result.

[80] The translation is that of Koester, *Word of Life*, 58. Cf. similarly: J. C. Poirier, "'Day and Night' and the Punctuation of John 9:3," *NTS* 42.2 (1996): 288–94; Keener, *Gospel of John*, 1:779; Burge, "Gospel and Epistles," 96. This reading: (1) takes John 9:3–4 as a single sentence, and removes the full stop from the end of John 9:3 as an unnecessary editorial insertion; (2) takes the δεῖ in 9:4 as the primary verb of the sentence; and (3) understands Jesus's statement—"that the works of God might be displayed in him [ἵνα φανερωθῇ τὰ ἔργα τοῦ θεοῦ ἐν αὐτῷ]"—to modify what follows rather than what precedes it.

[81] Koester, *Word of Life*, 58: "Jesus does not explain the cause of the blindness. He simply accepts it as a given and declares that he will deal with it in order to do God's work of healing."

[82] So also: NIV: "*this happened* so that"; CSB: "*this came about* so that." These translations imply that God directly *caused* the blindness *in order that* his works might be revealed through Jesus. In each case the italicized clause is not in the Greek and has been supplied. The ESV supplies no such phrase, but similarly takes Jesus's statement as implying that the man's blindness occurred for the purpose of God's works being displayed in him: "It was not that this man sinned, or his parents, but that the works of God might be displayed in him." These translations take the final ἵνα + subjunctive clause as indicating purpose rather than result, and follow the editorial decision of UBS4/5 to place a full stop at the end of verse 3.

[83] Cf. Turretin, *Institutes*, 1:635: "Therefore Christ, in order that no singular and personal sin might be imputed either to the blind man himself or to his parents, says that this happened in order that the works of God might be manifested (i.e., that God willed by this example to make known his works of justice and power in punishing and his works of mercy and omnipotence in healing)."

[84] David Rensberger, *Johannine Faith and Liberating Community* (Philadelphia: Westminster, 1988), 43–44, states the objection sharply: "Despite a hopeful beginning, as theodicy this is really worse yet. It seems to say that God did not even blind the man for his entire lifetime in order to punish some wrongdoing; he did it merely to show off his power by finally sending Jesus around to heal him."

God may be glorified through it [ἵνα δοξασθῇ ὁ υἱὸς τοῦ θεοῦ δι' αὐτῆς]"
(11:4).[85] Ultimately, John shows that only a God who is fully sovereign over
sin and suffering can provide any hope in the face of it.[86]

Thus, if John 5:14 teaches that personal sin can lead to personal suffering,
and John 9:3 teaches that not all personal suffering is the direct result of personal
sin, the larger reality is that God is utterly sovereign over all sin and suffering.
The God of the Bible is never "the author or approver of sin" (WCF 5.4, citing
James 1:13–14, 17; 1 John 2:16; Ps. 50:21). He does, however, directly cause
disaster and suffering for a range of good and holy purposes.[87] The humbling
reality is that God is the Creator, while we are mere creatures; he is "the potter,"
while we are "the clay" (Isa. 29:16; 41:25; 64:8; Jer. 18:6; Rom. 9:20–21). At the
same time, God's promise to his people is that "he works all things together for
good" so that they might be "conformed to the image of his Son" (Rom. 8:28–
29). If God sends suffering to his people, it is not to crush them but to conform
them to Christ. For this reason, the Heidelberg Catechism rightly encourages
Christian believers to confess with confidence that God "will make *whatever
evils he sends upon me*, in this valley of tears, *turn out to my advantage*; for he is
able to do it, being Almighty God, and willing, being a faithful Father."[88] According to John 9, the man born blind could certainly testify to this truth; it was in
and through his blindness—in and through his suffering—that God, at work in
his Son, "found" the blind man and enabled him to truly "see" (9:35–41).

3.2.3. Sin, Death, and Judgment: John 5

If John's Gospel relates sin to suffering in a complex manner, its teaching
about sin, death, and judgment is comparatively simple: sin inexorably leads
to death, and this is not merely the "natural" result of sin, but God's righteous
condemnation of it; while the final confirmation of God's condemnation of
sin is graciously delayed, Jesus will execute judgment on the final day.

First of all, the Gospel is clear that God's final condemnation is graciously
delayed. God's primary purpose in sending his Son into the world was *not* "to

---

[85] Contra Koester, *Word of Life*, 58: "Note that there is no speculation about the cause of the illness. Jesus does not say that God caused the illness in order to use it as an occasion for revealing his glory. Instead, he simply accepts the illness as a given and will work forward from there to bring glory to God by giving life."
[86] Carson, *Gospel according to John*, 362: "John certainly does not think that the occurrence of blindness from birth was outside the sweep of God's control, and therefore of his purpose."
[87] E.g., Deut. 32:39; 2 Sam. 12:10–12, 15; 1 Kings 11:14, 23; 12:15; 2 Chron. 10:15; Job 1:21; 2:10; Ps. 71:20; Isa. 45:7; Lam. 3:37; Amos 3:6.
[88] Heidelberg Catechism 26 (emphasis added). The reference to "evils" here, of course, cannot be taken to imply that God is the author of *moral* evil, i.e., sin.

condemn the world [οὐ . . . ἵνα κρίνῃ τὸν κόσμον]," but that "the world might be saved through him" (3:17; cf. 8:15, 50; 12:47).[89] Nevertheless, those who do not receive Jesus stand "condemned already [ἤδη κέκριται]" because they "have not believed [μὴ πεπίστευκεν] in the name of the only begotten Son of God (KJV)" who can save them (3:18);[90] "the wrath of God remains on them [ἡ ὀργὴ τοῦ θεοῦ μένει ἐπ᾽ αὐτόν]" because of their sin (3:36). Thus, in another sense, Jesus affirms that it was "for judgment [Εἰς κρίμα] I came into this world" (9:39). Speaking of the future, he declares emphatically that he has "much to judge [πολλὰ . . . κρίνειν]" (8:26), and that his very "word," spoken with the authority he received from the Father, "will judge" the one who rejects him "on the last day [κρινεῖ αὐτὸν ἐν τῇ ἐσχάτῃ ἡμέρᾳ]" (12:48–49).[91] God's final condemnation for sin is graciously delayed, but it will certainly come.

Second, the Gospel confirms that God's condemnation for sin takes the form of death. Jesus's warning to the Jews in John 8—"unless you believe that I am he, you will die in your sin(s)" (8:21, 24)—unmistakably evokes God's original decree in the garden of Eden, and the consistent biblical teaching thereafter, that the penalty for sin is death (Gen. 2:17; cf. Gen. 3:19, 22–23; Rom. 5:12, 16–18, 21; 6:23). More specifically, Jesus's warning alludes to Ezekiel 3:16–21, where the Lord three times declares that the wicked will "die in his sin(s)."[92] In this context, the prepositional phrase "in your sin(s)" (ἐν τῇ ἁμαρτίᾳ ὑμῶν [8:21]; ἐν ταῖς ἁμαρτίαις ὑμῶν [8:24]) is instrumental rather than locative. It carries the sense "you will die *on account of* your sin(s)." Sin is not merely the context in which death occurs, but the ground of God's judicial sentence of death.

Third, God's condemnation for sin will also take a more final form. In the crucial speech in John 5:19–29, Jesus affirms that the Father judges no one (ὁ πατὴρ κρίνει οὐδένα), but has "given all judgment to the Son [ἀλλὰ τὴν κρίσιν πᾶσαν δέδωκεν τῷ υἱῷ]" (5:22), because he is the "Son of Man" (5:27; cf. 8:26; 9:39; 12:48–49). Nevertheless, as Son of Man, Jesus does not judge independently of the Father, but according to the Father's will

---

[89] In John 3:17 the use of "save" (σῴζω) as an antonym for "judge" (κρίνω) indicates that in these texts "judge" has the sense of "condemn."

[90] Cf. Köstenberger, *John*, 130: "The two verbs in the perfect tense in 3:18, κέκριται . . . and μὴ πεπίστευκεν . . . , underscore the settled state of unbelievers' condemnation and unbelief."

[91] The expression "on the last day" (ἐν τῇ ἐσχάτῃ ἡμέρᾳ) is unique in the NT to the Gospel of John (6:39, 40, 44, 54; 11:24; 12:48). It draws on the OT "day of the Lord" tradition, and is unambiguously "the day" of the final resurrection and judgment.

[92] The Lord through Ezekiel speaks first of singular "sin" (Ezek. 3:18, בַּעֲוֺנוֹ יָמוּת [τῇ ἀδικίᾳ αὐτοῦ ἀποθανεῖται]; 3:19, בַּעֲוֺנוֹ יָמוּת [ἐν τῇ ἀδικίᾳ αὐτοῦ ἀποθανεῖται]) and then of plural "sins" (3:20, בְּחַטֹּאתוֹ יָמוּת [ἐν ταῖς ἁμαρτίαις αὐτοῦ ἀποθανεῖται]). Cf. Klink, *John*, 409.

(5:30; cf. 8:16).[93] At the climax of this remarkable passage, Jesus explains that the condemnation that already rests on those who reject God and practice evil (3:18, 36) will be confirmed when he calls them out of their graves "into the resurrection of condemnation [εἰς ἀνάστασιν κρίσεως]" (5:29, my translation).[94] The point could not be clearer: sin leads to death, and this is not merely a natural or organic process, but the direct result of God's judicial sentence, which Jesus himself will enact and confirm "on the last day [ἐν τῇ ἐσχάτῃ ἡμέρᾳ]" (12:48; cf. 6:39–40, 44, 54; 11:24). Thus, in addition to what we have seen already regarding sin, we can also now add that sin is *punishable*; it draws God's righteous condemnation.

At the same time, Jesus also makes it clear that those who hear him need not finally be condemned for their sin: "whoever hears my words," he declares, "and believes him who sent me has eternal life [ἔχει ζωὴν αἰώνιον]"; such a person "does not come into judgment, but has passed [μεταβέβηκεν] from death to life" (5:24). Those who come to God in Christ receive now, already, the affirmative judgment of the final day. John's Gospel confirms this teaching at multiple points. Those who come to Jesus, though they die physically, will never die in the fuller sense of facing God's final condemnation: the one who trusts in him "has eternal life" (3:15–16, 36; 4:14; 5:24; 6:27, 40, 47, 54; 10:28; 17:2–3); "whoever believes in him is not condemned" (3:18); those who "feed" on him will "not die," but will "live forever" (6:50–51); whoever "obeys" his "word" "will never see death" (8:51). Thus, as Jesus encourages Martha, even though believers die physically, "yet they will live," and so—in the final eschatological sense—will "never die" (11:25–26, my translations). Given this gracious promise of life to anyone who will receive him, we see again that sin, at its heart, is the utterly *personal* refusal to come to God in Christ.

3.2.4. Sin and God's Sovereignty as the Sinless One Dies: John 18–19

The Gospel's treatment of this thread of sin, suffering, death, and judgment within God's sovereignty is, again, Christologically focused. It receives its sharpest definition in the Gospel's presentation of Jesus, the sinless one, who is crucified and dies as a result of sin, according to God's sovereign plan.

---

[93] Cf. Turretin, *Institutes*, 3:599: "For although judiciary power is common to the whole Trinity, still it will be specially exercised by the incarnate Son."

[94] In John 5:29, the genitive phrases ἀνάστασιν ζωῆς ("resurrection of life") and ἀνάστασιν κρίσεως ("resurrection of judgment/condemnation") are probably best taken as genitives of destination, indicating both purpose and result: resurrection for the purpose, and with the result, of receiving either life or condemnation (cf. Wallace, *Greek Grammar*, 100–101).

The Gospel is clear that Jesus himself is sinless. If sin leads to suffering and death, which is God's righteous judgment, the one man who should *not* suffer, and who does *not* deserve to die, is Jesus himself. As "the light of the world," who embodies the very presence of God, Jesus has no darkness in him (8:12; 9:5; 12:46; cf. 1 John 1:5). Jesus himself explicitly testifies to this truth: his "food," he says, is to do "the will of the one who sent me [τὸ θέλημα τοῦ πέμψαντός με]" (4:34; cf. 5:30; 6:38); he is "true [ἀληθής]," and there is "no unrighteousness in him [ἀδικία ἐν αὐτῷ οὐκ ἔστιν]" (7:18) (my translations); despite their accusations that he is a "sinner [ἁμαρτωλός]" (9:16, 24), Jesus's opponents cannot "convict" him of sin (τίς ἐξ ὑμῶν ἐλέγχει με περὶ ἁμαρτίας [8:46]). Thus, when he dies on the cross, it is not—and cannot be—for his own sin. His death is, rather, the culmination of his perfect obedience to the "command" (ἐντολή) of the Father, who gave him "authority" to lay down his life, and also "to take it up again" (10:17–18). Jesus's initial vindication comes from the blind man, when he testifies that "God does not listen to sinners" but only to the one who "does his will [τὸ θέλημα αὐτοῦ ποιῇ]" (9:31). Further vindication comes when the Jewish leadership accuse Jesus of "doing evil [κακὸν ποιῶν]" (18:30), but Pilate three times declares that he finds "no cause [οὐδεμίαν αἰτίαν]" (my translation) to have Jesus crucified (18:38; 19:4; cf. 19:6, αἰτίαν). In the fulness of the Gospel, Jesus's vindication comes not merely in the course of his ministry and from human beings, but in his resurrection and from the Father.

Crucially, the Gospel emphasizes that the whole complex of sin that led to Jesus's death worked itself out under God's sovereign hand. At the climax of the Gospel, Jesus declares to Pilate, "You would have no authority over me at all unless it had been given you from above" (19:11). While the statement appears, in most English translations, to refer to Pilate's "authority" (ἐξουσίαν), the "it" which has "been given" (ἦν δεδομένον) to Pilate is not merely his "authority" (ἐξουσίαν) as governor, but the whole turn of events— the whole complex of sin—now unfolding before him.[95] Pilate's cowardice and injustice in condemning Jesus, the high priest's jealousy and hatred in handing Jesus over, Judas's treachery and greed in betraying Jesus, and even the devil's murderous plot to destroy Jesus—all of these wicked acts have "been given . . . from above." God's inscrutable sovereignty is such that this

---

[95] The participle δεδομένον is neuter and cannot take the feminine ἐξουσίαν as its antecedent. Correctly: M.-J. Lagrange, *Evangile selon Saint Jean* (Paris: J. Gabald, 1925), 483; E. C. Hoskyns, *The Fourth Gospel* (London: Faber and Faber, 1954), 524; Carson, *Gospel according to John*, 601–2.

complex of sin, like all others—perhaps *this* complex of sin *even more than all others*—serves his good purposes, because in and through it Jesus, "the Lamb of God . . . takes away the sin of the world!" (cf. 1:29). It is, therefore, not strong enough to say that God merely "permitted" the complex of sin that led to Jesus's death.[96] God proactively planned it, and purposely pursued it. At the same time, it is emphatically *not* God who is responsible for the wickedness that led to the cross. God planned it in such a way that those who sinned against Jesus are fully responsible for their own actions. This complex of sin, then—like all sin— stands against God's *moral* will, but works its way out in accordance with God's *decreed* will (cf. Luke 22:22).[97] As the Westminster Confession of Faith puts it, God's "providence . . . extends itself even to the first Fall, and all other sins of angels and men," but in such a way that the "sinfulness" of the sin "proceeds only from the creature, and not from God, who, being most holy and righteous, neither is nor can be the author or approver of sin" (WCF 5.4). This way of understanding the relationship between God and sin is certainly complex, but if we seek to maintain the Bible's teaching on God's sovereignty and human responsibility, there is no other alternative. On the one hand, if God did not plan Jesus's death, he is not really sovereign, and his gift of his Son as the Savior of the world was nothing more than a reaction to sin's initiative. On the other hand, if God's sovereign plan overrules real human responsibility, there is no real sin for which Jesus was sent to die.[98] We therefore need to reckon with multiple intentions in the one event: while Pilate, Caiaphas, Judas, and the devil planned Jesus's death *with wicked intent*, God planned it *for good*; while Pilate, Caiaphas, Judas, and the devil did their worst, God, through their sin, produced his best (cf. Gen. 50:19–20; Isa. 10:6–7; Acts 4:27–28).[99] In this important sense, Jesus teaches that while Pilate, and those who committed the "greater sin," remain fully accountable for their sin, the whole complex of sin that led to the cross was "given" by God (John 19:11). And this, of course, undergirds John's glorious affirmation that—in God's remarkable providence—this greatest of sins is also the means by which sin is overcome.

---

[96] WCF 5.4 distinguishes "a bare permission" from God's "most wise and powerful bounding, and otherwise ordering, and governing" of sin, "in a manifold dispensation, to His own holy ends." For extended discussion, see esp. Bavinck, *Reformed Dogmatics*, 3:62–63.

[97] For this distinction, see esp. Bavinck, *Reformed Dogmatics*, 2:242–45; 3:59–70.

[98] Cf. Carson, *Gospel according to John*, 600–601.

[99] Cf. Calvin, *Institutes*, 1.18.1: "The Jews intended to destroy Christ; Pilate and his soldiers complied with their mad desire; yet in solemn prayer the disciples confess that all the impious ones had done nothing except what 'the hand and plan' of God had decreed (Acts 4:28)."

3.2.5. Conclusion

The second major thread of sin in the Gospel of John relates sin to suffering, death, and judgment, and places all of these within the sovereign plan of God. On the one hand, while personal sin can lead to personal suffering (John 5:14), this is by no means necessarily or always the case (9:3). On the other hand, sin certainly does lead to death, and this is nothing less than God's judicial sentence for sin, which will be confirmed in its fullest sense when Jesus, his Son, executes the judgment of the final day (5:29). Sin is *punishable*; it renders those who practice it liable to God's righteous judgment; indeed, they are "condemned already" (3:18, 36; 5:29; 8:21, 24). Nevertheless, God's gracious provision in Jesus means that those who trust in him have already "passed from death to life" (5:24) and escape the condemnation they deserve (3:18); even though they die physically, they will live forever (3:36; 6:50; 8:51–52; 11:25–26). Within this complex of sin and its effects, Jesus appears as the sinless one who dies because of sin. He dies not for his own sin, but because of the sin of others, in a complex of events that has been "given" by God (19:11). And all of this gives reason to hope: for the God who gave his Son to suffer at the hands of sinners, also gave him with a greater purpose— to take their sin away.

3.3. SIN AND SACRIFICE: THE LAMB OF GOD TAKES AWAY SIN

3.3.1. Introduction

The Gospel of John presents a third and final thread within its doctrine of sin, which paradoxically begins to unravel the dark web we have traced so far. John's Gospel, that is, not only exposes the *nature* of sin, and explores the *effects* and *consequences* of sin, it also—especially—announces the final *removal* of sin.[100] This is the Johannine theme of sin and sacrifice, by which John shows that Jesus not only died *because of* sin, but *to take sin away*. This thread is introduced in the Gospel's first explicit reference to sin, which sets the trajectory for the whole Gospel (1:29), and is further emphasized in the Gospel's last explicit reference to sin (20:23), which sets the trajectory for the gospel-centered mission of the church. In the middle, the Gospel shows how Jesus's death was the means by which God defeated "the ruler of this

---

[100] For more extended treatment of this theme, see esp. J. R. Michaels, "Atonement in John's Gospel and Epistles: 'The Lamb of God Who Takes Away the Sin of the World,'" in *The Glory of the Atonement—Biblical, Historical, and Practical Perspectives: Essays in Honour of Roger Nicole*, ed. C. E. Hill and F. A. James (Downers Grove, IL: IVP Academic, 2004), 106–19.

world" and so opened the way to freedom for those who trust in him (12:31; 14:30; 16:11). This theme, without any doubt, is the most important thing that the Gospel has to say about sin: Jesus appeared in order to take it away.

3.3.2. The Lamb of God Takes Away the Sin of the World: John 1:29

The Gospel's teaching about the removal of sin is introduced in its first explicit reference to "sin," when John the Baptist declares that Jesus is "the Lamb of God who takes away the sin of the world ['Ἴδε ὁ ἀμνὸς τοῦ θεοῦ ὁ αἴρων τὴν ἁμαρτίαν τοῦ κόσμου]" (1:29; cf. 1:36).[101] John's identification of Jesus in these terms alludes to several important OT themes and texts, all related to God's provision of a sacrificial lamb to take away sin.[102] At the broadest level, John's declaration recalls the OT sacrificial system, in which God prescribed that "two lambs a year old [כבשים בני שנה שנים (ἀμνοὺς ἐνιαυσίους ἀμώμους δύο)]" were to be sacrificed daily on the altar as a "regular burnt offering [עלת תמיד (θυσίαν ἐνδελεχισμοῦ)]," making it possible for the holy God to dwell among his redeemed people (Ex. 29:38–46).[103] In addition, John's declaration that Jesus is "the Lamb of God" alludes to the account of the testing of Abraham at Mount Moriah (Gen. 22:1–19), when Abraham affirmed that "God will provide for himself the lamb [אלהים יראה לו השה ('Ὁ θεὸς ὄψεται ἑαυτῷ πρόβατον)]" (Gen. 22:8; cf. 22:13–14), by whose sacrifice Isaac's life was spared.[104] This connection is confirmed in John 3:16, which shows that what God spared Abraham from doing, God himself has done—he has given his "only begotten Son" (KJV [τὸν υἱὸν τὸν μονογεν]) for the life of the world.[105] Further, John the Baptist's declaration also casts Jesus as the fulfillment of the Passover lamb of the exodus (Ex. 12:1–51).[106] The Gospel as a

[101] Calvin, Gospel according to St. John 1–10, 32: "The chief office of Christ is explained briefly but clearly. By taking away the sins of the world by the sacrifice of His death, He reconciles men to God. Christ certainly bestows other blessings upon us, but the chief one, on which all the others depend, is that by appeasing the wrath of God He brings it to pass that we are reckoned righteous and pure. The source of all the streams of blessings is that by not imputing our sins, God receives us into favor. Accordingly John, that he may lead us to Christ, begins with the free pardon of sins which we obtain through Him."
[102] I take the genitive τοῦ θεοῦ ("of God") as a source genitive ("lamb from God"), with the sense of the lamb provided by God. The genitive could, in addition, have the sense of a simple possessive genitive ("lamb belonging to God"), but the fact that he "takes away the sins of the world" strongly suggests the idea of his being given by God for that purpose.
[103] Lambs were, of course, also designated for sacrifice in a number of other ways within the sacrificial system.
[104] The allusion is not significantly weakened by the observation that the Lord subsequently provides "a ram [איל (κριός)]" (Gen. 22:13).
[105] For the allusion, see Köstenberger, John, 129.
[106] Genesis 22:8 and Ex. 12:3–6 both use the more general term for "sheep" (שה [πρόβατον]) rather than specifically referring to a "lamb [(כבש (ἀμνός)]." The distinction, however, should not be pressed too strongly. Exodus 12:5 specifies that the "sheep" is to be "a year old [בן שנה (ἐνιαύσιος)]" and hence a lamb. The LXX is not consistent in its translation: Ex. 12:3, for example, translates שה with πρόβατον, while Isa. 53:7 translates שה with ἀμνός.

whole certainly presents Jesus as the fulfillment of the Passover,[107] and John's account of Jesus's crucifixion pointedly presents Jesus as the Passover lamb, who dies without one of his bones being broken (19:36; cf. Ex. 12:46; Num. 9:12; Ps. 34:20).[108] The Baptist's opening declaration, therefore, probably evokes not only the Lord's provision of sacrificial lambs, by which Israel's sins were taken away, and the Lord's provision of a sacrificial lamb (or ram), by which Isaac's life was spared, but also the Lord's provision of the Passover lamb, by which God simultaneously spared his people from his own righteous judgment, and delivered them from slavery under Pharaoh.

In addition to all of this, John the Baptist's declaration most specifically alludes to Isaiah 53, where "the servant of the Lord" is pictured as a "lamb" (ὁ ἀμνός) (Isa. 53:7 LXX) who "will bear" (ἀνοίσει) . . . "the sins" (τὰς ἁμαρτίας) (Isa. 53:11 LXX) of "many" (Isa. 53:12). This more specific allusion is established by the combination of the noun "lamb" (ἀμνός) with the idea of "bearing" (ἀναφέρω) or "taking away" (αἴρω) "sin(s)" (ἁμαρτία).[109] The verb in Isaiah 53:11 LXX is ἀναφέρω rather than αἴρω,[110] but the two verbs belong to the same semantic domain, expressing the idea of "carrying up or away" or "bearing away."[111] Indeed, John may well have chosen the verb αἴρω because, in a number of texts, the LXX uses it and its compounds to refer to the "taking away" of sin or of guilt.[112] In the most important of these texts, Exodus 34:5–7, the Lord reveals his "name" (שם יהוה [ὄνομα κυρίου])

---

[107] S. E. Porter, "Can Traditional Exegesis Enlighten Literary Analysis of the Fourth Gospel? An Examination of the Old Testament Fulfilment Motif and the Passover Theme," in *The Gospels and the Scriptures of Israel*, ed. C. A. Evans and W. R. Stegner, Journal for the Study of the New Testament Supplement Series 104 (Sheffield, UK: Sheffield Academic Press, 1994), 407–11, demonstrates significant Passover connections in John 1:29–36; 2:13–25; 6:1–14, 22–71; 11:47–12:8; 13:1–17:26; 19:13–42. See also Paul M. Hoskins, "Deliverance from Death by the True Passover Lamb: A Significant Aspect of the Fulfillment of the Passover in the Gospel of John," *JETS* 52 (2008): 285–99; Hoskins, "Freedom from Slavery to Sin," 47–53, who draws attention to further Passover symbolism in John 8:31–47.

[108] See M. J. J. Menken, "The Old Testament Quotation in John 19.36: Sources, Redaction, Backgrounds," in *The Four Gospels 1992: Festschrift Frans Neirynck*, vol. 3, ed. F. Van Segbroeck, et al., Bibliotheca Ephemeridum theologicarum Lovaniensium 100 (Leuven: Leuven University Press, 1992), 2101–18.

[109] The noun "lamb [ἀμνός]" occurs elsewhere in the NT only in Acts 8.32, which is a citation from Isa. 53:7, and in 1 Pet. 1:19, which also has strong connections to the Isaianic prophecy. For further arguments in favor of the allusion, see Carson, *Gospel according to John*, 150–51.

[110] D. A. Carson, "Adumbrations of Atonement Theology in the Fourth Gospel," *JETS* 57.3 (2014): 518–20, plausibly suggests that the Gospel faithfully preserves the testimony of John the Baptist, who may well have understood Jesus as the "warrior lamb/ram" of the Jewish apocalypses, who would "take away" sin by his judgment of the wicked (1 En. 9.9–12; T. Jos. 19.8; T. Ben. 3.8), but who also spoke better than he knew, like Caiaphas in John 11:49–52, and so spoke prophetically of Jesus's "taking away" of sin by the sacrifice of himself (John 6:51; 10:11, 15, 17–18; 11:50–52; 15:13; 17:19). The book of Revelation makes it clear that the "warrior lamb/ram" and "sacrificial lamb" imagery were compatible elements of John's theology (Rev. 5:5–6, 12–13; 7:17; 13:8; 17:14; 19:7, 9; 21:22–23; 22:1–3).

[111] See Johannes P. Louw and Eugene A. Nida, *Greek-English Lexicon of the New Testament Based on Semantic Domains*, 2nd ed., 2 vols. (New York: United Bible Societies, 1989), 1:207 (§ 15.203, 206).

[112] E.g., Ex. 28:38; 34:7; Lev. 10:17; 1 Sam. 15:25; 25:28; Mic. 7:18.

to Moses, and describes himself as "merciful and gracious," "abounding in steadfast love and faithfulness," perfectly just, and the one who *takes away . . . sins*" (ἀφαιρῶν . . . ἁμαρτίας) (Ex. 34:6–7 LXX). Given that the Gospel alludes, in its opening prologue, to this revelation of the divine name (John 1:14, 17), and is deeply concerned throughout with the climactic revelation of God's "name" in his Son, Jesus Christ,[113] the choice of this verb is unlikely to be accidental. John the Baptist's declaration of Jesus as "the Lamb of God who takes away the sins of the world" indicates that the Lord God, who abounds in love and justice, has now come to "take away sins" by the sacrifice of himself in the person of his Son.

The rich combination of ideas in this dense initial statement thus prepares the way not only for the multiple strands in John's dark web of sin, but also—especially—for John's presentation of Jesus's salvific mission. Since the people of the world are guilty and under wrath, God has provided the sacrifice needed to take their sins away. Since they are helpless and enslaved, God has provided the redemption they need. If the Gospel of John exposes the problem of sin as a dark web of many tangled threads, the first explicit reference to sin in the Gospel declares that God's grace in his Son is more than adequate to clear the whole web away.

3.3.3. The Son of Man Who Defeats "the Ruler of This World"

Jesus's victory over sin, especially by his sacrificial death, is further underlined in John's teaching regarding Jesus's victory over the devil. In particular, Jesus refers three times to the devil as "the ruler of this world [ὁ ἄρχων τοῦ κόσμου τούτου]" (John 12:31; 14:30; 16:11), and each time—paradoxically—emphasizes his own authority and victory over the evil one.[114]

Jesus's first reference to "the ruler of this world" (12:31) comes in the context of his "triumphal entry" into Jerusalem, when Jesus is hailed as "king of Israel" (12:13, 15; cf. Zech. 9:9), and is sought out by the nations (John 12:20). Jesus concludes that "the hour has come [Ἐλήλυθεν ἡ ὥρα] for the Son of Man to be glorified" (12:23; cf. 2:4; 7:30; 8:20), and this is confirmed by the voice from heaven (12:28). Jesus declares, "now [νῦν] is the judgment

[113] John 1:12; 3:18; 5:43; 10:25; 12:28; 14:13–14, 26; 15:16, 21; 16:23–24, 26; 17:6, 11–12, 26; 20:31. For this theme, see the works cited in note 39.
[114] The genitive τοῦ κόσμου is most likely a genitive of subordination ("ruler over this world"). Cf. Wallace, *Greek Grammar*, 103: "this genitive is a subset of the objective genitive, but not always." Harris, *John*, 234, on 12:31, suggests it could be an objective genitive ("over this world") or a possessive genitive ("possessed by the world" or "belonging to this world").

of this world; now will the ruler of this world be cast out [νῦν ὁ ἄρχων τοῦ κόσμου τούτου ἐκβληθήσεται ἔξω]" (12:31). The statement is emphatic: the great moment of eschatological fulfillment has arrived; the Son of Man— the true ruler of the world—will be glorified, the world will be judged, and the wicked pretender will be cast out. Jesus will win the victory over this "ruler" by his death on the cross, when he will be "lifted up from the earth" (12:32–33). The devil is a vanquished foe.

Jesus's second and third references to "the ruler of this world" also underline Jesus's superiority over him (John 14:30; 16:11). At his final meal with the disciples, Jesus tells them both that he is going away to the Father (14:28; cf. 7:33; 8:14, 21; 13:3, 33, 36; 14:2–4, 12; 16:5, 17, 28), and that "the ruler of this world is coming [ἔρχεται γὰρ ὁ τοῦ κόσμου ἄρχων]" (14:30). Jesus immediately, however, qualifies this ominous announcement by affirming that "he has no claim on me [καὶ ἐν ἐμοὶ οὐκ ἔχει οὐδέν]" (14:30). As the sinless one, who perfectly does the Father's will, Jesus is free from this ruler's power. His impending suffering and death are not to be understood as "the ruler of this world" exercising any power over him, but as Jesus willingly submitting to the Father's command, so that the world may know that he loves the Father (14:31). Again, Jesus speaks of "the ruler of this world" only to relativize his rule by placing it within the Father's authority, expressed through Jesus, his Son. Similarly, later at the same meal, Jesus comforts his disciples with the knowledge that the Spirit will "convict the world of sin and righteousness and judgment" (16:8). He grounds the last aspect of the Spirit's convicting work in the reality that "the ruler of this world is judged [κέκριται]" (16:11). Jesus's use of the perfect tense form underlines the certainty of the devil's judgment.[115] From Jesus's point of view, this judgment lies in the immediate future, but from the point of view of the Spirit's convicting work, it lies in the past. The Spirit, that is, will confirm the apostles' announcement of Jesus's victory over the devil at the cross (12:31–33). The devil's days are numbered. He is "the ruler of this world" only in a radically circumscribed sense. This is

---

[115] The perfect κέκριται is probably best taken as an intensive perfect, emphasizing the state resulting from the completed action of the cross. The devil "is judged" (ESV) or "now stands condemned" (NIV). The function of the Greek perfect remains a matter of debate. For recent discussion, see: Constantine R. Campbell, *Advances in the Study of Greek: New Insights for Reading the New Testament* (Grand Rapids, MI: Zondervan, 2015), 124–26; Robert Crellin, "The Semantics of the Perfect in the Greek of the New Testament," in *The Greek Verb Revisited: A Fresh Approach to Biblical Exegesis*, ed. S. E. Runge and C. J. Fresch (Bellingham, WA: Lexham, 2016), 430–57; Constantine R. Campbell, Buist M. Fanning, Stanley E. Porter, and D. A. Carson, *The Perfect Storm: Critical Discussion of the Semantics of the Greek Perfect Tense under Aspect Theory*, Studies in Biblical Greek 21 (New York: Peter Lang, 2020).

not only because the world ultimately belongs to God who made it, but also—especially—because Jesus has "overcome the world [νενίκηκα]" (16:33).[116] Nevertheless, John's Gospel is also clear that the devil will remain active in the world until the final judgment. In John 17, Jesus asks his Father not to take the disciples "out of the world" but to "keep them from the evil one [ἀλλ᾽ ἵνα τηρήσῃς αὐτοὺς ἐκ τοῦ πονηροῦ]" (17:15). The articular τοῦ πονηροῦ could be taken in the abstract sense "keep them from evil," but given Johannine usage elsewhere, Jesus almost certainly is referring to "the evil one" (cf. 1 John 2:13–14; 3:12; 5:18–19).[117] Although Jesus's death will be the decisive defeat of "the ruler of this world," Jesus shows by his prayer that the evil one will continue to attack his people, orchestrating the world in its hatred against them (cf. 1 John 5:19; Rev. 12:12–17). Jesus, therefore, prays for the Father's protection, which surely provides Christian believers with all the assurance they need; for even "if the Christian pilgrimage is inherently perilous, the safety that only God himself can provide is assured, as certainly as the prayers of God's own dear Son will be answered."[118]

3.3.4. The Risen Lord Who Declares Forgiveness of Sins: John 20:23

The very last reference to "sin" in the Gospel of John confirms that Jesus came to take sin away. In John 20, after his resurrection, Jesus appears to his disciples, and "sends them" out into the world, just as the Father "sent" him into the world (20:21; cf. 17:18). The mission on which Jesus sends the disciples has, at its heart, the declaration of what the Father has done in the Son to remove sin from the world. Jesus breathes on the disciples and charges them to "receive the Holy Spirit [Λάβετε Πνεῦμα Ἅγιον]" (20:22). He then invests them with his own authority to "forgive the sins [ἀφῆτε τὰς ἁμαρτίας]" of any and all who come to him (20:23). This is a remarkable charge, which establishes the apostles as Jesus's Spirit-enabled representatives in the world, and underlines that the church's apostolic mission, rooted in the Father's sending of the Son, is to declare the forgiveness of sins. Indeed, this very last reference to sin in the Gospel creates a kind of salvific *inclusio*: the Gospel's

---

[116] This, in turn, helps to explain why the Gospel of John, unlike the Synoptic Gospels, relates none of Jesus's exorcisms. It cannot be because the Fourth Gospel is uninterested in Jesus's authority over the powers of evil. On the contrary, this Gospel focuses attention on the climactic moment of Jesus's victory over the evil one, when "the ruler of this world" was judged in the "lifting up" of the Son of Man at the cross (3:14; 8:28; 12:32–33).
[117] In light of the Lord's Prayer (Matt. 6:13), John shows that what Jesus taught his disciples to pray for themselves and each other, he also already prayed for them himself.
[118] Carson, *Gospel according to John*, 565.

first and last references to sin point, above all, to Jesus as the Lamb of God who takes away the sin of the world (1:29), and who sends his disciples out into the world to declare the forgiveness of sins in his name (20:23). In John's theology, ruined sinners are not only reclaimed for God; they are recommissioned as his heralds, to announce God's forgiveness of sins in Christ.[119]

3.3.5. Conclusion

The Gospel of John thus weaves together multiple threads in its dark web of sin. Sin is the rejection of God in Christ, which springs from a perverted heart, results in a pattern of immoral behavior, enslaves those who practice it, and leads to their condemnation. This reality affects all people, and means that people find themselves under the power of the evil one, utterly unable to save themselves. Thus, in the Gospel of John, sin is *personal, perverted, practical, powerful, pervasive,* and *punishable.* In all of this, the Gospel's construction of sin, far from performing "no constitutive role" in its theology, is actually crucial for the Gospel's presentation of its central subject—Christ himself. Jesus is "the light of the world" who exposes sin, the sinless one who dies as a result of sin within God's sovereign plan, and—preeminently—"the Lamb of God" who "takes away sin." Thus, while the Gospel of John has a great deal to teach about sin, it is, after all, not a hamartiology but a *Gospel.* John therefore leaves his readers marveling at the sovereignty and grace of God. For while the Gospel paints a dark picture of humanity in sin—as hating God and hating his Son, as guilty, and enslaved, and under the sentence of death—it also draws attention to a deep and wonderful irony. In crucifying Jesus, those who sinned against him only served to enable his perfect obedience to the Father's command—that he would lay down his life for others (10:17–18). In hating God and his Son, those who did so only accomplished what God had planned in his love—that he would give his Son for the life of the world (3:14–16).

4. Sin in the Letters of John: Walking in the Light

4.1. INTRODUCTION

John's first letter further develops his doctrine of sin, and applies the truths revealed in the Gospel to the letter's Christian recipients. The letter, like the

---

[119] In the post-apostolic age, this commission applies primarily to the church's elder-overseers in their official capacity as God's "stewards" (Titus 1:7) and Christ's under-shepherds (Acts 20:28; Eph. 4:11; 1 Pet. 5:1–4). See WCF 30.2, which cites John 20:21–23 among its proof-texts.

Gospel, begins with God's "light," which exposes the darkness of human sin, but also provides the means for its removal (1 John 1:1–5; 2:8–11; cf. John 1:1–4, 14). As in the Gospel, John's affirmation that "God is light [ὁ θεὸς φῶς ἐστιν]" (1:5) has its roots in God's self-revelation throughout the Scriptures, and finds its climax in Christ, the "true light" which is "already shining" (2:8). The image refers, above all, to the perfection of God's character, "his moral excellence and efficacious purity,"[120] which is most fully revealed in Christ. This truth provides the context for John's teaching about God and sin throughout the whole letter, which is concentrated in four key passages. The first two key passages concern life "in the light," and address the problem of ongoing sin in the Christian life (1:7–10 and 2:1–12). The latter two passages concern life "in the darkness," and address the fundamental sin of rejecting God in Christ (3:4–9 and 5:16–21).[121] In the midst of this teaching, John again explores the nature, consequences, and removal of sin, and emphasizes Jesus's identity as the sinless one who takes away sin.

4.2. Sin in the Christian Life: 1 John 1:7–10 and 2:1–12

The first two key passages on sin apply the truth that "God is light" to the realities of ongoing sin in the Christian life (1 John 1:7–10 and 2:1–12). John affirms, first, that since "God is light," those who claim to have "fellowship with the Father and with his Son" must not "walk in the darkness" (1 John 1:3, 6; cf. John 8:12; 12:35); instead, they must "practice the truth [ποιοῦμεν τὴν ἀλήθειαν]" (1 John 1:6; cf. John 3:21), and "walk in the light [ἐν τῷ φωτὶ περιπατῶμεν]" (1 John 1:7; cf. John 8:12; 12:35). This cannot mean that those who have fellowship with God attain to some kind of sinless perfection in this life. John is clear: "If we say we have no sin [ἐὰν εἴπωμεν ὅτι ἁμαρτίαν οὐκ ἔχομεν], we deceive ourselves, and the truth is not in us" (1 John 1:8). Again, "If we say we have not sinned [ἐὰν εἴπωμεν ὅτι οὐχ ἡμαρτήκαμεν], we make him a liar, and his word is not in us" (1:10). Rather, to "walk in the light" refers, most fundamentally, to the life of open confession of sin before God, which embraces God's provision for sin in Christ. For those who "walk in the light," God's promise is that "the blood of Jesus his Son cleanses us from all sin [τὸ αἷμα Ἰησοῦ τοῦ υἱοῦ αὐτοῦ καθαρίζει ἡμᾶς ἀπὸ πάσης ἁμαρτίας]" (1:7). Thus,

---

[120] R. W. Yarbrough, 1, 2, and 3 John, BECNT (Grand Rapids, MI: Baker Academic, 2008), 50.
[121] Twenty-six out of the twenty-seven occurrences of the ἁμαρτ- root in 1 John occur in these four passages. The only remaining reference is 1 John 4:10, on which, see below. For related terms and concepts, see the survey of John's language in the Introduction to this chapter.

John affirms, "If we confess our sins [ἐὰν ὁμολογῶμεν τὰς ἁμαρτίας ἡμῶν], he is faithful and just to forgive us our sins [πιστός ἐστιν καὶ δίκαιος, ἵνα ἀφῇ ἡμῖν τὰς ἁμαρτίας] and to cleanse us from all unrighteousness [καὶ καθαρίσῃ ἡμᾶς ἀπὸ πάσης ἀδικίας]" (1:9). John's repeated references here to "cleansing [καθαρίζω]" characterize sin as an impurity or pollution which requires Jesus's sacrificial blood for its purification (1:7, 9).[122] These references recall Jesus's teaching in the Gospel that while those who belong to him are already "clean" (καθαρός), they also require ongoing "cleansing" (John 13:10–11; 15:2–3; cf. 1 John 3:3). In terms of John's doctrine of sin, then, we now learn that sin is *persistent*; it continues even in the Christian life, requiring those who have fellowship with God in Christ to continue to confess their sins and so be cleansed of them (cf. WCF 6.5, citing 1 John 1:8, 10).

Further, John affirms again that the problem of sin is *pervasive*. "Jesus Christ the righteous," he declares, "is the propitiation for our sins, and not for ours only but also for the sins of the whole world" (2:1–2). The contrast between "our sins" (τῶν ἁμαρτιῶν ἡμῶν) and those of "the whole world" (ὅλου τοῦ κόσμου) makes clear that sin is not a localized Jewish or Jewish-Christian problem, but one that extends to every corner of the globe.[123] This makes God's provision for sin in Christ all the more remarkable, since Jesus is "the propitiation [ἱλασμός]" for the "sins . . . of the whole world" (2:2).[124] Significantly, 1 John 2:1–2 combines Jesus's identity as the "advocate" (παράκλητος) with his identity as the "propitiation" (ἱλασμός) to emphasize that Jesus advocates with the Father on the basis of *his own* sacrifice on the cross. Lest it be thought, however, that Jesus advocates with an implacable Father, 1 John 4:10 makes clear that it is God, in his love, and not sinners in

---

[122] The Gospel of John employs the noun καθαρισμός ("purification") in relation to Jewish rites for purification from ritual impurity (John 2:6; 3:25). Revelation employs the adjective καθαρός in reference to the (symbolic) "pure" white linen worn by angels (Rev. 15:6), and by the saints (Rev. 19:8, 14), and the "pure" gold of the New Jerusalem (21:18, 21). The semantically related verb ἁγνίζω has a similar range of meanings: John 11:55 employs it to speak of ritual purification; 1 John 3:3 to speak of ongoing moral transformation (see Louw and Nida, *Greek-English Lexicon*, 1:535–36 [§ 53.28], which classifies καθαρίζω and cognates with ἁγνίζω and cognates in semantic domain 53: "Religious Activities," subsection C: "Purify, Cleanse").

[123] "The whole world" does not necessarily mean every individual; cf. 1 John 5:19, where the affirmation "the whole world [ὁ κόσμος ὅλος] lies in the power of the evil one" cannot mean that "every individual" is captive to the devil. For this reading of 1 John 2:2, see already Augustine, *Homilies 1 John* 1.8: the reference is to "the church throughout the whole world"; Calvin, *John 11–21 and 1 John*, 244: "John's purpose was only to make this blessing common to the whole Church. Therefore, under the word 'all' he does not include the reprobate, but refers to all who would believe and those who were scattered through various regions of the earth." For recent discussion, see Matthew S. Harmon, "For the Glory of the Father and the Salvation of His People: Definite Atonement in the Synoptics and Johannine Literature," in *From Heaven He Came and Sought Her: Definite Atonement in Historical, Biblical, Theological, and Pastoral Perspective*, ed. David Gibson and Jonathan Gibson (Wheaton, IL: Crossway, 2013), esp. 284–85.

[124] The key term ἱλασμός occurs only here and in 1 John 4:10 in the whole NT, but the context makes clear that John refers to a sacrifice designed to atone for sins (cf. Ezek. 44:27 LXX). For a thorough discussion of the whole word group, see esp. Silva, *NIDNTTE*, 2:531–41.

their sin, who provided for the removal of sin: it is "not that we have loved God but that he loved us and sent his Son to be *the propitiation for our sins* [ἱλασμὸν περὶ τῶν ἁμαρτιῶν ἡμῶν]" (4:10; cf. John 3:16). The Father's love, effective through the Son's sacrifice, is more than adequate to atone for all the sins of all of God's people; "your sins are forgiven for his name's sake [ἀφέωνται ὑμῖν αἱ ἁμαρτίαι διὰ τὸ ὄνομα αὐτοῦ]" (1 John 2:12). In the context of persistent and pervasive sin, then, Christians do not deal with ongoing sin in their lives by autonomous moral self-effort, but by repeatedly coming to God in Christ, receiving the purification he offers by his blood.

At the same time, John is equally clear that fellowship with God in Christ has ethical implications; it must work its way out in actual moral behavior. Thus John immediately affirms, "I am writing these things to you so that you may not sin [ἵνα μὴ ἁμάρτητε]" (2:1). Those who embrace the truth must keep Christ's "commandments" (2:3–4), and walk "in the same way in which he walked" (2:6; cf. John 3:21), which is to "abide in the light [ἐν τῷ φωτὶ μένει]" (1 John 2:10). Thus "walking in the light" involves not only the open confession of sin to God, and the embrace of God's provision for sin in Jesus's death, but also the life of moral transformation into the likeness of Christ, expressed both in love (2:7–11) and in doing God's will (2:15–17). "The true light is already shining [τὸ φῶς τὸ ἀληθινὸν ἤδη φαίνει]" (cf. John 1:5), "the darkness is passing away [ἡ σκοτία παράγεται]" (1 John 2:8), and "the world is passing away [ὁ κόσμος παράγεται] along with its desires" (2:17). Christian believers, therefore, cannot hate each other (2:9), and must not live for the fleeting "desires of the flesh and the desires of the eyes and pride of life" (2:16). They are, rather, to live for God's promised future by "purifying" themselves in an ongoing way, through confession and repentance, expressed in love and holiness, until Jesus returns (3:2–3). Here we see again that sin, and so also repentance from it, is thoroughly *practical*. Just as the fundamental sin of rejecting God in Christ expresses itself in actual immoral behavior, so fellowship with God in Christ must express itself in turning away from immoral actions, walking in obedience to God's commands, and practical love for fellow believers.

4.3. The Fundamental Sin of Rejecting God: 1 John 3:4–9 and 5:16–21

The third key passage, 1 John 3:4–9, clarifies the contrast between ongoing sin in the Christian life and the fundamental sin of rejecting God in Christ.

In particular, 1 John 3:4 provides what might be considered John's definition of sin: "everyone who makes a practice of sinning also practices lawlessness; sin is lawlessness [Πᾶς ὁ ποιῶν τὴν ἁμαρτίαν καὶ τὴν ἀνομίαν ποιεῖ, καὶ ἡ ἁμαρτία ἐστὶν ἡ ἀνομία]."[125] John's description of "everyone who makes a practice of sinning [Πᾶς ὁ ποιῶν τὴν ἁμαρτίαν]" parallels Jesus's teaching in John 8:34 and indicates that John's teaching is "in some measure an echo of Jesus's distinctive rhetoric."[126] Indeed, recognizing this parallel provides a crucial key to interpreting 1 John 3:4–9, since John here follows Jesus in drawing a sharp distinction between the children of God and the children of the devil (cf. John 8:31–47). Thus, John's teaching in this section of the letter emphatically and repeatedly affirms the incompatibility of "sin" with the Christian life: "no one who abides in him *keeps on sinning* [οὐχ ἁμαρτάνει]" (3:6); "*no one who keeps on sinning* [πᾶς ὁ ἁμαρτάνων] has either seen him or known him" (3:6); "*whoever makes a practice of sinning* [ὁ ποιῶν τὴν ἁμαρτίαν] is of the devil" (3:8); "no one born of God *makes a practice of sinning* [ἁμαρτίαν οὐ ποιεῖ], for God's seed abides in him; and *he cannot keep on sinning* [οὐ δύναται ἁμαρτάνειν], because he has been born of God" (3:9). These affirmations and denials cannot mean that those "born of God" will achieve sinless perfection in this life. As we have just seen, John straightforwardly affirms that Christians can and do sin, and that to claim otherwise is to deny the truth (1:8, 10; 2:1). In seeking to reconcile these realities, a common interpretation, reflected in the ESV and NIV translations, appeals to the continuous aspect of the present tense forms of ἁμαρτάνω and ποιέω and suggests that John refers to *ongoing* or *habitual* sin (e.g., 3:6–8 ESV and NIV: "keeps on sinning"; "makes a practice of sinning"; "continues to sin").[127] This reading is partly correct, but places too much weight on the present tense forms,[128] and—more importantly—does not yet get to the heart of the issue.

The key to understanding John's point is given in his definition of "sin" as "lawlessness" (ἡ ἁμαρτία ἐστὶν ἡ ἀνομία; 3:4)[129] The fact that both "sin"

---

[125] Augustine, *Homilies 1 John* 1.8. Turretin improves upon Augustine, recognizing that "lawlessness" includes sinful inclinations, and sins of omission. He defines sin as "an inclination, action or omission at variance with the law of God" (*Institutes*, 1:591); cf. Bavinck, *Reformed Dogmatics*, 3:135–36: "Throughout Scripture . . . the essential character of sin consists in lawlessness (ἀνομια; 1 John 3:4), in violating the law that God revealed in his Word"; cf. WSC Q14 and WLC Q24, which employ 1 John 3:4 in their definitions of sin.

[126] Yarbrough, *1, 2, and 3 John*, 181.

[127] For this interpretation, see, e.g., B. F. Westcott, *The Epistles of St. John: The Greek Text* (London: Macmillan, 1883), 104; Marianne M. Thompson, *1–3 John*, IVP New Testament Commentary (Downers Grove, IL: InterVarsity Press, 1992), 94–95; Gary M. Burge, *The Letters of John*, NIVAC (Grand Rapids, MI: Zondervan, 1996), 150.

[128] See Colin G. Kruse, "Sin and Perfection in 1 John," *Australian Biblical Review* 51 (2003): 66.

[129] Kruse, "Sin and Perfection in 1 John," 69–70.

and "lawlessness" have the article, but no clear antecedent, indicates that John speaks of a particular sin, which he defines as "lawlessness."[130] In biblical usage, this is covenant language and refers to those who reject God's covenant.[131] John thus contrasts "lawlessness [ἡ ἀνομία]" with "righteousness [ἡ δικαιοσύνη]" (3:7), and so indicates that "lawlessness" does not merely refer to acts which infringe God's law, but to the heart which refuses to recognize the law, and therefore to submit to the God who gave it.[132] This "lawlessness" was the original sin of Adam in the garden, when he followed the devil, who has been sinning in this way "from the beginning [ἀπ᾽ ἀρχῆς ὁ διάβολος ἁμαρτάνει]" (3:8; cf. John 8:44). Rather than humbly trusting God to teach him "good and evil," Adam asserted his own moral autonomy to determine the same (Gen. 2:9, 17; 3:5, 22; cf. 1 Kings 3:9); he rejected not only the law but also the lawgiver, God himself. In the same way, the apostle Paul characterizes the eschatological "Man of Lawlessness [ὁ ἄνθρωπος τῆς ἀνομίας]" by his resolute rejection of God (2 Thess. 2:3).[133] It is *this* sin of rejecting God which John refers to in 1 John 3, and it is therefore no surprise that John starkly declares that those who commit *this* sin are "of the devil [ὁ ποιῶν τὴν ἁμαρτίαν ἐκ τοῦ διαβόλου ἐστίν]" (1 John 3:8); indeed, they are his "children [τὰ τέκνα τοῦ διαβόλου]" (3:10). By contrast, those who are "born of God [ἐκ τοῦ θεοῦ γεγέννηται]" and are God's "children [τὰ τέκνα τοῦ θεοῦ]" cannot and do not sin *in this way* (3:9–10). Although God's children can, and often do, commit particular sinful acts, God's gracious gift of new birth has overcome their deep inner corruption and enabled them to receive God's gracious provision in his Son; moreover, the ongoing presence of God's "seed [σπέρμα]" in their lives—his renewing, life-giving power— enables them repeatedly to repent of their sins, "confess" them to God, and so be "cleansed" of "all unrighteousness" by "the blood of Jesus" (1:7, 9).[134] There is, therefore, a fundamental difference between "the sin" of "lawlessness" and the "sins" of the Christian life; the former involves a fundamental

---

[130] Karen H. Jobes, *1, 2, and 3 John*, ZECNT (Grand Rapids, MI: Zondervan, 2013), 147.

[131] Psalm 45:7 (44:8 LXX); Isa. 5:7; 33:15; Ezek. 33:13, 18; Matt. 7:23; 13:41; 23:28; Rom. 6:19; 2 Cor. 6:14; Heb. 1:9.

[132] Cf. Jobes, *1, 2, and 3 John*, 143–44.

[133] Cf. Yarbrough, *1, 2, and 3 John*, 182: in biblical thought, "lawlessness [ἡ ἀνομία]" "always refers to those who have resolutely turned away from God, to the point that they can no longer be regarded as his people but are in fact his enemies."

[134] Cf. Jobes, *1, 2, and 3 John*, 148: "The sin of a believer who acknowledges and confesses it is of a different type than the sin of those who refuse to confess and submit to God's authority. It is the *anomia* sin that leads to death that the one born of God is not able to commit because God's seed remains in them (σπέρμα αὐτοῦ ἐν αὐτῷ μένει) and they have been born of God (ἐκ τοῦ θεοῦ γεγέννηται)."

rejection of God in Christ; the latter are moral failures which—though they may be grave and prolonged—do not reflect such a fundamental rejection of "the light" (cf. WCF 17.2–3).

The fourth key passage further confirms this contrast between the "sins" of those who are "born of God" and "the sin" which is "lawlessness" (5:16–21). The "brother [ἀδελφός]" who "sins a sin not leading to death [ἁμαρτάνοντα ἁμαρτίαν μὴ πρὸς θάνατον]" (my translation) is in a very different situation than the person who commits "sin which leads to death [ἁμαρτία πρὸς θάνατον]" (5:16). While "all wrongdoing is sin [πᾶσα ἀδικία ἁμαρτία ἐστίν]," and even those who are "born of God" can and do sin in this sense, they do not, and cannot, sin in the more fundamental sense of rejecting God in Christ (5:17–18). The reason, again, is that they have been "born of God," and that "the One who was born of God [ὁ γεννηθεὶς ἐκ τοῦ θεοῦ]," that is, Jesus, "protects" or "keeps [τηρεῖ]" them, so that the evil one "does not touch" them (ὁ πονηρὸς οὐχ ἅπτεται αὐτοῦ) (5:18). There is, therefore, a fundamental distinction between those who are "from God" (ἐκ τοῦ θεοῦ ἐσμεν), and the rest of "the whole world," which "lies in the power of the evil one [ὁ κόσμος ὅλος ἐν τῷ πονηρῷ κεῖται]" (5:19). The "sin which leads to death" is the sin of rejecting the God of life, and his provision for eternal life in his Son (cf. 5:12).[135] For this reason, John closes his letter with the charge to God's children: "keep yourselves from idols" (5:21).

4.4. THE REMOVAL OF SIN

Finally, we cannot leave John's first letter without recognizing the most important thing the apostle has to say about sin, which is that Jesus came to "take away" sin. Just as the Gospel characterizes Jesus as "the Lamb of God who *takes away* the sin of the world [ὁ αἴρων τὴν ἁμαρτίαν τοῦ κόσμου]" (John 1:29), so John's letter declares the purpose of Jesus's life and mission in these terms: "he appeared in order to *take away* sins [ἵνα τὰς ἁμαρτίας ἄρῃ]" (1 John 3:5).[136] As in the Gospel, so in his letter, John draws on the Lord's self-revelation as the one who "takes away sins [ἀφαιρῶν . . . ἁμαρτίας]" (Ex. 34:7 LXX), by employing the verb αἴρω ("take away") to speak about Jesus's

---

[135] Cf. Calvin, *John 11–21 and 1 John*, 311: the sin which leads to death "is not what they call a partial Fall, or the transgression of a single commandment, but apostasy, men alienating themselves completely from God." Cf. Turretin, *Institutes*, 1:647–52; Bavinck, *Reformed Dogmatics*, 3:156–57. For recent discussion, see esp. Jobes, *1, 2, and 3 John*, 232–38.

[136] The textual variant, which reads "our sins" (ἁμαρτίας ἡμῶν), does not substantially affect the point.

comprehensive removal of sin from the world.[137] Again, as in the Gospel, John explains that Jesus was uniquely qualified for this mission because he himself was sinless: "in him there is no sin [καὶ ἁμαρτία ἐν αὐτῷ οὐκ ἔστιν]" (1 John 3:5); he is "the righteous [δίκαιον]" (2:1). Crucially, as we have already seen, it is Jesus's sacrificial death on the cross—his "blood" (1:7), his self-offering as a "propitiation [ἱλασμός]" (2:2; 4:10)—that is the means of sin's removal from the world. Moreover, as in the Gospel, the removal of sin is closely associated with the defeat of the devil: "The reason the Son of God appeared was to destroy the works of the devil" (3:8).

John makes clear, however, that this removal of sin, and the related defeat of the devil, is both now and not yet. He coordinates Jesus's mission to take away sin with Jesus's first and second "appearances": Jesus "appeared [ἐφανερώθη] in order to take away sins" (3:5); he "appeared [ἐφανερώθη]" in order to "destroy the works of the devil" (3:8);[138] but believers are still waiting for the day "when he appears [ἐὰν φανερωθῇ]," "at his coming [ἐν τῇ παρουσίᾳ αὐτοῦ]," when "we shall be like him, because we shall see him as he is" (2:28; 3:2). Jesus's mission to "take away" sin will be fully and finally complete only when he is revealed in all his glory. Indeed, John's decision to refer to Jesus "appearing" or "revealing [φανερόω]" himself, rather than to use the more common NT language of Jesus's "coming [ἔρχομαι, ἥκω, παρουσία]" may well be significant.[139] The verb φανερόω has obvious semantic overlap with John's "light" theme, and so underscores his teaching everywhere that God's revelation of his "light" in Christ will one day banish all the darkness.

5. Sin in Revelation: The Lord God Will Be Their Light

5.1. INTRODUCTION

The book of Revelation also holds out the promise—perhaps more vividly than any other book in the canon—of the complete removal of sin, and all of its effects, from the world. This glorious picture of the hope of those who have been freed from sin by the blood of Jesus, however, yet again shows the

---

[137] An allusion to Ex. 34:7 is suggested by: (1) the verb αἴρω, ἀφαιρέω with reference to "sin" (ἁμαρτία); and (2) reference to "lawlessness" (ἀνομία) in the immediate context (Ex. 34:7; 1 John 3:4).

[138] For Jesus's life, death, and resurrection as his first "appearance," described by the verb φανερόω, see also John 1:31; 2:11; 17:6; 21:1, 14; 1 John 1:2; 4:9.

[139] The NT texts employ a range of terms to speak about Jesus's second coming. For a comprehensive assessment, see Murray J. Smith, *Jesus, the Son of Man, and the Final Coming of God*, WUNT (Tübingen: Mohr Siebeck, forthcoming), ch. 8. First John does use the semi-technical term παρουσία, but only once (1 John 2:28).

darkness of human sin. While the explicit language of sin is less prominent in Revelation than in the Gospel or Letters of John, the book demonstrates the wickedness of those who reject God using a range of images and descriptions, and leaves no doubt about the ultimate consequences of sin for those who persist in it.[140] As in the Gospel and Letters, so in Revelation, it is "God's light," which will come to the world fully and finally when God dwells among his people in a "new heavens and new earth," that ultimately dispels the darkness of human sin and gives life to God's people from among "all nations" (Rev. 21:1–5, 23–24; 22:5).

5.2. The Nature of Sin

Revelation's account of the nature of sin is consistent with that of John's Gospel and Letters. Sin is, at its heart, a fundamental rejection of God in Christ. It involves a deep inner corruption, and personal enslavement to sin, expressed in discrete immoral actions. These elements of Revelation's teaching about sin can most helpfully be analyzed in reverse order.

To begin with, sin involves *sins*. The opening doxology—"To him who loves us and has freed us from our sins [Τῷ . . . λύσαντι ἡμᾶς ἐκ τῶν ἁμαρτιῶν ἡμῶν] by his blood" (1:5)—speaks of "sins" in the plural. This indicates multiple discrete acts, and thus a pattern of immoral behavior. At the other end of the book, in the climactic closing chapters, Revelation provides three lists of various kinds of "sinners," which give a clear picture of the "sins" that must be intended. It speaks of "the cowardly, the faithless, the detestable, the murderers, the sexually immoral, the sorcerers, the idolaters, and all the liars" (21:8; cf. 21:27; 22:15; also 9:20–21; 22:11). These catalogues speak directly into the context of Revelation's first hearers, who faced threats and persecutions for their loyalty to Christ. This explains some of the distinctive features of these lists, including the unusual fronting of "the cowardly" in the first list (21:8). Nevertheless, the immoral actions implied by these descriptors are, on the whole, common to biblical morality from Genesis to Revelation, summarized in the Ten Commandments. Sin here, as always in the Johannine literature, involves *sins* which transgress God's law; sin is eminently *practical*.

In addition, however, sin involves a form of personal enslavement. The opening doxology refers to Jesus as the one who "has freed us from our sins

---

[140] The ἁμαρτ– root occurs only three times in Revelation, always as the noun "sin" (ἁμαρτία) and always in the plural (Rev. 1:5; 18:4, 5); the other related Johannine terms do not appear (πονηρός; φαῦλος; ἀδικία; ἀνομία).

[λύσαντι ἡμᾶς ἐκ τῶν ἁμαρτιῶν ἡμῶν] by his blood."[141] This language un-mistakably echoes the exodus, and Isaiah's prophecy of a "second exodus" (Isa. 40:2 LXX). It characterizes sin as a tyrannical slave-master that enslaves those who practice it, and renders them helpless victims of their own wicked behavior, utterly unable to save themselves (cf. John 8:34). Thus sin is, again, a *powerful* reality against which human beings, on their own, are no match. Indeed, the extent of sin's mastery over the human race becomes clear in John's central vision of the heavenly throne room, when "the Lamb" who was "slain" is praised because he "purchased for God" (ἠγόρασας τῷ θεῷ), by his "blood" (ἐν τῷ αἵματί σου), people "from every tribe and language and people and na-tion" (5:6–10). The depiction of Christ's death as the means by which he has "purchased" or "ransomed" (ἀγοράζω) people for God confirms the depiction of sin as a slave-master. Revelation 5, however, adds the note that sin's power-ful hold on those who practice it extends to *all* kinds of people, and to *every* cor-ner of the globe. Thus, as we have seen throughout John's works, sin is not only *practical*, and *powerful*, but also utterly *pervasive* in its effects in the world.

Moreover, Revelation strongly implies that sin involves a deep, inner, personal corruption. The three climactic vice lists describe people by means of a series of substantives which indicate that sin, when persisted in, becomes determinative of a person's identity (21:8, 27; 22:15). The people described in these lists are not merely those whose lives include *episodes* of cowardice, or *instances* of immorality, no matter how frequent or flagitious. The corrup-tion of these people in sin has reached such an extent that it characterizes their whole being: they *are* "the idolaters" (εἰδωλολάτραις), "the murderers" (φονεῦσιν), "the sexually immoral" (πόρνοις), "the liars" (ψευδέσιν). While Revelation holds out the wonderfully liberating good news that sin *need not* define those who have succumbed to it, because Jesus has "freed us . . . by his blood" (1:5), it also holds out this stark alternative: those who refuse to come to God in Christ remain trapped in their sin and ultimately defined by it. Thus, again, as everywhere in John's works, sin's outward manifestations reflect a deep and pervasive personal corruption. Sin is *perverted*.

This personal corruption is closely related to the very essence of sin: the rejection of God in Christ. In this respect it is significant that all three vice

---

[141] The majority text and several other MSS and versions read λούσαντι ἡμᾶς ἀπό ("washed us from"). The UBS[5] editors rightly opt for λύσαντι ἡμᾶς ("freed us from"). This reading (1) has better support in the early MSS, (2) re-flects Isa. 40:2 LXX, and (3) comports well with the exodus imagery of Rev. 1:6.

lists end with references to those whose lives deny the truth: John speaks of "all the liars [πᾶσιν τοῖς ψευδέσιν]" (21:8); of "those who practice . . . falsehood [ὁ ποιῶν . . . ψεῦδος]" (21:27, my translation); of "everyone who loves and practices falsehood [πᾶς φιλῶν καὶ ποιῶν ψεῦδος]" (22:15). This fundamental rejection of God in Christ appears perhaps most starkly in the book's sharp distinction between true and false worship. On the one hand, the heavenly beings gathered around God's throne, and the faithful among the inhabitants of the earth, worship the one true God and him alone (4:8–11; 5:11–14; 7:9–12; 11:15–18; 14:6–7; 15:2–4; 19:1–10; 22:8–9). On the other hand, "the rest of mankind" worship "demons and idols of gold and silver and bronze and stone and wood" (9:20), and especially give themselves to worshiping "the dragon" (13:4) and "the beast" or its "image" (13:4, 8, 12, 15; 14:9, 11; 16:2; 19:20).[142] Rather than worshiping their Creator and Sustainer, the one who gives them life, human beings trapped in sin worship and serve false gods, and the devil who stands behind them. They "curse God," persist in sin, and refuse to "repent" (2:21; 9:20–21; 16:9, 11). Ultimately, it is this rejection of the truth of God, as he has revealed himself in his Son, that leaves sinners without hope in the world, and finally excluded from the life of "the new heavens and the new earth," where God dwells with his people (21:8, 27; 22:15). In this very strong sense, as we have seen throughout John's works, sin is deeply *personal*.

5.3. THE CONSEQUENCES OF SIN

Revelation depicts the consequences of sin in even more graphic terms than the Gospel and Letters: sin ultimately leads to God's righteous and eternal condemnation. This condemnation belongs first and foremost to the devil or Satan. Revelation, in fact, contains a more fulsome description of this malevolent spiritual being than we find anywhere else in Scripture: he is "the great dragon . . . that ancient serpent, who is called the devil and Satan, the deceiver of the whole world [ὁ δράκων ὁ μέγας, ὁ ὄφις ὁ ἀρχαῖος, ὁ καλούμενος Διάβολος καὶ ὁ Σατανᾶς, ὁ πλανῶν τὴν οἰκουμένην ὅλην]" (12:9). This characterization coordinates four descriptions of the devil. He is: (1) the "serpent" (ὁ ὄφις) from the garden of Eden (Gen. 3:1, 2, 4); (2) "the Satan" (ὁ Σατανᾶς),

---

[142] For the worship theme in Revelation, see further Murray J. Smith, "The Book of Revelation: A Call to Worship, Witness, and Wait in the Midst of Violence," in *Into All the World: Emergent Christianity in Its Jewish and Greco-Roman Context*, ed. M. Harding and A. Nobbs (Grand Rapids, MI: Eerdmans, 2017), 355–62.

that is, "the Adversary" of God, who "makes war" (ποιέω + πόλεμος) against God's people (Rev. 11:7–8; 12:7, 17; 13:4; 16:13–14; 17:14); (3) "the devil" (ὁ διάβολος), that is, "the slanderer," whose *modus operandi* is deceitful and destructive speech, which inspires the blasphemies and lies of "the beasts" and the "false prophet" and deceives "the whole world" (12:9; cf.13:5–6, 12–15; 16:13; 19:20; 20:10; cf. John 8:44); and (4) "the dragon" (ὁ δράκων), who throughout Scripture is closely associated with evil human authorities opposed to God,[143] and in Revelation stands behind the "beasts" (Rev. 13:1, 11), and the "false prophet" (16:13; 19:20; 20:10), which symbolize aspects of evil human empire. Thus, far from being a merely "spiritual" power that does not influence the concrete realities of life in the world, the devil is manifestly at work in and through them, and is especially focused on attacking the church (2:9–10, 13, 24; 3:9; 12:13–17).[144] The main point for our purposes, however, is that the devil is a defeated foe, awaiting final condemnation. In light of God's victory in Christ, the devil has been "thrown down to the earth [ἐβλήθη εἰς τὴν γῆν]" (12:9) and now wreaks havoc there, desperately working his "great wrath, because he knows that his time is short [θυμὸν μέγαν, εἰδὼς ὅτι ὀλίγον καιρὸν ἔχει]" (12:12). At the same time, the devil has been "bound [ἔδησεν]" for the "thousand years" between Christ's resurrection and return (20:2–3), so that while he causes serious problems for God's people, he does so only within the limits set by God himself.[145] Satan's end, therefore, is condemnation under God's eternal judgment: the devil, together with "the beasts" and "the false prophet," will be "thrown into the lake of fire and sulfur [ἐβλήθη εἰς τὴν λίμνην τοῦ πυρὸς καὶ θείου]," where "they will be tormented day and night forever and ever [βασανισθήσονται ἡμέρας καὶ νυκτὸς εἰς τοὺς αἰῶνας τῶν αἰώνων]" (20:10; cf. 19:20).

"The fire" of God's righteous condemnation is also reserved for all those who persist in rebellion against God and Christ. Each of the four cycles in the middle section of the book—the seven seals (6:1–8:5), seven trumpets

---

[143] Egypt and Pharaoh: Ps. 74:13–14 (LXX 73:13–14); Ezek. 29:3; 32:2–3; Nebuchadnezzar: Jer. 51:34 (LXX 28:34). Note esp. Ezek. 29:3 LXX, which describes Pharaoh as "the great dragon [Φαραω τὸν δράκοντα τὸν μέγαν]." This is the only occurrence of that phrase in the LXX. For further detail, including references in early Jewish literature, see G. K. Beale, *The Book of Revelation: A Commentary on the Greek Text*, NIGTC (Grand Rapids, MI: Eerdmans, 1999), 633; Smith, "Book of Revelation," 351–52.

[144] For the details, see Smith, "Book of Revelation," 347–55.

[145] I assume here the reading of Rev. 20:1–10 traditionally labeled "amillennial." For a recent defense of this view, suggesting "inaugurated millennialism" as a better description for the position, see G. K. Beale, "The Millennium in Revelation 20:1–10: An Amillennial Perspective," *Criswell Theological Review* 11.1 (2013): 29–62; cf. Meredith G. Kline, "First Resurrection," *WTJ* 37 (1975): 366–75; Kline, "First Resurrection: A Reaffirmation," *WTJ* 39.1 (1976): 110–19.

(8:1–11:19), seven signs (11:19–15:6), and seven bowls (15:7–16:21)—climaxes with a vision of final judgment, followed by a celebration of eternal salvation (6:12–8:1; 11:15–18; 14:14–15:4; 16:17–21).[146] These complementary visions of the final judgment depict God himself, "the one seated on the throne" and/or "the Lamb" coming to earth (Rev. 6:16, with Isa. 2:10, 19, 21; Rev. 14:14, with Dan. 7:13–14) to execute his righteous "wrath [ἡ ὀργή]" on those who have rejected him, persecuted his people, and destroyed the earth (Rev. 6:16–17; 11:18; 14:19; 16:19). The judgment is universal in scope, and eternal in duration (6:15; 11:18; 14:11, 15–16, 18–19; 15:3–4). This same final judgment is depicted in its full glory and terror in Revelation 17–20. These chapters do not provide a strict chronology of "the end," but present several complementary visions of the final judgment, and so reveal just how serious sin is. They describe, first, God's judgment on "Babylon," the great city opposed to God (17:1–19:5). While this applies, initially, to God's judgment on the Roman Empire, Revelation's imagery is not exhausted by that reference, and it extends to God's final judgment on all human empires and social systems that set themselves up against the Creator.[147] Revelation next depicts the final coming of the Lord Jesus, "the King of kings and Lord of lords," in full battle array, accompanied by the armies of heaven, to claim his own and to execute God's wrath on all of his enemies (19:11–21; cf. Isa. 63:1–6). As elsewhere in the book, this final eschatological judgment is universal in its scope and eternal in its duration (19:3, 18). The judgment is finally depicted in its fullest terms when the great enemies of God—the devil, the beast, and the false prophet—are "thrown into the lake of fire and sulfur . . . where they will be tormented day and night forever and ever" (20:10); and when the Lord comes to set up his "great white throne" on the earth and to judge all of humanity, according to whether their names were written in the Lamb's "book of life," and "according to their works" (20:11–15, my translation). As in the Gospel and the Letters, we see now in the most dramatic of terms—that sin is *punishable*.

Revelation's teaching regarding the *punishment* of sin raises at least three important interpretive and theological questions. First, Revelation 20:11–15

---

[146] For the "interlocking" technique which helps to structure this part of the book, see Adela Yarbro Collins, *The Combat Myth in the Book of Revelation*, Harvard Dissertations in Religion 9 (Missoula, MT: Scholars Press, 1976), 15–16; expanded by Beale, *Revelation*, 112–14. For the consummative judgment-salvation scenes, see Beale, *Revelation*, 122.
[147] For this perspective, see Beale, *Revelation*, 714, 869; Smith, "Book of Revelation," 347–55.

depicts the final judgment of all people, believers included, "according to their works [κατὰ τὰ ἔργα αὐτῶν]" (Rev. 20:12–13, my translation).[148] This final judgment of all people "according to works" is consistent with Jesus's teaching in John's Gospel (John 5:28–29),[149] with Revelation elsewhere (2:23; 11:18; 14:13; 21:8; 22:12), and with the rest of Scripture.[150] This teaching, however, must be carefully understood. The decisive reality at the final judgment is whether a person's name is written in "the book of life" (20:15), which is "the book of life of the Lamb who was slain" (13:8; cf. 3:5; 21:27): it is his "blood" that "freed" his people "from [their] sins" (1:5) and "purchased" them "for God" (5:9 NIV), and it is by his "blood" that they have "washed their robes and made them white" (7:14; 22:14). Moreover, if their lives exhibit good works, this is only because God has clothed them with "fine, bright and pure linen," which is the "righteous deeds of the saints [τὰ δικαιώματα τῶν ἁγίων]" (19:8).[151] Thus, while the evil works of those who reject God are rightly said to merit their condemnation, there is no sense in which the works of believers are meritorious, or provide any basis for their salvation. The final judgment is not *on account of works* (διὰ τὰ ἔργα) but *according to works* (κατὰ τὰ ἔργα), and the good works of believers are nothing more than the "fruits and evidences of a true and lively faith" (WCF 16.2; cf. 16.3–6 and 33.1).[152] In this way Revelation underscores its teaching that both faith in Christ, and the faithless rejection of him in sin, are thoroughly *practical*.

Second, Revelation depicts the judgment of the wicked as continuing into eternity. Although some have argued that the wicked are "annihilated" at the judgment,[153] the Reformed churches have long and rightly affirmed

---

[148] Beale, *Revelation*, 1037, suggests that the righteous are "spared from the judgment," but elsewhere acknowledges that "it is possible that the believing dead are included among those 'judged according to their works.'" (1034). This latter proposal is correct.

[149] John 3:18 affirms that "whoever believes in him [Christ] *is not condemned* [οὐ κρίνεται]." Similarly, in John 5:24, Jesus affirms that "whoever hears my words and believes him who sent me has eternal life. *He does not come into judgment* [εἰς κρίσιν οὐκ ἔρχεται]." In both cases, as Turretin recognizes, this does not mean that believers are exempt from judgment by Christ, but "is meant of the judgment of condemnation, which they do not dread" (*Institutes*, 3:600).

[150] For the specific phrase "according to his work" (κατὰ τὰ ἔργα αὐτοῦ): Ps. 62:12 (LXX 61:13); Prov. 24:12; Matt. 16:27 (some MSS); Rom. 2:6; cf. Pss. Sol. 2.16. For the general principle, in similar language, see: Ex. 20:5–7; Deut. 5:9–11; 7:9; 1 Kings 8:32, 39; Ps. 28:4 (LXX 27:4); Eccl. 12:14; Isa. 59:18; Jer. 51:56 (LXX 28:56); Ezek. 18:4, 30; Matt. 12:36–37; Rom. 14:10–12; 1 Cor. 3:12–15; 2 Cor. 5:10; Heb. 10:30; 1 Pet. 1:17.

[151] Cf. Calvin, *Institutes*, 2.5.2: "How often does this thought recur in Augustine: 'God does not crown our merits but his own gifts'"; "we call 'rewards' not what are due our merits, but what are rendered for graces already bestowed!" (also 3.18.7). Cf. Bavinck, *Reformed Dogmatics*, 4:729.

[152] For extended discussion of this point, see Turretin, *Institutes*, 2:710–24; 3:603; Bavinck, *Reformed Dogmatics*, 4:698–702.

[153] See esp. Edward Fudge, *The Fire That Consumes: A Biblical and Historical Study of the Doctrine of Final Punishment*, 3rd ed. (Cambridge: Lutterworth, 2012).

that the judgment of the wicked consists in their eternal conscious torment (e.g., WCF 33.2).[154] Revelation repeatedly employs the noun βασανισμός ("torment"), which consistently refers to conscious suffering (9:5; 11:10; 12:2; 18:7, 10, 15; 20:10).[155] The book, moreover, describes this "torment" of the wicked as continuing "forever and ever [εἰς τοὺς αἰῶνας τῶν αἰώνων]" (14:11; 19:3; 20:10), using language that demands to be read as a reference to ongoing, eternal condemnation. Certainly, the book employs the same language to describe the Lord's eternal life, glory, reign, and worship (1:6; 4:9–10; 5:13; 7:12; 10:6; 11:15; 15:7), and the blessed state of the saints (22:5), all of which unmistakably refer to realities that continue without end. Revelation further pictures the wicked as "outside" the "new Jerusalem" (21:2, 8; 22:14–15), and this also "implies that the existence of the wicked is coterminous with the eternal blessedness of the righteous."[156] As sobering as this reality is, Revelation affirms that the final condemnation of the wicked continues into eternity.[157] This is what Revelation calls "the second death [ὁ δεύτερος θάνατος]" (2:11; 20:6, 14; 21:8). It follows the wicked being called "into the resurrection of condemnation [εἰς ἀνάστασιν κρίσεως]" (John 5:29, my translation) and refers to the final, irreversible, permanent, and ongoing condemnation of those who reject the God who made them.[158]

Third, Revelation indicates that God's fearsome presence in judgment is the source of this eternal condemnation. There is a sense in which hell is "separation from God," and Revelation certainly pictures the wicked being excluded from the blessings of life with God in "the new heavens and new earth" (21:1, 8, 27; 22:15, 19; cf. Matt. 7:23; 25:41). The Scriptures also, however, emphasize that—above all—it is God's *presence* in judgment that is to be feared.[159] Consistent with this, Revelation depicts the coming of God

---

[154] See Calvin, *Institutes*, 3.25.12; Turretin, *Institutes*, 3:607; Bavinck, *Reformed Dogmatics*, 4:702–14; Charles Hodge, *Systematic Theology*, 3 vols. (Grand Rapids, MI: Eerdmans, 1952), 3:868–79. For a recent defense, see Michael S. Horton, *The Christian Faith: A Systematic Theology for Pilgrims on the Way* (Grand Rapids, MI: Zondervan, 2011), 974–84.

[155] Beale, *Revelation*, 762.

[156] Beale, *Revelation*, 762.

[157] Revelation's affirmation of judgment "according to works" provides a further indication that it does not teach annihilationism. A judgment "according to works" implies different degrees of punishment, while annihilation renders the same, undifferentiated judgment to all.

[158] In Revelation, "first" and "second" communicate, respectively, the present, impermanent state of things, and the final, permanent state. See "first resurrection" (20:5–6), "first heaven and first earth" (21:1), "second death" (2:11; 20:6, 14; 21:8).

[159] E.g., Pss. 96:13; 98:9; Isa. 2:10, 19, 21; 63:1–6; 66:15–19; Zeph. 1:2–18; Zech. 14:1–9; Matt. 10:28; 16:27; 25:31–46; 2 Thess. 1:9–10. On 2 Thessalonians 1:9 see esp. Charles L. Quarles, "The APO of 2 Thessalonians 1:9 and the Nature of Eternal Punishment," *WTJ* 59 (1997): 201–11; cf. Murray J. Smith, "The Thessalonian Correspondence," in *All Things to All Cultures: Paul among Jews, Greeks, and Romans*, ed. M. Harding and A. Nobbs (Grand Rapids, MI: Eerdmans, 2013), 296 n. 110.

in Christ as the source of final condemnation (2:16; 6:16; 14:10–11; 19:21; 20:11); when Christ comes, "he will tread the winepress of the fury of the wrath of God the Almighty" (19:15 with Isa. 63:1–6; cf. Rev. 14:19–20). We therefore cannot rightly speak of "hell" as a "place" or "state" outside of God's presence, or as a reality which is not upheld by his providence. "Hell," rather, is the terrifying prospect of exclusion from God's *favorable* presence, suffering the full force of his *condemning* presence in wrath and fury, for all eternity.[160] In all of these ways, Revelation underscores the immense gravity of sin, and God's righteous condemnation of it.

5.4. The Removal of Sin

These are sobering realities. We therefore cannot leave Revelation without noticing that the book also holds out the promise of the final removal of sin from the world, and does so in the most vivid of terms. As everywhere in John's works, this removal of sin is set within the frame of an inaugurated eschatology, and presented as the fruit of God's provision of a sacrifice for sin in the death of Jesus, his Son.[161]

In relation to the "now" of Revelation's eschatology, the opening doxology praises "Jesus Christ" as the one "who loves us and has freed us from our sins by his blood [Τῷ ἀγαπῶντι ἡμᾶς καὶ λύσαντι ἡμᾶς ἐκ τῶν ἁμαρτιῶν ἡμῶν ἐν τῷ αἵματι αὐτοῦ]."[162] The unmistakable allusion to the exodus pictures God's people as those who have been "freed" (λύω) from slavery to sin and who are now on their way to the fullness of freedom in the "promised land" of the new creation (cf. 1:6: "kingdom" and "priests" with 5:10; 20:6 and Ex. 19:4–6). Their redemption is grounded in Christ's "love" (ἀγαπάω),[163] and was effected "by his blood [ἐν τῷ αἵματι αὐτοῦ]," a reference to Christ's sacrificial death which reverberates throughout the book (Rev. 5:9; 7:14; 12:11; cf. 19:13).[164] The Lord Jesus's present victory

---

[160] Cf. Calvin, *Institutes*, 3.25.12: ". . . how wretched it is to be cut off from all fellowship with God. And not that only but so to feel his sovereign power against you that you cannot escape being pressed by it. . . . What and how great is this, to be eternally and unceasingly besieged by him?"

[161] For more extended discussion of this theme, see esp. Charles E. Hill, "Atonement in the Apocalypse of John: 'A Lamb Standing As If Slain,'" in *The Glory of the Atonement—Biblical, Historical, and Practical Perspectives: Essays in Honour of Roger Nicole*, ed. Charles E. Hill and F. A. James (Downers Grove, IL: IVP Academic, 2004), 190–208.

[162] Aune, *Revelation*, 46, notes that this is the first doxology in the NT addressed to Christ, and hence the earliest extant doxology addressed to him.

[163] For Christ's love for his people as the ground of his sacrifice of himself for them, see John 13:1, 34; 15:9, 12–13.

[164] Revelation 1:5 is the only use of λύω in connection with Christ's atoning work in the NT. The language is probably grounded in Isa. 40:2 LXX, which already uses λύω in connection with release from sins (λέλυται αὐτῆς ἡ ἁμαρτία). It is further linked to the commonly used cognates λύτρον (means of redemption) and ἀπολύτρωσις

over sin is further emphasized in the paradoxical vision of him as "the Lion of the tribe of Judah" and the "slain Lamb" (5:5–6; cf. 5:12; 13:8) who "has conquered" (ἐνίκησεν) and "ransomed" people "for God," by his "blood" (5:5–6, 9). God's people therefore also now "conquer" (νικάω) the devil, sin, and death "by the blood of the Lamb" (12:11; cf. 2:7, 11, 17, 26; 3:5, 12, 21; 15:2; 21:7), as they rely on him, "patiently enduring" (ὑπομονή) until he comes again (1:9; 2:2, 19; 3:10; 13:10; 14:12).[165] This strong note of present freedom from sin provides the basis for the Lord's repeated call for believers to "repent" of sin (2:5, 16, 22; 3:3, 19), as well as for his command to "come out" of "Babylon," "so that you will not share in her sins [ἵνα μὴ συγκοινωνήσητε ταῖς ἁμαρτίαις αὐτῇ]" (18:4 NIV), which are "heaped high as heaven [ὅτι ἐκολλήθησαν αὐτῆς αἱ ἁμαρτίαι ἄχρι τοῦ οὐρανοῦ]" (18:5). In stark contrast to those who align themselves with the wicked "harlot," "Babylon," and remain trapped in her sins, those who belong to Jesus are his "bride," the "new Jerusalem," whom he purifies from sin (7:14; 22:14) and adorns with "righteous deeds" (19:8).

In relation to the "not yet" of Revelation's eschatology, the book looks forward to the full and final removal of sin and all of its effects in the world. The stunning picture of Revelation 21–22 is anticipated in each of the seven letters to the churches (2:7, 10–11, 17, 26–28; 3:5, 12, 20–21), as well as in the final consummation scenes throughout the middle section of the book (6:12–8:1; 11:15–18; 14:14–15:4; 16:17–21). These scenes describe the final coming of God in Christ to renew his creation, remove all that is evil, perfect his people, and dwell among them forever. The final state of creation is, however, no mere repristination of the original. The "new Jerusalem" at the center of the "new heavens and new earth" is not a return to Eden, but a picture of Eden having reached its goal in the glorious Garden-City (21:1–2; cf. 3:12 with Isa. 65:17–25). The final coming of God in Christ, that is, creates a radical moral discontinuity between the present and the future: the devil and all his associates are defeated (Rev. 19:17–21; 20:10), sin and sinners are excluded (20:15; 21:8), death is done away with (20:14; 21:4), and all "mourning . . . crying . . . and pain" cease forever as God himself "wipes away every tear" (21:4; cf. 7:17 with Isa. 25:8). In this way God brings the entire created order to its appointed goal and makes "all things

---

(setting free/release); cf. Kertelge, "Revelation," in *Exegetical Dictionary of the New Testament*, ed. Horst Balz and Gerhard Schneider, 3 vols. (Grand Rapids, MI: Eerdmans, 1990–93), 2:368.

[165] Smith, "Book of Revelation," 365–71.

new" (Rev. 21:5).[166] In this (re)new(ed) creation, God himself will "dwell" among his peoples, in fulfillment of his covenant promise (21:3).[167] The removal of sin also means that human beings, redeemed in Christ, are finally free to fulfil God's purpose for Adam (Gen. 1:26–28), God's promise to Abraham (Gen. 12:3), and God's call to Israel (Ex. 19:6), as they "reign" on the earth, "a kingdom" and "priests"—the vast multitude of the fully perfected people of God (Rev. 1:6; 3:21; 5:9–10; 7:9–14; 20:6; 21:3; 22:5). Gloriously, in this God-centered Garden-City there is no possibility of a return to sin. As G. K. Beale notes, "The absence of liars in the new world shows that the coming order will exist on a higher moral level than even the cosmos before the Fall, where the Satanic liar was allowed entrance."[168] This is confirmed by the absence in the "new heavens and new earth" of the "sea" (21:1), and of the "night" (21:25; 22:5), both symbols of sin and its consequences; their removal indicates that "creation has been brought beyond any threat of future evil, chaos or judgement."[169] In the final analysis it is the bright "light" of the triune God's glorious radiance which expels the darkness of human sin, completes the perfection of his people, and renews the entire creation (21:23–24; 22:5).

6. Conclusion: The Anatomy of Sin in the Gospel, Letters, and Revelation of John

The Gospel, Letters, and Revelation of John present a dark web of sin and its effects and consequences. Sin is, in its essence, the *personal* rejection of God in Christ through unbelief. Sin is also, however: *practical*, being expressed in immoral action; *powerful*, in that it enslaves those who practice it; *perverted*, in that it involves a deep inner corruption; *pervasive*, affecting all kinds of people from every part of the world; *persistent*, continuing to affect the lives of believers until the return of Christ; and *punishable*, since

---

[166] See here esp. Bavinck, *Reformed Dogmatics*, 4:715–30. More recently, see: William J. Dumbrell, *The End of the Beginning: Revelation 21–22 and the Old Testament* (Eugene, OR: Wipf & Stock, 2001); Mark B. Stephens, *Annihilation or Renewal? The Meaning and Function of New Creation in the Book of Revelation*, WUNT 2/307 (Tübingen: Mohr Siebeck, 2011), 226–57; Brian J. Tabb, *All Things New: Revelation as Canonical Capstone*, NSBT 48 (Downers Grove, IL: InterVarsity Press, 2019), 165–80.

[167] For the central covenant promise, "I will be your God and you will be my people," or variations of it, see Gen. 17:7–8; 28:15; 31:3, 5, 42; 39:2–6, 21–23; Ex. 6:7; 29:45–46; Lev. 11:45; 25:38; 26:11–12; Deut. 23:15 (ET 23:14); 26:17–18; 29:12–13; 2 Sam. 7:23–24; 1 Chron. 17:22; Ps. 95:7; Jer. 11:4; 24:7; 30:22; 31:1, 33; 32:38; Ezek. 14:11; 34:24, 30–31; 36:28; 37:23, 27; Zech. 2:15 (ET 2:11); 8:8; 13:9; 2 Cor. 6:16; Rev. 21:3; cf. Hos. 1:8–2:23, where God rejects Israel as his people and yet promises restoration and reconciliation.

[168] Beale, *Revelation*, 1060.

[169] Jonathan Moo, "The Sea That Is No More: Revelation 21:1 and the Function of Sea Imagery in the Apocalypse of John," *NovT* 51 (2009): 167.

it draws God's righteous condemnation. This comprehensive presentation of the state of humanity in sin provides firm biblical support for the classic Reformed understanding of "total depravity." At the same time, as we have seen repeatedly, John's depiction of humanity's predicament in sin in such dark terms only serves to highlight the glorious gospel of Christ, in which he who is "Light from Light," by his death for sins, promises ultimately to dispel all the darkness.

15

"Wretched Man That I Am!"

SIN IN THE PAULINE EPISTLES[1]

Jonathan Gibson

All our knowledge, sense, and sight
Lie in deepest darkness shrouded,
Till your Spirit breaks our night
With the beams of truth unclouded.
Christ alone to God can win us;
Christ must work all good within us.

Tobias Clausnitzer (1663)

Introduction

A survey of Christian Scripture and church history reveals that the apostle Paul is known by many epithets, either through self-identification or through attribution from later students of his corpus. Paul describes himself as being an Israelite, a descendant of Abraham (Rom. 9:3–4; 11:1; 2 Cor. 11:22–23), from the tribe of Benjamin, a Hebrew of Hebrews, a zealot, a Pharisee, a persecutor of the church (Phil. 3:5–6), a diaspora Jew from Tarsus in Cilicia (Acts 21:39), a disciple of Gamaliel (Acts 22:3), a Roman citizen (Acts 22:25), a chief of sinners (1 Tim. 1:15), a convert to Christ (Phil. 3:8), a servant of Christ (2 Cor. 11:23), a preacher, an apostle, and a teacher (2 Tim. 1:11). Posthumously, the apostle has been called, positively: a "thaumaturge" (miracle worker),[2] "Paul

---

[1] My thanks to Richard Gaffin for feedback on this chapter, and to Jeremy Menicucci for his editorial assistance.
[2] Jennifer Eyl, "Divination and Miracles," in *Handbook to the Historical Paul*, ed. Ryan S. Schellenberg and Heidi Wendt (London: T&T Clark, 2022), 215–32.

the scribe,"[3] an "apostle-missionary,"[4] a "missionary theologian,"[5] "the patron saint of thought in Christianity,"[6] "the greatest constructive mind ever at work on the data of Christianity,"[7] "the first Christian theologian, the first theological thinker of Christianity,"[8] a "pastor-theologian,"[9] an "apostle of God's glory,"[10] and "the father of Christian eschatology."[11] Neutrally or negatively, the apostle has also been called "an anomalous diaspora Jew,"[12] a "radical Jew,"[13] a "militant disciple of Shammai" the first-century sage,[14] "the pagans' apostle,"[15] "the representative of the Platonic One,"[16] an "early Jewish apocalyptic mystic,"[17] a power-hungry priest,[18] and "the first corrupter of the doctrines of Jesus."[19] Missing from this litany of epithets, however, is the title "theologian of sin" or "father of Christian hamartiology." The appellation is apt. Among all the apostles, Paul speaks most extensively and incisively about sin. This chapter will aim to elucidate his doctrine of hamartiology and the system of thought that lies behind it.

The presentation will take the following shape: I. The Lexicon of Sin; II. The Canvas of Sin; III. The Context of Sin; IV. The Curriculum of Sin; V. The Consequences of Sin; and VI. The Christ of Sinners. The presentation will proceed in conversation with Geerhardus Vos,[20] Herman Ridderbos,[21]

---

[3] Peter Stuhlmacher, *Biblical Theology of the New Testament*, trans. Daniel P. Bailey (Grand Rapids, MI: Eerdmans, 2018 [German ed., 1999]), 276.

[4] Richard B. Gaffin Jr., *In the Fullness of Time: An Introduction to the Biblical Theology of Acts and Paul* (Wheaton, IL: Crossway, 2022), 276.

[5] Robert L. Reymond, *Paul: Missionary Theologian* (Fearn, Ross-shire, UK: Mentor, 2000).

[6] Albert Schweitzer, *The Mysticism of Paul the Apostle*, trans. William Montgomery (New York: H. Holt, 1931), 377.

[7] Geerhardus Vos, *The Pauline Eschatology* (Grand Rapids, MI: Eerdmans, 1972), 149.

[8] Gaffin, *In the Fullness of Time*, 232.

[9] Gaffin, *In the Fullness of Time*, 231; cf. also Todd D. Still, "Afterword: Tertullian and Pauline Studies," in *Tertullian and Paul*, ed. David E. Wilhite and Todd D. Still (London: T&T Clark, 2013), 283.

[10] Thomas R. Schreiner, *Paul, Apostle of God's Glory: A Pauline Theology*, 2nd ed. (Downers Grove, IL: IVP Academic, 2020).

[11] Vos, *Pauline Eschatology*, vi.

[12] John M. G. Barclay, *Jews in the Mediterranean Diaspora* (Edinburgh: T&T Clark, 1996), 381–96; cf. also Matthew V. Novenson, "Ioudaios, Pharisee, Zealot," in *Paul, Then and Now* (Grand Rapids, MI: Eerdmans, 2022), 24–45.

[13] Daniel Boyarin, *A Radical Jew: Paul and the Politics of Identity* (Berkeley: University of California Press, 1994).

[14] N. T. Wright, *Paul and the Faithfulness of God*, 2 vols. (London: SPCK, 2013), 1:80–90.

[15] Paula Fredriksen, *Paul: The Pagans' Apostle* (New Haven, CT: Yale University Press, 2017).

[16] Cavan W. Concannon, *Profaning Paul* (Chicago: University of Chicago Press, 2021).

[17] Alan F. Segal, *Paul the Convert: The Apostolate and Apostasy of Saul the Pharisee* (New Haven, CT: Yale University Press, 1990), following Schweitzer, *Mysticism of Paul the Apostle*.

[18] Friedrich Nietzsche, *The Antichrist*, trans. H. L. Mencken (Middlesex, UK: Echo Library, 2006), 42: "What [the apostle Paul] himself didn't believe was swallowed readily enough by the idiots among whom he spread his teaching. What he wanted was power; in Paul the priest once more reached out for power—he had use only for such concepts, teachings and symbols as served the purpose of tyrannizing over the masses and organizing mobs."

[19] Thomas Jefferson, in *The Writings of Thomas Jefferson: Being His Autobiography, Correspondence, Reports, Messages, Addresses, and Other Writings, Official and Private. Published by the Order of the Joint Committee of Congress on the Library, from the Original Manuscripts, Deposited in the Department of State, with Explanatory Notes, Tables of Contents, and a Copious Index to Each Volume, as Well as a General Index to the Whole*, ed. H. A. Washington, vol. 7. (Washington, DC: Taylor & Maury, 1853).

[20] Vos, *Pauline Eschatology*.

[21] Herman N. Ridderbos, *Paul: An Outline of His Theology*, trans. John Richard de Witt (Grand Rapids, MI: Eerdmans, 1966); Ridderbos, "The Redemptive-Historical Character of Paul's Preaching," in Ridderbos, *When the Time*

and Richard Gaffin,[22] whose seminal works on the deep structure of Paul's theology remain, at least within the Reformed tradition, unparalleled.[23]

We begin with a survey of the vocabulary of sin in the Pauline corpus.

I. The Lexicon of Sin

Paul's interest in and concern with hamartiology is seen in the extensive vocabulary that he employs throughout his corpus with respect to the subject. Paul refers to sin more than any other NT apostle, and especially so in his epistle to the Romans.

SPECIFIC AND GENERAL TERMS

At times, the apostle uses specific terms for individual sins, such as: "envy" (φθόνου); "murder" (φόνου); "deceit" (δόλου); "maliciousness" (κακοηθείας) (Rom. 1:29), etc. However, more often, he focuses on sin in general, employing about twenty words or so, several of which are the negation of a positive word via the prefix α-:[24] "unrighteousness" (ἀδικία; 12x); "unrighteous" (ἄδικος; 2x); "disobedience/to disobey" (ἀπείθεια/ἀπειθέω; 9x); "disobedience" (παρακοή; 2x); "uncleanness" (ἀκάθαρτος; 9x); "lawless" (ἄνομος; 6x); "ungodliness" (ἀσέβεια; 4x); "ungodly" (ἀσεβής; 3x); "unbelief/unfaithfulness" (ἀπιστία; 5x); "to disbelieve/to be unfaithful" (ἀπιστέω; 2x); "ignorance" (ἄγνοια; 1x); "error" (πλάνη; 4x); "vanity/futility" (ματαιότης; 2x); "to become futile" (ματαιόω; 1x); "lie" (ψεῦσμα; 1x); "liar" (ψεύστης; 1x); "to stumble" (προσκόπτω; 2x); "to cause to stumble" (σκανδαλίζω; 2x). Paul also uses phrases to convey the general category of sin: "to do wrong" (τὸ κακὸν ποιέω) (Rom. 13:4); "works of darkness" (τὰ ἔργα τοῦ σκότους) (Rom. 13:12); "do not know God" (μὴ εἰδόσιν θεόν) (2 Thess. 1:8);[25] and "do not obey the gospel" (μὴ ὑπακούουσιν τῷ εὐαγγελίῳ) (2 Thess. 1:8)

Had Fully Come: Studies in New Testament Theology (Eugene, OR: Wipf & Stock, 2001 [1957]).

[22] Gaffin, *In the Fullness of Time*, builds on the work of Vos and Ridderbos, providing further explanation and clarification. Gaffin also acknowledges dependence on John Murray, "Structural Strands in New Testament Eschatology," *Kerux: A Journal of Biblical-Theological Preaching/NWTS* 6.3 (December 1991): 19–26.

[23] Matthew Novenson, in his stimulating book *Paul, Then and Now* (Grand Rapids, MI: Eerdmans, 2022), says that he "can conceive of a Christian reading of Paul that grasped the nettle of thoroughgoing eschatology, but empirically . . . can think of almost none that do so" (161) besides Schweitzer, *Mysticism*; Krister Stendahl, *Final Account: Paul's Letter to the Romans* (Minneapolis: Fortress, 1995); and Fredriksen, *Pagans' Apostle.* Surprisingly, Novenson seems almost unaware of Vos's and Ridderbos's seminal contribution to the understanding of the apostle's eschatology.

[24] The following survey is indebted to Douglas J. Moo, "Sin in Paul," in *Fallen: A Theology of Sin*, ed. Christopher W. Morgan and Robert A. Peterson, Theology in Community (Wheaton, IL: Crossway, 2013), 107–31 (109–111); cf. also Reymond, *Paul: Missionary Theologian*, 317–18, for a similar list, though not as extensive or accurate as Moo's.

[25] Defined by Paul in Rom. 1:18ff. as a suppressing of the truth about God. This example is not counted in Moo's list.

FREQUENT TERMS

In addition to these terms, Paul uses four key words to capture and convey the general category of sin.[26] First, there is "sin / sinfulness / to commit sin / sinful / sinner"[27] (ἁμαρτία / ἁμάρτημα / ἁμαρτάνω / ἁμαρτωλός) (90x in Paul; 60x in Romans). The words translate the OT word for sin (noun: חַטָּאת, "sin"; verb: חטא, "miss a mark, to wrong, sin").[28] Paul most often uses the singular form of the noun rather than the plural,[29] which demonstrates that, at least for him, sin is to be understood in its totality more than in its variety.

Second, there is the word "trespass" / "a violation of moral standards" (παράπτωμα) (15x in Paul; 9x in Romans).[30] Paul speaks of sinners being dead in their "trespasses and sins" (τοῖς παραπτώμασιν καὶ ταῖς ἁμαρτίαις) (Eph. 2:1).

Third, Paul uses three words in relation to "desire/passions" (ἐπιθυμία, πάθος, and πάθημα).[31] The more prominent word is ἐπιθυμία (19x). It can be neutral (Phil. 1:23) or negative (2 Tim. 2:22) depending on the context, though Paul mainly employs it in a negative sense. It translates the OT word for "desire" (חמד), the verb being used to speak of covetousness in the Ten Commandments (Ex. 20:17).[32] Less frequent are the cognate nouns for "passions" (πάθος and πάθημα). The former, πάθος, is used 3x in Paul, two of which are in relation to sinful passions (Rom. 1:26; Col. 3:5; 1 Thess. 4:5); the latter, πάθημα, is used 16x in Paul, most often as "suffering" (Rom. 8:18), but in two cases as "passions" (Rom. 7:5; Gal. 5:24). In one case, "passions" (πάθημα) is coordinated with "desires" (ἐπιθυμίαις) (Gal. 5:24).

Fourth, there is the category of "transgression" / "act of deviating from an established boundary or norm" (παράβασις) (5x in Paul).[33] It translates the OT word for "transgression/crime/offense" (פֶּשַׁע).[34] In each instance, Paul employs the word in the context of God's law (explicitly or implicitly stated).

CONCLUSIONS

A few preliminary conclusions may be drawn from this survey.[35] First, the frequency of hamartiological words and phrases in the Pauline corpus

---

[26] Moo, "Sin in Paul," 109–110.
[27] BDAG 49–51.
[28] HALOT 1:305–306.
[29] For example in Romans, of the 48 occurrences of ἁμαρτία, 45 are in the singular (Moo, "Sin in Paul," 111). Moo notes that 2 of the 3 plurals occur in OT quotes: Rom. 4:7 (Ps. 31:1 [ET 32:1]); Rom. 11:27 (Isa. 27:9); Rom. 7:5.
[30] BDAG 770.
[31] BDAG 372, 747–48.
[32] HALOT 1:325.
[33] BDAG 758.
[34] HALOT 4:981–82.
[35] These are similar to those expressed by Moo, "Sin in Paul," 111.

indicate how serious a problem sin is in the mind of the apostle. Indeed, as we will see, it is from the plight of sin that Paul sees the solution in a Savior. Second, the extent of such words and phrases reveals the multidimensional character of sin in Paul. While the apostle is primarily concerned with sin in general, he also presents the many faces of sin. Third, given the prominence of sin words in Romans, that letter is most fruitful for gaining an insight into Paul's hamartiology.

BEYOND WORD STUDIES

Word studies and surveys, however, can take us only so far. The aim of this chapter is to investigate the *system* at work in Paul's thought with respect to sin. Of course, the Christian Scriptures in general, and the Pauline corpus in the NT in particular, do not provide a systematic theology of any one doctrine. Paul's letters are occasional letters, written to various churches in Asia Minor; their primary purpose is pastoral. And yet, the apostle's pastoralia reveals his theology.[36] As I argued in the first volume in this series, *From Heaven He Came and Sought Her*, a discernible system undergirds Paul's pastoral concerns for the churches with respect to the atonement.[37] The same is true with respect to his hamartiology. Being a biblico-systematic doctrine, Paul's doctrine of sin emerges from holding together various hamartiological texts while at the same time synthesizing internally related doctrines, such as covenant, anthropology, Christology, soteriology, and eschatology. That is to say, Paul's hamartiology is reached on the other side of a comprehensive synthesis of biblical texts and systematic doctrines. More narrowly, this chapter aims to understand Paul's hamartiology through the lens of his two-age eschatology.

II. The Canvas of Sin

ESCHATOLOGY AS CENTER

The major presupposition of this chapter, following Geerhardus Vos, is that Paul's eschatology serves as the controlling center of his theology. For Vos, eschatology is not a single item within Paul's theology, but rather "draws within its circle as correlated and eschatologically-complexioned parts practically all of

---

[36] Gaffin, *In the Fullness of Time*, 232: "In all their occasional character and pervasively doxological tone, the letters of Paul reflect a unified structure of thought, a coherence of theological thinking." Gaffin speaks of the pastoral applications in Paul's letters being like the tip of an iceberg, his system of theology sitting just below the surface of the text.

[37] Jonathan Gibson, "The Glorious, Indivisible, Trinitarian Work of God in Christ," in *From Heaven He Came and Sought Her: Definite Atonement in Historical, Biblical, Theological, and Pastoral Perspective*, ed. David Gibson and Jonathan Gibson (Wheaton, IL: Crossway, 2013), 331–73.

the fundamental tenets of Pauline Christianity."[38] Indeed, "to unfold the Apostle's eschatology means to set forth his theology as a whole."[39] Vos expands:

> It were far more accurate to say that the eschatological strain is the most systematic in the entire fabric of the Pauline thought-world. For it now appears that the closely interwoven soteric tissue derives its pattern from the eschatological scheme, which bears all the marks of having had precedence in his mind.[40]

Vos speaks of eschatology being "pre-determinative" for soteriology.[41] The argument contained herein is that this is also true for hamartiology.

However, some qualification is necessary. To assert the precedence of eschatology in Paul's thought is not to suggest that eschatology per se is the center of his theology. We know from other key texts that Christ's death and resurrection are the center of Paul's gospel,[42] at least as far as they relate to redemptive-historical, eschatological concerns. As Gaffin puts it,

> At the center of Paul's theology, constituting that center as much as anything, are Christ's death and resurrection—or, more broadly, messianic suffering and glory, his humiliation and exaltation, in their saving and Scripture-fulfilling, eschatological significance. The center of Paul's theology is determined by the triangulation of his Christology, soteriology, and eschatology.[43]

This chapter aims to advance this perspective by proposing that hamartiology is an underacknowledged but integral element in Paul's theology alongside Christology, soteriology, and eschatology. This is seen from the basic fact that Christology and soteriology presuppose hamartiology; indeed, without hamartiology, Christology and soteriology lack meaning and purpose. As Paul states regarding the things of first importance, Christ died "for our sins" (ὑπὲρ τῶν ἁμαρτιῶν) (1 Cor. 15:3). Also, the relationship between eschatology and soteriology—the former being predeterminative for the latter—is reflected in the relationship between eschatology and hamartiology. Vos's image of soteric tissue deriving its form from the eschatological skeletal

---

[38] Vos, *Pauline Eschatology*, 11.
[39] Vos, *Pauline Eschatology*, 11.
[40] Vos, *Pauline Eschatology*, 60.
[41] Vos, *Pauline Eschatology*, 60.
[42] First Corinthians 1:18–31; 2:2; 15:1–2; Gal. 6:4; 2 Tim. 2:8.
[43] Gaffin, *In the Fullness of Time*, 238: "An interwoven reciprocity between Christology, soteriology, and eschatology marks Paul's theology" (226).

frame is instructive for our investigation into the substance and form of Paul's doctrine of sin.

All told, at the heart of Paul's theology is an interplay between hamartiology, Christology, soteriology, and eschatology. That is to say, Paul's message about Christ (Christology) and his work (soteriology) is set against the backdrop of sin (hamartiology) and in the context of redemptive history (eschatology). Put differently, and in pictorial fashion, we might say that Paul paints his hamartiology, Christology, and soteriology on the canvas of a two-age, historical eschatology.

With this picture in mind, we turn now to Paul's two-age, historical-eschatological framework as it is revealed in his epistolary corpus.

Two Ages

Paul situates his ministry and message in a two-age, historical-eschatological framework. The two-age construction is seen in Ephesians 1:21, where Paul states that Christ has been exalted "far above all rule and authority and power and dominion, and above every name that is named, not only in this age but also in the one to come [οὐ μόνον ἐν τῷ αἰῶνι τούτῳ ἀλλὰ καὶ ἐν τῷ μέλλοντι]." According to Paul, there are two distinct ages: the present age and the future age. Paul sees himself as a minister of the gospel at the end of this first present age and at the dawning of the future age inaugurated by Christ in his first coming.[44] As Gaffin comments, Paul's "is an eschatological ministry. He ministers an eschatological *content* in an eschatological *context*."[45]

(1) The Present Age (Aeon)

Paul speaks explicitly of the present age (αἰών) in several places in his letters.[46] The apostle states that Christ gave himself for our sins to deliver us "from the present evil age" (ἐκ του αἰῶνος τοῦ ἐνεστῶτος πονηροῦ) (Gal. 1:4), and "from the domain of darkness" (ἐκ τῆς ἐξουσίας τοῦ σκότους) (Col. 1:13). Given Christ's deliverance from this age, Paul exhorts us not to be conformed "to this age" (τῷ αἰῶνι τούτῳ) (Rom. 12:2), an age in which we once walked

---

[44] Romans 1:1–2; 16:25–26; 1 Cor. 10:11; Col. 1:26–27; 2 Tim. 1:9–10.

[45] Gaffin, *In the Fullness of Time*, 261 (emphasis original).

[46] Romans 8:18; 11:5; 12:2; 1 Cor. 1:20; 2:6, 8; 3:18–20; 2 Cor. 4:4; Gal. 1:4; Eph. 2:2; 1 Tim. 6:17; 2 Tim. 4:10; Titus 2:12. Paul expresses the immediacy of the present age in different ways: by the attributive participle "to be present" (ἐνίστημι), by the demonstrative pronoun "this" (οὗτος), and by the adverb "now, present" (νῦν).

when we followed "according to the age of this world" (κατὰ τὸν αἰῶνα τοῦ κόσμου τούτου) (Eph. 2:2, my translation). Demas is an example of one who conformed to the world, seen in his forsaking Paul out of love for "this present age" (τὸν νῦν αἰῶνα) (2 Tim. 4:10, my translation).

(2) The Present World (Cosmos)

The temporal realm of this "age" (αἰών) is integrally connected to the physical realm of the "world" (κόσμος). Paul uses the term "world" in a neutral way as a spatial domain,[47] but he also employs it negatively as an ethical realm.[48] God will judge "the world" (τὸν κόσμον) (Rom. 3:6). "The wisdom of this world [τοῦ κόσμου τούτου] is folly with God" (1 Cor. 3:19a). Since it is fallen and foolish, "the present form of this world [τὸ σχῆμα τοῦ κόσμου τούτου] is passing away" (1 Cor. 7:31b).

(3) The Present World-Age (Cosmos-Aeon)

The temporal age-aeon and the spatial world-cosmos are so integrally connected that in reality, for Paul, they amount virtually to the same thing, what we might term, in the form of a compound hendiadys, the "world-age." The distinct-but-related connection between "this age" (temporal) and "this world" (spatial) is stated explicitly by Paul in Ephesians 2:2: "in which you once walked, following the [age] of this world [κατὰ τὸν αἰῶνα τοῦ κόσμου τούτου], following the prince of the power of the air, the spirit that is now at work in the sons of disobedience." In other words, for Paul the world-age is a spatiotemporal realm, one that is under the power of the devil and characterized by disobedience.

Although the descriptions of this world-age are generally negative in Paul's thought, the realm was not so from the beginning. The world-age began with the creation of the heavens and earth "in the beginning" (Gen. 1:1) and was described by God as "very good" (cf. Gen. 1:31). It was a period in which man enjoyed the state of innocence as a living being made in the image of God (cf. 1 Cor. 15:45) as he worshiped his Creator (cf. Rom. 1:25). However, soon after, the age became corrupted by Adam, the "one man" (ἑνὸς ἀνθρώπου) through whom sin and death entered the world (Rom. 5:12). Since the fall of Adam, the present world-age has been fundamentally

---

[47] Romans 1:8; 5:12; 1 Cor. 4:9; 7:31; 14:10; Eph. 1:4; Col. 1:6; 1 Tim. 6:7.
[48] Romans 3:6; 1 Cor. 1:20, 21; 2:12; 3:19; 7:31; 11:32; 2 Cor. 7:10; Phil. 2:15.

marked by the consequences of sin, misery, and death. If the first period was a short prelapsarian time of innocence, the subsequent period is a long postlapsarian time of disobedience that continues to the present. Broadly speaking, then, the age of the present world is a predominantly postlapsarian, pre- or sub-eschatological age.[49] This, however, is not the only age that Paul speaks about.

(4) The Future World-Age (Cosmos-Aeon)

For Paul, there is "this age" (αἰῶνι τούτῳ) and there is "the one to come" (τῷ μέλλοντι) (Eph. 1:21; cf. 1 Tim. 6:19: τὸ μέλλον). His talk of the "kingdom of God" (θεοῦ βασιλείαν) is also a reference to the future age, only in different terms.[50] The kingdom of God is something to be inherited in the future (1 Cor. 6:9; 15:50; cf. 2 Thess. 1:5); it is a "heavenly kingdom" (τὴν βασιλείαν . . . τὴν ἐπουράνιον) that one day we will be safely rescued into (2 Tim. 4:18). This future realm will be of a spatiotemporal nature, since the present (groaning) creation will be redeemed into a new (glorious) creation akin to the redemption of the sons of God (Rom. 8:23). Beyond these references, Paul does not mention the future world-age in his epistles. However, it is *everywhere assumed* when he speaks of the present world, especially in passages on deliverance. To be delivered from "the present evil age" (Gal. 1:4) implies transfer into another age—the age to come. As Paul says elsewhere, but in different terms, Christ "has delivered us from the domain of darkness and transferred us to the kingdom of his beloved Son [τὴν βασιλείαν τοῦ υἱοῦ τῆς ἀγάπης αὐτοῦ], in whom we have redemption, the forgiveness of sins" (Col. 1:13–14). Broadly speaking, then, the future world-age is an eschatological age in which we enjoy the benefits of the kingdom of God won for us by Jesus Christ, benefits that we enjoy now in a real-but-provisional sense and that we will enjoy then in a real-and-consummated sense.

(5) The Pre- and Post-Temporal "Periods"

In addition to the two ages, there is a pre-temporal "period" and a post-temporal "period" in Paul's theological framework. In the former, God established his saving purposes before the beginning of the present world-age. God

---

[49] *Pre*-eschatological refers to the *temporal* nature of the age, while *sub*-eschatological refers to the *qualitative* nature of the age.
[50] First Corinthians 6:9, 10; 15:50; Gal. 5:21; Eph. 5:5; 1 Thess. 2:12; 2 Thess. 1:5; 2 Tim. 4:18.

chose us "before the foundation of the world" (πρὸ καταβολῆς κόσμου) to be holy (Eph. 1:4); and he saved and called us according to his grace and purpose given in Christ "before the ages began" (πρὸ χρόνων αἰωνίων) (2 Tim. 1:9). In short, before the spatiotemporal realm of this world-age, God decreed our salvation. In the latter, the post-temporal "period," God will welcome into his new creation those who have waited for Jesus and have loved his appearing (Phil. 3:21; 2 Tim. 4:8); for those who do not know God and have refused to obey the gospel of Jesus, God will execute judgment as he shuts unbelievers out of his presence and glory (2 Thess. 1:8–10).

SUMMARY

In simple terms, then, there are two ages in Paul's thought: the present world-age and the future world-age. The one is historical and pre- or sub-eschatological, being comprised of two periods: a (short) prelapsarian period and a (long) postlapsarian period. The other is historical and eschatological, and, as we will see below, is also comprised of two periods: a provisional period (between Christ's two comings) and a consummated period (after Christ's second coming). This is the two-age, historical-eschatological context in which Paul situates his ministry and message; it is also the context within which we must understand his hamartiology.

BIFURCATION OF THE AGES

Contrary to Jewish thought, the relationship between these two ages is not a linear one of simple succession. Rather, the future age intruded into the present age at the coming of Christ, bifurcating history into the present world-age and the future world-age (see diagram 15.1).[51] In Paul's theological system, this new eschatological world-age was inaugurated by Christ in his person (as the Son of God) and in his work (his life, death, burial, resurrection, ascension, and his giving of the Spirit). For Paul, Christ's advent introduced a hitherto unseen vertical dimension into the horizontal dimension, what is called "inaugurated, provisional eschatology." However, the two ages or dimensions are not unrelated. The inaugurated eschaton introduced by Christ was not an unexpected intrusion into world history. As Paul explains in numerous places, the first, present

---

[51] This diagram, and the ones that follow, are expanded and developed from Geerhardus Vos's diagram of his basic two-age construction in *Pauline Eschatology*, 38.

DIAGRAM 15.1: Bifurcation of the Ages

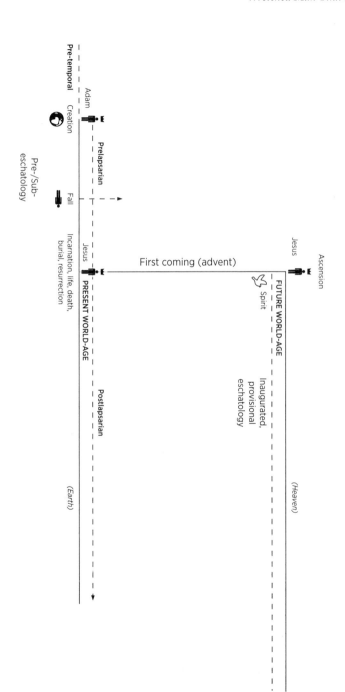

age, in which redemptive history plays out, contained a mystery waiting to be revealed.[52] The mystery was kept secret for "long ages" (χρόνοις αἰωνίοις) but has "now" (νῦν) been disclosed in the gospel of Jesus (Rom. 16:25–26). The timing of this full disclosure was at "the end of the ages" (τὰ τέλη τῶν αἰώνων) (1 Cor. 10:11), when "the fullness of the time" (τοῦ πληρώματος τῶν καιρῶν) had come (Gal. 4:4; Eph. 1:9–10). As Gaffin comments, "With the coming of Christ and his work in history, the time of the world has been 'filled up.' History, comprehensively considered, has reached its consummation, its telos."[53] And with the *telos* of the present age came the *initium* of the future age. Gaffin again: "'The fullness of time' is yet another way of signaling the end of this age and the dawning of the age to come."[54]

The beginning of this new future age erupted into redemptive history like a new creation, which is how Paul describes it in 2 Corinthians 5:17:

> Therefore, if anyone is in Christ, he is a new creation. The old has passed away; behold, the new has come.

> ὥστε εἴ τις ἐν Χριστῷ, καινὴ κτίσις· τὰ ἀρχαῖα παρῆλθεν, ἰδοὺ γέγονεν καινά.

Contrary to most lay (and some pastoral) readings, Paul is not primarily envisioning the new-creation change that occurs *inside* the believer. True as that is, Paul's concern is more eschatological than existential. Since there is no verb in the apodosis statement, a better translation is, "Therefore, if any-one is in Christ—new creation." In other words, the reference is, as Gaffin notes, "to the new creation, comprehensively considered, to which the one in Christ belongs, in which the one in Christ now exists."[55] That is to say, "it is a contrast between nothing less than two worlds—the old world order and the new world order."[56] Gaffin goes on to explain,

> The "old things" that have passed away are the things of the old fallen creation, the things of the unredeemed world in sin and misery—in other words, the things of this aeon, this present evil age. The "new things," in

---

[52] Romans 16:25–26; 1 Cor. 2:7; Eph. 1:9–10; 3:4–5; Col. 1:26; 2 Tim. 1:9–10; Titus 1:2, 3.
[53] Gaffin, *In the Fullness of Time*, 268. Other phraseology in Paul implicitly speaks to the "fullness of time" motif: for example, "last apostles" (τοὺς ἀποστόλους ἐσχάτους) (1 Cor. 4:9), "last enemy" (ἔσχατος ἐχθρός) (1 Cor. 15:26), "the Last Adam" (ὁ ἔσχατος Ἀδάμ) (1 Cor. 15:45); "last trumpet" (ἐσχάτῃ σάλπιγγι) (1 Cor. 15:52).
[54] Gaffin, *In the Fullness of Time*, 268.
[55] Gaffin, *In the Fullness of Time*, 256.
[56] Gaffin, *In the Fullness of Time*, 259.

contrast, are the things of the new creation, of the final eschatological order that has been inaugurated by Christ—in other words, the things of the aeon to come.[57]

For Paul, then, Christ's coming brought into existence a whole new world, one that stands in complete contrast to the first world and its present age (cf. Gal. 6:15). To be clear, Christ inaugurated this new world-age not simply in his coming as God's incarnate Son (Rom. 1:1–3; Gal. 4:4), but also in the work of his life (1 Tim. 3:16), death (Rom. 5:8; 8:32; 1 Cor. 1:17–18; 2:2; Gal. 3:1), burial (1 Cor. 15:4), resurrection (Rom. 1:4; 4:25; 8:34; 10:8–9; 1 Cor. 15:20, 23, 45), ascension (Rom. 8:34; Phil. 2:9), and his giving of the Spirit (Rom. 5:5; 8:9, 23; 1 Cor. 15:45; 2 Cor. 3:17; Eph. 1:13–14). In particular, the ascension of Christ shifts the eschatological "center of gravity" from earth to heaven, creating in effect "a cosmic dualism or bifurcation."[58] Paul reflects this dualism or bifurcation when he speaks of "the heavenly realms" (τοῖς ἐπουρανίοις), from which believers are abundantly blessed (Eph. 1:3, my translation) and where they are now seated with Christ (Eph. 2:6). Vos captures it as follows:

> Herein lies the inner significance of the repatriation of Christ into heaven, carrying thither with Himself all the historical time-matured fruit of his earthly stage of work, and now from there guiding with impartial solicitude the two lines of terrestrial and celestial development of his Church.[59]

For the Christian this means, he "has only his members upon the earth, which are to be mortified; himself, and as a whole, he belongs to the high mountain-land above."[60]

CONCURRENCE OF THE AGES

As just noted, the new-creation event wrought by Christ bifurcates world history into two ages: the present world-age and the future world-age. The horizontal dimension of the present age is linear, possessing a *terminus ad quo* (point from which) and a *terminus ad quem* (point to which). The *terminus ad quo* is the beginning of creation, which is then followed by a

---

[57] Gaffin, *In the Fullness of Time*, 260.
[58] Gaffin, *In the Fullness of Time*, 286.
[59] Vos, *Pauline Eschatology*, 41.
[60] Vos, *Pauline Eschatology*, 41.

(short) prelapsarian period. After the fall of Adam, the prelapsarian period is succeeded by a (long) postlapsarian period. The *terminus ad quem* of this latter period lies in the future but the terminus "begins" with the coming of Christ when he is revealed at "the fullness of the time" (Gal. 4:4; Eph. 1:9–10, my translation). With that climactic moment in redemptive history, the end of the present age is announced. Although the present age does not terminate at that point, it does become one that "is passing away" (παράγει) (1 Cor. 7:31), along with its rulers (1 Cor. 2:6). Indeed, for Paul, the coming of Christ is so definitive in its power that he can say that the end of this age has already "arrived" (κατήντηκεν) (1 Cor. 10:11, my translation), even though its end actually remains in the future. That end will occur at the second coming of Christ, when he will return to judge the living and the dead at his appearing and the coming of his kingdom (2 Tim. 4:1) and will deliver the kingdom to his Father, after destroying every rule and authority and power (1 Cor. 15:24). In this respect, for Paul, "there is one day of the Lord, one coming of the Messiah, one parousia of Christ, that occurs in two basic phases or stages."[61] That is, the advent of Christ and the parousia of Christ are two distinct moments of the one-event duplex; together they bring about the end of the present age in a now-not-yet tension. Until then, the two ages—the present evil age and the future eschatological age—run concurrently, the one in parallel to the other (see diagram 15.1). Paul refers to the overlap period of the two ages, as "this present age."[62] Since the present age has a distinct *terminus ad quem* (see diagram 15.2) and the future age does not, the latter may be said to be successive to the former.

SUCCESSION OF THE AGES

Paul makes the succession of the ages clear in his textus classicus for his two-age, historical-eschatological construction: Ephesians 1:21. There he speaks of "this age" (αἰῶνι τούτῳ) and "the one to come" (τῷ μέλλοντι), indicating that the latter succeeds the former. It is also implied when he writes of the kingdom of God coming in its consummate, final form after "the end" (τὸ τέλος) (1 Cor. 15:24–28). Thus, while the age to come has a distinct

---

[61] Gaffin, *In the Fullness of Time*, 279; "For Paul, the arrival of the Messiah has a dual character. It takes place not as a one-time coming but in two successive stages or epochs. The coming of the eschatological day of the Lord, the end of the age, the parousia of the Messiah, occurs in two installments" (282).

[62] First Timothy 6:17; 2 Tim. 4:10; Titus 2:12. Ridderbos, *Paul*, 87, calls it "the interim."

terminus ad quo in the first coming of Christ, it lacks any *terminus ad quem* due to its eternal nature. This is not to suggest, however, that the advent of Christ is its only deictic marker. The horizontal timeline is also demarcated by the parousia of Christ.[63] This event—viewed in Paul as the catalyst for a final resurrection (1 Cor. 15:23) and judgment of the living and the dead (2 Tim. 4:1)—marks the shift from the inaugurated, provisional, eschatological period to the consummated, final eschatological period in the age to come.[64] For the believer it will entail the transformation of "our lowly body to be like [Christ's] glorious body" (Phil. 3:21), when we will appear "with him in glory" (Col. 3:4). At this point in time, the present age will officially cease and the future age of "consummated, final eschatology" will succeed it (see diagram 15.2).

However, the succession of the ages should not be misunderstood to mean that Christ's second coming advances the *quality* of the inaugurated, eschatological age in its consummated, final period. The eschaton arrives in its real qualitative form at Christ's first coming—but provisionally so. Its arrival creates an antithesis between the two ages, an antithesis reflected in the warring of flesh and Spirit in the believer, as captured by Paul in Galatians 5:17:

> For the desires of the flesh are against the Spirit [κατὰ τοῦ πνεύματος], and the desires of the Spirit are against the flesh [κατὰ τῆς σαρκός], for these are opposed to each other [ἀντίκειται], to keep you from doing the things you want to do [ἵνα μὴ ἃ ἐὰν θέλητε ταῦτα ποιῆτε].

This conflict between flesh and Spirit continues in the present age but will eventually end at Christ's second coming. However, the end of the conflict, which is nothing less than the removal of the antithesis altogether, does not involve a new qualitative addition to the future age—only a quantitative consummation. Thus, the difference between the two periods of the eschatological age is that of inauguration and consummation, provision and finality. Keeping in mind the one-event-in-two-phases duplex of Christ's coming helps to avoid introducing a qualitative difference between inaugurated eschatology and consummated eschatology. However, until Christ's second coming, the antithesis between the ages does remain.

---

[63] First Corinthians 15:22–23; 1 Thess. 2:19; 3:13; 4:15; 5:23; 2 Thess. 2:1, 8; 2 Tim. 4:1.

[64] Between the two comings of Christ, Paul understands Christ to be seated at his Father's right hand, ruling in his session (1 Cor. 15:25–27; Eph. 1:20–23) and interceding for his people (Rom. 8:34).

DIAGRAM 15.2: Concurrence / Succession of the Ages

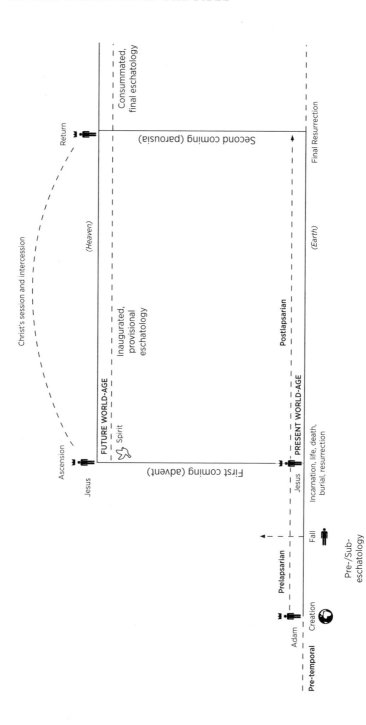

ANTITHESIS OF THE AGES

Upon Christ's inauguration of the future age in his first coming, the postlapsarian period of the first age and the provisional, eschatological period of the second age overlap and coexist in the sharpest antithesis. Considered as a whole, the antithesis between the ages has horizontal and vertical dimensions. Horizontally, the two ages are antithetical in their *temporal span*. The present age is finite and temporary (1 Cor. 2:6; 7:31); the future age is infinite and permanent (Eph. 1:21; 1 Tim. 6:19; 2 Cor. 5:17). As Vos comments, "The antithesis is between a world (age) that *is* and a world (age) that *is to come*."[65] Vertically, the ages are antithetical in their *ethical nature*. The present age is characterized by sin, condemnation, and death, under the sway of the world, the flesh, and the devil (Rom. 5:12–21; Eph. 2:1–3); the future age is characterized by righteousness, justification, and life, under the rule and reign of Christ (Rom. 5:15–21; 1 Cor. 15:24–28). For Vos, "the one great transcendental antithesis between this world and the world-to-come" is manifested in certain historic reflections, such as "the First Adam and the Last Adam, sin and righteousness, the flesh and the Spirit, law and faith."[66] Of these, the two Adams in particular present the antithesis sharply. In 1 Corinthians 15:45–47, Paul contrasts Adam as "the protos Man" (ὁ πρῶτος ἄνθρωπος) with Christ as "the eschatos Man" (ὁ ἔσχατος Ἀδάμ) and "the deuteros Man" (ὁ δεύτερος ἄνθρωπος). Since Paul's focus is Adam in his prelapsarian state as a living being, the contrast with Christ as the second and last Adam is primarily eschatological.[67] In Romans 5:12–21, however, the contrast between Adam and Christ is primarily ethical. Ridderbos captures the sharpness of the antithesis intended:

> Adam and Christ here stand over against each other as the two great figures at the entrance of two worlds, two aeons, two "creations," the old and the new; and in their actions and fate lies the decision for all who belong to them, because these are comprehended in them and thus are reckoned either to death or to life.[68]

In other words, the two giants of history—Adam and Christ—inaugurate two diametrically opposed worlds. As the protological giant of history, Adam

---

[65] Vos, *Pauline Eschatology*, 36.
[66] Vos, *Pauline Eschatology*, 60–61.
[67] Vos, *Pauline Eschatology*, 11, notes that "'Eschatos' here bears technical meaning; it designates not so much the Adam that belongs to the order of the 'eschata,' but pointedly the One who is the last in contrast to one other who is the first."
[68] Ridderbos, *Paul*, 61.

brings about the age of the world, the flesh, and the devil, in which sin, condemnation, and death reign; as the eschatological giant of history, Christ brings about the age of grace and the Spirit, in which righteousness, justification, and life reign. For the believer, it is the "once was" in Adam and the "now is" in Christ that creates the tension—the antithesis—of living between the ages.

TENSION OF THE AGES

The antithesis of the ages creates an existential tension for the believer in two dimensions. Horizontally, there is the tension of living between the now and the not yet of Christ's two comings, between the first installment of his advent and the second installment of his parousia. This is seen in Paul's letters where he speaks of his life being bound up in Christ *now* (Gal. 2:20–21; Phil. 1:21; Col. 3:3) and yet *still waiting* for Christ's appearing (Phil. 3:20–21; Col. 3:4; 2 Tim. 4:8). Vertically, there is the tension of living with the pull of the present evil age—externally from the world and the devil, internally from the flesh—and the pull of the future eschatological age—internally from the Spirit. In Gaffin's words, "Believers continue experiencing the tugs of conflicting attraction between the old, pre-eschatological order of sin and death and the new and final order of righteousness and life in Christ."[69] Life for the believer in these two ages is thus the "taseological" life—a life of tension.[70]

LIFE IN THE AGES

It is with respect to these two ages that Paul situates the life experience of the unbeliever and the believer: the unbeliever belongs to the first age; the believer, to the second age. Since believers were once unbelievers, their life experience is spoken of in terms of what they "once were" in Adam and outside of Christ and what they "now are" outside of Adam and in Christ. That is, the apostle tethers the life context of a person to one of two ages, inaugurated by one of two Adams.

On the one hand, for Paul, this world-age "constitute[s] the description of the totality of unredeemed life dominated by sin outside of Christ."[71] Two

---

[69] Gaffin, *In the Fullness of Time*, 283.
[70] I am playing off Oscar Cullman's descriptor for the overlap of the ages as "taseology," from the Greek τάσις, meaning "tension" (Cullman, *Salvation in History* [New York: Harper & Row, 1967], 172; cited in Gaffin, *In the Fullness of Time*, 283).
[71] Ridderbos, *Paul*, 91.

Pauline texts in particular demonstrate this clearly: in Galatians, Paul states that Christ gave himself to deliver us "from the present evil age" (ἐκ τοῦ αἰῶνος τοῦ ἐνεστῶτος πονηροῦ) (Gal. 1:4); and in Ephesians, he writes that we once walked "according to the age of this world" (κατὰ τὸν αἰῶνα τοῦ κόσμου τούτου) (Eph. 2:2, my translation). The outcome of such a world-age attachment leads only to condemnation (1 Cor. 11:32). In short, Paul understands human nature outside of Christ primarily in relation to this world-age.

On the other hand, for Paul, the world-age to come constitutes the description of the redeemed life dominated by the Spirit in Christ. Through faith-union with Christ, the "life-giving Spirit" as the apostle calls him (1 Cor. 15:45), we are regenerated by the washing of the Spirit (Titus 3:5) and filled by the Spirit (Eph. 5:18); we walk in accordance with the Spirit (Gal. 5:16); the Spirit dwells in us, testifying that we are indeed the children of God (Rom. 8:16). The Spirit also serves as a down payment, the guarantee, of our future inheritance in heaven (Eph. 1:14).

In sum, just as the present world-age is determinative for a true understanding of human nature in Adam by the flesh, so the future world-age is determinative for a true understanding of human nature in Christ by his Spirit. On this scheme, sin is not merely an individual condition or act, but a "supra-individual mode of existence"[72] that is intimately tied to the first age of the world inaugurated by Adam. As Ridderbos states, "in approaching the Pauline doctrine of sin, we must not orient ourselves in the first place to the individual and personal, but to the redemptive-historical and collective points of view."[73]

SUMMARY OF THE AGES

Paul's system of theology is informed and shaped by two ages: the present age and the future age. The one is historical and pre- or sub-eschatological, being comprised of two periods: a (short) prelapsarian period and a (long) postlapsarian period. The other is historical and eschatological and is also comprised of two periods: an inaugurated period (between Christ's two comings) and a consummated period (after Christ's second coming). The two ages are *comprehensive* (from creation to consummation), *concurrent* (they overlap between the first and second coming of Christ), *consecutive* (the one age

---

[72] Ridderbos, *Paul*, 93.
[73] Ridderbos, *Paul*, 91.

succeeds the other), *antithetical* (diametrically opposed in span and nature), and thus *taseological* (in tension, temporally and existentially).[74]

Tri-Directionalism of the Ages

Drawing together these threads of thought, Murray and Gaffin propose a tri-directional movement within Paul's two-age, historical-eschatological framework.[75] There is the *backward* movement, in which Paul looks back and sees the fulfillment of the ages in Christ's first appearing (Gal. 4:4; Eph. 1:9–10); the *forward* movement, in which the apostle looks toward the future appearing of Christ from heaven (Phil. 3:20–21; Col. 3:3–4); and the *upward* movement, in which he views the believer's orientation now being of a purely heavenly (that is, eschatological) focus (Eph. 2:6; Col. 3:1–2). It is within this tri-directional, two-age, historical-eschatological complex that Paul situates his ministry and message, a complex that is also predeterminative for his hamartiology.

Mapping Paul's Hamartiology

Paul's two-age, historical-eschatological framework aids our understanding of how he constructs his hamartiology within his theology. As noted above, Paul's eschatology is predeterminative for his Christology and soteriology.[76] The argument contained herein is that this is also true for his hamartiology. Paul's hamartiology maps onto the canvas of his two-age eschatology. The six states of man—categorized as innocence, sin, grace, intermediate, glory, and destruction—map neatly onto the temporal periods in Paul's two-age eschatological scheme (see diagram 15.3).

With respect to the present age of the world, there is the (short) prelapsarian period, when man enjoyed the *state of innocence* before the fall (1 Cor. 15:45); and the (long) postlapsarian period, when man endured the *state of sin* after the fall (Rom. 5:12), a period and state that continues to the present. With respect to the future age of the world, there are also two periods: the provisional, eschatological period, when man experiences the *state of grace* in the

---

[74] This summary is informed by Gaffin's own summary: "the two aeons are *comprehensive* (together they cover the entire flow of time, the whole of history, from its beginning at creation up to and including its consummation), *consecutive* (no other period intervenes between them), and *antithetical* (due to the entrance of sin with its effects into this age)" (Gaffin, *In the Fullness of Time*, 247, emphasis original).
[75] Gaffin, *In the Fullness of Time*, 291–93; cf. Murray, "Structural Strands in New Testament Eschatology," who labels the three movements respectively "anticipated," "prospective," and "projective."
[76] Vos, *Pauline Eschatology*, 60, comments: "the eschatological appears as pre-determinative [for] both the substance and form of the soteriological."

DIAGRAM 15.3: Mapping States of Man onto Ages

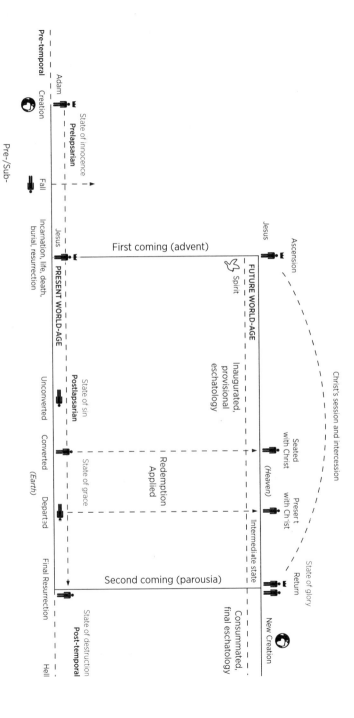

Spirit between the now and not yet of Christ's kingdom (Rom. 5:1–2, 5); and the final eschatological period, when man enjoys the *state of glory* in Christ's consummated kingdom (Rom. 8:29; 1 Cor. 15:28). During the provisional, eschatological period, man at his death enters the *intermediate state* between grace and glory, in which he experiences the state of sinless perfection as a righteous spirit (cf. Heb. 12:23). He is absent from the body but present with the Lord (2 Cor. 5:8), which is far better (Phil. 1:23), while still awaiting his glorified, resurrection body (1 Cor. 15:50–55). Those outside of Christ, who do not know God and who have refused to obey the gospel of Jesus, will experience the *state of destruction* in the post-temporal period of hell as they are shut out from the presence of God and his glory (2 Thess. 1:8–10).

This overview confirms what was proposed near the beginning of this chapter, that Paul's eschatology is predeterminative not only for his soteriology but also for his hamartiology. Before Paul paints his soteriology onto the canvas of his two-age eschatology, he first does so with respect to his hamartiology.[77] The eschatological canvas, however, is not the only backdrop against which we are to understand sin in Paul's thought.

III. The Context of Sin

Before and behind Paul's doctrine of sin is the presupposition of God as Creator. Without stating it explicitly, in the apostle's thought sin receives its ontology and definition only in the context of a Creator God who has revealed himself to his creatures externally through creation (nature around) and internally through conscience (law within). This truth about God is noticeable in Paul's presentation of the gospel to the Athenian philosophers and to the church in Rome.

In his Areopagus speech on Mars Hill, Paul addresses the problem of sin by speaking of the past times of ignorance (χρόνους τῆς ἀγνοίας) that God overlooked (Acts 17:30), the present command of repentance (μετανοεῖν) (17:30), and the future day of judgment for the world in righteousness (ἡμέραν ἐν ᾗ μέλλει κρίνειν τὴν οἰκουμένην ἐν δικαιοσύνῃ) (17:31). Underlying all these statements is the Creator-creature distinction and relation that he establishes earlier in his speech. Paul speaks of God as a Creator distinct from his creation and creatures (17:24–25), yet one who remains in relationship

---

[77] See diagram 15.4 in the last section of this chapter, "VI. The Christ of Sinners," for how Paul's eschatology is predeterminative for his soteriology.

with his creation, including mankind. As Creator, God made from one man all the nations on earth (17:26), determining their times and places of existence so that they might seek him (17:27). He is not far from any person; indeed, in him people live and move and have their being (17:28). Thus, in Paul's thought, the Creator-creature distinction and relation provide the context for man's sin and his responsibility and accountability before God.

This is also seen in Romans 1, where Paul explains that the main reason for God's wrath being poured out from heaven is the suppression of "the truth" (τὴν ἀλήθειαν) regarding God's divine nature and eternal power as Creator (vv. 18, 20). In sin, mankind suppresses this truth, even though it is plain and clearly perceived from the created order (v. 19). On this basis, Paul states that man is culpable and "without excuse" (ἀναπολογήτους). The apostle goes on to explain that, in his sin, man exchanges the worship of the Creator for worship of the creature (v. 25). In this regard, Paul's discussion on sin is predicated on the Creator-creature distinction and relation.

In sum, for Paul, the assumed context of any discussion of sin is God as Creator and man as creature. The Creator-creature distinction frames the whole discussion. As Ridderbos states, "Sin must be understood out of the relationship in which God has placed man to himself as his creature and in which he has given him and held out to him the prospect of life."[78]

Having established the canvas and context of sin, we turn now to the curriculum of sin in Paul, noting various elements.

IV. The Curriculum of Sin

ENTRANCE OF SIN

In Romans, Paul eliminates any possibility that sin is a given in the history of mankind. For him, sin has a clear entry point into the world that God created. There is a "historical before-and-after" with respect to creation and fall, rather than a quasi-eternal coexistence.[79] According to the apostle, the entrance of sin occurred through one man, the prototypical man, Adam. Paul affirms this truth within the larger context of assuring believers of God's future glory despite the trials and tribulations they face (Rom. 5:6–21). The key verse is Romans 5:12, which forms the protasis in Paul's extended comparison

[78] Ridderbos, *Paul*, 105.
[79] Richard B. Gaffin Jr., *No Adam, No Gospel: Adam and the History of Redemption* (Phillipsburg, NJ: P&R; Glenside, PA: Westminster Seminary Press, 2015), 16.

between the efficacy of the work of Adam on the one hand, and the work of Christ on the other hand.

The Point of Entry

For our purposes here, it is worth taking time to exegete Romans 5:12, given how crucial it is to the discussion of original sin. The verse reads,

> Therefore, just as sin entered into the world through one man, and death [entered] through sin, and so likewise death spread to all people because all sinned— (my translation)

> Διὰ τοῦτο ὥσπερ δι᾽ ἑνὸς ἀνθρώπου ἡ ἁμαρτία εἰς τὸν κόσμον εἰσῆλθεν καὶ διὰ τῆς ἁμαρτίας ὁ θάνατος, καὶ οὕτως εἰς πάντας ἀνθρώπους ὁ θάνατος διῆλθεν, ἐφ᾽ ᾧ πάντες ἥμαρτον.

The fronted prepositional phrase "through one man" (δι᾽ ἑνὸς ἀνθρώπου) provides focus on the *agent* through which sin entered the world—the one man. Ridderbos comments, "One man has given sin access into the world; he has, as it were, opened the gate of the world to sin."[80] The aorist tense of the verb "entered" (εἰσῆλθεν) gives a punctiliar character to sin's entrance, situating it at a *point* in the historical past. The object in the prepositional phrase (εἰς τὸν κόσμον) indicates *where* sin entered: the space of the created cosmos. The conjunctive "and" (καὶ) brings into play a second subject of the elided verb "entered" (εἰσῆλθεν): death. This subject is accompanied by a prepositional phrase (διὰ τῆς ἁμαρτίας) that describes the *means* of death's entrance into the world: "and death [entered] through sin."[81] Altogether, the language produces a summative allusion to the original transgression in the garden of Eden (Gen. 2:17; 3:19). For Paul, two realities (sin and death) came into the world by one man (Adam) at a single point in the historical past, the one the result of the other in "immediate sequence."[82]

A Continuative Comparison

The second half of Romans 5:12 introduces a "continuative comparison."[83] The conjunctive phrase "and so" (καὶ οὕτως) indicates that death spread to all

---

[80] Ridderbos, *Paul*, 96.
[81] By eliding the verb εἰσῆλθεν in the second main clause, Paul indicates that the entrance of sin and death are immediately sequential to each other, the latter following the former.
[82] Murray, *Romans*, 188.
[83] Murray, *Romans*, 184.

men (εἰς πάντας ἀνθρώπους ὁ θάνατος) in a way similar to one man bringing sin and death into the world. The verse concludes with a causal statement that grounds the universal spread of death to all people in the sin of all people: "because all sinned" (ἐφ' ᾧ πάντες ἥμαρτον). The prepositional phrase ἐφ' ᾧ has been interpreted as a reference back to Adam, the Vulgate opting for "in whom all sinned" (*in quo omnes peccaverunt*).[84] However, it is generally agreed among scholars that this is a poor rendering; the preposition plus relative pronoun can carry the force of the conjunction "because" (cf. 2 Cor. 5:14; Phil. 3:12): hence the popular translation, "because all sinned."[85]

On this reading, prima facie, it seems that Paul grounds the spread of death to all people *in the actual voluntary sin of all people.* The comparison in the verse thus reads as follows: just as sin and death entered the world through the sin of the one man, so likewise death spread to all people because all people sinned. However, as John Murray points out, this interpretation fails on factual, exegetical, and theological grounds.[86] Factually, the statement is not true: infants die without committing voluntary sin. Exegetically, two contextual factors point against it. (1) In verses 13 and 14 the apostle affirms the opposite, explicitly: death reigned over those who did *not* sin like Adam sinned. (2) In verses 15–19, Paul states five times (once in each verse) that death reigned over all due to the sin of the *one* man. Thus, to interpret Romans 5:12 as suggested above introduces a contradiction into a tightly argued passage in Paul's thought that is highly dependent on coherence for the argument to work. Finally, theologically, the interpretation contradicts the analogy at work across the whole passage. Paul's positive point is that all who believe are justified and attain life by the act of the one man, Jesus Christ. This is how justification and life "spread," so to speak, through the "all" united to Christ by faith. So likewise, the parallel to how death spread to all makes little sense if it is not grounded in Adam's sin but in their own individual, voluntary sins.

Solidarity in Sin

A better approach is to interpret Romans 5:12 in its wider context, along the lines of a solidarity between the one and the all/many, with respect to both

---

[84] This interpretation was followed by Augustine, *Against Two Epistles of the Pelagians* IV.4.7 (PL 44, col. 614), in his debates with Pelagius.

[85] Murray J. Harris notes that the relative pronoun is an abbreviated form of τούτῳ ὅτι ("upon this, that") (Harris, "Prepositions," in *New International Dictionary of New Testament Theology*, ed. Colin Brown, 4 vols. [Grand Rapids, MI: Zondervan, 1978], 3:1194–95).

[86] Murray, *Romans*, 185. The points that follow are all taken from Murray's exposition.

458 SIN AND DEPRAVITY IN THE BIBLE

Adam and Christ. Murray helpfully summarizes the context for us: "The central strand is the analogy that exists between the passing of condemnation and death to all by the sin of the one and the passing of justification and life to the justified by the righteousness of Christ."[87] This being so, the clause "all sinned" (πάντες ἥμαρτον) in verse 12 must match in meaning "the one man's trespass" (τοῦ ἑνὸς παραπτώματι) in verses 15–19; the same act of disobedience is in view: "the sin of the one may at the same time and with equal relevance be regarded as the sin of all."[88] Because of the solidarity at work between Adam and his descendants—a fundamental, federal solidarity, not a mere realistic, generational solidarity—the singularity and universality of sin must be held together. The real comparison at play in verse 12 is: just as sin and death entered the world through the sin of the one man, so likewise death spread to all people because (by the one man) all people sinned. Thus, while the Latin translation on Romans 5:12 ("in whom all sinned") might not be an accurate rendering of the Greek, the translation at least recognizes the "solidarity in sin"[89] that lies beneath the surface of the text.

In sum, undergirding Paul's whole argument in Romans 5:12–21 is a solidarity in action between the one man (Adam) and the all (sinners). If Paul can say, "As in Adam all die" (1 Cor. 15:22); equally so he can say, "As in Adam all sinned."[90] But Paul's point is that the conferral of sin from Adam to his posterity is not by imitation or generation but by imputation. Although this may be "an offense to reason," as Bernard Ramm states in the title of his book on original sin,[91] it is nevertheless the most logical implication of what the apostle argues in Romans 5. Adam's "all-embracing decision"[92] in the distant past was a sin-imputing, guilt-conveying, death-ensuing, epoch-inaugurating one that affected all those descended from him as a result of his federal representation of them. As such, it marked the historic entrance of sin into the world—a clear *terminus ad quo*, an entry point, from which sin came to do its deadly work.

This being so, what exactly *is* sin for Paul?

---

[87] Murray, *Romans*, 187.
[88] Murray, *Romans*, 187.
[89] Murray, *Romans*, 188.
[90] Murray, *Romans*, 188.
[91] Bernard L. Ramm, *Offense to Reason: A Theology of Sin* (San Francisco: Harper & Row, 1985), cited in Moo, "Sin in Paul," 125 n. 25.
[92] Ridderbos, *Paul*, 99.

ESSENCE OF SIN

As noted earlier, Paul situates sin in the context of the Creator-creature distinction in Acts 17 and in Romans 1. In Romans 2–3, he brings God's character and law into the orbit of discussion. As Ridderbos comments, "The consciousness of manhood is implied in the consciousness of God and of his law. Man is man in the relationship in which God has placed him to himself and to his law."[93]

God's Character

Although Paul rarely speaks of God's character in explicit terms, we may discern aspects of it from one or two of his comments. For example, God's holy character may be deduced from his "righteous judgment" (δικαιοκρισίας τοῦ θεοῦ) that will be revealed on his "day of wrath" (ἐν ἡμέρᾳ ὀργῆς) against the unrepentant (Rom. 2:5). For Paul, the sinner and his sin is understood in contrast to a holy God. Indeed, to sin is to fall short of "the glory of God" (τῆς δόξης τοῦ θεοῦ) (Rom. 3:23). This begins to move us toward a Pauline definition of sin.

God's Law

As the standard by which sinners are judged, Paul understands the law as holding everyone "accountable to God" (ὑπόδικος γένηται ... τῷ θεῷ) (Rom. 3:19); it is the means of producing the "knowledge of sin" (διὰ ... νόμου ἐπίγνωσις ἁμαρτίας) (v. 20). He later describes the law as "holy and righteous and good" (ἁγία καὶ δικαία καὶ ἀγαθή) (Rom. 7:12), which reflects the character of the God whose law it is. Thus, sin in Paul is to be understood in relation to a holy, righteous, and good God and his holy, righteous, and good law. In this regard, sin is a fleshly mind that is "hostile to God" (ἔχθρα εἰς θεόν) and refuses to submit to "God's law" (νόμῳ τοῦ θεοῦ) (Rom. 8:7).

Sin's Definition

In Paul's thought, then, whatever sin is, it is anti-God and anti-law. The "antichrist" figure in 2 Thessalonians 2 brings us close to a definition. Paul calls him "the man of lawlessness" (ὁ ἄνθρωπος τῆς ἀνομίας) (v. 3) and "the lawless one" (ὁ ἄνομος) (vv. 8, 9). Some translations render him "the Man of Sin" (KJV). The

---

[93] Ridderbos, *Paul*, 107.

disposition of his lawlessness is that he puts himself in the place of God (v. 4). But it is not just the "antichrist" figure whom Paul describes this way. The apostle speaks of all fallen people in similar terms. They are "the lawless" (ἀνόμοις), "disobedient" (ἀνυποτάκτοις), "ungodly" (ἀσεβέσι), "sinners" (ἁμαρτωλοῖς) (1 Tim. 1:9). And they have been like this since their first parents, when Eve was deceived and became a "transgressor" (παραβάσει) (1 Tim. 2:14).[94]

Sin, for Paul, is at heart a vertical issue between the creature and the Creator, or more specifically, between the subject and the Lawgiver. In sin, man tries to free himself from his Creator-Sovereign and his standards. He strives for an autonomy in which he gets to be his own god and write his own laws. Ridderbos captures it well: "One can define [sin] as man's willing-to-have-command-of-himself, wanting-to-be-as-God."[95] Precisely because he wants to be his own god, man rejects God's law and in turn trespasses his law—he becomes, *in essentia*, lawless. In short, "Sin is apostasy from God, refusal to be subject to him; it is also and for this reason lawlessness, disobedience, violation of the divine order. . . . Sin is in its essence transgression of the law appointed by God for man."[96]

ENVIRONMENT OF SIN

As noted above in the discussion on Paul's eschatology, the apostle frequently speaks of our "life-context" outside of Christ in terms of the present world-age. It is "the world turned away from God, rebellious and hostile toward [God],"[97] and which forms the environment in which sin flourishes. Ridderbos comments, "To belong to the world means to be a sinner, to participate in sin and to experience the judgment on sin."[98] As part of the world-age duplex, Paul speaks of three forces that are at work administering the reign of sin and death: the devil, the spiritual powers and authorities, and the flesh. The first two are external; the third, internal.

The Devil

According to Paul, the age of this present evil world is under the authority of the devil. Besides the term "devil" (διάβολος) (Eph. 4:27; 6:11; 1 Tim. 3:6, 7; 2 Tim.

---

[94] Besides these central ideas of enmity, lawlessness, disobedience, ungodliness, Paul employs other terms to convey sin: "foolishness" (see Rom. 1:22; 1 Cor. 1:19); "worthlessness, vanity, darkness, alienation from true life" (see Eph. 4:18); "without God," and therefore, "having no hope" (Eph. 2:12); and being "dead" (Eph. 2:1, 5; Col. 2:13; Rom. 7:10).
[95] Ridderbos, *Paul*, 105–106.
[96] Ridderbos, *Paul*, 107.
[97] Ridderbos, *Paul*, 92.
[98] Ridderbos, *Paul*, 92–93.

2:26), Paul uses other terms to describe him: he is "Satan" (σατανᾶς) (Rom. 16:20; 1 Cor. 5:5; 7:5; 2 Cor. 2:11; 11:14; 12:7; 1 Thess. 2:18; 2 Thess. 2:9; 1 Tim. 1:20; 5:15); "the evil one" (τοῦ πονηροῦ) (Eph. 6:16; 2 Thess. 3:3); "the prince of the power of the air" (τὸν ἄρχοντα τῆς ἐξουσίας τοῦ ἀέρος) (Eph. 2:2); and "the tempter" (ὁ πειράζων) (1 Thess. 3:5). Paul directly connects the devil with the present world-age: he is "the god of this world" (ὁ θεὸς τοῦ αἰῶνος τούτου) "who has blinded the minds of. . . unbelievers" (2 Cor. 4:4); "the spirit" (τοῦ πνεύματος) presently at work in the sons of disobedience (Eph. 2:2).

Spiritual Powers and Authorities

The devil, however, is not the only power at work in the realm of the world-age that stands in rebellion to God. Under the devil, various powers operate according to his direction and will, exerting influence on the human creature toward sin. In Ephesians 6, in the context of spiritual warfare, Paul speaks of the array of powers in the heavenly realms that wage war against the Christian. They are "the rulers" (τὰς ἀρχάς), "the authorities" (τὰς ἐξουσίας), "the cosmic powers" (τοὺς κοσμοκράτορας), "the spiritual forces" (τὰ πνευματικά) (Eph. 6:12).[99] Paul associates them with darkness (σκότος) and evil (πονηρία) (cf. also Col. 1:13). These powers, along with the devil, exert external influence in the environment of sin, lording it over the sinner. But, along with the devil, they are not the only force at work. There is also an internal force that influences the human creature toward sin, what Paul calls, "the flesh."

The Flesh

The word "flesh" (σάρξ) in Paul is a "polymorphous concept,"[100] with one Bible translation (NIV) using twenty-eight different words or phrases to translate the Greek word.[101] Ridderbos calls the relationship of identity between sin and flesh to be "one of the most distinctive and radical data of Pauline anthropology."[102] Douglas Moo outlines five basic uses of "flesh" in Paul's writings.[103] The apostle employs it for: (1) human or animal flesh as distinct from skeletal body (1 Cor. 15:39; Eph. 2:11; Col. 2:13; cf. Gal. 6:13); (2) the human body as a whole (2 Cor. 7:1); (3) the human being generally (1 Cor. 1:28–29); (4) the

---

[99] Cf. Rom. 8:38; 1 Cor. 15:24; Col. 1:13; 2:15.
[100] Anthony Thiselton, *The Two Horizons: New Testament Hermeneutics and Philosophical Description with Special Reference to Bultmann, Heidegger, Gadamer, and Wittgenstein* (Grand Rapids, MI: Eerdmans, 1979), 408–11.
[101] Noted by Moo, "Sin in Paul," 118.
[102] Ridderbos, *Paul*, 95.
[103] Moo, "Sin in Paul," 118–20.

human state or condition viewed "neutrally" as the life existence, communicating the weakness and dependence of the creature upon its Creator (1 Cor. 10:18; Rom. 8:3); (5) the fallen human condition (Rom. 8:4; Gal. 5:16–17). The last two uses touch on the life experience of the human creature, what Ridderbos describes as, "the coinciding of being human and being a sinner."[104] In short, for Paul, to be "in the flesh" is to be a creature of God living in sin.

Several Pauline texts bring this out. Paul characterizes life outside of Christ as living "in the flesh" (ἐν τῇ σαρκί) (Rom. 7:5), "according to the flesh" (κατὰ σάρκα) (Rom. 8:4–8), "in the passions of our flesh" (ταῖς ἐπιθυμίαις τῆς σαρκός) (Eph. 2:3). As such, it is a life fundamentally opposed to the Spirit (Gal. 5:16–17). Ridderbos provides a succinct summary:

> [T]o be "in the flesh," to be "carnal," and the like mean to sin, indeed to be under the power of sin. . . . there is here a new indication of the universality of sin, in that flesh on the one hand is a description of all that is man, and on the other of the sinful in man.[105]

To conclude: in Paul's thought, the world-age inaugurated by Adam produced an environment governed by the devil and spiritual powers and authorities (from the outside) and by the flesh (from the inside)—an environment in which sin flourishes. Through the one man, sin became the common experience of every man within the space-time environment of a fallen world-age.

EXPERIENCE OF SIN

While Paul refers to sin mainly in the singular (ἁμαρτία) in his writings, his vice lists demonstrate that he views sin as possessing many dimensions. Indeed, in several passages he lists multiple vices that reflect the many faces of sin. Two lists in particular are worth mentioning.

In Romans 1:24–32 Paul names the sins of idolatry (v. 24), sexual acts that are "contrary to nature" (v. 26), and a depraved mind (v. 28). The latter category he then unpacks in the longest of his "vice lists."[106] He provides a litany of all manner of sins: unrighteousness, evil, covetousness, malice; sinners are full of envy, murder, strife, deceit, maliciousness; they are gossips, slanderers, haters of God, insolent, haughty, boastful, inventors of evil, disobedient to parents,

---

[104] Ridderbos, *Paul*, 93.
[105] Ridderbos, *Paul*, 95.
[106] Cf. also Rom. 13:13; 1 Cor. 5:10–11; 6:9–10; 2 Cor. 12:20; Gal. 5:19–21; Eph. 4:19, 31; 5:3–5; Col. 3:5, 8; 1 Tim. 1:9–10; 6:4–5; 2 Tim. 3:2–5; Titus 3:3.

foolish, faithless, heartless, ruthless. The list ends with an observation about the nonchalant attitude of the perpetrators of these sins: "Though they know God's righteous decree that those who practice such things deserve to die, they not only do them but give approval to those who practice them" (v. 32).

In Romans 3:9–18 Paul argues that the common experience of sin, and its many faces, affects both Jews and Greeks. In arguing for the universality of sin, he brings together a mosaic of OT passages to communicate the multifaceted nature of sin. He covers mainly sins of speech and violence. Paul's extended quotation sets forth a fourteen-point indictment against mankind, each indictment but two being drawn from the Psalms:

> "None is righteous, no, not one;
>> no one understands;
>> no one seeks for God.
> All have turned aside; together they have become worthless;
>> no one does good,
>> not even one." [Ps. 14:1–3]
> "Their throat is an open grave;
>> they use their tongues to deceive." [Ps. 5:9]
> "The venom of asps is under their lips." [Ps. 140:3]
>> "Their mouth is full of curses and bitterness." [Ps. 10:7]
> "Their feet are swift to shed blood; [Prov. 1:16]
>> in their paths are ruin and misery,
> and the way of peace they have not known." [Isa. 59:7–8]
> "There is no fear of God before their eyes." [Ps. 36:1]

Paul opens the list with the emphatic statement of Psalm 14, in which positive characteristics are inverted by the negative indicative "no one is" (οὐκ ἔστιν). The inclusio of "not one" (οὐδὲ εἷς) and "not even one" (ἕως ἑνός) doubles the negative force and underlines the universality of sin. There is not one person who is righteous (δίκαιος), who understands (ὁ συνίων), or who seeks after God (ὁ ἐκζητῶν τὸν θεόν)—not even one!

This brings us to the extent of sin.

EXTENT OF SIN

Paul's argument that there is not a single righteous person among humanity (Jew or Gentile) speaks to the issue of the universality of sin. This is underscored most clearly in his letter to the Romans. Throughout, Paul addresses both Jews and Gentiles. For him, the gospel is the power of God for salvation "to everyone

[παντί] who believes, to the Jew first and also to the Greek" (1:16). This is because "all [πάντας], both Jews and Greeks, are under sin [ὑφ᾽ ἁμαρτίαν]" (3:9).
One of Paul's most frequently used words in Romans is the word "all" (πᾶς),
occurring about 70 times. He uses the adjective in different ways, but often with
respect to God's offer of salvation in the gospel to all, which arises out of the
universal guilt of all. For Paul, "all" (πάντες) have turned aside from God (3:12);
the law stops the mouth of "everyone" (πᾶν) and holds "the whole world" (πᾶς
ὁ κόσμος) accountable to God (3:19–20); "all" (πάντες) have sinned and fall
short of God's glory (3:23); death spread to "all people" (πάντας ἀνθρώπους)
because "all" (πάντες) have sinned (5:12); the one trespass led to condemnation
for "all" (πάντες) (5:18); God has consigned "all" (πάντας) to disobedience
(11:32). And yet despite this, there is good news for all, since "everyone [πᾶς]
who calls on the name of the Lord will be saved" (10:13).

The extent to which sin has affected mankind, however, is not only dis-
tributive; it is also intrusive.

EFFECTS OF SIN

In Paul, sin corrupts the whole man, inwardly and outwardly. The inner
corruption "asserts itself from within over the whole of human existence,"
affecting the will, desires, mind (e.g., Rom. 1:18ff.; Eph. 4:17–19); the outer
corruption of the body and its members "holds the inward man in its grasp
as a prisoner" (e.g., Rom. 7:14–25).[107]

The Inward Man

Paul uses a number of terms to describe the "inward man": "understanding"
(νοῦς), "mind" (φρόνημα), "heart" (καρδίας), "will" (θέλημα), "soul" (ψυχή),
"spirit" (πνεῦμα), and "conscience" (συνειδήσεως). Of these, Paul exhibits a
strong preference for "mind" (νοῦς/φρόνημα) and "heart" (καρδίας).

The Mind

The first term, νοῦς ("mind"), has no exact equivalent in English. In the Greek
NT it carries different shades of meaning: understanding, mind, disposition,
thought. One lexicon renders it as "the faculty of intellectual perception."[108]
Ridderbos comments,

---

[107] Ridderbos, *Paul*, 114.
[108] BDAG 680.

. . . *nous* on the one hand denotes the organ, the possibility, in which man is addressed as a thinking and responsible being by the revelation of God, and on the other hand constitutes as well the description of that by which he is most deeply determined in his thinking and acting.[109]

The word *nous* can be used both negatively and positively in Paul. Negatively, Paul speaks of God giving people up to "a debased mind" (ἀδόκιμον νοῦν) "to do what ought not to be done" (Rom. 1:28); he describes unconverted Gentiles as walking "in the futility of their minds" (ἐν ματαιότητι τοῦ νοὸς αὐτῶν) (Eph. 4:17). Elsewhere he speaks of sinners being "depraved in mind" (διεφθαρμένων ἀνθρώπων τὸν νοῦν) (1 Tim. 6:5) and "corrupted in mind" (ἄνθρωποι κατεφθαρμένοι τὸν νοῦν) (2 Tim. 3:8), their minds and consciences being "defiled" (μεμίανται) (Titus 1:15). But sin works more than a corruption or defilement in us; it also creates a hostile and insubordinate mind toward God and his law; indeed, the corruption is so deep that Paul can say that the mind is *unable* (οὐδὲ . . . δύναται) even to submit to God's law (Rom. 8:7–8). Positively, the mind is part of the renewal process that God works in us by his grace (Rom. 12:2; Eph. 4:23).

The Heart

The second term that Paul prefers to describe the inward man is "heart" (καρδίας). Ridderbos, again, provides a helpful definition: "[H]eart is the concept that preeminently denotes the human ego in its thinking, affections, aspirations, decisions, both in man's relationship to God and to the world surrounding him."[110] As with the "mind" (νοῦς), Paul uses the word "heart" (καρδίας) both negatively and positively. Negatively, the heart is "darkened" (ἐσκοτίσθη) by sin in its foolishness (Rom. 1:21); it is the locale of "the lusts" (ταῖς ἐπιθυμίαις) that lead to impurity (Rom. 1:24); it is "hard and impenitent" (τὴν σκληρότητά σου καὶ ἀμετανόητον καρδίαν) (Rom. 2:5; cf. Eph. 4:18). Positively, the heart is the spiritual organ that the Holy Spirit operates on (Rom. 5:5) and into which God pours the Spirit of his Son (Gal. 4:6).

In Ephesians 4:17–18 Paul makes a connection between the mind and the heart that is instructive for a discussion of sin and depravity. In speaking of the futility of the unbelieving mind and the darkened understanding that

---

[109] Ridderbos, *Paul*, 119.
[110] Ridderbos, *Paul*, 119.

accompanies it, Paul provides a sequenced double διά-causation: "*because of* [διά] the ignorance that is in them, *due to* [διά] their hardness of heart." In other words, the root cause of futility of mind and darkened understanding is a willful ignorance, and behind that, a hard heart.

The implications for a correct theological anthropology and soteriology are revealing. To Descartes's "I think, therefore I am," the apostle Paul replies, "I will, therefore I am." We are what we will, before we are what we think. For what we think is what we will. For this reason, Paul does not entertain any form of autosoterism or synergistic soterism. He is wholly committed to a monergistic soterism. In Paul's thought, man cannot think his way out of his sin, since his mind is clouded in its own futility and darkness; and even more significantly, man cannot *will* his way out of sin, since his heart is clogged with hardness and impenitence.

The Outward Man

Sin also corrupts the outward man. Paul speaks of ungodly people acting out of the lusts of the heart, which lead to "the dishonoring of their bodies among themselves" (τοῦ ἀτιμάζεσθαι τὰ σώματα αὐτῶν ἐν αὐτοῖς) (Rom. 1:24); the unbeliever carries out "the desires of the body and mind" (τὰ θελήματα τῆς σαρκὸς καὶ τῶν διανοιῶν) (Eph. 2:3).

In conclusion, given the fact that sin affects man in every faculty and sphere of his life, inward and outward, sin is a comprehensive problem. What compounds the problem is the enslaving power that sin possesses, so much so that it almost seems impossible to escape or conquer.

ENSLAVING POWER OF SIN

One of the striking things about sin in Paul's letter to the Romans is his personification of it.[111] Paul speaks of how sin "reigned" (ἐβασίλευσεν) in death (Rom. 5:17), and how, as those united to Christ in his death and resurrection, we are not to let sin "reign" (βασιλευέτω) in our mortal bodies (6:12). Paul describes us as once being "enslaved to sin" (δουλεύειν ... τῇ ἁμαρτίᾳ) (6:6) and "slaves of sin" (δοῦλοι τῆς ἁμαρτίας) (6:17). Under the law, sin holds us "captive" (ἐφρουρούμεθα), "imprisoning" (συγκλειόμενοι)

---

[111] Moo, "Sin in Paul," 111, makes the helpful distinction between personalization and personification. The former gives sin a personal ontology, like an evil spiritual power; the latter attributes personal qualities to sin.

us (Gal. 3:23). Sin pays the "wages" (τὰ ὀψώνια) of death (Rom. 6:23); it "seizes" (λαμβάνω) the opportunity to produce all manner of sins in us (7:8); it "deceives" (ἐξαπατάω) and "kills" (ἀποκτείνω) (7:11); it makes the sinner a "debtor" (ὀφειλέτης) (8:12).

These personifications paint a vivid picture of the encompassing power of sin. Although we are united to Christ by faith, sin remains a lively enemy that aims to lure us into the orbit of its influence and power. In Romans 6 Paul personifies the power of sin in three ways: (1) a master to whom we are enslaved; (2) a king to whom we must submit; and (3) an employer who pays our wage.

A Master

Paul employs the image of a master-slave relation to depict the life experience of a person outside of Christ. Sin is the master, and unbelievers are its slaves. Life under the master of sin is a life in bondage "to impurity and to lawlessness" (τῇ ἀκαθαρσίᾳ καὶ τῇ ἀνομίᾳ) (Rom. 6:19). But in Christ we "have been set free from sin" (ἐλευθερωθέντες δὲ ἀπὸ τῆς ἁμαρτίας) and "have become slaves of righteousness" (ἐδουλώθητε τῇ δικαιοσύνῃ) (6:18; cf. 6:6–7, 19, 20–22). Sin was an enslaving power, but Christ is a liberating power. Paul communicates the freedom we have experienced as believers through a once-were-but-now-are complex: we *once* were enslaved to sin (6:6, 17, 20), *but now* we have been set free from sin (6:7, 18, 22). For Paul, there is a "when" (ὅτε) state of enslavement, and a "but-now" (νυνὶ δέ) state of freedom. And Paul's point is that, having been liberated from the one master and joined to another, why would we go back to serve our old master? It would be bondage to do so.

A King

The second image that Paul employs to convey the power of sin is that of a tyrant king. Sin is personified as a dominating king ruling over his subjects in an oppressive manner. This is communicated through the language of "reign" and "dominion" in Romans 6. The first term, "reign" (βασιλεύω), means "to exercise authority at a royal level";[112] the second term, means "to be master of, dominate" (κυριεύω).[113] The apostle exhorts us not to let sin "reign" (βασιλευέτω) in our mortal body, exercising authority over us to the

---

[112] BDAG 170.
[113] BDAG 576.

point that it makes us obey its passions. Instead, we are to present ourselves to God as instruments of righteousness (Rom. 6:12–13). The reason? Because sin will "not have dominion" (οὐ κυριεύσει) over us (Rom. 6:14).[114] Through the use of these two words and the king-slave imagery that they convey, Paul aims to communicate the dominating power of sin.

An Employer

The third image is that of an employer paying out wages for services rendered. The idea in the term "wages" (ὀψώνια) is that of compensation. Sin is an employer, paying out a salary for our employment in its service (Rom. 6:23). The point of the personification is that sin is in charge. As slaves to sin, we receive the wage of death.

A Power over All

Finally, sin as master, tyrant, and employer shows no discrimination among its slaves, subjects, and workers—it dominates one and all. As Paul states in Romans 3:9b, "For we have already charged that all, both Jews and Greeks, are under sin [ὑφ' ἁμαρτίαν]." While Paul does not employ the word "power" in Romans 3:9, the preposition "under" communicates as much. Slaves, subjects, and workers are all *under* someone—so too those bound by sin.

Given that sin is an enslaving power, constantly seeking to draw us back under its bondage, dominion, and charge, what is the hope for mankind? For one thing, it is not found in the law. As Paul makes clear in Romans 7, the law only exacerbates sin.

EXACERBATION OF SIN

In his argument in Romans 7, Paul makes abundantly clear that the law is of no use when it comes to dealing with sin. To feel the force of the apostle's point, it is helpful to understand what the law meant to the Jew. For the Jew, the law was "the substance of life."[115] It was a means of life, "a protective and saving resource against the power of the evil impulse."[116] In other words, the

---

[114] An OT equivalent of this image is captured in Gen. 4:7: "And if you do not do well, sin is crouching at the door. Its desire is contrary to you, but you must rule over it" (Moo, "Sin in Paul," 111).

[115] Ridderbos, *Paul*, 132, citing W. Bousset, *Die Religion des Judentums*, 3rd ed. (Berlin: W. Peiser, 1926 [1903]), 119.

[116] Ridderbos, *Paul*, 133, citing H. J. Schoeps, *Paul: The Theology of the Apostle in the Light of Jewish Religious History* (Cambridge: Lutterworth, James Clarke, 1961), 168–218.

law was the way of justification before God and of victory over the power of sin. This points to the redemptive significance of the law in Judaism and sets the context for Paul's antithetical view of the law. The apostle presents four main uses of the law.

Uses of Law

First, *the law judges sin*. As Paul says, "all who have sinned under the law will be judged by the law" (διὰ νόμου κριθήσονται) (Rom. 2:12). As part of this judgment, the law holds the whole world "accountable to God" (ὑπόδικος γένηται . . . τῷ θεῷ) (Rom. 3:19). It is the standard by which God will judge and administer his just punishment; "the law brings wrath" (ὁ . . . νόμος ὀργὴν κατεργάζεται) (Rom. 4:15).

Second, *the law exposes sin*. It is the means by which sin becomes known: "through the law comes knowledge of sin" (διὰ . . . νόμου ἐπίγνωσις ἁμαρτίας) (Rom. 3:20). Indeed, as Paul even says, "I would not have known sin if it had not been for the law" (ἣν ἁμαρτίαν οὐκ ἔγνων εἰ μὴ διὰ νόμου) (Rom. 7:7, my translation).

Third, *the law exacerbates sin*. For Paul, our latent lusts are "aroused by the law" (τὰ διὰ τοῦ νόμου) (Rom. 7:5). The appearance of the law with its various commandments makes sin opportunistic to produce all kinds of sin in us (Rom. 7:8–11). Indeed, "through the commandment" (διὰ τῆς ἐντολῆς), sin increases "beyond measure" (καθ᾽ ὑπερβολήν) (Rom. 7:13).

All under Sin

For Paul, these purposes of the law coalesce to produce one overall purpose, and that is to show that *all* are under sin. It is not just the rebellious but also the religious who are guilty before God, as the law demonstrates. Romans 7 is crucial to Paul's point. The chapter forms the "culminating point" of Paul's doctrine of sin, as Ridderbos notes,

> in that it indicates that the corruption of sin in all its radicalness is not only to be sought in the blind heathen given up to all manner of perversity, but also in the man who lives under the strength of the law, who looks for his ideal and his moral strength in the law, and nevertheless must be brought to the recognition of having been sold under sin and of the "wretched man that I am, who will deliver me?"[117]

---

[117] Ridderbos, *Paul*, 130.

Impotence of the Law

The three uses of the law in Romans—of judging, exposing, and exacerbating sin—demonstrate the law's inability to help the sinner (even the so-called righteous) out of their sinful mode of existence in the world-age of Adam, a world-age influenced by the devil, the spiritual powers and authorities, and the flesh. Paul makes this clear in his writings in two ways. First, justification by the law is impossible since all—religious Jews as well as rebellious Gentiles—have broken the law (Rom. 2:1–3:20). Moreover, justification by works nullifies Christ's work: "if righteousness were through the law, then Christ died for no purpose" (Gal. 2:21). Second, victory over the power of sin by the law is impossible since the law can only expose and exacerbate sin; it does not ameliorate it (Rom. 7:5) or conceal it (Rom. 7:7). With the law comes only wrath (Rom. 4:15).

Ridderbos provides a helpful summary of Paul's overall point:

> . . . the law can offer relief and help in no respect whatever, indeed that it . . . makes the man who would be saved by the law sink down still more deeply into the morass of sin and sin's corruption. . . . In the struggle for redemption of life the law does not stand on the side of life, but on that of death. In place of being a champion for good the law has become a paladin of evil."[118]

This brings us to the fourth and ultimate use of the law in Paul's mind.

Pedagogy of the Law

While functioning negatively in relation to sin, the law is also employed positively in relation to grace. Negatively, the law imprisons the sinner and puts him to death; it arouses sin and increases its presence. But even with these condemning and killing effects, it "does not fall out of the control of the God and Father of Jesus Christ whom Paul preaches."[119] Even in the negative, the law achieves a positive: it points sinners to a Savior. As Paul puts it, the law becomes our "guardian," or better, our "tutor" (παιδαγωγός) to point us to Christ (Gal. 3:23–24).[120] The law does this, in one way, through

---

[118] Ridderbos, *Paul*, 131, 147.
[119] Ridderbos, *Paul*, 151.
[120] In this respect, some, like Ridderbos, have read Rom. 7 in terms of the *historia salutis* and not the *ordo salutis*. The "ego" that Paul speaks of is the unregenerate man—a religious man under the law, but not a converted man. Certainly the redemptive-historical concerns regarding the purpose of the law as a pedagogue to point to Christ would seem to favor this interpretation (see, e.g., Ridderbos, *Paul*, 126–30). In contrast, church history reveals another interpretation—a regenerate man struggling with sin as he lives between the two ages experiencing the "taseological" life (see, e.g., Murray, *Romans*, 244–66). For a helpful overview of each position, see Moo, *Romans*, 443–51. For an attempt at a via media, see Will N. Timmins, *Romans 7 and Christian Identity: A Study of the "I" in Its Literary Context*, Society for New Testament Studies Monograph Series 170 (Cambridge: Cambridge University

types and shadows (cf. 1 Cor. 5:7, for example). But that is not the use Paul has in mind here. For him, the law was added "because of transgression" (τῶν παραβάσεων χάριν προσετέθη) (Gal. 3:19). That is, the law serves as our pedagogue to convince and convict us of sin and therefore of our need for a Savior.

The necessity of a Savior implies that sin brings with it consequences from which we need to be rescued, to which we turn next.

V. Consequences of Sin

In several texts Paul demonstrates that sin carries consequences. For him, sin receives God's wrath and ends in death. These two consequences in Paul's thought map onto the eschatological canvas of sin, as described earlier, in a present-and-future pattern.

WRATH

In relation to the consequences of sin, God's wrath (ὀργή) is, as Ridderbos comments, "[t]he most inclusive and most radical idea."[121] Ridderbos expands: "On the one hand, with this term the punishment of sin is denoted in its whole extent; on the other hand, it is qualified in a pregnant manner as a personal expression of God himself."[122] This latter point must be carefully parsed, since God's wrath is not "a divine emotion" or "a movement within the divine being," as Ridderbos helpfully qualifies; rather, it is "the active divine judgment going forth against sin and the world."[123] God's wrath is also matched with his "indignation" (ὀργὴ καὶ θυμός) (Rom. 2:8 NASB). In Paul, the wrath of God not only speaks of what God *does* in response to sin, but also who God *is* in response to sin.

First, *God's wrath shows what he does.* God pours out his wrath from heaven on those "who suppress the truth [of his existence] in ungodliness" (τῶν τὴν ἀλήθειαν ἐν ἀδικίᾳ κατεχόντων) (1:18). God's wrath works its way out in his handing people over to their sin (παρέδωκεν αὐτοὺς ὁ θεός) (1:24, 26, 28). His wrath also results in "tribulation and anguish" (θλῖψις καὶ στενοχωρία) (Rom. 2:9, my translation) and in his "inflicting vengeance"

Press, 2017). For a review of Timmins's thesis, see Marcus A. Mininger, "Defining the Identity of the Christian 'I' between the Already and the Not Yet: In Review of Will N. Timmins's *Romans 7 and Christian Identity*," *Mid-America Journal of Theology* 31 (2020): 133–54.
[121] Ridderbos, *Paul*, 108.
[122] Ridderbos, *Paul*, 108.
[123] Ridderbos, *Paul*, 108.

(διδόντος ἐκδίκησιν) (2 Thess. 1:8). In a word, God's wrath shows that he does not sit idly by in response to the sin of his creatures.

Second, *God's wrath shows who he is*. Paul speaks of the judgment of God "rightly" (κατὰ ἀλήθειαν) falling on sinners (Rom. 2:2); he also calls God's judgment on sin a "righteous judgment" (δικαιοκρισίας) (Rom. 2:5; cf. 2 Thess. 1:5). The "righteousness of God" (θεοῦ δικαιοσύνην) is used synonymously with "the wrath" (τὴν ὀργήν) of God (Rom. 3:5). In other words, God's wrath is a function of his righteousness. Connected to this is the language of enmity and alienation to describe God's relationship to sinners. According to Paul, we are "alienated" (ἀπηλλοτριωμένους) from God (Col. 1:21; Eph. 2:12; 4:18); there is "enmity" (ἔχθρα) between God and us (Rom. 8:7, my translation; cf. Col. 1:21); we have become "enemies" (ἐχθροί), in both directions (Rom. 5:10; 11:28).

As mentioned earlier, in Paul's thought God's wrath maps onto his eschatological framework in a present-and-future pattern. God's wrath against sin is *already* being revealed from heaven, but it is *not yet* finally being revealed from heaven.

Various texts in Paul speak of the *present reality* of the wrath of God. The "wrath of God" (ὀργὴ θεοῦ) is already "revealed" (ἀποκαλύπτεται) from heaven on those who suppress the truth in unrighteousness (Rom. 1:18). This is expressed in God "handing over" (παρέδωκεν ... ὁ θεός) people to their sin (1:24, 26, 28, my translation). Paul describes the reprobate as "vessels of wrath" (σκεύη ὀργῆς), prepared beforehand for destruction (Rom. 9:22). While believers are not spoken of like this by Paul in Romans 9, he does give a similar description of the believer pre-conversion in Ephesians 2:3. We were once "by nature children of wrath [τέκνα φύσει ὀργῆς], like the rest of mankind [ὡς καὶ οἱ λοιποί]." Paul speaks of the government being God's servant to exact his "wrath" (ὀργήν) on the wrongdoer, which must refer to God's present wrath and not his future wrath (Rom. 13:4). Paul also mentions a present revelation of God's wrath for hindering the advance of the gospel (1 Thess. 2:16).

The present manifestation of God's wrath is also connected to its future manifestation. In Paul's gospel, the wrath of God, alongside the righteousness of God, is a future, eschatological reality that thrusts itself into the present. As Ridderbos notes, "The most central pronouncements of Paul on the wrath of God point to its revelation as eschatological reality already in the present, together with the revelation of the righteousness by faith."[124] For Paul, therefore, the process of final acquittal and final judgment has already begun.[125] This is important for the preaching of the gospel, since the wrath of God forms the backdrop for the grace of God revealed in Christ.

And yet the eschatological, while being thrust into the present, also remains "not yet." For Paul, there is a future "day of wrath" (ἡμέρᾳ ὀργῆς) (Rom. 2:5) on which God will render his righteous judgment (Rom. 12:19) for various vices (Eph. 5:3–6; Col. 3:5–6). As with the present day of God's wrath, this future day forms the backdrop for the salvation offered in the gospel. Paul speaks of our salvation in terms of being rescued from the future wrath of God: "Since, therefore, we have now been justified by his blood, much more shall we be saved by him from the wrath of God [ἀπὸ τῆς ὀργῆς]" (Rom. 5:9; cf. 1 Thess. 1:10; 5:9). This assurance is based on the fact that Christ has already anticipated the wrath of God on our behalf.

It is clear from these texts that God's wrath is very much a future reality as well as a present one in Paul's mind. There is a fixed day of wrath on which God will judge the world for its unrighteousness (Rom. 2:5).

DEATH

The other main consequence of sin is death, which Paul also handles along eschatological lines. As with God's wrath, the apostle maps death onto his eschatological framework in a present-and-future pattern. In several places, Paul indicates that death has *already* begun its deadly work in us. *Physically*, Paul speaks of "the body of sin" (τὸ σῶμα τῆς ἁμαρτίας) (Rom. 6:6) and "this body of death" (τοῦ σώματος τοῦ θανάτου τούτου) (Rom. 7:24), both phrases indicating that there is a corruption of the body by the twin agents of sin and death. Death is a condition that is already bearing fruit in the life of those who are living in the flesh (Rom. 7:5). Death has already begun to work itself out in the life of sin in man (Rom. 7:9–10). The flesh reaps corruption in us (Gal. 6:8). Ridderbos comments, "This 'dying' is not to be taken as introspection, acquiring an eye for guilt and punishment, but the sin-ruled condition of [man's] existence . . ." He goes on: "Sin brings death because it does not consist merely in separate acts whereby man remains himself, but is a power that corrupts him in his true manhood before God in such a way that he can

---

[124] Ridderbos, *Paul*, 109.
[125] Ridderbos, *Paul*, 109.

do nothing other than sin . . ."[126] Paul also views death (θάνατον) as a result of grief arising from the brokenness of this world (2 Cor. 7:10).

Besides the physical death that affects our bodies, *spiritual* death is already at work in us too. According to Paul, in our old life outside of Christ, we were spiritually "dead" (νεκρούς) in "trespasses and sins" (Eph. 2:1, 5). Elsewhere he speaks of the uncircumcision of our flesh as the means to our spiritual "death" (νεκρούς) (see Col. 2:13). Ridderbos provides a helpful summary of the physico-spiritual death in Paul's thought:

> Death is thereby not only a punishment that puts an end to life, but a condition in which the destiny of life outside Christ is turned into its opposite. It is corruption, destruction, in the active sense of the word, the absolute antithesis of life intended by God and saved by Christ.[127]

For Paul, the present reality of death in us, physical and spiritual, is not the only death we face as fallen creatures. There is still the final state of death. Several passages in Paul also present death as a *not-yet* reality. This future state is the ultimate consequence of the reign of death introduced by Adam in his fall (Rom. 5:14, 17, 21). Under the reign of death, all things end in "death" (θάνατος) (Rom. 6:21), and this is because "the wages of sin is death" (τὰ . . . ὀψώνια τῆς ἁμαρτίας θάνατος) (Rom. 6:23). As Ridderbos comments, "Death is therefore the end of sin, not simply as conclusion, but as result, as that in which sin reaches its objective."[128] Paul's pithy statement in 1 Corinthians 15 provides a succinct summary on the matter: "As in Adam all die" (ἐν τῷ Ἀδὰμ πάντες ἀποθνῄσκουσιν) (1 Cor. 15:22). That is, sin in Adam leads to death in Adam. Although death has already begun in our mortal bodies, Paul views it as "the last enemy to be destroyed" (ἔσχατος ἐχθρὸς καταργεῖται) (1 Cor. 15:26).

In sum, for Paul, death is a final state into which all sinners enter because of Adam's one trespass. Yet, while it is a final reality that awaits us, it is also a present reality that affects our current lives and bodies. We experience decay and corruption now, not just then.

Having analyzed the consequences of sin in God's wrath and human death, we turn finally to the good news of a Savior for sinners.

[126] Ridderbos, *Paul*, 113.
[127] Ridderbos, *Paul*, 112.
[128] Ridderbos, *Paul*, 112.

VI. The Christ of Sinners

From Plight to Solution

In Paul, man's predicament is dire. As a descendant of Adam, he has inherited by imputation the sin and guilt of his first father, and the consequence of death has begun to do its work in him. As part of the present world-age inaugurated by Adam, man lives out his mode of existence in the environment of sin, under the influence of the devil, spiritual powers and authorities, and the flesh. It is an age in which sin and death reign, affecting the inward man (in heart and mind) and the outward man (in body). He is slave to an irrepressible master, subject to a tyrant-king, and laborer to a cruel employer. He may still have the image of God in him, he may still live as a creature of God, but he is, as Paul says, "[without] hope and without God in the world" (Eph. 2:12). The situation is more dire still, since man lacks any will to obey God with his behavior, to understand God with his mind, or to seek after God with his heart (Rom. 3:10–11). Nevertheless, although man's plight is dire, the apostle does not despair. As he says elsewhere, "The saying is trustworthy and deserving of full acceptance, that Christ Jesus came into the world to save sinners" (1 Tim. 1:15).

God's Saving Work in Christ

As noted earlier, in Paul, the soteriological is shaped and informed by the eschatological. To quote Vos by way of reminder, "the closely interwoven soteric tissue derives its pattern from the eschatological scheme, which bears all the marks of having had precedence in his mind."[129] Here we return to the image of Paul's hamartiology being mapped onto his eschatology. If Paul's hamartiology is the first layer on his eschatological canvas, then his soteriology may be said to form a second layer, mapping onto the hamartiological and eschatological (see diagram 15.4). To be more specific, Paul's soteriology has four distinct-but-related moments, each of which answers to the problem of sin in its prospect, penalty, power, and presence.

Redemption Predestined

In the moment of redemption predestined, God deals with the *prospect* of sin before it becomes a reality. God chooses an elect number of people to salvation in Christ, to "be holy" (εἶναι … ἁγίους) (Eph. 1:4). The purpose

[129] Vos, *Pauline Eschatology*, 60.

DIAGRAM 15.4: Mapping Redemption onto Ages

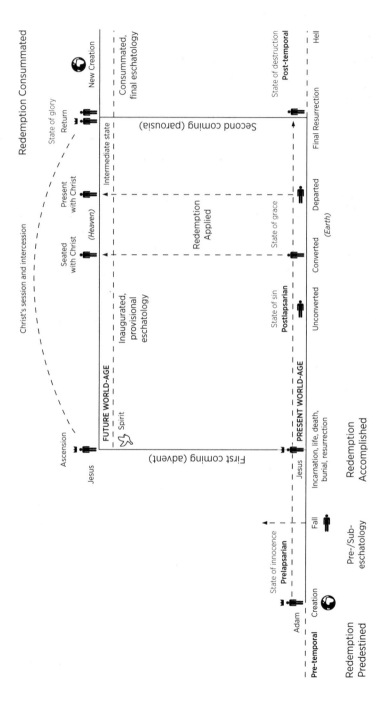

clause implies the prospect of sin in the human race. Having seen how Paul presents the effect of sin in human creatures, God's election cannot be based on his foreknowledge of any human will, faith, or work. As Paul affirms elsewhere, there is "none righteous, no, not one; no one understands; no one seeks for God" (Rom. 3:10–11). This being the case, God had to make the first move toward us in Christ. Paul explains that this occurred "before the foundation the world" (πρὸ καταβολῆς κόσμου) (Eph. 1:4), "before the ages began" (πρὸ χρόνων αἰωνίων) (2 Tim. 1:9).[130] Divine election is therefore a pre-temporal decision based on God's will not ours, the purpose of which is to make us holy. Given that God knew mankind would fall into sin, the goal of our election necessarily entails the eradication of sin.

REDEMPTION ACCOMPLISHED

In the moment of redemption accomplished, God dealt with the *penalty and power* of sin. With respect to the *penalty* of sin, when Christ died on the cross, God cancelled "the record of debt that stood against us with its legal demands" (ἐξαλείψας τὸ καθ᾽ ἡμῶν χειρόγραφον τοῖς δόγμασιν ὃ ἦν ὑπεναντίον ἡμῖν) (Col. 2:14). God turned aside his wrath by setting Christ forth as a "propitiation" (ἱλαστήριον) by his death (Rom. 3:25). With respect to the *power* of sin, God conquered it in the death of his Son. As Paul states, "We know that Christ, being raised from the dead, will never die again; death no longer has dominion over him [θάνατος αὐτοῦ οὐκέτι κυριεύει]. For the death he died he died *to* sin, once for all [τῇ ἁμαρτίᾳ ἀπέθανεν ἐφάπαξ], but the life he lives he lives to God" (Rom. 6:9–10, emphasis added). The dative case of τῇ ἁμαρτίᾳ is significant, highlighting a key aspect of Christ's death. On the cross, Christ was not just a vicarious sacrifice but also a victorious Savior, defeating the enslaving power of sin and bringing liberation to captives. The liberation from the power and reign of sin also included deliverance from the devil (Eph. 2:2, 6), spiritual powers and authorities (Col. 2:15), and the flesh (Rom. 8:3). Regarding the latter, Paul states that Christ came "in the likeness of sinful flesh" (ἐν ὁμοιώματι σαρκὸς ἁμαρτίας), and by his death "for sin" (περὶ ἁμαρτίας),[131] God "condemned sin in the flesh"

---

[130] Texts like these impinge on the order of the eternal decrees, a discussion of which is outside the remit of this chapter. The issues of supralapsarianism or infralapsarianism in Paul will be considered in my chapter on election and predestination in the next volume of "The Doctrines of Grace" series.

[131] The prepositional phrase "for sin" is best read as theological shorthand for "sin offering" (cf. Heb. 10:6, 8; 13:11). This is the common meaning of the Greek phrase in the LXX (Moo, *Romans*, 480 n. 48).

(κατέκρινεν τὴν ἁμαρτίαν ἐν τῇ σαρκί) (8:3). The word "likeness" is an important qualification. Christ himself did not *become* sinful flesh but rather became *like* sinful flesh, not in appearance but in participation. He came, as Murray notes, "into closest possible relation to sinful humanity without becoming himself sinful."[132] Indeed, it was more than a close relation to sinful humanity: "he also came into the closest relation to *sin* that was possible without himself becoming sinful."[133] That is, in becoming human, in being "in-fleshed," Christ "exposed himself to the power of sin,"[134] without succumbing to it. Indeed, on the contrary, he triumphed over it.

REDEMPTION APPLIED

In the moment of redemption applied, God deals with the *power* of sin in our lifetime experience. God overcomes the disinterest, hostility, and inability that sin creates in us. Being enslaved to sin, we lack any work to be righteous before God, a mind to understand God, or any desire to seek after God (Rom. 3:10–11). But the problem runs deeper still: we are "hostile" (ἔχθρα) to God and "unable to submit" (οὐχ ὑποτάσσεται, οὐδὲ γὰρ δύναται) to his law (see Rom. 8:7). Paul's soteric category of "calling"[135] answers to this problem. God's calling on our lives explains why we, who were once opposed to God and his Son, repent and turn to Christ. In Romans 8, Paul includes this "calling" as one of the key links in the golden chain of salvation: "And those whom he predestined he also called [ἐκάλεσεν], and those whom he called [ἐκάλεσεν] he also justified, and those whom he justified he also glorified" (Rom. 8:30).[136] As an integral link in the unbreakable chain, God's calling cannot but be effective. Those whom God foreloved, he called, and those whom he called, he justified and glorified. This is what overcomes our sin-entrenched, stubborn resistance to God's grace—his effectual call in the *ordo salutis*. Added to this is the fact that, once called and justified, we are raised with Christ and seated in the heavenly realms (Eph. 2:5–6). Our lives are now hidden with Christ in God (Col. 3:3–4; cf. Col. 1:27), and the powers of the future eschatological age are now at work in us, overcoming the power of sin as we walk by the Spirit (Rom. 8:10–11).

---

[132] Murray, *Romans*, 273.
[133] Murray, *Romans*, 273 (emphasis original).
[134] Moo, *Romans*, 479.
[135] Verb: καλέω; noun: κλῆσις (2 Tim. 1:9).
[136] For other texts concerning effectual calling in Paul, see Rom. 9:24; 1 Cor. 1:9; Gal. 1:6; 5:8, 13; Eph. 4:1, 4; 1 Thess. 2:12; 4:7; 5:24; 2 Thess. 2:14; 1 Tim. 6:12.

REDEMPTION CONSUMMATED

In the moment of redemption consummated, God deals with the *presence* of sin and its complete eradication from us, soul and body, forever. This is seen in the purpose of Christ's redeeming work, as stated by Paul. Negatively, our being crucified with Christ was "in order that the body of sin might be brought to nothing" (ἵνα καταργηθῇ τὸ σῶμα τῆς ἁμαρτίας) (Rom. 6:6). God's Son became like our sinful flesh "for sin" (περὶ ἁμαρτίας) (Rom. 8:3), namely, to deal with sin—in this text, to "condemn" (κατακρίνω) sin. Positively, the law of the Spirit of life has "set [us] free . . . from the law of sin and death" (ἠλευθέρωσέν σε ἀπὸ τοῦ νόμου τῆς ἁμαρτίας καὶ τοῦ θανάτου) (Rom. 8:2); the purpose of Christ reconciling us to God through his death was to present us "holy and blameless and above reproach before him" (ἁγίους καὶ ἀμώμους καὶ ἀνεγκλήτους κατενώπιον αὐτοῦ) (Col. 1:22). Paul ties our future, glorified state to the work of the Spirit in us now. The Spirit is the one who lives in us and who "will give life" (ζῳοποιήσει) to our mortal bodies (Rom. 8:11). Our faith-union with Christ means that we will be "glorified with him" (συνδοξασθῶμεν) (Rom. 8:17). The liberation from corruption is not just individual or personal; it is also universal. The whole of creation groans, longing to be released from its "bondage to corruption" (δουλείας τῆς φθορᾶς) and "to obtain the freedom of the glory of the children of God" (εἰς τὴν ἐλευθερίαν τῆς δόξης τῶν τέκνων τοῦ θεοῦ) (Rom. 8:21). We await "the redemption of our bodies" (τὴν ἀπολύτρωσιν τοῦ σώματος ἡμῶν) (Rom. 8:23), that is, our bodies of sin and death.

We may also deduce the end of sin by the fact that at his return Jesus will destroy death as "the last enemy" (ἔσχατος ἐχθρός) (1 Cor. 15:26). This must entail the destruction of sin too, since, as Paul states, "the wages of sin is death" (τὰ . . . ὀψώνια τῆς ἁμαρτίας θάνατος) (Rom. 6:23). The end of death will be the end of sin. If, at the final resurrection, death loses its sting, as Paul affirms will be the case with his two punchy rhetorical questions (1 Cor. 15:55), then sin and the law must also be rendered powerless. For, "The sting of death is sin, and the power of sin is the law" (τὸ δὲ κέντρον τοῦ θανάτου ἡ ἁμαρτία, ἡ δὲ δύναμις τῆς ἁμαρτίας ὁ νόμος) (1 Cor. 15:56). Thus, the crescendo of Paul's argument in 1 Corinthians 15 is a simple one: at the last trumpet, death will hold no sway; it will be a conquered foe—and therefore so too will sin and the law.

Paul's focus on "glory" (δόξα) in Romans 8 also implies the complete and final removal of sin in the moment of redemption consummated. In using the language of "glory," Paul indicates that our final state will not simply be a return to our original state of innocence, like Adam had in the prelapsarian period of the first age of the world (cf. 1 Cor. 15:45). In that state, Adam was both able not to sin (*posse non peccare*) and able to sin (*posse peccare*). His original righteousness was unstable because it was mutable. But in his redeeming work, Christ does more than take us back to Adam's mutable state of innocence. This is conveyed indirectly in how Paul speaks of us being "fellow heirs with Christ" (συγκληρονόμοι δὲ Χριστοῦ) (Rom. 8:17) who will one day "judge angels" (ἀγγέλους κρινοῦμεν) (1 Cor. 6:3). Christ in his glorification entered an immutable state of perfected righteousness, above the angels. By faith-union with him, we will one day be "fellow heirs" (συγκληρονόμοι) (Rom. 8:17), and so will enter that same state. This being so, sin will be eradicated from us completely, soul and body, forever. We will have attained a state higher and greater than the state into which Adam was created in the beginning. As Paul states, "Just as we have borne the image of the man of dust [τὴν εἰκόνα τοῦ χοϊκοῦ], we shall also bear the image of the man of heaven [τὴν εἰκόνα τοῦ ἐπουρανίου]" (1 Cor. 15:49).

In sum, Paul ties the entrance and end of sin and death, respectively, to the two figureheads of redemptive history: Adam and Christ. Through the first Adam, sin and death entered the present age of the world. Adam's fall divided the present age into a prelapsarian period (when Adam enjoyed the state of innocence) and a postlapsarian period (when Adam and his descendants experience the state of sin). But through the second and last Adam, sin and death were conquered, with an expiry date placed on them. In his resurrection and ascension Christ introduced a new, future age of the world, also divided into two periods: the inaugurated, provisional, eschatological period (when man experiences the state of grace and the intermediate state) and the consummated, final eschatological period (when man will enjoy the state of glory) (again, see diagram 15.4). If sin and death have their *terminus ad quo* in the first Adam, they will have their *terminus ad quem* in the last Adam. Through the first Adam, sin and death entered the world; through the second and last Adam, sin and death will exit the world—never to return.

Conclusion

In bringing this chapter to a close, we return to the opening remarks. Through self-identification or attribution by later students, the apostle Paul has acquired many epithets. This presentation has demonstrated that "theologian of sin" or "father of Christian hamartiology" should also be added to the extensive list. At the heart of Paul's theology is an interplay between hamartiology, Christology, soteriology, and eschatology. In pictorial fashion the apostle paints his hamartiology, Christology, and soteriology on the canvas of his two-age, historical eschatology. This is the framework at the center of Paul's theology. However, he does not "paint" (construct) it out of mere recreational or intellectual interest. Paul thinks and writes on the subject of sin first and foremost as a sinner, as one who has experienced the life of indwelling sin under the law as an unbeliever. Hence his exclamation and exasperation: "Wretched man that I am! Who will deliver me from this body of death?" But the apostle also thinks and writes on the subject as a Christian, as one who has experienced the life of imputed righteousness and internal regeneration in Christ by the Spirit. Hence his answer and exultation: "Thanks be to God through our Lord Jesus Christ."

16

"That None of You May Be Hardened by the Deceitfulness of Sin"

SIN IN HEBREWS, JAMES, 1–2 PETER, AND JUDE

Brandon D. Crowe

In this chapter I will investigate what Hebrews, James, 1–2 Peter, and Jude reveal about sin, its consequences, and its answer in Christ. These letters typically receive less attention than Paul's letters in secondary literature, and some aspects of these letters can be quite difficult to interpret. Yet collectively they reveal much about the depravity of the human heart. Sin and its pleasures are fleeting, and lead to enslavement and judgment. Sin is a serious problem from which we must be rescued. Sin is not only a danger for those outside the church, but also for those within the church. Jesus Christ is our deliverer, the faithful high priest who is holy, entirely separate from sin. Even some of the difficult passages in these letters make important contributions about the dangers of sin.

In this chapter I will discuss, first, the origins and nature of sin; second, the consequences of sin; third, sin in the new covenant; and fourth, Christ as the answer to sin.

1. The Origins and Nature of Sin
1.1. TRIALS AND TEMPTATIONS
The Epistle of James is concerned with the application of God's law, in light of the work of Christ, to the life of the new covenant community. As such, he has much to say about sin—including its origins.

James begins by encouraging his audience to consider it all joy when they face various *trials* (πειρασμοῖς) (1:2). The ESV is indicative of the way πειρασμοῖς is often translated: "when you meet *trials* of various kinds [ὅταν πειρασμοῖς περιπέσητε ποικίλοις]."[1] However, the KJV rendering is also possible: "*temptations.*" This is consistent with the use of the verbal form πειράζω a few verses later, which speaks of *temptations to sin* (James 1:13–15). Yet similar phrasing to James 1:2 is used in 1 Peter 1:6 (ποικίλοις πειρασμοῖς) to refer to *persecutions* facing God's people. Something similar to 1 Peter 1:6 seems to be operative in James 1:2. In both 1 Peter and James sufferings *test* faith, and an eschatological reward is in view (cf. James 1:4).[2]

Πειρασμός is also used in James 1:12: "Blessed is the man who remains steadfast under trial [πειρασμόν], for when he has stood the test he will receive the crown of life, which God has promised to those who love him." This text emphasizes the need to persevere in the face of πειρασμός (cf. 1:4). This macarism, "Blessed," recalls the beatitude from the Sermon on the Mount in which the one who is persecuted for Jesus's sake is blessed (Matt. 5:10–12). This echo further suggests that "trial" is the best translation of πειρασμός in James 1:2.

1.2. SIN AND INTERNAL PASSIONS

The emphasis is a bit different in James 1:13–15, where the verb πειράζω seems to refer to sinful, unlawful temptations. To be sure, trials may also cause us to turn away from God, which would be sinful. However, there is a long tradition understanding James 1:2–4, 12 and 1:13–15 differently. In his lengthy discussion of this issue, Dale Allison notes that in the history of interpretation most exegetes have seen 1:2–4 as "outer trial" and 1:13–15 as "inner temptation."[3] Whereas perseverance unto life is in view in 1:12, in 1:13–15 temptation yielding sin and death is in view (cf. Canons of Dort [hereafter CD] 1.1; 2.1). God is not susceptible to evil temptation (ἀπείραστος), and he never tempts anyone (James 1:13–14; cf. 1:17; cf. CD 1.5; HC 6–8; WCF 2.1; 3.1).[4] Sin does not come from God, but from one's

[1] See similarly CSB, NIV, NRSV.
[2] Compare Dale C. Allison Jr. *A Critical and Exegetical Commentary on the Epistle of James*, ICC (London: Bloomsbury T&T Clark, 2013), 159–60.
[3] See Allison, *James*, 214, along with the whole discussion (214–54). See also Douglas J. Moo, *The Letter of James*, PNTC (Grand Rapids, MI: Eerdmans, 2000), 72–73.
[4] Some argue that ἀπείραστος means that we ought not to test God (cf. Deut. 6:16). So, Peter H. Davids, "The Meaning of ΑΠΕΙΡΑΣΤΟΣ in James 1.13," *NTS* 24 (1978): 386–92; followed by Nicholas Ellis, *The Hermeneutics of Divine Testing: Cosmic Trials and Biblical Interpretation in the Epistle of James and Other Jewish Literature*, WUNT 2/396 (Tübingen: Mohr Siebeck, 2015), 160–61. While it is true that we must not test God, this is not the best rendering of ἀπείραστος in the context of James 1; see further Allison, *James*, 242.

own evil desire (CD 3–4.1, 3).[5] The term ἐπιθυμία has generated much discussion. In this case, it does not refer to desire in general but to *sinful* desire.[6] James also assumes we can be influenced toward sin by the devil and demons (cf. James 3:15; 4:7).[7] Even so, we are responsible for our own sin.

It is therefore best to understand different nuances between πειρασμός in James 1:2, 12 and πειράζω in James 1:13–14—the noun refers to trials, the verb to temptation. (This wordplay in Greek is difficult to capture in English.[8]) This means that sin comes from within us—from our sinful hearts. As I will argue later, in this sense our struggles with temptation are different than Christ's temptations.

James returns to our sinful hearts in 4:1–10, where he states that conflicts arise among the people because of their selfishness. These conflicts come "from your passions warring against your members" (James 4:1, my translation). This phrase most likely refers to the passions of individuals warring within themselves (cf. 3:14), though it could refer to the infighting of members of the community.[9] Here and elsewhere James critiques the double-minded (δίψυχος) (1:8; 4:8): those who doubt, are unstable (1:8), and their hearts need to be cleansed (4:8). The double-minded could refer to the ungodly among the covenant community—the hypocritical and wicked from the Psalms (e.g., Pss. 12:2; 119:113; cf. *2 Clem.* 11.2),[10] who are not pure in heart (Matt. 5:8; cf. Pss. 15; 24:4; 86:11; *2 Clem.* 11.1). If so, the term would refer to those who are not true believers.

Another possibility is that δίψυχος refers collectively to the covenant community, and James points out inconsistencies and ungodliness even among those who truly profess faith (cf. James 2:7). This would likely include true believers in the category of δίψυχος.[11] If so, then James uses strong language for the

---

[5] See Allison, *James*, 246–48.

[6] See John Calvin, *Institutes of the Christian Religion*, ed. John T. McNeill, trans. Ford Lewis Battles, 2 vols., LCC 20–21 (Louisville: Westminster/John Knox, 1960), 3.3.13 (1:606); Allison, *James*, 246–48. Many have correlated ἐπιθυμία to the Hebrew יֵצֶר, referring to the created thoughts of a person. Attention has especially been given to the dualism of "evil" יֵצֶר versus "good" יֵצֶר. See Joel Marcus, "The Evil Inclination in the Epistle of James," *Catholic Biblical Quarterly* 44 (1982): 606–21; Ellis, *Hermeneutics*, 51–56; Scot McKnight, *The Letter of James*, NICNT (Grand Rapids, MI: Eerdmans 2011), 118–22. However, Dan G. McCartney, *James*, BECNT (Grand Rapids, MI: Baker Academic, 2009), 106 n. 8, is likely correct that "the evil and good impulses within a person are not the focus of James's interest, and a reference to the evil impulse here, even if James concurred with the notion, would be a distraction from his main focus on the responsibility of the individual."

[7] See Ellis, *Hermeneutics*, esp. 180–84; Allison, *James*, 246–48.

[8] Notice, too, the consonance of π in James 1:2.

[9] "Division within the community is the product of division within individuals" (Allison, *James*, 598). See also Moo, *Letter of James*, 181, who notes the parallel in 1 Pet. 2:11.

[10] The verbal parallels, however, are not particularly close between James and Ps. 119:113. See also Francis Turretin, *Institutes of Elenctic Theology*, ed. James T. Dennison Jr., trans. George Musgrave Giger, 3 vols. (Phillipsburg, NJ: P&R, 1992–97), 15.15.7 (2:590).

[11] See G. K. Beale and Benjamin L. Gladd, *The Story Retold: A Biblical-Theological Introduction to the New Testament* (Downers Grove, IL: IVP Academic, 2019), 401–402. For a different view, see Allison, *James*, 45–46.

ongoing corruption and sinfulness in the community, which continues to affect even the regenerate. In support of this option, James refers to his audience as sinners (ἁμαρτολοί; 4:8) in need of cleansing. Though James does not say much about the mechanics of this cleansing, the possibility of cleansing is assumed, and James peppers his letter with God's grace (4:6) and mercy (2:13; 5:11, 15).

A choice between these options is difficult, though the first option seems to have more to commend it. It seems that "double-minded" properly refers to the ungodly, but James may use it improperly to urge believers not to behave as the double-minded. Either way, James warns against the danger of presumption and hypocrisy in the community. Our words and actions betray the nature of our faith. It is easy to talk religiously and avoid what God really requires (James 1:26–27; 2:1–13). At the same time, we may talk religiously but our idle words reveal the true state of our hearts (James 1:26; 3:1–12). Our words are a barometer of our hearts.[12] They are often more sinful than we care to admit, and we can even be deceived into thinking that dead faith is saving faith (James 2:17).

1.3. SIN AND THE LAW

The standard by which we should measure ourselves, and by which we will be judged, is the law of God (James 2:12; cf. 4:11). Though sin yields death and destruction (James 1:15; 5:3, 20), James has much that is positive to say about the royal law, the perfect law—the law of liberty (James 1:25; 2:8, 12). James must mean the (perfect) law of God from the OT. Yet he also views this law in relation to Christ, who fulfilled the law.[13] Yet even though Christ has fulfilled the law, James assumes the continuing validity of God's moral law.[14] The law reveals our sinfulness (cf. James 2:8–13). It shows us what we ought to do, but knowledge is not enough. We often know what we ought to do, but do not do it. This is transgression (cf. WSC Q&A 14).

James 4:17 states, "So whoever knows the right thing to do and fails to do it, for him it is sin." This raises an interesting question: Why does James write "for *him* it is sin"? This seems to relativize sin, at least to a degree. Is sin contingent upon a person's knowledge? Is it possible for something to be sin for one person, and not another? It seems that James is primarily concerned with highlighting the responsibility of his audience to act in accordance with

---

[12] See Richard J. Bauckham, *Wisdom of James: Disciple of Jesus the Sage*, New Testament Readings (London: Routledge, 1999), 101.

[13] See also Moo, *Letter of James*, 94; McCartney, *James*, 123.

[14] See similarly Bauckham, *Wisdom of James*, 149.

what they know: if they know that boasting in their supposed autonomy is evil (James 4:13–16), then they must act in accord with that knowledge. To do otherwise—to violate their conscience—is to sin.[15] James does not provide an extended exposition on the nature of sin. However, elsewhere we read that sin is the transgression of the law of God (1 John 3:4). James would agree with this. James addresses people who know the law of God and should be living in accord with it. James 4:17 also assumes that it is a sin not to do the *good* thing we ought to do; "sins of *omission* are as real and serious as sins of *commission*."[16]

1.4. SIN OF ANGELS AND SIN OF HUMANITY

Both Peter and Jude refer to the sin and punishment of angels to motivate faithful living (2 Pet. 2:4; Jude 6). This is another topic on which we may have many questions. What was the sin of angels? Does this reflect common Jewish interpretations of Genesis 6, in which angels copulated with women? How does this relate to the flood and the spread of sin in the world? Neither Peter nor Jude tells us what the angelic sin was specifically, though Jude indicates it was a rejection of authority (Jude 6). The comparison that Jude makes with Sodom and Gomorrah ("in the same way [ὅμοιον τρόπον]"; Jude 7, my translation) does not require that the angelic sin was sexual in nature, only that they rejected God's authority.[17]

This discussion is important for the doctrine of human depravity, since one of the key passages in the Bible about human depravity comes in Genesis 6:5, in a context that many think has in view the sexual sin of angels. Yet in Genesis the cause of the flood was not angelic sin, but human sin.[18] Today probably most NT scholars understand the sin of angels in 2 Peter and Jude (and perhaps the spirits in prison in 1 Pet. 3) to reflect Jewish interpretations of Genesis 6 that understood "the sons of God" to refer to angels who intermarried with human women and produced giant offspring. However, it is not clear that Genesis 6 refers to angelic-human marriages.[19] Nor is it clear

---

[15] Cf. Allison, *James*, 665.

[16] Moo, *Letter of James*, 208 (emphasis original).

[17] See similarly Geerhardus Vos, *Biblical Theology: Old and New Testaments* (Edinburgh: Banner of Truth, 1975), 49.

[18] See D. A. Carson, "Jude," in *Commentary on the New Testament Use of the Old Testament*, ed. G. K. Beale and D. A. Carson (Grand Rapids, MI: Baker Academic, 2007), 1070–72.

[19] The early Christian writing *Cave of Treasures* (possibly seventh century) argues that the sin in Gen. 6:4 cannot be angelic, sexual sin: "The former authors erred concerning this when they wrote that angels came down from heaven and mingled with the daughters of humankind, and that from them were born those famous heroes. It is not true . . . this does not lie within the nature of spiritual beings, nor in the nature of demons who are impure, evil-doers and lovers of adultery, because among them there is neither male nor female, and not a single one has been added to their number since they fell. If the devils could mingle with women they would not leave a single virgin in the

that "different flesh" (σαρκὸς ἑτέρας) in Jude 7 (cf. ESV mg.) refers to residents of Sodom, Gomorrah, *and* the surrounding cities lusting after angels.[20] It is more likely that the sons of God in Genesis 6 are humans.

Thus, despite the popularity of the angelic-sexual sin view today, it presents significant difficulties. I am not convinced it does justice either to Genesis or to the NT.[21] Neither 2 Peter nor Jude commit to non-biblical interpretive traditions of Genesis 6 that speak of the sexual sin of angels (such as is found in *1 Enoch*). It is therefore not clear that Genesis 6 is the requisite background for the angelic sin in Jude and 2 Peter. The focus is instead on human sinfulness and responsibility. Nevertheless, the sin of angels is real, and illustrates the real judgment that accrues to sin—whether angelic sin or human sin. If not even the angels were spared, why should we think we will be spared if we incorrigibly sin against God?

2. Consequences of Sin

2.1. DEATH

As we saw above with James, sin comes from within us and brings death. This is true both physically and spiritually. Perhaps both of these aspects of sin can be seen in James 1:13–15—especially if there is an allusion to Adam's first sin, which brought both physical and spiritual death (cf. CD 1.1; 2.1).[22] James later refers to the one who saves a sinner from error as someone who saves a soul from death (James 5:20).[23] Death here is not simply physical death (though it may include that), but must have in view ultimate, spiritual death.[24] Thus again we find a direct correlation between sin and death.

Similarly, Hebrews assumes that sin brings suffering, slavery, and death, and that the devil holds the power of death (Heb. 2:14–15). Sin brings wrath and punishment (e.g., Heb. 10:26–31). This biblical teaching is reflected in

---

whole human race whom they would not violate" (15:2–4) (translation [and dating] from Alexander Toepel, "The Cave of Treasures," *Old Testament Pseudepigrapha: More Noncanonical Scriptures*, ed. Richard J. Bauckham, James R. Davila, and Alesander Panayotov, vol. 1 [Grand Rapids, MI: Eerdmans, 2013], 551).

[20] See Herman Bavinck, *Reformed Dogmatics*, ed. John Bolt, trans. John Vriend, 4 vols. (Grand Rapids, MI: Baker Academic, 2003–8), 2:456–57; Kevin DeYoung, *What Does the Bible Really Teach about Homosexuality?* (Wheaton, IL: Crossway, 2015), 37–38. As DeYoung notes, there is no mention in the Genesis text of *other surrounding cities* seeking to engage in sexual activity with angels.

[21] See further Vos, *Biblical Theology*, 46–49, 52; Simon J. Kistemaker, *Exposition of the Epistles of Peter and the Epistle of Jude*, New Testament Commentary (Grand Rapids, MI: Baker, 1987), 377–88; John Murray, *Principles of Conduct: Aspects of Biblical Ethics* (Grand Rapids, MI: Eerdmans, 1957), 243–49.

[22] Though compare Allison, *James*, 253.

[23] Whoever is "saved" in James 5:20—whether the wayward or the one helping—cannot be saved by the actions of a sinful person. Only God can truly save (1 Pet. 1:18–19; see also James 4:12). See further below.

[24] See Peter H. Davids, *The Epistle of James: A Commentary on the Greek Text*, NIGTC (Grand Rapids, MI: Eerdmans, 1982), 200; Allison, *James*, 787.

the teachings of the Canons of Dort, which draw attention to the punishment God metes out against sin (CD 2.1), and the bondage that ensues on account of sin (CD 3/4.1, 3).[25] We need a rescuer, for since the days of Adam no one can free himself from the devil's grasp (CD 2.2).[26] Jesus's death is the climactic means by which sin was defeated (cf. Heb. 9:26–28; 10:10; 12:2–4), showing that only through death can the deathly power of sin be overcome (Heb. 2:14). Though Jesus defeated sin and helps us in our suffering (Heb. 2:18), sin continues to bring suffering and temptation in this age and can tempt us to fall away from the living God (Heb. 10:23–39; cf. 3:12).

Hebrews does not shy away from our culpability for sin or its continued dangers. Nevertheless, it does not facilely assume that all suffering is a direct result of our own sin. Sometimes, struggling against sin brings difficulty. Jesus's suffering was not a result of his own sin, but his obedience actually entailed suffering and difficulty (Heb. 5:8; 12:3–4). This should encourage us to struggle against sin. Difficulties in this age are God's fatherly discipline and indications of his paternal love (Heb. 12:5–10), which will yield the "peaceful fruit of righteousness" if we persevere (Heb. 12:11).

And persevere we must. Sin is an entanglement. It weighs us down (Heb. 12:1–2) and can hinder us from our eschatological goal of everlasting rest (cf. Heb. 4:1). Though we cannot save ourselves from sin, as we follow Christ we must take the initiative to lay it aside. The struggle will be long and fierce, illustrated in the way the Christian life is compared both to a race and to a boxing match (Heb. 12:1, 4).[27] William Lane observes, "The exhortation to run δι᾽ ὑπομονῆς, 'with endurance,' identifies the race not as a contest of speed, but of endurance."[28]

It is possible that Peter may speak, like Paul, of spiritual deadness (see Eph. 2:1). This possibility is seen in 1 Peter 4:6a: "For this is why the gospel was preached even to those who are dead." Yet here the focus does not seem to be on *spiritual* deadness. Instead, Peter has in view believers who have departed this life, but whose spiritual life comes by means of the gospel.[29] Suffering lasts only for a season, but yields glory for believers in Christ,

---

[25] See also WCF 6.6.

[26] Compare William L. Lane, *Hebrews 1–8*, WBC 47A (Nashville: Thomas Nelson, 1991), 61.

[27] See further William L. Lane, *Hebrews 9–13*, WBC 47B (Dallas: Word, 1991), 407–9, 417; Craig R. Koester, *Hebrews: A New Translation with Introduction and Commentary*, AB 36 (New York: Doubleday, 2001), 525.

[28] Lane, *Hebrews 9–13*, 409; see similarly Koester, *Hebrews*, 522.

[29] So, rightly, Thomas R. Schreiner, *1, 2 Peter, Jude*, NAC 37 (Nashville: Broadman & Holman, 2003), 205–8; see also Paul J. Achtemeier, *1 Peter*, Hermeneia (Minneapolis: Fortress, 1996), 290–91.

just as it did for Jesus himself (1 Pet. 4:1; cf. 2:21; 3:18–22).[30] In another passage Peter says that the one who suffers has stopped (πέπαυται) sinning (1 Pet. 4:1). This does not mean that Christians are entirely free from sin, but most likely that Christians who suffer, following in the steps of Christ, no longer walk contrary to the will of God (cf. 1 Pet. 4:2).[31] They no longer live according to the ignorance of their own passions (1 Pet. 1:14; 2:11; 4:2–8). Holiness is characterized by Christlikeness, whereas sin is characterized by self-indulgence. Suffering as a Christian need not be due to sin or due to a lack of faith, but is often indicative of obedience to the will of God in a sinful age. Jesus brings freedom from sin, and we must not distort that freedom into an excuse for evil deeds (1 Pet. 2:16).

2.2. DECEIT

Sin is also deceitful (Heb. 3:13); it tries to pull us away from what is good, and toward the easy and immediate. A danger for God's people is to know what we ought to do but then turn our backs when it is difficult to follow Christ. The example of Moses should encourage and instruct us, for he chose the difficult path of suffering and rejected the fleeting, sinful pleasures of Egypt (Heb. 11:25). The pleasures we may pursue apart from Christ do not last, whereas we will receive an eternal inheritance if we persevere by faith (Heb. 6:12; 9:15; 11:10, 16; 12:22; 13:14). Walking by faith may not be easy, especially since sin is deceitful (Heb. 3:13). Sin lies to us. It promises life and blessing, but instead delivers death and destruction (cf. James 1:15). This deception is one of the most practical aspects to remember about sin.

2.3. DEFILED CONSCIENCES

Not only does sin yield death, but sin defiles our consciences, which can be cleansed only by Christ (Heb. 9:9, 14; 10:2, 22). A clean conscience is important for finding freedom from the guilt and slavery of sin that Satan holds over us. Freedom in this sense comes objectively by the actions of Christ on our behalf, which is part of the greater fullness of access to God that we have in the new covenant era.[32] The word of God lays bare our sinfulness (Heb. 4:12–13), but Christ enables greater boldness and access to the living God

---

[30] Compare Schreiner, *1, 2 Peter, Jude*, 199. See also Brandon D. Crowe, *The Message of the General Epistles in the History of Redemption: Wisdom from James, Peter, John, and Jude* (Phillipsburg, NJ: P&R, 2015), 37–41.
[31] See Achtemeier, *1 Peter*, 279–80.
[32] WCF 20.1.

(cf. Heb. 4:14–16; 9:9, 14; 10:22).[33] Though Christ cleanses our conscience, Hebrews agrees with the broader NT witness that it is also our responsibility to live with a clear conscience before God (Heb. 13:18).[34] We must pursue righteousness, flee from sin, and avoid hypocrisy.

2.4. Spiritual Inability

As we have seen in some ways already, sin brings spiritual inability. Sin renders us unable to do anything truly spiritually good. In this light, 2 Peter 1:3 speaks of Jesus's divine power that grants us all we need for life and godliness.[35] This passage is invoked in the Canons of Dort to underscore our spiritual inability and God's omnipotence to grant us new life (CD 3–4.8).

However, modern-day commentators debate whether life and godliness (ζωὴν καὶ εὐσέβειαν) should be taken as a hendiadys (i.e., "a godly life"),[36] or whether ζωή refers to eternal life (beginning even now) and εὐσέβεια to a godly life in this age.[37] Reading 2 Peter in light of 1 Peter, where life sometimes refers to eternal life (1 Pet. 3:7; cf. 1:3; 4:6),[38] tips the scales in favor of the latter view, thus agreeing with the use of this text in the Canons of Dort to refer to God's power in granting eternal life.

Other texts also speak of our spiritual inability to save ourselves. For example, James, who understands the depths of human sinfulness, points to our need for salvation that comes from outside of ourselves. Those who have broken God's law are exposed to God's judgment (CD 3–4.1–3). Praise God that mercy triumphs over judgment (James 2:12–13)! Whereas sin begets death (James 1:15), God grants new life by his own will (James 1:18). For only God can save (James 4:12). James urges us to receive the "implanted word, which is able to save [our] souls" (James 1:21).[39] This implanted word is not some inherent quality that we have, but an alien word to be received by faith—most likely the gospel message and the law of the new covenant that it entails.[40]

---

[33] Compare Koester, *Hebrews*, 405.

[34] See, e.g., Acts 23:1; 24:16; Rom. 2:15; 9:1; 13:5; 1 Cor. 8:12; 10:28–29; 2 Cor. 1:12; 4:2; 1 Tim. 1:19; 3:9; 4:2; 2 Tim. 1:3; Titus 1:15; 1 Pet. 3:16.

[35] "His" divine power is ambiguous, but most likely refers to Jesus, who is the nearest antecedent. Cf. Schreiner, *1, 2 Peter, Jude*, 291; Richard J. Bauckham, *Jude, 2 Peter*, WBC 50 (Nashville: Thomas Nelson, 1983), 177.

[36] So, Bauckham, *Jude, 2 Peter*, 178; Peter H. Davids, *The Letters of 2 Peter and Jude*, PNTC (Grand Rapids, MI: Eerdmans, 2006), 168.

[37] So, Schreiner, *1, 2 Peter, Jude*, 291–92.

[38] 2 Peter does not use "life" anywhere other than 1:3. So notes Davids, *2 Peter and Jude*, 168.

[39] See further Crowe, *Message of the General Epistles*, 163–66.

[40] See also Moo, *Letter of James*, 87–88; McCartney, *James*, 118; contrast Allison, *James*, 311–16.

Likewise, 1 Peter assumes sinful humanity's inability to save itself. Near the opening of the letter, Peter speaks of Christians who have been born again through divine agency (1 Pet. 1:3; cf. 1:2, 22–23)—just as we cannot make ourselves be born, neither can we grant ourselves spiritual life.[41] Peter also says that to live in sin apart from Christ is to live in ignorance (1 Pet. 1:14; cf. 2:15), which also underscores our spiritual inability. Renewed people must walk in obedience, reflecting the holiness of God's character (1 Pet. 1:14–16). Since sin wages war against our souls, we must abstain from fleshly desires (1 Pet. 2:11–12).

Even so, our imperfect obedience does not save. Baptism does not wash away our sins like dirt but is an appeal (ἐπερώτημα) for a clean conscience before God.[42] Baptism symbolizes the cleansing of our consciences through the work of Christ, much like Hebrews 10:22 says.[43] However we interpret the difficult phrasing of 1 Peter 3:21, baptism does not ultimately save us from sin. Christ—crucified, resurrected, and ascended—does (1 Pet. 3:18–22).[44]

2.5. JUDGMENT

Consistently throughout Scripture—including in these letters—sin brings judgment. James speaks of the judgment that accrues to the ungodly wealthy who refuse to have compassion on those around them, in violation of God's law. They have ironically stored up treasure in the last days: they will be subject to judgment and will not profit from their riches (James 5:3).[45]

The dangers of sin are described acutely in 2 Peter and Jude. Not only is the world corrupted because of sin (2 Pet. 1:4), but punishment awaits those who walk the path of sin rather than the path of righteousness (2 Pet. 2:21). Jude even identifies Jesus as the one who destroyed the Israelites who did not believe, after delivering them from Egypt (Jude 5).[46] God knows how to

---

[41] See Schreiner, *1, 2 Peter, Jude*, 60–61.

[42] See Schreiner, *1, 2 Peter, Jude*, 195–96. This takes "good conscience" (συνειδήσεως ἀγαθῆς) as an objective genitive, rather than as a subjective genitive. The latter could be rendered "the good conscience's appeal." It is also possible, though less likely, to translate ἐπερώτημα as "pledge" (see BDAG s.v., #2; cf. NIV). See the discussion of possibilities in Schreiner, *1, 2 Peter, Jude*, 196.

[43] So, Schreiner, *1, 2 Peter, Jude*, 197.

[44] I will return to the work of Christ in 1 Peter in a later section.

[45] See Allison, *James*, 676–77.

[46] There is a well-known text-critical question here: Does Jude 5 read Ἰησοῦς or κύριος? The more likely reading is probably Ἰησοῦς, but even if it were κύριος, in the context of Jude this would refer to Jesus. See further Simon J. Gathercole, *The Preexistent Son: Recovering the Christologies of Matthew, Mark, and Luke* (Grand Rapids, MI: Eerdmans, 2006), 36–40; Bauckham, *Jude, 2 Peter*, 49; Tommy Wasserman, *The Epistle of Jude: Its Text and Transmission*, Coniectanea Biblica NT Series 43 (Stockholm: Almqvist & Wiksell, 2006), 262–66; Schreiner, *1, 2 Peter, Jude*, 444–45.

punish evil and has shown this throughout history (2 Pet. 2:4–9; cf. Jude 6). It is mistaken to conclude that there are no repercussions for sin. Judgment comes according to God's timeline (2 Pet. 3:1–10). We must not forget about the flood of Noah's day (2 Pet. 2:5), nor of the example of Sodom and Gomorrah (2 Pet. 2:6–10; Jude 7). In both cases judgment against sin in history prefigures God's final judgment. Likewise, when Jesus returns, there will be nowhere to hide (2 Pet. 3:10). It therefore matters how we live now. For those who disobey, "the gloom of utter darkness has been reserved forever" (Jude 13b). This is further addressed in Jude 14–15:

> It was also about these that Enoch, the seventh from Adam, prophesied, saying, "Behold, the Lord comes with ten thousands of his holy ones, to execute judgment on all and to convict all the ungodly of all their deeds of ungodliness that they have committed in such an ungodly way, and of all the harsh things that ungodly sinners have spoken against him."

Much is made about the source of Jude's quotation of Enoch, but regardless of where this quote comes from, the prophecy communicates the weightiness of sin: the Lord will come with ten thousands of holy angels to execute judgment on ungodly sinners.[47] To this warning we could again add Jude 5–7, which speaks about the destruction of the hard-hearted wilderness generation, the angels, and the residents of Sodom and Gomorrah when they did not believe. These are all warnings for us today about the dangers of sin. In fact, Jude 5–16 is largely a warning about the judgment that accrues to sin.

3. Sin in the New Covenant

3.1. THE WARNING PASSAGES IN HEBREWS

As we will see in more detail below, Hebrews teaches that the answer to sin is the high priestly work of Christ, who defeated sin on our behalf (CD 2.2–3). Yet that does not absolve us from the need to resist the ongoing dangers of sin. Though the end of the ages has come (Heb. 1:2; 9:26), we live with a "not-yet" reality in which sin continues to threaten.

The dangers of sin are apparent in the warning passages of Hebrews (Heb. 2:1–4; 3:7–4:13; 5:11–6:12; 10:19–39; 12:1–29). These passages speak not only of the ongoing threat of sin in general, but of its presence among the covenant community in particular. We must be vigilant, for sin leads to

---

[47] Compare Crowe, *Message of the General Epistles*, 111–12.

spiritual complacency, sluggishness, and atrophy (Heb. 2:1–3; 5:11; 6:12)—
even for those who have heard the gospel (Heb. 4:2, 6).

Much like Jude, these passages in Hebrews warn God's covenant people
using examples from biblical history. Participating in and benefiting from
God's mighty acts of deliverance does not guarantee a circumcised, believing
heart (Heb. 3:8, 10, 12; cf. 10:22). The danger for the covenant community is
to know the message of salvation but not truly believe (Heb. 3:12). We must
beware a sinful, unbelieving heart that has been "hardened by the deceitfulness of sin" (Heb. 3:13). The Canons of Dort recognize the hardness of heart
and will as a universal effect of the fall on human nature (CD 3–4.1), and
this is a danger even for the regenerate (CD 5.1–2, 4). Hardness of heart is
a persistent danger in the church, as it was for Israel (with whom there is a
close connection in Hebrews; cf. Heb. 4:2, 6). Hebrews warns those *in the
covenant community* not to fall away. If not even the miraculous deliverance
experienced by the Israelites immunized them from the dangers of sin (Heb.
3:16–19), neither will the experience of the "powers of the age to come"
in the new covenant era immunize anyone from the danger of falling away
(Heb. 2:4; 6:4–5).

This brings us to some of the most controversial aspects of the warning
passages. Do they teach that sin is so strong that true believers can lose their
salvation? This is sometimes understood to be the teaching of Hebrews 6:4–6:

> For it is impossible, in the case of those who have once been enlightened,
> who have tasted the heavenly gift, and have shared in the Holy Spirit, and
> have tasted the goodness of the word of God and the powers of the age to
> come, and then have fallen away, to restore them again to repentance, since
> they are crucifying once again the Son of God to their own harm and hold-
> ing him up to contempt.

Hebrews 6 does indeed speak of the danger of sin, and does so in extremely strong terms. However, the list of benefits experienced by the group
in question does not necessitate that we see them as having true, saving
faith.[48] Instead, these impressive experiences can be predicated of those who

---

[48] See John Calvin, *Commentaries on the Epistle of Paul to the Hebrews*, trans. John Owen (Grand Rapids, MI:
Baker, 1999), 136–38; John Owen, *An Exposition of the Epistle to the Hebrews*, ed. W. H. Goold, 7 vols. (1855; repr.
Grand Rapids, MI: Baker, 1980), 5:72–91; Turretin, *Institutes*, 15.15.4, 14 (2:588, 592–93); Roger Nicole, "Some
Comments on Hebrews 6:4–6 and the Doctrine of the Perseverance of God with the Saints," in *Current Issues in
Biblical and Patristic Interpretation: Studies in Honor of Merrill C. Tenney Presented by His Former Students*, ed.
Gerald F. Hawthorne (Grand Rapids, MI: Eerdmans, 1975), 355–64.

participate in the benefits of the covenant community.[49] It is impossible to renew them again to repentance if they turn away from and despise the Son of God—the only one who can take away sin. Reformed theologians have consistently identified the sin here with the blasphemy against the Holy Spirit in the Gospels (Matt. 12:31–32; Mark 3:28–29; Luke 12:10).[50] This is a sin of hard-heartedness, refusing to believe in Jesus even when confronted with the miracles of Jesus (in the Gospels), or when provided miraculous signs from heaven (assumed in Hebrews). Herman Bavinck discusses this sin in detail. Since this is such a widely discussed (and often misunderstood topic), I quote his trenchant observations at length:

> The blasphemy against the Holy Spirit . . . does not itself consist in doubt toward or the denial of that truth, but in a denial that contradicts the conviction of the mind, the illumination of the conscience, and the intuitions of the heart. It then consists in a conscious and deliberate attribution of what has been clearly perceived as God's work to the influence and activity of Satan, that is, in a deliberate blaspheming of the Holy Spirit, a defiant declaration that the Holy Spirit is the spirit from the abyss, that the truth is a lie, that Christ is Satan himself. Its motivation, then, is conscious and intentional hatred against God and what is recognized as divine; its essence is sin in its ultimate manifestation, the complete and consummate revolution, putting God in the place of Satan and Satan in the place of God. Its character is no longer human but demonic.[51]

In the Gospels, this sin is committed when the opponents of Jesus ascribe his mighty works to the devil (Matt. 12:24; Mark 3:22, 30; Luke 11:15). Jesus called his opponents' bluff when they asked for a sign, ostensibly in order to believe (Matt. 12:38–39; cf. Luke 11:16, 29). But it is clear in the Gospels, and in Hebrews, that even signs from heaven do not convince hard, uncircumcised, unbelieving hearts (cf. Acts 7:51)[52] To avoid this sin, we must receive with faith the message about Jesus and cling to him as our high priest, recognizing our need for deliverance (cf. esp. Matt. 12:29; Mark 3:27; Luke 11:22). A similar warning comes in Hebrews 10:19–39, where the covenant community is warned against trampling underfoot the blood of the Son of

---

[49] See Geerhardus Vos, *Reformed Dogmatics*, trans. and ed. Richard B. Gaffin Jr. et al., 5 vols. (Bellingham, WA: Lexham, 2012–16), 4:222–26.

[50] See, e.g., Bavinck, *Reformed Dogmatics*, 3:155–57; 4:268; Turretin, *Institutes*, 9.14 (1:647–52); 15.15.4 (2:588); Vos, *Reformed Dogmatics*, 2:72–75; Owen, *Exposition of the Epistle to the Hebrews*, 5:83.

[51] Bavinck, *Reformed Dogmatics*, 3:156.

[52] Bavinck observes that, "factually and materially," the sin in view in Heb. 6:4–8; 10:25–29 (and 1 John 5:16) "coincide[s] with the sin of blaspheming the Holy Spirit" (*Reformed Dogmatics*, 3:156–57 [157]).

God by which they were sanctified. This is an outrage to the Spirit of grace (Heb. 10:29). Again, the dangers of sin are for those who know the gospel message, and who have even been set apart from the world by means of their participation in the covenant community, but who turn their back on the means of forgiveness (Heb. 10:26).

Why would the early readers of Hebrews turn their backs? It was probably because of suffering. It is eminently likely that the audience of Hebrews was in danger of turning away from Christ because Christianity was proving to be a difficult path (cf. Heb. 10:32–38).[53] But to revert to the old ways would be a rejection of the only message that can save them. Salvation comes not from an obsolete (i.e., temporary) sacrificial system, but from the goal which the system anticipated. This is why it is imperative that they resist sin and persevere by faith; to turn back would be to perish (Heb. 10:39). Hebrews gives no ivory tower theology, but pastoral pleas for a people in danger of abandoning the message of salvation in the face of adversity.

But suffering does not entirely explain the dangers facing the community in Hebrews. Hebrews 12 adds to the warnings, including the danger of the "root of bitterness" that can grow up in the covenant community. This is more than an attitude of bitterness but alludes to Deuteronomy 29:18 (29:17 LXX) and refers specifically to the danger of idolatry in the covenant community. Moses warned the people, as they prepared to enter the promised land, about the dangers of unbelief in their midst. Even those who had been exposed to the word of God might fail to realize the goal in front of them due to hardness of heart.[54] So it is in Hebrews, where unbelief and disobedience are joined at the hip (cf. Heb. 3:18–19).

Hebrews therefore warns God's people that they are not immune from unbelief and turning aside from God's ways (CD 5.1–2, 4). Even God's people are too easily swayed and deceived by sin (Heb. 3:13). We therefore must press on in faith (Heb. 12:1–2), spurring "one another toward love and good deeds" (Heb. 10:24). Just as not all of those of Israel are true Israelites (Rom. 9:6), neither are all those in the new covenant community truly regenerate.

---

[53] I am inclined to see this passage as recalling the difficulties faced by Christians in Rome under the Emperor Claudius (reigned AD 41–54), when the Jews (certainly along with Christians) were expelled from Rome (see Suetonius, *Divus Claudius* 25.4). If so, then the author is perhaps addressing the Roman church's emerging conflict with Nero, somewhere during his reign of AD 54–68.

[54] Compare Lane, *Hebrews 9–13*, 453.

3.2. FORGIVENESS AND THE NEW COVENANT

The warnings in Hebrews thus assume a mixed community, even though the new covenant has already arrived. In fact, it is striking that the arrival of the new covenant is not given as a guarantee of faithfulness in the present age but is leveraged as a *warning* against the dangers of unbelief *in the new covenant community*. The new covenant passage from Jeremiah 31:31–34 (Jer. 38:31–34 LXX) is cited in Hebrews 8:8–12, and the author returns to it in 10:15–17. The audience of Hebrews participates in the new covenant. At the same time, the author warns covenant members not to trample the blood of the new covenant underfoot by despising the message about Christ (Heb. 10:26–29). The new covenant has truly come, but it is not yet fully here. In the meantime, the struggle against sin and unbelief, even in the covenant community, persists. We therefore should draw near in full assurance (Heb. 10:22), "hold[ing] fast the confession of our hope without wavering" (Heb. 10:23).

Hebrews does not teach radical discontinuity between the old covenant and the new covenant. The community dynamics are similar—both have had the gospel preached to them, and both are in danger of the sin of unbelief. The differences are relative rather than absolute.[55] If Hebrews warns those in the new covenant community against turning back and falling away from the grace of God (Heb. 3:12; 4:11; 6:6; 12:15), what then is new about the new covenant?[56] It cannot be that only in the new covenant is the law written on the hearts of God's people, for that was already true of regenerate members in the old covenant whose hearts were circumcised (cf. Deut. 10:16; Ps. 40:8).[57] It also cannot mean that there was no forgiveness objectively in the old covenant.[58]

Instead, the newness centers largely on the new way in which sin has been dealt with definitively. This is the context for the new covenant passage from Jeremiah quoted in Hebrews 8. The first covenant is obsolete because it could never definitively deal with sin; it was designed to be temporary. To cling to the old in the new day is to miss the goal to which the law (especially the sacrificial system) pointed all along. The author then discusses

---

[55] Cf. Calvin, *Institutes*, 2.10; Turretin, *Institutes*, 12.7.45–46 (2:231–32); WCF 7.5–6.
[56] Cf. CD 2, Error 2.
[57] Calvin, *Institutes*, 2.10.23; 2.11.7; Turretin, *Institutes*, 12.7.45–48 (2:231–33); 12.8.22 (2:239); Bavinck, *Reformed Dogmatics*, 4:135, 499, 659; Vos, *Reformed Dogmatics*, 5:163; G. K. Beale, *A New Testament Biblical Theology: The Unfolding of the Old Testament in the New* (Grand Rapids, MI: Baker Academic, 2011), 732.
[58] See, e.g., Ex. 34:7; Lev. 4:20, 26, 39; 5:10; Num. 14:19; 1 Kings 8:34–36, 46–51; 2 Chron. 7:14; Ps. 32:1, 5 (31:1, 5 LXX); 103:3, 12 (102:3,12 LXX); Isa. 1:18; 33:24; see also Turretin, *Institutes*, 12.7.45 (2:231–32); 12.10 (2:247–57).

the inefficacy of the old covenant sacrifices (Heb. 9:1–10), before discussing the better sacrifice offered by Christ (Heb. 9:11–28). He then returns to the inadequacy of the old (Heb. 10:1–4) and highlights the perfect obedience and sacrifice of Christ (Heb. 10:5–14).

This leads the author to quote Jeremiah 31 a second time, in Hebrews 10:15–17. First, he mentions the law being written on our hearts and minds (Jer. 31:33; Heb. 10:16). Since this follows the discussion of Jesus having the law written on his heart, delighting entirely to do the will of God, the emphasis seems to be on the Christological reality that underlies and secures the new covenant.[59] It is not that no one ever had the law of God written on their heart before Jesus, but this had never been true in the way that it is now that Christ has come and obeyed God entirely, perfectly. Now the law written on the heart is the law that Christ has fulfilled, and Jesus's work guarantees that the law will be written permanently on his people's hearts.[60]

Second, the quotation of Jeremiah 31:34 in Hebrews 10:17 emphasizes the true, full forgiveness of sins.[61] This refers to the definitive accomplishment of salvation that Christ has wrought. This also includes greater access to and boldness in approach to the throne of grace; the experience of new covenant believers is different than that of old covenant believers. But again, this difference is relative rather than absolute.

After this second quotation from Jeremiah 31 the author pivots to a warning (Heb. 10:19–39). In Hebrews 8 the focus is primarily on the work of Christ to put an end to sin, enacting a permanent covenant (Heb. 8:7, 13). The new covenant was necessary because, by their sin, the people had rejected the first covenant (Heb. 8:8–9). Yet this definitive work of Christ, in which God remembers our sins no more, does not obviate the need for the author to warn his audience, as he does in Hebrews 10:19–39. In Hebrews 10 the author invokes Jeremiah 31 to warn his audience against presumption and turning their backs on the message of salvation. By identifying with Christ, they had been set apart as the new covenant community. But where the sacrifice for sin is rejected, there is no forgiveness. Instead, there is judgment (Heb. 10:26–31). The superiority, permanence, and greater confidence of the

---

[59] See Sinclair B. Ferguson, *The Whole Christ: Legalism, Antinomianism, and Gospel Assurance—Why the Marrow Controversy Still Matters* (Wheaton, IL: Crossway, 2016), 167; cf. Bavinck, *Reformed Dogmatics*, 3:394–95; Turretin, *Institutes*, 11.24.30 (2:156); 14.13.18 (2:450–51).

[60] This particularly applies to the moral aspects of the law (cf. Ferguson, *Whole Christ*, 144–45).

[61] See also Wilhelmus à Brakel, *The Christian's Reasonable Service*, ed. Joel R. Beeke, trans. Bartel Elshout, 4 vols. (Grand Rapids, MI: Reformation Heritage, 1992–95), 1:435.

new covenant era (Heb. 10:19–25) do not guarantee true faith among the covenant community (Heb. 10:26–31).

If then the warnings remain, is not the new covenant just as unstable as the first covenant? Not at all! For now Christ has dealt definitively with sin, and now he ever lives to intercede for us (cf. Heb. 7:25–26). Jesus has completed his work of humiliation and understands and sympathizes with us. Jesus is a better, more effectual, more glorious, and more exalted priest than any priest of the old covenant. The structure of Hebrews highlights that the answer to the warnings comes not from ourselves—where sin remains a danger—but from the ministry of our great high priest—for each of the warning passages is closely related to a reflection of Jesus as high priest.[62] Jesus is the answer to the ongoing problem of sin for the believer.

3.3. The Slavery of False Teachers

We have seen that 2 Peter 1:3 teaches that Jesus's divine power has also given us all we need for a godly life. Godly living is an emphasis throughout 2 Peter.[63] In Peter's crosshairs are false teachers (2 Pet. 2:1) who blaspheme the way of truth (2 Pet. 2:2) and the holy commandment (2 Pet. 2:21)— those who pervert the gospel and lead others astray by their ungodly, licentious living (2:2, 18). Instead of following the law of God, they follow their own passions (2 Pet. 2:2, 10, 18; 3:3; cf. Jude 16).[64] They never stop sinning (ἀκαταπαύστους ἁμαρτίας) (2 Pet. 2:14). They preach freedom but are slaves to sin (2 Pet. 2:19; cf. 1 Pet. 2:16), which will bring judgment (2 Pet. 2:1, 3, 9, 12–13; cf. 1:4; 3:7, 16; CD 2.1). The Christian life must conform to the moral law of God, and to live in sin is to deny the gospel. Central to the understanding of sin in these letters is the casting off of the authority of God, following instead whatever one desires (e.g., 2 Pet. 2:2, 10, 18; Jude 8, 16).

Similarly, Jude writes to contend for the holiness of the gospel message (Jude 3) and warns against those who slip in among the community and deny Jesus by their sinful actions (Jude 4). Jude also seems to have false teachers in view (Jude 12). In both 2 Peter and Jude, sin is not primarily a danger that

---

[62] Hebrews 2:1–4 moves directly into a discussion of Jesus's victorious humanity (Heb. 2:5–18). Hebrews 3:7–4:13 moves directly to our great high priest who gives us confidence (Heb. 4:4–16). Hebrews 5:11–6:12 transitions to a discussion of Jesus as the anchor and high priest better than Melchizedek (Heb. 6:19–8:13). The warnings in Heb. 10:19–39 are preceded by a discussion of the perfect obedience of Jesus and his final sacrifice (Heb. 10:1–18). Hebrews 12 includes discussion of Jesus as our ἀρχηγός (Heb. 12:2) and the mediator of a better covenant (Heb. 12:24).
[63] Cf. WCF 16.3; WLC 57.
[64] See Bauckham, *Jude, 2 Peter*, 11.

comes from outside the covenant community but one that arises from within the community. By describing the false teachers as those who deny their master (2 Pet. 2:1; Jude 4), and as accursed children (2 Pet. 2:14), Peter and Jude warn of sinful, covenantal infidelity within the church.[65] Sin remains an ever-present danger, even in the covenant community. We need the grace of God in order that we might be kept from stumbling (Jude 24; cf. CD 2.1).

4. Christ as the Answer to Sin

4.1. Spiritual Inability and Need for Salvation

Despite the calls to faithful living in these letters, none of them teach salvation by our own works. Instead, Christ is the answer to our sinful hearts. The work of Christ is necessary for salvation because, as we have seen, we are spiritually unable to merit eternal life.

In this light, Peter says much about the sacrificial suffering of Jesus for us. He suffered for sin (1 Pet. 1:11, 19–21; 2:21–25; 3:18–22; cf. 1:2), which shows us the penalty for breaking the law of God. He suffered on our behalf (ὑπὲρ ὑμῶν) (2:21), which is explained succinctly in 1 Peter 2:24, quoting from Isaiah 53:5: "He himself bore our sins in his body on the tree, that we might die to sin and live to righteousness. By his wounds you have been healed" (cf. 1:19). Jesus rose again and ascended to heaven (1 Pet. 1:3, 11, 21; 2:7; 3:18, 22; cf. 2:23). Jesus thus defeated sin and death and offers forgiveness. Further, Jesus will return (1 Pet. 1:7, 13; 2:12; 5:1, 4), and sin will be judged (1 Pet. 4:1–6; cf. 1:17; 2:23; 3:19; 4:7). We therefore should do good, so that those around us may turn from sin and to Christ (1 Pet. 2:12, 20; 3:13; 4:19), looking ahead to the reward of righteousness (1 Pet. 1:4–9, 13; 5:10; cf. 5:1, 3). Life is difficult, but suffering is not necessarily attributed to our sin. Suffering may be (like it was for Jesus) an indication of our obedience as exiles (see esp. 1 Pet. 3:14, 17; 4:12–19; cf. 2:20).

4.2. Christology and Priesthood in Hebrews

Hebrews is unique in the NT for its extended discussion of Jesus as high priest. As high priest, Jesus alone deals definitively with sin. As high priest, Jesus is fully human, yet he does not share the sinful nature that characterizes all natural offspring of Adam. Only Jesus ministers in the heavenly sanctuary.

---

[65] The identity of the false teachers as "twice dead" (δὶς ἀποθανόντα) in Jude 12 may denote their spiritual deadness; cf. Schreiner, *1, 2 Peter, Jude*, 467; see also the possibility in Bauckham, *Jude, 2 Peter*, 88.

He provides freedom of conscience and greater access with boldness to the throne of grace. Even so, sin continues in the present age. We have not yet reached our heavenly rest. The incessant tug of sin is a danger within the church. Hebrews therefore warns God's covenant people against turning their backs on the message they have received.

Much of Hebrews's Christology centers on the humanity of Jesus as the great high priest. At the same time, the Christology of Hebrews is multifaceted. Hebrews begins not with the humanity of the Son, but with his divinity. The Son by whom God has spoken in the last days is the radiance of God's glory (ἀπαύγασμα τῆς δόξης) and the perfect representation of his being (χαρακτὴρ τῆς ὑποστάσεως αὐτοῦ) (Heb. 1:3a).[66] This ontological reality likely forms the center of a chiasm (Heb. 1:3a–b), which underlies the work of the Son in creation, providence, and redemption (Heb. 1:1–2, 3c–4). The Son's divinity ensures the efficacy of his sacrifice and fits the heavenliness of his ministry.[67] Further, the Son's radiance evokes brilliant light and points to his holiness. Elsewhere the NT teaches that God is light, and there is no darkness in him (1 John 1:5; cf. 1 Tim. 6:16; Heb. 6:18). The one who makes purification for sins is thus not only a perfect human (see below), but the preexistent, divine Son of God who is glorious in holiness. This divine Son will one day return to save those who eagerly await him (Heb. 9:28).[68]

Hebrews thus begins by underscoring the Son's divinity and his superiority to the angels (Heb. 1:4–14). After the Son deals with sin he enters into the heavenly world, where the angels worship him (Heb. 1:6; cf. 2:5).[69] The author cites Psalm 8:5–7 (ET 8:4–6) to show that the world is to be subject to a man (Heb. 2:5–8).[70] Psalm 8 recalls God's original created order, in which Adam stood as the first representative, with dominion over creation (Gen. 1:26–30). Adam was given a glorious goal of eschatological life, upon the condition of perfect obedience. Adam's sin disqualified him from realizing

---

[66] Compare BDAG "χαρακτήρ," 1077–78; "ὑποστάσεως," 1040.

[67] See Geerhardus Vos, "The Priesthood of Christ in the Epistle to the Hebrews," in *Redemptive History and Biblical Interpretation: The Shorter Writings of Geerhardus Vos*, ed. Richard B. Gaffin Jr. (Phillipsburg, NJ: P&R, 1980), 150–52.

[68] Note also WLC 38. One could also add Heb. 13:8, which assumes the divinity of the Son. Compare F. F. Bruce, *The Epistle to the Hebrews*, NICNT (Grand Rapids, MI: Eerdmans, 1964), 395; Lane, *Hebrews 9–13*, 528.

[69] On οἰκουμένη as the heavenly world, see Lane, *Hebrews 1–8*, 27; Koester, *Hebrews*, 193; Paul Ellingworth, *The Epistle to the Hebrews*, NIGTC (Grand Rapids, MI: Eerdmans, 2003), 117–18; David M. Moffitt, *Atonement and the Logic of Resurrection in the Epistle to the Hebrews*, Supplements to Novum Testamentum 141 (Leiden, Netherlands: Brill, 2011), 53–118.

[70] Bruce (*Hebrews*, 33 n. 18) and Lane (*Hebrews 1–8*, 45) argue that "the world to come" (τὴν οἰκουμένην τὴν μέλλουσαν) in 2:5 is virtually synonymous with "age to come" (μέλλοντος αἰῶνος) in 6:5, and refers to "the new creation inaugurated by the Son's enthronement" (Lane, *Hebrews 1–8*, 45).

the life offered to him, and frustration ensued in the created order (cf. Gen. 3:14–19). God's good creation has been corrupted by human sin. Thus we do not yet see all things under humanity's feet (Heb. 2:8).

Though we do not presently see the world subject to humanity, we do see Jesus, who has been crowned with glory and honor in his resurrection because of (διά) his suffering of death (Heb. 2:9).[71] Hebrews closely associates sin with suffering and death (e.g., Heb. 2:9, 14–15, 17–18; 3:17; 9:26–28; 10:11–12; 12:1–4; 13:12), reminding us of the consequences of sin stemming (ultimately) from Adam's sin.

In Hebrews 2 the author wrestles with the apparent embarrassment of the Son of God becoming low, subject even to death (v. 10). Yet it was fitting for Jesus to suffer, in order that he might defeat death and bring many sons to glory. Though for a time Jesus was made lower than the angels in his estate of humiliation (v. 7), the incarnate one's greatness is evident in his defeat of sin. This is something the angels could not do. Despite his inherent dignity, the Son was even made *perfect* through suffering (v. 10; 5:8–10). This cannot be perfection in an ontological sense, for Jesus is divine, which entails perfection. Instead, this must be a perfection in Jesus's priestly office, particularly with respect to his perfect, final sacrifice.[72] The priestly work of Christ in which he suffered was glorious, for it enabled him to become a source of eternal salvation (Heb. 2:9; 5:9). Jesus saves by suffering, defeating sin and death.

Hebrews highlights the solidarity between Jesus and his people in a number of ways, including Jesus's identity as the ἀρχηγός of salvation (Heb. 2:10).[73] This term, which is notoriously difficult to translate, is used four times in the NT, in each case with reference to Jesus's resurrection (Acts 3:15; 5:31; Heb. 2:10; 12:2).[74] As the one who has defeated death and entered eschatological life, Jesus is the pioneer, the champion, the forerunner who

---

[71] This "glory and honor" (δόξῃ καὶ τιμῇ) echoes Ps. 8:5 but may also recall the dignity of Aaron's high priesthood (Ex. 28:2, 40 LXX). So argues Lane, *Hebrews 1–8*, 49.

[72] See further Moisés Silva, "Perfection and Eschatology in Hebrews," *WTJ* 39 (1976): 60–71; Vos, "Priesthood of Christ," 144; Bavinck, *Reformed Dogmatics*, 3:476.

[73] Vos, "Priesthood of Christ," 133; contrast Colin Hickling, "John and Hebrews: The Background of Hebrews 2:10–18," *NTS* 29 (1983): 113.

[74] See also Ellingworth, *Hebrews*, 159; Craig S. Keener, *Acts: An Exegetical Commentary*, 4 vols. (Grand Rapids, MI: Baker Academic, 2012–15), 2:1098; Kevin L. Anderson, *"But God Raised Him from the Dead": The Theology of Jesus's Resurrection in Luke-Acts*, PBM (2006; repr., Eugene, OR: Wipf & Stock, 2006), 225; Paul-Gerhard Müller, ΧΡΙΣΤΟΣ ΑΡΧΗΓΟΣ, *Die religionsgeschichtliche und theologische Hintergrund einer neutestamentlichen Christusprädikation*, EHS.T 28 (Bern: Herbert Lang; Frankfurt: Peter Lang, 1973), 256–57; Richard Belward Rackham, *The Acts of the Apostles: An Exposition*, 11th ed., Westminster Commentaries (London: Muethen, 1930), 52; Keener, *Acts*, 2:1097–99.

brings many sons to glory. Jesus destroyed the one who has the power of death and frees those who are held in slavery to death (Heb. 2:14–15). Jesus experienced death, defeating sin and its consequences, in order to bring freedom. It was necessary for Jesus to become like his people in every respect, so that he could be a "merciful and faithful high priest" (Heb. 2:17). In a great twist of irony, Jesus by his death defeated the one who wielded death as a weapon against humanity.

4.3. THE SINLESS PRIEST

Jesus can do this on our behalf because he and his people—his brothers—are all "from one" (ἐξ ἑνός) (Heb. 2:11). This elliptical phrase is open to various interpretations: from one *what*? One option is "from one [man]," that is, from Adam.[75] This would cohere with the Adamic themes in this section of Hebrews, and would closely mirror Paul's language in Athens in Acts 17:26, where he most likely refers to Adam ("And he made from one man every nation of mankind to live on all the face of the earth, having determined allotted periods and the boundaries of their dwelling place [ἐποίησέν τε ἐξ ἑνὸς πᾶν ἔθνος ἀνθρώπων κατοικεῖν ἐπὶ παντὸς προσώπου τῆς γῆς]").

This interpretation of Hebrews 2:11 is quite possible, but it is not the most compelling. Nowhere else in the NT is Jesus said to have come *from* Adam.[76] Instead, Jesus stands parallel to Adam as one who was conceived supernaturally of a virgin.[77] This point requires further comment. For if Jesus would have come *from Adam* in the normal sense, he would have been implicated in the sin of Adam. But Hebrews makes it clear that though Jesus was made like his brothers in every way, he never sinned (Heb. 2:17; 4:15; cf. 5:1–3; 7:26–27). Jesus was not represented by Adam and was not therefore implicated in Adam's sin. Though Hebrews does not explicitly mention Jesus's virginal conception, the sinlessness of Jesus and the emphasis on the Son's preexistence in Hebrews coheres with the virginal conception.[78] If Jesus was born naturally "from Adam" he would have had an inclination toward sin, and it would be difficult to see how he could be described as holy, innocent, undefiled, separate from sinners (ὅσιος ἄκακος ἀμίαντος,

---

[75] See Moffitt, *Atonement*, 130–38; R. Kent Hughes, *Hebrews: An Anchor for the Soul*, Preaching the Word (Wheaton, IL: Crossway, 2015), 72.

[76] Luke 3:38 is not an exception, since Joseph is not the physical father of Jesus (Luke 1:30–38; 3:23).

[77] See esp. Rom. 5:12–21; 1 Cor. 15:44–49.

[78] See also J. Gresham Machen, *The Virgin Birth of Christ* (1930; repr., Grand Rapids, MI: Baker, 1965), 262–63.

504 SIN AND DEPRAVITY IN THE BIBLE

κεχωρισμένος ἀπὸ τῶν ἁμαρτωλῶν) (Heb. 7:26).[79] And crucially, if Jesus had been born with a sinful nature, then he would have a sin problem and would himself need to be rescued.[80] The Canons of Dort affirm that Jesus is the only perfectly holy man, which means he cannot be implicated in the sin of Adam (CD 2.4; 3–4.2; cf. 1.1; 2, Error 5). As the divine Son of God, it was not possible for Jesus to be tainted with sin.[81]

How then should we take "from one" in Hebrews 2:11? One possibility is that Abraham is in view, in light of his mention of Abraham's offspring in 2:16.[82] However, the best options are either (1) that "one" refers to God the Father,[83] or (2) a similar view is that Jesus shares the same humanity as his people.[84] A choice here depends in large measure on whether "one" (ἑνός) is masculine (in which case it would likely refer to God), or neuter (in which case it would likely refer to shared humanity).[85] The masculine reading seems to have more to commend it. This would emphasize that Jesus and his people share "the same trustful attitude towards God which marks them as children of God."[86]

If Jesus is not from Adam and does not share in sin, what does it mean for Jesus to be tempted in every way (κατὰ πάντα) just as we are (καθ' ὁμοιότητα) and yet not sin (Heb. 4:15)? We are limited in how far we can push the similarities between Jesus's temptations and our own. Since Jesus was not tempted by an internal pull toward sin,[87] his experience was different from ours. Geerhardus Vos makes an important point:

> Wherever the Epistle [of Hebrews] speaks of temptations of Christ, it always means to refer concretely and specifically to the temptations that arose from His call to suffer. Of temptations in general it never speaks in connection with Jesus. In thus doing it limits the sphere of the Saviour's

[79] Compare Turretin, *Institutes*, 13.12.2 (2:347); 14.9.3 (2:407).
[80] See, e.g., HC 15–16, 35; cf. HC 31; WCF 8.2; WLC 37.
[81] See WCF 8.3; WLC 38; Turretin, *Institutes*, 13.11 (2:340–47); Vos, *Reformed Dogmatics*, 3:47.
[82] See the discussion in Ellingworth, *Hebrews*, 164–65.
[83] See David deSilva, *Perseverance in Gratitude: A Socio-Rhetorical Commentary on the Epistle "to the Hebrews"* (Grand Rapids, MI: Eerdmans, 2000), 114; Vos, "Priesthood of Christ," 134, 144; Bavinck, *Reformed Dogmatics*, 3:469; Lane, *Hebrews 1–8*, 58; Koester, *Hebrews*, 229–30; Thomas R. Schreiner, *Hebrews*, Evangelical Biblical Theology Commentary (Bellingham, WA: Lexham, 2020), 97–98 and 98 n. 110.
[84] See Calvin, *Hebrews*, 64; Turretin, *Institutes*, 13.5.6 (2:307); Owen, *Exposition of the Epistle to the Hebrews*, 3:418; Philip Edgcumbe Hughes, *A Commentary on the Epistle to the Hebrews* (Grand Rapids, MI: Eerdmans, 1977), 105–6.
[85] For discussions of the options, see Ellingworth, *Hebrews*, 164–65; Owen, *Exposition of the Epistle to the Hebrews*, 3:417–18.
[86] Geerhardus Vos, "Hebrews, the Epistle of the Diatheke," in *Redemptive History and Biblical Interpretation: The Shorter Writings of Geerhardus Vos*, ed. Richard B. Gaffin Jr. (Phillipsburg, NJ: P&R, 1980), 206.
[87] Bavinck, *Reformed Dogmatics*, 3:315; cf. 3:252–53; 3:408; see also Calvin, *Institutes*, 2.16.12.

temptations to that class of experiences wherein a real appeal to His feelings and desires was possible, and yet the mere presence and force of such an appeal could not endanger His sinlessness. For the inclination to escape from suffering, which made the temptation a real one, is in itself a natural, innocent inclination. It could assert itself in the Savior's heart and require a positive choice of the will to overbear it and keep it down, without depending for its power on the presence of evil.[88]

Yet despite Jesus's lack of sin or inclination to sin, Hebrews leaves no doubt that Jesus understands us, sympathizes with us (Heb. 2:17; 4:15; 5:7–10), and helps us as the one who has defeated sin and death (Heb. 2:16–18; 4:16). Jesus knows what it is like to suffer, and he can help us face suffering when it threatens to, or actually does, lead us to sin.[89] Experiential knowledge of sin is not necessary for Jesus to help us in our struggle, nor is experience of sin necessary for him to sympathize with us (cf. Heb. 4:14–16; 5:7–10; 6:19–20; 7:19, 23–28). Jesus's temptation to avoid suffering is particularly pertinent for the probable background to the warning passages in Hebrews.[90]

Jesus's separation from sin is also seen in his one, final, perfect sacrifice (Heb. 7:27; 9:14, 25–28; 10:5–14). Jesus's full-fledged obedience is the answer to the problematic dichotomy between obedience and sacrifice that too often plagued God's people.[91] There is no hypocrisy in Jesus. He never sinned, either by omission or commission. The law requires not just avoidance of certain actions, but positive love for God and neighbor.[92] This is reflected in the quotation of Psalm 40:7–9 (ET 40:6–8) in Hebrews 10:5–7. Jesus delighted to do God's will in his body, which qualified him to offer himself as an effectual, bodily sacrifice (Heb. 10:5, 10). Like us, Jesus experienced suffering in a real body. Unlike us, Jesus did not sin in his body. The blood of Christ, without blemish (ἄμωμος), is sufficient to take away sin and cleanse our consciences (Heb. 9:14; cf. 1 Pet. 1:19).

Hebrews also makes much of the resurrection of Jesus, which correlates to the importance of Jesus's *heavenly* priestly ministry. The resurrection proves the sinlessness of Jesus, for if Jesus had been a sinner he would not

---

[88] Vos, "Priesthood of Christ," 149.
[89] Following Vos, "Priesthood of Christ," 145.
[90] Similarly, the trials and temptations of James 1 should point us to Christ, who was led by the Spirit into the wilderness in order to be tempted—not by God, but by the devil (Matt. 4:1; Luke 4:2; James 1:13). Yet unlike us, Jesus had no internal desire drawing him toward sin (James 1:14). He obeyed in the face of temptations (cf. James 4:7), refusing to put God to the test. The mature (τέλειος) man of James finds a model in Jesus himself.
[91] See the similar language of Lane, *Hebrews 1–8*, cxxxiv; Lane, *Hebrews 9–13*, 266.
[92] See, e.g., Matt. 7:12; 22:37–40; Rom. 13:10; Gal. 5:14; cf. Eph. 4:25–32.

have risen from the dead, nor would his offering be effectual. But Hebrews goes beyond this—not only has Jesus risen from the dead, but he has gone into the inner sanctum behind the veil (Heb. 6:19–20; cf. 9:12–14), and he ever lives to intercede for us (Heb. 7:25–26). The resurrection proves that the Son of God possesses "the power of an indestructible life" (7:16).[93]

In sum, Jesus our high priest is a person like us, yet without sin. He knows our weaknesses and is able to help us when we are tempted. By his obedience and sacrifice, he deals definitively with sin. It is therefore fitting that we have such a high priest: one who was lowly, who is now exalted in the heavenly places (Heb. 1:6; 2:10; 7:26). Jesus has realized the calling of humanity by full obedience and has put away sin at the end of the ages by his perfect sacrifice (Heb. 9:26). Jesus is the source of help in this age, and of eternal life to all who obey him (Heb. 5:9).

Though we cannot save ourselves from sin, practical holiness is necessary (cf. CD 3–4.9). We must strive for holiness, for without holiness no one will see the Lord (cf. Heb. 12:14).[94] This includes avoiding hard-hearted unbelief (Heb. 12:15) and sexual immorality (Heb. 12:16; cf. 13:4). Hebrews calls for ethical purity, especially in light of the greater day of redemptive history which has come in Christ.

5. Conclusion and Synthesis

Hebrews, James, 1–2 Peter, and Jude have a great deal to say about the problem of sin and its answer in Christ. The two issues are closely related—for the NT does not simply tell us our sin problem but speaks of the good news of sin's answer in Christ. I offer a few concluding thoughts by way of summary.

First, sin is a major problem for everyone. Sin leads to suffering, death, and judgment. Sin brings not freedom, but enslavement. Sin rejects God's authority and law, which leads to cursing and not to blessing.

Second, only Jesus, as perfect man and fully God, can suffer because of our sin and grant eternal life. No sinner can save himself or herself, since *perfect* obedience is necessary for eternal life. Sin renders us unable to attain eternal life on our own.

---

[93] This could refer to the resurrection (Moffitt, *Atonement*, 148, 203, 294; Lane, *Hebrews 1–8*, 184; Beale, *New Testament Biblical Theology*, 318–19) or to the divine sonship that lies behind the resurrection (so Vos, "Priesthood of Christ," 153); it may well refer to both, on which see Nick Brennan, *Divine Christology in the Epistle to the Hebrews: The Son as God*, Library of New Testament Studies 656 (London: Bloomsbury T&T Clark, 2022), 122, 142–44.
[94] See Bruce, *Hebrews*, 364; Turretin, *Institutes*, 17.3.12 (2:705); Bavinck, *Reformed Dogmatics*, 4:235–36, 253–54, 321–22.

Third, sin continues to be a clear and present danger in the new covenant community. Even the regenerate continue to struggle against sin, and we should not be surprised to find *unregenerate* persons within the covenant community. We must be vigilant over our own hearts, sensitive to our consciences, and cautious of those who would lead covenant members astray.

Fourth, the call to holiness is real, even for those who cannot obey the law of God perfectly. The Christian life is not characterized by sinfulness, but by Christlikeness, and therefore by holiness. Here is a standard that we, by the grace of God, must ever strive onward toward realizing more fully.

III

SIN AND DEPRAVITY
IN THEOLOGICAL
PERSPECTIVE

17

I and the Norm

COMPARATIVE RELIGIONS AND ALTERNATIVE PHILOSOPHIES OF SIN

Nathan D. Shannon

Introduction

Back in the mid-1990s, D. A. Carson made this troubling admission: "In my most somber moods I sometimes wonder if the ugly face of what I refer to as philosophical pluralism is the most dangerous threat to the gospel since the rise of the gnostic heresy in the second century."[1] Carson acted on his concern, penning a nearly 600-page tome in which he identifies and responds to several pluralistic themes which, concertedly, "tend toward the gagging of God" and a waning of Christian witness in the contemporary West.[2] The pluralistic challenge to the gospel, we now know, had not yet peaked, but was to become the new normal, as it is today for many Christians. In such a context, Christian attention to religions in their increasing social and political proximity is delayed only at great cost to the church. Theology of religions is the order of the day.

Fortunately, we do not have to reinvent the wheel. The demands of our own social and cultural contexts, and the challenges included therein for the church, are to a significant degree missiological. Increasing cultural and religious diversity in developed Western nations, and sober acknowledgment that the naïve safety of majority status as Christians is a thing of the past,

[1] D. A. Carson, *The Gagging of God: Christianity Confronts Pluralism* (Grand Rapids, MI: Zondervan, 1996), 10.
[2] Carson, *Gagging of God*, 37.

draw missiological reflection on the Christian encounter with non-Christian religions to the center of evangelical concern, and thus encourage the church on its way to a more sober take on its relationship to the present age. The gospel-and-culture question, in other words, cannot be only a hobby of urban church-planters or the theme of a poorly attended outreach event; it demands the careful attention of anyone charged with the care and shepherding of the body of Christ. And if we will learn from our times rather than hide from them, because we fear the Lord rather than men, let us acknowledge that the gospel-and-culture question must always now include the gospel-and-religions question—not only in the fabled mission field afar, but now at home as well.

I intend in what follows to take up this challenge, looking in particular to the doctrinal themes of the present volume: anthropology and sin. I first introduce a framework for comparative engagement; then survey relevant themes throughout the broadest possible collection of religious and non-religious traditions from around the world, engaging identifiable patterns in demonstration of select comparative themes; and, finally, offer concluding reflections. I hope, as much as possible in this context, to inform, equip, and encourage, so that "through the church the manifold wisdom of God might now be made known" (Eph. 3:10).

Framework for Comparative Engagement

Most readers are likely well enough informed to articulate classical Protestant or standard evangelical definitions of Christian anthropology and sin: image of God and transgression of the will of God. While the importance of such hard-won formulations can scarcely be overstated, it must be admitted that they manage little by way of engagement, dialogue, or Christian self-understanding in our pluralistic world. Catechesis is a sorry substitute for intelligent evangelism, or for what used to be called "elenctics."

Missiologist Johan Herman Bavinck claims that, at the end of the day, religion is essentially this: personal fellowship with the divine, with the absolute.[3] Religion seeks somehow to articulate or offer personal communion with an ontological self-existence, a being both independent of the world and at the same time everywhere indicated in human experience.[4] This religious

---

[3] In fact, he more often defines religion as response to revelation, but the two definitions are compatible.
[4] Notably, John Hick puts Wilfred Cantwell Smith's view in similar terms. See John Hick, *Problems of Religious Pluralism* (London: Macmillan, 1985), 29. According to Hick, this definition is key to Smith's advance beyond the

search, or the search that is religion, displays invariably—with the exception of the faith of the Bible—profound frustration with this idea of the absoluteness of divine personality and the personality of an absolute deity. Bavinck observes a universal human religiosity caught up in contradiction.[5]

Herman Bavinck, uncle to Johan Bavinck, argues that only in Christianity does one in fact find not only both the personality and the absoluteness of the self-existent being of universal religious attention, but also the essential coalescence of absoluteness and personality in the eternal life of a single, unique God. The triune God of the Bible is not absolute and yet somehow also personal—as all theisms are—but is, in himself, absolute personality.[6] No balancing act required, no mysticism of dark religious paradox; our God is the unchanging Father, Son, and Spirit, the Godhead three in one. Theology of religions begins with the immanent processions in the Godhead; only Christianity may claim religious fellowship with the absolute God; and the religion of the Bible is religion come to its own.

Accordingly, J. H. Bavinck and other neo-Calvinists conceive of the human creature itself in terms of consciousness of its relationship with the infinite personality of the Creator God, and of sin as moral wrong within that relational environment. Cornelius Van Til says that "God is man's ultimate environment."[7] As an earlier writer put it, "Against you, you only, have I sinned and done what is evil in your sight" (Ps. 51:4). Sin is human volitional self-expression which transgresses (or falls short of) an absolute moral standard personally and relationally expressed as moral norm for the creature.

J. H. Bavinck's claim is that religion is always and everywhere an attempt to make sense of human experience, even in particular moral experience, without reference to the triune God of the Bible. Religions everywhere betray the impossibility of making sense of human experience and sustaining

---

modern essentialist taxonomy of religions. Arguably, J. H. Bavinck has attempted much the same advance, with the important difference that by maintaining the antithesis of modern Calvinism he remains an exclusivist.

[5] For Example: J. H. Bavinck, *The Church between Temple and Mosque: A Study of the Relationship between the Christian Faith and Other Religions* (Grand Rapids, MI: Eerdmans, 1981), 185–93.

[6] Herman Bavinck and Cornelius Van Til signal this kataphatic emphasis when they speak of the personality of God in the singular. E.g., Cornelius Van Til, *Introduction to Systematic Theology: Prolegomena and the Doctrines of Revelation, Scripture, and God*, 2nd ed., ed. William Edgar (Phillipsburg, NJ: P&R, 2007), 363; Herman Bavinck, *God and Creation*, vol. 2 of *Reformed Dogmatics*, ed. John Bolt, trans. John Vriend (Grand Rapids, MI: Baker Academic, 2004), 30.

[7] Cornelius Van Til, *The Defense of the Faith*, 4th ed., ed. K. Scott Oliphint (Phillipsburg, NJ: P&R, 2008), 65. And elsewhere, "For man, self-consciousness presupposes God-consciousness. . . . Man's creature-consciousness may therefore be more particularly signalized as covenant-consciousness" (Van Til, *Christian Apologetics*, 2nd ed., ed. William Edgar [Phillipsburg, NJ: P&R, 2003], 115).

moral logic without an absolute God capable of engaging us and of rendering human experience meaningful and human volition morally significant.

Thus our comparative method: the impossibility of the contrary. The principal question here is man and his moral environment—as Bavinck puts it, "I and the norm"—and the survey that follows shall demonstrate that in seeking to make sense of human moral experience, religious systems are always involved in a tension between the absoluteness and the personality of man's moral environment. As a result, religious self-understanding is caught in a dialectic between an impersonal deism of sorts, in which human volition is expressed in a non-relational void, and pantheistic immanence, in which morality dissolves into ontology.

In what follows, we survey classical Indian, Chinese, and Greco-Roman thought in order to observe Bavinck's rule in action. The reader will note that this survey is criminally superficial. To conserve space, I omit material that can be easily acquired using one's preferred search engine; I forego as much as possible standard introductory material and get straight to the point. Still, expectations must be reasonable: nothing can here be argued, much less proven in the standard sense. My intention is to demonstrate a handful of missiological principles already well established in modern Calvinism, so that the reader may get a feel for how "it might work in real life" and perhaps be encouraged along the way to take up the theology of religions for the sake of the gathering and perfecting of the saints.

Ancient Religions of South Asia

From a doctrinal point of view, Hinduism is a polymorphic monotheism, or an overabundant modalism. Brahman, the ineffable unity and self-identity of all things, is believed to self-manifest in many gods, of whom some are represented again in yet further self-manifestations. This remarkable proliferation of anthropomorphic deities signals and may indeed still carry the syncretistic character of an especially extended process of development, dating as far back as the evidence goes—to the civilizations of the Indus river valley of the third millennium BC—of all that now goes by the name of Hinduism. And this anthropomorphic fertility against the backdrop of silent truth supplies the basic elements of the Hindu concept of man's moral environment. Human beings are consigned by the illusion of the self and of the world of experience to a cycle of birth, death, and reincarnation. Only by relinquishing these illusions, by means of moral living, ritual, and meditation, may a person experience release into the unity of divine truth and into the truth of an all-encompassing divine unity; and until this is accomplished an unbending and omniscient law of moral recompense, known as karma, determines one's lot in the next life.

This was the basic religious and philosophical environment when, in the sixth century BC, Siddhartha Gautama (c. 480–400 BC) was born into a royal family in the northeast of the Indian subcontinent. Struck by the pervasiveness of suffering, he renounced worldly privilege and devoted himself to pursuit of an answer to the problem of suffering. After deciding on the futility of asceticism and philosophical speculation, he turned to meditation, and achieved—if "achieved" is the best word—*nirvana*, release from the self as the seat of turmoil-inducing self-concern, as he sat under a Bodhi tree. The Buddha began preaching the four noble truths of suffering and the eightfold path to release, constituting what may be considered a pragmatic reform movement from within ancient Hinduism.

Buddhism and Hinduism have many things in common, including beliefs in *karma*, *samsara* (misery and cyclical reincarnation/rebirth), and an emphasis on meditation. Buddhism is distinguished by, among other things, rejection of the caste system and austerity in doctrine and practice. The Buddha was uninterested in philosophical or theological speculation, but was himself to become an object of worship. In both cases, existence as we experience it is hopelessly wretched and illusory. The primary predicament humans face is captivity to the illusion of self and individual experience and at the same time the suffering and cyclical misery induced by that very ignorance. Self-discipline and meditation (yoga, for the Hindu) are featured as the means to release.

J. H. Bavinck makes the striking observation that "[w]e look in vain for a people whose emotions have been more completely engaged with individual longing for deliverance than the people of India."[8] And both Hindu and Buddhist soteriologies concern themselves not only with moral wrongdoing but also no less with the wretched state of things which our complicity in deluded self-interest has brought about (cf. Rom. 8:20–23). Even Buddhism's strikingly empirical account of suffering combines metaphysics and morality (finitude and fragility, along with evil, both committed and suffered) to

---

[8] J. H. Bavinck, *The J. H. Bavinck Reader*, ed. John Bolt, James D. Bratt, and Paul J. Visser, trans. James A. De Jong (Grand Rapids, MI: Eerdmans, 2013), 188.

articulate the central predicament of human life. There is something terribly wrong—namely, everything—and human selfishness is the primary suspect.

Reformed folks are trained to emphasize the ethical character of sin and to deny it a metaphysical dimension. The fall was moral (or, better, covenantal) rather than metaphysical. To be a sinner is not to be less than human but rather to be at enmity with the personal origin of truth and life. This is an important emphasis, but underappreciation of the mutability of original righteousness lurks nearby. It is true that the first sin issued mysteriously from a righteous character; but it should be remembered that Adam's pre-fall person, though good, was changeable. He was able to sin (*posse peccare*) and able not to sin (*posse non peccare*). And we must suppose that Adam was aware of this instability and of the impending threat of divine justice should he sin. To put it more simply: Adam was created good, but he was incomplete—and he knew it. Even in the perfect days before sin, his heart was not fully at rest. The point is that biblical Christianity has the resources to affirm more than the moral despair of the sinful state; we ought also to appreciate an existential angst such as that which shakes so profoundly these religious traditions. They are certainly on to something.

In Hinduism and Buddhism, writes J. H. Bavinck, "[o]ne needs, once and for all, to be set free from the restrictive ties of *samsara* and be exalted into the glorious deliverance of being absorbed into divinity."[9] Notice that predicament and solution are interdependent notions. If the door is locked, only a key—and precisely the key for precisely this lock—is of any use. Here the predicament is the cyclical lot of all humans and the suffering that accompanies it. "It is important to notice," writes Marie Sabin, "that the Buddha is compelling precisely because, on one level he is describing psychological experience which all individuals can verify for themselves . . . he is simply describing what is observable within every human life."[10] Bavinck, too, commends the psychological sophistication of Buddhist thought, and all readers appreciate the candor and sobriety of the Buddha's observations. Bavinck notes furthermore an individualistic thread: "In India," he says, "*moksha* [deliverance] is predominantly considered as the liberation of the individual person. Each person must endeavor, through his or her own conduct, to become a participant in this escape."[11] One thus notices in this balance of corporate and individual themes a cyclical view of human life

---

[9] J. H. Bavinck, *J. H. Bavinck Reader*, 188.

[10] Marie Sabin, "The Liberating Experience in Buddhism and Christianity," *Dialogue* 18.1 (1991): 49–67 (50).

[11] J. H. Bavinck, *J. H. Bavinck Reader*, 188. Not to understate the role of gurus or mentors, who are key to spiritual progress.

standing in for the biblical notion of covenant and covenantal anthropology. One enters the world bearing the corporate guilt and corruption of Adamic origin from which one's own actual sins flow, or one re-enters a rehearsal of one's own experience of the universal but self-inflicted misery of *samara*.

Sabin, on the other hand, commends the Buddha's reluctance to theorize as a warning to all—especially Christians—who succumb to the urge to speculate: "This caution is necessary because the Christian tradition is more prone to interpret experience than to simply describe it."[12] In her view, our common plight is plain enough—"Christian 'sin,' like Buddhist 'suffering,' proceeds from self-delusion and the endless craving for happiness in illusory ways."[13] The difference lies in how or whether to explain it.[14] In contrast to the Christian, who "uses myth and metaphor to suggest a spiritual state of being that is otherwise perceived as ineffable," the Buddhist "is not using symbolic language and is not pointing to a mysterious truth. On the contrary, the Buddhist is using pragmatic, analytical language to describe a verifiable psychological phenomenon: get rid of your self-obsession and you will be free."[15]

Unfortunately for Sabin's account, to substitute description for definition, claiming only to describe and not to define, is in fact only to swap one definition for another.[16] So, while there is certainly a degree of similarity between Christianity and Buddhism in the experience of evil and the strain of finitude, whether the one experiencing is a bearer of the divine image accountable to his or her Creator God or is instead a ripple on the boundless surface of eternal change makes a great deal of difference. The biblical view of despair highlights guilt before God, whereas Buddhism conceives only of incidental accountability. One must escape, but not repent. "Self-delusion" is indeed a common theme, but in Buddhism one is simply a victim of one's misinterpretation. In Christianity, truth is a moral issue; reality indeed cares how it is being understood by its inhabitants; and conversion replaces a personally offensive lie with the truth that the whole realm of human experience is the Lord's and the fullness thereof. The resurrection broadcasts the fact that, due to the innocence of the Son, death had no claim on him; that

---

[12] Sabin, "Liberating Experience," 50.
[13] Sabin, "Liberating Experience," 50. More specifically, "Essentially, each seeks to break free of self-centeredness. Self-worship is the quintessential root of sin for the Christian and the quintessential root of suffering for the Buddhist" (51).
[14] Precisely John Hick's position.
[15] Sabin, "Liberating Experience," 52.
[16] See Cornelius Van Til, *Common Grace and the Gospel*, 2nd ed., ed. K. Scott Oliphint (Phillipsburg, NJ: P&R, 2015), 3–15. On the one hand, there is abundant metaphysical information in Buddhist thought, while on the other hand, the Buddha himself was notably unimpressed with speculation since it, he believed, is of no or even negative practical value.

because he obeyed, he was at peace with God and thus with creation; and that his suffering and death were superfluous from his own point of view. But all of this presupposes a sovereign work of creation *ex nihilo*, and the personal, covenantal immanence of the Creator. In Hindu and Buddhist traditions one encounters sober contemplation of the corporate misery of a thousand generations—"how long?"—in which, even of existence itself, one despairs.

Confucianism

Confucius (551–479 BC) would have sympathized with the Buddha's pragmatism;[17] he was similarly unimpressed with metaphysical or cosmological speculation, and even at times openly skeptical. But Confucius probably would have thought the Buddha's philosophy pointlessly nihilistic and, in the end, of little practical assistance. He was an advocate for a harmonious social and political order in which rulers were wise and benevolent and subjects content, cooperative, and fulfilled. He believed that such an order would promote and perfectly blend the honor of the individual with a just and seamless socio-political organism, where the grace and beauty of poetry and the arts would adorn a people, each one fulfilled in his or her givenness to the harmony of the whole. And Confucius had a special confidence that all this was achievable if one single element were firmly in place, that of filial piety. The parent-child or father-son relationship was to his mind the primary human relationship and the prototypical socio-political economy. A good son, who honors his parents privately, publicly, and sincerely, even after they are gone, is also a good citizen, and an agent of social flourishing and lasting harmony.

Although Confucius famously avoided theological issues, it is clear that he believed that the social order he envisioned had a heavenly origin and heavenly design. He believed himself to be a reformer, and claimed to invent nothing but only to promote a movement *ad fontes*,[18] so that what he hoped for was not eschatological arrival but reform and recovery of the peace and stability of a lost golden age. Indeed he speaks often and longingly of the

---

[17] Confucius's pragmatism is sometimes viewed as the East Asian counterpart to Western individualistic intellectualism. See Geung Ho Cho, "The Self and the Ideal Human Being in Eastern and Western Philosophical Traditions: Two Types of 'Being a Valuable Person,'" in *The Oneness Hypothesis: Beyond the Boundary of Self*, ed. Philip J. Ivanhoe, Owen J. Flanagan, Victoria S. Harrison, Hagop Sarkissian, and Eric Schwitzgebel (New York: Columbia University Press, 2018). A popular-level modern classic on the East/West question is Richard E. Nisbett, *The Geography of Thought: How Asians and Westerners Think Differently . . . and Why* (New York: Free Press, 2004).
[18] Such deference would have been characteristic: "Unlike the Western tradition, where philosophers often claimed their predecessors' ideas as their own, Chinese philosophers often credited their own creative ideas to 'old masters'" (Philip Ho Hwang, "A New Interpretation of Confucius," *Philosophy East and West* 30.1 [1980]: 45–55 [48]).

heroes of that forsaken heritage. But there is an important ambiguity here. Evidently, Confucius's aim was to *recover an ideal*—something of a contradiction. In this sense there is a curious undertone in his program of classical retrieval of hope in things unseen. Noteworthy as well is the fact that at the center of his aspiration is a rigorous program for individual moral self-cultivation. What the Christian might know as sanctification and spiritual discipline are at the center of Confucius's socio-political vision.[19]

There is no consensus on Confucius's view of human nature, and this may be, as many scholars suggest, because he did not have one.[20] Confucius was interested neither in a theory of human nature nor in metaethics—in accounting for moral obligation or moral predicates. He was interested primarily in the mechanics of right conduct.[21] There is a fine line here, which one scholar has articulated this way:

> Surprisingly . . . [Confucius] did not spell out how we could know whether a particular action is good or evil. . . . Is there any criterion or standard for it?[22]

In fact,

> Confucius held no one standard. . . . He did not believe that there is one standard for truths or that truths are fixed immutable.[23]

The task of sorting this out—unavoidable, it seemed—fell to a most devout and industrious disciple, Mencius (372–289 BC).

Mencius, set as he was on the faithful development of his master's teaching, "was forced to face the problem of why man ought to do good and act morally, and he attempted to solve this problem with his theory of human nature."[24] He "explicitly linked the task of self cultivation with the development of one's Heavenly conferred nature; he maintained the structure of

---

[19] Philip J. Ivanhoe, *Confucian Moral Self Cultivation*, 2nd ed. (Indianapolis: Hackett, 2000), xiv. "Cultivating the self in order to take one's place in this universal scheme describes the central task of life for . . . all Confucians."

[20] The absence of a clear theory of the human person in Confucius's teaching quickly proved provocative. See Maurizio Scarpari, "The Debate on Human Nature in Early Confucian Literature," *Philosophy East and West* 53.3 (2003): 323–39.

[21] A thesis clarified in Hwang, "New Interpretation."

[22] Hwang, "New Interpretation," 50.

[23] Hwang, "New Interpretation," 51–52. Hwang says elsewhere that "Confucius devoted his entire life to the task of explaining how a person might become a superior man or man of morality. But he did not explain *why* man ought to do good rather than evil and be a moral person" (Philip Ho Hwang, "What Is Mencius' Theory of Human Nature?" *Philosophy East and West* 29.2 [1979], 205).

[24] Hwang, "What Is Mencius' Theory of Human Nature?" 206. Hwang cites several sources expressing confidence in the idea that Mencius is a faithful formulator of Confucius's teaching (Hwang, "New Interpretation," 47–48).

Kongzi's [that is, Confucius's] original vision, but set it upon a new foundation, a subtle yet powerful theory about human nature."[25] Mencius was led
to affirm, first of all, that man *had* a nature, and then to attempt a distinction between true and false self: "to *develop* oneself according to one's true
nature is to fulfill a design inscribed by Heaven upon our human hearts. To
follow the nature, then, is to obey Heaven, and to develop oneself is to serve
Heaven."[26] In sum, Mencius taught that "man ought to do good because he
does good, and man does good because he ought to do good."[27]

   Underwhelmed, Christian reader? But what resemblance this bears to
the apostle Paul's doctrine of progressive sanctification, to be written five
thousand miles to the west and three hundred years later, in which Paul en-
joins every person called by God to "be who he is in Christ."[28] And one must
admire Mencius's metaethical candor: truly, at the end of the day, a moral
outlook exalts either God or man. Without a personal self-existent, to whom
shall Confucianism go? Mencius says: go nowhere; simply modulate the
grammar so that ontology *is* deontology. Lest we judge this artificial, and
unworthy of a great thinker, notice that this is precisely how the Christian
tradition has understood the fabric of human moral experience: ontology—
being—converted to moral norm. But of course in the Christian tradition
not the finite, fallen subject but personal *self-existence* is self-expressed as
moral norm for the world. And self-existence is the only sort of existence
that can vindicate the identification of *is* with *ought*. "Godliness is a moral
imperative," the so-called full-bucket problem, is a magical tautology at the
foundation of Christian-theistic ethics. The all-glorious and self-sufficient
God to whom nothing can be added created the world so that his glory would
increase to cover the earth from sea to sea.

   There is no single figure whose influence in the West even approaches
the stature of Confucius and the currency of his name in East Asia—where
the population of China alone is greater than that of North and South America
combined.[29] The breadth and persistence of his influence is truly beyond

---

[25] Ivanhoe, *Confucian Moral Self Cultivation*, 19.
[26] Ivanhoe, *Confucian Moral Self Cultivation*, 19–20.
[27] Hwang, "What Is Mencius' Theory of Human Nature?" 208.
[28] I borrow this wording from Richard B. Gaffin Jr., *By Faith, Not by Sight: Paul and the Order of Salvation*, 2nd ed. (Phillipsburg, NJ: P&R, 2013), 77–85.
[29] Ann-Ping Chin writes, "Until the mid-twentieth century, China was so inseparable from the idea of Confucius that her scheme of government and society, her concept of the self and human relationships, and her construct of culture and history all seemed to have originated from his mind alone" (*The Authentic Confucius: A Life of Thought and Politics* [New York: Scribner, 2007], 2).

calculation. It is therefore noteworthy that someone seeking fame and influence would, as a general rule, be ill-advised to repeat Confucius's professional choices. As one biographer put it, "Men like Confucius were not destined to have fame. Their concerns lacked immediate appeal."[30] One dare not attempt to explain all this, but we can hardly miss the fact that Confucius believed, effectively, in the kingdom of God, where self-realization and the benefit of all discover no conflict but mutually encourage; in eschatological hope, where now in principle the kingdom is within reach but in fact could come only by the help of heaven; and in an unwavering mandate to personal holiness. And there is something of a tension in the Confucian imperatives: on the one hand, he set the bar terribly high; but on the other, he had to preach it as though it could be attained. He leaves us wondering: who will ascend into heaven? Who can do it (Rom. 10:6–13). Without divine assistance and substitution passive and active, Confucius's Way is a heavy burden.[31] James Legge, the first to produce scholarly English translations of the Chinese classics, commended Mencius's (Confucian) view of man to Christians on the grounds that his theory is "as nearly as possible, identical with that of Bishop Butler."[32] Legge thus maps the theological field nicely: it is precisely Butler's belief in postlapsarian residual integrity with which the Calvinist takes issue, and where one finds the absolute bent irrecoverably toward the earth.[33] If the moral line is perfect holiness, as for Confucius's program it surely is, then only love and the Man from heaven can make us willing and able.

That brings our brief discussion of the religions of Asia to a close. Of all that we have seen, our guide in such matters, J. H. Bavinck, offers the following observation:

> The Christian church in Asia is involved in a life-and-death struggle in opposition to all these ideas. An invaluable privilege in that struggle is that

---

[30] Chin, *Authentic Confucius*, 1.

[31] The dehumanizing hierarchicalism to which Confucian ethics often gives way is well acknowledged—though to be fair there is no question of the master's intending it. See, e.g., Nam-Soon Kang, "Confucian Familism and Its Social/Religious Embodiment in Christianity: Reconsidering the Family Discourse from a Feminist Perspective," *Asia Journal of Theology* (2004): 168–189. Kang says, "It should be also noted that the Confucian concept of the person as a center of relationships rather than merely an isolated individual and its emphasis on family-centeredness and human relatedness have resulted in nepotism, favoritism, and provincialism" (179).

[32] James Legge, *The Chinese Classics, Volume 2: The Works of Mencius* (Hong Kong: Hong Kong University Press, 1960), 59, quoted in Hwang, "What Is Mencius' Theory of Human Nature?" 203.

[33] K. K. Yeo, "Chinese Christologies: Images of Christ and Chinese Cultures," in *Oxford Handbook of Christology*, ed. Francesca Aran Murphy (Oxford: Oxford University Press, 2015), 395: "Many Chinese Christians live in an oxymoronic state where they want to be faithful believers of Christ and also filial pietists. Many live in an impossible world of embracing the teaching of both Confucius and Christ. Does Christ, the New Law, annul or supplement and fulfill the Old Law, such as that of Confucian teachings?"

she is able to reach back to what the Christian church in previous centuries and other countries has thought and said about these matters. Why? Because the struggle we have in wrestling with Asian mysticism is comparable in a great many respects to what the church battled earlier. As similar as two drops of water, it is like the Hellenistic mysticism, Gnosticism, and neo-Platonism that as powerful philosophical systems held the early Christian centuries captive.[34]

Hellenistic Thought

The names of Plato (427–347 BC) and Aristotle (384–322 BC) are well enough known, but the apostolic church was met, some three and a half centuries after Aristotle's death, by a markedly different social, political, and philosophical environment. Those heroes of classical Greek philosophy were citizens of Greek city-states, and their philosophy was shaped accordingly. But Alexander the Great, whose conquests Aristotle personally encouraged in pointedly "classical" terms, would by force of ambition lead the Greek mind to contend with a bigger pond.[35] As city-state melted into empire, questions surrounding the changing realities of citizenship and human interaction began to eclipse metaphysical speculation and epistemological hairsplitting; ethics moved decidedly to the forefront of the philosophical agenda. And "the day was not far distant when Greece was to become but a Province of the Roman Empire."[36] Thus, by virtue of growing demand for ethical and political insight, philosophy increased its profile as an alternative to traditional religion, among various segments of the population. "[T]he ordinary person's agnosticism, bewilderment, or disenchantment with traditional gods and goddesses," writes one scholar, "fueled Stoicism and Epicureanism themselves."[37] Philosophy was not, as it often is in the West today, hostile to religious belief and practice, but it did begin more self-consciously to assume a role in meeting religious needs. We witness, accordingly, a fruitful shift of philosophical emphasis and an increase in philosophy's public profile as a path to the good life and to effective negotiation with the supernatural. Indeed, "[t]heology

---

[34] J. H. Bavinck, *J. H. Bavinck Reader*, 309.

[35] "In one celebrated fragment he [Aristotle] counsels Alexander to be 'a hegemon [leader] to the Greeks and a despot to the barbarians, to look after the former as after friends and relatives, and to deal with the latter as with beasts or plants'" (Peter Green, *Alexander of Macedon, 356–323 B.C.: A Historical Biography* [Berkeley: University of California Press, 1992], 59). And yet, "[t]o Alexander the sharp distinction between Greek and 'Barbarian' was unreal: he thought in terms of Empire, not in terms of the City" (Frederick Copleston, S.J., *A History of Philosophy*, vol. 1, *Greece and Rome* [New York: Doubleday, 1993], 379).

[36] Copleston, *Greece and Rome*, 379.

[37] A. A. Long, *From Epicurus to Epictetus: Studies in Hellenistic and Roman Philosophy* (Oxford: Oxford University Press, 2008), 115.

is central to both philosophies" to the extent that "[b]oth schools would be grossly misunderstood if we took their theological theses to be adventitious or some kind of sop to conventional expectations."[38] The intellectual backdrop to the conversion of one of Christianity's greatest teachers thus comes into view:

> And so it is that we can discern religious elements in such a predominantly ethical system as Stoicism, while in Neo-Platonism, the last flower of Ancient Philosophy, the syncretism of religion and philosophy reaches its culmination. More than that, we may say that in Plotinian Neo-Platonism . . . philosophy tends to pass over into religion.[39]

There was on the north side of the Agora in Athens a painted porch where Zeno of Citium (c. 335–263 BC) taught what would become Stoicism.[40] This school of thought would become widely known in the Graeco-Roman world and would even count the personal diary of a Roman Emperor, Marcus Aurelius, an example of its principles put to practice. *Orthos logos*, right reason, was the essence of the Stoic conception of moral good as well as the point of contact between Stoic ethics and theology. A. A. Long writes, "*Orthos logos* is defined as 'moral goodness,' 'universal law,' 'natural law prescribing what should and should not be done,' 'that in accordance with which the wise man always acts,' and other variants of these."[41] One detects indecision here with regard to an important distinction: is right reason a descriptive or a prescriptive notion? And in fact that is precisely the issue: "What complicates things is the fact that 'the law' and those who prescribe and obey it are not distinguished. God is *orthos logos* and *orthos logos* is also a description of the wise man's state of mind."[42] The vagueness one detects here signals an identification of law with moral reason and thus the fact that "the good man is not inferior to God," since "his *logos* is an instance of *orthos logos* in the larger sense."[43]

Evidently, there is no Creator-creature distinction here, and thus no divine law, as a given in the creature's moral environment, to which the

---

[38] Long, *From Epicurus to Epictetus*, 115.

[39] Copleston, *Greece and Rome*, 381.

[40] Stoicism takes its name from this "painted porch" (ἡ ποικίλη στοά [*the poikile stoa*]). Scholars distinguish early (300–50 BC), middle (50 BC–AD 250), and late Stoic thought (AD 250–550). It would have been during this middle period that Paul conversed with the Stoic and Epicurean philosophers in the marketplace of Athens. Copleston notes the eclecticism of the middle period, as does the text of Acts 17:21.

[41] A. A. Long, "The Stoic Concept of Evil," *Philosophical Quarterly* 18.73 (1968): 334.

[42] Long, "Stoic Concept of Evil," 334.

[43] Long, "Stoic Concept of Evil," 334.

creature's reason and conduct must be conformed. For the Stoics there is a simple identity between the objective moral law and subjective moral reason, so that a notion of "conformity to law" dissolves into the self-expression of a holy volition—how "the wise man always acts."

The natural order and course of things, being objectively determined and normative, in one sense takes on divine characteristics.[44] It is, from the human point of view, "given," or, if not to overstate, self-attesting. It is an immovable moral index of which serious persons will be ever mindful. And yet the human being lives and moves in this self-determined order in such a way that he "is himself a cause within the causal nexus."[45] That is, "[h]e consciously determines (*qua* the *logos* which is his as well as God's) what will happen, as well as being in some sense determined by what has happened."[46] The Stoic ethic is thus stretched between its hope of lighting the way to the good life through reliable moral guidelines and its deterministic monism, by virtue of which meaningful moral judgments are elusive.[47] The Stoics slip through this dilemma by relegating moral variation to the invisible sphere of subjective intention. Copleston explains: "The Stoics seem to have accepted—theoretically at least—the notion that no actions are wrong in themselves, as when Zeno admitted that not even cannibalism, incest or homosexuality are wrong in themselves. . . . he meant that the physical act is indifferent, moral evil pertaining to the human will and intention."[48] And A. A. Long: that "which bestows moral worth on an action" is "a disposition."[49]

The Stoics portrayed the ethical ideal personally, as a sage who acts according to nature—not mechanically, as one mindlessly observing traffic laws, but virtuously. That is, in Aristotelian fashion, the sage is the one who has acquired the virtues such that he *is* and not merely *has* them; he acts

---

[44] Long, "Stoic Concept of Evil," 332. "[T]he Stoics saw evidence of purpose in the regularity of natural phenomena and organic life," and "they attributed its cause to the conscious agency of God. Nature is not an unconscious final cause, accounting for the efforts of the individual organism to perfect itself, but matter informed by a rational efficient cause, God, who permeates all things in virtue of the *pneuma* they contain. . . . The Stoics identify God with the world, treating matter (*hyle*) as his body and *to poioun* as his *psyche*. As the human soul extends throughout the human body, so the moving principle in the world extends throughout its matter, endowing it with definite quality by variations of tension."

[45] Long, "Stoic Concept of Evil," 339.

[46] Long, "Stoic Concept of Evil," 339.

[47] For the Stoic, liberty meant "doing consciously, with assent, what one will do in any case" (Copleston, *Greece and Rome*, 389). Also, "Chrysippus, in his fourth book on Providence, argues that goods could not have existed without evils, on the ground that a pair of contraries neither can exist without the other, so that if you take away the one, you take away both" (*Greece and Rome*, 390).

[48] Copleston, *Greece and Rome*, 396.

[49] Long, "Stoic Concept of Evil," 335.

naturally and spontaneously according to nature. "Moral action then is consistent adherence to the principles which the good man's reason prescribes to him, and such principles are valid as laws of nature. The good man becomes the criterion, not 'reason' in general."[50]

In other words, there is no disconnect between the good and self-determined nature of things and the moral character of the sage. He exercises subtle moral reason consistently in accordance with law and nature, never succumbing to passion, whim, or attachment to inferior distractions. Interestingly, both the founding teacher of Stoicism and one of its most famous proponents took their own lives: Zeno reportedly strangled himself in order to show that he would be the one to give his life to the course of nature rather than have it taken from him; and Seneca bled himself to death in a sad but, shall we say, stoic submission to the force of events in his own life, namely, the crazed wrath of Nero.

Conversely, sin, for the Stoic, is any lack of conformity of the exercise of moral self-direction to nature or natural law.[51] This definition of sin is, again, indifferent to the mechanics of a given act: "Cosmic *kakia*," or natural evil, "is a necessary consequence of the divine plan for good," as pain is necessary for the protection of the body and so, while unpleasant, it is morally indifferent.[52] "Hence [natural evil] must not be confused, any more than pain, with moral *kakia*, the failure to act according to 'right reason' (*orthos logos*)."[53] "Seneca conceives of sin as fundamentally *noetic* and *anthropocentric*. The fundamental problem in the world is thus not suffering but ignorance . . . which prompts enslavement to vice rather than the true freedom offered by virtue."[54] And how does culpable ignorance come about? According to A. A. Long, "[t]he sources of corruption are firmly set in the environment."[55] As children grow, they are "provided with false conceptions of good."[56] "Evil then is a matter of misjudgment."[57] Evil is faulty inference to errant moral imperative. It is simply a matter of misinformation and misunderstanding,

---

[50] Long, "Stoic Concept of Evil," 335. Again, there is an intriguing ambiguity here, since the sage or the good man possesses subjectively a self-attesting moral reason, while he is at the same time a figment of moral imagination representing a principle of objectivity.

[51] Long, "Stoic Concept of Evil," 334.

[52] Long, "Stoic Concept of Evil," 334.

[53] Long, "Stoic Concept of Evil," 334.

[54] Brian J. Tabb, "Paul and Seneca on Suffering," in *Paul and Seneca in Dialogue*, ed. Joey Dodson and David E. Briones (Leiden, Netherlands: Brill, 2017), 98.

[55] Long, "Stoic Concept of Evil," 336.

[56] Long, "Stoic Concept of Evil," 336.

[57] Long, "Stoic Concept of Evil," 337.

There are rumblings in Stoic teaching of something like an enduring state for the soul of the sage, but the operative end or goal of Stoic ethics was surely *eudaimonia*, usually translated "happiness" or "flourishing"—"the good life," we might say. In this sense, peace and contentment are identified with successful pursuit of virtuous character and action. One self-liberates from the contortions and frustrations of a life stretched between shortsighted passions and desires, on the one hand, and the nature of things on the other, by working toward a deeper understanding of that natural order and course of things. "Transferring our moral language," erroneously, "to the pain itself . . . will not alleviate the pain. To realize that it is a necessary, though undesirable, feature of the human situation may do so."[58] As D. A. Russell comments, "Philosophy alone gives happiness; it does more than reproduce the bliss of the Golden Age, because it offers not innocent ignorance but virtue born of struggle."[59] Salvation by contemplation of idealized moral character is what we mean by a Stoicist "philosophical religion."

If accessibility indicates marketability, it is little surprise that Stoic ethics sold much better than Stoic metaphysics and cosmology. Liberation by practiced self-restraint has strong intuitive appeal; and this is an intuition (and an appeal) for which Scripture offers a compelling account. Stoic ethical thought honors a given or objective moral law which speaks to the personal subject from both within and without, and to which the human being is well advised to conform his will and personality. And although the Stoic theological account of the self-sufficiency of natural law forces upon Stoics an unwieldy determinism, spontaneity worked itself into their ethics by their insistence on the consciousness of God, so that the course of nature always reserved the right to make unpredictable, counterintuitive demands. Right behavior is whatever right reason recommends in a given situation—it is reason, after all. Zeno and Seneca, therefore, would have understood the idea that the transgression of Genesis 3:6 had nothing to do with fruit and everything to do with an unjustifiable transgression of good moral order and of Adam's own good character and his natural inclination to obedience. We may also expect that they would struggle less with the morality of the command to sacrifice Isaac than even many contemporary Christians.

---

[58] Long, "Stoic Concept of Evil," 330.
[59] D. A. Russell, "Letter to Lucilius," in *Seneca*, ed. Charles D. N. Costa (London: Routledge, 1974), 93, cited in Tabb, "Paul and Seneca," 97.

But the Stoic ethic cannot manage self-attesting moral authority that issues non-necessarily from a personal God, for outside of the circle of special
revelation, self-attestation draws its lifeblood from a self-existence allergic to
personality. There is some concern in Stoicism for the security of the distinction between right and wrong action, thus the givenness of the moral norm;
but without an objective expression of law, "objective" is a mirage, and sin
easily slips away from view into the uncertain sands of subjective character
and intention. Zeno proposed such a distinction between acts and intentions
which rendered incest and cannibalism, among other horrors, in and of themselves non-moral. One must see into the hidden intention in order to judge
even these moral horrors. This is a perverse self-consistency—were it not
for its absurdity, admirable for its theoretical courage. In spite of Stoicism's
popular reputation for practicality and utility, the fact is that it struggles to
substantiate moral predication; it cannot really identify and distinguish good
and evil:

> The Stoic concept of *kakia* belongs to a theory of ethics which raises inter-
> esting and important questions, but it contributes little to the practical analy-
> sis of moral conduct. *Kakia* is set firmly in the human sphere and shown to
> be quite independent of God's action and intentions. It is caused by men's
> misunderstanding of their own nature and the nature of the universe, and
> for this misunderstanding they are culpable. Unfortunately, all men, except
> the rare wise man, who intuits God's purposes, are in this condition. Thus
> *kakos* (morally bad) turns out to be more like a factual description of normal
> men than a way of placing the objects we ought not to desire or pursue. In
> practice the Stoics were forced to supplement their precious categorical
> distinctions by rules for judging the conduct of daily life.[60]

The Westminster Shorter Catechism claims that the chief end of man is
to glorify God and enjoy him forever. Proof texts are given separately for
each clause—glorify and enjoy—and those for the latter emphasize themes
such as: the Lord himself is the joy of his people; the Lord's protection means
rest, hope, and gladness; the presence of the Lord means fullness of joy and
pleasures evermore; and climactically, the Lord will wipe away every tear
and end suffering and sorrow forever. Striking are the theo-centrism of these
themes and the range of creaturely comforts envisioned—pleasure and absence of pain, the quietude of knowing that the Lord defends his people, even

[60] Long, "Stoic Concept of Evil," 343.

the Lord himself self-given is joy for those who are his. Of the parable of the wedding feast Charles Spurgeon said, "Gifts are lavishly bestowed and all that is requested of the subjects is that they . . . willingly come to the palace, not to labor or serve at the table, but to feast and to rejoice."[61] "Taste and see that the LORD is good" (Ps. 34:8) is an eschatological invitation displaying plainly the backbone of Christian theistic ethics from the original invitation signaled in the tree of life in the garden to the resurrection of Christ, in the flesh, the firstborn of the new creation. In these desolate ruins, "there shall be heard again the voice of mirth and the voice of gladness," and fixed on this very joy of restored communion, which he knew would surpass beyond measure the present sufferings, our Lord endured the cross (Jer. 33:10–11; Rom. 8:18; Heb. 12:2). Again Spurgeon: "Then it is for laughter, for happiness, for joy. . . . There is not a faculty of our nature which is not made to feel its need supplied when the soul accepts the provisions of mercy."[62]

Something of a malformed and disappointing knock-off of this is found in the ethics of the ancient hedonist, Epicurus (341–270 BC). Epicurus picked up the atomic materialism of Democritus (460–370 BC) and developed a rough calculus of human success accordingly. His assessment of the human situation is dreary. Martha Nussbaum puts it in striking terms:

> Epicurus invites us to look at ourselves, at our friends, at the society in which we live. . . . We see people rushing frenetically about after money, after fame, after gastronomic luxuries, after passionate love—people convinced by the culture itself, by the stories on which they are brought up, that such things have far more value than in fact they have . . . people convinced that they cannot possibly live without their hoards of money, their imported delicacies, their social standing, their lovers. . . . We see a sick society . . . that values money and luxury above the health of the soul. . . . We see a society, above all, whose every enterprise is poisoned by the fear of death, a fear that will not let its members taste any stable human joy, but turns them into groveling slaves of corrupt religious teachers.[63]

Nussbaum has her own take on things for which she is seeking to retrieve the therapeutic emphases of Hellenistic ethics. Nonetheless, Epicurus's concerns are sufficiently clear here. Human beings are "troubled" and

---

[61] C. H. Spurgeon, sermon 975, "The Parable of the Wedding Feast," delivered February 12, 1871.
[62] Spurgeon, "Parable of the Wedding Feast."
[63] Martha C. Nussbaum, *The Therapy of Desire: Theory and Practice in Hellenistic Ethics* (Princeton, NJ: Princeton University Press, 2009), 103.

"vulnerable to numerous pains and diseases" and cannot be trusted to reason their way to better conduct or a better life.[64] Evidently, they cannot be trusted with their own well-being, and the principal ailment, says Epicurus, is ignorance. Death, for example, is not to be feared. Since at the moment of death we cease to exist and are unable to feel or experience, there is no unpleasantness to speak of—literally nothing to fear. If people can be brought to understand this, they may be delivered from the fear of death and enjoy a sober peace in the face of fragility and finitude. Notice that Epicurus does not propose to eliminate the occasions for distress and sorrow; these are unavoidable. He focuses instead on peace of mind and tranquility of soul, first of all because by far the greater part of our duress is caused not by external affliction but by false belief regarding both what is good for us and what is harmful; and second because the state of the soul is far more important than that of the body. Soul experiences are more profound. And so, Epicurus's hedonism comes down to a program for the elimination of internal turmoil through a therapeutic practice of philosophical reflection aimed at the elimination of false desires, plus a moderate cultivation of intellectual enjoyment.

Epicurus's account of the source of moral confusion indulges somewhat in speculation regarding human infancy, the stage in life when every individual is still uncorrupted by the moral mistruths of cumulative culture. That is: each and every human enters life morally trustworthy, exercising sound instincts regarding the desirability of pleasure over pain. This Pelagian allegory stands for Epicurus as the key to his program of therapeutic reflection: "If we can really get ourselves to imagine a (mature) human being for whom all disturbance and impediment are removed—for whom the child's desires are truly satisfied—we will see, he claims, that this person lacks nothing and has no need to go after more."[65] Nussbaum continues: "*Ataraxia* (freedom from disturbance and anxiety) in the soul and freedom from pain in the body: these are the uncorrupted creature's goals."[66] Even more concretely: "[t]he goal seems to be . . . the continued undisturbed and unimpeded functioning of the whole creature"; this is "Epicurus's account of pleasure."[67]

Nussbaum believes that Epicurus highlights the hopelessness of moral reason, displayed in the dismal state of human affairs, as critique of the

---

[64] Nussbaum, *Therapy of Desire*, 104.
[65] Nussbaum, *Therapy of Desire*, 108.
[66] Nussbaum, *Therapy of Desire*, 109.
[67] Nussbaum, *Therapy of Desire*, 109.

Aristotelian dialectic and the suggestion that syllogistic moral reason is the way to better living. Epicurus famously said that, like a medical art that fails to expel sickness from the body, absurd is a philosophical art which fails to deliver the soul from suffering. Therapeutic payoff or nothing. Instead of the cold, naïve moral rationality of Aristotelian pedigree, Epicurus promotes his more practical method, a vision of therapeutic philosophical deliverance from stress-inducing ignorance. Nussbaum is no doubt correct; anyway, I lack the credentials to question her historical account. At the same time, displayed here in Epicurus's proposal is the recurring hubris of a philosopher claiming to know better than the rest of us—certainly a sorry sight, but not entirely misguided: moral clarity and assistance must indeed visit us from outside, from above; we need wisdom from heaven. If we are to be made willing and able, moral restoration must be granted, not achieved.

Epicurus applied the same paradigm to religion. He did not renounce belief in the gods, but was sure that they had no interest in human affairs. Fear of the gods and religious busyness were therefore, to his mind, both much ado about nothing and a sad scene of self-inflicted worry. Thus the theologically inclined reader of ancient thought faces an interesting question: "Is divine blessedness in the rational order pervading the entire world, as Stoics maintain? Or should one opt for the Epicurean conception of gods who are quite detached from the world and who provide no occupation for themselves or for anything else?"[68] This is, as we have seen, a dilemma with no claim on biblical religion.

Manichaeism, Neoplatonism, and Christianity's Greatest Conversion

It is customary to deploy one's finest superlative turns of phrase when approaching the person, mind, or influence of Augustine. Among the many reasons for this is that his biography is as endearing as his theology is momentous, and the volume and preservation of both his personal and professional production allow even modern readers to behold the striking unity of his person and work. Indeed we see in Augustine's rocky path to conversion, the bishopric of Hippo, and his theological prowess a concentrated retelling of the intellectual narrative of his day, the conclusion of which is yet to be written.

---

[68] Long, *From Epicurus to Epictetus*, 114. The latter (deistic) emphasis caught the attention of Guido de Brès. See the Belgic Confession, Article 13. On Calvinist interaction with Epicureanism, see the sources listed in Kirk M. Summers, *Morality after Calvin: Theodore Beza's Christian Censor and Reformed Ethics* (New York: Oxford University Press, 2017), 328 n. 89.

And you might say we owe it all to his mother. Monica was devout, even persistent, one might say perpetually panicked, about the faith of her son. Augustine would, after her passing, express regret for extending her angst unnecessarily and acknowledge her longsuffering with gratitude. Biographers suggest that Monica's preoccupation with her son's salvation and godliness instilled in him a lively consciousness of God and conscience that in one way or another pestered his wandering heart and mind until at last he returned to embrace his mother's confession as his own. That restlessness we all know—"our heart is restless until it rests in you"[69]—was the unstill concern of a loving mother. Fortunately for Augustine, he did not have a smartphone, or it might have been too much to bear!

When he was 17 years old, Augustine traveled nearly 300 kilometers from Thagaste, his provincial home in what is now northeastern Algeria, to Carthage, a bustling port town on the Bay of Tunis. He had come to study, and as he recounts in his *Confessions* (written roughly 25 years later), the *Hortensius* of Cicero made a great impression on him. We may put it this way: Augustine was introduced to the therapeutic if not soteric impulse of Hellenistic philosophy—and he was all in. "For centuries now," writes Peter Brown, "the idea of philosophy had been surrounded with a religious aura. It involved far more than an intellectual discipline. It was a love of 'Wisdom.' 'Wisdom' would console and purify its devotees; it demanded, in return, self-sacrifice and moral readjustment."[70] Reading Cicero, Augustine later wrote, "changed my feelings . . . it gave me entirely different values and priorities. Suddenly every vain hope became empty to me."[71]

Augustine's reflections on this time, and his embrace of pagan philosophy, are complex. When he read Cicero for the first time, he was 18 or 19 years old and unmarried but living with a young woman who, around the same time, gave birth to a son, Adeodatus. This situation would later be the subject of probing and remorseful reflections on sin, personal and doctrinal. To his mother's credit, Augustine was familiar with the Christian faith, but he was not faithful; he was catechized but not yet converted. Since he "was a boy from a Christian household," even when he was taken with the rhetoric and

---

[69] That duly famous line from the opening of the *Confessions*: "*inquietum est cor nostrum, donec requiescat in te.*" It is interesting that in his translation of the *Confessions*, Henry Chadwick appends to this statement a reference to Plotinus. This is a bit of speculative psychology, it seems, since Augustine certainly did not mean it that way.
[70] Peter Brown, *Augustine of Hippo: A Biography* (Berkeley: University of California Press, 2000), 29.
[71] Augustine, *Confessions* III.4.7. Quotations are from Henry Chadwick's translation.

virtue of Roman philosophy, "the precise form of 'Wisdom' that Augustine might seek, would, of course, be very different from what Cicero would have recognized as 'Wisdom'. . . a pagan wisdom, a wisdom without the 'name of Christ' was quite out of the question."[72] "One thing alone put a brake on my intense enthusiasm—that the name of Christ was not contained in the book."[73]

Again, this is a mixed bag. Augustine experienced his first philosophical awakening, one that united for him ever after intellect and discipline, heart and mind. Even today, no reader of Augustine—whether of the *Confessions* or the *De Trinitate*—misses out on the wondrous marriage of mind and heart in his work. And yet a dissonance lingers: Augustine says that Cicero set him on a path to seek the Lord, but it would be more than a decade before he would come to faith.

It is telling, then, that the absence of the "*nomen Christi*" irked him. In fact, it is more than the name of Christ that is missing from Hellenistic Wisdom. True theism is absent, and the gospel is grossly mimicked. And yet, the sincerity and utility of ancient therapeutic wisdom present us with what J. H. Bavinck calls "extremely embarrassing questions."[74] Nor is it "possible," he says, "to dispose of the problem by making the general statement that all the words of devotion in the non-Christian religions are to be regarded as mere hypocrisy."[75] When Augustine looks back, two and a half decades on, he sees his own sin and pride, and yet a sincerity in his restless search, and the patient but persistent invitation of the Lord—all these wound together in his slow but nervous progress toward rest. In fact, "the seriousness of the questions raised by Cicero . . . moved him to pick up a Latin Bible," but "he was repelled by the obscurity of its content" and its "barbarous style."[76]

Augustine's mind was busy and restless; he had a taste for self-improvement and indulged the allure of wisdom; and although his conscience was strained by his sexual sin, he nonetheless was not prepared to give it up. Manichaeism was a perfect fit. The Persian mystic Mani (216–277 AD) had founded a religion which "expressed in poetic form a revulsion from the material world."[77] "The Manichees regarded 'the lower half of the body' as the

---

[72] Brown, *Augustine of Hippo*, 30.

[73] Augustine, *Confessions* III.4.8.

[74] J. H. Bavinck, *The Impact of Christianity on the Non-Christian World* (Grand Rapids, MI: Eerdmans, 1949), 97.

[75] J. H. Bavinck, *Impact of Christianity*, 97.

[76] Henry Chadwick, *Augustine* (Oxford University Press, 1986), 11. Chadwick refers to the "barbarous style of the rather primitive version made by half-educated missionaries in the second century."

[77] Chadwick, *Augustine*, 11.

disgusting work of the devil, the very prince of darkness. Sex and the Dark were intimately associated in Mani's mind, and the Dark was the very essence of evil."[78] Fortunately for Augustine, the Manichees enforced celibacy only upon their most advanced practitioners, called "the elect." Renouncing sexual sin was therefore an honor to which this mere novice could yet only aspire.

Mani had rejected the OT on account of the shameful conduct of its protagonists and for its positive view of creation as such. And he contended with what for him was the central question of religious thought and moral living—the nature and origin of evil—with an elaborate cosmology:

> He explained evil as resulting from a primeval and still continuing conflict between Light and Dark, these terms being both symbol and physical reality. . . . In consequence of the damage inflicted by the powers of Dark on the realm of Light, little fragments of God, or Soul, have become scattered throughout the world in all living things, including animals and plants. . . . Above all, the Manichees urged that they had the only satisfactory answer to the problem of evil: it was an ineradicable force inherent in the physicality of the material world. No one could plausibly hold that the ultimate author of so uncomfortable a world could be both omnipotent and truly good.[79]

Thus the Manichees dealt with the problem of evil by making it a part of the universe and the realm of experience the field of invisible, cosmic conflict. "So convinced were they that evil could not come from a good God, that they believed that it came from an invasion of the good . . . by a hostile force of evil, equal in power, eternal, totally separate—the 'kingdom of Darkness.' "[80] They at once "flattered" Augustine's "intellectual preference for higher things by mocking the Old Testament," and offered him a moral high ground free of the inconvenience of repentance.[81] His sexual sin was now a foreign, even cosmic, force by which he was pitiably enthralled. Here again a bizarre mutation of Christian theism promised to put at ease his busy mind and troubled heart. Manichaeism, in this sense, was a timely intellectual distraction and the perfect religion for a young man with a lively sense of moral duty but an affection for pride and sin to match it. Portraying evil as equal to good, and the two as locked in conflict, achieves both theoretical elegance and unconfused moral urgency, all without a whisper of sorrow for sin.

---

[78] Chadwick, *Augustine*, 11.
[79] Chadwick, *Augustine*, 13–14.
[80] Brown, *Augustine of Hippo*, 36.
[81] Gillian R. Evans, *Augustine on Evil* (Cambridge: Cambridge University Press, 1993), 12.

The Manichees held that God contended imperfectly with a kingdom and force of darkness equal in power and eternity to himself. That is: their dualism robbed God of his nature. So the loss of divine transcendence meant that humans could not be expected to resist evil with greater success even than God. If God "could not even enter into conflict with the invaders, without undergoing a drastic and belated transformation of his being," his creature no less would be left to contend perpetually with darkness foreign to his person.[82] So Augustine heard, believed, and preached for nearly a decade. The Manichees

> took from Augustine his private responsibility for his own soul's health on which the philosophers insisted, and allowed him to cast his burden into the cosmic maelstrom. When he was young, he notes wrily, he was readier to believe that the universe was out of joint than that there was something wrong with himself.[83]

One might say that Augustine was at least for a time convinced that the Manichean cosmology made the most of all available data and of human experience. But Manichaeism was more than a compelling theory, weighed indifferently against the alternatives. It offered to do much more than scratch an itch for theoretical coherence; it offered nothing less than an explanation for the fact that "we are not merely a speck of dust or an ocean wave," that "we can make our own choices, that we are free."[84] Augustine, like all people, knew that "we are different from the stars, which can only run their prescribed courses," and that "[w]e are responsible—that is to say, we will have to give an account for our actions."[85] In Manichaeism, in other words, Augustine placed his hope of evading the law and justice of the high and holy God of history. Manichaeism entered his heart via his mind and conspired with his guilty conscience to obscure the truth of God and mitigate the wickedness of his sin.

More than a century previously, an Egyptian Greek by the name of Plotinus (205–270 AD) had taught in Rome and won notoriety for reviving the philosophy of Plato. His student Porphyry (233–305) would surpass him in productivity and clarity of thought—Peter Brown calls him "the first

---

[82] Brown, *Augustine of Hippo*, 41.
[83] Evans, *Augustine on Evil*, 13. Evans cites *Confessions* VII.3.4.
[84] J. H. Bavinck, *Church between Temple and Mosque*, 55.
[85] J. H. Bavinck, *Church between Temple and Mosque*, 55.

systematic theologian in the history of thought"[86]—and would help to ignite a lively interest in what we call "Neoplatonism." When Augustine moved from Carthage to Milan via Rome in 383/4, he would find himself immersed in Christian Neoplatonism through literature, friends, and the preaching of Ambrose. The excitement of a new intellectual environment, waning interest in Manichaeism, a bad break-up with his common-law wife, and all the trauma of relocation colluded to help Augustine further along the way toward his famous conversion of 386.

Augustine had grown increasingly frustrated with Manichaeism, even in particular with its view of evil and sin, and he had also entered the fray of contemporary discussions of the possibility of knowledge, predication, and aesthetic judgment. He wondered, that is, not only about good and evil, but also about knowledge, language, and beauty.[87] And Plotinus, remarkably, offered solace on all counts. Behind the instability of knower and known, the precariousness of matching subject to predicate, and the elusiveness of beauty and judgment, claimed Plotinus, lay the One—the "other world," which "provided the basis of the world of the senses. It charged the passing spectacle of material things with an intensity and a permanence that they could not possess in their own right."[88] On the One all things depend; the One depends upon nothing, and is self-caused. For Plotinus as for Plato, the One was also the Good, so that the possibility of evil and sin is in proportion to ontological descent from eternal unity. Plotinus identified material with sin. Evil presupposes good in the same way that a being presupposes Being itself.

Plotinus identified the human person with the immaterial soul. This immaterial person is, even while embodied, perpetually, even eternally, undescended, and so able to anchor knowledge of particulars in knowledge of the eternal forms. This also meant that attachment to material things was an impediment to cognitive purity, even to contemplation of the One, which may be understood as the soul returning to itself.

So, for the Neoplatonist, sin is ontological diminution, the soul or the mind burdened by the body and bodily appetites. Renunciation of these by mental effort was the recommended apophatic path to contemplation of the One, through which the soul could enjoy that natural return. Contemplative focus upon the divine One, with a well-deserved dose of self-denial, was "the

---

[86] Brown, *Augustine of Hippo*, 83.
[87] Brown, *Augustine of Hippo*, 86. Brown suggests that Porphyry's "On Beauty" "would have affected him intimately."
[88] Brown, *Augustine of Hippo*, 88.

very stuff of Augustine's own enquiry."[89] And with regard to "the relation-ship of Becoming and Being; and that of the manifold and the One," with Neoplatonism, "Augustine is given a framework within which to explore."[90]

Augustine would later record an account of a momentary but significant mystical experience he achieved by following the Neoplatonist practice of meditation. To his disappointment, afterward he found he was just as proud and burdened with sin as before. Thus the inadequacies of the philosophy he embraced at Milan would later be manifest, one might say, twice: first, Augustine's conversion would add to the high divine ontology of Neopla-tonism repentance and sorrow for sin. This would prove that ascending in a meditative mode an apophatic hierarchy of being does in fact little for the soul; it does not address sin as sin but as aggravating ontological deficiency, a metaphysical nuisance. Second, likely due to the influence of Plotinian Pla-tonism, Augustine would bequeath to Christendom the idea of evil as priva-tion, which, while affirming a priority of good and the parasitic nature of evil, could never produce a serious account of transgression and guilt—not with-out the inconvenient fact that "not being God" is in the end the real problem.

Ontological descent does not afford morally meaningful volition, as does ontological, Creator-creature distinction. When God creates, neither sin nor a tendency to sin appear, but only a relationally upheld possibility of sin. When Adam takes and eats, he does so as one who lives and moves and has his being in the presence of his Creator and Lord, the sustainer of all things. Adam is "lower" than the personal God by kind rather than by degree, so that as creature he is good, wholly good and inclined toward good—until he sins. Here, argue the Reformed, is the real problem of evil: a morally good will, a godly person, succumbing to temptation and transgressing the will of God. Herman Bavinck says that this mystery is second only to the mystery of existence itself. So Bavinck, Geerhardus Vos, and others see privation as a helpful corrective against Manichaean dualism, but argue that the historic Christian view, Augustine's included, is an active privation, a willful depar-ture—not mere ontological reduction—from goodness and godliness.[91] On an impersonal, ontological account, such as the Neoplatonist one, sin makes

---

[89] Evans, *Augustine on Evil*, 31.
[90] Evans, *Augustine on Evil*, 32.
[91] See Herman Bavinck, *Sin and Salvation in Christ*, vol. 3 of *Reformed Dogmatics*, ed. John Bolt, trans. John Vriend (Grand Rapids, MI: Baker Academic, 2003–8), 136–38; Geerhardus Vos, *Anthropology*, vol. 2 of *Reformed Dogmatics*, trans. and ed. Richard B. Gaffin Jr. (Bellingham, WA: Lexham, 2012–14), 56.

sense; it is understandable. And the human person is non-culpably burdened with it. But the orthodox idea of creation requires that we deny any precedent or anticipation of sin in God's good world before it actually takes place.

Conclusion

Clearly the world knows her Creator, and the image-bearer, individually and corporately, has been busy suppressing and replacing the truth about God (cf. Rom. 1:18). J. H. Bavinck writes, "In all these ideas we find that man is very conscious of the fact that the norm has binding religious authority which he cannot escape."[92] And Bavinck here says nothing more than what Paul teaches in Romans 1:32, or what we see in the panicked blame-game of Adam's botched apology (Gen. 3:12). To paraphrase B. B. Warfield, special revelation is designed to address the image-bearer in the actual circumstances in which he or she is found. And indeed, those circumstances are on the most important level always the same: under wrath and without God in the world, until feet quickened by mercy, and attended by the Spirit, bring good news.

---

[92] J. H. Bavinck, *Church between Temple and Mosque*, 65.

18

Whence This Evil?

TOWARD A BIBLICAL THEODICY

James N. Anderson

The problem of evil is often viewed primarily in the context of arguments against theism, but that is a relatively recent development in the history of human thought. Serious reflections on the problem of evil predate the rise of modern atheism by several millennia. For those who believe in a personal Creator God, the existence and extent of evil in the world—especially the ubiquity and depravity of human sin—present perplexing and often disturbing questions. This chapter will not seek to rebut the atheistic argument from evil, although what is said will certainly be relevant to that task. Rather, it will be an exercise in *faith seeking understanding*: a modest attempt to gain clarity on the questions and to outline a biblically faithful approach to developing answers.

1. Definitions and Distinctions

At a first approximation, evil may be simply defined as the opposite of goodness: something is evil to the extent that it is *not good*. This has the somewhat counterintuitive implication that everything bad is also evil. My tennis swing is bad, but is it really *evil*? This suggests that the general terms *good* and *bad* have broad semantic ranges, and we need to narrow things down. For our purposes it will be useful to define matters in Christian theistic terms. On the Christian view, God is good, but more than that: God is *the Good*, the ultimate source and standard of goodness. God alone is essentially and non-derivatively good; anything else is good to the extent that it reflects the character of God or conforms to the will of God. Consequently, something is evil to the extent that it *fails* to reflect the character of God or conform to the will of God.

We may put the matter thus: in God's universe, there are ways things *ought* to be and ways things *ought not* to be. Good and evil are the standard terms we use to describe these various ways things *ought* or *ought not* to be.

It is common in discussions of the problem of evil to define evil in terms of pain and suffering. This is understandable, since our paradigmatic cases of evil typically involve either instances of pain and suffering or the causes thereof. Even so, I want to resist that simple identification for two reasons. First, pain may not be *intrinsically* evil; it can sometimes have a positive utility, as we will consider in due course. Second, it seems possible for there to be evil without pain and suffering. Imagine an alternate universe in which God creates a single creature who (for whatever reason) rebels against God. At the first moment of rebellion, the creature might not immediately experience any pain or suffering (and neither would God, given divine impassibility). Nevertheless, that act of rebellion would be a clear instance of evil.

It is also commonplace to distinguish between *moral* and *natural* evil. Moral evil can be defined as any evil arising from the free action (or inaction) of moral agents, such as humans or angels. Christians have spoken of "sins of commission" (things done that should not have been done) and "sins of omission" (things not done that should have been done). Moral evil encompasses both types of sin. In contrast, natural evil is any evil that is *not* moral evil. For example, a tsunami that kills thousands of people and causes widespread devastation would be a case of natural evil.

The line between moral and natural evil is often blurred. Natural evils can be exacerbated or even triggered by moral evils, as in the case of a shoddily built apartment block that collapses during an earthquake, resulting in injuries and deaths. Nevertheless, the distinction is a useful one, and any satisfying discussion of the problem of evil must reckon with both kinds of evil, not least because the Bible speaks directly to both.

2. The Problems of Evil

Although we routinely speak of *the* problem of evil, as if there were a singular problem, further reflection reveals that there are *multiple* problems raised by the presence of evil, each of which invites a particular type of solution or response. In the first place, the **metaphysical problem of evil** concerns how evil could exist in any sense, given the biblical view of God. According to orthodox Christianity, God is perfect in goodness and the Creator of everything else that exists (i.e., everything other than God). If evil exists, it would seem to follow that God is the Creator of evil—but clearly that conflicts with God's perfect goodness. Christian theologians have traditionally appealed to the privation theory of evil, according to which evil has no existence in itself, but exists only as a corruption of what is good, to resolve the *prima facie* problem.[1]

Second, the **etiological problem of evil** concerns the *cause* or *origin* of evil in light of the original goodness of the creation. Scripture tells us that when the world was created it was, by the Creator's own judgment, "very good." How then could evil arise out of something that was wholly good? There is general agreement that the origin of moral evil must be resolved by an appeal to creaturely free will, although debate persists as to what *kind* of free will should be affirmed here.[2] As for natural evil, its origin can be subsequently explained as a consequence of moral evil (e.g., the divine curses in Gen. 3:14–19).

Third, the **moral problem of evil** is primarily concerned with how a holy and righteous God could permit—or even in some sense ordain—the occurrence of evil within his creation. This conundrum invites the task of *theodicy*: literally, "the justification of God." The justification in question is a *moral* one. On the face of it, a person who knowingly permits an evil when he has the power to prevent that evil bears some moral responsibility for that evil. An all-powerful God would be able to prevent any evil he wishes to prevent, and an all-good God would wish to prevent all evil. Yet God *does not* prevent all evil, including many evils that even a deity with limited power would be able to prevent. Naturally, that raises questions about God's moral goodness.

Last, the **eschatological problem of evil** focuses attention on the *future* existence of evil rather than its present existence. Will evil always exist in some form, or will it be completely eradicated at some point? Will the battle between good and evil continue indefinitely, or will good finally triumph

---

[1] For a classic articulation of this solution, see Augustine, *Confessions*, Book 7, chs. 12–13; Augustine, *Enchiridion*, chs. 3–4.

[2] For further discussion, see James N. Anderson, "Calvinism and the First Sin," in *Calvinism and the Problem of Evil*, ed. David E. Alexander and Daniel M. Johnson (Eugene, OR: Wipf & Stock, 2016), 200–32.

over evil? The eschatological problem is addressed by the person and work of Jesus Christ in his first and second advents. Christ has already triumphed decisively over sin, its causes, and its consequences, through his atoning death, resurrection, and ascension.[3] Although for various reasons evil is permitted by God to continue while the church pursues its Great Commission, the *de jure* victory has been won. The *de facto* victory will follow at the return of Christ, at which time the enemies of God and his people will be finally vanquished, and the redeemed will enjoy eternal communion with God in a renewed creation, with neither sin nor suffering to trouble them.[4]

Important as it is for Christians to reflect on all four of these problems, space constraints mean we must limit our discussion to the one that arguably attracts the greatest attention and concern: the moral problem. Thus, "problem of evil" will be used hereafter as shorthand for the *moral* problem of evil.

3. Parameters for a Biblical Theodicy

I assume that readers of this book will favor a biblical approach to the problem of evil. It hardly needs stating, however, that Christians have disagreed over what exactly constitutes a biblical approach (to this topic or any other). In this chapter, I will be unashamedly assuming a Reformed theological perspective on the issues. I will not rehearse the standard arguments for the distinctive doctrines of the Reformed faith, which have been more than adequately articulated elsewhere, although my citations of Scripture will give some indication of what I take to be the biblical basis for those Reformed distinctives.

Our first order of business will be to establish some basic theological parameters for thinking about the moral problem of evil—to lay down some doctrinal tracks for our theodical train to travel on. I will identify six parameters, briefly explaining the rationale for each one.

3.1. SOLA SCRIPTURA

The first parameter is an *epistemological* one, concerning the sources of knowledge that we bring to bear on the question. Christians standing in the Reformation tradition have been committed to the principle of *sola Scriptura*, which can be concisely stated as the conviction that the Bible alone is the word of God and the only infallible source and standard for Christian doctrine

---

[3] First Corinthians 15:20–28, 50–57; Col. 2:13–15.
[4] Revelation 19–22.

and practice.[5] *Sola Scriptura* does not exclude extrabiblical sources of knowledge, such as reason and experience, nor does it direct us to disregard noncanonical church traditions such as creeds and confessions. It does require us, however, to give the Bible primacy over all other sources of knowledge in our theological reflections.

A commitment to *sola Scriptura* has important implications for our approach to the problem of evil. First, it requires that our answers be *consistent* with the Bible. Any theodicy that appeals to notions at odds with Scripture must be rejected.

Furthermore, it demands that our answers be *primarily informed* by the Bible. We must look first to what Scripture says about evil and how it relates to God's purposes before we turn to extrabiblical sources. There is nothing inherently wrong in drawing on such sources, but they must play a secondary epistemic role. Scripture has much to say about the problem of evil, and what Scripture says must be given central place, because what Scripture says, God says.[6]

This leads to a third observation. *Sola Scriptura* must be accompanied by another Reformational principle: *tota Scriptura*. The *entire* Bible is the word of God, and thus our reflections on the problem of evil must be informed by "the whole counsel of God" in Scripture. We must resist the temptation to develop answers based on a small selection of texts or themes, failing to incorporate other biblical perspectives and principles that bear equally on the issues.

Finally, *sola Scriptura* entails that our theologizing must be *constrained* by God's word in the sense that we should resist speculations with little if any grounding in Scripture. Where the Bible speaks to an issue, we must listen and affirm; but where the Bible is silent, we should be hesitant to speak with confidence. Again, this does not mean that extrabiblical ideas are ruled out of court, only that they should not play a central and foundational role in our approach to the problem of evil.

3.2. DIVINE PERFECTION

The second parameter is a *metaphysical* one concerning the nature and attributes of God. If theodicy is the "justification of God," we must be clear

---

[5] For a recent exposition and defense of *sola Scriptura*, see Matthew Barrett, *God's Word Alone: The Authority of Scripture*, The 5 Solas Series (Grand Rapids, MI: Zondervan, 2016).
[6] Benjamin B. Warfield, *The Inspiration and Authority of the Bible* (Philadelphia: Presbyterian & Reformed, 1948), 299–348.

about the nature of the God whose ways are justified. Christian theologians have almost unanimously affirmed that God is a *perfect* being—that is to say, God possesses all "great-making attributes," and he possesses them to the greatest possible degree.[7] Thus, God is not merely wise, but *maximally* wise; God is not merely powerful, but *maximally* powerful; and so on for every great-making attribute. The absolute perfection of God is often expressed in terms of the *infinitude* of his attributes, as the Westminster Shorter Catechism illustrates:

> Q 4. What is God?
> A. God is a spirit, infinite, eternal, and unchangeable, in his being, wisdom, power, holiness, justice, goodness, and truth.

The implication is that God is not *finite* or *limited* in his attributes, as if it were possible for there to exist a being who possesses *greater* attributes (or the same attributes to a greater degree).

The notion of divine perfection is arguably definitional of God, at least in the classical theistic tradition, and it has considerable intuitive support. Even more decisive, however, is the consistent scriptural testimony speaking of the perfections of God.[8]

The relevance of this parameter for a biblical theodicy should be obvious. Any satisfying account of why God permits evil within his creation must be consistent with his absolute perfection. Any theodicy that seeks to make room for evil by conceding limits on God's power, wisdom, or goodness, cannot be regarded as authentically biblical or Christian.

3.3. DIVINE SOVEREIGNTY AND ASEITY

The third parameter may be viewed as an extension of the second. If God is absolutely perfect in all his attributes, it follows that God must have the attributes of *sovereignty* (comprehensive authority and control over his creation) and *aseity* (absolute self-existence and independence). If any elements of the creation were beyond God's control, and thus able to constrain or frustrate his will or his purposes, that would constitute a limitation of God's power and thus an imperfection. Similarly, if God were dependent upon his

---

[7] Katherin A. Rogers, *Perfect Being Theology* (Edinburgh: Edinburgh University Press, 2000).
[8] A sampling of texts: Deut. 32:4; Pss.18:30; 145:17; Jer. 32:17; Hab. 1:13; Matt. 5:48; Luke 1:37; Rom. 16:27; Rev. 1:8.

creation in any respect—for his existence, his attributes, or the fulfillment of his purposes—that would amount to a limitation of God's being and thus an imperfection. In short, an absolutely perfect God could not be subject to, constrained by, or dependent upon any *other* being in any respect.

Although some may consider this a questionable theological deduction, Scripture speaks quite directly and forcefully about God's sovereignty over his creation and his absolute independence.[9] Once again, these divine attributes have crucial implications for developing a biblical theodicy. Any account of God's relationship to evil that compromises his sovereignty and aseity must be regarded as unacceptable for the Christian committed to *sola Scriptura* and *tota Scriptura*.

3.4. DIVINE GLORY

A biblical theodicy should take into account not only what Scripture teaches about the *attributes* of God, but also what it teaches about the *purposes* of God. Answers to the question "Why does God allow evil?" must be placed in the broader context of God's general purposes for his creation. Why did God create the world? Why did God permit the world to fall into sin and corruption? Why did God implement a plan of redemption and restoration for that fallen world? What are God's *ultimate* purposes in all these acts?

Scripture often tells us why God does what he does. God commands his people to be holy because he is himself holy.[10] God delivered Israel from slavery in Egypt because he loved them.[11] God sent his Son into the world because he loved the world.[12] Examples could be multiplied. But does God have one *overarching and unifying purpose*, to which all other purposes are subordinated? The apostle Paul indicates in Ephesians 1 that God's ultimate end in the redemption of his elected people is "the praise of his glory" (Eph. 1:12, 14). Similarly, Paul argues in Romans 9 that God's purpose in choosing some to be "vessels of mercy" is so that he might "make known the riches of his glory" (Rom. 9:23). Paul's stunning doxology in Romans 11:33–36 further reinforces the idea that God's ultimate end in redemption is his own glory.

This observation about the ultimate purpose of God's redemptive acts can be straightforwardly extended to all God's works of creation and providence.

---

[9] Exodus 3:14; Job 42:2; Pss. 33:10–11; 115:3; Isa. 46:8–11; Acts 17:24–25; Eph. 1:11.
[10] Leviticus 11:44–45.
[11] Deuteronomy 7:6–8.
[12] John 3:16.

Jonathan Edwards persuasively argued that God's ultimate end in the creation of the world is the manifestation of his glory.[13] The refrain that God does all things for his own glory—for his own name's sake—is pervasive in the biblical narrative.

Furthermore, that God's ultimate purpose is the manifestation of his own glory coheres profoundly with what we noted earlier about divine perfection, sovereignty, and aseity. If God alone possesses all perfections, then he alone is worthy of all praise, honor, and glory. For God to act so as to glorify *another* being would amount to a denial of his divine nature—but God cannot deny himself.[14] By the same token, if God were dependent on *another* being in any respect, that other being would have the right to share in God's glory—but God will not share his glory.[15] Indeed, the very fact that God will not share his glory confirms that he is committed exclusively to his self-glorification.

God's ultimate aim of self-glorification serves as another important constraint on a biblical theodicy. Whatever explanation we offer regarding God's relationship to evil, and whatever justification we offer regarding God's permission of evil, must cohere with what Scripture teaches about God's overarching purpose in creation and redemption.

3.5. DIVINE INCOMPREHENSIBILITY

A biblical epistemology is founded on two pillars. First, we *can* know many important truths about God and his purposes, on account of God's gracious self-revelation. Second, there are many things about God and his purposes that we *cannot* know because God has not revealed them to us and because (in the vast majority of cases) our limited creaturely minds are simply incapable of grasping them. Thus, while God is not *inapprehensible* (utterly beyond human knowledge) we acknowledge that he is *incomprehensible* (beyond our understanding in countless respects). This follows from the simple fact that God is God and we are not. There is a vast ontological and epistemological chasm between the Creator and his creatures. It comes as no surprise, then, that the inscrutability of God and his ways is another theme that recurs in Scripture.[16]

The doctrine of divine incomprehensibility thus serves as another parameter for a biblical approach to the problem of evil. Although God has revealed

---

[13] Jonathan Edwards, *A Dissertation concerning the End for Which God Created the World* (1765).
[14] Second Timothy 2:13.
[15] Exodus 34:14; Isa. 48:11; cf. Rom. 1:21–23.
[16] Deuteronomy 29:29; Ps. 139:6; Isa. 55:8–9; Job 38–41; Rom. 11:33–35.

many important truths about his attributes and purposes, we are often left in the dark with respect to precise details. We know in general terms what God's purposes are in the world, but in the absence of special revelation about particular evils, we are rarely able to discern God's *specific* purposes in doing or permitting such-and-such. A biblical theodicy must be prepared to accommodate the epistemic implications of the Creator-creature distinction and the limitations of human knowledge and understanding.

3.6. A REDEMPTIVE-HISTORICAL PERSPECTIVE

One further factor ought to be acknowledged by any distinctively Christian approach to the problem of evil. Christianity, in contrast to many other religious faiths, is irreducibly historical. The Christian worldview is not merely an assemblage of eternal theological truths and universal moral principles. It incorporates a *story*—indeed, the story of all stories, the story of the world. It presents a concrete philosophy of history, offering an account of how events have unfolded, and will continue to unfold, under the providential direction of the Creator.

The biblical view of history is often summarized in four epochal categories: creation, fall, redemption, and consummation. Reformed theologians have further refined this fourfold scheme by paying close attention to the central and unifying role that the *divine covenants* play in the biblical narrative. They have spoken of three overarching covenants that characterize God's dealings with man: (1) a covenant of *works*, established at creation with all mankind through Adam as the covenant head, but broken by Adam, resulting in the calamitous fall of the human race; (2) a covenant of *redemption*, established in eternity between the three persons of the Trinity, consisting of a plan to save an elect people from divine wrath and judgment through an atoning sacrifice by the incarnate Son of God; and (3) a covenant of *grace*, established between God and his elect people, with Christ as the covenant head, and administered through the ages as a progression of historical-redemptive covenants.[17] This covenantal scheme thus supplies a theological lens through which to interpret not only the more obviously redemptive acts of God in history, but also by extension all historical events under the providential hand of God.

---

[17] Herman Bavinck, *Reformed Dogmatics: Sin and Salvation in Christ*, ed. John Bolt, trans. John Vriend, 4 vols. (Grand Rapids, MI: Baker Academic, 2003–8), 3:193–232.

This has significant implications for developing a biblical theodicy. Evil is not an ahistorical or transhistorical phenomenon. Just as the creation is inherently temporal, so is the corruption of that creation. The problem of evil is prompted by the *present* reality of evil in the world—if there were no evil *now*, then the problem of evil would not seem nearly so pressing! Nevertheless, how we understand evil *in the present* must be informed by what has taken place *in the past* and what will take place *in the future*. Thus, the task of theodicy must be guided by a Christian philosophy of history, and if the Reformed tradition has it right, a biblical theodicy should be formulated from a covenantal, redemptive-historical perspective.

4. A Survey of Proposed Theodicies

The literature on Christian theodicy is vast, and nothing close to a comprehensive survey can be attempted here. Instead, I will summarize nine noteworthy proposals and offer a brief assessment of each in light of the preceding discussion of biblical parameters.

4.1. FREE WILL

The free-will theodicy has a long pedigree but has enjoyed increased popularity in the last half-century or so.[18] According to this account, God has bestowed some of his creatures with the power of free choice; not only is this highly valuable in itself, it also enables these creatures to be morally responsible agents who enter into authentic love relationships with God and one another, not to mention other cooperative social relationships that bring about great goods in the world. However, there is a price to pay: if God's creatures are to have genuine free will, they must be able to choose evil as well as good, and their choices must be *autonomous* in the sense that they cannot be determined or directed by God. If God were somehow to *ensure* that his creatures made only good choices, and engaged only in loving relationships, they would not truly be free and morally responsible. God has therefore accepted a kind of trade-off. Although he does not *want* his creatures to rebel against him, God is willing to allow it for the greater good of granting them free will and honoring their decisions. Even if God were to counteract the consequences of their evil choices—for example, by vaporizing the bullets from

---

[18] For two prominent examples, see Richard Swinburne, *Providence and the Problem of Evil* (Oxford: Clarendon, 1998); William Hasker, *The Triumph of God over Evil* (Downers Grove, IL: IVP Academic, 2008).

an assassin's rifle—that would erode the value of creaturely free will, because choices without weighty consequences cannot be morally significant choices.

In sum, the free-will theodicy maintains that a world with creaturely free will that also allows for evil as a consequence of that free will is *more valuable overall* than a vapid world with no evil but also no morally responsible agents or significant love relationships. For that reason, God is justified in permitting evil.

While the free-will theodicy is undoubtedly popular among both academics and lay Christians, it is noteworthy that none of the biblical authors ever appeals to creaturely free will to get God "off the hook" for the evil in the world. Furthermore, there are several reasons why Christians should find this theodicy less than satisfying. Here I will mention only three. In the first place, God has free will but cannot choose evil, and thus the capacity for choosing evil cannot be necessary for the possession of free will.

Second, as it is typically developed, this theodicy depends on a libertarian view of free will, according to which God cannot determine or exercise sovereign control over the free actions of his creatures. Not only is this contrary to many biblical texts which imply that God foreordains all things, including human free choices; it also runs into conflict with many orthodox Christian doctrines such as divine foreknowledge, the impeccability of Christ, and salvation by grace alone.[19]

Last, the claim that morally significant relationships must entail the possibility of evil choices is undermined by the biblical teaching about the new creation. The redeemed in the eschaton will still be moral agents with the capacity for love relationships, but they will be unable to do evil. Indeed, the glorified saints will enjoy *more* freedom and blessedness than before, yet without the ability to sin. It seems that it is indeed within God's power to keep his creatures from committing sin without undermining their freedom, which casts doubt on the foundational assumption of the free-will theodicy.

4.2. Natural Laws

A second theodicy, offered most notably by C. S. Lewis, appeals to the idea of natural laws to help explain God's permission of moral and natural evil.[20] The argument runs as follows: it is a necessary condition for meaningful moral

---

[19] David E. Alexander, "Orthodoxy, Theological Determinism, and the Problem of Evil," in *Calvinism and the Problem of Evil* (Eugene, OR: Pickwick, 2016), 123–43.
[20] C. S. Lewis, *The Problem of Pain* (London: Geoffrey Bles, 1940), 25–27.

choices that we inhabit a world with a stable environment governed by natural laws which allow us to predict (for the most part) the immediate consequences of our actions. For example, if I put up an umbrella over my wife's head, I need to know that it will block the raindrops, but not prevent air from reaching her lungs. Were we to live in a chaotic, unpredictable world, we simply could not tell whether our actions would have helpful or harmful consequences.

Even so, this stability and law-governed regularity comes at a cost. The same natural laws that enable us to build houses also mean that those houses can be destroyed by tornados. The laws of physics that allow us to create nuclear power stations also permit the manufacture of nuclear weapons. Like the free-will theodicy, the natural-law theodicy maintains that God has made a morally justifiable trade-off: a robust physical environment comes at a price—the potential for physical harms—but the price is worth it.

Scripture acknowledges that God has created a stable, law-governed universe and that he is to be praised for doing so.[21] But does this mean God had to permit the entrance of moral and natural evil into the world? Not obviously so. On the contrary, the biblical narrative presents two scenarios that serve as counterexamples: the garden of Eden and the new creation. The garden of Eden was a stable physical environment where man was able to flourish in the absence of evil. There is no indication that Adam would have been exposed to the painful consequences of natural laws even if he had not sinned. Similarly, the new creation will be a stable physical environment where, by God's providence, there will be no suffering or any other harm.[22]

The natural-law theodicy invites us to think that a law-governed physical world will almost inevitably involve natural evils. But could not a sovereign God providentially arrange things so that harmful events never actually occurred? Even if we grant that they sometimes have to occur, surely it would be within God's power to mitigate their painful consequences. Moreover, if natural evil is a consequence of moral evil, as Scripture indicates, this theodicy cannot provide a general explanation of God's permission of evil.

4.3. DIVINE PUNISHMENT

The divine-punishment theodicy asserts that God permits, and in many cases inflicts, suffering as a just penalty for the sins of his creatures. There is little

---

[21] See esp. Pss. 19, 65, and 104.
[22] Revelation 21:1–4; 22:1–5.

question that Scripture endorses a retributive account of justice, and that many instances of creaturely suffering are depicted as divine punishment, from Genesis 3 to Revelation 22.[23] Even so, while this explanation does have strong biblical warrant, it cannot serve as a one-size-fits-all theodicy. In the first place, Scripture also tells us that some instances of suffering are not to be understood as divine punishments.[24] Second, this theodicy fails to explain why God permitted moral evil in the first place. Yes, the curse was a punishment for Adam's sin—but why did God allow Adam to sin at all? The divine-punishment answer is at best a partial theodicy that needs to be supplemented by other answers.

4.4. SOUL-MAKING

Inspired by the writings of second-century Christian bishop Irenaeus, the British philosopher John Hick brought to prominence a response to the problem of evil that has become known as the *soul-making theodicy*.[25] Hick argued that evil is a necessary component of an environment in which free creatures can exercise significant moral choices and thereby become spiritually mature. In other words, facing and wrestling with evil is necessary to develop moral and spiritual character, and such character-building is a great good that justifies God's permission of evil. A world containing evils, but also creatures who have developed mature souls through confronting and overcoming those evils, is a better world—all things considered—than one without evil but also without mature souls.

Scripture certainly teaches that facing suffering and overcoming evil are important means by which God develops our character.[26] The soul-making theodicy is founded on some genuine insights. It falls short as a comprehensive theodicy, however, because it suggests that God could not fulfil his purposes for his creation *without* evil. There is no indication in the Bible that in the absence of evil and suffering Adam could not have become the spiritually mature person God intended him to be. We can recognize that Adam had to be confronted with a *moral choice* between good and evil without granting that Adam had to commit or experience an actual evil. In addition, the idea that every evil has a character-building purpose not only lacks biblical warrant but

[23] Note esp. Paul's argument in Rom. 1:18–2:11.
[24] Job 1:1, 22; John 9:13; 1 Pet. 3:14.
[25] John Hick, *Evil and the God of Love* (London: Macmillan, 1966).
[26] Romans 5:3–5; James 1:2–4; 1 Pet. 1:6–9.

also conflicts with our experiences. It is not hard to point to cases where those who have encountered evil or experienced pain have become *less* virtuous as a consequence, rather than more so.

4.5. DIVINE GLORIFICATION

Another line of response to the moral problem has been to argue that some evils are necessary conditions for the manifestation of God's glory, specifically the divine attributes of mercy and justice.[27] Although God is merciful and just by his very nature, and thus would possess those attributes regardless of whether evil existed, those attributes can be exercised only if there are sinful creatures who can be the proper objects of divine mercy and justice. Since such attributes reflect the essential goodness of God, the *demonstration* of those attributes has great value. God is therefore justified in permitting moral evils so that he can exercise mercy (in some cases) and justice (in other cases) toward the creatures who freely commit those evils.

This theodicy can also be applied indirectly to natural evils, insofar as those natural evils are a consequence of moral evils. For example, if sinful creatures *deserve* to be afflicted by diseases, God's mercy may be demonstrated through his healing of diseases and his justice may be demonstrated through his refraining to do so. But neither would be possible in a world without disease.

The apostle Paul gestures toward such a theodicy in his discussion of divine election in Romans 9:22–24:

> What if God, *desiring to show his wrath and to make known his power*, has endured with much patience vessels of wrath prepared for destruction, *in order to make known the riches of his glory for vessels of mercy*, which he has prepared beforehand for glory—even us whom he has called, not from the Jews only but also from the Gentiles?

Paul's point is clear enough: God has prepared some for glory and others for destruction for the specific purpose of demonstrating his wrath, power, and mercy—all of which reflect his glorious divine perfections. Other biblical texts also indicate that one of the reasons God permits evil is to demonstrate his attributes.[28]

---

[27] For a rather triumphalist example, see Jay E. Adams, *The Grand Demonstration: A Biblical Study of the So-Called Problem of Evil* (Santa Barbara, CA: EastGate, 1991).
[28] Romans 3:1–8, 25–26; 5:8.

While this argument can serve as one important element of a biblical theodicy, it cannot bear the entire weight on its own. For one thing, there are instances of horrific evil that seem to go far beyond what would be needed to manifest God's attributes. Take the Holocaust as an obvious example. Could not God have demonstrated his power, mercy, justice, and so forth, *without* permitting such a grievous evil? If such is the case, this theodicy fails to explain why God allowed *that particular evil*—and many other comparable cases—and thus it needs to be supplemented by other lines of response.

4.6. Human Virtues

Just as it has been argued that evil is necessary for the manifestation of certain divine attributes, something similar has been argued with respect to human virtues. Without fear, there could be no courage. Without frustration, there could be no patience. Without wrongdoing, there could be no forgiveness. Without suffering, there could be no compassion.

It is generally conceded that the most praiseworthy of human characteristics and accomplishments can be demonstrated only in the face of significant pain, adversity, and deprivation. This suggests in turn that a world in which there is fear but also courage, frustration but also patience, wrongdoing but also forgiveness, suffering but also compassion, and so forth, is *overall more valuable* than a morally bland world in which all these things are absent. Consequently, God is justified in permitting these moral and natural evils because they provide opportunities for great moral goods that could not otherwise exist.

Scripture offers positive support for this line of reasoning. For example, in 2 Corinthians 1:3–7 Paul gives a twofold explanation for the fact that Christians experience afflictions even though their sins have been fully forgiven by God: (1) they can experience the comfort of God as they share in the sufferings of Christ, and (2) they can comfort *other believers* who are also experiencing afflictions. We see here a remarkable symbiosis of affliction and comfort involving both divine and human agency, with glory being given ultimately to God (2 Cor. 1:3).

Once again, this is at best a partial theodicy. Surely there are instances of great evil that seem to go far beyond what would be strictly necessary for the demonstration of human virtues. Worse still, there are some moral and natural evils that turn out to be an occasion for human vices rather than virtues—which is just as we would expect, given the biblical doctrine of human depravity. Despite such limitations, however, this partial theodicy takes us some way toward explaining why God permits suffering in the lives of his children.

4.7. GOD'S MEGAPHONE

We often assume that pain always has negative value: that for any given pain, it would be better not to suffer it than to suffer it. This can mask the fact that the experience of pain often has positive effects, such as increasing our spiritual sensitivity and turning our thoughts toward God. For this very reason, pain can be a very effective instrument in God's hands for gaining our attention and reordering our priorities. As C. S. Lewis memorably put it, "God whispers to us in our pleasures, speaks in our conscience, but shouts in our pain: it is His megaphone to rouse a deaf world."[29]

The argument is not that some pains are good in themselves, but rather that they can be *instrumentally* good inasmuch as they have beneficial consequences that outweigh the negative value of the pains themselves. Some have objected that pain is not strictly necessary for such purposes; the mere attenuation or absence of pleasure could accomplish the same results. Nevertheless, Lewis's argument that pain has the power to bring us to our senses, in a way that the mere privation of pleasure cannot, resonates with many of us.

A number of biblical texts can be cited in support of this theodicy. Jesus indicated to his disciples in Luke 13:1–5 that one reason some people suffer calamities is so that other people will be prompted toward repentance. The so-called parable of the prodigal son in Luke 15 provides an object lesson in how the turn from sensual pleasures (Luke 15:13) to suffering (vv. 14–16) serves as a spur toward genuine repentance (vv. 17–19). The psalmist testifies to how afflictions in his life served to draw him closer to God (Ps. 119:67, 71). One could argue that much of the history of Israel in the OT illustrates how God mercifully sends afflictions to shake his people from their wayward courses.

While this explanation may apply to much of the suffering that God permits, there are too many counterexamples for it to serve as a complete theodicy. Some experiences of pain only harden people's hearts and dull their spiritual senses (although, we should note, even this can serve God's good purposes). Moreover, as with the preceding theodicies, it falls short

[29] Lewis, *Problem of Pain*, 74.

when applied to the two ends of the Bible's redemptive-historical narrative: the garden of Eden and the new creation. Do we want to say that Adam's attention was not sufficiently directed toward God before the fall, or that pain might occasionally be necessary in the eschaton to keep us fully devoted to our Lord?

4.8. O FELIX CULPA

On the biblical Christian view, the evil in the world is a consequence of the fall. Moral evil is rampant because of original sin: we have all inherited a morally and spiritually corrupt nature from our forefather Adam, and thus we are inclined by nature toward selfishness and ungodliness. Natural evil is largely due to the curse placed on the natural world as a result of Adam's sin.

But what of the fall itself? So much evil could have been avoided had God not permitted Adam's sin, and surely the omniscient Creator knew that Adam *would* sin. Why then did God allow it? One powerful answer to the question comes in the form of the "O-Felix-Culpa" theodicy (literally "blessed fall" or "happy fault"), which was suggested by the medieval theologian Thomas Aquinas and has been revived more recently by Alvin Plantinga.[30]

The reasoning behind the theodicy runs as follows. It is true that, all things being equal, a world *with* sin would be worse than a world *without* sin. But not all things are equal, because that simplistic comparison fails to take into account some of the features of this world that would be absent had sin never entered the world. For this world is not only a world with sin, but also a world in which God in his great mercy took on human flesh in the person of his Son, Jesus Christ, and made an atoning sacrifice in order to redeem a people for himself so that they would enjoy eternal blessedness in fellowship with the triune God.

In short, our world is not simply a Genesis 1–3 world; it is also an Ephesians 1, Philippians 2, and Romans 3 world. Consequently, we have the privilege of knowing God not only as our Creator but also as our Redeemer. Our knowledge of God is more profound, and our relationship with God more precious, because we have been redeemed from our sins and know God not merely as creatures but as *forgiven sinners* reconciled to him through Christ. None of that would be possible had God not permitted the fall.

---

[30] Thomas Aquinas, *Summa Theologiae* 3a, 1, 3; Alvin Plantinga, "Supralapsarianism, or '*O Felix Culpa*,'" in *Christian Faith and the Problem of Evil*, ed. Peter Van Inwagen (Grand Rapids, MI: Eerdmans, 2004), 1–25.

For the sake of abbreviation, let us call a world in which there is not only a fall but also an incarnation and an atonement (and everything else that follows from these two great redemptive acts of God) an "FIA" (fall-incarnation-atonement) world. The central insight of the "O-Felix-Culpa" theodicy is that an FIA world is *overall more valuable*—and more glorifying to God—than a *non*-FIA world.

The logic of this theodicy is attractive and consistent with what Scripture teaches about the glories of the incarnation and the atonement, both of which presuppose the fallenness of mankind.[31] It is entirely plausible that the praise and thankfulness of redeemed, sinful humans will exceed that of the unfallen angels who are mere spectators to God's work of redemption. This answer therefore supplies an important component of a broader biblical theodicy.

Even so, it cannot serve as a stand-alone theodicy because it fails to explain why God has not mitigated many of the consequences of the fall. We can grant that an FIA world is more valuable, all else being equal, than a non-FIA world. But would not an FIA world with far fewer diseases, rapes, and murders be a better world overall than *this* FIA world? The "O-Felix-Culpa" theodicy sheds little if any light on why God has permitted so many *other* evils in this world.

4.9. Best Possible World

The word *theodicy* was brought to prominence as the title of a work by the German rationalist philosopher G. W. Leibniz (1646–1716), which attempted to reconcile the existence of an all-good, all-powerful, all-knowing God with the reality of evil in the world—not merely the existence of evil, but the amounts and types of evil we encounter in the world. Even if it does not rule out the *existence* of God, the sheer quantity and intensity of evil we observe at least seems to raise doubts about the *perfection* of God. Leibniz's response is both elegant and highly controversial: despite appearances, this world is in fact the *best possible world*, and thus no imperfection can be ascribed to God for bringing about this world.

Leibniz's reasoning is straightforward. If God is all-powerful, he is *able* to create the best possible world, and if God is all-good, he *will* create the best possible world if he is able to do so. Indeed, it would be a kind of moral

---

[31] Some theologians have argued that God the Son would have become incarnate even if there had been no fall, but that is a speculation without any biblical support.

failing on God's part to create any world less than the best. It follows that God *must* create the best possible world.

One retort is that, quite evidently, this is *not* the best of all possible worlds. It seems easy to imagine a world better than this one (e.g., a world in which the 9/11 attacks were thwarted). But Leibniz has a forceful rebuttal: this objection fails because we are in no position to say with confidence that there could have been a better world than this one. For one thing, we cannot be sure what criteria God uses to judge the relative goodness of possible worlds. Furthermore, we are largely ignorant about how all the goods and evils in this world are interconnected. For any given evil E, we might imagine there is some possible world *without* E that is better than this world. Yet for all we know, removing E would have consequences such that any possible world without E inevitably would have some *greater* evil than E or would lack some good that outweighs E. Thus, for all we know, there is no possible world without E that is *altogether* better than this world.

The Leibnizian defense comes to this: God alone is in a position to make reliable judgments about the relative goodness of possible worlds—and we are not God. But if we already know that God exists and created the world, we can infer that this must be the best possible world after all.

Leibniz's theodicy can be commended for seeking to uphold divine perfection, sovereignty, and aseity, and also for recognizing our epistemic limitations. Nevertheless, there are at least three reasons to doubt the claim that this must be the best of all possible worlds.

First, Leibniz's argument seems to compromise God's freedom to create. If God is obligated to create the best possible world, then God cannot refrain from creating the best possible world, in which case God cannot *not* create.

Second, there may be no *single* best possible world. Perhaps for any possible world there is at least one possible world that is better, in which case there is no more a best possible world than there is a highest possible number. Or perhaps there are many possible worlds that are *equally* good—that is, equally glorifying to God—and God is free to create any one of them.

Third, there may be no single metric by which to compare the value of worlds. After all, there are different *kinds* of value: moral value, aesthetic value, economic value, numerical value, and so forth. Perhaps asking whether there is a best possible world is like asking whether there is a best possible song or a best possible novel. What kind of best is best?

5. Toward a Biblical Theodicy

In this final section, I propose to outline an approach to the moral problem of evil that not only honors the parameters set out in section 3 but also incorporates insights from many of the partial theodicies discussed in section 4. In my judgment, a biblical theodicy will require at least the following components: (1) a recognition that God not only permits evil but ordains it; (2) a distinction between proximate and ultimate agency; (3) a greater-good rationale for God's permission of evil; and (4) an honest acknowledgment of the limits of divine revelation and human knowledge. Each of these four points will be supported with reference to three biblical "case studies": the story of Joseph, the book of Job, and the crucifixion of Jesus.[32]

5.1. PERMITTING AND ORDAINING

Every Christian recognizes that God *permits* evil. Clearly there are countless evils in the world that God *could* eradicate or prevent, but he does not do so; thus, God permits them. But what kind of permission is this? Is it like the passive "hands-off" permission of a government that allows people to make choices that sometimes harm themselves and others? Or is it better characterized as an *active* permission, an exercise of God's sovereign control over his creation?

To bring the issue into clearer focus, consider this scenario. Suppose a father allows his children to play in the sea, but his attention is directed elsewhere and one of the children is swept away by strong currents. Whether or not the father would be blameworthy for the death of his child, this is not properly analogous to divine permission because the father was not aware of the evil as it happened. Since God is omniscient and omnipresent, his permission of evil cannot be an "out-of-sight" permission. God must *knowingly* and *willingly* allow any evils that he could have prevented.

Some theologians have been content to go so far but no farther, insisting that while God knowingly permits evil, we must not say that he *ordains* evil—in the sense that the evils in the world are part of a divine plan or decree—because that would make God culpable for evil. They prefer to affirm a kind of *passive* permission, like that of a father who knowingly allows his child to fall off his bicycle as he learns to ride it. The father does not *intend*

---

[32] I am indebted to Greg Welty for bringing this conveniently alliterative triad to my attention. For his own exposition, see Greg Welty, *Why Is There Evil in the World (And So Much of It)?* (Fearn, Ross-shire, UK: Christian Focus, 2018).

for the child to fall, but he permits it by deliberate non-intervention. It is far from clear, however, that this model of divine permission absolves God of culpability for the evils in the world in the way its advocates think. Return to the scenario above and suppose instead that the father is watching his children as they play in the sea. Seeing that one of them has been caught by the current, he could intervene and save the child but chooses not to. Can we say that the father is blameless because he did not *intend* the death, but only knowingly permitted it?

The point is this: the crucial issue in theodicy is not so much *how* God permits evil—whether it is active or passive, intended or unintended—but rather *what justifies* God's permission of evil. If God has a sufficient moral justification for permitting some particular evil, would not that license his *actively* permitting it? An active divine permission is no less suited for a biblical theodicy than a passive one. Indeed, if God is justified in *permitting* some particular evil, then he is justified in *ordaining* that evil, for the outcome is exactly the same: the occurrence of the evil.

Moreover, Scripture is quite explicit about the sovereign control God exercises over both natural and moral evils. Since God directs *all things* according to his sovereign will, that must include instances of sin and suffering.[33] Consider the first of the three biblical case studies mentioned above. After recounting the sins his brothers committed against him, Joseph declares, "You meant it for evil, but God meant it for good."[34] Notice that Joseph does not say that God *allowed* it, but that God *intended* it.[35] The evil committed by Joseph's brothers was indeed part of a divine plan. Of course, it is correct to say that God *permitted* their sin. But it was not a merely passive permission. It was an *ordaining* permission.

Consider, second, the case of Job. It is true that the Lord *permitted* Satan to afflict Job (Job 1:12; 2:6). Even so, it is evident from the narrative that the Lord knew what would happen and that there was a divine purpose behind the evils. This was a *purposeful* permission. Indeed, we must not miss the striking fact that Job attributed his afflictions ultimately to the hand of God (Job 1:21, 2.10; 12:9; 19:21), and he was not at fault in so doing (Job 1:22).

However, it is the crucifixion of Jesus—the greatest moral evil in history, the most heinous crime ever committed—that decisively establishes the

[33] Isaiah 45:7; Lam. 3:37–38; Rom. 8:28; 11:36; Eph. 1:11.
[34] Genesis 50:20; cf. Gen. 45:5–7.
[35] As the ESV translation reflects, the same Hebrew verb is used for the brothers' intending and for God's intending.

point. On the one hand, it is not wrong to say that God knowingly permitted the death of his Son at the hands of wicked men. God could have intervened and prevented it. Yet by no means was this a "hands-off" permission. On the contrary, Scripture is clear that the crucifixion was part of a divine *plan*—indeed, a plan established before the creation of the world.[36] The crucifixion of Christ was divinely orchestrated. It was *predestined*.[37]

The broader implications should not be missed. If God's absolute holiness does not preclude him from ordaining evil in these three cases, there is no reason to think it precludes him from ordaining evil more generally. Thus, given Scripture's consistent testimony regarding God's sovereignty over his creation, a biblical theodicy must acknowledge that God not only permits evil but ordains it. Hard as it may be to accept, every evil in the world is part of a divine plan. The Bible does not offer a "hands-off" defense of God, and neither should we.[38]

5.2. PROXIMATE AND ULTIMATE AGENCY

When discussing the relationship between God and events within his creation, theologians routinely appeal to a distinction between primary and secondary causality. God is the *primary* (or ultimate) cause of all things, whereas creatures are the *secondary* (or proximate) causes of many things. The two types of causality are not mutually exclusive: for any event in the creation, God is necessarily the first cause, but there may also be creaturely second causes. God's primary causality has been further distinguished into three categories: *creation*, *conservation*, and *concurrence*.[39] God is the first cause of all things insofar as he (1) actively brings things into existence in the first place, (2) actively sustains their existence, and (3) actively upholds their causal powers and relations. According to the doctrine of concurrence, creatures are real secondary causes—when I raise my hand, it is literally true that *I* am the immediate cause of the raised hand—but creaturely cause-and-effect relationships obtain only because God is upholding them as the first cause.

---

[36] Acts 2:23; 1 Pet. 1:20.
[37] Acts 4:27–28.
[38] For a helpful discussion of the language of divine permission, see Guillaume Bignon, *Excusing Sinners and Blaming God: A Calvinist Assessment of Determinism, Moral Responsibility, and Divine Involvement in Evil*, Princeton Theological Monograph Series (Eugene, OR: Pickwick, 2018), 211–26.
[39] Francis Turretin, *Institutes of Elenctic Theology*, ed. James T. Dennison Jr., trans. George Musgrave Giger, 3 vols. (Phillipsburg, NJ: Presbyterian & Reformed, 1992), 1:501–11. Some theologians have spoken of divine *preservation* rather than *conservation*.

The distinction between primary and secondary causality is consistent with a natural reading of Scripture, and it comports well with biblical teachings about divine perfection, sovereignty, and aseity, according to which everything other than God is absolutely dependent upon God and nothing takes place apart from the power and will of God. Nevertheless, as we seek to develop a theodicy that closely tracks biblical descriptions of God's relationship to moral and natural evil, it may be more helpful to distinguish between *proximate agency* and *ultimate agency*. Accordingly, we should say that for every instance of evil in the world, creatures are typically the *proximate* agents—always in the case of moral evils and sometimes in the case of natural evils—whereas God is the *ultimate* agent.

One advantage of speaking in terms of agency rather than causality is that it requires us to consider the *intentions* of the agents involved. God's intentions are necessarily good; they are always righteous, holy, and wise. The intentions of creatures may be good or evil—or a mixture of the two. Drawing these distinctions will help us toward an understanding of how a good God can permit evil; indeed, how a sovereign God can ordain evil without thereby being guilty of evil.

The notion of dual agency is far from an extrabiblical speculation or philosophical imposition. It appears on the very surface of numerous biblical texts. Consider three particularly striking examples:

(1) In 1 Samuel 4:10–11, we are told that the Philistines attacked Israel, killing the two sons of Eli in the process. This was moral evil on the part of the Philistines, yet it was ordained by God, "for it was the will of the LORD *to put them to death*" (1 Sam. 2:25). Who then killed the sons of Eli? Scripture gives a double answer: the Lord *and* the Philistines. But while the Philistines acted wickedly, the Lord's intentions were wholly righteous.

(2) First Chronicles 10 recounts the death of Saul. Verse 4 tell us that "Saul took his own sword and fell upon it." But according to verse 14, "the LORD put him to death." Who then killed Saul? Again, Scripture gives a double answer: the Lord *and* Saul himself. But while Saul acted sinfully in taking his own life, the Lord did not.

(3) Isaiah 10:5–19 describes how the Lord will use the Assyrians as a rod (vv. 5, 15) to chastise the nation of Israel. The dual agency cannot be missed here. The Assyrians are the proximate agents of the destruction of Israel; they act with evil intentions and thus will be punished in due

course (vv. 12–19). Yet in the very same passage the Lord is clearly depicted as the ultimate agent of judgment, the one who *wields* the rod of discipline in his righteousness.

The distinction between proximate and ultimate agency is also evident in the cases of Joseph, Job, and Jesus. When Joseph says to his brothers, "You meant evil against me, but God meant it for good," not only does he acknowledged two *agencies*—God and the brothers—he also explicitly distinguishes between their *intentions*. The brothers' intentions were evil, whereas God's intentions were good. Thus, although God ordained their sinful actions, he himself committed no evil.

In the case of the disasters that befell Job, multiple proximate agents are involved: Satan, the Sabeans, and the Chaldeans.[40] All had evil intentions in their actions. Even so, as we noted previously, Job himself takes God to be the ultimate agent behind these events.[41] Although Job is ignorant and perplexed about *why* God has afflicted him, he never ascribes evil intentions to God, and the prologue makes clear that God and Satan have antithetical motivations.

Finally, consider the dual agency in the death of Christ. The proximate agents of Jesus's crucifixion were the Romans and the Jews; they acted with evil intentions and thus were morally culpable.[42] Even so, there was a divine agency behind the human agency. The death of Christ was not merely permitted but was predestined by God. God *sent* his Son into the world to die as an atoning sacrifice. Indeed, Scripture goes so far as to assert that Christ was "smitten by God," that it was "the will of the LORD to crush him."[43] Yet God ordained this terrible injustice to accomplish a tremendous good: the glorious demonstration of his justice and his mercy in the redemption of sinners.

In light of these and many other scriptural examples, it seems that a biblical theodicy must accommodate the dual agency involved in (all) moral evils and (some) natural evils. Not only does this honor the sovereignty of God by recognizing that nothing takes place apart from the will of God; it also goes some considerable way toward preserving the righteousness of God by allowing us to contrast God's intentions (always good) with those of the creatures who actually commit the moral evils.

---

[40] Note that here we have an example of a proximate agent (Satan) causing various *natural* evils (Job 1:16, 19; 2:7).
[41] Interestingly, the fire from heaven (Job 1:16) is described by the messenger as "fire from God," even though the implication of the narrative is that Satan is the proximate agent (Job 1:12).
[42] Acts 2:23, 36; 3:14–15; 4:10, 27–28.
[43] Isaiah 53:4, 10.

5.3. The Greater-Good Justification

Theodicy concerns the justification of God—more precisely, the justification of the *ways* of God, insofar as God not only permits but ordains the moral evils committed by his creatures and the natural evils that follow them. We have reached the point where we must directly address the question of divine justification.

Let us begin by noting that, despite the diversity of the nine theodicies surveyed earlier, a common thread runs through all of them. In each case, it is argued that God is justified in permitting evil (either evil in general or some particular type of evil) because it is necessary for him to do so in order to allow or attain some *greater good* that outweighs the evil. The difference between the theodicies lies primarily in the identification of that greater good: for the free-will theodicy, the greater good is significant moral agency and genuine love relationships; for the natural-law theodicy, a stable environment for moral choices; for the divine-punishment theodicy, the execution and demonstration of justice; and so on. A greater-good principle is assumed by Leibniz's argument that God has created the best possible world, for if any evil in this world were *not* necessary to attain some greater good (or to prevent some greater evil, which comes to the same thing), then a world without that evil would be a *better* world than this one.

It is widely accepted in our own experience and moral reasonings that one can be morally justified in permitting an evil, even in causing a harm, in order to bring about a greater good that could not be otherwise attained. Consider the case of a surgeon who amputates an infected limb in order to save a patient's life. The loss of a limb, considered as such, is hardly a *good* thing—but clearly the surgeon is justified in removing the limb. Or consider a sting operation in which police officers knowingly allow a gang to commit a crime in order to catch them red-handed and prosecute them, thereby preventing further (and possibly greater) felonies. Examples can be multiplied and drawn from various areas of life: law enforcement, government foreign policy, medical treatment, parental discipline, and so on. Every one of us has, at some time or other, knowingly allowed some evil to occur and justified our actions (or inactions) by reasoning that it was necessary for the sake of some greater good.

Such being the case, it is entirely reasonable to hold that God's permission of evil is justified on account of some greater good that could not otherwise be obtained. Moreover, as we noted earlier, if God's *permitting* evil can be justified on those grounds, there is no reason in principle why his *ordaining* evil could not be justified on the same grounds.

But is this rationale supported by Scripture? While the Bible never explicitly states that God allows or ordains evil for the sake of a greater good, there are certainly texts that imply such a principle. Consider for instance the argument of Hebrews 12:3–11. God disciplines his children, and that discipline is *painful*—it typically involves suffering and deprivation—but God does it because it is necessary to bring about a greater good for those he loves: "the peaceful fruit of righteousness." Indeed, one of the most prominent themes of the NT is that believers suffer not because afflictions are good *in themselves*, but because they accomplish a multiplicity of goods that outweigh the negative aspects of those afflictions (e.g., 2 Cor. 4:7–18).[44]

Once again, our three case studies illustrate the point. In the story of Joseph, the greater-good justification is explicitly articulated by the victim himself: "You meant evil against me, but God meant it for good, *to bring it about that many people should be kept alive, as they are today*" (Gen. 50:20). In the case of Job's ordeals, the greater-good justification may be less obvious, but the prologue indicates that God's rationale for allowing Satan to afflict Job is twofold: first, it serves to vindicate Job's own integrity; but more importantly, it serves to vindicate God's truthfulness, justness, almightiness, and worthiness to be worshiped because of who he is and not merely because of the earthly blessings he bestows.[45] (We might also note a *third* good: the accumulated benefits that millions of people have experienced through reading the story of Job!)

As for the third case—the crucifixion of Christ—the greater-good justification is explicit throughout the NT. The crucifixion was unquestionably a great moral evil, but it was necessary for a greater good: the redemption of God's people through a perfect atoning sacrifice. Indeed, it accomplished an *even greater good* insofar as it continually demonstrates to all creation the glory of God in the manifestation of his immeasurable wisdom, power, justice, and mercy.

We therefore find compelling support in Scripture for a greater-good theodicy. Indeed, in light of the perfections of God, it is hard to see what logical alternatives there could be. What *other* kind of rationale could an all-powerful, all-good God have for permitting evil? At the same time, we should

---

[44] For other examples implying a greater-good principle, see Matt. 4:1–11; Rom. 8:18–30; 11:11–36.
[45] Job 1:9–11; 2:4–5.

be careful not to overextend the theodicy. The greater-good principle entails that, for every evil, God permits it only because he knows it is necessary for some greater good. It does *not* follow, however, that we will normally be in a position to discern *what that greater good is*. In some cases, the Bible tells us—at least in general terms—the greater goods for which God permits certain evils. But the Bible leaves us in the dark in other cases, particularly with respect to *why the evils in question were necessary*; that is, why the goods could not have been obtained without those evils. All we can know, in those difficult and often distressing cases, is that God knows.

5.4. THE NECESSITY OF MYSTERY

The Bible does not leave us unarmed and uninformed in the face of the problem of evil. Scripture affirms that God's original creation was completely good. Evil has no original or independent existence; it exists only as the corruption of what is good. Moral evil entered the world through the free actions of God's creatures, and natural evil is a consequence of moral evil. Nevertheless, God is absolutely sovereign over moral and natural evil. His permission of evil is not merely passive, but active and purposeful. God ordains the evil actions committed by his creatures, but only for the sake of greater goods that could not otherwise be obtained. Since God's intentions are entirely holy and wise, and he has the right to do with his creation as he wills, God cannot be properly charged with evil.

Nevertheless, as we have noted, Scripture does not answer every question raised by the problem of evil and by the biblical theodicy outlined here. There are at least three respects in which a residue of mystery remains.

(1) We are ignorant about God's *means* in ordaining evil. How can God be the ultimate cause of all things, including the sinful actions of his creatures, without being tainted by evil himself? If I cause someone else to sin, I am thereby guilty of sin.[46] Why not so for God? The nature of God's causal relationship with his creation is a tricky one in its own right, even before the problem of evil is raised. Indeed, the nature of causation itself has generated no end of philosophical debate! Perhaps the best we can say here is that, because of the ontological Creator-creature distinction, divine causation is *sui generis* and operates at a different level than intramundane causation (i.e., causal relationships *within* the creation). Divine causation is

[46] Cf. Mark 9:42; Rom. 14:21.

thus merely *analogous* to creaturely causation; there are points of similarity but also points of dissimilarity.[47] We must rest in the conviction that God has the causal means at his disposal to *ordain* evil without thereby *committing* evil, even if those means remain mysterious to us. The secret things belong to God.

(2) We are ignorant about God's *motives* in ordaining evil. As we have seen, Scripture gives us general answers as to why God permits various kinds of evils. It also gives us more detailed explanations in some particular cases. But for many of the evils we encounter in the world, we are at a loss to say anything more than that God allowed it for *some* greater good. (To insist that God ordained it for his own glory, while true, sheds no further light.) Thus, God's specific motivations are often beyond our ken if not beyond our comprehension. We must rest in the conviction that our God is righteous in all his ways and wise beyond all human measure, and therefore God must *have* justifying reasons for his actions even if we cannot identify those reasons. The secret things belong to God.

(3) We are ignorant about God's *mechanisms* in ordaining evil for the greater good. We can sometimes see (or at least imagine) how an instance of moral or natural evil was necessary to bring about a greater good, but that may be the exception rather than the rule. In reality, we grasp very little about the way billions of individual events are interconnected in our world, including the complex connections between moral actions and the (often unpredictable) consequences of those actions. Thus, while we can be confident that God is always accomplishing some greater good whenever he permits an evil, we cannot expect to see precisely *how* or *why* that is the case. But it also follows that when we cannot see the connections, we are in no position to conclude that there *could not* be any such connections. The secret things belong to God.

We should not be the least bit embarrassed about these elements of mystery. Such gaps in our knowledge do not present any objection to the biblical worldview, because they are *implied* by that worldview. Mystery is a feature of the Christian faith, not a bug. While the Bible does not answer all our questions about the problem of evil, it does answer the most important ones, including the question of why the Bible does not answer all our questions.

---

[47] For an extended discussion, see Anderson, "Calvinism and the First Sin," 204–10.

19

Total Depravity and God's Covenant with Adam (1)

A CASE FOR THE COVENANT

Garry Williams

Introduction

When we come to understand that we are totally unable to respond to the grace of God apart from the irresistible regenerating work of the Holy Spirit, we naturally ask about the origin of the fallen condition in which we now find ourselves. Tracing the thread of our lives down the corridors of memory, we realize that we cannot recall a day when we were free from temptation and lived without sin. Taking upon our lips the Psalms, we confess with David that we were brought forth in iniquity and conceived in sin (Ps. 51:5). At that point the thread runs out. We are left wiser by the enquiry: we now understand not only the synchronic extent of sin pervading our entire human constitution in any one moment, but also its diachronic reach back to the root of our own existence in the womb. But the question has not been answered, it has simply been relocated and expanded. Having traced the thread step by step, we now ask about the origin of the whole ruined thread itself. Granted that depravity afflicts the entirety of my existence in this space and time, where did it come from? How did I come to be conceived in this fallen condition?

Enter Adam. His role has perhaps never been more vividly illustrated than by Thomas Goodwin when he comments on Paul using the role of "the first man" as a public person to illustrate the influence of "the second man" (1 Cor. 15:47):

> He calls Adam "the first man," and Christ our Lord, "the second man," and both for that very purpose and respect which we have in hand. For, first, he speaks of them as if there had never been any more men in the world, nor were ever to be for time to come, except these two. And why? but because these two between them had all the rest of the sons of men hanging at their girdle; because they were both common persons, that had the rest in like (though opposite) considerations included and involved in them.[1]

It is to Adam that Scripture leads us in the search for the root of our sinfulness. And so our enquiry into our total depravity morphs to focus not just on ourselves, but on Adam and his role (the subject of this chapter), and on our relation to him (the subject of the next chapter). Who was Adam? And how did he come to have such a determinative place in human history? Toward the end of the sixteenth century, Reformed theology came to explain that God established Adam as the first head of the human race in a covenant. This chapter will make the case for the existence of this covenant with Adam, and for Adam's representative role within it. The entire chapter is occupied with this single task. The rejection of the idea of a covenant with Adam in evangelical and broadly Reformed circles necessitates what is in effect an extended prelude to my next chapter, in which a covenantal understanding of Adam is deployed to explain our relation to him.

The basic claim that God made a covenant with Adam did not emerge for the first time among the Reformed in the sixteenth century. Augustine writes about "the first covenant (*testamentum*), made with the first man" and "the original sin by which God's covenant was first broken."[2] This does not necessarily mean that Augustine taught the same covenant as later Reformed theology. It is one thing—itself a significant thing—to hold that Adam was in a covenant with God, but the details of that covenant might be underdeveloped or might take many forms.[3]

When the idea of God's covenant with Adam reached its mature form in the sixteenth and seventeenth centuries, it came to be known by differ-

---

[1] Thomas Goodwin, *Christ Set Forth*, in *The Works of Thomas Goodwin*, vol. 4 (Edinburgh: James Nichol, 1861–66), 31.
[2] Augustine, *The City of God*, ed. John O'Meara, trans. Henry Bettenson (London: Penguin, 1984), xvi.27 (688, 689).
[3] Aaron C. Denlinger, *Omnes in Adam ex pacto Dei: Ambrogio Catarino's Doctrine of Covenantal Solidarity and Its Influence on Post-Reformation Reformed Theologians*, Reformed Historical Theology 8 (Göttingen, Germany: Vandenhoeck & Ruprecht, 2010), 235.

ent names: *foedus creationis* (covenant of creation), *foedus naturae* (covenant of nature), the covenant of life (Westminster Larger Catechism 20; Westminster Shorter Catechism 12), *foedus amicitiae* ("covenant of friendship"), and perhaps its most widespread label, *foedus operum* ("covenant of works," used in the Westminster Confession of Faith vii. 2). It has also been called the Adamic or Edenic covenant. This covenant with Adam took its place within the wider scope of Reformed covenant theology. Historically speaking, it is fair to say with Mark Karlberg that "Reformed theology is the theology of the covenants."[4] And yet, despite its remarkable lineage, not just the covenant with Adam but covenant theology as a whole has lost the place it once had. J. I. Packer wrote in 1990, "in modern Christendom covenant theology has been unjustly forgotten."[5] Thirty years on the situation has improved, but covenant theology is still beset by both ignorance and criticism. The criticism of the older covenant theology falls most heavily on the idea of an eternal covenant between the divine persons (the covenant of redemption) and on the covenant with Adam. Aaron Denlinger cites several examples: Stephen Strehle regards the covenant with Adam as "a divine fabrication" which involves God "relating the unrelated" to bring about relationships that "exist only within this divine fantasy."[6] Jürgen Moltmann argues that the covenant with Adam was projected back onto the first man from Sinai, with the result that the Lutheran law-gospel distinction entered Reformed theology.[7] In rejecting the covenant of works as an example of "covenant overload" in Reformed theology, John H. Stek believes that he is following Scripture rather than the unbiblical accretions of the Reformed tradition.[8]

The Absence of the Term "Covenant" in Genesis 1–3

The most obvious point made against the idea of a covenant with Adam is the absence of the term "covenant" (בְּרִית) in Genesis 1–3. While the presence of the term would of course be decisive, its absence is in fact irrelevant to

---

[4] Mark W. Karlberg, "Reformed Theology as the Theology of the Covenants: The Contributions of Meredith G. Kline to Reformed Systematics," in *Creator, Redeemer, Consummator: A Festschrift for Meredith G. Kline*, ed. Howard Griffith and John R. Muether (Eugene, OR: Wipf & Stock, 2000), 252.

[5] In the introduction to Herman Witsius, *The Economy of the Covenants between God and Man*, ed. and trans. William Crookshank, 2 vols. (London: R. Baynes, J. Maitland, T. Lochhead, T. Nelson, 1822; repr. Escondido, CA: The den Dulk Christian Foundation, 1990), § 1.

[6] Denlinger, *Omnes in Adam*, 64.

[7] Denlinger, *Omnes in Adam*, 38.

[8] John H. Stek, " 'Covenant' Overload in Reformed Theology," *CTJ* 29 (1994), 12–41, passim.

determining whether or not God made a covenant with Adam. What matters is the thing, not the word, and the thing can be present without the word. Later biblical passages often apply terms to the persons and events of earlier episodes that were not originally used of them, despite being available. A pertinent example is the fact that Genesis 3 does not use any of the Hebrew terms for "sin" to describe what Adam did, even though a few verses later God warns Cain that "sin" (חַטָּאת) is crouching at his door (4:7). Despite this, the apostle Paul felt able to apply several Greek terms to Adam's deed in Romans 5: "sin" (ἁμαρτία) (vv. 12, 13, 20, 21), "transgression" (παράβασις in v. 14, and παράπτωμα in vv. 15ff.), and "disobedience" (παρακοή; v. 19). The absence of "covenant" is used to argue against the idea of a covenant with Adam, but surely no one would take seriously the suggestion that it would be wrong to say that Adam "sinned"?

But in fact, they *would*! So committed is James Barr to denying the traditional reading of the fall that he actually argues from the absence of the terms for sin, evil, rebellion, transgression, and guilt in the Eden narrative.[9] This is the same Barr who is renowned for so effectively warning against the identification of a concept with a specific term.[10] When Barr falls short of his own semantic standards and contradicts the apostolic exegesis of Genesis, we may safely regard his argument as a salutary warning rather than as an example to follow. The implications here extend not only to sin; similar arguments apply to other ways in which the NT coins new terminology for Adam. He is described by Luke as "the son of God" (3:38) and by Paul as "a type [τύπος] of the one who was to come" (Rom. 5:14), neither of which are descriptions found in Genesis.[11] The apostles drew out the divinely intended meaning of Genesis with retrojected terminology. We dare not think that we are better exegetes of the OT than the designated apostles of the Lord Jesus Christ, who were promised the assistance of his own Spirit (John 14:26). Nor may we claim that they could do it because they were apostles, while we may not. That sounds pious but might just as well be restated thus: "The apostles read the Old Testament in this way, but I am not going to. I will read it my way."

---

[9] James Barr, *The Garden of Eden and the Hope of Immortality* (London: SCM, 1992), 6.
[10] This irony is noted by C. John Collins, *Genesis 1–4: A Linguistic, Literary, and Theological Commentary* (Phillipsburg, NJ: P&R, 2006), 155.
[11] Richard Barcellos, *The Covenant of Works: Its Confessional and Scriptural Basis*, Recovering Our Confessional Heritage 3 (Palmdale, CA: RBAP, 2016), 61.

Nor do we have to wait for the apostles to find the retrojective use of terminology. There are specific examples even of covenant terminology being read back into earlier situations within the OT itself. In Genesis 15 God does not tell Abram that he is making a covenant with him; the word בְּרִית does not pass between them. It is only the narrator who states that "the LORD made a covenant with Abram" (v. 18).[12] When David becomes king and God makes promises to him in 2 Samuel 5 and 7, and 1 Chronicles 17, the texts do not describe what is happening as a covenant. Later, in 2 Samuel 23, David reflects at the end of his life that God "has made with me an everlasting covenant, ordered in all things and secure" (v. 5). In 2 Chronicles 13:5 Abijah challenges Jeroboam and all Israel with these words: "Ought you not to know that the LORD God of Israel gave the kingship over Israel forever to David and his sons by a covenant of salt?" And Psalm 89 describes God as saying, "I have made a covenant with my chosen one" (v. 3).[13] The same applies to other elements of covenantal terminology, most notably the retrospective designation of an earlier word as a sworn oath. For example, it is only after God tells Moses that he will not enter the promised land (Num. 20:12; 27:13–14; Deut. 1:37; 3:26–27) that the statement is described as God swearing an oath (וַיִּשָּׁבַע; Deut. 4:21). Further examples include the announcement of judgment on Eli's family (1 Sam. 2:27–36, described as an oath in 3:14); David's plan to build a house for the Lord (2 Sam. 7:2, described as an oath in Ps. 132:2); and Shimei's agreement not to leave Jerusalem (1 Kings 2:38, described as an oath by Solomon in 2:42–43).[14] The absence of the *signum* is not the absence of the *res*, and so it is no bar to the existence of a covenant.

It may nonetheless be puzzling. Can we explain why Genesis 1–3 does not use the vocabulary of covenant? Some exegetes seem to expect a biblical author to communicate everything he wants to say on the very surface of his text, to make his meaning leap off the page to wrestle into submission with body-blows of overt terminology even the most skeptical reader, compelling him to tap out, admitting the sense of the mighty meaning. Such expectations

---

[12] Brian Habig, "Hosea 6:7 Revisited," *Presbyterion*, 42.1–2 (2016): 15.

[13] Noted by many, including O. Palmer Robertson, *The Christ of the Covenants* (Phillipsburg, NJ: Presbyterian & Reformed, 1980), 18.

[14] These examples are identified by Stek, " 'Covenant' Overload," 36 n. 71, who nonetheless rejects a covenant with Adam. Gordon Hugenberger notes further examples: 2 Sam. 3:9; Isa. 54:9; Ezek. 16:8; 20:5–6; and more than forty texts which speak of the Lord's oath concerning the promised land (even though the oath in Gen. 22:16 does not mention the land). See Hugenberger's *Marriage as a Covenant: A Study of Biblical Law and Ethics Governing Marriage, Developed from the Perspective of Malachi*, VTSup 52 (Leiden, Netherlands: Brill, 1994), 187 n. 86.

seem to make a virtue of the stubborn resistance of the reader to persuasion, and they expect as little literary art of the author as there is in the instructions for assembling flat-pack furniture.[15] Along with many who rightly take a more literary approach to the Bible, Tryggve Mettinger argues the opposite, that the absence of overt terms is the very genius of Genesis:

> The Eden Narrative is a sophisticated piece of literary art. It is a story about the divine commandment, without using any of the Hebrew words for commandment; about a divine test, without the Hebrew term [*nissâ*]; and about sin, without any of the central terms for sin [verbs such as *pāša*, *ḥāṭā'*, *āwâ*, etc.].

He goes on to cite Gunnar Ekelöf's poem "Poetics":

> It is to the silence you should listen
> the silence behind invocations, allusions
> the silence of rhetoric . . .
> What I have written
> I have written between the lines.[16]

We would do well to learn this lesson and to be done once for all with the wooden reading of biblical texts that refuses the conclusion to which the details are pointing but which none of them names. There is nothing exegetically faithful about missing the subtly expressed point of a biblical text. A reluctance to be persuaded may feel like exegetical virtue, but to fail to notice what is truly there below the surface is to refuse to hear what the text is actually saying.

The Possibility of Covenants before the Fall

There are also ways of defining "covenant" that rule out the possibility of a covenant between God and Adam. The most significant is the argument that covenants are only necessary, and therefore only exist, subsequent to the entrance of sin into the world.[17] The difficulty for this claim is that there are two examples of prelapsarian covenants.

---

[15] Or perhaps less: might not the surprisingly still unnamed figure who appears in the Ikea instructions be, like the furniture itself, a work of art?
[16] Tryggve N. D. Mettinger, *The Eden Narrative: A Literary and Religio-Historical Study of Genesis 2–3* (Winona Lake, IN: Eisenbrauns, 2007), 135; the poem is quoted from the 1959 collection *Opus Incertum*.
[17] So, e.g., Stek, "'Covenant' Overload," summarized on 39–40; Paul R. Williamson, *Sealed with an Oath: Covenant in God's Unfolding Purpose*, NSBT 23 (Leicester, UK: Apollos, 2007), 72.

In Jeremiah 33 God attests to the certainty of his promises to his people by twice pointing them back to the creation itself:

> Thus says the LORD: "If you can break my covenant [בְּרִיתִי] with the day and my covenant with the night, so that day and night will not come at their appointed time, then also my covenant with David my servant may be broken, so that he shall not have a son to reign on his throne, and my covenant with the Levitical priests my ministers" (vv. 20–21). . . .

> Thus says the LORD: "If I have not established my covenant with day and night and the fixed order [חֻקּוֹת] of heaven and earth, then I will reject the offspring of Jacob and David my servant and will not choose one of his offspring to rule over the offspring of Abraham, Isaac, and Jacob. For I will restore their fortunes and will have mercy on them." (vv. 25–26)

This is sometimes mistaken for a reference to God's promise of nature's stability after the flood in Genesis 8:22, but closer attention to the texts suggests otherwise. These verses in chapter 33 are related to 31:35–36 by the shared terms "day," "night," and "fixed order," and that passage in turn suggests a connection back to Genesis 1, not 8:

> Thus says the LORD,
> who gives the sun for light by day
>   and the fixed order [חֻקֹּת] of the moon and the stars for light by night,
> who stirs up the sea so that its waves roar—
>   the LORD of hosts is his name:
> "If this fixed order [הַחֻקִּים] departs
>   from before me, declares the LORD,
> then shall the offspring of Israel cease
>   from being a nation before me forever."

Whereas the language of chapter 33 considered alone could refer to the Noahic covenant, chapter 31 further details the created phenomena in view as the sun, moon, and stars. These are not mentioned in Genesis 8, but they are all mentioned on day four of the creation narrative (Gen. 1:14–19).[18] The masculine term for "fixed order" in 31:36 is used of the initial creation of the sun, moon, stars, and heavens in Psalm 148:6: "he established them for ever and ever; he gave a decree [חָק] and it shall not pass away." Jeremiah 31

---

[18] Robertson, *Christ of the Covenants*, 19–21. Paul Williamson is thus wrong to dismiss the connection between Jer. 31:35–37 and Gen. 1 as "an argument from silence"; see *Sealed with an Oath*, 74.

shows us how to read Jeremiah 33: this covenant was made with the lights in the heavens when God created them, prior to the entrance of sin.[19]

Second, the bond of marriage is spoken of as a covenant in Malachi 2:14: "she is your companion and your wife by covenant." Marriage is a creation ordinance. It might be argued that this did not apply to Adam and Eve's marriage, because theirs did not need to be a covenant, in the absence of sin. However, the language of Genesis itself suggests that the first marriage was a covenant. Adam's one-flesh union with Eve is the basis for the declaration that a man will leave his father and mother and "cleave" (דָּבַק) to his wife (Gen. 2:24 KJV, RSV).[20] This verb has covenantal overtones because it is used extensively to describe the loyalty of Israel to her God in the Sinai covenant (e.g., Deut. 10:20; 11:22; 13:4; 30:20; Josh. 22:5; 23:8), the covenant that would have been ringing in the ears of Moses's audience as they heard the text of Genesis. Gordon Hugenberger finds the covenantal obligations of the first pair also stated in the narrative. Eve is to be Adam's helper, and Adam is to treat her in a way that reflects her origin as "bone of my bone and flesh of my flesh."[21] As Craig Bartholomew states, even in an unfallen world a covenant would have been the appropriate way to create the new special relationships that would have been necessary for fulfilling the cultural mandate.[22] The marriage of Adam and Eve is therefore a second example of a prelapsarian covenant.

Defining Elements of a Covenant

Another way to restrict the extent of covenant theology in the Bible is to adopt a definition of covenant so stringent that few relationships can fulfil its requirements. The appeal here is not to the absence of terminology for covenants, but to the absence of their necessary constituent parts. A broader definition of those parts will inevitably yield fewer covenants; a narrower definition, more.

My own view, in brief, is that the biblical usage evidences a considerable degree of latitude in the application of the term בְּרִית, and that we ought not to reduce it to a single core element.[23] At one end of the spectrum, we

---

[19] On this reading, the Jeremiah texts are further examples of retrojected covenant terminology in addition to the ones cited in the previous section.

[20] Meredith G. Kline, *Kingdom Prologue: Genesis Foundations for a Covenantal Worldview* (Eugene, OR: Wipf & Stock, 2006), 71.

[21] Hugenberger, *Marriage as a Covenant*, 182.

[22] Craig C. Bartholomew, "Covenant and Creation: Covenant Overload or Covenantal Deconstruction," *CTJ* 30 (1995): 26–27.

[23] Hugenberger, *Marriage as a Covenant*, 171.

find the full set of elements often present in ancient Near Eastern treaty texts and manifest in the structure of Deuteronomy: preamble (Deut. 1:1–5), historical prologue (1:6–4:49), stipulations (chs. 5–26), curses and blessings or covenant ratification (chs. 27–30), and succession arrangements or covenant continuity (chs. 31–34).[24] This pattern is highly significant where we can find it, but it cannot be used to provide a list of elements that must be present in any covenant, because not all covenants were written treaties.[25] At the other end of the spectrum, we find an example such as Jeremiah 33 where the term בְּרִית is applied to the Lord's unilateral and unconditional commitment to inanimate objects such as the sun and moon. Other instances of a "covenant" involving non-sentient partners are Job's covenant with his eyes (Job 31:1), and Israel's prophesied covenant with the animals (Hos. 2:18). The breadth of biblical usage favors a more minimal definition of covenant. Good examples are proposed by Bruce Waltke, "a solemn commitment of oneself to undertake an obligation," and Thomas McComiskey, "a relationship that involves obligation."[26] Such definitions open the way to a freer and more expansive application of the term "covenant" in Christian theology more generally, and to God's relationship with Adam in particular.

Even if we were to insist on a more detailed and specific definition of covenant, we would still find a covenant between God and Adam in Genesis 1–3 because the principal elements commonly specified are present. The two parties are described clearly. The giver of the covenant is God, who is both Elohim, the creating, ordering, filling, and resting suzerain of heaven and earth (1:1–2:3); and YHWH Elohim, the Lord who fashions Adam (2:4–25). The receiver of the covenant is Adam, created in God's image from the dust of the ground as his vassal and deputy. There are clear stipulations commissioning Adam to his kingly (1:26–28) and priestly (2:15) tasks (discussed below), and warning him away from the tree of the knowledge of good and evil (2:17). Adam has set before him the blessing of life and a growing reign beyond the garden, and the curse of death should he disobey, with these alternatives symbolized by the two trees. Adam's consent to these terms is evident both by the absence of his objecting, and by his passing on the terms to Eve

[24] Meredith G. Kline, *Treaty of the Great King: The Covenant Structure of Deuteronomy: Studies and Commentary* (Eugene, OR: Wipf & Stock, n.d.), 28.
[25] Hugenberger, *Marriage as a Covenant*, 172.
[26] Bruce K. Waltke, *An Old Testament Theology: An Exegetical, Canonical, and Thematic Approach* (Grand Rapids, MI: Zondervan, 2007), 287; Thomas E. McComiskey, *The Minor Prophets: An Exegetical and Expository Commentary*, ed. Thomas Edward McComiskey, 3 vols. (Grand Rapids, MI: Baker, 1998), 1:95.

(3:2–3).[27] Here are the constituent parts of a typical ancient Near Eastern covenant treaty: parties, stipulations, blessings, and curses.

There remains, however, a case against the covenant with Adam based on the absence of one recurring feature of covenants: a self-binding oath. As Hugenberger notes, there is a "widespread scholarly consensus" on the "relative indispensability" of an oath for ratifying a covenant. Indeed, Norbert Lohfink defined covenant as oath; G. M. Tucker has argued that it is the oath pattern that distinguishes a covenant from a contract; and Moshe Weinfeld avers that "*berith* as a commitment has to be confirmed by an oath."[28] Many passages in the OT closely connect בְּרִית with "oath" (אָלָה), and making a covenant (most commonly כָּרַת בְּרִית) with swearing an oath (שָׁבַע).[29] The connections are clear, but it would be wrong to conclude that we can find a covenant only if there is an explicit oath present in the text. As Hugenberger notes, in the extant extrabiblical treaty texts an oath of ratification is "only rarely stipulated."[30] We have already seen how, just as the term בְּרִית could be used later of an earlier episode, so too could the vocabulary of oath swearing. John Stek, who uses the absence of an oath to deny a covenant with Adam, argues that the term could be applied retrospectively.[31] Paul Williamson also denies a covenant with Adam and argues that a biblical covenant "comprises an elective relationship formalized by means of a solemn obligation or oath." But he too grants that this is sometimes "not expressly mentioned" and may be implicit.[32] We need not find an explicit oath in Genesis 1–2 to understand that the Lord was binding himself to Adam. Self-binding is exactly what the solemn words of the text communicate. This is true both of God's speech generally ("let there be"; "let us make"), and of the words that pertain to the covenant with Adam: "you shall surely die." So sure was God's creation plan that Jeremiah could argue from the "covenant" and "fixed order" of creation to the stability of the covenant with Israel (33:20–21, 25–26).

---

[27] Thomas Boston argues from the silence, in *A View of the Covenant of Works from the Sacred Records*, in *The Complete Works of the Late Rev. Thomas Boston*, ed. Samuel M'Millan, 12 vols. (Wheaton, IL: Richard Owen Roberts, 1980), 11:179; Collins argues from the speech, in *Genesis 1–4*, 138.

[28] See Hugenberger, *Marriage as a Covenant*, 182–183, and also G. M. Tucker, "Covenant Forms and Contract Forms," *VT* 15.4 (1965): 487–503.

[29] Tucker's examples include: Gen. 21:31–32; 26:28, 31; Josh. 9:15; 2 Kings 11:4; Ezek. 17:13, 16, 18–19 (all covenants between people), and Deut. 4:31; 29:12–14; Ezek. 16:8 (covenants between God and his people) (Tucker, "Covenant Forms," 488–89); Hugenberger gives instances of the terms connected in hendiadys, synonymous parallelism, functional parallelism, and in multiple shared syntagms (Hugenberger, *Marriage as a Covenant*, 183 n. 74).

[30] Hugenberger, *Marriage as a Covenant*, 186, following Kenneth Kitchen.

[31] See Stek, " 'Covenant' Overload," 36 n. 71.

[32] Williamson, *Sealed with an Oath*, 39, 43.

"YHWH Elohim"

Alongside the presence of the elements of a covenant, there are several other lines of evidence within Genesis 1–3 that demonstrate the existence of God's covenant with Adam. One of the notable features is the way in which God's name changes from Elohim ("God") in 1:1–2:3 to YHWH Elohim (usually "the LORD God") in 2:4–3:24. This pairing never occurs again in the Pentateuch, apart from a single instance in Exodus 9:30.[33] At the very point when the narrative turns to the detail of the creation of Adam, the new name used for God combines his identity as both the Creator of all things and the God of the covenant, YHWH being the name under which he later reveals himself to Israel as his chosen people (Ex. 6:2–3). Adam is thus the representative of the whole human race that has God as its Creator (Elohim), and the man who in the pattern of his life foreshadows the people of Israel who have God as their covenant Lord (YHWH).[34] With the use of the covenant name, vistas of parallels open up: Israel, like Adam, will be put in a land, given a law to keep, and will be expelled upon breaking it. Short of using the term "covenant" itself, it is hard to think of a clearer way for the text to signal that God is the covenant God of Adam than by using his covenant name at the exact point when it narrates their dealings.[35] The name is omitted in these chapters only by the serpent and the woman as they negotiate the first sin (Gen. 3:1–6): in other words, to sin is to turn from the covenant.

Adam the Representative Man

God is depicted as the covenant God, and Adam is depicted as more than just an individual man when he is created in God's image. The first man's own name, "Adam" (אָדָם), bespeaks his significance. The word occurs initially in 1:26 as the collective "man." Opinions vary on when it transitions from "the man" to the proper name "Adam." (For example, the AV first uses "Adam" in 2:19, the NIV and ESV in 2:20, the RSV in 3:17, the CSB in 4:25.) The ambiguity, as Gordon Wenham notes, may be a deliberate way of stressing that Adam is the "representative of humanity."[36] Adam, the usage suggests, is The Man.

---

[33] Gordon J. Wenham, *Genesis 1–15*, WBC 1 (Milton Keynes, UK: Word, 1991), 56.
[34] Mettinger, *Eden Narrative*, 57.
[35] This is central to Bartholomew's case for a creation covenant in "Covenant and Creation," 29.
[36] Wenham, *Genesis 1–15*, 32. This point is made as early as Catarino; see Denlinger, *Omnes in Adam*, 194–95.

Adam the Covenantal King

The mandate Adam was given when he was created in the image of God was unmistakably royal, which identifies him as a kingly figure and thereby contributes to the case for his being in a covenant with God like the later biblical kings. He was to "have dominion" (רָדָה) over the creatures of the three zones created in Genesis 1: sea, air, and land (1:26, 28). The language of dominion is used of Solomon's rule over all the land and kings west of the Euphrates (1 Kings 4:24) and in his prayer for "dominion from sea to sea, from the River to the ends of the earth" (Ps. 72:8). This is the dominion that is promised to the Lord in Psalm 110:2. Adam was charged to fill the earth with his children, and with them to "subdue it" (Gen. 1:28). The verb used here (כָּבַשׁ) has military overtones. The driving out of the Canaanites would see the land "subdued" before YHWH (Num. 32:22), and before the Hebrews (v. 29; so too in Josh. 18:1). Later in Israel's history King David "subdued" nations (2 Sam. 8:11).[37] In addition to the language in Genesis itself, Psalm 8 reflects on the creation status of mankind in royal terms. Man is "crowned" with "glory and honor" (v. 5). He is given "dominion" or "rule" over the works of God's hands (v. 6, using מָשַׁל, a different term from Genesis 1, but also used for the rule of kings, in 2 Sam. 23:3; Ps. 103:19; Isa. 19:4; and Mic. 5:2).[38]

Adam is created in God's image as his son, which again suggests that he is a king. When Luke calls Adam "the son of God" (Luke 3:38) he is drawing out the significance of the divine image rather than imposing an alien idea on the text of Genesis. The connection of image with sonship is reflected in Genesis 5:1–3, where we read that Adam's son Seth is in his father's likeness (דְּמוּת) and according to his image (צֶלֶם), just after the statement in verse 1 that Adam himself was created in God's likeness (דְּמוּת). The Adam-like Seth is Adam's son, and the God-like Adam is God's son. The link from image and son to kingship has been explored by Stephen Wellum and Peter Gentry. They have shown how in the ancient Near East kings bore the likeness of gods as sons bear the likeness of fathers. For example, in Egyptian usage from 1630 onward, during the time when Israel was in Egypt, the kings were described as "living statues" of the gods.[39] The king was like his god

---

[37] Seth D. Postell, *Adam as Israel: Genesis 1–3 as the Introduction to the Torah and Tanakh* (Eugene, OR: Pickwick, 2011), 131, 89.

[38] Peter J. Gentry and Stephen J. Wellum, *Kingdom through Covenant: A Biblical-Theological Understanding of the Covenants* (Wheaton, IL: Crossway, 2015), 196.

[39] Gentry and Wellum, *Kingdom through Covenant*, 191.

as a son is like his father. The language of image and likeness applied to the king in the Tel Fakhariyeh Inscription even uses the Aramaic equivalents of "דְּמוּת" and "צֶלֶם" to denote respectively the king as servant of the god and as ruler of the people.[40] For my purposes here, the important lesson of Wellum and Gentry's work is that the image-son-king complex was covenantal. Both the upward and downward relationships of the king are "relationships characterised by faithfulness and loyal love, obedience and trust—exactly the character of relationships specified by covenants after the Fall."[41] It is no surprise that the later kings of God's people became kings in covenant both with the people themselves (2 Sam. 5:1–3) and with God (Ps. 89). Adam the king in the image of his Father is Adam the son in covenant.

Adam the Covenantal Priest

Many details of the Genesis narrative identify Eden as the first sanctuary and Adam as its priest. The extensive parallels between Eden and Israel's later tabernacle and temple are well-established.[42] Adam was the sanctuary's priest. God placed him in the garden "to work it and keep it" (Gen. 2:15). This pairing of the verbs עָבַד and שָׁמַר would bring to the Mosaic mind of the Israelite reader the work of the Levites and the priests. This was their role in the tabernacle (Num. 3:7–8; 8:25–26; 18:2–6), and later in the Solomonic and eschatological temples (1 Chron. 23:32; Ezek. 44:14). The Aaronic priests were to guard their priesthood and to serve (Num. 18:7).[43]

There is further, indirect evidence for identifying Adam as a priest via the gemstones worn by the king of Tyre in Ezekiel 28. Even as he is described as being an Adam "in Eden," the king of Tyre is adorned with gemstones that evoke the attire of the high priest. In Exodus, the breastplate for the high priest Aaron is to be decorated with four rows of three gemstones each (Ex. 28:17–20; cf. 39:10–13). In Ezekiel, the king of Tyre is described as wearing

---

[40] Gentry and Wellum, *Kingdom through Covenant*, 193.
[41] Gentry and Wellum, *Kingdom through Covenant*, 195.
[42] See, for example: G. K. Beale, *The Temple and the Church's Mission: A Biblical Theology of the Dwelling Place of God*, NSBT 17, ed. D. A. Carson (Downers Grove, IL: InterVarsity Press, 2004), 66–80; Richard Davidson, "Earth's First Sanctuary: Genesis 1–3 and Parallel Creation Accounts," *AUSS* 53.1 (2015): 65–89; L. Michael Morales, *Who Shall Ascend the Mountain of the Lord? A Biblical Theology of the Book of Leviticus*, NSBT 37 (Nottingham, UK: Apollos, 2015), ch. 2; Gordon Wenham, "Sanctuary Symbolism in the Garden of Eden Story," in *I Studied Inscriptions from before the Flood: Ancient Near Eastern, Literary, and Linguistic Approaches to Genesis 1–11*, ed. Richard S. Hess and David Toshio Tsumura, Sources for Biblical and Theological Study 4 (Winona Lake, IN: Eisenbrauns, 1994), 399–404; Gentry and Wellum, *Kingdom through Covenant*, 211–16. Among these sources, Beale makes the most of ancient Near Eastern parallels and Davidson is the most comprehensive.
[43] So, Kline, *Kingdom Prologue*, 85–86; Beale, *Temple and the Church's Mission*, 66–68; Davidson, "Earth's First Sanctuary," 72; Morales, *Who Shall Ascend?*, 53.

three triads of precious stones (Ezek. 28:13). The first two stones listed in Exodus and Ezekiel are the same and the fourth triad for Aaron is the same as the second for the king. Emerald and sapphire occur together in both lists, though reversed.[44]

Like the monarchy, the priesthood was covenantal. Part of its role was to deal with the sin that threatened the survival of the people of Israel within the Sinai covenant. The people depended on the faithful operation of the priesthood and its sacrificial system to make atonement. At the ironic nadir of their spiritual declension, witnessed in a vision by Ezekiel, the priests in Jerusalem turned to idolatry the very institution that was meant to preserve their nation, leading to the departure of the Lord's glory (anticipated in 8:6, enacted in ch. 10). The priesthood began with its own distinct covenant (cf. Ex. 28–29; 32:25–29), God's "covenant of salt" with the house of Aaron (Num. 18:19). The corruption of the priesthood was therefore a sin against its own founding covenant, so that as part of his reformation Nehemiah called on God to remember those who had "desecrated the priesthood and the covenant of the priesthood and the Levites" (Neh. 13:29). In pronouncing judgment on the priests of his day through Malachi, the Lord speaks of his covenant with Levi being a covenant of life, peace, and fear that will, despite their disobedience, be upheld (Mal. 2:1–9; cf. 3:3–4).

Adam the Covenantal Prophet

Some who recognize Adam as king and priest deny that he also exercised a prophetic office before the fall. Meredith Kline allows only a postlapsarian prophetic office, arguing that a prophet must have a mediatorial and "even a certain antithetical stance" toward his own community.[45] James Jordan also rejects the idea of Adam as a prelapsarian prophet, maintaining that a prophet is someone with whom God consults.[46] This is a rare example of unwarranted exegetical minimalism from Jordan and Kline. Given that Klineans are the avowed enemies of the "federal vision" at a systematic theological level, the resemblance between their maximal reading of many biblical texts is uncanny. It is therefore all the more strange to find at this point their founding

---

[44] For these details, see Daniel I. Block, *The Book of Ezekiel: Chapters 25–48* (Grand Rapids, MI: Eerdmans, 1998), 106.
[45] Kline, *Kingdom Prologue*, 89.
[46] James B. Jordan, *Through New Eyes: Developing a Biblical View of the World* (Eugene, OR: Wipf & Stock, 1999), 139.

fathers embracing the same minimalist eschewal of a prelapsarian prophetic office. It is true that some of the prophets are depicted as consulting with God, but that is far from always the case. It may also be that there is, as Mettinger suggests, a hint of Adam's presence in the divine consultations when the king of Tyre is called a cherub (Ezek. 28:14, 16).[47] A more prevalent feature of the prophetic office was mediation of the knowledge of God's will, something that Adam did when he taught the commandment of God to Eve. She did not exist when Adam was told about the permitted and forbidden foods (Gen. 2:16–17), but when she speaks with the serpent, she knows what was commanded (Gen. 3:2–3). Dietrich Bonhoeffer comments that this detail is "undoubtedly wrong" in terms of the narrative and "has no inner meaning at all," but he misses the significance of it for our understanding of Adam's own role.[48] Adam had evidently mediated to Eve the knowledge of God's law, showing that he is a prophet and her representative in receiving the law, as Moses would be for Israel. She herself seems to recognize her husband's representative function: when the commandment is spoken to Adam, God uses a singular verb for "you shall not eat" (לֹא תֹאכַל; 2:17), but when Eve repeats it she uses a plural verb for the same phrase (לֹא תֹאכְלוּ; 3:3).[49] Perhaps Adam's warning Eve will suffice for Kline's antithetical stance.

Like the kings and priests, the prophets too held a covenantal office, not because they were in distinct individual covenants with God, but because their entire ministry involved being prosecutors of the old covenant and predictors of the new. The covenant was the sphere of their activity. Thus the Adam of the covenant occupies his *munus triplex*, his threefold office: he is a king to rule the creation, a priest to guard the garden, and a prophet to speak God's word. Here is the first man who anticipates the second, the Christ who will be the great King, Priest, and Prophet.

Paradigmatic Transgression: Hosea 6:7

We have seen abundant evidence for the covenant of life within the narrative details of Genesis 1–3, but there are also two later OT texts that attest the covenant, both from eighth-century prophets.[50]

[47] Mettinger, *Eden Narrative*, 92.
[48] Dietrich Bonhoeffer, *Creation and Fall: A Theological Interpretation of Genesis 1–3*, trans. John C. Fletcher (London: SCM, 1959), 57.
[49] The significance of the change is noted by Collins, *Genesis 1–4*, 114.
[50] Readers familiar with debates surrounding the covenant of life may wonder why I am not exploring Gen. 6:18 in this section. The verse does indeed speak of God establishing a preexisting covenant with Noah, as Gentry and

Hosea 6:7 is perhaps the most noted and debated example of retrojected covenantal language for God's relationship with Adam. The prophet's words describe the sin of Ephraim (Israel) and Judah: "But like Adam [כְּאָדָם] they transgressed the covenant; there they dealt faithlessly with me." The three main interpretations of the verse are based on different understandings of the word כְּאָדָם, rendered by the ESV "like Adam." The geographical reading (favored by the RSV, NJB, and NRSV) takes "Adam" to be a place, perhaps the place mentioned in Joshua 3:16, translating the verse, "At Adam they transgressed the covenant." The Septuagint represents a generic reading that takes the Hebrew to mean "like a man [ὡς ἄνθρωπος]." This sense is assumed by Theodore of Mopsuestia, defended by Calvin, and then adopted in the Geneva Bible and the Authorized Version.[51] A third, specific individual interpretation finds a reference to God's covenant with the first man Adam: "Like Adam they transgressed the covenant." This reading is found in Jewish sources and the Vulgate (*sicut Adam*).[52] It is adopted by Cyril of Alexandria, Rashi, Martin Luther, Hugo Grotius, and increasingly by Reformed writers until the critical era.[53]

In favor of the geographical interpretation is its fit with the statement in the second half of the verse that the people dealt faithlessly "there" (שָׁם), taking the locative to have the place Adam as its antecedent. It is not, however, difficult for the other readings to explain the significance of the שָׁם. As Robertson argues, it could simply have been the moment of a dramatic prophetic gesture as Hosea pointed toward the place not of past but of present idolatry.[54] Or it might have a non-geographical sense, as in Psalm 14:5.[55] The fatal problem for the geographical interpretation is that there is no notorious sin associated with the place Adam in the whole of Scripture. In fact the Adam

---

Wellum have argued (see *Kingdom through Covenant*, ch. 5), but the work of showing how it relates to the covenant of life specifically is beyond the scope of this chapter. The possible antecedents established by God in 6:18 include the creation-stability covenant of Jeremiah, the cultural mandate, the covenant of life, and the promise of Gen. 3:15. My understanding is that it refers primarily to the promise of 3:15, providing an indirect argument for the covenant of life because the promise anticipates a seed who will be the last Adam, obeying where the first Adam disobeyed.

[51] Byron G. Curtis, "Hosea 6:7 and Covenant Breaking Like/At Adam," in *The Law Is Not of Faith: Essays on Works and Grace in the Mosaic Covenant*, ed. Bryan D. Estelle, J. V. Fesko, and David VanDrunen (Phillipsburg, NJ: P&R, 2009), 177–78.

[52] For an example from Jewish literature see *Genesis Rabbah* 19:9. Gregory Beale notes several others in *A New Testament Biblical Theology: The Unfolding of the Old Testament in the New* (Grand Rapids, MI: Baker Academic, 2011), 43 n. 46.

[53] Benjamin B. Warfield covers some of the historical figures supporting this reading, including Francis Turretin, Jonathan Edwards, Herman Bavinck, and Geerhardus Vos, in Warfield, *Hosea VI.7: Adam or Man?*, in *Selected Shorter Writings*, ed. John E. Meeter, 2 vols. (Phillipsburg, NJ: P&R, 1970–1973; repr. 2005), 1:116–29.

[54] Robertson, *Christ of the Covenants*, 22 n. 2.

[55] McComiskey, *Minor Prophets*, 1:95.

of Joshua 3:16 is associated more clearly with the initial obedient, triumphant crossing of the Jordan. As an explanation for the reference to transgression in the verse, the obscure place Adam is a feeble contender against the man with whom sin itself began. A further weakness is that the geographical translation requires an emendation to the text, reading the inseparable preposition בְּ instead of כְּ, an amendment apparently first suggested by Julius Wellhausen.[56] This is an emendation that lacks support, as Warfield insists when he affirms the received text: "Neither the MSS nor the versions nor the quotations made from it suggest the currency, at any time accessible to our observation, of any other reading."[57]

Byron Curtis has recently proposed a complex variation on the geographical reading that finds a reference to both the first man and the physical town. He argues that the ambiguity of "Adam" creates a "Janus" or "asymmetrical pivotal polysemous parallelism."[58] In other words, the polysemous term "Adam" pivots and should be taken one way with the first line and another with the second. Curtis translates the noun twice to bring out the two senses:

> Like [their ancestor] Adam, they broke [עבר] the covenant;
> Like [the residents of the town of] Adam, they double-crossed [בגד] me
>   there.[59]

The double sense that this creates is further strengthened by the verb עָבַר, which can also be read two ways, as "transgress" or "cross." The verse thus parallels the first man's breaking of the covenant, a later disobedient crossing of the Jordan at the place Adam that double-crossed God, and Israel's current breaking of the Sinai covenant. Israel now breaks the covenant as it was broken by the man Adam *and* by the people of the crossing place. Curtis tentatively identifies the covenant breaking event at Adam as a reference to the assassination of the northern king Pekahiah by Pekah (2 Kings 15:23–26), a recent event in Hosea's time that might have involved Pekah crossing the Jordan at Adam on his way from Gilead to Samaria.

Difficulties beset this subtle reading, all pertaining to its geographical aspect. The first is that, according to Joshua 3:16, Adam was not the place

---

[56] So, Byron Curtis, "Hosea 6:7 and Covenant Breaking," 181.
[57] Warfield, *Hosea VI.7: Adam or Man?*, 1:125.
[58] The parallelism is asymmetric because the pivotal term is in one of two lines rather than in the middle of three (see Curtis, "Hosea 6:7 and Covenant Breaking," 206).
[59] Curtis, "Hosea 6:7 and Covenant Breaking," 207.

where the Hebrews crossed the Jordan but the "very far away" upstream limit of the water piling up. Adam is twenty-six miles north of Jericho, which means that it is ill-suited as an image for crossing the Jordan.[60] Curtis's reading may avoid this problem by positing a later treacherous crossing that did take place at Adam, but the reconstruction of Pekah's route from Gilead to Samaria is in fact wholly speculative; Curtis himself offers it as "the most tentative of hypotheses."[61] Last, I find it hard to see how the reconstruction makes internal sense: Curtis's translation speaks of the residents of the town Adam sinning, but the crime he references was committed by Pekah in Samaria, around twenty-five miles away.

Unlike the geographical, the generic interpretation requires no emendation, but it does point beyond itself toward the specific individual reading, inviting us to identify its Everyman with Adam. The translation "like men" implies a covenantal transgression not just on the part of Israel, but typical of mankind as a whole, which in the Scriptures point us back beyond Abraham to the father of the race, the archetypal transgressor.[62] The more we reckon with the singular generic "man," the more he comes into focus as Adam, the Bible's paradigmatic transgressor. The way in which the generic interpretation flows into the individual suggests that Francis Turretin is most likely right to find both in the verse: the words may refer to "the inconstancy of men" and yet "nothing prevents them being referred also to Adam."[63]

It should be salutary for conservative interpreters to note that much of the resistance to finding the individual Adam in Hosea 6:7 arises from critical reconstructions of OT origins. At the risk of oversimplifying these byzantine schemes (which is itself an argument against them; recall the risible hubris with which diagrams map the relationships of J, E, JE, D, P, Dtr1, Dtr2, DH, and R), the higher critics generally judge that the Torah was based on the Prophets and not vice versa. As such, Hosea could not have referred to the man Adam because he knew no Adam. As Warfield notes, it is "inductions as to the history of religious thought in Israel" that generate "a large part of the difficulty of the passage" for the critics. It is a difficulty that not all

---

[60] As noted by Curtis, "Hosea 6:7 and Covenant Breaking," 186. As Brian Habig points out, this counts against Curtis's own reading (see Habig, "Hosea 6:7," 19).
[61] Curtis, "Hosea 6:7 and Covenant Breaking," 196.
[62] So, Robertson, *Christ of the Covenants*, 23.
[63] Francis Turretin, *Institutes of Elenctic Theology*, ed. James T. Dennison Jr., trans. George Musgrave Giger, 3 vols. (Phillipsburg, NJ: P&R, 1992–97), 8.3.8 (1:576).

critics share (some date the supposed J source of Gen. 2:4b–3:24 earlier than Hosea), and one that certainly ought not to be shared.[64]

A great advantage of the specific individual reading is that it fits with the way in which Hosea makes other references to biblical history, most significantly, events recorded in Genesis. He uses the language of beasts of the field, birds of the heavens, and fish of the sea (Hos. 4:3), thorns and thistles (10:8), the covenant with Abraham (1:9–10), Ishmael as a donkey wandering alone (8:9), Admah and Zeboiim (11:8; from Gen. 14:2, 8, and Deut. 29:23), and the story of Jacob (12:2–6, 12).[65] Most importantly, the interpretation makes good literary and theological sense because of the parallel between Adam and Israel. As Jerome saw, both were given a land to live in and a law to keep, and both transgressed that law: "they imitated *Adam*, so that what he did in paradise, they did on earth, disregarding my *pact* and law."[66] As Hosea diagnoses sin, a reference to the initial creation follows on well from the way he has articulated hope in terms of the re-creation: "I will make for them a covenant on that day with the beasts of the field, the birds of the heavens, and the creeping things of the ground" (Hos. 2:18). Just as the sin of God's people resembled Adam's creation-spoiling sin, so their restoration will bring a harmony with the creation that resembles the pre-fall world.[67]

Turretin argues for a reference to the individual Adam from the "similar locution" in Job 31:33, which he thinks refers back to Genesis 3:12 (ESV mg.): "if I have concealed my transgressions as Adam did by hiding my iniquity in my heart."[68] The Hebrew is the same here as Hosea 6:7 (כְּאָדָם) and is rendered "as Adam" in the AV and "like Adam" in the ASV, but more recent translations prefer the generic "as others do" (ESV; CSB) or "as people do" (NIV), relegating Adam to a footnote. Thomas Boston argues for a reference to Adam in Hosea on the basis of Psalm 82:7: "like Adam you shall die, and fall like any prince."[69] The Hebrew is the same again, but here Adam does not even make it into the footnotes of the ESV or the CSB. Perhaps, given the foundational place of Adam in biblical history and the abundance of

---

[64] Warfield, *Hosea VI.7: Adam or Man?*, 1:125.
[65] Curtis lists sixteen allusions to Genesis in Hosea (including these) and a further seventeen to Exodus–Deuteronomy (see "Hosea 6:7 and Covenant Breaking," 189–91 and 192–93).
[66] Jerome, "Commentary on Hosea," in *Commentaries on the Twelve Prophets*, ed. Thomas P. Scheck, vol. 2 (Downers Grove, IL: InterVarsity Press, 2016–17), 195.
[67] Curtis, "Hosea 6:7 and Covenant Breaking," 195.
[68] Turretin, *Institutes*, 8.3.8 (1:576).
[69] Boston, *View of the Covenant of Works*, 11:182.

connections to the later kings and priests, we ought to expect him to loom larger in the pages of the OT than many in the post-critical era have allowed.

The Everlasting Covenant: Isaiah 24:5

The second example of a later text referencing a covenant with Adam is Isaiah 24:5. The penultimate verse of Isaiah 23 says that Tyre "will prostitute herself with all the kingdoms of the world on the face of the earth" (v. 17), establishing a global reference for the term אֶרֶץ, which is then used throughout the eschatological prophecies of chapter 24 (vv. 1, 3, 4, 5, 6, 11, 13, 16, 17, 18, 19, 20). This wide scope is confirmed by the use of the term "world" (תֵבֵל) in verse 4, and by statements such as verse 13: "thus it shall be in the midst of the earth among the nations." Within this global context we find the charge of verse 5:

> The earth lies defiled
> under its inhabitants;
> for they have transgressed the laws,
> violated the statutes,
> broken the everlasting covenant.

What is this "everlasting covenant [בְּרִית עוֹלָם]" with the inhabitants of the earth? The phrase itself does not tell us, because it is used so widely of biblical covenants (of the Noahic covenant in Gen. 9:16; the Abrahamic in Ps. 105:10; the Mosaic Sabbath in Lev. 24:8; the Davidic in 2 Sam. 23:5; and the new covenant in Isa. 55:3 and 61:8). While there is language in Isaiah 24 that alludes to Noah, for example the phrase "windows of the heaven" (v. 18; cf. Gen. 7:11; 8:2), the difficulty with limiting the reference here to the Noahic covenant is that the covenant in view in Isaiah has been comprehensively broken by mankind. J. A. Motyer explains that the verb used here for covenant breaking (פָּרַר) is "deeper than transgressing or disobeying, actually annulling, nullifying or setting aside the whole concept of covenant relationship and life."[70] Hence Isaiah speaks in the next verse of the ensuing disaster:

> Therefore a curse devours the earth,
> and its inhabitants suffer for their guilt;
> therefore the inhabitants of the earth are scorched,
> and few men are left. (Isa. 24:6)

---

[70] J. A. Motyer, *The Prophecy of Isaiah* (Leicester, UK: Inter-Varsity Press, 1993), 199, comparing Deut. 31:20.

By contrast, according to most interpreters the covenant with Noah was an unconditional covenant, perhaps even the paradigmatic unconditional covenant. Even if the Noahic covenant was not entirely unconditional, the comprehensive brokenness described in Isaiah 24 contradicts its permanence. As Motyer puts it, the ambience of the prophecy starts with Noah but cannot be limited to him.[71] Isaiah's picture does, however, fit with the sin of Adam subsequently reiterated throughout human history. As E. J. Young argues, "the eternal covenant here spoken of designates the fact that God has given His Law and ordinances to Adam, and in Adam to all mankind."[72]

The Apostle Paul's Covenantal Adam

A covenant with Adam is rightly inferred from the way in which he is used in the NT to interpret the covenantal Christ and his work, most notably in Romans 5:12–21 and 1 Corinthians 15:20–28 and 42–49. In these passages Adam is not just an illustration for Christ: Adam is the type of whom Christ is the eschatological antitype. Christ acts as a representative like Adam but reverses his work, replacing condemnation and death with justification and life—resurrection life. In Paul's theology Christ is conceived in covenantal terms. He is the singular seed who inherits the promises of the Abrahamic covenant (Gal. 3:16), and whose obedience is, therefore, framed by the covenant. As Kline comments, "If the role of Christ as the second Adam is recognized as covenantal, this scheme provides further clear warrant for classifying the arrangement made with the first Adam as covenantal."[73]

Headship Is Federal

Some have already given up so much that they can abandon the idea of a covenant with Adam at little dogmatic cost, because there is not much of a building left for their foundation to support. For those who hold to the idea of Adam as humanity's representative, the price is higher. They should grasp the need to maintain that Adam was in a covenant with God because it is covenant that constitutes representative headship. This is why Adam's headship is termed "federal" (from the Latin *foedus*, "covenant"). Unless we reduce the headship of Adam solely to his place as progenitor of the race, then his

---

[71] Motyer, *Prophet of Isaiah*, 199.
[72] Edward J. Young, *The Book of Isaiah: The English Text, with Introduction, Exposition, and Notes*, 3 vols. (Grand Rapids, MI: Eerdmans, 1965), 2:158.
[73] Kline, *Kingdom Prologue*, 20.

headship needs to have been formed within the framework of divine appointment. Some who profess to reject the covenant with Adam effectively affirm it in their teaching on Adam's headship. To describe God making Adam the representative of his people so that he would bring on them blessing or curse is to describe the substance of the covenant of works. Is the debate then merely verbal? If we love the thing but not the name, may we not say, like Shakespeare's Juliet,

> What's Covenant? it is nor party, nor stipulation,
> Nor curse, nor blessing, nor any other part
> Belonging to a relationship. O! be some other name:
> What's in a name?

We may not, because in God's world names are rather more significant than they are in Juliet's. If in texts such as Hosea 6:7 God has given this relationship the name "covenant," then we are not free to deny it.

Is there a viable alternative path of non-covenantal natural headship? Might Adam's representative role be constituted by his biological paternity alone, sans covenant? That Adam was the first father of the race is indeed an aspect of his position as head, but it is not sufficient to establish it. If anyone argues that it is sufficient, they prove too much, because nothing would then prevent all of Adam's sins being passed down to his descendants. Indeed nothing would prevent all of the sins of all fathers throughout history being passed to their descendants, in an ever-accumulating *massa horribilis*. A divine appointment is needed both to establish and to limit Adam's headship. This is why Thomas Boston resisted criticisms of the idea of a covenant with Adam: "If the covenant made with Adam was not a proper covenant, he could not be a proper representing head; and if he was not, then there cannot be a proper imputation of Adam's sin unto his posterity."[74] More on this in the next chapter.

Conclusion

There are so many issues that merit sustained attention within the theology of the covenant with Adam. They include the timing of the covenant's initiation, the relationship between Eve and the garden sanctuary, the function of the life and death trees, Adam's eschatology, the identity of the serpent, the

---

[74] Boston, *View of the Covenant of Works*, 180–81.

nature and origin of the first sin, and the role of grace and faith in the garden. They are vital for a broader theology of the first man, and therefore of the second, but for my present purposes the point has been established: Adam and his role are to be understood in terms of God's covenant with him and his threefold office within it as representative king, priest, and prophet. This conclusion concerning Adam's relationship to God provides a vital foundation as we turn in the next chapter to consider our relationship to Adam. How was it that Adam's sin became ours?

20

Total Depravity and God's Covenant with Adam (2)

THE IMPUTATION OF ADAM'S SIN

Garry Williams

The Definition and Scope of Original Sin

"Repent and believe in the gospel" (Mark 1:15). The centrality of the call to repentance in gospel preaching tells us that fundamental to conversion is a realization that we are spiritually sick and in need of the great physician (Mark 2:17). It is not long before convicted sinners come to ponder the origin of our depraved nature and to trace its root back to the beginning of our lives. Inevitably we then ask how we came to be born in this condition. Scripture points us for our answer to Adam, and invites us thereby to ask how we relate to him. Francis Turretin states that "Adam in a certain manner included the whole human race,"[1] but in what manner did he do so? The best minds of the church have long puzzled over this question at the heart of the doctrine of original sin. Finding an answer is a step toward understanding the origin of our total depravity.

"Original sin" (*peccatum originale*) is a confusing term. Technically, it does not refer to the original sin committed by Adam himself, but to the inherited depravity of the human heart in all of us (*corruptio haereditaria*).

---

[1] Francis Turretin, *Institutes of Elenctic Theology*, ed. James T. Dennison Jr., trans. George Musgrave Giger, 3 vols. (Phillipsburg, NJ: P&R, 1992–97), 8.3.11 (1:576).

As John Calvin defines it, original sin is "a hereditary depravity and corruption of our nature, diffused into all parts of the soul."[2] In practice, the term is used more loosely. Jonathan Edwards agrees with Calvin when he defines original sin as the *"innate sinful depravity of the heart"* but recognizes that the term "vulgarly understood" includes not only the depraved heart but also the imputation of Adam's sin.[3] For the sake of clarity, I will use the term "original sin" only when referring broadly to this *locus* of doctrine, preferring the more specific term "primal sin" for Adam's own sinful act, "imputed sin" for the reckoning of that act to his descendants, and "birth sin" for the depravity of the heart.[4]

One of the great controverted issues in the doctrine of original sin concerns the relationship between imputed sin and birth sin. Is Adam's primal sin first imputed to us, so that we are then born with a depraved heart? Or is the depraved heart itself the *basis* of the primal sin being reckoned ours? No one should pretend that these are easy questions to answer. They provoke different responses not only across confessional boundaries but also within them. The fact that the difficulty in answering them is as universal as the sin itself may both comfort and concern us. Comfort, because we know that greater minds and souls have struggled before us; concern, because it can be hard to abide the puzzle. There are some theological questions that can remain unanswered without affecting the Christian life, but this is not one of them. It is central to our experience as moral agents. Blaise Pascal expresses very well the existential discomfort of the perplexity. He acknowledges that "nothing shocks our reason more than to say that the sin of the first man made guilty those who, so far from that source, seem incapable of having taken part in it." And yet this mystery is a "gnarled chasm" within which "lie the twists and turns of our condition." It is "the one thing without which we can have no understanding of ourselves." Perplexing as it is, we need it more than we can understand it: "humanity is more inconceivable without this mystery than this mystery is conceivable to humanity."[5]

---

[2] John Calvin, *Institutes of the Christian Religion*, ed. John T. McNeill, trans. Ford Lewis Battles, 2 vols., The Library of Christian Classics 20–21 (Philadelphia: Westminster, 1960); 2.1.8 (1:251).
[3] Jonathan Edwards, *Original Sin*, ed. Clyde A. Holbrook, vol. 3 of *The Works of Jonathan Edwards*, 26 vols. (New Haven, CT: Yale University Press, 1970; repr. 1997), 107.
[4] This terminology is not original. Augustine debates with Pelagius the effect of the *primum peccatum* of Adam (*De gratia Christi et de peccato originale* ii.15). The Thirty-Nine Articles speak of "birth-sin" (art. 9). Technically, we might more accurately speak of "conception" rather than "birth" sin, but I am a moth to the lamp of historical precedent.
[5] Blaise Pascal, *Pensées and Other Writings*, ed. Anthony Levi, trans. Honor Levi (Oxford: Oxford University Press, 1995; repr. 2008), 42–43.

As we step into the gnarled chasm, we do well to remember that sin is first and foremost not a theological puzzle but a spiritual reality for every person. Sin is more pressing as an existential enemy to fight than as a technical question to ponder. As William Perkins comments, when you find that your town is on fire, your first concern is to extinguish the fire, not to find where it started.[6] Investigating the origin of our depravity is not an exercise that can be conducted at arm's length. When I write and you read about original sin, we are not like veterinary scientists studying a disease that afflicts another species. We are more like convicted criminals considering how we came to commit our crimes.

The Fact of Birth Sin

It is appropriate to begin with birth sin, the depravity of the heart, because it is closest to our experience. The brute fact of birth sin should be beyond dispute. That all human beings apart from Jesus Christ are corrupt from conception is arguably the most empirically attested doctrine of the Christian faith. Despite romantically idealized views of children and childhood, no parent will believe they have a sinless child for long. At some point the conclusion of universal depravity must follow from the sad consistency of our experience of others, and of ourselves. As Edwards argues, it is observation that proves a tendency, and "a steady effect argues a steady cause."[7] The fact that the individual sinful tendency is observed in the context of human society does not disprove the inference that we incline to sinful acts because of a moral disposition that precedes social influence. Societies are made up of people, and societies that corrupt every child born into them reveal the prior nature of the people who compose them. Consistent societal sin reveals consistently fallen human nature.

Even anti-theist philosophers retain a bleak assessment of human nature. Writing in *The Guardian*, John Gray speaks of how we can now understand what used to be called "evil" as "a natural tendency to animosity and destruction, co-existing in human beings alongside tendencies to sympathy and cooperation." Gray does not believe that human progress will overcome the negative tendency. He cites an exchange of letters between Sigmund Freud

---

[6] Quoted by Donald Macleod in "Original Sin in Reformed Theology," in *Adam, the Fall, and Original Sin: Theological, Biblical, and Scientific Perspectives*, ed. Hans Madueme and Michael Reeves (Grand Rapids, MI: Baker Academic, 2014), 130.

[7] Edwards, *Original Sin*, 121.

and Albert Einstein in 1931–32. Einstein asks Freud, "Is it possible to control man's mental evolution so as to make him proof against the psychosis of hate and destructiveness?" Freud replies that "there is no likelihood of our being able to suppress humanity's aggressive tendencies." Gray attempts to recast Freud's mythology in materialist terms:

> Rather than psychoanalysis, it may be some version of evolutionary psychology that can best illuminate the human proclivity to hatred and destruction. The point is that destructive behaviour of this kind flows from inherent human flaws. Crucially, these defects are not only or even mainly intellectual. No advance in human knowledge can stop humans attacking and persecuting others.[8]

The aetiology of evil here is wrong, but the conclusion regarding inherent flaws is realistically bleak. It is a conclusion that Gray reaches even though he has ruled out of consideration the most serious human flaw, animosity toward God himself.

Scripture attests the universality of human corruption, with a particular focus on the human heart as its source. The flood is sent by God because "the LORD saw that the wickedness of man was great in the earth, and that every intention of the thoughts of his heart was only evil continually" (Gen. 6:5). Even at the spiritual high point of the dedication of the temple, Solomon asks the Lord to forgive those who repent, because "there is no one who does not sin" (1 Kings 8:46). This is echoed in Ecclesiastes: "Surely there is not a righteous man on earth who does good and never sins" (7:20). Like Genesis, Ecclesiastes traces the problem to the human heart: "the hearts of the children of man are full of evil, and madness is in their hearts while they live, and after that they go to the dead" (Eccl. 9:3). The prophet Jeremiah agrees: "The heart is deceitful above all things, and desperately sick" (Jer. 17:9). In the NT, the great catena of quotations in Romans 3:10–18 pronounces a devastating verdict on humanity, especially in the quotations from Psalms 14 and 53: "None is righteous, no, not one; no one understands; no one seeks for God. All have turned aside; together they have become worthless; no one does good, not even one" (Rom. 3:10–12). Scripture is also clear that the human heart disease can be traced back to the beginning of our existence. Speaking of man born of woman, Job asks, "Who can bring a clean thing out of an unclean?

---

[8] John Gray, "The Truth about Evil," *The Guardian*, October 21, 2014, http://www.theguardian.com/news/2014/oct/21/-sp-the-truth-about-evil-john-gray.

There is not one" (Job 14:4; cf. Eliphaz in 15:14). Folly, Proverbs tells us, "is bound up in the heart of a child" (Prov. 22:15). And of course there is David's prayer in Psalm 51:5, "Behold, I was brought forth in iniquity, and in sin did my mother conceive me," and the similar thought in Psalm 58:3, "The wicked are estranged from the womb; they go astray from birth, speaking lies." Paul echoes the verdict of the OT writers when he writes to the Ephesians: "we . . . were by nature children of wrath, like the rest of mankind" (Eph. 2:3). Given the reference to being "children," the phrase "by nature" (φύσει) suggests by birth, as it does in Galatians 2:15 ("Jews by birth"). This is birth sin.

When he states that we are "children of wrath," Paul shows that birth sin is damnable: we are conceived in a state of enmity with God. We should not be surprised to find the unborn child taken seriously as a moral person because Scripture attests the spiritual capacity of even pre-verbal infants. In Psalm 22 David tells God, "you made me trust you at my mother's breasts," and "from my mother's womb you have been my God" (vv. 9, 10). John the Baptist was filled with the Holy Spirit "even from his mother's womb" (Luke 1:15), and he leapt at the approach of the unborn Jesus (1:41). Clearly, infants can have a kind of faith even before they are capable of deliberative mental acts. This is termed the "seed" of faith by Calvin, and "a seminal or radical and habitual faith" by Turretin.[9] The heart exists with all its habits from the moment of conception, and it is from the heart that all later acts spring. It is the source of "evil thoughts, sexual immorality, theft, murder, adultery, coveting, wickedness, deceit, sensuality, envy, slander, pride, foolishness" (Mark 7:21–22). According to our fallen nature, apart from the gracious work of the Spirit of God, the spiritual habits of infants are habits of unbelief, of God-hating. Boston draws the awful conclusion:

> Suppose you had never sinned in your own persons, but had perfectly obeyed since you were capable of keeping or breaking God's law; yet being under that covenant you should still be under the curse, as being born under it, on the account of Adam's first sin.[10]

To hold that all infants are damnable for the mere possession of a fallen nature is not to say that all or even any who die in infancy are eternally condemned; but saved infants are saved by grace, not because they were sinless.

[9] Calvin, *Institutes*, 4.16.20 (2:1343); Turretin, *Institutes*, 15.14.2 (2:583).
[10] Thomas Boston, *A View of the Covenant of Works from the Sacred Records*, in *The Complete Works of the Late Rev. Thomas Boston*, ed. Samuel M'Millan, 12 vols. (Wheaton, IL: Richard Owen Roberts, 1980), 11:334.

Birth sin condemns us all. Both experience and Scripture attest that sin is universal in all people from conception. Nevertheless, we should remember that, while sin now permeates the fallen human heart, it is not, properly speaking, essential to created human nature. As Robert Dabney explains, depravity is technically "not an attribute" but an "*accidens,*" an accidental (as in non-essential) property of the human soul.[11] We see this from the fact that Jesus Christ did not have a sinful heart and yet was the most truly human man, *der rechte Mann* ("the right man"), as Martin Luther calls him.

Moral Individualism

Is birth sin inherited from Adam? Some, like Rudolf Bultmann, believe that the question can be answered with a peremptory wave of the enlightened hand:

> Nor can we understand that in consequence of the guilt of our ancestors we should be condemned to the death of a natural being, because we know of guilt only as a responsible act and therefore regard original sin, in the sense of a quasi-natural hereditary illness, as a submoral and impossible concept.[12]

Bultmann states here the cardinal objection to any conception of Adam's sin bringing death on others: individuals can only be held responsible for what they themselves have done in their own bodies. This continues to be a common objection in modern theology. For example, Richard Swinburne opposes the idea that anyone could be guilty for another's sin: "a person is surely not responsible for, not guilty in respect of, the acts of others; above all, he is not guilty for the acts of others which he could not have influenced."[13] A report of the Church of England's Doctrine Commission, *The Mystery of Salvation,* states that "moral responsibility is ultimately incommunicable."[14]

The objection based on individual responsibility rose to prominence in the eighteenth century, for example in the work of John Taylor of Norwich:

> That any Man, without my Knowledge or Consent, should so represent me, that when he is guilty I am to be reputed guilty, and when he transgresses I shall be accountable and punishable for his Transgression, and thereby subjected to

---

[11] Robert L. Dabney, *Systematic Theology* (Edinburgh: Banner of Truth, 1985 [1871]), 322.
[12] Rudolf Bultmann, *New Testament and Mythology and Other Basic Writings,* ed. and trans. Schubert M. Ogden (London: SCM, 1985), 7.
[13] Richard Swinburne, *Responsibility and Atonement* (1989; repr., Oxford: Clarendon, 1998), 91.
[14] *The Mystery of Salvation* (1995; repr., London: Church House Publishing, 1997), 212.

the Wrath and Curse of God; nay further, that his Wickedness shall give me a *sinful Nature*, and all this before I am born, and consequently while I am in no Capacity of knowing, helping or hindering what he doth; surely any one, who *dares* use his Understanding, must clearly see this is unreasonable, and altogether inconsistent with the Truth and Goodness of God.[15]

Theological individualism took hold in Taylor's century, but it had its roots long before in the controversies of Augustine with the Pelagians. As Augustine reports, Pelagius himself held that it is only our own deeds that can make us good or evil: "Everything good, and everything evil, on account of which we are either laudable or blameworthy, is not born with us but done by us."[16] This means that the sin of Adam is injurious to us "not by transmission, but by example."[17] For the Pelagian Coelestius, each infant has a fresh beginning and chooses whether or not to reenact Adam's sin: "infants at their birth are in the same state that Adam was in before his transgression."[18] Augustine rejected this as a "deadly heresy," which every catholic must oppose with all his energy.[19] This is not, he is clear, an area where doubt is compatible with soundness.

Contrary to Pelagians ancient and modern, Adam was not an island. Moral individualism is incompatible with the teaching of Holy Scripture on multiple fronts, including protology, hamartiology, Christology, and soteriology. Paul's teaching on Adam and Christ in Romans 5:12–21 shows that our salvation itself depends on moral individualism being false: while we may lament the sin of Adam that condemns us, our only hope is the righteousness of Christ that justifies. The parallel between Adam and Christ begins in verse 12, breaks off, and is resumed in verse 18. In the midst of the similarities that Paul identifies between Adam and Christ there are vital differences, most notably the sustained contrasts between the moral character of their actions and their effects: "the free gift is not like the result of that one man's sin" (Rom. 5:16). But for our purposes it is the similarity that matters. As John Murray argues, the "sustained emphasis not only upon the one man Adam and the one man Christ but also upon the one trespass and the one righteous act points to a basic identity in respect of *modus operandi*."[20] The passage

[15] John Taylor, *A Supplement to the Scripture-Doctrine of Original Sin* (London: Mary Fenner, 1741), 109.
[16] Augustine, *On the Grace of Christ, and Original Sin* ii.14, in *NPNF*[1] 5:241.
[17] Augustine, *On the Grace* ii.16, in *NPNF*[1] 5:242.
[18] Augustine, *On the Grace* ii.2, in *NPNF*[1] 5:237.
[19] Augustine, *On the Grace* ii.25, in *NPNF*[1] 5:245.
[20] John Murray, *The Imputation of Adam's Sin* (Phillipsburg, NJ: P&R, 1959), 33.

teaches that Adam and Christ both acted as representatives. This argument does not depend on a particular reading of verse 12. Many in history have understood the verse as Augustine did when he rendered ἐφ᾽ ᾧ πάντες ἥμαρτον as "in quo omnes peccaverunt" ("in whom all sinned").[21] If the verse did say that, it would indeed confirm the idea of all humanity sinning in Adam. The difficulty with that reading is the distance between the phrase ἐφ᾽ ᾧ and its presumed antecedent "through one man." The more likely sense of the phrase is "because" or "in that," which is how it is used in 2 Corinthians 5:4: "because we do not want to be unclothed [ἐφ᾽ ᾧ οὐ θέλομεν ἐκδύσασθαι]" (CSB). The translation "because all sinned" leaves open the question of *how* all sinned, whether in Adam's sin or in their own. Does Paul mean that all sinned when they themselves sinned in their own bodies, or that they sinned when Adam sinned?

While in Romans 3:23 the phrase "all have sinned [πάντες ἥμαρτον]" clearly refers to individual sin, in chapter 5 Paul emphasizes the decisively instrumental role of Adam:

> The free gift is not like the result of that one man's sin. For the judgment following one trespass brought condemnation, but the free gift following many trespasses brought justification. For if, because of one man's trespass, death reigned through that one man, much more will those who receive the abundance of grace and the free gift of righteousness reign in life through the one man Jesus Christ. Therefore, as one trespass led to condemnation for all men, so one act of righteousness leads to justification and life for all men. For as by the one man's disobedience the many were made sinners, so by the one man's obedience the many will be made righteous. (5:16–19)

The same point is made several times throughout these verses: the one man's sin, trespass, and disobedience brought judgment, led to condemnation and the reign of death, and made many sinners. As Douglas Moo comments on verse 17, "This emphasis on the 'one man Adam' and his sin as the instrument by which death exercises its rule reveals again the concern of Paul to tie the fate of all people in some direct way with the sin of Adam."[22]

Paul's reading of Adam reflects the teaching of Genesis itself. As Thomas Boston points out, all of the verbs in the command and warning given to Adam in Genesis 2:16–17 are singular, pertaining particularly to Adam

---

[21] See Augustine, *Against Two Epistles of the Pelagians* iv.7, in *NPNF*¹ 5:419.
[22] Douglas J. Moo, *The Epistle to the Romans* (Grand Rapids, MI: Eerdmans, 1996), 339.

himself. Adam alone was the representative actor. His single sin resulted in all of his natural descendants being born outside of Eden in a fallen state. Boston argues that even the sins of any children born to Adam during his probation would only have affected the children themselves: Adam alone is, as he puts it, "a public person," "the compend of the whole world."[23] Following the lead of the Eden narrative, Paul is clear: the one act of the one man Adam condemns us. The later verses clarify the sense in which "all sinned" in verse 12.[24] Paul means neither that Adam sinned and we copy him, nor that Adam sinned and passed on to us a sinful nature so that we sinned and were then condemned for it, but that *when Adam sinned, there and then we sinned in him and were condemned.* We do sin in our own bodies and we do inherit a corrupt nature from Adam, but neither of those facts is in view here. No stages are interposed. There is an "immediate conjunction" of the sin, death, and condemnation of Adam with the sin, death, and condemnation of all.[25] The parallel with Christ implies nothing less: just as we are justified by the one act of Christ apart from our own deeds, so we are condemned by the one act of Adam apart from our own deeds.

Mediate Imputation

Romans 5:12–21 teaches a stronger immediacy than the advocates of a mediate imputation would allow. There are different versions of mediate imputation, but they share in common the claim that each person's inherited corruption precedes and mediates the imputation of sin. The mediate view was propounded in the French Reformed church at the Academy of Saumur by Joshua Placaeus (Josué de la Place, 1596–1655), who held that each individual inherits corruption from Adam, and on that basis is condemned for Adam's sin.[26] The Third Synod of Charenton in 1645 rejected the view that "restraineth the Nature of Original Sin to the sole Hereditary Corruption of *Adam's* Posterity," most likely a description of Placaeus's early teaching, which he then refined to include the idea of Adam's sin being imputed, but only mediately, by way of inherent corruption.[27]

---

[23] Boston, *View of the Covenant of Works*, 11:186.
[24] Murray, *Imputation of Adam's Sin*, 8, 19–21.
[25] Murray, *Imputation of Adam's Sin*, 65–68.
[26] The key work by Placaeus is *De Imputatione Primi Peccati Adami* (1655).
[27] *Synodicon in Gallia Reformata: Or, the Acts, Decisions, Decrees, and Canons of Those Famous National Councils of the Reformed Churches in France*, ed. and trans. John Quick, 2 vols. (London: T. Parkhurst and J. Robinson, 1692), 2:473. For this reading of the history, see Murray, *Imputation of Adam's Sin*, 42–46.

We do indeed inherit corruption, but, given Paul's teaching on the immediacy of Adam's relation to our condemnation, the corruption inherited (the *macula*) cannot be an intermediary basis for inheriting the guilt of Adam. Even as Paul underlines the universal effect of Adam's own deed, he denies that the personal sin of his descendants up to the time of Moses is the cause of their death: their "sinning was not like the transgression of Adam," and yet "death reigned" over them (5:14).[28]

Even if mediate imputation were exegetically feasible, its theological advantages are illusory. It is thought by its proponents to account for individual moral responsibility because it locates my corruption between Adam's sin and my condemnation: I incur primal sin only through the instrumentality of my own corrupt nature. But the moral question occurs again, only further back: on this scenario, you should ask not what you did to have primal sin imputed to you without personal guilt, but what you did to inherit a corrupt nature without any personal guilt in view. If birth sin precedes imputed sin, then what is the just basis for birth sin itself inhering in us? The mediate scheme affirms the inheritance of birth sin but refuses to turn to imputed sin to explain the moral basis of that inheritance. The principle that "like begets like" is invoked to explain how we come into the world in a fallen state, but while it may explain the mechanism of inheritance, it does nothing to explain the justice of it. So far as the moral question is concerned, it simply obtrudes "the fact itself as an explanation of the fact."[29]

A further problem with the mediate scheme is that, by basing the imputation of primal sin on the prior possession of a corrupt nature, it supposes a moment of existence for the sinner in a corrupt nature prior to condemnation. Yet this stage does not exist: there is not even a notional instant in which every person conceived in corruption is deemed innocent prior to the imputation of primal sin. Fallen human beings are condemned from the very beginning of their existence. The sentence has already been passed, and is contemporary with our existence itself.[30]

This is a point of wider spiritual significance when we look to understand the justice of the imputation of sin to us. When I ponder the origin of my own

---

[28] Thomas Schreiner makes this point against Henri Blocher's account of original sin. For Blocher, see *Original Sin: Illuminating the Riddle* (Leicester, UK: Apollos, 1997); for Schreiner's objection, see Macleod, "Original Sin and Original Death," 277.

[29] A criticism made by Dabney in *Systematic Theology*, 341, though he identifies the whole mediate-immediate distinction as one that "should never have been made" (342), favoring an agnostic position.

[30] Dabney, *Systematic Theology*, 341.

sinfulness, I am tempted to imagine a scenario in which an innocent Williams had Adam's sin imputed to him. Picturing it like that aggravates the difficulty with original sin because it leaves me feeling its injustice all the more acutely: why would I, an innocent person, have been burdened with Adam's guilt? But as Murray argues, sinners are "not conceived of in the mind and purpose of God except as one with Adam."[31] To suppose my momentary innocent existence would also enable me to exculpate myself from imputed sin, as if it were *peccatum alienum* in the sense that I am the innocent victim of it. As Berkouwer warns, "our confession of original sin may not function and cannot function as a means of *excusing ourselves* or of *hiding behind another man's guilt*."[32] The pictured scenario is all wrong. There never was an innocent Williams to whom sin was subsequently imputed. As Murray explains, the posterity of Adam were only ever contemplated by God as "members of the race in solidaric union with Adam." We were never regarded as potentially one with Adam, but always as actually one with him. It is, therefore, a "capital mistake" to ask, "when does each member of the race *become* actually sinful?"[33] The fact that I never existed as an innocent person means that I have no basis for accusing God of imputing sin to me when I was innocent. There was no person prior to the imputation of sin who did not deserve it. I never walked in the garden under a covenant yet unbroken.

Birth Sin without Imputed Sin

Oliver Crisp has recently proposed a view that goes a step beyond mediate imputation. Crisp works in the sphere of "analytic theology," a method applying the tools of analytic philosophy to explicate theological problems. Analytic theology is not rationalistic, because it assigns to reason a procedural role within a given theology rather than a substantive role building a theology from scratch.[34] It can therefore function as a tool within confessional systems, much like the scholastic method, of which it is arguably a modern development. We will meet Crisp again below as a proponent of a helpfully suggestive version of federalism, but here we find him on another, more recent track, advocating what he describes as a retrieval of a modified

---

[31] Murray, *Imputation of Adam's Sin*, 90.
[32] G. C. Berkouwer, *Sin*, trans. Philip C. Holtrop (Grand Rapids, MI: Eerdmans, 1971), 435, emphasis original.
[33] Murray, *Imputation of Adam's Sin*, 90, emphasis original.
[34] The procedural-substantive distinction is drawn by Paul Helm in *Faith and Understanding* (Edinburgh: Edinburgh University Press, 1997), ch. 1.

Zwinglian account of original sin.[35] Unlike the Salmurians, he does not use inherited corruption to explain how we become guilty of Adam's primal sin, because he holds that "fallen humans are not culpable for Adam's sin."[36] Crisp has come to accept moral individualism, at least within the doctrine of original sin: "to be the proper subject of culpability for the primal sin or the guilt of that sin one would have to be the person who committed the primal sin."[37] Crisp agrees with Huldrych Zwingli that "original sin is not sin but disease."[38] He concludes that we inherit "a moral condition from fallen Adam that includes no guilt at all."[39] Nevertheless, Crisp affirms that, from the moment of their generation, human beings do face "death and separation from God irrespective of actual sin," not because they are guilty, but because they are diseased, and because they inevitably commit sinful acts.[40] Crisp's view bears some similarity not only to Zwingli but also to the historic teaching of the Eastern church, with its emphasis on the transmission of corruption to Adam's descendants as the reason we bear the punishment of death. There are Greek fathers who teach that we share in primal guilt, but many, especially among the modern Orthodox, are eager to repudiate forensic imputation and to emphasize individual inherited corruption. The anti-forensic tendency even reaches Pelagian proportions in some recent writers like John Romanides, who reads his teaching back into the fathers:

> The Fathers stress that everyone is born like Adam and Eve, and everyone goes through the same fall. Darkening of the nous happens to each one. The nous that exists in the embryo is not yet darkened. Each one suffers the fall of Adam and Eve on account of his surroundings.[41]

This is both un-Orthodox and un-orthodox.

Crisp's Zwinglian scheme and the more traditional end of the Orthodox spectrum face the same moral problem as Salmurian mediate imputation, with slight adjustment. They differ from the Salmurians in that they deny the imputation of primal sin and guilt, but they share the emphasis on inherited

---

[35] Crisp himself notes the change in his own thinking in "On Original Sin," *IJST* 17.3 (2015): 258 n. 12.
[36] Oliver D. Crisp, "Retrieving Zwingli's Doctrine of Original Sin," *JRT* 10 (2016): 352.
[37] Crisp, "On Original Sin," 261.
[38] Cited in Crisp, "Retrieving Zwingli's Doctrine," 345.
[39] Oliver D. Crisp, "Sin," in *Christian Dogmatics: Reformed Theology for the Church Catholic*, ed. Michael Allen and Scott R. Swain (Grand Rapids, MI: Baker Academic, 2016), 212; cf. Crisp, "On Original Sin," 264.
[40] Crisp, "On Original Sin," 264; cf. Crisp, "Retrieving Zwingli's Doctrine," 352.
[41] John Romanides, *Empirical Dogmatics of the Orthodox Catholic Church*, ed. Effie Mavromichali, trans. Pelagia Selfe, 2nd ed., 2 vols. (Levadia, Greece: Birth of Theotokos Monastery, 2011), 2:184.

corruption and the problematic failure to explain the moral basis for that inheritance. The problem with the Salmurian teaching is the order: the imputation of primal sin is located subsequent to the inheritance of a corrupt nature, removing the moral basis for the corrupt generation. The problem with the Zwinglian and some of the Orthodox schemes is not order (because the imputation of primal sin is denied), but the resulting difficulty is the same: on what moral basis are sinners conceived with a corrupt nature? In fact, by denying original guilt Crisp takes off the table anything outside ourselves as the moral basis for inheriting a fallen condition. It has become a matter of principle that moral explanation stops with me, which means that a position that sprang from a desire to alleviate the moral difficulty with imputed sin is left with as serious a moral difficulty of its own regarding birth sin. As the Formula Consensus Helveticus states,

> There appears no way in which hereditary corruption could fall, as a spiritual death, upon the whole human race by the just judgment of God, unless some sin of that race preceded, incurring the penalty of that death. For God, the most supreme Judge of all the earth, punishes none but the guilty.[42]

Without implying that advocates of mediate imputation are themselves Pelagian, I do fear that the moral problem might keep pressing upon them until they deny not only imputed guilt but also inherited corruption, because the moral problem keeps returning and the Pelagian account is the only one that will truly secure individual self-determination. This is why the Formula states that to deny the moral role of imputed sin is actually to "expose the doctrine of hereditary corruption to grave danger."[43] We are compelled by both exegesis and moral reasoning to conclude that we are deemed guilty immediately on the basis of the one act committed by the one man Adam, not only through or in birth sin.

Distinguishing Realism and Federalism

If accounts that prioritize birth sin fail to explain the moral basis for it, do schemes that posit an immediate connection between Adam and his descendants fare any better? There are two main ways in which Reformed theology

---

[42] Translated in Martin Klauber, "The Helvetic Formula Consensus (1675): An Introduction and Translation," *TJ* 11.1 (1990): 118 (canon 10).
[43] Klauber, "Helvetic Formula Consensus (1675)," 118 (canon 12).

has sought to establish such immediacy: by means of either a realism that locates the sinner somehow in Adam when he sinned; or a federalism that identifies Adam as our divinely appointed head in the covenant of life, the covenant I argued for in the previous chapter. Realists hold that we were present in Adam, while federalists maintain that he acted on our behalf.

The distinction between realism and federalism needs to be articulated with care. As the opposite of federalism, realism could easily be mistaken for a complete rejection of the covenant of life or even of covenant theology as a whole, but many Reformed realists affirm that God made a covenant with Adam. They are opposed not to federal theology per se but to the specific claim that the imputation of Adam's sin to his descendants rested on God's constituting him as our federal head. Nor, conversely, are federalists uninterested in the real bond between Adam and his descendants. The Westminster Larger Catechism Q&A26 teaches that natural generation is the means by which birth sin is conveyed. Francis Turretin affirms a twofold bond with Adam: the one natural, making him our common father; the other forensic, making him the head who acted for us.[44] Similarly, Thomas Boston explains that Adam was "fittest to be our federal head" because he was our natural head.[45] Bavinck can affirm that Adam "was not a private person, not a loose individual alongside other such loose individuals, but a root-source, the base, the seminal beginning of the whole human race, our common natural head," and yet also that "realism by itself is insufficient as an explanation of original sin."[46] Murray rejects "any incompatibility between natural headship and representative union."[47] The precise point of disagreement between realists and federalists concerns not the reality of a natural or a covenantal connection between Adam and his posterity, but which of these provides the moral basis for Adam's sin being ours.

Realism: Augustine and Shedd

The great concern of realism is to vindicate the justice of God by showing how we sinned and became guilty in Adam. Different varieties of realism attempt to show this in different ways. In *The City of God* Augustine explains

---

[44] Turretin, *Institutes*, 8.3.11 (1:577).
[45] Boston, *View of the Covenant of Works*, 11:189.
[46] Herman Bavinck, *Reformed Dogmatics*, ed. John Bolt, trans. John Vriend, 4 vols. (Grand Rapids, MI: Baker Academic, 2003–8), 3:102.
[47] Murray, *Imputation of Adam's Sin*, 37.

that, while at the time of the fall "we did not yet possess forms individually created and assigned to us to live in them as individuals," our "seminal nature" already existed. It was this nature that was "vitiated through sin, and bound with death's fetters in its just condemnation" when Adam fell. His action affected the entire race because "we were all in that one man, seeing that we all *were* that one man."[48] It is from the likeness of the earthly man that we are born, so sin and death are then passed down to us by generation.[49] Adam and Eve's descendants would be like them because "whatever was born from them could not have been different from what they themselves had been."[50]

There can be no doubt about Augustine's realism or his belief in the propagation of human nature from Adam, but when it comes to the moment of propagation he is unable to decide if each human soul is created out of nothing (creationism) or is born of the souls of its parents (traducianism).[51] As John Rist explains, Augustine seems to have inclined to traducianism because of his negative view of sex. He believed that male erection and ejaculation had been designed to be under Adam's rational control in Eden, but are now involuntary and thus an instance of the disordered relationship between the body and the will. As a result of this disorder, sin is always present at the origin of the seed. On the other hand, it was also the physicality of propagation that kept Augustine from settling decisively on traducianism, because he could not grant that sinfulness could be a physical property of the seed.[52] Given that Augustine expresses uncertainty on the question of the soul's origin but certainty on our sinning in Adam, it is clear that his conviction on the latter does not depend on any particular answer to the former.

There is a marked contrast between Augustine's separation of these two questions and the way in which traducianism is deployed as a basis for realism by a number of prominent nineteenth-century American theologians. While there are Baptists like Augustus Strong who hold to this type of position, its best-known proponent is the presbyterian William Shedd. Shedd believes that his own tradition lacks an account of original sin that could

---

[48] Augustine, *The City of God*, ed. John O'Meara, trans. Henry Bettenson (London: Penguin, 1984), xiii.14 (523), emphasis original.

[49] Augustine, *City of God* xiii.23.

[50] Augustine, *City of God* xiii.3 (512).

[51] See Augustine, *The Retractations* ii.82, in *Fathers of the Church: A New Translation*, vol. 60, ed. R. J. Deferrari, trans. M. I. Bogan (Washington, DC: Catholic University of America Press, 1968), 244, where Augustine describes the uncertainty he had expressed in an earlier work on the origin of individual souls.

[52] John M. Rist, *Augustine: Ancient Thought Baptized* (1994; repr., Cambridge: Cambridge University Press, 1996), 319.

vindicate the justice of God. He argues that, without any prior liability of personal guilt (*reatus culpae*), any kind of liability to punishment (*reatus poenae*) attributed to Adam's descendants is "putative and fictitious, not real," involving an arbitrary "constructive guilt" imposed by a sovereign. And it is imposed with grave consequences: "this confounds all moral distinctions and destroys all ethics by annulling the difference between righteousness and unrighteousness and putting each in precisely the same relation to divine sovereignty and agency."[53] His own position is that everyone can be punished for Adam's sin only because everyone committed it. The first sin, common rather than individual, is imputed to Adam's descendants for the same reason as any sin is justly imputed, "that it was committed by those to whom it is imputed."[54]

How could this be? Shedd's answer is that Adam and his descendants "existed together and sinned together as a unity." He does not mean by this that a great number of individual preexistent souls was present in Adam. Adam was not "a mere receptacle containing millions of separate individuals" but one, simple essence.[55] He carried in him the whole genus of human nature as a single, specific reality, not as a multiplicity of individual persons or even portions of nature.[56] His will was not just the will of an individual but was also the will of the whole species.[57] Shedd believes that this essence-realism solves the problem of the justice of original sin because it shows that no one is punished for a sin that he has not committed: "The doctrine of the specific unity of Adam and his posterity removes the great difficulties connected with the imputation of Adam's sin to his posterity that arise from the injustice of punishing a person for a sin in which he had no kind of participation."[58] Shedd even denies that Adam vicariously represented his descendants, because that would imply their absence from him.[59]

An obvious reply to such a realist scheme is that, even though the generic will of the species may have been in Adam, *my* individual will was not, and therefore did not act consciously in him when he sinned. If individual consciousness of action is a prerequisite for moral responsibility, then we cannot be held responsible for what Adam did even if he carried the generic will

---

[53] William G. T. Shedd, *Dogmatic Theology*, ed. Alan W. Gomes, 3rd ed. (Phillipsburg, NJ: P&R, 2003), 456–57.
[54] Shedd, *Dogmatic Theology*, 561.
[55] William G. T. Shedd, *Discourses and Essays* (Andover, MA: Warren F. Draper 1870), 259.
[56] Shedd, *Dogmatic Theology*, 448.
[57] Shedd, *Discourses and Essays*, 260.
[58] Shedd, *Dogmatic Theology*, 445.
[59] Shedd, *Dogmatic Theology*, 435.

of our species in him. Shedd answers this criticism by deploying a brilliant analysis of the deep recesses of human action. He identifies the decisive role of the human heart "below all the conscious exercises and operations" of the soul.[60] Shedd grants that the heart cannot be directly observed but insists that we must infer its existence, much like a postulate in mathematics, because only this inference enables us to understand our own experience.[61] The heart is traditionally identified in Reformed theology as a cognitive-volitional-affective complex, but there are different views of the relative positions of the understanding and the will within that complex.[62] Shedd prioritizes the will: "Man at bottom is a Will—a self-determining creature—and his other faculties of knowing and feeling are grafted into this stock and root."[63] The depth of the human will within the person means that many of its acts are not conscious to the mind. Shedd suspects that people pass whole days, weeks, and even months without being conscious for a moment of the workings of their moral agency.[64] He insists that even without such consciousness the will is still active and morally responsible, as when we find ourselves in a sinful train of thought without consciously intending it.[65]

Shedd applies this praxiology to defend a realist hamartiology. Since responsible presence does not entail consciousness, the fact that none of us recalls the fall does not mean that our wills were not involved in it. Even Adam himself was not conscious of the origination of the first sin in him, because his conscious transgression arose from an evil nature that had been generated unconsciously deep in his will.[66] Thus Shedd believes that he has removed "the only serious objection" to our unity with Adam in his sin.[67]

The brilliance of this argument lies in the identification of the depth-structure of the human person, the profound observation, incontestable upon reflection, that so much of who we are is unconscious. This is a claim worth pondering in its own right, apart from the doctrine of original sin. It is relevant to a number of contemporary issues, such as the continuity of personal identity in those suffering from dementia. It would be going too far to say that

---

[60] Shedd, *Discourses and Essays*, 230.
[61] Shedd, *Discourses and Essays*, 233.
[62] For a treatment of this issue through the lens of Jonathan Edwards, see Brad Walton, *Jonathan Edwards*, Religious Affections, *and the Puritan Analysis of True Piety, Spiritual Sensation, and Heart Religion*, Studies in American Religion, 74 (Lewiston, NY: Edwin Mellen, 2002).
[63] Shedd, *Discourses and Essays*, 242.
[64] Shedd, *Discourses and Essays*, 252.
[65] Shedd, *Discourses and Essays*, 253–54.
[66] Shedd, *Discourses and Essays*, 255–56.
[67] Shedd, *Discourses and Essays*, 257.

Shedd's position mandates the depth psychology of any particular psycho-analytical or other psychodynamic school, all of which have their problems from a Christian perspective, but it does indicate that we should accept a basic insistence on the role of the unconscious in the human psyche. Indeed, Shedd may have been ahead of his time in his observations on the human will, and he may point us toward a properly theological analysis of the psyche.

A last element is still required to explain how, for Shedd, the one human nature found in Adam comes in due course to be the human nature of each of his individuated descendants. Shedd holds that God created in Adam and Eve the "specific psychico-physical nature from which all the subsequent indi-viduals of the human family are procreated both psychically and physically."[68] Every time a person is created, a part of the "primitive nonindividualized human nature" is separated off and constituted a new individual, resulting in the "constant diminution" of the "original mass" so that the remaining nature from that point "would not yield so many individuals" as the nature of Adam.

It is evident that Shedd's doctrine of original sin requires a very particu-lar set of convictions. Realism and traducianism might exist separately, as in Augustine, but for Shedd traducianism is necessary to sustain his particu-lar version of realism. Without traducianism there would be no ontological bridge between the essence of human nature in Adam and his descendants. Shedd also has to affirm the responsible agency of an un-individuated and unconscious will. It would be possible to agree with parts of Shedd's scheme and not to embrace the realist whole. For example, one might hold that Adam carried the entire soulic mass of humanity for the purpose of procreating souls but not in such a way that it could sustain moral responsibility. Or one might agree that souls are procreated somewhat like bodies but deny that par-ents therefore carry the entire soulic mass of their descendants, any more than they carry their entire physical mass: perhaps souls are somehow multiplied from the parental spiritual stock. Shedd holds together a sophisticated scheme constructed from a very specific combination of convictions.

Critique of Realism

For my present purposes the question of the origin of the soul, a very difficult question, can be left open. The deeper problem with Shedd's realism is not his

---

[68] Shedd, *Dogmatic Theology*, 431.

traducianism but the fact that it establishes the involvement of only human nature and not of human persons in the sin of Adam. The involvement of our species-will in Adam, unconsciously willing to sin in him, does not amount to Adam's descendants acting culpably in him. Shedd posits our real numerical identity with Adam at the level of the single human essence, but it is human persons who sin, not human nature. Dabney puts the problem succinctly: "we cannot attach the idea of sin, morality, responsibility, and guilt to anything but a personal being."[69] Shedd's defense of the significance of the unconscious will does not address the real challenge to his realism at this point. The difficulty his scheme faces is not that the single human essence in Adam was unconscious—a difficulty to which he has indeed provided an instructive reply—but that it was anhypostatic, or as we might put it (with apologies to John Donne), "un-personed," at least with regard to all persons not yet born.

This difficulty might be addressed by pushing the realist account so far that persons in Adam become sufficiently agential as to bear moral responsibility *qua* persons. This is, rightly, something that Shedd himself would not countenance. To summon individual souls into Adam would be like seeing the cyborgs of fiction rising from a pool of molten metal to take human shape. By supposing that the soulic mass is somehow already enhypostatized for all humanity, we would secure moral responsibility for all, but only by embracing a theory of the preexistence of individual souls. This was taught by Origen, who used the theory to resolve, as David Weaver describes it, "the paradoxical situation of a state of present culpability for a fault antecedent to one's own existence."[70] It is a view lacking biblical support and condemned by the church at the Second Council of Constantinople in 553.

A second major problem with realism is that, as Boston argued long before Shedd, it risks proving that not only Adam's first disobedience but all of his subsequent sins were passed on until "his whole guilt contracted all his life over had disburdened itself upon us."[71] We may go further: if sin is inherited for purely natural reasons, why would the disburdening stop with Adam's sins? Apart from the fact that the human essence is diminished and divided each time a person is conceived from it, the situation would remain

---

[69] Dabney, *Systematic Theology*, 340. Many others make the same point, e.g., James Henley Thornwell, "Original Sin," in *Lectures in Theology*, in *The Collected Writings of James Henley Thornwell*, 4 vols. (1974; repr., Edinburgh: Banner of Truth, 1986), 1:334 (lecture 13); Bavinck, *Dogmatics*, 3:102; Blocher, *Illuminating the Riddle*, 115.
[70] David Weaver, "From Paul to Augustine: Romans 5:12 in Early Christian Exegesis," *St. Vladimir's Theological Quarterly* 23.3 (1983): 197.
[71] Boston, *View of the Covenant of Works*, 11:188.

the same in later transitions as it was in the first. Each individual would carry in himself the as yet un-individuated essence of the remaining generic human will from which his descendants would be formed. The human nature would continue to accumulate every sin committed by each of its carriers in an ever-growing hideous mass of sin for which the later generations would be responsible. This is a consequence of traducian essence-realism.[72]

The realist scheme can avoid this implication only by introducing some kind of limit on Adam's representative function. The obvious kind of limit that might prove viable is a federal arrangement that defines the boundaries of Adam's representative capacity, an arrangement appointing Adam to represent thus far only. Even Murray, who rejects a covenant with Adam and prefers an "Adamic administration," thinks that the imputation of sin was limited by "a special act of providence by which a special relationship was constituted" (a relationship which we might call a . . . ?).[73] Such a scheme Shedd cannot embrace because it involves introducing the federal to tidy up a loose end in the natural. That would be to concede the federalist's point that the natural cannot suffice to explain the transmission of sin. It is also hard to see how a lately invoked federalism would actually restrain the force of the natural, given the impetus with which it has been propelled on its way by Shedd's realism. The only sure way would be to make the federal instrumental to establishing the natural in the first place, but then the natural would be established on the basis of the federal, and realism would be framed by and founded upon federalism. Shedd could hardly approve.

A third problem with the realist account is that it threatens to compromise the sinlessness of Christ. So long as Christ receives his human nature ultimately from Adam, he receives a human nature responsible for the sin that Adam committed because it existed in Adam. Bavinck concludes that, on the realist view, it is "impossible" to see how Christ is free from original sin.[74] In the face of this criticism, Shedd alarmingly concedes that Christ's un-individuated nature sinned in Adam and needed to be sanctified: "as the guilt of Adam's sin rested upon that unindividualized portion of the common fallen

---

[72] This criticism is widely made, for example, by Thornwell, "Nature of Our Interest in the Sin of Adam: Being a Review of Baird's Elohim Revealed," in *Lectures in Theology*, 1:540 (lecture 16); Bavinck, *Reformed Dogmatics*, 3:103; Murray, *Imputation of Adam's Sin*, 39; Blocher, *Illuminating the Riddle*, 115.

[73] Murray, *Imputation of Adam's Sin*, 39.

[74] Bavinck, *Reformed Dogmatics*, 3:103. Thornwell uses this argument against Samuel Baird ("Nature of Our Interest," 1:557). For a more developed and recent critique of the Christological problems caused by Shedd's realism, see Oliver D. Crisp, *An American Augustinian: Sin and Salvation in the Dogmatic Theology of William G. T. Shedd* (Milton Keynes, UK: Paternoster, 2007), 68–73.

nature of Adam assumed by the Logos, it was expiated by the one sacrifice on Calvary."[75] The idea of Christ's human nature being cleansed by his own subsequent work is temporally contorted, like the defense of the doctrine of the immaculate conception which holds that Jesus is so much his mother's redeemer that she never sins in the first place. More serious still is the fact that, on Shedd's scheme, the cleansing happens too late: no matter what the retroactive effect of the atonement, Christ's human nature was once sinful. Perhaps a realist might say that because Christ's nature was cleansed at his conception, he remained sinless because he never actually existed as an individual. This argument might protect the sinlessness of Christ, but only at the cost of over-turning the realist argument itself. Any successful distancing of Christ from the sin of Adam on the ground that he did not share in it as an individual person has implicitly granted that no descendant was responsible for what Adam did because no descendant participated in it as an individual person. If Christ is innocent of Adam's sin because he did not yet exist as a person in Adam, then so am I. Conversely, if, as Shedd believes, my nature's presence in Adam is sufficient to make me responsible for his sin, then so is Christ's.

Maintaining the Sin-Guilt-Punishment Nexus

Realism is unsuccessful, but its instinct is good: to preserve the sin-guilt-pun-ishment nexus, and thus to uphold the justice of God in imputing Adam's sin to his descendants. Most Reformed writers maintain the sin-guilt-punishment nexus because, as Calvin puts it, "without guilt there would be no accusa-tion [*non esset reatus absque culpa*]."[76] Turretin insists that imputation must come with participation: "no one can in anyone deserve the punishment of death unless he had with him and in him a common sin, the cause of death."[77] Edwards agrees: "certainly the righteous Judge of all the earth won't bring death on thousands of millions, not only that are not worthy of death, but are worthy of no punishment at all."[78] The principle is stated by Boston: God "can never impute to men the sin of which they are not guilty."[79] This is not a constraint imposed on God from without but a reflection of his own inher-ent justice. The covenant of life was not a blank sheet on which a capricious

[75] Shedd, *Dogmatic Theology*, 476.
[76] Calvin, *Institutes*, 2.1.8 (1:251); CR 30:183.
[77] Turretin, *Institutes*, 9.9.18 (1:620).
[78] Edwards, *Original Sin*, 209.
[79] Boston, *View of the Covenant of Works*, 11:187.

God could write whatever he wanted. As James Henley Thornwell states, "if there were not a real unity betwixt Adam and the race, the covenant of works could not, by an arbitrary constitution, treat them as one."[80]

There is, it must be noted, a problematic version of federalism that makes a point of not maintaining the sin-guilt-punishment nexus. Charles Hodge argues that we are one with Adam only in his penalty and not also in his sin. On the question of imputed guilt, he distinguishes between guilt as "criminality or moral ill-desert," which we do not share with Adam, and guilt as "the judicial obligation to satisfy justice," which we do share with him.[81] Hodge thinks that it is a point agreed among Calvinists that the guilt imputed to us for Adam's sin is only the latter, the liability to punishment (known as *reatus poenae*).[82] I shall term Hodge's position "consequence-only federalism" to distinguish it from a federalism that affirms our share in Adam's sin and ill-desert (*reatus culpae*; liability to guilt).

The attraction of Hodge's position is that it does not rest the weight of the entire nexus upon our connection to Adam. The problem with it is that the weight is only reduced by separating punishment from sin and guilt.[83] This inflames the moral difficulty. We cannot be related to Adam's legal liability to punishment without any connection to the sin for which he was liable. It is hard to see how consequence-only federalism does not imply that we are punished for something with which we were utterly uninvolved. As Crisp says, Hodge's scheme appears to be "monumentally unjust."[84] Although there are important differences between mediate models of imputation and consequence-only federalism, both alike fail to show how the sinner commits the sin that is imputed to him. Ironically, given their right criticism of Hodge, Shedd and Crisp (in his Zwinglian mode) also succumb to the same problem, that neither successfully posits individual involvement in Adam's sin as a basis for sharing his corruption.

The Requisite Unity

Eschewing Hodge's consequence-only federalism, we must seek an account of the unity between Adam and his descendants that would suffice

---

[80] Thornwell, "Original Sin," 1:346.
[81] Charles Hodge, *Systematic Theology*, 3 vols. (1952; repr., Grand Rapids, MI: Eerdmans, 1989), 2:194.
[82] Cited in Murray, *Imputation of Adam's Sin*, 74 n. 119.
[83] Murray offers a sustained critique of Hodge on exegetical and historical grounds in *Imputation of Adam's Sin*, 72–85.
[84] Crisp, *American Augustinian*, 53.

to make them "justly participant" in his sin and *reatus culpae*.[85] The unity must suffice, but it must not go so far as to nullify the reality of imputation. While Adam's sin is in a sense mine, there must remain another sense in which it is his and not mine: "in respect of posterity, Adam's trespass was both *peccatum alienum* and *peccatum proprium*."[86] Press solidarity too far, and it comes into conflict with Paul's repeated emphasis on the one man Adam who acts for others: "many died through one man's trespass" (Rom. 5:15); "one man's sin" (Rom. 5:16); "because of one man's trespass, death reigned through that one man" (Rom. 5:17), and "by the one man's disobedience the many were made sinners" (Rom. 5:19). As Hodge says, "a thing cannot represent itself."[87] We need a unity more germane to moral action than the substance unity posited by realism, a unity of persons that suffices for justly participant representation, but not a unity so invasive that it collapses the persons into one and undermines representation and imputation.

Edwards: Occasionalism as the Basis of Unity

I believe that we can find such an account by reflecting on the ontologically constitutive power of the will of God in appointing Adam as the head of the race in the covenant of life. My line of thought begins with Jonathan Edwards. There has been widespread hostility to Edwards as a thinker and a man. Mark Twain famously describes him as a "resplendent intellect gone mad."[88] Charles Angoff denounces him as "the most bitter hater of man the American pulpit ever had," "a pathetic, sickly, angry, Puritan."[89] This type of verdict is provoked by the view that Edwards took of human depravity and destiny, with the negative comments often focusing on his works discussing the fall and its effects. W. E. Lecky describes Edwards's *Original Sin* as "one of the most revolting books that have ever proceeded from the pen of man."[90] *Caveat lector*, says Oliver Wendell Holmes, because "the idea that a

---

[85] The phrase "justly participant' is used by George Hutchinson in *The Problem of Original Sin in American Presbyterian Theology*, 2nd ed. (Toccoa, GA: Sola Fide, 2014), 107.

[86] So, Murray, *Imputation of Adam's Sin*, 86.

[87] Charles Hodge, "Review of an Article in the June Number of the Christian Spectator, entitled, 'Inquiries Respecting the Doctrine of Imputation,'" *Biblical Repertory and Theological Review* 2.3 (NS) (1830): 437. Bavinck says the same of imputation; see *Reformed Dogmatics*, 3:102.

[88] Cited in M. X. Lesser, *Reading Jonathan Edwards: An Annotated Bibliography in Three Parts, 1729–2005* (Grand Rapids, MI: Eerdmans, 2008), vii.

[89] Cited in Clyde A. Holbrook, "Jonathan Edwards and His Detractors," *TT* 10.3 (1953): 387.

[90] Cited by Clyde A. Holbrook in the introduction to Edwards, *Original Sin*, 99.

descendant of Adam can in any way be guilty or reckoned guilty of his sin" will "injure the mind as a habit of gross sin injures the type of the character."[91]

Edwards wrote *Original Sin* to refute a treatise by John Taylor, whose individualism we encountered earlier.[92] It is summed up well in these words: "A *Representative* of moral Action is what I can by no means digest."[93] For Taylor, the claim that God could constitute a representative whose guilt and corruption are imputed to us "is one of the greatest Absurdities in all the System of *corrupt Religion*." He finds that it is "absolutely *impossible*" to prove the righteousness of such a constitution.[94] Taylor's commitment to individual self-determination even leads him to exclude righteousness and holiness from the image of God in which Adam was first created. Adam could not yet have had these moral properties because "he must exist, and use his intellectual Powers before he could be righteous."[95] Taylor concludes: "*Original Righteousness* in *Adam* turns out full as bad as *Original Sin* in his Posterity."[96]

By contrast, Edwards does not think that belief in original sin depends on finding a solution to its difficulties. He writes that if we cannot solve the difficulties then we must simply accept original sin as a "plain fact" and get over it "by shutting our mouths, and acknowledging the weakness and scantiness of our understandings."[97] He does, however, think that moral representation is possible and real: "God, in each step of his proceeding with Adam, in relation to the covenant or constitution established with him, looked on his posterity as being one with him."[98] Edwards focuses on unity with Adam as the key issue. He thinks that resistance to the idea of our oneness with Adam stems from a failure to grasp "the degree, in which created identity or oneness with past existence, in general, depends on the sovereign constitution and law of the Supreme Author and Disposer of the universe."[99] Edwards claims that there is just as much basis for our oneness with Adam as there is for my oneness with myself over time. In dialogue with John Locke's emphasis on

---

[91] Cited in C. Samuel Storms, *Tragedy in Eden: Original Sin in the Theology of Jonathan Edwards* (Lanham, MD: University Press of America, 1985), 80–81.

[92] Taylor's work was published in multiple and expanding editions (as he responded to his critics: Isaac Watts in the 1741 edition and John Wesley in 1767). Taylor did not know that Isaac Watts wrote the book he was criticizing, *The Ruin and Recovery of Mankind*; see Taylor, *Supplement*, iii–iv. For the publication history, see Storms, *Tragedy in Eden*, 34–35.

[93] Taylor, *Supplement*, 108, emphasis original.

[94] Taylor, *Supplement*, 109, emphasis original.

[95] Taylor, *Supplement*, 161.

[96] Taylor, *Supplement*, 165, emphasis original.

[97] Edwards, *Original Sin*, 394, 395.

[98] Edwards, *Original Sin*, 389.

[99] Edwards, *Original Sin*, 397.

consciousness as the basis for identity, he argues that all oneness depends simply on God's sovereign constitution.[100]

When Edwards says that all identity depends on divine constitution, he means that it does so exclusively. Edwards is an occasionalist, which means that for him there is no ground for identity in created reality itself because no created thing has any causal power to continue its own existence from one moment to the next. The relation of a thing at T1 and the same thing at T2 is properly speaking an occasion rather than a cause.[101] The cause of the thing existing at T2 would be either the *"antecedent existence* of the same substance, or else the *power of the Creator*." But the antecedent substance at T1 cannot be its own cause at T2, because it does not exist at T2 to do the causing: "no cause can produce effects in a *time* and *place* in which itself is *not*."[102] In fact Edwards denies any causal function for the thing at T1: "antecedent existence is nothing, as to any proper influence or assistance in the affair." It is "as if there had been nothing *before*."[103] Every dependent thing is therefore in a "constant flux," created only for an instant before collapsing back into nonexistence.[104] What we see as identity through time is really a succession of creations out of nothing. Since everything comes into existence afresh in each moment, what exists now is a *"new effect."* While something may be like what previously existed, "simply and absolutely considered," it is "not the same with any past existence."[105]

How then do things continue to exist, if they have no causal power? The later moment of existence is entirely from God and is "not in any part, or degree, from its antecedent existence."[106] Edwards believes that this is what it means for us to live and move and have our being in God (Acts 17:28).[107] He reaches a radical metaphysical conclusion: "God's *preserving* created things in being is perfectly equivalent to a *continued creation*, or to his creating those things out of nothing at *each moment* of their existence."[108] The only difference between the first and subsequent acts of creation is the

---

[100] For the interaction with Locke, see Edwards, *Original Sin*, 398–99. Edwards argues that even if consciousness is necessary for identity, it depends in turn on sovereign constitution.
[101] Jonathan Edwards, *Freedom of the Will*, ed. Paul Ramsey, vol. 1 of *The Works of Jonathan Edwards*, 26 vols. (New Haven, CT: Yale University Press, 1957), 180–81.
[102] Edwards, *Original Sin*, 400, emphasis original.
[103] Edwards, *Original Sin*, 402, emphasis original.
[104] Edwards, *Original Sin*, 404.
[105] Edwards, *Original Sin*, 402.
[106] Edwards, *Original Sin*, 402.
[107] He quotes the text in Edwards, *Original Sin*, 404.
[108] Edwards, *Original Sin*, 401, emphasis original.

circumstance of later moments having acts of God's power that precede them.[109] For Edwards, this universal metaphysic means that personal identity "depends on an arbitrary divine constitution."[110]

Edwards does not conclude from his occasionalism that there is no continuity of identity in created things. Rather, "a *divine constitution* is the thing which *makes truth*, in affairs of this nature."[111] Specifically, it makes it true that we are one with Adam. The divine will establishes such a remarkable unity between Adam and his descendants that it is as if they existed somehow conjoined at the same time:

> Let us suppose, that Adam and all his posterity had *coexisted*, and that his posterity had been, through a law of nature established by the Creator, *united* to him, something as the branches of a tree are united to the root, or the members of the body to the head; so as to constitute as it were *one* complex person, or *one* moral whole: so that by the law of union there should have been a *communion* and *coexistence* in acts and affections; all jointly participating, and all concurring, as *one whole*, in the disposition and action of the head: as we see in the body natural, the whole body is affected as the head is affected; and the whole body concurs when the head acts.[112]

Later, Edwards adds the image of Adam's descendants being "somehow grown out of him" and remaining "literally united to him."[113]

On the basis of this tree analogy, Edwards argues that the sin-guilt-punishment nexus is isomorphic for Adam and his descendants. In Adam there was first a rising evil inclination and then the sinful act, after which God handed him over to an evil disposition of the heart. There are three stages here: rising disposition, sinful act, and abiding disposition. The pattern is the same for us: "in each branch, as in the root."[114] Some readers have wrongly thought that Edwards teaches mediate imputation here because he argues that the pattern of disposition followed by sin is the same in us as it was in Adam.[115] This sounds like the Salmurian claim that the corrupt nature precedes the imputation of sin. But when Edwards says that the disposition precedes the sin, he means not the abiding but the rising disposition. And the tree analogy

---

[109] Edwards, *Original Sin*, 402.
[110] Edwards, *Original Sin*, 399, cf. 403–4.
[111] Edwards, *Original Sin*, 404, emphasis original.
[112] Edwards, *Original Sin*, 391 n. 1, emphasis original.
[113] Edwards, *Original Sin*, 405 n. 6.
[114] Edwards, *Original Sin*, 392 n. 1.
[115] For the mediate reading, see for example Bavinck, *Reformed Dogmatics*, 3:100; and Hodge, *Systematic Theology*, 2:207.

shows that he is not discussing what happens when we are conceived but how we shared in Adam's act just as if we had been there coexisting with him as one moral person at the time when he sinned, like a branch coexisting with and conjoined to its root.[116] In fact Edwards is so far from teaching mediate imputation that Paul Helm suggests that even "immediate imputation" is "perhaps too *weak* an expression to convey Edwards's view accurately," such is our oneness with Adam.[117] As Edwards himself says, imputation is based on participation: "the sin of the apostasy is not theirs, merely because God *imputes* it to them; but it is *truly* and *properly* theirs, and on that ground, God imputes it to them."[118]

The Failure of Occasionalism

Many modern readers are surprised by the occasionalism of Edwards, especially if they have encountered him first as a late proponent of Puritan spirituality and a defender of the Great Awakening. For his supposed evangelical heirs, it is strange enough to find him engaged in philosophy; even more strange is his defense of this philosophy in particular. And I have not mentioned yet that he denied the existence of matter. Yet in the eighteenth-century context, occasionalism makes much more sense because it enabled Edwards to insist on the complete dependence of the creation on God against those who were increasingly propounding its independence.[119] So too immaterialism, which Edwards embraced in *Of Being* in order to argue the radical dependence of creation on the mind of God: "I demand in what respect this world has a being, but only in the divine consciousness. Certainly in no respect. There would be figures and magnitudes, and motions and proportions—but where? Where else but in the Almighty's knowledge."[120] Edwards, like Nicolas Malebranche and George Berkeley, was employing what appear to us to be exotic metaphysical positions to resist arguments that would ascribe self-existence to physical matter. Stephen Holmes highlights the threat posed by the teaching of Thomas Hobbes, who argued that matter is the

---

[116] For this reading, see esp. Murray, *Imputation of Adam's Sin*, 56–62; so too Benjamin B. Warfield, "Edwards and the New England Theology," in *The Works of Benjamin B. Warfield*, 10 vols. (Grand Rapids, MI: Baker, 1978), 9:530; and Blocher, *Illuminating the Riddle*, 117.

[117] Paul Helm, "The Great Christian Doctrine (*Original Sin*)," in *A God-Entranced Vision of All Things: The Legacy of Jonathan Edwards*, ed. John Piper and Justin Taylor (Wheaton, IL: Crossway, 2004), 196, emphasis original.

[118] Edwards, *Original Sin*, 408, emphasis original.

[119] So, Stephen Holmes, *God of Grace and God of Glory: An Account of the Theology of Jonathan Edwards* (Edinburgh: T&T Clark, 2000), 93.

[120] Jonathan Edwards, "Of Being," in *Scientific and Philosophical Writings*, ed. Wallace E. Anderson, vol. 6 of *The Works of Jonathan Edwards*, 26 vols. (New Haven, CT: Yale University Press, 1980), 204.

only genuine substance, and that "incorporeal substance" is an "insignificant sound" like "round quadrangle."[121] On such a basis God must either not exist, or he too must be reduced to matter. Edwards counters this philosophy with a denial of any ultimate underlying created reality that can keep itself in being. The substance of bodies is in fact "either nothing, or nothing but the Deity acting in that particular manner in those parts of space where he thinks fit." With respect to physical bodies, "there is no proper substance but God himself," who is the "*ens entium*" ("being of beings").[122]

While there are serious problems with both occasionalism and immaterialism, the instinct behind both should be attractive to any Christian: to deny to matter self-existence and self-preservation, and to question the ontological ultimacy of any created thing. In the seventeenth century the debate concerned atoms. Today we might recast it in terms of fermions and bosons, the elementary subatomic particles of matter and force, but the issue remains the same: does the universe rest on its own bottom? Can it explain itself? Or is it utterly dependent on God?

The apologetic gain from Edwardsean occasionalism for defending original sin would be considerable: it would prove that there is no more secure basis for identifying any other created entity as one with itself than there is for identifying humanity as one with Adam. If occasionalism is true, then when I wake up in the morning and believe that I am the same person who fell asleep the night before, I have in effect conceded the justice of Adam's sin being reckoned mine. Adam-humanity is as much one as I am one, because everything is one in exactly the same way.

There are, however, two insurmountable problems with occasionalism. The first, set out succinctly by Crisp, is that it implies that "God *is* the proximate, not just the ultimate cause of sin, because no other being has causal power."[123] The very strength of occasionalism in demonstrating a single basis for all identity is its weakness when it comes to construing God's relation to evil. Because there are no secondary causes, God has become both "the necessary and sufficient cause of sin."[124] To my mind, Edwards is bafflingly indifferent to this issue in both *Original Sin* and *Freedom of the Will*, but it is

---

[121] Holmes, *God of Grace and God of Glory*, 82 n. 15, referencing Hobbes's *Leviathan*, i.4.
[122] Jonathan Edwards, "Of Atoms," in *Scientific and Philosophical Writings*, ed. Wallace E. Anderson, vol. 6 of *The Works of Jonathan Edwards* (New Haven, CT: Yale University Press, 1980), 215.
[123] Oliver D. Crisp, *Jonathan Edwards and the Metaphysics of Sin* (Aldershot, UK: Ashgate, 2005), 50, emphasis original.
[124] Crisp, *Jonathan Edwards*, 92.

fatal for his occasionalism. The second problem is that, while Edwards finds a common ground for all unity, the unity his account sustains is very thin indeed. I do not say this because his account bases unity in the will of God— that is in fact its strength—but because even on its own terms occasionalism turns Adam into a series of Adams, each created out of nothing and then collapsing back into nothing at the end of his own moment. In what Philip Quinn terms a "charming irony," Edwards has employed occasionalism to establish the identity of Adam-humanity when in fact it undermines it because the Adam who sinned was annihilated.[125] Everything has the same basis of unity, but, given the cessation of every moment *in nihilum*, it is no unity at all.

Contemporary Philosophies of Persistence

In one of his earlier treatments of original sin, Crisp proposes to take from Edwards what is now known as a "perdurantist" theory of identity without the problematic occasionalism.[126] Perdurantism is a philosophical account of how things persist through time. Perdurantists hold that as an individual object is made up of parts spread out in space, so it is made up of parts spread out through time. Much as I have fingers and hips and toes, so I have a yesterday part and a today part and a tomorrow part. An object itself is therefore the sum of all its temporal parts. This means that the Williams you meet in any particular moment is but a temporal part of Williams. Applied to the doctrine of original sin, perdurantism yields the idea of God forming a "temporally scattered object" composed of not just Adam himself but also his descendants. These temporal parts, scattered through space and time, are "gerrymandered" by God as a single object, a space-time worm that Crisp terms "Perdurantist Humanity."[127]

Michael Rea finds two significant problems with this "Organic Whole Theory" that Crisp finds in Edwards. The first is that it would imply that Adam-humanity is responsible as a whole for all of the acts done by all of its parts, not just for Adam's first sin. The second is that it seems to identify "Humanity" itself as a moral agent, which Rea rightly says would be "wholly inappropriate."[128] How can an entity that has multiple brains, each

---

[125] Quinn is cited in Crisp, *Jonathan Edwards*, 132–33.
[126] Crisp, *Jonathan Edwards*, 104.
[127] Crisp, *Jonathan Edwards*, 106.
[128] Michael C. Rea, "The Metaphysics of Original Sin," in *Persons: Human and Divine*, ed. Peter Van Inwagen and Dean Zimmerman (Oxford: Clarendon, 2007), 341.

with multiple acts of will, itself be understood as the agent of those acts? Crisp himself notes the "problem of ascribing moral properties to an abstract object."[129] His solution is to adopt a more complex account of the object. Instead of the object itself having sin and guilt, it is described as having temporal parts, all of which have original guilt after the primal sin. Perdurantist humanity does not have sin, but it has parts that have sin.[130] This defense feels like a step toward Rea's own alternative interpretation of Edwards as not a perdurantist but a stage theorist.[131] Stage theory is also a four-dimensional view of objects existing through space and time, but it would not identify Adam and his posterity as a single object. Instead, they are viewed as "distinct individuals who share a common temporal stage or set of temporal stages."[132] Stage theory has the advantage that each stage can be regarded as a complete person, whereas perdurantism makes the whole object the true individual. Stage theory avoids the problem of statements about the parts having to be predicated of the whole and the characterization of the many-brained Adam-humanity as a moral agent, because the stages exist properly as objects, in this case persons, in themselves. Rea holds that God's decisions about which stages form a whole generally reflect our intuitions, but in the case of Adam and his posterity "we learn from revelation (plus, perhaps, a bit of systematic theologizing) that a rather unexpected set of temporal predications is true of each of us," namely, that each of us has as a counterpart stage, the Adam who sinned. This means that "*I was Adam.*"[133] Rea even thinks that on this basis I could have prevented Adam's sin, which makes me responsible for it. The strangest aspect of the stage theory analysis is that it identifies Adam-humanity as a unity only for a defined period: "Adam undergoes fission at the time of his first sin, splitting into billions of different people."[134] As Crisp notes, stage theory comes with the price of making most people's existence extremely "gappy," because it entails there being a huge temporal gap between each person's Adam stage and his or her own conception.[135]

Crisp and Rea have explored how the doctrine of original sin might function in terms of contemporary philosophies of persistence. Their

---

[129] Crisp, *Metaphysics*, 124.
[130] Crisp, *Metaphysics*, 124–25.
[131] Major defenses of stage theory are Theodore Sider, *Four-Dimensionalism: An Ontology of Persistence and Time* (Oxford: Oxford University Press, 2001); and Katherine Hawley, *How Things Persist* (Oxford: Clarendon, 2001).
[132] Rea, "Metaphysics," 334.
[133] Rea, "Metaphysics," 342, emphasis original.
[134] Rea, "Metaphysics," 334.
[135] See Crisp, "Sin," 208.

proposals may serve both to develop the way in which we conceptualize the ontology implied by the doctrine and to defend it against its philosophically minded critics. However, even a brief foray into the philosophical literature on persistence reveals the extent to which Crisp and Rea have to presume answers to perennial and possibly irresolvable metaphysical questions regarding the nature and persistence of things.[136] They have had to make choices between presentism and eternalism, three-dimensionalism and four-dimensionalism, perdurantism, endurantism, and exdurantism, worms and slices. While philosophy can be a useful clarifying tool, I am wary of constructing the truths of Scripture on the basis of a particular philosophy, classical, mediaeval, or modern, both because the philosophical issues have proved so intractable, and because philosophical foundations have a tendency to wash away over time, taking any theological superstructure with them. There are some philosophical questions where a particular answer is implied by the teaching of Scripture, even if the question is not overtly addressed in Scripture, but in many cases, it is difficult or even impossible to settle philosophical debates by reference to biblical teaching, even if we rightly extend the definition of "biblical" to include the logical implications of the text's explicit statements.

Rather than the doctrine of original sin depending on the philosophy of persistence, it is the philosophy that needs the metaphysical foundation that only theology can supply. Perdurantism in and of itself can only articulate a way of conceiving scattered temporal parts as making up a single object. It cannot explain how the parts are one. Stage theory has the same problem with aggregating its stages. The need is not unnoticed in the literature. Ludwig Jaskolla contends that stage theory faces "the challenge of the insufficient binding of temporal parts," a failure to articulate sufficient "intrinsic carriers" for the persistence relation.[137] His own solution is a form of panpsychism, the doctrine that all the basic physical constituents of the universe themselves have non-physical mental properties. This seems to me to be a desperate expedient. Katherine Hawley adopts a more agnostic position, positing unknown relations that somehow underpin the causation essential to

---

[136] An introduction can be gained from Sally Haslanger, "Persistence through Time," in *The Oxford Handbook of Metaphysics*, ed. Michael J. Loux and Dean W. Zimmerman (Oxford: Oxford University Press, 2003); and a more detailed sense of the range of positions from Sally Haslanger and Roxanne Marie Kurtz, eds., *Persistence: Contemporary Readings* (Cambridge, MA: Bradford, 2006).

[137] Ludwig Jaskolla, *Real Fourdimensionalism: An Essay in the Ontology of Persistence and Mind*, Philosophical Studies Series 130 (Cham, Switzerland: Springer, 2017), 123.

persistence.[138] Hawley thinks that the posited relations are "unmysterious," but they seem to me (as to others) to be wholly mysterious and posited merely because they have to be.[139] Secular theories of persistence cannot account for the unity of the different parts or stages of things, nor do they tell us why these parts or stages form this single object and those do not. It should be open season for a searching presuppositionalist critique of this major gap in the contemporary philosophy of persistence.[140]

A Divine-Word Ontology

The struggle to ground accounts of persistence warns us that even as we reject occasionalism we must not lose the vital insight that it is God who creates and sustains the identity of things. As Edwards states, "a *divine constitution* is the thing which *makes truth*, in affairs of this nature."[141] We can reject the end- less creation of all things *ex nihilo*, affirm the continuation of matter through moments of time, and still hold that the identity of objects depends on God calling them into being and keeping them in being. God alone can answer the problem of insufficient binding. Nevertheless, with regard to original sin the challenge is to show how the divine constitution ensures that Adam's descendants are justly participant in the primal sin without collapsing them into one and losing the federalist truth of representation and imputation. Can we really meet this challenge with nothing better than the assertion that God just wills that Adam shall be the representative of the entire race? Is there really no more to identity than "God just says so"?

As soon as we articulate the questions like that, we should hear the theo- logical problem with them: the word "just." Given what we know of the word of God, how could it ever be appropriate to refer to God "just" saying anything? If we do, then we need to deepen our grasp of the power of the word of God, and thereby to strengthen our ontology. Consider the causal power of divine speech. By his word God created the universe out of nothing: "The universe was created by the word of God, so that what is seen was not made out of things that are visible" (Heb. 11:3). By his word God sustains all

---

[138] In more technical terms, they are "non-supervenient relations" that are not based in the properties of the stages or the spatio-temporal relations between them yet underpin immanent causation (see Hawley, *How Things Persist*, 72).
[139] Hawley, *How Things Persist*, 71. The "others" include Karen Bennett, "Review of Katherine Hawley, *How Things Persist*," *Philosophy and Phenomenological Research*, 69.1 (2004): 231.
[140] Though the task should come with a health warning, since the literature on persistence can leave the head spin- ning, like a rotating disc.
[141] Edwards, *Original Sin*, 404, emphasis original.

things: "he upholds the universe by the word of his power" (Heb. 1:3). By his word God brings us out of death into new life: "you have been born again, not of perishable seed but of imperishable, through the living and abiding word of God" (1 Pet. 1:23). A divine-word ontology is more robust than one based ultimately on the properties of things themselves because it is as robust as the word of God that created and sustains the universe. A thing is the thing that it is because God's word has created and sustained it. Underpinning all the reality and identity evident in phenomena is the word of God, so if we find that we must ascribe the existence of something to the word of God we have not thinned the ice of its ontology. Nor is the word of God regarding Adam simply a creative word of divine command. This is where the conclusion of my previous chapter helps us again: that the word constituting Adam as head of the race is a covenantal word of divine self-binding. The self-binding word created the solidarity that brought the immediate imputation of sin, guilt, and punishment on the human race.

This is not a new explanation of the basis for imputing Adam's sin. Robert Rollock expressed it right back at the beginning of the Reformed formulation of the covenant of life:

> Whence proceeds this efficacy or power of that first sin, to engender, as it were, and to derive sin into all and every one of Adam's progeny? I answer; This efficacy of that sin is by reason of that word and covenant which God made with Adam in his creation.[142]

In our own time, J. V. Fesko has defended the doctrine of imputation on the basis of God's "*covenantal* declarations."[143] When some federalists resist the idea of a covenant with Adam, they weaken their own position. Murray, for example, appeals to the "constitutive ordination" of God as the basis for representation, but his refusal to classify God's relationship with Adam as a covenant does nothing to help him express the certain efficacy of that ordination.[144]

The emphasis on a constitutive covenantal word is a promising strand of the Reformed tradition, but in our day even the use of the terms "federalism" and "realism" to characterize the debate is misleading. The terms became

---

[142] Robert Rollock, *A Treatise of God's Effectual Calling*, trans. Henry Holland, in *Select Works of Robert Rollock*, ed. William M. Gunn, 2 vols. (Grand Rapids, MI: Reformation Heritage, 2008), 1:175.
[143] J. V. Fesko, *Death in Adam, Life in Christ: The Doctrine of Imputation* (Fearn, Ross-shire, UK: Mentor, 2016), 243.
[144] Murray, *Imputation of Adam's Sin*, 39. For the eschewal, see Murray, "The Adamic Administration," in *Collected Writings of John Murray*, 4 vols. (Edinburgh: Banner of Truth, 1976–82), 2:47–59.

standard centuries ago, and they pervade Reformed literature. For example, in his *Studies in Dogmatics* volume on sin G. C. Berkouwer has two chapters entitled "Realism" and "Federalism." J. V. Fesko contrasts the "ontological" and the "legal."[145] Even when Crisp adverts to federalists who seek to "augment" their scheme with realist considerations, the basic dichotomy is still implied, as when he contrasts those who "opt for a real union between Adam and his progeny rather than a union that is a moral and legal construct."[146] The problem with these ways of speaking is that the federal and legal is contrasted with the real and ontological, as though the federal and legal has no reality or being. Historically, the *real* of "realism" would have been understood to refer to the essence, the nature of Adam, but in contemporary ears it lacks that specificity and too easily suggests that there is something *unreal* about covenantal ontology. This matters, because one of the major objections to federalism is what Crisp terms *"the fiction objection."*[147] Perhaps this objection has had the currency it has because the proponents of federalism have accepted terminology that suggests it. Realism would be better termed "essentialism" to narrow its reference more clearly.

The Wisdom of the Divine Constitution

Does a divine-word ontology mean that God could constitute any random collection of unrelated persons as a unity to which he might impute sin? This is the freakish outcome that leads Robert Chisholm to reject the Edwardsean claim that God "makes truth in affairs of this nature":

> God could regard temporally scattered individuals—you this year, me last year, and the vice-president the year before that—as comprising a single individual. And then he could justly punish you this year and me last year for the sins that the vice-president committed the year before that.[148]

Paul Helm defends Edwards against this charge by pointing out that even his occasionalism does not imply that God could constitute a single object consisting of "my left shoe today, the Taj Mahal ten years ago, and my favourite cherry tree tomorrow."[149] God is always wise, and in his wisdom he

---

[145] As used by Fesko, *Death in Adam*, 77.
[146] Crisp, "Sin," 205 n. 19, 206.
[147] Crisp, "Sin," 204, emphasis original.
[148] Cited in Crisp, *Metaphysics*, 97.
[149] Helm, *Faith*, 171; so too Crisp, *Metaphysics*, 99, 117.

would not gerrymander randomly or constitute irrational unities. As Edwards argues, when we speak of the "arbitrary constitution" of God we mean that his purposes rest on his will, his *arbitrium*, and his will "depends on nothing but the divine wisdom."[150] There is a way, a manner, a *modus* by which God in his wisdom treats things as one, "a certain established method" by which a new effect follows its past existence.[151] I do not even think it would be true to say that God could constitute anything according to his absolute power but does not. A widely borrowed phrase from Augustine, *potuit, sed noluit* ("he was able to, but he was not willing"), is not applicable here.[152] Insofar as such a description envisages God's power operating in isolation, it is theologically nonsensical, because God is simple and none of his attributes can ever be set aside to allow his power to act alone.

What can we say about the *modus*? As Edwards observes, God treats things as one "by communicating to them like properties, relations, and circumstances" which "leads us to regard and treat them as one."[153] There are certain signs of unity present in the creation to render it comprehensible to its inhabitants. From observing these signs, we rightly conclude that God acts in such a way that he would not constitute a single object out of just any scattered items or persons with no manifest identity or connection. The outward manifestations of the unities in creation function like sacraments in redemption: they are visible signs of a unity based in the invisible will and word of God.

What are these conventional signs of identity? This is not a question to be answered by working out a list of properties or relations in advance of any particular examples. The boundaries of sapiential divine constitution have to be discerned from the given facts of creation as interpreted by revelation. This is an exercise in the patient observation and description of creational and biblical data. Such an exercise would only ever produce limited results, because many of the secondary causes that manifest the unity of things are beyond our powers of observation. Indeed, there are many created things that are themselves entirely beyond our perception. A great deal of what God has made, both spirit and matter, cannot ordinarily be perceived. The heavenly

---

[150] Edwards, *Original Sin*, 403.
[151] Edwards, *Original Sin*, 402.
[152] Used by Augustine in *On Nature and Grace* (ch. 8), differently from its afterlife as a version of the now more familiar *potentia absoluta / ordinata* distinction (absolute / ordained power).
[153] Edwards, *Original Sin*, 406.

realm around us can be seen only if our eyes are opened to it, like Elisha's servant who saw the fiery chariots present around the prophet only when his eyes were opened (2 Kings 6:17). Even the lowest common denominators of material things cannot be seen. The most powerful particle accelerator detects but cannot actually see subatomic particles. Pulsars, some of the densest things in creation, have been located only by their radio emissions and not by sight, leading to the first being called for a time LGM-1, Little Green Man 1. With so much invisible in the creation, it would be a foolhardy theologian who ruled out the possibility of undisclosed realities that encode unities without being perceptible to us. Thornwell candidly admits that it is hard to define the basis of moral unity and avows an appropriate humility: "We accept whatever God has thought proper to reveal, and whenever the curtain drops upon His revelation, we lay our hands upon our mouth."[154]

What then can we legitimately discern from the perceptible facts of creation as interpreted by revelation? While the category of shared substance cannot carry the weight that essentialism places upon it, it is not irrelevant to discerning unity. We do not have to be proponents of an un-individuated soulic mass to think that it matters that Adam and his descendants share human nature. Indeed, commonality of kind may be the starting point for discerning most unities. In addition to that, there is much to learn from Thornwell's emphasis on a unity grounded in "the relations of individual beings." He argues that our common life springs from "the intimate connection between the parts," evidenced in the organization of society.[155] So strong is the bond formed by the relations that "what a man does by his agent he as truly does as if he did it in his own proper person." Applying this to punishment, Thornwell holds that I can be punished only if I am guilty, but denies that I can be held guilty only for what I myself have caused. The question is not whether someone can be punished for what is not his own deed, "but whether there is only one way of a thing's being his own."[156] Thornwell holds that the covenant creates for the descendants of Adam a "moral history" and "moral relations" even before their existence.[157] Their interest in the covenant means that it is "just the same as if they had already received an actual existence."[158]

---

[154] Thornwell, "Nature of Our Interest," 1:553.
[155] Thornwell, "Nature of Our Interest," 1:552.
[156] Thornwell, "Nature of Our Interest," 1:545. He cites the maxim *qui facit per alium, facit per se* (he who acts through another, himself acts).
[157] Thornwell, "Original Sin," 1:303.
[158] Thornwell, "Nature of Our Interest," 1:561.

Thornwell's emphasis on relations is instructive because relations, unlike many substances or natures, are not objects. Representation in a political system, for example, is a relation constituted by the words at a coronation, election, or induction. "Be thou anointed, blessed, and consecrated Queen over the Peoples"; "And I hereby declare that the said Boris Johnson is duly elected"; "I do solemnly swear that I will support and defend the Constitution of the United States against all enemies." Even these merely human words create relations. In the case of Adam's federal headship, the word that constituted his relation to us was the always efficacious word of God himself (e.g., Gen. 2:16–17).

Cataloguing the extent of even the known signs of unity in creation would be a task beyond Carl Linnaeus himself. In this exercise, priority must be given to the many instances in Scripture where God relates to groups of individuals in a representative. These matter most because they are indisputable instances of moral unity mandated by God, rather than just examples from human societies. Some biblical scholars have begun the exegetical work on these episodes as instances of collective responsibility, but too much of their energy has been consumed by fanciful reconstructions of the text's supposed pre-history rather than theological construction on the basis of the given and received text.[159] Not enough attention has been given to such texts by analytic theologians working on original sin, with the result that they have favored more individualistic accounts of moral responsibility in a way that problematizes many biblical passages besides Genesis 3. Analytic theologians need to pay closer attention to the evidence that can be drawn from descriptions of the divine economy in the biblical text itself. We need the careful dissective methods of analytic theology, but they must be subordinated more rigorously to the conclusions of exegesis and biblical theology that are themselves the fruit of submissive listening to the inspired text in its canonical form. The claim that analytic theology is procedural rather than substantive will prove empty if in practice the biblical text is ignored in analytic writing, or is addressed in a single footnote. On some topics it might be feasible to take exegetical conclusions as read, for example when working within a Chalcedonian Christology. But on a topic as disputed as the imputation of sin, the analytic cannot be separated from the exegetical, nor can the exegetical be

---

[159] The best recent work I have seen is Joel Kaminsky, *Corporate Responsibility in the Hebrew Bible*, JSOTSup 196 (Sheffield, UK: Sheffield Academic Press, 1995).

sidestepped by appealing to the fact that "commentators disagree" or that "there are other ways of reading this text." That is true of every text. Exegetical debate invites vigorous engagement, not avoidance. If analytic theology is to find its proper place within the church's dogmatics, it needs to be integrated with a sustained, disciplined listening to the biblical text. Otherwise, the risk is that analytic theology will make categorical assertions that cannot be maintained in the face of exegesis.

An example of such an assertion is the axiom that the imputation of sin requires personal action or at least personal consent to representation.[160] This is one of the darlings of much theology, but I cannot see how it can be maintained in the face of the biblical data. Cited in its favor are passages such as Deuteronomy 24:16: "Fathers shall not be put to death because of their children, nor shall children be put to death because of their fathers. Each one shall be put to death for his own sin." But this was a law regulating the conduct of Israel's rulers, not that of God himself. Another passage often used is Ezekiel 18, with its assertion that "the soul who sins shall die" (Ezek. 18:4, 20), but this was a statement specific to a context in which the children were wrongly trying to exculpate themselves by blaming their parents. Alongside such texts is a recurring pattern of divinely approved but humanly unauthorized moral representation in Scripture. I can here point only to some of the relevant passages (ironic, I know). As we have seen, Adam was both father and king, and in the rest of Scripture the punishment for the sins of fathers and kings repeatedly falls on children and people. Major penal examples include Ham and Canaan (Gen. 9:20–27), Achan and his family (Josh. 7), the second commandment (Ex. 20:5), Saul and his descendants (2 Sam. 21), David and his people (2 Sam. 24), Jeroboam and his house (1 Kings 14:7–11), and Manasseh and his people (2 Kings 21:1–18). There are similar examples of representative blessing, most notably Abraham. Edwards notes how, when God spoke to Abraham, he spoke in the second person singular "but meant chiefly his posterity." The same pattern occurs with the promises to Isaac and Jacob, in Isaac's blessing of Esau and Jacob, and Jacob's blessing of his sons.[161] Such episodes demonstrate that neither personal action, simultaneous contiguity, nor consent to representation are prerequisites of imputation in the

---

[160] Labeled "the authorization objection" by Crisp and endorsed by him in his 2016 chapter "Sin," 203 (see note 39, above). Fesko criticizes Crisp for the absence of any "substantial exegetical argumentation" in his more recent work on original sin (see Fesko, *Death in Adam*, 269).

[161] Edwards, *Original Sin*, 253.

biblical narrative. In God's economy representation is usually given, not chosen. The reality of representation and the resulting imputation is not limited to biblical instances. Solidaric relationships pervade human life, especially the state. As Murray argues, we reject the imputation of sin from a vicarious representative only when "we fail to take account of the pervasiveness of corporate responsibility."[162]

The Unique Adam, Known through Christ

Even later biblical examples such as these are only fading echoes of the representative role of Adam. All other representative relationships in the family, society, state, or nation are useful as illustrations, but they can serve only as lesser instances that fall short of both heads of the race. As Bavinck puts it, Adam and Christ together occupy "a totally exceptional position."[163] The unity of Adam with humanity might at first glance appear minimally inscribed in outward signs, since, when he transgressed, none of his descendants had yet lived. Adam and Eve were utterly alone, she his only companion. Contemporaneous spatio-temporal contiguity did not pertain to Adam and his descendants at the moment when he sinned. And yet in Scripture Adam is, after Christ, the preeminent representative. His preeminence is made clear in particular by his position as the Alpha Man, the first bearer of our nature, the one from whom all other human persons are descended (cf. Acts 17:26). Strangely, this position, which by definition isolates him from others, is itself the sign that he represents them, the outward manifestation of the covenantal word spoken over him. Contained as they are as derivatives within this Adamic family tree, it is inevitable that other instances of representation prior to the coming of the last Adam will be lesser examples than the first. The position of Adam-humanity above other unities makes it *sui generis*. As a result, it is harder to criticize than if it were a commonplace, as Dabney explains:

> Man reasons chiefly by parallel instances; his reasoning is comparison. Consequently, in a case wholly unique, where there is no parallel, while he may not comprehend, he cannot convict of injustice. The case is above his grasp; he has no experimental scales in which to weigh it.[164]

---

[162] Murray, *Imputation of Adam's Sin*, 36.
[163] Bavinck, *Reformed Dogmatics*, 3:105.
[164] Dabney, *Systematic Theology*, 349.

And yet, when compared to Christ, Adam himself is merely a type of the great father and king to come. Adam is a king who is echoed by later kings, who points ahead to the antitypical king, and is himself surpassed by him.

A fruit of the parallel between Adam and Christ is that it helps the believer understand something of Adam's role from within his or her own spiritual experience. By the Spirit, the believer enjoys union with Christ as head and with the other members of his body. It is in the life of the church, especially at the Lord's table, that we should find the most persuasive argument for and instructive reflection of our union with Christ as our head. (That we do not do so is either because our eyes are not open to it, or because the reality of the church is so different from what it should and could be in the power of the Spirit.) At its best, the unity of the body is a lived, conscious experience. As we have seen, Paul parallels Adam and Christ with specific reference to their representative roles, in each case the one acting for the many. Something of the Christ-church representative relationship thus pertains to Adam-humanity. Adam and his descendants are not united by the Holy Spirit, but the parallel nonetheless elevates our unity with Adam above other unities and lifts it toward our unity with Christ. We can therefore learn something of our oneness with Adam through the daily lived experience of our oneness with Christ. Every time one member suffers with another, we experience a dimension of our shared union with Christ (1 Cor. 12:26), himself persecuted in our suffering (Acts 9:4), and, reasoning *a maiore ad minus*, something of the oneness we had with Adam.

No Adam, No Christ

C. S. Lewis advised a young aspiring writer not to tell people how to feel but to write in such a way as to evoke feeling: "Don't say it was 'delightful'; make *us* say 'delightful' when we have read the description."[165] My aim has been the same when it comes to maintaining Adam's historicity. While I have not argued that he existed, I hope to have shown that he must have existed by explaining how much rested on his shoulders. If we deny that Adam existed, then Paul's entire summary of the two great epochs of human history is nonsense: there would then be no one transgression committed by the one man. And if there is no transgression . . . The deletion of Adam, including his

---

[165] C. S. Lewis, *Letters to Children*, ed. Lyle W. Dorsett and Marjorie Lamp Mead (New York: Simon & Schuster, 1995), 64.

reduction to a literary cypher, threatens to infect Christ, and thus to undermine Christianity itself. Adam and Christ in biblical theology are too intertwined for us to separate them. As Augustine stated, "it is in what concerns these two men that the Christian faith properly consists."[166] The close connections between them as type and antitype have long been noticed not just by Origenist allegorists but also among the Reformed, for example by Boston:

> Adam's preposterous love to his wife made him sin; Christ's love to his spouse made him suffer and satisfy. In a garden Adam sinned, and therefore in a garden Christ was buried. Eating ruined man, and by eating he is saved again. By eating the forbidden fruit all died; and by eating Christ's flesh and drinking his blood by faith, the soul gets life again.[167]

Erase one husband, one garden, one meal, and the others will soon be in question. To threaten Christ, we need not go so far as to deny Adam's existence. Arguments adduced against Adam's headship would suffice to deny the representative work of Christ. If Adam cannot by his one deed condemn many, then nor can Christ by his one deed justify many. The moral objection to representation cuts both ways. The consequence of moral individualism is ultimately despair, because we will be left believing that as only we could bring ourselves down into the mire of sin and death, so only we can lift ourselves out of it.

Conclusion

The Pauline baseline on representation is clear: the one sin of the one man Adam condemns us all. Different theories attempt to explain how that is so, and how it can be just. Mediate imputation holds that we are condemned for Adam's sin because we have birth sin, but this inverts the proper relation between sin and punishment, as does Crisp's revival of Zwingli. Hodge's minimalist consequence-federalism wrongly detaches imputed punishment from imputed sin and guilt. The fully developed essentialism of Shedd seeks to maintain the sin-guilt-punishment nexus but actually fails to show how the descendants of Adam were morally responsible for his action. Edwards rightly identified the constitutive power of the will of God, but his account was marred by its occasionalism. Crisp has taken from Edwards an emphasis

---

[166] Augustine, *On the Grace of Christ, and Original Sin* ii.28, in *NPNF*¹ 5:247.
[167] Boston, *View of the Covenant of Works*, 11:232–33.

on the constitutive power of God sans occasionalism, with an alternative model suggested by Rea. This recent analytic work is, to my mind, the most stimulating line of argument that we have seen for the metaphysics of imputed sin in the recent literature, but it needs to be more closely integrated with biblical, covenantal, and systematic theology. I have sought to begin this work by reflecting on the ontologically constitutive power of the word of God, the representative relationships of kings and fathers, the created features that signify identity, and an account of the constitutive word as specifically the word of the covenant of life.

The position that I have outlined is a species of federalism because the moral unity of Adam-humanity is constituted from above by the will of God in the covenantal word, not from below by nature. The primal sin of Adam is imputed to his descendants on the basis of their being constituted one by the word of God. With that constitution in place and on the basis of it, we come into existence with birth sin. Apart from the constituting covenant, Adam would not have been the representative head of his people, merely their father and grandfather and great-grandfather. The natural matters, but it is downstream from the federal. God in his wisdom has chosen to make ordinary generation the way in which imputation is worked out and signified. Underlining the constitutive power of the word of God as a deeper moral basis than even natural descent highlights the true ontological depth of federalism. It shows that the contrast between federalism and *real*-ism is easily mistaken. The federal could not be more real. A federal account of imputed sin affirms the highest conceivable ontological basis for the unity of Adam and his descendants in their fall into total depravity, "And God said . . . And it was so."

21

The Heart Wants What It Wants

A PROTESTANT ASSESSMENT OF THE
DOCTRINE OF CONCUPISCENCE

Steven Wedgeworth

One of the more unexpected side effects of recent debates over human sexuality in evangelical churches has been the reemergence of a somewhat archaic word: *concupiscence*. Writing in Public Discourse, Denny Burk and Rosaria Butterfield emphasize the doctrine of concupiscence as a dividing line between Protestant and Roman Catholic understandings of illicit desire.[1] Likewise, the term concupiscence appeared in "The Ad Interim Committee Report on Human Sexuality" prepared for the forty-eighth General Assembly of the Presbyterian Church in America,[2] a study report concerning LGBTQ-related issues. A word that had been largely unused now has a new sort of relevance, and so it is important that Christian ministers and teachers have a proper understanding of the concept.

Connecting concupiscence to debates over sexuality makes a good deal of sense, particularly in light of the way Saint Augustine discussed the concept. As we will see, in the thought of Augustine, concupiscence was profoundly connected to sexual activity. The doctrine itself, however, is much broader and indeed more basic than that. Most fundamentally, concupiscence

---

[1] Denny Burk and Rosaria Butterfield, "Learning to Hate our Sin without Hating Ourselves," Public Discourse: Journal of the Witherspoon Institute, https://www.thepublicdiscourse.com/2018/07/22066/ (accessed June 29, 2020).

[2] https://pcaga.org/wp-content/uploads/2020/05/AIC-Report-to-48th-GA-5-28-20-1.pdf (accessed March 10, 2023).

is an implication of the doctrine of original sin. Because of this, the doctrine of concupiscence played a key role in the debates between Augustine and the various advocates of Pelagianism, as well as the Reformation debates over justification.

This essay will define concupiscence and then survey its relationship to the Christian doctrine of sin throughout various periods of church history. Particular emphasis will be placed on the significance of the morality of concupiscence, whether it is itself sin. In doing so, this chapter will also demonstrate the magisterial Protestant position on the topic and how it applies to the doctrine of justification. Finally, having provided a proper understanding of what concupiscence is, as well as its sinfulness, we will return to those contemporary moral questions that evangelical churches are now asking. The heart wants what it wants, as the old saying goes. But the doctrine of concupiscence can help us see *why* the heart wants what it wants, and whether that wanting is indeed good.

What Is Concupiscence?

The reason that the term concupiscence sounds so foreign to a contemporary reader is that it is itself but an English rendering of the Latin term *concupiscentia*. Its Greek counterpart, which appears in the NT, is ἐπιθυμία. The most basic definition for all of these words is simply "desire." This need not immediately imply an immoral desire.[3] For example, 1 Timothy 3:1 uses the term when it speaks of the desire for church office, a desire which Paul says is for "a good work." And when Thomas Aquinas defines concupiscence, he appeals to Aristotle, saying, "concupiscence is a craving for that which is pleasant."[4] In this sense, concupiscence is not a problematic or sinful thing at all. It is simply the faculty of desire.

But the more common use of concupiscence, and the sense which this essay will take up, is what could be called *carnal desire* or lust. In this specified sense, concupiscence is directly associated with the commandment against covetousness. It refers to the pervasive tendency which arises from our sinful natures to desire the wrong thing or to desire the right thing in the wrong way.

---

[3] BDAG 372. BDAG defines ἐπιθυμία in two ways: (1) "a great desire for something, *desire, longing, craving*," used neutrally (e.g., Mark. 4:19) or positively (e.g., 1 Thess. 2:17); (2) "a desire for something forbidden or simply inordinate, *craving, lust*" (e.g., Rom. 7:8).

[4] Thomas Aquinas, "Question 30: Concupiscence," New Advent, https://www.newadvent.org/summa/2030.htm (accessed June 29, 2020); *Summa Theologiae* I–II.q30.a1.

Common passages from Scripture which speak of this problem are Exodus 20:17, Matthew 5:28, Galatians 5:17, James 1:15, and 1 John 2:16.

Perhaps the most important biblical passage for this stipulated understanding of desire is found in the seventh chapter of Romans. There, the apostle Paul discusses the "law of sin" which dwells in the flesh. Importantly, Paul connects this to covetousness: "For I would not have known what it is to covet if the law had not said, 'You shall not covet.' But sin, seizing an opportunity through the commandment, produced in me all kinds of covetousness" (Rom. 7:7–8). The term "covetousness" in Romans 7:8 is often translated as "desires" in modern English translations. In the old King James Version, however, the word was translated as "concupiscence."

This concupiscence, for Paul, might almost be subconscious. He says, "For I do not understand my own actions. For I do not do what I want, but I do the very thing I hate" (Rom. 7:15). It becomes clear that Paul writes these words as a Christian, as a believer, because he agrees with the law of God (Rom. 7:16), even on this point of coveting. He even later speaks of his "inner being," which "delights in the law of God" (Rom. 7:22), something an unregenerate person could never say.[5] So, the problem for Paul is not intellectual agreement. It is, instead, the fact that his "flesh" continues to serve sin quite apart from his rational consent. This internal warfare is so pronounced that Paul speaks of it as if there were two different people within himself:

> Now if I do what I do not want, I agree with the law, that it is good. So now it is no longer I who do it, but sin that dwells within me. For I know that nothing good dwells in me, that is, in my flesh. For I have the desire to do what is right, but not the ability to carry it out. For I do not do the good I want, but the evil I do not want is what I keep on doing. Now if I do what I do not want, it is no longer I who do it, but sin that dwells within me. (Rom. 7:16–20)

Paul draws the lines of opposition between his "members" and "body" on the one side, and his "inner being" and "mind" on the other. The former two are still subjected to sin, while the latter two have been redeemed, and so Paul cries out to be delivered from "this body of death" (Rom. 7:24).

The "body of death," understood as a whole, is what later Christian writers mean by the doctrine of concupiscence. It is not merely desire but

[5] John Murray provides a typical example of this interpretation, following in the general Reformed tradition (*The Epistle to the Romans*, NICNT [Grand Rapids, MI: Eerdmans, 1973], 259–264).

disordered desire. It is a constant covetousness. Concupiscence is distinct from any actual sin in particular; but it is distinct because it is always the desire which stands behind and before every actual sin. Therefore, it is also frequently described as the "tendency to" or "affection toward" sin.

The Meaning of Concupiscence in Church History

One cannot get far in any discussion about concupiscence without having to interact with a number of traditional authorities. For most Western Christians over the years, Augustine of Hippo has provided the interpretive paradigm for understanding concupiscence. The conversation did not end with Augustine, however, since a sort of scholastic tradition developed in the following centuries. Martin Luther challenged this tradition on many points, and, as we will see, he attempted to draw upon Augustine's teaching on concupiscence to do so. Following Luther, the Reformed scholastics continued to refine the doctrine of concupiscence and apply it to the believer's ongoing struggle against sin. To better understand this history of development, we will consider how a number of key historical figures taught the doctrine of concupiscence.

AUGUSTINE OF HIPPO

Augustine writes extensively about concupiscence. He addresses the topic in detail in one of his most famous works, the *City of God*, but it also appears in his moral treatises and especially in his anti-Pelagian writings. For Augustine, concupiscence is connected to sex. He emphasizes the debilitating reality of sexual lust and its effect on all sex. This connection between lust and sex is, in Augustine's mind, so thoroughly entwined that all sexual activity after the fall of Adam is sinful, though sex within marriage is forgiven because of the presence of the original good goal of producing offspring.[6] For all of this, however, it is important to note that Augustine still understands concupiscence in a broader sense: "lust may have many objects."[7]

Augustine locates concupiscence's most basic aspect in the body's rebellion against the mind, and indeed even the mind's own rebellion against its original goal, the pure contemplation of God.[8] He explains it this way:

[6] See, for example, Augustine, *On Marriage and Concupiscence*, in *NPNF*¹ 5:267, 270–71; Augustine, *City of God*, in *NPNF*¹ 2:276–77, 281–82.
[7] Augustine, *City of God*, in *NPNF*¹ 2:275.
[8] Augustine, *City of God*, in *NPNF*¹ 2:279–82.

... this lust, of which we at present speak, is the more shameful on this account, because the soul is therein neither master of itself, so as not to lust at all, nor of the body, so as to keep the members under the control of the will; for if they were thus ruled, there should be no shame. But now the soul is ashamed that the body, which by nature is inferior and subject to it, should resist its authority.[9]

Also:

... in weakness, that is, *not of the flesh only*, as this man supposes, but both of the flesh and of the mind; because *the mind, too, was, in comparison of that last stage of complete perfection, weak*, and to it also was assigned, in order to check its elation, that messenger of Satan, the thorn in the flesh; although it was very strong, in contrast with the carnal or animal faculties, which as yet understand not the things of the Spirit of God.[10]

Concupiscence, then, is the basic war that man now recognizes within himself after Adam's introduction of sin into the world and his passing it down to his posterity through natural generation.[11] Thus, for Augustine, concupiscence applies to every kind of sin. Indeed, after the fall, concupiscence is the starting condition for all humans, "the root of all evil things."[12]

As mentioned above, concupiscence is not limited to the body for Augustine. He will describe it as "heat"[13] and attribute it to the "lust of the flesh, against which the lust of the spirit fights."[14] In this respect, concupiscence bears a particular relationship to the body and bodily appetites. However, Augustine denies that concupiscence is simply to be identified with the bodily senses: "The bodily senses, without which no man living in the body ever has been or is or will be, are not the same as the concupiscence by which the flesh lusts against the spirit."[15] Rather, concupiscence is the wrongful use of any and all goods. It is a false love, love turned to covetous desire. As such, it affects the body more directly and powerfully than the mind, but Augustine is clear that the whole of man is now cursed with this inordinate lusting.

[9] Augustine, *City of God*, in *NPNF*[1] 2:279.
[10] Augustine, *On the Grace of Christ, and Original Sin*, in *NPNF*[1] 5:222, emphasis added.
[11] Augustine, *On the Merits and Forgiveness of Sins, and On the Baptism of Infants*, in *NPNF*[1] 5:20–21, 22, 59; see also Augustine, *On Continence*, 18–21, in *NPNF*[1] 3:386–88.
[12] Augustine, *On the Grace of Christ*, in *NPNF*[1] 5:225.
[13] Augustine, *City of God*, 2:281–82; Augustine, *On Marriage and Concupiscence*, in *NPNF*[1] 5:293.
[14] Augustine, *On Continence*, 3:381.
[15] Augustine, *Against Julian*, in *The Fathers of the Church: A New Translation*, vol. 35, ed. H. Dressler, trans. M. A. Schumacher (Washington, DC: Catholic University of America Press, 1957), 295–96.

DOCTRINAL IMPLICATIONS

Augustine's understanding of concupiscence has a number of implications, both doctrinal and practical. Since all people have fallen in Adam, they all possess concupiscence. None can be considered without sin. This is true even before they commit actual sins.[16] Since Augustine believes this original sin is passed down through ordinary human generation, it extends even prior to the actual birth.[17]

This original sin is distinct from actual sins, though actual sins will invariably follow from it.[18] But actual sins will invariably follow because concupiscence is also passed down through ordinary generation, as an effect of original sin.[19]

The "law of sin," which Augustine identifies with "the rebellious motion of the flesh,"[20] is concupiscence, and it is "passed on from the first pair to their posterity."[21] The only man to ever be born without this concupiscence, Augustine argues elsewhere, is Jesus Christ: "excepting His flesh, all other human flesh is sinful flesh."[22] Therefore, all humans possess original sin, and all are sinners—by their very nature.

DOES AUGUSTINE BELIEVE THAT CONCUPISCENCE IS SIN?

Augustine's account of the "sinfulness" of concupiscence is quite complicated. In his earlier writings he had stated that "sinning therefore takes place only by exercise of will."[23] Critics, particularly Pelagian critics, reasonably pointed out how this would seem to rule out the sinfulness of original sin. Rather than simply retract his early claims, Augustine attempted to harmonize the tensions. In the *Retractions*, he writes,

> Even those sins which are not unjustly called involuntary, because they are committed by those who are ignorant or constrained, cannot be committed entirely without the will, since, in truth, he who sins through ignorance in any case sins voluntarily, because he thinks he should do something that should not be done. He who does not do what he wills because "the flesh

---

[16] Augustine, *On the Merits*, in *NPNF*[1] 5:19.
[17] Augustine, *On the Grace of Christ*, in *NPNF*[1] 5:252–53.
[18] Augustine, *On the Merits*, in *NPNF*[1] 5:19, 20–21.
[19] Augustine, *On the Merits*, in *NPNF*[1] 5:59.
[20] Augustine, *On the Merits*, in *NPNF*[1] 5:59.
[21] Augustine, *On the Merits*, in *NPNF*[1] 5:59.
[22] Augustine, *Against Julian*, 293.
[23] Augustine, *On Two Souls, Against the Manichaeans*, in *NPNF*[1] 4:102; see also Augustine, *Concerning the Nature of Good, Against the Manichaeans*, in *NPNF*[1] 4:357.

lusts against the spirit," certainly lusts without the will and, therefore, does not do what he wills. If, however, he is overcome, he yields to concupiscence voluntarily, and, therefore, does only what he wills, free, so to speak, "as regards justice" and "a slave of sin." And what is called original sin in infants, for they do not as yet use free choice of the will, is not improperly called voluntary also, because, inherited from man's first evil will, it has become, in a certain sense, hereditary.[24]

Thus, Augustine believes that original sin can indeed be said to be voluntary, even in the case of infants, because it is inherited from man's original will. This is a stipulated definition, to be sure, but Augustine believes he has resolved the apparent contradiction by reaffirming the voluntary nature of all sin, including original sin.[25]

A similar tension arises with concupiscence, but with an even more complex explanation. Again, in the *Retractions*, Augustine writes,

> My statement thus expressed: "Sin is not except in the will," can, indeed, be judged false on the ground that the Apostle says: "Now if I do what I do not wish, it is no longer I who do it, but the sin that dwells in me," for this sin is in the will to the degree that he says: "I do what I do not wish." How, then, is there never sin but in the will? But this sin about which the Apostle spoke in this way is called sin because, by sin, it was committed and is the penalty of sin, inasmuch as this is said about concupiscence of the flesh, as he makes clear. . . . This is the perfection of good, when this concupiscence of sin is not in man, to which, in truth, when one lives a good life, the will does not consent. But, nevertheless, man does not fully accomplish the good because he still remains in the concupiscence that the will resists. The guilt of this concupiscence is remitted by baptism, but there remains the weakness against which, until he is cured, every faithful man who advances in the right direction struggles against most earnestly. Sin, however, which is "never except in the will" must especially be understood as that which is followed by just condemnation . . . although, indeed, that sin whereby consent is given to the concupiscence of sin is not committed except by the will.[26]

Unlike the previous dilemma, Augustine does not attempt to argue that concupiscence is voluntary. Instead, he argues that concupiscence is not

---

[24] Augustine, *The Retractions*, in *The Fathers of the Church: A New Translation*, vol. 60, ed. R. J. Deferrari, trans. M. I. Bogan (Washington, DC: Catholic University of America Press, 1968), 53–54.

[25] Several critics maintain that Augustine did not, in fact, resolve this contradiction in any satisfactory way; see Robert F. Brown, "The First Evil Will Must Be Incomprehensible: A Critique of Augustine," *Journal of the American Academy of Religion* 46.3 (1978): 315–29; and William S. Babcock, "Augustine on Sin and Moral Agency," *The Journal of Religious Ethics* 16.1 (1988): 28–55.

[26] Augustine, *Retractations* 65.

properly sin but rather is "called sin" because it is committed "by sin" and is "the penalty of sin." This is indeed an argument that Augustine makes in other places, but he does not appear to be consistent in how he argues. In the *Retractions*, he implies that this is a sort of improper use of speech, and that concupiscence is not therefore truly sin but only called so because of close association. Elsewhere, however, Augustine speaks differently. In at least two other places, Augustine argues that certain penalties of sin, including the darkening of the mind and concupiscence, are themselves sin. For instance, "This darkening was, of course, already their punishment and penalty; and yet by this very penalty . . . they fell into more grievous sins still. . . . Here is the punishment of iniquity, which is itself iniquity."[27] And,

> In like manner, the concupiscence of the flesh against which a good spirit lusts is *not only a sin*, because it is disobedience against the dominion of the mind—as well as punishment for sin, because it has been reckoned as the wages of disobedience—but also a cause of sin, in the failure of him who consents to it or in the contagion of birth.[28]

In these quotes we see Augustine calling concupiscence a sin. In the former, he mentions that the darkening of the human mind was both "punishment of iniquity" and "itself iniquity." In the latter, he says that concupiscence is "not only a sin . . . as well as punishment for sin . . . but also a cause of sin." This assertion, it should be noted, appears in Augustine's final work, *Against Julian*, and was written after the *Retractions*.[29]

Thus, interpreters of Augustine are faced with a dilemma. They must explain how these particular instances of sin are volitional, something Augustine appears to deny; or they must modify Augustine's claim that all sin requires consent. A third explanation is more likely. Augustine uses the term "sin" in equivocal ways. Some things can be sinful and even be called "sin," but yet not be "a sin"—a sin in the sense of a particular actual sin. An equivocal use of this sort would explain Augustine's apparent contradictions, as well as how both Protestant and Roman Catholic heirs of the Augustinian tradition could so confidently claim him for their competing positions.

A similar equivocation occurs in Augustine's explanation of guilt. He seems to say that concupiscence brings guilt prior to baptism. Even in his

---

[27] Augustine, *On Nature and Grace*, in *NPNF*¹ 5:129.
[28] Augustine, *Against Julian*, 249.
[29] Augustine, *Against Julian*, xi.

statement in the *Retractions* this is emphasized: "The guilt of this concupiscence is remitted by baptism."[30] This claim also appears throughout Augustine's writings on concupiscence.[31] It is precisely the *guilt* of concupiscence that is taken away in baptism, for Augustine.[32] If something brings guilt, would it not therefore be itself a sin? Augustine has a rather subtle answer to this question. We can see his logic in a passage on original sin and baptism. Augustine writes,

> The fault of our nature remains in our offspring so deeply impressed as to make it guilty, even when the guilt of the self-same fault has been washed away in the parent by the remission of sins—until every defect *which ends in sin by the consent of the human will* is consumed and done away in the last regeneration. This will be identical with that renovation of the very flesh itself which is promised in its future resurrection, when we shall not only commit no sins, but be even free from those corrupt desires which lead us to sin *by yielding consent to them.*[33]

Original sin itself does indeed bring guilt, but concupiscence is an effect—or a defect—of original sin rather than original sin itself. It is a punishment for original sin and necessarily leads man to sin, but the new sin does not actually occur until it is given consent. Considered simply in itself, then, concupiscence is a weakness, a corrupt desire, and it will lead to sin unless God intervenes; but the sin, and thus the guilt, requires consent.

This distinction would appear to resolve the difficulty, and in favor of concupiscence not being, in itself, sin, but rather being both the punishment of original sin and the means by which every actual sin occurs. And yet, there are still complicated passages in Augustine's writings that resist full harmonization. For instance, Augustine discusses the different effects of concupiscence in the baptized and the unbaptized:

> Concupiscence, therefore, as the law of sin which remains in the members of this body of death, is born with infants. In baptized infants, it is deprived of guilt, is left for the struggle [of life], but pursues with no condemnation, such as die before the struggle. Unbaptized infants it implicates as guilty and as children of wrath, even if they die in infancy, draws into

---

[30] Augustine, *Retractations* 65.
[31] Augustine, *On the Merits*, in *NPNF*[1] 5:45, 62–63; *On Marriage and Concupiscence*, in *NPNF*[1] 5:275; *On Continence*, in *NPNF*[1] 3:386.
[32] Augustine, *On the Merits*, in *NPNF*[1] 5:63; *On Marriage and Concupiscence*, in *NPNF*[1] 5:275, 278; Augustine, *On Man's Perfection in Righteousness*, in *NPNF*[1] 5:176.
[33] Augustine, *On the Grace of Christ*, in *NPNF*[1] 5:253, emphasis added.

condemnation. In baptized adults, however, endowed with reason, whatever consent their mind gives to this concupiscence for the commission of sin is an act of their own will. After all sins have been blotted out, and that guilt has been cancelled which by nature bound men in a conquered condition, it still remains—but not to hurt in any way those who yield no consent to it for unlawful deeds.[34]

Here, again, we see the requirement of consent for concupiscence to bring about guilt, but, according to Augustine, such a distinction applies only to the baptized. In the case of unbaptized infants, concupiscence "implicates [them] as guilty" and "draws [them] into condemnation." An unbaptized infant would not be able to properly yield consent to anything, and so this appears to be a true inconsistency for Augustine.

This statement that concupiscence is sin in the unbaptized but not sin in the baptized appears in several places throughout Augustine's writings. In *On Marriage and Concupiscence* he argues,

If it may be[,] in the case of a baptized parent[,] concupiscence and not be sin, why should this same concupiscence be sin in the offspring?—The answer to be given is this: carnal concupiscence is remitted, indeed, in baptism; not so that it is put out of existence, but so that it is not to be imputed for sin. Although its guilt is now taken away, it still remains until our entire infirmity be healed by the advancing renewal of our inner man.[35]

He goes on to add, "For not to have sin means this, not to be deemed guilty of sin."[36] Thus the "sin" is present in both parent and child, but it is only imputed to the unbaptized.

A similar series of equivocal statements appears in *Against Two Letters of the Pelagians*:

But although this [concupiscence] is called sin, it is certainly so called not because it is sin, but because it is made by sin, as a writing is said to be some one's "hand" because the hand has written it. . . . And this very concupiscence of the flesh is in such wise put away in baptism, that although it is inherited by all that are born, it in no respect hurts those that are born anew. And yet from these, if they carnally beget children, it is again derived; and again it will be hurtful to those that are born, unless . . . its guilt, derived by generation, has been put away by regeneration; and thus it is now no more

[34] Augustine, *On the Merits*, in *NPNF*¹ 5:45.
[35] Augustine, *On Marriage and Concupiscence*, in *NPNF*¹ 5:275.
[36] Augustine, *On Marriage and Concupiscence*, in *NPNF*¹ 5:275, 278.

sin, but is called so, whether because it became what it is by sin, or because it is stirred by the delight of sinning, although by the conquest of the delight of righteousness consent is not given to it.[37]

In this case, Augustine says that concupiscence is not sin but is rather called sin by metonymy, similar to what he said in the *Retractions*, and yet he goes on to say that concupiscence is *"now no more* sin" in the baptized, unless they give consent. But would not the matter of consent apply equally to the unbaptized as well? And could not metonymy be equally invoked in the case of the baptized? It seems that Augustine is offering two different explanations for why concupiscence is not sin—it is not sin unless paired with consent, and baptism takes away its guilt until additional consent is added.

A third place where concupiscence is said to bring about guilt prior to baptism is found in *Against Julian*:

> Although man's body . . . is sanctified so that through the remission of sins he is not bound by any guilt for past sins, nor for the concupiscence of the flesh which exists in him. Every man at birth is necessarily answerable by the guilt of this concupiscence, and will be until death, if he is not reborn.[38]

Here again, the difference is not volition, but baptism.

One way to resolve the inconsistency would be to classify concupiscence as a subset of original sin, as distinct from actual sins. Augustine does not quite do this, however, as his different explanations in the *Retractions*, cited earlier, indicate. Another way would be simply to concede that not all sin requires true or full volition, again an option Augustine rejects.

This point of dispute proved quite significant for later church history, but within Augustine's own writing it does not amount to much. In no case is concupiscence a good or even neutral thing, for him. It is always described as evil.[39] It is a war of rebellion within the soul.[40] Augustine even says that concupiscence cannot be sanctified.[41] It "must rather be made void lest it hold the sanctified liable to eternal death."[42]

---

[37] Augustine, *Against Two Letters of the Pelagians*, in *NPNF*[1] 5:385.
[38] Augustine, *Against Julian*, 352.
[39] Augustine, *On the Merits*, in *NPNF*[1] 5:37; *Against Two Letters*, 384; *Against Julian*, 272, 356.
[40] Augustine, *Against Julian*, 261.
[41] Augustine, *Against Julian*, 361.
[42] Augustine, *Against Julian*, 362.

So, is concupiscence sin for Augustine? No and yes. No, in that, it is rhetorically called sin, by way of metonymy, rather than properly sin in and of itself. Yes, in that, concupiscence does bring about a guilt that needs to be taken away in baptism. Further, concupiscence remains in the baptized. Its guilt is taken away, but it nevertheless remains as "the law of sin" in the Christian's body.[43] It is "removed" only in the sense that it is "not imputed as sin to the person."[44]

SALVATION BY GRACE

And so, with this lengthy explanation of the sinfulness of concupiscence in Augustine's writings, what does it mean for Augustine's doctrine of salvation? The most immediate implication is that it reinforces man's innate inability. Concupiscence explains why unregenerate man will invariably sin. Until his nature is changed, he cannot hope to make progress in righteousness. Even the things he believes to be good are tainted by inordinate desires.

Augustine maintains that concupiscence remains in the baptized, but it is not imputed to them as sin.[45] And so while Christians are not "hurt" by concupiscence in the sense that they are made guilty before God, they are, nevertheless, harmed by it in the sense that they are weak, and will continue to be throughout their life.[46] The continuing presence of concupiscence in the lives of believers ensures that no believer will be perfect until death.[47] This means that believers are only ever found righteous by God's forgiveness:

> In such judgment all will be found righteous who with sincerity pray: "Forgive us our debts, as we forgive our debtors." For it is through this forgiveness that they will be found righteous; on this account that whatever sins they have here incurred, they have blotted out by their deeds of charity.[48]

And also, "Hence indeed 'they are without fault'; for as they have forgiven those who have done them wrong, so are they purified by God's forgiveness of themselves."[49]

---

[43] Augustine, *On Man's Perfection in Righteousness*, in *NPNF*[1] 5:170.
[44] Augustine, *On Man's Perfection in Righteousness*, in *NPNF*[1] 5:176; *On Marriage and Concupiscence*, in *NPNF*[1] 5:275; *Against Julian*, 360.
[45] Augustine, *On Man's Perfection in Righteousness*, in *NPNF*[1] 5:176; *On Marriage and Concupiscence*, in *NPNF*[1] 5:275, 278.
[46] Augustine, *On Man's Perfection in Righteousness*, in *NPNF*[1] 5:164.
[47] Augustine, *On Man's Perfection in Righteousness*, in *NPNF*[1] 5:164–65, 168–70; *Against Two Letters*, 386.
[48] Augustine, *On Man's Perfection in Righteousness*, in *NPNF*[1] 5:167.
[49] Augustine, *On Man's Perfection in Righteousness*, in *NPNF*[1] 5:169–70.

This sort of "justification by forgiveness" still involves works of charity for Augustine,[50] but the pervasive reality of concupiscence means that not even those works can make a person truly good, in and of themselves, for "the very sons of God . . . are good in such a way that they still remain also evil."[51] This then leads Augustine to state that man must always be dependent on God's grace, knowing that some evil remains and can be forgiven only by God's free pardon. Even when man's will is active in the process of sanctification, his knowledge of concupiscence and indwelling sin means that he is dependent on God's free mercy:

> For all this is accomplished by the will, by the exercise of faith, hope, and love . . . by this process, it is certainly brought about that our heart is cleansed, and all our sin taken away; and what the righteous King, when sitting on His throne, *shall find concealed in the heart and uncleansed as yet, shall be remitted by His mercy*, so that the whole shall be rendered sound and cleansed for seeing God.[52]

Indeed, after all the good that an upright man does, "what remains may be forgiven him by free pardon."[53]

In fact, Augustine takes this thought so far as to contrast a man's standing in Christ over and against his standing in Adam.[54] In himself, he is a sinner. In Christ, he is righteous:

> Now it follows from the whole of this, that in so far as we are born of God we abide in Him who appeared to take away sins, that is, in Christ, and sin not,—which is simply that "the inward man is renewed day by day"; but in so far as we are born of that man "through whom sin entered into the world, and death by sin, and so death passed upon all men," we are not without sin, because we are not as yet free from his infirmity.[55]

Because of this abiding tension, the Christian must ask God not to be judged according to the full standard of justice,[56] and he must not trust "in his own resources."[57] He must not be judged "in himself."[58] Instead, he must "glory in the mercy of the Judge Himself."[59]

---

[50] See also Augustine, *On the Merits*, in *NPNF*¹ 5:45.
[51] Augustine, *On Man's Perfection in Righteousness*, in *NPNF*¹ 5:171.
[52] Augustine, *On Man's Perfection in Righteousness*, in *NPNF*¹ 5:171, emphasis added.
[53] Augustine, *On Man's Perfection in Righteousness*, in *NPNF*¹ 5:172.
[54] Augustine, *On Man's Perfection in Righteousness*, in *NPNF*¹ 5:169.
[55] Augustine, *On Man's Perfection in Righteousness*, in *NPNF*¹ 5:173.
[56] Augustine, *On Man's Perfection in Righteousness*, in *NPNF*¹ 5:173.
[57] Augustine, *On Man's Perfection in Righteousness*, in *NPNF*¹ 5:175.
[58] Augustine, *On Man's Perfection in Righteousness*, in *NPNF*¹ 5:169.
[59] Augustine, *On Man's Perfection in Righteousness*, in *NPNF*¹ 5:171.

Thus, the doctrine of concupiscence, in Augustine's thought, is a constant reminder that a man must be saved by the grace of God and not by his own merit, not even the inherent righteousness worked in him by God's grace. In one place, Augustine says that inherent but partial righteousness must be counted as "dung" compared to the full righteousness which awaits us in the future state.[60] In another place, he even contrasts man's inherent nature against God's gracious imputation.[61] And since man will never be perfect in this life, the Christian must rely on the judgment of mercy, his identity in Christ, and the non-imputation of guilt. This is salvation by grace.

PRACTICAL APPLICATIONS

In addition to these theological claims, Augustine believes his understanding of concupiscence has a number of practical implications. Several of them have to do with sexual intercourse. Augustine does not believe that sex is inherently sinful, at least not in its original state in Eden, but he does believe that it is always sinful in a fallen world. In several places, Augustine speculates about what sexual reproduction would have been like in the garden of Eden. He says that it would have been purely rational, with the bodily members obeying the mind, as it commanded them to reproduce. This explanation can strike the modern reader as nearly comical, but Augustine is willing to think about it in some detail.[62] After the introduction of sin, however, our members ceased to obey our mind and can only obey with the incitement of lust.[63] This is what brings about sex's tragic condition.

This means that, for Augustine, all sexual reproduction is now dependent, in some sense, upon sinful concupiscence:

> When it must come to man's great function of the procreation of children the members which were expressly created for this purpose will not obey the direction of the will, but lust has to be waited for to set these members in motion, as if it had legal right over them, and sometimes it refuses to act when the mind wills, while often it acts against its will![64]

---

[60] Augustine, *On the Grace of Christ*, in *NPNF*¹ 5:235.
[61] Augustine, *On Marriage and Concupiscence*, in *NPNF*¹ 5:278.
[62] Augustine, *City of God*, in *NPNF*¹ 280–82; *On the Good of Marriage 2*, in *NPNF*¹ 3:399–400; *On the Grace of Christ*, in *NPNF*¹ 5:251–52; *On Marriage and Concupiscence*, in *NPNF*¹ 5:304–5.
[63] Augustine, *City of God*, in *NPNF*¹ 275–76, 277, 281–82.
[64] Augustine, *On Marriage and Concupiscence*, in *NPNF*¹ 5:266.

All sex is therefore sinful, unless enjoyed within marriage and for the purpose of bringing about godly offspring.[65] The institution of marriage is given so that "evil" may be "turned to a good use."[66]

It follows from this that all sexual activity outside of marriage is sinful, as is all intentionally contraceptive activity.[67] Augustine even extends this rule so as to prohibit sex during pregnancy.[68] Recreational sex within marriage, so long as it is open to procreation, is also a sort of sin, but it is a pardoned sin allowed by way of permission.[69] Augustine even suggests that after bearing a certain number of children, husbands and wives might be able to "ascend unto a higher degree of holiness" and live in physical continence.[70]

Because of this close relationship between sexual intercourse and concupiscence, all children are born in sin. They thus stand in need of forgiveness, which Augustine believes comes to them through baptism. If they are not baptized, then Augustine believes that such infants are damned.[71]

Martin Luther, the Council of Trent, and the Lutheran Confessional Position

The beginnings of Martin Luther's Reformation have understandably been contextualized according to his critique of indulgences. This was indeed the popular catalyst and the practical catalyst which went on to highlight the related doctrinal concerns. But it is important to note that Luther was also, from those early years, actively engaged in investigating and revising the particulars of scholastic theology, especially as it related to the reception of Augustine's doctrines of nature and grace.[72] In fact, Luther published his *Disputation against Scholastic Theology* in September of 1517, a month before posting his *Ninety-Five Theses*.[73] Central to his argument in that disputation is Luther's interpretation of Augustine on original sin and concupiscence.

[65] Augustine, *On Marriage and Concupiscence*, in *NPNF¹* 5:401, 404; *On the Grace of Christ* 251; *Against Two Letters* 387; *Against Julian*, 301–2.
[66] Augustine, *On the Grace of Christ* 252.
[67] Augustine, *On Marriage and Concupiscence*, in *NPNF¹* 5:271.
[68] Augustine, *On the Good of Marriage 5*, 401.
[69] Augustine, *On the Good of Marriage 5*, 401.
[70] Augustine, *On the Good of Marriage 5*, 406.
[71] Augustine, *On the Merits*, in *NPNF¹* 5:22–23, 45.
[72] Heiko Oberman, *Luther: Man between God and the Devil* (New Haven, CT: Yale University Press, 1989), 158–61; Oberman, *The Dawn of the Reformation* (Grand Rapids, MI: Eerdmans, 1992), 39–83.
[73] Oberman, *Luther*, 356.

Luther begins this disputation with a strong defense of Augustine and then applies certain points of Augustine's teaching on original sin to the work of various medieval theologians, especially Duns Scotus and Gabriel Biel.[74] In his fourth thesis, Luther argues, "It is therefore true that man, being a bad tree, can only will and do evil," and then in his seventh, "without the grace of God the will produces an act that is perverse and evil."[75] Whereas a modern reader might expect Luther to rest these claims simply on certain biblical proof texts, Luther himself is willing to invoke the doctrine of concupiscence: "No act is done according to nature that is not an act of concupiscence against God," and, "Every act of concupiscence against God is evil and a fornication of the spirit."[76]

Luther is willing to make qualifications. He maintains that the will is not evil by nature, not "essentially evil," but nevertheless it is so corrupted by the fall that it is innately evil until changed by God's grace.[77] Because of this, Luther can argue that no virtue is without sin,[78] and that "he who is outside the grace of God sins incessantly, even when he does not kill, commit adultery, or become angry."[79] Luther is here speaking of man considered apart from any grace, in the flesh, and his argument is that concupiscence so thoroughly pervades man's nature that even works that would otherwise be good are evil.

This theme would become a constant one throughout Luther's theology in the following years. In the 1518 Heidelberg Disputation, he says, "the works of man . . . are . . . likely to be mortal sins."[80] In that thesis, Luther was speaking of man apart from grace, but in the seventh thesis he extends this same principle to believers: "The works of the righteous would be mortal sins if they would not be feared as mortal sins by the righteous themselves out of pious fear of God."[81] In fact, Luther continues to press the implications of concupiscence to the point where he can say, "there is no righteous person on earth who in doing good does not sin."[82] Then, appealing to Isaiah 64:6, he proclaims, "righteous deeds are unclean."[83]

---

[74] Martin Luther, "Disputation against Scholastic Theology," in *Luther's Works*, ed. J. J. Pelikan, H. C. Oswald, and H. T. Lehmann, vol. 31, *Career of the Reformer* (Philadelphia: Fortress, 1999), 9.

[75] Luther, "Disputation against Scholastic Theology," 9.

[76] Luther, "Disputation against Scholastic Theology," 10 (theses 21 and 22).

[77] Luther, "Disputation against Scholastic Theology," 9 (theses 8, 9, and 7, respectively).

[78] Luther, "Disputation against Scholastic Theology," 11 (thesis 38).

[79] Luther, "Disputation against Scholastic Theology," 13 (thesis 62).

[80] Martin Luther, "Heidelberg Disputation," in *Luther's Works*, vol. 31, *Career of the Reformer*, 39 (thesis 3).

[81] Luther, "Heidelberg Disputation," 40.

[82] Luther, "Heidelberg Disputation," 59.

[83] Luther, "Heidelberg Disputation," 59.

It could be argued that Luther is expanding Augustine's doctrine of concupiscence.[84] Whereas Augustine had attempted to restrict the title of "sin" to each volitional act, considered individually, Luther asserts that since the will is itself distorted through concupiscence, every deed is necessarily also distorted as a rule. And any moral imperfection is sin: "Whoever does less than he ought, sins."[85] This does not mean, however, that Christians cannot do good works. Instead, Luther argues that every good deed is both accepted and not accepted, depending on its relationship to God through the work of Christ. In and of itself, it is tainted with sin, but God chooses to accept the believer's good works through pardon: "I therefore say that every good deed is both accepted and not unaccepted, and, on the other hand, that it is not accepted but unaccepted. It is accepted through pardon, and thus not rejected, for he forgives through mercy that which is less worthy of being accepted."[86]

Here we see an early version of Luther's *simul iustus et peccator*. The good works are sinful in one way, but they are acceptable to God in another way. When read in light of Augustine's "righteous dung" (in *On the Grace of Christ, and Original Sin* [1.53.48]) and his insistence on the need for gracious divine imputation (in *On Marriage and Concupiscence* [1.37.32]), the potential discrepancies between Luther and Augustine look to be Luther's resolution of Augustine's complex thought in one particular direction.

Luther continued to emphasize the radical nature of sin on human nature and the effects of concupiscence on every human work. In the *Explanations of the 95 Theses*, written in 1518, Luther, having not yet rejected the notion of purgatory, wrote that even concupiscence, called "the tinder of sin," will "delay entrance into the kingdom of heaven."[87] And in the 1519 Leipzig Debate, he argued that, "To deny that man sins even when doing good; that venial sin is pardonable, not according to its nature, but by the mercy of God; or that sin remains in the child after baptism; that is equivalent to crushing Paul and Christ under foot."[88] These would prove to be explosive theological positions.

---

[84] Luther does not explicitly criticize Augustine here, though he is willing to make critical remarks about Augustine in later writings. See Martin Luther, "Defense and Explanation of All the Articles," in *Luther's Works*, 32:27; "Against Latomus," in *Luther's Works*, 32:204.

[85] Luther, "Heidelberg Disputation," 61.

[86] Luther, "Heidelberg Disputation," 64.

[87] Luther, "Explanations of the 95 Theses or Explanations of the Disputation concerning the Value of Indulgences," 153.

[88] Martin Luther, "Leipzig Debate," in *Luther's Works*, vol. 31, *Career of the Reformer*, 317.

THE PAPAL CRITIQUE AND LUTHER'S RESPONSE

Pope Leo X responded to Luther in 1520, not merely to his protesting over indulgences but also to his theological positions. Writing in *Exurge Domine*, Leo lists particular teachings from Luther, including teaching on original sin and concupiscence, which he then condemns:

> 2. To deny that sin remains in a child after baptism is to disregard both Paul and Christ alike.
> 3. The tinder of sin hinders a soul departing from the body from entering into heaven, even though there is no actual sin.
> 31. In every good work the just man sins.
> 32. A good work perfectly performed is a venial sin.
> 35. No one is certain that he is not always sinning mortally because of the most hidden vice of pride.
> 36. After sin, free will is a reality in name only; and when it does what is in its power, it sins mortally.
> . . . All and each of the above-mentioned articles or errors, as set before you, we condemn, disapprove, and entirely reject as respectively heretical or scandalous or false or offensive to pious ears or seductive of simple minds and in opposition to Catholic truth.[89]

When Luther received the bull, he did not recant his teachings but rather reasserted them vigorously.[90] One of his responses was the treatise *Grund und Ursach*, translated in English as "Defense and Explanation of All the Articles."[91] There Luther explains and defends his earlier teachings, insisting on their foundation not only in Augustine but also in the Scriptures. Citing Romans 7:7, Galatians 5:17, and Romans 7:18, Luther insists that concupiscence remains in the baptized, and that the Scriptures call it sin.[92] He points out that Colossians 3:5 lists concupiscence alongside other sins like fornication and avarice.[93] Luther notes that his opponents argue that the Scriptures call concupiscence sin in an improper sense because it is a penalty for sin. It does not itself bring guilt, they say, echoing one strand of Augustine's thought.[94] Luther has little patience for this sort of moral parsing, disclaiming it as "arbitrarily fabricated without any basis or reason in Scripture."[95] For Luther, the fact

---

[89] Heinrich Denzinger, *Compendium of Creeds, Definitions, and Declarations on Matters of Faith and Morals*, 43rd ed., ed. P. Hünermann, R. Fastiggi, and Anne Nash (San Francisco: Ignatius, 2012), 363, 366–67.
[90] Roland Bainton, *Here I Stand* (1950; repr., Nashville: Abingdon, 1978), 154–57.
[91] Luther, "Defense and Explanation of All the Articles," 5.
[92] Luther, "Defense and Explanation of All the Articles," 19.
[93] Luther, "Defense and Explanation of All the Articles," 20.
[94] Luther, "Defense and Explanation of All the Articles," 27.
[95] Luther, "Defense and Explanation of All the Articles," 27.

that the Scriptures call concupiscence sin is good enough, as is the fact that the Decalogue positively names lust as a violation of God's commandments.

It is interesting that Luther does not criticize Augustine on this point. He would surely be aware of his opponents' ability to call upon Augustine's distinctions. Instead, Luther claims Augustine for his own position, conceding that the "guilt" of original sin passes away in baptism but the "work" of original sin remains. Luther quotes Augustine here, saying, "it [the work of original sin] lives, twists, turns, raves, and assails us until our physical death, and only then is it destroyed."[96] Luther continues to employ Augustinian categories when he says that while this sin remains in the baptized, it is not imputed to the believer by God but rather is pardoned.[97]

This distinction will become Luther's—and Lutheranism's—primary one. Sin remains in believers, but God graciously chooses not to impute it, forgiving it for the sake of Christ. Even though "a righteous man sins in all his good works,"[98] believers can be saved and accepted, "solely on the mercy of God, putting all confidence and trust in him."[99] Their good works are accepted by God only because God has first forgiven them all their faults, and therefore they can claim no merit in them, only gratitude for divine grace.

A final important work by Luther on the doctrine of concupiscence is *Against Latomus*, published in 1521. Here Luther again defends his previous writings on the subject and reaffirms his developing theology. Familiar statements are found: "sin remains after baptism,"[100] and "every good work is sin."[101] Luther then makes a more complicated argument:

> For I meant and now [expressly] say (what makes every hair of our professors stand on end) that sin, as long as we live, inheres essentially in good works, just as the ability to laugh inheres in man. (I speak after the fashion of Aristotle, not of the sophists, for they still don't know what is an essential or proper attribute according to Aristotle.) [In contrast], food, sleep, and death are attributed to man by accidental predication. Consequently, just as it does not follow that because a man is always capable of laughing, therefore he always laughs, so it does not follow that because a man lives, therefore he is always awake, eating, or dying.

[96] Luther, "Defense and Explanation of All the Articles," 5.
[97] Luther, "Defense and Explanation of All the Articles," 28.
[98] Luther, "Defense and Explanation of All the Articles," 83.
[99] Luther, "Defense and Explanation of All the Articles," 83.
[100] Martin Luther, "Against Latomus," in *Luther's Works*, 32:157. Latomus was the Latin name used by Jacobus Masson, a member of the theological faculty of the University of Louvain in Belgium; see introduction to "Against Latomus," 135.
[101] Luther, "Against Latomus," 161.

However, this does follow: a man lives, therefore he is capable of laughter, of eating, of sleeping, of dying, etc. In the same way, this follows: a man does good and therefore sins, because a man doing good is a subject which has sin as its attribute, just as was postulated on the basis of what Solomon says.[102]

Luther's statement that "sin inheres essentially in every good work" indeed shocked his opponents. They interpreted him as saying that good works are essentially sin. Luther's point, however, was that because of the inordinate desire which always exists within man, even in the believer, good works have some measure of concupiscence in them. Luther believes that he is the one properly using Aristotelian categories. He believes that this point means that every potentially good work would still be judged sinful if measured by strict divine justice. Later on, he explicitly affirms that virtues are not "evil . . . in themselves, for they are the gifts of God."[103] It is because of concupiscence, "that deeply hidden root of sin,"[104] that virtuous things are sinful.

By this point in the debate, Luther feels confident that Augustine is on his side, but he is willing to grant that Augustine is at times inconsistent: "However, as I said, I do not entirely believe Augustine, so that my opponents cannot say that I base myself on him only when he agrees with me—it may be that he is as thoroughly inconsistent as Latomus infers, but that is no concern of mine."[105] Such a statement does not seem entirely sincere, as Luther overwhelmingly cites Augustine for support. However, it is true that Luther thinks many of the technicalities are of no real significance. He argues that the Scriptures know nothing of "nonmetaphorical sin" that is not "in its nature truly sin."[106] Indeed, " 'sin' is used in Scripture in a single, very simple way, not in many different ones."[107] Augustine is good, but Scripture is better. Concupiscence violates God's law, God's word calls concupiscence sin, and so, for Luther, concupiscence is sin.

A final point of distinction is worth noting here, as it will reappear in later Reformed writers. Luther maintains that while sin *remains* in the believer, it no longer *reigns*. "The whole of sin is truly annulled so that it definitely no

---

[102] Luther, "Against Latomus," 186–87.
[103] Luther, "Against Latomus," 226.
[104] Luther, "Against Latomus," 226.
[105] Luther, "Against Latomus," 204.
[106] Luther, "Against Latomus," 202.
[107] Luther, "Against Latomus," 195.

longer reigns."[108] This "non-reigning sin" or "reigned-over sin"[109] is real but is not imputed as sin. It remains in the flesh, but is condemned.[110] Luther adds that, "through baptism, sin in us is arrested, judged, and wholly incapacitated so that it can do nothing, and is appointed to complete annihilation."[111] This sin remains sin, "but only according to substance, and not in its quantity, quality, or action, for it is wholly passive."[112] Here, it seems, Luther is approximating Augustine's distinction about the role of consent in making concupiscence liable. For Luther, however, consent does not make concupiscence sin. It makes it reigning sin: "If you consent to this [sin], you have made sin to reign, you serve it and have sinned mortally."[113]

Thus, for Luther, concupiscence is always to be understood as sin, and it would always condemn the sinner were it not for God's gracious choice not to impute it as sin. This sinful concupiscence continues to exist in the believer, even after regeneration, and so the believer must know that he is always both a sinner and a righteous man, in each and every deed that he does. This means that he can never rely on his own works. He must always turn away from them and look to the grace of God found in Christ. If the believer resists concupiscence and reigns over it, then the remaining concupiscence is not counted against him. If the believer consents to concupiscence, then it has reigned over him. He must confess it as new sin needing forgiveness.

THE COUNCIL OF TRENT AND THE LUTHERAN CONFESSIONAL CONCLUSION

Having doubled down on his theological project, Luther was indeed excommunicated on January 3, 1521.[114] The Reformation continued apace, and so the Roman Catholic Church was compelled to make its most authoritative response by way of the Council of Trent, held from 1545–63. In its fifth session, Trent addressed original sin and concupiscence. There it states, "If anyone denies that the guilt of original sin is remitted by the grace of our Lord Jesus Christ given in baptism or asserts that all that is sin in the true and proper sense is not taken away but only brushed over or not imputed, let him

---

[108] Luther, "Against Latomus," 204.
[109] Luther, "Against Latomus," 213.
[110] Luther, "Against Latomus," 206.
[111] Luther, "Against Latomus," 206.
[112] Luther, "Against Latomus," 207.
[113] Luther, "Against Latomus," 214.
[114] Oberman, *Luther*, 358.

be anathema."[115] This is clearly a condemnation of Luther's position. Trent goes on to explain why it is unacceptable to merely state that original sin is "not imputed." It is unacceptable because "in those who are reborn God hates nothing . . . innocent, unstained, pure, and guiltless, have become the beloved sons of God, 'heirs of God and fellow heirs with Christ' (Rom. 8:17), so that nothing henceforth holds them back from entering into heaven."[116]

What is unstated here is the implication that as soon as the baptized give consent to their concupiscence, something would indeed give them a blame and thus "hold them back from entering into heaven" until it was dealt with by subsequent penance. Thus, the one point about concupiscence directly ties into the larger soteriological system. This condemnation certainly applies to Luther, but it also seems to apply to Augustine. After all, Augustine had said that concupiscence was "not imputed,"[117] and that man considered "in himself" was not faultless.[118]

Moving to the specific issue of concupiscence, Trent declares,

> The holy council, however, professes and thinks that concupiscence or the tinder of sin remains in the baptized. . . . Of this concupiscence, which the apostle occasionally calls "sin" (cf. Rom. 6:12–15; 7:7, 14–20), the holy council declares: The Catholic Church has never understood that it is called sin because it would be sin in the true and proper sense in those who have been reborn, but because it comes from sin and inclines to sin. If anyone thinks the contrary, let him be anathema.[119]

Thus, Trent resolves Augustine's thought entirely in the direction of concupiscence being called sin by metonymy only. For Trent, concupiscence does not possess the nature of sin. This is no mere wrangling over words, because, again, it directly affects the rest of the soteriological system. If concupiscence has the nature of sin, then the baptized cannot truly be said to be righteous. They must be deemed so only forensically, not actually being so in and of themselves. Therefore, the way a theologian interprets the meaning of concupiscence will commit him or her to either the Lutheran or the Catholic position on the doctrine of justification.

---

[115] Denzinger, *Compendium of Creeds*, 373.
[116] Denzinger, *Compendium of Creeds*, 373.
[117] Augustine, *On Man's Perfection in Righteousness*, in *NPNF*[1] 5:176; *On Marriage and Concupiscence*, in *NPNF*[1] 5:275; *Against Julian*, 321, 359–60.
[118] Augustine, *On Man's Perfection in Righteousness*, in *NPNF*[1] 5:169, 170–72; *On Marriage and Concupiscence*, in *NPNF*[1] 5:278.
[119] Denzinger, *Compendium of Creeds*, 373–74.

The Lutheran churches responded to the Catholic formula in a number of ways. Martin Chemnitz penned a magisterial work, *The Examination of the Council of Trent*, in 1565. In it, he devotes an entire chapter to the topic of original sin after baptism as it relates to concupiscence. He summarizes the main contention in this way:

> Lest we be led away from the point at issue by strange arguments, the question is not whether these remnants of original sin make the regenerate, who through baptism have been implanted and remain in Christ through faith, hateful to God and condemn them, for there is now no condemnation for them (Rom. 8:1). Neither is this the proper place to dispute about cases where these remnants of original sin rule in the mortal body in such a way that we do not fight against the desires of concupiscence, but obey them (Rom. 6), for then sin, when it is finished, brings forth death (James 1:15), and Rom. 8:13. . . . But this is the question, what this concupiscence which remains in the regenerate in this life after their baptism is, when it is not obeyed; what, I say, it is per se, in itself, of itself, and by its nature.[120]

The root issue, as is here shown, is not whether God condemns the believer because of the remaining sin of concupiscence but whether concupiscence has the nature of sin.

The Lutheran Confessions also address this question. The Augsburg Confession treats original sin and concupiscence quite simply. In its second article it states, "since the Fall of Adam all men who are born according to the course of nature are conceived and born in sin. That is to say, they are without the fear of God, without trust in God, and are concupiscent. And this disease or vice of origin is truly sin, which even now damns and brings eternal death to those who are not born again through Baptism and the Holy Spirit."[121] Such a statement actually says nothing about the implications of original sin and concupiscence after baptism, and so it does not directly affect the debate between Lutheranism and Catholicism.[122] More significant is the *Apology of the Augsburg Confession*, which rejects the argument that concupiscence is only a penalty and not sin.[123] It concludes by maintaining that those who say concupiscence is only

---

[120] Martin Chemnitz, *Examination of the Council of Trent, Part 1*, in *Chemnitz's Works*, vol. 1, trans. Fred Kramer (St. Louis: Concordia, 2007), 338–39.
[121]"Augsburg Confession," in *The Book of Concord: The Confessions of the Evangelical Lutheran Church*, trans. and ed. Theodore G. Tappert (Philadelphia: Fortress, 1959), 29 (art. 2).
[122] Though even here, many detailed arguments can be made about what is and is not said by both parties; see Chemnitz, *Examination of the Council of Trent*, 312–21.
[123] "Apology of the Augsburg Confession," in *Book of Concord*, 105 (art. 2.38).

a penalty and not sin teach that man can "obey the commandments of God by his own powers,"[124] whereas the Lutherans confess that man is captive to the evil until redeemed by Christ. This topic is immensely practical because "we cannot know [Christ's] blessings unless we recognize our evil."[125]

The Lutheran churches make their final statement on the matter of concupiscence in the "Formula of Concord," and it largely repeats the earlier statements. In the first part, "The Epitome of the Formula Concord," they distinguish between man's nature as he was originally created and how he is after the fall, possessing then original sin.[126] The document goes on to say, "On the other hand, we believe, teach, and confess that original sin is not a slight corruption of human nature, but that it is so deep a corruption that nothing sound or uncorrupted has survived in man's body or soul, in his inward or outward powers."[127] Thus, Luther's position on concupiscence became the Lutheran position: concupiscence is sin.

To summarize the Lutheran position, we can say that concupiscence is one aspect of original sin. It is a constant lusting and a disposition toward sin. Because it is in its nature sin and always present in man, concupiscence means that people cannot please God in and of themselves. They cannot obey God or keep God's commands, even if they conform in outward action. Rather, even deeds which seem righteous will be sinful. This means that we always stand in need of divine grace, for God to forgive our concupiscence and not impute the guilt to us. This concupiscence remains after baptism, and it remains sin in its nature, but God does not count it as sin against the believer.

When it comes to the relationship between concupiscence and sexual intercourse, Luther largely follows Augustine.[128] It is worth noting that the *Apology of the Augsburg Confession* distinguishes between the sexual appetite in itself and the lustful distortion of it after the fall:

> Gen. 1:28 teaches that men were created to be fruitful, and that one sex in a proper way should desire the other. For we are speaking not of concupiscence, which is sin, but of that appetite which was to have been in nature in its integrity [which would have existed in nature even if it had remained

---

[124] "Apology of the Augsburg Confession," 106.
[125] "Apology of the Augsburg Confession," 106.
[126] "Epitome of the Formula Concord," in *Book of Concord*, 466.
[127] "Epitome of the Formula Concord," 467.
[128] Martin Luther, "Lectures on Genesis," in *Luther's Works*, ed. J. J. Pelikan, H. C. Oswald, and H. T. Lehmann, vol. 1, *Lectures on Genesis: Chapters 1–5* (St. Louis: Concordia, 1999), 116; "The Estate of Marriage," in *Luther's Works*, vol. 45, *Christian in Society II*, 45.

uncorrupted], which they call physical love. And this love of one sex for the other is truly a divine ordinance.[129]

Reformed Scholasticism

The Reformed theologians, many of whom began as Lutherans, followed Luther on the question of concupiscence. They all agreed that original sin consists in both the loss of original righteousness and the added propensity toward evil. Writing of the effects of original sin, John Calvin says, "even infants . . . have the seed [of sin] enclosed within themselves. Indeed, their whole nature is a seed of sin." He adds, "this perversity never ceases in us, but continually bears new fruits . . . just as a glowing furnace continually emits flame and sparks, or a spring ceaselessly gives forth water."[130]

Calvin is more willing than Luther to point out a potential disagreement with Augustine on this question: "But between Augustine and us we can see that there is this difference of opinion: he dare not call this disease 'sin.'"[131] But like Luther, Calvin also points out that Augustine is inconsistent on the question: "Augustine does not always refrain from using the term 'sin.'" After the words are carefully examined, Calvin believes that Augustine means the same thing as he and Luther: "By these words he admits that in so far as believers are subject to the inordinate desires of the flesh, they are guilty of sin."[132]

Subsequent Reformed writers feel less need to explain themselves in relation to Augustine, simply asserting the Protestant position as correct. Thus, Zanchi says,

> But like as the corruption of our whole nature immediately by God's just judgment took hold on the person of Adam for that actual disobedience called of the Apostle concupiscence, which is both a punishment of the former sin, a sin, and a cause of other sins, even so being taught by the holy scriptures.[133]

And,

> concupiscence of its own nature is a sin, fighting against the law of God and making men subject to condemnation . . . yea, that in the regenerate

---

[129] "Apology of the Augsburg Confession," *Book of Concord*, 240.

[130] John Calvin, *Institutes of the Christian Religion*, ed. John T. McNeill, trans. Ford Lewis Battles, 2 vols. (Louisville: Westminster/John Knox, 1960), 2:1311–12.

[131] Calvin, *Institutes*, 1:602.

[132] Calvin, *Institutes*, 1:602.

[133] Girolamo Zanchi, *Confession of the Christian Religion*, vol. 1, ed. R. Bast, L. Baschera, and C. Moser (Leiden, Netherlands: Brill, 2007), 169b.

themselves, though the guiltiness being taken away by faith in Christ, it be not imputed unto them anymore, yet we doubt not but it is a sin, yea, and that worthy of eternal death.[134]

John Davenant writes similarly: "this inbred propensity or habit of inordinate concupiscence . . . makes man prone to transgress the law of God."[135] Davenant is more than willing to distinguish proper forms of desire, non-sinful concupiscence, from coveting or lust: "we must understand that the word concupiscence sometimes denotes the mere faculty of desire . . . we grant that it is a good creature of God."[136] Yet when paired with sin, "it denotes the contagion or unruly tendency, which has infected the faculty itself; and this disorder, we say, is formally repugnant to that rectitude which God has impressed upon the same faculty."[137]

This position on concupiscence is mostly constant throughout the Reformed scholastics.[138] There is some difference between the categorization of concupiscence as merely original sin or as a sort of actual sin. Summarizing the Reformed tradition, Herman Bavinck points out that the Reformed rejected the argument that sin had to be voluntary to be sin, but he notes that this meant only that some sins can precede the exercise of the will, not that they would ever exist wholly apart from the will. Bavinck invokes the distinction between original sin and actual sin to account for this. Concupiscence prior to consent is sin, but in the category of original sin. After receiving consent, concupiscence becomes a particular actual sin.[139] Davenant had given a similar explanation: "the corrupt disposition, which inclines internally to actual sin, is most properly Original Sin . . . so although the faculty of desire itself is not sin, yet the inclination and propensity of it to evil is sin; even in one asleep, when it does not at all actually incline to sin."[140]

Zacharias Ursinus, however, is willing to consider concupiscence a sort of actual sin, but of the "non-reigning" variety. Here he continues Luther's categories of "reigning sin" and "reigned-over sin." Ursinus writes,

[134] Zanchi, *Confession of the Christian Religion*, 171.
[135] John Davenant, *A Treatise on Justification*, vol. 1, trans. Josiah Allport (London: Hamilton, Adams, 1844), 126.
[136] Davenant, *Treatise on Justification*, 126.
[137] Davenant, *Treatise on Justification*, 126.
[138] Francis Turretin, *Institutes of Elenctic Theology*, ed. James T. Dennison Jr., trans. George Musgrave Giger, 3 vols. (Phillipsburg, NJ: P&R, 1997) 1:637, 639–40; Witsius, *Economy of the Covenants*, trans. William Crookshank (London: T. Tegg, & Son, Cheapside, 1837), 60–62; Heinrich Heppe, *Reformed Dogmatics*, ed. Ernst Bizer (Grand Rapids, MI: Baker, 1950), 331–41; Herman Bavinck, *Reformed Dogmatics*, ed. John Bolt, trans. John Vriend, 4 vols. (Grand Rapids, MI: Baker, 2003–8), 3:142–44.
[139] Bavinck, *Reformed Dogmatics*, 3:143.
[140] Bavinck, *Reformed Dogmatics*, 3:127.

Sin which does not thus reign, is that which the sinner resists by the grace of the Holy Spirit. It does not, therefore, expose him to eternal death, because he has repented and found favor through Christ. Such sins are disordered inclinations and unholy desires, a want of righteousness, and many sins of ignorance, of omission, and of infirmity, which remain in the godly as long as they continue in this life; but which they, nevertheless, acknowledge, deplore, hate, resist, and earnestly pray may be forgiven them for the sake of Christ, the Mediator, saying, forgive us our debts. Hence the godly retain their faith and consolation, notwithstanding they are not free from these sins. "If we say we have no sin, we deceive ourselves, and the truth is not in us." "It is no more I that do it, but sin that dwelleth in me." "There is no condemnation to them that are in Christ Jesus, who walk after the Spirit." "Who can understand his errors? Cleanse thou me from secret faults" (1 John 1:8. Rom. 7:18; 8:1. Ps. 19:13.).[141]

Notice that Ursinus includes "disordered inclinations and unholy desires" in this category of "sin which does not thus reign." This all follows an earlier distinction Ursinus made between original and actual sin. Concupiscence, for Ursinus, is a kind of actual sin but a non-reigning sin, and "it does not . . . expose him to eternal death." In fact, Ursinus is even willing to use the language of "venial" sin in this respect, though he cautions that such can easily be misunderstood.

John Owen referred to this "non-reigning sin" simply as "indwelling sin." Owen writes,

And this also lies in it as it is enmity, that every part and parcel of it, if we may so speak, the least degree of it that can possibly remain in any one, whilst and where there is any thing of its nature, is enmity still. It may not be so effectual and powerful in operation as where it hath more life and vigour, but it is enmity still. As every drop of poison is poison, and will infect, and every spark of fire is fire, and will burn; so is every thing of the law of sin, the last, the least of it—it is enmity, it will poison, it will burn.[142]

Owen believes that "the meanest acting, the meanest and most imperceptible working of it, is the acting and working of enmity."[143] Concupiscence is, then, always moving from original to actual sin. Importantly, the believer

---

[141] Zacharias Ursinus, *Commentary on the Heidelberg Catechism* (Phillipsburg, NJ: P&R, repr. of 1852 ed.), 45. Q. 7.
[142] John Owen, "The Nature, Power, Deceit, and Prevalency of the Remainders of Indwelling Sin in Believers," in *The Works of John Owen*, ed. William H. Goold and Andrew Thomson, 16 vols. (Carlisle, PA: Banner of Truth, 1966), 6:177.
[143] Owen, "Nature, Power, Deceit," 177.

can mortify this sin, as the grace of God makes it so that "the heart is not habitually inclined unto evil by the remainders of indwelling sin."[144] Thus it is not reigning sin. But concupiscence itself remains "a constant, habitual propensity unto evil in itself or its own nature,"[145] and so the believer must constantly be engaged in the mortification of the flesh, throughout his or her entire life.

Owen also contributes an answer to the popular question, "Is temptation sin?" He answers that external temptations are not sin, but internal temptations are. Owen writes, "Now, when such a temptation comes from without, it is unto the soul an indifferent thing, neither good nor evil, unless it be consented unto; but the very proposal from within, it being the soul's own act, is its sin."[146] This follows from the fact that concupiscence is sin. Internal temptations are effects of the disordered desires of the soul.

Concupiscence in the Reformed Confessions

Concupiscence is explicitly present in at least three Reformed Confessions. The Thirty-Nine Articles of the Church of England state that original sin brings about concupiscence and that concupiscence "hath of itself the nature of sin."[147] The Irish Articles state that original sin includes a "bent unto sin" and then repeats that concupiscence is sin by nature.[148] Finally, this same line of argument appears in the Westminster Confession of Faith:

> From this original corruption, whereby we are utterly indisposed, disabled, and made opposite to all good, and *wholly inclined to all evil*, do proceed all actual transgressions. . . . This corruption of nature, during this life, doth remain in those that are regenerated; and although it be through Christ pardoned and mortified, *yet both itself and all the motions thereof are truly and properly sin.*[149]

The Westminster Confession is describing concupiscence when it says that the sinner is "wholly inclined to all evil" and the "motions" of the corrupt nature are sin. Therefore, the Westminster Confession declares concupiscence to be "truly and properly sin."

---

[144] Owen, "Nature, Power, Deceit," 191.
[145] Owen, "Nature, Power, Deceit," 191.
[146] John Owen, "Temptation and Sin," in *Works of John Owen*, 6:194.
[147] Thirty-Nine Articles of the Church of England, Article 9, in *Documents of the English Reformation*, ed. Gerald Bray (Cambridge: James Clarke, 2004), 290.
[148] Irish Articles of Religion, Articles 23 and 24, in *Documents of the English Reformation*, ed. Bray, 441.
[149] WCF 6.4, 5.

Contemporary Applications

Having now demonstrated the biblical and historical meaning of concupiscence, we can return to our current day and evaluate how concupiscence might apply to contemporary debates. Concupiscence is a corruption caused by original sin which pervades the whole of the human person and inclines them toward sin. It exists particularly as inordinate desire, and it constantly wars against the leading of the Spirit of God. Concupiscence is also the source of internal temptation toward sin. For Protestants, concupiscence is always sin, whereas for Roman Catholics it is sin in the unbaptized and potential sin in the baptized. What might this mean for ongoing discussions in the contemporary evangelical church?

The first thing we should note is that concupiscence is a universal problem. While it does indeed apply to things like homosexuality, it also applies to a great many heterosexual sins. Any form of lusting or coveting is sinful concupiscence. The desire to have sexual relations with someone other than one's spouse is concupiscence (Matt. 5:28), as is any desire to have multiple spouses (Matt. 19:5). Further, even certain sexual activity within marriage can be considered concupiscence. We do not have to fully agree with Augustine's view that excitement and great pleasure are necessarily forms of concupiscence.[150] Indeed, there would seem to be some biblical reason to disagree; for example, Proverbs 5:19 encourages a husband to be "intoxicated" or "enraptured" by romantic love for his wife.[151] Still, any pursuit of sexual pleasure that sacrificed or violated other goods would be a sort of concupiscence. Thus, all selfish and self-centered sexual actions would be sinful, as well as immoderate or overindulgent ones. Always having "sex on the brain," so to speak, or prioritizing the physical aspects of sex over the emotional and spiritual good of oneself or others would also be a form of concupiscence. The fact that such desires seem to be instinctual is no vindication. Given what we know of concupiscence, that is precisely what we would expect. The heart wants what it wants, but it is deceitful and desperately sick; who can understand it? (Jer. 17:9).

The question of contraception is another place where the doctrine of concupiscence can help to clarify categories. For Augustine, and indeed for the overwhelming majority of the Christian tradition, contraception was simply

---

[150] Augustine, *On the Merits*, in *NPNF*¹ 5:59; *Against Julian*, 284.
[151] The Hebrew word used in this verse is שָׁגָה, which literally means to "stagger because of . . . wine" (*HALOT* 2:1413).

off-limits. It was considered sin because it prevented the procreational end of sex, which was the primary if not the only truly legitimate end. Later Protestant thinkers were willing to discuss multiple legitimate ends of sex, but none advocated for contraception until the twentieth century. It is beyond the limits of this essay to mount any kind of case for or against contraception, but we can say that the doctrine of concupiscence teaches that any potential use of contraception would have to be justified as a rational and temperate means to other compelling goods. It could never be used simply to allow for pleasure without consequence, and it could never be used so thoroughly as entirely to prevent procreation. All intentionally child-free marriages would be condemned as justifying concupiscence.

So then, what of the debates around "LGBTQ" or "Side-B" Christianity, as it has become known in some circles? Again, concupiscence would apply to any and all inordinate or disordered desires. Such desires are an effect of original sin, and their earliest motions are themselves a species of actual sin. The desires themselves and internal temptations, not merely the outward actions, are sinful. This also applies to the matter of "orientation." Mark Yarhouse explains that a homosexual or "gay" orientation means an "enduring same-sex attraction . . . when same-sex attraction is strong and persists over time."[152] He distinguishes this from particular same-sex attractions themselves, as well as from any particular social or political "identity" that a person may choose to claim. Orientation is, thus, a prior tendency or inclination. The doctrine of concupiscence is immediately relevant to these same categories. The particular attractions would be clear forms of lust, specific and actual motions of concupiscence, even to the point of being sorts of active or actual sins. The ongoing orientation, however, would be more like the "habit" or "propensity" toward the evil lusting. It would therefore be considered the "tinder" of sin in the Catholic system or "abiding" sin in the Protestant system—in either sense, it would be concupiscence. The challenge for the Christian struggling with an orientation of same-sex attraction would be for the individual so affected to mortify such sin, to make sure that it remains "reigned-over" sin rather than "reigning-over sin," to use Luther's and Ursinus's categories. If not acted upon, such an orientation would still be understood to be sin, but sin forgiven in Christ. If it were acted upon (even mentally), however, it would become a new actual sin, in need of new repentance.

[152] Mark Yarhouse, *Sexual Identity and Faith* (Conshohocken, PA: Templeton, 2019), 61.

This historical framework can also help us evaluate certain popular contemporary articulations of the moral status of same-sex temptation from evangelical writers. For instance, Sam Allberry writes,

> Same-sex temptations (along with any other kind of temptation to sin) reflect our own fallenness. But this is not the same as saying *the presence of temptation* itself is a sin to be repented of. Scripture makes a distinction between temptation and sin. . . . But we need to be careful not to imply that a Christian who is faithfully resisting temptation is in sin merely for experiencing the temptation. . . . The sincere Christian who is deeply distressed at the temptations he or she is facing may be crushed by the idea that, merely having the capacity to be tempted in this way, they are thereby sinning.[153]

Allberry's book is otherwise commendable, but his statement here stands in contradiction to the historical Protestant case presented in this chapter. It is important to note at the outset that temptations per se do not necessarily reflect fallenness, as is seen in the case of Christ and his temptations. Related to this, Allberry's failure to explain the difference between external temptations from the world and the devil and internal temptations arising from our own sinful nature leads him to collapse a necessary distinction: the same-sex temptations or homosexual attraction that he speaks of are *internal* temptations that arise from a sinful human nature. By collapsing internal temptations into external temptations, and then distinguishing temptation in general from sin, Allberry in effect recategorizes same-sex attraction as an amoral entity—a "temptation"—and thus not a sin. But as the discussion above has demonstrated, same-sex attraction, biblically understood, *is* a sin, not merely a temptation. Indeed, it is not even merely a "consequence of the fall," as Allberry contends, something akin to getting "sick."[154] These points of confusion arise from the fact that Allberry's book lacks any discussion on the nature of concupiscence. While a short popular book might be excused for neglecting a scholastic doctrine, in this case the deficiency puts Allberry in contradiction to the larger Protestant moral tradition.

Another example of this muddled confusion in some evangelical circles is Wesley Hill's book *Spiritual Friendship*. Hill writes,

---

[153] Sam Allberry, *Is God Anti-Gay? And Other Questions about Jesus, the Bible, and Same-Sex Sexuality* (Epsom, Surrey, UK: Good Book Company, 2023), 60–61 (emphasis original).
[154] Allberry, *Is God Anti-Gay?*, 41: "It is not un-Christian to experience same-sex attraction any more than it is un-Christian to get sick."

Being gay is, for me, as much a sensibility as anything else: a heightened sensitivity to and passion for same-sex beauty that helps determine the kind of conversations I have, which people I'm drawn to spend time with, what novels and poems and films I enjoy, the particular visual art I appreciate, and also, I think, the kind of friendships I pursue and try to strengthen. I don't imagine I would have invested half as much effort in loving my male friends, and making sacrifices of time, energy, and even money on their behalf, if I weren't gay. My sexuality, my basic erotic orientation to the world, is inescapably intertwined with how I go about finding and keeping friends.[155]

Hill is clear in other places that he views sexual activity between persons of the same sex to be sinful,[156] but he is not so clear on the status of the orientation itself. In the above quote, he seems to be combining his "basic erotic orientation to the world" with his sociability. His propensity toward friendship, a natural and good tendency, is "inescapably intertwined" with his disordered sexual tendencies, that is, with concupiscence. He does not present this as a sort of corruption of the original good, though he notes the dangers that are always present. Hill's solution is to "channel" or "sublimate" his "longings for same-sex intimacy in the direction of chaste friendship."[157] While the goal here is consistent with the historic Christian ethic, the classical Protestant tradition would explain these concepts differently. The same-sex orientation, "being gay," would be an aspect of original sin; its remaining presence as an ongoing pre-volitional inclination would be concupiscence.

A 2022 podcast with Ed Shaw and his "Living Out" ministry team also highlights a number of confusions which older dogmatic categories and distinctions could correct.[158] Shaw and his team are seeking to answer the question "Is same-sex attraction inherently sinful?" Their proposed answer is "no." They initially try to explain that the act of being attracted to someone is complex. One might be attracted to virtues within the other person, or the attraction might be mixed with a desire for their friendship. But Shaw understands that this is not the root issue, and so he proposes a distinction between the temptation and the desire: "Alongside good things like friendship, there

---

[155] Wesley Hill, *Spiritual Friendship: Finding Love in the Church as a Celibate Gay Christian* (Grand Rapids, MI: Brazos, 2015), 80–81.

[156] Wesley Hill, *Washed and Waiting: Reflections on Christian Faithfulness and Homosexuality* (Grand Rapids, MI: Zondervan, 2016), 65–72.

[157] Hill, *Spiritual Friendship*, 81.

[158] "Is Same-Sex Attraction Inherently Sinful? (Questions No One Wants to Answer #4)," https://www.livingout .org/resources/podcasts/36/is-same-sex-attraction-inherently-sinful-questions-no-one-wants-to-answer-4 (accessed February 24, 2022).

will be a temptation to sin, it seems to me; it will be a part of the experience."[159] In this quote, Shaw is demonstrating the relationship between internal temptation and concupiscence. He appears to see them as distinct, with only the latter being sinful. One of Shaw's cohosts then expands upon this thought and takes it in a direction which runs contrary to the Protestant understanding of concupiscence:

> I've got this instinctive, in a sense, human response, and yes, we're fallen humans, so that might be shaped, impacted, distorted by sin, but there's an innate human experience happening. I've got to choose. Do I let that entice me into sin, as James 1 talks about, or do I let that lead me somewhere good and do something healthy with it?[160]

We can see here an assumption that "fallen" desires are "distorted by sin" but not necessarily sinful until acted upon, at least volitionally. A Protestant could agree that the original "innate human experience" would have been good, but after man's fall into sin, the experience is filled with concupiscence. The distortion is precisely within the desire.

Shaw admits that these various phenomena are not easily separable:

> I'd love to be able to say that my instinctive response, when experiencing attraction to another guy, is automatically to go towards praising the Lord for beauty, but there's probably something else because of the reality of sinful desire within us wanting to take me in a different direction . . .[161]

He recognizes that the intermixture of original good desire and distorted fallen desire is so thorough as to be experientially inseparable. However, he resolves this dilemma by arguing that the desire is not yet itself sinful:

> One of the key moments for me was wrestling with [the question] "What is Jesus thinking at the moment when I'm seeing an attractive guy, what am I going to do with that?," and feeling the pressure to go in a bad direction with it, [then] seeing Jesus as one who is fundamentally sympathetic, that he's looking down and saying, "I sympathize. I know what temptation is like and was able to resist it." Actually seeing Jesus, in that moment, as sympathetic is fundamentally useful in not turning same-sex attraction into a sinful pattern of thinking and behavior.[162]

---

[159] 13:47 time-mark of the above podcast.
[160] 16:11 time-mark.
[161] 16:42 time-mark.
[162] 17:21 time-mark.

This quote again shows the distinction between the temptation and the sin. Shaw further argues that Jesus is "sympathetic" to the one being tempted, invoking Hebrews 4:15. Here there is a potential equivocation. Jesus can indeed sympathize with the experience of temptation, but only external temptation, since he was always "yet without sin." He does not, therefore, share the internal temptations characterized by concupiscence. Given this, we may say that Jesus sympathizes with us as humans going through temptation, but he never experienced inordinate desires or misdirected loves. Jesus can share the common experience of being tempted without sharing all particular temptations. Insofar as Shaw means to discuss a misplaced erotic attraction, then, his argument does not acquit such a desire from being sinful. Jesus, capable of external temptations, never had an illicit internal attraction. To argue otherwise would be to deny the perfect righteousness of Christ in his life under the law.

With a proper understanding of the Protestant tradition, the "Living Out" team should say that same-sex erotic attraction is indeed sinful, because it is an expression of concupiscence, but that it can become a "reigned-over sin" through the transformative grace of God, repentance, and a life of Christian discipline. Even if the pull of such an internal desire is never fully extinguished in this life, its power can be greatly reduced. It need not bring eternal guilt upon believers. This is true not because same-sex attraction lacks the nature of sin, but rather because it can be forgiven and conquered through the atoning work of Christ. As the apostle Paul affirms, Christ died *for* sin (1 Cor. 15:3) and *to* sin (Rom. 6:10); that is, in his death Christ paid the *penalty* of sin and conquered the *power* of sin. These older dogmatic categories and distinctions can bring clarity to an ongoing debate, and they may even provide the means for certain authors to sharpen their understanding and improve their articulation of their position, so that they become more consistent with their overarching goals.

As relevant as discussions over sexuality currently are, we should also remember that concupiscence is a form of coveting, a violation of the tenth commandment. As such, it is not limited to sex but applies to every manner of consumption. Cultures of excess or greed are guilty of concupiscence. Any economic strategy or system which separates profit from the common good—the love of God and the love of one's neighbor—would fall under such condemnation. This even applies to popular sorts of self-help and self-discovery. Adopting boutique lifestyle choices or going on adventurous trips to "find oneself" can often be ways of indulging inordinate desires and sacrificing other compelling duties. "Gap years" and "midlife crises" are very often euphemisms for concupiscence. A deeper interrogation of our goals and desires would humble us all. The mere fact that a desire "comes from the heart" does not make it good, whether it be sexual love, professional vocation, or self-discovery.

Conclusion

This brings us back to the relationship between concupiscence and justification by faith alone. Since concupiscence is so deeply rooted within us, it is simply not possible to consider any aspect of our nature as being without blame. Even our best deeds have some level of false motivation, selfishness, or inordinate desire. Therefore, concupiscence must humble us to the point where we cry out for mercy. No flesh can be justified "by the works of the law" (Rom. 3:20; Gal. 2:16). No one can be truly righteous "in themselves" (see Rom. 3:10; Phil. 3:9). The only way that any of our works could be accepted by God is if we are first forgiven of our sins, and if our inherent guilt is not imputed (Ps. 143:2; Rom. 3:22–26). And this requires an atonement found only in the work of Christ. Indeed, the more we understand the doctrine of concupiscence, the more we understand the gospel. That is surely the most relevant, and the most practical, application of all.

22

On Revelation and the Psychical Effects of Sin

TOWARD A CONSTRUCTIVE PROPOSAL[1]

Nathaniel Gray Sutanto

[Bonaventure has] an uncluttered sense that created intelligence is *flooded by divine light*, and by the simple fact that it never occurs to him to think that the arts of the mind may be secular. . . . Bonaventure is a positive divine, one for whom the mind's powers are encompassed and *accompanied by* a gift and light which are not of the mind's invention.[2]

The theory of the unconscious finds support in Holy Scripture insofar as it definitely takes the view that the soul is much richer and deeper than the consciousness . . . and it posits this thought as basic to its doctrine of sin . . .[3]

[To suppress the truth] need not be understood as a conscious action. It can be developed in total silence in the human heart. I am inclined to understand this in the sense of repression, as the concept of repression has been developed in recent psychology. As a rule, repression occurs unconsciously, but that makes it no less real.[4]

Talk of the effects of sin on the mind and will tend to focus on how we are willfully resistant to God's revelation, or how we fail to infer the proper

---

[1] My thanks to Michael Allen for reading an earlier draft of this paper.
[2] John Webster, "*Regina Atrium*: Theology and the Humanities," in *The Domain of the Word: Scripture and Theological Reason* (London: T&T Clark, 2012), 174, emphasis added.
[3] Herman Bavinck, "The Unconscious," in Bavinck, *Essays on Religion, Science, and Society*, ed. John Bolt, trans. Harry Boonstra and Gerrit Sheeres (Grand Rapids, MI: Baker Academic, 2008), 197.
[4] J. H. Bavinck, "Religious Consciousness in History," in *The J. H. Bavinck Reader*, ed. John Bolt, James Bratt, Paul J. Visser, trans. James De Jong (Grand Rapids, MI: Eerdmans, 2008), 242.

things about God from that revelation, or how we fail to come to know God at all, becoming ignorant. Instead of focusing on these effects of sin, however, this chapter focuses on how sin has corrupted the soul—the seat of the will and the intellect. As such, the *psychical* effects of sin have caused creatures to suppress the knowledge of God in a way that is pre-theoretical and pre-volitional—it is an act of second nature that requires no conscious action or reflection. In order to do this, however, one needs first to attend to how it is, precisely, that God's revelation impacts the human soul in general.

This chapter takes its cue from particular moves in Herman and Johan Bavinck, the medieval theologian Bonaventure, and the contemporary work in cognitive and behavioral philosophy represented by Hubert Dreyfus. My purpose here is not historical; the aim is not to argue that there is a direct line of dependence that can be traced among these thinkers; nor is my purpose here merely conceptual, that is, merely to establish that there are concep-tual overlaps between these thinkers; neither am I making the case that my proposal here is simply identical with the neo-Calvinists, Bonaventure, or Dreyfus. Rather, I attempt to build a constructive sketch about the psychical effects and location of sin that stands on these thinkers eclectically.

First-generation neo-Calvinists characterized general revelation as a pre-theoretical and primordial reality that impacts human consciousness: God is known not by way of propositions inferred from nature by reason, but by way of pre-predicative *feeling or awareness*. God himself implants this revelatory pressure on every human being, resulting in this affective aware-ness. Bonaventure, in a conceptually overlapping fashion, sketched a view of illumination that is presupposed by and is the context of the mind's rational capacity. Intuitive awareness of God is ever-present to the human creature. Herman Bavinck and Bonaventure both followed the Augustinian method of ascending to God by turning inward by the divine light: God is found in the depths of the soul. God's revelation penetrates deep within the human self.

Building on these two accounts of the primordial character of God's revelation, I propose a sketch of the psychical effects of sin along these lines: in correspondence with general revelation's primordial and pre-cognitive re-ception in the unconscious, the suppression of that revelation in sin consists not merely in an inferring of wrong conclusions about God or a conscious act of the will, but firstly in the unconscious and intuitive ways in which the heart suppresses the truth. That is, just as the *givenness* of God's revelation penetrates sinners in the *psyche*, the soul that is the seat of the will and the intellect, so should we understand the psyche as the primary locus of sin's effects that inhibits the proper reception of the givenness of that revelation. Sin, then, affects not only the intellectual capacity of creatures to apprehend the givenness of God's general revelation and the clarity of special revelation.[5] As James K. A. Smith has observed, just as "there are cognitive or noetic effects of sin upon 'understanding,' there are also affective effects of sin upon aesthetic 'perception.'"[6]

This essay fleshes out how it is that sin is carried out on the level of *psychical* knowing and perception. Drawing from contemporary work on the unconscious nature of skillful coping as carried out by second-nature habits (in Hubert Dreyfus), this chapter argues that the suppression of the truth is a function of the sinful nature, and as such is a *species of skillful coping*—namely, it is an ingrained and natural act of sinful human beings that needs *no willful consciousness* to carry out—we suppress the truth in the same way as a jazz musician skillfully improvises without consciousness, or in the same way as it is second nature for trauma victims to avoid certain triggers and patterns of thought. Common grace thus allows unbelievers to function properly despite their skilled suppression of the truth, and allows for "moments" in which suppression fails to arise, allowing that unconscious awareness to become consciously present in an unbeliever's mind. In this way, my proposal goes well with Alan Noble's call for Christians to perform habits that become "disruptive witnesses" to challenge the second-natured way in which nonbelievers ignore God.[7]

To these ends, then, this chapter proceeds in four steps. First, I draw from Herman and Johan Bavinck on the primordial way in which revelation penetrates the human psyche, and that suppression of the truth is *psychical* rather than merely epistemological. Second, I retrieve Bonaventure's claim that God is the first being known by human beings as the fount of all knowledge,

---

[5] The givenness of which I speak here is not to be confused with the "myth of the given" that has been disputed by philosophers like Wilfred Sellars and more recently by John McDowell. While more needs to be said about Herman Bavinck's representationalist epistemology and the current phenomenological accounts of McDowell, the focus on the psychical and unconscious knowing here, in my view, is compatible with Sameer Yadav's constructive account that builds on McDowell and Nyssa, to the effect that the world is primordially meaningful to us precisely because it is the theater of God's revelation (see Sameer Yadav, *The Problem of Perception and the Experience of God: Toward a Theological Empiricism* [Minneapolis: Fortress, 2015]; Nathaniel Gray Sutanto, "Review of *The Problem of Perception and the Experience of God: Toward a Theological Empiricism*," *Journal of Theological Studies* 67.2 [October 2016]: 875–77).

[6] James K. A. Smith, "Questions about the Perception of 'Christian Truth': On the Affective Effects of Sin," *New Blackfriars* 88 (2007): 592.

[7] Alan Noble, *Disruptive Witness: Speaking Truth in a Distracted Age* (Downers Grove, IL: InterVarsity Press, 2018).

and that one ascends to God by way of attending to the divine illumination provided within the soul.[8] Third, I then argue that Hubert Dreyfus's account of skillful coping in reference to daily acts of habit is an apt way to describe our skilled ability to suppress our ever-present knowledge of God. Finally, in a brief conclusion, I shall revisit the *locus classicus* of Romans 1 to show the explanatory power of this proposal as a way of reading some of the more perplexing portions of this passage.

I. Herman and Johan Bavinck on General Revelation, the Psyche, and Suppression[9]

In a chapter of *Philosophy of Revelation* that dealt with the *locus* of revelation's impact on human beings, Herman Bavinck observed that revelation is "the secret of the mind."[10] This observation is the conclusion to a train of reasoning that investigated the inner depths of one's consciousness. Prompted by Augustine, Bavinck argued that the knowledge of God is somehow apprehended precisely by looking within, by piercing that which is behind conscious thinking and willing:

> Thus Augustine went back behind thought to the essence of the soul, and found in it not a simple unity but a marvelously rich totality; he found there the ideas, the norms, the laws of the true and the good, the solution of the problem of the certainty of knowledge, of the cause of all things, of the supreme good; he found there the seeds and germs of all knowledge and science and art; he found there even, in the triad of *memoria*, *intellectus*, and *voluntas* . . . a reflection (*afdruk*) of the triune being of God. Augustine was the philosopher of self-examination, and in self-consciousness he discovered the starting point of a new metaphysics.[11]

In other words, in the depths of self-consciousness, "we find at its very root the consciousness of dependence. In our self-consciousness we are not only conscious of being but also of something definite, of being the very

---

[8] Despite my focus on Bonaventure here, I have argued that Bavinck's construal of revelation, feeling, and reason conceptually meshes the accounts of illumination offered by Bonaventure *and* Aquinas. See my *God and Knowledge: Herman Bavinck's Theological Epistemology* (London: Bloomsbury T&T Clark, 2020), ch. 7.

[9] This section is a revision of particular parts of my "Neocalvinism on General Revelation: A Dogmatic Sketch," *IJST* 20 (2018): 495–516.

[10] Herman Bavinck, *Philosophy of Revelation: A New Annotated Edition*, ed. Cory Brock and Nathaniel Gray Sutanto (Peabody, MA: Hendrickson, 2018), 59.

[11] Bavinck, *Philosophy of Revelation*, 55. On Bavinck's use of Augustine in conjunction with Romantic thought in a way that complements this present essay, see Cory Brock and Nathaniel Gray Sutanto, "Herman Bavinck's Reformed Eclecticism: On Catholicity, Consciousness, and Theological Epistemology," *SJT* 70 (2017): 310–32; and Cory Brock, *Orthodox Yet Modern: Herman Bavinck's Use of Friedrich Schleiermacher* (Bellingham, WA: Lexham, 2020).

thing we are."[12] Creatures always feel their dependence on external objects (relatively) and on God (absolutely). As Bavinck wrote explicitly, Schleiermacher was quite right in his claim that consciousness of self involves a consciousness of one's dependence:

> And this definite mode of being, most generally described, consists in a dependent, limited, finite, created being. Before all thinking and willing, before all reasoning and action, we are and exist, exist in a definite way, and inseparable from these is a consciousness of our being and of its specific mode. The core of our self-consciousness is, as Schleiermacher perceived much more clearly than Kant, not autonomy, but a feeling of dependence. In the act of becoming conscious of ourselves we become conscious of ourselves as creatures. . . . We feel ourselves dependent on everything around us; we are not alone.[13]

What Bavinck maintains, then, is the claim that there is something "immediate" about the "existence of both the world and God."[14] Indeed, "in self-consciousness both the existence and the specific mode of existence of the self, the ego, are revealed."[15] Bavinck is here arguing that there is a bond between self and reality, between the self and its knowledge of the self as a unified whole, that is obtained prior to "all thinking." This is a knowledge in consciousness not reducible to the conscious entertaining of propositions that are believed—it is an assumed consciousness that is part and parcel of one's existence in the world.

Bavinck grounds these claims not in the innate powers of the human soul, but in the reality of divine revelation. Again, "revelation, is the secret of the mind; in our self-consciousness, independently of our co-operation and apart from our will, the reality of our ego and of the world is revealed to us."[16] Evoking Acts 14 and 17, Bavinck ties self-consciousness with the general revelation of God:

> God, the creator of all nature, has not left himself without witness but through all nature, both that of man himself and that of the outside world,

---

[12] Bavinck, *Philosophy of Revelation*, 56.
[13] Bavinck, *Philosophy of Revelation*, 56–57.
[14] Bavinck, *Philosophy of Revelation*, 57.
[15] Bavinck, *Philosophy of Revelation*, 58.
[16] Bavinck, *Philosophy of Revelation*, 59. So, Schleiermacher: "If man is not one with the Eternal in the unity of intuition and feeling which is immediate, he remains, in the unity of consciousness which is derived, forever apart" (Schleiermacher, *On Religion: Speeches to Its Cultured Despisers*, trans. John Oman [Louisville: Westminster/John Knox, 1994], 40).

speaks to him . . . revelation alone accounts for the impressive and incontrovertible fact of the worship of God. In self-consciousness God makes known to us man, the world, and himself.[17]

In his treatment on the unconscious life, Bavinck relates these moves to Kant's notion of intuition and to Augustine's inner sense of the self:

> [In consciousness, there is] observing, remembering, judging, knowing; but also feelings, both sensory and spiritual. . . . Consciousness is knowledge, and awareness, "knowing" what goes on inside of me. And second, it is an immediate awareness. It is a knowledge obtained not through external sense organs or through deliberate research and serious study but directly through immediate experience, through an "inner sense" [inneren Sinn], as Kant called it, in imitation of the *sensus interior* of Augustine and the Scholastics. . . . This immediate awareness, which is part of and is produced by certain psychic phenomena, has an attendant character: it is a direct and concomitant consciousness.[18]

But how, exactly, is something known apart from all thinking and willing? These claims are illumined when they are situated alongside other texts in Bavinck's corpus. In Bavinck's treatment of the knowing faculty in his *Beginselen der Psychologie*, Bavinck argues that feeling is not a separate faculty, but a specific activity of the knowing faculty in the psyche. After summarizing the contemporary positions that describe the faculty of feeling (*gevoelvermogen*), Bavinck argues that it is a mistake to locate feeling as a separate faculty alongside other faculties (of knowing and desiring): "feeling . . . taken in the subjective sense and as an immediate sensation or consciousness of agreeable or unagreeable states, is not a particular faculty, nor can it be." Rather, "As sensation or consciousness [feeling] belongs with all intuitions [beseffen], impressions [indrukken], perception, concepts, and so on, to the knowing faculty [kenvermogen]."[19] Feeling considers the same objects

---

[17] Bavinck, *Philosophy of Revelation*, 66.

[18] Bavinck, "Unconscious," 176. The gloss for the original German is included in the translation cited. It should be clear here that Bavinck's sense of the word "immediate," as reflected in these passages, does not refer to the acceptance of the notion that creatures can know God in his essence. Bavinck accepts that creatures know God immediately in the sense that this knowledge of God obtains directly because of God's revealing action, but mediately in the sense that revelation never grants us unmediated knowledge of God's essence. "Even in cases where he reveals himself internally in the human consciousness by his Spirit, this revelation always occurs organically and hence mediately. The distance between the Creator and creature is much too great for human beings to perceive God directly" (*Reformed Dogmatics*, ed. John Bolt, trans. John Vriend, 4 vols. [Grand Rapids, MI: Baker Academic, 2004], 1:309–10). Where most relevant, I draw the original texts from Herman Bavinck, *Gereformeerde Dogmatiek*, 3rd ed, 4 vols. (Kampen, Netherlands: Kok, 1918).

[19] Bavinck, *Beginselen der Psychologie* (Kampen, Netherlands: Bos, 1897), 55. Unless indicated otherwise, translations are my own.

of knowledge as the intellect, but knows them in a different mode—again, a knowledge prior to thinking and willing. Appealing to Arthur Schopenhauer, Bavinck makes the significant move in *locating feeling as a function of the knowing faculty*. In his words,

> Through feeling, we indicate, as Schopenhauer rightly said, all immediate and direct *knowing that precedes thinking and reflection, which is in contrast to knowledge in abstract concepts and in the state of reasoning.* Just as when something is told, we feel instinctively whether [that which is said] is true or untrue. From here it is decisive that feeling in this sense is not a special [separated] faculty, but a special activity within the knowing faculty.[20]

This articulation of feeling as an immediate awareness, sensation, or perception, however, should again not be mistaken to be a detached and reflective contemplation on the truth of particular propositions. It is more akin to the knowledge about our sense of touch and of the inner states of the soul. Bavinck argues clearly that it is a knowledge that may obtain apart from conscious reflection, and it is here that he specifies that feeling indicates an inner certainty because it is a knowledge without concepts: "This way of taking cognizance is of the highest significance . . . it is not less certain than [reasoning and thinking], but exceeds far above them in certainty. But it is indeed less clear and conscious, *precisely because it is not a knowledge in concepts* [*juist omdat zij geen kennis in begrippen*], and is not the fruit of deliberate reflection and reasoning."[21]

Herman Bavinck, then, opened up the possibility of holding that there is an unconscious knowledge that is felt rather than articulated—an immediate awareness that is known by the body and is not reducible to the forms of justified true belief. One might come to know God, then, without entertaining an explicit proposition—knowledge of God remains ubiquitous and universal, rendering all humankind without excuse in a manner not contingent on explicit forms of propositional belief.[22]

---

[20] Bavinck, *Beginselen der Psychologie*, 57, emphasis added; in the original Dutch, "Door het gevoel duiden wij, zooals Schopenhauer terecht zeide, al die onmiddellijke, rechtstreeksche, aan alle denken en reflectie voorafgaande kennis aan, welke tegen de kennis in abstracte begrippen en redeneeringen overstaat. Zoodra ons iets verteld wordt, voelen wij instinctief, dat het waar of onwaar is. Maar daarmede is dan ook beslist, dat het gevoel in dezen zin geen bijzonder vermogen is, maar eene bijzondere werkzaamheid van het kenvermogen."

[21] Bavinck, *Beginselen der Psychologie*, 57–58, emphasis added. These claims are related to Bavinck's understanding of revelation as received *prior to* innate and acquired knowledge, creating impressions and intuitions, in his *Reformed Dogmatics*, 2:68–73.

[22] For a fuller explication of this line of reasoning, see esp. Cory C. Brock and N. Gray Sutanto, *Neo-Calvinism: A Theological Introduction* (Bellingham, WA: Lexham Press, 2023), ch. 4 on revelation and reason.

These claims, taken from works that pre-date and post-date the *Reformed Dogmatics*, reveal a strongly Romantic strand in Bavinck's thinking on general revelation. Revisiting his claims in the *Reformed Dogmatics* in light of the above analysis would thus prove illuminating, while also providing a fuller picture of his dogmatic thought. His *God and Creation* followed the classical Reformed understanding of general revelation, and thus that God reveals himself through nature and the human conscience. Bavinck, however, went on to argue that this revelation had both an objective and a subjective side.[23] On the objective side, rational agents perceive God through the things that are made.[24] On the other hand, he argued that the objective side of revelation "only highlighted one side of the truth" and required an analysis of the subjective side of revelation.[25] This included affirming the classical understanding that humans are born equipped with the apparatus required to reason unto God: "we possess both the capacity (aptitude, faculty) and the inclination (*habitus*, disposition) to arrive at some firm, certain, and unfailing knowledge of God."[26] But, more so, in the subjective side of revelation Bavinck also affirmed that God reveals himself primordially and internally, arguing that there is an "interior impact of revelation upon [humanity's] consciousness"[27] that "precedes" both the implanted and acquired knowledge of God.[28] God exerts a "revelatory pressure."[29]

It is this revelatory pressure that forms the basis for all cognitive acts. "Accordingly, the innate knowledge of God is not opposed to the acquired knowledge of God, for, in a broader sense, also the former can be called acquired. In fact, *God's revelation precedes both*, for God does not leave himself without a witness."[30] This revelation creates impressions (*indrukken*)

---

[23] Bavinck, *Reformed Dogmatics*, 1:586. This coheres with Bavinck's emphasis throughout his works on the correspondence between subject and object: "All life and all knowledge is based on a kind of agreement between subject and object."

For more on the subject-object relationship in Bavinck, see Henk van den Belt, *The Authority of Scripture in Reformed Theology: Truth and Trust* (Leiden, Netherlands: Brill, 2009), 233ff.; Nathaniel Gray Sutanto, "Herman Bavinck and Thomas Reid on Perception and Knowing God," *HTR* 111.1 (January 2018): 115–34, esp. 124–31; Cory Brock and Nathaniel Gray Sutanto, "Herman Bavinck's Reformed Eclecticism: On Catholicity, Consciousness, and Theological Epistemology," *SJT* 70 (2017): 310–32.

[24] Bavinck, *Reformed Dogmatics*, 2:69.

[25] Bavinck, *Reformed Dogmatics*, 2:70.

[26] Bavinck, *Reformed Dogmatics*, 2:71.

[27] Bavinck, *Reformed Dogmatics*, 2:72.

[28] Bavinck, *Reformed Dogmatics*, 2:73.

[29] Bavinck, *Reformed Dogmatics*, 2:73.

[30] Bavinck, *Reformed Dogmatics*, 2:73. Though Nicholas Wolterstorff, "Herman Bavinck—Proto Reformed Epistemologist," *CTJ* 45 (2010): 139, cites this passage, he takes no notice of this statement and focuses instead only on the immediately formed beliefs of which Bavinck speaks. Insofar as Wolterstorff and Plantinga focus solely on knowledge as involving warranted (or justified) true belief, Bavinck's articulation of feeling as knowledge remains elusive. Indeed, if feeling is an activity of knowing, then Bavinck is open to the possibility that knowledge can be had without there being an explicit proposition to be believed. Romantic presence is irreducible to propositional belief.

and intuitions in a manner that correlates with Bavinck's comments on feeling in his analysis of the psyche. These impressions, then, are cognized and thematized by the conscious workings of the mind:

> And humans, having been created in the divine image, were gifted with the capacity to receive the impressions [*indrukken*] of this revelation and thereby to acquire some sense and knowledge of the Eternal Being. The innate knowledge of God, *the moment it becomes cognition and hence not only cognitive ability but also cognitive action, never originated apart from the working of God's revelation from within and without, and is to that extent therefore acquired.*[31]

In a manner consistent with his *Beginselen der Psychologie* and *Philosophy of Revelation*, Bavinck's *Reformed Dogmatics* contained a strand of Romanticism in his understanding of general revelation even while he sought to preserve classical Reformed lines of reasoning on this dogmatic locus. Though Bavinck included both nonconceptual and conceptual awareness under the definition of "knowledge," it might be useful to refer to the former as a kind of *phenomenological* awareness that precedes explicit conceptual forms of knowledge, for clarity's sake.[32]

If Herman Bavinck argued that revelation is initially received in the psyche, known by way of feeling rather than cognition, J. H. Bavinck, too, articulated general revelation along these lines.[33] God's general revelation does not imply that humanity ought to know him by the "natural light of reason" alone.[34] In this regard, Bavinck argues that one must "disentangle" general revelation from the "abstract philosophical accretions" that attended its articulations, and must set it "in terms of biblical reality."[35] Thinking,

---

[31] Bavinck, *Reformed Dogmatics*, 2.73 (*Gereformeerde Dogmatiek*, 2.51). Bavinck expresses this same thought consistently in his Stone lectures: "For revelation always supposes that the human is able to receive impressions or thoughts or inclinations from another than this phenomenal world, and in a way other than that usually employed" (*Philosophy of Revelation* 175)

[32] As implied in this analysis, this pre-theoretical revelation of God does not mean that reason is denigrated or rendered wholly passive in Bavinck's thought. It is reason's role to bring about clear concepts out of these impressions. I explore the implications of these claims to natural theology, and the scholarship on the continuity between Herman and J. H. Bavinck, in "Neocalvinism on General Revelation: A Dogmatic Sketch," 509–16. For further clarifications on the matter, see as well my "*Gevoel* and Illumination: Bavinck, Augustine, and Bonaventure on Awareness of God," *Pro Ecclesia* (Online First, 2021): 1–14.

[33] This reception of general revelation, it should be noted, is due wholly to the reliable and dynamic action of God as the subject, rather than the human agent.

[34] This is not to claim that reason ought to play no role in articulating those beliefs. Indeed, the neo-Calvinists argued that reasoning had an appropriate place—the point, however, is that revelation is a primordial feature of creaturely existence precisely because God never leaves himself without a witness, and that revelation precedes and is independent of human reasoning.

[35] J. H. Bavinck, "Religious Consciousness in History," 238.

reasoning, observing, and conscious reflection are not "where God meets" humankind. Rather, "the meeting point of general revelation," J. H. Bavinck writes, is "first of all in the problems inherent in being human, that is, in being a fallen human being."[36] In his reflections on the matter, he surveys a few biblical texts before homing in on the classical locus of Romans 1. Commenting on Psalm 19, Bavinck observes that general revelation is paradoxical precisely because God reveals without words: "This passage is all about speech without words, witness without words, that makes an impact on people with invisible force and against which they have no defense because it engulfs them all around in its silent majesty."[37] From Amos 4:13, he argues that there is a direct revealing act of God upon what he interprets to be the self-consciousness in human beings. If God "makes known his thoughts to men," then, he reasoned, something "of God also exists in the great mystery of that double effect on our self-consciousness. It is directly connected to God."[38] In Psalm 139 and Job 33:14–17, he surmises, revelation is intrinsically personal—an encounter that pervades the individual's conscience. Acts 17, further, teaches that this "language without speech" is intended by God to evoke a response—the universal religious consciousness that produces the pagan religions forms precisely that response to general revelation when special revelation is rejected or unavailable.

Finally, J. H. Bavinck argues that Romans 1 declares that God makes himself "manifest" through "voiceless speech."[39] General revelation occurs not so much in the propositions that philosophers infer from an active reflection on nature; it is more primitively related to the relations that image-bearers have with their environment and with each other, along with the direct workings of God in their consciousness. The force of the text, in God making it "plain" to all of humankind (Rom. 1:19), is that it is this revelation that "grips them in their inner lives."[40] That this revelation is described as being "understood" (Rom. 1:20 NIV) indicates that God's revelation truly penetrates into every human being: "The apostle wants to show clearly here that it is not only possible, but that it actually happens."[41] This, in turn, renders intelligible why humanity is said to be without excuse. That general

---

[36] J. H. Bavinck, "Religious Consciousness and Christian Faith," in *J. H. Bavinck Reader*, 279.
[37] J. H. Bavinck, "Religious Consciousness in History," 235.
[38] J. H. Bavinck, "Religious Consciousness in History," 236.
[39] J. H. Bavinck, "Religious Consciousness and Christian Faith," 277.
[40] J. H. Bavinck, "Religious Consciousness in History," 242.
[41] J. H. Bavinck, "Religious Consciousness in History," 244.

revelation does not produce true worship, then, is not because of a failure for humans to reason unto God, so that they are ignorant of him; rather, it is because they suppress this unconscious knowledge in a similarly unconscious fashion.[42] This "repression," J. H. Bavinck reasons, is psychological in nature and irreducible to erroneous epistemological inferences that lead to false beliefs. As cited in the beginning of this chapter, suppression

> need not be understood as a conscious action. It can develop in total silence in the human heart. I am inclined to understand this in the sense of repression, as the concept of repression has been developed in recent psychology. As a rule, repression occurs unconsciously, but that makes it no less real.[43]

To be sure, J. H. Bavinck's appeal to psychology is not meant to suggest that he adopts uncritically a kind of Freudian emphasis according to which the act of repression so submerges a particular subconscious state or memory such that one can be totally unaware of it. The categories of unconscious knowledge and suppression here are used precisely to argue that it is a "real" suppression by the sinful psyche—the innermost beings of the image-bearers. As such, it is a responsible suppression and repression of that which is clearly revealed. Knowledge of God "actually happens" because God's revelation is penetrative and pervasive—suppression's unconscious character emphasizes not our lack of responsibility but exactly our culpability. Suppression has become so second nature that its occurrence needs no conscious action.[44] In this, Johan Bavinck's analysis of the psyche complements his uncle's, especially as the latter judges that the unconscious is to be related to the soul. A "theory of the unconscious finds support in Holy Scripture insofar as it definitely takes the view that the soul is much richer and deeper than the consciousness . . . and it posits this thought as basic to its doctrine of sin."[45]

---

[42] J. H. Bavinck's reading of Rom. 1:19–21 seems to conflict with Rik Peels, particularly when the latter claims that the text refers to a merely "*propositional* knowledge that there is such a being as God and that he exemplifies certain properties" in contrast to "having experiential knowledge or knowledge *by acquaintance* of God and living in thankful response to God" (Rik Peels, "Sin and Human Cognition of God," *SJT* 64 [2011]: 403, emphases original). J. H. Bavinck's reading, in other words, argues that unbelievers, too, have an intimate knowledge of and acquaintance with God irreducible to propositional knowledge: but it is an intimate knowledge of their relational break with their Creator and their failure to live in proper response to God's glory. Peels's reading is certainly a strong dogmatic account of general revelation, because it upholds that all creatures know God—but in his reading he would have to account for the empirical observation that nonbelievers often do not consciously (at least in a way that we have access to) believe that they hold to be true certain propositions about God.
[43] J. H. Bavinck, "Religious Consciousness in History," 242.
[44] For a recent philosophical exposition of unconscious knowledge and knowing via a kind of "second nature" compatible with the sketch I offer here, see, e.g., Andrew Inkpin, *Disclosing the World: On the Phenomenology of Language* (Cambridge, MA: MIT Press, 2016).
[45] Herman Bavinck, "Unconscious," 197.

This emphasis on the holistically personal character of revelation's en-counter with the human psyche brings into view the primordial relationship that image-bearers have with the created world around them. There is a bond that connects subject-and-object—a bond through which general revelation comes. General revelation "must be understood more existentially."[46] Speak-ing in a Romantic fashion, Johan Bavinck writes,

> General revelation occurs in the living connection between people and the world around them, in what one could call the symbiotic relationship be-tween people and the world. Older philosophy was once inclined to isolate people too much from the world and to consider humanity in isolation. *It regarded humanity as a subject over against the world. And when it made humanity the object of its study, it placed primary emphasis on humanity's observational and thinking relationship to the world.* We need to keep in mind that humanity exists in an unbreakable and living relationship with the world and that it can never be isolated from it for even one moment.[47]

The upshot seems clear: humanity's reception of general revelation is not contingent on their active use of reasoning, nor is it contingent on their developing an active *habitus* so that they can infer the existence of God from contingent things.[48] As Paul Visser notes, this does not rule out an appropriate place for conscious reflection: "the structured religions demon-strate this reflection" on divine revelation.[49] It does, however, resist a confla-tion between revelation and the conscious use of natural reason. A focus is then placed on the relational and holistic accounts of knowing that might be

---

[46] J. H. Bavinck, "Religious Consciousness and Christian Faith," 278.

[47] J. H. Bavinck, "Religious Consciousness and Christian Faith," 278, emphasis added. Paul Visser, in the introduc-tion to the reader, observes that J. H. Bavinck's doctoral thesis argued that "the processes of thinking and learning, far from occurring autonomously, are closely tied to an intuitive apprehension of given reality. It is precisely the operation of this feeling in the process of human reasoning that points to the influence of the human self" (Visser, "Introduction," in *J. H. Bavinck Reader*, 8).

[48] J. H. Bavinck regards this to be in tension with the thought of Roman Catholicism (see esp. "Religious Conscious-ness in History," 25–68). Matthew Levering's description of Thomas Aquinas seems relevant: "Unlike Anselm, then, Aquinas does not think that the fool is actually, in the strict sense, a fool; the fool's statement is not, as Anselm thinks it to be, logically nonsensical. Rather, the fool, due ultimately to the effects of original sin, lacks the specula-tive *habitus* that would enable him to reason to God from contingent things" (Levering, *Scripture and Metaphysics: Aquinas and the Renewal of Trinitarian Theology* [Oxford: Blackwell, 2004], 59).

J. H. Bavinck further suggested that the Reformed account of missions and general revelation were thus dif-ferent from Thomas. In J. H. Bavinck's interpretation, Thomas "clearly distinguishes between truths that can be understood through the natural light of human reason and those that must be revealed to humans as mysteries of faith. He proposed that missionaries should first build on general concepts that could be derived from natural the-ology when they encountered paganism and then seek ways to teach the mysteries of faith from this foundation" ("General Revelation and the Non-Christian Religions," in *J. H. Bavinck Reader*, 97).

It might be illuminating here to consider the neo-Calvinists as upholding a (Romantic) mixture of what Lydia Schumacher has described as the *concursus* and *influentia* models of divine illumination. See esp. her *Divine Illumination: The History and Future of Augustine's Theory of Knowledge* (Oxford: Blackwell, 2011), 142–78.

[49] Vissers, "Introduction," 45.

eclipsed by an emphasis on explicit awareness and reflection. Image-bearers "have a permanent fellowship with God, *even when we are not aware of it.* Human life consists of a continual dialogue with God, a conversation that God continues to initiate. This I-Thou relation comprises the core of our existence."[50]

II. Bonaventure on Illumination: A *Concursus* Model

Commenting on John 1:5, Johan Bavinck remarks that the author "is thinking here of the ever-present revelation of the Logos in the world, in human consciousness."[51] Indeed, the neo-Calvinistic emphasis of revelation's precognitive and primordial character highlights the presence and action of God who reveals himself to the human psyche rather than the innate powers of the human self to know God. To emphasize this dimension further, Bonaventure's account of illumination is helpful in stressing the dependence we have on God to know all things and his ever-present light in creatures, both pre-fall and post-fall. As one shall see, retrieving Bonaventure's account along with the neo-Calvinistic sketch I have provided above depicts a powerful picture of divine revelation as a primordial feature of human cognition, even as the fall has corrupted the human soul.

Bonaventure argues in his *Itinerarium mentis in Deum* that creatures, in order to know particulars and mutable objects, need a knowledge of that which is immutable and exemplary. Rather than moving from mutable things to the immutable in a movement of mere ascent, he argues that human beings require a knowledge of pure being in order to comprehend finite and mutable beings. The anagogical ascent toward the knowledge of God, therefore, is a tracing back to *a priori* knowledge that God has imparted of himself to every human being: "being is that which first comes into the intellect, and this being is that which is pure act."[52] Commenting on this specific passage, Christopher Cullen observes that, for Bonaventure, "the intellect could not attain a single concept unless it knew what being is per se, and being cannot be known unless it is grasped together with its essential predicates—simplicity, necessity,

---

[50] Visser, "Introduction," 44, emphasis added. Visser notes that J. H. Bavinck, too, was influenced by Schleiermacher in his account of humanity's religious response to God: "Bavinck had serious reservations about much of Friedrich Schleiermacher's theology. Yet he was influenced by Schleiermacher's notion of religion as the 'feeling of dependence' and wholeheartedly agreed with Schleiermacher's rejection of the rationalistic construct of *religio naturalis*, adopting this as a point of departure for his own work" (Visser, "Introduction," 34).

[51] J. H. Bavinck, "Religious Consciousness in History," 247.

[52] Bonaventure, *Itinerarium mentis in Deum*, ed. Philotheus Boehner and Sr. M. Frances Laughlin, trans. Philotheus Boehner, vol. 2 (St. Bonaventure, NY: Franciscan Institute, 1956), ch. 5 (308b).

absoluteness, and eternity."[53] In short, human beings first know God, and it is through this knowledge of God that they come to know created things.

Bonaventure specifies that it is specifically Christ, as the eternal divine wisdom, that is the precondition of our knowing. By virtue of the doctrine of appropriation, according to which the three persons of the Godhead share the same essential properties but those properties can be predicated properly of each person distinctly, Bonaventure ascribes "efficiency to the Father, exemplarity to the Son, and finality to the Spirit."[54] Illumination, therefore, reveals that the Son is the exemplar to which all things point. The Son is wisdom, light himself, in whom the ontological principles of creation and redemption subsist, and in his light do we see light:

> Not only is Wisdom capable of knowing [all things]: it is the very principle of knowing. Therefore, it is called "light," as being the principle of knowing all that is known; "mirror," as being the principle of knowing all that is seen and approved; "exemplar," as being the principle of knowing all that is foreseen and disposed; "book of life," as being the principle of knowing all that is predestined and reprobated.[55]

Bonaventure's argument here is not that creatures are thus left to themselves to look for patterns of God's wisdom in creation. His doctrine of illumination is more direct, and involves the active involvement of the divine word in aiding every creature. God's light is present with and attends the human mind at every point, such that "there is an intuitive grasp of the divine being . . . the condition for the possibility of grasping finite being in the first place is that there is an intuitive grasp of infinite being. God is the light in which the intellect sees."[56]

In other words, there is no conflation in Bonaventure's mind between created reason and the divine light that illumines. The divine light is *not* creaturely reason, but aids it at every point.[57] It is present concurrently with

---

[53] Christopher Cullen, *Bonaventure* (Oxford: Oxford University Press, 2006), 61; cf. Peter S. Dillard, *A Way into Scholasticism: A Companion to St. Bonaventure's The Soul's Journey to God* (Eugene, OR: Cascade, 2011), 557.

[54] Bonaventure, *Breviloquium*, ed. Dominic Monti (St. Bonaventure, NY: Franciscan Institute, 2006), 1.6.4. On appropriation, Bonaventure writes, ". . . regarding the plurality of appropriations, Holy Scripture teaches us to hold the following: that even though all the essential attributes apply equally and without distinction to all the persons, yet oneness is appropriated to the Father, truth to the Son, and goodness to the Holy Spirit. . . . in the Father is the efficient principle, in the Son the exemplary principle, and in the Holy Spirit the final principle" (*Breviloquium*, 1.6.1).

[55] Bonaventure, *Breviloquium*, 1.8.2.

[56] Cullen, *Bonaventure*, 62.

[57] Bonaventure, *Disputed Questions on the Knowledge of Christ*, ed. George Marcil, trans. Zachary Hayes (St. Bonaventure, NY: Franciscan Institute, 1979), 4.

every act of creaturely cognition. Lydia Schumacher sums up this argument in this way:

> [Bonaventure] maintains that the Son exerts a direct influence on the human agent intellect through the eternal reasons, which supervise and sustain the work of human reason. Because of those reasons, the active work of the intellect is a cooperative effort or concursus on the part of the human mind and its "inner teacher," Christ.
>
> Without the supernatural support for natural cognition that is received from Christ, human beings would be unable to know reality with complete certainty.[58]

There is, in a sense, an *a priori* structure to Bonaventure's doctrine of illumination—but it is important here to stress that he is not advocating a rationalist theory of innate ideas, nor is his insistence on God's illumination as a precondition for knowing reducible to or identical with Immanuel Kant's categories—something that Bavinck himself recognized about Bonaventure.[59] Efrem Bettoni's remark regarding the difference between Bonaventure and Kant is worth heeding:

> For St. Bonaventure the "a priori" is merely a human participation in the divine thought which has created things according to the archetypes eternally generated with and in the word. Kant ends in the absolute subjectivity while St. Bonaventure guarantees the objectivity of our thought by basing it on the absolute objectivity of divine knowledge. And thus the abyss between the two thinkers remains intact: the abyss between immanence and transcendence.[60]

Bonaventure follows Augustine's modifications of Plato's doctrine of reminiscence here and grounds this "primordial awareness of God" in the "presence of God to the soul."[61] Again, Lydia Schumacher: "it is His light that supplements or concurs with the human cognitive light so that it can truly illumine reality."[62]

As such, it is unclear that Schumacher's conclusion is warranted when she infers that, for Bonaventure, it is the "human mind," which "is adequate

[58] Schumacher, *Divine Illumination*, 130. See also Dominic Monti, "Introduction," in Bonaventure, *Breviloquium*, ed. Dominic Monti (St. Bonaventure, NY: Franciscan Institute, 2006), xli–xlii.
[59] Bavinck defends Bonaventure from the charge that he advocated a theory of innate ideas, while suggesting that, as previously noted, Bonaventure's explicit treatment of Scripture as a starting point to the *Breviloquium* is worthy of emulation (Bavinck, *Reformed Dogmatics*, 2:65 and 1:97, respectively).
[60] Efrem Bettoni, *Saint Bonaventure*, trans. Angelus Gambatese (Westport, CT: Greenwood, 1981), 103, cited in Cullen, *Bonaventure*, 62–63.
[61] Cullen, *Bonaventure*, 63.
[62] Schumacher, *Divine Illumination*, 142.

to acquire accurate and absolutely certain understanding of all things," from Bonaventure's claim that Christ aids the mind at every point.[63] It seems, rather, that the argument establishes precisely the opposite case: that the mind's turn inward marks not that it is a self-sufficient foundation for knowing but that it is radically dependent on God's ever-present illumination.[64] Further, that human beings continue to enjoy an intuitive knowledge of God after the fall highlights, again, not primarily humanity's innate intellectual prowess post-fall but God's faithful action.[65] Objectively, the knowledge of God is self-evident and ever-present, but subjectively, "from the deficiency of reason," God may be doubted "because of a threefold defect in the mind of the knower: in the act of apprehending, in the act of judging, or in the act of analyzing."[66] This internal illumination, in turn, requires the clarifying illumination of the superior light of Scripture: "Thus it follows that Holy Scripture, even though it is concerned mainly with the works of restoration, must necessarily also deal with the works of creation, insofar as they lead to the knowledge of the first effective and recreating principle."[67]

Bonaventure's theory of illumination is a *concursus* model, in contrast to an *influentia* one. A *concursus* model argues that God instills his light in the human mind in such a way that it is ever-present; it attends every cognitive act, is distinguished from reason, and is that which directly aids reason, concurring with it toward certitude, apprehension, and wise judgment. An *influentia* model, by contrast, argues that the divine light in us *is* our created reasoning capacity. God is said to be our light by virtue of creating us with the capacity of reasoning. One participates in the divine

---

[63] Schumacher, *Divine Illumination*, 145. For more on Bonaventure's understanding of the noetic effects of sin, see my "Questioning Bonaventure's Augustinianism?: On the Noetic Effects of Sin," *New Blackfriars* 102 (2021): 401–17.

[64] Cf. Schumacher, *Divine Illumination*, 132. Schumacher seems to conflate the ground for the intuitive knowledge of God in fallen humans, however, at times attributing this to God's illumination and at other times to fallen humanity's innate intellect. Later, Schumacher argues that Bonaventure's proposal that Christ "intervenes in human cognitive processes" somehow means that the mind "discovers itself as the perfectly adequate foundation for all knowledge" (*Divine Illumination*, 146 and 149, respectively). Schumacher makes this inference to argue the controversial case that Bonaventure began a trajectory of a kind of rationalist subjectivism that departs from Augustine. While this might have been an unintended consequence in later Franciscan theology, it remains unclear, however, that Bonaventure, on his own terms, could be read in this fashion. Rather, I remain persuaded in Cullen's observation that the proper conclusion from Bonaventure's analysis of God's knowledge as primordial is that "all knowledge is a form of enlightenment and that all light flows from the fontal source of light" (Cullen, *Bonaventure*, 30 [see also pp. 63–64 on reason's deficiency]).

[65] "Without the illumination of the Word, humanity would know nothing of the underlying structures of the universe, and yet sinful human beings have failed to recognize the source of their knowledge and trace it back to its First Principle. As such, they can no longer read 'the book of creation' effectively" (Dominic Monti, "Introduction," XLII; contra Schumacher, *Divine Illumination*, 149).

[66] Cullen, *Bonaventure*, 64. On this, see esp. Bonaventure, *Disputed Questions on the Mystery of the Trinity*, ed. George Marcil, trans. Zachary Hayes (St. Bonaventure, NY: Franciscan Institute, 1979), Q. 1.

[67] Bonaventure, *Breviloquium*, 2.5.2.

light just as one uses reason rightly. In a *concursus* model, the divine light is an extrinsic force that thus aids human reasoning directly from above. An *influentia* model, instead, posits that what "comes from above . . . is not the mind's ideas themselves but the *ability* to form ideas on the basis of things below. Put differently, the divine light is an intrinsic as opposed to extrinsic force."[68]

This ever-present character of illumination—ever-present due to God's active revealing work, not due to the innate power of the human mind—informs the shape of Bonaventure's account of the arts.[69] As divine illumination is the fount out of which all human knowledge comes to be, all of the arts can be traced back to its divine origins, as God's being and the human's unification with God encircles creation's beginning and end. The title of Bonaventure's "companion piece to the *Itinerarium*,"[70] *On the Reduction of the Arts*, signals these moves: the arts can be reduced, not in the sense that the work of scholarship is insignificant or of only peripheral importance, but in the sense that they inescapably reveal vestiges of God's self to the contemplative mind.[71] Bonaventure is keen on emphasizing, however, that the arts are reduced back to God precisely because divine illumination attends every act of human knowing and is ever present in the human mind.[72] As such, "to lead the arts back to theology means, for Bonaventure, to show the organic connection between all the arts and the central concern of the Scriptures or theology. None of the arts, including philosophy, ought to be allowed to stand as an independent and self-sufficient discipline."[73] The movement of reduction is a "movement of knowledge" which raises our awareness of reality to a more explicit, "conscious, cognitive level."[74] Failure to trace all things back to God would be a fundamental failure to understand the objects under study, as every object of human knowledge is patterned after divine ideas that preexist them in God.

---

[68] Schumacher, *Divine Illumination*, 176. Schumacher identifies *concursus* with Bonaventure's account of illumination while distinguishing that from Aquinas's *influentia* model (cf. Cullen, *Bonaventure*, 62). In *God and Knowledge*, ch. 7, I argue that Bavinck meshes Bonaventure and Aquinas precisely in the sense that he adopted both *concursus* and *influentia* patterns of reasoning with respect to divine revelation and illumination.

[69] These next few paragraphs borrow from *God and Knowledge*, 166–67.

[70] Cullen, *Bonaventure*, 30. Cullen provides a succinct summary of the *Reduction* and the scholarly impact of the work on pp. 30–35. See also Webster's elegant close reading in his *"Regina Atrium*," 174–82.

[71] "Bonaventure speaks of the philosophical disciplines and states that there is nothing in these disciplines which does not imply a vestige of the Trinity" (Zachary Hayes, "Introduction," in Bonaventure, *On the Reduction of the Arts to Theology*, trans. Zachary Hayes [St. Bonaventure, NY: Franciscan Institute, 1996], 3).

[72] Hayes, "Introduction," 3.

[73] Hayes, "Introduction," 2.

[74] Hayes, "Introduction," 8.

The *Reduction* opens with James 1:17, which Bonaventure takes to refer to "all illumination."[75] A single "fontal" light produces many lights, and even "though every illumination of knowledge is internal," Bonaventure continues to make a distinction between the exterior, inferior, interior, and superior lights.[76] The exterior lights refer to the mechanical arts, which have to do with the domestic life: weaving, agriculture, hunting, and so on. The inferior light refers to sense perception, while the interior refers to philosophical knowledge. The superior light is the light of grace and Holy Scripture.

The light of Scripture is "superior" as it reveals truths "which transcend reason," and as such cannot be acquired by human reason, but comes down from God himself "by inspiration."[77] But here, it is key not to miss that the superior light is not just the apex of human knowledge, but is that on which all of knowledge rests:

> And as all those lights had their origin in a single light, so too all these branches of knowledge are ordered to the knowledge of sacred Scripture; they are contained in it; they are perfected by it; they are ordered to the eternal illumination by means of it. Therefore all our knowledge should come to rest in the knowledge of Scripture, and particularly in the *anagogical* understanding of Scripture through which any illumination is traced back to God from whom it took its origin.[78]

This understanding of Scripture's integral and foundational role for knowledge of God and the rest of the sciences informs Bavinck's (controversial) judgment that Thomas's organization of his *Summa* is "inferior" to Bonaventure's, as the latter included a doctrine of Scripture in the prologue to his *Breviloquium*.[79] In Bavinck's perspective, Bonaventure's organization prevented him from structuring reason and revelation as merely two forms of knowing side by side in a dualist fashion.

John Webster, commenting on Bonaventure's view of Scripture in the *Reduction*, describes it this way:

---

[75] Bonaventure, *On the Reduction of the Arts*, § 1.
[76] Bonaventure, *On the Reduction of the Arts*, § 1.
[77] Bonaventure, *On the Reduction of the Arts*, § 5.
[78] Bonaventure, *On the Reduction of the Arts*, § 7, emphasis original. Schumacher, commenting on the *Reduction*, puts it rather starkly: "If the sciences through which the external world is studied (weaving, metal-working, architecture, agriculture, hunting, navigation, medicine, and drama) and the philosophical lines of inquiry pursued by the intellect (natural philosophy, rational philosophy, and moral philosophy) are not evaluated in reference to the superior light, or the attendant forms in the mind of Christ, any inquiry into them will not result in wisdom. It will fail to illumine the true nature of the realities that are under consideration. If Christ is not given his place at the center of all areas of study, in summary, then study has no meaning whatsoever" (Schumacher, *Divine Illumination*, 142–43).
[79] Bavinck, *Reformed Dogmatics*, 1:98–99.

> The light of Scripture is superior because it is not simply one of the set of other illuminations of the arts of the mind, but that which affords comprehensive illumination of technical, intellectual and moral culture in its entirety. The illumination given by Scripture pervades and interpenetrates the whole of creaturely knowing; it is its surrounding atmosphere, not simply another set of materials on which to go to work. . . . This is why the light of Holy Scripture is not commensurate with the other lights, but the light upon which their particular lights depend.[80]

The reduction proper, then, finds that all of the arts conform to a pattern that befits the eternal generation of the word of God, the ordained pattern of human life, and the soul's unification with God. Hence, for example, just as the word of God is eternally begotten, so sense perception manifests how objects stimulate a "similitude," which proceeds from the object by way of a sense.[81] The delight that we find in particular objects, as well, mirrors the soul's delight in having God as their object. And so on.

The key here is not that Bonaventure's reductions are convincing at every point, but to note simply what he does: every form of human knowledge can be traced back to a contemplation of God's being, the source of illumination. Bonaventure repeats the same point in various ways: divine wisdom "lies hidden in sense knowledge,"[82] "the illumination of the mechanical arts is a path to the illumination of sacred Scripture,"[83] "all natural philosophy . . . presupposes the Word of God as begotten and incarnate,"[84] such that "the wisdom of God lies hidden in natural philosophy."[85] If for Bavinck revelation is the "secret of the mind," so in Bonaventure illumination is what lies beneath the arts. The Scriptures manifest in a greater light what humans had already known by illumination: "it is evident that the *manifold wisdom of God*, which is clearly revealed in sacred Scripture, *lies hidden in all knowledge and in all nature.*"[86] Cullen's summary here is apt: "All knowledge must be 'reduced' to the one truth of Christ. Indeed, there can be no truth apart from Christ, the

---

[80] Webster, *"Regina Atrium,"* 176.

[81] Bonaventure, *On the Reduction of the Arts*, § 8.

[82] Bonaventure, *On the Reduction of the Arts*, § 10.

[83] Bonaventure, *On the Reduction of the Arts*, § 14.

[84] Bonaventure, *On the Reduction of the Arts*, § 20.

[85] Bonaventure, *On the Reduction of the Arts*, § 23. Behind this is Bonaventure's logos-centric understanding of the Word as the divine exemplar of all things. See, e.g., *Breviloquium*, 1.6.1–5, 1.8.2, 2.1.4; Schumacher, *Divine Illumination*, 122, 126; Cullen, *Bonaventure*, 71–77.

[86] Bonaventure, *On the Reduction of the Arts*, § 26, latter emphasis added. Etienne Gilson's comment here is relevant: "Thus, for him [Bonaventure], the philosophy of St. Albert and St. Thomas was of necessity in error because, while it situated Christ in the center of theology, it did not situate Him in the center of philosophy" (Gilson, *The Philosophy of St. Bonaventure*, trans. Dom Illtyd Trethowman and Frank J. Sheed [Paterson, NJ: St. Anthony Guild Press, 1965], 28).

Metaphysical Center."[87] As a result, "all knowledge and art reflect the font of intelligibility."[88]

Sin inhibits creatures from contemplating the arts in a way that traces them back to God.[89] Thus, it is not as if the noetic effect of sin here is in causing creatures to become unaware of God, and henceforth they are to become aware of God through reasoning. Not so: Bonaventure's project forms a circle. Precisely because the mind is already illumined by a light that discloses God's pure and unchangeable being, the reduction of the arts to theology is not merely about coming to know the higher truths of God in Scripture. Again, Webster's observation here is apt: "creatures illuminate the world only insofar as their acts are themselves illuminated. Only as acts of knowing are bathed in light can they be the means of seeing our way around the world or of giving ourselves a truthful picture of it."[90] Prior divine illumination is a precondition of creaturely knowing, and thus sin does not strip creatures of God's illumination, but rather inhibits them from properly recognizing what is always there. Creatures know things just *as* they know God, and they come to know things because of God's prior action. Restorative grace aids reason: "The rational power needs help in considering, choosing, and following the truth: through the gift of understanding it is directed to the consideration of the truth; through the gift of counsel, to choose the truth; and knowledge to carry out what has been chosen."[91]

Like Bavinck, Bonaventure followed the Augustinian logic of ascending upward by attending to the depths of the soul, guided by the reality of God and his light:

> The journey of the mind in each step is made possible by divine illumination. He follows the Augustinian method of ascent to God in the *Confessions*, in which Augustine speaks of returning to himself and then entering into his inward self in order to behold the inner light. From within, he looks above.[92]

---

[87] Cullen, *Bonaventure*, 32. See also Therese Scarpelli, "Bonaventure's Christocentric Epistemology: Christ's Human Knowledge as the Epitome of Illumination in 'De Scientia Christi,'" *Franciscan Studies* 65 (2007): 68–69, which reinforces the same observation.

[88] Cullen, *Bonaventure*, 90.

[89] Bonaventure, *On the Reduction of the Arts*, § 12. Though Bonaventure argues that the contamination of sin involves the absence of original justice, causing our "souls to incur a four-fold penalty: weakness, ignorance, malice, and concupiscence," he nonetheless highlights that every *actual* sin is located primarily in the will: "Therefore every sin is a disorder in the mind, or more precisely in the will, which is the source of both virtue and vice" (*Breviloquium*, 2.5.2, 2.8.2, respectively).

[90] Webster, "*Regina Atrium*," 176.

[91] Bonaventure, *Breviloquium*, 5.5.4.

[92] Cullen, *Bonaventure*, 87.

III. Suppression as *Skillful Coping*: A Theological Reinterpretation of Dreyfus's Model

The previous two sections highlight the pervasiveness of God's revelation and its inescapability. Instead of offering an account of revelation that focuses on the propositions apprehended by reason or accepted by the will, they make a case that revelation penetrates the inner depths of the *soul*—that seat of the will and reason.[93] Here, I suggest that Hubert Dreyfus's work on skillful coping as the primordial context in which reasoning and willing occur fits well with the accounts offered by the Bavincks and Bonaventure above, and that his account can also be reinterpreted theologically in the context of the doctrine of sinful humanity's suppression of the truth, as outlined in Romans 1. I will begin by summarizing the broad strokes of Dreyfus's project, before giving a theological re-appropriation of his model.

Dreyfus's project is extensive in scope, so we can highlight only the most relevant features for our purposes here. Dreyfus's account of skillful coping contains at least these three interrelated features: (1) Conceptual reasoning and conscious acts of the will are not the main ways in which human beings exhibit expertise. (2) Human skillfulness, instead, manifests itself in the intuitive, noncognitive, and non–volitionally responsive ways in which one copes with environmental affordances. (3) Skillful coping marks not only the master's expertise but also everyday existence. Willful action and conceptual reflection, then, always take place in the context of "everyday practice" that lies beneath "our theoretical presuppositions and assumptions."[94]

First, then, Dreyfus situates his argument against the backdrop of the Platonic and Western philosophical tradition that privileged the intellect. Human beings, intellectualists argued, act according to explicit or implicit conceptual rules, and practical knowledge itself could be extracted into a set of maxims one can then replicate and follow. Whether it was in the case of Plato himself, who argued that "[e]xperts had once known the rules they used . . . but then they had forgotten them,"[95] or, more recently, in John McDowell's model,

---

[93] I follow Bonaventure here, who argued that "a joint capacity of will and reason [form] the principal faculties of the soul," such that "the entire soul has a two-fold capacity: cognitive and affective" (*Breviloquium*, 2.9.1 and 2.9.6, respectively). This agrees with Bavinck's analysis in "Primacy of the Intellect or the Will," in Bavinck, *Essays on Religion, Science, and Society*, ed. John Bolt, trans. Harry Boonstra and Gerrit Sheeres (Grand Rapids, MI: Baker Academic, 2008), 199–205.

[94] Hubert Dreyfus, *Skillful Coping: Essays on the Phenomenology of Everyday Perception and Action*, ed. Mark A. Wrathall (Oxford: Oxford University Press, 2014), 134.

[95] Dreyfus, *Skillful Coping*, 27.

according to which all human expertise and perception are always at least implicitly conceptual, the Western tradition prioritized the conceptual over the phenomenological.[96]

This prioritization of the mental over the phenomenological, however, is mistaken. Two lines of argument support Dreyfus's thesis. First, Dreyfus observes that the hope that artificial intelligence can replace human expertise, if only it had all of the same information and rules, has been dashed. Current cognitive and technological research continue to produce evidence that artificial, computer intelligence simply cannot reproduce, say, the chess master's ability to intuit, anticipate, and creatively respond to the opponent's challenges. Nor could artificial intelligence replicate the simple ways in which children seem to be able to intuit stories, or sense the social climate of a relational interaction. In either case, though human beings are often incapable of articulating how precisely they can sense the particular moves they ought to make, they are able to perform with fluid coping in ways that machines cannot.

The second line of evidence is our second point: a human becomes skilled at something precisely when that "skill has become so much a part of him that he need be no more aware of it than he is of his own body."[97] Dreyfus's argument here explicates the relevant phenomenological data. Consider the chess master or driver:

> The expert chess player, classed as an international master or grandmaster, in most situations experiences a compelling sense of the issue and the best move. Excellent chess players can play at the rate of 5–10 seconds a move and even faster without any degradation in performance. At this speed they must depend almost entirely on intuition and hardly at all on analysis and comparison or alternatives. . . . The expert driver, generally without any awareness, not only knows by feel and familiarity when an action such as slowing is required, but he generally knows how to perform the act without evaluating and comparing alternatives. He shifts gears when appropriate with no conscious awareness of his acts . . . our description of skill acquisition counters the traditional prejudice that expertise necessarily involves inference.[98]

Experts not only need no awareness to perform, they are also often incapable of describing all that they do, nor are they conscious of particular steps of these acts. Crucially, this characterization of expertise does not just cover the

---

[96] Dreyfus, *Skillful Coping*, 105–11.
[97] Dreyfus, *Skillful Coping*, 34.
[98] Dreyfus, *Skillful Coping*, 35.

professional technicality of specific tasks, but also *everyday practice*. Human beings require no conscious reflection or willing in most of their everyday decisions, and it is precisely when a disturbance occurs that our fluid coping is turned into conscious reflection. In Dreyfus's words, there is a kind of intentionality in everyday coping and expertise that is *meaningful* but yet *nonconceptual*:

> Thus, the pure perceiving of the chess master, as well as that of the *phronimos* [phenomenological appearance] and, indeed, the expert in any skill domain, even everyday coping, has a kind of *intentional* content; it just isn't conceptual content. A "bare Given" and the "thinkable" are not our only alternatives. We must accept the possibility that our ground-level coping opens up the world by opening us up to a *meaningful* Given—a Given that is *nonconceptual* but not *bare*.[99]

Everyday coping involves the intuitive ways in which one responds to the *affordances* of the world: features of our environment that elicit our responses. The chair is *for* sitting, the hammer is *for* hammering nails, and specific people *require* specific social interactions. Here, Dreyfus signals his indebtedness to Heidegger and Aristotle specifically: "It is this necessary situational specificity of skillful coping that Aristotle and Heidegger noted in the case of the *phronimos*, and which led Heidegger to conclude that skillful coping is nonconceptual."[100] The space of reason and conscious reflection does have its place—it can help us reorient ourselves to the world—but everyday coping requires not the conscious use of reason, but the primordial instincts of the self, whether social, intuitive, or physical.

In this regard, Dreyfus's account finds an ally in the Bavincks, who, as indicated above, argued that the soul and the knowledge of God lie underneath conscious willing and acting. As Herman Bavinck wrote in another place, "Understanding and reason [indicate] so little of the essence of man and the whole of the content of the faculty of knowing; rather they are merely particular activities of the knowing faculty that first began their work as the fundamentals of human knowledge that lie broad and deep in the unconscious."[101] The unconscious, in other words, is not merely that which

---

[99] Dreyfus, *Skillful Coping*, 116, emphases original.
[100] Dreyfus, *Skillful Coping*, 116.
[101] Bavinck, *Beginselen der Psychologie*, 82. In the original Dutch, "Zoo weinig zijn verstand en rede het wezen van den mensch en de gansche inhoud van het kenvermogen, dat ze daarvan veeleer slechts bijzondere werkzaamheden zijn, die dan eerst hun arbeid beginnen, als de fundamenten der menschelijke kennis reeds breed en diep, tot in het onbewuste toe, gelegd zijn."

characterizes technical expertise and skills that become second nature to us, but also that from which most of our everyday behavior stems.

The third point follows naturally from the previous two: reflection and conscious acts both always occur in a primordial context of skillful coping. We are always already skillfully coping as we think and consciously will. Dreyfus draws from two Heidegerrian terms: *Vorsicht* and *Vorhabe*. *Vorsicht*, the theoretical circle of human reflection and interpretation, always takes place in the context of *Vorhabe*, the "background of practices."[102] This background of practices is itself rooted in ontology, and ontology, here, does not refer to a *theory of being*, as commonly understood, but to the way *humans are*. Theoretical, conceptual reflection, "is always already shaped by what might be called our implicit ontology, an 'ontology' which is in our practices as ways of behaving toward things and people, not in our minds as background assumptions which we happen to take for granted."[103] Intentions do indeed direct these practices, but they are not conceptually or consciously directed—they are moved "by the *perceived conditions*, not by one's *volition*."[104] The self is always moving toward particular horizons, even while our conscious acts of the will or conceptual reflection lie elsewhere.

The yield of Dreyfus's analysis, reinterpreted theologically for our purposes, is the following: Analyses of the noetic effects of sin that focus on whether the intellect is apprehending particular propositions about God, inferred from nature or Scripture, or on the willful acts of inference and suppression, do not go deep enough. Though they may be illuminating, focusing merely on the apprehension of the intellect or the conscious acts of the will do not yet penetrate to the deepest level of where sin's effects are most present. In fact, the conscious reflection and acts of the sinner are always already being performed within the context of unconscious, skilled behavior in response to the affordances of the world.

Theologically, we have observed from the Bavincks and Bonaventure above that the primordial context in which humanity lives is *precisely God's self-revelation*. That is, in a manner more pervasive than any social or physical environment in which we exist, the human self is always living in the context of divine action. In God we live and move and have our being. Since that is the case, the human self is always already skillfully coping with this

---

[102] Dreyfus, *Skillful Coping*, 134.
[103] Dreyfus, *Skillful Coping*, 134.
[104] Dreyfus, *Skillful Coping*, 148, emphases original.

primordial environment. God's self-revelation is the primary *affordance* that elicits our fluid coping, and it is the context out of which we reflect and make conscious decisions.[105]

Skillful coping is not just the assimilation of learned techniques that then become second nature, but also the very way in which human beings live in the everyday. Suppressing this primordial environment, then, is not something we need to learn. It is *not* a second-nature skill that we have learned to master in a progression that moves from explicit learning to implicit expertise. Rather, the Scriptures say that we are "by nature children of wrath"—we come into the world walking in trespasses and sins (Eph. 2:1–3), and along with the darkening of our "understanding," we also "practice every kind of impurity" (Eph. 4:17–19). Sinfully suppressing God's self-revelation is our nature's fallen skill. It need not be taught, for in sin were we conceived (Ps. 51). As I will further argue below, our lives are marked by the ruptured relationship that we have with God, and just as trauma victims learn skillfully to suppress the memories of their traumatic events, so do sinners come forth already, by nature, suppressing their relationship with God.

IV. Revisiting Romans 1

With the sketch of skillful coping now at hand, we can revisit the *locus classicus* of Romans 1:18–21 in an attempt to elucidate the theological and exegetical yield of the observations above. The notion of skillful coping complements well J. H. Bavinck's exegesis of the relevant passage, so that's where we'll begin:

> For the wrath of God is revealed from heaven against all ungodliness and unrighteousness of men, who by their unrighteousness suppress the truth. For what can be known about God is plain to them, because God has shown it to them. For his invisible attributes, namely, his eternal power and divine nature, have been clearly perceived, ever since the creation of the world, in the things that have been made. So they are without excuse. For although they knew God, they did not honor him as God or give thanks to him, but they became futile in their thinking, and their foolish hearts were darkened.

Theologians and exegetes alike puzzle over the seemingly paradoxical way in which this passage speaks of the natural person's knowledge of God. Gleaning

---

[105] In this sense, my argument here complements James K. A. Smith, especially in his *Imagining the Kingdom: How Worship Works* (Grand Rapids, MI: Baker Academic, 2013).

from other passages in Scripture, it is clear that the unregenerate do not know God—they worship what they fail to know (e.g., Acts 17:23–28), and yet Romans 1 speaks of a clear knowledge of God that is suppressed. As J. H. Bavinck surmises, human beings "proceed as unknowing knowers."[106] Objectively, God's revelation is utterly clear such that it penetrates into every psyche, yet they suppress that knowledge. It is tempting to argue here that God's revelation is available in nature, and human beings are rendered "without excuse" because they fail to reason unto him. But this, I think, misses the force of this passage: the knowledge of God is not a bare *possibility* conditioned upon whether we actively infer properly from creation to God, but an *actual fact* that obtains in human beings because of God's action. Given the sketch of illumination above, the knowledge here is not incrementally gained by way of a process of reasoning, but rather by way of the primordial "given" of existing in the context of God's revelation. As the Bavincks and Bonaventure make clear, there is no circumstance in which human beings do not know God or do not enjoy his gracious, ever-present illumination. Failure to honor God or give thanks to him (v. 21b) occurs *in the context of knowing God* (v. 21a).

Hence, the word "suppress" (v. 18) here deserves close attention, for it cannot be a suppression that results in a lack of knowledge. Here is where our account of skilled coping is helpful—humans suppress that knowledge so skillfully that it is an unconscious act. Again, J. H. Bavinck argues that this has to be couched in terms of the psyche, underneath willing or thinking:

> Suppression occurs so directly, so spontaneously, so simultaneously with the "understanding and seeing clearly" that at the precise moment that people see, they no longer see; at the exact moment that they know, they already no longer know. Psychologically considered, this is in and of itself entirely possible. . . . In this connection one could even say that human beings, in being addressed by the world around them, always suppress an instance of their becoming aware as an instance in which God, who is present everywhere and in everything, presents himself and manifests himself to them in a very evident way.[107]

In short, "God definitely reveals himself, but people immediately push it away, repress it, suppress it."[108] It would be a mistake to infer here that

---

[106] J. H. Bavinck, "Religious Consciousness and Christian Faith," 284.
[107] J. H. Bavinck, "Religious Consciousness and Christian Faith," 284.
[108] J. H. Bavinck, "Religious Consciousness and Christian Faith," 285.

Bavinck therefore actually diminishes the noetic effects of sin, as if his focus of repressing here renders sin's effects to be only primarily on the will, or that affirming the noetic effects of sin strongly means that one becomes unaware of God. Sin's effects on the mind and the will are so pervasive that the mind and will *fail to apprehend and respond* to what is *known and the God who is acting upon them*. To make sense of this paradoxical claim, J. H. Bavinck turns to the reality of the unconscious:

> we need to keep a sharp eye on the fact that there is something distorted in the human condition. People have been resisting, suppressing. They have done so unconsciously. But they do so all the time, moment by moment *always unaware that they are doing so*. But at the same time, there is always a definite unsettledness deep within them as a consequence of that suppression . . . the engine of this suppressing process runs noiselessly, but not so noiselessly that they never feel it running now and then and thereby realize that something is amiss in their lives. People play hide-and-seek with God.[109]

As argued above, the environment of God's revelation is an *affordance* that constantly requires our responses. It is the environment that culls our skilled apprehension and action, which in turn requires no conscious thought or volition. Unlike Dreyfus's account of skilled coping, however, where the focus is on positive expertise—the adult's ability to sense the room for proper social behavior, or the chess-master's hyper-speed response-rate—J. H. Bavinck here is suggesting a kind of skillful coping in a *negative* direction. To explicate this aspect further, I turn to phenomenological accounts of trauma, where skillful coping is developed in order to *avoid* or mitigate particularly difficult affordances.

Consider, first, the dysfunctional family in which an estranged child, now an adult, receives daily texts from a sibling that their mother has been diagnosed with a fatal disease. Their mother has only a few more years to live. These texts beckon the child to come home, but the child has become so accustomed to living on his own and ignoring the family that he refuses to respond or read the daily text messages. After a few months, the text messages are treated no longer as minor nuisances that require conscious deleting, but become ignored altogether, grouped together with all of the other unread messages he receives, receding into the back of his subconscious

---

[109] J. H. Bavinck, "Religious Consciousness and Christian Faith," 285, emphasis added.

(think about how many emails or text messages we receive from people that we daily ignore, though, when asked, we know that we have received them). The estranged child can go about his daily business without even once consciously thinking about the messages or his mother, despite it being there in his subconscious—that is, of course, until that distant sibling shows up on his doorstep, forcing him to recall all of the messages he had so skillfully and successfully (in self-deception) coped with in suppression.

Think also of a party at which a person, say, John, notices a person he has tried to avoid for a long time—perhaps it was someone with whom he had an awkward past. John finds ways to avoid making eye-contact with the person, and in doing so perhaps he rushes ahead to another friend group or some distant area of the party in which he thinks he is less likely to encounter him or her. He may make it through the evening successfully, not bringing the person to his conscious attention, only to be forced to do so when someone notifies him again of the person's presence. And in that moment of panic, John falsely declares that he was totally unaware that he or she was at this party.

In both of the above cases, ignoring, self-deceiving, suppression, have become internalized performances of skillful coping. Painful, dysfunctional, and at first requiring much effort, they have become part and parcel of the countless daily things that we are rarely, if ever, conscious about—but that yet are still instances of knowledge, indeed, unconscious knowledge.

So it is, I am suggesting, in a manner I think consistent with the neo-Calvinists, with the creaturely dysfunctional relationship with God outside of Christ. Here, general revelation is that visceral perception or feeling or unconscious knowledge of God that all creatures experience by virtue of God's revealing act. In this construal, it is a mistake to think that the solution to bring about the sinner's acknowledgment of God is to present some arguments based on a few premises. Rather, just as in the case of the estranged child or the eye-contact-avoiding man, attention must be given to the subconscious suppression involved.

The crucial differences between our main theme and the examples of the dysfunctional family or of John and his awkward acquaintance above, of course, is that our skilled avoidance of God is neither learned nor progressively acquired: *it is innate within the sinner's psyche*. One is born skilled at not-apprehending and avoiding the obvious and most pervasive affordance: God himself (cf. Eph. 4:17–19). Conversion, therefore, requires a heart surgery that often involves painful reflection on the wrongs we have done and the memories we have so skillfully submerged. We have a traumatic relationship with God as covenant breakers. "They are people with a wound that cannot be closed—they suppress."[110]

This reading of Romans 1 arms us with considerable benefits. First, we can affirm that the knowledge of God is ever-present without denigrating the effects of sin that cause us to fail to apprehend God properly. Second, following from the first, we can maintain the paradox of knowing-yet-not-knowing that we have seen is the condition of sinners living in God's good world. Third, we can capture a deeper sense of sin's pervasiveness that goes beyond mere analyses of the intellect or the will.

V. Conclusion: *Common Grace and Acts of Disruption*

The bleak picture of the pervasiveness of sin's effect on the psyche sketched above can discourage us from being proper witnesses in God's world. But all is not lost. In this era of redemptive history, before Christ's second coming, God continues to uphold creation for the purposes of the gospel. God gifts common grace into the created order, restraining nonbelievers' sinful selves so that they are never as bad as they could be, and so that their unconscious and conscious acts of rebellion never come to eschatological fruition. J. H. Bavinck himself recognized this when he argued that there are "moments" where nonbelievers are confronted viscerally by how they have been suppressing the very ground of their being.[111] These moments could be triggered by the gospel itself, or by an existential crisis where they are called truly to see themselves, as they become "aware of the horror of this suppressing process and realize that they have always known but have never wanted to know."[112]

Other moments of disruption, however, do take place. The suppression, in God's providence, never takes place equally in all people. In some, the suppression is so skilled and unconscious that it never enters into their consciousness. In others, the suppression easily rises up to the surface, triggering them to ask questions about their existence. Others are overwhelmed by God's presence such that they cannot but see that they have been unconsciously

110 J. H. Bavinck, "Religious Consciousness and Christian Faith," 286.
111 J. H. Bavinck, "Religious Consciousness and Christian Faith," 285.
112 J. H. Bavinck, "Religious Consciousness and Christian Faith," 285.

suppressing, triggering them to enter into times of crisis—for such people, "suppressing only takes place accompanied by a great deal of unsettledness."[113]

Christian witness is crucial in the world precisely because God never leaves himself without a witness, and his sheep will ultimately recognize his voice. Common grace exists for the purposes of redemptive grace. As J. H. Bavinck continues to emphasize, these "moments" of recognition and consciousness are due to God, and not human creatures themselves: "This is due to no human virtue. It proves nothing about the nobility of human nature. It is only due to God's personal involvement with people and to the overpowering force with which he has clearly made himself known to people."[114] Hence, "deep within the hidden recesses of people's beings, that repressed and suppressed truth is still present. It has never simply disappeared but has always been alive and active."[115] On this, Herman Bavinck agrees:

> God did not leave sin alone to do its destructive work. He had and, after the Fall, continued to have a purpose for his creation; he interposed common grace between sin and the creation—a grace that, while it does not inwardly renew, nevertheless restrains and compels. All that is good and true has its origin in this grace, including the good we see in fallen man. . . . *Consequently*, traces of the image of God continued in mankind.[116]

Common grace, therefore, prevents humanity from totally nourishing their deep suppression of God's general revelation, and allows for sinners to recognize disruptions to that skilled coping underneath all of their thinking and willing. Christians should thus pursue to be faithful witnesses, conduits of disruption that beckon the recognition of transcendence that continues to pervade God's creation and point to our need for reconciliation.

An implication of this study, critically, is that this calls not just for Christians to engage the intellect of our unbelieving neighbors, but to *expose* the skilled ways in which we have been repressing our ruptured relationship with God. Effective witness should emphasize not just the dissemination of new information to the unbeliever, but an existential encounter that confronts their unconscious dysfunction and their ruined natures. This is the message of the gospel: "we implore you on behalf of Christ, be reconciled to God" (2 Cor. 5:20).

---

[113] J. H. Bavinck, "Religious Consciousness and Christian Faith," 286. Here, Bavinck cites Calvin's doctrine of the *semen religionis*.

[114] J. H. Bavinck, "Religious Consciousness and Christian Faith," 286.

[115] J. H. Bavinck, "Religious Consciousness and Christian Faith," 286.

[116] Herman Bavinck, "Common Grace," trans. Raymond C. Van Leeuwen, *CTJ* 24 (1989): 64, emphasis added.

23

Original Sin in Modern Theology

CHARLES HODGE AND HERMAN BAVINCK ON FRIEDRICH SCHLEIERMACHER

Nathaniel Gray Sutanto

I. Introduction

Commenting on Charles Hodge's critical reception of Friedrich Schleiermacher, Brian Gerrish observed that "It can safely be said that [Hodge] traced all Schleiermacher's mistakes to two sources: a defective method and commitment to a pantheistic philosophy."[1] Writing under the new pressures of biblical criticism and the reformulations of the doctrine of original sin in the modern era, Charles Hodge (1797–1878) sought to defend the doctrine under the conditions of the classical Reformed tradition on which he stood. Yet, it has been observed that Hodge, in his attempt to retrieve the doctrine in the context of modern deviations, ended up with a doctrine of original sin that was rather "idiosyncratic" within the Reformed tradition.[2] The key and oft-quoted text that signaled Hodge's modification could be found in the second volume of his *Systematic Theology*:

---

[1] Brian A. Gerrish, *Thinking with the Church: Essays in Historical Theology* (Grand Rapids, MI: Eerdmans, 2011), 151.
[2] Oliver D. Crisp, "Federalism vs. Realism: Charles Hodge, Augustus Strong, and William Shedd on the Imputation of Sin," *IJST* 8 (2006): 66; Crisp, *The Word Enfleshed: Exploring the Person and Work of Christ* (Grand Rapids, MI: Baker Academic, 2016), 129 n. 20; see also John Murray, *The Imputation of Adam's Sin* (Grand Rapids, MI: Eerdmans, 1959), 77; Annette G. Aubert, *The German Roots of Nineteenth-Century American Theology* (Oxford: Oxford University Press), 194–219.

> To impute sin, in Scripture and theological language, is to impute the guilt
> of sin. And by guilt is meant not criminality or moral ill-desert, or demerit,
> much less moral pollution, but the judicial obligation to satisfy justice.
> Hence, the evil consequent on the imputation is not an arbitrary infliction;
> not merely a misfortune or calamity; not a chastisement in the proper sense
> of that word, but a punishment, *i.e.*, an evil inflicted in execution of the
> penalty of law and for the satisfaction of justice.[3]

The idiosyncrasy of Hodge's view is as follows. According to the mainstream
Reformed-federal position on original sin, Adam's first sin resulted in a twofold curse upon humanity: original guilt and original pollution, with total depravity as an inherited result of his sin.[4] God immediately imputed this curse
on Adam's progeny on the basis of Adam's natural and representative bond
with them. Francis Turretin's delineation of this was typical of this federalist
view: "For the bond between Adam and his posterity is twofold (1) natural,
as he is the father, and we are his children; (2) political and forensic, as he
was the prince and representative head of the whole human race."[5] That is,
God imputes the sin of Adam to his progeny because Adam was the father
of all human beings, and Adam represents them, as the actions of a prince
represent his people.[6]

Regarding this first aspect, original guilt, it was commonplace to make a
further distinction concerning the guilt imputed. The liability that humanity
inherited is twofold: the liability to guilt (*reatus culpae*) and liability to punishment (*reatus poenae*).[7] In line with this distinction, the majority report of

---

[3] Charles Hodge, *Systematic Theology*, 3 vols. (London: Thomas Nelson, 1872), 2:194.

[4] As codified in the Westminster Confession of Faith 6.2–4: "2. By this sin they fell from their original righteousness and communion with God, and so became dead in sin, and wholly defiled in all the parts and faculties of soul
and body. 3. They being the root of all mankind, the guilt [original guilt; the first aspect of the curse] of this sin
was imputed; and the same death in sin, and corrupted nature, conveyed to all their posterity descending from them
by ordinary generation. 4. From this original corruption [the second aspect], whereby we are utterly indisposed,
disabled, and made opposite to all good, and wholly inclined to all evil, do proceed all actual transgressions."

[5] Francis Turretin, *Institutes of Elenctic Theology*, ed. James T. Dennison Jr., trans. George Musgrove Giger, 3 vols.
(New Jersey: Presbyterian & Reformed, 1992), 1:616. Hodge, too, shared this concern to uphold the natural and
representative bond of Adam's headship: "The union between Adam and his posterity which is the ground of the
imputation of his sin to them, is both natural and federal" (Hodge, *Systematic Theology*, 2:196).

[6] Hodge added a biologically tinged description of Adam's natural headship, namely, that Adam and the human
race are the same species (see *Systematic Theology*, 2:77–91). As we shall see, however, Hodge distinguished this
view from what he considered to be the realist-organic position of Schleiermacher, according to which, he thinks,
humanity is a singular substance and individuals are reducible to modes of existence of that substance.

[7] Though it is beyond the scope of the present chapter, it is worth exploring Bavinck's reservations concerning this
distinction as utilized in Roman Catholic theology: "The Roman Catholic Church makes a distinction between
'being accused of a fault' (*reatus culpae*) and 'judged fit for a punishment' (*reatus poenae*). But this distinction
obviously betrays the intent to justify the 'satisfactory' punishments for believers here on earth and in purgatory and
is directly at variance with the nature of guilt and punishment" (Herman Bavinck, *Reformed Dogmatics*, ed. John
Bolt, trans. John Vriend, 4 vols. [Grand Rapids, MI: Baker Academic, 2004], 3:171). As we shall see, Bavinck saw
such a vital connection between guilt and punishment that he does not explicitly utilize this distinction in discussing
the definitions of either category.

the federal position argued that image-bearers of Adam are guilty of Adam's sin and must be punished, for an inseparable logical connection bonds guilt and punishment: one cannot bear a punishment if one is innocent, and likewise one cannot be held responsible to make a satisfaction for a violation if one is not the agent guilty of such a violation. God imputes the sin of Adam to them, and they are liable to punishment because of it. Hodge, however, argued that a more rigorous distinction between the two should be made, and that the responsibility for one to make satisfaction or to bear a punishment can be unlinked from personal demerit. Guilt, then, means

> . . . the obligation to satisfy justice. This may be removed by the satisfaction of justice personally or vicariously. It may be transferred from one person to another, or assumed by one person for another. . . . It is in this sense that it is said that the guilt of Adam's sin is imputed to us. . . . *This is very different from demerit or personal ill-desert.* The ordinary theological word guilt is well expressed by the German word *Schuld*, which means the responsibility for some wrong, or injury, or loss; or, the obligation to make satisfaction. It, therefore, includes the meaning of our words guilt and debt.[8]

While punishment or satisfaction is transferable from one person to another (for a punishment can be borne by someone else "vicariously"), personal guilt, merit, or demerit are not:

> It assumes that guilt, Schuld, *reatus*, in the sense of the obligation of the sinner to satisfy divine justice, may be removed, may be transferred from one person to another, or assumed by one in the place of another. In perfect consistency with this doctrine it is maintained that guilt or *reatus* in the sense of demerit or ill-desert does not admit of removal or transfer.[9]

In part, Hodge was motivated to make this distinction to emphasize the parallel between Adam and Christ: just as Christ was not really (or personally) guilty for Adam's sin, but was punished as a substitute for sinners, so those who remain outside of Christ are punished for Adam's sin, not because they are personally guilty for Adam's sin, but simply because the punishment of his sin is imputed to them. Likewise, God considered Christ's righteousness to be ours, not because we have personally merited righteousness, but simply because God transfers the rewards of Christ's merits, and so considers his

---

[8] Hodge, *Systematic Theology*, 2:476, emphasis added.
[9] Hodge, *Systematic Theology*, 2:477.

merit to be ours.[10] In other words, the relation between Adam and humanity, and Christ and the redeemed, respectively, has to be conceived in federalist rather than realist terms. Annette Aubert clearly demarcates the difference between Hodge and the majority-federalist view in the following way:

> In contrast to Reformed scholastic theologians (who maintained that punishment [*poena*] and guilt [*culpa*] cannot be separated in the doctrine of imputation), Hodge makes the scholastic "distinction" between liability to guilt (*reatus culpae*) and liability to punishment (*reatus poenae*). Hodge attains this distinction by adopting German terms; specifically in the work of traditional German scholarship he finds help in defining the concept of "guilt" (*Schuld*).[11]

Hodge's modification of the majority federalist view seems to generate various problems.[12] First, it seems to exacerbate the common charge that the federalist position renders God unjust, for one person cannot be justly punished for the guilt of another. Second, it further lends credence to the objection that the federalist account involves merely legal fictions of transferring guilt and righteousness—legal declarations that seem arbitrary rather than based on something metaphysically real.[13]

---

[10] "It is in this sense that it is said that the guilt of Adam's sin is imputed to us; that Christ assumed the guilt of our sins; and that his blood cleanses from guilt" (Hodge, *Systematic Theology*, 2:476). Crisp likens the federalist account to the imputing of legal fictions: "Like the imputation of sin, this too is a species of legal fiction according to the federalist account. Christ does not literally take on the sins of all Adam's posterity. He is their substitute, but this does not entail taking on their sin and guilt" (Crisp, "Federalism vs. Realism," 69).

[11] Aubert, *German Roots of Nineteenth-Century American Theology*, 201. Likewise, Crisp: "Hodge sees that if he concedes that God imputes guilt immediately, then it might appear that I am somehow guilty of Adam's sin. He averts this outcome by denying that immediate imputation has this consequence. All that guilt involves in this case, he claims, is liability to punishment, not, in addition, liability to guilt (because the guilt of the first sin was Adam's guilt, not mine). But this is just to say God imputes someone else's sin to me and treats me as the sinner, punishing me for it. . . . In order to avoid falling into the arms of realists, Hodge claims that the legal fiction of imputation extends to sin and only that aspect of guilt that is compatible with imputation being a legal fiction" (Crisp, "Federalism vs. Realism," 70). "Immediate" imputation is in contrast to the "mediate" account, according to which the transmission of Adam's guilt is imputed not directly to his descendants solely by God's decree, but rather that, having inherited original corruption, creatures inevitably sin and are then considered guilty. For a brief summary of the history of the debate between the two views, see Donald Macleod, "Original Sin in Reformed Theology," in *Adam, the Fall, and Original Sin: Theological, Biblical, and Scientific Perspectives*, ed. Hans Madueme and Michael Reeves (Grand Rapids, MI: Baker Academic, 2014), 140–42. The mediated imputation view seems to imply a further distinction between original sin and actual sin: "Whereas original sin is that inherited moral corruption with which we are all generated, and for which we are not responsible or culpable, actual sins are those particular things we are disposed to do because we are born in a morally vitiated state" (Oliver D. Crisp, "On Original Sin," *IJST* 17 [2015]: 261; see also Douglas Sweeney, " 'Falling Away from the General Faith of the Reformation'? The Contest over Calvinism in Nineteenth-Century America," in *John Calvin's American Legacy*, ed. Thomas J. Davis [Oxford: Oxford University Press, 2009], 111–46).

[12] For a further exposition of Hodge in context, see Ryan McGraw's chapter, "Old Princeton and the Imputation of Adam's Sin," in the present volume. Note McGraw's observation as well, that Hodge's view "raises numerous problems in light of historic Reformed views on imputation. Restricting 'imputation' to punishment appears to deny imputation altogether" (see the section on "The Doctrine of Sin" in McGraw's chapter in this volume [ch. 8]).

[13] Crisp echoes both of these objections in "Federalism vs. Realism," and "On Original Sin." I have tried to show how Bavinck's Trinitarian and organic account of the image of God and original sin evade both objections in Nathaniel Sutanto, "Herman Bavinck on the Image of God and Original Sin," *IJST* 18 (2016): 174–90. Further,

Now, what does this have to do with Gerrish's observation, quoted in the beginning of this chapter? The subject of this chapter is original sin in modern theology, and it seeks to explicate modern Reformed accounts of the doctrine. I intend to do this by examining two modern Reformed responses to Schleiermacher's doctrine of original sin, in Charles Hodge and Herman Bavinck.

My argument is that Hodge was further motivated to dislodge the imputation of punishment from that of Adam's guilt because he was concerned to counter what he considered to be Friedrich Schleiermacher's organic and realist (and thus pantheistic) vision of humanity and the transmission of sin.[14] There is a certain irony to this: in seeking to retrieve a traditional federalist account from what he considered to be adverse modern modifications epitomized in the father of liberal theology, Hodge ended up modifying the doctrine himself.[15] As an alternative, I seek to show that Herman Bavinck (1851–1921) provided a better course of direction—he was better able to preserve the central tenets of the majority federalist position precisely because he did not reject aspects of a realist account of original sin—even those realist moves made by Schleiermacher. Further, Bavinck provided a better model to follow because, in his commitment to irenic criticism and catholicity, he was able to appreciate Schleiermacher's account, and in admitting some points at which Schleiermacher was correct, Bavinck did not compromise but rather preserved and advanced a robustly orthodox, Reformed, federalist *and* realist, organic vision of humanity and the imputation of sin. Brian Gerrish's comment, then, does not merely explicate Hodge's objections against Schleiermacher, but also illumines the theological motivations of Hodge's account of the imputation of original guilt.

The rest of this chapter, then, moves in three steps. First, I exposit the moves that characterize modern accounts of original sin before zooming in

---

defending the Lutheran (and Reformational) account of imputation from the charge that it renders God's declarative word to be a legal fiction, Robert Kolb argued thusly: "Such critics ignore the fact that in another sense of the word 'forensic,' God's justification of sinners takes place just as his creation of the reality of his entire universe took place, by virtue of—that is, by the power of—his Word. His re-creation happens, Luther asserted, when God gives his promise of new life in Christ to his chosen people. . . . This promise, God's regard or reckoning (imputation), creates and determines reality, including the reality of the new state of the sinner forgiven and given new birth (John 3:5–8)" (Robert Kolb and Carl R. Trueman, *Between Wittenberg and Geneva: Lutheran and Reformed Theology in Conversation* [Grand Rapids, MI: Baker Academic, 2017], 124).

[14] While Crisp uses Hodge as a foil to more orthodox Reformed-realist accounts of the imputation of sin that postdate Hodge's work (in Shedd and Strong), Crisp did not note that Hodge himself was self-consciously responding to the realist accounts of Schleiermacher.

[15] The contours of the narrative thus mirrors rather starkly Hodge's dispute with Nevin on the Lord's Supper and the reception of Hodge's sacramentology in general. See esp. Sweeney, " 'Falling Away from the General Faith of the Reformation,' " 111–46; and J. Todd Billings, *Remembrance, Communion, and Hope: Rediscovering the Gospel in the Lord's Supper* (Grand Rapids, MI: Eerdmans, 2018), 122–28.

on Schleiermacher's reconstruction of original sin and total depravity. This shows how Schleiermacher sought to inherit and creatively rethink the traditional Reformed views he received. Second, I shall show more closely Hodge's explicit objections to Schleiermacher's views, and show that those worries also motivate his emphasis on the strictly legal character of the imputation of sin. Finally, I move to Bavinck's account of the image of God and the imputation of sin, showing that his construction allowed him to be charitable to Schleiermacher's moves, while perhaps hinting that he was indebted to Schleiermacher in building his own account. In so doing, this chapter will have explicated two modern Reformed accounts of the imputation of sin (in Hodge and Bavinck), that are logically connected by how they interacted with the account of the father of modern theology, Friedrich Schleiermacher.

II. Friedrich Schleiermacher on Original Sin and Total Depravity

The modern era followed the trajectory established in the Enlightenment, questioning the legitimacy of theology as an appropriate academic discipline. Currents in the natural sciences and biblical criticism that were emancipated from confessional commitments nurtured a skepticism that doubted whether theology can be considered a proper science (*Wissenschaft*).[16] The doctrine of original sin (or the fall) seemed to be a paradigmatic example of why theology's content ought to be revised if it were to be made sensible to modern ears. The doctrine, in other words, was thought to be in need of reconstruction in a manner consistent with the priorities of the newly recognized sources of authority outside of the traditional sources of faith in Scripture or tradition, that is, in the sources provided by reason, new empirical data, religious phenomenology, psychology, or sociology.[17] Hence, the modern era and modern

---

[16] See Thomas Albert Howard, *Protestant Theology and the Making of the Modern German University* (Oxford: Oxford University Press, 2006); Johannes Zachhuber, *Theology as Science in Nineteenth-Century Germany: From F. C. Baur to Ernst Troeltsch* (Oxford: Oxford University Press, 2013); Zachary Purvis, *Theology and the University in Nineteenth-Century Germany* (Oxford: Oxford University Press, 2016). Herman Bavinck comments on the impact of these intellectual currents from within the Dutch context in *Verslag der Handelingen van de Eerste Kamer*, March 12, 1913, 432–33; Bavinck, *Reformed Dogmatics*, 1:49; and "Theology and Religious Studies," in Bavinck, *Essays on Religion, Science, and Society*, ed. John Bolt, trans. Harry Boonstra and Gerrit Sheeres (Grand Rapids, MI: Baker Academic, 2008), 49–60.

[17] As Ian McFarland summarized, "belief in a historical Fall . . . was widely accepted by Christians of all stripes well into the nineteenth century. Today there are still vehement defenders of the historical accuracy of Gen. 1–3, but the picture of the natural history of the human species in particular and the cosmos in general produced over the last two centuries by a convergence of data from geology, biology, paleontology, and genetics has strained the credibility of literal readings of the biblical creation stories past the breaking point" (McFarland, *Adam's Fall: A Meditation on the Christian Doctrine of Original Sin* [Oxford: Blackwell, 2010], 143). For a recent attempt to reconcile the plausibility of a historical fall with both monogenism and polygenism, see Matthew Levering, *Engaging the Doctrine of Creation: Cosmos, Creatures, and the Wise and Good Creator* (Grand Rapids, MI: Baker Academic, 2017), 227–72.

theologians seemed to take for granted that (1) the fall cannot have its basis in a real historical event, and that (2) the notion that one can be held responsible for the sins of another is morally atrocious, despite the emphasis on the social dimensions of sin that the modern era presented. Sin, or at least the capacity to sin (or the inability to attain the good), then, is not an intrusion to an otherwise good creation, but a primordial feature of human existence, and the biblical narrative of the fall is simply a paradigm that is enacted and experienced by every person. Another consequence of these two premises is (3) that knowledge of sin is dependent on knowledge of the process and presence of redemption.[18] In each of these emerging moves, the era produced theologies that cannot

> be brought into easy harmony with the traditional faith of Nicaea or Chalcedon. Indeed, it is clear that some of the theologies surveyed would resist such conformity on a point of principle, seeking to distance themselves from bare formulations and cold abstractions for a livelier doctrine that attends in a more explicit manner to themes of encounter, relationship, and empowerment.[19]

Friedrich Schleiermacher stood as a central figure within these academic debates. Indeed, he set himself the task of reasserting Protestant theology, but in a manner that would be fresh and accommodating to his intellectual milieu. His *Brief Outline of the Study of Theology* (1811/1830) delineated not merely a theological curriculum for within the academy but also argued that theology should simultaneously be guided by the goals of church ministry and the new scientific methods of the philosophical and historical departments.[20] His *Christian Faith* followed this approach, and his account of original sin exhibits the twin desire of creative innovation and faithful reception [21]

---

[18] Paul Nimmo, "Sin and Reconciliation," in *Oxford Handbook of Nineteenth Century Theology*, ed. Joel D. S. Rasmussen, Judith Wolfe, and Johannes Zachhuber (Oxford, Oxford University Press, 2017), 655–57; Carl R. Trueman, "Original Sin in Modern Theology," in *Adam, the Fall, and Original Sin*, 183–85.

[19] Nimmo, "Sin and Reconciliation," 657. Speaking specifically on Schleiermacher on p. 648, "his conception of sin sits uneasily with the forensic aspect of traditional views, and his view of redemption distinctly relativized both the ontological claims of the Christian creeds and the salvific centrality of the events of cross and resurrection."

[20] Friedrich Schleiermacher, *Brief Outline of Theology as a Field of Study: Revised Translation of the 1811 and 1830 editions*, trans. Terrence N. Tice, 3rd ed. (Louisville: Westminster/John Knox, 2011). See esp. pp. 1–14. Zachary Purvis clarified that this ecclesial purpose "underscored training for leadership more than edification in divine wisdom" ("Education and Its Institutions," in *Oxford Handbook of Nineteenth Century Theology*, 310).

[21] Friedrich Schleiermacher, *Christian Faith: A New Translation and Critical Edition*, ed. Catherine L. Kelsey and Terrence N. Tice, trans. Terrence N. Tice, Catherine L. Kelsey, and Edwina Lawler, 2 vols. (Louisville: Westminster/John Knox, 2016 [hereafter *CF*]). So, Walter E. Wyman: "[Schleiermacher's] discussion of sin and redemption exhibits his dual commitment to revision and fidelity to the Christian (specifically, Protestant) tradition" (Walter E. Wyman Jr., "Sin and Redemption," in *The Cambridge Companion to Friedrich Schleiermacher*, ed. Jacqueline Mariña [Cambridge: Cambridge University Press, 2005], 129). See also Daniel Pedersen, *Schleiermacher's Theology of Sin and Nature: Agency, Value, and Modern Theology* (New York: Routledge, 2020).

One ought to keep in mind Schleiermacher's basic definition of sin before we explicate his account of original sin and total depravity. For Schleiermacher, sin arises developmentally. Human creatures began to exist with a sensuous consciousness[22] and later developed the capacity for a religious consciousness, a consciousness of God as the *Whence* on which creatures are absolutely dependent.[23] Sin occurs when the sensible (that is, sensuous) self-consciousness obstructs the presence of the higher self-consciousness.[24] In other words, sin emerges when the consciousness of our absolute dependence on God, or our "God-consciousness," is forgotten due to our preoccupation with the mundane tasks and ends of ordinary (sensuous) life. Sin is all "that has hindered the free development of God-consciousness."[25] The result is what Schleiermacher terms *Gottvergessenheit*—a God-forgetfulness, or, better, a state of consciousness that represents an "obliviousness as to God."[26] The rupturing of God-consciousness by way of preoccupation with sensible life leads to an experiencing of life as "pervaded with oppositions," that is, an opposition between our freedom in action, on the one hand, and our dependence on the objective factors of sensible life that impinge upon us, and which are not due to our choices, on the other hand.[27]

The sensible self-consciousness, which represents Schleiermacher's interpretation of the flesh, has an advantage over the higher consciousness

---

[22] As Schleiermacher, *CF*, § 4.3–4 indicates, the sensible life or self-consciousness is the sphere of relative freedom and dependence. Or, as Kevin Hector aptly summarized, "Schleiermacher understands the world, and our place in it, in terms of the relative opposition between freedom and dependence, and so recognizable *as* relative, in light of that which absolutely transcends both. . . . Schleiermacher gathers the entire realm of relative freedom and dependence into the category of 'sensible life', and terms one's awareness of this realm 'sensible self-consciousness'" (Hector, *The Theological Project of Modernism: Faith and Mineness* [Oxford: Oxford University Press, 2015], 105).

[23] It is worth noting that Schleiermacher's account of sin is highly Christocentric, and can be comprehended only in relation to sin's opposition to the redemption found in Christ. An explication of Schleiermacher's doctrine of sin in relation to the atonement would bring this out more explicitly, but is not within the scope of the present chapter. "Thus sin and grace are indissolubly linked in Schleiermacher's thought. Even while sin is discussed apart from grace for the sake of presentation, the treatment always remains proleptic—a reflection of the condition anterior to redemption, in which sin still holds sway" (Kevin M. Vander Schel, "Friedrich Schleiermacher," in the *T&T Clark Companion to the Doctrine of Sin*, ed. Keith L. Johnson and David Lauber [London: Bloomsbury, 2016], 254). Bavinck highlights and actually commends this nuance in Schleiermacher's doctrine of sin: "Schleiermacher, Ritschl, and others correctly stressed that sin only comes to its most appalling manifestation vis-à-vis the gospel of the grace of God in Christ and hence within the boundaries of Christianity. Scripture itself testifies to this when especially in the New Testament it repeatedly discusses at length the sins of unbelief, offense, apostasy, and particularly the blasphemy of the Holy Spirit and brings to light its great culpability and punishability" (Bavinck, *Reformed Dogmatics*, 3:141).

[24] "This means that we become conscious in such a way that just as God-consciousness is awakened in a human being, sin will also come into consciousness" (Schleiermacher, *CF*, § 67.2).

[25] Schleiermacher, *CF*, § 66.1.

[26] Schleiermacher, *CF*, § 11.2. As the editors helpfully explain, "This word could be rendered literally as 'God-forgetfulness' but in German *Vergessenheit* means 'oblivion', i.e., left completely out of mind. Something simply 'forgotten' (*vergessen*) would have to have been somehow in mind, somehow consciously noticed and acknowledged, in the first place." This is not a requirement here.

[27] Hector, *Theological Project of Modernism*, 106, 110–11.

(or, the Spirit) because it precedes it in the order of human evolution.[28] Sin thus emerges not only when the capacity for God-consciousness has developed, but specifically when "the self is unable to integrate the religious self-consciousness with the lower ones."[29]

Implicit in the above definition is the rejection of a historical fall from which an alteration of human nature was the result. Though we are aware that sin was indeed inherited and perpetuated in us through something outside of us, it is unnecessary to attribute this inheritance to a first sin by an original human couple. Schleiermacher rejects the historicity of a fall for several reasons, not least because he held that exegesis is outside the bounds of the dogmatician's terrain.[30] First, he argued that denying a primal transition from innocence to depravity is required to explain why it is that the original pair would sin in the first place. If the first human beings truly did have a nature free from the seeds of sin, then why would they have listened to Satan's "whispering innuendos?"[31] Indeed, it seems logical to infer that "such an inclination toward sin would therefore have to have existed in the first human beings already before the first sin, because otherwise no susceptibility to temptation could have taken place."[32] Hence, though one might maintain that the original human beings were culpable for perpetuating sin's influence to future generations, "nothing new or special" happened to their natures as a result of the "first sin."[33] Again, "Adam would have to have broken away from God already before his first sin," such that "one could not say that nature had been altered by the first sin."[34] It might be tempting at this point to infer that this makes God the author of an original sinfulness, creating humanity as sinners

28 ". . . the strength of resistance that flesh produces and that is expressed in consciousness of sin depends on the head start which flesh would already have gained at that earlier time. Yet, by all means, the extent of that head start also would have its basis in connection with collective life" (Schleiermacher, *CF*, § 67.2). Here, Derek Nelson describes the flesh's advantage as a kind of "'squatter's rights' on the territory of the self" due to its "developmental anteriority" (Nelson, "Schleiermacher and Ritschl on Individual and Social Sin," *Journal for the History of Modern Theology* 16 [2009]: 135). It is important to note that the mundane activities of the sensuous consciousness are not sinful in themselves, however, but only become an occasion for the consciousness of sin when they obstruct the vitality of God-consciousness.
29 Nelson, "Schleiermacher and Ritschl on Individual and Social Sin," 135. B. A. Gerrish warns against the mistake of thinking that Schleiermacher's view consists in defining sin as only present alongside the consciousness of sin: "he obviously did not mean to say that sin is purely subjective—without source or ground. The 'germ' of sin is everything that arrests the development of the consciousness of God, whether acknowledged as sin or not (§ 66)" (Gerrish, *Christian Faith: Dogmatics in Outline* [Louisville: Westminster/John Knox, 2014], 83 n. 9). This is in response to a reading in Hodge, *Systematic Theology*, 2:140; cf. Aubert, *German Roots of Nineteenth-Century American Theology*, 49, 198.
30 Schleiermacher, *CF*, § 72.5.
31 Schleiermacher, *CF*, § 72.2.
32 Schleiermacher, *CF*, § 72.2. "Accordingly, Schleiermacher finds no true explanation for the beginnings of sin in the narrative of the first pair in the Garden, since their susceptibility to the serpent's temptation still implies some prior inclination to sinfulness" (Vander Schel, "Schleiermacher," 255).
33 Schleiermacher, *CF*, § 72.3.
34 Schleiermacher, *CF*, § 72.3. So, Nimmo: "[Schleiermacher] does . . . suggest that nothing peculiar or novel took place in Adam and Eve; in the first sin, 'they were simply the first born of sinfulness'" ("Sin and Reconciliation,"

to begin with. But this is to miss that Schleiermacher redefined the "original perfection of humanity" as simply the innate capacity to "appropriate grace."[35] Schleiermacher argues that the capacity to sin is innately within every human creature—a capacity not introduced by a fall—and takes this to be relatively compatible with the supposition of the catholic Christian faith, according to which the original human beings were able either to sin or not to sin.[36]

Second, Schleiermacher thinks it irrational to claim that individuals can be held responsible for an alien and imputed sin. Here, Schleiermacher explicitly critiques both classically realist and federalist accounts of the imputation and transmission of Adam's sin as "entirely arbitrary and wholly groundless":[37]

> we can be glad to dispense with all of those artificially constructed theories, which also chiefly bear the tendency to focus on divine justice in the imputing of Adam's sin to his descendants and thereby on assigning punishment for it. To dispense with them is all the more warrantable for two reasons. First, they can be dispensed with, in part, insofar as they would also have added to their account of all human beings' participating in Adam's sin by referring to a specific theory concerning how individual souls originated— as in that which assumes that all human beings are included in the very existence of Adam—whereas in our own domain of existence we would lack all grounds or means for setting forth such a theory. Second, they can be dispensed with, in part, insofar as, in an extremely arbitrary manner, these theories consider God's command to be a covenant contracted with the entire human race but embraced in the person of Adam. In these theories, thus the judicial consequences of violating the covenant would fall on Adam's heirs as well, a process that subsumes human beings' relationship with God and God's reckoning under the concept of an external, judicial relationship, and thereafter that view has also borne a most deleterious influence on people's conception of how redemption works.[38]

---

647). Nimmo is citing pp. 295 and 299 of the earlier edition of *Christian Faith* (Friedrich Schleiermacher, *Christian Faith*, ed. H. R. Mackintosh and J. S. Stewart [Edinburgh: T&T Clark, 1991]).

[35] Schleiermacher, *CF*, § 69 n. 14, § 59–60.

[36] As Nelson tersely summarized, for Schleiermacher "[t]o say that creation is 'good' is basically to affirm that God has made creatures that can come to know and love God. That is to say, goodness is not a state of moral activity, but a framework for moral possibility. Creation is 'perfect' when it is, in principle, perfectible" (Nelson, "Schleiermacher and Ritschl on Individual and Social Sin," 134). By contrast, confessional Reformed theology recognized a distinction between humanity in the state of integrity and fallen humanity, and saw that in the former there was not a "germ" or "seed" of sin (contra Schleiermacher), but simply the *possibility* of sin, which in turn corrupted human nature. See, here, Bavinck, *Reformed Dogmatics*, 3:66–69.

[37] Schleiermacher, *CF*, § 72.4.

[38] Schleiermacher, *CF*, § 72.4. In that same section, he went on, "if the first human beings had laudably withstood the first test, no second one would have been laid before them, but at that point they, and we with them, would have remained exempt from all temptation forevermore. Rather, it is the case that . . . the temptation indicated in the Mosaic narrative is very skimpy."

Indeed, the Berliner thought that placing the weight of the entire human race and history on two individuals would be an unreasonable act. Why should God place the direction of human nature "within one small sphere of activity," indeed, on two "inexperienced individuals who would also have had no presentiment whatsoever regarding any such importance of that event?"[39]

What, then, is the message communicated by the Mosaic narrative? The story of the fall is a paradigmatic account of how sin is perpetuated, inherited, and actualized. Adam and Eve demonstrated that, everywhere, sin always "had the same features."[40] Eve represented the domination of the sensible consciousness, blocking God-consciousness, while Adam represented "how sin comes to be taken up in an imitative process . . . and yet how this activity presupposes a God-forgetfulness, even if it be based on a mere distraction."[41] In short, Eve was a paradigm of a kind of originating and actual sin, whereas Adam displayed an originated sin, indicating that the influence of sin preexists actual acts and perpetuates it. This was no state of integrity, but rather the state of every human "nature apart from the process of redemption, a human nature that is exactly the same throughout, with no exception."[42]

There is then a deeply social and ethical explanation for original sin in Schleiermacher's model.[43] Denying a historical fall means significantly redefining the meaning of the term "original" in original sin. Originating original sin, then, does not refer to the primal act that led to the guilt and corruption of humanity, but rather to the sins of a previous generation that led to the imitation of those sins in the succeeding generation. Originated original sin is that propensity to sin in the latter generation which has an external ground.[44] Hence, sin spirals forward through the proceeding of sinful generations and social influence.[45]

---

[39] Schleiermacher, *CF*, § 72.4.

[40] Schleiermacher, *CF*, § 72.5.

[41] Schleiermacher, *CF*, § 72.5.

[42] Schleiermacher, *CF*, § 72.6.

[43] Nimmo compares Schleiermacher's account of sin with other modern accounts which highlight "the corporate dimension of creaturely sinfulness, corrupting not only atomized individuals but also social communities and human institutions" (Nimmo, "Sin and Reconciliation," 656).

[44] Schleiermacher, *CF*, § 71.1. "Until then, and only to that degree, original sin is rightly called 'originated' because it has its cause outside the individual."

[45] Schleiermacher, *CF*, § 71.2. "If, on the one hand, the susceptibility to sin that precedes every deed is effected in each individual by the sin and susceptibility of sin of others, but if, at the same time, it is also propagated in others and secured in them by each individual through one's own free actions, then sinfulness is of a thoroughly collective nature." Despite this emphasis on the "shared environment," McFarland insists (in contrast to Hodge's reading) that Schleiermacher's account still makes "each person's Fall ultimately his or her own affair . . . modern versions cut us loose from Adam and one another in a way that makes original sin *only* our own" (McFarland, *Adam's Fall*, 154).

It follows that original sin does not refer to the imputation of Adam's sin in guilt or punishment, but rather to the collective guilt of all.[46] Humans stand in solidarity in perpetuating sin, and thus are collectively guilty as a single unity. As Schleiermacher claimed in an oft-cited statement, "in each individual susceptibility to sin is the work of all, and in all individuals it is the work of each. Indeed, susceptibility to sin is to be understood rightly and fully in this commonality."[47] Again, our guilt "is called a *fault* [*Schuld*] with complete correctness only if it is absolutely considered to be the collective deed of the entire human race in that it cannot likewise be a fault of an individual, at least to the extent that it is engendered in that individual."[48]

We can now come to understand Schleiermacher's retrieval of "total depravity."[49] God-forgetfulness spreads from one generation to another, exacerbating our incapacity to do good:

> In any given individual a susceptibility to sin is present in that individual before any deed of the individual's own, one that is even based beyond the individual's own existence, consists of a complete incapacity for good, which incapacity is removed, in turn, only through the influence of redemption.[50]

There is no perfect action. We strengthen the germ of sin by habitually sinning, and we are mired in the sins of previous generations: "In all human beings actual sin is continually issuing from original sin."[51] Humans unfailingly (or inevitably) sin. Redemption is necessary, and it is precisely the work of Christ and his Spirit that counteracts the pervasiveness of humanity's obliviousness vis-à-vis God.

III. Hodge's Critique of Schleiermacher Revisited

With Schleiermacher's account of original sin and total depravity in hand, we can make some more sense of Hodge's critique against him. Hodge discerned

---

[46] So, Wyman: Sin "is inherited, not in a biological or Augustinian sense, but socially and historically: individuals are raised by families and in cultures and nations where the common life is shaped by individuals and groups whose God-consciousness is always already deficient" ("Sin and Redemption," 135–36).

[47] Schleiermacher, *CF*, § 71.2.

[48] Schleiermacher, *CF*, § 71.2. It follows, then, that the redemptive activity of Christ also has a deeply social dimension: ". . . the totality of sin is the collective act of the whole human race from the very first human being onward. Moreover, this collective act could be overcome only through Christ's efficacious activity also being spread across the entire human race" (*CF*, § 72.4).

[49] Wyman, "Sin and Redemption," 136. Total depravity is Wyman's description of Schleiermacher's account, which shows that Schleiermacher advocated for a revised version of total depravity, rather than a total repudiation of the doctrine.

[50] Schleiermacher, *CF*, § 70.

[51] Schleiermacher, *CF*, § 73.

in Schleiermacher an overtly communal account of sin that seemed to him to swallow up the individuality or agency of individual sinners into a single generic humanity. He is already concerned to critique various forms of realistic accounts of sin, regarding them to be philosophically untenable and overtly subjectivist. The principle behind realism, Hodge reasoned, is the supposition that moral agents are responsible only for those acts that they themselves *personally* commit, and thus realism wrongly infers that for us to be held accountable for Adam's sin, then his sin must really be our sin, and therefore we are substantially (and not merely federally) one with Adam.[52] But this, for Hodge, is to impose an alien philosophical principle into the text of Scripture: "The assumption that we acted thousands of years before we were born, so as to be personally responsible for such act, is a monstrous assumption."[53] Recall, then, that for Hodge it does not follow that we are guilty for Adam's sin, though we *are* to be punished for it.

Hodge seems to think that realism commits one to the view that individuals and Adam "are numerically the same substance."[54] This aversion to realism fuels his reaction to Schleiermacher, as he thinks that Schleiermacher's anthropology and hamartiology represent a particularly insidious form of realism:

> The German theologians, particularly those of the school of Schleiermacher, use the terms life, law, and organic law. Human nature is a generic life, *i.e.*, a form of life manifested in a multitude of individuals of the same kind. In the individual it is not distinct or different from what is in the genus. It is the same organic law. A single oak may produce ten thousand other oaks, but the whole forest is as much an inward organic unity as any single tree.[55]

Hodge repeats this line of reasoning, too, in his commentary on Romans:

> According to the realistic doctrine, revived by the modern speculative theologians of the school of Schleiermacher, humanity existed as a generic life in Adam. The acts of that life were therefore the acts of all individuals to whom, in the development of the race, the life itself was communicated. All men consequently sinned in Adam, by an act of self-determination. They are punished, therefore, not for Adam's act, but for their own; not simply for their innate depravity, nor for their personal acts only, but for the act

---

[52] Hodge, *Systematic Theology*, 2:225–26.
[53] Hodge, *Systematic Theology*, 2:223.
[54] Hodge, *Systematic Theology*, 2:222.
[55] Hodge, *Systematic Theology*, 2:54.

which they committed thousands of years ago, when their nature, i.e., their intelligence and will were determined to evil in the person of Adam.[56]

Hodge is alarmed by this, and thinks that these commitments seem to resemble an even more problematic doctrine, that of pantheism, as humans are considered merely as modes of an individual substance.[57] The Princetonian was motivated, then, to construe a doctrine of sin that eludes realism and the seemingly subjectivist and pantheistic implications of Schleiermacher's account.[58] It was these kinds of comments that lead Aubert to conclude that Hodge's doctrine of the atonement (and its concomitant claims concerning original sin) "reveals his reactions to Schleiermacher and mediating theology."[59]

Despite Schleiermacher's clear rejection of classically realist models of the transmission of sin noted above, an initial reading of Schleiermacher seems to vindicate Hodge's worry. Indeed, Schleiermacher often claims that humanity hangs together as a singular whole, and further that humans are in some way one with the whole of creation. These claims, in turn, might explain why Schleiermacher describes the origin and transmission of sin in such pervasively communal terms. In the *Speeches*, Schleiermacher claimed that an individual's "inner nature is a necessary complement of a complete intuition of humanity" and that we can perceive the "whole" and reach "unity with it in fellowship with others, by the influence of those who have long been freed from dependence on their own fleeting being, and from the endeavor to expand and isolate it."[60] Moreover, he argues that a human being is a kind of microcosm in which the entirety of human nature is perceived: "You are a compendium of humanity. In a certain sense your single nature embraces all human nature."[61]

But to infer from these claims that Schleiermacher considered all individuals to be merely modes of a single substance, or that creation and humanity are somehow identical, is to conflate epistemological and ethical claims

---

[56] Charles Hodge, *A Commentary on Romans* (Carlisle, PA: Banner of Truth, 1972), 182.

[57] Hodge, *Systematic Theology*, 2:57–59.

[58] Aubert, *German Roots of Nineteenth-Century American Theology*, 204. Aubert observes that Hodge's view of Christ's work of salvation as an imputation of his merits is also in response to that of Schleiermacher: "Hodge's statement stands in contrast to the theologies of Schleiermacher, mediating theologians, and Gerhart, which all teach that Christ introduces a new life which conflicts with the sin of man, and after the contest conquers sin" (204).

[59] Aubert, *German Roots of Nineteenth-Century American Theology*, 225.

[60] Friedrich Schleiermacher, *On Religion: Speeches to Its Cultured Despisers*, 3rd ed., trans. John Oman (London: Paul, Trench, Trubner, 1893), 76, 78.

[61] Schleiermacher, *On Religion*, 79.

with ontological ones. Schleiermacher's claims concerning the transmission of sin emphasize the ethical and socially mediated bonds that bind humanity rather than essential ones. Further, he established firm distinctions between selves, world, and God, by clearly demarcating between relative and absolute dependence. Human beings are aware of their relative dependence on the objects of the world, and they are in absolute dependence only on God. Being "at one with the world in self-consciousness," then, does not mean being metaphysically identified with it, but rather it means

> . . . nothing other than our being conscious of ourselves as a living part that coexists within that whole, and this cannot possibly be a consciousness of absolute dependence. Rather, since all coexisting, living parts are in a state of reciprocal action among themselves, in every such part this being-one-with-the-whole essentially bears a twofold character. It contains a feeling of dependence, to be sure, inasmuch as the other parts bear an effect on oneself out of their own self-initiated activity, but it likewise contains a feeling of freedom, inasmuch as one also bears an effect on other parts out of one's own self-initiated activity. The two factors, moreover, are not to be separated from each other. Thus, the feeling of absolute dependence is not to be explained as a way the world is composed but is to be explained only as a way God is composed, viewing God as the absolute undivided unity.[62]

Creation consists of parts within a whole not because the parts are interchangeable with the whole, but in the sense that there is a reciprocal relationship of spontaneity (freedom) and reception (dependence) between those parts. We are aware of the choices we make that impact others and objects in the world, and are simultaneously aware of how the choices of others and external objects affect us. God, however, is the higher (absolute) unity that transcends both subject and object, as all things in creation are absolutely dependent on God. As Schleiermacher himself notes in his marginalia, "It is almost inconceivable how people can have ascribed pantheism to me, since I completely sunder the feeling of absolute dependence from any relation to the world."[63]

The seemingly (and possibly) unsettling conclusion to infer from the above observations is this: Hodge did not merely deviate from the accounts of original sin and guilt articulated by the majority federalist reports in large part

---

[62] Schleiermacher, *CF*, § 32.2.
[63] This note was helpfully provided by the editors in *CF*, § 4.4 n. 22.

because he was concerned to critique Schleiermacher's realism; his critiques also reveal a possibly substantial misreading of Schleiermacher's account. In sum, Hodge had rendered himself vulnerable in two major ways. First, in dislodging punishment from guilt, he is vulnerable to charges concerning the rationality and justice of God for God's decision to punish humans for Adam's sin, also exacerbating the legal-fiction critique often charged against federalism. Second, Hodge made himself vulnerable in that first way because he was motivated to critique and distance himself from Schleiermacher, a move that revealed a rather tenuous reading of Schleiermacher's anthropology and hamartiology. Might there be a more tenable presentation of an orthodox Reformed doctrine of original sin in the modern period that takes into account Schleiermacher's major revisions? For this, I suggest one ought to consider the contributions of Herman Bavinck.

IV. Herman Bavinck's Doctrine of Original Sin and Reception of Schleiermacher

> The world, the earth, humanity, are one organic whole. They stand, they fall, they are raised up together.[64]

> Not only does the Christian worldview seek to restore the harmony between the natural and moral orders in the objective side, but also thus in the subjective it seeks to bring together a wonderful unity between our thinking and our doing, and our head and our heart. . . . Intellectual, mystical, and ethical elements hold together in a balance, and Hegel, Schleiermacher, and Kant have reconciled the one with the others.[65]

As is often observed, Herman Bavinck's work is characterized by a remarkable breadth of knowledge and depth of insight. He engaged his interlocutors so carefully that often readers of Bavinck are hard pressed to decide where in the text we might find his own voice. Like Hodge, he stood for confessional Reformed orthodoxy in a time when the theological landscape was shifting, but, perhaps unlike Hodge, Bavinck was specifically concerned to take into consideration what he considered to be real advancements made

---

[64] Bavinck, *Reformed Dogmatics*, 3:588.

[65] Herman Bavinck, *Christelijke wereldbeschouwing*, 3rd ed. (Kampen, Netherlands: Kok, 1929), 84–85. In the original Dutch, "En niet alleen herstelt de Christelijke wereldbeschouwing objective de harmonie tusschen natuurlijke en zedelijke orde, maar daardoor brengt zij ook subjective tusschen ons denken en ons doen, tusschen ons hoofd den ons hart eene heerlijke eenheid tot stand. . . . Intellectueele, mystische, en ethische elementen houden elkander in evenwicht, en Hegel, Schleiermacher, en Kant worden de een met den ander verzoend."

by Schleiermacher. Reformed theology, he wrote, "is sufficiently pliant and flexible to appreciate and appropriate what is good in our age."[66]

Bavinck's simultaneous openness to modern theology and insistence on the truth of Reformed orthodoxy is perhaps exemplified in his attitude toward and treatment of Schleiermacher—a theologian that he regarded to be both often erroneous but yet deeply misunderstood. Despite the errors that Bavinck judged to reside in Schleiermacher's works, Bavinck thought that there was no going back behind the Berliner: "Schleiermacher has exerted incalculable influence. All subsequent theology is dependent on him . . . he has made his influence felt on all theological orientations—liberal, mediating, and confessional—and in all churches—Catholic, Lutheran, and Reformed."[67] While it is beyond the scope of the current chapter, what has clearly emerged in recent scholarship is Bavinck's keen desire simultaneously to distance himself from and yet to charitably appropriate the Berliner's work, especially in the loci of prolegomena, general revelation, and the nature of religion—a utilization of Schleiermacher that Cory Brock has aptly characterized as neither mere "demonization" nor "dependence."[68] This chapter continues within that trajectory. As we shall see, Bavinck's treatment of original sin and interaction with Schleiermacher is consistent with the observation that he was keen not to demonize Schleiermacher's work, but charitably to appropriate his model while staying within the bounds of confessional Reformed orthodoxy.[69]

This section, then, seeks to show Bavinck's appropriation and critique of Schleiermacher in the doctrine of original sin while also displaying the inner logic

---

[66] Herman Bavinck, "The Future of Calvinism," trans. Geerhardus Vos, *The Presbyterian and Reformed Review* 17 (1894): 21. For more on Herman Bavinck's insistence on the truth of Calvinism and its simultaneous openness, see Nathaniel Gray Sutanto, "Confessional, International, and Cosmopolitan: Herman Bavinck's Neo-Calvinistic and Protestant Vision of the Catholicity of the Church," *JRT* 12 (2018): 22–39.

[67] Bavinck, *Reformed Dogmatics*, 1:165–66.

[68] Cory Brock, "Between Demonization and Dependence: Bavinck's Appropriation of Schleiermacher," *Ad Fontes* 7 (2018): 1–6. See also the evidence collated in Cory Brock and Nathaniel Gray Sutanto, "Herman Bavinck's Reformed Eclecticism: On Catholicity, Consciousness, and Theological Epistemology," *SJT* 70 (2017): 310–32; Sutanto, "Confessional, International, and Cosmopolitan"; Sutanto, "Herman Bavinck and Thomas Reid on Perception and Knowing God," *HTR* 111 (2018): 115–34; and esp. Cory Brock, *Orthodox Yet Modern: Herman Bavinck's Use of Friedrich Schleiermacher* (Bellingham, WA: Lexham, 2020). On Herman Bavinck's critical appropriation of the German absolute idealist Eduard von Hartmann, which overlaps rather considerably with his own usage of Schleiermacher, see Sutanto, *God and Knowledge: Herman Bavinck's Theological Epistemology* (London: Bloomsbury T&T Clark, 2020), ch. 6.

[69] Other than Schleiermacher, Bavinck's interaction with other modern theologians in relation to original sin is also worth investigating. He would argue that "The philosophy of Kant, Schelling, Schopenhauer, and others; the theory of [human] heredity and [human] solidarity; a spectrum of historical and sociological studies—all have offered unexpected but significant support for the dogma of original sin. After theology rejected it, philosophy again took it up" (Bavinck, *Reformed Dogmatics*, 3:100).

of Bavinck's account, rooted as it is in his organic conception of the image of God and the realistic and ethical bonds that unite humanity as a singular whole.[70]

Bavinck was content to uphold the central strands of the confessional Reformed tradition with regard to original sin. The fall was a historical reality on which the doctrines of Christianity stand, and which makes Christianity quite unique.[71] Significantly, it communicates "the organic connectedness of the human race" and eschews any theory of sin that renders humanity merely into an "aggregate of individuals" that do not have a "common head in Adam nor in Christ."[72] Sin, then, does not merely denote specific acts but a state of guilt and corruption into which one is born, and from which actual sin arises. Bavinck includes Schleiermacher among those who attribute guilt only to personal and actual sins, rather than its being a state into which we are born—a move that interestingly exacerbates the independence and individuality of the human person rather than considering that person to be connected with the human race.[73] Indeed, Schleiermacher highlights the *ethical* nature of the *imago Dei* in emphasizing the free personality of the individual in a manner that complements his denial of a historical fall. Schleiermacher and other modern theologians "deny the reality of a state of integrity and locate the image of God solely in man's free personality, his rational or moral nature, in a religious-ethical bent, in man's vocation to enter communion with God."[74] As one shall see, though Bavinck recognized that Schleiermacher's emphasis on the communal guilt and social influence of sin were accurate, he thought that Schleiermacher's account inevitably rendered sin into a merely personal affair because there was no transition from a state of integrity into a fallen state in his account.

Likewise, Bavinck maintained the distinction between originating and originated original sin, arguing that the former referred to Adam's first sin

---

[70] It is beyond the scope of this essay to outline in detail the whole of Bavinck's thought on these issues. I have attempted to expound Bavinck's doctrines of original sin and the image of God more expansively (though without explicitly noting the modern/Schleiermacherian influences in them) in Nathaniel Gray Sutanto, "Herman Bavinck on the Image of God and Original Sin," *IJST* 18 (2016): 174–90; and "Egocentricity, Metaphysics, and Organism: Sin and Renewal in Bavinck's *Ethics*," *Studies in Christian Ethics* 34 (2021): 223–40.

[71] Bavinck, *Reformed Dogmatics*, 3:38.

[72] Bavinck, *Reformed Dogmatics*, 3:73. This underlies Bavinck's critique against Albrecht Ritschl, who, in Bavinck's reading, conceived the transmission of sin only in terms of imitation rather than imputation and an inheritance of corruption: "This total universality of sin cannot be explained in terms of imitation. It is anterior to every conscious and intentional act of the will and is in every one of us a state long before it turns into deeds. That Ritschl does not recognize this is due in his case to nominalism. He regards humanity as the sum of all individuals, not an organism. Sin is not a state but consists only in acts of the will" (Bavinck, *Reformed Dogmatics*, 3:89).

[73] Bavinck, *Reformed Dogmatics*, 3:92. "Also Schleiermacher, therefore, rejected the notion that original sin cannot be guilt until it breaks out in actual sins."

[74] Bavinck, *Reformed Dogmatics*, 2:535. Recall McFarland's observation that Schleiermacher and others in the modern tradition ultimately cut "us loose from Adam and one another in a way that makes original sin *only* our own" (McFarland, *Adam's Fall*, 154, emphasis added).

in both a realistic and a federalist-ethical sense, while the latter referred to the inherited guilt, punishment, and corruption that humanity receives from Adam. Indeed, despite the various intellectual difficulties that this doctrine might produce, Bavinck held that this traditional doctrine of original sin is necessary not only to explain the present condition of humanity but also to satisfy the witness of the guilty human conscience:

> Much misunderstanding could be avoided if, in original sin, we differentiated between an originating sin (*peccatum originans*; imputed guilt) and the sin originated (*peccatum originatum*; inherent punishment). Actually, by original or hereditary sin, one should understand only the moral depravity that people carry with them from the time of their conception and birth from their sinful parents.
>
> But this moral depravity, which is characteristic of all people by nature and does not just arise later as a result of their own misguided deeds, certainly must have a cause. According to Scripture and for Christian thought, this cause can be no other than the first trespass of the first human, by which sin and death entered the world. Adam's disobedience is the originating sin. Scripture plainly says it (Rom. 5:12; 1 Cor. 15:22), and experience confirms it every minute: all people are conceived in sin and born in iniquity.[75]

One should thus not vitiate the connection between guilt and punishment: "Sin and guilt are inseparable,"[76] Bavinck wrote, and the original Dutch is more forceful: "Sin and guilt are inextricably (or inseparably) linked with one another [*Zonde en schuld zijn onlosmakelijk aan elkander verbonden*]."[77] This claim went alongside a central tenet of realism, as he considered humanity to be like "branches in a trunk, a mass at its beginning, members in a head, so all of us were germinally present in Adam's loins, and all proceeded from that source. In a sense it can be said that 'we were that one human,' that what he did was done by us all in him."[78] The maintenance of sin, guilt, and punishment as linked concepts preserves the justice of God: "Otherwise God would be unjust for punishing with death, the wages of sin (Rom. 6:23), that

---

[75] Bavinck, *Reformed Dogmatics*, 3:101.
[76] Bavinck, *Reformed Dogmatics*, 3:92.
[77] Bavinck, *Gereformeerde Dogmatiek*, 5th ed., 4 vols. (Kampen, Netherlands: Kok, 1929), 3:69. The third to fifth editions are identical, except for pagination. Unless otherwise noted, translations are my own.
[78] Bavinck, *Reformed Dogmatics*, 3:102. The English translation unfortunately veils how the original text strings together unattributed uses of Latin terms, likely signifying Bavinck's adherence to classical teachings of realism: "Gelijk rami in radice, massa in primitiis, membra in capite, zoo waren alle menschen in Adams lendenen begrepen en zijn zij allen voortgekomen uit zijne heup. Hij was geen privaat person, geen los individu naast anderen, maar hij caput natural; in zekeren zin kan gezegd worden, dat nos omnes ille unus homo fuimus, dat wat hij deed dor ons allen gedaan werd in hem" (*Gereformeerde Dogmatiek*, 3:80).

which *is* no sin and does not deserve death. . . . fellowship with God would be withheld where there was no guilt."[79]

It is thus not surprising that Bavinck was unsatisfied with Schleiermacher's redefinition of original sin. Bavinck was keen to affirm, with Schleiermacher, that human solidarity and the transmission of originated sin are certainly experienced and perpetuated by way of social influence: "the sinful deeds and inclinations of humans exert mutual influence as well and promote and confirm each other. In human society, consequently, there arises a 'law of sin' [*Gezetz der Sünde*], a realm of sin, a common sinfulness," but this law of sin by virtue of our shared environment is distinct from original sin proper "and was wrongfully so called by Schleiermacher."[80]

Bavinck's organic understanding of humanity explains this mutual influence and the solidarity of the human race in sin.[81] Here, it is important to note that after the above comment concerning the existence of a law of sin that permeates the human race, Bavinck located the emergence of an organic consciousness among his current intellectual milieu. "The sense of history that awakened after the Revolution," Bavinck wrote, rejuvenated an appreciation for the "incalculable value of community, society, and state," and "the organic understanding" of religion and morality in an unprecedented manner.[82] These cumulative achievements have "collectively put an end to the individualistic and atomistic view of humanity and of the sin dominant in it. If anything is certain, it is that sin is not an accidental phenomenon in the

---

[79] Bavinck, *Reformed Dogmatics*, 3:92, emphasis original. In his treatment of the punishment for actual sins, Bavinck argued that guilt "is an obligation incurred through a violation of the law to satisfy the law by suffering a proportionate penalty" (Bavinck, *Reformed Dogmatics*, 3:170–71); and further, "Guilt and pollution always go together as the two inseparable sides of sin; where the one is, the other is as well. . . . Guilt obligates us to [endure] punishment; pollution renders us unclean" (Bavinck, *Reformed Dogmatics*, 3:174). Compare this with Aubert's observation concerning Hodge and Turretin: "According to Hodge, imputation deals only with the *reatus poenae*; and he believed that the word 'guilt' denotes 'the relation which sin bears to justice.' Here he differed from Francis Turretin, who insisted that punishment (*poena*) is always based on guilt (*culpa*). This implies that humanity partakes in the liability (*reatus*)—'the obligation to penalty'—of the sin of Adam and denotes that humanity partook also in the guilt (*culpa*) of his sin. Hodge's departure from Turretin's view can be explained in terms of his dependence on and interaction with modern German biblical scholarship" (Aubert, *German Roots of Nineteenth-Century American Theology*, 202). Aubert cites Hodge, *Systematic Theology*, 2:189; and Turretin, *Institutes*, 1:620.

[80] Bavinck, *Reformed Dogmatics*, 3:88 (*Gereformeerde Dogmatiek*, 3:65). The English translation veils Bavinck's allusion to the German phrase.

[81] For a fuller treatment of Bavinck's organic worldview, see esp. James Eglinton, *Trinity and Organism: Toward a New Reading of Herman Bavinck's Organic Motif* (London: Bloomsbury T & T Clark, 2012); and my own *God and Knowledge: Herman Bavinck's Theological Epistemology* (London: Bloomsbury T&T Clark, 2020).

[82] Bavinck, *Reformed Dogmatics*, 3:88. For more on Bavinck and the French Revolution, see George Harinck, "Herman Bavinck and the Neo-Calvinist Concept of the French Revolution," in George Harinck and James Eglinton, eds., *Neo-Calvinism and the French Revolution* (London: Bloomsbury T&T Clark, 2015), 13–31.

life of individuals, but a state and manner of life involving the whole human race, a property of human nature."[83]

In other words, in consonance with this view of sin as a property of human nature and of the human race as a single entity, Bavinck held that the *imago Dei* referred not merely to human individuals but to the entirety of the human race:

> [the *imago Dei*] can only be somewhat unfolded in its depth and riches in a humanity counting billions of members. Just as the traces of God (*vestigia Dei*) are spread over many, many works, in both space and time, so also the image of God can only be displayed in all its dimensions and characteristic features in a humanity whose members exist both successively . . . and contemporaneously side by side.[84]

The human individual is thus a "compendium, the epitome of all of nature, a microcosm, and, precisely on that account, also the image and likeness of God, his son and heir, a micro-divine-being (*mikrotheos*)."[85] Human beings are connected to one another in such a manner that the individual is not comprehensible without the whole, and the whole is illumined by the individual.

The unity of the image of God in the human race, then, explains why sin inflicts the entirety of Adam's race—the parts are affected because they are comprehended in the whole, and the diversity of individuals is vitiated by sin because Adam is the head of humanity. Simultaneously, we are "seminally . . . comprehended" in Adam and yet "it was he who broke the probationary command, and not we."[86] There was a real imputation, such that it is not enough to say that in some sense we were germinally present in Adam, but federalism "certainly does not rule out the truth contained in realism; on the contrary, it fully accepts it."[87] Underneath this claim is Bavinck's provocative understanding that creation, and humankind in particular, are patterned after the Trinity. Because the triune Creator is an absolute unity-in-diversity, his creation is marked by unities-in-diversities, and all the more clearly so for the image-bearers of God.[88]

[83] Bavinck, *Reformed Dogmatics*, 3:88; see also 1:260, 521, on Bavinck's comments concerning the role Schleiermacher (or Romanticism) played in reinvigorating a fresh appreciation for an organic worldview.

[84] Bavinck, *Reformed Dogmatics*, 2:577.

[85] Bavinck, *Reformed Dogmatics*, 2:562. One cannot help but hear an echo of Schleiermacher here. Recall, above, "You are a compendium of humanity. In a certain sense your single nature embraces all human nature" (Schleiermacher, *On Religion*, 79).

[86] Bavinck, *Reformed Dogmatics*, 3:102.

[87] Bavinck, *Reformed Dogmatics*, 3:104.

[88] I explicate the logic, textual evidences, and fruits of this claim (especially against the common charges that federalism renders God arbitrary and imputes merely legal fictions) in Sutanto, "Herman Bavinck on the Image of God and Original Sin."

Hence, the covenant of works, in which God considers Adam as the representative head of the human race, is a *fitting* arrangement that corresponds to humanity's organic shape—it is a special act of God that comports with the organic makeup of the human race as a unity-in-diversity.[89] The imputation of Adam's sin, in other words, respects the ethical connectedness and the ontology of humanity.[90] The relational, legal, and ethical bond that connects humanity to two federal heads (in Adam, or in Christ) reflect the organic makeup of an ectypal humanity created by a Trinitarian God. In a word, the unity and solidarity brought about by the headship of Adam or Christ "constitutes the organism of humanity."[91] A key passage is as follows:

> If humanity, both in a physical and an ethical [*ethischen*] sense, were to remain a unity, as it was intended to be . . . if in that human race there were to exist, not just community of blood, as in the case of the animals, but on that basis also community of all material, moral [*zedelijke*], and spiritual goods, then that could be brought about and maintained only by judging all in one person. As things went with that person, so they would go with the whole human race. If Adam fell, humanity would fall; if Christ remained standing, humanity would be raised up in him. The covenant of works and the covenant of grace are the forms by which the organism of humanity is maintained also in a religious and an ethical [*ethischen*] sense. Because God is interested, not in a handful of individuals, *but in humanity as his image and likeness*, it had [*moest*] to fall and be raised up again in one person.[92]

If Bavinck is right, realism and federalism complement each other and need not be presented as a binary. I suggest that Ian McFarland's critique of Herman Bavinck, to the effect that Bavinck failed to provide a "rationale" by which "*Adam* can be described" as a federal head, then, does not take

---

[89] Bavinck also argued that the covenant of works accommodated the basic insights of Schleiermacher and Kant, in the sense that a covenantal arrangement maintained both the dependence of humankind on the God who establishes the covenant and the freedom of the human personality in relative self-determination: "The covenant of works, accordingly, does justice to both the sovereignty of God—which implies the dependence of creatures and the nonmeritoriousness of all their works—and to the grace and generosity of God, who nevertheless wants to give the creature a higher-than-earthly blessedness. It maintains both the dependence as well as the freedom of mankind. It combines Schleiermacher [dependence] and Kant [freedom]. The probationary command relates to the moral law as the covenant of works relates to man's creation in God's image. The moral law stands or falls in its entirety with the probationary command, and the image of God in mankind in its entirety stands or falls with the covenant of works" (Bavinck, *Reformed Dogmatics*, 2:572).
[90] Bavinck argued that pushing realism to its logical consequences (without adhering to federalism) would render imputation (mediate or otherwise) wholly unnecessary to account for the transmission of sin and guilt. Realism would hold that we inherited a corrupted nature from Adam (as we are somehow metaphysically one with him), and we would then inevitably sin, thus incurring guilt for our own sin.
[91] Bavinck, *Reformed Dogmatics*, 3:106.
[92] Bavinck, *Reformed Dogmatics*, 3:106 (*Gereformeerde Dogmatiek*, 2:96), emphasis added. The language implies that the modality of necessity, however weakly or strongly interpreted, is invoked.

into sufficient account the Trinitarian and realist underpinnings of Bavinck's theological anthropology.[93] Bavinck did not merely ground Adam's representative status on his being a *"first* in a series," but on the organic (and Trinitarian) makeup of humanity, just as Christ is the unity that undergirds the diversity of renewed humanity.[94] Neither, then, could Bavinck be charged with presenting a legal-fiction account of original sin or the atonement, since the imputation of Adam's sin (or Christ's righteousness) recognizes and comports with humanity's organic shape.[95] These ethical bonds that unite humanity render responsibility an inherently communal affair.

However, it is a mistake to infer from this that human individuality is unimportant. After Bavinck's presentation of this organic account of the imputation of Adam's sin, Bavinck was keen to maintain the balance between communal guilt—which acknowledges the reality of inherited sin as a law and reality—and the individual guilt that accrues from actual sin. Here, Bavinck appealed to Schleiermacher after a prefatory comment, agreeing that humanity is caught up in one another's guilt:

> It is . . . completely true that we can never with complete accuracy indicate the boundaries that separate personal guilt from communal guilt. What Schleiermacher says of original sin is something very different from what Scripture and the church say concerning it, but by itself is completely true of sin in general that it is the collective deed and collective guilt of the human race as a whole. In other words, the sinful state and sinful deeds of each individual are, on the one hand, conditioned by those of the previous generation, and, on the other, they in turn condition the sinful state and acts of later descendants. Sin is "in each the work of all and in all the work of each."[96]

Significant in this passage, then, is that despite Bavinck's lingering suspicion as to whether Schleiermacher ultimately subscribes to a kind of "pantheism,"[97] Bavinck recognized that the communal and social emphasis that Schleiermacher placed on the transmission of guilt represented an *ethical* rather than *ontological* claim. That is, despite the suggestive claims that Schleiermacher makes that might make him susceptible to charges of

---

[93] McFarland, *In Adam's Fall*, 153, emphasis original.
[94] McFarland, *In Adam's Fall*, 153.
[95] It is worth mentioning here that Bavinck remained a creationist, despite holding to some central tenets of realism: "Creationism preserves the organic—both physical and moral [*beide physische en moreele*]—unity of humanity and at the same time it respects the mystery of the individual personality" (Bavinck, *Reformed Dogmatics*, 2:587 [*Gereformeerde Dogmatiek*, 2:634]).
[96] Bavinck, *Reformed Dogmatics*, 3:116, quoting Schleiermacher, *CF*, § 71.1.
[97] E.g., Bavinck, *Reformed Dogmatics*, 2:613.

pantheism, a charitable reading allows one to read Schleiermacher differently—indeed—in the way that he himself intended. His focus was on the ethical bonds that constitute humanity's makeup, rather than a substantial one.

Let us take stock of the above exposition. Bavinck was critical of Schleiermacher's doctrine of original sin in the sense that, in denying a historical fall, and thus a transition from a human nature in a state of innocence to a fallen human nature, Schleiermacher rendered original sin and guilt into a merely personal affair. For Schleiermacher, there was no federal head, and thus no unity undergirds the diversity of the human race. Bavinck was, however, appreciative of Schleiermacher's emphasis on the social and communal aspects of the transmission of sin. Ethical bonds connect all of humanity, and each individual is involved in the organism's sins. Personal responsibility is insufficient to account for the pervasiveness and perpetuation of sin. Far from decrying realism or Schleiermacher's emphasis on the communal, then, Bavinck argued that a properly Reformed and federalist model of original sin stands on important strands of the realist model.

Important for our purposes here, too, is the observation that Bavinck upheld the *organic unity* of the human race without *reducing* the individuals into mere modes of a singular substance. The ethical bonds that unite the human race into a single head do not necessarily betray a commitment to pantheism. In recognizing this possibility, Bavinck was able to accommodate what he considered to be genuine insights made by Schleiermacher into a confessionally Reformed model of original sin, all the while advancing that model into new directions that push beyond the language of mere legal fictions or the posing of federalism and realism as two opposing sides of a debate. Indeed, Bavinck's organic model of original sin is arguably a meshing of both federalist and realist instincts.[98]

V. Conclusion

The modern revisions of the doctrine of original sin are far-reaching and serious, and Christian theologians should be vigilant in attending to the argumentation, lest the doctrines as taught in Scripture be compromised and the faith of the church be vitiated. In attending to this call to be vigilant, however,

---

[98] Though outside the scope of this chapter, it is worth considering a close comparison and analysis between Bavinck's organic account here and what Oliver Crisp has called a "union" account of the atonement (and original sin) in *The Word Enfleshed*, 130–40.

it has perhaps been the case that some theologians have been tempted simply to respond to or react intemperately against present oppositions. Ironically, such attitudes might actually endanger us into writing a kind of theology that is disordered precisely because it is driven by reaction. Hodge might serve as a warning sign for this, as his rather stark opposition against Schleiermacher may have led him both to misread his opponent and to construct a rather unique approach to original imputation himself.

What I have tried to show is that Herman Bavinck perhaps modeled a better direction. While continuing to preserve orthodox commitments, he was keen to accommodate the opposing views of his interlocutors, and in doing so actually advanced his own Reformed tradition. This has the effect not merely of creating a sense of profundity, but also the performance of the conviction that Christian orthodoxy truly is an all-encompassing worldview—one inevitably echoes it, if only by borrowed capital. Christian theologians are required to model the intellectual patience requisite to listen well and to respond in a manner that exposes that echo. One embodies this mode in the hope of persuading the interlocutor into seeing that one inevitably stands upon Christian orthodoxy even while one might think himself or herself to be revising or opposing it.[99]

---

[99] On intellectual patience, see John B. Webster, "Intellectual Patience," in *God without Measure: Working Papers in Christian Theology*, vol. 2, *Virtue and Intellect* (London: Bloomsbury, 2016), 173–88.

24

Incurvatus Est in Se

TOWARD A THEOLOGY OF SIN

Andrew Leslie

I. Naming and Knowing "Sin"

So much effort has gone into trying to capture a satisfactorily coherent and co-hesive definition of sin, that we may wonder if it is best to abandon the quest altogether, heeding the potentially sage advice of Heinrich Vogel, who once remarked that "[s]in cannot be defined but can only be opposed."[1] There are good reasons to press on, however, as notorious and confronting as the terrain may be. For as we shall see, sin cannot and, indeed, must not entirely elude definition, even if we find that no account will ever be able to render an expla-nation for the evil that lies at its heart, a mystery that simply "posits itself."[2]

In raising the question of definition, we are at the outset pressed to con-sider the very possibility of naming and knowing "sin" in the first place. An obvious place to begin is with a name given to sin by Scripture. Inhabiting the logic of a biblical name for a moment may allow us then to work backwards from there and address the possibility of speaking meaningfully about this reality from the perspective of those to whom the scriptural language and description of sin is directed.

[1] Cited in G. C. Berkouwer, *Sin*, trans. Philip C. Holtrop (Grand Rapids, MI: Eerdmans, 1971), 283. Some of the material in the following chapter overlaps with Andrew M. Leslie, "Retrieving a Mature Reformed Doctrine of Original Sin: A Conversation with Some Recent Proposals," *IJST* 22 (2020): 336–60, with permission.
[2] Reinhold Niebuhr, *The Nature and Destiny of Man: A Christian Interpretation*, vol. 1, *Human Nature* (New York: Scribner, 1942), 181; David H. Kelsey, *Eccentric Existence: A Theological Anthropology* (Louisville: Westminster/John Knox, 2009), 410–11, 420–21. The notion is traced back to Søren Kierkegaard's *Concept of Anxiety*.

There are, of course, a variety of terms used in Scripture to portray the character of sin,[3] but perhaps the most straightforward depiction is given by the apostle John, who refers to it simply as "lawlessness" (ἀνομία) in 1 John 3:4. Not surprisingly, this definition has virtually acquired textbook status. So, for instance, the Westminster Shorter Catechism captures the succinctness of John's diagnosis by describing sin as "any want of conformity unto, or transgression of, the law of God" (Q&A 14); and many others more or less follow suit.[4] But the definition offered by the Catechism adds an important clarification. The law against which sin is a violation is not some transcendental and abstract set of universal principles, but specifically the law *of God*. This is precisely what distinguishes sin from the Kantian notion of radical evil. Where Kant famously defends the concept of "God" as an extrapolation from the subjective, rational intuition of a universal moral law, the specific law against which *sin* offends finds its content and authority grounded in the objectively self-sufficient God from whom it is issued.[5] As John Webster puts it, the divine law is no less than "the imperative extension of God's being and works."[6] Consequently, a sufficiently "thick" exposition of sin as "lawlessness" presses us to account for the parameters of the divine-human relationship in which the law is at once situated, expressed, and infringed upon by its creaturely subjects. What kind of God does his law disclose? What does it mean to be human subjects of this God, bound to honor him in a particular way, through obedience to the specificity of his law? In appreciating exactly what is entailed in sin's lawlessness, we must have a constant eye to these twin dimensions of the relationship in which it is located. Quoting James 4:12, Petrus van Mastricht expresses the point with sharpness in his reminder that the law against which sin chafes is "not that of just anyone [*cuiusvis*]," but of "that one lawgiver who is able to save and destroy."[7] In other words,

---

[3] For a survey of the biblical vocabulary, see, e.g., Herman Bavinck, *Reformed Dogmatics*, ed. John Bolt, trans. John Vriend, 4 vols. (Grand Rapids, MI: Baker Academic, 2003–8), 3:129–33; Marguerite Shuster, *The Fall and Sin: What We Have Become as Sinners* (Grand Rapids, MI: Eerdmans, 2004), 263–65.

[4] E.g., Augustine, *Answer to Faustus, a Manichean*, trans. Roland J. Teske, in *The Works of Saint Augustine: A Translation for the 21st Century*, vol. I/20 (New York: New City Press, 2007), XXII.27 (317); Francis Turretin, *Institutes of Elenctic Theology*, ed. James T. Dennison Jr., trans. George Musgrave Giger, 3 vols. (Phillipsburg, NJ: P&R, 1992–97), 9.1.3 (1:591); Petrus van Mastricht, *Theoretico-practica theologia*, 7 vols. (Utrecht: W. van de Water, 1724), IV.ii.4 (443a); Bavinck, *Reformed Dogmatics*, 3:133–36; John Murray, *The Collected Writings of John Murray*, 4 vols. (Edinburgh: Banner of Truth, 1977), 2:77–79; Wolfhart Pannenberg, *Systematic Theology*, trans. Geoffrey W. Bromiley, 3 vols. (Grand Rapids, MI: Eerdmans, 1991–93), 2:239–40; Shuster, *Fall and Sin*, 102–10.

[5] On this, compare, for instance, Pannenberg, *Systematic Theology*, 2:246; Shuster, *Fall and Sin*, 103.

[6] John B. Webster, *God without Measure: Working Papers in Christian Theology*, vol. 2, *Virtue and Intellect* (London: Bloomsbury, 2016), 123.

[7] Mastricht, *Theologia*, IV.ii.4. All Latin translations in this chapter are mine.

as Webster puts it, "Christian teaching about sin" is, "in short, . . . a function or extension of the Christian doctrine of God."[8]

Consequently, when referring to sin as "lawlessness," it is inadequate to think purely in terms of what Paul Ricoeur calls a "closed morality,"[9] or a set of discrete infractions against some finite moral code, albeit a divinely revealed one. It is not merely an isolated, unhinged ethical code that names various human states and actions as "sin," insofar as they are violations of that code. That prerogative must ultimately lie with the God whose will is expressed through that code. Which is to say, sin can be named and defined as such only in the context of divine judgment. Before the fact, such naming takes the shape of divine threat: "for in the day that you eat of it you shall surely die" (Gen. 2:17). Here "sin" is not yet an actuality; it remains a mere possibility. But once sin has occurred, its divine identification necessarily arises in the context of a curse: "to dust you shall return" (Gen. 3:19). In other words, in naming some actuality as "sin," God simultaneously reveals himself as the offended other. The divine identification of sin is at once a disclosure of his wrath. And yet, in judging something as an offense, neither God, the sinner, nor the offense itself is somehow obscured beneath a blaze of infinite and all-consuming holy terror. Bridging God's infinite holiness and the creaturely offender is the finite command, the accommodated expression of the infinite will. Through its finite form, divine law gives enumerable specificity to the naming and identification of sin—disobedience, idolatry, deceit, adultery, covetousness, and so on—while at the same time mediating the curse of its infinite legislator.

Ricoeur shrewdly detects here an irreducible dialectic at the heart of the biblical language of sin, between the "open morality" of an infinitely holy God and the "closed morality" of his finite law.[10] Regardless of the form, whether Law or Prophet, woven through the fabric of the entire biblical canon is a juxtaposition between the unrelenting indignation and limitless demand of prophetic denunciation and the concrete specificity of the legal code. That way, the "fracture"—the separation and distance implied by the curse—does not annul a real relationship of explicit and enumerable accountability between God and the sinner, a relationship which Ricoeur suggests is best described as a "covenant."

---

[8] Webster, *God without Measure*, 123; cf. David Kelsey's remark: "Sin . . . is defined by direct reference to God. It is defined theocentrically; it is always 'against God.' It is not fundamentally constituted by a mis-relating to ourselves and to our neighbors but by a mis-relating to God" (Kelsey, *Eccentric Existence*, 409–10).

[9] Paul Ricoeur, *The Symbolism of Evil* (Boston: Beacon, 1967), 58.

[10] On this, see Ricoeur, *Symbolism of Evil*, 50–70.

All this is to say that human consciousness of "sin" depends on the God who alone possesses the right to name and judge it to be so. Therefore, to speak meaningfully about sin implies we are conscious of that judgment, of divine law. But just as divine law cannot be abstracted from the divine lawgiver, or from the one to whom it is addressed, so too consciousness of its judgment cannot occur in an abstract or neutral fashion. It arises only in the context of relationship with God. And to sinners, that consciousness necessarily takes the form of a covenantal curse, a punitive sentence through which the God they have offended holds them to account.

Yet a difficulty remains. A sinner's consciousness of divine judgment need not entail full acknowledgment of fault, or the assumption of any responsibility for the offense. If we may borrow from the apostle Paul, it is quite possible to "know God's righteous decree that those who practice such things deserve to die," while not only continuing to do "such things" but even giving "approval to those who practice them" (Rom. 1:32). To that extent, the sinner's knowledge of sin remains intractably deficient, however alert they may be to the divine sentence. For the sinner to know the full truth about their sin entails no less than an admission which unreservedly accords with the truth of God's judgment: "Against *you*, you only, have I sinned and done what is evil in *your sight*" (Ps. 51:4). In other words, for the sinner, true knowledge of sin necessarily begins with repentance. It is an act of confession, a wholehearted renunciation of this state. Anything less than this, and some form of deception has entered the picture.

The trouble is, to be cursed as a sinner does not necessarily offer any mode of deliverance from this state. That is to say, there is no reason to believe the mere revelation of God's judgment, of divine law, will itself lead to repentance. In fact, the Scriptures consistently pose the reverse. There is surely a certain culpable folly and ignorance—defiance, even—that pretends to "hide" in the presence of divine judgment. And yet invariably that is the pattern, from beginning to end, from garden to judgment day. The same instinct that led Adam to hide among the trees of the garden will one day lead people to say to the mountains, "Fall on us!" (Luke 23:30).[11] When sinners are faced with just judgment, evasion, suppression, and even an intensification of culpability is the standard order of affairs.

---

[11] This is not the place to question speculations about the likelihood of repentance in hell, but it is certainly a relevant extension of this point.

Paul famously puts further analytical flesh on this dynamic when re-counting the impact of divine law on the sinner. In his letter to the Galatians, he refers to the imprisoning effect of "the paidagogos," the law given in Scripture as a guardian to "imprison everything under sin" (Gal. 3:22; cf. Rom. 5:20). In imagining what Paul intends here by portraying the law as a guardian or schoolmaster, we are not to think of some "tranquil" progression "from childhood to adulthood," as Ricoeur puts it, but of "a sort of *inversion through excess*."[12] Indeed, in Romans 7 the picture is more vivid still. Here Paul zeroes in on a perverse collusion between sin and the law (vv. 7–12). Far from arresting sin in its tracks, the commandment—in itself "holy and righteous and good"—merely affords the opportunity for sin to multiply its evil, making the sinner "sinful beyond measure" (ὑπερβολὴν ἁμαρτωλὸς) (v. 13).

For this reason, G. C. Berkouwer rightly insists we misappropriate the so-called "elenctic" or "pedagogical" use of the law if we naïvely presume it is capable of inducing true (that is, repentant) knowledge of sin, sheerly through its bludgeoning force. On its own, the force of divine judgment communicated through the law simply magnifies and intensifies guilt.[13] Indeed, here it is worth recalling Paul's distinction between a "worldly grief [that] produces death" versus the "godly grief [that] produces a repentance" (2 Cor. 7:10). There is a kind of guilty conscience that serves only to make matters worse. Not unlike the tortured personal perspective of Augustine's *Confessions*, Ricoeur strikingly portrays a "phenomenology" of guilt where any dim and unfocused sense of conviction a sinner may experience under the weight of divine curse quickly descends into an enslaving and counter-productive project of self-justification—a project that at once domesticates the law by atomizing and multiplying its demands into manageable portions, while evading its call for genuine and radical obedience through scrupulous attention to the endless rituals of cleansing, excusing, and justifying oneself.[14] The inevitable "failure of this undertaking," he writes, simply exacerbates the "feeling of guilt," and "the integral observance by which the conscience seeks to exculpate itself" only "increases the indictment."[15] This is the "real meaning of the curse of the law."[16]

[12] Ricoeur, *Symbolism of Evil*, 149.
[13] For his extended discussion of this, see Berkouwer, *Sin*, 166–86.
[14] See Ricoeur, *Symbolism of Evil*, 118–50, esp. 139–50.
[15] Ricoeur, *Symbolism of Evil*, 145.
[16] Ricoeur, *Symbolism of Evil*, 143.

In view of all this, if we are to speak accurately about sin, there are really only two scenarios before us. On the one hand, sin might be known and defined as a mere possibility, something that may or may not occur, but that is clearly foreshadowed by divine sanction: "for in the day that you eat of it you shall surely die." This is to know sin from the vantage point of uninterrupted fellowship with God; a fellowship as yet untouched by what is merely prefigured in the form of a warning. But once sin has entered the picture, once that fellowship suffers the rupture of divine curse, a true perception of sin can now emerge only from the perspective of wholehearted repentance. And this, of course, is where a properly Christian doctrine of sin begins.

But for the reasons we have seen, Christianity's confessional clarity about sin cannot chiefly arise from an experience of the curse. It is true that older writers would sometimes speak of the need for "legal conviction"— an awareness and admission of guilt, even a repentance of sorts—before a sinner can arrive at the point of authentically *Christian* repentance. To make repentance possible, so the logic goes, the law must first do its work, "so that every mouth may be stopped, and the whole world may be held accountable to God" (Rom. 3:19).[17] Such conviction might emanate simply from an apprehension of the law within the conscience (so, Rom. 2:14–15). It may be further reinforced by the formal proclamation of the law. Ultimately, however, it might arise only from a special, illuminating work of the Holy Spirit, who brings its searing judgment to bear on the "mind of sin"; after all, widespread indifference to the law among sinners only underlines an existing hardness to its curse, which may not be surmountable by conscience and proclamation alone. All manner of effects may result from this conviction, such as a sense of guilt, grief, humiliation, reformation of behavior, and even a longing for deliverance. Yet, as John Owen points out, all these consequences of the law's conviction are not so much a "duty" to be fulfilled as a reinforcement of its curse.[18] And therefore, however constructive such conviction may be in silencing the sinner's excuses and prompting him or her to inquire after deliverance, it "doth not suffice to give a man a true and

---

[17] So, e.g., Richard Sibbes, *The Complete Works*, 7 vols. (Edinburgh: J. Nichol, 1862–64), 6.176.

[18] "That perturbations, sorrows, dejections, dread, fears, are no duty unto any; only they are such things as sometimes ensue or are immitted into the mind upon that which is a duty indispensable, namely, conviction of sin. They belong not to the precept of the law, but to its curse. They are no part of what is required of us, but of what is inflicted on us" (John Owen, *The Works of John Owen, D.D.*, ed. William H. Goold, 24 vols. [Edinburgh: Johnstone & Hunter, 1850–1855], 3:360).

thorough conviction of sin."[19] Indeed, consistent with Ricoeur's "pathology" noted above, someone like Owen readily agrees that mere "legal conviction" *alone* ultimately serves the perversity of further entrenching existing patterns of sin. Perhaps Kierkegaard (under the pseudonym Anti-Climacus) captures something like the equivocal effect of this legal conviction when he compares the banal, "spiritless" existence of those who for the most part remain ignorant and indifferent to sin with the "spirited" despair of those who have become conscious of its real possibility, power, and culpability before God. To be spirited might seem like an advance, a move closer to the truth about sin, toward repentance. In reality, it proves only to be a step further away, toward ever-greater defiance until it finally reaches the fag end of the demoniac's *conscious* rage.[20] After all, is it not so often the case in the Gospels, that the demoniac is both closest to the truth yet furthest away?

Properly Christian clarity about sin must, then, find its origin in a source other than divine law. Commenting on John 16:8, Owen points to a unique kind of conviction the Holy Spirit delivers directly from Christ and the divine wisdom peculiarly summed up in him.[21] Ironically, it is in the very act of redeeming sinners that Christ transpires to possess an unequalled capacity to expose the true depravity of sin. So scandalously and irretrievably wicked is sin that it took no less than the blood of the divine Son to bear its curse in opening space for redemption. If sin itself debases God's honor, through the law he puts it to the higher end of upholding his vindicatory justice through the recompense of the curse. But in Christ, God puts sin to a higher end still, namely the praise of his glorious grace in the sinner's pardon and deliverance.[22] And having put sin to this glorious end, Christ therein uniquely exposes its true depths. To that degree Karl Barth was right to insist upon

---

[19] Owen, *Works*, 2:95. Karl Barth clearly has a kind of legal "preparationism" in mind when critiquing the seventeenth-century Protestant orthodox tendency to define sin by reference to the law (note, e.g., his remarks on Rom. 3:20: Karl Barth, *Church Dogmatics*, ed. Geoffrey W. Bromiley and Thomas F. Torrance, 4 vols. [Edinburgh: T&T Clark, 1956–69], IV/1.395, cf. 369–72). While Barth's critique is exaggerated in service of his idiosyncratic Christocentric method, it is noteworthy that Owen himself consciously cautions against the danger of confusing true repentance with the mere pangs of a conscience troubled by preaching that has dealt with it "severely" (Owen, *Works*, 3:362).

[20] For this interpretation of Kierkegaard's notoriously difficult text, *The Sickness unto Death*, see the extended discussion in Jason A. Mahn, *Fortunate Fallibility: Kierkegaard and the Power of Sin* (New York: Oxford University Press, 2011), 87–131. Mahn sees the paradox captured in a remark like the following, when Kierkegaard is describing the stronger form of despair called "defiance": "But just because it is despair through the aid of the eternal, in a sense it is very close to the truth; and just because it lies very close to the truth, it is infinitely far away" (Søren Kierkegaard, *The Sickness unto Death: A Christian Psychological Exposition for Upbuilding and Awakening*, trans. Howard V. Hong and Edna H. Hong [Princeton, NJ: Princeton University Press, 1980], 67). Note too Kierkegaard's conclusions about "defiance" at the end of Part I of *Sickness unto Death* (72–74).

[21] For this, see Owen, *Works*, 2:94–101; cf. also Sibbes, *Complete Works*, 6:169–72.

[22] Owen, *Works*, 2:100–101.

this point,[23] even if he was not quite as original in making this observation as he might have supposed. It is not that Christ somehow invalidates the law's sentence against sin; far from it. His cross confirms and heightens its judgment, while at the same time eliminating its curse, subordinating it to the gracious end of forgiveness and a full-scale redemption from all of sin's devastating consequences.

Thus it is only in the context of divine mercy—a new word from God, a covenant *of grace*—that a sinner may properly know the truth about sin. Bathing the sinner in the gracious light of the cross, the gospel allows the law's so-called elenctic and pedagogical use to come into its own, while adding fresh clarity about sin in the face of Christ's atoning death. By holding out the prospect of pardon and thoroughgoing deliverance from sin, the gospel at once liberates the sinner and compels him to own the law's sentence against sin.[24]

This is why Christians have traditionally regarded repentance as something inseparably coordinate with faith. Just as the gospel proclamation itself embraces both the promise of forgiveness and a call to repentance (Luke 24:46–47; Acts 2:37–38; 5:31; 20:21; Heb. 6:1), so too is it grasped by a kind of trust that cannot but entail a wholesale renunciation of sin. Such renunciation consents to God's sentence against sin meted out at the cross—"we know that our old self was crucified with him"—as well as the gradual outworking of that sentence in the mortification of sin within our members—"in order that the body of sin might be brought to nothing, so that we would no longer be enslaved to sin" (Rom. 6:6).

At the very least, then, faith and repentance are intimately and inseparably entwined, as John Murray readily insists. But is Murray right to dismiss any question of priority between the two?[25] Owen hints at a subtler answer, which sheds light on the important theological dynamic between them. On the one hand, the gospel command to repent necessarily implies the prospect of mercy and forgiveness, lest God deceive sinners through a futile call. True

---

[23] Cf. Barth, *Church Dogmatics*, IV/1.412: "The serious and terrible nature of human corruption, the depth of the abyss into which man is about to fall as the author of it, can be measured by the fact that the love of God could react and reply to this event only by His giving, His giving up, of Jesus Christ Himself to overcome and remove it and in that way to redeem man, fulfilling the judgment upon it in such a way that the Judge allowed Himself to be judged and caused the man of sin to be put to death in His own person."

[24] See Bavinck's apposite remark: "Christian faith is needed to rightly know sin, but that faith also looks back toward the law, discovers its spiritual character, and thus receives insight into the true nature of sin. The gospel would not be gospel if it did not include forgiveness of all those transgressions we have committed against the law of God. Just as grace presupposes sin, forgiveness, and guilt, so the gospel presupposes law" (Bavinck, *Reformed Dogmatics*, 3:141).

[25] John Murray, *Redemption: Accomplished and Applied* (Edinburgh: Banner of Truth, 1979), 113.

repentance, then, is not the Judas-like compelled confession of a soul tortured beneath the weight of sin's consequences, but a free and full admission that cannot but emerge from faith's joyful sense of divine mercies.[26] In "order of nature," we may say that authentically Christian repentance is a fruit of faith—not just faith "in general," but faith in the "special object" of God's mercy manifest in Christ.[27] But in "order of confession," it may normally be that penitent sinners are first led to confront the horror of their sin, assuming full responsibility for it as they gaze mournfully on "him whom they have pierced" (Zech. 12:10). And with a cry "from the depths," as it were, only thence does the true brilliance of God's pardoning grace emerge in full focus: "For with the LORD there is steadfast love, and with him is plentiful redemption" (Ps. 130:7).

In any event, as Martin Luther famously began his *Ninety-Five Theses*, Christian faith never outgrows the demand for repentant clarity about sin. Confession is not a fitful and traumatic affair, merely restricted to moments of notorious lapse, but the natural register of a faith that is marked by constant attentiveness to the evil of sin, together with its ongoing power and possibility.[28] Until the reality and threat of sin entirely disappears, the joy of Christian assurance is paradoxically juxtaposed against the sorrow of penance. Christian faith only ever leaves off at the point where it confronts the real truth about our fallibility. It is as if Christian experience is perpetually suspended between the total eclipse of Good Friday and the glorious dawn of Easter Sunday—for now, at least. Grace will shine more brilliantly within Christian consciousness only as the threat of sin appears more menacing. Perhaps it is in this sense that sin is best described as a "happy fault" (*felix culpa*), what Jason Mahn calls "fortunate fallibility" as he recounts Kierkegaard's vivid treatment of this paradox.[29]

A Christian exploration of sin and its lawlessness is no theoretical abstraction, then. It is an exercise in penitent and honest self-reflection before Christ; a fitting, Spirit-led, and necessary response to the gracious covenantal blessing we have experienced in him. If the cursed sinner instinctively "hates the light," scurrying for the cover of darkness "lest [their] works should be

---

[26] Owen, *Works*, 6:373–74, 438–39.

[27] Owen, *Works*, 22:32–33. Owen elsewhere writes, "No comfortable, refreshing thoughts of God, no warrantable or acceptable boldness in an approach and access unto him, can any one entertain or receive, but in this exercise of faith on Christ as the mediator between God and man" (Owen, *Works*, 1:134).

[28] See, e.g., Owen, *Works*, 6:547–51; 22:31–32.

[29] Mahn, *Fortunate Fallibility*.

exposed" (John 3:20), Christians are drawn to face up to sin in the light of one to whom the Father has entrusted all judgment, with all fear of condemnation vanquished in the knowledge that they have already "passed from death to life" (John 5:24). Indeed, a Christian theology of sin ought to be something all believers can recognize and embrace as a kind of approach to Christ which echoes the invocation of the psalmist—"search me," "try me," "know my thoughts," "see if there be any grievous way in me, and lead me in the way everlasting!"—in full consciousness of his omniscient gaze (Ps. 139:23–24).[30]

Guided by the "Spirit of truth," what the perspective of penitent faith provides, then, is a kind of "confessional" hermeneutic that drives us back to Scripture as the divine diagnosis and interpretation of our plight in retrospect of our redemption in Christ. It is in the fullness of what we know of God's mercy to us in Christ that we can now proceed to hear Scripture speak of sin's origin; its character; its immediate and ongoing effects on ourselves, our relationship with God, and our descendants; as well as the place God has allowed it in his redemptive plans and purposes for creation.

II. *Unde Malum?* Accounting for the Existence of Sin

As natural and logical as it may seem to proceed from here in our theological description of sin by turning first to the question of its origin, theologians have often lingered over the validity of the question itself, or at least the possibility of finding an answer. If true knowledge of sin arises only through confession of our guilt, Berkouwer insists, "we do not, and we cannot, yearn for an 'explanation' of our sins."[31] His point is simply that what looks like the honest pursuit of an explanation—for a "cause" or "origin" of sin—all too easily disguises a dubious evasion of responsibility, a quest to locate the blame somewhere else. If we are to speak of a true "explanation" for sin's origin at all, perhaps we should only venture to say that any account must ultimately cease with ourselves. Yet even here significant difficulties remain. To point to my own individual responsibility as the explanation of sin begs the question, who is responsible for me and my actions? And as soon as I attempt to answer that question, another like it will ensue. In other words,

---

[30] See McFadyen's apposite remark: "Sin can only responsibly be faced through grace and only responsibly brought to speech in a language, the predominant modality of which is confession conjoined with thanks and praise offering all back to God" (Alistair McFadyen, *Bound to Sin: Abuse, Holocaust, and the Christian Doctrine of Sin* [Cambridge: Cambridge University Press, 2000], 249).

[31] Berkouwer, *Sin*, 19.

as David Kelsey rightly maintains, explanations for sin so often merely shift the question back a step.[32] Indeed, perhaps the foremost challenge we face when accounting for the existence of sin arises from a sense that sinners are at once entirely responsible for their sin, while at the same time they are not the final cause of their own existence and actions *in every respect*. Consequently, when it comes to locating a "final cause" for sin—if any—we are bound to encroach upon infamously complex and controversial terrain. In navigating this terrain, the tradition has typically sought to draw out a number of theological inferences that stem from a foundational biblical conviction concerning the character of God.

A. The Biblical *"A Priori"*: The Goodness of God and His Creaturely Analogue

The Scriptures are so emphatic in upholding both the unadulterated goodness of God and his utter distance from and aversion to any declension from that goodness, that Berkouwer calls it a cardinal "a priori" to any theological exploration into the origins of sin and evil. The conviction could not be expressed more succinctly than it is by the apostle John: "God is light, and in him is no darkness at all" (1 John 1:5). So emphatic are the Scriptures on this point that very often the goodness and perfection of God is explicitly defined in opposition to what is deemed sin and evil (e.g., Num. 23:19; Deut. 32:4; 1 Sam. 15:29; 2 Chron. 19:7; Job 34:10; Ps. 92:15; Hab. 1:12–13; James 1:13). Indeed, the sheer impossibility of any fellowship between God and the sinner underlines a fundamental aspect of his holiness, an obstacle that cannot be overcome without a thoroughgoing satisfaction of his righteous anger against the abomination he so resolutely hates (Isa. 6:1–7; cf. Deut. 25:16; Pss. 5:4; 11:5; Zech. 8:17; Luke 16:15).

If God is the exclusive reference point for what is "good" (cf. Pss. 118:1; 136:1), his works of creation cannot be supposed to make up for some moral deficit or imperfection in his character, as if he somehow needs creation to vindicate himself from any possible threat or accusation. Rather, the sheer redundancy of creation to his moral purity makes it entirely necessary for creation to express that purity, albeit in a finite and creaturely way. In other words, the very gratuity of creation relative to God's eternally free, perfect, and self-sufficient existence ineluctably testifies to its essential goodness.

---

[32] Kelsey, *Eccentric Existence*, 410.

That was always the point of the Thomistic *analogia entis*; not to commit the intolerable blasphemy of placing God and his creation on some emana-tionist continuum of relative ontological perfections, as Barth so feared, but to make the simple observation that whatever God is *in himself* (the "*esse ipsum subsistens*"), his creation must also be via *participation* ("*ens per par-ticipationem*"), in the radical otherness of its creaturely form. Indeed, not only is the gift-like existence of creation a derived and contingent expres-sion of his eternal existence, so too must any real, intelligible truth about its essential character be a contingent expression and derivation of the truth that is eternally summed up in God himself. If it is true that God embraces the very essence of goodness, then any truth about his works must entail a finite communication of that eternal goodness. Jonathan Edwards captured the point memorably in comparing our own impelled acts of benevolence with God's free, creative benevolence. On the one hand, even the "most gra-cious" of creatures, he writes, are "not so independent and self-moved in their goodness" that they are not "excited by some object that they find: something appearing good, or in some respect worthy of regard," presenting itself and moving their kindness. God, on the other hand, "being all and alone is ab-solutely self-moved," so that rather than finding objects of his benevolence, he creates them as the very expression of his benevolence. Hence "all that is good and worthy in the object, and the very being of the object" merely proceeds "from the overflowing of his fullness."[33]

Of course, the needless "surplus" or superabundance of God's goodness in creation need not manifest itself in wooden uniformity. There is, as Aqui-nas reminds us, a dynamic diversity within creation precisely because mere uniformity clearly could not adequately reflect God's goodness.[34] Likewise, the creaturely analogue of divine goodness need not unfold at once in all its actualized perfection. Even at "the end," creation will never cease to remain contingent on God's eternal perfection. But what was "good," or indeed "very good" at the beginning need not entail the complete disclosure of everything creation can possibly attest to concerning God's goodness. Only in its total-ity does creation comprehensively glorify God. The point is often made with

---

[33] Jonathan Edwards, *Ethical Writings*, ed. Paul Ramsey, vol. 8 of *The Works of Jonathan Edwards*, 26 vols. (New Haven, CT: Yale University Press, 1989), 462–63.
[34] Thomas Aquinas, *Summa Theologiae* I.q47.a1. On this point, see Michael Hanby, "Creation as Aesthetic Analogy," in *The Analogy of Being: Invention of the Antichrist or the Wisdom of God?*, ed. Thomas Joseph White (Grand Rapids, MI: Eerdmans, 2011), 373–74.

reference to the unfolding plotline of biblical history. In light of the end—
that "enduring city" to come—the garden paradise could only have been a
provisional expression of God's goodness, however unspoiled its excellence.

The same observation regarding the differentiated expression of God's
goodness becomes all the more vivid by zeroing in on what is undeniably
the pinnacle of creation, or what God uniquely designates as his "image." Of
course, the notorious elusiveness of this title is only matched by a universal
sense of its significance. For all the scarcity in biblical reference, let alone
elaboration of its essence, the occasions where it is mentioned are highly suggestive indeed. And among the multitudes of portraits vying for attention, the
most uncontested observation is undoubtedly that which is articulated best by
the apostle Paul himself: "*He* is the image [εἰκὼν] of the invisible God, the
firstborn of all creation" (Col. 1:15). Anything else that is said about the title
must be relative to this, to the concrete existence of the incarnate Son. Barth,
of course, famously went so far as insisting the title is properly a prerogative
of the Son alone. To the extent that any other human being bears the title, it
is only ever "according to" him who *is* the image of God *sui generis*.[35] Even
if Barth's observation is tied up with his unique methodological convictions
concerning election and the like, more recent explorations of the designation
insist upon a similar conclusion even where the hermeneutical standpoint
is rather more traditional.[36] Whatever it meant for Adam to be created "in
the image of God" in the beginning (Gen. 1:26–27), that must ultimately
give way to the full "glory of God" uniquely unveiled in the "face of Jesus
Christ" (2 Cor. 4:6; cf. 3:18–4:6). As someone like Kilner is keen to point
out, where the NT uses the language of "image" (εἰκὼν, χαρακτὴρ) in reference to Christ, it is closely associated with the reflection of God's "glory,"
or the visible, concrete, and incarnate manifestation of his attributes (cf.
Heb. 1:1–3). Moreover, to the extent that the members of Christ's "body"
may eventually be transformed into that likeness and glory, it will always
be subordinate to what is uniquely summed up in its "head." In "the end"
there will be only the "man of heaven" and those who are raised to "bear"
his image (1 Cor. 15:49).

---

[35] E.g., Barth, *Church Dogmatics*, III/1.197–206.

[36] Notably, John F. Kilner, *Dignity and Destiny: Humanity in the Image of God* (Grand Rapids, MI: Eerdmans,
2015). Kelsey's extensive treatment of the title in the "Coda" to his *magnum opus* bears a distinctly Barthian accent, notwithstanding his own "triple helix" approach to defining human identity with reference to Christ (Kelsey,
Eccentric Existence, 893–1051).

The point of this is simply to say that the summit of God's creative goodness and glory is uniquely concentrated in the incarnate Son, the "image of God" par excellence. To use Hans Urs von Balthasar's expression, he is "the concrete analogia entis," the supreme *creaturely* analogue or ectype of essential divine goodness.[37] As David Bentley Hart observes, this claim is animated by Chalcedonian logic, which at once affirms that God has never drawn closer to his creation than he has in Christ, without ever endangering the integrity of those natures in all their radical difference;[38] a point Owen also recognized when he carefully sought to ground the incarnate Son's superlative status as the "representative" image of God in his eternal procession from the Father as the "essential" image of God.[39]

Frankly, it must be said, while the Western Catholic tradition is frequently derided for privileging functional or ontological descriptions of the *imago Dei* such as "dominion," or the soul's "rational" and "moral" capacities, this fundamentally Christological orientation has always been primary. Indeed, there can be no doubt that the very reason theologians have classically attended to the qualitative notion of Adam's "original righteousness" as the chief expression of the divine image—something that was to play out concretely through his embodied relations to God, his fellow human beings, and the rest of creation—is because of what redeemed humanity is destined to become in Christ, a reflection of the qualitative divine-likeness or glory that is embodied uniquely and perfectly in him (cf. Rom. 8:29; Eph. 4:24; Col. 3:10; 2 Cor. 3:18–4:6).[40]

B. The Existence of Sin: A Necessary or Unpreventable Foil to God's Glory?

Be that as it may, the real elephant in the room here is the seemingly indispensable role sin plays in the complete manifestation of God's creative good-

---

[37] Hans Urs von Balthasar, *Theo-Drama: Theological Dramatic Theory*, trans. Graham Harrison (San Francisco: Ignatius, 1988–98), II.267.

[38] David Bentley Hart, "The Destiny of Christian Metaphysics: Reflections on the *Analogia Entis*," in *The Analogy of Being: Invention of the Antichrist or the Wisdom of God?*, ed. Thomas Joseph White (Grand Rapids, MI: Eerdmans, 2011), 409–10. See Thomas Joseph White, "'Through Him All Things Were Made' (John 1:3): The Analogy of the Word Incarnate according to St. Thomas Aquinas and Its Ontological Presuppositions," in *The Analogy of Being: Invention of the Antichrist or the Wisdom of God?*, ed. Thomas Joseph White (Grand Rapids, MI: Eerdmans, 2011), 251–59.

[39] See Owen, *Works*, 1:71–72, 78, 79–80.

[40] If Kilner is right to insist that, strictly speaking, human beings always exist "according to" or with an intended destiny in reference to the true image of God in Christ—regardless of how well they reflect his likeness and glory—his critique of the tradition is fair enough. An absence of "original righteousness," then, may have nothing to do with a person's created status vis-à-vis the image of God. But the tradition's emphasis on "original righteousness" arguably intends to represent precisely the point Kilner himself makes, namely, that we only "live up to" our image-status to the extent that we reflect what is uniquely summed up in Christ (cf. Kilner, *Dignity and Destiny*, 147). For Kilner's arguments against the tradition on this point, see *Dignity and Destiny*, 189–99.

ness. Since God is glorified only in the totality of creaturely life and history, the concentrated expression of that glory in the incarnate Son necessarily embraces the totality of his specific redemptive mission in both its earthly and heavenly states. But here is the conundrum: While the work of Christ clearly does not entail any divine approval of sin, does not the presence of sin in human history—even as an obstacle to be overcome—suggest its existence is an unpreventable or necessary foil to the magnification or vindication of God's attributes in the Son? There is a kind of theodicy which unashamedly embraces this kind of conclusion, whether in the form of something like Hegel's idealism, or the so-called "Irenaean theodicy" which has gained traction as an answer to the challenge of modern palaeoanthropology,[41] or the kenotic eschatological vision of Jürgen Moltmann.[42] More classically, however, theologians have intensely resisted that inference, perhaps even in the strongest possible terms. Aside from its impact on more abstract metaphysical questions concerning divine aseity and the like, ascribing any unavoidability or necessity to the presence of sin would appear to entail a straightforward encroachment upon the goodness of God and its unalloyed expression within creation. At best, it seems to concede that evil and sin are an unpreventable dualistic intrusion, an alien threat to divine honor that God is compelled to vanquish. At worst, it gives the perverse impression that evil and sin are somehow necessary or determined to enhance God's being or a specific attribute such as his love.

Yet before hastening to cast aside these conclusions, the scope and seriousness of the challenge sin poses should at minimum make us wonder if this kind of theodicy, with its dualistic or deterministic implications, is not so absurdly unreasonable after all. Even traditionally infralapsarian and supralapsarian accounts of the Son's incarnate advent surely at least tend in the direction of the two outcomes we may instinctively wish to avoid (dualism and determinism). At one end, the protological thrust of the infralapsarian could imply that the Son's appearance is somehow necessary to polish off the unwanted tarnish that sin has introduced to the original glory of creation in all its unspoiled perfection. Alternatively, the eschatological thrust

---

[41] See, e.g., Mark Harris, *The Nature of Creation: Examining the Bible and Science* (Durham, UK: Acumen, 2013). For the classic modern deployment of the so-called Irenaean theodicy, see John Hick, *Evil and the God of Love* (Basingstoke, UK: Palgrave Macmillan, 2007 [1977]), 211–15.

[42] E.g., Jürgen Moltmann, *The Trinity and the Kingdom of God: The Doctrine of God* (Tübingen: SCM, 1981), 21–60; 108–11; 114–19.

of the supralapsarian might suggest that sin was a necessary, divinely ordained prelude to all that the Son uniquely has unfolded and will unfold in his redemptive mission. It is easy to caricature, of course, but the point is simply this: the challenge of narrating the Son's full disclosure of divine glory in a way that does not entail an admission that sin is an unpreventable (dualistic) or necessary (deterministic) foil is acute, however unwanted that admission may be.[43]

Barth, for one, attempts to sidestep the admission through his radical revision of election, insisting that we define human nature strictly by reference to the God-man alone. To his mind, the concrete existence and perfection of Christ compels us to see that authentic humanity is ontologically oriented toward God, not against him: "To be man," he writes, "is to be with God."[44] Consequently, humanity realizes its "ontological possibility" only in "the doing of the will of God."[45] That is to say, whatever else we say about genuine human "freedom"—so called *liberum arbitrium*—it must, at heart, encapsulate the sheer "impossibility" of sin (*non potest peccare*).[46] Long before Barth, Maximus the Confessor famously rejected the potential for any conflict between Christ's human and divine wills by arguing that our creaturely freedom is most truly human when it submits willingly to God without any trace of deliberation (*gnome*). Yet, for Maximus, and the orthodox tradition more generally, besides Christ himself, the indefectible will is only ever an eschatological reality. In the beginning, the historical advent of sin manifestly points to the original possibility of sin (*potest peccare*), even if that sin was never a constitutional inevitability (*potest non peccare*). Barth rejects this way of squaring things not only because he wishes to uphold a strictly Christological definition of authentic human nature, but perhaps even more fundamentally because the ontological goodness of our creaturely nature can never allow room for any freedom to sin. To embrace sin is not to enact some God-created potential but to do what Christ reveals to be impossible, to undo

---

[43] Although Kelsey and others accuse Schleiermacher of effectively veering in the more deterministic direction of sin as a kind of necessary fault, Schleiermacher himself feels this dilemma acutely, labeling the two extremes as a form of "Manichaeism" (dualism), where God's will is trumped by the human will, or "Pelagianism" (determinism), where the distinction between the Redeemer and the redeemed, grace and sin is effectively collapsed (Friedrich Schleiermacher, *Christian Faith* [Edinburgh: T&T Clark, 1999], 269–70, 326–30, 335; cf. Kelsey, *Eccentric Existence*, 411; see too, Mahn, *Fortunate Fallibility*, 102–3).

[44] Barth, *Church Dogmatics*, III/2.139. "As he dwells in this sphere [in Christ], man is so with God that he derives solely and exclusively from Him. . . . It means that it is only with Him and not without Him or against Him that he can exist, and think and speak, and work and rest, and rejoice and mourn, and live and die" (Barth, *Church Dogmatics*, III/2.142).

[45] Barth, *Church Dogmatics*, III/2.142.

[46] Barth, *Church Dogmatics*, IV/2.494–95; cf. III/2.197.

our creaturely integrity by enslaving ourselves to an unreality, a *nichtige* outside of him (*servum arbitrium*).[47]

There is no doubt that Barth has exposed one of the chief problems in defining human freedom as pure "indifference" to the effectual influence of any cause or moral object, even where it is ostensibly put to the service of exonerating God from any part in sin and evil, as it often is in the Molinist-Arminian tradition. By seeking to circumvent the Scylla of determinism through the notion of pure indifference, a dualistic Charybdis invariably follows in its wake. Yet, as Barth himself readily admits, for all its apparent "impossibility" and irrational "nothingness," sin really "exists." And more to the point, one way or another God has not prevented its existence. To that extent, Berkouwer is right to infer that Barth has merely shifted the general problem "to other ground."[48] The capacity to contradict the divine will, and even our own ontology, appears to be an all-too-evident possibility of our created natures after all.[49] And therefore it is hard to see how the Christological revision of election and anthropology avoids the spectre of sin as a necessary or unpreventable foil; the "No" that forms the inevitable backdrop to the "Yes" of his universal grace revealed in the faithfulness of the human Christ.

C. *"Posse Peccare"*: A Way Forward?

As Berkouwer rightly observes, the "posse peccare" of the Augustinian tradition is really just a self-evident admission arising from a straightforward interpretation of the biblical witness concerning our plight: for whatever their ontological goodness as creatures of an all-benevolent God, human beings are manifestly capable of sin.[50] Perhaps we may chart a way forward by exploring the theological principles which have traditionally brought some clarity to this observation, with all its attending challenges.

At the outset, such an observation is, as we would expect, traditionally set against a caveat, or what Berkouwer calls "the biblical a priori": *Deus non est causa, auctor peccati* (God is not the cause, the author of sin). Anything less than this and all the biblical refrains concerning the goodness of God,

---

[47] Barth, *Church Dogmatics*, IV/2.494–96; cf. III/2.146–67.
[48] G. C. Berkouwer, *The Triumph of Grace in the Theology of Karl Barth*, trans. Harry R. Boer (London: Paternoster, 1956), 233.
[49] "Real man can deny and obscure his reality. This ability for which there is no reason, the mad and incomprehensible possibility of sin, is a sorry fact. And since man is able to sin, and actually does so, he betrays himself into a destructive contradiction in which he is as it were torn apart" (Barth, *Church Dogmatics*, III/2.205).
[50] Berkouwer, *Triumph of Grace*, 233.

his creation, and his uncompromising judgment against evil would seem to be mere farce. Scripture undeniably assumes that men and women are the deserving objects of God's wrath (and, we might add, the needy objects of his merciful redemption), because it is they who are ultimately accountable for their sin. However much an already-fallen angelic realm may have been implicated in their fall (or in any subsequent sin), there is no absolution of responsibility on this score. And certainly, Scripture will permit neither human nor demon to deflect any of this blame back onto their Maker. That is to say, for whatever else we might wish to say about the human ability to sin, the nature of our full accountability for this fall is such that there is nothing inevitable about our God-given natures, no inherent design flaw, no hairline fracture, let alone any fatalistic divine determination, that would make our fall physically necessary or unpreventable, and therein somehow excusable. And yet we fell.

To account for this anomaly—or what Kierkegaard may call a paradox—a series of further distinctions needs to come into play. First, the manifestly obvious phenomenological observation, "posse peccare" (able to sin), is clarified by an important qualification that, at least in the beginning, "potuit non peccare" (he was able not to sin), Adam was *genuinely* able not to sin. In other words, at the outset, human nature was not in a state of disorder, of "pure nature," that needed the correction of some subsequent gift of grace (*donum superadditum*). Nor was it in a state of pure indifference, as if the inherent God-given goodness of its embodied existence, its intellectual capacities, desires, and appetites, provided absolutely no positive check or effectual influence on the human will.[51] The notion of Adam's freedom to sin may entail the capacity for moral deliberation—what Maximus called the "gnomic will," with its powers of *bouleusis* and *prohairesis*—but it does not imply a state of absolute volitional neutrality.[52] Indeed, if theologians have traditionally emphasized Adam's "original righteousness" as the chief expression of the divine image, the point of that observation is not to accent some abstract moral capacity but to underline his eminent fitness for the task at hand: to "fill and subdue," to represent and glorify God by enacting

[51] Interestingly, McFarland questions Augustine's consistency on this score, detaching will from his nature: e.g., Ian A. McFarland, *In Adam's Fall: A Meditation on the Christian Doctrine of Original Sin* (Chichester, West Sussex, UK: Wiley-Blackwell, 2010), 71–74, 78–79. For Aquinas, pre-fall will was sovereign over the bodily appetites, but that is not to say that the appetites did not in some way confirm and strengthen the will's choices.
[52] So, Francis Turretin, *Opera* (Edinburgh: John D. Lowe, 1847–48), VIII.i.8–9; cf. Lars Thunberg, *Microcosm and Mediator: The Theological Anthropology of Maximus the Confessor*, 2nd ed. (Chicago: Open Court, 1995), 218–26.

and enabling creation's God-given potential.[53] Properly understood, then, the claim "posse peccare" should not suggest the actualization of some "potential" that was always naturally inherent to human existence. Everything about Adam's original nature meant that sin was not at all inevitable but entirely preventable, and more to the point, entirely unnatural and at odds with the end for which he was made. Of course, this theological inference remains one of the most decisive obstacles to any straightforward rapprochement between a biblical account of human origins and modern palaeoanthropology, where the biological conditions of our irretrievably mortal existence would seem to render sin or at least a tendency to violence a perpetually emergent, even necessary, feature of our evolving natures themselves.[54]

But leaving that question to one side for now, by emphasizing Adam's genuine ability to prevent sin we can also get to the heart of what is meant by another clarificatory distinction, namely the concept of "privation." Since the advent of sin cannot be explained as the actualization of any capacity inherent within his essentially good nature, the "essence" of sin itself must be understood as a kind of privation. It has no material substance. It is not something created by God, nor is it something that emerges or evolves naturally, potentially, or unavoidably from his creation. Even less is it some kind of alien intrusion, a foreign entity that suddenly and inexplicably materialized with an altogether different substance of its own. Rather, it is a negation of being; an absence of what is good, and therefore, something that defies truth and rational explanation. Indeed, Kierkegaard was probably right that it is only as we come to grasp the total unnecessity of sin that we grasp the character of its

---

[53] E.g., here is Jerome Zanchi: "For this is the truth on the earth: in it a visible image was made—not by any painter or sculptor—but by God himself, who fashioned man with his own hands, endowing him with body and soul, and bringing him to life in this state. And therefore he wished to be visible in the midst of the world so he could be contemplated by all things. . . . You see, after founding some great city, great princes are accustomed to establish an image of themselves in the midst of it, in ongoing memory of its foundation, so that all future generations may discern from the semblance and features of the figure what the founder of that city was like in spirit, and that they too might love him in spirit. Similarly, after making the world, God fashioned his own visible image in it so that man himself as a representative of God might also rule it, and that God in him, as in his image, by certain means might be seen and loved" (*De operibus Dei* III.1, in Girolamo Zanchi, *Omnium operum theologicorum* [Geneva: Samuel Crispin, 1619], tIII [c. 690]).

Similarly, here is Owen: "They [other creatures] could not any way declare the glory of God, but passively and objectively. They were as a harmonious, well-tuned instrument, which gives no sound unless there be a skilful hand to move and act it. What is light, if there be no eye to see it? Or what is music, if there be no ear to hear it? How glorious and beautiful soever any of the works of creation appear to be, from impressions of divine power, wisdom, and goodness on them; yet, without this image of God in man, there was nothing here below to understand God in them—to glorify God by them. This alone is that whereby, in a way of admiration, obedience, and praise, we were enabled to render unto God all the glory which he designed from those works of his power" (Owen, *Works*, 1:183).

[54] A point Daniel W. Houck readily concedes in his own recent constructive response to this challenge: Daniel W. Houck, *Aquinas, Original Sin, and the Challenge of Evolution* (Cambridge: Cambridge University Press, 2020), 185–89, 205.

true depravity in all its inexplicability. In this sense Barth certainly had a point when referring to sin as an "ontological impossibility." But to think of sin like this is only to do so in the abstract. Concretely, our dilemma is—as we have said before—sin actually exists. And so long as it exists, we cannot speak of it as "pure privation," as if it somehow defies reality altogether.[55] Indeed, most prefer to think of sin as some real thing that suffers from a kind of defect or declension. Whatever the defect is—the "evil" that makes something "sin"— that which remains is unquestionably real and *actual*. As Kelsey admits, even if we are to say that the "evil" which makes for sin is not a "reality in its own right"—that it is a "negative mystery"—it nevertheless has a genuine "reality" that is only ever "parasitic on creatures' reality."[56] Older writers make the same point by distinguishing between the sin itself, which in essence is not something positive or real—an ontological impossibility—and the "substratum" that gives sin its real, concrete existence.[57] Hence, as Herman Bavinck remarks, sin does not amount to an alteration in human "substance" itself; rather, it entails a parasitic moral privation which deforms that substance to a fundamentally odious and corrupt end, liable to the curse of divine judgment.[58]

All this is to say that the privation at the heart of sin has no good cause, no rational explanation. It is an absurd mystery that certainly must never be described as a necessary or unpreventable part of God's creation or human existence. Indeed, this is part of the reason Berkouwer insists we should entirely dismiss any quest to find a cause for sin. Sin is simply a "riddle," an irrational mystery that refuses explanation.[59] Kelsey takes a similar view, following Kierkegaard's famous cue by insisting that sin is a circularity which simply "posits itself."[60] In neither case should the appeal to mystery be read as a lazy shortcut out of a complexity that can be resolved with a little more effort; a temptation theologians sometimes face.[61] Rather, the refusal to grant

---

[55] For an extended critique of the way evil has sometimes been interpreted as "pure privation," see, e.g., Charles Hodge, *Systematic Theology*, 3 vols. (New York: Scribner, 1872–73), 2:133–37, 157–59.

[56] Kelsey, *Eccentric Existence*, 405; cf. Bavinck, *Reformed Dogmatics*, 3:138, 210: "[S]in cannot have its own principle and its own independent existence; it only originated *after* and exists only *by* and in connection *with* the good."

[57] E.g., Mastricht, *Theologia*, IV.ii.21 (446b–47a): "The Reformed certainly acknowledge that sin is grounded in a certain substratum, namely a power or action in which the evil inheres, since it is not a substance which subsists through itself. They acknowledge, then, that sin is not a [merely] negative thing. But they deny that it is some real, substantial or positive thing. Truly, it is a certain privation which consists only in *anomia*, or an absence of moral rectitude in the bearing subject" (my translation).

[58] Bavinck, *Reformed Dogmatics*, 3:139–40.

[59] See Berkouwer, *Sin*, 11–66, 130–48.

[60] Kelsey, *Eccentric Existence*, 410–11, 420–21. See also Emil Brunner's remark: "Only he who understands that sin is inexplicable knows what it is" (Emil Brunner, *Man in Revolt*, trans. Olive Wyon [London: Lutterworth, 1939], 132).

[61] Both Berkouwer and Kelsey are clearly conscious of this temptation (Berkouwer, *Sin*, 130–31; Kelsey, *Eccentric Existence*, 411).

sin any explanation is a principled one, stemming from the conviction that it is and will always be utterly absurd.

There is an important truth to this. Yet so long as we admit that the privation of sin and evil only ever coincide with what actually exists, we cannot totally evade questions of explanation and causality by taking refuge in its mystery.[62] Indeed, as much as we may instinctively recoil at the thought, the real existence of sin in human history means it cannot be decoupled from good causes that must ultimately find their terminus in God alone. Not only did God create a world in which sin is a possibility, the actualization of that possibility in human history is also nested within the scope of his providential concursus. Certainly, there is enough *prima facie* evidence to suggest that the Scriptures would not be troubled by this inference. Aside from more general affirmations of universal divine sovereignty, one only needs to refer to the hardening of Pharaoh's or Sihon's heart (Ex. 9:12; Deut. 2:30; cf. Josh. 11:20; 1 Kings 12:15), the evil spirit that so troubled Saul (1 Sam. 16:14–15), or Shimei's curse (2 Sam. 16:10). Indeed, perhaps the most striking allusion to this reality is the very passion of our Lord, with its repeated refrains of divine intention and scriptural fulfillment (e.g., Matt. 26:24, 31, 53–54, 56; 27:9–10; Luke 22:31–42; John 12:27; 13:18; 19:11, 24, 28, 36–37; Acts 2:23; 4:28).

Classically, theologians have attempted to circumvent the thorny dilemmas in this concurrence through several further, admittedly technical and abstruse distinctions. First of all, to avoid suggesting that the moral privation in any sinful act naturally proceeds from some innate God-created volitional capacity, someone like Aquinas will deny that a person's will is the "direct efficient cause" of the privation itself. Strictly speaking, the moral privation of sin is its own cause. It has no good cause. Yet, because that moral privation must be inalienably coupled to some natural accidents to elicit a real sinful act, the privation is dependent upon the "accidental efficient cause," or an "indirect" "deficient cause," which is the human will.[63] In that way the sinner's will becomes the "direct efficient" cause of the sinful act itself, while only indirectly triggering the moral privation nested within the act.[64]

---

[62] Schleiermacher undoubtedly seeks to face this conundrum squarely, even if Kelsey is justified in feeling that his solution makes sin a divinely ordained, necessary prelude to redemption (Schleiermacher, *Christian Faith*, 335–37; cf. Kelsey, *Eccentric Existence*, 411).
[63] See Augustine, *The City of God against the Pagans* (Cambridge: Cambridge University Press, 1998), XII.7 (507–8).
[64] Aquinas, *Summa Theologiae* I–II.q75.a1.

The bigger problem, of course, is the divine concurrence in the act. Augustinians have resisted the more strongly libertarian accounts of human freedom which limit God's influence on the will to a mere "general" concurrence, as opposed to an "effectual" concurrence with each human act or choice itself, not least because of the dualistic implications that inevitably follow, as we hinted above. If God only concurs with the will in general (rather than with its specific choices), he would seem to have no efficient control over the existence of sin in his world. On the other hand, of course, to say that God somehow efficiently determines an act of sin would seem to be no less problematic. To avoid this suggestion, Aquinas will simply repeat our "biblical a priori" and refuse to say that God is in any way a "cause" of sin, whether directly or indirectly. Properly speaking, the human will is the direct efficient cause of any volitional act. As we saw above, in the case of sin, the will indirectly triggers a moral privation or defect nested within the act, making it a sinful act. It is true, Aquinas says, that God efficiently concurs with such an act, inasmuch as it is a volitional act. But in no way is he the direct or even indirect cause of the defect or privation which makes that act sinful.[65] To translate his observation into more concrete terms, this is really his way of saying that God retains effectual control over the existence of sin and evil in his world while insisting that he only ever puts it to his good ends (cf. Gen. 50:20; Isa. 10:5–7).

Theologians have also deployed the language of "permission" in similarly subtle ways to account for this asymmetry between human and divine purposes in sin.[66] Take, for instance, the Reformed thinker Gisbertus Voetius. He points out that when it comes to the abstract moral privation of sin itself, God merely permits, or does not will to prevent, its existence, without positively causing it in any way. Yet, in terms of the real concrete act in which that privation is nested, he contends that "mere permission" is insufficient to capture God's effectual concursus over the human will. Instead, like many others before him, he insists upon God's *active* or willing permission of the concrete act itself.[67]

---

[65] Aquinas, *Summa Theologiae* I–II.q79.a1. To this extent, Berkouwer is probably correct to question Bavinck's hint that God might be the deficient cause of sin (Berkouwer, *Sin*, 54–55). In a Reformed adaptation of this kind of casuistry, Mastricht speaks of God as the cause of the physical substrata of the sinful act, but not the cause of the sinful privation itself (Mastricht, *Theologia*, III.x.34 [399b–400a]; IV.i.7 [430a]; i.12 [432a]; IV.ii.5 [443b]).
[66] D. A. Carson, *How Long, O Lord? Reflections on Suffering and Evil* (Grand Rapids, MI: Baker, 1990), 213.
[67] Gisbertus Voetius, *Selectarum disputationum theologicarum*, 5 vols. (Utrecht: J. a Waesberge, 1648–67), 1:1132–34; see also, e.g., Aquinas, *Summa Theologiae* I.q19.a9.

Finally, Early Modern Catholic and Reformed theologians would also draw upon finely honed scholastic vocabulary to bring further clarity to God's asymmetrical concursus with sin.[68] While rejecting the notion of pure indifference, as if human beings can actually defy the positive will of God at any given moment (in the so-called "compound sense"), they were equally eager to account for our created volitional agency in such a way that our choices, not least the choice to sin, remain *genuinely ours*. Consequently, there is what they call a "necessity of consequence," where all our choices are enabled and determined by God according to the good ends of his providence. But since God achieves his purposes through the genuine agency of our wills—not in spite of them—the determination of his providence does not necessitate the outcome of our choices themselves ("necessity of the consequent"). That way, the existence of sin is always necessarily dependent on the will of God, who sovereignly puts it to his good purposes, without in any way making it necessary to those purposes in itself.

With all this, we have marshalled the best efforts of the tradition to understand how it is that God can allow and actively permit the existence of sin in his world according to the benevolent ends of his secret providence, without in any way making it necessary or unpreventable in accomplishing those good purposes. Hence, for whatever his own ends in allowing its existence, he may justly subject it to his public judgment, condemning its perpetrators in the strongest possible terms. No doubt we are only glimpsing here the dim outline of something that remains largely shrouded in mystery. Even the most eloquent advocates like Francis Turretin are quick to admit that our language and understanding is strained to its limits.[69] Yet, for want of providing a clearer alternative, it would seem that Berkouwer, and Barth before him, are a little too hasty in sweeping this kind of careful casuistry aside.

Of course, it is still the case that God has chosen to glorify himself in creation *through Christ*; that is to say, not just in spite of, but through the presence of sin. As Voetius puts it, sin brings God certain "accidental advantages" (*usus per accidens*), namely, "the illustration of his glory, wisdom, power,

---

[68] On the Reformed appropriation of this vocabulary, see Willem J. van Asselt et al., eds., *Reformed Thought on Freedom: The Concept of Free Choice in Early Modern Reformed Theology* (Grand Rapids, MI: Baker Academic, 2010). Recently, however, Richard Muller has fairly questioned the degree to which this terminology necessarily represents a distinctively "Scotian" accent in Early Modern Reformed thought (Richard A. Muller, *Divine Will and Human Choice: Freedom, Contingency, and Necessity in Early Modern Reformed Thought* [Grand Rapids, MI: Baker, 2017]). For an example of the following terminology being used in this context, see Turretin, *Institutes*, 6.7.23, 35 [1:523, 528]; 9.7.17 [1:611].

[69] "It is not to be denied that here we truly meet the depth (*bathos*) of the wisdom of God—rather to be wondered at than to be pried into, far surpassing the reach of reason" (Turretin, *Institutes*, 9.7.16 [1:610]).

mercy, and justice"; things so inimical to the purpose of sin itself yet so essential to God's design in actively allowing it to occur (cf. Prov. 16:4; Rom. 11:36; Eph. 1:11).[70] However much theologians might legitimately speak of God's intention to permit sin as a kind of probation, to test Adam's obedience before promoting him to a fully indefectible glory, neither infralapsarian nor supralapsarian can deny that God eternally willed to reserve the full disclosure of his goodness for the most blessed work of glorifying redeemed sinners in Christ.[71] But that is not at all to say that sin was either unpreventable or necessary to the complete manifestation of his glory. In other words, in addressing the question, *unde malum?*, we quickly discover that the answer bursts the boundaries of any attempted theodicy in the strict sense. It turns out that God does not need justification for his actions after all: the fact that in his infinite wisdom he has chosen to do things *this way* does not mean it was the *only way* he could do things, nor even the *only wise way* of doing things.[72]

III. A Taxonomy of Sin and Its Effects

Moving on from the question of sin's existence, we are now in a position to expand on a description or taxonomy of sin itself. Having established that the depravity of sin is parasitic on reality, in the context of God's gracious disclosure in Scripture, it is possible and, indeed, necessary to find language to describe its character, even if we cannot ultimately penetrate the inexplicable mystery of its wickedness.

A. The "Lawlessness" of Sin

In discerning the framework of a biblical taxonomy of sin, we begin by returning to inhabit the deceptively straightforward logic of the Johannine diagnosis: "sin is lawlessness." The elusive complexity of this definition partly arises from the theologian's sense that whatever it is that John has in mind, the "lawlessness" of sin cannot be reduced to the mere binary infraction of some objective code of "dos" and "don'ts," of commands and prohibitions. As we noted above, the thing that establishes and shapes human relationship with God is the finite accommodation of his infinite and sovereign will

---

[70] Voetius, *Selectarum disputationum theologicarum*, I.1071.

[71] In this respect Kelsey misrepresents the tradition by caricaturing its representation of Adam and Eve as "ideal types," and that the eschaton entailed some return to that pre-fall paradisaical "ideal" (Kelsey, *Eccentric Existence*, 206–7, 297–98).

[72] Modern advocates of the so-called Irenaean theodicy are right in what they affirm—this is the best possible world—but wrong in what they implicitly deny—this is the *only* best possible world.

into a form that human beings can readily comprehend, and to which they can respond as creatures uniquely called into covenant with him. For all the qualitative difference that exists between God and his human covenant partners, it is the finite, contingent expression of his eternal will that makes this relationship irreducibly personal and particular.

On the one hand, the "open morality" of his holy and immutable character furnishes an organic unity to the accommodated expression of his will. The Scriptures point to this, of course, in the way specific injunctions and prohibitions are integrated within the more comprehensive command to "love": to love God above all else, and as a nonnegotiable expression of that allegiance, to love your neighbor "as yourself" (Mark 12:29–31; John 13:34–35; 14:15, 21, 23–24; Rom. 13:8–10; Gal. 5:14; 1 John 4:7, 20–21; 5:2–3).[73] On the other hand, as an accommodation, the objective creaturely expression of his will is necessarily particular or contingent upon the historical existence of human beings in all their individuality, variety, and connection, with the vast array of unique daily circumstances they face. In a sense, then, any objective expression of God's will through the "closed morality" of discrete promises, commands, and prohibitions is already a kind of divine casuistry. It is already an application of God's single and immutable will, refracted across the mutable terrain of particular persons and nations, and, not least, distinct concrete situations, perhaps even of differing moral consequence.[74]

Indeed, it is for this reason that, however necessary it may be, a purely objective iteration of the divine will—whether enclosed within nature itself, or expressed in the natural form of human language—cannot alone suffice to enact the kind of accountability that animates a properly personal covenantal relationship between God and an individual human being. For a person to "know the will of God" for their own life, it is not enough that they can recite a set of instructions or a code—albeit a divinely revealed one—since any code is already a diversification, an application of the divine will to discrete cases, which may or may not mirror the concrete daily circumstances a particular individual might face. What is also needed is for that diversified

---

[73] In dialogue with Ulrich Luz, Kelsey provides an exploration of this principle vis-à-vis the Ten Commandments and the way they are exposited and exemplified in the Sermon on the Mount (Kelsey, *Eccentric Existence*, 741–827). Of course, that general observation is nothing new (cf. John Calvin, *Institutes of the Christian Religion*, ed. John T. McNeill, trans. Ford Lewis Battles, 2 vols. [Philadelphia: Westminster, 1960], 2.8 [1:367–423]).

[74] This seems to be part of Kelsey's point in relation to the Sermon on the Mount: that its normative force can be understood only as it exemplifies what it means to love God and one's neighbor in concrete situations (e.g., Kelsey, *Eccentric Existence*, 781–82).

revelation of God's will to come together in the person's own subjective will and consciousness in a manner analogous to the way it comes together in the divine mind. In its analogous and creaturely form, that coming together, or subjective knowledge of the divine will, takes the shape of a particular orientation to God, his world, and its future—something akin to what Kelsey calls our "basic personal identity"—as well as a capacity to discern how that will should apply, or be diversely expressed in a person's immediate or "proximate" context.[75] In other words, if on the God-ward side it is the eternal will that forms and establishes all the historical particularities of the divine-human covenant, on the side of the creature, a person's situation within that covenant, as well as his or her capacity to attend to all its particularities, are only ever contingent realities, received from God as a gift. Traditionally, theologians have spoken of this subjective, God-given capacity under the rubric of "illumination." That is to say, it is not simply that God has shed light or truth upon his world, he also furnishes his covenant partners with the very eyes they need to see it, a point famously captured in the psalmist's acknowledgment, "in your light do we see light" (Ps. 36:9).

Classically, the Augustinian tradition has insisted that this was the context in which humanity was originally set. As we saw above, to speak of Adam's "original righteousness," as the tradition generally has (following the cue of Eccl. 7:29), deliberately cuts against the fiction of viewing his pre-fall state as one of absolute volitional neutrality or indifference. It is to claim that he was created upright, divinely attuned to his gifted context, instinctively aware of his unique creaturely orientation as God's covenant partner and image-bearer, with all that that entailed for his agency in the world. That is why theologians have tended to define Adam's original righteousness as the habitual conformity of all his faculties to God's will.[76] Adam had, as it were, the law of God written on his heart. Indeed, in an observation that was carried over into the Protestant tradition without hesitation, Aquinas infers that Adam possessed every gift or "virtue," the summit of which are, of course, the so-called "theological" virtues: faith, hope, and love.[77] It is not that Adam

---

[75] Where Kelsey speaks of our "basic personal identity" as something given to us by God's particular way of relating to us as creatures, he does not intend to exclude our own response to that mode of relation (e.g., *Eccentric Existence*, 591, 864).

[76] E.g., Mastricht, *Theologia*, III.ix.33 (380a).

[77] E.g., Aquinas, *Summa Theologiae* I.q95.a3; Mastricht, *Theologia*, III.ix.37 (381b). See, too, Calvin, *Institutes (1559)*, 2.2.12 (1:270–71); Peter Martyr Vermigli, *Commentary on Aristotle's Nicomachean Ethics*, ed. Emidio Campi and Joseph C. McLelland, vol. 73 of Sixteenth Century Essays and Studies (Kirksville, MO: Truman State University Press, 2006), 296–97.

necessarily possessed these qualities in all their actualized perfection, but he did so in a manner that enabled him to recognize his contingent identity and fully equipped him to enact his agency as an authentic image or creaturely analogue of God's eternal will.[78]

In other words, the important thing to see here is that Adam's upright, God-given conformity to the "law" needs to be understood as the harmonious alignment of an objectively revealed divine intention for his life and future in the garden, alongside a fitting subjective mode of being through which he might instinctively recognize and positively enact that intention. Objectively, the divine intention can be iterated in the casuistry of particular promises, commands, and prohibitions, as it was in the garden, throughout Israel's history, in the ministry of Christ and the apostles, and as it is for us now in inspired Scripture. Subjectively, it takes shape as a habitual conformity, which above all would manifest itself in the exercise of faith, hope, and love, all directed toward the God who not only sustained Adam's life in the garden, but also held out the prospect of an even fuller eschatological reward.[79]

All this is to say that, when we speak of sin as "lawlessness," it primarily needs to be understood as a declension from all that Adam's original conformity to God's will implied. As Genesis describes it, the specific proscription concerning the tree, together with the already-fallen serpent's temptation, provided the occasion for Adam's fall. Yet, given the upright integrity of his created state, for Adam to steal the fruit, or indeed to violate any divine command, would require no less than an entire disruption of that created integrity with all that it entailed, not least his instinctive, habitual orientation to God and his will. In that sense, well before the transgression of the concrete command, there had to have been a violation of the entire law in the form of a willful disorientation and surrender of his integrity, a wholescale relinquishment of righteousness, of faith, hope, and love.

B. THE ROOT OF SIN'S LAWLESSNESS: UNBELIEF

But is there a logic or order to this relinquishment? In asking this we face a similar conundrum to the one we have seen before. Kelsey strongly resists

---

[78] See Kelsey, *Eccentric Existence*, 303: "The only relevant sense of 'perfection' here is 'defined in terms of the appropriateness of personal bodies' response to God's relating to them.'"

[79] Note, for instance, how Mastricht traces the sequence of these virtues in relation to the promise of life in the garden. To his mind, faith, hope, and love for God are the basic instruments of natural worship, and the root of all piety (Mastricht, *Theologia*, III.ix.37 [381b]).

any attempt to identify some sin beneath all sins. The irrational mystery of sin defies systematization, and therefore, we cannot speak of any single "root," but only of "rough typologies," he says.[80] Certainly, the fundamental evil in sin will always defy any *good* explanation. But sin's parasitic existence means it cannot defy logic and explanation altogether. So long as it exists, it can be described "logically"—in some measure at least—however irrational and mysterious its evil intent. Indeed, even Kelsey concedes that all sin has at least one thing in common: it is "against God."[81] For Aquinas, the "beginning" (*initium*) of Adam's sin was pride, which led to a covetous or inordinate desire for the spiritual good of "God-likeness" that was expressly forbidden in the command.[82] Not only is there solid precedent for this suggestion in Augustine,[83] it has a sound rationale inasmuch as he—like the Catholic tradition in general—regards charity or love for God as the root of all virtues. By displacing charity with a form of self-love, Adam expelled all the theological virtues, overturning his God-ward orientation and relinquishing his original righteousness.[84]

Following Luther's lead, however, Protestants have classically preferred to regard faith as the root virtue, not to rob love of its crowning significance but partly in recognition that hope and love can emerge only from a fiduciary apprehension of the truth about God and his will toward us. Consequently, the Protestant tradition has classically insisted that Adam's sin had to begin with unbelief.[85] Even to entertain the serpent's temptation required an illegitimate equivocation over the truthfulness of God's will and sanction that would allow him to lust after some self-designated, pretended good in substitution for all the God-given, God-centered bounty he enjoyed in the garden. In other words, a proud and contemptuous reversal of loves from God to the self was undeniably part of the mix, but such a reversal could not occur without prior consent to some deception or untruth about God and his creation.[86] Or, to put

---

[80] Kelsey, *Eccentric Existence*, 420–21, 587.

[81] David H. Kelsey, "Response to the Symposium on *Eccentric Existence*," *Modern Theology* 27 (2011): 84.

[82] Aquinas, *Summa Theologiae* I–II.q84.a1, 2. Note that Aquinas distinguishes "pride" ("turning away from God"), as the "beginning" of sin, from "covetousness" (turning toward a "mutable good"), which he calls the "root" of all sin (taking his cue from 1 Tim. 6:10).

[83] See Augustine, *City of God against the Pagans* XIV.xiii (608).

[84] So, Aquinas, *Summa Theologiae* I–II.q81.a2; q85.a1, 3.

[85] While Barth retains "pride" as a description of sin's "totality," he nonetheless defines pride as the "concrete form" of unbelief (Barth, *Church Dogmatics*, IV/1.414–16).

[86] So, e.g., Martin Luther, *The Freedom of a Christian* (*LW* 31, 350); Calvin, *Institutes (1559)*, 2.1.4 (1:244–46); André Rivet et al., *Synopsis Purioris Theologiae: Latin Text and English Translation* (3 vols.), vol. 1, *Disputations 1–23*, ed., Dolf (Roelf T.) te Velde, trans. Riemer A. Faber (Leiden, Netherlands: Brill, 2015), XIV.10–18 (341–43); Turretin, *Institutes*, 9.6.6–13 (1:605–6); cf. McFarland, *Original Sin*, 200–203.

things the other way around, as soon as there is a dissonance between what a person believes to be true about their "personal identity"—about God and their place in the world—and the real truth that originates with God himself, there will be an inevitable disorientation of loves and hopes away from God and his will. Such disorientation binds a person in a course that can only lead to a plurality of concrete violations of God's will along the lines of Adam's specific transgression against the command concerning the tree.

In summary, then, before "lawlessness" describes any circumstantial violation of God's will or law, there has to be a more fundamental subjective rupture, the displacement of covenantal intimacy with a posture of self-determined rebellion against the lawgiver that originates with unbelief or a denial of the divine truth that shapes and regulates the character of that relationship. Surely that is the point of James's observation, after all (James 2:8–11)? Behind the multitude of commands there is a single lawgiver, and thus to stumble "at one point" is only ever indicative of a more deep-seated insurgence against him and all that he stands for.

For all its idiosyncratic brilliance, perhaps Kelsey's typology of sin resonates more with his Protestant tradition at this point than he may wish to concede. Aside from discrete "sins in the plural," or the multitude of concrete practices in our "proximate" daily contexts that are distortions of "how" we are called to be, Kelsey refers to a more rudimentary kind of "sin in the singular" which is a distortion of our "basic personal identity," or "who" we are in our "ultimate" context as constituted by God. In Kelsey's proposal, our "basic personal identity" has three discrete dimensions that reflect three modes in which the triune God relates to us: as the creative source of life; as the guarantor of a future glorified life; and as our un-estranged Father. Leaving aside the notably Barthian accents regarding election and reconciliation that undergird his proposal, the way Kelsey thinks that we are to "live out" this identity in our proximate or quotidian contexts is consistent with the manner in which theology has traditionally sought to describe humanity in its originally upright state. To Kelsey's mind, faith, hope, and love toward God are the only "appropriate" ways of honoring the discrete senses in which our reality is grounded in him who is our Creator, Consummator, and eternal Father. While Kelsey believes our "basic personal identity" is inalienable because it is "eccentrically" constituted by God, he is well aware that it is possible to live inappropriately or "at cross-grain" to that identity: "sin in the singular." Faith in God as Creator and Preserver of our life and identity can readily give way to a trust in some aspect of creation itself or, indeed, to self-reliance.[87] Hope in God as the one who will bring creation's radical eschatological consummation can easily be displaced by nihilistic despair, or narratives that locate our identity in the fulfillment of static roles and traditions, or in human achievement.[88] And finally, love for God can easily be displaced by forms of self-love that are self-justifying, leading to abuse or resentment.[89] Yet, although Kelsey actively resists integrating these discrete distortions into a single pathology (just as he is opposed to uniting the three modes of divine relation into a single narrative), the language he uses to describe the cause of these distortions is remarkably uniform across all three. In each case, he says, it is to "live at cross-grain," to "self-contradict," "to misconstrue," to "respond inappropriately" to one's basic personal identity as it is eccentrically established by God. In other words, in each case, some untruth or dissonance with reality shapes the way a person conceives their identity. In fact, Kelsey also uses similar language to describe the character of concrete sinful practices ("sin the plural"), namely, they are "inappropriate" or "distorted responses to the Triune God."[90]

Arguably, this is not terribly distant from what Protestants have classically intended by isolating "unbelief" as the root of all sin. Of course, Kelsey is right to insist that distortions of faith, hope, and love, cannot be conflated into one overarching pathology any more than the dynamic, eschatologically oriented created ideal for humanity—roughly parallel to what he calls our eccentric identity—can be reduced to one single dimension. In that respect, his Protestant forebears would readily agree. Turretin, for instance, sees a toxic amalgam of many "sins" in that "original sin." "It is certain," he writes, "that we must not regard that Fall as any particular sin, such as theft or adultery, but as a general apostasy and defection from God." In other words, the fall was "a complicated disease," "a total aggregate of various acts, both internal and external, impinging against both tables of the law."[91] But there is a common

---

[87] Kelsey, *Eccentric Existence*, 422–38.

[88] Kelsey, *Eccentric Existence*, 590–602.

[89] Kelsey, *Eccentric Existence*, 864–89.

[90] Kelsey, *Eccentric Existence*, 567; cf. 412–21, 567–89, 847–63.

[91] Turretin, *Institutes*, 9.6.3 (1:604). Mastricht describes it like this: "In it there was pride, ingratitude, unbelief, idolatry, disobedience, negligence, an unreasonable desire for understanding, most evil desire, a felony against the truth of things, want of natural affections (*astorgia*), homicide against the whole world, a perfidy and violation of the covenant. Most of all, in the violation of this sacrament, there was essentially a universal profession of disobedience, contempt of the covenant, rebellion, and total apostasy from God" (Mastricht, *Theologia*, IV.i.15 [433a]).

thread to the way Kelsey describes this complex amalgam of distortions—both of "identity" or orientation and of "acts"—that resonates with the tradition's emphasis on unbelief. Perhaps that privileges "faith" as the root virtue after all. That is not to say that unbelief tells the whole story, it is simply to claim that, at heart, all sin is animated by a kind of commitment to an untruth, a dissonance that distorts a natural orientation of dependence on God as Creator, hope in his promised future, and a love directed toward his fatherly goodness.

C. THE ESSENCE OF SIN'S LAWLESSNESS: FALSE WORSHIP

To retain "unbelief" as the root of sin's lawlessness seemingly cuts against a widespread modern preference for the root metaphor of "idolatry." Indeed, Kelsey himself has made some penetrating observations about this popular choice of metaphor. When it is dislocated from its biblical and specifically cultic context, he observes, the metaphor typically narrates a conscious attempt to resolve some anxiety over one's "meaningfulness, authenticity, or sheer reality."[92] Such a project may be defined in terms of an ultimately self-defeating, self-alienating attempt to build a stable identity through seeking to transcend our creaturely finitude, or, conversely, through overdependence on some aspect of finite existence.[93] Taken this way, Kelsey shrewdly detects a migration of sin away from its traditional doctrinal home in creation to theological anthropology.[94] Sin is no longer chiefly a culpable offense "against God" as the good Creator; it is now primarily an offense "against oneself." God only necessarily enters the picture in the soteriological domain, where faith in him functions as the solution to the self-justifying, self-alienating bind of attempting to construct one's own identity. As such, Kelsey observes, guilt may be reinterpreted along a purely subjective horizontal axis, in psychological terms with therapeutic solutions, rather than as an objective status before God.

Of course, Kelsey's point is not to say that God *cannot* enter the picture as the offended Creator when sin is construed as idolatry, only that he *need not*. The question, then, is whether or not idolatry can be retrieved as a general metaphor for sin, while retaining sin's primary orientation as an offense against God. Certainly, there are those who have made constructive

---

[92] Kelsey, "Response to the Symposium," 85. As Kelsey alludes, there is no doubt that Reinhold Niebuhr, with his appropriation of Kierkegaard's concept of "anxiety," has been influential in this way of construing the sin of idolatry. See, e.g., Niebuhr, *Nature and Destiny of Man: A Christian Interpretation*, vol. 1, *Human Nature*, 166–77, 251–54, cf. 178–240.
[93] David H. Kelsey, "Whatever Happened to the Doctrine of Sin?," *TT* 50 (1993): 172–73.
[94] For this and the following, see, "Whatever Happened to the Doctrine of Sin?," 172–75; "Response to the Symposium," 84–85.

suggestions along these lines. Someone like Alistair McFadyen, for instance, takes the traditional notions of both "pride" and "sloth" as root sins, and characterizes them in a manner resembling the modern deployment of the "idolatry" metaphor. On the one hand, pride represents the quest to over-inflate the finite: it "elevates oneself (or that with which one identifies one-self: class, race, sex, political movement) to the ultimate good, the arbiter and criterion of the worth of everything else, the good towards which all other goods . . . are to be dedicated."[95] On the other hand, "sloth" represents the escape to false transcendence. It exchanges the transcendence of the dynamic, life-giving God, preferring instead to ground "personal energies" in a static "transcendent orientation which is self-dissipating."[96] Even still, McFadyen is keen to retain the distinctive character of sin as an offense "against God." Indeed, echoing the observations of Kelsey, he is keenly aware of the way in which metaphors like pride and sloth can be cashed out in purely immanent terms to describe imbalances in relational dynamics with other human beings, as he suggests is the tendency in certain feminist accounts of sin.[97] In other words, pride and sloth are not inherently theological terms, and without being deliberately placed in that context they can easily "function as ways of nam-ing disorders of selfhood unplugged from the ecology of relation to God."[98]

For this reason, McFadyen consciously seeks to transpose these root metaphors into the normative frame of idolatrous worship. Drawing on the observations of Moshe Halbertal and Avishai Margalit, McFadyen observes that the biblical language of idolatry is frequently tied up with images of infidelity to Yahweh such as adultery, lust, and prostitution (e.g., Ex. 34:12–17; Lev. 20:5; 1 Chron. 5:25; Hos. 1:9; 2:9–15; 3:1; Ezek. 16:15–34; Jer. 2:18–28).[99] Idolatry or false worship, then, may well be a matter of perform-ing illicit cultic acts (making "graven images"). In that case, it is primarily a question of "how" we worship (the second commandment). But idolatry can also embrace the more fundamental question of "who" or "what" we wor-ship (the first commandment). It can indicate an unfaithful misrelation to the living God, a turning away from him as the center of personal allegiance and covenantal dependence to something false and lifeless. Since pride and sloth

---

[95] McFadyen, *Bound to Sin*, 217.
[96] McFadyen, *Bound to Sin*, 219.
[97] McFadyen, *Bound to Sin*, 164–65.
[98] McFadyen, *Bound to Sin*, 164.
[99] For this and the following, see McFadyen, *Bound to Sin*, 221–26; cf. Moshe Halbertal and Avishai Margalit, *Idolatry* (Cambridge, MA: Harvard University Press, 1994).

entail a redirection of personal energies away from "God's abundance and plenitude" toward "other forces which de-energise and disorient from the abundance, fullness, and freedom of life with God,"[100] McFadyen thinks we may aptly call them species of idolatry, or *false worship*, albeit of a non-ritual kind. And therefore, to the extent that all sin embraces misrelation in the form of either pride or sloth, McFadyen detects the fundamental sin of idolatry. But here idolatry is not characterized chiefly as a self-defeating attempt to construct one's own identity, but in the more immediately biblical sense of false worship which always entails culpable infidelity to the living God.

More recently, Richard Lints has argued that the paradigm of "false worship" as a universal defining characteristic of sin is underlined by the liturgical shape of the so-called "first table" of the Genesis creation account (Gen. 1:1–2:3), which is suggestive of a cosmic "temple in which the glory of God is reflected and the divine presence rests."[101] If this observation is correct, the creation of man and woman in the image of God (Gen. 1:26) takes on a specific cultic significance, where the Creator establishes that image to be his visible reflection, illuminating the cosmic temple with divine likeness as they enact their vocation to "fill and subdue."[102] As we noted above, the notion of image as a visible reflection of God's likeness or glory is not a new observation and is basic to the tradition's emphasis on Adam's "original righteousness." The suggestion that Adam's placement in the garden had a special cultic significance is not particularly groundbreaking either.[103] Nonetheless, it is certainly a perspective that has regained favor, particularly as interpreters attend to the close parallel between "image" (*tselem*; צֶלֶם) and "likeness" (*Demuth*; דְּמוּת) or even their interchangeability, suggested both by the biblical text (Gen. 1:26; 5:1, 3; 9:6; Ezek. 23:14–15; cf. 1 Cor. 11:7; James 3:9), and by ancient Near Eastern parallels.[104]

---

[100] McFadyen, *Bound to Sin*, 226.
[101] Richard Lints, *Identity and Idolatry: The Image of God and Its Inversion* (Nottingham, UK: Apollos, 2015), 53; cf. Richard M. Davidson, "Earth's First Sanctuary: Genesis 1–3 and Parallel Creation Accounts," *AUSS* 53 (2015): 65–89.
[102] Lints, *Identity and Idolatry*, 57–75.
[103] So, Mastricht, *Theologia*, III.ix.37 (381b); Owen, *Works*, 17:40–42; 19:344–45.
[104] See J. Richard Middleton, *The Liberating Image: The Imago Dei in Genesis 1* (Grand Rapids, MI: Brazos, 2005), 89–90; Kilner, *Dignity and Destiny*, 124–33. Contrary to Kilner's insinuation (127 n. 180), Early Modern Protestant interpreters typically preferred to regard the terms in Gen. 1:26 as roughly cognate, as contemporary exegetes do (e.g., Calvin, *Institutes [1559]*, 1.15.3 [1:186–89]); Rivet et al., *Synopsis Purioris Theologiae: Latin Text and English Translation (Volume 1: Disputations 1–23)*, XIII.36 (329); Mastricht, *Theologia*, III.ix.28 [378b–379a]). Hence, they typically inferred that with the fall, only a fraction of divine likeness—that is, of the *image*—remains in the natural structure and gifts of sinful human beings. Certainly this observation is true of Reformed thinkers. Some Lutherans went so far as saying the image was entirely extinguished on precisely these grounds. See the exhaustive discussion of the *imago Dei* in Zanchi's *De operibus Dei* III.1 (Zanchi, *Operum*, tIII [cc. 677–93]).

Furthermore, Lints brings the cultic significance of the image into sharper focus by observing how the positive connotations of the concept in the early chapters of Genesis (*tselem elohim*; צֶלֶם אֱלֹהִים) are eclipsed by the more typical association of *tselem* with idolatry throughout the rest of Israel's history (e.g., Num. 33:52; 2 Kings 11:18; 2 Chron. 23:17; Amos 5:26; Ezek. 7:20). When deploying this or other cognate terms for idolatrous images, the Scriptures often underline and mock the dependence of an image on its craftsman (Ex. 20:4; Deut. 4:16; 27:15; Judg. 17:5; Pss. 106:19–20; 115:4–8; 135:15–18; Amos 5:26; Ezek. 7:20; Jer. 10:3–5). Whereas an image is intended to represent some deity and function as an object of worship, in reality it is merely the fragile projection of some human artist fashioned from lifeless materials they might otherwise use for fuel (cf. Isa. 40:18–20; 44:10–20). But it is not just that the image itself is lifeless and worthless. By depending on the idol, the one who fashions it as an object of worship actually begins to resemble it in all its lifelessness (Pss. 115:4–8; 135:15–18), an irony that G. K. Beale has discussed extensively as well.[105]

Lints sees a number of implications in all this. First, the biblical prohibition against "image-making" is not a simple rejection of "images" *tout court*. While it is true that no human fabrication can possibly do justice to the living God (Isa. 40:18–20), God is manifestly capable of fabricating his own image to reflect his likeness, as he has in the creation of humanity. Yet the striking and sudden eclipse of that image so early in the biblical narrative beneath the proliferation of idols implies that the story of fallen humanity outside the garden is essentially a story of false worship. Not only does the identity of the nations coalesce around idols of their making, so too do the very people of God repeatedly demonstrate their infidelity to Yahweh as they embrace the identity and false worship of their neighbors. Tragically, then, the image of God is itself turned "upside down" as human beings begin to resemble the falsehoods they worship, robbing God of his glory in creation. Indeed, the problem is not just that counterfeit gods "receive the praise and worship that belong to God," Kilner says, but also that "those intended to be God's own images, whom God created for God's glory, are the very ones undermining that glory and thereby forfeiting their own."[106] Both

---

[105] Intriguingly, Lints does not make much of the striking statement of this outcome in the Psalms. On this reference and its textual parallels elsewhere, notably Deut. 4:28–29; 29:4, 17; and Isa. 6:9–10, see G. K. Beale, *We Become What We Worship: A Biblical Theology of Idolatry* (Downers Grove, IL: IVP Academic, 2008), 44–46, 53, 75–76, 142, 148.
[106] Kilner, *Dignity and Destiny*, 156.

Lints and Beale draw attention to the graphic illustration of the problem in the account of the golden calf, where God pointedly judges his idolatrous people as "stiff-necked," not unlike the calf itself (Ex. 32:9; 33:3, 5). Yet, strikingly, this judgment becomes paradigmatic of Israel's general unfaithfulness throughout the OT, where it is often described by further metaphors of lifelessness (hard-heartedness, eyes that do not see, ears that do not hear, etc.: cf. Deut. 4:28; 10:16; 2 Chron. 30:8; 36:13; Neh. 9:16–17; Job 41:24; Pss. 95:8; 115:5–6; Isa. 6:9–10; 32:3; 44:18; Jer. 5:21; 7:26; 17:23; Ezek. 3:7; 12:2; Zech. 7:11). In other words, what is always seemingly implied in Israel's general infidelity is the sin of idolatry, not just in terms of diverted allegiances or a "misrelation" to Yahweh (as McFadyen puts it), but also in a misrepresentation of God himself as his defective covenantal image-bearers. Of course, Israel's covenant infidelity is merely a replication of that paradigmatic act of unfaithfulness, that *original* sin where God's created image, that human analogue or reflection of divine-likeness, was first defaced in the garden.

Consequently, to the extent that all sin replicates that original infidelity to God, we might attempt to draw all these observations together by concluding that sin is always a species of idolatry or false worship along both axes proscribed by the first two commandments. If, on the one hand, infidelity entails a diversion of personal allegiance away from the life-giving God, a reorientation of faith, hope, and love toward some other, finite center of dependence, it inevitably displaces the object of worship for another "who" or "what" (the first commandment). But in violating the first, we violate the second, the "how" of worship. Through infidelity we make *ourselves* into that graven image of God. Perhaps, then, this is why Paul can universalize the problem of idolatry in Romans 1–3. With or without the Torah, regardless of its motivation or presenting pathology, sin always entails a violation of God's honor (cf. Rom. 1:23; 2:23–24; 3:23), and to that extent it is a failure in worship that incurs guilt before God.[107]

---

[107] Kilner's reflections on this passage are apropos: "Though all are in God's image and are intended to reflect God's attributes, all in actuality lack the glory God intends them to have. . . . To be precise, images point to something else, of which they are images. Whether the image is a statue of a 'god' or a picture of a 'successful' (wealthy, powerful, good-looking, etc.) person, the image in effect encourages people to worship something. When people orient themselves to such objects of worship, they, too, become like and glorify those objects. A powerful dynamic overpowers the dynamic of being in the image of God. People, since they are inescapably in God's image, should exclusively be living out God's intentions for them to reflect godly attributes, to God's glory. Yet they instead live out the implications of their identification with counterfeit gods. Such is the power and tragedy of sin. People become more like what they worship" (Kilner, *Dignity and Destiny*, 157–58).

But to say that idolatry is something endemic to sin's lawlessness does not necessarily turn it into a controlling metaphor—*the sin* beneath all sins—as it functions in some modern accounts along the lines that Kelsey describes. Nor should it dilute the variegated complexity of sin's many concrete presentations. In commenting on the way Paul deploys the metaphor in Romans 1, for instance, Lints remarks that his point is not so much to provide an "exhaustive account of human corruptions" as to furnish a "large conceptual framework" that captures the general moral degradation and infidelity of sin as a species of false or defective worship.[108] Indeed, even if the general depiction of all sin as false worship or idolatry is sound, it remains the case that beneath this disorientation of worship is a commitment to a lie, a dissonance with the truth about God, his world, and our place within it. And therefore, the classical Protestant contention that "unbelief" is the root animating all sin and its fundamental distortion of worship remains intact.

IV. Human Solidarity in Sin and Its Effects

In claiming that sin is in essence a kind of false worship fundamentally animated by unbelief, we encounter a complexity that we have thus far left to one side. McFadyen contends that sin's basic infidelity to God is primarily a matter of (dis)orientation to God (our "ultimate" context, in Kelsey's terms), which plays out in a distorted set of practices in our "proximate" contexts.[109] In other words, it is chiefly a failure in "active relationality" before it is an explicit failure in creed or propositional belief. Yet as McFadyen readily implies, this is not to say that our orientation is devoid of truth commitment altogether. There are what he calls "operational beliefs" which are "embedded" in our orientation and practices. The complexity is, these "operational beliefs" need not be explicit; indeed, they may well contradict one's explicit beliefs.[110] That is why the problem of sin in practice proves much more intractably obstinate than a mere deficiency in stated beliefs. It is also why Ricoeur can intimate that the experience of sin's effects in the form of some defilement is more basic and immediate than any consciousness of it *as sin* or any sense of personal guilt, let alone the clarity that arises from

---

[108] Lints, *Identity and Idolatry*, 110; cf. Kilner, *Dignity and Destiny*, 156–58, 244.
[109] McFadyen, *Bound to Sin*, 222: "Both worship and therefore idolatry in the Bible are not primarily ideational realities, but pertain to the fundamental orientation of human lives in practice: whether or not they are oriented towards the blessing, glory and majesty of the true God. Idolatry has to do primarily with active relationality, with behavior; only secondarily with ideas."
[110] McFadyen, *Bound to Sin*, 224.

repentance.[111] Kelsey similarly acknowledges that to live at cross-grain to one's basic identity (sin in the singular), or to engage in distorted practices in our daily contexts (sin in the plural) need not entail any conscious act of rebellion or explicit and deliberate rejection of "who" we were made to be and "how" we are called to be. In other words, the unbelief or dissonance with truth and reality that lies at the heart of all sin may well be implicit rather than explicit. But the fact that it is implicit does not make it any less real or consequential.

A. "Bound to Sin": Some Contemporary Augustinian Voices

When speaking of implicit unbelief, what is lurking in the shadows, of course, is the suggestion that people may somehow be implicated in a broader system of unbelief that is bigger than themselves, and that has already disoriented them from God quite apart from any sinful practice or, indeed, any stated beliefs. In other words, to the extent that it is implicit, we may infer that the unbelief which lies at the root of their sinful misrelation to God, or distorted quotidian identity (to use Kelsey's term), is a given; it is beyond their explicit control. Both McFadyen and Kelsey are certainly keen to admit as much, or at least to affirm that people might find themselves already intractably bound in misrelation to God. Indeed, for them it is not just a possibility, but what they call a universal "de facto" reality.[112] In other words, with the Augustinian tradition in general, both authors emphatically insist that not only does a corporate solidarity in human sin really exist, but that such solidarity cannot adequately be explained in terms of mere "imitation."

McFadyen, for instance, traces the way "modernity" has typically rejected the Augustinian heritage from a sense that any notion of a "bound" will compromises authentic human agency, depersonalizes guilt, and attributes guilt in circumstances over which one has no control.[113] Against this tendency, McFadyen seeks to defend the classical position by testing and illustrating its superior explanatory power over more fashionable libertarian, act-centered accounts of sin in the concrete scenarios of child sex abuse and the Holocaust.

Kelsey likewise resists the reductionism of defining sin purely in terms of repeated, discrete activity. For instance, he suggests that, rather than

---

[111] Ricoeur, *Symbolism of Evil*, 7–8, 30–33.
[112] See McFadyen, *Bound to Sin*, 248; Kelsey, *Eccentric Existence*, 845.
[113] McFadyen, *Bound to Sin*, 14–42.

trusting in God as Creator, one way a person may live out their daily existence at "cross-grain" to their "basic personal identity" as a human creature is by "passively accepting his fellow creatures' [false] stereotypes of him as definitive of who he is."[114] But as he admits, acquiescing in some creaturely standard or good as the ultimate source of one's identity (rather than God as Creator) elides any binary, active-versus-passive pattern.[115] More to the point, though, Kelsey reflects on the moral ambiguity of the quotidian as a broader reality and concludes that its existing patterns of sin, deceit, and evil are sufficiently entrenched and obdurate that no one "born" into them can escape their distorting effects.[116] This is more than just the ambiguity of "finitude," anxiety over which inevitably leads free agents to sin by seeking false transcendence (so, Niebuhr). It is even more than a social ambiguity along the lines proposed by Schleiermacher, where the sins of a generation inevitably replicate themselves in the next through a kind of universal participation in a psychological "incapacity for good."[117] Indeed, Kelsey is critical of the way Schleiermacher readily associates this condition with our created state, as something divinely imposed and necessary to enable the "progressive development" of humanity toward a state of mature and redeemed God-consciousness.[118] Rather, Kelsey's claim arises from a principled decision to derive the doctrine of creation from the wisdom literature (rather than from Gen. 1–3), where it is seemingly impossible to extricate oneself from inexplicable evils and injustices that characterize Qohelet's "life under the sun."[119] Hence, for whatever "freedom" a person may have to "choose among alternative possible practices and actions, objects and relations . . . , they are not free to enact such choices as enactments of trust in and loyalty to the triune God relating to them creatively."[120] For Kelsey, then, this "sin in the singular," or a life oriented at "cross-grain" to our "basic personal identity" is a pathology in which all people are bound, not in a way that disables their wills or even threatens their natural integrity as human beings, but in a fashion that prevents them from extricating themselves from that distortion.[121]

---

[114] Kelsey, *Eccentric Existence*, 423, 424, 425.
[115] Kelsey, *Eccentric Existence*, 426.
[116] So, Kelsey, *Eccentric Existence*, 432–38.
[117] Schleiermacher, *Christian Faith*, 285–91, 301–4.
[118] Kelsey, *Eccentric Existence*, 411; cf. Schleiermacher, *Christian Faith*, 330–38. The expression "progressive development" is Schleiermacher's (*Christian Faith*, 288).
[119] Kelsey, *Eccentric Existence*, 208–12.
[120] Kelsey, *Eccentric Existence*, 434.
[121] See Kelsey, *Eccentric Existence*, 845–46.

There are significant contemporary theological voices, then, like McFadyen and Kelsey (along with numerous others), who explicitly wish to stand with the Augustinian tradition in maintaining that there is corporate solidarity to human sin that is far stronger than mere imitation.[122] In some fashion, socially and even biologically, every individual is inevitably caught up in a system of sin that is bigger than themselves and their own choices.

If this theological instinct remains an accurate one, the scriptural images of sickness, brokenness, or stain provide a fitting vehicle for picturing this solidarity. While it is easy to deploy these metaphors in ways that would end up characterizing pathologies in an entirely non-theological fashion,[123] the Scriptures do frequently utilize them as general descriptions of sin. Most famously of all, Christ likens his own redemptive ministry toward sinners to that of a physician (Mark 2:17; Matt. 9:12; Luke 5:31). Moreover, while the Bible does not always ascribe a direct causal link between a specific sickness and sin, on occasion it does (Ps. 107:17; John 5:1–15; James 2:14–16; 1 Cor. 11:29–30), and there are certainly suggestions that one can at least be symbolic of the other (Lev. 14; Isa. 2:5–6; Mark 2:1–12). Even more pointedly still, it frequently associates sin with physical defilement and pollution (Job 15:14; Isa. 1:15–16; 53:4; 59:3; 64:6; 65:5; Matt. 7:16–20; 15:10–20; Rev. 22:11), an association which is often grasped most vividly by the penitent (Isa. 6:5; Ps. 51:2, 7, 9–10, 17). Yet the language of sickness and defilement conjures up a solidarity in sin that extends beyond discrete sinful acts. A person may well act in a particular way because he or she is already sick and defiled (so Matt. 7:16–20). As Ricoeur suggests, the Bible's appropriation of these metaphors in the context of sin—as in David's confession of his adultery (Ps. 51)—drags the problem of sin backward from any specific transgression toward something more primal and basic, hinting at "an enveloping situation, like a snare in which man is caught."[124]

Even still, the symbols of sickness and defilement rekindle an ambiguity in this solidarity that has proven to be a particularly fraught one. Taken literally, they are, of course, conditions which arise through some physical contagion. They are conditions which suggest both bondage and infection

---

[122] Other notable studies include: Henri Blocher, *Original Sin: Illuminating the Riddle* (Leicester, UK: Apollos, 1997); McFarland, *Original Sin*; Jesse Couenhoven, *Stricken by Sin, Cured by Christ: Agency, Necessity, and Culpability in Augustinian Theology* (Oxford: Oxford University Press, 2013).

[123] See Shuster's comments on this score: Shuster, *Fall and Sin*, 117–19.

[124] Ricoeur, *Symbolism of Evil*, 90, 93.

from without, through contact with some external source. While the Bible may typically intend something chiefly metaphorical rather than literal in this language, at times the Scriptures deploy the images in ways that deliberately seem to blur the lines between a physical and spiritual solidarity in human sin. If the "quasi-physical" allusion is not already apparent in Psalm 51 by the fact "that the fault confessed be itself of the sexual order," as Ricoeur observes,[125] it is unmistakable in David's sense that his sin must be traced back to his conception in his mother's womb (Ps. 51:5). But the lines are most starkly blurred, of course, in the language of corruption and death, neither of which can easily be reduced to mere spiritual symbols,[126] and both of which the NT clearly depicts as inevitable consequences of sin's equally inescapable "reign" (Rom. 5:12–21; cf. John 3:6; Rom. 3:23; 6:12, 20–21; 8:10; 1 Cor. 15:21–26, 45–56).

The seemingly physical dimension to human solidarity in sin has proven to be the thorniest complexity in the theological history of this doctrine. The complexity plays out on two related axes. At one end, likening human solidarity in sin to a quasi-physical disease threatens to reintroduce the kind of dualism that the tradition has assiduously sought to avoid when describing the nature of sin. If depravity and corruption is a quasi-physical reality into which we are "born," a state in which we are seminally bound through the "magic" of touch, to use Ricoeur's expression, does that not reify and depersonalize sin into its own independent "thing" after all? At the other end, there is the perennial question of the justice in all this. Can such a diseased state, an affliction over which we have no control, rightly be described as "sin" for which God fairly holds us to account? In addressing these questions, the Augustinian tradition has not always spoken unanimously, and that, along with the continued equivocation over these issues in recent theological treatments of the subject, only attests to their genuine complexity.[127]

---

[125] Ricoeur, *Symbolism of Evil*, 90.

[126] Niebuhr, who like Kelsey wishes to mount a biblical case for human mortality as a pre-fall reality rather than a punishment for sin, nevertheless admits that "[d]espite St. Paul's symbolic use of the term death . . . it is probable that St. Paul followed the rabbinic teaching of his day in the belief that death was the consequence of Adam's sin" (Niebuhr, *Nature and Destiny of Man: A Christian Interpretation, vol. 1, Human Nature*, 174).

[127] In the following, I do not consider the distinctively Catholic approach to resolving these dilemmas, which would involve a departure from the Protestant confessional conviction that original sin is a state worthy of damnation. For a more pointed discussion of the differences, see Leslie, "Retrieving a Mature Reformed Doctrine of Original Sin." Even so, it is worth noting that several contemporary Protestant contributions deliberately move in this direction, most notably Houck, *Original Sin*. One even seeks to suggest there is a minority Reformed and confessional precedent for this move: see Oliver D. Crisp, "On Original Sin," *IJST* 17 (2015): 252–66; Oliver D. Crisp, "Retrieving Zwingli's Doctrine of Original Sin," *JRT* 10 (2016): 340–60; Oliver D. Crisp, "Sin," in *Christian Dogmatics: Reformed Theology for the Catholic Church*, ed. Michael Allen and Scott R. Swain (Grand Rapids, MI: Baker, 2016), 194–215. See further below, n. 138.

Even still, there are resources within the tradition that attempt to carve a way forward, and it is worth examining their coherence in dialogue with some of these challenges.

B. "Flesh Gives Birth to Flesh": The Intergenerational Propagation of Corruption and Sin

In his recent work on original sin, Ian McFarland eloquently attests to the intractable difficulties associated with any doctrine of sin that heavily relies on some notion of biological transmission to underwrite our solidarity in this state. It is true, as McFadyen points out, that where modern thinkers hesitate at this point, assumptions of human origins vis-à-vis palaeoanthropology are often lurking in the background.[128] Apart from anything else, the viability of finding some single origin or cause of something akin to a biologically transmitted "disease" is, for many like McFarland, simply fanciful.[129] But leaving that to one side, McFarland points to a more serious and ultimately insurmountable challenge related to an ambiguity he detects in Augustine's tendency to rely on distorted bodily desires (concupiscence), a "sinful nature" per se, as the mode through which human solidarity in sin is intergeneration-ally mediated. While Augustine works hard to maintain that the postlapsar-ian human will is enmeshed and bound in a nature that inevitably leads to acts of sin, McFarland thinks that Augustine does not entirely escape the Pelagian dualism he wishes to avoid, where a person's agency and will ef-fectively hovers above their nature as a distinct, quasi-sovereign entity. This ambiguity is especially apparent, he feels, in Augustine's exegesis of Romans 7:14–20. When reflecting on verse 20, Augustine entertains the possibility that a regenerate person may have concupiscent desires in their nature ("sin that dwells within me") from which their will is now disengaged ("it is no longer I who do it"). McFarland's basic contention here is that any bifurcation of personal agency from a so-called "sinful nature" runs the risk of deper-sonalizing sin and veers toward the kind of "ontological dualism" that was not only a hallmark of Pelagian anthropology, but is "deeply engrained in the sensibilities of Western culture."[130] And to his mind, traditional Augustinian accounts of original sin inevitably tend in this direction when one sin at the

---

[128] McFadyen, *Bound to Sin*, 22–25.
[129] McFarland, *Original Sin*, 143–44, 148–49, 153, 165.
[130] McFarland, *Original Sin*, 158.

head of humanity—Adam's—is somehow transmitted by way of the "nature" we inherit, quite apart from our own personal agency, so that effectively we become responsible for a sin we did not *actually* commit. As McFarland points out, Augustine himself may have stopped short of a strongly seminal and traducianist account of sin's transmission (whether through the soul or the body), akin to the "realism" William Shedd famously proposed in the nineteenth century,[131] but to his mind the difficulties remain wherever sin is conceived as a quasi-"thing" that can be passed on biologically from one generation to another.

Instead, McFarland draws on the anthropological insights Maximus refined in the context of the dyothelite controversies in the seventh century, especially Maximus's careful delineation between "person" (*hypostasis*) and "nature" (*ousia*).[132] To uphold the integrity of Christ's divine and human wills, Maximus concluded that "will" is a function of "nature" rather than "person." This way the notion of "person" was clarified to be the singular concrete subject or agent of any particular instantiation of nature (the "mode" or *tropos*), without filling it up with ontological characteristics which properly belong to the nature itself (the "what" of any given person). In other words, it is not the "person" who has a will distinct from and somehow hovering above their nature. Rather, the will is embedded within their nature, which concretely exists only insofar as that nature is individually hypostasized. Appropriating it to our context, McFarland believes that it is possible then to speak of a corrupted or "fallen" nature in terms of a will and bodily desires that are in some way distorted and broken by the effects of sin without in any way saying the nature itself is "sinful." God creates our "natures," so that, whatever their susceptibility to corruption and disorder, they must remain something ontologically "good." Sin cannot exist or even be conceived of abstractly in the form of a "nature." Rather, what makes any given instantiation of nature *actually* sinful is the concrete subject or hypostasis. By sheer dint of being a living agent with a "fallen" nature, McFarland contends, that nature is concretely energized in a sinful way, even before any specifically sinful and blameworthy acts.

With this revision, McFarland believes he has avoided the pitfalls of more traditional models of original sin. He still wishes to speak of human

---

[131] William G. T. Shedd, *Dogmatic Theology*, 3 vols. (New York: Scribner, 1891), 2:3–94. On the ambiguities in Augustine's own position, see Couenhoven, *Stricken by Sin*, 26–45.
[132] For the following, see McFarland, *Original Sin*, 88–116.

solidarity in sin, of course. The natures we possess—while not sinful in themselves—are inextricably bound in a biological and social network of sin's destructive effects. But the actual unity in sin itself is not conveyed or transmitted by natural means but arises simply because there is a kind of hypostatic solidarity to the race, the exception being Christ himself, who shared the same corruptible nature but hypostasized it in his own sinless way.[133] In other words, much like Kelsey, McFarland is entirely happy to affirm that all human beings are "born into" a socially and biologically interdependent state of sin, without wanting to attribute any single "cause" for this solidarity.

Here it needs to be said that there are voices in the Augustinian tradition which resonate with some of McFarland's concerns.[134] As he readily admits, the mature Reformed doctrine of original sin deliberately eschewed a realist or traducianist model in favor of an immediate imputative model, and in doing so avoided some of the serious pitfalls he has identified. In fact, when examined more closely, there can be no doubt that when describing human solidarity in sin, the Reformed model preserves the sort of personal integrity and responsibility that McFarland is eager to keep intact. Mastricht's discussion is a notable case in point. Like McFarland, Mastricht insists that the nature we have inherited through biological generation is vitiated and depraved. Of course, McFarland is uneasy with the typically Reformed conviction that this nature is a divinely imposed punishment for Adam's sin, a point to which we shall return shortly. Even still, for precisely the same reasons as McFarland, Mastricht is very careful to avoid any notion that the vitiated nature we inherit is somehow ontologically "sinful"—for that would make God the author of an evil "thing,"[135] or any suggestion that sin and corruption itself

---

[133] On these grounds, McFarland wants to make a case for Christ possessing a "fallen" nature (susceptible to corruption, prone to experiencing the effects of sin), but with Maximus he agrees that Christ's divine hypostasis prevented that nature from possessing the deliberative faculties (*gnome, bouleusis*, and *prohairesis*) that it does when hypostatized by all other humans before the eschaton. In that way, McFarland's suggestion is not especially radical (cf. McFarland, *Original Sin*, 117–40).

[134] See, e.g., Bavinck, *Reformed Dogmatics*, 3:103; Hodge, *Systematic Theology*, 2:51–64, 216–27, John Murray, *The Imputation of Adam's Sin* (Phillipsburg, NJ: P&R, 1959), 32–33; Geerhardus Vos, *Reformed Dogmatics*, trans. and ed. Richard B. Gaffin Jr. et al., 5 vols. (Bellingham, WA: Lexham, 2012–16), 2:37–39. More recently, Michael Rea has expressed similar concerns about Shedd's proposal along with "organic whole" theories he ascribes to Aquinas and Jonathan Edwards (Michael C. Rea, "The Metaphysics of Original Sin," in *Persons: Human and Divine*, ed. Peter van Inwagen and Dean Zimmermann [Oxford: Clarendon, 2007], 328–31, 338–41).

[135] In responding to the objection that the doctrine makes God the "author of sin, insofar as he is not only the author of generation, but also of the privation of original justice" (i.e., that God has created the corrupt nature we are born with), Mastricht writes, "He is certainly the author of generation, and of what is born as to the kind (*talis*)—as something physically good, but not as something morally evil" (Mastricht, *Theologia*, IV.ii.23 [448a]). Likewise, he insists that God is the creator of the "corrupted habit (*habitus corrupti*)," but "not of the corruption and lawlessness (ἀνομίας) itself, which enters the habit from the creature through original unrighteousness" (Mastricht, *Theologia*, IV.ii.26 [450a]; cf. Mastricht, *Theologia*, IV.ii.33 [453a–b]).

is somehow traduced through seminal generation.[136] Indeed, commenting further on seminal traducianism, he observes how the Reformed will readily admit that "defective temperaments" pass on physically through "seminal traduction," undoubtedly giving rise to a certain "proclivity for this or that actual sin." In that way, generation is a kind of *conditio sine qua non*, which allows corruption to spread throughout the race. Nonetheless, he says, the Reformed "absolutely deny" that the evil or "corruption itself" is somehow traduced through insemination, not least because sin cannot be abstracted from a person's psychosomatic unity and somehow passed through the body, which on its own is a brute entity incapable of bearing moral good or evil.[137]

Even further precision comes when Mastricht speaks of the interface between a person's will and the depraved nature they have received by generation. Drawing upon a number of subtle scholastic distinctions regarding the will, Mastricht clarifies the way in which a person can receive a vitiated nature through generation and yet remain personally responsible for this state and the sin that inevitably ensues, even from infancy. Various Catholics had argued that both the state and the very first (*primo-primum*) motions of concupiscence are devoid of all voluntary consent and therefore cannot be classed as "sin."[138] But in responding to this, Mastricht says that the Reformed draw a distinction between two kinds of voluntary consent: "antecedent" or "prior" consent, and "concomitant" consent. Concupiscence is certainly devoid of prior consent. Since it is a reality present from conception in the fallen person, there is no sense in which he or she plays any part in inducing the condition. Nevertheless, the vital corruption of concupiscence relies on concomitant consent, which is another way of saying that

---

[136] Sin is not propagated through either the body or the soul "distinctly" since (1) the body "when abstracted from the soul is something brute and unable to convey within it (*penitus incapax*) good or evil," and (2) every soul is "concreated by God" (Mastricht, *Theologia*, IV.ii.19 [446a]; cf. Mastricht, *Theologia*, IV.ii.35 [454a–b]).

[137] Mastricht, *Theologia*, IV.ii.35 (454a–b). Using an old distinction which Bonaventure seemingly attributes to Hugh of St. Victor (see, Bonaventure, II *Sent.* d33.a2.q2. conc.), Mastricht remarks that our corruption is the same "in species" (*specie*) to Adam's, but not the same "in number" (*numero*) (Mastricht, *Theologia*, IV.ii.35 [454b]); cf. Aquinas, *Summa Theologiae* I–II.q82.a2.

[138] As Johann Gerhard notes, the Catholic position holds that, on its own, original sin with its attendant concupiscence is merely an "idle evil, resting tinder, and a paralysed quality" (Johann Gerhard, *Loci Theologici*, 5 vols. [Berlin: Gust. Schlawitz, 1863–1885], II.x.10 [2:193a]). As noted already, there are modern Protestant voices in this discussion who quite explicitly wish to move in a more classically Catholic direction on this score by limiting "sin," more strictly understood, to the point at which depraved concupiscence coincides with conscious deliberation: e.g., Couenhoven, *Stricken by Sin*, 211–12; and extensively, Houck, *Original Sin*. Quite apart from the details of Zwingli's own position, Crisp's claim that there is minority Protestant confessional precedent for this move is implausible, especially considering that it was widely rejected by Early Modern Protestants for much the same reasons as McFadyen objects to the modern preference for "act centered" accounts of sin (Crisp, "Original Sin," 258–60; cf. Crisp, "Zwingli's Doctrine"; Crisp, "Sin," 197–200, 212–14; see, e.g., Turretin, *Institutes*, 9.2.5 [1:593–94]; 11.21.12 [2:136–37]; cf. Leslie, "Retrieving a Mature Reformed Doctrine of Original Sin," 347).

the state of concupiscence depends on the concomitant presence of an active will, even in its very first motions, before the will begins to engage rationally with these disordered desires to elicit a properly sinful "act" (the so-called *secundo-primum* and *secundum* motions of concupiscence).[139] In other words, as Turretin puts it, the will is always "radically" implicated in original sin, and in that broad sense it is "voluntary," even if it is not yet voluntary in the stricter sense of a sin actually committed.[140] That being so, it is concomitant, not prior, consent which is sufficient to render the corrupted habit (part of the depraved, but physically good nature we receive) an actual evil reality.[141] Indeed, as Martin Chemnitz points out, Luther would go so far as insisting that even the "tinder" (*fomes*) of concupiscence can be classed as "actual sin" in the sense that it is always a "most energetic and restless origin of actual sins."[142] Certainly, all Early Modern Protestants would agree that infants are not yet guilty of "actual sin" in the proper sense of that which embraces rational consent.[143] Even still, the "radical" dependence of both the state and the first motions of concupiscence on the will is an adequate means of understanding how Scripture can readily hold even infants personally to account for their share in original sin.[144]

Arguably, then, the Protestant tradition has developed its own resources to avoid the risk of reifying and depersonalizing sin when explaining human solidarity in the condition. However much the solidarity can be likened to

---

[139] Mastricht, *Theologia*, IV.ii.22 (447a–b); cf. Martin Chemnitz's reference to five stages of sin in gradual progression from habitual and original sin to fully consensual acts: "1. Fomes, sive depravatio inhaerans, quae complectituretiam defectus. 2. Suggestiones cogitationum & affectuum, id est, quando depravatio originalis movet se aliquae inclinatione. 3. Delectatio. 4. Consensus. 5. Ipsum opus. Ex his gradibus primi duo pertinent ad originale, reliqui tres ad actuale peccatum" (Martin Chemnitz, *Loci Theologici* [Frankfurt & Wittenberg: Sumptibus D. Tobiae Mevii & Elerdi Schumacheri, 1653], tl.de pecc.c8.iv [1:239a]; see also, Turretin, *Institutes*, 11.21.10 [2:136]; or Bavinck's discussion of these distinctions [Bavinck, *Reformed Dogmatics*, 3:142–44]).

[140] Turretin, *Institutes*, 9.2.9; cf. 1–10 (1:593–4); cf. Bavinck, *Reformed Dogmatics*, III.144: ". . . the sins of the human state and involuntary sins still do not totally occur apart from the will."

[141] For this reason, Mastricht will quite readily class Paul's unwanted desires (Rom. 7:15–17; cf. Gal. 5:17) as "sin," even where the will does not *previously* consent to them. Likewise, sins of ignorance, illness, and inadventure need to be explained in this way (cf. Num 15:27; Ps, 19:13; Gen. 12:17; Gen. 20:2; Acts 3:17; 1 Tim. 1:13) (Mastricht, *Theologia*, IV.ii.22 [447a–b]). Note also Gerhard's extensive response to Robert Bellarmine, defending the proposition that both the state and the first motions of concupiscence are sinful, even after a person is regenerate (Gerhard, *Loci Theologici*, II.x.11 [2:193a–219b]).

[142] Chemnitz, *Loci*, tl.de pecc c8.iv (239a–b); cf. c8.iii–iv (237b–239b). See also Mastricht's comments on the Lutheran position. He states that, while the Reformed agree that "original corruption is active in infants (*infantibus actu inesse corruptionem originalem*)," they prefer not to say that infants are guilty of "actual sin" since they are rationally incapable of grasping the law's demands. However, bearing Chemnitz's careful qualifications in mind, the difference between the Reformed and Lutheran positions appears to be only a subtle one (Mastricht, *Theologia*, IV.iii.24 [468b]).

[143] So, Mastricht, *Theologia*, IV.iii.8 (460a); IV.iii.24 (468b).

[144] So, e.g., Turretin, *Institutes*, 9.2.8–9 (1:594); Mastricht, *Theologia*, IV.ii.28 (450b–451a); cf. IV.ii.23 (448a); IV.ii.34 (454a); cf. Henri Blocher's apposite remark: "We underline the fact that original sin so conceived is not only 'potential' but *actual*, from the start, as is foetal and infant life itself. The will, though undeveloped, does exist, and its anti-God tendency already constitutes a wilful exercise" (Blocher, *Sin*, 128–89).

a disease with an undeniably physical dimension, the solidarity needs to be cashed out in a way that does not undo the ontological integrity and goodness of human nature itself, nor deprive someone of their personal responsibility for this state, without which McFarland is right to say that any meaningful notion of accountability or guilt before God would surely unravel. This coheres with the kinds of observations McFadyen and Kelsey make above, and which McFarland himself takes up toward the end of his study.[145] Patterns of "depravity"—e.g., distorted temperaments, addictive proclivities, and psychological disorders—can readily exchange between generations, not simply as social or systemic phenomena but also at the level of biology and genetics, as evidence seems to attest.[146] But however much a person finds himself "bound" up in this depravity, it is not a bondage that incapacitates his will. Nor is it "magic," some independent evil thing that somehow lurks in the shadows independently from a person's, or indeed, a collection of persons', active wills. Rather, to speak of "total depravity" is to refer to a universal condition which inevitably bends the will in a distorted, lawless direction. It is life "in the flesh" (Rom. 8:5–8), an orientation of false worship marked by enmity toward God and an inability to please him that concretely manifests itself in countless and, indeed, morally variable ways. For all the radical qualitative differences in their *actual* sins, it is a condition that afflicts all people equally, victim and perpetrator, infant and adult alike, and to that extent, all are equally responsible for it before God. In that way, Ricoeur is right to insist that, whatever else we may say about this condition of "defilement," it is bondage that is self-inflicted.[147] We may find ourselves trapped in this disorientation, irretrievably disfigured by the effects of sin and evil that stubbornly persist from generation to generation. But at the heart of this defilement is a "servile will"; a will that is at once bound in a "state" and yet

---

[145] McFarland, *Original Sin*, ch. 7. See too, "The Fall and Sin," in *The Oxford Handbook of Systematic Theology*, ed. John Webster, Kathryn Tanner, and Iain Torrance (Oxford: Oxford University Press, 2007).

[146] Shuster, *Fall and Sin*, 117–27; cf. Dean Hamer and Peter Copeland, *Living with Our Genes: The Groundbreaking Book about the Science of Personality, Behavior, and Genetic Destiny* (New York: Doubleday, 1998). As a contemporary Reformed thinker, Blocher makes some important suggestions along these lines, although it is not altogether clear whether or not he moves closer toward bodily traducianism than Turretin (whom he quotes) would willingly grant. It is not helped by a mistake in his translation where he renders Turretin's remark that the "tinder" (*fomes*) of sin is "impressed upon the fetus through the vital and animal spirits" (*fomes hujus peccati hauritur in ipsa conceptione, et foetui mediantibus spiritibus vitalibus et animalibus imprimitur*), as "'through the vital and animal spirits of the foetus' sin may be imprinted upon the soul." In describing the body's role in sin's propagation, Turretin is not intending any kind of bodily traduction of sin as a "formal" thing itself that impresses itself on the soul so much as the "tinder" or fomes of sin, or the kinds of depraved dispositions which are only actualized as sin in psychosomatic unity (Blocher, *Sin*, 126, cf. 122–31; for Turretin, see English translation: *Institutes*, 9.11.8 [1:641]; Latin: *Opera*, IX.xii.8 [1:579]).

[147] Ricoeur, *Symbolism of Evil*, 152–54.

is "in act."[148] And to that degree, each individual is personally accountable for his or her solidarity in this state. No one can "blame" their own share of it on the sin of another, whether neighbor, parent, or grandparent.

For all that, it is hard to escape a lingering sense of dissatisfaction with this admission, however true it may be. For all our active compliance with this state, it is still a state of *bondage*. And to the extent that it is bondage, the question of contagion—some external infliction, an imposition or constraint from without—cannot so easily be set aside. As we might expect, both Kelsey and McFarland vigorously dismiss any talk of a cause. If there is an "original sin," it is simply the "first in a series," no more or less bound than all the sins that follow. In other words, it is a sin which already finds itself to be in solidarity with the whole.[149] But the solidarity itself has no cause: it simply is and always has been. Right from the outset, human beings have always been *non posse non peccare* (not able not to sin). The trouble is, however, while human solidarity in sin should be explained as an active and not merely passive affair, beneath our "concomitant" compliance with the state, already implied is a *created* disorder within our nature over which we have no control. To comply with that disorder and make it *my own sin* is one thing. But why there is or should be some sort of physical depravity in the first place is a question that surely remains. The disorder itself may not be "sin" or an ontological evil per se, nor even some efficient or physical cause of sin, but it is a condition so intractably severe that we cannot comply with it in any other way than to embrace it as *our own sin*.

C. "As in Adam All Die": The Propriety of Human Solidarity in Sin

Cast in this light, the obstinate matter of the propriety and justice in all this rears its head yet again. To retrace what is now familiar ground, there is no way of sidestepping questions of causality, so long as this disorder is something that really exists. And unless this disorder, the ontological substrata of our solidarity in sin, is an entity outside God's active providential concursus—a kind of dualistic intrusion[150]—it is none other than a reality he has both created and deliberately inflicted upon us as a *conditio sine qua non*

---

[148] Ricoeur, *Symbolism of Evil*, 154.
[149] McFarland, *Original Sin*, 160.
[150] It is hard to see how Kelsey does not at least flirt with this possibility (Kelsey, *Eccentric Existence*, 212).

of our universal bondage in sin. If so, we are on the face of it left with a highly curious situation indeed. Right from the beginning, it would seem, God has furnished human beings with a nature that from a purely metaphysical, ontological perspective may well be classified "good," but which proves entirely inadequate to prevent any hypostatic individual (aside from Christ) from resisting something that is most definitely "not good." Technically it may be true that neither nature nor God himself is the efficient cause of the sinful solidarity that inevitably ensues. But in failing to furnish human beings with adequate ontological conditions for an end he legally demands at the very best suggests some kind of deficiency in his creative power, or at worst, the moral farce of imposing on his creatures an unattainable, and therefore inherently unjust demand, lending a haunting credibility to the clay's protest, "why have you made me like this?" (cf. Rom. 9:20).[151]

It is for this reason that the Augustinian tradition has isolated the vital theological significance of what the Bible attributes singly to Adam, not as some fictional or mythical cypher for the universal inevitability of sin but as a real historical act, a first sin that had to have arisen in Edenic conditions so unlike ours, but that, once committed, wreaked havoc on the whole. As we argued above, Adam's conditions—the conditions in which humanity was originally set by God—were such that there was nothing unattainable or unrealistic about the divine command, "do this and you will live." Lawlessness was not an inevitability. His sin was at once an entirely possible, yet at the same time an utterly inexplicable, inversion of the orientation in which he was set. If, as we have said, the root sin of unbelief—that fundamental dissonance with the truth—is already implied in our concomitant consent to the bondage in which we are born, Adam's unbelief was unique. That is to say, if we find ourselves already "locked" in a state of unbelief, as McFarland puts it,[152] for Adam it was an entirely free, deliberate, "antecedent" act, without any trace of concomitant bondage or estrangement. And therefore, the irretrievable disorientation, bondage, deprivation of righteousness, or *pollutio*, that immediately ensued for Adam was a divine imposition, a curse leading to death, and yet at the same time, it was something entirely *self*-imposed, a fitting and inevitable consequence of a prior act, in a way that it has not been for any sinner since.

---

[151] Houck states this dilemma, which he perceives in "modern Augustinian accounts of original sin," even more starkly: "By implying or stating directly that God creates the creature in opposition to himself, modern Augustinianism implies that God hates God" (Houck, *Original Sin*, 177).
[152] McFarland, *Original Sin*, 205.

In other words, by interpreting Adam's fall as a genuinely historical event, the tradition is in a very real way attempting to safeguard God's integrity with respect to the unadulterated goodness of human nature at its outset, the propriety of the specific expectations he placed upon those first human beings, and the fitting consequences that would flow from any failure on their part.

But here is the nub of the problem, of course. Adam is clearly an isolated case. How is it right for God to curse the entire race with the same effects of Adam's fall, saddling every other human being with a deprivation and corruption of nature to which we cannot but give our sinful consent? It is one thing to suffer collateral damage from another person's sin. To admit that the effects of any malevolence may have unpredictable and far-reaching consequences does not pose a great challenge, although most would surely still recognize an injustice here. Even where a victim of another's sin may find themselves bound to cooperate with that sin in some destructive way, to deny that a genuine injustice has been perpetrated through this imposition would level the distinction between perpetrator and victim way too far, in a manner that is morally intolerable and repugnant. So, to say that Adam's sin had far-reaching effects is one thing, an injustice of its own for which he is squarely responsible. But it is another thing altogether to be "born into" those effects, to have them deliberately imposed upon us by a benevolent Creator, and imposed in such a way that we cannot but consent to and comply with those effects *as our own sin*. In that case it is not just an imposition from Adam, but a direct imposition by God, a punishment of sorts.

In this regard, the Reformed tradition was right to detect a principle of justice at stake here. Turretin states the dilemma plainly: "[I]t is repugnant to divine justice to punish anyone for another's sin (which is simply and in every way another's)."[153] To be "worthy of punishment" (*reatus poenae*) cannot justly arise without foundation, without some genuine "condition of guilt" (*reatus culpac*).[154] In other words, the universal imposition of punishment needs a legal foundation in some real and universally representative sin, otherwise it is profoundly unjust. Of course, precisely this dilemma led Reformed thinkers to conclude that Adam's unique sin and guilt had to have been something God immediately

---

[153] Turretin, *Institutes*, 9.9.31 (1:625). Blocher casts the question clearly: "Can we see how it is *right*, under the righteous God's sovereign rule, that Adam's descendants find themselves deprived of the gift of divine fellowship, and therefore enmeshed in a destructive disorder at all levels of their nature, which affects heredity; and that they find themselves the slaves of their own pride, greed, lies and fears, under the tyranny of the Evil One?" (Blocher, *Sin*, 129).
[154] Owen, *Works*, 5:199.

imputed to the whole race, in "order of nature" prior to the natural corruption, the deprivation of righteousness that now binds us all in sinful solidarity.[155] Without this, there is no good and just reason why anyone should be "born into," punished with the malevolent effects of another's sin, created by God in such a way that those effects are only ever embraced as *their own sin and guilt*.

The Reformed recognized that the imputation of Adam's sin was a necessary clarification of precisely what is entailed in the biblical allusions to his so-called "headship" over the human race. As someone like Henri Blocher argues, whatever else may be said about the details of Paul's famous appeals to Adam (Rom. 5:12–20 or 1 Cor. 15:21–22, 48–49), there can be little doubt that some notion of Adamic headship is conspicuously on view in these appeals, analogous to that of Christ, as the tradition has widely recognized. But against the instincts of his Reformed forebears, Blocher feels it is simply not possible to find the notion of an "imputed" Adamic sin in a text like Romans 5, or indeed, anywhere else in Scripture.[156] Instead, he thinks it is sufficient to underwrite our share in the effects of Adam's sin through an "organic solidarity of the race," a "capitate structure" of human nature in him.[157] But there are difficulties here. Irrespective of how this organic solidarity happens to play out from generation to generation—and Blocher cashes it out in terms not terribly dissimilar to someone like Turretin[158]—it cannot perpetuate itself in some quasi-deistic fashion.[159] As Blocher readily admits,

---

[155] Turretin, *Institutes*, 9.9.14 (1:617). We leave it to others in this volume to discuss the historical origins of this development in Reformed theology and its association with an Adamic covenant, with its notable Renaissance Catholic precedent in the ingenious contribution of Ambrosius Catharinus (1483–1553). Cf. Aaron C. Denlinger, *Omnes in Adam ex pacto Dei: Ambrogio Catarino's Doctrine of Covenantal Solidarity and Its Influence on Post-Reformation Reformed Theologians* (Göttingen, Germany: Vandenhoeck & Ruprecht, 2010).

[156] Blocher carves out his own position on Rom. 5:12–20, distinguishing his position from "looser" realist accounts of solidarity and federalist accounts which detect the immediate imputation of Adam's sin. To his mind, the passage simply does not speak to the means by which Adam's "original" sin becomes the sin of all (see Blocher, *Sin*, 63–81; likewise, James D. G. Dunn, *Romans 1–8*, WBC 38A [Waco, TX: Word, 1988], 274). A classic defense of the federalist reading is still Murray, *Imputation*. Thomas Schreiner, who reads 5:12–14 differently from Murray, believes the forensic domain of the verb κατεστάθησαν in 5:19 means the immediate imputation of Adam's sin is decisively on view in 5:15–19 (Thomas R. Schreiner, "Original Sin and Original Death, Romans 5:12–19," in *Adam, the Fall, and Original Sin*, 273–74; likewise, Brian Vickers, *Jesus' Blood and Righteousness: Paul's Theology of Imputation* [Wheaton, IL: Crossway, 2006], 140).

[157] Blocher, *Sin*, 129.

[158] Although, see n. 146, above.

[159] Intriguingly, Houck's discussion of what he calls "disease theories" of original sin (such as Aquinas's own position, Crisp's, and, we might add, Blocher's) virtually implies that they do work in this way, where the corrupt nature somehow perpetuates itself intergenerationally by obligating God to withhold sanctifying grace. His objection to these theories is not so much that solidarity in sin perpetuates itself like this, but rather his objection stems in part from the intolerable corollary that, had Adam not sinned, the solidarity of his descendants in grace would have to have arisen from some obligation arising from the uncorrupted nature itself. Houck's own modification of Aquinas's position admits that God does actively create the descendants of the first humans in a state of original sin, deprived of the supernatural grace their parents once had, while insisting that God does not in any way "impute" Adam's sin to his descendants (presumably because he hesitates over "legal" or "federal" accounts of original sin [cf. Houck, *Original Sin*, 29–30]). The key piece here is that the only reason Adam's descendants might

it remains the case that "[w]e are created 'in Adam.'" However much God may fashion the whole lump "through" the nature of one, our share in that lump is still manifestly *his creation*.[160] And therefore, the propriety for this created "solidarity" in nature is not an issue that can be swept aside as easily as Blocher maintains, through a looser concept of Adamic headship that involves no imputation of his sin.[161] Nevertheless, Blocher is right to hint that any reliance on "imputation" as the solution to the dilemma merely shifts the problem back a step. How is it right that God would hold anyone *to account*, to be considered guilty and liable to punishment for another's sin, as the legal foundation for their share in that sin's punishing effects? On the face of it that would appear no less "repugnant to common moral taste" than anything else we have seen thus far.[162] On that basis Blocher joins those outside the Reformed tradition who continue to find the notion of an immediately imputed Adamic sin troubling to say the least.[163] In any event, it seems to stand in direct violation of straightforward biblical affirmations of individual accountability for sin, the most famous being in Ezekiel 18.

We leave it to others in this volume to defend the biblical viability of a universally imputed Adamic sin as something stemming from his unique public headship over the race.[164] Suffice it to say, as Reformed writers have long argued, there are numerous cases in Scripture where it seems entirely possible for the iniquity and guilt of one to be justly counted as another's, notwithstanding the teaching of a text like Ezekiel 18.[165] In other words, although a principle of individual accountability is certainly upheld in

---

be deprived of supernatural grace is the fact that those descendants themselves willfully persist in disobedience. In other words, to cut the nexus with Adam's sin requires a view of original sin where some measure of "natural" obedience to God remains theoretically possible and intact in pre-rational infants deprived of supernatural grace, so that any so-called "mortal sin" which might eventually ensue is not an inevitability of that state. Such a position is a decidedly non-Augustinian way of resolving the justice dilemma, but also involves an emphatic departure from the inescapably Augustinian Protestant confessional tradition. Even so, Houck does seem to want to retain some sense in which the inherited nature is "sinful" and a consequence of Adam's sin, which leads him to wrestle with the very conundrum of God's concursus in its perpetuation (see Houck, *Original Sin*, 74–87, 200–220, 244–54).

[160] Blocher, *Sin*, 130. This seems to be parallel to Crisp's preference for an Edwardsean perdurantist or "participation argument" (Crisp, "Sin," 208–11).

[161] Likewise Crisp, who is overly hasty in dismissing the moral issue here ("Sin," 210–11, 212–13); cf. Garry William's observations on this score, ch. 20 in this volume. Rea tacitly admits that this dilemma also remains with his ingenious "fission theory" alternative (Rea, "Original Sin," 343; cf. 341–45).

[162] Blocher, *Sin*, 130; similarly, McFarland, *Original Sin*, 152–153; Crisp, "Original Sin," 257–258; Crisp, "Sin," 202–5; and Thomas H. McCall, *Against God and Nature: The Doctrine of Sin* (Wheaton, IL: Crossway, 2019), 164–65.

[163] E.g., McFarland, *Original Sin*, 152–53.

[164] Cf. Garry Williams's two chapters in this volume. See too, J. V. Fesko, *Death in Adam, Life in Christ: The Doctrine of Imputation* (Fearn, Ross-shire, UK: Mentor, 2016), 175–96.

[165] Aside from Rom. 5:12–20, which remains a disputed *dictum* for this principle, some of the usual texts cited in support of it include Ex. 20:5; Josh. 7:10–26; 1 Sam. 15:2, 3 (cf. Ex. 17:8–16); 2 Sam. 21, 24; 1 Kings 14:9, 10; 21:21, 22; Matt. 23:25; cf. Turretin, *Institutes*, 9.9.19 (1:620–21). This fairly standard appeal to biblical evidence is surprisingly overlooked in recent critiques of the federalist position, such as those of Blocher, McFarland, Crisp, and McCall.

Scripture (cf. Ezek. 18:20), this is not the only way God's justice appears to play out in his relationship with human beings. There is nothing "arbitrary" about this admission.[166] It simply means that the biblical account of divine justice is sufficiently nuanced to recognize that God sometimes deals with people in corporate or federal relationships, so that the acts of one are counted as implicating another, or indeed, whole families and nations, in their guilt. Indeed, without this admission, suspicions of a "legal fiction" lurking beneath the solidarity that exists between a righteous Savior and the sinners to whom God imputes that righteousness, would surely carry a weight they do not otherwise have.[167]

If all this is true, the notion of a covenant with Adam as the head of the human race, in which God deems his obedience (or lack thereof) a representative and universally imputable act, is not so fanciful as its detractors sometimes self-evidently suppose.[168] It is not that the universal imputation of Adam's unique sin somehow undoes the principle of individual accountability: "the one who sins is the one who will die." As we have seen, Adam's sin and its effects always receive our concomitant consent; it is voluntarily "owned" as the personal sin of every individual to whom it is imputed. But the uniquely representative and immediately imputable character of that one act is the only just foundation for the divine infliction of a natural corruption and deprivation which binds the rest of the race in that same sinful disorientation.

Of course, much more needs to be said on this score than is possible here. If the typical objection that some historical, Edenic covenant with a representative, unfallen Adam is a "text-less" doctrine is relatively straightforward to contest,[169] the challenge it poses to the claims of modern palaeoanthropology

---

[166] Contra McFarland, *Original Sin*, 153; or Crisp, "Sin," 202–5.

[167] The point here is not derived exclusively from a disputed interpretation of Rom. 5:12–19, but from a theological conviction that God's justice is not in fact arbitrary, but manifests itself consistently in creation and redemption. Indeed, one of Crisp's objections to this claim rests on the mistaken assumption that Christ's headship over his body entails neither legal nor realist dimensions. In a manner that is parallel to the immediate imputation of Adam's sin, Protestants have classically held that the forensic entitlement enshrined in the doctrine of justification is the immediate legal ground for the organic participation in Christ's resurrection life that the elect experience in regeneration, as Vos rightly recognizes (Vos, *Reformed Dogmatics*, 2:40; contra Crisp, "Sin," 205 n. 18). For a similar response to Crisp on this score, see Fesko, *Death in Adam*, 266–69. Note too Williams's perceptive comments about a false dichotomy that is all-too-readily implied in the distinction between "Realism" and "Federalism," as if it equates to a distinction between what possesses ontology and what is purely arbitrary (ch. 20 in this volume).

[168] For a classic defense of the concept arising out of the specific doctrinal context of original sin, see Vos, *Reformed Dogmatics*, 2:31–49.

[169] Mastricht, *Theologia*, III.xii.23 (421a). Mastricht, for instance, makes the fair (if predictable) observation that to exclude the "substance" (*res*) of a doctrine simply because it is not explicitly mentioned in Scripture would create difficulties for a number of other important doctrines, such as the Trinity. In any event, as Richard Muller has shown, the biblical case typically developed for an Edenic covenant was extensive and rigorous. By no means did it depend entirely on any proof text such as the famous (but disputed) reference in Hos. 6:7 (Richard A. Muller,

is undeniably acute. Yet, in formalizing and defending the biblical foundations of this doctrine, Reformed writers recognized that a great deal was
at stake. Mastricht, for instance, can remark that in denying a covenant of
works it becomes that much harder to do justice to numerous Christian doctrines, not least the "propagation of original corruption" or the "satisfaction
of Christ."[170] If that is the case, regardless of any remaining quibbles over
terminology—"covenant," "administration," or otherwise—the historical
and representative character of Adam's unique fall is something integral to
the so-called analogy of faith, a foundational or confessional principle which
cannot but regulate the way Christian readers of Scripture should attempt any
dialogue or rapprochement with the modern scientific consensus.

V. Conclusion: The Mystery of Sin in the Clarity of God's Goodness

If describing the character of sin is an inherently murky business, it is so only
because it is murky by nature. How is it even possible to describe something
through necessary deployment of creaturely goods like language and logic
when the very thing being described defies all that is good? Barth surely
captured the weight of this dilemma when insisting that sin is an "ontological
impossibility." Even so, as is all too readily apparent, sin really does exist.
And the real, concrete existence of sin, like the existence of anything, is intelligible only in light of God's sovereign goodness, apart from which nothing
exists. If the sinner by instinct evades a true assessment of sin's presence in
his or her life and in the surrounding world, it begins to become intelligible in
that divine light—not the light of judgment but the light of grace refracted to
us in the glorious face of Christ, the image of God par excellence. Apart from
restoring broken image-bearers into his likeness, what the light of the gospel
affords the sinner is the unspeakably wondrous gift of being able to step out
from beneath the consuming fire of divine judgment to view the veracity of
that judgment without quite as much evasion and denial as before.

But the intelligibility that this gracious vantage point provides extends
only so far. It would surely mark a perverse return of that evasion to conclude from sin's existence that God somehow needed it so that he could

---

"The Covenant of Works and the Stability of the Divine Law in the Seventeenth-Century Reformed Orthodoxy: A
Study in the Theology of Herman Witsius and Wilhelmus à Brakel," *CTJ* 29 [1994]: 91–93).
[170] Mastricht, *Theologia*, III.xii.23 (421a).

glorify some attribute that was missing in the beginning—say, his love and mercy—in the redemptive work of Christ. Hardly less perverse is the conclusion that sin was some unpreventable alien intrusion, a threat to divine honor that God was compelled to vanquish through the death and resurrection of his Son. Suffice to say that, for whatever God's good purposes in actively permitting the entrance of sin into his world, the evil that lies at its heart will always remain an entirely unnecessary and unfathomable mystery, a "riddle" without any good cause, for which God's image-bearers are forever, irreducibly to blame.

25

"Distinguished among Ten Thousand"

THE SINLESSNESS OF CHRIST

Mark Jones

What appears to be a rather straightforward explanation of the biblical witness concerning the person of Jesus as the sinless Son of God cannot be assumed today because of the various positions regarding his humanity that have been put forward by Christian theologians over the past few hundred years. Ecclesiastical history concerning dogmatic accounts of various theological loci has never been straightforward, though one may expect the confession that Jesus was (and still is) sinless to be rather obvious and necessary for the maintenance and advancement of the Christian religion.

Like any other major confessions in the Christian faith, Christ's sinlessness requires explanation, usually in response to certain questions that arise from the possible implications of the doctrine under examination. Why was Jesus sinless? What did it mean for him to be sinless? Was it possible for him to be sinful? In what sense does he identify with sinful humanity? While there is near unanimity in the Christian church on the confession that Jesus was sinless during his life on earth, the details of that confession are not so straightforward.

The Biblical Witness

Pagan observers of Christ's character knew there was something peculiar about his moral dignity. Pilate asks before the crowd of Jews who demanded his crucifixion, "Why? What evil has he done?" (Matt. 27:23). No doubt Pilate felt the burden of his actions given that his wife had earlier said to him, "Have nothing to do with that righteous man" (Matt. 27:19). At Christ's crucifixion, the Roman centurion made the startling confession, "Truly this was the Son of God!" (Matt. 27:54), a confession echoed by one of the dying thieves, who publicly proclaimed, "This man has done nothing wrong" (Luke 23:41). What were these people saying? They were simply echoing the confession of Judas Iscariot that Jesus was innocent (Matt. 27:4). These testimonies are, of course, not decisive by any stretch of the imagination. But they are noteworthy in terms of how innocent bystanders, pagans, enemies, and rulers viewed Jesus of Nazareth, and especially at the end of his life when he was being treated like a guilty criminal.

Righteous witnesses of Christ's life give us an even clearer picture of the reality and nature of his sinlessness. Peter calls Jesus "the Holy and Righteous One" (Acts 3:14; see 7:52; 22:14). He informs his readers that they were bought with the "precious blood of Christ, like that of a lamb without blemish or spot" (1 Pet. 1:19). With even greater clarity, in the context of explaining why Jesus is able to save (1 Pet. 2:24), Peter says that Jesus "committed no sin, neither was deceit found in his mouth" (1 Pet. 2:22). Likewise, the apostle John says that in Jesus "there is no sin" (1 John 3:5). The author of Hebrews, speaking of Christ's ability to be tempted like us, also makes the salient point that Jesus was nonetheless "without sin" (Heb. 4:15), and later speaks of him in his high priestly role as "holy, innocent, unstained, separated from sinners" (Heb. 7:26). And the apostle Paul also says that Jesus "knew no sin" (2 Cor. 5:21).

Jesus himself leaves us in no doubt about his own consciousness of being a sinless person. In John 8:46 he asks a rhetorical question: "Which one of you convicts me of sin?" Frédéric Godet makes the point worth stating:

> The *perfect* holiness of Christ is in this passage demonstrated, not by the silence of the Jews, who might have chosen to ignore the sins of their questioner, but by the assurance with which His direct consciousness of the purity of His whole life is in this question affirmed.[1]

A holy man, ordinarily speaking, would never make such a claim about himself; but the Holy One of God does so because he came to testify to the

---

[1] Frédéric Godet, *Commentary on the Gospel of St. John* (Edinburgh: T&T Clark, 1881), 348.

truth about himself and God. There is a holy confidence evident in Christ's ministry, and particularly in his intense theological debates with the Jewish religious leaders of his day, that either explicitly or implicitly affirms everything that has been said so far about the sinless holiness of his nature. For example, when the Jews picked up stones to stone him, Jesus makes a statement about himself followed by a (rhetorical) question: "I have shown you many good works from the Father; for which of them are you going to stone me?" (John 10:32). The truth is, there are no grounds upon which Jesus can be lawfully condemned.

The biblical witness seems straightforward enough. Why go on? What else needs to be said? Should we not simply content ourselves with these perspicuous statements concerning the sinlessness of Jesus of Nazareth? First, we need to understand *why* the biblical witness presents us with a sinless man from Nazareth. Second, there remain, even with this confession, a host of unanswered questions regarding the purity of Christ's nature. For example, to what extent, if any, did the divine nature influence Christ's human nature? Was the human nature of Christ identical with Adam's nature in the garden, or was it, as some theologians have argued, "fallen" human nature? Following from this, how can we affirm the reality of Christ's temptations if we also affirm that it was not possible for him to sin? Or was it possible for him to sin, even though he remained sinless? As Gerald O'Collins notes,

> Was he immune from sin—sinless not merely *de facto* but also *de jure*? Such an absolute impeccability in principle seems like a contradiction in terms. But how could we reconcile an absolute, intrinsic impeccability with Christ's complete humanity—in particular, with his genuine human freedom?[2]

These and other questions need to be addressed so that our understanding of Christ's sinlessness is not reduced to a piling up of (allegedly) self-interpreting proof texts on such a crucial doctrine.

Chalcedon

Who is Jesus? The affirmation of Jesus's sinlessness is simply the affirmation of his person. In 325, Nicaea made the catholic confession that Jesus is the

---

[2] Gerald O'Collins, *Christology: A Biblical, Historical, and Systematic Study of Jesus* (Oxford: Oxford University Press, 1995), 268.

divine Son. But this Jesus is a man, and thus the Nicene Creed affirms his incarnation: "Who for us men, and for our salvation, came down and was incarnate and was made man." Following from the confession offered at Nicaea were intense Christological conflicts that would be partly resolved at Chalcedon in 451. Even Chalcedonian orthodoxy, for all its details, does not resolve a number of important Christological questions; it nonetheless does establish a basic view on Christ's person that helps us to understand why he is the sinless Savior.

Twenty years before Chalcedon, Nestorianism[3] was defeated at the Council of Ephesus (431). There is one subject ("hypostasis"), the second person of the Trinity: the Son of God. Obviously, this was affirmed at Nicaea, but Cyril of Alexandria (376–444) was all too willing to put more nails in the coffin of a two-subject Christology. At Ephesus the title belonging exclusively to Mary as *Theotokos* (the God-bearer) was affirmed. Ephesus did not solve every problem, since Eutyches and his followers embraced monophysitism,[4] which was not, in their minds, opposed to Nicaea since the Nicene Creed spoke only of Christ as consubstantial with the Father but not consubstantial with humanity. Thus Chalcedon was necessary to combat the rising Eutychianism[5] and also to provide yet another blow to Nestorianism. This, as far as it goes, is about as neat as we can make the history sound. Despite the "good order" at such a large assembly of bishops, further Christological controversy remained not only during but also after Chalcedon. Still, what we have as a result of Chalcedon provides a basic confession regarding Christ's person that not only does justice to the biblical data but also helps us understand why an affirmation of Christ's sinlessness is a *sine qua non* of the Christian faith.

Even if the Creed does not give a resounding victory to either the Alexandrians or the Antiochenes, it does state that Jesus is both "perfect in Godhead and also perfect in manhood." His manhood consists of a "reasonable soul and body." The Son of God must be

---

[3] Ascribed to Nestorius of Constantinople, Nestorianism affirms there were two separate persons in Christ. Nestorius did not teach this crass view, but over time his name was attached to the concept of Christ whereby he was a divine person and a human person, sometimes also known as "Two Sons" Christology.

[4] From the Greek, "one nature," monophysitism refers to those who seemingly rejected the conclusions of Chalcedon (451), which is "diphysite" (two nature). Monophysites affirmed two perfect natures (divine and human), but the harmonizing or blending of these natures sometimes led to problems concerning the true humanity of Christ, as in the case of Eutyches.

[5] Referring to the theology of Eutyches, Eutychianism is the belief that there is a "mixture" of divinity and humanity in Christ. Similar to monophysitism, but different in some ways, Eutychianism denies that Jesus was consubstantial with the human race.

... recognized in two natures, unconfusedly, unchangeably, indivisibly, inseparably; the difference of natures being by no means taken away by the union, but rather the distinctive character of each nature being preserved, combining in one Person and hypostasis; not divided or separated into two persons, but one and the same Son and Only Begotten God, Word, Lord Jesus Christ . . .[6]

Chalcedon provides the Creedal basis for the affirmation, based on the Scriptures, that Jesus was not only sinless but, if we are to make sense of the claims of the Creed, *non posse peccare* (not able to sin).

"And the Word Became . . ."

The Son of God was a perfect person before the incarnation. He remained what he was and is and will always be, but he was also made flesh (what he was not). The Son of God was required, if he was to save humanity, to assume a true human nature consisting of a body and soul. Otherwise, he could not have saved those who are body-soul composites with identities. The English Puritan and member at the Westminster Assembly John Arrowsmith (1602–59), argued, "With us, the soul, and body, being united, make a person. But in Christ, the soul and body were so united, as to have their subsistence not of themselves (as in us) but in the Godhead."[7] The assumption of a human nature by the eternal Son led to what has been called a hypostatic union. The humanity of Christ is "enhypostatic" insofar as it subsists only in the person of the Son.

Thus in the person of Christ we believe in a union between the divine and the human. Just as he is very God of very God, so also he is very man of very man. Indeed, in terms of our salvation, his humanity is as important as his divinity. According to his divinity, he has infinite knowledge (omniscience); he is omnipresent, eternal, unchangeable, and so on. According to his humanity, he obeyed, died, and rose again. Yet these natures never "do things" in the abstract. Jesus died on the cross; Jesus ate bread; Jesus forgives sins; Jesus will return to judge all mankind. He does these things according to his human or divine nature, but the important point is that he is the subject.

---

[6] John Anthony McGuckin, *The Westminster Handbook to Patristic Theology* (Louisville: Westminster/John Knox, 2004), 80.

[7] John Arrowsmith, *Theanthropos, or, God-Man, Being an Exposition upon the First Eighteen Verses of the First Chapter of the Gospel according to St. John* (London: Printed for Humphrey Moseley and William Wilson, 1660), 207.

Affirming Christ's two natures provides the ontological basis for the affirmation of his sinlessness as the Son of God. He is a divine being. The apostle John calls him the Alpha and the Omega (Rev. 1:8, 17; 22:13). John assumes Christ's preexistence in the opening words of his Gospel (John 1:1; see also 8:58; 17:5). Jesus is called by the name "God" (John 1:1; 20:28; Rom. 9:5; Heb. 1:8–9; 2 Pet. 1:1). Likewise, the evidence for his true humanity is also clear and persuasive. Matthew records his human descent (Matt. 1); John declares that Christians confess that Jesus has come in the flesh (1 John 4:2); and the Gospel authors all make it crystal clear that Jesus died on the cross, which is possible only if he has a true human nature. Moreover, in the Gospel accounts, Jesus eats, drinks, weeps, walks, talks, etc. When all the Scriptures are reckoned with, there is never the slightest hint that Jesus is not truly human, but there is also never the slightest hint that he is simply a human. He is the God-man.

"Flesh"

But the assumption of a true human nature has raised a number of questions by theologians over the "type" of humanity assumed by the Son. Even in the seventeenth century, long before Edward Irving (1792–1834) and Karl Barth (1886–1968), Arrowsmith deals with the question of whether the Son assumed a human nature in its perfection—such as Adam possessed in the garden—or a human nature clothed with infirmities that are a result of the fall.

Arrowsmith acknowledges that Christ's humanity was not strictly similar to that of Adam's before the fall. Christ assumed a human nature "clothed with infirmities, as after the fall; which is implied in the word Flesh."[8] The Scriptures do not say that the Word became man, but rather "flesh." Thus,

> when it would speak contemptibly of man, and shew him to be the lowest Creature, to call him, flesh, when it would set forth the weaknesse, that man is subject to. . . . So then the word was made flesh, that is, took not onely man's nature, but man's infirmities.[9]

In typical scholastic fashion, Arrowsmith makes another distinction in order to clarify his position. While Christ did assume a nature with infirmities, the nature assumed was not a sinful human nature and the infirmities that naturally

---

[8] Arrowsmith, *Theanthropos*, 208.
[9] Arrowsmith, *Theanthropos*, 208.

result from sin. Thus he distinguishes between "painful infirmities" and "sinful and culpable infirmities," the latter of which Christ did not take and the former of which he took only a part.[10] The "painful infirmities" fall under a twofold consideration, namely, those that are "personal" and proper to some men and women, such as various diseases (e.g., leprosy), and those that are "natural," such as pain, grief, sorrow, hunger, and thirst. The former Christ did not take, but he certainly experienced the latter.[11] Arrowsmith further qualifies his position later by stating that Christ did in fact take the sinful infirmities of man by way of imputation, for because of his divine nature he was protected from any inherent sin.[12] John Owen, also affirming the basic view of Arrowsmith, posits that certain infirmities (e.g., "inordinate inclinations" and sickness) "would have absolutely impeded the work he had to do."[13]

In the NT, "flesh" (*sarx*) has a basic twofold meaning. It may refer either to human weakness, and all that that means (e.g., perishableness), or to mankind in sin. Sometimes Paul refers to "flesh" in a sense that is morally neutral insofar as he is speaking about concrete material corporeality. Hence we are body-soul composites; we are humans, as distinguished from angels and God. Yet Paul also uses the word "flesh" to describe mankind in his sin and depravity (Rom. 7:5, 14; Gal. 5:19; 6:8). Sin and flesh come into the closest identity at times when describing man. The question before us concerns what specific type of human flesh Christ assumed.

Was the flesh the Son assumed practically the same as that which Adam was created with before the fall? Or did the Son assume a fallen human nature? This question has been vigorously debated in the past few hundred years, apparently having its genesis in Britain via the Scottish theologian Edward Irving.

Fallen Humanity?

While Edward Irving may have been the first Christian theologian to give a somewhat sophisticated defense of the fallen humanity view of Christ's human nature, Karl Barth likely gave it the popularity that it has enjoyed

---

[10] Arrowsmith, *Theanthropos*, 209. Thomas Watson also distinguishes between sinful and painful infirmities; see *A Body of Practical Divinity* (Glasgow: James Tweedie, 1759), 116. See also George Smeaton, who argues that Jesus did not assume individual infirmities such as "disorderly mental conditions or any of the germs of sickness" (*The Doctrine of the Atonement* [Edinburgh: T&T Clark, 1868], 95).
[11] Arrowsmith, *Theanthropos*, 209.
[12] Arrowsmith, *Theanthropos*, 217.
[13] John Owen, *An Exposition of the Epistle to the Hebrews*, 7 vols. (Edinburgh: Johnstone & Hunter, 1854–62), 3:468.

since, with Thomas F. Torrance (1913–2007), Colin Gunton (1941–2003), and Thomas Weinandy all allegedly advocating for some versions of the "fallen" view. Yet, Barth's view does not appear to have always been well understood.

In a fascinating and penetrating study on Barth, Shao Kai Tseng refutes the so-called fallenness view of Christ's human nature often read into Barth. According to Tseng, "Barth makes it unequivocal that Christ's human nature as distinct from the sinful flesh is without sin."[14] Tseng adds,

> Whenever Barth speaks loosely of Christ's assumption of fallen human nature in his later writings, therefore, we have to bear in mind his own qualification that properly speaking this is not human nature, but rather un-nature. Grasping his dialectical treatment of sin and human nature as two contradictory determinations of the human being would help us understand Van Kuiken's observation of Barth's later distinction between Christ's "human nature" and "sinful flesh." The former is an ontological category and the latter an existential/historical one.[15]

Jesus enters a context in which he may be said to participate in the world of sinful flesh, but unlike Adam he triumphs over this world through his faithful obedience toward God. Tseng adds,

> Barth stresses that Christ did not assume and enter into a historical condition of sinlessness. Sin is of course foreign to Christ's human nature (strictly defined), but this has no direct soteric import as far as the historical economy of salvation is concerned, for the nature of all sinners remains uncorrupted in the condition of fallenness. Christ took on the world-historical condition of fallenness to be under the sway of that evil determination "from below" by the actuality of nothingness. Just as for every other human being, sin is an ontological impossibility for Christ because it is absolutely alien to his human nature, but at the same time his being, like ours, is totally determined by the historical condition of original sin.[16]

Considering these findings, this view espoused by Barth turns out to be not so radical at all, since sin is an ontological impossibility in the person of Christ, properly speaking. The existential identification with fallen humanity

---

[14] Shao Kai Tseng, *Barth's Ontology of Sin and Grace: Variations on a Theme of Augustine* (New York: Routledge, 2018), 111.

[15] Tseng, *Barth's Ontology of Sin and Grace*, 111. The work Tseng refers to by Van Kuiken also provides an even-handed look at the topic of Christ's so-called "fallen human nature." See Jerome Van Kuiken, *Christ's Humanity in Current and Ancient Controversy: Fallen or Not?* (London: Bloomsbury T&T Clark, 2017).

[16] Tseng, *Barth's Ontology of Sin and Grace*, 111–12.

is something that, properly understood, has a strong Reformed pedigree when one looks at exegetical considerations arising out of Christ's baptism of repentance by John the Baptist.

Irving, on the other hand, adopts a more radical view than Barth. His view may involve for Christ a sort of existential awareness of his "fallenness," but that is because it is indeed ontologically true. He affirms that Christ took our fallen nature since "there was no other in existence to take."[17] For Irving, it was impossible, because the fall of Adam affected the rest of humanity, to find flesh on earth that was not fallen. So Christ assumes our nature, which is necessarily fallen human nature. This nature is both "mortal and corruptible."[18] With all of the possible dilemmas arising from such a view, Irving felt that his robust doctrine of the Spirit's work on and in Christ was a sufficient safeguard for maintaining the "sinlessness" of Christ, despite the fact that the Son assumed a corrupt human nature that, apart from the Spirit, would have been internally inclined toward evil temptations. Thus, because he assumed a fallen human nature, he was also legitimately tempted, which otherwise could not have been the case, according to Irving.

The distinction made by Arrowsmith between "painful infirmities" and "sinful and culpable infirmities" would not be sufficient for Irving. All the effects of the fall must be predicated of the human nature of Christ, not just suffering and death, but also internal "evil propensities." Irving boasts that in his view, "I have the Holy Ghost manifested in subduing, restraining, conquering, the evil propensities of the fallen manhood, and making it an apt organ for expressing the will of the Father."[19] There is yet a further consideration regarding Irving's view. He asserts that "Christ had a body and soul of man's substance, without thereby having a human person; and, therefore, we can assert the sinfulness of the whole, the complete, the perfect human nature, which he took, without in the least implicating Him with sin."[20] He distinguishes substance from person so that when he speaks of Christ's fallen humanity, he is arguing that the sinful inclinations are true only of the nature apart from his identity as the God-man.

Thus, as Van Kuiken notes, "To preserve Christ's personal sinlessness despite his sinful substance, Irving idiosyncratically differentiates three kinds

---

[17] Edward Irving, *The Collected Writings of Edward Irving*, 5 vols. (London: Alexander Strahan, 1865), 5:116.
[18] *Collected Writings of Edward Irving*, 5:116.
[19] *Collected Writings of Edward Irving*, 5:170.
[20] *Collected Writings of Edward Irving*, 5:565.

of sin: original sin, constitutional sin, and actual sin."[21] Typically among Reformed theologians, they distinguish between original sin and actual sin. But Irving speaks of constitutional sin, which is usually explained in the context of original sin. According to Van Kuiken's analysis of Irving, by assuming a fallen human nature,

> Christ apportions to himself a part of the common mass of sinful human nature, thereby sharing in the collective sins and carnal temptations of the whole race, as well as in the guilt of having a fallen nature. Yet the divine will in Christ, being immutably immune from temptations, ever wills the will of his Father, while the Holy Spirit continuously neutralizes the sinful impulses of Christ's flesh, converting them into holy thinking, willing, and doing. By these means, Christ never falls into actual sin, which is the voluntary transgression of God's law.[22]

Irving's view is so idiosyncratic that one would be hard pressed to link it to any one ancient heresy. Just as Irving was fond of accusing his critics of heresies, there appears to be traces of both Eutychianism and Nestorianism in his portrait of Christ. He asserts that Jesus possesses a fallen human nature but does not wish to attribute that to the person of Christ. To speak of Christ as "fallen," he must abstract the humanity of Christ in such a manner that vestiges of Nestorianism quickly creep into his Christology. Marcus Dods (1834–1909), a critic of Irving, rightly argues,

> If a fallen nature exist at all, it can exist only as the nature of a fallen person. If then there was a fallen nature, or a nature in a fallen state existing in Christ, the conclusion is inevitable, that there was a fallen person in him; and consequently that either the humanity was a person or the second person of the Holy Trinity was fallen. In every point of view therefore in which the question as to a fallen nature can be placed, it appears to me clear as the light of day, that he who persists in saying that our Lord took a fallen human nature, or human nature in a fallen state, has just to choose whether he will preach the impiety of a fallen God, or the heresy of a distinct human personality, in the one mediator between God and man.[23]

To put the matter rather bluntly, for all of the pretended advantages that an assumption of Christ having a fallen human nature gets for us

---

[21] Van Kuiken, *Christ's Humanity*, 16.
[22] Van Kuiken, *Christ's Humanity*, 17.
[23] Marcus Dods, *On the Incarnation of the Eternal Word* (London: R. B. Seely & W. Burnside, 1831), 377–78.

believers, the fatal flaw in this model is the unavoidable conclusion that Christ is sinful. Irving may not agree that that is the logical implication of his position, but a Chalcedonian view of Christ really can admit no other conclusion.

There are other implications for the "fallen humanity" view. First, for many in the Reformed tradition, original corruption and original guilt go hand in hand. So, if Christ assumes a fallen human nature, he is also at the same time guilty before God, even if he has not committed a personal sin. Second, assuming a fallen nature cannot, particularly in the Reformed theological tradition, be understood apart from the implication that the person is responsible for the natures. Impeccability, which necessarily results from the identity of the person as one person, who is fully divine, would be compromised, since the assumption of a fallen nature destroys the grounds for impeccability because the *person* would be identified as fallen, not simply the nature. Third, because fallen nature is "odious" to God, the Son would be odious to God. A fallen nature is the penalty we have incurred by virtue of our union with Adam. We have sinned in Adam and thus are, by nature, odious to God and have incurred the penalty of a fallen nature. Since Christ was not "in Adam" like we are, and thus not a sinner in Adam, there are no justifiable grounds for his assumption of a fallen human nature. It would be unjust of God to do that.

Returning to the view put forth by Arrowsmith, this view appears to be the safest insofar as we can maintain Chalcedonian orthodoxy, biblical fidelity, and theological consistency. Herman Bavinck (1854–1921) speaks of Christ assuming a "weak human nature," which was different from Adam's created nature in innocence. Bavinck also appears to be affirming Arrowsmith's distinction between painful infirmities that are personal (e.g., leprosy) and painful infirmities that are natural (e.g., hunger):

> But one may not infer from this that Christ was also susceptible to all kinds of illness, for though he did take upon himself the general consequences of sin—suffering and death—that now belong to human nature, he did not assume every particular illness, which is the consequence of special circumstances, a weak constitution, an irregular or imprudent lifestyle.[24]

---

[24] Herman Bavinck, *Reformed Dogmatics*, ed. John Bolt, trans. John Vriend, 4 vols. (Grand Rapids, MI: Baker Academic, 2003–8), 3:311.

Importantly, Bavinck makes a key observation concerning Christ's human nature, namely, that it was "much more highly developed than was Adam's, for in the state of integrity there was simply no occasion for many emotions, such as anger, sadness, pity, compassion, and so on."[25]

Most theologians in the tradition have, therefore, maintained this basic understanding of Christ's humanity, namely, that it was not protected from the weaknesses of certain painful infirmities. But at the same time it was not possible for Christ to be leprous and therefore ceremonially unclean according to the OT Scriptures (Lev. 13–14).

Christ's Impeccability

The sinlessness of Christ cannot be adequately understood apart from the reality of his temptations on earth as mediator. The first question to ask is whether Christ could have possibly sinned under the force of temptation. If so, what are the implications for our doctrine of Christ and God? If not, what are the implications concerning the realities of Christ's temptations?

Christ was either peccable (able to sin = *posse peccare*) or impeccable (not able to sin = *non posse peccare*). Those affirming peccability usually do so because they cannot conceive how a temptation would have any real force apart from the possibility of giving in to such a temptation. Despite this protestation, the implications of affirming peccability of Christ are so significant that one cannot go down that path without potentially doing great harm to the Christian religion.[26] O'Collins rightly notes that we have to affirm that Christ was impeccable *de jure* because, if this were not so, we would "face the situation of God possibly in deliberate opposition to God; one divine person would be capable (through his human will) of committing sin and so intentionally transgressing the divine will."[27]

Similarly, in the nineteenth century, W. G. T. Shedd (1820–94) leaves us with little doubt that an impeccable Christ is essential to the Christian faith: "When the logos goes into union with a human nature, so as to constitute a single person with it, he becomes responsible for all that this person does

---

[25] Bavinck, *Reformed Dogmatics*, 3:311.

[26] Charles Hodge affirmed the peccability of Christ, though his argument is not very developed. He affirms that Christ's sinlessness "does not amount to absolute impeccability. It was not a non potest peccare. If He was a true man He must have been capable of sinning. . . . Temptation implies the possibility of sin. If from the constitution of his person it was impossible for Christ to sin, then his temptation was unreal and without effect . . ." (Charles Hodge, *Systematic Theology*, vol. 2 [London: James Clarke, 1960], 457).

[27] O'Collins, *Christology*, 269.

through the instrumentality of this nature. . . . Should Jesus Christ sin, incarnate God would sin."[28] We should tremble to conceive of God (the Son) waging an unholy war against God (the Father).

Moreover, if Christ could sin, why could the Spirit not keep him from such an action? How does the Spirit's role factor into this monstrosity?

Picking up on the idea of a God at war with himself, Thomas Torrance claims that the question of whether Jesus could have sinned if he had wished is

> irrelevant and absurd, for the whole point of the matter is that he would not have liked to. It was just because sin was so loathsome to him that he could not have sinned. There is no freedom apart from character; there is no "can" apart from "like." Christ could not have sinned because he loved God. He loved God and did what he liked; but what he liked, he did, and what he liked was to love God. He could not sin against what he was, the very Love of God incarnate. The fact that Christ is one with God in Will and Purpose and Love means that he could not have sinned any more than God could have sinned. . . . To sin is to move against and away from God. But as one with the Word, as Word of God moving from God into time, Christ could not have moved against God; that is an absurdity.[29]

This gets us closer to a resolution insofar as we are not simply asserting that Christ's person keeps him from sin, but his sinless nature means that he was necessarily drawn to God, not away from him. In John 5:19, Jesus says, "Truly, truly, I say to you, the Son can do nothing of his own accord, but only what he sees the Father doing. For whatever the Father does, that the Son does likewise." This shows not only that Christ was drawn to God, but that the Father was drawn to Christ's works in such a way that to argue that Christ could sin is to argue that the Father could, in a certain sense, will the Son to sin, since Jesus can only do what the Father does. But since Jesus does nothing of his own accord, but only acts in accordance with the will of the Father, he could not have sinned. Proponents of the peccability view, in their rush to insist on how temptations must be real for Christ, rarely consider the implications of Christ's words in John 5:19.

In connection with the relation between the works of the Father and of the Son, Christological orthodoxy insists that Jesus possesses two wills, not

---

[28] W. G. T. Shedd, *Dogmatic Theology*, ed. Alan W. Gomes, 3rd ed. (Phillipsburg, NJ: P&R, 2003), 661.
[29] Thomas F. Torrance, *The Doctrine of Jesus Christ* (Eugene, OR: Wipf & Stock, 2002), 128–29.

one. Now, following from this, we may argue that if Jesus could have sinned, then a problem emerges regarding the precise relationship between his human and divine wills. The Definition of Faith of the Sixth Ecumenical Council says, "And these two natural wills are not contrary the one to the other (God forbid!) as the impious heretics assert, but his human will follows and that not as resisting and reluctant, but rather as subject to his divine and omnipotent will."[30] There is a principle of subjection, but not contrariety, between the two wills of Christ.

Now, a human may be created in holiness and righteousness, as Adam was, and so be able to resist temptation but nevertheless be able to sin. Adam was not, as history shows us, impeccable. But in the case of Jesus, he is different. As Shedd says, Jesus is different "in that he was not only able to resist temptation, but it was infallibly certain that he would resist it: the holy energy of his will was not only sufficiently strong to overcome, but was so additionally strong that it could not be overcome."[31]

Bruce Ware claims that Christ, in his theanthropic person, is impeccable, "but his impeccability is quite literally irrelevant to explaining his sinlessness."[32] After offering a few analogies, Ware adds, "Although Christ was fully God, and as fully God he could not sin, he deliberately did not appeal, as it were, to his divine nature in fighting the temptations that came to him."[33] Ware is trying to make the point that, in his struggle against true temptation, Jesus was the submissive servant who relied on the Spirit and the word to fight his battles. True enough. But here is the fatal flaw in Ware's argument: Christ's fight against sin was not as an abstract human being, but as the God-man. In other words, Jesus not only could never act apart from his identity of who he is, but he necessarily fought temptation by a constant appeal to who he is. As the eternal Son, he resisted temptation not only because of the power of the Spirit working upon his humanity, but also because of his identity shaping his actions, thoughts, and emotions. Christians, too, can successfully fight temptation not only because they possess the Spirit, but also because of their identity in Christ.

---

[30] From the Council of Constantinople (680–681). See Steven D. Cone and Robert F. Rea, *A Global Church History: The Great Tradition through Cultures, Continents, and Centuries* (London: Bloomsbury, 2019), 570.
[31] Shedd, *Dogmatic Theology*, 659.
[32] Bruce Ware, *The Man Christ Jesus: Theological Reflections on the Humanity of Christ* (Wheaton, IL: Crossway, 2012), 81.
[33] Ware, *Man Christ Jesus*, 83.

"Tempted as We Are"

What is temptation? Christ's impeccability must be maintained, but temptation must also be understood. In his work on the sinlessness of Jesus, Carl
Ullmann (1796–1865) speaks of temptation as

> every influence by which a personality intended for moral action may re-
> ceive an impulse from good towards evil, every enticement to sin produced
> by any kind of impression, and especially such a one as, proceeding from
> some other person, is purposely designed to lead to sin. That which tempts
> may lie either in the man himself, in the form of disorderly desire or inclina-
> tion; or be presented from without, in the shape of a motive to sinful action.[34]

However, while he admits that a temptation may approach a person from
without, the outward temptation must nevertheless

> enter the mind through the medium of thought or fancy or sensuous impres-
> sion, or else it is as good as not present. It must also exhibit the appearance
> of good; for mere evil, as such, does not tempt any but natures already
> Satanic. If evil is to tempt at all, it must appear as good; it must take the
> illusory form of a desirable possession, enjoyment, or other coveted result.[35]

As we shall see below, this was precisely the case in terms of Christ's temptations. They were obviously "from without," but they still presented themselves to Christ's soul as something, in the abstract, that was "good." Thus
his desire to have the cup (of wrath) removed from him was, in the abstract,
a good thing.

Admittedly, Christ's personal temptations are filled with mystery and
awe. One can certainly say too little and another can easily say too much. The
fact of his temptation cannot be disputed, since we are told explicitly that he
was tempted (Luke 4:1–2; Heb. 4:15). But the nature of Christ's temptations
have occasioned a great deal of discussion, and rightly so! Generally, the
Reformed interpretative tradition has affirmed and denied very specific ways
in which Christ was tempted. Owen claims that our temptations mostly arise

---

[34] Carl Ullmann, *The Sinlessness of Jesus: An Evidence for Christianity* (Edinburgh: T&T Clark, 1870), 127–28.
[35] Ullmann, *Sinlessness of Jesus*, 128. Ullmann speaks of two ways in which Jesus was tempted: "On the one hand,
allurements were presented which might have moved Him to actual sin; and, on the other hand, He was beset by
sufferings which might have turned Him aside from the Divine path of duty. These temptations, moreover, occurred
both on great occasions and in minute particulars, under the most varied circumstances, from the beginning to the
end of His earthly course. But in the midst of them all, His spiritual energy and His love to God remained pure
and unimpaired. Temptations of the first order culminated in the attack made on Jesus by Satan; temptations of the
second order assailed Him most severely during the struggles of Gethsemane, and when He felt Himself forsaken
by God on the cross" (*Sinlessness of Jesus*, 129–30).

from within, "from our own unbelief and lusts."[36] But Jesus was "absolutely free" from the internal temptations that arose from unbelief or lust; "for," says Owen, "as he had no inward disposition or inclination unto the least evil, being perfect in all graces and all their operations at all times, so when the prince of this world came unto him, he had no part in him."[37]

Amandus Polanus (1561–1610), in his *Syntagma theologiae christianae*, speaks of a threefold difference between our temptations and Christ's:

> (1) It is taken from a different principle from whence they [temptations] arose. Our affections arise from flesh that has been corrupted, and arise before the judgment of reason and do not always conform to reason. Now in fact these affections existed in Christ in the sensitive appetite, but because he was without sin and always conformed to right reason, thus these affections were stimulated by right reason instead of by the sensitive appetite. Take note of John 11:33 which reads, "he groaned in spirit and was troubled," but with right reason and without sin.
> (2) It is taken from the diversity of objects. Our affections tend toward illicit and evil things for the most part. But Christ's affections never tended toward the evil, but rather tended always toward the good.
> (3) It is taken from defect and repugnance. Our affections often fall short of right reason, and oppose it, and bring it down to themselves. But in Christ, just as they are stimulated by right reason, so also they are always conformed to right reason.[38]

Christ's temptations therefore are not strictly synonymous with ours, even though we can posit that we are both tempted in every way. The account of Christ's temptation in Luke 4 helps us understand the nature of his temptation and his sinlessness in light of the various trials he suffered at the hands of Satan. While Adam experienced his temptation in the garden of Eden, Jesus was tempted in the difficulty of the wilderness. Jesus, unlike Adam, is in a state of humiliation and suffering. Already he is in a more difficult state.

---

[36] Owen, *Exposition of the Epistle to the Hebrews*, 3:468.
[37] Owen, *Exposition of the Epistle to the Hebrews*, 3:468.
[38] Amandus Polanus, *Syntagma theologiae christianae ab Amando Polano a Polansdorf: Juxta leges ordinis Methodici conformatum, atque in libros decem digestum jamque demum in unum volumen compactum, novissime emendatum*, vol. 2 (Hanau, Germany: Wechel, 1609); lib. VI, cap. XV (2403–4): "1. Sumitur principio diverso un de oriuntur. Nostri affectus proveniunt a carne corrupta, & preveniunt judicium rationis & rationi non semper obtemperant: in Christo autem erant quidem in appetitu sensitivo, sed quia sine peccato erat & semper obtemperabat rectae rationi ideo a recta potius ratione quam ab appetitu sensitivo excitabantur. Huc facit quod legitur John 11.33. Infremuit spiritu & turbavit seipsum, recta nimirum ratione, & sine peccato. 2. Sumitur ab objectorum diversitate. Nostri affectus ferunt plerunq; in objecta illicita & mala: Christi autem affectus nunquam ad malum ferebantur, sed semper ad bonum. 3. Sumitur a defectu & repugnantia. Nostri affectus saepe deficiunt a recta ratione, ei repugnant eamq; ad se trahunt: at in Christo dicut a recta ratione excitabantur, ita etiam rectae rationi semper obtemperabant."

When Satan tempted Jesus, it would be a matter of whether Jesus would live by faith in obedience to the will of God or whether he would pursue glory through the (easier) means offered to him by the devil.

Satan knew the types of temptations that would be real for Christ. The temptations were not for things overtly sinful, such as a night with a prostitute. First, he tempted Jesus to command a stone to become bread in order to prove he is the Son of God (Luke 4:3). Would Jesus trust his Father's words (Luke 3:22) or would he perform a miracle at the request of the devil in order to assure himself of his identity? The force of the temptation is clear: eating is not, in and of itself, necessarily sinful, but may be done as an act of righteousness (i.e., keeping the sixth commandment). Yet, Jesus answers, quoting from Deuteronomy 8:3, "It is written, 'Man shall not live by bread alone'" (Luke 4:4). His reference to this OT passage is crucial: in the original context, the Israelites needed to trust that God would supply their needs, even apart from natural processes. Would Jesus live by God's power or by his own? Would he live by faith or by sight? For a man so naturally powerful because of his Messianic power, this was a real temptation for Christ, namely, to depend upon himself, since he could so easily depend upon his natural resources.

Second, the devil also promised Jesus authority and glory over the kingdoms of the world if Jesus would worship him (Luke 4:5–7). On the surface, this does not seem much of a temptation. But considering how difficult the path ahead was for Christ, and all that would mean in terms of his cry of dereliction, Jesus had to ask himself whether he would be God's Messiah by following the path of suffering or would he be Satan's Messiah by simply bowing down to him? The easier path is a temptation for all human beings, but Christ chose instead the difficult path (see Luke 4:8, quoting Deut. 6:13).

Third, the final temptation recorded by Luke involved the question of whether Christ would try to "prove God." The Israelites, in unbelief, doubted God and his ability to bring them into the promised land (Ex. 17:7). Satan tempted Christ to cast himself down so that God would prove himself to Christ by protecting him via angels (Luke 4:9–11). Yet Christ knew that he was not allowed to put God to the test (Luke 4:12). Christ had to trust in God's fatherly care and protection without trying to prove it in a way that was unlawful.

Would Jesus live by God's power or his own? Would Jesus choose the easy path to glory or the difficult road of suffering? Would Christ try to prove that God cared for him or would he trust that God would take care of him even when it appeared Christ was being treated harshly (starvation)? So while Jesus did not have any sinful impulses toward evil, he nevertheless felt the pull of these temptations because they carried a certain natural appeal to any person.

Jesus, as we have said, had certain infirmities (i.e., human weaknesses, appropriate to humanity) that made him subject to hunger and thirst, for example. So the temptation to eat when hungry was a "natural" temptation insofar as it was a real temptation to someone who is hungry. Jesus understood that every act must be on God's terms and so there are no "neutral" acts for God's Messiah.

Sinlessness heightens, not lessens, temptation. As Leon Morris (1914–2006) has said,

> The man who yields to a particular temptation has not felt its full power. He has given in while the temptation has yet something in reserve. Only the man who does not yield to a temptation, who, as regards that particular temptation, is sinless, knows the full extent of that temptation.[39]

As one who persevered to the end without sinning, Jesus felt the full force of various temptations much more strongly than we do. His temptations were more difficult because he did not and could not give in to them. His impeccability, far from destroying the reality of temptation, heightens the force of the temptation.

Sinlessness as Obedience

Jesus as a sinless person should not be understood as someone who simply refrained from evil, but also as someone who perfectly fulfilled the will of the Father by keeping the laws imposed upon him in his role as mediator (prophet, priest, and king). The author of Hebrews speaks of Jesus as one who "learned obedience" (Heb. 5:8). Commenting on this passage, Owen makes a distinction between Christ's general obedience, which refers to the whole pattern of his life on earth, and Christ's peculiar obedience, which refers specifically to his obedience unto death.[40] The verse in question has in view particularly the latter understanding of obedience:

---

[39] Leon Morris, *The Lord from Heaven: A Study of the New Testament Teaching on the Deity and Humanity of Jesus Christ* (Grand Rapids, MI: Eerdmans, 1958), 51–52.
[40] Owen, *Exposition of the Epistle to the Hebrews*, 4:523.

Following from that, to learn obedience has a threefold sense:

1. To learn it materially, that is, to be taught by God to obey him, which we were at some time ignorant of. This does not apply to Christ, for he knew what was required of him.
2. To learn it formally, which has in view God's instruction, help, and direction of us in our acts of obedience because we are weak and unskillful. Again, this could not be true of Christ since he always had a fullness of grace, and so constantly knew what he had to do and was perfectly willing to do what was required of him.
3. To learn obedience through experience. By undergoing such severe trials of hardship, even death on a cross, Christ learned suffering-obedience. This type of obedience required suffering so that his knowledge of suffering might be of great value to the church.[41]

Christ's life was, in a manner of speaking, a "perpetual Gethsemane," that is, a continued oblation to God and one marked by a daily cross. Owen remarks that in his sufferings Christ "had occasion to exercise those graces of humility, self-denial, meekness, patience, faith, which were habitually present in his holy nature, but were not capable of the peculiar exercise intended but by reason of his sufferings."[42] Hebrews 10:5 draws on Psalm 40:6 to address the body that was prepared for Christ by the Father. God prepared a sinless body, and fitted Christ with the requisite gifts and graces to perform the work of mediator. Owen makes two important observations: first, that we should praise the Father for the "holy properties" of Christ's human nature;[43] and, second, in connection with the first point, it was the Father who not only "prepared" the Son's body, but also "filled it with grace . . . strengthened, acted, and supported it in [Christ's] whole course of obedience."[44] Thus as we consider the sinlessness of Christ we must keep in mind not only the role of the Spirit but also the role of the Father, who prepared a body for his Son and provided him with the requisite graces to maintain not just a sinless but a positively righteous estate.

In terms of Christ's "positive" obedience, we can look at the way in which he kept the moral law, the Decalogue. He brought glory to God on earth (John 17:4), thus keeping the first commandment. He believed and

[41] Owen, *Exposition of the Epistle to the Hebrews*, 4:524.
[42] Owen, *Exposition of the Epistle to the Hebrews*, 4:525.
[43] Owen, *Exposition of the Epistle to the Hebrews*, 6:461.
[44] Owen, *Exposition of the Epistle to the Hebrews*, 6:461.

feared God (Heb. 2:13; 5:7; Luke 4:1–12). He was zealous for God's glory (John 2:17) and thanked God his Father constantly (John 11:41). He yielded complete obedience to him in all things (John 10:17; 15:10). With clean hands and a pure heart (Ps. 24:4), Jesus kept the second commandment. He worshiped God (Luke 4:16); he condemned false worship (John 4:22; Matt. 15:9). As the visible image of God, he did not need to make unlawful images of God. In his sinless moral purity, he is the true image of God. As God's image-bearer (Col. 1:15), he kept the third commandment. He revealed the Father (John 14:9), spoke the words the Father gave to him (John 12:49), and did the will of the Father (John 6:38). As such he did not take God's name in vain, but brought glory to God. Not only did he keep the fourth commandment by going to the synagogue on the Sabbath day (Luke 4:16), but he also did works of piety and mercy on the Sabbath (Mark 2:23–3:6). Following from that, the Lord of the Sabbath secured our eternal Sabbath rest through his death on the cross, resting in the grave on the Sabbath, and rising to usher in the Lord's Day whereby the people of God gather to worship.

Jesus always pleased his Father (John 8:29), thus keeping the fifth commandment. On the cross, even as he was dying, he aimed to take care of his mother (John 19:27). In terms of the wider application of the fifth commandment, the Lord kept the laws of the land (Mark 12:17; Matt. 17:24–27). By preserving life, he kept the sixth commandment. He preserved people, both spiritually and physically. He healed many (Matt. 4:23). Positively, he was meek, gentle, kind, loving, and peaceable (Matt. 11:29). By his showing mercy and compassion (Luke 18:35–43) we see the positive application of the commandment not to murder. As the bridegroom to the church, Jesus showed the consummate act of love: he laid down his life for his bride (Eph. 5:25). Besides that, Jesus gave freely (John 2:1–11) and opposed robbery (John 2:13–17). He thus kept the eighth commandment, which was really symbolic of his entire life, namely, that the one who was rich became poor so that we, in our poverty, might become rich (2 Cor. 8:9). The Truth always spoke the truth (John 8:45–47) because he spoke only the words the Father had given to him (John 12:49). He stood for the truth because he is the Truth (John 1:14, 17; 14:6). He did not flatter (Matt. 23) or speak the truth unseasonably or conceal the truth (Matt. 26:64). At bottom, the ninth commandment for Jesus was a matter, principally, of speaking the words the Father gave to him. Finally, as one who "owns" the universe, he could have supplied his every need and desire, but instead he received only that which came from his Father's hand (Luke 4:1–12). He did not covet; he did not need to covet. Rather, on God's terms, through patient endurance, he received his reward at the appropriate time according to God's will.

Whatever command Christ gave as the prophet-priest-king, he kept himself. He did not require of his followers any more than what he was prepared to do himself. His sinlessness was decisive action; it was the perpetual willingness of the Savior to submit his will to the will of God and to delight to do so.

Conclusion

G. C. Berkouwer (1903–96) rightly claimed that the church's belief in Christ's sinlessness involves "both his not-having-sinned in fact and his not-being-able-to-sin."[45] Similarly, Herman Bavinck argued that the Scripture "prompts us to recognize in Christ, not just an empirical sinlessness, but a necessary sinlessness as well."[46] Our confession that Christ is and was sinless is not a confession that he was the successful Pelagian who managed to overcome from within. Rather, even the possibility of Christ sinning is, by virtue of his identity, an ontological impossibility.

The identity of Christ as the God-man is the single greatest (and most decisive) factor in the doctrine of his sinlessness. The Holy One of God is not a title he earns so much as a title he possesses. That is the confession of the church. The Holy One became flesh, and as a man he never lost sight of his identity in relation to himself, the Father, the Spirit, and the church. Everything was at stake for us and our salvation in the person of Christ. And as grueling and difficult as his life was—utterly beyond our ability to comprehend—there was no doubt that his coming into the world would result in the salvation of his Bride. The sinless one could not fail and did not fail. He is "distinguished among ten thousand" (Song 5:10).

---

[45] G. C. Berkouwer, *The Person of Christ* (Grand Rapids, MI: Eerdmans, 1955), 263–64.

[46] Bavinck, *Reformed Dogmatics*, 3:314.

IV

SIN AND DEPRAVITY IN
PASTORAL PRACTICE

26

Losing Our Religion

THE IMPACT OF SECULARIZATION
ON THE UNDERSTANDING OF SIN

David F. Wells

The Secular Context

The emergence of a modernizing world is imposing a new kind of pressure on Christian faith. In the past, many of the most serious challenges came from alternative philosophies or religions. In the early church, it was Gnosticism. Much later in Europe, in the eighteenth century, it was the Enlightenment with its array of hostile philosophies. In the nineteenth century, the opposition to Christian belief was swelled by the arrival of Marxism. Each of these philosophies had its own way of thinking about human nature, human failure, and what, if anything, is ultimate.

Today, though, we are seeing something a little different. It is not so much a coherent philosophy that is putting pressure on Christian faith as it is a diffuse, cultural environment. This is what is now mounting the most significant challenge, certainly in the West, but also in other parts of the world that are also modernizing. In these societies, a public environment emerges that inclines those who breathe its air to make certain assumptions about the nature of reality. This cultural context is not itself a religion, but because it has the power to shape how people construe the whole meaning of life, it functions like one.

One of the most striking things about this, though, is how unaware most people are of the dangers inherent within these cultures. We see and want all of the benefits of living in modernized societies but we do not see the shadows that so often follow these benefits. We see the spectacular cities, the inventive technologies, the endless products and services, and the educational institutions. We relish all of the choices and options that we have. However, living in these contexts exposes us both to being emptied out and to having our worldview changed in deleterious ways. There is, in fact, an internal and psychological cost to be paid when we are part of these modernized contexts. Never have people had so much, but never have they had so little. This is what David Myers calls the "American paradox."[1] It is, though, a paradox seen throughout the West. Along with our extraordinary technology and virile capitalism, along with our global connections and a multitude of products and options, we have levels of anxiety that have never been higher, a drug culture that is growing more invasive, a level of incarceration that is unparalleled, and our marriages are not doing well.[2] Beneath all of the spectacular accomplishments on the surface, and despite the remarkable benefits that our modern world indeed offers us, there is an aching void.

Although we today are quite nonchalant about all of this, others have not been. They have viewed the emergence of this modernized world with some alarm. Among the most interesting were Karl Marx and Friedrich Engels. In 1848, Marx and Engels provided quite a prescient perspective on this world that was just coming into view at that time. What they saw was that capitalism was reordering the whole of life and, they thought, reducing all human relations merely to cash value.[3] It was expanding the number and size of cities and greatly diminishing rural populations.[4] And what they saw coming has, of course, only continued. It has become a defining mark of the modernized world. Today we have dense urbanization and a growing number of megacities. They argued that, because of mechanization, the modern world would be one where craft is lost, and work becomes monotonous. The worker becomes just "an appendage of the machine."[5] And the need

---

[1] David G. Myers, *The American Paradox: Spiritual Hunger in an Age of Plenty* (New Haven, CT: Yale University Press, 2000).

[2] Mary Eberstadt makes the argument that it is the decline of the family in the West that is key to the decline of Christianity and this, in turn, is a significant factor in the emergence of secularism. See her *How the West Really Lost God* (Conshohocken, PA: Templeton, 2013). In the US, according to the Census Bureau, the percentage of children born out of wedlock has increased from below 10% in the 1960s to 40.8% in 2010. This is but one symptom of the slow death of marriage.

[3] Karl Marx and Friedrich Engels, *The Communist Manifesto* (New York: Modern Reader Paperbacks, 1968), 3–5.

[4] Marx and Engels, *Communist Manifesto*, 9.

[5] Marx and Engels, *Communist Manifesto*. A century later, Reinhold Niebuhr was to make the same observation, though he was writing about the United States. See his *Reflections on the End of an Era* (New York: Scribner, 1934), 99–104.

for "a constantly expanding market," they argued, sends people "over the whole surface of the globe" in search of materials and markets. This gives "a cosmopolitan character to production and consumption in every country."[6] In short, they saw coming what we now call globalization. Today, people, materials, products, and, of course, information move around the world as if national borders were not there. And they saw with startling clarity the turbulence in life that all of this would bring, although they mistakenly thought its cause was just class warfare. Nevertheless, they did see that gone would be the old stable communities where people were known and where lives overlapped. Gone would be connections to the past. Gone would be a settled condition to life. It would all be replaced by stress and disorder. "The bourgeoisie cannot exist without constantly revolutionizing the instruments of production," and this leads to "uninterrupted disturbance" and "everlasting uncertainty and agitation."[7] And today, there is an enormous literature analyzing and often bemoaning the pace and stress of modern life. There is an equally large quantity of literature of self-help books for people trying to cope with it all.

Marx and Engels then proposed, among other things, a radically anti-modern agenda[8] that would spike this whole development. Like King Canute, they stood together on the seashore and commanded the incoming tide of modernization to stop and go back out. To bring this about they proposed banning private property, all inheritance, and capitalism in an effort to move toward a classless society.[9] They set out to keep all people equally poor for ideological reasons rather than allowing some to become well off. In the end, this turned out to be a brutal, inhumane experiment. In time it collapsed— a collapse symbolically marked by the opening of the Berlin Wall in 1989— but not before it had inflicted a lot of damage. Nevertheless, their description of a world that was modernizing was, in quite a few ways, very accurate.

---

[6] Marx and Engels, *Communist Manifesto*, 7–8.

[7] Marx and Engels, *Communist Manifesto*, 7.

[8] The same sense of unease with modernization was evident in America, too. Here, though, an answer was sought that was not political and structural as in Marxism but, rather, personal. It emerged, Jackson Lears has said, among "simple-lifers, militarists, mind-curists, mystics. Whether they focused on premodern character or on more recent models, all these disparate pilgrims sought 'authentic' alternatives to the apparent unreality of modern existence." This search was driven by a revulsion at the way all of life was organized around the production of goods and services, all subjected to the same dehumanizing search for efficiency, all kept in check by the same rational controls, and all of it leading to the "disenchantment" of the world, meaning that it was stripped of all mystery (T. J. Jackson Lears, *No Place of Grace: Antimodernism and the Transformation of American Culture* [Chicago: University of Chicago Press, 1981], 5).

[9] This experiment was also predicated on the idea that human nature is malleable, that it is always subject to change and, indeed, that it can be changed. Their proposal, therefore, was "a secular form of human salvation" (Leslie Stevenson and David L. Haberman, *Ten Theories of Human Nature* [Oxford: Oxford University Press, 2009], 163).

There is, though, an even larger question about the consequences of living in such a world that Marx and Engels never even considered because of their atheism. It is the fate of religion. What is going to happen to religion when societies begin to modernize? Can it flourish amid the dense cities that we now have where a multitude of worldviews and religions jostle together side by side and rub shoulders with each other every day? Will it become lost amid the barrage of information and images, from around the world, that daily empty into our minds through our brilliant technology? Will its character be changed by the habits of consumption that become ingrained in those who live in societies shaped by capitalism? What happens, in other words, when people consume religion as they might any other product? And will it be overshadowed by the multitude of tensions in our modern life? Today, many feel insecure, stressed out, and overworked. Can Christian faith survive in a world like this?

This question has been debated energetically by social scientists for more than four decades. Some have argued that as a society becomes more modernized it becomes irreversibly more hostile to all religions, Christianity included.[10] Modernization in this view "is the causal engine dragging the gods into retirement"[11] as Rodney Stark put it. Many of the studies done at ground level last century in Europe seemed to bear this out.[12] The more Europe modernized, the less religious it became and the more secularized.

However, it has also become clear that the destruction of belief in the West is not the only story that has been taking place. Early on, a counter literature emerged arguing, almost paradoxically, that despite the undoubted and growing secularization, much believing was also occurring.[13] In other words, the fact that societies are being secularized does not automatically mean that all private consciousness will be secularized as well. There is no

---

[10] The most vigorous defender of this view today is Steve Bruce. See his *Secularization: In Defense of an Unfashionable Theory* (Oxford: Oxford University Press, 2011); and *God Is Dead: Secularization in the West* (Oxford: Blackwell Publishing, 2002). For an overview, see Callum G. Brown, *The Death of Christian Britain: Understanding Secularization 1800–2000* (London: Routledge, 2001).

[11] Rodney Stark, "Secularization, R. I. P.," in *The Secularization Debate*, ed. William H. Swatos and Daniel V. A. Olson (New York: Rowman & Littlefield, 2000), 43.

[12] See, e.g., Grace Davie, "Europe: The Exception That Proves the Rule," in *The Desecularization of the World: Resurgent Religion and World Politics*, ed. Peter L. Berger (Grand Rapids, MI: Eerdmans, 1999), 65–83. Davie notes the extraordinary decline in church attendance and religious commitment in the 1980s and 90s but concludes that churches still retain a role of "vicarious memory." That is, Europeans delegate to churches functions that most of them in their indifference do not want to do themselves. For more recent statistics, see Marion Burkimsher, "Is Religious Attendance Bottoming Out? An Examination of Current Trends across Europe," *Journal for the Scientific Study of Religion*, 53.2 (2014): 432–45.

[13] Andrew M. Greeley, *Unsecular Man: The Persistence of Religion* (New York: Schocken, 1985); Berger, *Desecularization of the World*; Robert Royal, *The God That Did Not Fail: How Religion Built and Sustains the West* (New York: Encounter, 2006).

determinism at work here. Peter Berger, in fact, argued that the world today "is as furiously religious as it ever was, and in some places more so than ever."[14] And John Micklethwait and Adrian Wooldridge said that "religion has always thrived in the world's most modern country," which they see as the United States, and that "it is also thriving in much of the modernizing world too, from Asia to the Middle East."[15]

Ironically, today it is the secular outlook itself that is suffering from some internal doubts. While "there has been a crisis of religion in the modern world," Berger has said, "there now appears to be a crisis of secularity as well."[16] This does not mean, of course, that the currents of a this-worldly, skeptical, and nonbelieving society are any less swift or any less powerful than they were in earlier decades. Rather, it is the self-assurance of the secular outlook that is now in a little jeopardy.

Certainly since the 1960s, the idea of inevitable social progress,[17] which was at the heart of the Enlightenment outlook and of what a secular world has come to mean, is far less certain. After all, what kind of progress is it that has given us a world of such conflict, uncertainty, and striving, a place where even terrorists now dream of being able to use a nuclear device in a heavily populated city? And the Enlightenment's confidence in reason's objectivity, which became a hallmark of secular-humanism, has been widely abandoned. Postmoderns are far more likely to think that the use of reason is but a cover for private agendas and that those agendas are simply about achieving dominance. Some of the original beliefs that were central in the Enlightenment's secular mentality, then, are being shaken. Nevertheless, despite the emergence of this postmodern mood, the social machinery of secularization is still everywhere present in the West. It is still very powerful.[18]

There is a reason this debate has gone on for so long. It is that both sides have a leg on which to stand. On the one hand, it is fallacious to say that religion cannot survive in modernized contexts. It is surviving, and this despite several centuries in which Enlightened and secular attitudes have spread throughout

---

[14] Berger, *Desecularization of the World*, 2.

[15] John Micklethwait and Adrian Wooldridge, *God Is Back: How the Global Revival of Faith Is Changing the World* (New York: Penguin, 2009), 354–55.

[16] Peter L. Berger, "From the Crisis of Religion to the Crisis of Secularity," in *Religion and America: Spirituality in a Secular Age*, ed. Mary Douglas and Steven M. Tipton (Boston: Beacon, 1983), 14.

[17] For the history and outworking of this belief, see Christopher Lasch, *The True and Only Heaven: Progress and Its Critics* (New York: W. W. Norton, 1990).

[18] I have explored this transition from the modern to the postmodern world in a little more detail in my *Above All Earthly Pow'rs: Christ in a Postmodern World* (Grand Rapids, MI: Eerdmans, 2005), 60–90.

the West. On the other hand, it is also the case that these Western contexts do ooze the "acids of modernity," to use Walter Lippman's phrase. These acids corrode religious belief and practice, though they corrode some religions more than others. They are especially destructive of historic Christian faith.

The most important question we need to think about, then, is the one Charles Taylor recently asked.[19] Five hundred years ago in Europe it was almost impossible not to believe in God's existence, the supernatural, absolute moral norms, and the existence of religious authority. Today, by contrast, it is hard for Westerners to believe any of these things. Such belief is an uphill struggle in our modernized, affluent cultures. It goes counter to all that is taken for granted and therefore assumed to be normal. Why is this? What has happened? The answer, of course, is that secularization—the inevitable concomitant to modernization—has taken root.

Modernizing societies create public environments. These are what give people their taken-for-granted assumptions about reality. And in our time it is assumed that the whole meaning of life should be construed without reference to God. This is the "normal" way of thinking. Our public square, as a result, becomes "naked." It has been stripped of any active divine presence or religious truth, as Richard John Neuhaus argued.[20] This absence potentially exerts a powerful shaping force on the way that even Christian faith is articulated. The reason is that the price of survival in a secularized context is that faith must disguise the fact that it is religious. If it refuses, it must face the consequences.

Under this pressure, Christian faith becomes prone, as Bruce notes, to being "increasingly privatized and divorced from the public world." It does so as an act of self-preservation, however unconsciously. Its preoccupation,

---

[19] Charles Taylor, *A Secular Age* (Cambridge, MA: Harvard University Press, 2007), 1–13. Taylor discusses two other ways of thinking about secularization, but it is what he says about "the immanent frame" that is my focus here (*Secular Age*, 539–93).

[20] Richard John Neuhaus, *The Naked Public Square: Religion and Democracy in America* (Grand Rapids, MI: Eerdmans, 1984). Some years after the publication of this book, Stephen D. Smith suggested that it was mainly concerned with the question as to how it was that America had "come to its current embrace of secularism? The Constitution does not dictate any such position; . . . And contrary to the predictions of the countless eager prophets of secularization, the American people persist in being as devout as they have ever been" (Stephen D. Smith, "On the Square," *First Things* 192 [April 2009]: 84). What Neuhaus discussed has, of course, spawned a whole series of conflicts along several lines that divide Christian faith from a secular world. On politics, e.g., see Kent Greenawalt, *Religious Convictions and Political Choice* (Oxford: Oxford University Press, 1988); and Christopher Eberle, *Religious Conviction in Liberal Politics* (Cambridge: Cambridge University Press, 2002). On the matter of sexuality, Gabriele Kuby has argued that cultural elites in Europe and the United States, with help from their governments, are enforcing the new ideologies of sexual and gender freedom. These are profoundly and aggressively secular. They are doing so over Christian resistance (see Kuby, *The Global Sexual Revolution: Destruction of Freedom in the Name of Freedom*, trans. James Patrick Kirchner [Kettering, OH: Angelico, 2015]).

therefore, shifts "from the next life to this life."[21] But more than that, it shifts from the outside world, which is unfriendly to it, to an inside world. And this is followed by another change. It is that, whereas once the great depths in life were sought in the cosmos, and in God himself, now they are increasingly sought in ourselves. Consequently, as Taylor puts it, there is now "a rich vocabulary of interiority, an inner realm of thought and feeling to be explored."[22] What is unseen becomes unreal but what is experienced within, privately and personally, is the touchstone of reality. Exploring this inner realm is what life is all about, for it is from here that there arises the only mystery we can access and the only set of morals we can find. Taylor calls this a "self-sufficient immanent order."[23]

In the absence of a supernatural framework to life, as Walker Percy saw, the self instead becomes "sovereign." All reality contracts into this miniature world within. The self has no other universe of meaning than its own internal world. In this universe, it rules. The self is therefore "free to pursue its own destiny without God."[24] In fact, it is oblivious to the God who is objective to it and morally other. That is, the self shields itself off from the One who stands outside of it and who is the standard by which all good is judged as good and all evil is exposed as evil. It finds "God," instead, in its own inner depths, but those depths are indistinguishable from the depths of its own self. And this, of course, is what leads to the functional atheism so evident in all of our secularized, Western societies.

There is, of course, much more that can be said about the shift in perspective that our experience in the modern world facilitates. But the changes I have tried to describe are sufficient for us to see what kind of framework has now emerged. It is within this framework that we so often understand Christian faith, including its doctrine of sin. This framework does not force itself on us irresistibly. It can be resisted. But it is a powerful, coercive, and corrosive force. Its effects are seen in three main ways when it comes to the matter of sin, and these are what I now wish to explore.

First, sin is no longer defined in relation to *God* but, rather, it is thought of only in terms of the self. Second, because of this change, we have come to

---

21 Bruce, *God Is Dead*, 182. This shift is also, of course, taking the first steps down a road that, if followed, eventually leads to a full-blown secular outlook, which is life only in the "here and now." Phil Zuckerman, a self-defined secularist, has said that "to be secular ultimately means living in the here and now—with exuberance, relish, passion, and tenacity—because this is the only existence we'll ever have" (Phil Zuckerman, *Living the Secular Life: New Answers to Old Questions* [New York: Penguin, 2014], 7).
22 Taylor, *Secular Age*, 539.
23 Taylor, *Secular Age*, 543.
24 Walker Percy, *Lost in the Cosmos: The Last Self-Help Book* (New York: Farrar, Straus, & Giroux, 1983), 13.

understand ourselves more in terms of the self than of human nature. Third, the effect of these two changes is that guilt, in a biblical sense, disappears and is replaced by shame in a psychological sense.[25]

The Doctrine of Sin

I. GOD

In our Western secularized cultures, the understanding of sin has both contracted and lost its reference point. It has contracted in the sense that many of the failures and moral breaches previous generations recognized as sins are now seen as simply crimes. No one any longer calls them sins even though many are, in fact, violations of one or more of the Ten Commandments. And the same kind of process has happened at a psychological level. Many of the things that used to be sins are now only diseases.[26] And sometimes these are not even clinically recognized diseases but simply maladies of the psyche. But all of this has happened because we are understanding all human behavior along a flat, horizontal level. We are not thinking of it vertically in relation to God. Sin, in consequence, "disappears." After all, actions that are the fruit only of psychological illness, or unstable homes, or even poor self-esteem, no longer are viewed as having moral weight.

What language, then, are we to use when atrocities happen, or dark corruption is exposed? We do, of course, use our most serious word. We say that what has taken place is *evil*. Were we to call these moral breaches "sin" instead, it would seem as if we were trivializing them. The reason, of course, is that the word *sin* has been emptied of any serious moral meaning today. Because it has been stripped of its religious significance, sin is never more than just a small breach, the breaking of some inconsequential rule.

The reality, of course, is quite the opposite. Sin is a much deeper, more serious word than evil, at least as evil is understood today. Today, evil is simply badness, the assault on human well-being, but it is badness that has no moral framework to interpret it and give it weight. How could it, in secularized societies where there are no ultimate rights and wrongs and where God has disappeared from view? In Christian faith, though, the word *sin* puts that badness, that assault on human well-being, back into a theological

---

[25] I initially explored these themes in my *Losing Our Virtue: Why the Church Must Recover Its Moral Vision* (Grand Rapids, MI: Eerdmans, 1998), 81–178.

[26] Karl Menninger made this argument in his *Whatever Became of Sin?* (New York: Hawthorn, 1973), 50–93.

framework. Now it is badness, not only in relation to the other person who is damaged, but also in relation to *God*. More than that, it is badness in relation to God as judge and sovereign Lord. This is what gives to sin its depth of meaning and its gravity. "Only when we are confronted with God in his holiness," Michael Horton correctly says, "do we really understand something of the weight of sin (Isa. 6:1–7)."[27]

In the NT, the nature of sin emerges through the different language used to describe it as well as the different contexts in which it is discussed. Sin is missing a target, abandoning a path, breaking the moral law, going against truth, and defying what is right. It is doing what is wrong, and this can be done in a multitude of ways. The important thing to see here, though, is that the target missed, the law defied, the path abandoned, and the truth rejected, are in each case *God's*. All sin is born in the primary action of the sinner's fist being raised against God in rebellion. Sin, then, attempts to usurp the place of God and puts the sinner in God's place. It writes its own script for life. Self-interest therefore takes the place of God's truth and of his moral norms. And sin sees, quite correctly, that submission to God is the mortal enemy of its own, self-seized freedom. In Western cultures, there is no higher value than that of self-autonomy.

At the fall, an element alien to God's creation intruded into it. This alien element brought with it death. In place of the original uprightness in the human soul, there is now an array of dark, self-focused, lawless, and sometimes destructive passions. The inner world of human consciousness after the fall is, therefore, completely transformed. But because God has disappeared from our secular cultures today, there is no way for people to understand themselves or their own (sinful) self-experience. Where do the mists of uneasiness, of emptiness, come from that hang over their consciousness? What are they to make of their apprehension, their sense of disorder within, their fear, anxiety, and sometimes despair? There is now no coherence to this inner life. What once gave it coherence was the inner righteousness, the orientation to God that was there at creation. All of this has been lost. It is all gone. That is why we experience in ourselves such confusion. There are no explanations for this from within ourselves. There is, as Berkouwer said, only a "senselessness"[28] to sin.

---

[27] Michael S. Horton, *The Christian Faith: A Systematic Theology for Pilgrims on the Way* (Grand Rapids, MI: Zondervan, 2011), 428.

[28] G. C. Berkouwer, *Studies in Dogmatics: Sin*, trans. Philip C. Holtrop (Grand Rapids, MI: Eerdmans, 1971), 140.

What secularization does is eliminate the vertical dimension to our understanding and transform everything into what is just horizontal and private.[29] Where the language of God is still retained, its meaning is now sought in the sinner's consciousness.[30] And this interior world is what frames the meaning of sin. "Sin" now is just inward dysfunction. It is about being emotionally closed, being repressed, not being self-actualized or self-differentiated, and being crippled by various maladies such as poor self-esteem. From another angle it is, as Philip Cushman puts it, about being "lonely, undervalued, 'unreal,' fragmented, diffuse, obsessed with gaining personal recognition, and lacking in guidance."[31] And salvation, of course, is then understood therapeutically as being all of the ways in which this inward dysfunction and pain are healed.

What makes our cultural context so powerful, of course, is that it is also reinforcing the essential impulses of sin that are within. What I have described as having taken place in our modernized societies is, in fact, exactly parallel to what Paul says has taken place in sinful human nature as a whole. It is that people have turned from "the truth about God" and they have believed "the lie."[32] They serve the creature rather than God (Rom. 1:25). It was freedom that was seized. And the seeds of freedom are still seen lying in the soil of this self-world. But, from a Christian angle, this supposed freedom has resulted in nothing but servitude. More than that, it is a servitude shrouded in darkness. If any of us, Ted Peters says, "initiates evil, we also discover evil; we find it already there. Evil exists within us, outside of us, and before us."[33]

Sin and today's Western culture, therefore, have now coalesced in saying that there are no ultimate rights and wrongs. There are just private preferences which have no ultimate moral weight. In these ways, our secularized, postmodern culture dissolves the meaning of sin and makes righteousness, including righteous thinking, look strange and even offensive.

---

[29] Lears, *No Place of Grace*, 41.

[30] There are, of course, many other changes that follow. This shift inward is one that invariably makes of the sinner a consumer even in church. God becomes the product, the preacher the salesperson, and the churchgoer the consumer whose power of choice is sovereign. The nature of the local church therefore changes, as does its function, because it is now defined by its role in this cycle of consumption. See Stefan Paas, *Church Planting in the Secular West: Learning from the European Experience* (Grand Rapids, MI: Eerdmans, 2016), 192–97.

[31] Philip Cushman, *Constructing the Self, Constructing America: A Cultural History of Psychotherapy* (Reading, MA: Addison-Wesley, 1995), 67.

[32] It is "*the* lie," since Paul uses a definite article here. This appears to be an allusion to the first sin, in which Satan interposed himself between God and Adam and Eve and then lured Adam and Eve away from obedience (Gen. 3:1–13). An avalanche then fell between the Creator and his human creation, and it is in this environment that Satan works to undo all of the good that God does.

[33] Ted Peters, *Sin: Radical Evil in Soul and Society* (Grand Rapids, MI: Eerdmans, 1994), 25.

II. Self

The turn inward that I have been describing, the loss of the vertical and the relocation of reality only along the horizontal line has made another change necessary. It is that human nature has been replaced by the self in our understanding. I have already mentioned this in terms of how we think about sin. But we need to pursue this thought a little further.

It is no easy task to explain exactly what is entailed in this transition from nature to self, from thinking that there is a common, internal shape to all human beings, to thinking of each as being a stand-alone and unique person. The difficulty, of course, is that there have been multiple understandings as to what human nature is. And for a long time, even those who still used this language rarely did so with the belief that all human nature is in the image of God. Furthermore, quite diverse understandings of the self have emerged as well. Explaining how, in our understanding, we have moved from nature to self is thus quite complicated. However, this complexity should not be allowed to obscure the simple fact that in modernized societies we are now much inclined to think about ourselves only in terms of our own unique interior rather than, as was once the case, in terms of a nature which is shared with, and common to, all human beings.

The idea that there is such a thing as human nature has, in fact, been falling apart, bit by bit, over a long time. At first it was under philosophical attack. But now it is under siege from a different direction. The secularization of modern cultures strongly militates against the Christian understanding of human nature in the *imago Dei*. The reason, quite simply, is that this is a religious idea, and in secularized culture, religious ideas have no grounding. There is nothing out there to authorize them.

Nevertheless, let us begin with what has been lost. It is the understanding of what it means to be in the image of God. But what does this mean?

For a truth that is so important to Christian understanding, it is perhaps surprising that Scripture leaves it a bit unexplained in Genesis, where it first appears.[34] There are, in fact, only three OT passages that speak of being in the image or likeness of God (Gen. 1:26–28; 5:1–3; 9:6). The first two have generated a lot of suggestions.[35] The third, though, is rather more specific.

---

[34] For a succinct review of biblical teaching and historical reflection on the *imago Dei*, see Anthony A. Hoekema, *Created in God's Image* (Grand Rapids, MI: Eerdmans, 1986), 11–65. See also Henri Blocher, *In the Beginning* (Downers Grove, IL: InterVarsity Press, 1984), 79–94.

[35] See the exhaustive discussion in J. Richard Middleton, *The Liberating Image: The Imago Dei in Genesis 1* (Grand Rapids, MI: Brazos, 2005).

A murderer, it affirms, is liable to the forfeiture of his or her own life since the person killed is one whom God "made in his own image" (Gen. 9:6). Much the same kind of thought also appears in the NT. James chides those who use abusive language because the people verbally abused "are made in the likeness of God" (James 3:9). Clearly, these two statements—one about murder and the other about verbal abuse—ground the ethical standards that are in play on the fact that all people are made in the image of God.

Scripture, of course, makes a somewhat varied use of this language. In order to develop an understanding that can include the different ways in which the *imago Dei* is viewed, we need to make some distinctions. A useful place to start is by distinguishing, as Augustus Strong did a long time ago, between the "natural image" and the "moral image."[36] The former speaks of the natural capacities that are there by creation. They include reason, will, creative ability, aesthetic sense, conscience, and the emotions.[37] The latter, the moral image, speaks of the inner righteousness, the holiness, which was original to both Adam and Eve in the beginning. It was this righteousness that gave direction to all of the inner faculties such that life was God-centered and lived entirely on his terms and for his glory.[38]

It is, of course, the moral likeness to God that was lost at the fall. The "image of God was not utterly effaced and destroyed," Calvin says, but what remained is a "fearful deformity." Deliverance from our inward corruption begins only with "that renovation we obtain from Christ."[39] This restoration slowly enables the natural image to function as God intended. It is in Christ that God's original creational intent for us is restored. In him, we see all that we were intended to be but never were, subsequent to, and because of, the fall.

This, however, is not the only usage of the image-of-God language. What we also need to see is that Christ himself is "the image of God" (2 Cor. 4:4). He is "the image of the invisible God" (Col. 1:15), and the "exact imprint of his nature" (Heb. 1:3). Being redeemed, therefore, means being "conformed to the image of his Son" (Rom. 8:29) and so having the moral image restored

---

[36] Augustus Strong, *Systematic Theology: A Compendium* (Old Tappan, NJ: Fleming H. Revell, 1907), 515–23.

[37] Indeed, it is the existence of this capacity that enables even unbelievers, those with no knowledge of God's revelation in Scripture, to be able to receive his revelation of himself in nature. "[God's] invisible attributes, namely his eternal power and divine nature," Paul says, "have been clearly perceived, ever since the creation of the world, in the things that have been made." Unbelievers, therefore, "are without excuse" (Rom. 1:20).

[38] Similarly, Emil Brunner distinguishes between the "structure" of the image of God and its "content." See his *The Christian Doctrine of Creation and Redemption*, trans. Olive Wyon, 3 vols. (London: Lutterworth, 1952), 2:77–78.

[39] John Calvin, *Institutes of the Christian Religion*, trans. Henry Beveridge, 3 vols. (London: James Clarke, 1953), 1:164.

by him. Indeed, Paul says explicitly that redemption's "new self" is "created after the likeness of God in true righteousness and holiness" (Eph. 4:24; see also Col. 3:9–10; Eph. 1:4). This new nature, of course, lives side by side with the old nature. Christian believers, then, are hybrid creatures, partly tied by their old nature into a world that is passing away, and partly anchored by the new nature in a world that will never pass away.

Using the language of "human nature" to think about what humans have in common, then, is best understood when we are looking at it through the lens of the *imago Dei*. This human nature is not just a more developed, more complex form of reason, will, and emotions than is seen in animals.[40] Rather, human beings are by creation related to God as echo is to sound, and this happens through their divinely given nature. It is this that distinguishes humans from animals. And when redeemed, it is this that enables people to be God's footprint in the world, his representatives in whom the Holy Spirit has applied Christ's redemption.[41]

It is in this sense that I am using the word *nature* here. It is nature that even in its fallenness still retains a natural likeness to God, though no longer a moral likeness. How else can we understand both Genesis 9:6 and James 3:9?[42] The fact that all people are in the image of God, not just those in a saving relation with God through Christ, is what gives to all people their intrinsic worth as human beings. This is why murder is forbidden. It is also why so many of the social reform movements that have emerged in the past have predicated their action—be it in the exercise of compassion for those in need or in the pursuit of justice for those to whom it has been denied—on the

---

[40] Richard Lints makes this distinction by arguing that this image must be conceived "from above," where it reflects the reality of the triune God rather than "from below," where it is thought of only by way of comparison to animals (Richard Lints, "Imaging and Idolatry: The Sociality of Personhood in the Canon," in *Personal Identity in Theological Perspective*, ed. Richard Lints, Michael S. Horton, and Mark R. Talbot [Grand Rapids, MI: Eerdmans, 2006], 205–6). However, Lints then goes on to argue that Gen. 1:26 means that "humankind does not have the image of God, nor is it made in the image of God, but is itself the image of God" (Richard Lints, *Identity and Idolatry: The Image of God and Its Inversion* [Downers Grove, IL: InterVarsity Press, 2015], 60). The *imago Dei*, he contends, has to do with personhood, and that in relation to the Trinity. Indeed, he specifically contrasts the idea of "human identity" or "personal identity" with that of "human nature." The *imago* speaks not of any internal structure to the human being but only of a relationship to God. The difficulty with this is that Gen. 1:26 indicates that, from the very instant of creation, the *imago Dei* was present. There was no interlude after creation during which time self-understanding emerged to produce self-identity and the understanding of meaning. Furthermore, in Scripture, only Christ himself is said to *be* the image of God. We are always said to be *in* God's image or likeness.

[41] Jeffrey J. Niehaus, *Ancient Near Eastern Themes in Biblical Theology* (Grand Rapids, MI: Kregel, 2008), 99, 113–14.

[42] G. C. Berkouwer, for example, tries to restrict the image of God only to believers when they are acting in God's service and reflecting his character. He is opposed to thinking that all people are in the image of God because, he says, that violates the prohibition against idol making. That prohibition, though, was one that was issued to human beings. We are not to make idols for the purpose of engaging in false worship, of turning away from God. God, though, can make people in his own image without being guilty of idolatry. See G. C. Berkouwer, *Man: The Image of God*, trans. Dirk W. Jellema (Grand Rapids, MI: Eerdmans, 1962), 54–57, 81–82.

belief of the worth of each person regardless of how poor, powerless, or insignificant he or she might be. Each is in the image of God.

All of this, though, is now lost in modern understanding. In place of nature, we have the self. That is, in each person is a unique, inner core. This is found at the confluence of gender, ethnicity, cultural understanding, education, and life experiences. All of these contribute to what is a person's inner core. And this psychological core is different in each person. It is from this center that there emerge each person's unique perceptions. Every era, Cushman has written, "has a predominant configuration of the self, a particular foundational set of beliefs about what it means to be human."[43] This is ours. It all rests on a self-sufficient individualism together with the belief that inner feelings are the essence of being human.

An important social consequence of this is not only that it heightens the importance of diversity but, in fact, it leaves us with the situation in which diversity is all that there is. There is no human nature that is at the core of all human experience. Rather, we are just our skin color, ethnicity, and sexual orientation. These are what say who we are, and therefore it is these things that drive our public debates and divisions.

Understanding the modern self is not, of course, quite as simple as this brief description suggests. Especially in our postmodern context, the self is no longer seen as a single, static thing. Rather, it moves "through a multiplicity of changing profiles."[44] It changes itself, or it is changed, as it moves through different social settings. While in an earlier time this "inconsistency" would have been seen as a serious flaw, it is now celebrated as a reflection of our diversity. Indeed, it has even been argued that there are different kinds of self in the same person at the same time.[45] And sometimes, as Carl Goldberg notes, people experience internal suffering because they feel "the self is crumbling away without a new, valued self emerging to replace it."[46] The self, then, is a multifaceted, mobile, and even malleable thing. In that sense it is quite different from human nature in the *imago Dei*. And this is the important point.

The fact that the self is always in motion does, though, raise an important question. If the self does indeed change, or if there are multiple selves, or if

---

[43] Cushman, *Constructing the Self*, 3.
[44] Calvin O. Schrag, *The Self after Postmodernity* (New Haven, CT: Yale University Press, 1997), 17.
[45] Raymond Martin and John Barresi, *The Rise and Fall of Soul and Self* (New York: Columbia University Press, 2006), 198–200. For a history of how the self has been conceived across time, see Teodros Kiros, *Self-Construction and the Formation of Human Values: Truth, Language, and Desire* (Westport, CT: Praeger, 1998).
[46] Carl Goldberg, *Understanding Shame* (Northvale, NJ: Jason Aronson, 1991), 51.

the self can disintegrate, is the person whose self it is the same person across time? Is there a clothesline over which all of the garments of experience hang, an identity that is preserved through all of our experiences as we move through life? We seem to assume that there is. We remember ourselves in our past; we are aware of ourselves as engaging in the present; and we project ourselves into the future. But we do not assume that we have become different people in these different phases of our lives. We grow up and grow old, but we still identify ourselves with the whole of our past. We use the word "I" across all the phases of our lives, from our first days to our last. And yet, in what does that single identity, this "I," consist, if the self is always mutating? That is a vexed and unsolved philosophical problem today.

It is at least clear, though, that, in passing from the thought of human nature to that of the self, we have passed from the moral world that we once inhabited into one that is now only psychological. As the vertical aspect in our understanding breaks down under the weight of secularism, all that remains is the horizontal.

These two worlds, of course, foster entirely different understandings of life. A moral world is one in which there are enduring rights and wrongs. These moral norms are our virtues, and when these virtues become habituated, they produce character. In a moral world there is always moral accountability, and this accountability is sharpened when it is understood within a Christian framework. The point is that we are not simply accountable but we are accountable before *God*, who is utterly holy, ablaze in pure light.

In a psychological world, things are quite different. Moral norms disappear and are replaced simply by preferences. What were once virtues now become "values." They are not enduring moral requirements but simply the inward rules by which we have chosen to live. These values, therefore, are really value-free. And accountability is often no higher than simply to ourselves. The importance of character now is replaced by the importance of personality. It now becomes less important to be "good" than it is to be liked or, better still, to be envied.

Once, when we lived in the moral world, the repair of human life came through redemption. Now, in our psychological world, repair is self-originated, and it comes in the form of healing. Once we stood before God. Now, we only stand before each other. Once we lived in a house that had skylights. Now our house has none. All that it has are windows from which we look out onto our world. Some evangelicals have begun to cast their message more in terms of the psychological world than that which is moral. There is no question that secularized societies are now understanding all of life within a framework that is private, internal, and psychological. And, more and more, it is this world that is present in the minds of many who go to church.[47]

What has happened, of course, is that the tensions that are always present in biblical faith, one way or another, between Christ and culture, Christian belief and the world, have dissipated. When this happens, sin becomes merely ignorance or dysfunction, grace cannot be distinguished from self-effort, and God is reduced into being simply our best self. This was the path walked by classical Protestant liberalism in an earlier time. It is what Richard Niebuhr, following Karl Barth, called "Culture-Protestantism."[48] Evangelicalism of the kind I have been describing has started down this road. In the next generation, if the development is not arrested, it will end up as a full-blown liberalism.

III. SHAME

If it is the case that the idea of human nature has been replaced by that of the self, then it follows, as night follows day, that the idea of guilt will be replaced by that of shame. Here I am thinking of guilt as what results when our thoughts and actions are lined up vertically and measured against God's character and law. In that moment, we know ourselves to have fallen short, wandered off the path, disobeyed God, and rebelled against him. The emotion that follows this knowledge is often complex: we are disappointed with ourselves, frustrated, dismayed, depressed, and embarrassed.

What is interesting here is that the same emotions also make up shame. And this is why in our language we often use guilt and shame as synonyms. We might say something like, "I felt so guilty and so ashamed when . . ." However, I am here distinguishing between them in the sense that, whereas our actions are lined up vertically in guilt, they are lined up *only* horizontally in shame.[49] We are guilty before God, but today in our secularized societies we are ashamed *only* before others.

---

[47] This is the kind of analysis developed by Todd M. Brenneman in his *Homespun Gospel: The Triumph of Sentimentality in Contemporary Evangelicalism* (New York: Oxford University Press, 2014). He uses the ministries of three pastor-writers as a prism in which to see the broader evangelical impulses. The pastors are Joel Osteen, Rick Warren, and Max Lucado.

[48] H. Richard Niebuhr, *Christ and Culture* (New York: Harper & Brothers, 1951), 84.

[49] Psychologists have struggled hard to differentiate guilt and shame too, but typically not in the way I am suggesting here. They think of guilt as shame over a moral action, but they don't think of the moral action as having violated God's command. See Gershen Kaufman, *The Psychology of Shame: Theory and Treatment of Shame-Based Syndromes* (New York: Springer, 1989), 26–27.

Shame is a powerful emotion that enters into the heart of our self-understanding. It arises when, for some reason, we are seen by someone to be other than what we want to be, or thought we were, or presented ourselves as being. In that moment, a disconnect happens. That disconnect brings a sense of shame. There are many ways in which this might come about, and some have no moral connections at all. Someone, for example, might be ashamed of their parents who are uneducated. Some are ashamed of where they grew up because the neighborhood was very poor. In that case, who this person wants to be is suddenly called into question by where they have come from. They feel ashamed.

At other times, though, shame does have a moral connection. A person who sees him or herself as being honest—or who wants others to think that they are honest—will be deeply ashamed if it becomes known that all the while this image was being presented to others, this person was, say, systematically looting a business or defrauding customers. The point here is that shame arises from what *others* come to know about us.

In a Christian understanding, a person will feel guilty before God for acts of moral failure. Where these acts have social consequences, this person will also feel ashamed before others. But in this psychological world in which we now live, people feel no guilt before God but only shame before others. And what they might be ashamed about varies from person to person.

The secularization of our understanding, then, has profoundly changed the way we understand ourselves. It has also profoundly changed how we think about the meaning of life. The easiest way to sum all of this up is to say that today, side by side in our Western cultures, can be seen two entirely different and contradictory understandings of justification.

In the one, the biblical understanding, we who are in God's image and who are sinners are made right before *God*. In the other, we who are only selves and often depleted are made right within *ourselves*. In the one, we are guilty for moral offenses. In the other, we are ashamed for psychological reasons. In the one, our moral failures are lined up vertically in relation to God's character and law. In the other, they are lined up only against others and what they will think of us. In the one, we are incapable of giving ourselves right standing before God. That is the work of God's grace alone. In the other, there are many psychological resources and self-help techniques that are offered to bring about right standing before our self and others. In

820 SIN AND DEPRAVITY IN PASTORAL PRACTICE

the one, our sin is imputed to Christ and his righteousness is imputed to us. In the other, we try to abandon our painful, negative memories and then to discover more positive, uplifting feelings. In the one, we look for redemption. In the other, we seek healing. One is Christian and the other is modern, therapeutic understanding.

It seems rather clear, then, that Christian faith now finds itself in a rather new situation. Today, it is not simply this or that doctrine that is being contested in our modern world. Rather, it is the *whole* Christian worldview within which those doctrines belong. Our modernized cultures are producing ways of perceiving reality that are far removed from what God has revealed that reality to be, and far removed from what historic Christian faith has understood reality to be. This is true of the typical modern ideas about God, truth, right and wrong, sin and guilt, and redemption. The gospel, for this reason, is often incomprehensible to modern people. The Western church is now truly in a missionary, not only an evangelistic, context.

27

An Apology for *Elenctics*

THE UNMASKING OF SIN IN THE RETRIEVAL
OF A THEOLOGICAL DISCIPLINE

Daniel Strange

The very concept of *"elenctics"* is out of accord with the diffident, tolerant mood of today. But no Christian who accepts the biblical view of the evil of idolatry on the one hand and the finality of Jesus Christ on the other can escape it. Further, only those who see the need for *elenctics* can also see the need for dialogue and can understand its proper place.[1]

In all *elenctics*, the concern is always with the all-important question: "What have you done with God?"[2]

Introduction

Elenctics, which derives from the Greek ἐλέγχω ("convict" or "unmask"), can be defined in the words of its greatest twentieth-century advocate, J. H. Bavinck, as "the science which is concerned with the conviction of sin . . . it is the science which unmasks to heathendom, all false religions as sin against God, and it calls heathendom to a knowledge of the only true God."[3] *Elenctics* has a missiological drive because it is not primarily concerned with an "on the back foot" defense of the faith, but rather goes on the offensive, attacking unbelief: "*Elenctics* calls the non-Christian religions to a position of responsibility, and attempts to convince their adherents of sin and

---

[1] John Stott, *Christian Mission in the Modern World* (Downers Grove, IL: InterVarsity Press, 1975), 107.
[2] J. H. Bavinck, *An Introduction to the Science of Missions* (Grand Rapids, MI: Baker, 1960), 223.
[3] Bavinck, *Introduction to the Science of Missions*, 222. The concept is older than Bavinck and reaches back into Reformed history, being used by figures such as Gisbertus Voetius, Francis Turretin, and later, Abraham Kuyper.

to move them to repentance and conversion."[4] In rather more prosaic terms, Paul Visser summarizes Bavinck's understanding of *elenctics* as

> a two-pronged activity: scholarly reflection on the religions, and theological reflection on the apologetic approach to the religious person. These two elements of *elenctics* can be distinguished but never detached from each other: they serve one another, are the two sides of the same coin.[5]

In this chapter, I wish to make a case, or better, a passionate plea, for the rehabilitation of the "lost" theological discipline known as "*elenctics*." Its inclusion in this volume is apposite given the focus on hamartiological aspects of theological anthropology. I say *elenctics* has been "lost," but one might well argue that trying to revive it is a lost cause. The influential evangelical missiologist David Hesselgrave has noted that *elenctics* is a "neglected subject in contemporary theology,"[6] and, as noted above, John Stott highlighted the discipline and its neglect in his *Christian Mission in the Modern World*. However, that "modern" world of Stott and Hesselgrave was the 1970s. In the forty-plus years since, *elenctics* has remained buried, with no popular or mainstream revival forthcoming.[7] And one can see why. *Elenctics* would be a nightmare for any communication department dealing with positioning, branding, and public relations. First, the name is not catchy and does not roll off the tongue. Second, although its disciplinary home has been within missiology (*elenctics* being sometimes referred to as "missionary apologetics"), its relationship to and reliance on dogmatics, religious studies, and apologetics proper has not always been clearly defined. Third, and most importantly, is the subject matter of *elenctics*. To reiterate, if Stott refers to the 1970s as "diffident" and "tolerant," consider how the combative mood of *elenctics* scans in the 2020s, not simply to culture in general, but within missiology in particular, even within sectors of *evangelical* missiology. And the audacity to call it a "science"? Surely *elenctics* must be described as an antiquated subject in a church history course and not prescribed as a contemporary theological, let alone a "scientific," discipline.

---

[4] Bavinck, *Introduction to the Science of Missions*, 232.
[5] Paul J. Visser, *Heart for the Gospel, Heart for the World: The Life and Thought of a Reformed Pioneer Missiologist Johan Herman Bavinck (1895–1964)* (Eugene, OR: Wipf & Stock, 2003), 257.
[6] David Hesselgrave, *Communicating Christ Cross-Culturally: An Introduction to Missionary Communication* (Grand Rapids, MI: Zondervan, 1978), 419.
[7] I say mainstream, because there have been some who have endeavoured to keep the elenctic flame alive, most importantly, Harvie Conn at Westminster Theological Seminary, Philadelphia. I should also mention Cornelius J. Haak, "The Missional Approach: Reconsidering *Elenctics*. Part 1," *CTJ* 44.1 (2009): 37–48; and "The Missional Approach: Reconsidering *Elenctics*. Part 2," *CTJ* 44.2 (2009): 288–304; Carl J. Bosma, "Jonah 1:9—An Example of Elenctic Testimony," *CTJ* 48.1 (2013): 65–90. It is disappointing, however, that Christopher J. H. Wright's 2015 updated and expanded edition of *Christian Mission in the Modern World* has taken out Stott's section on elenctics.

However, I wish to argue that, whatever one calls it, and however it is categorized, *elenctics* has a vital place within the theological encyclopedia. Moreover, even discussing *elenctics* has a catalyzing effect, as it will be shown to be at the nexus of a number of knotty and seemingly intractable relationships between the squabbling siblings that are the "scientific" study of religion/religious studies, the theology of religions, and missiology. In what follows I will argue that there can be harmony, complementarity, and interdependence between these disciplines, with *elenctics* providing a necessary missiological momentum and *telos*, which can and must focus both academy and church on the claims and call of Jesus Christ. As Bavinck argues, "missions is not simply a by-product of ecclesiastical life and theology. Missions belongs to the very essence of the church and therefore always pushes itself to the fore in all theological reflection."[8]

In order to build the case for *elenctics*, it is necessary first to establish a strong *theological* foundation on which *elenctics* follows as its natural and necessary missiological corollary. This will be done in two parts: first, by making some comments on the need for theological religious studies; second, by outlining a "subversive fulfillment" theology of religions on which *elenctics* rests. Having laid these foundations, I will then describe the *elenctic* task, stressing areas which need particular emphasis if the discipline is to be accepted in the twenty-first century.

As a final introductory comment, I must declare my continued reliance on and inspiration from the work of J. H. Bavinck, nephew to Herman Bavinck, whose own exposition of *elenctics* in his magnum opus, *An Introduction to the Science of Missions*, remains its seminal treatment. While I will continue to draw from Bavinck's own exposition of *elenctics* in this work, I recognize that sixty years have passed since its publication. Therefore, what is needed is not simple regurgitation but rather a retrieval, bolstering, and recontextualization.

I. Releasing Religious Studies

In a number of his writings, the conservative Catholic theologian Gavin D'Costa describes quite brilliantly a genealogy that charts the Oedipal nature of religious studies in parallel with theology's "Babylonian captivity" in the modern university.[9] Much of the realm of religious studies has presupposed an

---

[8] Bavinck, *Introduction to the Science of Missions*, 233.
[9] Gavin D'Costa, *Theology in the Public Square: Church, Academy, and Nation* (Oxford: Blackwell, 2005).

alleged "neutral" and "objective" scientific positivism which does not comport well with the confessional theological task. Ninian Smart has declared theology as the "conceptual albatross around the neck of religious studies."[10] Anecdotally, in my own undergraduate work in "theology *and* religious studies" (the conjunction "and" here hinting at an awkward estrangement) I witnessed this unequal yoking. As a young evangelical student, learning about the phenomenological method and being asked to practice *epoché* (that process within phenomenology of blocking biases and suspending judgment in order to explain a phenomenon accurately) always sat uneasily with me. The work of D'Costa, MacIntyre, and others within the post-liberal tradition have debunked some of this, but it is still prevalent in religious studies.[11] Unashamedly, D'Costa argues that, contra modernity's construal of the academic study of "religion," the fullest understanding and interpreting of the religions are seen "in the light of the triune God who is the fullness of truth. Only from this theological narrative can other religions be truly understood, simply because Christianity is true."[12] Likewise John Milbank has stated more generally that,

> The pathos of modern theology is its false humility. For theology, this must be a fatal disease, because once theology surrenders its claim to be a meta-discourse, it cannot any longer articulate the word of the creator God, but is bound to turn into the oracular voice of some finite idol, such as historical scholarship, humanist psychology, or transcendental philosophy. If theology no longer seeks to position, qualify or criticize other discourses, then it is inevitable that these discourses will position theology: for the necessity of an ultimate organizing logic . . . cannot be wished away.[13]

I would add to Milbank's list of "finite idols" the study of religion.

As a cobelligerent in fighting against the forces of the modernistic scientific study of religions, post-liberal/postmodern theologies have been helpful. However, such post-liberal/postmodern theologies cannot truly be allies because often they have an epistemological foundation or rather, non-foundation,

---

[10] Ninian Smart, "Religious Studies in the United Kingdom," *Religion* 18 (1998): 8.

[11] The evangelical religious studies scholar Terry Muck writes, "I remember having a conversation a number of years ago with such a scholar of religion about this very topic. At one point in our conversation he said, 'What really scares me about evangelical Christians is that they bring a theology to the study of religion.' My response was this: 'What really scares me are scholars who study religion and think that they don't bring a "theology" to their study of religion'" (Muck, "The Study of Religion," in *Handbook of Religion: A Christian Engagement with Traditions, Teachings, and Practices*, ed. Terry C. Muck, Harold A. Netland, and Gerald R. McDermott [Grand Rapids, MI: Baker Academic, 2014], 16).

[12] Gavin D'Costa, *Christianity and World Religions: Disputed Questions in the Theology of Religions* (Chichester, West Sussex, UK: Wiley-Blackwell, 2009), 91.

[13] John Milbank, *Theology and Social Theory: Beyond Secular Reason*, 2nd ed. (New York: Wiley, 2006), 331.

which makes difficult any universal claims of the human religious condition that might lead to legitimate comparisons between Christian faith and the "Other." Rather, for these theologians, "religion" and "religions" (terms which some of these thinkers reject as a Western social construct) are incommensurable. While this is argued as being the only way to truly respect the Other—in other words, not forcing them into a controlling, Western narrative—it means that "religions" cannot easily be judged as false, opposed to, or anti-Christian. From an evangelical point of view, this is problematic, since evangelicals do want to make universal claims and do not want to end up with only a fideistic apologetic. As a result, evangelicals are stuck between the incommensurability of religions—which undermines evangelism and the universalism of the gospel call—and the religious bigotry of the Western metanarrative.

Therefore, what is needed is an evangelical "*theological* religious studies" or "*theological* comparative religions." A few key evangelicals in the field are starting to address this, but there is much work to be done, particularly when it appears that there is a social science hegemony in evangelical missiology.[14] There needs to be a detailed intra-evangelical debate concerning the relationship between the theology of religions, theological religious studies, and the implications for an evangelical ethnography and phenomenology which is not "neutral," but which is still concerned with careful listening to how others understand themselves from the inside, before outside interpretation can proceed. In other words, how can one reach a partisan objectivity?[15]

As will be seen, the *elenctic* task and its effectiveness will depend upon the breadth and depth of such *theological* religious studies in all its sub-divisions: history of religions (which itself will need a resurrection from the dead); psychology, anthropology, philosophy, phenomenology, and ethnography. The crucial point is that, rather than being an albatross in leading these disciplines, it is theology that *liberates* them and allows them to flourish and fly.

II. Rebuilding on a "Subversive Fulfillment" Base[16]

Although the Christian church has always reflected upon and engaged "religious" alterity, and although it is now firmly established in the theological

---

[14] One volume that attempts a more theological religious studies approach is Muck, Netland, and McDermott, *Handbook of Religion.*

[15] See Terry Muck, "The Christian Study of World Religion," in *Handbook of Religion*, 4.

[16] Parts of this section are a summary of Daniel Strange, *For Their Rock Is Not as Our Rock: An Evangelical Theology of Religions* (Nottingham, UK: Apollos, 2014; Zondervan 2015, published as *Their Rock Is Not Like Our Rock:*

firmament, the birth of a distinct discipline known as the "theology of religions" is still within living memory. While I have already indicated how one's theology of religions might impact religious studies, what about the relationship between the theology of religions and missiology? The Reformed missiologist Johannes Verkuyl writes,

> Theology of religions and missiology, both being branches of theology, also complement each other. If a theologian of religions lacks missionary motivation and perspective, he has actually traded in the real foundation of his discipline for something which provides no basis at all. On the other hand, if a missiologist both in his method and his conclusions fails to take theology of religions into account, he will be blind to what is actually transpiring among human beings and religions and thus talk only in thin air and grope about in a fog.[17]

If *elenctics* resides within the discipline of missiology, then it is founded on one's theology of religions. A weakness in J. H. Bavinck's treatment of *elenctics* in his *Introduction to the Science of Missions* is that his theology of religions is assumed rather than articulated.[18] Even in other writings which are firmly within the area of the theology of religions, Bavinck's impressionistic (albeit rich and evocative) writing style means he does not give a detailed dogmatic articulation of his theology of religions.

Drawing on Bavinck and others within the Reformed tradition, I attempted such a detailed dogmatic construction in my 2015 monograph *Their Rock Is Not as Our Rock: A Theology of Religions*. The distillation of my theology of religions can be articulated thus:

> From the presupposition of an epistemologically authoritative biblical revelation, non-Christian religions are sovereignly directed, variegated and dynamic, collective human idolatrous responses to divine revelation, behind which stand deceiving demonic forces. Being antithetically against yet parasitically dependent upon the truth of the Christian worldview, non-Christian religions are "subversively fulfilled" in the gospel of Jesus Christ.[19]

A Theology of Religions); Strange, "For Their Rock Is Not as Our Rock: The Gospel as the 'Subversive Fulfillment' of the Religious Other," *JETS* 56 (2013): 2; Strange, "An Unholy Mess," *Primer* 7 (2019): 6–19.

[17] Johannes Verkuyl, *Contemporary Missiology* (Grand Rapids, MI: Eerdmans, 1978), 362.

[18] This is echoed by Visser in *Heart for the Gospel*, 280.

[19] Strange, *Their Rock Is Not Like Our Rock*, 42. The actual term "*subversive fulfillment*" is not original to me but is used by Hendrik Kraemer, albeit only once, in an essay he wrote in 1939: "This apprehension of the essential 'otherness' of the world of divine realities revealed in Jesus Christ from the atmosphere of religion as we know it in the history of the race, cannot be grasped merely by way of investigation and reasoning. Only an attentive study of the Bible can open the eyes to the fact that Christ, 'the power of God' and 'the wisdom of God' stands in contradiction to the power and wisdom of man. Perhaps in some respects it is proper to speak of contradictive or *subversive*

It is worth re-rehearsing the key elements of this theology of religions, given its importance in justifying the *elenctic* approach.

A "subversive fulfillment" theology of religions contends that the conceptual category of *idolatry* is the most accurate "container" in explaining the anthropological complexity of human religiosity, allowing for both radical discontinuity and formal/structural continuity between Christian faith and the religious Other. Hence Jesus Christ both "subverts" and "fulfills" them simultaneously. Not only is idolatry the prevalent "biblical" category in which to interpret the religious Other, but historically, with the notion of religious "diversity," "subversive fulfillment" has decidedly negative connotations:

> In the context of pre-modern discussions on religion, and the diversity of religions, the notion of idolatry is omnipresent. We must remember that "Religion", in the singular, essentially refers to Christianity, as the worship of the true God who revealed himself to mankind through the Gospel. In the fourth century, Lactantius famously argued that the word *religio* derived from *religare*, "to bind," explaining: "It is by the bound of piety that we are bound [*religati*] and attached to God. From this religion derives its name." Christian authors defined religion as the intimate knowledge of God embodied in the Christian faith, the *sole vera religio*. Everything else could be described as "idolatry," or "superstition," the inappropriate worship of pretence divinities.[20]

The apostle Paul's attitude, approach, and appeal in his encounter with the Athenians recorded in Acts 17 is a microcosm of a "subversive fulfillment" approach. The discursive framing of the pericope begins with the apostle's paroxysm over a city submerged in idolatry, and ends with a call to repentance in light of coming judgment, for which Jesus's resurrection is the proof. Within these bookends is Paul's description of the Athenians being "very religious" (δεισιδαιμονέστερος):[21]

> It is not beyond possibility that Paul cleverly chose this term precisely for the sake of its ambiguity. His readers would wonder whether the good or bad sense was being stressed by Paul, and Paul would be striking a double blow: men cannot eradicate a religious impulse within themselves (as the Athenians demonstrate), and yet this good impulse has been degraded by

---

fulfilment" (Kraemer, "Continuity or Discontinuity," in *The Authority of Faith: International Missionary Council Meeting at Tambaram, Madras*, ed. G. Paton [London: Oxford University Press, 1939], 5).

[20] Daniel Barbu, "Idolatry and Religious Diversity: Thinking about the Other in Early Modern Europe," *Revue Genevoise D'anthropologie et D'histoire des Religions* 9 (2014): 39–50 (42).

[21] A hapax legomenon.

rebellion against the living and true God (as the Athenians also demonstrate). Although men do not acknowledge it, they are aware of their relation and accountability to the living and true God who created them. But
rather than come to terms with him and his wrath against their sin (cf. Rom.
1:18), they pervert the truth. And in this they become ignorant and foolish
(Rom. 1:21–22).[22]

Deisidaimonesterous neatly encapsulates the anthropological ambiguity
and complexity of religious alterity. We might summarize it as human beings
both "knowing" and not knowing God, and simultaneously running to God
and running away from God. From Genesis 3:15 onward, God's sovereign
judicial curse is to put enmity between the "seed of the woman" and the "seed
of the serpent": two streams of humanity diametrically opposed to each other.
Reformed theologians call this the doctrine of the "antithesis" (lit., "to set
against"). This antithesis is captured in a wealth of stark biblical contrasts
seen genealogically and typologically in the OT (immediately in terms of
Adam to Seth/Cain to Lamech), and described in the NT as the stark difference between death and life, darkness and light, blindness and sight, being
in Adam and in Christ, goats and sheep, covenant breakers and covenant
keepers. Jesus declared that "no one can serve two masters" (Matt. 6:24), and
so "Whoever is not with me is against me" (Matt. 12:30). Colossians 2:6–8
describes these two forms of existence when it speaks of those "rooted and
built up in [Christ]" and those captive to "hollow and deceptive philosophy,
which depends on human tradition and the elemental spiritual forces, *and not
according to Christ.*" This is the "radical difference"[23] between the Christian
faith and the religious Other.

The antithesis is comprehensive, and extends to all areas of human life:
head, heart, and hands. There is nothing that remains untouched or untainted.
A "religious" antithesis generates an epistemological and intellectual antithesis: "because the mind of the flesh is enmity against God; for it is not subject
to the law of God, neither indeed can it be" (Rom. 8:7, ASV), and "once you
were alienated from God and were enemies in your minds because of your
evil behavior" (Col. 1:21 NIV).

While *deisidaimonesterous* connotes radical difference and discontinuity,
it also connotes a commensurability of formal similarity, which (and contra

[22] Greg L. Bahnsen, *Always Ready: Directions for Defending the Faith* (Nacogdoches, TX: Covenant Media: 1996), 254.
[23] Hendrik Kraemer, *The Christian Message in a Non-Christian World* (London: Edinburgh House Press, 1938), 300.

post-liberal/postmodern theology of religions) recognizes shared territory as a precondition of judgment, evaluation, and comparison. Consequently, this legitimates the Other being called "false" and its worshipers being called to repentance. In this sense religion, either true or false, is a genus. How, theologically, does one account for this continuity?

In terms of general theological anthropology, we might say that, just as those rooted and built up in Christ still struggle with the sinful nature (producing "fruit" that looks like it belongs to a different tree), so, analogously, those "not according to Christ" (those unregenerate, "in Adam" and captive to the suppressive compulsion) are kept from fully realizing their rebellion and hatred of him. Cornelius Van Til states this well:

> The natural [unregenerate] man, "sins against" his own essentially Satanic principle. As the Christian has the incubus of his "old man" weighing him down and therefore keeping him from realizing the "life of Christ" within him, so the natural man has the incubus of the sense of Deity weighing him down and keeping him from realizing the life of Satan within him. The actual situation is therefore always a mix of truth with error. Being "without God in the world" the natural man yet knows God, and, in spite of himself, to some extent recognizes God. By virtue of their creation in God's image, by virtue of the ineradicable sense of deity within them and by virtue of God's restraining general grace, those who hate God, yet in a restricted sense know God, and do good.[24]

It is the perpetuity of the *imago Dei* and the *sensus divinitatis*, together with God's common grace, that must be held in tension with the doctrine of the antithesis: "the Prodigal cannot altogether stifle his Master's voice."[25]

Again, the concept of idolatry gives us the heuristic tool to contain and explain this anthropological mix. Idols and idolatry are not created *ex nihilo* but are the work of human hands, constructed out of the physical and mental created world. They are counterfeits and are parasitic on the truth. In this sense we can define idolatrous religion as *a response to divine revelation*.

III. Recognizing the Magnetic Points

"Very religious" captures the response to divine revelation well, but it is somewhat vague in terms of detail. Are we able to give any more analytical

---

[24] Cornelius Van Til, *An Introduction to Systematic Theology* (Phillipsburg, NJ: P&R, 2007), 27.

[25] Cornelius Van Til, *The Defense of the Faith* (Phillipsburg, NJ: P&R, 1967), 190. Quoted in Greg L. Bahnsen, *Van Til's Apologetic: Readings and Analysis*, 459. Original in Van Til.

and phenomenological definition to Paul's term "very religious"? And if this were possible, then would we be able to say more precisely how Jesus is the "subversive fulfillment" of the idolatrous Other?

In what might be called a religious morphology or a Reformed view of comparative religions, J. H. Bavinck posits a universal "religious consciousness" that can be described in a series of "magnetic points":

> It appears that humanity always and everywhere has fallen back on definite ideas and presumptions, and that these ideas and presumptions always resurface in surprising ways whenever they may have been temporarily repressed for various reasons. . . . This is a universal religious consciousness that remains indestructible in the midst of all disturbing and confusing developments.[26]

> There seems to be a kind of framework within which human religions need to operate. There appear to be definite points of contact around which all kinds of ideas crystallize. There seem to be quite vague feelings—one might better call them direction signals that have been actively brooding everywhere. . . . Perhaps this can be expressed thus: there seem to be definite magnetic points that time and again irresistibly compel human religious thought. Human beings cannot escape their power but must provide an answer to those basic questions posed to them.[27]

The first "magnetic point" Bavinck calls "*I and the Cosmos.*" Human beings have an innate sense of totality, "the feeling of communion with the cosmic whole."[28] We know we do not stand alone as islands in the universe; we sense that we somehow belong. With this, though, comes a tension, since, in the face of the cosmos, we simultaneously experience that we are insignificant nothings but also that we are "so powerful as to experience all things converging and uniting within oneself."[29]

In the second point, "*I and the Norm,*" we discern, however vaguely, that there are rules to be obeyed that do not originate with ourselves. With this comes a sense of responsibility to live up to those norms: "life is a dialogue between law and reality, between natural self-fulfilment and the moral

---

[26] J. H. Bavinck, "Religious Consciousness and Christian Faith," in *The J. H. Bavinck Reader*, ed. John Bolt, James D. Bratt, and Paul J. Visser (Grand Rapids, MI: Eerdmans, 2013), 150–51.
[27] Bavinck, "Religious Consciousness," 226–27. Bavinck describes these magnetic points in two places using different orderings: "Religious Consciousness," 151–98; and J. H. Bavinck, *The Church between Temple and Mosque* (Grand Rapids, MI: Eerdmans, 1966), 37–106. The same points are also described in a less schematic way in Bavinck's *Introduction to the Science of Missions*, 247–72.
[28] Bavinck, "Religious Consciousness," 160.
[29] Bavinck, "Religious Consciousness," 162.

demand for self-restraint. People chafe against the law and they want to be enveloped by it, carried by it."[30]

The third magnetic point Bavinck calls "*I and Salvation*," and it is concerned with deliverance. We know there is something not right with the world. There is finitude, brokenness, and wrongdoing in the world, and the problem of suffering and death consistently confronts us. We mourn for a "paradise lost" and yearn for deliverance from these evils, craving redemption: "man has that remarkable tendency not to accept reality as it presents itself to him, but he always dreams of the better world in which life will be healthy and safe."[31]

The fourth point Bavinck calls "*I and the Riddle of my existence*." Humans are active doers and passive victims; they lead but they also undergo their lives. As a result, an existential tension is created between human freedom and boundedness.

The fifth and final point may be called "*I and the Higher Power*." People everywhere perceive that behind all realities stands a greater reality. This greater reality is variously conceived but is always a superior power. There is also a sense that humans stand in some sort of relationship to this higher power, or at least they should. This understanding creates the expressed desire to seek connection with this power, but what is it? Who is it?

These five magnetic points are all connected and demonstrate a particular interrelationship, in that "totality" and "destiny" focus on human insignificance and boundedness, while "norm" and "deliverance" focus on human significance and freedom:

> at the intersection of these two lines of thoughts . . . lies the awareness of being related to a higher power. The higher power is at the same time the deepest meaning of the whole, the bearer of cosmic laws, the energiser of the norm, the helper toward salvation. That intersection of these two lines is obviously the heart of religious consciousness.[32]

As we come to discuss *elenctics*, I will demonstrate that there is great potential for further exploration and analysis of these points, albeit with one observation: It may be for presentational and even apologetic reasons that

---

[30] Bavinck, "Religious Consciousness," 293–94. I should note that it is this magnetic point which forms the basis for Nathan D. Shannon's chapter in this present volume, "I and the Norm: Comparative Religions and Alternative Philosophies of Sin."
[31] Bavinck, *Church between Temple and Mosque*, 33.
[32] Bavinck, "Religious Consciousness," 203.

Bavinck's book *Religious Consciousness* begins with a phenomenological description of these points as evidenced in the Vedas, the Qur'an, mystic practices, and personal-anecdote religious traditions. In these sections, there is no theological justification or biblical exegesis. From a strictly methodological perspective, such an ordering is unfortunate, as it leaves Bavinck open to the charge that the magnetic points are inductive, suggesting a natural theology. However, as one reads to the end of the work, Bavinck's biblical exegesis, theological anthropology, and commitment to *sola Scriptura* becomes clearer as he tethers the idolatrous religious consciousness in a thick and psychoanalytically tinged exegesis of Romans 1:18–32, and in particular, the "invisible qualities" of God's "eternal power" and "divine nature" (Rom. 1:20), which, for Bavinck, pertain to our *dependence* on God and our *accountability* to him.[33] The magnetic points, therefore, are nothing more than particular (or religion-specific) expressions of the themes of dependence and accountability. Therefore, and ironically, the religious consciousness evidenced in the magnetic points are anything but "natural," being abnormal or "made-up," both in the sense of being fantastical or, even better, caked-on and disfiguring "makeup" that masks and obscures the natural face. Bavinck himself uses the evocative illustration of dreaming to describe this process in the non-Christian:

> that revelation impinges on them and compels them to listen, but it is [at] the same time pushed down and repressed. And the only aspects of it that remain connected to human consciousness, even while torn from their original context, become seeds of an entirely different sequence of ideas around which they crystallize.[34]

In terms of nomenclature for the dogmatic theology of religions emerging from the above analysis, Hendrik Kraemer's term "subversive fulfillment"

---

[33] Bavinck, "Religious Consciousness," 243.

[34] Bavinck, "Religious Consciousness," 290. In Strange, *Their Rock Is Not Like Our Rock*, I delineate several revelatory categories out of which idolatry is fashioned. Historically and phenomenologically, it is hard to disentangle these categories (hence the need for the scientific study of religion in terms of the history of religions and phenomenology), but they can be distinguished. "*Imaginal* revelation" is the category I refer to in this chapter in terms of the magnetic points. However, one can also talk about "*remnantal* and *influental* revelation," both of which could be classed as idolatrous responses to, or better, memories of, *special* revelation. *Remnantal* revelation recognizes knowledge of primeval events such as fall and flood, which, though entropically distorted over time, give us a comparative theological explanation of "commonalities" and "continuities" between religious traditions, for example, certain events, themes, and archetypes. *Influental* "revelation" refers to the impact or "influent" of the Judeo-Christian worldview on living religious traditions, both historically and presently. It is the variegated admixture of these revelatory categories (imaginal, remnantal, and influental) together with variegated "levels" of suppression and divine judicial "giving over" across cultures and across history that accounts for idolatrous and counterfeiting religious diversity. For more detail, see Strange, *Their Rock Is Not Like Our Rock*, ch. 2, and 254–58.

accurately describes the relationship between Christian faith and the religious Other. The gospel of Christ confronts and subverts idolatrous religious consciousness and its historical manifestations, but it is also its fulfillment. As we will see shortly, the magnetic points which we have just described are subversively fulfilled in Jesus Christ.

What is required is a missiological approach that complements a "subversive fulfillment" theology of religions. It is to this we now turn.[35]

IV. Retrieving *Elenctics* for the Twenty-First Century

In the first half of this chapter, I have argued for a *theological* religious studies and then have summarized a "subversive fulfillment" theology of religions. Both of these strands are brought together as we come to their missiological conclusion: *elenctics*. But what is *elenctics*, and how does one do it?

In his *Christian Mission in the Modern World*, Stott briefly mentions *elenctics* in his chapter on dialogue:

> Although there is an important place for dialogue . . . there is also a need for "encounter" with [those of other faiths], and even for "confrontation," in which we seek to both disclose the inadequacies and falsities of non-Christian religion and to demonstrate the adequacy and truth, absoluteness and finality of the Lord Jesus Christ.[36]

Stott then proceeds to refer us back to J. H. Bavinck's treatment, highlighting some of the main points of his thesis. I too wish to refer back to Bavinck but in a way that will promote and recontextualize *elenctics* and its study to a new generation of Christian believers. This will mean accentuating some features, making explicit what in Bavinck is, at best, suggestive and opaque, and, at worst, missing.

---

[35] J. H. Bavinck and Hendrik Kraemer are not the only ones to speak in these terms. As J. H. Bavinck's more famous uncle Herman Bavinck writes, "All the elements and forms that are essential to religion . . . though corrupted, nevertheless do occur in pagan religions. Here and there even unconscious predictions and striking expectations of a better and purer religion are voiced. Hence Christianity is not only positioned antithetically toward paganism; it is also paganism's fulfillment. Christianity is the true religion, therefore also the highest and purest; it is the truth of all religions. What in paganism is the caricature, the living original is here. What is appearance there is essence here. What is sought there can be found here. Christianity is the explanation of 'ethnicism.' Christ is the Promised One to Israel and the desire of all the Gentiles. Israel and the church are elect for the benefit of humankind. In Abraham's seed, all the nations of the earth will be blessed" (Herman Bavinck, *Reformed Dogmatics*, ed. John Bolt, trans. John Vriend, 4 vols. [Grand Rapids, MI: Baker Academic, 2004], 1:319–20). Similarly, Cornelius Van Til, writing a few decades after Kraemer, notes, "In false theophanies, prophecies and miracles, we have an indication of man's deepest needs. Christianity stands, to be sure in antithetical relation to the religions of the world, but it also offers itself as the fulfilment of that of which the nations have unwittingly had some faint desire" (Van Til, *Introduction to Systematic Theology*, 2nd ed. [Phillipsburg, NJ: P&R, 2007], 204–5).

[36] Stott, *Christian Mission in the Modern World*, 105.

We will achieve this by unpacking a statement from Bavinck at the beginning of three chapters on *elenctics* in his *Introduction to the Science of Missions*. Having listed the occurrences of the verb *elengchein* (ἐλέγχειν) in the NT,[37] Bavinck writes,

> From these texts it is clear that the word in the New Testament is regularly translated as rebuking, but then in the sense that it includes the conviction of sin and a call to repentance. When we speak of *elenctics* we do well to understand it in the sense that it has in John 16:8. The Holy Spirit will convince the world of sin. The Holy Spirit is actually the only conceivable subject of the verb, for the conviction of sin exceeds all human ability. Only the Holy Spirit can do this, even though he can and will use us as instruments in his hand. Taken in this sense, *elenctics* is the science which is concerned with the conviction of sin. In a special sense then it is the science which unmasks all false religion as sin against God and calls people to the knowledge of the one, true God. To be able to do this well and truthfully it is necessary to have a responsible knowledge of false religions, but one must be able to lay bare the deepest motifs which are therein expressed. This can actually occur only if one recognizes and unmasks these same undercurrents within himself. *Elenctics* is possible only on the basis of a veritable self-knowledge, which is kindled in our hearts by the Holy Spirit.[38]

First, *elenctics* is *pneumacentric*, in that, in the deepest sense the Holy Spirit is "subject" and "author" of *elenctics*. In what no doubt comes from a Reformed monergistic confessional stance, Bavinck stresses the sovereign agency of the Holy Spirit in the work of the conviction of sin: "he alone can call to repentance and we are only means in his hand."[39] While we must work hard within the *elenctic* science, our role is instrumental, being totally reliant on the Spirit's role in awakening an awareness of guilt and shame: "this

---

[37] Jude 14–15; Rev. 3:19; John 16:8; 1 Tim. 5:20; Matt. 18:15. Strangely, Bavinck does not mention Titus 1:9.

[38] Bavinck, *Introduction to the Science of Missions*, 222. Although not directly relevant to this chapter, I need to note that I am aware of the important debate as to whether the primary reference of "unmasking" and "convicting" of *elenctics* is that of "guilt" or "shame." Bavinck himself believes the Homeric meaning of *elenghos* was that of shame but that in the NT the focus had moved to that of guilt (*Introduction to the Science of Missions*, 221). Subsequent advocates of *elenctics*, including David Hesselgrave and Cornelius Haak, follow Bavinck on this. However, this has recently been questioned by Chris Flanders, who contends that shame is focused in terms of semantic range, believing Bavinck et al. have wrongly interpolated a Western guilt framework (see Flanders, "Conviction and Elenctics: Bringing Shame upon an Honored Missiological Paradigm," *International Journal of Frontier Mission* 37 (2020): 121–31. Flanders notes the peculiarity of Bavinck referencing Büchsel's "ἐλέγχω" dictionary entry in the *Theological Dictionary of the New Testament*, even though Büchsel does not mention guilt but does mention shame. Flanders also notes that both Liddell-Scott and *The New International Dictionary of New Testament Theology* do not mention guilt or guiltiness in their treatments of ἐλέγχω. See also Robert J. Priest, "Missionary *Elenctics*: Conscience and Culture," *Missiology: An International Review* 22.3 (1994). Here, I simply make two observations. First, in Gen. 3 guilt and shame appear in tandem, as mutually implicatory. Second, in many contexts/cultures these notions do not appear, on a practical level at least, to be separable.

[39] Bavinck, *Introduction to the Science of Missions*, 229.

knowledge gives us the comfort that in the last instance the results do not depend on our weak powers, but that it is the Holy Spirit who would make us powerful in Christ."[40]

Second, I note the necessity of *"a responsible knowledge of false religions, but one must be able to lay bare the deepest motifs which are therein expressed."*[41] *Elenctics* requires both *professional* expertise and *personal* relationship. Concerning the former, although Bavinck does not refer to the *insider-outsider* debate or distinctions between *emic* and *etic*,[42] he notes the need for what we would call religious studies, or, as I have argued, a *theological* religious study:

> To be able to approach effectively, to be able to convince of sin, a certain knowledge of the phenomenon of non-Christian religions is indispensable . . . *elenctics* must first of all begin with the precise and calm knowledge of the nature of the religion with which it is concerned. It must do this honestly and calmly; that is to say, it must not be too quick to interrupt, it must listen to this religion state its case. . . . In the very nature of the case *elenctics* makes thankful use of the data provided by the science of religion and by the history of religion. These two subjects constitute the building blocks with which it works.[43]

However, such scientific awareness must be complemented by a "living" approach:

> *Elenctics* as the science of *elengchein*, the conviction of sin, can actually be exercised only in living contact with the adherents of other religions. Each generalization, every systematization, carries within itself the danger that one will do injustice to the living person. In practice I am never concerned with Buddhism, but with a living person and *his* Buddhism, I am never in contact with Islam but with a Moslem and *his* Mohammedanism. . . . *Elenctics* as a science, in other words, can never make superfluous the sensitive probing of the hidden depths of a person, a probing of his inner existence.[44]

This balancing of rigorous scientific study and relational encounter should be the aspirational goal of theological religious studies. Certainly,

---

[40] Bavinck, *Introduction to the Science of Missions*, 229. For more on the role of the Holy Spirit in *elenctics*, see Brian A. DeVries, "The Evangelistic Trialogue: Gospel Communication with the Holy Spirit," *CTJ* 44.1 (2009): 49–73.
[41] Bavinck, *Introduction to the Science of Missions*, 222.
[42] In anthropology and ethnography, the *emic* refers to the perspective of the studied culture, and the *etic* the perspective of the observer.
[43] Bavinck, *Introduction to the Science of Missions*, 241.
[44] Bavinck, *Introduction to the Science of Missions*, 241.

considering the way some teach other religions in schools and at an undergraduate and postgraduate level in colleges and seminaries, they would do
well to take this construal on board. As Terry Muck has written recently,

> Religion must be increasingly seen as a dynamic quality of the human
> experience: people and cultures change the way they embrace and express
> their religions. To use a mathematical analogy, this means the introductory
> course in the religion will need to become more of a calculus capable of
> observing constantly changing dynamics than either an arithmetic (just the
> facts, please) or an algebra (religion as symbol systems).[45]

Third, *elenctics* is properly *presuppositional*, and vice versa. If we acknowledge the Spirit's agency, we must still speak of the human *elenctic* task
in the unmasking of false religion. Although *elenctics* has been described as
"missionary apologetics," in Bavinck's treatment the relationship between
elenctics and apologetics is a little strained because Bavinck appears to associate apologetics with a rationalistic starting point and an overreliance on
philosophical persuasion, which does not deal with deeper moral and religious motivations and "the magnetic power of sin": "We can never employ
philosophical argumentation to build a bridge from a non-Christian religion
to the Christian faith, a bridge which would make an inner change unnecessary, and would make superfluous a call to repentance."[46] It seems that, for
Bavinck, rational argument has a place but by itself fails to penetrate the
idolatrous heart. With a Pauline zeal and "provocation" (cf. Acts 17:16), there
is a viscerality in Bavinck's description of idolatry: "Idolatry is despicable,
a terrible rebellion against the only true God; it is satanic pride, self-idolatry,
self-deification, an attempt to pull God down to the world, and to make God
a servant of one's self."[47]

While some apologetic methods may have an overly rationalistic emphasis, this is not true of *all* apologetic methodologies. At the heart of a presuppositional apologetic methodology is a "transcendental thrust": "Properly
understood, presuppositional apologetics is transcendental in its thrust. That
is to say, it seeks to do justice to the intellectual and spiritual conditions
whereby anything has meaning."[48] In his presuppositional primer, *Every*

[45] Muck, "Christian Study of World Religion," 9.
[46] Bavinck, *Introduction to the Science of Missions*, 229.
[47] Bavinck, *Introduction to the Science of Missions*, 226.
[48] William Edgar, "Without Apology: Why I Am a Presuppositionalist," *WTJ* 58.1 (1996): 18.

Thought Captive, Richard Pratt helpfully speaks of the "two-step" strategy of presuppositionalism based on Proverbs 26:4–5:

> Answer not a fool according to his folly,
>   lest you be like him yourself.
> Answer a fool according to his folly,
>   lest he be wise in his own eyes.

Verse 4 encapsulates the "argument from truth."[49] Like one standing on the rock of God's word (cf. Matt. 7:24–25), the Christian must not reason with the assumptions of the non-Christian or else they will become like the fool who does right in his own eyes. Apologetically, this will not help anyone. Rather, the Christian is one who in his heart reveres Christ as Lord (1 Pet. 3:15). We argue *for* Christianity *from* Christianity.

Verse 5, meanwhile, encapsulates the "argument from folly."[50] For the sake of argument, we must rehearse what it is like to stand on the sinking sand of our own autonomous commitments, judgments, and the authorities we put in place of the living God (cf. Matt. 7:26–27). We want fools to see the error of being wise in their own eyes. We must show them the outcome of what happens when their commitments are fully realized. In all of this we are appealing to what unbelievers know but have suppressed in their rebellion.

While we are not to have a rationalistic apologetic, in Acts the apostles are seen to refute, argue, and prove, "drawing things together" (Acts 9:22). Paul at the Areopagus demonstrates this par excellence when he appeals to the suppressed truth of the pagan poets, clearly setting side by side the transcendently unique Creator Yahweh and the nature of his creation, in contrast to the worldview of the Athenians.[51] Acts seems to be full of transcendental thrust and two-step strategy, not as a substitute for preaching Christ, but as a support.

Where presuppositional apologetics and *elenctics* converge can be summed up by William Edgar who has, in his long career, championed both J. H. Bavinck and Cornelius Van Til:

> Presuppositional apologetics, I believe, recognizes the religious core of our natures better than other systems do, because it understands that we are

---

[49] Richard L. Pratt Jr., *Every Thought Captive: A Study Manual for the Defense of Christian Truth* (Phillipsburg, NJ: P&R, 1980), 86.
[50] Pratt, *Every Thought Captive*, 92.
[51] For more on this, see Flavien Pardigon, *Paul against the Idols: A Contextual Reading of the Areopagus Speech* (Eugene, OR: Pickwick, 2019).

united, and that our dispositional complex, however individual and diverse, is always directed towards a goal, be it the true hope of the gospel or the deceptive promise of the idol.[52]

Bavinck would, I hope, think it legitimate here to substitute "presuppositional apologetics" for *"elenctics."* We might usefully think of presuppositions as commitments, ultimate commitments, which are not simply *a priori* ideas. Yes, we have presuppositions (beliefs) but also predispositions (patterns of life) and predilections (feelings). This is important, because it means that the dissonance of antithesis and image-bearer is not only cognitive. The *sensus divinitatis* (Rom. 1:18–20) is *the suppressed awareness of a broken relationship.* This is at the heart of *elenctics*: "In all *elenctics*, the concern is always with the all-important question: 'What have you done with God?' "[53]

Biblically speaking, the cracked cisterns of idolatry which bring only disillusionment, despair, and unfulfilled desires are wonderfully fulfilled and surpassed in the fount of Living Water, Jesus Christ the Lord. Therefore, practically, the apologetic, that is to say, the *elenctic* task is to demonstrate the "appallingness" of idolatry and the "appealingness" of Christ. In the area of cultural apologetics, I have broken this down into a replicable four-stage process based on Acts 17:

1. ENTERING: *Stepping into* the world and listening to the story: "For as I walked around and looked carefully at your objects of worship" (v. 23 NIV).
2. EXPLORING: *Searching for* elements of grace and the idols attached to them: "People of Athens! I see that in every way you are very religious. For as I walked around and looked carefully at your objects of worship, I even found an altar with this inscription: to an unknown god" (vv. 22–23 NIV).
3. EXPOSING: *Showing up* the idols as destructive frauds: "Therefore since we are God's offspring, we should not think that the divine being is like gold or silver or stone—an image made by human design and skill" (v. 29 NIV).
4. EVANGELIZING: *Showing off* the gospel of Jesus Christ as "subversive fulfillment": "So you are ignorant of the very thing you worship—and this is what I am going to proclaim to you" (v. 23 NIV).[54]

---

[52] Edgar, "Without Apology," 20.
[53] Bavinck, *Introduction to the Science of Missions,* 223.
[54] Daniel Strange, *Plugged In: Connecting Your Faith with What You Watch, Read and Play* (Epsom, Surrey, UK: Good Book Company, 2019), 119.

Again, these stages are, I believe, appropriate to the *elenctic* task. As Bavinck writes,

> In the darkness of human existence, where repressing and replacing focus their empty work day and night, only the proclamation of the gospel of Jesus Christ can bring light. Truth is found in him. This is the complete and living power for people, the power long repressed and rejected. Contained in his words is always something of the "I was always with you, but you were not with me." "I am the Christ whom you have repressed." "I am the one with whom you have struggled and whom you have assaulted." "It is hard for you to kick against the pricks."[55]

Offering Jesus to religious alterity means both connection and confrontation. He is the subversive fulfillment of idolatry. He is the subversive fulfillment of the magnetic points. The *elenctic* question "What have you done with God?" finds its complement in the question that Jesus himself asked while he was on earth: " 'But what about you?' he asked. 'Who do you say I am?' " (Mark 8:29 NIV).

Demonstrating Jesus Christ as the subversive fulfillment of religious alterity can be taken on a further level of analysis and specificity by showing how not simply the Christian faith as a worldview but the person of Christ is the subversive fulfillment of Bavinck's magnetic points. He is the magnetic Person whom we present to people. This connection is implied in Bavinck's *Introduction to the Science of Missions* but never fully developed. I maintain that it has great potential as a schema for "traction" in apologetics, cultural apologetics, and discipleship.[56]

To the magnetic point of *I and the Cosmos* we proclaim Jesus as subversive fulfillment. The *imago Dei* affirms both our insignificance (we are *not* God), and significance (we are images *of God*). We are *Adam*—ones "from the earth," and so our need for connection is natural. However, we need to realize that we are disconnected: from ourselves, from each other, from the creation, and, most of all, from the Creator against whom we have rebelled. Being connected to this world means being connected to a world that is under judgment and perishing. Jesus, the second Adam, offers a new kingdom in which we enter by repentance and faith. This kingdom is both "now and

---

[55] Bavinck, *Introduction to the Science of Missions*, 290.
[56] In Bavinck's more extensive treatment of the magnetic points, he does show how the Christian faith answers the magnetic points, but *elenctics* is not mentioned.

840 SIN AND DEPRAVITY IN PASTORAL PRACTICE

not yet," but it is inexorable: "That kingdom comes by grace, and through grace draws all dimensions of creation together into one great whole, into a symphony of divine domination."[57] For those entering this kingdom, it means death and sacrifice but not a loss of self in terms of individuality and responsibility. Rather, it means a rebirth and resurrection, communion with God in our union with Christ, and community in the body of Christ, the church.[58]

To the magnetic point of *I and the Norm*, we proclaim Jesus as subversive fulfillment. Jesus offers himself as both the standard and the Savior. The world is not as it should be, and we cannot save it ourselves:

> Transgression of the law is not an assault on good order or an agreement, but it is very definitely rebellion against God and an attempt to pry oneself loose from God's grip and to attack the image of God. That law is Jesus Christ, in whom the entire law is fulfilled and who kept every commandment in our place out of the depths of his divine love . . . outside of him safety is nowhere and never found.[59]

To the magnetic point of *I and Salvation*, we proclaim Jesus as subversive fulfillment. The enmity within ourselves, between ourselves, and with the spiritual and natural realms from which we seek deliverance are the fruit of the root cause—enmity with God, his righteous wrath, and an eternity in hell. Deliverance can be found only through a work outside of us through one mediator, the God-man Jesus Christ—*and him alone*. In him there is not only escape but restoration, in which we are God's agents and ambassadors.

To the magnetic point of *I and the Riddle of my existence*, we proclaim Jesus as subversive fulfillment. The world is not governed by a grinding fate or malevolent forces but by a sovereign God who is Lord over all creation, both natural and supernatural. This sovereignty does not take away human freedom but is its precondition. As Bavinck notes,

> the lot that is assigned a person is not some dark fate, nor is it cosmic determinism. But in the deepest sense it is the unfolding plan of God. The dialogue

---

[57] Bavinck, "Religious Consciousness," 292.
[58] I have filled these points out more fully in "The Magnetic Person: The Doctrine of Missions," in *Theology for Ministry*, ed. William R. Edwards, John C. A. Ferguson, and Chad Van Dixhoorn (Phillipsburg, NJ: P&R, 2022). For an attempt to apply the magnetic point to "secular" culture, see my *Making Faith Magnetic: Five Hidden Themes Our Culture Can't Stop Talking About—And How to Connect Them to Christ* (Epsom, Surrey, UK: Good Book Company, 2021).
[59] Bavinck, "Religious Consciousness," 294.

that a person experiences between his or her activity and his or her destiny increasingly takes on the character of a dialogue between a child and its father.[60]

To the magnetic point of *I and Higher Power*, we proclaim Jesus as subversive fulfillment. We do not worship a non-Absolute deity, or an impersonal force but a Someone, maximally Absolute and maximally Personal, one who is both transcendent and immanent, Judge and Savior. We worship One who has reached down to us in grace, the Word made flesh: "That Higher Power is the one that came into the world in the form of Jesus Christ and removed the veil over his face so that we might see the Son and the Father. 'Whoever has seen me has seen the Father.' "[61]

In summary here, I think there is a mutually beneficial rapprochement and enrichment between *elenctics* and the resources of a presuppositional apologetic methodology in that both draw from the same theological anthropology. Making this association for *elenctics* is important if it is to be revived. First, given Bavinck's ambivalence to apologetics and rational argument; second, given a paucity of specific practical guidance as to how to "do" *elenctics* in his *Introduction to the Science of Missions*; and third, given what Bavinck says about the role of the Holy Spirit, one might be driven (wrongly but understandably) overly to fideistic conclusions. Presuppositionalism can be a bulwark against this happening. Making this association for presuppositional apologetics is important as *elenctics*, particularly in Bavinck's rendition, has a wholistic, one might say, human "earthiness," and evangelistic drive. This would prevent two tendencies of which presuppositionalism has been guilty. The first is that it can become too intellectualized, abstruse, and, ironically, rationalistic. Second, and related, it has been overly fascinated with methodological exercises and in-house bickering, at the expense of practice. *Elenctics* can be a bulwark against these apologetic dangers because of its wholistic theological anthropology, together with its outward and applied focus.

Conclusion

Finally, and in conclusion, *elenctics* can occur "only if one recognizes and unmasks these same undercurrents within himself. *Elenctics* is possible only on the basis of a veritable self-knowledge, which is kindled in our hearts by

[60] Bavinck, "Religious Consciousness," 296.
[61] Bavinck, "Religious Consciousness," 294.

the Holy Spirit."[62] Here I note the *posture* and *place* of *elenctics*. There is something uncomfortably "hard-edged" about *elenctics* (even pronouncing the term!), and the *elenctic* task. The unmasking of sin, antithesis, idolatry, confrontation, and the call to repentance have never been winsome doctrines, but they are at the heart of a biblical theology of religions and the missionary task. However, with these vital doctrines and their practical applications, the attendant temptations of malice and vain glory are ever present, individually and "tribally." Bavinck's writings (and by all accounts his life too),[63] exude the adage *suaviter in modo, fortiter in re* ("gentle in persuasion, powerful in substance") and what he himself calls the warm undertone of meeting-in-love: "the recognition of myself in the other person, a sympathetic feeling of his guilt and a sincere desire in Christ to do with this man what Christ has done with me."[64]

In 1 John 5 we are exhorted to keep ourselves from idols. Although I have never formerly called it *elenctics*, my seminary teaching in modules on apologetics, cultural apologetics, and the theology of religions have been heavily influenced by this discipline, particularly as articulated by J. H. Bavinck. In recent years, and because of the increasingly post-Christian and pagan culture in which I teach, both myself and my students have realized that *elenctics* is not simply an outward focus on the Other, but also an inward focus on ourselves and our Christian spirituality, discipleship, and formation:

> *Elenctics* receives the greatest support from its repeated awareness that the sharpest weapons must in the first place be turned against ourselves. . . . Anyone who knows himself to any extent knows the finesse with which a man can escape from God, and wrestle free from his grasp. To be really able to convict anyone in sin, a person must know himself, and the hidden corners of his heart very well. There is no more humbling work in the world than to engage in *elenctics*. For at each moment the person knows that the weapons which he turns against another have wounded himself. The Holy Spirit convicts us, and then through us he convicts the world.[65]

Moreover, for myself and our seminarians, we are recognizing that it is *elenctics* that will be needed for our discipling and catechizing of *believers* under our pastoral care. How do our gatherings and the means of grace keep

[62] Bavinck, *Introduction to the Science of Missions*, 222.
[63] See Visser, *Heart for the Gospel*. A shorter account of Bavinck's life and work can be found in Bolt, Bratt, and Visser, eds., *J. H. Bavinck Reader*, 1–92.
[64] Bavinck, *Introduction to the Science of Missions*, 127.
[65] Bavinck, *Introduction to the Science of Missions*, 272.

us magnetized by Jesus and not pulled away by the magnetic power of sin, pious self-excitement, and religious inventiveness?

Therefore, as we continue to reflect (and agonize) on the whys and wherefores of theological education in terms of curriculum, pedagogy, and disciplines, we would do well to consider *elenctics*, not only as a discrete course in the missiological curriculum, but as an attitude diffused throughout our institutions:

> It would be too much to say that all of theology ought to be more mission-ary directed, but it is a fact that each department of theology also has a missionary function to fulfil. In theology, the church of our day must again direct itself to its exalted task of proclaiming the holy gospel in the midst of a world gripped by evil. It is here that the church must issue its call to repentance and confessions of guilt, the call also to faith in Jesus Christ.[66]

---

[66] Bavinck, *Introduction to the Science of Missions*, 246.

28

Evangelizing Fallen People

APOLOGETICS AND THE DOCTRINE OF SIN

James N. Anderson

Apologetics is the vindication of the Christian philosophy of life against the various forms of the non-Christian philosophy of life.[1]

The sinner has cemented colored glasses to his eyes which he cannot remove. And all is yellow to the jaundiced eye.[2]

Christian apologetics (from Greek, *apologia*: answer, defense) is commonly defined as *the rational defense of the Christian faith*.[3] Apologetics has been an important aspect of the witness and ministry of the Christian church from its very inception.[4] A comprehensive Christian apologetic will set forth the intellectual virtues of Christian beliefs, rebut objections to those beliefs, and expose the irrationality and absurdity of opposing belief systems. As such, apologetics is beneficial both to believers, in serving to protect and strengthen their faith, and to nonbelievers, by removing intellectual obstacles to faith and exposing the errors of unbelief.

---

[1] Cornelius Van Til, *Christian Apologetics* (Phillipsburg, NJ: P&R, 1976), 1.

[2] Van Til, *Christian Apologetics*, 45.

[3] C. Stephen Evans, *Pocket Dictionary of Apologetics and Philosophy of Religion* (Downers Grove, IL: InterVarsity Press, 2002), 12. As I use the term in this chapter, "rational" simply means "in accord with reason" or (more precisely) "in accord with proper norms of reasoning." Cognate terms ("rationality," "irrational," etc.) should be understood along similar lines. That the task of apologetics includes a defense or demonstration of the *rationality* of the Christian faith should not be taken to imply that Christian beliefs must conform to (supposedly) external, neutral, or autonomous standards of reason, only that Christian beliefs are consonant with the *proper* norms of reason. The latter is quite consistent with the claim, made by Van Til and others, that reason itself rests upon the truth of the Christian worldview.

[4] For a historical survey, see Benjamin K. Forrest, Joshua D. Chatraw, and Alister E. McGrath, eds., *The History of Apologetics* (Grand Rapids, MI: Zondervan Academic, 2020).

The burden of this chapter is (1) to lay some biblical foundations for thinking about apologetics, (2) to review several major approaches to apologetics in the Christian church, and (3) to advocate for one particular approach. But the reader might well ask, Why would a book devoted to the doctrine of sin include a chapter on apologetics? Here are two reasons to justify its inclusion: First, Christian apologetics can be viewed as a subdivision of Christian theology. John Frame has observed that Christian theology is "the application of Scripture to all of life," and Christian apologetics is specifically "the application of Scripture to unbelief."[5] Unbelief has its roots in *sin*—specifically, it is a manifestation of the intellectual rebellion of creatures against their Creator's clear self-revelation. Hence, there is a close connection between the task of apologetics and the doctrine of sin; the former cannot be properly understood without due reflection on the latter.

Second, as I will argue below, there is a biblical mandate for the practice of apologetics, both for the church corporately and for believers individually. If such is the case, it will be important for us to reflect on what Scripture teaches with regard to *how* we should engage in apologetics: the nature of apologetic encounters, the basis on which we should defend the truth and rationality of the Christian faith, the causes of doubt and denial, the obstacles we typically face, the goals we seek to accomplish, and so forth. It takes little reflection to see that what the Bible says about the nature, extent, and consequences of human sin will have a major bearing on those topics. To give one example: if our intellectual faculties have been affected by sin, such that our reasoning has been corrupted in significant respects, that will have important implications for how we approach the task of apologetics.

1. The Biblical Mandate for Apologetics

Is apologetics a task for all Christians or only for those with a special gifting and enthusiasm for it? It is true that God has distributed various gifts and callings among his people, and he has been pleased to raise up specially gifted apologists in every generation, just as he has raised up exceptional preachers, teachers, evangelists, and reformers. Nevertheless, just as every Christian is called to be an *evangelist* in the broad sense—one who proclaims the gospel

---

[5] John M. Frame, *The Doctrine of the Knowledge of God* (Phillipsburg, NJ: P&R, 1987), 87.

and bears witness to Jesus Christ—so every Christian is also called to be an *apologist* in the broad sense—one who makes a defense (*apologia*) of the faith when the opportunity arises.

It could be argued that the entire Bible serves as both an *apologia* and a mandate for apologetics. But let us focus on two specific kinds of support for apologetics in the NT. First of all, there are *exhortations* to defend the faith. Consider these words from Peter:

> In your hearts honor Christ the Lord as holy, always being prepared to make a defense [ἀπολογία] to anyone who asks you for a reason [λόγος] for the hope that is in you. (1 Pet. 3:15)

The apostle is addressing Christians who are enduring suffering because of their faith and yet continue to trust and hope in Christ amid their trials. Unbelievers, not surprisingly, find this perplexing! They want to know *why* these Christians have such hope, and Peter exhorts them to give these unbelievers an answer in the form of a *reason* for their hope.[6]

Another exhortation comes from the punchy little epistle of Jude:

> Beloved, although I was very eager to write to you about our common salvation, I found it necessary to write appealing to you to contend for the faith that was once for all delivered to the saints. (Jude 3)

Jude is concerned about the threat of false teachers within the church (v. 4) and so he exhorts his readers—and by extension, all Christians (see v. 1)—to "carry on the fight for the faith," that is, for the apostolic message of salvation through Jesus Christ.[7] In contrast to Peter's exhortation, the defense is directed more toward protecting believers than answering unbelievers.

In addition to these exhortations, we also find various *examples* of apologetics in the NT. According to the book of Acts, the apostle Paul not only *proclaimed* the gospel to the unbelievers he encountered, but also *reasoned* and *debated* with them, whether Jews or Gentiles.[8] Paul was an apologist-evangelist, and a model for Christians in that regard. The author of the fourth

---

[6] John Frame thus offers an alternative definition of apologetics: "the discipline that teaches Christians how to give a reason for their hope" (John M. Frame, *Apologetics: A Justification of Christian Belief*, ed. Joseph E. Torres [Phillipsburg, NJ: P&R, 2015], 1).

[7] Richard J. Bauckham, *Jude, 2 Peter*, WBC 50 (Nashville: Thomas Nelson, 1996), 31–34.

[8] Acts 9:22; 17:2–3, 17; 18:4, 19; 19:8–9; 24:25.

Gospel, "St. John the Evangelist," was likewise an apologist. Consider how John characterizes his purpose in writing his account:

> Now Jesus did many other signs in the presence of the disciples, which are not written in this book; but these are written so that you may believe that Jesus is the Christ, the Son of God, and that by believing you may have life in his name. (John 20:30–31)

John wrote to persuade his readers *to believe* that Jesus is the Christ, the Son of God, and he provided *reasons* for them to believe (specifically, his own eyewitness testimony to the "signs" Jesus performed, and above all, to his resurrection). To the examples of Paul and John we could add the Lord Jesus himself, who frequently engaged in debate with his opponents, refuting their criticisms and exposing the hypocrisy of their refusal to believe in him.[9]

John Frame has helpfully distinguished three aspects of the task of apologetics: *proof, defense,* and *offense.*[10] Each can be found in the practice of the apostles and the early church:

> *Proof* involves giving positive arguments to set forth the truth and rationality of the defining tenets of the Christian worldview, such as the existence of the biblical God, the divine inspiration of Scripture, and the resurrection of Christ. We see this aspect illustrated by Peter, Paul, and Apollos, among others, as they argued from the Hebrew Scriptures that Jesus was the Messiah.[11]

> *Defense* (sometimes called "negative apologetics") involves rebutting objections to the truth and rationality of the Christian worldview. One example can be seen in Jesus's response to the Sadducees' skepticism about the doctrine of the resurrection (Luke 20:27–40). Paul also alludes to the defensive aspect of apologetics in his second letter to the Corinthians: "We destroy arguments and every lofty opinion raised against the knowledge of God" (2 Cor. 10:5).

> *Offense* involves arguing *against* the truth and rationality of competitors to the Christian worldview. Paul's subtle internal critique of pagan Greek worldviews in his Areopagus sermon is a fine illustration of "going on the offense" in apologetics (Acts 17:22–31).

Thus we see that a balanced biblical apologetic ought to integrate all three aspects: proof, defense, and offense.

[9] Luke also fits the category of apologist-evangelist: see Luke 1:1–4 and Acts 1:1–3.
[10] Frame, *Apologetics*, 1–3.
[11] Acts 2:14–36; 3:11–26; 9:22; 17:2–3; 18:24–28.

The biblical mandate for apologetics can also be seen indirectly by way of the mandate for *evangelism*. While some Christians are specially gifted and appointed to serve the church as evangelists, all are called to bear witness to their faith in Christ and to share the good news of salvation with the lost. But in an increasingly secular and post-Christian culture, effective evangelism will require apologetics, just as it did in the pre-Christian culture of the first century. When we call on people to believe in the Lord Jesus Christ for salvation, the typical response is: *Why?* Why should we believe in Jesus? Why do we need this "gospel"? Why should we accept these "strange things" (Acts 17:20)? The moment we begin to address these *why* questions, we are stepping onto the field of apologetics. If only for this reason, it is important for Christians to reflect upon the task of apologetics.

2. Apologetics, Epistemology, and Theology

Not only does the Bible give us a strong mandate for apologetics, it also has much to tell us about the task and practice of apologetics. We should not imagine that Scripture merely directs us to "defend the faith" while leaving the *how* entirely up to our discretion. On the contrary, there is much to be learned from God's word about the *how* of apologetics if we will pay close attention to its teachings. In this section, I will argue that a biblical *methodology* for apologetics must be undergirded by a biblical *epistemology*, which in turn should be informed by a biblical *theology*.[12]

It should not be controversial to say that how we practice apologetics ought to be directed and constrained by a biblical Christian worldview. In the first place, the truth-claims we seek to defend—what we might call the *content* of our apologetic—should be consistent with a Christian worldview and also should represent the *entirety* of a Christian worldview. We ought not be satisfied with contending for an attenuated version of the Christian faith. Second, the way we defend those truth-claims—the *method* of our apologetic—should also be consistent with and informed by a Christian worldview. This method will cover matters such as the authorities to which we appeal, the criteria of truth and rationality we assume, the kinds of arguments we use, and the rhetorical strategies we employ. Third, the manner in which we

---

[12] Epistemology is the study of knowledge and related concepts such as truth, evidence, perception, and rational justification. By "biblical theology" I mean a system of theology based on the teachings of the Bible, rather than the more technical usage referring to the discipline of theology that emphasizes the progressive nature of biblical revelation, commonly associated with scholars such as Geerhardus Vos, Herman Ridderbos, and Meredith Kline.

defend the faith—the *ethic* of our apologetic—should likewise reflect our Christian convictions. Consistency demands that we behave in a Christlike manner as we defend the gospel of Christ.

Unlike the first and third, the second point—the issue of apologetic methodology—has engendered an enormous amount of controversy within the church in recent decades, and thus demands special attention. At the risk of oversimplifying a multifaceted debate, I suggest that disputes over apologetic methodology ultimately boil down to disagreements (whether recognized or not) over *epistemology*: what we know and how we know it, how we should reason and evaluate truth-claims, what sources and authorities we should recognize, what standards of rationality we should accept, and so forth. After all, apologetics is largely concerned with *epistemological* matters. It offers a *rational* defense of Christian *beliefs*. In its strongest forms, it seeks to vindicate Christian claims to *knowledge*: we can *know* that there is a God, that the Bible is the word of God, that Jesus is the Son of God, and so on. A flawed epistemology will therefore lead to a compromised apologetic methodology.

Apologetic methodology is thus downstream from epistemology in the sense that one's approach to apologetics will be significantly shaped and directed by one's theory of knowledge and rationality. Yet epistemology itself is not the fountainhead; it also lies downstream from even more foundational commitments. Our epistemology should not be formulated in a vacuum, isolated from our Christian convictions. A truly Christian epistemology should be embedded in a broader Christian worldview, with its distinctive doctrines of God, creation, mankind, revelation, sin, and salvation. In other words, a self-consciously Christian *epistemology* must be informed by a self-consciously Christian *theology*. What the Bible tells us about God and his self-revelation, his works of creation and redemption, the nature of man and his relationship to God, the consequences of sin on our various faculties, the differences between believers and unbelievers, and many other matters besides, will have significant implications for our epistemology. It follows that there can be no such thing as a *religiously neutral* epistemology. An epistemology informed by a Christian worldview will differ markedly from one informed by a non-Christian worldview.[13]

---

[13] In speaking of a "Christian epistemology," I do not mean to suggest that the Bible addresses all the questions epistemologists have traditionally asked, such as, "What distinguishes knowledge from mere opinion?" and, "How do we refute various skeptical challenges?" What I do claim is that the Bible speaks, both directly and indirectly, to

We may therefore summarize the proper order of reflection as follows:

THEOLOGY → EPISTEMOLOGY → APOLOGETICS

Or more precisely, recognizing that we approach these issues from a stance of Christian conviction:

CHRISTIAN THEOLOGY → CHRISTIAN EPISTEMOLOGY → CHRISTIAN APOLOGETICS

The lesson is this: if we are to think responsibly about the *how* of apologetics, we must first reflect on matters of epistemology—sources and criteria of truth and knowledge, norms of reasoning, proper authorities, the reliability of various human cognitive faculties, and so forth. But even those epistemological reflections should be directed by our prior *theological* convictions, derived first and foremost from God's authoritative revelation in Scripture. As has often been said, *theology matters*. A holistic biblical theology should inform every area of our lives, not least how we approach the important task of defending the faith in an increasingly anti-Christian culture.

3. Some Important Biblical Texts

We have considered matters in rather general terms thus far, so let us now turn to specifics. We cannot explore every biblical text with significant epistemological implications—that would demand an entire book.[14] We will therefore content ourselves with some brief observations about a selection of texts with particular bearing on the subject of apologetics, arranged under five headings: (1) natural revelation; (2) special revelation; (3) the lordship and authority of Christ; (4) the noetic (i.e., intellectual) effects of sin; and (5) the antithesis between believers and unbelievers

3.1. NATURAL REVELATION

Genesis 1:1–31; Psalm 19:1–6; Hebrews 11:3; Revelation 4:11. Scripture is unambiguous in its basic doctrine of creation. All things were created *ex nihilo* by God alone; they were created good and for God's own glory. We should therefore expect the creation to testify unmistakably to its Creator—

---

many of the issues that fall under the purview of epistemology. Scripture has important things to tell us about the nature, extent, sources, and limitations of human knowledge and reason.

[14] For a far more extensive treatment of biblical epistemology, see Frame, *Doctrine of the Knowledge of God*.

to bear the Maker's stamp. It is unthinkable that God would fashion a universe that failed to manifest its origins in his wisdom and power, a cosmos that appeared to be self-sufficient and self-contained. On the contrary, "the heavens declare the glory of God"!

Romans 1:18–32. This text is arguably the *locus classicus* of the doctrine of natural revelation. Foundational to Paul's argument that "all have sinned and fall short of the glory of God" (3:23) is the premise that God's existence and attributes "have been clearly perceived, ever since the creation of the world, in the things that have been made" (1:20). God has not concealed himself from his creatures. On the contrary, "what can be known of God is manifest to them, for God has made it manifest to them" (1:19, my translation). Consequently, people are "without excuse" (ἀναπολογήτους: literally, "without an apologetic"). Paul is crystal clear about the fundamental sin of mankind. Even though everyone *knows* at some basic level that there is a Creator to whom they owe honor and thanks, they have failed to give him his due (1:21). Instead, they suppress the truth in unrighteousness (1:18)—implying, of course, that they already *possess* the truth (cf. v. 25). Moreover, in addition to knowledge of God, they also possess (to some degree) knowledge of God's moral requirements and the penalty for flouting them (1:28–32).[15]

Romans 2:14–15. In arguing that the Gentiles, who do not have the written Mosaic law, are nonetheless guilty of sin before God, Paul affirms what theologians have called *natural law*: moral principles knowable by natural revelation alone, specifically through the conscience. Thus, there is an internal as well as an external aspect to natural revelation that serves to render sinners "without excuse" before God. In a sense, Paul is not introducing a new thought here, but rather is developing his earlier remark (1:32) about all people knowing not only God but also his righteous ordinance (δικαίωμα).

Genesis 1:27. One crucial aspect of natural revelation is rooted in the doctrine of the *imago Dei*. We alone among God's creatures are made "in the image of God," uniquely bearing the special stamp of our Creator.[16] As such, human nature is perhaps the element of natural revelation that most powerfully bears witness to the Creator of the cosmos. Although human nature

---

[15] Paul's primary targets in 1:18–32 are pagans rather than Jews, but what he argues about knowledge of God applies *a fortiori* to the Jews, since they possess special revelation *in addition to* natural revelation.

[16] Herman Bavinck observes that mankind does not merely *bear* the image of God, but rather *is* the image of God (Herman Bavinck, *Reformed Dogmatics: God and Creation*, ed. John Bolt, trans. John Vriend, 4 vols. [Grand Rapids, MI: Baker Academic, 2003–2008], 2:533).

has been corrupted by the fall, the *imago Dei* has not been eradicated, only obscured and suppressed (Gen. 9:6; James 3:9). This ontological fact thus provides a universal point of contact for apologetics.

3.2. SPECIAL REVELATION

By definition, special revelation is *not general*, that is, not available to all mankind through the created order and human nature. Special revelation is typically *verbal* in character: God *speaks* to people (individually or in groups) at various times and by various means, either immediately, as in the case of the words of Christ, the incarnate Son of God, or through intermediaries such as prophets and apostles (Heb. 1:1–2). For Protestants who accept the doctrine of *sola Scriptura*, the Bible alone is God's word (special revelation) for God's people in the post-apostolic, pre-consummation age.[17]

Second Timothy 3:16. In this supremely important text for the doctrine of special revelation, Paul declares that "all Scripture is breathed out [θεόπνευστος] by God." The implication is that Scripture is no less than *divine speech*—the very words of God—and thus it carries all of the authority of God, which is to say, the *highest possible* authority. No other source of truth (intuition, experience, tradition, etc.) is described in the NT in equivalent terms, and thus Scripture must be understood as uniquely infallible and authoritative.[18] It is striking that even the Lord Jesus, despite speaking with his own divine authority, referred and appealed to no authority other than Scripture as the verbal revelation of God.[19]

John 1:1–18. The stunning opening of the fourth Gospel presents Jesus Christ as the incarnate Son of God, the eternal Word of God become flesh, who uniquely reveals the Father to us. Every word of Christ is thus *divine testimony*: it is special revelation in the most direct sense. But where do we find the authoritative words of Christ preserved for us today? In the Bible alone. Christ continues to speak, testifying to his redemptive work through the Scriptures of the Old and New Testaments, written under the inspiration of the Holy Spirit (2 Pet. 1:21). The word of God is the word of God the Son.[20]

---

[17] For a robust contemporary defense of *sola Scriptura*, see Matthew Barrett, *God's Word Alone: The Authority of Scripture*, The 5 Solas Series (Grand Rapids, MI: Zondervan, 2016).

[18] Although Paul has in view the OT in this text, his affirmation of the divine inspiration of Scripture applies by extension to the NT as well, insofar as the latter is also regarded as Scripture (2 Pet. 3:16).

[19] John W. Wenham, "Christ's View of Scripture," in *Inerrancy*, ed. Norman L. Geisler (Grand Rapids, MI: Zondervan, 1979), 3–36.

[20] As many commentators on this passage have noted, the revelatory work of the Son includes a *cosmic* aspect (John 1:4–5, 9) indicating that Christ speaks to his creatures through natural revelation as well as special revelation.

John 17:17. "Your word is truth," declared Jesus in his high priestly prayer to the Father, before making a perfect atonement for the sins of his people. We should not miss the strength of this simple statement. It is not merely that God's word is *true* (adjective) but rather that it is *truth* (noun). That is to say, God's word has the *very essence* of truth.[21] Given that Scripture is God's word, it serves as the ultimate standard of truth (cf. Isa. 8:20). Scripture is infallible and supremely authoritative. Its veracity is not—and cannot be—subject to evaluation by any higher standard.

Hebrews 6:13. When God made a promise to Abraham, "he swore by himself"—by his own authority—because there is no greater authority. This irreproachable theological principle undergirds the Reformed doctrine of "self-attesting Scripture." On pain of contradiction, God's word must attest to its own authority, rather than appealing to some other authority, for no other reason than that it is *God's* word.[22] Any biblical epistemology worth its salt must accommodate this crucial aspect of the doctrine of Scripture.

3.3. THE LORDSHIP AND AUTHORITY OF CHRIST

"Jesus is Lord" is the primary confession of the NT (Rom. 10:9; 1 Cor. 8:6; 12:3; Phil. 2:11; Eph. 4:5). This simple-yet-world-shaking credo identifies Jesus with the one true God of the OT, affirming his equality with God the Father in his authority over all creation (Matt. 11:27; 28:19–20). The lordship and authority of Christ have important *epistemological* implications regarding how we approach truth-claims in general and Christ's self-attestation in particular.

Colossians 1:15–20; 2:1–15. Paul affirms in superlative terms the full deity of Christ and his sovereign authority over the entire creation (1:16–18; 2:9–10). Christ thus possesses absolute lordship over all creatures, including all human beings—*whether they acknowledge it or not.* This lordship extends to the epistemological or intellectual realm. Paul declares that "all the treasures of wisdom and knowledge" are "hidden" in Christ (2:3). Accordingly, he draws a sharp contrast between "philosophy and empty deceit" that is "according to human tradition [and] the elemental spirits of the world," and philosophy that

---

As such, this text should be viewed in tandem with the texts discussed under the previous heading, esp. Rom. 1:18–32.

[21] Commentators have noted the grammatical parallel with John 1:1: "The Word was God." The eternal *Logos* has the very essence of God, in the sense that he is fully divine and equal with God (Daniel B. Wallace, *Greek Grammar beyond the Basics* [Grand Rapids, MI: Zondervan, 1996], 266–69).

[22] As the first chapter of the Westminster Confession of Faith puts it, "The authority of the Holy Scripture, for which it ought to be believed, and obeyed, dependeth not upon the testimony of any man, or church; but wholly upon God (who is truth itself) the author thereof: and therefore it is to be received, because it is the Word of God."

is "according to Christ" (2:8). It follows from the lordship of Christ that every human faculty—including every human intellect—ought to be submitted to the authority of Christ. In Paul's mind, there is no middle ground: either one is reasoning under the lordship of Christ or one is reasoning in rebellion.

John 14:6. "I am the way, the truth, and the life." The familiarity of this verse should not obscure the sheer magnitude of its claims. Jesus is not merely one who bestows life, but the very source of life itself (John 5:26; 17:2; Acts 3:15). By the same token, Jesus is not merely one who gives true testimony, but the very source of truth itself. Thus, there is no higher epistemic authority than the word of Christ.

Second Corinthians 10:4–5. In this text, Paul draws a striking connection between the spiritual warfare in which we engage and the basis on which we confront unbelieving thought. Not only do we "destroy arguments and every lofty opinion raised against the knowledge of God," but we also "take every thought captive to obey Christ." This vivid metaphor powerfully conveys the lordship of Christ over the *intellectual* realm: the realm of arguments, opinions, knowledge, and thoughts.

Matthew 6:24; 12:30. For Christians, there can be no divided loyalties. This is a principle that applies to every area of life, including the realm of intellectual authorities. We cannot serve two "epistemological masters." If Christ is Lord at all, he must be Lord of all. With respect to the authority of Christ, there is no neutral stance, no position of indifference. In the end, either we are submitting our thoughts to his authoritative revelation or we are not.

3.4. The Noetic Effects of Sin

Romans 1:18–32. This text is significant not only for its strong doctrine of natural revelation, but also for its diagnosis of how fallen humans respond to that revelation and the effects of sin on how they think about themselves and the world. Rebellious people simply do not approach God's revelation from a neutral, objective, rational stance. Rather, the unregenerate "suppress the truth in unrighteousness" (v. 18 NASB). Despite the "clearly perceived" revelation of their Creator, they do not honor or give thanks to him, and thus become "futile in their thinking" (v. 21) and "fools" who—with tragicomic irony—consider themselves "wise" (v. 22). Consequently, God in his wrath has "given them up" to depraved practices and darkened, corrupted thoughts (vv. 21, 28). A complex psychological dynamic has to be acknowledged here.

On the one hand, unbelievers cannot eradicate their knowledge of God and his laws; on the other hand, their "default setting" is one of sinful suppression, intellectual idolatry, and confusion.

Romans 8:5–8. The same stance of intellectual rebellion is reflected in these later verses. Unlike the "spiritual mind," the "fleshly mind" (i.e., the mind of the unregenerate unbeliever) is by nature "hostile to God" and *cannot* submit to God's law. Paul's repeated use of the term "mind" (φρόνημα) makes clear that he is speaking primarily of a corrupted intellect, not merely a corrupted will (although, in a biblical anthropology, the two are integrally related).

Ephesians 4:17–19. Paul's grim view of the noetic effects of sin is on full display in this text, with its unmistakable echoes of Romans 1. The believers in Ephesus are exhorted not to live as the unbelieving Gentiles do, "in the futility of their minds" (ἐν ματαιότητι τοῦ νοὸς) and "darkened in their understanding" (ἐσκοτωμένοι τῇ διανοίᾳ).[23] The cognitive afflictions of the unregenerate have a double cause: their internal suppression of the truth ("the ignorance that is in them") and their moral and spiritual sclerosis ("their hardness of heart"). While his vocabulary may allow for distinctions between human faculties, such as the intellect and the will, Paul's statements leave no room for separation or compartmentalization. In short, the apostle's doctrine of sin is one of *total* (i.e., all-encompassing) depravity.

First Corinthians 1–2. The opening chapters of Paul's first letter to the Corinthians present a very similar assessment of the effects of sin on how unregenerate people think about God's self-revelation in Christ. The message of the cross is "foolishness" to those who are outside of Christ, even though they consider themselves the "wise" of the world (1:18–21). Only those whose minds have been enlightened by the Spirit can truly understand the things of God (2:11–16).

Luke 16:19–31. While this parable may not speak directly about the noetic effects of sin, as the preceding passages do, its sobering conclusion makes a pertinent point. Jesus tells us that if someone has already rejected the testimony of God's word through his prophets, even personally witnessing a man risen from the dead will not be sufficient to change his or her mind.[24] What this indicates is that the root problem of unbelief is not *external*, such

---

[23] Compare Rom. 1:21: "they became futile [ἐματαιώθησαν] in their thinking, and their foolish hearts were darkened [ἐσκοτίσθη]."

[24] It is worth noting that this direct experience would be even stronger evidence of a resurrection than the documentary historical evidence offered in the apologetic arguments of contemporary evidentialists.

as a lack of sufficient empirical evidence, but rather *internal*. Unbelief is a fundamentally spiritual problem—a problem of the *heart*. Unbelievers are inclined by nature to interpret what they observe in the world in ways that *reinforce* their rejection of the truth.[25] The striking conclusion of the parable also underscores what we noted earlier about the authority of special revelation and the self-attesting nature of Scripture.

3.5. THE BELIEVER-UNBELIEVER ANTITHESIS

A biblical epistemology should also recognize the stark antithesis between Christian thought and non-Christian thought, that is, between believers and unbelievers with respect to their intellectual orientation and outlook. This antithesis finds particular emphasis in the Pauline epistles.

Romans 12:1–2. After exhorting his readers to submit their bodies as "living sacrifices" in the service of God, Paul encourages them also to be "transformed" by the renewal of their minds.[26] Rather than being "conformed" to *worldly* patterns of thought, Christians are to pursue *godly* patterns of thought, for the purpose of discerning the "good and acceptable and perfect" will of God. No doubt Paul is drawing an implicit contrast with the intellectual futility of the unregenerate (Rom. 1:21–22).[27]

First Corinthians 1–2. We observed previously how this passage speaks in forceful terms about the noetic effects of sin. But we should also recognize the antithesis Paul draws between the "wisdom of God" revealed in Christ and the "wisdom of the world," and correlatively between the "spiritual person" and the "natural person," regarding how they think about God and the gospel. In Paul's mind, there is simply no middle way. There is no neutral ground, no intellectual "demilitarized zone."[28]

Ephesians 4:17–24. Once again, we find Paul's remarks about the epistemic consequences of human fallenness (vv. 17–19) coupled with expressions of the believer-unbeliever antithesis. The way of the unregenerate Gentiles (v. 17) is contrasted with "the way you learned Christ" (v. 20).

---

[25] Cf. Matt. 12:22–24; John 9:13–16; 11:45–53; 12:37–40.

[26] We should not read too much into the distinction between "bodies" and "minds" in this verse, as though Paul were leaning heavily on a dualistic anthropology. "Body" is likely a synecdoche representing the entire person (see Thomas R. Schreiner, *Romans*, BECNT [Grand Rapids, MI: Baker Academic, 1998], 646–47).

[27] "The downward spiral of thinking traced in Rom. 1:18–32 is reversed in those who are redeemed from sin. Their minds are not given over to futility but are renewed to understand the truth" (Schreiner, *Romans*, 647).

[28] For further discussion of the epistemological implications of 1 Cor. 2:6–16, see Richard B. Gaffin Jr., "Epistemological Reflections on 1 Corinthians 2:6–16," in *Revelation and Reason: New Essays in Reformed Apologetics*, ed. K. Scott Oliphint and Lane G. Tipton (Phillipsburg, NJ: P&R, 2007), 13–40.

Similarly, the "old self," representing "your former manner of life," is opposed to "the new self, created after the likeness of God" (vv. 22–24).[29] This is a *categorical* difference, not merely one of degree.

Colossians 2:6–8. It comes as no surprise to find the same antithetical contrast reflected in another Pauline epistle where the authority and supremacy of Christ is front and center. Having exhorted his readers to continue to walk under the lordship of Jesus, Paul warns them not to be taken captive by worldly philosophies that are "according to human tradition" rather than "according to Christ."[30] The fundamental opposition between Christian and non-Christian thought could hardly be more apparent. Believers are called to "philosophize" in a consistently *Christian* fashion.

4. A Brief Survey of Apologetic Approaches

We have considered the connection between theology, epistemology, and apologetics, and briefly reviewed a selection of biblical texts that ought to inform a Christian epistemology. We are now better placed to evaluate some of the options on the menu of apologetic methods. In this section, I will survey three major approaches to apologetics advocated by evangelical Protestants, attempting to draw out their distinguishing features by way of contrast. Space constraints preclude anything close to a comprehensive survey, and thus some generalization will be unavoidable.[31] Nevertheless, we should be able to see that the debate over methodology in apologetics is not "much ado about nothing."

4.1. CLASSICAL APOLOGETICS

The classical approach to apologetics maintains that the Christian faith can be defended by appealing primarily to the "book of nature," that is, to natural revelation and natural reason. The book of nature can be construed in fairly broad terms so as to include self-evident principles of reason, commonsense

---

[29] Note likewise the contrast between "in the futility of their minds [τοῦ νοὸς αὐτῶν]" (v. 17) and "in the spirit of your minds [τοῦ νοὸς ὑμῶν]" (v. 23).

[30] The Greek participle συλαγωγῶν connotes the idea of being carried away as spoils or as a captive of war (Johannes P. Louw and Eugene A. Nida, eds., *Greek-English Lexicon of the New Testament Based on Semantic Domains*, 2nd ed., 2 vols. [New York: United Bible Societies, 1989], 1:473 [§ 37.10]).

[31] For this reason, I will not discuss here the "cumulative case" approach (which I do not consider significantly different from the classical and evidentialist approaches) or the "Reformed epistemology" of Alvin Plantinga and others (which is not itself a distinctive approach to apologetics, although it does have some implications for apologetics). For a useful overview of the debate over apologetic methodology, see William Lane Craig et al., *Five Views on Apologetics*, ed. Steven B. Cowan (Grand Rapids, MI: Zondervan Academic, 2000).

intuitions, empirical scientific data, historical facts, and other generally available sources of evidence.

The classical approach typically adopts a linear two-stage method.[32] First, various theistic arguments are deployed to demonstrate the existence of God, where God is understood to be the perfect, transcendent, spiritual, personal Creator of the universe. These would include versions of the *ontological argument* (the very possibility of God implies his necessary existence), the *cosmological argument* (the contingent universe requires a self-existent first cause), the *teleological argument* (apparent design or purpose in nature points to a supernatural intelligent Creator), and the *moral argument* (transcendent moral laws require a transcendent moral Lawgiver). In modern classical apologetics, the theistic arguments will often combine philosophical and scientific considerations (e.g., arguments based on the fine-tuning of the physical constants of the universe). The goal of this first stage is to reduce the field of competitors to only *monotheistic* worldviews, and also to establish the *possibility* of supernatural interventions in the natural course of events (i.e., miracles), thus preparing the ground for the second stage.[33]

The second stage then aims further to narrow the field to specifically *Christian* theism, mainly by way of historical evidential arguments. After defending the knowability of the past through ordinary historical research, and rebutting objections to miracle claims, classical apologists argue that the NT documents can be accepted as *generally reliable historical sources* based on eyewitness testimonies. From this baseline it is argued that Jesus was a real historical figure who claimed to be not only the Messiah prophesied in the OT, but also the incarnate Son of God, and that he provided decisive evidence for these claims by performing miraculous signs and rising from the dead. Indeed, the resurrection of Christ is taken to be the "super-miracle" that vindicates Christianity over against competing theistic religions such as Islam.

Classical apologetics has been closely associated with the Thomist tradition in Christian theology and philosophy, not least because the first stage of its method deploys classical theistic arguments from natural reason such as Aquinas's famous "Five Ways."[34] That said, cosmological arguments can

---

[32] R. C. Sproul, John Gerstner, and Arthur Lindsley, *Classical Apologetics: A Rational Defense of the Christian Faith and a Critique of Presuppositional Apologetics* (Grand Rapids, MI: Zondervan, 1984), 137; William Lane Craig, "Classical Apologetics," in *Five Views on Apologetics*, 48.

[33] Sproul, Gerstner, and Lindsley, *Classical Apologetics*, 146–52; Norman L. Geisler, *Christian Apologetics* (Grand Rapids, MI: Baker Academic, 1976), 61, 95–97, 265.

[34] Thomas Aquinas, *Summa Theologiae* Ia.q2.a3.

be traced back to ancient Greek philosophy (Thomas himself being an Aristotelian), and contemporary classical apologists do not restrict themselves to specifically Thomistic arguments.[35] Moreover, a wide range of theological positions can be found among proponents of the classical approach. There are Reformed classical apologists, such as R. C. Sproul and John Gerstner, who explicitly advocate a two-stage approach, starting with traditional natural theology (ontological, cosmological, and teleological arguments) before moving to historical arguments for miracles that validate specifically Christian claims about special revelation.[36] There are also non-Reformed advocates, such as self-described "evangelical Thomist" Norman Geisler and the philosopher-apologist William Lane Craig (an evangelical Molinist, who has been critical of Reformed theology).[37] In fact, the resurgence of enthusiasm for natural theology in the evangelical world can be credited in large measure to the Arminian philosopher Stuart Hackett.[38] One of the attractions of the classical approach is its compatibility with a broad base of theological convictions. It aims at nothing more than "mere Christianity" and thus it demands nothing more.

Three distinctives of the classical approach should be noted. First, it takes for granted that the natural reasoning faculties of unbelievers are competent to judge whether the claims of divine revelation (such as Scripture) are worthy of acceptance. Those claims should be embraced if—and only if—they pass the tests of reason and empirical investigation. While some (usually Reformed) classical apologists acknowledge the noetic effects of sin, it is often hard to discern what impact this has on their apologetic methodology.[39]

Second, the classical approach requires that the evidence of natural revelation be considered and interpreted without any reference to special revelation. Although Christians affirm both natural and special revelation, the latter has to be "bracketed out" when engaging in apologetics with unbelievers. John Calvin famously remarked that due to the noetic effects

---

[35] William Lane Craig, for example, defends two versions of the cosmological argument, neither of which is Thomistic. William Lane Craig, *Reasonable Faith: Christian Truth and Apologetics*, 3rd ed. (Wheaton, IL: Crossway, 2008), 106–56.

[36] Sproul, Gerstner, and Lindsley, *Classical Apologetics*, 137. For a more recent defense of the classical approach (and critique of presuppositionalism) by a Reformed scholar, see J. V. Fesko, *Reforming Apologetics: Retrieving the Classic Reformed Approach to Defending the Faith* (Grand Rapids, MI: Eerdmans, 2019). See also my chapter-by-chapter review of Fesko's book: https://www.proginosko.com/2021/07/reforming-apologetics-wrap-up/.

[37] Geisler, *Christian Apologetics*; Craig, *Reasonable Faith*.

[38] Stuart C. Hackett, *The Resurrection of Theism: Prolegomena to Christian Apology* (Chicago: Moody, 1957). Geisler and Craig have both acknowledged their intellectual debt to Hackett.

[39] Frame, *Apologetics*, 228–33.

of sin, we need the "spectacles" of Scripture to rightly read the book of nature.[40] But the classical approach supposes that the book of nature can be read perfectly well without the corrective lenses of special revelation. Sproul and Gerstner claim that their two-stage method considers "natural revelation" in the first stage and "supernatural revelation" in the second.[41] But this is rather misleading because, in the second stage of their argument, special revelation is not treated *as* special revelation. When they appeal to the evidence of the biblical documents, they invite the unbeliever to treat them as "any other historical record," "uninspired," and "merely human and historical."[42] Special revelation *as such* makes its appearance only at the final conclusion of the entire argument. It is but the punctuation mark at the end of the sentence.

Third, although rarely acknowledged directly, classical apologetics requires that any common ground between the believer and the unbeliever be regarded as *religiously neutral* ground. The classical method supposes that the case for the Christian worldview can be built upon a foundation of *worldview-neutral* first principles such as the laws of logic, the reliability of sense perception, the uniformity of nature, the scientific method, the historical method, and so forth. This foundation is understood to be neither Christian nor non-Christian, and thus it avoids the cardinal sin of "begging the question" against the unbeliever.[43] In effect, the classical apologist is committed to engaging with the unbeliever on the basis of a *neutral epistemology* with criteria for knowledge, rationality, and verification that, they assume, do not depend on any worldview commitments. But a neutral epistemology must be a *secular* epistemology; it must be free of any theological (let alone Christian) presuppositions. The classical approach thus requires the Christian to adopt a different epistemology in *apologetics*—an attenuated, religiously neutral epistemology—than he would in any other field (theology, ethics, history, psychology, sociology, etc.). That classical apologists are committed to the notion of neutral common ground is evident from the fact that they insist so strongly on a "linear argument" that avoids any hint

---

[40] "Just as old or bleary-eyed men and those with weak vision, if you thrust before them a most beautiful volume, even if they recognize it to be some sort of writing, yet can scarcely construe two words, but with the aid of spectacles will begin to read distinctly; so Scripture, gathering up the otherwise confused knowledge of God in our minds, having dispersed our dullness, clearly shows us the true God" (John Calvin, *Institutes of the Christian Religion*, ed. John T. McNeill, trans. Ford Lewis Battles, 2 vols. [London: Westminster/John Knox, 1960], 1.6.1; cf. 1.14.1).

[41] Sproul, Gerstner, and Lindsley, *Classical Apologetics*, 137.

[42] Sproul, Gerstner, and Lindsley, *Classical Apologetics*, 141, 144, 152, 155.

[43] Sproul, Gerstner, and Lindsley, *Classical Apologetics*, 155, 188, 318–38; Geisler, *Christian Apologetics*, 56–58, 61.

of "circular reasoning" (i.e., appealing to authorities that unbelievers do not accept). Indeed, it is this third distinctive of the classical approach that ultimately explains the first two.

4.2. EVIDENTIALIST APOLOGETICS

Although the evidentialist approach is similar in many respects to the classical approach, there are some distinctive features that we will note here. At the heart of the evidentialist method is the conviction that, as a general rule, truth-claims should be evaluated by considering the evidence for and against them, and therefore the Christian worldview should be defended primarily by appealing to various evidences that favor it over the alternatives. For most evidentialists, empirical facts (i.e., facts about the external world known through sense perception) will bear the greatest weight in the argument, although "evidence" can be understood more broadly to include other data such as philosophical intuitions and religious experiences. In any event, the basic idea is this: if we consider—as objectively as we can—all the available and relevant evidence, we can show that the Christian worldview is *probably* true, or at least more probable than any competing worldview, and thus reasonable to believe. Put simply, our beliefs should *follow the evidence*—and the overall evidence supports Christianity.

In practice, evidentialist apologetics can appear very similar to classical apologetics, frequently deploying the same arguments in much the same fashion. There are, however, some methodological differences. Whereas the classical approach is characterized as a *two-stage* method, the evidentialist method is (at least in principle) a *one-stage* method, where that one stage consists in adjudicating the entire field of competing worldviews in light of our total evidence. Classical apologists characteristically hold that one cannot begin by appealing to historical evidence for miracles; one has to establish the existence of God, and thus the *possibility* of miracles, before making a historical case for *actual* miracles. Evidentialists, on the other hand, maintain that any historical evidence for miracles can serve as *indirect* evidence for the existence of God. In theory, one can mount an immediate evidential case for specifically *Christian* theism by way of a historical evidential argument for the veracity of the resurrection accounts in the NT. There is no need first to lay a generically theistic foundation based on natural theology.[44]

---

[44] Gary R. Habermas, "Evidential Apologetics," in *Five Views on Apologetics*, 92, 98.

Despite this subtle point of difference, the evidentialist shares with the classicalist an underlying commitment to the idea of *religiously neutral* common ground and engagement with unbelievers on the basis of a neutral (secular) epistemology. Thus, for example, the influential evidentialist John Warwick Montgomery contends that the authenticity of the NT, including its miracle claims, can be demonstrated "on the basis of the accepted canons of historical method" and by applying "the tests of reliability employed in general historiography and literary criticism."[45] Gary Habermas, another leading evidentialist, claims that by the "careful application of historical principles, tempered by various sorts of critical analysis," it is possible to "reach sturdy conclusions within the canons of historical research."[46] In other words, we can apply standard historiographical methods—methods approved by historical scholars regardless of their worldview commitments—in the defense of the Christian faith.

A recent example of the evidentialist approach can be found in Greg Gilbert's book *Why Trust the Bible?* Gilbert is concerned to distance himself from a presuppositionalist approach that is vulnerable to "the charge of unwarranted circularity."[47] His alternative is to argue first for the general reliability of the NT, then for the historicity of the resurrection, and finally for the divine inspiration of the Bible based on the authoritative testimony of Jesus. Gilbert summarizes his approach as follows:

> [L]et's approach the documents that make up the New Testament not *first* as the Word of God but simply as historical documents, and then on that basis, let's see if we can arrive at a confident conclusion that Jesus rose from the dead. Even someone who's not a Christian should have no objection to this. After all, to approach the New Testament simply as a collection of historical documents involves no special pleading, no special status, no special truth claims. Let's let them speak for themselves in the "court of historical opinion," as it were.[48]

> If the resurrection happened, then our trust of the Bible is actually catapulted to a whole new level of confidence, far beyond the mere historical

[45] John Warwick Montgomery, *History and Christianity* (Downers Grove, IL: InterVarsity Press, 1965), 43, 26.

[46] Habermas, "Evidential Apologetics," 95. For a sophisticated application of the evidentialist approach by a former student of Habermas, see Michael R. Licona, *The Resurrection of Jesus: A New Historiographical Approach* (Downers Grove, IL: IVP Academic, 2010).

[47] Gregory D. Gilbert, *Why Trust the Bible?* (Wheaton, IL: Crossway, 2015), 18.

[48] Gilbert, *Why Trust the Bible?*, 19, emphasis original.

kind. If Jesus was really resurrected from the dead, then the Bible is the Word of God.[49]

As with the classical approach, we can see the driving concern to avoid even the hint of Christian presuppositions and to appeal to neutral, secular criteria for evaluating the truth-claims of the Christian faith ("the court of historical opinion").

4.3. Presuppositional (Covenantal) Apologetics

Presuppositional apologetics is most associated with Cornelius Van Til, long-time professor at Westminster Theological Seminary, Philadelphia, although Van Til confessed that he was merely standing on the shoulders of Christian thinkers who preceded him.[50] Van Til's work has been carried forward by other Reformed scholars such as John Frame, Greg Bahnsen, William Edgar, and K. Scott Oliphint. Although one finds different emphases among these apologists, and even some substantive disagreements, presuppositionalists are united in their view of apologetics by two foundational convictions.

The first is this: *There can be no intellectual or epistemological neutrality.* No one can approach any issue in Christian apologetics—the existence of God, the inspiration of Scripture, the resurrection of Christ, the problem of evil, and so on—from a neutral or unbiased perspective. Both believers and unbelievers come to the table with an array of presuppositions that condition how they reason, how they interpret evidence, how they evaluate truth-claims, what authorities they recognize, what ultimate standards they apply, and what they consider probable, plausible, and possible *even before considering any specific arguments or evidences.* In short, everyone brings to the table a *worldview*, whether or not they are aware of it, and that worldview will reflect substantive metaphysical and epistemological presuppositions.

It follows that no one can adopt a *worldview-neutral* perspective with respect to any topic in apologetics. No one can reason in a "presuppositional vacuum." For the same reason, we cannot naïvely appeal to *worldview-neutral* criteria—whether "self-evident principles of reason," "empirical data," "historical facts," etc.—to adjudicate between competing worldviews. We cannot simply "step outside" our worldview or "bracket out" our presuppositions

---

[49] Gilbert, *Why Trust the Bible?*, 124, cf. 141–42.
[50] The term *presuppositionalist* has also been applied to Gordon Clark and Francis Schaeffer, although their approaches differ in significant respects from Van Til's.

when engaged in debates over which worldview we *should* hold. Presuppositionalists therefore maintain that Christians should neither *attempt* nor *purport* to adopt a neutral perspective or epistemology when defending the faith. Rather, we must argue with our feet firmly planted in the very worldview we seek to vindicate; we must *presuppose* that which we aim to *prove*.

The second, closely related conviction is this: *There can be no intellectual or epistemological autonomy.* Presuppositionalists argue that, from the standpoint of a biblical epistemology, the human mind is not autonomous. It is not a "law unto itself" or the final judge of what is true and reasonable. As creatures designed to think God's thoughts after him, we are not meant to reason independently of God's revelation (both natural and special). The Greek philosopher Protagoras famously declared that "man is the measure of all things." Such a stance of autonomy is anathema to a Christian worldview, which affirms that *God* is the measure of all things. If we are rightly to reason about the world, we must reason in submission to the authority of God as he has revealed himself in Christ and his word. Simply put: if Jesus is Lord of all, then he is Lord of the human intellect, and thus there can be no intellectual autonomy. This applies not only to believers but also to unbelievers, whether they recognize it or not. Furthermore, any attempt to reason autonomously—to treat our own minds as independent judges—will not lead to knowledge of the truth but rather to suppression and distortion of the truth. Pressed to its self-stultifying conclusion, an autonomous epistemology invites relativism, skepticism, and ultimately nihilism.

In sum, the presuppositional approach is concerned to avoid putting "God in the dock," to use C. S. Lewis's memorable phrase; indeed, to avoid any *pretense* of doing so. Rather than determining whether God's word can be pronounced "not guilty" at the bar of autonomous human reason, the presuppositionalist contends that we are able to reason at all only because the absolute, transcendent, personal, triune God of the Bible exists and upholds all things by his powerful word (cf. Heb. 1:3). The only way to reason *successfully* is to reason *submissively*, recognizing who we truly are before God. Whereas the classical and evidentialist approaches seek to vindicate the Christian faith by appealing to reason and evidence, the presuppositional approach aims to demonstrate something more profound and more consistent with a biblical worldview, namely, that *our use of reason and evidence is ultimately vindicated by the Christian faith.*

Presuppositional apologetics is more closely associated with Reformed theology than classical and evidentialist apologetics. This is not a historical accident. The Reformed tradition is known for emphasizing the sovereignty of God, the lordship and authority of Christ, the self-attesting nature of Scripture, and the noetic effects of sin. In addition, presuppositionalism is well fitted to the bicovenantal framework of confessional Reformed theology. Every fallen human being is either under the covenant of works (with Adam as head) or under the covenant of grace (with Christ as head)—which is to say, either a rebel at enmity with God or an ex-rebel now reconciled to God. This explains, on a covenantal basis, the believer-unbeliever antithesis. For such reasons, presuppositionalism has also been dubbed "covenantal apologetics."[51]

The contention that people reason and interpret evidence within the context of some presuppositional framework (or worldview) has raised concerns about whether apologetics is possible at all. If there is no worldview-neutral stance from which we can adjudicate between competing worldviews, how do we avoid a "presuppositional stand-off" that collapses into mere fideism? How can we make a *rational* defense of Christian presuppositions over against non-Christian presuppositions?

Van Til's answer was to advocate a "transcendental" form of argument. Despite our opposing presuppositions, both Christians and non-Christians, in order to engage in any kind of meaningful discussion, must assume on a *practical* level that we can reason intelligibly about our experiences of the world. Any meaningful discussion must take for granted that truth is real, that there are laws of logic, that our cognitive faculties are generally reliable, that some of our beliefs can be rationally justified, and that the world we experience is generally stable, orderly, and intelligible. But the crucial question is this: *Whose presuppositions are consistent with these inescapable assumptions?* Which worldview—the Christian's or the non-Christian's—can account for our ability to engage in rational thought and discussion? Which worldview can adequately account for the possibility of human knowledge?

The central presuppositionalist argument is that the Christian and the non-Christian can engage in a reasoned debate *only because the Christian*

---

[51] K. Scott Oliphint, *Covenantal Apologetics: Principles and Practice in Defense of Our Faith* (Wheaton, IL: Crossway, 2013).

worldview is true. Human reason and knowledge *presuppose* the God of the Bible. As Van Til put it,

> It is the firm conviction of every epistemologically self-conscious Christian that no human being can utter a single syllable, whether in negation or affirmation, unless it were for God's existence. Thus the transcendental argument seeks to discover what sort of foundations the house of human knowledge must have, in order to be what it is.[52]

> [T]he argument for Christianity must therefore be that of presupposition. With Augustine it must be maintained that God's revelation is the sun from which all other light derives. The best, the only, the absolutely certain proof of the truth of Christianity is that unless its truth be presupposed there is no proof of anything. Christianity is proved as being the very foundation of the idea of proof itself.[53]

How then does this translate into an apologetic strategy? Generally speaking, presuppositionalism adopts a two-step approach that focuses on an *internal critique* of the competing worldviews. The first step is to assume the unbeliever's worldview "for the sake of argument" and show that *if* the unbeliever's worldview *were* true, it would be impossible for anyone—including the unbeliever—to know or reason about anything at all. The second step is to invite the unbeliever to assume the *Christian* worldview "for the sake of argument" and show that our worldview *can* account for human knowledge and rational discourse.[54]

Greg Bahnsen provides a helpful summary of the presuppositional approach:

> To put it in compressed form, apologetical disputes hinge on the conflicting presuppositions (worldview) of the believer and the unbeliever, but the believer can argue for the rationality of his presuppositions (and demonstrate the irrationality of the opposing outlook) by means of an "internal comparison and critique" of the two contrary sets of presuppositions. This is what is known as an indirect argument—an argument "from the impossibility of the contrary." . . . The two fundamental theories or worldviews must be compared, being analyzed "from within" themselves, with a view to reducing to

---

[52] Cornelius Van Til, *A Survey of Christian Epistemology* (Phillipsburg, NJ: P&R, 1969), 11.

[53] Cornelius Van Til, *The Defense of the Faith*, 4th ed., ed. K. Scott Oliphint (Phillipsburg, NJ: P&R, 2008), 381.

[54] Note that these two steps are very different from the two stages of the classical approach. In principle, either step can be performed first, although for rhetorical purposes it is usually more effective to deconstruct the non-Christian worldview before contrasting it with the Christian worldview.

absurdity the position that opposes your own. The autonomous position of the unbeliever must be shown to be untenable on its own grounds.[55]

In practice, the presuppositionalist approach can be broadened to encompass a range of features of human thought and action that both believers and unbelievers routinely take for granted: the existence of truth, the laws of logic, intelligible experiences of the world, objective moral standards, moral responsibility, aesthetic values, the uniformity of nature, human dignity, human rights, and the like. The Christian worldview can account for these features, and integrate them into a unified view of thought and life, in a way that no competing worldview can. What is more, the presuppositional apologist will contend that, inasmuch as the unbeliever relies on any of these things—as he must do—he is unwittingly living off "borrowed capital" from biblical theism.[56] Ironically, this becomes particularly evident when the unbeliever raises objections against the Christian faith. He complains that the God of the Bible behaves immorally, all the while relying on a moral system co-opted from the Christian worldview. He insists that modern science has refuted the biblical account of creation, yet his own worldview cannot account for the orderliness and rational intelligibility of the universe that makes science possible in the first place. And so on.

5. In Defense of Presuppositional Apologetics

It should be apparent from the foregoing survey that the differences between these apologetic approaches are not merely matters of semantics or emphasis but concern significant matters of epistemology and argumentative methodology. In this section, I will offer a compact defense of the presuppositional approach. My aims here are relatively modest: I will argue that the presuppositional approach is *biblical* and *effective*, and that the most common objections to this approach carry little, if any, weight. For more detailed treatments of the principles and practical application of presuppositionalism, the reader is encouraged to consult other works.[57]

---

[55] Greg L. Bahnsen, *Van Til's Apologetic: Readings and Analysis* (Phillipsburg, NJ: P&R, 1998), 484–85; cf. 512–15.

[56] Cornelius Van Til, *An Introduction to Systematic Theology* (Phillipsburg, NJ: P&R, 1974), 84–85.

[57] Frame, *Apologetics*; John M. Frame, *Christianity Considered: A Guide for Skeptics and Seekers* (Bellingham, WA: Lexham, 2018); Bahnsen, *Van Til's Apologetic*; Oliphint, *Covenantal Apologetics*; K. Scott Oliphint, *Know Why You Believe* (Grand Rapids, MI: Zondervan, 2017); Richard L. Pratt Jr., *Every Thought Captive: A Study Manual for the Defense of Christian Truth* (Phillipsburg, NJ: P&R, 1980); James N. Anderson, "Presuppositionalism and Frame's Epistemology," in *Speaking the Truth in Love: The Theology of John M. Frame*, ed. John J. Hughes (Phillipsburg, NJ: P&R, 2009), 431–59; James N. Anderson, *Why Should I Believe Christianity?* (Fearn, Ross-shire, UK: Christian Focus, 2016).

5.1. Presuppositional Apologetics Is Biblical

One cannot simply cite chapter and verse of the Bible in order to defend one particular apologetic method over others. Scripture does not *directly* address this issue any more than it directly addresses, say, the extent of the atonement or the ethics of contraception. A naïve proof-texting approach will not settle a debate where thoughtful Christians, equally committed to the authority of the Bible, can be found on all sides. I therefore suggest that the question of which approach is "most biblical" is better viewed as the question of which method is *most consistent with* and *most informed by* a comprehensive biblical worldview. With that caveat in place, I offer six reasons why I believe presuppositional apologetics fits the bill.

1. *Presuppositional apologetics recognizes the importance of a biblical epistemology.* One of the virtues of presuppositionalism is its clear recognition that *epistemology precedes apologetics* and *theology precedes epistemology*.[58] Presuppositionalism is therefore especially attentive to what the Bible teaches about the relationship between divine and human knowledge, divine revelation in its various forms, the natural knowledge of God, the noetic effects of sin, and the proper epistemic authorities for believers and unbelievers. For this reason, presuppositionalism—in contrast to other approaches—repudiates the notion of a neutral or secular epistemology on the basis of which the Christian faith can be defended. A Christian worldview cannot be vindicated on the basis of a non-Christian epistemology. To adopt such an epistemology, even inadvertently, is to nullify the very worldview we seek to defend.

2. *Presuppositional apologetics honors the self-attesting nature of Scripture and avoids separating natural revelation from special revelation.* Presuppositionalism does not attempt to validate Scripture on the basis of autonomous human reason and experience, as if the latter were a more reliable and authoritative standard of truth. Nor does it appeal to natural revelation isolated from special revelation, as though the book of nature can be rightly read apart from the book of Scripture. Rather, presuppositionalism seeks to defend the Christian faith as a cohesive, integrated worldview—"Christianity as a unit," as Van Til put it—where natural revelation and special revelation work together to give us a reliable knowledge of God, ourselves, and the

---

[58] Recall the discussion in section 2: apologetic methodology is downstream from epistemology, which is itself downstream from theology.

world. In short, presuppositionalism refuses to separate the God of the Bible from the Bible of the God of the Bible.

3. *Presuppositional apologetics honors the comprehensive lordship of Christ.* Abraham Kuyper's famous declaration perfectly captures one of the driving motivations for presuppositionalism: "There is not a square inch in the whole domain of our human existence over which Christ, who is Sovereign over *all*, does not cry: 'Mine!'"[59] Christ is Lord over all, including the intellectual realm—the realm of truth, reason, and knowledge. That applies to all human beings, regardless of whether they acknowledge it. Presuppositionalism therefore rejects the notions of intellectual neutrality and autonomy. Either one takes every thought captive in submission to Jesus Christ, or one does not. The conviction of the presuppositionalist is that autonomy is not only opposed to Christ, but also a recipe for relativism, skepticism, and nihilism.

4. *Presuppositional apologetics acknowledges the biblical antithesis between believers and unbelievers.* Every approach to apologetics affirms—or at least assumes—that Christians and non-Christians are made in the image of God, equally exposed to natural revelation, and able to communicate and reason with one another due to God's common grace. But not every approach acknowledges alongside these truths the fundamental differences in the spiritual orientation and intellectual outlook of believers and unbelievers.[60] Any approach that fails to grapple with this equally significant dimension of the apologetical situation falls short of biblical teachings. Scripture is clear: the difference between believing and unbelieving is the difference between light and darkness, wisdom and foolishness, even life and death.

5. *Presuppositional apologetics gives serious attention to the noetic effects of sin.* Reformed theologians are usually quick to emphasize the impact of sin on the human intellect, but not all take it into account in their approach to apologetics. According to God's word, the "natural man" is unable to engage in a neutral, objective, reasonable evaluation of the Christian faith. While many unbelievers have sharp intellects, by nature they will use their intelligence to rationalize their unbelief and suppression of God's revelation.[61] The

---

[59] Abraham Kuyper, "Sphere Sovereignty," in *Abraham Kuyper: A Centennial Reader*, ed. James D. Bratt (Grand Rapids, MI: Eerdmans, 1998), 488, emphasis original.

[60] Recall the discussion of the believer-unbeliever antithesis in section 3.5.

[61] Van Til likened the intellect of fallen man to "a buzz-saw that is sharp and shining, ready to cut the boards that come to it," but having a misaligned blade such that "every board he saws is cut slantwise and thus unusable . . ." Van Til concludes, "As long as the set of the saw is not changed, the result will always be the same. So also whenever the teachings of Christianity are presented to the natural man, they will be cut according to the set of sinful human personality" (Van Til, *Defense of the Faith*, 97).

apologist's task is not to accommodate the intellectual rebellion of unbelievers, but to challenge it head-on and expose its self-defeating consequences.

6. *Presuppositional apologetics affirms a more biblical view of common ground.* Any attempt to engage in meaningful debate presupposes that there is some common ground between the two disputants, some shared experiences and points of agreement. Presuppositionalism readily affirms that there is common ground between the believer and the unbeliever, but in keeping with a biblical epistemology it denies that the common ground is *religiously neutral* ground, i.e., that it does not presuppose any theistic or specifically Christian commitments. The distinctive claim of presuppositionalism is that the common ground is actually *Christian* ground; to be more precise, it is *Christ's* ground. Thus, non-Christians are able to engage in reasoned debate with Christians *only because the word of Christ is true*—in other words, only because reality is what the Bible says it is and because Christ is the eternal *Logos* (Word) who gives light to everyone (John 1:9).

5.2. Presuppositional Apologetics Is Effective

The danger in arguing that one approach to apologetics is "more effective" than others is like the danger in arguing that one approach to evangelism, preaching, or counseling is "more effective" than others. Such claims tend to shift the focus unhelpfully toward perceived results and pragmatic factors. Does the approach "get results"? Does it "work in practice"?

While I do believe that presuppositionalism "works in practice," I want to consider here its effectiveness primarily in terms of (1) whether it is well-calibrated to the biblically defined goals of apologetics; (2) whether it rightly diagnoses the situation that the apologist-evangelist faces; and (3) whether it is flexible enough to deal with a wide range of issues and challenges. I therefore offer seven reasons why presuppositional apologetics is especially effective in the increasingly post-Christian culture that we inhabit today.[62]

1. *Presuppositional apologetics properly diagnoses and addresses the fundamental causes of unbelief.* It is common for skeptics to say things like, "There's not enough evidence for the existence of God!" or "There are no good arguments for the existence of God!" Even if offered sincerely, such

---

[62] To these seven points, one might add that presuppositionalism is equally well-equipped to deal with *modernist* and *postmodernist* manifestations of unbelieving thought, because it strikes at their common root, namely, an anti-theistic commitment to human autonomy (both intellectual and moral). On the basis of this insight, both modernism and postmodernism can be subjected to a presuppositional critique and "reduced to absurdity."

self-reports are entirely contrary to the Bible's diagnosis of unbelief. Every aspect of the creation clearly testifies to its transcendent Creator and sustainer. In God's universe, there can be no *rational* excuse for failing to acknowledge God (Rom. 1:20). The problem is not an external one (insufficient evidence) but rather an internal one (sinful suppression of the evidence). Hence, presuppositional apologetics does not seek to persuade people of something they do not already know, but rather to expose the fact that they have been suppressing what they *do* know, and that suppression is betrayed by the fact that they *tacitly presuppose* the reality of God whenever they rely on their intellectual faculties, their moral sensibilities, and their assumption of an orderly, intelligible universe.

2. *Presuppositional apologetics strikes at the root of the disagreement between believers and unbelievers.* We should not imagine that the Christian and the non-Christian have the same basic outlook on reality, with a shared base of assumptions about how to determine what is true and right, but simply disagree on what conclusions to draw when they examine the evidence. Presuppositionalists understand that the apologetic encounter involves a clash of entire worldviews—a conflict between two fundamentally opposed belief systems and authority claims. It is ultimately a dispute over conflicting presuppositions, and thus any effective apologetic strategy must engage with the unbeliever *at the presuppositional level*, defending the integrity of Christian presuppositions and exposing the intellectual futility of non-Christian presuppositions.

3. *Presuppositional apologetics directly confronts the myths of autonomy and neutrality.* As we have seen, rather than ignoring or (worse) accommodating the unbeliever's assumptions about the independence of human reason and the feasibility of evaluating religious claims from a neutral perspective, presuppositionalism challenges those assumptions by arguing that (1) if the Christian worldview is true, autonomy and neutrality are impossible, and (2) human reason is reliable only because it is *not* autonomous but rather is continually dependent on God's providence and revelation.

4. *Presuppositional apologetics recognizes that evidences are always subject to interpretation.* Contrary to some popular misconceptions, presuppositionalism is not opposed to the use of evidences in apologetics.[63] It does,

---

[63] Cornelius Van Til, *Christian Theistic Evidences*, 2nd ed. (Phillipsburg, NJ: P&R, 2016); John M. Frame, *Cornelius Van Til: An Analysis of His Thought* (Phillipsburg, NJ: P&R, 1995), 177–84; Bahnsen, *Van Til's Apologetic*, 634–48; Thom Notaro, *Van Til and the Use of Evidence* (Phillipsburg, NJ: P&R, 1980).

however, challenge the naïve idea of *brute uninterpreted* evidence. All experiences of the world are interpreted through the lens of a worldview: basic presuppositions about what is real, possible, plausible, probable, valuable, and so forth. It is therefore futile to pile up evidence upon evidence, in the hope of changing the unbeliever's mind, without challenging the worldview in terms of which he or she reasons about that evidence.[64] Scripture gives us numerous examples of unbelievers who "reasoned away" the evidences presented to them because of a deep-seated precommitment to a false worldview.[65]

5. *Presuppositional apologetics balances the three aspects of apologetics: proof, defense, and offense.* The presuppositional approach naturally incorporates all three elements of a holistic biblical apologetic. *Proof*: it makes a positive case for the Christian worldview by arguing that only biblical theism can account for the intelligibility of the universe and our ability to reason reliably about it, as well as appealing to the abundant evidence (historical, scientific, psychological, sociological, etc.) supporting that worldview. *Defense*: it contends that objections to the Christian worldview either misrepresent that worldview (thus missing the target) or tacitly depend on non-Christian presuppositions (thus begging the question). *Offense*: it argues against competing worldviews by way of internal critiques, exposing their self-stultifying implications and their failure to account for the very things they take for granted, such as objective truth, reason, and morality, in order to make their claims.

6. *Presuppositional apologetics can be applied to any topic of conversation.* Since nothing in human experience makes sense apart from God and his word, it is possible to begin a fruitful conversation with any subject of interest or concern to the unbeliever: the desire for justice or social reform, the importance of human rights, the benefits of modern science, the problem of "fake news," the beauty of the natural world, the alleged irrationality of

---

[64] "Every bit of historical investigation, whether it be in the directly biblical field, archaeology, or in general history, is bound to confirm the truth of the claims of the Christian position. But I would not talk endlessly about facts and more facts without challenging the unbeliever's philosophy of fact" (Cornelius Van Til, *A Christian Theory of Knowledge* [Phillipsburg, NJ: P&R, 1969], 293). Van Til speaks elsewhere of the traditional apologist "throwing facts to his non-Christian friend as he might throw a ball." The unbeliever obligingly receives all these facts, tossing them casually over his shoulder into "the bottomless pit of pure possibility." The point is the same: facts are meaningless when divorced from the system of thought (worldview) in terms of which they have significance (Van Til, *Defense of the Faith*, 260–61).

[65] Consider, for example, Ex. 7:20–23; 8:17–19; Matt. 12:22–24; John 9:13–16; 10:24–26; 11:45–53. One might argue that the problem in each of these cases was hard-heartedness rather than a false worldview. However, the two are not mutually exclusive. According to a biblical anthropology, the mind and the heart are tightly integrated. In each case, we can discern an intellectual rationalization driven by an attachment to false views of God, the world, and oneself.

religious beliefs—even the simple fact that we expect the lights to come on when we flip the switch. Whatever the topic, the basic strategy is the same: "You take X for granted, but X makes sense only in the context of a Christian worldview. If your worldview were true, there would be no X!"

7. *Presuppositional apologetics helps keep the gospel at the center of the conversation.* As I have emphasized, presuppositionalism avoids separating natural revelation and special revelation, and defends "Christianity as a unit"—an integrated, all-encompassing worldview that alone makes sense of our experiences of the world. The good news of salvation—the redemptive work of the triune God—lies at the very heart of the Christian worldview. Hence, one cannot talk about the Christian worldview without talking about *the gospel*: the world-shaking, life-transforming message that God sent his own Son into the world to save sinners. Whatever arguments we present for the essential tenets of a Christian worldview, these will always be offered in the broader context of the redemptive-historical storyline of Scripture.

5.3. OBJECTIONS TO PRESUPPOSITIONAL APOLOGETICS

It is no secret that presuppositional apologetics has been subject to controversy and has been the target of a wide range of criticisms, although I would suggest that the majority of the criticisms are based on misunderstandings or misrepresentations of the approach that can be easily corrected. By way of illustration, here are brief responses to four of the most common objections.

1. *"Presuppositional apologetics involves fallacious circular reasoning."* This is arguably the most serious criticism of presuppositionalism. It is true that Van Til held that one must *presuppose* the Christian worldview in order to *prove* the Christian worldview. His critics therefore complain that presuppositionalism "begs the question" by assuming the very propositions in dispute. Is it not obviously fallacious to presuppose what you are supposed to be proving?

Van Til openly admitted that his method involved a kind of circular reasoning.[66] But it is crucial to understand that this is not the kind of vicious circularity involved in a *petitio principii* fallacy, where the conclusion of

---

[66] Van Til, *Survey of Christian Epistemology*, 10–13; Van Til, *Defense of the Faith*, 123; Van Til, *Introduction to Systematic Theology*, 146–47; Frame, *Cornelius Van Til*, 301–9; Frame, *Apologetics*, 10–15; Bahnsen, *Van Til's Apologetic*, 483, 518–20 (esp. n. 122). Let the record show that even though Van Til and other presuppositionalists have repeatedly refuted this objection, it continues to be brandished by his critics as though it had never been adequately addressed.

the argument is trivially assumed in one of its premises (e.g., "The Bible says it is God's Word and whatever God says must be true!").[67] Rather, Van Til's profound insight is that *human reasoning in general* presupposes a biblical theistic worldview, and thus any kind of argumentation—including argumentation for the truth of Christianity—must presuppose that worldview, on pain of self-contradiction. This kind of presuppositional circularity is necessarily involved in *all* transcendental arguments (i.e., arguments that seek to disclose the preconditions of human knowledge and reasoning). Transcendental arguments would not be treated as a subject of serious discussion by philosophers if they were as patently fallacious as critics of presuppositionalism suggest.

It should also be recognized that any argument offered in defense of one's ultimate presuppositions, including one's ultimate epistemic authorities, must rely on the very same presuppositions and authorities—again, on pain of self-contradiction. It would be self-defeating to appeal to Authority B to vindicate Authority A as one's ultimate authority![68] This is precisely why Van Til insisted that "the argument for Christianity must therefore be that of presupposition." The only way to resolve disagreements at that ultimate level is by an internal comparison and critique of competing presuppositions (worldviews).

2. *"Presuppositional apologetics is fideistic."* This objection is closely tied to the previous one. Since presuppositionalism rejects the idea of a neutral starting point in apologetics, critics have suggested that it ultimately reduces to a form of fideism.[69] If we have to argue on the basis of a *Christian* epistemology, we have no choice but to make an arbitrary "leap of faith" to accept *Christian* presuppositions at the outset; we cannot *argue* for those presuppositions from some worldview-neutral foundation. Put simply, if we have to *presuppose* Christianity in order to *prove* it, we are not proving it at all—we are merely presupposing it! Is that not the epitome of fideism?

---

[67] Contra Sproul, Gerstner, and Lindsley, *Classical Apologetics*, 322. The mistake of these authors is to confuse a *presupposition* of an argument with a *premise* of an argument. For further explanation, see James N. Anderson, "Does Presuppositionalism Engage in Question-Begging?" *Analogical Thoughts* (blog), https://www.proginosko .com/2012/03/does-presuppositionalism-engage-in-question-begging/ (accessed July 12, 2021).

[68] Recall the statement from the Westminster Confession of Faith quoted in footnote 22. It is worth noting that a similar "circular reasoning" objection has been raised routinely since the sixteenth century by Roman Catholic critics of the Reformed doctrine of self-attesting Scripture. The core issue is the same: any ultimate authority must, in the nature of the case, be *self*-authenticating. Van Til's apologetic method is merely the consistent outworking of Reformed orthodoxy regarding the sources of divine revelation.

[69] Sproul, Gerstner, and Lindsley, *Classical Apologetics*, 184, 211, 308–9; Geisler, *Christian Apologetics*, 56–58. "Fideism" refers here to the idea that one's position must be taken entirely "on faith," without any rational or evidential support.

The objection assumes that one must either argue from a neutral starting point or give up argument altogether. But this is a false dilemma, for there is a third option: to argue "from the impossibility of the contrary." In other words, the presuppositionalist argues that if the Christian worldview were *not* true, we would not be able to reason cogently or make sense of anything at all. Only the Christian worldview can account for the features of human life and experience we take for granted, including our intellectual faculties. This is as far from fideism as can be imagined!

3. *"Presuppositional apologetics denies any common ground between the believer and the unbeliever."* It should be apparent by now that nothing could be further from the truth. Presuppositionalism readily affirms that there is abundant common ground in apologetics: believers and unbelievers are both made in the image of God, created to think God's thoughts after him, able to reason about the world, and continually exposed to natural revelation. What presuppositionalism denies is that this common ground is *religiously neutral* ground, for that would be a *de facto* denial of the Christian worldview. The apologist's task is not to build a case for the Christian faith on a secular foundation—to build Solomon's temple out of mud bricks, as it were—but rather to show that the unbeliever has been unwittingly standing on the solid ground of the Christian worldview the whole time.

4. *"Presuppositional apologetics downplays the book of nature."*[70] One often hears that presuppositionalists are opposed in principle to natural theology and appeals to natural revelation. But this is based on a caricature of presuppositionalism. Van Til had a robust doctrine of natural revelation—as robust as any Reformed theologian—and only objected to conceptions of natural theology that appeal to *autonomous* human reason and sever natural revelation from special revelation.[71] Presuppositionalists are more than ready to point unbelievers to the book of nature, but only insist that the book of nature cannot be rightly interpreted apart from the book of Scripture.[72] These two divinely authored books are designed to be read *together*. The presuppositional approach aims to defend the Christian worldview as an integrated unit, without "bracketing out" special revelation for the purposes of apologetics.

[70] For a recent instance of this objection, see Fesko, *Reforming Apologetics*, 193–219.
[71] Cornelius Van Til, "Nature and Scripture," in *The Infallible Word: A Symposium by the Members of the Faculty of Westminster Theological Seminary*, ed. N. B. Stonehouse and Paul Woolley (Philadelphia: P&R, 1946), 263–301; Van Til, *Introduction to Systematic Theology*, 75–109.
[72] For a recent example, see John M. Frame, *Nature's Case for God: A Brief Biblical Argument* (Bellingham, WA: Lexham, 2018).

6. Conclusion

The question of how Christians should make a rational defense of the faith is not a trivial one, but neither does it lie at the center of the circle of Christian orthodoxy. Although I have defended a presuppositional approach here, disagreements over apologetic method should not be a cause of division in the church. My hope is that those who have never encountered presuppositionalism before will give it a closer look, and that those who have previously dismissed it will give it a second look. At the very least, I trust that readers have been encouraged to reflect more deeply on the connections between evangelism, apologetics, and the doctrine of sin. Whatever view we take of apologetics, let us rejoice above all that Christ is proclaimed (Phil. 1:18).

29

Counseling Fallen People

APPLYING THE TRUTH OF *SOLA SCRIPTURA*

Heath Lambert

Counseling fallen people requires the Bible because all counseling problems are sin problems, which the Bible alone understands.[1] I plan to defend that conviction in this chapter. But first, we need a bit more explanation about the nature of counseling conversations.

Counseling is a conversation where a person with questions, problems, and trouble seeks assistance from someone they believe has answers, solutions, and help.[2] Counselors are the persons in a counseling conversation who are believed to be the ones with the answers, solutions, and help to address the questions, problems, and trouble of the people who approach them for assistance. For the purposes of this chapter, it is important to know that counselors do not create their answers, solutions, and help out of thin air. They do not dispense them as disconnected bits of wisdom. Instead, counselors provide answers, solutions, and help that are built on a foundation of wisdom and theory.

Upholding every answer to complex questions, undergirding every solution to difficult problems, and supporting every practical effort of care amid serious trouble is a fabric of beliefs and convictions about how life works.

---

[1] Faithful biblical counsel engages the counselee as a sinner and/or saint and a sufferer. You can read about my research concerning this development within the biblical counseling movement in Heath Lambert, *The Biblical Counseling Movement after Adams* (Wheaton, IL: Crossway, 2010), 49–80.
[2] Heath Lambert, *A Theology of Biblical Counseling: The Doctrinal Foundation of Counseling Ministry* (Grand Rapids, MI: Zondervan, 2016), 13.

This fabric of beliefs and convictions is called a worldview. All counsel, from every counselor, is built on a worldview that describes at least three realities: who we are, what is wrong with us, and how to fix it. Because the work of counseling engages people who have problems and seeks to help them move toward solutions, the task of counseling is simply impossible without a worldview that understands these three realities.

However, that a counselor's approach to help includes these three components does not necessarily mean that a counselor's worldview is correct or consistent. In fact, the presence of a worldview does not even require the counselor to know they have a worldview. The worldview of any counselor may be more or less sophisticated. It may be acknowledged or ignored. It may be right or wrong. But every counselor builds his or her counsel on the foundation of *some* worldview.

The Bible alone contains God's worldview. As such, it is the *true* worldview. It is the Bible that sets forth God's understanding of who we are, what is wrong with us, and how to fix it. Faithful counsel must use the Bible's worldview as the foundation for faithful counseling practice.

Counseling and Sin

Every counseling practitioner does his or her work out of the overflow of a worldview that answers who we are, what is wrong with us, and what it would take to fix it. Counseling people means the counselor has an understanding of who people are. Counseling people also means having an understanding of what is wrong with people, since the work of giving counsel assumes the existence of a problem. Counseling people also means understanding what it takes to fix those problems, since counseling moves toward solutions. Each of these three elements in the required counseling worldview is crucial, but the focus of this chapter is the second element: an understanding of what is wrong with us.

Every counseling practitioner has an understanding of what is wrong with the people who seek out counseling services. Things get complicated at this point because there are nearly as many different understandings of what is wrong with people as there are counseling practitioners. There are a variety of explanations for why people have problems that require counseling, including parental influences from early childhood, genetic influences, chemical influences in the brain, habituated behaviors, negative responses to traumatic experiences, unmet needs, and many, many others. Very thick books have been written engaging the corpus of explanations for what is wrong with people who seek counseling help.

The examples that I have listed, like the many I have not listed, are not wrong but are incomplete. Counseling systems that seek to answer what is wrong with people are often correct as far as they go. The problem is that they address only a narrow slice of human difficulties; they fail to account for other manifestations of difficulty outside of the specific area they address, and they fail to understand the genesis of the problem in the first place. One of the ongoing problems in the counseling world is that there is no grand unifying theory that explains what is ultimately wrong with people.

This is not a problem for Christians. As believers we have God's authoritative word, the Bible, that tells us what is wrong with us. In the Bible God reveals the master category for all counseling problems. More than that, he describes the various manifestations of that master category. In Scripture God makes clear that what explains every counseling dilemma, every problem in living, is the tragedy of sin.

Sin as the root of all counseling problems is one of the most important contributions to the counseling field from counseling practitioners who are committed to the authority and sufficiency of Scripture. The biblical doctrine of total depravity teaches that, while God's common grace protects human beings from performing the maximum amount of sinful acts (cf. Gen. 4:15; 11:6–9; 20:6; 2 Thess. 2:7), sin has completely corrupted each person. Human beings are not just touched by sin. They are not merely tainted. They are ruined.

This sinful ruin devastates our standing before God. Humans are separated from God because of sin, and their consciences convict them of it (Rom. 5:12–14; 2:14–15). There is no aspect of our humanness that has not been affected by sin. This sinful ruin devastates our volition. Sin distorts our motivations, corrupting our ability to choose what is right (James 1:14–15). Sin has calamitous effects on our thinking. Because of our rebellion against God, the cognitive abilities of our minds are severely damaged (Rom. 1:18ff.; Col. 1:21; Eph. 4:17–18). Sin also disrupts our emotions. The destructive effects of sin corrupt God's good gift of emotion, rendering us unable to feel as we should (Prov. 2:14). Sin impacts our bodies, so that what God made perfect is now weak (1 Cor. 15:42–44). Sin impacts our relationships, so that good fellowship between persons is corrupted (Titus 3:3). Sin is so devastating that its consequences corrupt even the entire created order (Rom. 8:20–22). This is a brief summary of the effects of human sinfulness.[3] All of this sinful corruption touches down in the practice of counseling in three specific ways.

Cosmic Corruption

The Bible makes clear that, when Adam sinned, he plunged the entire cosmos into a state of ruin along with him (Gen. 3:17–19). The entire created order was devastated by Adam's disobedience, and a limitless buffet of terror has followed in its wake. Cells grow at unnatural and unprecedented rates; animals develop a predatory instinct and attack; demonic forces are on the prowl, looking to devour; weather systems develop into deadly forces that wipe out entire cities; genes mutate, leading to babies with any number of congenital abnormalities.

These manifestations of the cosmic consequences of sin—combined with many, many others—lead to counseling problems that are all incredibly painful but for which no living person is accountable. Of course, these problems trace back to the fall of Adam, but no person in the counselee's life is responsible; not themselves, and not anyone they know. Hurting men and women seek out counseling care because they are overwhelmed by a terminal cancer diagnosis after living a healthy life, or a loved one was killed in a hurricane, or their family has welcomed the birth of a precious baby with all the challenges of a trisomy 13 diagnosis. Sin is at the root of these kinds of counseling problems, but the focus of counseling is not to locate responsibility for sin on the hurting person but rather to help them trust God amid the excruciating consequences of living life in a world devasted by the cosmic results of sin.

Individual Corruption

Sin has cosmic consequences, but it has individual effects as well. Living in a sinful world means each individual person sins in very specific ways. Individuals damage their lives through the abuse of chemicals like alcohol and tobacco. They destroy their bodies through self-mutilating acts like cutting. They isolate themselves from others to focus on pornography addictions. They lose their jobs after misappropriating funds. Such manifestations of sinfulness fill up countless counseling hours.

---

[3] Lambert, *Theology of Biblical Counseling*, 214–46.

In these cases, the responsibility for sin is much more personal than in the consequences of sin that flow from Adam's disobedience alone. Our individual corruption proves that each human being is a sinner in his or her own right, and is happy to choose actions that lead to destruction (Rom. 1:32). Counseling in such situations seeks to love people by helping them see their sin, take responsibility for it, seek the forgiveness of God in Christ to atone for it, and put off earthly practices in pursuit of putting on the practices of God's chosen ones (Col. 3:1–17).

Relational Corruption

Because every sinful individual lives life with other sinful individuals, sin always has a relational impact. The sin of one person impacts another and creates pain. Friends quit speaking to one another, spouses divorce, parents abuse their children, Christians gossip about one another, and people sue their bosses for wrongful termination. In these as well as in other countless examples, we see the moral friction caused as sinners live together in a corrupt world.

Counseling in a world of relational brokenness is about walking with people who have sinned in their relationships, assisting them in seeing where they have wronged another person, and helping them to take responsibility through confession of sin and satisfaction of any restitution that may be required (Matt. 7:3–5). It is also about helping them to know what forgiveness and reconciliation look like when others have sinned against them (Matt. 18:15–35).

These three categories are commonplace for most Christians. Believers are accustomed to thinking about them. But they are absolutely revolutionary in the field of counseling. They are revolutionary for secular counseling practitioners who lack this organizing principle from God himself that arranges every single counseling problem. These categories are also revolutionary for many Christians who do not appreciate how comprehensive these categories are and how relevant they are to the counseling problems people face.

In instructing his people about sin, God has provided an incredible gift. There is no place else besides the Bible that includes such crucial information. There is no research study that demonstrates this truth, and there is no secular theorist who describes it. Ever since the scientific revolution touched the field of psychology in the late 1800s, the gathered forces of the Western scholarly world have struggled to describe what the nature of human problems is.[4] God alone tells us. And he tells us in shockingly moral categories: humans have defied God, leading to earth-shaking consequences. That defiance destroys our relationships and our lives, and ultimately ends in death.

This is the key to unlocking every counseling problem in the universe. And only those with access to God's special revelation know it. Christians know it from studying the Bible. And so we must conclude that counseling fallen people requires the Bible, because all counseling problems are sin problems, which the Bible alone understands. Any approach to counseling that is ignorant of the Bible's teaching on sin—or, which refuses to implement the Bible's teaching on sin—will be insufficient and, ultimately, unhelpful as a counseling resource. That is the argument contained herein.

The rest of this chapter will illustrate the argument in a specific counseling context. First, I will introduce you to a troubled young man I met several years ago whom I will refer to as Tyler. Next, I will introduce you to a Christian who has created a counseling system to help Tyler which does not understand the Bible's teaching on sin as a controlling reality for people like Tyler. The goal is to use an illustration to demonstrate the truth of my argument that counseling fallen people requires the Bible, which alone understands sin.

Counseling Tyler

I met Tyler several years ago when a lady in our church asked me to reach out to a man whom she knew who was struggling with his sexuality. She did not know what to say or do to help him with his problem. She did not even understand his problem, but she asked if he would be willing to meet with me, and he agreed.

On the appointed day, I arrived at Tyler's house and rang the bell. I was surprised by the figure who greeted me. The person standing in the door appeared to be a man who was making every effort to adopt the appearance of a woman. He had long, stringy blonde hair, his nails were manicured as a woman's might be, and he was wearing a very effeminate top, that was more blouse than shirt. When I asked for Tyler, the person facing me let me know in an artificially high voice that Tyler was the person with whom I was speaking; but, he added, he preferred to be called Tiffany.

---

[4] Lambert, *Biblical Counseling Movement after Adams*, 30–32.

I extended my hand, and the man I was invited to visit asked me in. As we sat down, I told him how happy I was to be able to spend time with him. I mentioned the name of our mutual friend and he smiled. He made clear that he knew that she had asked me to visit him because she thought he was "messed up." He disagreed with her opinion but really loved her, nevertheless.

Within a matter of moments Tyler and I were talking about his life. He began to share a painful story of always believing he was a girl trapped in a man's body. For as long as he could remember he wanted to be a girl, dress in girl's clothing, act like a girl, and play with girls. These intense desires and feelings were the source of tremendous pain. He did not fit in with any social group—not boys, not girls. He had conflicts at home with his parents and siblings. He had conflicts in his own heart every time he changed clothes, took a shower, used the restroom, or looked in the mirror. Tyler's strong internal sense of self was powerful. The shape of his body was also powerful. The two, however, were at odds and Tyler was miserable.

He spent years of his childhood in dark depression. As he moved into adolescence, the depression turned even darker as he began to contemplate suicide. He began to fantasize—even obsess—over his own death. It was at this point that Tyler's parents began to admit to themselves that the child they thought was strange was actually in trouble and needed a lot of help.

They began to seek help together and were connected with a network of therapists who identified Tyler's problem with the diagnosis of gender dysphoria, which refers to the emotional pain stemming from the disjunction between a person's perceived gender and biological sex. In therapy, Tyler discovered that a potential solution to his problem was gender reassignment surgery. Tyler could bring alignment between his physical body and his internal sense of self through a course of treatment, beginning with hormone therapy to alter the biological function of testosterone in his body and culminating in gender reassignment surgery.

As I sat with Tyler that afternoon at his house, he was in the advanced stages of hormone therapy, had finished the psychological evaluation required for approval of his gender reassignment operation, and was weeks away from surgery. He was ecstatic. Tyler's parents were a bit more dubious, but nobody could deny that, for the first time in his life, Tyler seemed truly happy, expectant, and content. Perhaps his life of sorrow was about to end.

Tyler's story is crushing. Any person of compassion is heartbroken by his experience of pain and his parents' sense of helplessness, and thus understands the desire to offer care and help. The issue of concern, however, is how to understand Tyler's problem and, based on that understanding, how to offer care. The care Tyler was receiving from secular professionals is understandable in the world in which we live. Christians must be concerned about how to engage that care from a biblical perspective, and must understand that the core issue is not change in and of itself but change that glorifies God.[5]

What is a Christian response to Tyler and the care he is receiving? The answer to that question is more complicated than you might imagine. Christians have disagreed for many decades about how to evaluate the standards of counseling care. The most significant approach to providing and evaluating counseling care, as noted above, rejects the authority and sufficiency of Scripture for counseling, and is called integrationism. That voice is the dominant one, and it is that voice on the issue of transgenderism that we must evaluate here.

Counseling and Integration

It is obvious to anyone reading Tyler's agonizing story that there is something wrong with his experience. It is plain that he feels life is not working out for him. As I have argued, any counseling approach that would help Tyler must not only acknowledge that something is wrong with Tyler's experience but must also understand what it is that is wrong. From a Christian perspective, which sees the Bible as authoritative for life and godliness, it is clear that sin looms large in Tyler's life. All three manifestations of sin in counseling are apparent. We see the cosmic corruption of sin in a world of such painful suffering, the individual corruption of sin in Tyler's willful rejection of who God made him to be, and relational corruption in the relationships that have been broken and strained in this situation. Sin is obviously at the root of every element of Tyler's struggle. That means that the Bible is required to make sense of Tyler's situation and to chart a course toward change.

But this conviction is quite controversial. Most believers in Christian higher education practice and teach an approach to counseling that does not

---

[5] Heath Lambert, "95 Theses for an Authentically Christian Commitment to Biblical Counseling," *Association of Certified Biblical Counselors*, https://s3-us-west-2.amazonaws.com/acbcdigitalresources/resources/2017%2C+95 +Theses+of+Biblical+Counseling/95+Theses+-+Heath+Lambert.pdf.

see Scripture as authoritative and sufficient for counseling conversations. Many of those Christians confess the authority of Scripture over all of life, but they do not embrace Scripture as a sufficient source of wisdom for counseling. They believe the Bible to be inspired and precious, but argue that it is a revelation of limited scope in need of crucial augmentation by sources from secular psychology. The worldview foundation that upholds their counseling is thus an integration of material from Scripture and various secular sources.[6]

A crucial book which relates an integrationist perspective on the transgender issues that constitute Tyler's struggle is *Understanding Gender Dysphoria: Navigating Transgender Issues in a Changing Culture*, by Mark Yarhouse.[7] Yarhouse seeks to explain a Christian understanding of gender dysphoria and transgender issues using three frameworks of understanding.

Yarhouse first discusses the integrity framework:

> From this perspective same-sex sexual behavior is sin in part because it does not "merge or join two persons into an integrated sexual whole"; the "essential maleness" and "essential femaleness" is not brought together as intended from creation. When extended to the discussion of transsexuality and cross-gender identification, the theological concerns rest in the "denial of the integrity of one's own sex and an overt attempt at marring the sacred image of maleness or femaleness formed by God."[8]

Yarhouse suggests that this framework is preferred by theologically conservative Christians. Yarhouse discusses Deuteronomy 22:5 and 23:1 as frequently cited biblical texts to support this framework. He also subsumes what he calls the "four acts of the biblical drama," namely, creation, fall,

---

[6] Many different labels exist for those who engage in such work, including integrationists, Christian counselors, Christian psychologists, and transformational psychologists. There are important distinctions between these and other labels, but they are all united around the view that the truths of Scripture must be augmented with findings from other areas to create a full-orbed foundation for counseling wisdom. I have written about this project in many places. See Stuart Scott and Heath Lambert, eds., *Counseling the Hard Cases: True Stories Illustrating the Sufficiency of God's Resources in Scripture* (Nashville: B&H, 2012), ch. 1.

[7] Mark A. Yarhouse, *Understanding Gender Dysphoria: Navigating Transgender Issues in a Changing Culture* (Downers Grove, IL: IVP Academic, 2015). Yarhouse writes from a distinctively integrationist perspective, provides a helpful survey of the issues in the transgender debate, and received a great deal of attention with the release of his book. *Christianity Today* even ran a cover story: "Understanding the Transgender Phenomenon," *Christianity Today*, June 8, 2015, https://www.christianitytoday.com/ct/2015/july-august/understanding-transgender-gender -dysphoria.html. Many books have been written in addition to Yarhouse's, however, which have received much less attention: Andrew Walker, *God and the Transgender Debate: What Does the Bible Actually Say about Gender Identity?* (Epsom, Surrey, UK: Good Book Company, 2017); Vaughan Roberts, *Transgender* (Epsom, Surrey, UK: Good Book Company, 2016); Denny Burk and Heath Lambert, *Transforming Homosexuality: What the Bible Says about Sexual Orientation and Change* (Phillipsburg, NJ: P&R, 2015); Denny Burk, *What Is the Meaning of Sex?* (Wheaton, IL: Crossway, 2013); R. Albert Mohler Jr., *Desire and Deceit: The Real Cost of the New Sexual Tolerance* (Colorado Springs: Multnomah, 2008).

[8] Yarhouse, *Gender Dysphoria*, 46, quoting Robert A. J. Gagnon, "Transexuality and Ordination" (2007): www.rob gagnon.net/articles/TransexualityOrdination.pdf.

redemption, and consummation in this framework.[9] But he uses only the first of the four "frameworks." Yarhouse highlights the disability framework next:

> A second way to think about gender dysphoria is with reference to the mental health dimensions of the phenomenon. I refer to this as the disability framework. For Christians who are drawn more to this framework, gender dysphoria is viewed as a result of living in a fallen world in which the condition—like so many mental health concerns—is a nonmoral reality. Whether we consider brain-sex theory or any other explanatory framework for the origins of the phenomenon, the causal pathways and existing structures are viewed by proponents of the disability framework as not functioning as originally intended.[10]

This framework, quite different from the integrity framework, understands transgender behavior to be part of a fallen world that, nevertheless, is not sinful itself but is a nonmoral mental health problem. Yarhouse finally discusses the diversity framework:

> A third way to think about transgender issues is to see them as something to be celebrated, honored or revered. The sociocultural context in which we live in the West is rapidly moving in this direction. I think of this as a diversity framework. The diversity framework highlights transgender issues as reflecting an identity and culture to be celebrated as an expression of diversity. Current models that celebrate a transgender identity and community reflect this framework.[11]

Where the integrity framework views transgenderism as wrong, and the disability framework views transgenderism as a nonmoral problem, this framework understands transgenderism as an expression of human nature that is to be embraced and celebrated. It is the framework adopted by the LGBTQ movement and, Yarhouse notes, is the framework that is becoming the most popular in developed countries in the West.

With three different frameworks the question becomes: Which framework should guide an authentically Christian understanding? Yarhouse provides his answer:

> My concern is that any one of these three frameworks—to the exclusion of the best the others have to offer—will likely be an inadequate response for the Christian community. My own leaning is to identify strengths in each

---

[9] Yarhouse, *Gender Dysphoria*, 31–46.
[10] Yarhouse, *Gender Dysphoria*, 48.
[11] Yarhouse, *Gender Dysphoria*, 50.

framework, to essentially see these as lenses through which we see the topic under discussion. Rather than select one lens to look at gender dysphoria, we can look through all three, identify the strengths of each framework and apply it to how we approach the topic and the person who is navigating this terrain. What we have then is what I refer to as an integrated framework that draws on the best of each existing framework.[12]

This is where we see the integrationism of Yarhouse. He starts with the teaching of Scripture but, finding it insufficient as a guide on these issues, augments the teaching of Scripture with secular resources that he arranges in two other categories.[13]

Yarhouse's integrated approach to gender dysphoria and transgenderism comprises the foundational worldview upon which he builds a system of counseling care. Yarhouse makes his system of counseling care clear. After engaging in an informative survey of the available options, from a wait-and-see approach for younger persons, to cross-dressing, and from hormone therapy to gender reassignment surgery, Yarhouse acknowledges that such procedures exist on a continuum from least to most invasive. When it comes to making recommendations about those interventions, Yarhouse says,

> On a continuum from least to most invasive [this approach] recognizes that hormonal treatment and sex reassignment would be the most invasive. This is not to say a Christian would not consider the most invasive procedures; I know many who have. But they would not begin there, nor would they take such a decision lightly. Ideally, they would consider options based upon the input and recommendations from experts in this area, as well as thoughtful and prayerful consideration with a discernment group of those whose perspectives they respect.[14]

Yarhouse's counseling approach is very carefully stated and is framed by his commitment to a worldview that integrates the teachings of Scripture with the findings of secular professionals.

---

[12] Yarhouse, *Gender Dysphoria*, 53.
[13] One fascinating observation about Yarhouse's attempt to integrate these frameworks comes in the fact that secular proponents of the disability and diversity frameworks profoundly disagree with one another's positions. For example, Paul McHugh, former Chief of Psychiatry at John's Hopkins, profoundly disagrees with the LGBTQ movement as to how transgender behaviors should be addressed. LGBTQ leaders have, in turn, objected to McHugh's work in the strongest possible terms. Below, I shall argue that Yarhouse's attempt to integrate the biblical and secular teachings on transgenderism is fatally flawed. The point here is that the competing secular approaches would argue the same thing against Yarhouse, that the different frameworks cannot be integrated. Such widespread disagreement raises serious questions about the ability to integrate any of these approaches, as Yarhouse is so inclined to do. See, e.g., Paul McHugh, "Transgender Surgery Isn't the Solution," *Wall Street Journal*, June 12, 2014.
[14] Yarhouse, *Gender Dysphoria*, 124.

On the one hand, Yarhouse's commitment to the integrity framework leads him to a preference for the least invasive means to resolve gender dysphoria, like cross-dressing. He is not eager to alter permanently the bodies of human beings through hormone therapy or surgery. On the other hand, Yarhouse's commitment to the disability and diversity frameworks prohibit him from absolutely ruling out the most invasive options, like surgery. Indeed, Yarhouse argues that people who choose these options must, ultimately, be embraced by the Christian community.[15]

Yarhouse represents an integrative approach to counseling "Tyler." Yarhouse, who in early engagements with Tyler may have encouraged a very slow approach, would ultimately not have refused but embraced Tyler's decision to attempt to change his biological sex with a surgical procedure.

Counseling Ruined Sinners

My goal in this chapter is to argue that counseling fallen people requires the Bible because all counseling problems are sin problems, which the Bible alone understands, and to illustrate that conviction with a specific counseling engagement. It is the goal of Scripture to illuminate all areas of life and expose us to God's perspective on each area (Ps. 119:105). When the light of Scripture's teaching on sin is held up to Tyler's situation and to Yarhouse's counsel, it alone illuminates the situation to help us see as we should.

Scripture Alone Illuminates the Sinful Ruin of Tyler's Problem

Scripture shines on Tyler's situation and helps us understand his trouble from the perspective of God's worldview.

First, sin has corrupted Tyler's thinking. Scripture is clear that God made Tyler as a man and not as a woman (Gen. 1:26–27). In a fallen world the physical consequences of sin can create biological problems, like intersex, where it is challenging to discern whether a person is a man or a woman. The problem of intersex, however, is very different than transgenderism, and it is not Tyler's difficulty. Tyler, like every other male, has X and Y chromosomes and can never be anything different, no matter what kind of surgical mutilations he endures. This is what is true and, deep down, Tyler knows it

---

[15] Later Yarhouse adds, "The Christian community would do well to recognize the conflict [faced by persons dealing with transgender struggles] and try to work with the person and with those who have expertise in this area to find the least invasive ways to manage the dysphoria and to offer compassion and mercy when that has not been possible" (Yarhouse, *Gender Dysphoria*, 144).

to be true (Rom. 2:14–15). But in his sin, Tyler suppresses the truth and tells himself lies (Eph. 4:17–18).

This is the information illuminated for Christians by the light of Scripture. Standing on the sufficient authority of Scripture, Christians are not confused by Tyler's distorted thinking. We are not tempted to compromise simply because a psychiatric community is supporting his distorted thinking. The Bible exposes the situation and clarifies our thinking. It lights up the darkness. Such illumination leads to a stunning amount of clarity in a world where some of the most educated professionals on the planet are unwilling and unable to declare what Tyler's gender is. They have to listen to him say what he thinks it is. As they listen to him, they are cooperating with his fallen assessment as a man whose thinking is corrupted by sin.

Second, Tyler's emotions have been corrupted by sin. Because Tyler suppresses the truth in unrighteousness, his heart is not wired to be appropriately thrilled by the truth and saddened by falsehood. His heart, instead, malfunctions and works in reverse. Tyler is devastated by the truth of who God made him to be and rejoices at a futile effort to change it. Christians who know the truth see his pain and weep with him; but we weep for different reasons. These Christians and Tyler will both have tears, but those tears will spring from very different wells, and flow in opposite directions. Tyler weeps because he hates the truth; Christians, standing on the authority and sufficiency of Scripture, must weep because Tyler cannot see the truth. Tyler's tears lead him to increasingly extreme efforts to conceal the truth. The tears of a faithful Christian will lead to efforts to expose and embrace the truth.

Scripture Alone Illuminates the Sinful Ruin of the Unbelievers Trying to Help Tyler

Scripture shines on the counsel Tyler is receiving from a team of medical and therapeutic professionals and helps us understand their counsel from the perspective of God's worldview.

Tyler has a team of abundantly educated, highly trained, and expertly certified professionals. They are offering him counsel, dispensing drugs and hormones, evaluating his psyche, and planning to remove parts of his body in a highly sophisticated operation costing hundreds of thousands of dollars. But with all their education, all their training, and with all the cultural approval they have to engage in acts that are, candidly, shocking, they still have the same problem Tyler has. Their thinking is corrupted by the fall (cf. Eph. 4:17–18), and their separation from God has blinded their eyes so that they cannot know the truth. All of the information they have about the human body and Tyler's situation just gives them more knowledge to sin against.

Sinning against such a vast body of knowledge actually thickens the plot for Tyler. In Scripture, when someone possesses more knowledge and uses that increased knowledge to help others live faithlessly, they compound their own sin and guilt (cf. 2 Pet. 2). Tyler is sinful in his own right, but he has found a group of other sinners who are helping him to live against the word of God. Furthermore, this group of people helping him down the path of sin are doing so at Tyler's most crucial moment of need. Instead of pointing him to hope and life, they are leading him to death and destruction. The consequences of sin are thus compounded. It is important to note that this is of course what we expect from ruined sinners who do not believe in Jesus's death and resurrection. The light of Scripture, however, shines bright clarity on a matter such as this for the Christian.

Scripture Alone Illuminates the Sinful Ruin of the Believers Offering Distorted Care to Tyler

Scripture shines on the perspective on transgenderism offered by Christians like Mark Yarhouse and helps us understand his integrative approach from the perspective of God's worldview.

For all the sophistication in Yarhouse's attempt to integrate three different frameworks on this issue, his integrated worldview still has him conceding to the process of grossly extreme practices like sex-reassignment surgery. This reality places him in the same place as radical LGBTQ activists and dramatically to the left of conservative Christians embracing the so-called integrity framework. It even places him to the left of many conservative secularists embracing the disability framework. To call this a serious problem is to say the absolute least.

Yarhouse gestures in the direction of Scripture when he evaluates a handful of texts that address gender and surveys the four acts of the biblical drama. But Yarhouse will not give Scripture the final word on issues of gender and biological sex. The problem is not merely that he listens to other perspectives outside of Scripture. The problem is that, when all is said and done, Yarhouse's diversity framework ends up exerting a controlling influence over his self-styled integrity framework. Yarhouse, in other words, allows those who advocate for hormonal therapy and sex reassignment surgery to win the day over what God says in his word. Yarhouse unfortunately is plagued by the same impact of sin on his thinking as the unbeliever who is about to have sex reassignment surgery and the secular professionals who will do the work.

Such significant error in the thinking of a Christian causes serious concern. After all, Christians have been redeemed by Christ. The apostle Paul makes clear that Christians are not to think the same way that unbelievers think, in the futility of their minds (Eph. 4:17–18). But the apostle Paul also teaches that Christians still struggle with sin (Rom. 6:12–14), are growing in grace by degrees (2 Cor. 3:18), and that the renewal of our minds is an ongoing process (Col. 3:9–10). Salvation in Christ does not effect the full and final release from all the presence and consequence of sin.

Yarhouse is on the same journey to be rid of the presence of sin that all Christians are on. And yet, his error is not restricted to himself, but is also in print. This places Yarhouse in the same situation as the other experts mentioned above and means that Yarhouse is sinning against increased knowledge. But the problem is worse in Yarhouse's case because he is a believer in Christ. In the Bible, when people in the believing community sin against increased knowledge, and help others sin against that knowledge, it creates a very serious problem: that of the false prophet, as discussed in 2 Peter 2. Christians are not allowed to say "peace" when there is no peace. We are not allowed to agree, however tentatively, with the most radical secularists in the culture who undermine the truth of God. When the impact of sin in the lives of believers is compounded with the sins of others, the consequences for people like Tyler and, indeed, for our entire culture, are serious in the extreme.

Counseling and Good News

I sat with Tyler for a long time at his house that afternoon. I listened carefully to his painful story and felt badly for all the suffering he had experienced in his life. When he finished his story, I requested permission to ask him a question, which he granted. I pointed out that the narrative that controlled his life was the fight to transform his body into what he sensed it ought to be in his mind. His life was controlled by the desire to look like a woman. He nodded that that was true. Then I posed the question: In light of the fact that he was preparing to endure a surgery that would permanently alter his appearance to resolve the conflict between his mind and his body, how could he be sure that it was not his body that was the problem, but rather the way he was thinking about his body? Tyler could not answer my question.

I pointed out that there was another narrative that controlled his life besides the one to become a woman. Then I told Tyler about Jesus Christ. I shared with him about how human beings have sinned against a God who is holy and righteous. I told him how he sent his Son to obey the law throughout his life and to suffer the penalty for our disobedience on the cross. I told him that Jesus rose from the dead and ascended to heaven, where he is reigning on his throne. I told Tyler that one of his sins was that he wanted to be different than what God made him to be. And I told him that he could repent of all of his sin and trust in Jesus Christ and that Jesus would forgive him, change him, and give him eternal life with him. And then I asked Tyler if he wanted to turn from his sin to trust in Jesus.

Tyler's answer was fascinating. For our entire conversation, Tyler had been falsely raising his voice to an unnaturally high pitch in an effort to make his inherently low voice sound more feminine. But it took work to keep his voice that high, and as he talked, his register would slip lower and lower. After a time, Tyler would eventually notice that his voice was getting lower and he would quickly jerk it up into a high falsetto. Tyler's voice thus modulated through the octaves for our entire time together. But when I asked him about repenting of his sins and trusting in Christ, he looked at me, sat for a moment, and then in a low, flat, baritone voice simply said, "No."

It was the most honest he had been during our entire conversation. Unfortunately, even his honest expression of a lack of interest in Christ was further evidence of a heart devastated by sin. The same person who found it impossible to embrace his manhood also found it impossible to embrace the most glorious man in history, the only Savior from sin.

And this gets to another important lesson about counseling in general and counseling Tyler in particular. That lesson is that people who seek out counseling care are hurting, and all counseling seeks to deliver good news. Tyler was looking for good news. The message of judgment that had come to him was that there was a terrible conflict between his sense of self and the image reflected in the mirror. Then he received "good news." Secular professionals shared a message that he could be different by submitting to a battery of psychiatric evaluations, hormones, and, ultimately, a knife. Tyler embraced the good news he heard and was happy. But Christians standing on the authority and sufficiency of Scripture know that that good news is not truly good because that good news will not last.

The only good news that lasts is the good news of Jesus Christ crucified, buried, and risen for sinners. He is the good news regardless of the corruption that sinners face, whether cosmic, relational, or individual. If you reject the Bible's message about sin you can never hope to embrace in counseling the good news that saves from sin. The Bible alone understands the problem of sin. And the Bible alone understands that the solution to sin is in Jesus's perfect sacrifice. That is why counseling people in a fallen world requires the Bible.

30

Preaching to Sinners
in a Secular Age

R. Albert Mohler Jr.

Whatever Happened to Sin?

The modern preacher confronts an immediate perplexity—the doctrine of sin is absolutely essential to Christianity, but it is increasingly foreign if not noxious to our modern age. There is no Christianity without a biblical doctrine of sin, and yet that doctrine and the fundamental understanding of sin are now largely absent from our society in any explicit form. Beyond that, a consciousness of sin is increasingly undermined by the massive shift in worldviews that has taken place in the last few centuries, in particular from 1900 to the present. Preachers now confront the reality that much of our theological vocabulary stems from a language that is currently missing from so many of those who live around us. We have now reached the point that sin and its related biblical truths are no longer a part of what we will see described as the "social imaginary" of an increasingly secular people.

The project of eliminating sin as a meaningful category in our society has been intentional, in the sense that the modern mind is increasingly committed to structures of thought that eliminate any theological referent at all, and especially any notion of human moral responsibility combined with the inevitability of divine judgment. The great therapeutic and intellectual turns of the twentieth century have now given birth to the abundant confusions of the twenty-first century. We confront millions of human beings who lack a

898 SIN AND DEPRAVITY IN PASTORAL PRACTICE

knowledge of the one true God and, quite inevitably, also lack a knowledge of themselves. One thing many moderns seem absolutely convinced of, is that whatever they may be, they are *not* sinners. The modern project is thus celebrated as an achievement of human liberation. We have now liberated ourselves from the repressive and unhealthy notion of sin, but the truth is we are no happier. The liberation from sin has turned out to be far less fulfilling than its prophets will admit. Christians now face the challenge of contending for the reality of sin, not only as a meaningful category with therapeutic implications, but as an objective truth without which we can understand neither ourselves as individuals nor the reality of human society. Of course, this comes hand in hand with the truth that the entire Christian worldview based upon Holy Scripture is now *terra incognita* to millions of our neighbors. Furthermore, as we shall see, we also face the fundamental fact that many of our own church members and those who identify as fellow believers also lack any biblical notion of sin. This means, therefore, that they also do not understand the gospel. Actually, that is one of the most bracing realizations that the gospel-committed preacher must now confront. When we use the language of sin, so essential to the gospel and to the description of the human predicament, we are using language that will be met with both resistance and befuddlement. And, compounding the problem, many of those who hear our messages will believe themselves to be in agreement with what we are saying about sin, without fully taking into account what such a theological affirmation would mean.

Much of this was apparent by the year 1973 when psychiatrist Karl Menninger wrote an unexpectedly influential book with an attention-getting title, *Whatever Became of Sin?*[1] Menninger was one of the nation's most preeminent psychiatrists as well as a professing Christian. The Menninger Clinic, then located in Topeka, Kansas, was one of the most respected psychiatric treatment centers in the United States. Menninger's book caught many by surprise because of his frankness in posing the question. After all, what *had* become of sin? Interestingly, Menninger's book was influential, at least in part, precisely because he was speaking as a psychiatrist rather than as a theologian. The society might have given scant attention to a work of a theologian inquiring into the disappearance of sin. But by 1973, the ascent of both the therapeutic and the medical in the hierarchy of expertise meant

[1] Karl Menninger, *Whatever Became of Sin?* (New York: Hawthorn, 1973).

that Menninger's posing of the question caught attention. Menninger's point was that he saw the practice of psychiatry as hopeless without the category of sin. Even then, Menninger was convinced that treating human behavior and the most basic human problem merely as psychiatric pathology was not enough. Nevertheless, by the time Menninger wrote his book and posed his question, sin had disappeared to the extent that very few saw any hope of its reappearance.

It is interesting to note that sin could not disappear alone. Christian doctrines are not isolated propositions, for Christianity is a comprehensive system of truth. Thus, sin could only disappear because other major Christian doctrines also vanished from much of the national consciousness. The British novelist David Lodge noticed the absence of hell by the decade of the 1960s: "At some point in the nineteen-sixties, Hell disappeared. No one could say for certain when this happened. First it was there, then it wasn't."[2] Similarly, writing roughly a decade after Menninger had noted the disappearance of sin, University of Chicago historian Martin Marty noted that hell was also missing from the modern consciousness. "Hell disappeared. No one noticed," he observed.[3]

Addressing the issue in a more explicitly theological frame, Thomas G. Long of Princeton Theological Seminary observed, "The word 'sin' has experienced a serious deflation in the working vocabulary of our culture. Once upon a time, 'sin' was a majestic word, a necessary word, a word without which we could not describe our humanness, a word that, in a single syllable, could both climb giddily to the heights of human folly and crawl into the depths of human ruination. In the last few decades, however, the meaning of sin has diminished and deteriorated; sin has been demoted."[4] Long accurately described the demotion of sin, suggesting that by the 1990s, sin was "forced to walk the streets on the seamy side of town, left to describe those obvious, and in some way, most superficial frailties of the flesh."[5] Clearly, Long saw that sin had not completely escaped modern reference, but, having been demoted to far less than its biblical reality, sin was something that brought a smirk to the face, rather than contrition to the heart. How did this happen?

---

[2] David Lodge, *Bodies and Souls* (New York: Penguin, 1980), 1. Interestingly, the novel was originally entitled *How Far Can You Go?* (London: Martin Secker & Warburg, 1980).
[3] Martin E. Marty, "Hell Disappeared. No One Noticed. A Civic Argument," *HTR* 78 (1985): 381–98.
[4] Thomas G. Long, "God Be Merciful to Me, a Miscalculator," *TT* 50.2 (July 1993): 165.
[5] Long, "God Be Merciful to Me, a Miscalculator," 165.

A Secular Age

Our ability to describe the modern mind is conscribed by our own ability to trace intellectual currents and how the basic worldview of entire societies can be transformed. By any measure, the most fundamental transformation of the human mind in the West is described as secularization. Nevertheless, secularization (and the condition of being secular) does not mean what either the original prophets of secularization or many modern people assume. The original prophets of secularization, coming fast on the heels of the development of sociology as a way of explaining the world without theological referent, assumed that modernity would inevitably mean the decline of all religious forms and belief in God. Figures such as Emile Durkheim and Max Weber argued that the modern world was, to use Weber's term, "disenchanted." The loss of enchantment meant that societies and the people who comprised them would lose all necessity of religious reference and all substance of religious intuition and belief. As it happens, secularization has meant exactly that, but in a limited frame. The prophets of secularization were right that the society would move in a secular direction, but they were wrong about the shape secularity would take.

In some parts of the world, and in some social sectors of our world, secularization has indeed meant the disappearance of belief in God and, in some cases, a complete loss of theological memory. Thus, much of Western Europe has depopulated churches and empty cathedrals. These structures have become the physical fulfillment of Shakespeare's vision of "bare ruined choirs."[6] Shakespeare's tragic vision has become a reality throughout much of what sociologist Peter Berger calls, "Eurosecularity."[7] Nevertheless, as Berger noted, much of the rest of the world has seen "a veritable explosion of religious faith."[8] But this explosion has taken place outside of modern Western nations, for the most part. At the same time, one of the most interesting intellectual reassessments of our times is the way Berger and others have had to reassess the theory of secularization. As far back as the 1960s, Berger had argued for the classical theory of secularization—that religious belief, practice, and intuition would simply disappear in the face of modernity. By the 1990s, Berger was ready to reassess the theory. With bracing intellectual

[6] William Shakespeare, "Sonnet 73."
[7] Peter L. Berger, "Secularization Falsified," *First Things* 180 (February 2008), https://www.firstthings.com/article/2008/02/secularization-falsified.
[8] Berger, "Secularization Falsified."

honesty, Berger concluded that he and his fellow sociologists, in the main, had been wrong to believe that modernity would mean secularization, pure and simple. By 2008, Berger would argue for a fundamental reconsideration of secularization, that modernity is "characterized by an increasing plurality," rather than pure secularity.[9] One of the problems the prophets of secularization faced at the end of the twentieth century was the fact that American religion appeared to be quite robust. Even as Europe was increasingly marked by vacant cathedrals, the United States saw a nearly endless construction of mega-churches. At first glance, this would appear to completely refute the idea of secularization. On the other hand, as Berger understood, secularization could take different forms. In the world of "Eurosecularity," the classical theory of secularization actually followed its predicted course. Berger would quip that the classical theory of secularization failed except in two places— Western Europe and on American university campuses. There was considerable truth in his sarcasm. But the most important issue in Berger's analysis is to understand that he saw secularization, especially in the United States, as allowing for the continuation of religious belief, but with those beliefs largely evacuated of the cognitive content and moral demand understood by previous generations. Pluralization created a platform of tentativeness and qualification, for every theological claim and what Berger memorably named "plausibility structures" had shifted. Put another way, much of American Christianity, and the larger American culture, became not so much *anti-theological* as *non-theological*. Furthermore, as we shall see, many of those who considered themselves Christian believers were (and are) actually operating under fundamentally secular categories.

The most important analysis of the secular condition was offered by Canadian philosopher Charles Taylor in his magisterial work, *A Secular Age*.[10] Taylor asked the question bluntly: "What does it mean to say that we live in a secular age?"[11] Taylor asserted that, beyond doubt, we live in a secular age, but he went on to say, "It is not so clear in what this secularity consists."[12] On the one hand, religious belief is now seen as an option for many, but the very fact that it is optional means that it is no longer a religious belief in the classic sense. Taylor's insights are incredibly important for modern ministry

[9] Berger, "Secularization Falsified."
[10] Charles Taylor, *A Secular Age* (Cambridge, MA: Belknap/Harvard University Press, 2007).
[11] Taylor, *Secular Age*, 1.
[12] Taylor, *Secular Age*, 1.

and the modern preacher. In one of his most important arguments, Taylor described the secular condition of our society as "one which takes us from a society in which it was virtually impossible not to believe in God, to one in which faith, even for the staunchest believer, is one human possibility among others."[13] In other words, "Belief in God is no longer axiomatic. There are alternatives. And this will also likely mean that at least in certain milieu, it will be hard to sustain one's faith. There will be people who feel bound to give it up, even though they mourn its loss. . . . There will be many others to whom faith never seems an eligible possibility."[14]

Taylor traced the development of Western cultures through a succession of what he calls "conditions of belief." Actually, the very notion of "conditions of belief" is one of Taylor's most important contributions. He reminds us that beliefs are always set upon a certain set of intellectual presuppositions and conditions that must be observed and acknowledged. A change in those fundamental conditions means that the entire superstructure of belief is transformed. Taylor traces Western thought through three major conditions of belief, in historical succession. First came the condition in which it was *impossible not to believe*. In this condition, unbelief was simply an option unavailable to people of the time. Prior to 1500, for example, unbelief in the form of anything like atheism or agnosticism was simply intellectually impossible because it was missing from what Taylor terms the "social imaginary"—the sum total of available ideas at any given cultural moment.[15] Unbelief was simply not an option, intellectually speaking. All that began to change with the advent of the transitions to modernity and eventually with the arrival of the modern age itself. The second major condition of belief was one in which it became *possible not to believe*. In this transitional stage (in which many societies may now be found) the social imaginary begins to include secular and nontheistic options. Unbelief becomes a choice, an available option in one form or another. The third condition of belief is what we now find in the context of late modernity—the condition in which it is *impossible to believe*. This describes much of Western Europe and many sectors of society in the United States, particularly associated with modern academic culture, high technology, urbanization, and the so-called cultural creatives. In Taylor's words,

---

[13] Taylor, *Secular Age*, 3.
[14] Taylor, *Secular Age*, 3.
[15] See Charles Taylor, *Modern Social Imaginaries* (Durham, NC: Duke University Press, 2004).

We have also changed from a condition in which belief was the default option, not just for the naïve but also for those who knew, considered, talked about atheism; to a condition in which for more and more people unbelieving construals seem at first blush the only plausible ones.[16]

Under this third condition of belief, theistic belief becomes intellectually, socially, politically, and individually impossible. Unbelief becomes the only plausible position.

Our challenge in preaching to sinners in a secular age is certainly complicated by the arrival of this third condition of belief. Nevertheless, many of the people to whom we preach will actually be operating under the *second* condition of belief. They may well acknowledge that unbelief is a possibility, but they consider themselves to be *believers*. The problem is, as Charles Taylors understands, that belief in God does not mean in the twenty-first century what it meant in previous intellectual epochs. As Taylor states,

> To put the point in different terms, belief in God isn't quite the same thing in 1500 and 2000. I'm not referring to the fact that even orthodox Christianity has undergone important changes (e.g., the "decline of hell," new understandings of the atonement). Even in regard to identical creedal propositions, there is an important difference. This emerges as soon as we take account of the fact that all beliefs are held within a context or framework of the-taken-for-granted, which usually remains tacit, and may even be as yet unacknowledged by the agent, because it was never formulated.[17]

Thus, many of those who hear us preach will understand themselves to be believers, but in an oddly modern sense in which belief has now become their *choice*, and to some extent, the expression of the self, rather than a confession of objective and revealed truth.

For our purposes, the analysis of Charles Taylor is incredibly helpful. His tracing of secularization in terms of the successive conditions of belief, his notion of the social imaginary, and his understanding of how belief has changed in the modern era, all help us to understand both the thinking of those who hear us preach and the challenge of preaching faithfully in this context. One other crucial category from Taylor is especially helpful. In the transition to modernity, Taylor traces the shift from the "porous self" to the "buffered self." Prior to the arrival of late modernity, the self in society was

---

[16] Taylor, *Secular Age*, 12.
[17] Taylor, *Secular Age*, 14.

"porous," meaning that the self was understood to be vulnerable to external realities, such as moral scrutiny, the affirmation of an objective morality, and the eventual judgment of God. But the modern self is a "buffered self" that is protected by the lineaments of the modern mind and the ubiquity of therapeutic categories. The buffered self is largely impervious to external scrutiny and protected from external evaluation, the threatened authority of objective truth, and any sense of a divine Judge and Lawgiver. Again, we have to take into consideration the fact that many people who consider themselves Christian believers actually define their own self, explicitly or not, as a "buffered self." They are actually hiding behind therapeutic categories and have shielded themselves, morally, theologically, and spiritually, from external scrutiny and judgment.

Finally, we have to consider the contribution of sociologists such as Robert Bellah. In 1985, Bellah and a team of co-researchers released a major study on American religion and, citing Alexis de Tocqueville, the American heart. The product of their work was *Habits of the Heart: Individualism and Commitment in American Life*.[18] Bellah was already well known for his description of American "civil religion," by which he meant a vaguely nontheistic but culturally unifying form of religion, borrowed explicitly from Christianity, that became something of the glue that held American society together. By the last quarter of the twentieth century, Christian theologians and preachers often observed what is rightly described as "cultural Christianity," which is what Bellah was describing as civil religion. In *Habits of the Heart*, Bellah and his team demonstrated that modernity had brought a fundamental change in the American mode of thinking, and they pointed to a rather radical individualism as one of the defining marks of the American heart. Their research took the form of thousands of interviews with a cross section of Americans. Famously, one of their interviews was with a woman who, for the purposes of the research, was identified as Sheila. Sheila had taken American individualism to the extreme, explaining, "I believe in God. I'm not a religious fanatic. I can't remember the last time I went to church. My faith has carried me a long way. It's Sheilaism. Just my own little voice."[19]

While few Americans would go so far as to describe their religious convictions as their individualized form of "Sheilaism," the fact is Sheila was

---

[18] Robert N. Bellah, Richard Madsen, William M. Sullivan, Ann Swidler, and Steven M. Tipton, *Habits of the Heart: Individualism and Commitment in American Life* (Berkeley: University of California Press, 1985).
[19] Bellah, et al., *Habits of the Heart*, 221.

hardly alone in describing her religion almost exclusively in terms of herself. Any biblical notion of sin is fundamentally absent without leave from many modern minds and hearts. This presents the thinking Christian, and especially the Christian preacher, with an enormous challenge.

The debate about secularization will continue, but the fundamental reality is undeniable. A seismic shift has taken place in the thinking of those who inhabit the cultures of modernity. It is a phenomenon that is both secular and plural, marked by disenchantment and disengagement. These same societies and the inhabitants of these societies can also demonstrate a remarkable religiosity, sometimes channeled into forms that are recognizably religious, while at other times they take the form of political energy or absorption of the self—or some combination thereof.

I contend for an understanding of secularization as a process and of the secular condition as a reality by underlining the fact that *to be secular is to live without a sense of the binding authority of theism*. It is not that no form of religiosity, religious practice, or religious belief is present. It is rather the condition marked by the absence of the *binding authority* of theism. What is missing is the very character of biblical religion as found in God's relationship with Israel, and most consummately, in the gospel of Christ. In this sense, oddly enough, millions and millions of people are both religious and secular. But in that combination, the most important reality is the secular.

Theological Transitions

The larger sociological shifts would be quite sufficient to underline the depth of our challenge. Nevertheless, we also have to recognize that significant theological transitions also contributed to the eclipse and demolition of sin. Much of this can be traced back to the origins of modern theology, particularly to the emphasis on religious experience and subjectivity made by figures such as Friedrich Schleiermacher. Protestant liberalism redefined sin as the inevitable consequence of redefining the doctrine of God. Following the course of the Enlightenment, the progenitors of theological liberalism saw the traditional Christian doctrine of sin, quite rightly, as part of the larger framework of theological orthodoxy. This was the very framework that Protestant liberals sought to overcome. Enlightenment philosophers had already dismissed sin as an ontological category. Immanuel Kant rejected the doctrine of original sin as "an affront to human freedom."[20] In the United States, the founding fathers of Protestant liberalism argued, in essence, for the rescue of Christian morality at the expense of orthodox Christian theology. Those early liberals of the late nineteenth and early twentieth centuries had no intentions of dethroning sin as a moralistic category, but their redefinition of God at the expense of divine holiness, righteousness, and justice, and their redefinition of the gospel meant that they were undermining any absolute and stable foundation for morality. Add to this the revolution brought by figures such as Walter Rauschenbusch and other promoters the Social Gospel. Rauschenbusch, appalled by the conditions of evil in society, largely (if not exclusively) transformed the doctrine of sin from an individual's offense against a holy God to injustice in social structures and the larger society. Even where the Social Gospel was not explicitly affirmed, its presuppositions and intuitions became deeply imbedded in much of twentieth-century Protestantism. By the midpoint of the twentieth century, a theologian such as H. Richard Niebuhr would rightly define Protestant liberalism as preaching that "a God without wrath brought men without sin into a kingdom without judgment through the ministrations of a Christ without a cross."[21] Notice that key phrase, "men without sin."

Even more significantly, it was Richard Niebuhr's more famous brother, Reinhold Niebuhr, whose affirmation of theological and moral "realism" supposedly represented a recovery of an Augustinian notion of sin. Actually, it was only a very partial recovery. Niebuhr's realism represented an Augustinian turn insofar as he affirmed the reality of human evil in the face of modern sophisticated denials. As Niebuhr bore witness to the twentieth century, it was fundamentally dishonest and dangerous to deny the human capacity for evil. At the same time, however, Niebuhr transferred almost exclusive concern to the sinfulness of society rather than the sinfulness of human individuals. This found its clearest expression in the title of Niebuhr's most famous work, *Moral Man and Immoral Society*.[22] Even those who did not read the book, but saw the title, got the point. The shift from a concern for individual sin to a near exclusive concern for sin in structural and systemic manifestations marked what was celebrated as the recovery of "realism" in theology. As such assumptions filtered down through society, sin became associated with particularly scandalous behavior, behavior that could be dismissed as unseemly

---

[20] Mark Lilla, *The Stillborn God: Religion, Politics, and the Modern West* (New York: Vintage, 2007), 144.
[21] H. Richard Niebuhr, *The Kingdom of God in America* (New York: Harper & Row, 1957).
[22] Reinhold Niebuhr, *Moral Man and Immoral Society* (New York: Scribner, 1932).

and embarrassing, and systemic or social sin that was the inevitable result of corporate human evil. When it came to individuals, sin was continually discounted. Or, as Thomas Long argued, the sinner became merely a "miscalculator." Humans make mistakes. Who needs the category of sin?

The Modern Reduction

Modernity has also brought a radically redefined concept of humanity, and of our place in the cosmos. Worldviews based in naturalism and materialism became, as Charles Taylor would remind us, *possible* in the modern age. For many people in modern society, especially those who operate from a scientific, technological, or humanistic perspective, a naturalistic and materialistic understanding of humanity (and the entire cosmos) is the only *possible* affirmation. All of this would be impossible without the Darwinian revolution and the unwinding of the consequences of naturalistic evolution. A universe without a Creator is a universe without any practical notion of sin. In any worldview that is honestly and consistently materialistic, morality is nothing more than a survival mechanism among human beings. Indeed, honesty should compel the naturalist and the materialist to admit that morality is nothing but fictive. Nevertheless, it turns out the notions of morality are rather indispensable—in social terms—even if fictional. (Try parenting a toddler while trying to deny the reality of human agency.) Few are so direct and candid as Sean Carroll, professor at the California Institute of Technology. In his book *The Big Picture*, Carroll argues that the cosmos is inherently meaningless, and that the laws of physics eliminate any possible meaning in the cosmos at large or in our own lives lived on a smaller frame.[23] In his book, Carroll offered a bit of "existential therapy."[24] He went on to say, "I want to argue that, though we are part of a universe that runs according to impersonal underlying laws, we nevertheless matter."[25] Rather pathetically, he also attempted to argue that the meaning "we find in life is not transcendent, but it's no less meaningful for that."[26] It seems unlikely that many can be convinced that life has meaning if that meaning is not transcendent. On the other hand, many modern people probably seek to avoid asking the question altogether. When it comes to morality, Carroll admits that the pressing

[23] Sean Carroll, *The Big Picture* (New York: Dutton, 2016).
[24] Carroll, *Big Picture*, 3.
[25] Carroll, *Big Picture*, 3.
[26] Carroll, *Big Picture*, 6.

question is this: "Can we bring meaning and morality to our lives, and speak sensibly about what is right and what is wrong?"[27] Eventually, he comes to the conclusion that ideas like morality "are nowhere to be found in the Core Theory of quantum fields, the physics underlying our everyday lives."[28] In other words, morality is completely fictional, and sin is therefore fictional as well. Nevertheless, since human beings have evolved as existential creatures, we are hungry for meaning and thus we must rely on some artificial sense of meaning in order to get along. Morality, meaning, and purpose, "though not built into the architecture of the universe," nevertheless "emerge as ways of talking about our human-scale environment."[29] In the end, "The universe doesn't care about us, but we care about the universe. That's what makes us special, not any immaterial souls or special purpose in the grand cosmic plan."[30] And in such a universe, the accidents of evolution we know as human beings must grapple with meaning and morality, even as these existential impulses can be only artificial and therapeutic.

Similarly, at least some serious thinkers have acknowledged that the prevailing materialistic understanding of the universe renders the affirmation of human moral agency impossible. Using the language of "free will" is thus illusory, even if necessary. This is the point essentially made by philosopher Stephen Cave.[31] Cave acknowledges that science has become increasingly committed to determinism in some form: "The sciences have grown steadily bolder in their claim that all human behavior can be explained through the clockwork laws of cause and effect."[32] Cave explicitly traces this way of thinking to the revolution that began with Charles Darwin. He also acknowledges that the denial of human moral agency comes with enormous problems:

> This development raises uncomfortable—and increasingly nontheoretical—questions: If moral responsibility depends on faith in our own agency, then as belief in determinism spreads, will we become morally irresponsible? And if we increasingly see belief in free will as a delusion, what will happen to all those institutions that are based on it?[33]

[27] Carroll, *Big Picture*, 222.
[28] Carroll, *Big Picture*, 389.
[29] Carroll, *Big Picture*, 389.
[30] Carroll, *Big Picture*, 422.
[31] Stephen Cave, "There's No Such Thing as Free Will: But We're Better Off Believing in It Anyway," *The Atlantic*, June 2016, https://www.theatlantic.com/magazine/archive/2016/06/theres-no-such-thing-as-free-will/480750/.
[32] Cave, "There's No Such Thing as Free Will."
[33] Cave, "There's No Such Thing as Free Will."

Cave goes on to cite psychological studies indicating that individuals who lack belief in moral agency tend, unsurprisingly, to misbehave. What would Cave propose as a remedy for an inevitable moral catastrophe if human moral agency were widely undermined? In the end, his argument is that we should continue to act *as if* we believe in human moral agency and responsibility, even as we simultaneously affirm that there can be *no reality* to either human moral agency or moral responsibility. The title of his article expresses the argument perfectly: "There's No Such Thing as Free Will: But We Are Better Off Believing It Anyway." We immediately suspect that such an effort is doomed to failure, and we have to suspect that Cave and others who share his worldview understand that living *as if* the universe has meaning and *as if* human moral responsibility is real is an exercise in self-delusion that is destined to fail, and to fail miserably.

The implausibility of these proposals takes us even further back in intellectual history to the haunting fears of Fredrich Nietzsche, who feared that the modern age would leave human beings in the excruciating predicament of having the experience of shame but no hope of redemption. As Douglas Murray explains,

> The consensus for centuries was that only God could forgive the ultimate sins. But on a day-to-day level the Christian tradition, among others, also stressed the desirability—if not the necessity—of forgiveness. Even to the point of infinite forgiveness. As one of the consequences of the death of God, Fredrich Nietzsche foresaw that people could find themselves stuck in cycles of Christian theology with no way out. Specifically, that people would inherit the concepts of guilt, sin and shame but would also be without the means of redemption which the Christian religion also offered. Today we do seem to live in a world where actions can have consequences we could never have imagined, where guilt and shame are more at hand than ever, and where we have no means whatsoever of redemption. We do not know who could offer it, who could accept it, and whether it is a desirable quality compared to an endless cycle of fiery certainty and denunciation [34]

In a similar vein, Mark Lilla remembered the haunting fear of the German poet Johann Wolfgang von Goethe that a twisted form of the Christian tradition might survive but without the gospel and Christian hope. Lilla understands the psychological catastrophe this would bring: "Psychologically

---

[34] Douglas Murray, *The Madness of Crowds: Gender, Race, and Identity* (London: Bloomsbury Continuum, 2019), 182.

speaking, however, Goethe was right: 'if Protestants bereft of God retain consciousness of sin, the weight will be crushing and the despair complete.' "[35]

The modern reduction—specifically the modern *theological* reduction— does not mean that religious impulses have disappeared. To the contrary, as Joseph Bottum has rightly observed, political ideas simply take on a spiritual shape. Bottum described the collapse of mainline Protestantism and then observed,

> And with that mainline collapse, a set of spiritual concerns, once contained and channeled by the churches, was set free to find new homes in our public conflicts. We live in a highly spiritualized age, I argue, when we believe that our ordinary political opponents are not merely mistaken but actually evil. We live with religious anxiety when we expect our attitudes towards social questions to explain our goodness and our salvation.[36]

Bottum's keen observation is that one dimension of our contemporary reality, not wrongly described as a consequence of secularization, is that theological energy is now expressed through political means. All the fervor is there, but it is now about politics as the ultimate concern. Once again, sin becomes an issue of political policy debates, not a matter of transgression against a holy God.

The Triumph of the Therapeutic

By the midpoint of the twentieth century many people in the West no longer believed that they were sinners, but they were quite certain that they were sick. And this sickness was not so much a condition of the body, as of the soul. More explicitly, not even so much a troubling of the soul as an affliction of the psyche. The most insightful observer of this crucial turn in Western consciousness was Philip Rieff, then University Professor of Sociology at the University of Pennsylvania. In *The Triumph of the Therapeutic: Uses of Faith after Freud*,[37] Rieff pointed to the eclipse of Christian theology and the rise of the modern culture of therapy, the psychologization of human life from top to bottom—a comprehensive reordering of the human understanding toward the concerns of the self and the promise of liberation by therapy. The entire culture was reoriented into the contours of therapeutic thought. Rieff, by the way, noted that Christian theologians in mainline Protestantism

---

[35] Lilla, *Stillborn God*, 149.
[36] Joseph Bottum, "The Spiritual Shape of Political Ideas," *The Weekly Standard*, December 1, 2014.
[37] Philip Rieff, *The Triumph of the Therapeutic: Uses of Faith after Freud* (New York: Harper & Row, 1966).

had already lost their confidence in any doctrine of sin. Even before writing *The Triumph of the Therapeutic*, Rieff had written an incredibly honest and bracing assessment of Sigmund Freud in *Freud: The Mind of the Moralist*.[38] In that work, Rieff described Freud's corpus as "perhaps the most important body of thought committed to paper in the twentieth century."[39] Rieff also understood and was quite alarmed by the realization that Freud offered no consolation. As Rieff explained, the hopes of religion are absent in Freud. When it comes to Freud's theoretical work, "There are truths in these texts, but no truth; helps but no help."[40] The consequences of Freud's work include the shaping of the modern understanding of sin, in a way that Rieff clearly perceived:

> A culture in which Freud is the presiding figure appears very different from any that have preceded it. He is not only the first irreligious moralist, he is a moralist without even a moralizing message. Man is tied to the weight of his own past, and even by a great therapeutic labor little more can be accomplished but a shifting of the burden. Freud's case histories are apologues that teach nothing; every case is different—or, what amounts to the same thing, could have been interpreted differently. It is exhilarating and yet terrifying to read Freud as a moralist, to see how compelling can be the judgment of a man who never preaches, leads us nowhere, assures us of nothing except perhaps that, having learned from him, the burden of misery we must find strength to carry will be somewhat lighter. To be less vulnerable to the arrows of sickness that fortune inevitably shoots at us, and that we, by virtue of our particular constitution, invite—this is as much good health as any of us educated by Freud can wish for.[41]

The therapeutic revolution would not affect only the secular sphere. Increasingly, it crept into institutional Christianity. First, it appeared in the message preached by paragons of Protestant liberalism such as Harry Emerson Fosdick, pastor of New York City's Riverside Church. Fosdick worked to harmonize the insights of Freud and the therapeutic revolution with a religious message, but that message was stated in opposition to historic orthodox Christianity. Fosdick saw Protestant orthodoxy as essentially anti-therapeutic and harmful. In a softer and more popular form, this same message was translated to the ministry of another New York City preacher, Norman Vincent

---

[38] Philip Rieff, *Freud: The Mind of the Moralist* (New York: Viking, 1959).
[39] Rieff, *Freud: Mind of the Moralist*, x.
[40] Rieff, *Freud: Mind of the Moralist*, x.
[41] Rieff, *Freud: Mind of the Moralist*, xi.

Peale. Peale's famous philosophy of the "power of positive thinking" represented the triumph of a rather superficial and popular psychology over the traditional Christian message. Peale's pop psychology, marketed as positive thinking, mixed with his association with mainline Protestantism and American patriotism, was deeply seductive to many middle-class American Christians, who failed to recognize the theological revolution Peale was projecting.

Taking the movement even further, a generation later televangelist Robert Schuller would amplify and transform Peale's message of positive thinking into Schuller's own "possibility thinking." From the pulpit of his Crystal Cathedral in Orange County, California, Schuller exceeded even Peale in amplifying popular psychology at the expense of traditional Christian doctrine. Schuller went so far as to offer what he called a "New Reformation," which would consist of redefining basic Christian doctrines, most importantly the doctrine of sin. Schuller began by defining sin as "any human condition or act that robs God of glory by stripping one of his children of their right to divine dignity."[42] Note carefully that Schuller begins with language that might have been drawn from the Heidelberg Catechism, only to turn to language that is focused on humanity rather than the holiness of God. Shortly after making that statement, Schuller amplified his transformation of the Christian doctrine of sin to this definition: "Sin is any act or thought that robs myself or another human being of his or her self-esteem."[43] The shocking nature of Schuller's "New Reformation" was not missed by the evangelical establishment, but it was eagerly absorbed by millions who watched Schuller on television, flocked to his Crystal Cathedral, and eagerly embraced Schuller's combination of self-esteem and economic aspiration as a new gospel. We must also observe that Harry Emerson Fosdick, Norman Vincent Peale, Robert Schuller, and their colleagues were not alone in advancing the triumph of the therapeutic in American religion. In the second half of the twentieth century, many theological seminaries exhibited a transformed understanding of ministry as "pastoral care," and that pastoral care represented an infusion of the therapeutic at the expense of theology in the seminary curriculum. Liberal Protestantism had basically redefined Christianity as a therapeutic message, and ministry was reconceived as a religious form of a "helping profession." The traditional Christian doctrine of sin was, on terms set by the therapeutic

---

[42] Robert Schuller, *Self-Esteem: The New Reformation* (Waco, TX: Word, 1983), 21.
[43] Schuller, *Self-Esteem*, 21.

revolution, repressive, dangerous, outdated, and sick. To much of the Protestant mainstream, sin had become an embarrassment.

Moralistic Therapeutic Deism

If the triumph of the therapeutic was clear by the middle of the twentieth century, the beginning of the twenty-first century brought the realization that the therapeutic had now been combined with other minimal theological beliefs into a new American religion that threatened to become dominant. The best analysis of this new American religion, something similar to what Robert Bellah described as a civil religion, came from sociologist Christian Smith and his team of researchers. Together, they followed a generation of young people from early adolescence to young adulthood in a series of reports. The most important book from their project is *Soul Searching: The Religious and Spiritual Lives of American Teenagers*.[44] Smith and his colleagues detected among American adolescents a basic religiosity that took the form of an exceedingly vague theology. Interview by interview, the shape of this new religion became evident. Smith and his team named this new religion "Moralistic Therapeutic Deism." The three words that name this new religion also describe it well. Like any religion, Moralistic Therapeutic Deism has its own creed. As described in *Soul Searching*,

> The creed of this religion, as codified from what emerged from our interviews, sounds something like this: 1. A God who created and orders the world and watches over human life on earth. 2. God wants people to be good, nice, and fair to each other, as taught in the Bible and by most world religions. 3. The central goal of life is to be happy and to feel good about one's self. 4. God does not need to be particularly involved in one's life except when God is needed to resolve a problem. 5. Good people go to heaven when they die.[45]

Clearly, this new religion is *moralistic* in that it assumes that there is a moral order to the universe and that it has some binding authority on human beings. It is *deistic* in the sense that it acknowledges that the cosmos can be explained only by a divine Creator, but like the deists of the eighteenth century, these teenagers assumed that God is neither in control of the universe nor

---

[44] Christian Smith with Melinda Lundquist Denton, *Soul Searching: The Religious and Spiritual Lives of American Teenagers* (New York: Oxford University Press, 2005).
[45] Smith and Denton, *Soul Searching*, 162–63.

particularly concerned about what human beings are up to. God is there to be called upon in an emergency, and he intervenes when called upon, except when he does not. God is a problem solver, and the teenagers hope that he would be accessible and amenable to solving their problems, but on an as-needed basis. On the other hand, a lot of the teenagers seemed to have little divine reference to their actual problems. Most importantly, the new religion is *therapeutic* because it could scarcely be anything else—the religious impulse is one of focus on the self and its security and happiness. Having considered the appearance of Moralistic Therapeutic Deism among American adolescents, including a large percentage of whom identified as Christian, Christian Smith and his associates acknowledged that these teenagers could have developed this theological understanding only by receiving it from their parents, their churches, and the larger culture. This research also produced an indictment:

> But we can say here that we've come with some confidence to believe that a significant part of Christianity in the United States is actually only tenuously Christian in any sense that is seriously connected to the actual historical Christian tradition, but has rather substantially morphed into Christianity's misbegotten step cousin, Moralistic Therapeutic Deism. This has happened in the minds and hearts of many individual believers and, it also appears, within the structures of at least some Christian organizations and institutions. The language, and therefore experience, of Trinity, holiness, sin, grace, justification, sanctification, church, Eucharist, and heaven and hell, appear, among most Christian teenagers in the United states at the very least, to be supplanted by the language of happiness, niceness, and an earned heavenly reward.[46]

They conclude: "It is not so much that American Christianity is being secularized. Rather, but more astutely, Christianity is either degenerating into a pathetic version of itself, or, more significantly, Christianity is actively being colonized and displaced by a quite different religious faith."[47]

With terrifying precision, Christian Smith and his team have described this new American religion that is indeed colonizing much of American Christianity. Rightly, they note that Moralistic Therapeutic Deism is "a quite different religious faith." Our horror is the realization that it is nonetheless preached in many pulpits considered to be Christian and affirmed in the hearts of many individuals who believe themselves to be Christians.

[46] Smith and Denton, *Soul Searching*, 171.
[47] Smith and Denton, *Soul Searching*, 171.

Preaching to Sinners in a Secular Age

So what is the preacher to do? What message are we to preach? If the ministry is not a helping profession committed to some form of therapeutic intervention, then what is the sum and substance of the Christian ministry?

Thankfully, historic biblical Christianity answers those questions conclusively. Nevertheless, the recovery of the Christian doctrine of sin and an effective and faithful means of communicating the biblical doctrine of sin in a secular age are daunting. But the Christian preacher must be fully aware that the power of the gospel infinitely eclipses all human confusions and obstacles to gospel ministry. Put simply, the only means of recovery is to preach the word in season and out of season (2 Tim. 4:1–2), with the full measure of conviction, and with a passion to see sinful human beings come to Christ and be reconciled to God, their sins forgiven, and the righteousness of Christ imputed to them.

One immediate realization that must come to the preacher is that there is no mediating position between the rejection of the concept of sin and its biblical affirmation. A little bit of the doctrine of sin will do no one any good. Recovery will be found—and salvation of sinners can come—only when the word is rightly preached and when sin is powerfully demonstrated in its biblical fullness—and its biblical horror. At the same time, the task of Christian apologetics is underlined by our acknowledgment that most, if not all, modern ears offer resistance to preaching about sin. On the other hand, as Christians we already know that the natural man and woman is resistant to the gospel. So what do we do? We preach Christ, fully confident that the gospel is more powerful than the comprehensive challenge of modern secularism.

A recovery of the biblical doctrine of sin will require exegetical, biblical, historical, pastoral, and systematic theological work. It will be demonstrated in a theology that also functions as apologetics. We must also understand, quite constantly, that sin is inherently a theological category and that we should never expect the secular mind to find the biblical notion of sin acceptable, attractive, or satisfactory. Seen in this secular light, the notion of sin is an affront to modern humanity. And yet, Christians must not shrink from sin's essentially theological nature as a category. As Cornelius Plantinga rightly observed,

> In biblical thinking, we can understand neither shalom nor sin apart from reference to God. Sin is a religious concept, not a moral one. Sin is lawlessness,

culpable folly, moral wandering, faithlessness, and much more. But, we call these moral misadventures sin because they offend and betray God.[48]

Plantinga continues:

> All sin has first and finally a Godward force. Let us say that *a sin* is any thought, desire, emotion, word, or deed—or its particular absence—that displeases God and deserves blame. Let us add that *sin* is the disposition to commit sins. And let us use the word *sin* for instances of either. Sin is a personal affront to a personal God.[49]

We should also note that Plantinga, in a longer consideration of sin and the preacher's challenge, noted that "anyone who tries to recover the knowledge of sin these days must overcome long odds."[50]

Essentially, all authentic preaching is about *God*. A lack of attention to the character of God, as revealed to us in Holy Scripture, renders any preaching about sin incoherent and insubstantial. John Portman puts the issue clearly: "Can you sin if you don't believe in God? It makes no sense to say that you have offended someone you do not know, someone you can't even fathom."[51]

Philosopher Alasdair MacIntyre puts it this way: "What Christians require is a conception, not only of defects of character, or vices, but of breaches of divine law, of sin."[52] David Kelsey, quite bravely in his context, went so far as to argue that the eclipse of the wrath of God meant the eclipse of sin as a rational category. As he explained, we may be facing "not so much a disuse of the concept of sin, as it is an abandonment of the concept of divine wrath, for, if there is no need to talk about the wrath of God, then there is not much need to talk about the sin that incurs the wrath."[53]

Of course, the Christian preacher also understands the absolute necessity of seeing Christianity as a theological whole, and not merely the sum of its parts. The doctrine of sin is not merely a "part" of Christian theology and the consequence of sin is not merely a "part" of the Holy Spirit's work of conviction. We must see Christian theology as comprehensive biblical truth, as whole and undivided, and our preaching challenge as systematic and holistic.

---

[48] Cornelius Plantinga, *Not the Way It's Supposed to Be: A Breviary of Sin* (Grand Rapids, MI: Eerdmans, 1996), 12.
[49] Plantinga, *Not the Way It's Supposed to Be*, 13.
[50] Plantinga, *Not the Way It's Supposed to Be*, x.
[51] John Portman, *A History of Sin: Its Evolution to Today and Beyond* (Lanham, MD: Rowman & Littlefield, 2007), 27.
[52] Alasdair MacIntyre, *After Virtue* (Notre Dame, IN: University of Notre Dame Press, 1984), 168.
[53] David Kelsey, "Whatever Happened to the Doctrine of Sin?" *TT* 50.2 (July 1993): 219.

I like the way Joseph Bottum speaks of the coherence of Christian doctrine: "The individual bits of Christian theology don't actually work all that well when they're broken apart from one another."[54]

Honesty also compels us to acknowledge that no Christian preacher is up to this challenge alone. Not one of us has the power, authority, persuasive ability, or rhetorical skill to bring about the conviction of sin. We are preaching to people who are carrying an overwhelming burden of shame, precisely because they are guilty of sin against God. As sinners, there is only one hope for their salvation, but Christ is a sure and certain hope. We are called to preach the gospel and the entirety of biblical truth faithfully and compellingly, but only the Holy Spirit can convict of sin. As Christ told his disciples, the Holy Spirit "will convict the world concerning sin and righteousness and judgment" (John 16:8). That is the preacher's confidence. We are to preach Christ, we are to preach the word of God, and the Holy Spirit will do what we ourselves cannot do—convict sinners of their sin and draw them to Christ.

In conclusion, we do well to be reminded that this is not the first time the Christian church has confronted a society with no biblical notion of sin. Indeed, long before we arrived on the scene, the early Christians in the Roman Empire knew the experience of preaching sin to a society that knew only shame and guilt. The power of the Christian message is demonstrated in the fact that Christians were responsible for transforming the worldview of the Roman Empire in a short time from a culture of shame to one with a consciousness of sin. A merely earthly reference of moral misbehavior that produced sin gave way to an understanding of the human moral problem as sin against a transcendent Creator. This came about only through Christian preaching and Christian witness. In his book *From Shame to Sin: The Christian Transformation of Sexual Morality in Late Antiquity*, Kyle Harper traces this theological transformation.[55] As Harper explains,

> Shame is a social concept, instantiated in human emotions; sin is a theological concept. They represent different categories of moral sanction. That is the point: "the transition from a late classical to a Christian sexual morality marked a paradigm shift, a quantum leap to a new foundational logic of sexual ethics, in which the cosmos replaced the city as the framework of morality."[56]

[54] Bottum, "Spiritual Shape of Political Ideas," 2014.
[55] Kyle Harper, *From Shame to Sin: The Christian Transformation of Sexual Morality in Late Antiquity* (Cambridge, MA: Harvard University Press, 2013).
[56] Harper, *From Shame to Sin*, 7.

Harper's point is this: By the preaching of the gospel, early Christians in the Roman Empire shifted the understanding of morality (and sexual morality, in particular) from behaviors that would produce either honor or shame within a merely human perspective to behaviors that would be judged by a holy God. The Christian doctrine of sin was understood to be of cosmic significance. The previous culture of shame saw moral misbehavior merely as significant in social terms. Ending with reference to Harper's work is meant as encouragement. For, if Christians preaching the gospel could bring about a transformation from shame to sin in the early Christian centuries, we have hope that the preaching of the gospel may bring about the same in our own time. That is our hope. We preach in a secular age, but our task is to preach the very same gospel as handed down by Christ to the apostles and by the apostles on to us. In it is the power of God for salvation (Rom. 1:16)—and that is enough.

Appendix

Scripture Versions Cited

Select Bibliography

À Brakel, Wilhelmus. *The Christian's Reasonable Service.* Edited by Joel R. Beeke. Translated by Bartel Elshout. Vol. 1. Grand Rapids, MI: Reformation Heritage, 1992.

Adams, Jay E. *The Grand Demonstration: A Biblical Study of the So-Called Problem of Evil.* Santa Barbara, CA: EastGate, 1991.

Alexander, David E. "Orthodoxy, Theological Determinism, and the Problem of Evil." Pages 123–144 in *Calvinism and the Problem of Evil.* Eugene, OR: Pickwick, 2016.

Allberry, Sam. *Is God Anti-Gay?* Updated edition. Epsom, Surrey, UK: Good Book Company, 2023.

Allen, Michael. "Jonathan Edwards and the Lapsarian Debate." *SJT* 62.3 (2009): 299–315.

Anderson, James N. "Calvinism and the First Sin." Pages 200–32 in *Calvinism and the Problem of Evil.* Edited by David E. Alexander and Daniel M. Johnson. Eugene, OR: Wipf & Stock, 2016.

Anderson, William H. U. "The Curse of Work in Qoheleth: An Exposé of Gen. 3:17–19 in Ecclesiastes." *Evangelical Quarterly* 70 (1998): 99–113.

Aquinas, Thomas. "Question 30. Concupiscence," New Advent, https://www.new advent.org/summa/2030.htm (accessed June 29, 2020).

Arminius, James. *The Works of James Arminius (1560–1609) (Complete).* Library of Alexandria. Grand Rapids, MI: Baker, 1956.

Armstrong, B. G. *Calvinism and the Amyraut Heresy: Protestant Scholasticism and Humanism in Seventeenth-Century France.* Madison: University of Wisconsin Press, 1969.

Arnoldus Corvinus, Johannes. *Defensio Sententiæ D. Iacobi Arminij.* Leiden, Netherlands, 1613.

Assis, Elie. *Self-Interest or Communal Interest: An Ideology of Leadership in the Gideon, Abimelech, and Jephthah Narratives (Judges 6–12).* VTSup 106. Leiden, Netherlands: Brill, 2005.

Augustine. *Against Julian.* In *The Fathers of the Church: A New Translation.* Vol. 35. Edited by H. Dressler. Translated by M. A. Schumacher. Washington, DC: Catholic University of America Press, 1957.

Augustine. *Answer to Faustus, a Manichean.* Translated by Roland S. J. Teske. In *The Works of Saint Augustine: A Translation for the 21st Century.* Vol. I/20. New York: New City Press, 2007.

Augustine. *Answer to the Pelagians: The Punishment and Forgiveness of Sins and the Baptism of Little Ones.* Edited by John E. Rotelle. Translated by Roland J. Teske. New York: New City Press, 1999.

Augustine. *The City of God.* Edited by John O'Meara. Translated by Henry Bettenson. London: Penguin, 1984.

Augustine. *The Nature of the Good.* In *The Manichean Debate*, Part I. Vol. 19. In *The Works of Saint Augustine: A Translation for the 21st Century.* Edited by Roland J. Teske. Hyde Park, NY: New City Press, 2006.

Augustine, *Enchiridion on Faith, Hope, and Love.* In *St. Augustine. The Enchiridion on Faith, Hope, and Love.* Edited by Henry Paolucci. Chicago: Regnery, 1961.

Augustine. *On Marriage and Concupiscence.* Edited by Philip Schaff and Henry Wace. T&T Clark, Grand Rapids, MI: Eerdmans, 1991.

Augustine. *The Retractations.* Edited by R. J. Deferrari. Translated by M. I. Bogan. Vol. 60. Washington, DC: Catholic University of America Press, 1968.

Augustine. *Saint Augustin: Anti-Pelagian Writings.* Vol. 5. of *NPNF*[1].

Augustine. *St. Augustin: The Writings against the Manichaeans and against the Donatists.* Vol. 4 of *NPNF*[1].

Augustine. *Miscellany of Questions in Response to Simplican.* In *Responses to Miscellaneous Questions*, Part I. Vol. 12. In *The Works of Saint Augustine: A Translation for the 21st Century.* Edited by Boniface Ramsey. Hyde Park, NY: New City Press, 2008.

Augustine. *Unfinished Work in Answer to Julian.* In *Answer to the Pelagians*, III, Part I. Vol. 25. In *The Works of Saint Augustine: A Translation for the 21st Century.* Edited by Roland J. Teske. Hyde Park, NY: New City Press, 2015.

Babcock, William S. "Augustine on Sin and Moral Agency." *The Journal of Religious Ethics* 16.1 (1988): 28–55.

Bahnsen, Greg L. *Always Ready: Directions for Defending the Faith.* Nacogdoches, TX: Covenant Media Press, 1996.

Bahnsen, Greg L. *Van Til's Apologetic: Readings and Analysis.* Phillipsburg, NJ: P&R, 1998.

Ballor, Jordan J. *Covenant, Causality, and Law: A Study in the Theology of Wolfgang Musculus.* Refo500 Academic Studies (R5AS) 3. Göttingen, Germany: Vandenhoeck & Ruprecht, 2012.

Ballor, Jordan, Matthew Gaetano, and David Sytsma. *Beyond Dordt and De Auxiliis: The Dynamics of Protestant and Catholic Soteriology in the Sixteenth and Seventeenth Centuries.* Leiden, Netherlands: Brill, 2019.

Bangs, Carl. *Arminius: A Study in the Dutch Reformation.* Nashville: Abingdon, 1971.

Barbu, Daniel. "Idolatry and Religious Diversity: Thinking about the Other in Early Modern Europe." *ASDIWAL. Revue Genevoise D'anthropologie et d'histoire des Religions* 9 (2014): 39–50.

Barcellos, Richard. *The Covenant of Works: Its Confessional and Scriptural Basis.* Recovering Our Confessional Heritage 3. Palmdale, CA: RBAP, 2016.

Barr, James. *The Garden of Eden and the Hope of Immortality.* London: SCM, 1992.

Barrett, Michael. "The Danger of Heartless Religion: An Exposition of Isaiah 1:2–18." *Puritan Reformed Journal* 6.2 (2014): 5–15.

Barth, Karl. *Church Dogmatics.* Edited by G. W. Bromiley and T. F. Torrance. Vol. I/2. Edinburgh: T&T Clark, 1956.

Baschera, Luca. "Total Depravity? The Consequences of Original Sin in John Calvin and Later Reformed Theology." Pages 37–58 in *Calvinus Clarissimus Theologus: Papers of the Tenth International Congress on Calvin Research.* Edited by Herman J. Selderhuis. Göttingen, Germany: Vandenhoeck & Ruprecht, 2012.

Baumann, Gerlinde. *Love and Violence: Marriage as Metaphor for the Relationship between Yhwh and Israel in the Prophetic Books.* Collegeville: Liturgical Press, 2003.

Bavinck, Herman. "The Future of Calvinism." Translated by Geerhardus Vos. *The Presbyterian and Reformed Review* 17 (1894): 1–24.

Bavinck, Herman. *Philosophy of Revelation: A New Annotated Edition.* Edited by Cory Brock and Nathaniel Gray Sutanto. Peabody, MA: Hendrickson, 2018.

Bavinck, Herman. "Primacy of the Intellect or the Will." Edited by John Bolt. Translated by Harry Boonstra and Gerrit Sheeres. In *Essays on Religion, Science, and Society.* Grand Rapids, MI: Baker Academic, 2008.

Bavinck, Herman. *Reformed Dogmatics.* 4 vols. Grand Rapids, MI: Baker Academic, 2003.

Bavinck, Herman. "The Unconscious." In Herman Bavinck, *Essays on Religion, Science, and Society.* Edited by John Bolt. Translated by Harry Boonstra and Gerrit Sheeres. Grand Rapids, MI: Baker Academic, 2008.

Bavinck, J. H. *The Church between Temple and Mosque: A Study of the Relationship between the Christian Faith and Other Religions.* Grand Rapids, MI: Eerdmans, 1981

Bavinck, J. H. "General Revelation and the Non-Christian Religions." Pages 95–109 in *The J. H. Bavinck Reader.* Edited by John Bolt, James Bratt, and Paul J. Visser. Translated by James De Jong. Grand Rapids, MI: Eerdmans, 2008.

Bavinck, J. H. "Religious Consciousness and Christian Faith." In *The J. H. Bavinck Reader.* Edited by John Bolt, James Bratt, and Paul Vissers. Translated by James De Jong. Grand Rapids, MI: Eerdmans, 2008.

Bavinck, J. H. "Religious Consciousness in History." In *The J. H. Bavinck Reader.* Edited by John Bolt, James Bratt, and Paul J. Visser. Translated by James De Jong. Grand Rapids, MI: Eerdmans, 2008.

Beach, J. Mark. *Christ and the Covenant: Francis Turretin's Federal Theology as a Defense of the Doctrine of Grace.* Göttingen, Germany: Vandenhoeck & Ruprecht, 2007.

Beale, G. K. "An Exegetical and Theological Consideration of Pharaoh's Heart in Exodus 4–14 and Romans 9." *TJ* 5 (1984): 129–54.

Beale, G. K. *A New Testament Biblical Theology: The Unfolding of the Old Testament in the New.* Grand Rapids, MI: Baker Academic, 2011.

Beale, G. K. *We Become What We Worship: A Biblical Theology of Idolatry.* Downers Grove, IL: IVP Academic, 2008.

Beatrice, Pier Franco. *The Transmission of Sin: Augustine and the Pre-Augustinian Sources.* Translated by Adam Kamesar. Oxford: Oxford University Press, 2013.

Beeke, Joel R., and Paul M. Smalley. *Reformed Systematic Theology.* Vol. 2, *Man and Christ.* Wheaton, IL: Crossway, 2020.

Bellah, Robert N., Richard Madsen, William M. Sullivan, Ann Swidler, and Steven M. Tipton. *Habits of the Heart: Individualism and Commitment in American Life.* Berkeley: University of California Press, 1985.

Bellarmine, Robert. *De controversiis Christianae fidei.* Vol. 4.1. Naples: J. Giuliano, 1856.

Berger, Peter L. "From the Crisis of Religion to the Crisis of Secularity." In Mary Douglas and Steven M. Tipton, eds. *Religion and America: Spiritual Life in a Secular Age.* Boston: Beacon, 1983.

Berger, Peter L. "Secularization Falsified." *First Things* 180 (October 2008): 23–27.

Berger, Peter L., ed. *The Desecularization of the World: Resurgent Religion and World Politics.* Grand Rapids, MI: Eerdmans, 1999.

Berkouwer, G. C. *Studies in Dogmatics: Man: The Image of God.* Translated by Dirk W. Jellema. Grand Rapids, MI: Eerdmans, 1962.

Berkouwer, G. C. *Studies in Dogmatics: The Person of Christ.* Grand Rapids, MI: Eerdmans, 1955.

Berkouwer, G. C. *Studies in Dogmatics: Sin.* Translated by Philip C. Holtrop. Grand Rapids, MI: Eerdmans, 1971.

Berman, Joshua. "The Making of the Sin of Achan (Joshua 7)." *BibInt* 22 (2014): 115–31.

Bierma, Lyle. "The Canons of Dordt as a Missional Document." *Pro Rege* 48.1 (September 2019): 1–6.

Bignon, Guillaume. *Excusing Sinners and Blaming God: A Calvinist Assessment of Determinism, Moral Responsibility, and Divine Involvement in Evil.* Princeton Theological Monograph Series. Eugene, OR: Pickwick, 2018.

Blocher, Henri. *In the Beginning: The Opening Chapters of Genesis.* Downers Grove, IL: InterVarsity Press, 1984.

Blocher, Henri. *Original Sin: Illuminating the Riddle.* NSBT 5. Grand Rapids, MI: Eerdmans, 1997.

Boda, Mark J. *A Severe Mercy: Sin and Its Remedy in the Old Testament.* Literature and Theology of the Hebrew Scriptures 1. Winona Lake, IN: Eisenbrauns, 2009.

Bonner, Gerald. *Church and Faith in the Patristic Tradition: Augustine, Pelagianism, and Early Christian Northumbria.* Collected Studies Series. Brookfield, VT: Variorum, 1996.

Bosma, Carl J. "Jonah 1:9—An Example of Elenctic Testimony." *CTJ* 48.1 (2013): 65–90.

Boston, Thomas. "Covenant of Works." Pages 173–338 in vol. 11 of *The Complete Works of Thomas Boston.* 12 vols. Grand Rapids, MI: Reformation Heritage, 2022. See esp. pages 232–33.

Bounds, Christopher. "Tertullian's Doctrine of Christian Perfection and Its Theological Context." *Wesleyan Theological Journal* 51.2 (2016): 130.

Brenneman, Todd M. *Homespun Gospel: The Triumph of Sentimentality in Contemporary Evangelicalism.* New York: Oxford University Press, 2014.

Brian, Rustin E. *Jacob Arminius: The Man from Oudewater.* Eugene, OR: Cascade, 2015.

Brock, Cory. "Between Demonization and Dependence: Bavinck's Appropriation of Schleiermacher." *Ad Fontes* 7 (2018): 1–6.

Brock, Cory. "Herman Bavinck's Reformed Eclecticism: On Catholicity, Consciousness, and Theological Epistemology." *SJT* 70.3 (2017): 310–32.

Brown, Robert F. "The First Evil Will Must Be Incomprehensible: A Critique of Augustine." *Journal of the American Academy of Religion* 46.3 (1978): 315–29.

Bruce, Steve. *God Is Dead: Secularization in the West.* Oxford: Wiley-Blackwell, 2002.

Brueggemann, Walter. *In Man We Trust.* Richmond, VA: John Knox, 1972.

Burk, Denny, and Rosaria Butterfield. "Learning to Hate Our Sin without Hating Ourselves." Public Discourse: Journal of the Witherspoon Institute. https://www.thepublicdiscourse.com/2018/07/22066/ (accessed June 29, 2020).

Burk, Denny, and Heath Lambert. *Transforming Homosexuality: What the Bible Says about Sexual Orientation and Change.* Phillipsburg, NJ: P&R, 2015.

Burns, Lanier. "From Ordered Soul to Corrupted Nature: Calvin's View of Sin." Pages 85–106 in *John Calvin and Evangelical Theology: Legacy and Prospect.* Edited by Sung Wook Chung. Louisville: Westminster/John Knox, 2009.

Calvin, John. *Institutes of the Christian Religion.* LCC 20. Edited by John T. McNeill. Translated by Ford Lewis Battles. 2 vols. Philadelphia: Westminster, 1960.

Calvin, John. *The Bondage and Liberation of the Will: A Defence of the Orthodox Doctrine of Human Choice against Pighius.* Edited by A. N. S. Lane. Translated by G. I. Davies. Grand Rapids, MI: Baker, 1998.

Canons and Decrees of the Council of Trent, with the Antidote. Braunschweig, Germany: C. A. Schwetschke, 1863.

Carson, D. A. *The Gagging of God: Christianity Confronts Pluralism.* Grand Rapids, MI: Zondervan, 1996.

Cave, Stephen. "There's No Such Thing as Free Will: But We're Better Off Believing in It Anyway." *The Atlantic,* June 2016.

Charles, J. D. "Vice and Virtue Lists." In *Dictionary of New Testament Background: A Compendium of Contemporary Biblical Scholarship.* Edited by Stanley E. Porter and Craig A. Evans. Downers Grove, IL: InterVarsity Press, 2000.

Chemnitz, Martin. *Examination of the Council of Trent, Part 1.* Vol. 1 of *Chemnitz's Works.* Translated by Fred Kramer. St. Louis, Concordia, 2007.

Cho, Geung Ho. "The Self and the Ideal Human Being in Eastern and Western Philosophical Traditions: Two Types of 'Being a Valuable Person.'" In *The Oneness Hypothesis: Beyond the Boundary of Self.* Edited by Philip J. Ivanhoe et al. New York: Columbia University Press, 2018.

Clark, David K. "Warfield, Infant Salvation, and the Logic of Calvinism." *JETS* 27.4 (1984): 459–64.

Clark, R. Scott. *Caspar Olevian and the Substance of the Covenant: The Double Benefit of Christ.* Grand Rapids, MI: Reformation Heritage, 2008.

Clark, R. Scott. "Christ and Covenant: Federal Theology in Orthodoxy." Pages 403–28 in *A Companion to Reformed Orthodoxy.* Edited by Herman J. Selderhuis. Leiden, Netherlands: Brill, 2013.

Cocceius, Johannes. *The Doctrine of the Covenant and Testament of God.* Translated by Casey Carmichael. Vol. 3 of Classic Reformed Theology. Grand Rapids, MI: Reformation Heritage, 2016.

Coles, Gregory. *Single, Gay Christian: A Personal Journey of Faith and Sexual Identity.* Downers Grove, IL: InterVarsity Press, 2017.

Collins, C. John. "The Place of the 'Fall' in the Overall Vision of the Hebrew Bible." *TJ* (2019): 171–80.

Couenhoven, Jesse. *Stricken by Sin, Cured by Christ: Agency, Necessity, and Culpability in Augustinian Theology.* Oxford: Oxford University Press, 2013.

Crisp, Oliver D. *An American Augustinian: Sin and Salvation in the Dogmatic Theology of William G. T. Shedd.* Milton Keynes, UK: Paternoster, 2007.

Crisp, Oliver D. "Federalism vs. Realism: Charles Hodge, Augustus Strong, and William Shedd on the Imputation of Sin." *IJST* 8.1 (2006): 55–71.

Crisp, Oliver D. *Jonathan Edwards among the Theologians.* Grand Rapids, MI: Eerdmans, 2015.

Crisp, Oliver D. "Jonathan Edwards on the Imputation of Sin." In *Retrieving Doctrine: Essays in Reformed Theology.* Downers Grove, IL: IVP Academic, 2010.

Crisp, Oliver D. *Jonathan Edwards on the Metaphysics of Sin.* Abingdon-on-Thames, UK: Routledge, 2017.

Crisp, Oliver D. "Retrieving Zwingli's Doctrine of Original Sin." *JRT* 10 (2016): 340–60.

Crisp, Oliver D. "Sin." Pages 194–215 in *Christian Dogmatics: Reformed Theology for the Church Catholic.* Edited by Michael Allen and Scott R. Swain. Grand Rapids, MI: Baker Academic, 2016.

Curtis, Byron G. "Hosea 6:7 and Covenant Breaking Like/At Adam." Pages 170–209 in *The Law Is Not of Faith: Essays on Works and Grace in the Mosaic Covenant.* Edited by Bryan D. Estelle, J. V. Fesko, and David VanDrunen. Phillipsburg, NJ: P&R, 2009.

Cushman, Philip. *Constructing the Self, Constructing America: A Cultural History of Psychotherapy.* Reading, MA: Addison-Wesley, 1995.

Davies, John A. " 'Discerning between Good and Evil': Solomon as a New Adam in 1 Kings." *WTJ* 73.1 (2011): 39–57.

D'Costa, Gavin. *Christianity and World Religions: Disputed Questions in the Theology of Religions.* Chichester, West Sussex, UK: Wiley-Blackwell, 2009.

De Campos, H. C. *Doctrine in Development: Johannes Piscator and Debates over Christ's Active Obedience.* Reformed Historical-Theological Series. Grand Rapids, MI: Reformation Heritage, 2018.

De la Place, Josué. *De imputatione primi peccati Adami . . . disputatio.* Saumur, France, 1655.

Den Boer, William. *God's Twofold Love: The Theology of Jacob Arminius.* Reformed Historical Theology 14. Göttingen, Germany: Vandenhoeck & Ruprecht, 2010.

Denlinger, Aaron C. *Omnes in Adam Ex Pacto Dei: Ambrogio Catarino's Doctrine of Covenantal Solidarity and Its Influence on Post-Reformation Reformed Theologians.* Reformed Historical Theology 8. Göttingen, Germany: Vandenhoeck & Ruprecht, 2010.

Dennison, James T. Jr., ed. *Reformed Confessions of the 16th and 17th Centuries in English Translation.* 4 vols. Grand Rapids, MI: Reformation Heritage, 2014.

DeYoung, Kevin. *What Does the Bible Really Teach about Homosexuality?* Wheaton, IL: Crossway, 2015.

Didymus the Blind. *Against the Manichaeans.* PG 39.1096B.

Douma, J. *The Ten Commandments: Manual for the Christian Life.* Translated by Nelson D. Kloosterman. Phillipsburg, NJ: P&R, 1996.

Dumbrell, William J. *Covenant and Creation: A Theology of Old Testament Covenants.* Eugene, OR: Wipf & Stock, 1984.

Duncan, J. Ligon. "Common Sense Realism and American Presbyterianism: An Evaluation of the Impact of Scottish Realism on Princeton and the South." MA thesis, Covenant Theological Seminary, 1987.

Edwards, Jonathan. *A Dissertation concerning the End for Which God Created the World,* 1765.

Edwards, Jonathan. *Freedom of the Will.* Edited by Paul Ramsey. Vol. 1 of *The Works of Jonathan Edwards.* 26 vols. New Haven, CT: Yale University Press, 1957.

Edwards, Jonathan. "Of Being." In *Scientific and Philosophical Writings.* Edited by Wallace E. Anderson. Vol. 6 of *The Works of Jonathan Edwards.* 26 vols. New Haven, CT: Yale University Press, 1980.

Edwards, Jonathan. *Original Sin.* Edited by Clyde A. Holbrook. Vol. 3 of *The Works of Jonathan Edwards.* 26 vols. New Haven, CT: Yale University Press, 1997.

Edwards, Jonathan. *Ethical Writings.* Edited by Paul Ramsey. Vol. 8 of *The Works of Jonathan Edwards.* 26 vols. New Haven, CT: Yale University Press, 1989.

Ellis, Mark A. trans and ed. *The Arminian Confession of 1621.* Princeton Theological Monograph Series. Eugene, OR: Pickwick, 2005.

Ellis, Mark A. *Simon Episcopius' Doctrine of Original Sin.* American University Studies 240. New York: Peter Lang, 2006.

Erasmus. *A Warrior Shielding a Discussion of Free Will against the Enslaved Will by Martin Luther* (Part 1, February 1526; Part 2, September 1527), *CWE* 76:91–297; 77:333–749.

Evans, Caleb. *The Deceitfulness of Sin.* Bristol, UK: W. Pine, 1792.

Evans, Gillian R. *Augustine on Evil.* Cambridge: Cambridge University Press, 1993.

Evans, Robert F. *Pelagius: Inquiries and Reappraisals.* Eugene, OR: Wipf & Stock, 2010.

Ferguson, Sinclair B. *The Whole Christ: Legalism, Antinomianism, and Gospel Assurance — Why the Marrow Controversy Still Matters.* Wheaton, IL: Crossway, 2016.

Fesko, J. V. *Death in Adam, Life in Christ: The Doctrine of Imputation.* Geanies House, UK: Christian Focus, 2016.

Fesko, J. V. *Reforming Apologetics: Retrieving the Classic Reformed Approach to Defending the Faith.* Grand Rapids, MI: Eerdmans, 2019.

Frame, John. *Cornelius Van Til: An Analysis of His Thought.* Phillipsburg, NJ: P&R, 1995.

Frame, John. *Nature's Case for God: A Brief Biblical Argument.* Bellingham, WA: Lexham, 2018.

Frame, John. *The Doctrine of the Knowledge of God.* Phillipsburg, NJ: P&R, 1987.

Frame, John. *Systematic Theology: An Introduction to Christian Belief.* Phillipsburg, NJ: P&R, 2013.

Gaffin, Richard B., Jr. *By Faith, Not by Sight: Paul and the Order of Salvation.* 2nd ed. Phillipsburg, NJ: P&R, 2013.

Gaffin, Richard B., Jr. "Epistemological Reflections on 1 Corinthians 2:6–16." Pages 13–40 in *Revelation and Reason: New Essays in Reformed Apologetics.* Phillipsburg, NJ: P&R, 2007.

Gaffin, Richard B., Jr. *In the Fullness of Time: An Introduction to the Biblical Theology of Acts and Paul.* Wheaton, IL: Crossway, 2022.

Gaffin, Richard B., Jr. *No Adam, No Gospel: Adam and the History of Redemption.* Phillipsburg, NJ: P&R; Glenside, PA: Westminster Seminary Press, 2015.

Gagnon, Robert A. J. "Transexuality and Ordination," 2007. www.robgagnon.net/articles/TransexualityOrdination.pdf.

Gerhard, Johann. *On Sin and Free Choice.* Theological Commonplaces XII–XIV. Translated by Richard J. Dinda. Edited by Benjamin T. G. Mayes and Heath R. Curtis. St. Louis: Concordia, 2014 [1611].

Gibson, David, and Jonathan Gibson, eds. *From Heaven He Came and Sought Her: Definite Atonement in Historical, Biblical, Theological, and Pastoral Perspective.* Wheaton, IL: Crossway, 2013.

Godfrey, W. Robert. "Popular and Catholic: The Modus Docendi of the Canons of Dordt." Pages 243–60 in *Revisiting the Synod of Dort.* Edited by Aza Goudriaan and Fred van Lieburg. Leiden, Netherlands: Brill, 2011.

Goldberg, Carl. *Understanding Shame.* Northvale, NJ: Jason Aronson, 1991.

Gordon, Christopher J. "Dead in Sin: The Utter Depravity of Mankind." In *A Faith Worth Defending: The Synod of Dort's Enduring Heritage.* Edited by Jon D. Payne and Sebastian Heck. Grand Rapids, MI: Reformation Heritage, 2019.

Greeley, Andrew M. *Unsecular Man: The Persistence of Religion.* New York: Schocken, 1985.

Greene, G. R. "God's Lamb: Divine Provision for Sin." *PRSt* 37 (2010): 147–64.

Haak, Cornelius J. "The Missional Approach: Reconsidering Elenctics. Part 1." *CTJ* 44.1 (2009): 37–48.

Haak, Cornelius J. "The Missional Approach: Reconsidering Elenctics. Part 2." *CTJ* 44.2 (2009): 288–304.

Halbertal, Moshe, and Avishai Margalit. *Idolatry.* Cambridge, MA: Harvard University Press, 1994.

Hamer, Dean, and Peter Copeland. *Living with Our Genes: The Groundbreaking Book about the Science of Personality, Behavior, and Genetic Destiny.* New York: Doubleday, 1998.

Hampton, Stephen. "Sin, Grace, and Free Choice in Post-Reformation Reformed Theology." Pages 228–41 in *The Oxford Handbook of Early Modern Theology, 1600–1800.* Edited by Ulrich L. Lehner, Richard A. Muller, A. G. Roeber. Oxford: Oxford University Press, 2014.

Hanley, Ryan C. "The Background and Purpose of Stripping the Adulteress in Hosea 2." *JETS* 60.1 (2017): 89–103.

Hannah, John D. "Doctrine of Original Sin in Postrevolutionary America." *BSac* 134.535 (1977): 238–56.

Harper, Kyle. *From Shame to Sin: The Christian Transformation of Sexual Morality in Late Antiquity.* Cambridge, MA: Harvard University Press, 2013.

Hasker, William. *The Triumph of God over Evil.* Downers Grove, IL: IVP Academic, 2008.

Helm, Paul. "The Great Christian Doctrine (Original Sin)." Pages 175–200 in *A God Entranced Vision of All Things: The Legacy of Jonathan Edwards.* Edited by John Piper and Justin Taylor. Wheaton, IL: Crossway, 2004.

Helm, Paul. "Nature and Grace." In *Aquinas among the Protestants.* Edited by M. Svensson and D. VanDrunen. Hoboken, NJ: Wiley-Blackwell, 2018.

Heppe, Heinrich. *Reformed Dogmatics.* Edited by E. Bizer. Grand Rapids, MI: Baker, 1950.

Hick, John. *Evil and the God of Love.* London: Macmillan, 1966.

Hill, Wesley. *Spiritual Friendship: Finding Love in the Church as a Celibate Gay Christian.* Grand Rapids, MI: Brazos, 2015.

Hoekema, Anthony A. "The Missionary Focus of the Canons of Dordt." *CTJ* (November 1972): 209–22.

Hoekema, Anthony A. *Created in God's Image.* Grand Rapids, MI: Eerdmans, 1986.

Hoitenga, Dewey J., Jr. *John Calvin and the Will: A Critique and Corrective.* Grand Rapids, MI: Baker, 1997.

Holbrook, Clyde A. "Jonathan Edwards Addresses Some 'Modern Critics' of Original Sin." *The Journal of Religion* 63.3 (1983): 211–30.

Horton, Michael S. *The Christian Faith: A Systematic Theology for Pilgrims on the Way.* Grand Rapids, MI: Zondervan, 2011.

Hoskins, Paul M. "Freedom from Slavery to Sin and the Devil: John 8:31–47 and the Passover Theme of the Gospel of John." *TJ* 31 (2010): 47–53.

Houck, Daniel W. *Aquinas, Original Sin, and the Challenge of Evolution.* Cambridge: Cambridge University Press, 2020.

Hunnius, Aegidius. *Articulus de peccato etc.* Vol. 1. In *Operum Latinorum.* Edited by H. Garthius. Wittenberg: G. Muller, 1607–9.

Hutchinson, G. P. *The Problem of Original Sin in American Presbyterian Theology.* International Library of Philosophy and Theology: Biblical and Theological Studies Series. Phillipsburg, NJ: P&R, 1972.

Ilić, Luka. *Theologian of Sin and Grace: The Process of Radicalization in the Theology of Matthias Flacius Illyricus.* Göttingen, Germany: Vandenhoeck & Ruprecht, 2014.

Image, Isabella C. *The Human Condition in Hilary of Poitiers: The Will and Original Sin between Origen and Augustine.* Oxford: Oxford University Press, 2017.

Irenaeus. *Against Heresies.* In vol. 2 of *Libros quinque adversus haereses.* Edited by W. Wigan Harvey. Cambridge: Cambridge University Press, 1857.

Ivanhoe, Philip J. *Confucian Moral Self Cultivation.* 2nd ed. Indianapolis: Hackett, 2000.

Jedin, Hubert. *A History of the Council of Trent.* Translated by E. Graf. 2 vols. London: Thomas Nelson, 1957.

Johnson, Greg. *Still Time to Care: What We Can Learn from the Church's Failed Attempt to Cure Homosexuality.* Grand Rapids, MI: Zondervan, 2021.

Johnson, Keith L., and David Lauber, eds. *T&T Clark Companion to the Doctrine of Sin.* London: Bloomsbury T&T Clark, 2016.

Kaufman, Gersken. *The Psychology of Shame: Theory and Treatment of Shame-Based Syndromes.* New York: Springer, 1989.

Kelsey, David H. *Eccentric Existence: A Theological Anthropology.* Louisville: Westminster/John Knox, 2009.

Kelsey, David H. *Self-Construction and the Formation of Human Values: Truth, Language, and Desire.* Westport, CT: Praeger, 1998.

Kiros, Teodros. "Whatever Happened to the Doctrine of Sin?" *TT* 50.2 (July 1993): 169–178.

Knox, John S. *Jacobus Arminius Stands His Ground.* Eugene, OR: Wipf & Stock, 2018.

Kolb, Robert. *Bound Choice, Election, and Wittenberg Theological Method: From Martin Luther to the Formula of Concord.* Grand Rapids, MI: Eerdmans, 2005.

Kruse, C. G. "Sin and Perfection in 1 John." *Australian Biblical Review* 51 (2003): 60–70.

Kuby, Gabriele. *The Global Sexual Revolution: Destruction of Freedom in the Name of Freedom.* Translated by James Patrick Kirchner. Kettering, OH: Angelico, 2015.

Lambert, Heath. *A Theology of Biblical Counseling: The Doctrinal Foundation of Counseling Ministry.* Grand Rapids, MI: Zondervan, 2016.

Landis, Robert W. *The Doctrine of Original Sin as Received and Taught by the Churches of the Reformation, Stated and Defended, and the Error of Dr. Hodge in Claiming That This Doctrine Recognizes the Gratuitous Imputation of Sin, Pointed Out and Refuted.* Richmond, VA: Whittet & Shepperson, 1884.

Lane, A. N. S. "Albert Pighius's Controversial Work on Original Sin." *Reformation and Renaissance Review* 4 (2000): 29–61.

Lane, A. N. S. "Did Calvin Believe in Freewill?" *Vox Evangelica* 12 (1981): 72–90.

Leith, John H. "The Doctrine of the Will in the *Institutes of the Christian Religion.*" Pages 49–66 in *Reformatio Perennis: Essays on Calvin and the Reformation in Honor of Ford Lewis Battles.* Edited by Brian A. Gerrish and Robert Benedetto. Pittsburgh Theological Monograph Series. Pittsburgh, PA: Pickwick, 1981.

Leslie, Andrew M. "Retrieving a Mature Reformed Doctrine of Original Sin: A Conversation with Some Recent Proposals." *IJST* 22.3 (2020): 336–60.

Lints, Richard. *Identity and Idolatry: The Image of God and Its Inversion.* Nottingham, UK: Apollos, 2015.

Lints, Richard. "Imaging and Idolatry: The Sociality of Personhood in the Canon." Edited by Richard Lints, Michael S. Horton, and Mark R. Talbot. Grand Rapids, MI: Eerdmans, 2006.

Long, A. A. "The Stoic Concept of Evil." *Philosophical Quarterly* 18.73 (1968): 329–43.

Long, Thomas G. "God Be Merciful to Me, a Miscalculator." *TT* 50.2 (July 1993): 165–68.

Lopes Pereira, Jairzinho. *Augustine of Hippo and Martin Luther on Original Sin.* Göttingen, Germany: Vandenhoeck & Ruprecht, 2013.

Luther, Martin. *The Bondage of the Will* (1525), *LW* 33:294.

Luther, Martin. *The Freedom of a Christian* (1520), *LW* 31:361.

Machen, J. Gresham. *Christianity and Liberalism.* Grand Rapids, MI: Eerdmans, 2009.

Macleod, Donald. "Original Sin in Reformed Theology." Pages 129–46 in *Adam, the Fall, and Original Sin: Theological, Biblical, and Scientific Perspectives.* Edited by Hans Madueme and Michael Reeves. Grand Rapids, MI: Baker Academic, 2014.

Madueme, Hans, and Michael Reeves, eds. *Adam, the Fall, and Original Sin: Theological, Biblical, and Scientific Perspectives.* Grand Rapids, MI: Baker, 2014.

Mahn, Jason A. *Fortunate Fallibility: Kierkegaard and the Power of Sin.* New York: Oxford University Press, 2011.

Marcus, Joel. "The Evil Inclination in the Epistle of James." *Catholic Biblical Quarterly* 44 (1982): 606–21.

Martin, Raymond, and John Barresi. *The Rise and Fall of Soul and Self: An Intellectual History of Personal Identity.* New York: Columbia University Press, 2006.

Mastricht, Petrus van. *Theoretical-Practical Theology: The Works of God and the Fall of Man.* Vol. 3. Edited by Joel R. Beeke. Translated by Todd M. Rester. Grand Rapids, MI: Reformation Heritage, 2021.

McCall, Thomas H. *Against God and Nature: The Doctrine of Sin.* Wheaton, IL: Crossway, 2019.

McFadyen, Alistair. *Bound to Sin: Abuse, Holocaust, and the Christian Doctrine of Sin.* Cambridge: Cambridge University Press, 2000.

McFarland, Ian. *In Adam's Fall: A Meditation on the Christian Doctrine of Original Sin.* Oxford: Blackwell, 2010.

McGraw, Ryan M. *Reformed Scholasticism: Recovering the Tools of Reformed Theology.* Edinburgh: T&T Clark, 2019.

McSorley, H. J. *Luther: Right or Wrong?: An Ecumenical-Theological Study of Luther's Major Work, The Bondage of the Will.* New York: Newman, 1969.

Mendoz, Fernando. "El pecado original en la Homilía sobre la Pascua de Melitón de Sardes." *Scripta Theologica* 2 (1970): 287–302.

Menninger, Karl. *Whatever Became of Sin?* New York: Hawthorn, 1973.

Middleton, J. Richard. *The Liberating Image: The Imago Dei in Genesis 1.* Grand Rapids, MI: Brazos, 2005.

Milbank, John. *Theology and Social Theory: Beyond Secular Reason.* 2nd ed. Oxford: Wiley-Blackwell, 2006.

Mininger, Marcus A. "Defining the Identity of the Christian 'I' between the Already and the Not Yet: In Review of Will N. Timmins's *Romans 7 and Christian Identity.*" Mid-America Journal of Theology 31 (2020): 133–54.

Mohler, R. Albert, Jr. *Desire and Deceit: The Real Cost of the New Sexual Tolerance.* Colorado Springs: Multnomah, 2008.

Moo, Douglas J. *The Epistle to the Romans.* Grand Rapids, MI: Eerdmans, 1996.

Moo, Douglas J. "Sin in Paul." Pages 107–31 in *Fallen: A Theology of Sin.* Edited by Christopher W. Morgan and Robert A. Peterson. Wheaton, IL: Crossway, 2013.

Morales, L. Michael. *Who Shall Ascend the Mountain of the Lord? A Biblical Theology of the Book of Leviticus.* NSBT 37. Nottingham, UK: Apollos, 2015.

Morgan, Christopher W. and Robert A. Peterson, eds. *Fallen: A Theology of Sin.* Theology in Community. Wheaton, IL: Crossway, 2013.

Morris, Leon. *The Lord from Heaven: A Study of the New Testament Teaching on the Deity and Humanity of Jesus Christ.* Grand Rapids, MI: Eerdmans, 1958.

Moxon, R. S. *The Doctrine of Sin: A Critical and Historical Investigation into the Views of the Concept of Sin Held in Early Christian, Medieval, and Modern Times.* London: George Allen & Unwin, 1922.

Muller, Richard A. "The Covenant of Works and the Stability of Divine Law in Seventeenth-Century Reformed Orthodoxy: A Study in the Theology of Herman Witsius and Wilhelmus à Brakel." *CTJ* 29.1 (1994): 75–101.

Muller, Richard A. "Divine Covenants, Absolute and Conditional: John Cameron and the Early Orthodox Development of Reformed Covenant Theology." *Mid-America Journal of Theology* 17 (2006): 11–56.

Muller, Richard A. *Divine Will and Human Choice: Freedom, Contingency, and Necessity in Early Modern Reformed Thought.* Grand Rapids, MI: Baker Academic, 2017.

Muller, Richard A. "The Federal Motif in Seventeenth-Century Arminian Theology." *Nederlands Archief voor Kerkgeschiedenis* 62.1 (1982): 102–22.

Muller, Richard A. "Fides and Cognitio in Relation to the Problem of Intellect and Will in the Theology of John Calvin." *CTJ* 25.2 (1990): 207–224.

Muller, Richard A. "Goading the Determinists: Thomas Goad (1576–1638) on Necessity, Contingency, and God's Eternal Decree." *Mid-America Journal of Theology* 26 (2015): 59–75.

Muller, Richard A. *God, Creation, and Providence in the Thought of Jacob Arminius: Sources and Directions of Scholastic Protestantism in the Era of Early Orthodoxy.* Grand Rapids, MI: Baker, 1991.

Muller, Richard A. "Jonathan Edwards and the Absence of Free Choice: A Parting of Ways in the Reformed Tradition." *Jonathan Edwards Studies* 1.1 (2011): 3–22.

Murray, John. *Collected Writings of John Murray.* 4 vols. Edinburgh: Banner of Truth, 2009.

Murray, John. *The Epistle to the Romans.* NICOT. Grand Rapids, MI: Eerdmans, 1973.

Murray, John. *The Imputation of Adam's Sin.* Grand Rapids, MI: Eerdmans, 1959.

Murray, John. *Principles of Conduct: Aspects of Biblical Ethics.* Grand Rapids, MI: Eerdmans, 1957.

Murray, John. "Structural Strands in New Testament Eschatology." *Kerux: A Journal of Biblical-Theological Preaching/NWTS* 6.3 (December 1991): 19–26.

Niebuhr, Reinhold. *The Nature and Destiny of Man: A Christian Interpretation.* Vol. 1, *Human Nature.* New York: Scribner, 1942.

Nietzsche, Friedrich. *The Antichrist.* Translated by H. L. Mencken. Middlesex, UK: Echo Library, 2006.

Nimmo, Paul. "Sin and Reconciliation." Pages 655–57 in *Oxford Handbook of Nineteenth Century Theology.* Edited by Joel D. S. Rasmussen, Judith Wolfe, and Johannes Zachhuber. Oxford: Oxford University Press, 2017.

O'Donovan, Oliver. *Resurrection and Moral Order: An Outline of Evangelical Ethics.* 2nd ed. Leicester, UK/Grand Rapids, MI: Apollos/Eerdmans, 1994.

Oliphint, K. Scott. *Covenantal Apologetics: Principles and Practice in Defense of Our Faith.* Wheaton, IL: Crossway, 2013.

Ortlund, Raymond C., Jr. *God's Unfaithful Wife: A Biblical Theology of Spiritual Idolatry.* NSBT 2. Nottingham, UK: Apollos/Downers Grove, IL: InterVarsity Press, 1996.

Owen, John. *The Nature, Power, Deceit, and Prevalency of the Remainders of Indwelling Sin in Believers.* In *The Works of John Owen.* Vol. 6. Carlisle, PA: Banner of Truth, 1966.

Pardigon, Flavien. *Paul against the Idols: A Contextual Reading of the Areopagus Speech.* Eugene, OR: Pickwick, 2019.

Pascal, Blaise. *Pensées and Other Writings.* Edited by Anthony Levi. Translated by Honor Levi. Oxford: Oxford University Press, 2008.

Peels, Rik. "Sin and Human Cognition of God." *SJT* 64 (2011): 390–409.

Pelagius. *Pelagius' Commentary on St. Paul's Epistle to the Romans.* Translated by Theodore De Brun. Oxford: Clarendon, 1993.

Pelikan, Jaroslav. *Development of Christian Doctrine: Some Historical Prolegomena.* New Haven, CT: Yale University Press, 1969.

Perkins, William. *The Works of William Perkins.* 10 vols. Edited by Joel R. Beeke and Derek W. H. Thomas. Grand Rapids, MI: Reformation Heritage, 2020.

Peters, Ted. *Sin: Radical Evil in Soul and Society.* Grand Rapids, MI: Eerdmans, 1994.

Pitkin, Barbara. "Nothing but Concupiscence: Calvin's Understanding of Sin and the Via Augustini." *CTJ* 34.2 (1999): 347–69.

Plantinga, Cornelius. *Not the Way It's Supposed to Be: A Breviary of Sin.* Grand Rapids, MI: Eerdmans, 1996.

Portman, John. *A History of Sin: Its Evolution to Today and Beyond.* Lanham, MD: Rowman & Littlefield, 2007.

Pratt Richard L., Jr. *Every Thought Captive: A Study Manual for the Defense of Christian Truth.* Phillipsburg, NJ: P&R, 1980.

Prosper of Aquitaine. *De gratia Dei et libero arbitrio liber contra collatorem.* PL 51:221–22, 227, 243, 259.

Ramm, Bernard L. *Offense to Reason: A Theology of Sin.* San Francisco: Harper & Row, 1985.

Rees, B. R. *Pelagius: A Reluctant Heretic.* Suffolk, UK: Boydell, 1988.

Ricoeur, Paul. *The Symbolism of Evil.* Boston: Beacon, 1967.

Ridderbos, Herman N. *The Gospel according to John: A Theological Commentary.* Translated by John Vriend. Grand Rapids, MI: Eerdmans, 1997.

Ridderbos, Herman N. *Paul: An Outline of His Theology.* Translated by John Richard de Witt. Grand Rapids, MI: Eerdmans, 1966.

Ridderbos, Herman N. *When the Time Had Fully Come: Studies in New Testament Theology.* Eugene, OR: Wipf & Stock, 2001.

Rieff, Philip. *Freud: The Mind of the Moralist.* New York: Viking, 1959.

Rieff, Philip. *The Triumph of the Therapeutic: Uses of Faith after Freud.* New York: Harper & Row, 1966.

Riggan, George A. "Original Sin in the Thought of Augustine." PhD diss., Yale University, 1949.

Rist, John. *Augustine Deformed: Love, Sin, and Freedom in the Western Moral Tradition.* Cambridge: Cambridge University Press, 2016.

Rivet, André. *Decretum synodi nationalis ecclesiarum in Gallia reformatum . . . De imputatione primi peccati omnibus Adami posteris etc.* Geneva: Chouët, 1647.

Roberts, Matthew P. W. *Pride: Identity and the Worship of Self.* Fearn, Ross-shire, UK: Christian Focus, 2023.

Roberts, Simon. *Order and Dispute: An Introduction to Legal Anthropology.* Harmondsworth, UK: Penguin, 1979.

Rosenberg, Stanley P., ed. *Finding Ourselves after Darwin: Conversations on the Image of God, Original Sin, and the Problem of Evil.* Grand Rapids, MI: Baker Academic, 2018.

Rosner, B. S. "Idolatry." In *New Dictionary of Biblical Theology.* Edited by T. D. Alexander et al. Downers Grove, IL: IVP Academic, 2000.

Scarpari, Maurizio. "The Debate on Human Nature in Early Confucian Literature." *Philosophy East and West* 53.3 (2003): 323–39.

Schrag, Calvin O. *The Self after Postmodernity.* New Haven, CT: Yale University Press, 1997.

Schubert, Anselm. *Das Ende der Sünde: Anthropologie und Erbsünde zwischen Reformation und Aufklärung.* Forschungen zur Kirchen und Dogmengeschichte. Göttingen, Germany: Vandenhoeck & Ruprecht, 2002.

Schuller, Robert. *Self-Esteem: The New Reformation.* Waco, TX: Word, 1983.

Scott, Stuart, and Heath Lambert, eds. *Counseling the Hard Cases: True Stories Illustrating the Sufficiency of God's Resources in Scripture.* Nashville: B&H, 2012.

Sell, Alan P. F. *The Great Debate: Calvinism, Arminianism, and Salvation.* Eugene, OR: Wipf & Stock, 1982.

Shaw, Ed. *The Plausibility Problem: The Church and Same-Sex Attraction.* Nottingham, UK: Inter-Varsity Press, 2015.

Sherwood, Yvonne. *The Prostitute and the Prophet: Reading Hosea in the Late Twentieth Century.* London: T&T Clark, 2004.

Shuster, Marguerite. *The Fall and Sin: What We Have Become as Sinners.* Grand Rapids, MI: Eerdmans, 2004.

Squires, Stuart. *The Pelagian Controversy: An Introduction to the Enemies of Grace and the Conspiracy of Lost Souls.* Eugene, OR: Pickwick, 2019.

Stanglin, Keith D., and Thomas H. McCall. *Jacob Arminius: Theologian of Grace.* New York: Oxford University Press, 2012.

Stevens, John. *The Fight of Your Life: Facing and Resisting Temptation.* Fearn, Ross-shire, UK: Christian Focus, 2019.

Stevenson, Leslie, and David L. Haberman. *Ten Theories of Human Nature.* Oxford: Oxford University Press, 2009.

Storms, C. Samuel. *Tragedy in Eden: Original Sin in the Theology of Jonathan Edwards.* Lanham, MD: University Press of America, 1985.

Strange, Daniel. *For Their Rock Is Not as Our Rock: An Evangelical Theology of Religions.* Nottingham, UK: Apollos, 2014.

Strange, Daniel. "For Their Rock Is Not as Our Rock: The Gospel as the 'Subversive Fulfillment' of the Religious Other." *JETS* 56.2 (2013).

Strange, Daniel. "An Unholy Mess." *Primer* 7 (2019): 6–19.

Stump, J. B., and Chad V. Meister, eds. *Original Sin and the Fall: Five Views.* Downers Grove, IL: IVP Academic, 2020.

Sutanto, Nathaniel Gray. "Egocentricity, Metaphysics, and Organism: Sin and Renewal in Bavinck's Ethics." *Studies in Christian Ethics* 34 (2021): 223–40.

Sutanto, Nathaniel Gray. "Herman Bavinck on the Image of God and Original Sin." *IJST* 18 (2016): 174–90.

Swierenga, Robert P. "Calvin and the Council of Trent: A Reappraisal." *Reformed Journal* 16.3 (1966): 35–37.

Taylor, A. E. *The Faith of a Moralist.* London: Macmillan, 1930.

Taylor, Charles. *A Secular Age.* Cambridge: Harvard University Press, 2007.

Thunberg, Lars. *Microcosm and Mediator: The Theological Anthropology of Maximus the Confessor.* Chicago: Open Court, 1995.

Toews, John E. *The Story of Original Sin.* Cambridge: James Clarke, 2013.

Trapé, A., and L. Longobardo. "Original Sin." In *Encyclopedia of Ancient Christianity.* Edited by Angelo di Berardino et al. Vol. 3. Nottingham, UK: IVP Academic, 2014.

Tseng, Shao Kai. *Barth's Ontology of Sin and Grace: Variations on a Theme of Augustine.* Abingdon-on-Thames, UK: Routledge, 2018.

Turretin, Francis. *Institutes of Elenctic Theology.* 3 vols. Phillipsburg, NJ: P&R, 1992.

Ullmann, Carl. *The Sinlessness of Jesus: An Evidence for Christianity.* Edinburgh: T&T Clark, 1870.

Van Asselt, Willem J., J. Martin Bac, and Roelf T. te Velde, eds. *Reformed Thought on Freedom: The Concept of Free Choice in Early Modern Reformed Theology.* Grand Rapids, MI: Baker Academic, 2010.

Van Kuiken, E. Jerome. *Christ's Humanity in Current and Ancient Controversy: Fallen or Not?* London: Bloomsbury T&T Clark, 2017.

Van Til, Cornelius. *A Christian Theory of Knowledge.* Phillipsburg, NJ: P&R, 1969.

Van Til, Cornelius. *The Defense of the Faith.* Edited by K. Scott Oliphint. 4th ed. Phillipsburg, NJ: P&R, 2008.

Van Til, Cornelius. *An Introduction to Systematic Theology.* Phillipsburg, NJ: P&R, 2007.

Vermigli, Peter Martyr. *On Original Sin.* Translated and edited by Kirk Summers. Leesburg, VA: Davenant, 2019.

Vööbus, Arthur. "Regarding the Theological Anthropology of Theodore of Mopsuestia." *Church History* 33 (1964): 115–24.

Vorster, Nico. "Calvin's Modification of Augustine's Doctrine of Original Sin." *In Die Skriflig* 44, Supplement 3 (2010): 71–89.

Vos, Geerhardus. *Biblical Theology of the Old and New Testaments.* Carlisle, PA: Banner of Truth, 2007.

Vos, Geerhardus. *The Pauline Eschatology.* Grand Rapids, MI: Eerdmans, 1972.

Vos, Geerhardus. *Reformed Dogmatics.* 5 vols. Translated by Richard B. Gaffin Jr. et al. Bellingham, WA: Lexham, 2012.

Walker, Andrew T. *God and the Transgender Debate: What Does the Bible Actually Say about Gender Identity?* Epsom, Surrey, UK: Good Book Company, 2017.

Warfield, B. B. *Selected Shorter Writings*. Phillipsburg, NJ: P&R, 2001.

Wells, David F. *Above All Earthly Pow'rs: Christ in a Postmodern World.* Grand Rapids, MI: Eerdmans, 2005.

Wells, David F. *Losing Our Virtue: Why the Church Must Recover Its Moral Vision.* Grand Rapids, MI: Eerdmans, 1998.

Welty, Greg. *Why Is There Evil in the World (And So Much of It)?* Fearn, Ross-shire, UK: Christian Focus, 2018.

Wenham, Gordon. "Original Sin in Genesis 1–11." *Churchman* 104.4 (1990): 309–21.

Wiley, Tatha. *Original Sin: Origins, Developments, Contemporary Meanings.* New York: Paulist, 2002.

Williams, Norman Powell. *The Ideas of the Fall and of Original Sin.* The Bampton Lectures, 1924. New York: Longmans, Green, 1927.

Yarbrough, Robert W. "Sin in the Gospels, Acts, and Hebrews to Revelation." Pages 83–106 in *Fallen: A Theology of Sin.* Theology in Community. Edited by C. W. Morgan and R. A. Peterson. Wheaton, IL: Crossway, 2013.

Yarhouse, Mark A. *Sexual Identity and Faith.* Conshohocken, PA: Templeton, 2019.

Yarhouse, Mark A. *Understanding Gender Dysphoria: Navigating Transgender Issues in a Changing Culture.* Downers Grove, IL: IVP Academic, 2015.

Zumstein, Jean. "Die Sünde im Johannesevangelium." *Zeitschrift für Neues Testament* 12 (2009): 27–35.

Index of Biblical References

Index of Names

Aaron, 269, 502n71, 579–80
Abel, 259, 287n115, 310n35
Abel, Douglas Stephen, 342n71
Abelard, Peter, 143
Abernethy, Andrew T., 331n33
Abijah, 571
Abraham (Abram), 45, 45n12, 157, 188,
    262–68, 263n39, 266n51, 268n56, 277,
    285–86, 290, 291, 310, 390n43, 391n45,
    408, 430, 433, 504, 571, 573, 584, 585, 628,
    833n35, 854
À Brakel, Wilhelmus, 207, 218, 229, 254n10
Achan, 279, 628
Achtemeier, Paul J., 489n29, 490n31
Adam. *See* Index of Subjects
Adams, Jay E., 552n27
Adeodatus (son of Augustine), 531
Adrian VI (Pope), 106
Ahab, 288, 339, 339n58
Akers, Matthew R., 334n43
Albertus Magnus, 149
Alexander, Archibald, 195, 196, 213–19,
    213n143, 215n159, 228
Alexander, David E., 549n19
Alexander, James W., 213n145
Alexander, T. Desmond, 261, 266n49
Allberry, Sam, 663
Allen, Michael, 160n140, 669n1
Allison, Dale C., 484, 485n9
Aloisi, J., 395n58, 395n60
Ambrose, 63, 119, 535
Amyraut, Moïses, 156, 157, 159, 159n136
Andersen, Francis I., 307n31, 340n62
Anderson, James N., 539–66, 845–77
Anderson, Kevin L., 502n74
Anderson, Owen, 210n118
Anderson, William H. U., 316n48
Andrew (NT disciple), 376
Angoff, Charles, 613

Anselm of Canterbury, 136, 141, 150, 150n89,
    155, 170n33, 680n48
Antic, Radiša, 316n48
Apollinaris, 47
Aquinas, Thomas. *See* Index of Subjects
Aristotle, 139, 152n100, 522, 522n35, 634,
    651, 691
Arius, 47
Arminius, James (Jacob). *See* Index of Subjects
Armstrong, Brian G., 158n133
Arnobius (the Younger), 83, 83n1, 90–91,
    90nn25–26, 92–94
Arnold, Brian J., 28n41
Arrowsmith, John, 783–85, 787, 789
Ash, John, 246, 247n72
Assis, Elie, 282n101
Aubert, Annette G., 702, 712, 712n58, 718n79
Augustine of Hippo. *See* Index of Subjects

Babcock, William S., 639n25
Bahnsen, Greg L., 864, 867
Bainton, Roland, 650n90
Ballor, Jordan J., 153n105
Bangs, Carl, 170n35
Barbu, Daniel, 827n20
Barcellos, Richard, 570n11
Barclay, John M. G., 434n12
Barker, Margaret, 253n7
Barlaeus, Caspar, 179
Barnabas, 86, 95–96
Barnard, L. W., 22n4, 24n14
Barnes, Albert, 222
Barr, James, 570
Barresi, John, 816n45
Barrett, C. K., 389n40
Barrett, Matthew, 543n5, 853n17
Barrett, Michael, 333n38
Barth, Karl, 731, 731n19, 732n23, 736, 737,
    740–41, 740n44, 741n49, 744, 747, 752n85,
    777, 784, 785–87, 818

Eve, 7, 57, 71n124, 88, 91, 136, 140, 168, 179,
    188, 215–16, 220n185, 225, 232, 255–61,
    336–37, 337n48, 341n68, 393n54, 399, 400,
    460, 574, 575, 581, 588, 602, 605, 608, 629,
    707n34, 709, 748n71, 812n32, 814; see also
    Adam, in Index of Subjects
Eve, John, 240
Eyl, Jennifer, 433n2

Fabri, Johannes, 113
Fabry, Heinz-Josef, 334n42
Fairbairn, Donald, 83n1
Fanning, Buist M., 411n115
Fenner, Dudley, 154
Fensham, F. C., 343n82
Ferguson, Everett, 32n63
Ferguson, Sinclair B., 498nn59–60
Fesko, J. V., 623–24, 628n160, 776n167,
    860n36, 876n70
Fidus, 31, 31n56
Fisher, John (Ioannis Fischerii), 105, 115n55
Flacius (Matthias Flacius Illyricus), 142, 143n44
Flanders, Chris, 834n38
Florus of Lyons, 84
Fohrer, G., 328n21
Fokkelman, J. P., 284n104
Forman, Charles C., 316n48
Fornecker, Samuel David, 169n31, 172n42
Fosdick, Harry Emerson, 911, 912
Foster, Paul, 24n14
Fox, Mary, 232
Fox, Michael V., 298n15, 315
Fox, William, 232
Frame, John M., 356, 364, 846, 847n6, 848,
    851n14, 864
Frederick, Daniel, 315n46
Fredriksen, Paula, 151n94, 434n15, 435n23
Freedman, David Noel, 340n62
Freud, Sigmund, 593–94, 911
Fudge, Edward, 426n133
Fulgentius of Ruspe, 83
Fuller, Andrew, 233–34nn12–13, 234–36, 238,
    240–41
Futato, Mark D., 337n48
Fyall, Robert, 309n34, 312n39

Gaffin, Richard B., Jr., 433n1, 435, 435n22,
    437n36, 438, 438n43, 439, 444, 446n61,
    450, 452, 452n74, 857n28
Gagnon, Robert A. J., 887n8
Garrett, Duane A., 339n58, 340n62, 341n70

Gathercole, Simon J., 492n46
Gatiss, Lee, 11, 156n122, 163–93
Gaventa, B. R., 373n58
Geisler, Norman, 860, 860n38
Geldenhouwer, Gerard, 106
Gemser, B., 325n5
Gentry, Peter J., 578–79, 581–82n50
George, David, 232
Gerhard, Johann, 175, 185, 191n139, 192,
    768n138, 769n141
Gerrish, Brian A., 699, 703, 707n29
Gerstner, John H., 860, 861, 875n67
Gese, Hartmut, 293n1
Gibbs, Philip, 237–38, 237n26, 241
Gibson, David, 1–18
Gibson, Jonathan, 1–18, 256n18, 285n106,
    336n47, 433–81
Gideon, 280, 282
Gilbert, Gregory D., 863
Gill, John, 233, 234
Gillmayr-Bucher, Susanne, 280n92
Gladd, Benjamin L., 485n11
Godet, Frédéric, 780
Godfrey, W. Robert, 2n2, 9n27, 165n12,
    167n21, 175n61
Goldberg, Carl, 816
Golding, Arthur, 151n96
Goldsworthy, Graeme, 294
Golitzin, Alexander, 33n72, 34n76, 36nn92–93,
    36n96, 38n111
Gomarus, Franciscus, 172n43, 178, 197,
    200–201, 204, 206, 207, 211, 219, 221, 228
Goodwin, Thomas, 567
Gordis, Robert, 309n33
Gordon, Christopher J., 175n58
Goudriaan, Aza, 179, 182
Grane, Leif, 138n20, 139n26
Grant, Robert M., 22n4
Gray, G. Buchanan, 307n31
Gray, John, 593–94
Greeley, Andrew M., 806n13
Green, Ashbel, 195
Green, Bradley G., 41–82
Green, Joel B., 369n39
Green, Peter, 522n35
Greenawalt, Kent, 808n20
Greene, G. R., 381n3, 382n6
Greer, Rowan A., 30
Gregory of Nazianzus, 63
Gregory of Nyssa (Nyssen), 32, 671n5
Gregory of Rimini, 138, 155

Index of Subjects